"The tide is definitely turning. No longer can it be taken for granted that the New Perspective has the last word on the 'chief article.' With essays by specialists in various fields, this volume is a wonderful defense of the gospel, and I heartily recommend it."
    Michael Horton, J. Gresham Machen Professor of Systematic Theology and Apologetics, Westminster Seminary California; author, *Justification* (New Studies in Dogmatics)

"A thoughtful, thorough, and important set of essays on the current 'state of the union' on the perennial issue of justification by faith. The introductory essay by Matthew Barrett is worth the price of admission itself—outlining in detail the wide range of biblical-theological issues at stake in the current discussions about the nature of justification, now forty years on from the advent of the New Perspective on Paul. It is hard to imagine a single volume covering virtually every single aspect of the controversy surrounding Protestant—and, to a lesser extent, Roman Catholic—scholarship on the doctrine, but this large collection of essays comes very close. This volume reflects well a core conviction throughout Reformed Protestantism that the Word must be heard afresh in every generation, most especially because it is the Word of Life. This book takes seriously and graciously the voices of opposition. If you want to dive deep into the doctrine of justification, this volume ought to be at the top of your list."
    Richard Lints, Andrew Mutch Distinguished Professor of Theology, Gordon-Conwell Theological Seminary

"*The Doctrine on Which the Church Stands or Falls* is a sterling contribution to a biblically informed, theologically deep, historically sensitive, and pastorally astute engagement with the doctrine of justification by faith alone—*sola fide*. Controversies past and present relating to the doctrine are deftly explored, whether it is the Council of Trent on view or the New Perspective on Paul or the apocalyptic reading of Paul. An invaluable resource and stimulus to careful thought about a crucial doctrine provided by a galaxy of eminently able scholars."
    Graham A. Cole, Dean, Senior Vice President for Education, and Professor of Biblical and Systematic Theology, Trinity Evangelical Divinity School

"Into a world literally hell-bent on self-justification through better performance, the biblical doctrine of justification of sinners through faith in Jesus Christ brings a refreshing, ever re-creating breeze. In this volume, twenty-seven essays examine this doctrine from exegetical, systematic, historical, and practical perspectives. The authors stimulate readers to return to the rich resources of Scripture and enable them to proclaim God's way of restoring sinners to their God-given relationship with their Creator. This volume provides readers with insights mined from the Bible and from the pastoral needs of people today, aiding personal reflection and material for bringing the saving presence of Christ into everyday life."
    Robert Kolb, Emeritus Professor of Systematic Theology, Concordia Seminary

"The breadth and depth of this new work on justification is quite astonishing. An array of scholars from various backgrounds assess the biblical witness, the theological profile, the historical backdrop, and the pastoral application of justification. A most impressive achievement."
    Thomas R. Schreiner, James Buchanan Harrison Professor of New Testament Interpretation, The Southern Baptist Theological Seminary

"We've just celebrated the five hundredth anniversary of the Protestant Reformation and at the same time have passed through about fifty years of questioning (and reformulation) of the classic Reformation doctrine of justification by grace alone through faith alone in Christ alone. This makes *The Doctrine on Which the Church Stands or Falls* timely indeed. As someone who has been engaged in both the academic and ecclesiastical defense of the historic Reformation doctrine, I welcome this sturdy volume. I have already learned much from the authors and will return to this book again as a resource as I continue to explain and address this crucial topic."

J. Ligon Duncan III, Chancellor, CEO, and John E. Richards Professor of Systematic and Historical Theology, Reformed Theological Seminary

"With a distinguished cast of scholars representing a wide range of competencies and traditions, this book ices the cake of the five hundredth anniversary of the Protestant Reformation. Not only are the biblical data (Old and New Testaments) and Second Temple writings thoroughly covered, topics like the New Perspective, justification in Patristic writings, the Reformation, Roman Catholic teaching on justification, and justification since the rise of the Enlightenment all come under careful scrutiny. No new book can be declared a classic. Yet in an era when post-Christian Westerners—even in the church—have tended to devalue doctrine in exchange for the worship of experience, this book's timely and skilled affirmations of doctrine generally and justification in particular make it a contender for classic status in coming years. It will not only inform but reinvigorate all careful readers desiring to plumb the depths of justification's priceless truth."

Robert W. Yarbrough, Professor of New Testament, Covenant Theological Seminary

"Thoroughly rooted in Scripture and classical Protestant theology, the essayists in *The Doctrine on Which the Church Stands or Falls* passionately and accessibly demonstrate the truth manifest in the classical Reformers' commendation of the doctrine of justification by grace alone: God imputes Christ's righteousness to sinners for Jesus's sake. In light of current obfuscations of this doctrine from so many quarters—misplaced ecumenism, liberal Protestantism, and faulty exegesis—this book is a welcome, indeed vital, resource for all gospel preachers and teachers. This volume promises to carry forward the achievements of the Reformers beyond the five hundredth anniversary of the Reformation to future generations."

Mark Mattes, Department Chair and Professor of Theology and Philosophy, Grand View University

"Justification is 'the heart of the matter,' as Luther called it in his debate with Erasmus. Faith, church, and theology all depend on this doctrine. This topic thus needs attention and—although it sounds odd—deserves a great book like this one edited by Matthew Barrett. The wide spectrum of issues surrounding justification is opened up by a team of top scholars and is written down in a clear and sound biblical style. This book is a very helpful guide for students and pastors but will also help the Christian church rediscover why there is a church and what her core business is all about."

Herman Selderhuis, Professor of Church History, Theological University Apeldoorn; Director, Refo500

"The doctrine of justification by faith alone was not invented by the Reformers of the sixteenth century, but it was the centerpiece of their program to renew the church on the basis of the Word of God. It remains no less crucial today. I welcome this new collection of essays—scholarly, substantial, engaging—which moves the discussion forward in a helpful way."

Timothy George, Dean, Beeson Divinity School, Samford University; general editor, Reformation Commentary on Scripture

"*The Doctrine on Which the Church Stands or Falls* is a robust survey of the doctrine of justification. Assembled is an outstanding team of scholars and pastors whose research and reflection afford rich fare to readers hungering to know more of the grace of justification. Whether you want to know more of the doctrine's foundations in biblical teaching, the relationship of justification to other theological doctrines, the ways in which the doctrine has been formulated throughout the history of the church, the ancient and modern controversies and disagreements concerning the doctrine, or justification's implications for Christian life and ministry, you will find yourself informed and challenged by the servings of this volume. *The Doctrine on Which the Church Stands or Falls* is nothing less than a full-course meal, well served. *Bon appétit!*"
    Guy Prentiss Waters, James M. Baird Jr. Professor of New Testament, Reformed Theological Seminary

"How can a person be right with God? In this stellar, well-conceived volume, the contributors' collective answer to this question is, 'One is right with God only by trusting in the righteousness of another, namely, in the sinless substitute, Christ Jesus, alone'—the 'great exchange.' In this, they stand in a powerful biblical and historical tradition, as the volume amply demonstrates. Highly recommended!"
    Andreas J. Köstenberger, Director of the Center for Biblical Studies and Research Professor of New Testament and Biblical Theology, Midwestern Baptist Theological Seminary; Founder, Biblical Foundations

"Obscuring the doctrine of justification has been one of the devil's most effective weapons against the church. This landmark study calls us back to a God-glorifying, loving, missional faith in the God who justifies. As justification depends on and determines so much of life and theology, it is only fitting that this book so ably incorporates wide-ranging exegesis, church history, doctrine, and pastoralia. I warmly commend it to all who wish to be better equipped for life and ministry."
    Peter Sanlon, Director of Training, The Free Church of England

"Intrinsic to the heart of the Protestant tradition is the confession of justification by faith alone. Rooted in the Reformation response to the faith-and-works orientation of the basis of salvation, this doctrine has been rightly seen as utterly biblical. Matthew Barrett also knows that this core doctrine of true Christianity can never be taken for granted—hence this excellent treatment of what this doctrine entails and how it relates to other areas of the Christian life. Warmly recommended."
    Michael A. G. Haykin, Professor of Church History and Biblical Spirituality, The Southern Baptist Theological Seminary

"In *The Doctrine on Which the Church Stands or Falls*, Matthew Barrett and more than twenty other capable and gifted thinkers have offered a thorough and persuasive case for the doctrine of justification by grace through faith. Exploring this vital theological concept from the perspective of the Hebrew Scriptures, the teaching of the New Testament, and the history of Christian doctrine, as well as from the vantage point of systematic and pastoral theology, the authors offer a comprehensive and symphonic chorus for readers of this outstanding volume. The exposition, explication, and application of this essential Christian teaching found in this impressive book should become essential reading for theologians, biblical scholars, pastors, students, and interested laypersons. Barrett is to be commended and congratulated for putting together this much-needed work at this important time."
    David S. Dockery, President, Trinity International University / Trinity Evangelical Divinity School

"Since justification by grace alone through faith alone on account of Christ alone is truly that doctrine on which Christ's church stands or falls, this wonderful doctrine cannot be studied enough or too deeply. Barrett has assembled a solid group of faithful and first-rate scholars to tackle this subject from biblical, theological, historical, and pastoral perspectives. While some ask the question, 'Why the Reformation?' this volume provides the answer. This is the doctrine by which the church stands or falls because this doctrine is the gospel! A feast awaits the reader."

Kim Riddlebarger, Senior Pastor, Christ Reformed Church, Anaheim, California

"Looking at this substantial work, the expression 'kid in a candy store' comes to mind—at least if the candy you seek is a thorough, in-depth, sophisticated, and biblically faithful treatment of the doctrine of justification. I commend Matthew Barrett for assembling a team of exceedingly competent biblical scholars, church historians, and theologians who have canvassed this enormously important doctrine from multiple angles, theoretical and practical. I highly recommend this book to scholars and pastors alike who are looking for the latest thinking on justification from an orthodox Protestant perspective. This book has it all!"

Alan W. Gomes, Professor of Theology, Talbot School of Theology; Senior Research Fellow, Phoenix Seminary

The Doctrine on Which the Church Stands or Falls

Justification in Biblical, Theological, Historical, and Pastoral Perspective

Edited by Matthew Barrett

Foreword by D. A. Carson

WHEATON, ILLINOIS

The Doctrine on Which the Church Stands or Falls: Justification in Biblical, Theological, Historical, and Pastoral Perspective

Copyright © 2019 by Matthew Barrett

Published by Crossway
    1300 Crescent Street
    Wheaton, Illinois 60187

All rights reserved. No part of this publication may be reproduced, stored in a retrieval system, or transmitted in any form by any means, electronic, mechanical, photocopy, recording, or otherwise, without the prior permission of the publisher, except as provided for by USA copyright law. Crossway® is a registered trademark in the United States of America.

Cover design: Jordan Singer

Cover image: Wikimedia commons

Note on the cover: The cover depicts the Frauenkirche in Dresden, once rooted in the Reformation theology of Luther but later compromised by its defense of Nazi Germany. The top image portrays the church as it stood before World War II and the bottom image, after it had fallen during the Allied offensive on the city.

First printing 2019

Printed in the United States of America

Unless otherwise indicated, Scripture quotations are from the ESV® Bible (The Holy Bible, English Standard Version®), copyright © 2001 by Crossway, a publishing ministry of Good News Publishers. Used by permission. All rights reserved. Note that some chapters use a different default version, as indicated in those chapters.

Scripture quotations marked CSB have been taken from the Christian Standard Bible®. Copyright © 2017 by Holman Bible Publishers. Used by permission. Christian Standard Bible® and CSB® are federally registered trademarks of Holman Bible Publishers.

Scripture quotations marked KJV are from the *King James Version* of the Bible.

Scripture quotations marked NASB are from *The New American Standard Bible*®. Copyright © The Lockman Foundation 1960, 1962, 1963, 1968, 1971, 1972, 1973, 1975, 1977, 1995. Used by permission.

Scripture references marked NIV are taken from The Holy Bible, New International Version®, NIV®. Copyright © 1973, 1978, 1984, 2011 by Biblica, Inc.™ Used by permission. All rights reserved worldwide.

Scripture references marked NRSV are from *The New Revised Standard Version*. Copyright © 1989 by the Division of Christian Education of the National Council of the Churches of Christ in the U.S.A. Published by Thomas Nelson, Inc. Used by permission of the National Council of the Churches of Christ in the U.S.A.

All emphases in Scripture quotations have been added by the author.

Hardcover ISBN: 978-1-4335-5541-1
ePub ISBN: 978-1-4335-5544-2
PDF ISBN: 978-1-4335-5542-8
Mobipocket ISBN: 978-1-4335-5543-5

Library of Congress Cataloging-in-Publication Data

Names: Barrett, Matthew, 1982– author.
Title: The doctrine on which the church stands or falls : justification in biblical, theological, historical, and pastoral perspective / edited by Matthew Barrett; foreword by D. A. Carson.
Description: Wheaton, Illinois : Crossway, 2019. | Includes bibliographical references and index.
Identifiers: LCCN 2018014927 (print) | LCCN 2018042280 (ebook) | ISBN 9781433555428 (pdf) | ISBN 9781433555435 (mobi) | ISBN 9781433555442 (epub) | ISBN 9781433555411 (hardcover) | ISBN 9781433555442 (ePub) | ISBN 9781433555435 (mobipocket)
Subjects: LCSH: Justification (Christian theology)
Classification: LCC BT764.3 (ebook) | LCC BT764.3 .B37 2019 (print) | DDC 234/.7—dc23
LC record available at https://lccn.loc.gov/2018014927

Crossway is a publishing ministry of Good News Publishers.

SH		28	27	26	25	24	23	22	21	20	19
15	14	13	12	11	10	9	8	7	6	5	4	3	2	1

Contents

List of Illustrations 11

Foreword 13
    D. A. Carson

Abbreviations 17

Introduction 23
    The Foolishness of Justification
    Matthew Barrett

PART ONE
JUSTIFICATION IN BIBLICAL PERSPECTIVE

1. "He Believed the Lord" 41
   The Pedigree of Justification in the Pentateuch
   Stephen Dempster

2. Singing and Living Justification by Faith Alone 67
   The Psalms and the Wisdom Literature
   Allan Harman

3. Salvation Is the Lord's 99
   Prophetic Perspectives
   Willem A. VanGemeren

4. Setting the Record Straight 147
   Second Temple Judaism and Works Righteousness
   Robert J. Cara

5. What Does Justification Have to Do with the Gospels? ... 179
   Brian Vickers

6. The Righteous God Righteously Righteouses the Unrighteous ... 213
   Justification according to Romans
   Andrew David Naselli

7. By Grace You Have Been Saved through Faith 239
   Justification in the Pauline Epistles
   Brandon Crowe

8   An Epistle of Straw? 273
    Reconciling James and Paul
    DAN MCCARTNEY

9   The New Quest for Paul 295
    A Critique of the New Perspective on Paul
    TIMO LAATO

10 What's Next? 327
    Justification after the New Perspective
    DAVID A. SHAW

PART TWO
JUSTIFICATION IN THEOLOGICAL PERSPECTIVE

11 "Behold, the Lamb of God" 351
    *Theology Proper and the Inseparability of Penal-Substitutionary Atonement
    from Forensic Justification and Imputation*
    STEPHEN J. WELLUM

12 Raised for Our Justification 387
    *The Christological, Covenantal, Forensic, and Eschatological Contours of an
    Ambiguous Relationship*
    MATTHEW BARRETT

13 The Theology of Justification by Faith 419
    The Theological Case for Sola Fide
    MARK THOMPSON

14 The Passive *and* Active Obedience of Christ 441
    Retrieving a Biblical Distinction
    BRANDON CROWE

15 A Contested Union 469
    Union with Christ and the Justification Debate
    DAVID VANDRUNEN

16 Faith Works 505
    Properly Understanding the Relationship between Justification and Sanctification
    R. LUCAS STAMPS

17 Justification, the Law, and the New Covenant 533
    JASON MEYER

PART THREE
JUSTIFICATION IN CHURCH HISTORY

18 Reformation Invention or Historic Orthodoxy? 563
    Justification in the Fathers
    GERALD BRAY

19 The Evolution of Justification 587
    Justification in the Medieval Traditions
    NICK NEEDHAM

20 Can This Bird Fly? 623
    The Reformation as Reaction to the Via Moderna's Covenantal, Voluntarist Justification Theology
    MATTHEW BARRETT

21 The First and Chief Article 657
    Luther's Discovery of Sola Fide *and Its Controversial Reception in Lutheranism*
    KOREY MAAS

22 The Ground of Religion 701
    Justification according to the Reformed Tradition
    J. V. FESKO

23 Not by Faith Alone? 739
    An Analysis of the Roman Catholic Doctrine of Justification from Trent to the Joint Declaration
    LEONARDO DE CHIRICO

24 The Eclipse of Justification 769
    Justification during the Enlightenment and Post-Enlightenment Eras
    BRUCE P. BAUGUS

PART FOUR
JUSTIFICATION IN PASTORAL PRACTICE

25 Justification and Conversion 811
    Attractions and Repulsions to Rome
    CHRIS CASTALDO

26 The Ground on Which We Stand 839
    The Necessity of Justification for Pastoral Ministry
    SAM STORMS

Contributors 867
General Index 871
Scripture Index 895

Illustrations

FIGURES

1.1 The Structure of the Torah 60
6.1 The Frequency of the Δίκ Word Group in Sections of Romans 215
21.1 Intellectualist Schema of Thomas Aquinas 628
21.2 Voluntarist Schema of Gabriel Biel 630

TABLES

1.1 Structure of Genesis 15 52
3.1 Symbolic Significance of Hosea's Children 130
6.1 The Δίκ Word Group in Romans (76x) 214
6.2 Two Kinds of Righteousness in Romans 9:30–10:6 229
6.3 Contrasts between Justification and Progressive Sanctification 234
17.1 Faith Path and Works Path in Galatians 3 538
17.2 Law Not Made to Justify 540
17.3 Correlation of Old and New Covenants 552
21.1 [Oberman's] Schema 1: A Chart of the Interrelation of Justification
     and Predestination 636
23.1 Causality in Trent's View of Justification 706
23.2 Westminster Assembly's Rejection of Errors 718
23.3 Westminster Assembly's Revision of Thirty-Nine Articles, Article 11 720

Foreword

D. A. CARSON

The title of this book, *The Doctrine on Which the Church Stands or Falls*, referring to justification, has been an axiom in Protestant circles since the time of Luther; the subtitle, *Justification in Biblical, Theological, Historical, and Pastoral Perspective*, indicates the scope of the project, fully justifying (that word again!) its nine-hundred-page heft.

Many, of course, have vigorously challenged the claim that justification is the doctrine on which the church stands or falls. After all, they say, justification is primarily a Pauline notion, and even then, it is very unevenly distributed in the Pauline corpus. Some argue that reconciliation is more central to Paul than is justification. Moreover, justification is not central to the Synoptics or to the Johannine corpus. Hebrews is more interested in priestly notions of sacrifice than in the forensic categories of justification. What about the Old Testament? A large part of it is made up (it is alleged) of Deuteronomistic theology, which is certainly not pulsing to vindicate justification by grace alone through faith alone. Even if one could make a case for the centrality of justification at the time of the Protestant Reformation, isn't that because of the particular focus of the most contested points in the sixteenth century? But in the fourth century the focus of debate was Christology; in the eighteenth century it was the nature and locus of revelation. So doesn't it follow, then, that a fixation on justification betrays both a misunderstanding of Scripture and a hopelessly naive and reductionistic reading of historical theology?

So the first place to reenter the debate, then, is to review afresh what Scripture says. Here it is important not to focus undue attention on "righteousness" words (as important as they are): the central question is how human beings this side of Genesis 3 can be brought back to the holy God who is their Maker, Redeemer, and Judge. Not surprisingly, then, this book devotes several substantial chapters to probing this theme in the Old and New Testaments, beginning with the Pentateuch, the Psalms and Wisdom Literature, and the Prophets. Words have not been ignored: one writer unpacks Romans by arguing that in this epistle "the righteous God righteously righteouses the unrighteous," thereby indicating his understanding of Romans 3:21–26 while hinting at the challenges of translation (and not leaving much scope for Ernst Käsemann either).

Competent probes examine the justification theme in the Gospels and in James; two chapters evaluate the "New Perspective" and its aftermath. One could wish for more; nevertheless, one must applaud the choices that were made.

Part of the problem with the debates over the significance of justification is that they have often been conducted in atomistic fashion—that is, various doctrines have been enumerated, and then several questions are posed: Which individual doctrines surface most frequently in the biblical texts? Comparing them two or three at a time, which one is the most important, once all the comparisons have been made? This approach is fundamentally misguided. The Bible is not to be treated like a theological smorgasbord, where all the offerings are presented on separate platters, each dish inviting individual evaluation. The Bible invites—indeed, it demands—appropriate theological integration. How is justification tied to the atonement and to the resurrection of Jesus ("raised for our justification," Paul says)? What other Christological emphases, apart from Jesus's death and resurrection, are tied to justification? Can one sustain a robust grasp of justification without a reflective grasp of the active and passive obedience of Christ? How are justification and faith properly tied together? Justification and sanctification? (And in this case, one must specify whether one means "sanctification" in the dominant Pauline sense or in the dominant confessional sense: the latter is narrower than the former.) How is justification related to the law, to the new covenant, to union with Christ, to eschatology? What ties these doctrines together? Does any other doctrinal element tie together such disparate theological loci in quite the way justification does? Don't such realities expose the artificiality of arguments that deploy mere counting techniques to relegate justification to some inferior role in the constellation of biblical theology?

Indeed, there is a bigger theological issue at stake, a worldview issue, one that is hinted at in two of the essays in this book. Consider the various forms of Buddhism. Strictly speaking, Buddhism does not confess a personal, transcendent God with whom one must be reconciled. The notion of justification is entirely alien to it. Hinduism does not envisage a *telos* to which history is rushing. It depicts cyclical patterns in which individuals hop on and off the eternal spiral ("up" or "down"). Neither of these perspectives envisages the *summum bonum*, the supreme good, to be the deep knowledge of the holy and transcendent God, personally knowing him and being known by him, both in time and in eternity, which anticipation drives the question, How can a man be just before God? Nor does the contemporary Western passion for self-definition and self-chosen identity fuss very much about whether there is a God to whom we must render account. But if we are dealing with the God of the Bible, to know this God who is there and to enjoy him forever depend utterly on whether or not this God declares us *just* before him. If he does not, we are damned. If he does, we are saved. In other words, justification is a category that is tied to a particular worldview, the biblical worldview. We claim that this worldview, in which the biblical content explains how God's rebellious image bearers may be reconciled to their Maker by means of the sacrifice God himself has provided through the death and resurrection of his Son, is not merely "true for us" because we have accepted it as true but is *true*, and therefore hugely important. We cannot dismiss it without breaking ourselves on it: we will give an answer to this God. Thus our status before God, our justfication, is of fundamental significance; it is the "ground of religion" (as one writer in this book has put it); it is the doctrine on which the church stands or falls. It is a worldview question.

As for the historical argument that justification has not always had the controlling importance it had in the sixteenth century, well, that much at least is true. But that's a different matter from deciding whether it *should* have had greater importance in any particular age. The existential importance of a doctrine in a particular century often turns on what is most disputed, what is most denied (and therefore affirmed by others)—not by the fundamentally systemic question about whether the church lives and dies, stands or falls, by a particular complex theological construction. The essays in the historical section of this volume helpfully explore what was understood about justification in the Patristic era, how that understanding evolved in the medieval traditions, and how it broke out in the Reformation and beyond. Precisely *because* it was most heavily disputed at the time of the Reformation, more clarifying attention was devoted to it.

The issues treated in this important volume are not only confessional, then, but have to do with our well-being both in this life and in the life to come. They have to do with God and our relationship to him; they turn on what the gospel is, how human beings may be right with God. Nothing, nothing at all, is more important than such matters.

Abbreviations

AB	Anchor Bible
ABR	*Australian Biblical Review*
ACT	Ancient Christian Texts
ACW	Ancient Christian Writers
AnBib	Analecta Biblica
ANF	*Ante-Nicene Fathers*. Edited by Alexander Roberts and James Donaldson. 1885–1896. Reprint, Grand Rapids, MI: Eerdmans, 1985–1987.
ARG	*Archiv für Reformationsgeschichte*
ASBT	Acadia Studies in Bible and Theology
ATDan	Acta Theologica Danica
AThR	*Anglican Theological Review*
BBM	Baker Biblical Monograph
BCCT	Brill's Companions to the Christian Tradition
BCR	Biblioteca di cultura religiosa
BDAG	Danker, Frederick W., Walter Bauer, William F. Arndt, and F. Wilbur Gingrich. *A Greek-English Lexicon of the New Testament and Other Early Christian Literature*. 3rd ed. Chicago: University of Chicago Press, 2000.
BDF	Blass, Friedrich, Albert Debrunner, and Robert W. Funk. *A Greek Grammar of the New Testament and Other Early Christian Literature*. Chicago: University of Chicago Press, 1961.
BECNT	Baker Exegetical Commentary on the New Testament
BHR	Bibliotheca Humanistica et Reformatorica
BJRL	*Bulletin of the John Rylands University Library of Manchester*
BNTC	Black's New Testament Commentaries
BOC	*The Book of Concord: The Confessions of the Evangelical Lutheran Church*. Edited by Robert Kolb and Timothy J. Wengert. Minneapolis: Fortress, 2000.
BRS	Biblical Resource Series
BSCH	Brill's Series in Church History

BTCP	Biblical Theology for Christian Proclamation
BZAW	Beihefte zur Zeitschrift für die alttestamentliche Wissenschaft
BZNW	Beihefte zur Zeitschrift für die neutestamentliche Wissenschaft
CBET	Contributions to Biblical Exegesis and Theology
CCR	Cambridge Companions to Religion
CCT	Contours of Christian Theology
CGTC	Cambridge Greek Testament Commentary
Chm	*Churchman*
CLRC	Courtenay Library of Reformation Classics
ConBOT	Coniectanea Biblica: Old Testament Series
COQG	Christian Origins and the Question of God
CR	*Corpus Reformatorum*. Edited by C. G. Bretschneider and H. E. Bindseil. Halle and Brunswick: Schwetschke, 1834–1860.
CS	*Christianity and Society*
CSMLT	Cambridge Studies in Medieval Life and Thought
CTHP	Cambridge Texts in the History of Philosophy
CTJ	*Calvin Theological Journal*
CTQ	*Concordia Theological Quarterly*
CurTM	*Currents in Theology and Mission*
CV	*Communio Viatorum*
DBSJ	*Detroit Baptist Seminary Journal*
DHWC	Documentary History of Western Civilization
DSD	*Dead Sea Discoveries*
EC	*Early Christianity*
EJL	Early Judaism and Its Literature
Eng.	English
ERT	*Evangelical Review of Theology*
EuroJTh	*European Journal of Theology*
EUSLR	Emory University Studies in Law and Religion
EvQ	*Evangelical Quarterly*
EvT	*Evangelische Theologie*
FAT	Forschungen zum Alten Testament
FR	*Fac-Réflexions*
FRLANT	Forschungen zur Religion und Literatur des Alten und Neuen Testaments
GH	Gorgias Handbooks
HBT	*Horizons in Biblical Theology*
HS	*Hebrew Studies*

HThKNT	Herders Theologischer Kommentar zum Neuen Testament
HTR	*Harvard Theological Review*
IBC	Interpretation: A Bible Commentary for Teaching and Preaching
ICC	International Critical Commentary
IJST	*International Journal of Systematic Theology*
Int	*Interpretation*
ITQ	*Irish Theological Quarterly*
JBL	*Journal of Biblical Literature*
JBQ	*Jewish Bible Quarterly*
JES	Jonathan Edwards Studies
JETS	*Journal of the Evangelical Theological Society*
JR	*Journal of Religion*
JSJ	*Journal for the Study of Judaism*
JSJSup	Supplements to the Journal for the Study of Judaism
JSNT	*Journal for the Study of the New Testament*
JSNTSup	Journal for the Study of the New Testament Supplement Series
JTISup	Journal of Theological Interpretation Supplements
JTS	*Journal of Theological Studies*
KEK	Kritisch-exegetischer Kommentar über das Neue Testament
KNTTM	Kommentar zum Neuen Testament aus Talmud und Midrasch
LCC	Library of Christian Classics
LCL	Loeb Classical Library
LEH	Library of Ecclesiastical History
LF	*Lutheran Forum*
LHBOTS	The Library of Hebrew Bible / Old Testament Studies
LNTS	Library of New Testament Studies
LQ	*Lutheran Quarterly*
LSJ	Liddell, Henry George, Robert Scott, Henry Stuart Jones. *A Greek-English Lexicon*. 9th ed. with revised supplement. Oxford: Clarendon, 1996.
LW	Luther, Martin. *Luther's Works*. Edited by Jaroslav Pelikan, Helmut T. Lehmann, and Christopher Brown. American ed. 82 vols. (projected). Philadelphia: Fortress; Saint Louis, MO: Concordia, 1955–.
LXX	Septuagint
MAS	Middle Ages Series
MJT	*Mid-America Journal of Theology*
MNTC	Moffatt New Testament Commentary
MST	Mediaeval Sources in Translation
MT	Masoretic Text

NAC	New American Commentary
NACSBT	NAC Studies in Bible and Theology
NIBC	New International Biblical Commentary
NICNT	New International Commentary on the New Testament
NICOT	New International Commentary on the Old Testament
NIDNTT	*New International Dictionary of New Testament Theology*. Edited by Colin Brown. 4 vols. Grand Rapids, MI: Zondervan, 1975–1978.
NIDOTTE	*New International Dictionary of Old Testament Theology and Exegesis*. Edited by Willem A. VanGemeren. 5 vols. Grand Rapids, MI: Zondervan, 1997.
NIGTC	New International Greek Testament Commentary
NIVAC	NIV Application Commentary
NovT	*Novum Testamentum*
NPNF1	*Nicene and Post-Nicene Fathers of the Christian Church*. 1st ser. Edited by Philip Schaff. 1886–1890. Reprint, Grand Rapids, MI: Eerdmans, 1956.
NPNF2	*Nicene and Post-Nicene Fathers of the Christian Church*. 2nd ser. Edited by Philip Schaff and Henry Wace. 1890–1900. Reprint, Grand Rapids, MI: Eerdmans, 1987.
NPP	New Perspective on Paul
NSBT	New Studies in Biblical Theology
NSD	New Studies in Dogmatics
NTOA	Novum Testamentum et Orbis Antiquus
NTS	*New Testament Studies*
NTSI	New Testament and the Scriptures of Israel
OBT	Overtures to Biblical Theology
OSHT	Oxford Studies in Historical Theology
ÖTKNT	Ökumenischer Taschenbuch-Kommentar zum Neuen Testament
OTL	Old Testament Library
OTM	Oxford Theological Monographs
PBM	Paternoster Biblical Monographs
PBT	Piccola biblioteca teologica
PE	*Pro Ecclesia*
PL	Patrologia Latina (or Patrologiae Cursus Completus: Series Latina). Edited by Jacques-Paul Migne. 217 vols. Paris, 1844–1864.
PNTC	Pillar New Testament Commentary
PPS	Popular Patristics Series
QD	Quaestiones Disputatae

RAS	Refo500 Academic Studies
RD	Religions and Discourse
REC	Reformed Expository Commentary
REDS	Reformed, Exegetical and Doctrinal Studies
RevExp	*Review and Expositor*
RFN	Religionsgeschichte der Frühen Neuzeit
RHT	Reformed Historical Theology
RHTS	Reformed Historical-Theological Studies
RRef	*La Revue Réformée*
RRJ	*Reformation and Revival Journal*
RRR	*Reformation and Renaissance Review*
RTR	*Reformed Theological Review*
RTRSup	Reformed Theological Review, Supplement Series
SBJT	*Southern Baptist Journal of Theology*
SBLMS	Society of Biblical Literature Monograph Series
SBLSS	Society of Biblical Literature Symposium Series
SCBC	*Sources and Contexts of the Book of Concord.* Edited by Robert Kolb and James A. Nestingen. Minneapolis: Fortress, 2001.
SCES	Sixteenth Century Essays and Studies
SCHT	Studies in Christian History and Thought
SCJ	*Sixteenth Century Journal*
SdT	*Studi di teologia*
SFSHJ	South Florida Studies in the History of Judaism
SHCT	Studies in the History of Christian Thought
SHCTr	Studies in the History of Christian Traditions
SJT	*Scottish Journal of Theology*
SMRT	Studies in Medieval and Reformation Thought
SNTSMS	Society for New Testament Studies Monograph Series
SP	Sacra Pagina
SSBT	Short Studies in Biblical Theology
STR	Studies in Theology and Religion
SubBi	Subsidia Biblica
SUNT	Studien zur Umwelt des Neuen Testaments
TB	Theologische Bücherei: Neudrucke und Berichte aus dem 20. Jahrhundert
TDNT	*Theological Dictionary of the New Testament.* Edited by Gerhard Kittel and Gerhard Friedrich. Translated by Geoffrey W. Bromiley. 10 vols. Grand Rapids, MI: Eerdmans, 1964–1976.
TGST	Tesi Gregoriana, Serie Teologia

Them	*Themelios*
THR	Travaux d'humanisme et Renaissance
TJ	*Trinity Journal*
TNTC	Tyndale New Testament Commentaries
TOTC	Tyndale Old Testament Commentaries
TSRPRT	Texts and Studies in Reformation and Post-Reformation Thought
TynBul	*Tyndale Bulletin*
UT	Universo teologia
VT	*Vetus Testamentum*
VTSup	Supplements to Vetus Testamentum
WA	*D. Martin Luthers Werke, Kritische Gesamtausgabe*. 73 vols. Weimar: Hermann Böhlaus Nachfolger, 1883–2009.
WABr	*D. Martin Luthers Werke, Kritische Gesamtausgabe: Briefwechsel*. 18 vols. Weimar: Hermann Böhlaus Nachfolger, 1930–1983.
WARF	Westminster Assembly and the Reformed Faith
WBC	Word Biblical Commentary
WMANT	Wissenschaftliche Monographien zum Alten und Neuen Testament
WSAMA	Walberberger Studien der Albertus-Magnus-Akademie
WTJ	*Westminster Theological Journal*
WUNT	Wissenschaftliche Untersuchungen zum Neuen Testament
ZAW	*Zeitschrift für die alttestamentliche Wissenschaft*
ZECNT	Zondervan Exegetical Commentary on the New Testament
ZNW	*Zeitschrift für die neutestamentliche Wissenschaft und die Kunde der älteren Kirche*

Introduction

The Foolishness of Justification

MATTHEW BARRETT

How can a person be right with God? Few questions have so vigorously arrested the attention of the Protestant church. From this one question was birthed the Reformation itself, forever changing the way Christians interpreted Scripture, perceived a holy God, and applied the mediating work of Christ. From this one question, evangelicals—as the Reformers were first called—were forced to reconsider the relationship between redemption accomplished and redemption applied. If the obedience and sacrifice of Christ was sufficient, then no longer could one's merits in any way contribute to one's right standing with God. One is right with God only by trusting (*sola fide*) in the righteousness of another, namely, in the sinless substitute, Christ Jesus, alone (*solus Christus*).

The Covenant of Creation and Federal Headship

To articulate the doctrine of justification, one naturally must move from drama to doctrine. Justification is positioned within the Spirit's variegated application of redemption, the order of salvation (*ordo salutis*), yet it stems from and is inseparably tied to the objective and historic work of Jesus Christ (*historia salutis*). In the beginning, our triune God created the world good, a goodness that reflected his inherent, immutable, eternal, and ethical holiness. The unstained beauty of his righteousness was manifested in the original state of the created order, which he declared good from the start.

Nowhere did such goodness reside with conspicuous radiance than in man and woman, for they alone were made in the image of their Creator (Gen. 1:27). While they were created to enjoy communion with their Creator, that *imago Dei* and the communion it promised were put to the test when God presented Adam and Eve with certain covenant stipulations that would define his loving, personal relationship with them

(2:16–17). This covenant at creation placed before the first couple life eternal if they would listen, trust, and obey.[1] Never would the tree of life be far from their lips if they would not stray from the benevolence of their covenant Maker.

Yet such covenant stipulations also threatened death, physical as well as spiritual, should they defy their Maker, rebel against his commands, defile the purity of his Edenic temple, and elevate their autonomy in the treason of idolatry. The tragedy of Genesis 3 is just such a transgression. Yet such a transgression was disastrous not for them alone but for the entire human race to come. As Paul tells the church in Rome (Rom. 5:12–21), Adam represented mankind, so that his transgression against the covenant of creation resulted in his guilt and corruption being imputed to his progeny. Adam's federal headship was legal in every sense of the word, so that all his children stood condemned in him. His guilt and condemnation thus resulted in a nature polluted by sin, so that no one after him was exempt from those sinful inclinations rooted deep within human nature. The fall of Adam was the fall of humanity because all people share covenant solidarity with their first father. Physical death was the most immediate consequence: "In Adam all die" (1 Cor. 15:22). However, death goes beyond the flesh, a visual parallel to the spiritual death within: "You were dead in the trespasses and sins in which you once walked" (Eph. 2:1–2).

Theologians of Glory or the Crucified Lord of Glory?

Although it may seem odd that Adam is rarely mentioned in the drama that unfolds, humanity's solidarity with him is glaringly present with each new Adam. God's promise to raise up an offspring of the woman that would redeem the children of Adam became increasingly urgent with each new misstep east of Eden. The depravity rooted in man's nature was so pervasive that it took little time at all for humanity collectively to hold up its fist in the air, screaming out in defiance against God. From Adam to Cain, from the flood to Babel, and from Sodom to Israel's exile, the history of humanity can be summed up concisely: in Adam, man strives to justify himself. Theologians of glory, to borrow from Martin Luther, will always build a tower into the heavens as if they can climb their way up into glory and claim the throne of the one who made them. "Let us make a name for ourselves" (Gen. 11:4) is their battle cry, and the history of mankind from Adam to Israel is full of judicial bloodshed since no man stands righteous before him whose justice knows no imperfection: "For the wrath of God is revealed from heaven against all ungodliness and unrighteousness of men" (Rom. 1:18).

Israel should be the exception to this tragedy, but unfortunately, she is the exemplar. God's special, called-out covenant people were even given the law, the constitution of the covenant written on tablets of stone by the very finger of God, revealing to them exactly how they could live in communion with him. As perfect as that law was, the children

---

1. For a more detailed description of the covenant of creation, see Peter J. Gentry and Stephen J. Wellum, "The Covenant with Creation in Genesis 1–3," chap. 6 in *Kingdom through Covenant: A Biblical-Theological Understanding of the Covenants*, 2nd ed. (Wheaton, IL: Crossway, 2018).

of Abraham were still children of Adam, plagued by the same evil desires. Not even supernatural liberation from Egypt could keep this people from prostituting themselves in idolatry. As long as Israel remained in Adam, it would jump at the first opportunity to act on the corruption within and break the covenant its God had so graciously made in the first place. Such idolatry resulted in physical death but also, worse still, spiritual condemnation. No Israelite could obey the law perfectly; no Israelite would obey the law flawlessly. Under the law came judgment. In that sense, "all, both Jews and Greeks, are under sin, as it is written: 'None is righteous, no, not one'" (Rom. 3:9–10; cf. Ps. 14:1–3). Naturally, Paul could conclude, "For by works of the law no human being will be justified in his sight, since through the law comes knowledge of sin" (Rom. 3:20).

Yet when all the world had gone astray, divine light shined bright into a dark madness. That light was none other than Jesus Christ (John 1:9; 8:12; 2 Cor. 4:3–6). Predicted by the prophets, foreshadowed in Israel's array of types, the offspring of the woman had at long last arrived to redeem Adam's fallen race. Finally, those in Adam could find redemption—in Christ, the last Adam. As announced at his birth, his name is Jesus, "for he will save his people from their sins" (Matt. 1:21). Clarifying the single passion of his divinely ordained mission, Jesus declared, "For the Son of Man came to seek and to save the lost" (Luke 19:10). Or as Matthew's Gospel stresses, the Son of God himself had become incarnate and tabernacled among his people (Matt. 1:23), fully intending in the end to give his life as "a ransom for many" (20:28). "I have not come to call the righteous," Jesus proclaimed, "but sinners to repentance" (Luke 5:32).

Unthinkable, however, was the *means* by which the Son of Man would accomplish such a salvation. The Lord of glory would be crucified (1 Cor. 2:8). He did not climb Babel into the heavens but descended from the heavens to endure the death Babel's citizens deserved. To succeed in his Father's eyes, he would have to fail in the eyes of the world.

From Eternal Son to Last Adam: Covenant of Redemption, Recapitulation, and Active Obedience

Jesus did not believe, however, that his mission was accidental; rather, his mission was from his Father. Turning to the Gospel of John, theologians have long observed that the Son's salvific mission stemmed from an eternal, intra-Trinitarian covenant, one that defines the soteriological intentions of the economic Trinity.[2] As the one eternally generated by the Father, the Son voluntarily accepted the Father's plan of redemption. The Son became the surety of this *pactum salutis*, a *pactum* that commissioned the Son to secure the eternal destiny of God's elect.

---

2. See John Owen, *The Mystery of the Gospel Vindicated*, in *The Works of John Owen*, ed. William H. Goold, vol. 12, *The Gospel Defended* (Edinburgh: Banner of Truth, 1991), 497; J. V. Fesko, *The Covenant of Redemption: Origins, Development, and Reception*, RHT 35 (Göttingen: Vandenhoeck & Ruprecht, 2015), 15; Fesko, *The Trinity and the Covenant of Redemption* (Fearn, Ross-Shire, Scotland: Mentor, 2016); Matthew Barrett, *40 Questions about Salvation* (Grand Rapids, MI: Kregel Academic, 2018), 68–70; Scott R. Swain, "Covenant of Redemption," in *Christian Dogmatics: Reformed Theology for the Church Catholic*, ed. Michael Allen and Scott R. Swain (Grand Rapids, MI: Baker Academic, 2016), 107–25.

In the economy of salvation, this *pactum salutis* is assumed in the many ways Jesus reveals that his mission is not his own but comes directly from his Father: "For the works that the Father has given me to accomplish, the very works that I am doing, bear witness about me that the Father has sent me" (John 5:36). Again, Jesus says,

> For I have come down from heaven, not to do my own will but the will of him who sent me. And this is the will of him who sent me, that I should lose nothing of all that he has given me, but raise it up on the last day. For this is the will of my Father, that everyone who looks on the Son and believes in him should have eternal life, and I will raise him up on the last day. (6:38–40)

As Jesus approaches the cross, his High Priestly Prayer to his Father reveals the same:

> I glorified you on earth, having accomplished the work that you gave me to do. . . .
> I have manifested your name to the people whom you gave me out of the world. Yours they were, and you gave them to me, and they have kept your word. Now they know that everything that you have given me is from you. For I have given them the words that you gave me, and they have received them and have come to know in truth that I came from you; and they have believed that you sent me. (17:4–8)

What are these "works" (5:36) that the Father has sent his Son to accomplish? Evangelicals have been quick to answer that question by turning to the cross. That is a biblical instinct yet one that needs some nuance lest the whole life of Christ be considered irrelevant to the Son's mission. If Jesus is the second Adam (Romans 5), then it is not only his death but also his whole life that is redemptive in nature. Here the church father Irenaeus is insightful, reminding Gospel readers that Matthew, Mark, Luke, and John, in all their diverse emphases, agree that the Son recapitulates the work of Adam and Israel but with an entirely different outcome than what Adam and Israel achieved. His mission is not only to die on behalf of sinners but to live on their behalf as well. Adam failed to obey, to fulfill the stipulations of the covenant at creation, but the Son listens to his Father, fulfilling every covenant stipulation so that those in Christ will eat from the tree of life eternally. If the first Adam failed to uphold the covenant of creation, the second Adam will establish a new covenant ratified not only by his sacrificial blood but in and through his obedience. Not only has he come to suffer and pay Adam's debt, but as Jesus reveals at his own baptism, he has also come to "fulfill all righteousness" (Matt. 3:15). Such righteousness by the last Adam matches the state of the first Adam even before the fall. Prior to Genesis 3, Adam was not only characterized by the absence of sin but was simultaneously defined by the presence of an original righteousness.[3] The fall, therefore, not only introduced the presence of sin, and with it sin's penalty (death), but also resulted in the loss of that original righteousness. Nevertheless, in Christ not only is such a penalty paid, but also righteousness is gained.

---

3. J. V. Fesko, *Justification: Understanding the Classic Reformed Doctrine* (Phillipsburg, NJ: P&R, 2008), 152.

Adam is not the only one Christ recapitulates in his obedience. Israel could not, and indeed would not, keep the law at Sinai, but Jesus enters the scene as the true Israel, an obedient son, born under the law, so that he might fulfill the law for all those to be adopted into the family of Abraham (Gal. 4:3–5). Jesus recapitulates the history of Israel when he is driven into the wilderness to be tempted by the devil (Matt. 4:1). Israel's forty years of wandering are pictured in Jesus fasting forty days and nights (4:2). But this time, when the tempter comes, the true Israel does not fall down to worship the devil in exchange for the world's glory; instead, he rebukes Satan—"Be gone, Satan!" He knows what "is written" by his Father, and in every temptation, he stands by his Father's word (4:10). Yet such temptations are necessary. Only if Christ is "tempted as we are" but is "without sin" can Adam's children "with confidence draw near to the throne of grace" (Heb. 4:15–16). Throughout the ministry of Jesus, then, it would prove necessary for Christ to learn "obedience through what he suffered" so that he might become "the source of eternal salvation" (5:8–9).

For Christ, the covenant of redemption and the covenant of creation are not unrelated in his act of recapitulation. "When we place the person and work of Christ in the context of the covenant of redemption (*pactum salutis*)," says Michael Horton, "we underscore his identity as the eternal Son, and in the context of the covenant of creation, his identity as the second Adam."[4] We might also add that it is only because he is the eternal Son that he can be sent by the Father to fulfill the covenant of creation as the second Adam. How necessary, too, since Adam's children need not only forgiveness, for breaking the law, but also righteousness, for failing to uphold the law. Apart from the eternal Son of God's incarnational active obedience as the last Adam, the justification of the ungodly is an impossibility; the covenant of redemption is void.[5]

The Form of a Servant and the Price of Liberation

As critical as recapitulation is for the fulfillment of the covenant of redemption and the justification of the ungodly, such recapitulation is designed to accompany the passive obedience that Christ endures by his suffering. His suffering does not start at the cross, however, but pervades his entire life. "From the time he took on the form of a servant," Calvin asserts, "he began to pay the price of liberation in order to redeem us."[6]

Nevertheless, it is at the cross that his whole life of suffering is brought to its culmination. At the cross Christ dies to make atonement, and such an atonement is penal to the core. The eternal Son of God has become incarnate not only to fulfill all righteousness as the last Adam but also to endure Adam's penalty for breaking the commands of his covenant Maker. Such a penalty is deserved by all those in Adam. For not only has the guilt of Adam's sin been imputed to his progeny, but also, because of the corrupt

---

4. Michael S. Horton, *Lord and Servant: A Covenant Christology* (Louisville: Westminster John Knox, 2005), 171–72.
5. For a full presentation of active obedience, see chap. 14, by Brandon Crowe, in this volume. Also see his book *The Last Adam: A Theology of the Obedient Life of Jesus in the Gospels* (Grand Rapids, MI; Baker Academic, 2017).
6. John Calvin, *Institutes of the Christian Religion*, trans. Henry Beveridge (Grand Rapids, MI: Eerdmans, 1957), 2.16.5.

nature that every child of Adam has received as a result, every person has acted corruptly, defying his or her Creator. Since we are curved in, entertaining the idols of our adulterous hearts, our guilt and condemnation increase. But even one transgression against the loving and personal God who made us would justify his wrath for eternity. Those outside Christ disagree, believing their sin to be of little consequence. Yet that is only because they compare their sin with that of other transgressors, as if the scales of justice turned on the horizontal plane. In Scripture, justice hangs vertically. On the last day, God will not divide the righteous from the wicked by contrasting whether one is as wicked as his or her neighbor; rather, each person will stand trial before God's infinite holiness and the beauty of his impeccable righteousness.

Positioned against God himself, no one will be able to excuse himself or herself but will realize that every single idolatrous thought deserves the unending wrath of retributive justice. Nevertheless, those in Christ fear no such wrath. For the Son of God himself has stepped down from the heavens and become incarnate, and "being found in human form, he humbled himself by becoming obedient to the point of death, even death on a cross" (Phil. 2:8). As much as the cross showcases the penal nature of Christ's suffering, even there Christ is active in his obedience to the Father. As Jesus prays after agonizing over the cup he is to drink, "Not my will, but yours, be done" (Luke 22:42).

Drinking the cup was, as Jesus himself testifies, to fulfill the Scriptures. As foretold by Isaiah, the suffering servant is a "man of sorrows" (Isa. 53:3):

> Surely he has borne our griefs
>   and carried our sorrows;
> yet we esteemed him stricken,
>   smitten by God, and afflicted.
> But he was pierced for our transgressions;
>   he was crushed for our iniquities;
> upon him was the chastisement that brought us peace,
>   and with his wounds we are healed. (53:4–5)

Isaiah has no hesitation interpreting such suffering in forensic categories. Transgressions, iniquities—these are the legal barriers that make justification an impossibility, that is, unless this man of sorrows is qualified and willing to be pierced for our lawbreaking, crushed for our hideous injustices.

The representation evident in this wrath-bearing substitute is foreshadowed by the prophets but brought into full view by the apostles. John, who is no stranger to the priestly, sacrificial language Jesus used in his Gospel, writes in his first letter, "In this is love, not that we have loved God but that he loved us and sent his Son to be the propitiation for our sins" (1 John 4:10; cf. 2:2). The author of Hebrews, whose entire letter revolves around the priestly office of Christ, can similarly say, "Therefore he had to be made like his brothers in every respect, so that he might become a merciful and faithful high priest in the service of God, to make propitiation for the sins of the people" (Heb. 2:17). As one would expect, such vernacular is not foreign to Paul either, who confesses Jesus to be the one "whom God put forward as a propitiation by his blood, to be received by faith" (Rom. 3:25). In case one doubts that Paul's use of "propitiation" is rooted in the justice of God, Paul then concludes, "This was to show God's righteousness, because in his divine forbearance he had passed over former sins" (3:25).

Despite ongoing controversy over the atonement, the New Testament is clear, especially in its use of the Old Testament, that Christ redeems by substituting himself for sinners and absorbing the wrath they deserve as a punishment for their sins. That affirmation does not preclude other biblical atonement motifs but makes them possible in the first place. The reason, for example, that Christ is victorious over the evil powers is because he has taken away the power Satan has over man, namely, the penalty of sin itself. By paying the sinner's debt, Christ liberates the sinner from Satan's accusation. Only by Christ's suffering the penalty of divine judgment is Satan stripped of his weapons of mass destruction; only by Christ's drinking the cup of wrath in full in our place is Satan relinquished of his condemning power. Even the resurrection, which is the ultimate signal of Satan's demise, is grounded in the payment for sin. By raising Christ from the dead, the Father is essentially announcing to the whole world that he is fully satisfied with the payment offered at the cross by his own Son. Jesus cries, "It is finished," as he breathes his last, but when he breathes resurrection air on the third day, it is the Father, now, who shouts, "It is finished." The resurrection *is* the vindication of Christ, and his empty tomb announces justification for all those in Christ. Undoubtedly, he "was delivered up for our trespasses," says Paul, but he was also "raised for our justification" (Rom. 4:25).[7]

A Marvelous Exchange

Justification, then, is grounded on the work of Christ *in toto*. Neither good merits nor faith itself can be the *basis* of right standing with God if Christ's obedience and sacrifice are sufficient. The believer's assurance rests not in himself but in an alien righteousness, one that is *extra nos*. Theologians of glory seek a righteousness within, by works of the law, but theologians of the cross turn entirely to the righteousness God gives *sola gratia*. They understand that "the righteousness of God has been manifested apart from the law" because it is a "righteousness of God through faith in Jesus Christ for all who believe" (Rom. 3:22). Relying on works is a fool's errand since "all have sinned and fall short of the glory of God" (3:23). Condemnation alone awaits those exposed by divine glory. However, justification awaits anyone who looks outside himself to Christ. He is "justified by his grace as a gift, through the redemption that is in Christ Jesus, whom God put forward as a propitiation by his blood, to be received by faith" (3:24–25; cf. 4:2–6).

A great, marvelous exchange has taken place: our guilt and with it the penalty our transgressions deserve have been transferred to Christ and paid in full; his obedience,

---
7. See chap. 12 in this volume, where I discuss further implications of resurrection and justification.

that is, his impeccable righteousness, has been imputed to us. As a result, we stand not only forgiven in the sight of a holy God but righteous: "For our sake he made him to be sin who knew no sin, so that in him we might become the righteousness of God" (2 Cor. 5:21). That righteousness is not inherent in us but is none other than the righteousness of our Savior credited to our account. Paul confesses that he does not have "a righteousness of [his] own that comes from the law, but that which comes through faith in Christ, the righteousness from God that depends on faith" (Phil. 3:9). On that basis, the righteous Judge of all the earth declares us righteous in his sight.

This great exchange is legal—"There is therefore now no *condemnation* for those who are in Christ Jesus" (Rom. 8:1)—but it could not be more personal. Far from some abstract transaction, the Father has so loved the sinner that he gave up his own Son, who himself weeps over Jerusalem before he brings his righteous obedience to its consummation at the cross. In Adam, "one trespass led to condemnation for all men," but Christ's "one act of righteousness leads to justification and life for all men" (5:18). Such righteousness is ours only through the obedience of our Lord: "For as by the one man's disobedience the many were made sinners, so by the one man's obedience the many will be made righteous" (5:19). Rather than reading 5:19 restrictively, as if only the penal nature of Christ's suffering is in view, one should instead understand Paul to say that the cross is "the *climax* of a course of obedience extending throughout [Christ's] entire earthly life and encompassing his fulfillment of every aspect of the law."[8]

Again, we are reminded of Paul's letter to the Philippians: "And being found in human form, he humbled himself by becoming obedient to the point of death, even death on a cross" (Phil. 2:8). The cross, therefore, is not where the obedience of Christ ends and his suffering begins; rather, the whole life of obedience Christ lived is brought to its defining moment as Jesus obeys the will of his Father in all its bitterness. Apart from the active obedience of Christ reaching its culmination at the cross and finding its judicial confirmation in the resurrection, Paul could not then rejoice in Christ's exaltation to the right hand of the Father. But he does, as indicated by his emphatic διό: "Therefore God has highly exalted him and bestowed on him the name that is above every name, so that at the name of Jesus every knee should bow, in heaven and on earth and under the earth, and every tongue confess that Jesus Christ is Lord, to the glory of God the Father" (2:9–11).[9] Apart from the obedience of Christ, the exaltation of Christ is unjustified, and consequently, so are we guilty sinners.

---

8. David VanDrunen, "To Obey Is Better Than Sacrifice: A Defense of the Active Obedience of Christ in the Light of Recent Criticism," in *By Faith Alone: Answering the Challenges to the Doctrine of Justification*, ed. Gary L. W. Johnson and Guy P. Waters (Wheaton, IL: Crossway, 2006), 145. See VanDrunen's extended exegetical discussion listing many reasons why this is the case.

9. VanDrunen explains, "Crucial for the present discussion is that Paul makes the exaltation the consequence of the obedience and the obedience the cause of the exaltation. Paul does this by connecting the conclusion of his description of Christ's obedience in [Phil.] 2:8 and the beginning of his description of Christ's exaltation with the strong causal conjunction διό: Christ 'was obedient unto death, even the death of the cross, *therefore* God exalted him' (AT). God exalted Christ on the basis of his obedience." VanDrunen, "To Obey Is Better Than Sacrifice," 146. Also see R. Scott Clark, "Do This and Live: Christ's Active Obedience as the Ground of Justification," in *Covenant, Justification, and Pastoral Ministry: Essays by the Faculty of Westminster Seminary California*, ed. R. Scott Clark (Phillipsburg, NJ: P&R, 2007), 230.

Faith as Instrumental

If Christ alone is the basis for justification, then his active and passive obedience are the object of saving faith. Faith itself is not the basis of justification, but it is the instrumental cause of justification. Paul articulates such theological nuance when he not only stresses that the "righteousness of God has been manifested apart from the law" (Rom. 3:21), eliminating works from justification entirely, but then adds that such righteousness comes "*through faith* in Jesus Christ for all who believe" (3:22). God is "just and the justifier of the *one who has faith* in Jesus" (3:26).

If justification occurs through faith in the redemptive work of Christ alone, then faith and works in the justification event are entirely antithetical to one another. To attempt, as so many have, to insert works, even Spirit-wrought works, into this forensic declaration would undermine the sufficiency and efficacy of Christ's propitiation. As Paul tells the Galatians, "If righteousness were through the law, then Christ died for no purpose" (Gal. 2:21). Additionally, the incorporation of works into justification would give the believer something to boast about. Even if the smallest contribution is added to Christ's finished work, justification would no longer be by grace *alone* through faith *alone*. But if faith alone is the channel through which our justification is pronounced, then boasting is an impossibility: "Then what becomes of our boasting? It is excluded. By what kind of law? By a law of works? No, but by the law of faith. For we hold that one is justified by faith apart from works of the law" (Rom. 3:27–28).

In Paul's context, *sola fide* is the hinge on which his mission endeavor turns. For Jew and Gentile are accepted by God just the same: through faith in the crucified and risen Lord:

> We ourselves are Jews by birth and not Gentile sinners; yet we know that a person is not justified by works of the law but through faith in Jesus Christ, so we also have believed in Christ Jesus, in order to be justified by faith in Christ and not by works of the law, because by works of the law no one will be justified. (Gal. 2:15–16)

Those righteous in God's sight, then, are not those who "rely on works of the law" (3:10) but those who "live by faith" (3:11; cf. Hab. 2:4).

The Revolution Caused by Justification

Like the apostle Paul, Martin Luther put forward his doctrine of justification, but it was not long until the antinomian objection surfaced. If the basis of justification excluded good works, how would the Christian life not be emptied of sanctifying transformation? If faith relied not on works but on Christ alone, how could faith not be severed entirely from the renewal that holiness brings?

Such an objection, however, fails to distinguish justification from sanctification. Justification is an instantaneous declaration by God that is possible due to the imputation (not infusion) of Christ's righteousness, whereas sanctification is a process that spans the Christian life in which the Spirit works internally to conform one to the image of Christ. The former is judicial, but the latter is sanative. This distinction Rome could neither conceive nor accept.

Yet such an objection also fails to see that justification and sanctification, distinguishable as they may be, are nevertheless inseparable. They are a double grace, a *duplex gratia*, which stems from union with Christ. In Calvin's words, "By partaking of him, we principally receive a double grace: namely, that being reconciled to God through Christ's blamelessness, we may have in heaven instead of a Judge a gracious Father; and secondly, that sanctified by Christ's spirit we may cultivate blamelessness and purity of life."[10] For the Reformers, as for the apostles, the sinner is justified by faith alone, but that faith is never alone.

The twofold gifts that stem from union with Christ, however, are not arbitrarily related or unrelated, which would only give the antinomian objection legitimacy.[11] For those in Christ, the forensic gives birth to the transformative; the legal grounds the relational (Rom. 5:16; 8:1–17; Gal. 3:14). One is not justified because he is sanctified, but he is sanctified because he is justified.[12] The new life the Spirit imparts is an impossibility if not grounded in the righteous status the Father imputes from his Son. Imitation of Christ turns Pelagian if not established by the imputation of Christ's righteousness. We dare not base the indicative of the gospel of our Lord Jesus Christ on the imperatives of the Christian life.[13] Geerhardus Vos writes, "The mystical is based on the forensic, not the forensic on the mystical."[14] Calvin before him says something similar: "For since we are clothed with the righteousness of the Son, we are reconciled to God, and renewed by the power of the Spirit to holiness."[15] The word "since" is critical, grounding the Spirit's work of renewal (holiness) on the righteousness of the Son (imputation).

Hence Paul can say that there is "no condemnation for those who are in Christ Jesus" and then turn to confidently assert that "if Christ is in you, although the body is dead because of sin, the Spirit is life because of righteousness" (Rom. 8:1, 10). With a new legal status in hand, the believer is no longer under the law; liberated from its power, he now sets his mind on the things of the Spirit. Paul could not more strongly

---

10. Calvin, *Institutes*, 3.11.1.
11. We should never set union with Christ over against the benefits of the *ordo salutis*. Such a false dichotomy is unnecessary and dangerous: "Reformed theologians have never felt any sense of self-contradiction in saying that justification and sanctification are twin benefits of union with Christ and that within the *ordo* sanctification depends on justification. The very notion of an *ordo* requires logical dependence." Michael Horton, *Justification*, NSD (Grand Rapids, MI; Zondervan Academic, 2018), 2:469.
12. J. V. Fesko, *Beyond Calvin: Union with Christ and Justification in Early Modern Reformed Theology (1517–1700)*, RHT 20 (Göttingen: Vandenhoeck & Ruprecht, 2012), 29–30.
13. On this point, see chap. 15, by David VanDrunen, in this volume.
14. And again: "Paul consciously and consistently subordinated the mystical aspect of the relation to Christ to the forensic one.... Paul's mind was to such an extent forensically oriented that he regarded the entire complex of subjective spiritual changes that take place in the believer and of subjective spiritual blessings enjoyed by the believer as the direct outcome of the forensic work of Christ applied in justification." Geerhardus Vos, "The Alleged Legalism in Paul's Doctrine of Justification," in *Redemptive History and Biblical Interpretation: The Shorter Writings of Geerhardus Vos*, ed. Richard B. Gaffin Jr. (Phillipsburg, NJ: P&R, 1980), 384.
15. Calvin, *Institutes*, 3.11.17. See Michael Horton, "Calvin's Theology of Union with Christ and the Double Grace: Modern Reception and Contemporary Possibilities," in *Calvin's Theology and Its Reception: Disputes, Developments, and New Possibilities*, ed. J. Todd Billings and I. John Hesselink (Louisville: Westminster John Knox, 2012), 72–96.

ground the Spirit's work in sanctification on the foundation of justification than when he transitions from the objective to the subjective in Romans 8:3–6:

> For God has done what the law, weakened by the flesh, could not do. By sending his own Son in the likeness of sinful flesh and for sin, he condemned sin in the flesh, in order that the righteous requirement of the law might be fulfilled in us, who walk not according to the flesh but according to the Spirit. For those who live according to the flesh set their minds on the things of the flesh, but those who live according to the Spirit set their minds on the things of the Spirit. For to set the mind on the flesh is death, but to set the mind on the Spirit is life and peace.

If these two graces are inseparable, justification grounding and causing sanctification, then it should be little surprise to discover in the Scriptures that the doctrine of justification leads to authentic, sanctifying change in people, reorienting their personal identity, reconstituting the purpose for which they live. Called to a land he had not seen, promised an heir born from a body long expired, Abraham was told to number the stars, for that was how numerous his offspring would be. "And he believed the LORD, and he counted it to him as righteousness" (Gen. 15:6). Counted righteous, Abraham became the patriarch of God's covenant people. Not only was *sola fide* instrumental to receiving a new status (righteousness), but Abraham's faith in the promises of God would be exemplary for the true spiritual heirs to come, as the apostle Paul demonstrates in his letter to the Romans (4:1–25).

But Abraham never saw those covenant promises fulfilled. That privilege would be for his offspring instead. Nevertheless, justification by faith alone not only generated a new forensic identity for the patriarch but from that moment forward reconfigured the way he perceived his God-given mission. Submitting to circumcision (Gen. 17:1–14), interceding for Sodom (18:22–33), sacrificing Isaac (22:1–19), recruiting a wife for the heir of the promise (24:1–28)—these are not the works of a man seeking a justification otherwise uncertain; rather, these are the works that stem from faith. Here is the fruit of a sinner already declared righteous; on display are the sanctifying deeds of a man justified and reconciled with God.

The apostle Paul was no stranger to the revolution that justification could effect. The persecutor of Christ's church believed himself to be entirely secure, asserting the credentials of his Judaic zeal, with every reason to take pride in the national identity he inherited and the works of the law that gave him confidence in the flesh:

> If anyone else thinks he has reason for confidence in the flesh, I have more: circumcised on the eighth day, of the people of Israel, of the tribe of Benjamin, a Hebrew of Hebrews; as to the law, a Pharisee; as to zeal, a persecutor of the church; as to righteousness under the law, blameless. (Phil. 3:4–6)

However, when confronted by the risen, vindicated, justified Christ, Paul abandoned any trust in himself, looking instead to a righteousness alien to himself, that is, a righteousness found in Christ:

> But whatever gain I had, I counted as loss for the sake of Christ. Indeed, I count everything as loss because of the surpassing worth of knowing Christ Jesus my Lord. For his sake I have suffered the loss of all things and count them as rubbish, in order that I may gain Christ and be found in him, not having a righteousness of my own that comes from the law, but that which comes through faith in Christ, the righteousness from God that depends on faith. (3:7–9)

For the apostle, the "righteousness from God that depends on faith" is Abrahamic through and through. Like Abraham, Paul was declared righteous through faith *alone*, and the righteous status reckoned to him was not his own. While Abraham trusted in God's promise to give him an heir, that heir had come in and through Christ, so that "if you are Christ's, then you are Abraham's offspring, heirs according to promise" (Gal. 3:29; cf. 3:9). After the Damascus road, there was no question that Paul was Christ's.

Also, as with Abraham, Paul's new judicial status—being clothed in the righteousness of Christ—resulted in, produced, and caused a lifelong transformation. He counted "everything as loss because of the surpassing worth of knowing Christ," so that he "may know him and the power of his resurrection, and may share his sufferings, becoming like him in his death," so that "by any means possible" Paul "may attain the resurrection from the dead" (Phil. 3:8, 10–11). And know Christ's sufferings he did, imprisoned repeatedly until he suffered the same fate as his Savior.

The Organic Connection between the *Historia Salutis* and *Ordo Salutis*

Yet we would be mistaken to think that Paul somehow moved past the imputed righteousness of Christ he claimed in his letter to the Philippians. While we might overreach to conclude that it was the center of his thought, there can be no denying that it was essential to Paul's understanding of "the Way" (Acts 9:2). As Romans, 2 Corinthians, and Galatians demonstrate, Paul found it impossible to define union with Christ apart from the believer's new forensic identity, an identity (status) grounded in the perfect obedience of the crucified, risen, and righteous one himself (e.g., Rom. 3:21–26; 2 Cor. 5:21; Gal. 3:10–14). Today many are persuaded by those who claim that the gospel is to be kept away from the domain of justification. While Paul refused to confuse the two, nevertheless, his rebuke of the Galatians assumes an organic and necessary connection between the two. To abandon justification *sola fide* and the free imputation of Christ's righteousness to those who believe is to forfeit the gospel itself (Gal. 1:6–9).

Paul undoubtedly knew the difference between the *historia salutis* and the *ordo salutis*, a distinction that pervades Romans. Yet it was precisely because Paul understood the difference between redemption accomplished and redemption applied that he found it inconceivable to consider one without the other. God has "put forward" Christ "as a propitiation" so that he would be "received by faith" and we would be "justified by his grace as a gift" (Rom. 3:24–25). "For our sake" God "made him [Christ] to be sin"—why?—"so that in him we might become the righteousness of God" (2 Cor. 5:21).

The inseparable link between the *historia salutis* and the *ordo salutis* is not uniquely Pauline either but permeates Johannine thought as well:

> For God so loved the world, that he gave his only Son, that whoever believes in him should not perish but have eternal life. For God did not send his Son into the world to condemn the world, but in order that the world might be saved through him. Whoever believes in him is not condemned, but whoever does not believe is condemned already, because he has not believed in the name of the only Son of God. (John 3:16–18)

Apparently, forensic categories are not only vital to Paul's gospel (Gal. 1:6–9; 2:15–3:29) but are also just as critical to John's gospel (see also 1 John 1:1–9; 2:2; 4:9–10).

Witnessing the corrosion of justification and imputation, the Reformers grieved that the gospel of free judicial grace had been so corrupted in their day. Like Paul's tone with the Galatians, Martin Luther, Philipp Melanchthon, John Calvin, and others were outraged at doctrinal infidelity in the church, especially on something as central as soteriology. Like Paul (and John), the Reformers saw no disconnect between the cross and faith. To segregate redemption accomplished from redemption applied would have undermined the intrinsic connection between *solus Christus* and *sola fide*. Misconstruing one leads to the fatality of the other, a reality by no means hypothetical to the Reformers, who were products of Rome's soteriological misconception.

Justification Centrality

When the Reformers were enlightened by the Scriptures, their eyes having been opened to the forensic nature of justification and imputation over against Rome's sanative view of infused grace, they were unembarrassed to stress that justification is central not only to a biblical view of the gospel but also to the entire Christian faith. Luther labeled the evangelical doctrine of justification "the first and chief article" in the Smalcald Articles.[16] Calvin said that justification "is the ground on which religion must be supported," warning that "unless you understand first of all what your position is before God, and what the judgment which he passes upon you, you have no foundation on which your salvation can be laid, or on which piety towards God can be reared."[17] Peter Martyr Vermigli was convinced that justification is "the head, fountain, and mainstay of all religion."[18] And though it was not the Reformers but Johann Heinrich Alsted (1618) who said that justification is "the doctrine on which the church stands or falls," nevertheless, the Reformers would certainly have agreed.[19]

Yet again, the revolution justification would cause was not foreign to the Reformers. As with Abraham and Paul, so too did the Reformers believe that the divine declaration

---

16. "Smalcald Articles," 2, in *BOC*, 301.
17. Calvin, *Institutes*, 3.11.1.
18. Peter Martyr Vermigli, *Predestination and Justification: Two Theological Loci*, trans. and ed. Frank A. James III, Peter Martyr Library 8 (Kirksville, MO: Thomas Jefferson University Press, 2003), 96.
19. See Alister E. McGrath, *Iustitia Dei: A History of the Christian Doctrine of Justification*, 2nd ed. (Cambridge: Cambridge University Press, 1998), 448n3.

of new forensic status in Christ would acutely produce the fruits of sanctification, contrary to popular antinomian accusations. For example, at the start of his 1535 *Lectures on Galatians*, Luther accentuated not only what's at stake in the doctrine ("If it is lost and perishes, the whole knowledge of truth, life, and salvation is lost and perishes at the same time") but also what is gained:

> But it is because, as I often warn you, there is a clear and present danger that the devil may take away from us the pure doctrine of faith and may substitute for it the doctrine of works and of human traditions. It is very necessary, therefore, that this doctrine of faith be continually read and heard in public. No matter how well known it may be or how carefully learned, the devil, our adversary, who prowls around and seeks to devour us (1 Peter 5:8), is not dead. Our flesh also goes on living. Besides, temptations of every sort attack and oppress us on every side. Therefore this doctrine can never be discussed and taught enough. If it is lost and perishes, the whole knowledge of truth, life, and salvation is lost and perishes at the same time. But if it flourishes, everything good flourishes—religion, true worship, the glory of God, and the right knowledge of all things and of all social conditions.[20]

In Luther's mind, as in Paul's, everything flourishes if justification is rightly understood, including worship and society itself. The Reformers not only feared what would be lost if justification *sola fide* vanished but rejoiced at the prospects of what might be gained should it be embraced.

The Foolishness of Justification

Understandably, heirs of the Reformation today envy the task of the sixteenth century. What appeared to be chaos to the Reformers—facing as they did opposition from Rome and certain radicals—was but bijou compared to the onslaught of ambiguity over justification that would circulate the modern and postmodern eras. This side of the sixteenth century, the evangelical doctrine faces challenges not only from Rome but also from movements as influential, variegated, and evolving as Protestant liberalism, neoorthodoxy, New Finnish Lutheranism, post-Vatican II Catholicism, Newman's *via media*, the Federal Vision, and the New Perspective on Paul. In the eyes of many, the material principle of the Reformation, and the doctrine of imputation it brings with it, is considered foolishness. So normal is it to criticize the Reformation doctrine that it takes courage to be Protestant in the twenty-first century.

The contributors to this volume, however, welcome the opportunity to be named fools if it means being identified with the "foolishness of God" (1 Cor. 1:25). Such foolishness is wiser than the cleverness of humanity's most *en vogue* justification theories. If "Christ crucified" continues to be a "stumbling block" (1 Cor. 1:23) today, as it was in Paul's day, then it should not surprise us that the justification secured at the cross and

---

20. Martin Luther, *Lectures on Galatians* (1535), LW 26:3.

resurrection (Rom. 4:25) would be a stumbling block in our own day, "folly" (1 Cor. 1:23) to its critics and revisionaries.

That justification and imputation are considered folly to many today might lead some evangelicals to put their heads in the sand—along with their doctrine of justification. Paul took a different approach. Being named a fool did not lead him to retreat into intellectual isolationism but emboldened him to rearticulate his justification theology for a brave new theological world. He was impelled to stand in the Areopagus and converse with the philosophers, all in order to explain, clarify, and defend the faith. He was pressed to rebuke the Galatians—or even Peter himself—whenever he saw the gospel being tarnished by modifications or revisions of justification *sola gratia* and *sola fide*. No one can accuse Paul of not understanding just what was at stake, nor of forgetting just what might be gained.

So, too, does this volume wade into the deep waters of the doctrine of justification sensing the weightiness of what is at stake. In the twenty-first century, challenges to justification are legion. No longer do they surface from one or two disciplines, but they can be seen in nearly every field of study. For any treatment of justification to be taken seriously, therefore, it must provide a robust articulation, explanation, and defense of justification within the contours of biblical, theological, historical, and pastoral studies. To meet that challenge, *The Doctrine on Which the Church Stands or Falls* brings together a community of scholars, some of the most outstanding evangelical thinkers in their respective disciplines, so that the next generation of evangelicals will remain faithful, equipped to contend for the faith once for all delivered to the saints (Jude 3). Our hope, indeed, our prayer, is not merely that such a doctrine might reconfigure the believer's personal identity in union with the risen Christ but that this material principle might reconstitute the purpose for which the Christian and the church exist, recognizing that only in a God who justifies the ungodly will it live, move, and have its being.

PART ONE

JUSTIFICATION IN BIBLICAL PERSPECTIVE

1

"He Believed the Lord"

The Pedigree of Justification in the Pentateuch

STEPHEN DEMPSTER

It is indisputable that the Pauline doctrine of justification is grounded in a reading of the Old Testament.[1] The apostle did not create the doctrine *ex nihilo*. As with other doctrines formulated by New Testament authors, they have their start in Genesis if not in other parts of Israel's Scriptures. These sacred writings gave Paul common ground with his theological opponents. They never argued over the fact of their authority or their extent, but they did argue about their interpretation.

Paul uses a number of texts in seeking to prove his doctrine that God justifies the wicked through faith in Christ. But the most important for him is Genesis 15:6, where we read these words: "He [Abram] believed in the Lord, and he reckoned/credited it to him for righteousness."[2] Paul cites this verse three times (Rom. 4:3, 22; Gal. 3:6; cf. Rom. 4:9), and it provides the conceptual substructure for his discussion of faith, grace, works, and law. In fact, one commentator's statement could be viewed as representative of many: "For Paul this Old Testament verse is the classic passage for justification by faith alone apart from the works of the law."[3] And another is not far off the same mark: "Genesis 15:6 is the hermeneutical key for Paul's reading of Abraham's story, and the

---

1. I would like to thank the following scholars for reading this essay and supplying helpful insight: Craig Carter, Stan Fowler, Peter Gentry, Steven Kempf, Byron Wheaton, and Walter Moberly. While we may have disagreements, I deeply appreciate their interaction. I would also like to dedicate this essay to one of my former students, Daniel Cooper, who presented a memorable paper on this topic in a class presentation.
2. Unless otherwise noted, Scripture quotations in this chapter are my own translations.
3. Manfred Oeming, "Ist Genesis 15:6 ein Beleg für die Anrechnung des Glaubens zur Gerechtigkeit," *ZAW* 95, no. 2 (1983): 182. The original reads, "Für Paulus ist dieser Vers der alttestamentliche locus classicus für die Rechtfertigung allein aus Glauben ohne Werke des Gesetzes."

one act of Abraham that Paul ever emphasizes is Abraham's faith."[4] Still another scholar in no way understates the significance of this verse: "No other Old Testament text has exercised such a compelling influence on the New Testament."[5]

It is often mentioned in this discussion that James uses the same text to prove that with God justification is by works, not by faith (James 2:23), a distinctive early Christian perspective that seems to directly contradict Paul's view. A significant number of modern scholars would agree that Paul has essentially distorted the meaning of Genesis 15:6 in the interest of his view of justification by faith. Reinhard Feldmeier and Hermann Spieckermann write in their magisterial *God of the Living*, "Neither does God make Abraham just, nor does Abraham effect anything for other people through his faith."[6] Another commentator states explicitly, "The verse [Gen. 15:6] has no relation to the dogma of 'justification by faith.'"[7] Paul thus reads this verse "through Christian glasses."[8] James Barr, ever the contrarian, argues that

> the most prominent example of Christianizing [the Old Testament] . . . lies in the conception of justification by faith. . . . Justification by faith is, among the convictions that Christian Old Testament theologians have most often held, the one where they have been most reluctant to give up the "Christianizing" of the Hebrew Bible.[9]

Part of Barr's argument is that the entire doctrine may be based on a mistranslation of the Hebrew of Genesis 15:6[10] and that another "correct" translation has developed somewhat of a following and provides "a new perspective" on this Old Testament text.[11]

Along with Barr's criticism coming from a Christian direction in Old Testament studies, another comes from a more Jewish angle. In an important essay, Jon Levenson criticizes the traditional Christian reading as exemplified in Gerhard von Rad's exegesis of Genesis 15:6.[12] He argues that such a reading privileges a part of the narrative and is essentially in conflict with another part, Genesis 26:5, where it states that Abraham kept the law—that is, Abraham had established a reservoir of merit through his good deeds and was therefore justified in God's sight. Von Rad thus is accused of taking 15:6 in "isolation from the rest of the Abraham material in the Hebrew Bible and indeed

---

4. Orrey McFarland, "Whose Abraham, Which Promise? Genesis 15.6 in Philo's *De Virtutibus* and Romans 4," *JSNT* 35, no. 2 (2012): 119.
5. Walter Brueggemann, *Genesis*, IBC (Louisville: Westminster John Knox, 2010), 146.
6. Reinhard Feldmeier and Hermann Spieckermann, *God of the Living: A Biblical Theology* (Waco, TX: Baylor University Press, 2011), 293.
7. Benno Jacob, *The First Book of the Bible: Genesis*, ed. Ernest I. Jacob and Walter Jacob (Jerusalem: KTAV, 2007), 100.
8. Lloyd Gaston, "Abraham and the Righteousness of God," *HBT* 2, no. 1 (1980): 40.
9. James Barr, *The Concept of Biblical Theology: An Old Testament Perspective* (Minneapolis: Fortress, 1999), 261–62.
10. Similarly, for example, Thomas Römer remarks, "If this understanding is right, Genesis 15:6 has nothing to do with 'justification by faith.'" "Abraham's Righteousness and Sacrifice: How to Understand (and Translate) Genesis 15 and 22," *CV* 54, no. 1 (2012): 14.
11. This is, of course, a wordplay on the New Perspective in Pauline theology and not to be confused with it. See Benjamin Schliesser, *Abraham's Faith in Romans 4: Paul's Concept of Faith in Light of the History of Reception of Genesis 15:6*, WUNT, 2nd ser., vol. 224 (Tübingen: Mohr Siebeck, 2007), 115.
12. Gerhard von Rad, "Faith Reckoned as Righteousness," in *The Problem of the Hexateuch and Other Essays*, trans. E. W. Trueman Dicken (London: Oliver and Boyd, 1966), 125–30.

"He Believed the Lord"   43

from the Hebrew Bible itself."[13] Thus, we have two types of interpretation, "a Pauline type which takes the verse in isolation and insists on the autonomy of faith and a Philonic type, in which faith and the observance of commandments are each predicated of Abraham on the basis of texts in Genesis."[14] Indeed, this "rabbinic"[15] view has received further support from Walter Moberly, who argues that, contrary to von Rad, the best way to interpret Genesis 15 is through the lens of another text, Psalm 106:30–31, where Phinehas is credited with righteousness as a reward for his act of zeal on behalf of Yahweh.[16] Thus, Abram's faith is more about his faithfulness than his faith, more about obedience than any one act of faith, and this provides a solid basis for this text to be understood in line with the rabbinic doctrine of merit. Thus, Moberly accounts for a significant Jewish strand of interpretation that connects Abram's faith in Genesis 15 with his act of obedience in Genesis 22.[17] While Moberly still believes that the Pauline understanding has a place at the interpretive table, it is only one option.

In light of these concerns, this essay seeks to examine the evidence afresh and explore this influential text to determine its meaning and significance *within the Pentateuch*.

The Significance of Genesis 15

Genesis 15 is a pivotal text in the Abraham story, and of course, the Abraham narrative is crucial for the book of Genesis and the Torah as a whole, because it is the first of the so-called patriarchal narratives, which describe the beginning of the nation of Israel. This chapter contains the first account that formalizes the divine-human relationship between Abram and God in the form of a covenant, it is the first major dialogue that takes place between these two "partners,"[18] and it is in this text that Abram for the first time speaks directly with God.[19] Before this time, he has heard the word of God and simply obeyed, but now for the first time he actually addresses God. From a narrative point of view, the first time that a speaker talks in a story is often considered revelatory of the person and his or her state of mind and is extremely significant for the events as they unfold.[20] God is the first speaker in Genesis, and his words are "Let there be light!"

---

13. Jon D. Levenson, *The Hebrew Bible, the Old Testament, and Historical Criticism: Jews and Christians in Biblical Studies* (Louisville: Westminster John Knox, 1993), 60.
14. Levenson, *Hebrew Bible*, 59.
15. It is not completely accurate to call this a Jewish view, since Paul, for example, was definitely a Jew, and so were most of the first Christians.
16. R. W. L. Moberly, "Abraham's Righteousness (Genesis Xv 6)," in *Studies in the Pentateuch*, ed. J. A. Emerton, VTSup 41 (Leiden: Brill, 1990), 103–30.
17. E.g., see 1 Macc. 2:52: "Was not Abraham found faithful in testing [Genesis 22] and it was credited to him for righteousness [Genesis 15]"; Sir. 44:19–20: "Abraham was a great father of many people . . . who kept the law of the most High, and was in covenant with him: he established the covenant in his flesh; and when he was proved [Genesis 22], he was found faithful [Genesis 15]."
18. So also Victor P. Hamilton, *The Book of Genesis, Chapters 1–17*, NICOT (Grand Rapids, MI: Eerdmans, 1995), 334.
19. John H. Sailhamer, *The Pentateuch as Narrative: A Biblical-Theological Commentary* (Grand Rapids, MI: Zondervan, 1995), 127. It can be assumed that Abram speaks with God before this time, but no explicit words of his are recorded. See Gen. 12:8 and 13:18, where one could assume that Abram spoke to God.
20. As Robert Alter notes, "In any given narrative event, and especially at the beginning of any new story, the point at which dialogue first emerges will be worthy of special attention, and in most instances, the initial words spoken by a personage will be revelatory, perhaps more in manner than in matter, constituting an important moment in the expression of character." *The Art of Biblical Narrative*, 2nd ed. (New York: Basic Books, 2011), 94.

(1:3). The serpent's first words are "Has God really said . . . ?" (3:1). Cain's first words are "Am I my brother's keeper?" (4:9). In this text, Abram, the prospective father of the nation of Israel, speaks his first words to God, and they reveal an anxious state of mind that has been bothering him for some time (15:2–3), and his second word to God, a year before Isaac will be born, amplifies this anxiety (17:17–18). So, obviously, this text is a critical one in the Abraham story.

Moreover, in this text there are some significant differences from the surrounding context. It is the first example in the Abraham narrative where the author uses asyndeton to indicate a major break in the flow (15:1 begins without a conjunction), and the text contains another example at the ending of the episode (15:18), which functions to explain what happened in this particular section.[21] This text in a sense functions as an important transition marker in the narrative. Before this time, the narrative has focused explicitly on the promise of land. This text formalizes that promise with a covenant and a divine oath that secures the future land for Abraham's descendants, but it also introduces the theme of the next chapters that focus on seed and concludes with another divine oath securing the future for the seed.[22] Unlike many of the narratives in Genesis, chapter 15 contains explicit theological reflection, or narrative explanation. The events in the story are not just left to explain themselves, as one finds in many of the stories of the patriarchs; the narrator provides commentary: "This means that . . ."[23] Moreover, here appear the only reference to faith and righteousness in the Torah and the first mention of the Abrahamic covenant, both of which become important themes in the Scriptures. Furthermore, in this text the writer is aware of the remainder of the Pentateuch, as there is a prophecy of the nascent Israel's descent into Egypt, an allusion to the burning bush, and predictions of the liberation from Egypt and even the conquest of Canaan (Gen. 15:13–16)![24] Moberly's comments in no way understate the significance of Genesis 15: "Genesis xv gives the impression of being the fullest and most formal portrayal of Yahweh's commitment to Israel (both people and land) in the whole Abraham cycle, a portrayal of unusual and imaginatively suggestive character."[25]

The Abraham Narrative in the Torah

In the larger story of the Torah, the patriarchal narratives, of which the Abraham story is the first, "are set within the framework of the primaeval history on the one side (Gen 1–11), and the establishment of the nation [of Israel] on the other [Ex–Deut]."[26] Abram

---

21. These represent the two major functions of asyndeton within Hebrew *narrative*: a new start and an explanation. See Stephen G. Dempster, "Linguistic Features of Hebrew Narrative: A Discourse Analysis of Narrative from the Classical Period" (PhD diss., University of Toronto, 1985), 40–47.

22. That second oath is found in Gen. 22:16–18. For an insightful analysis, see Byron Wheaton, "Focus and Structure in the Abraham Narratives," *TJ*, n.s., 27, no. 1 (2006): 143–62.

23. Cf. esp. Gen. 15:6, 18–21. See also 22:1, 18–19.

24. See also the work of John Ha, *Genesis 15: A Theological Compendium of Pentateuchal History*, BZAW 181 (Berlin: de Gruyter, 1989).

25. Moberly, "Abraham's Righteousness," 119.

26. Brevard S. Childs, *Old Testament Theology in a Canonical Context* (Philadelphia: Fortress, 1985), 218.

has been called out of Mesopotamia by God (Gen. 12:1–3). He has been promised that he will become a great nation, receive a great name, and be blessed, as well as be a source of universal blessing. Those who bless Abram will in turn be blessed, and the one who curses him will be cursed. All this suggests that Abram and his future descendants are set on an unstoppable mission of universal blessing.

The syntax of Abram's call is straightforward: two imperatives to Abram followed by three promises each:[27]

> Go from your country and your kindred and your father's house to the land I will show you.
> I will make of you a great nation,
> I will bless you,
> I will make your name great. (12:1–2a)
>
> Be a blessing—
> I will bless those who bless you,
> I will curse the one who curses you,
> All the families of the earth will be blessed in you. (12:2b–3)

Thus, there are two distinct sections, each introduced by an imperative followed by a trio of verbs. The first trio emphasizes becoming a great nation, and the second stresses a role among the nations, culminating in the mother of all blessings—blessing for the entire world. In other words, the promise to Abram reaches its goal "when it includes all the families of the earth."[28]

These two sections anticipate two "panels" in the Abraham narrative, the first one focusing on land and concluding with a covenant in response to the patriarch's great faith (12:4–15:21) and the second one focusing on descendants and the patriarch's great act of obedience (16:1–22:23). Moreover, the beginning of the Abraham narrative is echoed near the end of the story, when his second call, to offer his son as a holocaust offering, uses the same language of divine demand as his first call, to depart Mesopotamia (Genesis 22). These are the only times this linguistic construction occurs in the Bible, and thus it provides bookends for the Abraham story.[29] Thus, the first divine call commands the patriarch to give up his past, represented by three descriptors: country, kindred, and father's house (12:1). The second call asks him to give up his future and raises the stakes with four descriptors of Abraham's miracle heir: your

---

27. For full discussion, see Peter J. Gentry and Stephen J. Wellum, *Kingdom through Covenant: A Biblical-Theological Understanding of the Covenants* (Wheaton, IL: Crossway, 2012), 230–35.

28. Ralph W. Klein, "Call, Covenant, and Community: The Story of Abraham and Sarah," *CurTM* 15 (1988): 121. This is true whether one understands the final *niphal* stem verb as reflexive or passive. The passive emphasizes more the agency of Israel. For extended discussion and the various options, see Gentry and Wellum, *Kingdom through Covenant*, 233–41. Gentry emphasizes the use of a passive meaning for the *niphal* stem and a middle meaning for the *hithpael* stem of the relevant verb. Walter Moberly highlights the reflexive meaning of the verb and consequently downplays its missional significance, seeing Abram as a model for blessing rather than a mediator of blessing. But as Klein argues above, while the reflexive meaning downplays the mediator role, the universal significance is not affected. See R. W. L. Moberly, *The Theology of the Book of Genesis* (Cambridge: Cambridge University Press, 2009).

29. The construction is found in Gen. 12:1 and 22:2: לֶךְ־לְךָ. Many commentators make this observation.

son, your only son, the one whom you love, Isaac (22:2).³⁰ Significantly, the second call reemphasizes that Abraham's descendants will be the means of universal blessing, this time because of Abraham's obedience (cf. 12:3; 22:18).

This call to personal and universal blessing at the beginning and ending of the Abraham story, of course, is set against the backdrop of a world gone awry. The world in fact lies under curse and not under blessing. The pristine world of harmony and goodness that was created for the first human couple to thrive in and be blessed has turned into a world of sin, death, and alienation. The stunning world of harmony and wonder whose goodness filled God's vision with delight has become a horror show that tears apart the divine heart as he sees his creation being violated.³¹ Adam and Eve have sinned and been sent into exile from the garden (3:23–24), Cain has killed his brother and been exiled (4:10–16), and the flood has "exiled" a sinful human race from existence (Genesis 6–9). Even after the flood, the human community *en masse* has revolted by seeking to storm heaven and make a name for itself, and it has in turn been exiled from that location and scattered across the face of the earth (11:8–9). In each example, with the exception of the last, God has shown grace—in providing clothes for the first couple and giving them a promise, in providing Cain with a mark of protection, in saving Noah and his family and the creatures of the earth in an ark.³² And this salvation is because Noah, the tenth generation from Adam, is clearly a righteous person (6:9; 7:1). Because of this righteousness, God has made a covenant with all creation.

Righteousness is absolutely central to covenant and creation, and without it the created order cannot continue. Yet it is clear that after the flood and the covenant with Noah, nothing has changed in terms of the general human condition. Humanity is as evil after the flood as it was before, although Noah, the world's savior, is righteous (6:5–8; 8:21; see also 6:9; 7:1). Although God promises that he will never destroy the world by flood again, humans continue to rebel, the paradigmatic example being the Tower of Babel, where the building of this huge tower is a gargantuan expression of human hubris to make a name for itself (11:1–9). Yet even here, God disperses the builders of the tower across the face of the earth. In many of these cases, God has been concerned with "damage control."³³ But it is with Abram that God makes a significant new start, moving beyond "damage control" to decisively restore the lost conditions of Paradise and reverse the curses of Adam.³⁴

Whereas the presence of curse has been explicitly mentioned five times in the narrative of Genesis 3–11 (3:14, 17; 4:11; 5:29; 9:25), with the call of Abram in 12:2–3,

---

30. Jon D. Levenson shows that the descriptors in the second story recall those in the first, but he does not make the point about the escalation of the cost of obedience. See his fine study *Inheriting Abraham: The Legacy of the Patriarch in Judaism, Christianity, and Islam* (Princeton, NJ: Princeton University Press, 2012), 67.
31. Cf., e.g., the repetition of "goodness" in Genesis 1 with the repetition of "violence" in Genesis 6.
32. Gerhard von Rad, *Genesis: A Commentary*, trans. John H. Marks (Philadelphia: Westminster, 1973), 152–55.
33. Levenson, *Inheriting Abraham*, 20.
34. Levenson, *Inheriting Abraham*, 20.

blessing appears in a rapid-fire succession of phrases, in fact, five times.³⁵ Moreover, the promise of universal blessing is repeated another four times in the narrative of Genesis (18:18; 22:18; 26:4; 28:14), matching the fivefold blessing in 12:2–3! Against a context of death and disorder, God decisively blesses Abram; against a backdrop of people questing for fame and glory in the construction of a tower, Abram will receive a great name; against a backstory of exile and alienation, Abram is going to get land and become a great nation; against the dark canvas of a world that has descended once again to being תֹהוּ וָבֹהוּ (1:2: "without form and void" [KJV]; "formless and empty" [NIV]; "a formless void" [NRSV]), God is going to shine his light of universal blessing through Abram.

But it is extremely significant that as Noah represented the tenth generation from Adam, Abram is the tenth from Noah. Noah's righteousness saved not the world of his time but only his own family and the animals, but it is said of Abram that through him all the families of the earth will be blessed—not just one. Yet as the story unfolds, nothing is heard about Abram's righteousness, nor about a covenant. Not only do the questions about Abram's progeny and possession of the land drive the narrative forward to seek an answer, but also do the closely related questions of righteousness and covenant. Prior to his call, given the context, it can be assumed that Abram can be classed as unrighteous just as everyone else was, with the exception of Noah in the distant past, with whom a covenant with creation had been made. Although he is never called "unrighteous," that is a clear implication of his backstory.³⁶ But if he is to be the savior of the world in a far greater sense than Noah, will God work differently now because of the problem of sin? What about another covenant, and what about righteousness? The reader must wait to hear the answers to these questions.

As the story unfolds, Abraham experiences many trials. His journey to the land of Canaan is derailed in Haran for a while until after his father dies (11:31–32).³⁷ When he arrives at his destination in Canaan, it is occupied by Canaanites, and the promises of land and nationhood seem a remote reality. To make matters worse, as soon as he enters the land, he makes a hasty exit because of a severe famine (12:6, 10–20). In fact, the only land that Abram will personally own in Canaan will be a graveyard for his wife, purchased for an outrageous sum of money (Genesis 23). The delay in land possession requires an explanation.

Moreover, "the facts on the ground" about future progeny for the future patriarch and matriarch are not auspicious either. Their biological clocks are ticking. They are not

---

35. See Hans Walter Wolff, "The Kerygma of the Yahwist," in Walter Brueggemann and Hans Walter Wolff, *The Vitality of Old Testament Traditions*, 2nd ed. (Atlanta: John Knox, 1982), 54–55.

36. See McFarland, who cites Schliesser regarding Paul's use of the Abraham story: "Nowhere does Scripture call Abraham (anything like) 'ungodly,' yet it is impossible *not* to deduce from the apostle's line of thought that he *de facto* does so." McFarland, "Whose Abraham, Which Promise?," 115n43. See further Schliesser, *Abraham's Faith*, 345. To be sure, humanity as ungodly is seen as an ontological state apart from God's righteousness. For other biblical evidence regarding Abram's backstory, one has to go no further than Josh. 24:2–3 to see an almost casual reference to his idolatry.

37. There is a problem in the chronology here, which can be rectified if Terah died at the age of 145 (Samaritan Pentateuch). See Gen. 11:27 and 12:4. There are other problems regarding the call as well, which some translations rectify by rendering God's speech to Abram as pluperfect, "had said," in 12:1. These issues do not impinge on the issues relevant to this essay.

getting any younger. Abram was called at the age of seventy-five, and his wife was sixty-five, with no prospect of an heir, except perhaps Lot, Abram's nephew, and he has now departed (13:12–13). And although Abram rescues him from Mesopotamian armies, Lot returns to Sodom (Genesis 14; 19). Now—perhaps a decade after Abram's initial call[38]—there has been no progress in fulfillment. If the promise of receiving land seems a bit of a stretch, the prospect of descendants and becoming a great nation is doubly so. Later it will seem ludicrous and laughable, as Sarai's womb is considered "dead" at the age of eighty-nine; the aged couple then will laugh incredulously at the reiteration of the divine promise (17:17; 18:12).[39]

As one reads through the first half of the Abram story, Abram's situation has begun to change. He has just recently won a major battle in which he was vastly outnumbered by Mesopotamian armies (Genesis 14). In defeating four kings and their armies, his royal status has begun to emerge. He has rescued his nephew and his family along with a number of Canaanite kings—and has done so with only 318 armed men (14:14). On his way home from his triumph, he is met by an enigmatic figure, a king of Salem, named Melchizedek, who appears out of nowhere to invoke a divine blessing on him:

> Blessed be Abram by God Most High,
>   Creator of heaven and earth.
> Blessed be God Most High,
>   who delivered your enemies into your hand. (14:19–20)

Abram gives him a tithe and refuses to accept any wealth from his conquest, letting God be the sole source of his blessing. But this blessing from the Most High God, Creator of heaven and earth, and therefore the source of all blessing, is a signal of something important that is going to happen in the text, as such events often are in Hebrew narrative. It is thus not insignificant that such an "incidental" occurrence by someone representing the Most High God, whose name represents both royalty and righteousness, would bless the future father of Israel before a crucial chapter in the Abraham narrative.

Genesis 15

The striking use of asyndeton combined with disjunctive clauses (x + *qatal*) both at the beginning of Genesis 15 (15:1) and at the end (15:18) serve to set off this text formally from its surrounding context. The syntactic breaks highlight the semantic importance

---

38. The next chapter indicates Abram's and Sarai's ages as ten years older. This assumes that, chronologically, Genesis 15 is tied closely to chap. 16. There is a Jewish exegetical tradition that understood chap. 15 to be chronologically prior to chap. 12. This does not seem to account for the fact that the context of the passage suggests that Abram is actually living in the land of Canaan after he has responded to the call. Note the fact that he has already been called out of Mesopotamia (15:7) and has been given "this land" (15:7). Moreover, the divine oath granting Abram the land assumes that he is in it (15:18). Of course, this view is wrestling with the fact that for Abram to respond to the call of God, his faith must have been there from the beginning, not appearing for the first time halfway through the story. For an exposition of this Jewish view, see Edward Adams, "Abraham's Faith and Gentile Disobedience: Textual Links between Romans 1 and 4," *JSNT* 19, no. 65 (1997): 47–66.

39. While some commentators think that Abram's laughter was not inspired by doubt, the context clearly shows otherwise: "Will a hundred-year-old man have a child? Will a ninety-year-old woman give birth?" (Gen. 17:17). Indeed, this is also Sarah's reason for her laughter in the next chapter: "After I and my husband are old, will I have pleasure?" (18:12).

"He Believed the Lord" 49

of the units for the Abraham narrative, for this is the only time in the narrative that such striking usage occurs at the beginning and ending of an episode. The first asyndetic clause signals a new start in the narrative, and the second provides a narrative explanation for the events that have transpired in the text.

This is not to discount the importance of the previous events narrated in chapter 14, some of which have already been noted. Although chapter 15 opens with a standard formula that indicates an uncertain amount of time after the previous events (אַחַר הַדְּבָרִים הָאֵלֶּה) and a new start in the narrative, there are some significant links with the previous chapter. A similar formula is used at the end of the second major section of the narrative in Genesis 22, and there are also significant echoes with chapter 21.[40] The opening transitional temporal framework is followed by a divine word being given to Abram in the form of a prophetic oracle. But as has been noted, there are not only prophetic motifs, such as prophetic terminology (15:1, 4)[41] and long-range prediction (15:13–16), but there are also theological concepts, such as faith and righteousness (15:6), a formula of divine identification similar to one that will be used later regarding the exodus and Sinai (15:7), and the formalization of a covenant (15:18).

Moreover, this is the first sustained dialogue that takes place between God and Abram, and the text itself is divided into two units based on clear differences in content: 15:1–6 deals with the issue of an heir for the patriarch and climaxes with a divine verdict on the patriarch's faith; 15:7–21 treats the theme of land and concludes with a divine covenant with Abram that guarantees him the land of Canaan. In each section, an initial statement of God leads to a burning question of Abram, followed by an action, which leads to a divine verdict. In fact, the questions of Abram are crucial—they are essential for providing "the necessary backdrop for the central issue of this chapter, that is, the apparent delay in fulfilling his promises."[42]

The first divine statement (15:1) seeks to allay Abram's fear, stressing that God is a defender (a shield) who provides a rich reward, while the second assures Abram that God has brought him to the land of Canaan from Ur (15:7) to possess the land. The first is expressed in a "fear not" oracle for a reason—Abram has apprehension—and the concept of divine defense and divine reward is an answer. The apprehension may deal with the previous battle, in which he has trusted God for both the outcome and the reward, but Abram's response reveals his real concern—the delay in fulfilling the promise of an heir. The second divine statement is simply a divine identification formula regarding Yahweh as the God who caused Abram's exodus from Ur in order for him to possess the land of Canaan. This second statement is addressing the delayed fulfillment of this promise as well, which Abram's question makes explicit: "How can I know that I will inherit the land" (15:8) since it is now occupied (15:7)? Both answers to Abram's queries take place during the night, and in each case he does something to which God responds.

---

40. For some of the connections between chaps. 21 and 22, see Römer, "Abraham's Righteousness and Sacrifice."
41. This terminology is a hallmark of prophecy; cf. Jer. 14:1; Ezek. 1:3; Zech. 1:1; 7:1.
42. Sailhamer, *Pentateuch as Narrative*, 149.

In the first section of Genesis 15, Abram hears God in a prophetic vision: "Do not be afraid! I am your shield—your reward will be very great" (15:1). These verses pick up themes from the previous narrative in which Abram was delivered from his enemies by God and in which he had refused wealth from the king of Sodom. The Hebrew word for "shield," stressing God's protection, is from the same root as the verb "delivered" in 14:20, and the issue of wealth is found in Abram's tithe to Melchizedek and his rejection of being enriched by any human agency (14:23). Now he is told that God will give him a great wage. In light of the context, Abram is being told that God has not only been his protection in the recent past but will also be his protection in the future, specifically dealing with the promise of becoming a great nation, which includes both descendants and land. Not only will God have Abram's back, he will also give him a very great reward. The intensifier "very" (מְאֹד) amplifies the promise, and it will be amplified even more in 17:6, where the word is doubled (מְאֹד מְאֹד) to emphasize again the magnitude of the promise of descendants.

But Abram is left wondering. He wonders not just about the promise of becoming a great nation but also about having even one descendant to populate it. What about that promise? He argues that the present inheritor of his estate will be a servant from his household since he has no heir. The identity of Abram's servant is a bit unclear. He seems to be called the son of his possession (a son acquired by purchase) or the one in charge of his possession (household). He is further identified as Eliezer, the Dammeseq, a word that could be possibly understood as a location (Damascus) or as "the one of Meseq," which is similar to the earlier word for "possession," which could then be simply a further amplification: "Eliezer, the one over the acquisition." Although the exact identity of this servant is unclear, what is certain is that Abram is viewing the servant as a surrogate for an heir; it is as if he is saying, "Look, you have not given me a descendant [clearly 'seed' is used in the singular sense here]. Look, the son of my house will be my heir ['will heir me']. That is, Eliezer will be my heir."

Undoubtedly, Abram is attempting to "help" God out with the fulfillment of his promise: "I do not currently have an heir, so perhaps I am misunderstanding things." The use of the presentative particle הֵן ("Look!" Gen. 15:3) invites the divine interlocutor as well as the narrative audience to actually see Abram's "answer" up close: Eliezer. If Abram "domesticates" the promise here and seeks for his servant to be a surrogate heir, his wife will do the same thing in the next chapter when she seeks to make her servant, Hagar, a surrogate wife for Abram, so that the promise can be fulfilled in a more "sensible" way (Genesis 16).

The narrator in 15:4 uses a similar presentative, וְהִנֵּה, to contrast the word of God with Abram's "answer": "Look—the word of Yahweh came to him!" The actual words of Yahweh highlight this disjunction even more: "This one will not be your heir! But the one who comes forth from your loins will be your heir!" The use of an envelope structure points to the two different answers—Abram's and God's:

לֹא יִירָשְׁךָ זֶה כִּי־אִם אֲשֶׁר יֵצֵא מִמֵּעֶיךָ הוּא יִירָשֶׁךָ׃

Moreover, the use of "right" dislocation—that is, the use of a cleft structure—puts to the forefront of the discourse the identity of the real heir as someone who comes from Abram's own body:[43]

הוּא יִירָשֶׁךָ ⟵	כִּי־אִם אֲשֶׁר יֵצֵא מִמֵּעֶיךָ
"He will heir you!" ⟵	"But the one who comes from your loins . . ."

Thus, the grammar stresses in the strongest possible way the fact that the heir will *not* be the servant but will come from Abram's own body. Then Yahweh takes Abram out (presumably in the vision) under the night sky and shows him the heavens and tells him to count the stars if he is able. Then he pauses and tells Abram in no uncertain terms, "Thus will be your descendants!" This promise reiterates an earlier one in similar language when Abram was told that he would have as many descendants as the dust of the land of Canaan (13:14–17). Abram presumably looks up at the heavens, and the text simply says, "He believed in Yahweh." The text adds a description: "He considered/reckoned it to him (as) righteousness" (15:6). That is, Abram is considered righteous, just as Noah was in his generation. Before looking at this verse in more detail to determine the possibility of another translation, the remainder of the chapter needs to be examined.

That Genesis 15:6 forms a climax dealing with the issue of a descendant for Abram is clear because 15:7 begins a new section with the theme of land. Yahweh identifies himself as the one who brought Abram up from Ur of the Chaldees to possess the land of Canaan, and this statement elicits Abram's question why he lacks possession of this land. A powerful object lesson taking the form of a covenant rite is performed by Abram, and another nocturnal vision assures Abram of his eventual possession of the land. A blazing fire moves through dismembered animals and makes a divine oath, assuring Abram of the promise of the land.

Therefore, in chapter 15 there are two clear themes dealing with progeny and land, two essential components of the earlier promise of blessing. In an in-depth study of the text, John Ha reaches this conclusion: "At both levels of theme and literary composition, Gen. 15 is a coherent and closely-knit whole, whose unity has been remarkably worked out by its author."[44]

The structure of the text is lucid (see table 1.1).[45] In the second passage, 15:7–21, the divine verdict takes the form of two sections, first a prophecy to Abram cast in the first and second person and then a reflection on the meaning of the ritual and what actually happened. The last comment regarding the covenant (15:18–21) is probably relevant not only to 15:7–17 but to the entire chapter. The divine speech unites both units into a

---

43. Paul Joüon and T. Muraoka, *A Grammar of Biblical Hebrew*, 2nd ed., SubBi 27 (Rome: Gregorian University Press, 2006), 551–54. These structures are usually understood as focus structures, providing a topic on which the rest of the sentence serves as a comment. See T. Muraoka, *Emphatic Words and Structures in Biblical Hebrew* (Leiden: Brill, 1985), 93–97.
44. Ha, *Genesis 15*, 58.
45. This table is based on my own analysis, but John Ha's is much more detailed. See Ha, *Genesis 15*, 59–62.

coherent whole: "To your *seed*, I will give this *land*" (15:18).[46] Thus there is a logic to the entirety. The covenant is given because of righteousness, which is given because of faith. With this general structure in mind, we can consider the exact nature of Abram's response to God's promise of an heir and the divine counterresponse in 15:6.

Table 1.1 Structure of Genesis 15

	15:1–6	15:7–17
Divine oracle	15:1	15:7
Human questioning	15:2–3	15:8
Divine instruction	15:4–5	15:9
Human response	15:6a	15:10–12
Divine verdict	15:6b	15:13–17
Final verdict	15:18–21	

Genesis 15:6

The First Clause

The first clause, "He believed in Yahweh," has few major exegetical issues. Although the subject has changed from the previous narrative verb, where it was Yahweh, it is clear that *Abram* believed, since the object ("in Yahweh") clarifies the subject clearly. The Septuagint makes the subject explicit by mentioning Abram.

What does the word "believe" actually mean? It comes from a root meaning "firm" and "reliable," something that can be depended on. When it is used in this basic form in Hebrew, it means essentially an agreement with the content of a previous speech: it is trustworthy, reliable.[47] In *qal* stem participial forms, it is used for "doorposts" (2 Kings 18:16) or personal "caregivers" (Ruth 4:16; 2 Kings 10:1). It reflects some of this usage when it becomes a loanword in English for strong assent to a statement ("Amen!"), essentially affirming that the statement is correct. Relevant noun forms for the Hebrew roots stress reliability (Prov. 14:5). A craftsman is someone whose work is reliable (Song 7:1).

When the verb occurs in the *niphal* stem, it means "that which can be relied on." Thus, Joseph will know that his brothers' words can be trusted if they bring their youngest brother back to Egypt (Gen. 42:20). Moses is the most reliable of Yahweh's servants (Num. 12:7), and God is reliable precisely because he keeps his covenant for a thousand generations (Deut. 7:9). In the *hiphil* stem it means "to declare someone (or his words) to be reliable." In the only other example of this form of the verb in Genesis, a dramatic counterexample to Abram is provided. Thus, Jacob cannot believe his sons when they tell him the news that Joseph is alive and is a prince in Egypt; it is too incredible for the old man to believe, given what his sons have already put him through (Gen. 45:26). It

---

46. See Ha, *Genesis 15*, 62.
47. For oaths, see Num. 5:22; Deut. 27:15–26; for simple agreements, see 1 Kings 1:36; Neh. 5:13; Jer. 11:5.

is only when he realizes the import of what his eyes see, when he considers all the wagons loaded with goods from Egypt, that he accepts their report and his spirit is revived. Later in the Torah, when the Israelites experience deliverance at the Red Sea and see the Egyptian bodies washed up on the shore, they believe in Yahweh and his servant Moses (Ex. 14:31). Clearly, belief is more than mental assent. It calls for commitment, a placing of trust in someone. In both of the above examples, it changes the perspective of the subject and leads to commitment to act on the belief. Another example shows what it is at stake. When Achish, the king of Gath, asks David where he has been raiding, David lies and tells him that he is pillaging Israelite towns and villages. Achish believes him and concludes that this means that David will be forced to be his servant since his own people will view him as a traitor (1 Sam. 27:12). His attitude toward David is changed because he believes David's words.

It should be mentioned that in all the above examples except in the case of Jacob, the verb is used with the preposition ב. These examples correlate with Ernst Jenni's exhaustive study indicating that "to believe in" indicates an enduring quality attached to the belief. When belief is collocated with the preposition ל, it has a more occasional nature.[48]

Thus, Abraham believes in Yahweh here: he believes his statement, not only that he will have an heir (an individual seed) but also that he will have as many descendants as the stars of heaven. In a very real sense, Abram is saying "Amen!" to God's promise.[49]

The use of the particular verb form here for "believed" has suggested to some scholars a number of possibilities in meaning. Since one expects another preterite—a *waw*-consecutive form, or *wayyiqtol*—one must explain the use of the *weqatal* form. Some scholars, like R. Meyer, believe that this is simply a stylistic variation for *wayyiqtol* since there are similar forms found in other contexts—it is thus a *waw*-copulative form and not a *waw*-consecutive, and the *waw*-copulative form is found in the oldest Hebrew texts.[50] Others argue that it is a frequentative form since in many contexts *weqatal* has this function, especially in procedural or predictive discourse or in descriptive discourse in narrative.[51] Thus, in this text the passage would be translated "He kept on believing" or "He continued to believe" rather than simply "He believed."[52] The context lends support for this translation since it can be assumed that Abram first believed when he left Mesopotamia and that he believed at other

---

48. Ernst Jenni, *Die Hebräischen Präpositionen*, vol. 1, *Die Präposition Beth* (Stuttgart: Kohlhammer, 1992), 254. I am thankful to Peter Gentry for this information.
49. Thus one can accept the result of Meredith Kline's study without necessarily agreeing with his argument that the verb here is declarative. See Meredith G. Kline, "Abram's Amen," *WTJ* 31, no. 1 (1968): 1–11.
50. R. Meyer, "Auffallender Erzählungstil in einem angeblichen Auszug aus der 'Chronik der Könige von Juda,'" in *Festschrift: F. Baumgartel*, ed. J. Hermann and L. Rost (Erlangen: Universitatsbund Erlangen, 1959), 114–23. Meyer notes in particular the *waw*-copulative use in the song of Deborah (Judg. 5:26). Some scholars would attribute such *waw*-copulative usage to late Aramaic influence, but this is not necessary, particularly for such early texts as Genesis. If Aramaic influence was present, one would expect to find many more examples.
51. Wilhelm Gesenius, *Gesenius' Hebrew Grammar*, ed. E. Kautzsch, trans. A. E. Cowley (1861–1931; repr., Mineola, NY: Dover, 2006), 122ss.
52. Gesenius, *Gesenius' Hebrew Grammar*, 190; Max Frederick Rogland, "Abram's Persistent Faith: Hebrew Verb Semantics in Genesis 15:6," *WTJ* 70, no. 2 (2008): 239–44; Oeming, "Ist Genesis 15:6?," 195–96; Ha, *Genesis 15*, 23; Moberly, "Abraham's Righteousness," 105–6.

times before this period (Gen. 12:4; 13:18). Thus, Genesis 15:6 is simply saying that he continued to believe as he has always done.

Yet linguistically, a *weqatal* with frequentative or durative force usually occurs in the context of other imperfective forms or in a literary context indicating that a habitual action is occurring. But there is little in this context except the verb form itself to indicate such force. In fact, there is only one other similar verbal form in the entire Abraham narrative (21:24). Others suggest that the form may indicate a significant break in the narrative, isolating it from the previous statement to show that it did not depend solely on it.[53] Still others suggest that it may have climactic meaning in the narrative.[54] In this context, it is probably best to understand it in line with the other preterites as a simple one-time act. The use of the variant form occurs in a significant number of other places where it suggests simple preterite meaning, and here it is probably intended to highlight an act—a climactic act in the narrative. The fact that this is a dense theological text suggests that Abram decisively got this right. He trusted in Yahweh—that is, his word of promise (15:5)—in a way that his very life depended on it. This is a grammatical way of stating that his life was bound up with the promise (e.g., 44:30–31). So the disjunctive verb form highlights Abram's faith. As Elizabeth Robar mentions, "From the perspective of the broader context, then, we may see the unexpected *we + qatal* in Gen 15:6 as a thematic marker that the role played by Abraham's believing in the Lord and being considered righteous is integral to the highest level developing themes."[55]

Although Abram's faith may have been present before (how else would he have left Mesopotamia?), the text does not mention it explicitly. It leaves the explicit mention of it to this passage because in some ways, here is the defining moment of his faith. In the midst of a crisis of profound proportions, he trusts in Yahweh and his promise.[56]

The Second Clause

The next clause, "He reckoned it to him [as] righteousness" (Gen. 15:6), is fraught with exegetical issues. Who is the subject of the verb? What is the reference to the third feminine singular pronominal suffix attached to the second verb ("it")? Does it refer to the verbal idea expressed in the previous verb ("believed") or simply to the promise of a child in the previous five verses? Or is it cataphoric, referring to the word "righteousness," with which it agrees grammatically? Moreover, what is the meaning of "righteousness"? Does it refer to a state of being before God (e.g., that Abram is righteous as

---

53. Allen P. Ross, *Creation and Blessing: A Guide to the Study and Exposition of Genesis* (Grand Rapids, MI: Baker, 2000), 309–10. Therefore, it could have any number of meanings: parenthetic, summary, frequentative, or characteristic.
54. Robert E. Longacre, "Weqatal Forms in Biblical Hebrew Prose," in *Biblical Hebrew and Discourse Linguistics*, ed. Robert D. Bergen (Winona Lake, IN: Eisenbrauns, 1994), 50–98. While Longacre does not make this suggestion for Gen. 15:6 in his article, it could be implied there from his study of other occurrences of these forms. By contrast, Sailhamer argues that the syntax of the verse suggests it is to be read as background for 15:7. This is highly unlikely. Sailhamer, *Pentateuch as Narrative*, 151.
55. Elizabeth Robar, *The Verb and the Paragraph in Biblical Hebrew: A Cognitive-Linguistic Approach*, Studies in Semitic Languages and Linguistics 78 (Leiden: Brill, 2014), 179.
56. Adams, "Abraham's Faith and Gentile Disobedience," 61. This has "the character of a decisive turning point in the story." Walter Eichrodt, *Theology of the Old Testament* (Philadelphia: Westminster, 1967), 2:278.

Noah was [6:9]), or does it refer to a merit or reward that Abram receives for his faith? The translation options can be enumerated as follows:

1. "And he [Abram] believed in Yahweh, and he [Yahweh] credited it [the act of believing] to him [as] righteousness/merit."
2. "And he [Abram] believed in Yahweh, and he [Yahweh] credited it—namely, righteousness/merit—to him."
3. "And he [Abram] believed in Yahweh, and he [Abram] credited it to him [Yahweh] [as] righteousness [i.e., considered him (Yahweh) gracious (for giving the promise)]."

It is probably best to deal with this text as a unit rather than dividing it into its constituent parts. Although this text is a syntactic *hapax legomenon*,[57] it is not a semantic *hapax legomenon*, for there are enough parallels to understand what is transpiring. The verb here translated "to credit" or "to reckon" often indicates attributing a quality to someone. It can be used in various contexts: accounting, moral situations, cultic worship, and everyday life. In the *qal* stem, it can have but does not require a double accusative, in which "something is reckoned to someone (as . . .)."[58] Thus, in a near parallel in Genesis, Judah considers Tamar to be a harlot because of her dress (38:15). In a strikingly similar example, Eli considers the desperately praying Hannah to be drunk (1 Sam. 1:13). In another case, Shimei desperately pleads with David not to attribute to him sin for cursing the king in his flight from his son Absalom (2 Sam. 19:19). David speaks of the joys of forgiveness belonging to the one to whom Yahweh does not attribute sin (Ps. 32:2). Job complains that God considers him to be an enemy (Job 13:24; 19:11; cf. 33:10), while his family members consider him to be a stranger (19:15). The *niphal* stem usage is simply a transformation of the *qal* stem in which the object becomes the grammatical subject. Thus, Jacob's wives are considered to be strangers by their father because of his actions (Gen. 31:15). Job's friends are considered to be senseless beasts by Job (Job 18:3). Even a fool is viewed as wise if he keeps his mouth shut (Prov. 17:28). In a cultic context, the offering one person brings to Yahweh is either credited to the suppliant as acceptable or not, depending on the type of offering it is (Lev. 7:18; 17:4).[59] In an almost exact semantic parallel with Genesis 15:6, it is said that because of Phinehas's act of zeal for Yahweh, righteousness was reckoned to him by Yahweh (Ps. 106:31). This clause is essentially a passive transformation of Genesis 15:6:

Gen. 15:6 וַיַּחְשְׁבֶהָ לּוֹ צְדָקָה "He [Yahweh] credited it to him as righteousness."
Ps. 106:31 וַתֵּחָשֶׁב לוֹ לִצְדָקָה "It was credited to him for righteousness."

If the verb in the psalm were active, the construction would probably be the same as that in Genesis 15:6, with the object being Phinehas's act of zeal and the subject being Yahweh.

---

57. Oeming, "Ist Genesis 15:6?," 191.
58. W. Schottroff, "Ḥšb: To Think," in *Theological Lexicon of the Old Testament*, ed. Ernst Jenni and Claus Westermann, trans. Mark E. Biddle (Peabody, MA: Hendrickson, 1997), 2:481.
59. In both of these cases, the offering is not accepted either because it was not eaten within three days or because it was not presented at the correct location.

And there is another point of similarity in both contexts. In the Psalms text, because of Phinehas's zeal, God not only attributes to him righteousness but also makes a covenant with him. Similarly, after Abram's faith, God makes a covenant with him.[60] In other words, it would be highly incongruous of Abram to be rewarding God for a divine act (i.e., attributing to him righteousness). Rather, God is rewarding Abram for a human act.[61]

The Achilles' heel for any understanding that sees Abram as the one who credits Yahweh for his righteousness in making the promise to Abram is a matter of context and linguistics. God has done nothing yet except make a promise to Abram. He has not fulfilled it, so why would Abram credit him with an act of righteousness? Moreover, the act of crediting someone with righteousness is not the same as praising someone. While form critically this passage is often seen as a salvation oracle given to someone who is lamenting his fate of childlessness, it has been argued that one expects a vow of praise.[62] Even if one grants the assumption, such vows of praise do not always follow in laments, and this is a strange verb to use for declaring praise to God. Moreover, while the subject of the verb can be a human, such a person is invariably a social superior. The reverse side of the coin of crediting someone with righteousness is to forgive them, or not credit them with sin (cf. 2 Sam. 19:19; Ps. 32:2). Again, this is done by someone with a higher social status.

One further point to be established is the meaning of "righteousness." The root meaning indicates conformity to a standard. Thus, weights and measures must have this quality. When used in a religious context, it carries the same idea of conforming to the divine will. Thus, Noah is righteous (Gen. 6:9; 7:1), and the hypothetical members of Sodom who will be spared judgment are righteous, and it would be unthinkable of God to destroy the righteous with the wicked (18:23–33). Righteousness is a state that conforms to God's will, and it specifically has to do with relationships. Thus, when Israelite creditors return a garment used as collateral for a loan so that debtors do not sleep without clothing in the cold, this is regarded as righteousness before God (Deut. 24:13). Living a righteous life by keeping the Shema and the commandments—which are all about proper relationships—results in righteousness (6:25). Consistently, judgment is rendered according to one's righteousness (i.e., according to how one has met God's standards). Hence, biblical texts speak of the righteous being declared righteous because of their righteousness. Solomon thus prays that the wicked might be rendered according to their wickedness and "the righteous declared righteous" (וּלְהַצְדִּיק צַדִּיק) "according to their righteousness" (לָתֶת לוֹ כְּצִדְקָתוֹ), that is, their life of righteous deeds (1 Kings 8:32). When Isaiah says that

---

60. It was precisely this point that convinced the great Italian scholar Samuel Luzzatto to change his understanding of this verse. See Daniel A. Klein, "Who Counted Righteousness to Whom? Two Clashing Views by Shadal on Genesis 15:6," *JBQ* 36, no. 1 (2008): 30–31.

61. Of course, the Septuagint eliminates any ambiguity about the subject with the passive transformation of the verb ("It was counted to him for righteousness"). Although the verb's semantic range also includes "to think," "to intend," and "to plan," it is quite a stretch to argue with Horst Seebass that 15:6 means that "Abram relied on Yahweh and Yahweh planned for him a saving event." Here Seebass argues that there is an eschatological thrust with Yahweh's decision and that righteousness refers to a future saving act of Yahweh, as it frequently does in Isaiah. H. Seebass, *Genesis: Vätergeschichte I* (Neukirchen-Vluyn: Neukirchener, 1997), 71–72." Yohan Hwang takes up Seebass's argument in the general context of Genesis, but the meaning "plan" seems counterintuitive in the context of Genesis 15, and this is a unique meaning for "righteousness" in the Pentateuch. See Yohan Hwang, "Eschatology in Genesis 15:6," *HS* 55 (2014): 19–41, esp. 28.

62. Gaston, "Abraham and the Righteousness of God," 46–47.

Yahweh sought "righteousness" (צְדָקָה), he was looking for a life corresponding to his will. When instead he received the "cries" (צְעָקָה) of the oppressed, it was clear that his people were committed to their own advantage (Isa. 5:7). Ezekiel emphasizes that the righteous are precisely so because they do righteousness (Ezek. 18:5–27). Synonymous expressions for people characterized by righteousness are "(morally) clean hands" (2 Sam. 22:21), an "upright heart" (1 Kings 3:6), and a "person of faithfulness" (1 Sam. 26:23). In other texts, particularly the latter half of Isaiah, and in many of the psalms, righteousness means Yahweh's salvation for his people (e.g., Isa. 46:13; 51:8; cf. Pss. 88:12; 98:2; Mic. 6:5).

Within Genesis, the word for "righteousness" is used to depict Jacob's honesty in his dealings with Laban. It is also used as part of the fixed expression "justice and righteousness" to explicate God's requirements for relationships that Abram will teach his children (Gen. 18:19). And it is precisely because Abram will be concerned with "righteousness" that he debates with God about the possibility of the righteous—that is, those who practice righteousness—being swept away with the wicked in the judgment of Sodom. Repeatedly this word, "righteous," appears in that discussion (18:23, 24 [2x], 25 [2x], 26, 28). Previous to the time of Abram, the epithet "righteous one" is used only of Noah, and thus, he and his family were saved from the judgment of the flood. To have righteousness reckoned to one, then, is remarkable, and it means that one is viewed as Noah—as a righteous one. An alternative translation of Genesis 15:6b would then be "God said to Abram because of his faith in the divine promise, 'You are righteous.'"[63]

The larger context of Genesis confirms this reading. As mentioned before, Noah has a covenant made with him because he alone is righteous in his generation; his righteousness qualifies him to be the savior of the then-known world. He represents the tenth generation from Adam. But he is able to save only his family and representative animals. Abram is the tenth generation from Noah, and a covenant is made with him on the basis of his righteousness, which is credited to him because of his faith in the divine promise. Moreover, he is later called to walk before God and be perfect (17:1), language that is also used of Noah (6:9), and as such, he becomes the father of many nations and thus is able to save the world, not just his own family.

It would seem, then, that a natural reading of this text is that Abram is being *constituted as being reckoned righteous not for anything else but for his faith* (i.e., believing in the promise despite the natural evidence). This is his *new status*, based not on a meritorious act but simply on his faith in the divine promise.

As for the question whether the "it" is cataphoric for righteousness rather than anaphoric for Abram's faith, a cataphoric reference is not the most natural reading. Cataphora are relatively rare in Hebrew, and in the two identical linguistic examples to this construction, the pronoun is anaphoric (Gen. 38:15; 1 Sam. 1:13).[64] Thus, the best translation is "He believed in Yahweh, and he [i.e., Yahweh] counted his faith for righteousness."

---

63. See, e.g., Moberly, "Abraham's Righteousness," 104.
64. Examples with other pronominal suffixes are also anaphoric: Ps. 144:3; Isa. 53:3–4. One particular type of cataphora that is frequent is the use of the demonstrative singular and plural pronouns: "this" and "these." See Gen. 2:4, 23; 5:1; 6:9; 10:1; 11:27; 17:10.

As the text continues, Abram raises the question of land, and then God makes a covenant with him. Usually in the ancient world, a land grant was made with an individual because of a deed of service. Here the covenant is made because of Abram's "deed of service": his faith that is reckoned to him as righteousness. Abram is given a vision that provides the reason for the delay of the land promise, and this is enough for Abram. Moreover, by passing between the ritually slaughtered animals, Yahweh invokes a self-malediction if he does not fulfill his word. Thus, this chapter is about Abram trusting in God and about a God who can be trusted absolutely, at the cost of God's own life.[65] Abram's "very great reward" (Gen. 15:1) is far greater than he ever thought. Not only will God shield (protect) the patriarch's future, but also the stars are a sign of his progeny. And the sign of the future gift of the land is Yahweh passing between the carcasses of animals, graphically showing by a sign the lengths—and depths—to which he will go to fulfill this covenant.

Beyond Genesis 15 in the Torah

As the narrative continues, Abram is tempted to domesticate the promise again; this time his wife makes the suggestion of a surrogate replacement for him to have an heir (Genesis 16). As a result, Ishmael is born through Hagar. Ishmael is clearly not the child of promise, and as Genesis 17 makes clear, thirteen years later, that child will be named Laughter. Here the first parents in the new covenant have their names changed to reflect their new destiny as father and mother of many nations and even royal progeny! The expansion of Abram's name to Abraham means an expanded posterity. He will become the father of many nations. In a special way, this chapter seeks to show the fulfillment of the promise to bless all nations. In addition, Abram is given a covenant sign, and the covenant sign is something that he does, marking his house and descendants: circumcision. It is a sign of cutting, and it is a sign on the flesh of every male that God has cut a covenant with his people. What does it signify? That the sign marks the sexual organ reminds the Israelites that their first father depended on God for progeny and that through this seed, all families of the earth will be blessed. And it is a sign of the patriarch's faith and dedication to God. It represents the cutting away of human endeavor and the importance of trusting in God.[66] And consequently, in the next chapter, an annunciation takes place as divine visitors meet Abraham and Sarah and announce Sarah's "impossible" birth of Isaac to an "impossible" matriarch.[67]

One could argue that at times Abraham loses faith in God's promise. It might seem that this is the case when he laughs about the possibility of having a child, and God says that the child will thus be called Laughter. But the fact is that Abraham persists in the life of

---

65. Brueggemann, *Genesis*, 150.
66. Circumcision was a reminder "that human nature alone was unable to generate the promised seed if God was not willing to grant such fruitfulness." Ross, *Creation and Blessing*, 333. This should not be misconstrued as the total elimination of human effort but rather viewed as its transformation by faith. In fact, the new man (Abraham) will still have sexual relations with the new woman (Sarah). I would like to thank Walter Moberly for this important nuance, gleaned during a personal communication with the author, May 24, 2018.
67. On the theme of the "impossible" in the Abraham narrative, see in particular Walter Brueggemann, "'Impossibility' and Epistemology in the Faith Tradition of Abraham and Sarah (Gen 18:1–15)," *ZAW* 94, no. 4 (1982): 615–34.

faith. He has honest doubts, but they do not lead him to despair. This all leads up to the climax of the Abrahamic narrative. Isaac, the miracle child, is now born, and sometime later Abraham is told to sacrifice his son as a burnt offering on a mountain specified by God. That this represents Abraham's greatest test is an understatement. As commentators have noted, it echoes his first call in chapter 12. There Abram was told to give up his past; now he is told to give up his future—the future promised to him by God. This laconic description of the dark night of the patriarch's soul is an absolute masterpiece of Hebrew narrative art.[68] Abraham does not question or hesitate here as he does in Genesis 15; he arises early in the morning to do the will of his "Father." On the third day of his journey, he sees the mountain of the holocaust. He leaves his servants behind at the foot of the mountain, telling them that he and his son will go up and worship on the mountain and return later. Meanwhile, the son and the father embark on their ascent of the mountain in the most tender and dramatic fashion, each speaking affectionately to one another. The son is old enough to carry the wood for a sacrifice, so he is at least an adolescent. In a touching moment, the son asks his father where the lamb for the burnt offering is. The father's answer that God will provide seems harmless enough, perhaps as a way to put off the question or to "stickhandle" his way around the real issue. But seen from the context of the entire narrative, the father's response as well as his alacrity to do God's bidding and the certainty of belief in his return with the boy shows a faith that even transcends the amazing faith of Genesis 15:6. There he believed, *after questioning* against all odds, that he would have an heir from his own loins; here he believes, *without questioning* at all the divine promise, that he and his son will endure the test. God will provide the sacrifice. Thus, when Isaac is bound, Abraham is binding his beloved son, Isaac.

At the last possible moment, when Abraham raises the knife, an angel intervenes to save the son, and he provides the animal for the sacrifice. Abraham hears the angel declare a second time—this time in a divine oath (the first explicit example in the Bible)—that Abraham will be the recipient of immense blessing because he did this (i.e., he obeyed the divine word). But what must have been the driving force of Abraham's action in supremely obeying the will of God? What led him to obey the divine voice come hell or high water? This was not an arbitrary belief based on whim; it was a faith whose seeds were sown at his call, it was a faith that when tested proved triumphant regarding the birth of an heir, and it was a faith that believed in the resurrection of that same heir—if necessary! Abraham believed in a faithful Yahweh right to the end. That meant obedience. Again, it is important to stress "that Abraham's faith cannot be understood apart from his whole life of obedient response to God."[69]

Consequently, it is interesting that in Genesis, when Abraham is remembered in the next generation, the narrator uses language to show that, in his eyes, Abraham kept the Torah before it was ever given:

---

68. Erich Auerbach, *Mimesis: The Representation of Reality in Western Literature* (Princeton, NJ: Princeton University Press, 1953), 3–23.
69. Moberly, "Abraham's Righteousness," 129.

I will fulfill the oath that I swore to your father Abraham. I will make your offspring as numerous as the stars of heaven and will give to your offspring all these lands. And all the nations of the earth shall gain blessing for themselves through your offspring, because Abraham obeyed my voice and kept my charge, my commandments, my statutes, and my laws. (Gen. 26:3–5)[70]

Noticing the striking use of the language describing obedience to the Torah, early Jewish interpreters explained this parallel by concluding that the Torah must have in fact already been given to Abraham. But might the text suggest that Abraham kept what was later to become the law before it was given because he was supremely the person of faith?

Torah

This emphasis on faith, of course, is often overlooked in the Pentateuch because of the massive corpus of legal texts that constitute the Sinai covenant and its reconfiguration on the plains of Moab in Deuteronomy.[71] Essentially, the narrative of the Torah can be pictured in the diagram in figure 1.1:[72]

Figure 1.1 The Structure of the Torah

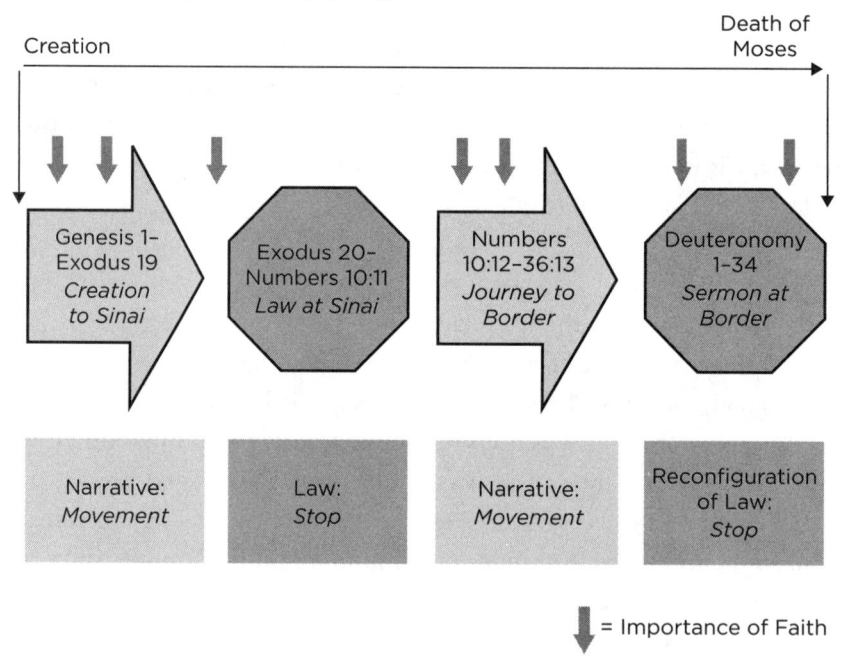

Genesis 1–Exodus 19 Creation to Sinai	Exodus 20–Numbers 10:11 Law at Sinai	Numbers 10:12–36:13 Journey to Border	Deuteronomy 1–34 Sermon at Border
Narrative: Movement	Law: Stop	Narrative: Movement	Reconfiguration of Law: Stop

↓ = Importance of Faith

---

70. Cf. Deut. 11:1, where very similar phraseology stands for the commandments of the Torah.
71. For the convincing analysis of Deuteronomy in this understanding, see Scott Hahn, *Kinship by Covenant: A Canonical Approach to the Fulfillment of God's Saving Promises* (New Haven, CT: Yale University Press, 2009), 67–92.
72. It is actually more complex than this since there are small narrative sections within the law at Sinai (e.g., Exodus 24; 32–34; Lev. 9–10; 24:10–14). There are also small legal sections within the overall narrative (e.g., Numbers 15; 18–19).

It is particularly in the narrative sections that faith is accentuated. Thus there is a focus on faith immediately before the exodus when Moses is called. He lacks the faith to go down to Egypt and stand before Pharaoh because he is convinced that the people will not believe him. It is in these contexts that faith and the signs to stimulate and nourish faith are developed in the text as crucially important for Israelite salvation, just as they were in Genesis 15 (Ex. 4:1, 5, 8 [2x], 9). When Moses shows the people the signs, they believe in him. And immediately before that salvation takes place, with Israel caught between the Pharaonic devil and the deep Red Sea, the people are called to stand still and watch the salvation of God (14:14). After the miracle of the exodus, with Israel on the other side of the Red Sea and the Egyptian army washed up on the shore, the people believe in Yahweh and his servant Moses (14:31). Immediately before the covenant at Sinai, God envelops Moses in his glory cloud in front of all the people gathered at the base of the mountain, so that they will always believe in Moses (19:9).

After Sinai, when the people head to the Promised Land, again the presence or absence of faith determines whether the people enter the land or are exiled from it. An entire generation is condemned to wander in the wilderness until they all die because of their lack of faith, because, Yahweh says, "they refused to believe in me" (Num. 14:11). When the people's rebellion is remembered later, it is clearly viewed as an act of unbelief in the promise of God (Deut. 9:23). Even the great Moses and Aaron do not enter the land because of a failure in faith—"because," God says, "you did not believe in me" (Num. 20:12).

When the old generation has passed away, Moses makes a new covenant with the people as they are on the plains of Moab, on the verge of entering Canaan. The covenant that the book of Deuteronomy presents is really a reconfiguration of the covenant at Sinai.[73] In some ways it has to reconfigure the original design, for it is made for the life of the people in the land of promise and not in the desert. And it is a readjustment in many ways to the sinfulness of the people. There is the stark awareness of their sin, with concessions to their sinful propensities. The law concerning the king recognizes the desire for the people to have a king "like all the other nations" but presents them with a compromise: the people can have a king, but he must not be like foreign rulers (Deut. 17:14–20). The law effectively strips the king of any illusions of power that he might have and makes him a servant of the people and preeminently a servant of God. Similarly, the provision for divorce seeks to curtail abuses (24:1–5), as does the law regarding the treatment of women taken in war (21:10–14). In some ways, these are not ideal laws, but they are realistic, working with people where they are. But repeatedly in the text, God is looking for something more. The Shema presents the big picture, boiling down all the later commands into a few verses: "Yahweh our God is one, and you will love Yahweh your God with all your heart, soul, and strength" (6:4–5). Thus, Yahweh is looking for not only a circumcised body but a circumcised heart (cf. 30:6;

---

73. For the full development of this interpretation, see Hahn, *Kinship by Covenant*.

Ezek. 11:19–21; 36:26). The circumcision in the flesh of Abraham is not enough. What is important is what the circumcision stood for—a life consecrated to God, a life that lives by faith in the promises of God.[74] Where was that life first depicted in detail and theological reflection? In Abram, when he believed in God. There he trusted not in himself to have a child but in the Lord God.

Thus, this circumcision of the heart is what the Torah really demands. Note that Moses makes this point, intentionally alluding to the Shema:

> And now, Israel, what does the LORD your God ask of you but to fear the LORD your God, to walk in obedience to him, to love him, to serve the LORD your God with all your heart and with all your soul, and to observe the LORD's commands and decrees that I am giving you today for your own good? . . . Circumcise your hearts, therefore, and do not be stiff-necked any longer. (Deut. 10:12–13, 16)

The aged Moses realizes that Israel will not be able to keep the law but that they are going to bring the curses of the covenant down on themselves. Yet this is not a spiritual dead end. In exile, if they turn back to God, God will hear them and perform on them what they could never do for themselves: circumcise their hearts so that they will desire to do the will of God: "The LORD your God will circumcise your hearts and the hearts of your descendants, so that you may love him with all your heart and with all your soul, and live" (Deut. 30:6). Thus, Israel will, in fact, obey the Lord from the heart.

It is apparent, then, that John Sailhamer and Hans-Christoph Schmitt, from different perspectives, are correct when they argue that the macrostructure of the Torah is designed to show the importance of faith.[75] What is required is a circumcised heart (i.e., faith so that one can keep the law like Abraham). But this faith should not be understood simply as mental assent.

For example, consider the many places in the Pentateuch where faith is found in the context of hearing the voice of Yahweh or obedience: In Exodus 4, Moses anticipates the people objecting to his leadership and says, "What if the people do not believe me or listen to my voice?" (Ex. 4:1). God gives him signs for the people, and it is clear that believing Moses and listening to (obeying) his voice are inextricably related (4:8 [2x], 9). Later, when Moses is reflecting on the failure of the first generation of Israelites to enter the land of Canaan, he says about them, "You did not believe in him or obey his voice" (Deut. 9:23). In 2 Kings the Deuteronomistic historian provides the theological rationale for the demise of the northern kingdom, associating the failure to believe with being stiff-necked and refusing to listen (17:14). It is thus interesting in Genesis 22 that when Abraham has passed the test in offering up Isaac on the altar, the divine word does not

---

74. Ross, *Creation and Blessing*, 333. Circumcision is a rite that Israel probably borrowed from Egypt, where it likely indicated devotion to the deity or king. Thus, it is a sign of dedication to the deity in Israel, that is, a marker of righteousness. For a study of all the ancient evidence, see John D. Meade, "The Meaning of Circumcision in Israel: A Proposal for a Transfer of Rite from Egypt," *SBJT* 20, no. 1 (2016): 35–54.
75. Sailhamer, *Pentateuch as Narrative*; Sailhamer, *The Meaning of the Pentateuch: Revelation, Composition, and Interpretation* (Downers Grove, IL: IVP Academic, 2010); Hans-Christoph Schmitt, "Redaktion des Pentateuch im Geiste der Prophetie: Beobachtungen zur Bedeutung der 'Glaubens'-Thematik innerhalb der Theologie des Pentateuch," *VT* 32, no. 2 (1982): 170–89.

say that it was because he believed in Yahweh but because he heard (obeyed) his voice (22:18). This is because "believing" and "hearing (obeying)" were correlative terms in the author's mind: one was inward, the other was outward. When Nehemiah is reflecting on Abraham's belief in Yahweh and the latter's decision to make a covenant with him, he simply says, "You found his heart faithful [נֶאֱמָן] to you, and you made a covenant with him to give to his descendants the land of the Canaanites . . . because you are righteous [כִּי צַדִּיק אָתָּה]" (Neh. 9:8).

Abraham's faith resulted in faithfulness (i.e., he believed in the promises of God even when they were delayed). Thus God reckoned to him righteousness. But this righteousness in a sense gave him no "free pass." It was not to be a legal fiction. He was called to live into that righteousness and teach his children the way of Yahweh, which was essentially a way marked by justice and righteousness. But from where did this righteousness originate? A righteous God considered him righteous (צַדִּיק) because he had thrown himself on his promise.[76]

Conclusion

Thus, the "new perspective" on Abraham's faith and his justification of God (and not by God), which was set forth by James Barr as a better alternative to the traditional view of Genesis 15:6, is exegetically tenuous. It is possible grammatically, but so is the famous sentence "Colorless green ideas sleep furiously." In terms of the context, both local and global, righteousness is required for human salvation. It happened to save the world *in nuce* in the tenth descendant from Adam (Noah), and it will save the world *en masse* in the tenth descendant from Noah (Abraham). Within the local story, it is one of the exceeding great rewards that Abram is given—before a covenant is made with him. Moreover, an inferior never reckons anything to a superior.

Also found wanting is Levenson's reading, which has received support from Moberly, that the isolation of Genesis 15:6 "from the rest of the Abraham material in the Hebrew Bible and indeed from the Hebrew Bible itself"[77] has produced a "Pauline type [of exegesis] which takes the verse in isolation and insists on the autonomy of faith" as opposed to a "Philonic type in which faith and the observance of commandments are each predicated of Abraham on the basis of texts in Genesis."[78] It is an exegetical fact that Genesis 15 precedes Genesis 26, in which it states that Abraham kept all the commandments of God, as well as Genesis 22, not only in the text but in the chronology of the text. The same is true for the Sinai narrative as well as for its Deuteronomic reconfiguration on the plains of Moab. By virtue of its narrative prominence, Sinai (Exodus 19–Numbers 10) clearly dwarfs the Abraham story (Genesis 12–22), but Israel

---

76. *Pace* Hans Wildberger, who argues that the sense of the Genesis passage has been significantly altered. Hans Wildberger, "'*mn*: Firm, Secure," in Jenni and Westermann, *Theological Lexicon of the Old Testament*, 1:141. Note that Ezekiel explicitly connects righteousness with the righteous. The righteous one lives by his righteousness (Ezek. 14:14; 18:5–9, 14–17, 20). See further Klaus Koch, "*Ṣdq*: To Be Communally Faithful, Beneficial," in Jenni and Westermann, *Theological Lexicon of the Old Testament*, 3:1059.
77. Levenson, *Hebrew Bible*, 60.
78. Levenson, *Hebrew Bible*, 59.

(i.e., the father of Israel) is born in Canaan, not at Sinai, and he exercises faith *before* he receives the ratification of that faith in what was to become the quintessential mark of Jewishness—circumcision. In a later work, Levenson makes the point that "Abraham does not observe the great bulk of the commandments of the Torah . . . with the glaring exception of circumcision."[79] But even circumcision comes *after*, and it is the sign of faith. All these facts require explanation. Could this be the reason why Abraham fulfilled the law even before it was given, as noted in Genesis 26:5? Most commentators understand a passage like Genesis 26:5 to be the work of a redactor, who is seeking to revise Abraham in light of the law. Rabbinic interpreters often understood a text like this to imply that Abraham must have known the law.[80] However, taking the text as it stands, it is clear that "Abraham was dust long before Moses [the great lawgiver] was born."[81] Was it not also the case that Abraham's heart was circumcised well before his body and that to live by faith in God's promise was what keeping the Torah was all about?[82] Could this be the reason why the righteous Abraham would become the father of many nations instead of saving only his own family, as Noah did? The narrative structure of the text provides the major clue to this exegetical problem. This is shown clearly by Levenson in a later work when he states that in the rabbinic estimation, Sinai so overshadows Abraham that their "paradigm is not Abraham pronounced righteous while still uncircumcised and in that sense more a Gentile than a Jew."[83] Rather, their paradigm is determined by Sinai. From a larger canonical perspective, it is significant that the first link between faith and righteousness, and the only one in the Torah, is found in the Abraham story, well before Sinai, and it must be borne in mind that the writer of Genesis 15 is probably aware of the entire Torah and even the story of the conquest (see 15:11–16).[84]

From a larger biblical perspective, then, Abraham, like Noah, is a new Adamic figure. The first Adam did not believe in the word of God and disobeyed: he was not righteous. The tenth from Adam, Noah, believed in the word of God and was righteous, and in a sense he saved the world, preparing it for a universal salvation. Abraham, the tenth from Noah, is another step in this universal plan for people to believe in the divine promise, become righteous, and obey the divine word.[85]

The Abraham story is also lucid in showing that faith issues in obedience. As Moberly comments, "Abraham's faith cannot be understood apart from his whole life of obedi-

---

79. Levenson, *Inheriting Abraham*, 3.
80. See, for example, the various rabbinic responses in Levenson, *Inheriting Abraham*, 142–68. Note, for example, Mishnah Kiddushin 4:14: "We find that Abraham our father performed the entire Torah before it was given, as it says, 'Abraham listened to My voice, and he observed My statutes, commandments, laws and teachings'" (Gen. 26:5).
81. David C. Steinmetz, *Luther in Context*, 2nd ed. (Grand Rapids, MI: Baker Academic, 2002), 32.
82. See, for example, the insightful comments by Sailhamer on connecting Gen. 15:6 and 26:5: "Be like Abraham. Live a life of faith and it can be said that you are keeping the Law." Sailhamer, *Pentateuch as Narrative*, 71.
83. Levenson, *Inheriting Abraham*, 169.
84. It is also significant that Phinehas is *already* a member of the covenant community when he is credited with righteousness for his action. Cf. Brian Vickers, *Jesus' Blood and Righteousness: Paul's Theology of Imputation* (Wheaton, IL: Crossway, 2006), 82.
85. I would like to thank Byron Wheaton for the reference to Adam and unbelief.

ent response to God."[86] Nevertheless, the two *can* be distinguished in the sense that a root can be distinguished from the tree. Or perhaps the better analogy is that of the distinction between the seed and the mature person. Abram believed in the wild promise of God that he would have an heir despite its human impossibility, and the *result* was righteousness—and Laughter. Good news indeed.[87]

Recommended Resources

Adams, Edward. "Abraham's Faith and Gentile Disobedience: Textual Links between Romans 1 and 4." *Journal for the Study of the New Testament* 19, no. 65 (1997): 47–66.

Brueggemann, Walter. "'Impossibility' and Epistemology in the Faith Tradition of Abraham and Sarah (Gen 18:1–15)." *Zeitschrift für die alttestamentliche Wissenschaft* 94, no. 4 (1982): 615–34.

Gaston, Lloyd. "Abraham and the Righteousness of God." *Horizons in Biblical Theology* 2, no. 1 (1980): 39–68.

Gentry, Peter J., and Stephen J. Wellum. *Kingdom through Covenant: A Biblical-Theological Understanding of the Covenants.* Wheaton, IL: Crossway, 2012.

Ha, John. *Genesis 15: A Theological Compendium of Pentateuchal History.* Beihefte zur Zeitschrift für die alttestamentliche Wissenschaft 181. Berlin: de Gruyter, 1989.

Hahn, Scott. *Kinship by Covenant: A Canonical Approach to the Fulfillment of God's Saving Promises.* New Haven, CT: Yale University Press, 2009.

Jacob, Benno. *The First Book of the Bible: Genesis.* Edited by Ernst I. Jacob and Walter Jacob. Jerusalem: KTAV, 2007.

Klein, Daniel A. "Who Counted Righteousness to Whom? Two Clashing Views by Shadal on Genesis 15:6." *Jewish Bible Quarterly* 36, no. 1 (2008): 28–32.

Klein, Ralph W. "Call, Covenant, and Community: The Story of Abraham and Sarah." *Currents in Theology and Mission* 15 (1988): 120–27.

Kline, Meredith G. "Abram's Amen." *Westminster Theological Journal* 31, no. 1 (1968): 1–11.

Koch, Klaus. "Ṣdq: To Be Communally Faithful, Beneficial." In *Theological Lexicon of the Old Testament*, edited by Ernst Jenni and Claus Westermann, translated by Mark E. Biddle, 2:1046–62. Peabody, MA: Hendrickson, 1997.

Levenson, Jon D. *The Hebrew Bible, the Old Testament, and Historical Criticism: Jews and Christians in Biblical Studies.* Louisville: Westminster John Knox, 1993.

———. *Inheriting Abraham: The Legacy of the Patriarch in Judaism, Christianity, and Islam.* Princeton, NJ: Princeton University Press, 2012.

Longacre, Robert E. "Weqatal Forms in Biblical Hebrew Prose." In *Biblical Hebrew and Discourse Linguistics*, edited by Robert D. Bergen, 50–98. Winona Lake, IN: Eisenbrauns, 1994.

---

86. Moberly, "Abraham's Righteousness," 129.
87. Thus, these analogies are helpful when discussing some of the issues in New Testament theology regarding the difference between Paul and James. Paul looks at the beginning, James the end. Or as Douglas Moo helpfully puts it, Paul uses a telephoto lens, James a wide-angle lens. See Douglas J. Moo, "Genesis 15:6 in the New Testament," in *From Creation to New Creation: Biblical Theology and Exegesis*, ed. Daniel M. Gurtner and Benjamin L. Gladd (Peabody, MA: Hendrickson, 2013), 162.

McFarland, Orrey. "Whose Abraham, Which Promise? Genesis 15.6 in Philo's *De Virtutibus* and Romans 4." *Journal for the Study of the New Testament* 35, no. 2 (2012): 107–29.

Meyer, R. "Auffallender Erzählungstil in einem angeblichen Auszug aus der 'Chronik der Könige von Juda.'" In *Festschrift: F. Baumgartel*, edited by J. Hermann and L. Rost, 114–23. Erlangen: Universitätsbund Erlangen, 1959.

Moberly, R. W. L. "Abraham's Righteousness (Genesis Xv 6)." In *Studies in the Pentateuch*, edited by J. A. Emerton, 103–30. Supplements to Vetus Testamentum 41. Leiden: Brill, 1990.

Moo, Douglas J. "Genesis 15:6 in the New Testament." In *From Creation to New Creation: Biblical Theology and Exegesis*, edited by Daniel M. Gurtner and Benjamin L. Gladd, 147–62. Peabody, MA: Hendrickson, 2013.

Oeming, Manfred. "Ist Genesis 15:6 ein Beleg für die Anrechnung des Glaubens zur Gerechtigkeit?" *Zeitschrift für die alttestamentliche Wissenschaft* 95, no. 2 (1983): 182–97.

Rogland, Max Frederick. "Abram's Persistent Faith: Hebrew Verb Semantics in Genesis 15:6." *Westminster Theological Journal* 70, no. 2 (2008): 239–44.

Römer, Thomas. "Abraham's Righteousness and Sacrifice: How to Understand (and Translate) Genesis 15 and 22." *Communio Viatorum* 54, no. 1 (2012): 3–15.

Sailhamer, John H. *The Pentateuch as Narrative: A Biblical-Theological Commentary*. Grand Rapids, MI: Zondervan, 1995.

Schliesser, Benjamin. *Abraham's Faith in Romans 4: Paul's Concept of Faith in Light of the History of Reception of Genesis 15:6*. Wissenschaftliche Untersuchungen zum Neuen Testament 224. Tübingen: Mohr Siebeck, 2007.

von Rad, Gerhard. "Faith Reckoned as Righteousness." In *The Problem of the Hexateuch and Other Essays*, 25–30. Translated by E. W. Trueman Dicken. London: Oliver and Boyd, 1966.

Wheaton, Byron. "Focus and Structure in the Abraham Narratives." *Trinity Journal*, n.s., 27, no. 1 (2006): 143–62.

2

Singing and Living Justification by Faith Alone

The Psalms and the Wisdom Literature

ALLAN HARMAN

The Poetical Books form a distinct group of literature within the Old Testament, though there are many differences within the group as a whole or, in the case of the Psalms, within one book. In this chapter we explore the theme of justification by faith alone especially in the Psalter but also in the Old Testament Wisdom Literature as a whole.

The Psalter is unique in that it incorporates songs that date from the time of Moses (Psalm 90) to the postexilic period (e.g., Psalms 74; 126). It constitutes an important part of the Old Testament Scriptures as it brings together in one book the faith of Israel. It is not the content but rather the format that is new. As the psalmists sang their songs, they expressed the doctrinal affirmations of God's people. In fact, communal songs like Psalm 44 or 78 gave the people, as a whole, the opportunity to express their collective memory of God's dealings with them or their hopes for his future interventions on their behalf. Principal James Denney of Glasgow once wrote, "The Confession of faith is to be sung, not signed."[1] While his comment was, unfortunately, a reflection of the changing attitudes to creedal subscription at the end of the nineteenth century, it is a very apt description of the Psalter. There was no formal creed in Israel to which assent was required in written form, but what the people believed was expressed in songs of

---

1. *The Letters of Principal James Denney to Family and Friends*, ed. James Moffat (London: Hodder & Stoughton, 1922), ix.

religious devotion. Many of those songs are incorporated into the book of Psalms, and they reveal much of the content of Israel's faith.

One passage of Old Testament Scripture that did become almost a formal creed was God's own declaration of his person and character as set out in Exodus 34:6–7. After the sin of the people lapsing into idolatry at Sinai, Moses requested that God would reveal his ways to him (33:13). God's promise was that he would proclaim his name "The LORD," saying, "And I will be gracious to whom I will be gracious, and will show mercy on whom I will show mercy" (33:19). Moses was placed in a cleft of the rock, and as God's after-glory passed by,[2] he proclaimed his own character:

> The LORD, the LORD, a God merciful and gracious, slow to anger, and abounding in steadfast love and faithfulness, keeping steadfast love for thousands, forgiving iniquity and transgression and sin, but who will by no means clear the guilty, visiting the iniquity of the fathers on the children and the children's children, to the third and fourth generation. (34:6–7)

The repetition of the divine name "the LORD" is unusual, but it served to concentrate attention on the fact that it was the covenantal God of Israel who was declaring his character. He was both merciful and gracious (רַחוּם וְחַנּוּן).

That this statement became, in essence, a creed is shown by the number of times it is quoted in the rest of the Old Testament. There are at least eight instances: Numbers 14:18; Nehemiah 9:17; Psalms 86:15; 103:8; 145:8; Joel 2:13; Jonah 4:2; and Nahum 1:3. The Psalter passages are significant for the present discussion because they show how this creed was incorporated into song and became part of the confessional testimony of Israel. Psalm 86 is remarkable in that every verse is an echo of some other part of the Old Testament. Well-known passages of Scripture have been brought together to form a new song. The psalmist, in appealing to God, uses the vocabulary of Exodus 34. He appeals to him as being "good and forgiving, abounding in steadfast love" (Ps. 86:5). "Forgiving" (סַלָּח) occurs in Exodus 34:9 in Moses's appeal to God to forgive the sin of the people, while "abounding in steadfast love" comes in the opening declaration of God's character (Ps. 86:5). The fuller quotation from Exodus 34 comes in Psalm 86:15, where the psalmist employs the creedal statement to reinforce his confident trust in God's forgiving grace. In Psalm 103, the anonymous psalmist refers to God's self-revelation of himself to Moses in response to his request, "Please, show me your glory" (Ex. 33:18). The psalmist writes,

> He made known his ways to Moses,
> > his acts to the people of Israel.
> The LORD is merciful and gracious,
> > slow to anger and abounding in steadfast love. (Ps. 103:7–8)

---

2. This is the suggestion of Walter C. Kaiser Jr., *Exodus*, in *Genesis–Leviticus*, vol. 1 of *The Expositor's Bible Commentary*, 2nd ed. (Grand Rapids, MI: Zondervan, 2010), 484. Kaiser expressed the same view in *Hard Sayings of the Old Testament* (Downers Grove, IL: InterVarsity Press, 1988), 83–84.

This repetition of the creed introduces an extended section that rejoices in the reality of God's forgiveness, so much so that he is able to remove sin as far as the east is from the west (103:12). The final Psalter quotation of the Exodus creed occurs in Psalm 145:8, where the words are repeated with only a slight alteration (גְדָל־חָסֶד instead of רַב־חֶסֶד) that does not alter either the translation or the meaning.

These Psalter examples show how the formula of Exodus 34:6 became part of the thought of Israel and formed a convenient expression of confidence in God's character, especially as it was displayed in forgiving the sins of the people. What the people knew as part of their piety was integrated into their song.

Continuity of Covenantal Relationships in the Psalter

Just as the covenantal relationship forms the background of the ministry of the Old Testament prophets, so it also forms the background of the songs that Israel sang. They are based on the great themes of God's intervention in human history, first in choosing Abraham and then in redeeming a people for himself out of bondage and slavery in Egypt. At the heart of the covenant was God's grace and mercy. God established the bond between himself and Israel unilaterally, and it was an expression of his gracious favor to an undeserving people. Israel was not chosen because of size, importance, or moral stance before God but simply because he set his sovereign love on her (Deut. 7:7–8). The theme of covenant appears explicitly in the Psalter. The Abrahamic covenant is expounded in psalms such as Psalm 105, while the Sinai covenant features prominently in many psalms through references to experiences in Egypt, the Red Sea, and the desert. The Davidic covenant is the central focus of Psalms 89 and 132. In addition, the covenantal theme also appears implicitly in words and expressions that are used to reflect the relationship.[3] These include the declaration "I am your servant and your son" (עַבְדְּךָ וּבֶן־אֲמָתֶךָ), which was clearly a standard way of expressing allegiance to a sovereign (cf. Ahaz's words to Tiglath-pileser, 2 Kings 16:7).

Under the Mosaic law, the failure to attain to God's standard of obedience was met by the sacrificial system established at Sinai. The sacrifices were to be offered by a people already in a special relationship with God. The people offered sacrifices not to obtain God's grace but to retain it. The sacrificial offerings, whether for an individual or for the people as a whole, did not commence fellowship but maintained it. What disturbed the fellowship between the Lord and his people was removed by sacrifice. No more graphic ceremony could illustrate both the means of forgiveness and the reality of sins forgiven than that of the Day of Atonement (Leviticus 16). Two goats were selected, and the first one was offered as a sin offering. The other goat, after the sins of the people were transferred to it symbolically, was led away into the wilderness. The second goat made the point that the people's sin was forever removed.

---

3. See my discussions in Allan M. Harman, "The Abrahamic Covenant in the Psalter," in *An Everlasting Covenant: Biblical and Theological Essays in Honour of William J. Dumbrell*, ed. John A. Davies and Allan M. Harman, RTRSup 4 (Melbourne: Reformed Theological Review, 2010), 83–99; Harman, "The Exodus and the Sinai Covenant in the Book of Psalms," *Festschrift in Honor of Dr. Prof. In Whan Kim* (Seoul: Chongshin University, 2011), 128–69.

The earlier Old Testament teaching on God's nature and the means by which sinners could be reconciled to him are evident in the Psalms. Their teaching is a reflection of the covenantal relationship as displayed in the lives of individual believers. The verb "to atone," כִּפֶּר, occurs frequently in the book of Leviticus but only three times in the Psalter (Pss. 65:3; 78:38; 79:9). In each of these instances, the subject who atones is God himself. In Psalm 65:3, the psalmist declares, "When iniquities prevail against me, you atone for our transgressions" (פְּשָׁעֵינוּ אַתָּה תְכַפְּרֵם). In the context, this divine action is linked to God's choice (בָּחַר) of those whom he brings near to his courts (65:4). Psalm 78 is a historical retrospect of Israel's history that recounts many of the occasions on which Israel sinned against the Lord; 78:38 notes how God's merciful character was displayed in that "he, being compassionate, atoned for their iniquity and did not destroy them." The divine characteristic to which the psalmist appeals is God's compassion (רַחוּם), which may well be an echo of Exodus 34:6. It is significant that the psalmist goes on immediately to speak of the exodus experience, repeating so many of the distinctive expressions used in the book of Exodus to describe God's power in delivering his people from slavery in Egypt. He "redeemed them from the foe" (78:42), bringing out "his people like sheep" (78:52) and "to his holy land" (78:54). The final occurrence of "atone for" in the Psalms occurs in 79:9:

> Help us, O God of our salvation,
>   for the glory of your name;
> deliver us, and atone for our sins,
>   for your name's sake!

Like other similar appeals in the Old Testament, such as Micah 7:18 ("Who is a God like you, pardoning iniquity and passing over transgression for the remnant of his inheritance?"), the appeal in Psalm 79:9 is based on a comprehensive view of God's being and character. Because of his intrinsic nature, he intervenes between his anger and men's sins and removes transgression. The motives flow from his own nature, and the initiative is on his part.

The Concept of Justification in the Psalms

The concept of justification in the Psalter has to take into account two great doctrines. The first is God's character, especially his holiness, and the second is human sinfulness. The first of these aspects features prominently in the Psalter. So many attributes of God occur in the Psalms because the majority of the psalms are either prayers addressed to God or declarations about him, in which various aspects of his character are highlighted.

God's Holiness

When God gives the detailed instructions regarding worship in the book of Leviticus, his own self-declarations include the repeated affirmation, or a near variation, "For I [the

Lord] am holy" (Lev. 11:44–45; 19:2; 20:7, 26; 21:8). This concept was fundamental for Israel because it determined many aspects of the people's life. They had to reflect his holiness (Lev. 11:44–45; 19:2; 20:7, 26; 21:6), and it determined how they could approach him.

The Psalms teach about God's holiness in several ways. First, they have in common with the book of Isaiah the phrase "the Holy One of Israel." Of the twenty-six times this phrase appears in the Old Testament, only six occur in books other than Isaiah, three of which appear in the Psalms. In Psalm 71, the psalmist concludes by addressing praise to his God for his faithfulness and calls him, "O Holy One of Israel" (71:22). In a long historical review, Asaph recounts numerous occasions on which Israel rebelled against the Lord, and one of his summaries is that "they tested God again and again and provoked the Holy One of Israel" (78:41). The final occurrence in the Psalter is in a psalm that expands on the content of the Davidic covenant (2 Samuel 7) and in so doing extols the character of Israel as a people whose shield "belongs to the Lord, [whose] king to the Holy One of Israel" (Ps. 89:18). What these occurrences show is that the title "the Holy One of Israel" was quite widely known and used in Israel, whatever its origins may have been. While the vast majority of its occurrences are Isaianic, the expression was clearly part of Israel's praise.

The holiness of God is presented in other ways in the Psalter as well. The psalmist rarely attributes holiness directly to God, but one place where he does so is Psalm 22:2–3: "O my God, I cry by day, but you do not answer, and by night, but I find no rest. Yet you are holy, enthroned on the praises of Israel."[4] More common is the ascription of holiness to things belonging to or associated with the Lord. For example, the city of God is called "the holy habitation of the Most High" (46:4), his temple is holy (65:4), and his name is both holy and awesome (111:9). In regard to this last case, the "name" most probably stands for God's own self-revelation, so that there is little difference between saying "he is holy" and "his name is holy" (cf. 33:21; 103:1; 105:3; 106:47; 145:21).

The fact that God's earthly dwelling place, the temple, was holy, affords another significant aspect, because more than once the Psalter raises the question of how sinful humans can make their approach into his presence. Two psalms that address this question are Psalms 15 and 24. In Psalm 15, the psalmist commences by asking who can take up his abode and dwell in God's sanctuary, on his holy hill. The answer is a long list of moral characteristics that no one can measure up to (15:2–5). Anyone who looks at this list will notice that Psalm 24 is similar but with differences. The opening query is extended to a double question: "Who shall ascend the hill of the Lord? And who shall stand in his holy place?" (24:3). The idea is both of going up onto the mount of God and of having the ability to stand one's ground there. But the answer to the questions dispels any confidence that a person can do that, for the psalmist says, "He who has clean hands and a pure heart, who does not lift up his soul to what is false and does not

---

4. The expression "holy is he" comes three times in Psalm 99, and this is discussed later in this chapter, in the section "God's Justification in the Psalter."

swear deceitfully" (24:4). However, what is impossible for any human is not impossible with God, who is able to make provision for sinners to approach him: "He will receive blessing from the LORD and righteousness from the God of his salvation" (24:5). Old Testament believers had the message of grace, and it was to be expanded and explained further in the New Testament. God saves us,

> not because of works done by us in righteousness, but according to his own mercy, by the washing of regeneration and renewal of the Holy Spirit, whom he poured out on us richly through Jesus Christ our Savior, so that being justified by his grace we might become heirs according to the hope of eternal life. (Titus 3:5–7)

Another aspect of God's holiness presented repeatedly in the Psalter is God's "righteousness" or "justice." If holiness is the characteristic of God that sets him apart from us, then justice is a demonstration of that holiness, for it simply means to do what is right always and in all circumstances. That is revealed in God's actions as Lawgiver, Judge, promise keeper, and, especially, the one who pardons sin. While there are many references in the Psalms to God as the vindicator of his people against their enemies, the major significance here is the use of "righteousness" in relation to salvation of individuals. No passage is more relevant than Psalm 51, where David prays, "Deliver me from bloodguiltiness, O God, O God of my salvation, and my tongue will sing aloud of your righteousness'" (51:14). This is not a plea for vindication, as is shown by the use of the synonyms "salvation" and "righteousness." What the psalmist needs is unmerited forgiveness. The basis for such forgiveness lay in what Moses had long before declared about God: "Know therefore that the LORD your God is God, the faithful God who keeps covenant and steadfast love with those who love him and keep his commandments" (Deut. 7:9). In a psalm such as this, "righteousness" has become a redemptive attribute of God. The same use of this term can also be found in Psalms 31:1; 85:9–11; 89:16; 103:17; and 143:1.

Human Sinfulness

Discussion of justification in the Psalms has to be set against the Psalter's teaching on the universality of human sinfulness. When Paul wanted to show that both Jews and Gentiles were under the power of sin, he cited passages from the Old Testament as proof of his assertion. It is notable that most of the quotations are from the book of Psalms. This is the list, with the passages from the Psalter in italics:

> "*None is righteous, no, not one;*
>   *no one understands;*
>   *no one seeks for God.*
> *All have turned aside; together they have become worthless;*
>   *no one does good,*
>   *not even one."*

"Their throat is an open grave;
   they use their tongues to deceive."
"The venom of asps is under their lips."
   "Their mouth is full of curses and bitterness."
"Their feet are swift to shed blood:
   In their paths are ruin and misery,
and the way of peace they have not known."
   "There is no fear of God before their eyes." (Rom. 3:10–18)

The whole catena of passages is from the Psalter, with the only exception being Romans 3:15–17, where a passage from Isaiah 59:7–8 is inserted before the final quotation, which points to the origin of sin in the human heart.[5] The opening quotation from Psalm 14 depicts the condition of the whole world, a passage that has few equals in the Old Testament in relation to the universality and depth of human corruption. The following verses illustrate the general principle through quotations that demonstrate how sin affects speech in particular (Rom. 3:13–14) and then how it disturbs human relationships, even leading to murder (3:15–17).

The final quotation from Psalm 36:1 in Romans 3:18 is important since it states a general principle. It draws a sharp distinction between those who display the type of characteristics that have just been described in the quotations and those who fear God. The concept of fearing God is significant in the Psalms and Wisdom Literature, though the psalmist here does not use the normal expression (יִרְאַת יְהוָה) but rather one that speaks more of terror than loving veneration (פַּחַד אֱלֹהִים). But the point of the quotation is clear. No more apt verse could have been quoted to conclude the indictment of all men as being under sin. As John Murray comments, "The absence of this fear means that God is excluded not only from the centre of thought and calculation but from the whole horizon of our reckoning; God is not in all our thoughts. Figuratively, he is not before our eyes. And this is unqualified godlessness."[6]

The universal application of these quotations is made explicit in the words of Romans 3:19: "Now we know that whatever the law says it speaks to those who are under the law, so that every mouth may be stopped, and the whole world may be held accountable to God." The law condemns not only the Jews but the Gentiles as well. The implication is that the preceding quotations were characteristic of the Gentiles even though they did not have the Old Testament law. God's demands would confront them with judgment, so that all would be without excuse. The universality of sin is given expression emphatically in the words "every mouth" and "the whole world."

The whole section in Romans 3 is brought to a conclusion by a statement that presents another Psalter quotation: "For by works of the law no human being will

---

5. This listing of passages by Paul has often been referred to as an exhibition by him of rabbinic practice. However, no examples can be quoted of rabbis joining together passages such as Paul does here in order to reassert a particular aspect of teaching.
6. John Murray, *The Epistle to the Romans: The English Text with Introduction, Exposition and Notes*, NICNT (Grand Rapids, MI: Eerdmans, 1960), 1:105.

be justified in his sight, since through the law comes knowledge of sin" (3:20). The introductory words, "For by works of the law," are not actually part of the quotation from Psalm 143:2, though they appear here and in Galatians 2:16, where Paul uses the same quotation. By this introductory comment, Paul intends to define the scope of the negative expressed in the psalm. This definition is a correct interpretation of the psalm, for in the first clause of Psalm 143:2, "Enter not into judgment with your servant," the psalmist recognizes that if he were put on trial, he would be sentenced because of his deeds. The general statement that no one can be justified before God means that the psalmist did not expect justification to accrue through the works of the law. The thought of the quotation was well paraphrased by James Denney long ago: "Let mortal man, clothed in works of law, present himself before the Most High, and his verdict must always be: Unrighteous."[7]

A final comment on this passage with these numerous Psalms quotations is necessary. The indictments place in stark relief the utter sinfulness of all. However, they go further, for they form part of a section that has an integral place in the argument in Romans. In order to lay the foundations for the doctrine of justification by faith, the apostle Paul presents the whole world as guilty and condemned by God. Consequently, no one is able to achieve justification by keeping the law. That fact must be accepted before we are in a position to appreciate and embrace the grace shown in the gospel that Paul goes on to expound.

These quotations in Romans 3 merely give a sample of the Psalter's teaching regarding sin.[8] Throughout the Psalms both individual and corporate sin loom large. Psalms such as 78; 105; and 106 reflect on the communal exhibition of sinful behavior. A good illustration comes in the confession in Psalm 106:6: "Both we and our fathers have sinned; we have committed iniquity; we have done wickedness." Then there follows a catalog of offenses that Israel committed against their sovereign Lord. Songs such as these were meant to recall for the people their own willful rebellion, while at the same time remembering God's gracious adherence to his covenantal promises.

It is against this background that God's justifying grace has to be considered. The picture the Psalter presents is that God does not leave mankind in "the miry bog" (40:2) or crying "out of the depths" (130:1). Rather, he intervenes to save and in doing so blots out transgressions.

God's Justification in the Psalter

The term "justification" is not common in the Psalter, though the wider concept is. Justification is an act of God's free grace in forgiving sin. It shows that pardon is not dependent on man's ability to perform actions pleasing to God but rather is based on God's initiative in graciously removing iniquity.

---

7. James Denney, "St. Paul's Epistle to the Romans," in *The Expositor's Greek Testament*, ed. W. Robertson Nicoll (London: Hodder & Stoughton, 1917), 2:608.

8. For an excellent summary of the teaching on sin in the Psalter, see Geoffrey Grogan, *Psalms*, Two Horizons Old Testament Commentary (Grand Rapids, MI: Eerdmans, 2008), 326–41.

The New Testament usage of the verb "justify" (δικαιοω) has its background in the Old Testament.⁹ That usage stands over against the indictment against all mankind, expressed in the words "There is none who does good, not even one" (Pss. 14:3; 53:3; see also Paul's use of this verse in Rom. 3:12 as he begins his list of passages from the Old Testament proving universal guilt). The Hebrew verb "justify" (צָדַק) is not common in the Psalms, and at times, especially with *qal* forms, it is hard to decide whether the meaning is forensic or stative. This is so in passages like Psalms 51:4 and 143:2, where the context is not absolutely decisive, but usage elsewhere tends to suggest that the forensic meaning is intended.

Several other verbs are listed as meaning "to forgive" in the *Dictionary of Classical Hebrew*.¹⁰ These are כָּסָה, מָחַל, נָשָׂא, סָלַח, עָרַב, and סָכַךְ, though מָחַל can be disregarded since it does not appear in the Masoretic Text, while עָרַב and סָכַךְ do not appear with this meaning in the Psalms. The other three, while infrequent, are significant, especially with the occurrence of both סָכַךְ and נָשָׂא in Psalm 32 (see the discussion on this psalm on p. 77 below). In Psalms 25:11 and 103:3, סָלַח designates God's action in forgiving human sin, while the noun derived from the root סלח, סְלִיחָה, "forgiveness," comes in a significant context in Psalm 130:4. These, however, do not form the full vocabulary of forgiveness in the Psalter. In particular, Psalm 51 contains a cluster of expressions that all relate to removal of sin, and they seem to be virtually synonymous:

מָחָה	"blot out"	51:1, 9
כָּבַס	"wash"	51:2, 7
טָהֵר	"purify"	51:2, 7

The first of these verbs, מָחָה, occurs thirty-three times in the Old Testament, and practically all of them are theologically significant. When Israel sinned so grievously against the Lord at Sinai, Moses pled for forgiveness to be shown them. If the Lord would not, then he asked God to "please blot me out of your book that you have written" (Ex. 32:32). It is uncertain whether Moses was thinking about a stain or a debt in a ledger. In Psalm 51, the idea of a stain is prominent, as the synonym for "blot out" is "wash." David asks for cleansing so that his iniquity will be removed. The reverse request (i.e., "do not blot out") can be seen in Psalm 109:14, as in Nehemiah 4:5.

The second of these verbs, כָּבַס, "to wash," is not primarily a verb related to remission of sin, but it is used twice in this way in Psalm 51, as well as in Jeremiah 2:22 and 4:14. It is usually employed in reference to whitening cloth (as very frequently in Leviticus), and though in the passages in Jeremiah it refers to washing of the body, the usage is clearly metaphorical for cleansing from sin. No doubt exists about the usages in Psalm 51:2, 7, because the occurrences are in a context dealing with forgiveness and have the verb טָהֵר, "to cleanse," as a synonym.

---

9. For a discussion of the Old Testament background, see Murray, "Appendix A: Justification," in *Romans*, 1:336–47.
10. David J. A. Clines, ed., *Dictionary of Classical Hebrew*, vol. 9, *English-Hebrew Index; Word Frequency Table* (Sheffield: Sheffield Phoenix Press, 2016), 172.

The third verb, טָהַר, "to cleanse," is frequently used to describe the ritual cleansing of priests and people. It is made clear, however, that what was ultimately important was not ritual cleansing by the priest but God's action in cleansing from sins. This is the point that comes out in Hezekiah's prayer for those who may not have kept all the rules relating to ceremonial cleansing. He prays, "May the good LORD pardon everyone who sets his heart to seek God, the LORD, the God of his fathers, even though not according to the sanctuary's rules of cleanness" (2 Chron. 30:18–19). Likewise, in Psalm 51, when the root טהר appears three times (Ps. 51:2, 7, 10), it is pointing to divine action in removing sin.

One psalm that crystallizes the teaching of the Psalter on both God's holiness and his forgiving mercy is Psalm 99. Not only is he referred to as "holy" three times, and not only is worship at "his holy mountain," but also he is the God who has established equity and who executes justice and righteousness. The psalm is structured around a threefold refrain, all calling for praise of the holy God:

> Let them praise your great and awesome name!
>   Holy is he! (99:3)

> Exalt the LORD our God;
>   worship at his footstool!
>   Holy is he! (99:5)

> Exalt the LORD our God,
>   and worship at his holy mountain;
>   for the LORD our God is holy! (99:9)

There is a striking progression of thought to which the altered and expanded refrain corresponds. The two opening verses extol the Lord, who reigns over all, for though he is over Zion, he is also exalted over all peoples. Then comes the call for acknowledging his great and awesome name, with the declaration "Holy is he!" What follows is reference to the demonstration of God's holiness as shown by his justice (mentioned twice), his equity, and his righteousness, all of which have been displayed to his people ("in Jacob," 99:4). Then comes the second call to respond to his revelation by worshiping at his footstool and so acknowledging his holiness. The final part of the psalm instances three leaders in Israel—Moses, Aaron, and Samuel—who called on God and found him a ready help in time of trouble. In addressing God, the psalmist makes a wonderful statement: "O LORD our God, you answered them; you were a forgiving God to them, but an avenger of their wrongdoings" (99:8). The Hebrew text says, "You were the God taking away their iniquities." The final occurrence of the refrain expands it further: "Exalt the LORD our God, and worship at his holy mountain; for the LORD our God is holy!" (99:9). The climax is reached after linking together the concepts of God's holiness and his forgiving mercy. No other passage in the Psalter brings these two aspects into juxtaposition like this. Though sinful persons like the three mentioned knew full well of God's holiness, yet they also were deeply conscious of grace manifested to them. This latter fact is stressed by the use of the pronominal suffix in the phrase "*their* iniquities" and by the assertion that "*to them*" God was the one who could, and did, remove sin.

Luther's "Pauline Psalms"

It was the book of Psalms linked with Paul's teaching in Romans that brought Martin Luther to a living faith and to an assurance that in Christ he was forgiven all his sins. It is not surprising that the Psalter remained his favorite book all his life. Much later, long after his conversion, as recorded in the *Table Talk*, he was asked by his students on which books of the Bible they should preach. He gave priority, he said, to the Pauline psalms (Lat. *psalmi paulini*). They knew that the apostle did not compose any psalms, and hence they had to ask for an explanation. He indicated that he was referring to those such as Psalms 32; 51; 130; and 143, in which the teaching was identical to that in the Pauline Epistles.[11] Forgiveness of sins was not by human righteousness or achievements but solely from the free grace of God. Comment is needed on these psalms as they set out so clearly the expressions for sin and forgiveness that are typical of Old Testament teaching.

Psalm 32

Before reviewing the expressions in Psalm 32:1–2, it is necessary to take note of what the psalmist says in 32:3–4 concerning his spiritual condition. Here are his words:

> For when I kept silent, my bones wasted away
>   through my groaning all day long.
> For night and day your hand was heavy upon me;
>   my strength was dried up as by the heat of summer.

It is easy to see why a passage such as this appealed to Luther, for he had suffered physically while under God's heavy hand. He once reflected on his experience and wrote,

> Though I lived as a monk without reproach, I felt that I was a sinner before God with an extremely disturbed conscience. . . . I did not love, yes, I hated the righteous God who punishes sinners, and secretly, if not blasphemously, certainly murmuring greatly, I was angry with God.[12]

In the psalmist's experience, however, he was brought to the point where he knew that self-realization of his state was not sufficient. He had to confess his sins to his sovereign, "to the Lord" (לַיהוָה):

> I acknowledged my sin to you,
>   and I did not cover my iniquity;

---

11. Martin Luther, *D. Martin Luthers Werke, Kritische Gesamtausgabe: Tischreden* [Table Talk]. (Weimar: Hermann Böhlau Nachfolger, 1912–1921), 1:790–91.
12. Martin Luther, "Preface to the Complete Edition of Luther's Latin Writings," in *LW* 34:336–37.

I said: "I will confess my transgressions to the LORD,"
    and you forgave the iniquity of my sin. (32:5)

These words contain not only three of the basic terms for sin but also different expressions for confession and forgiveness. These can be tabulated in this way:

I *acknowledged* my *sin*.
I *did not cover* my *iniquity*.
I will *confess* my *transgressions*.
You *forgave* the *iniquity of my sin*.

Three common terms for wayward behavior are used. The first of these, "sin" (חֲטָאָה), describes missing the mark, while the second, "iniquity" (עָוֹן), usually denotes activity that is crooked or wrong, distorted behavior. These two terms are combined in the expression "the iniquity of my sin," one that is so unusual that many scholars have proposed some emendation. However, it may just be a case of hendiadys ("iniquity *and* sin"), or possibly an example of a double-duty suffix, "my sin," which would yield the translation "my iniquity, my sin."[13] The double expression shows how close the terms are in meaning, and it serves to emphasize the reality of God's actions toward him. The third term, "transgression" (פֶּשַׁע), speaks of rebellion or revolt.[14]

It is significant that the three terms used here in Psalm 32 for "sin" constitute a significant part of the Old Testament terminology for sin. It is not surprising that because of the strong moral basis for Old Testament religious faith, there is richness about the vocabulary for sin. While at least ten terms are evidenced, the three here are the most common, occurring together thirteen times as a combined cluster.[15] The order may vary, but the remarkable combination is clearly intended to point to the totality of human sin. What is true for Psalm 32 will be seen to be true also for Psalm 51.

Psalm 32:5 contains terms that can be set out as parallels:

| sin | iniquity | transgression |
| acknowledge | not cover | confess |

Both sets of parallels provide terms that are virtually synonymous. There are different aspects to sin and forgiveness, yet these expressions can often be interchanged as here.

While 32:3–5 sets out the personal experience of the psalmist, the opening verses formulate the same truths in doxological fashion for all mankind. Instead of the pronouncement of a single blessing, as at the opening of the Psalter (1:1), here there is a twofold blessing:

---

13. See Mitchell Dahood, *Psalms I: 1–50: A New Translation with Introduction and Commentary*, AB 16 (New York: Doubleday, 1965), 165.
14. For a discussion of the Old Testament terms for "sin," see Alex Luc, in *NIDOTTE*, 2:87–93.
15. Cf. the listing of the Old Testament language for "sin" in four groups as set out by Christopher R. North, *The Thought of the Old Testament: Three Lectures* (London: Epworth, 1948), 44–45.

> Blessed is the one whose transgression is forgiven,
>   whose sin is covered.
> Blessed is the man against whom the Lord counts not iniquity,
>   and in whose spirit there is no deceit (32:1–2).

The parallels here are as follows:

transgression	sin	iniquity
forgiven	covered	not counted

The first expression for forgiveness, at the opening of this psalm, is a regular one in the Hebrew Bible and one that occurs in very significant contexts. In particular, the usage of the phrase "to bear sin" (נָשָׂא חֵטְא) in Isaiah 53:12 must be taken into consideration, along with the parallel expression "to carry iniquity" (סָבַל עָוֹן) in 53:11. In his important study of these expressions in Isaiah 53, the late Alan Groves pointed out that these verbs signifying "to carry" or "to bear" can be followed by any of the three synonyms for sin: פֶּשַׁע, עָוֹן, or חֵטְא.[16] An examination of the usage of נשא plus one of the standard expressions for sin reveals that five categories can be isolated.[17] The fifth one, in which Yahweh is the subject, followed by one of the synonyms for sin, is the relevant category for Psalm 32:1, though with one qualification. The syntax is different in that a passive participle of נָשָׂא is used (נְשׂוּי), but the forgiver is clearly God, thus putting the term in the same category as those in which a finite verb is used. The opening of this psalm focuses immediately on the reality that transgression can be removed by the one to whom confession of it is made (32:5).

The second expression in Psalm 32:1 also uses a passive participle in noting that sin is covered (כְּסוּי חֲטָאָה). The verb כָּסָה occurs 155 times in the Hebrew Bible, usually in the literal sense of covering parts of the body, buildings, or natural objects. But here, as in Psalm 85:2, the expression "to cover sin" clearly is synonymous with "forgiving sin," as the contexts make plain.

The third expression is preceded by another pronouncement of blessing, with the declaration that this applies to the man to whom the Lord does not reckon iniquity (לֹא יַחְשֹׁב עָוֹן). The verb used here (חָשַׁב) is the same one that appears in Genesis 15:6 in reference to Abraham: "And he believed the Lord, and he *counted* it to him as righteousness." This verb comes from the field of accounting, though its semantic range widens to include "think," "consider," or "plan." When followed by the Hebrew preposition לְ, it indicates for whose benefit the action is intended. Here in Psalm 32, it is the "blessed man," whose transgressions are forgiven and whose sin is covered, who does not have his iniquity reckoned to his account.

---

16. J. Alan Groves, "Atonement in Isaiah 53: 'For He Bore the Sins of Many,'" in *The Glory of the Atonement: Biblical, Historical, and Practical Perspectives; Essays in Honor of Roger R. Nicole*, ed. Charles E. Hill and Frank A. James III (Downers Grove, IL: InterVarsity Press, 2004), 61–89.

17. Groves, "Atonement in Isaiah 53," 69–75.

The opening verses of Psalm 32 summarize biblical teaching about the nature of sin but also about the reality of God's forgiving grace. The terms "forgiven," "covered," and "not counted" likewise summarize the teaching on the removal of human rebelliousness toward God.

Psalm 51

The superscription to Psalm 51 is one of the longest in the whole collection. It runs as follows: "To the choirmaster. A Psalm of David, when Nathan the prophet went to him, after he had gone in to Bathsheba." This heading, together with the content of the psalm, certainly fits in with the record of the incident in 2 Samuel 11–12. Certainly, David's confession to Nathan, "I have sinned against the LORD" (12:13), agrees with the words in the psalm that it was against the Lord, and him only, that he had sinned (Ps. 51:4). His confession in 2 Samuel is all the more potent as it consists in Hebrew of just two words (חָטָאתִי לַיהוָה).

Just as with Psalm 32, it is easy to see why Martin Luther turned to this psalm. He could share with David the consciousness of sin that was pervasive. He felt plagued by his sin, having no rest day or night because of his terror of God's wrath and judgment. But more particularly, he could share in the graciousness of God in showing mercy to him and cleansing him from his sin. God heard his cry for mercy, washed him whiter than snow, and created in him a clean heart. David's experience was replicated in Luther's.

It is significant that the same three words for sin are employed in Psalm 51:1–2 as were used in 32:1–2: "transgression," "iniquity," and "sin." Once more the same cluster of terms is used, though in a variant order as compared with Psalm 32. However, the expressions for the removal of sin differ. Instead of "forgiven," "covered," and "not counted," David uses "blot out," "wash," and "cleanse." These are three standard terms for removal of sin,[18] but it is also relevant to note that they are repeated later in the psalm. "Wash" and "cleanse" appear together again in 51:7, while "blot out" appears in 51:9.

Bruce Waltke has provided an excellent summary of David's petitions in 51:1–2:

> On the basis of God's forgiving character, David boldly makes his double petition. First, he asks God to blot out (*mâhâ*, i.e., wipe the slate clean and remove God's wrath) his transgressions, one of several metaphors for forensic forgiveness in the Old Testament. And second, he requests that God "launder" him (*kâbas*) so as to "cleanse" him (*hâttâ'*, i.e., "de-sin") and purify him (*tâhêr*, i.e., make him fit for temple worship). God's forgiveness is required because David has violated God's standard of holiness. David's three words in the semantic domain of sin assume this standard: he fell short of it (*hâttâ'*, "sin"), rebelled against it (*pesaʿ*, "transgression") and deviated from it or perverted it and so incurred guilt (*ʿâwôn*, "iniquity").[19]

---

18. See the earlier discussion on these terms, in the section "God's Justification in the Psalter."
19. Bruce K. Waltke, "Atonement in Psalm 51: 'My Sacrifice, O God, Is a Broken Spirit,'" in Hill and James, *Glory of the Atonement*, 55–56.

Other teaching in Psalm 51 is also highly relevant. First, David speaks of his own sin in connection with Bathsheba and Uriah in its primary orientation as sin against God. This was not to deny that he sinned against others, but in pleading for mercy he says, "Against you, you only, have I sinned and done what is evil in your sight, so that you may be justified in your words and blameless in your judgment" (51:4). The ESV translation brings out well the force of the Hebrew word order. The primary focus of sin is against God. Men might have acquitted David,[20] yet he knows that before God he is guilty of adultery and murder. The final words of 51:4 are quoted by Paul in Romans 3:4. God is true to his pledged word. He is "justified" when he hears the cry for mercy and then acts in accordance with his covenantal promises.

Second, David traces his sinfulness back to the point of his conception in his mother's womb (Ps. 51:5). In this verse he is speaking of the inborn bias that affects all of us by nature. Sin inevitably appears in each new life. Paul's explanation of this is that "sin came into the world through one man, and death through sin, and so death spread to all men because all sinned" (Rom. 5:12).

Third, in Psalm 51:7–10, David invokes the language of priestly cleansing. Hyssop, a common plant, was used at the Passover (Ex. 12:22) but also in connection with purificatory procedures carried out by the priests (see Lev. 14:4, 6, 49, 51, 52). In addition to his earlier pleas, he now seeks that God would sprinkle him so that he might become whiter than snow. It is probable that this imagery is echoed in Isaiah's words to the sinful people of his day when the Lord says, "Though your sins are like scarlet, they shall be as white as snow" (Isa. 1:18).

Fourth, the psalmist realizes that offering sacrificial worship by itself is insufficient to cleanse him from the guilt of his sins. What is needed is something deeper accompanying any other formal act of contrition. He needs to offer "a broken spirit," "a broken and contrite heart" (Ps. 51:17).

Psalm 130

In the history of the Christian church, Psalm 130 has often been known by its opening words in Latin, *De profundis*. It is not difficult to understand how Luther was able to identify so strongly with the words of this psalm. He, too, knew what it was like to pass through depths of despair. Based on this psalm he composed an evangelical hymn, *Aus tiefer schrei ich zu dir* ("From Depths of Woe I Cry to Thee").

Most probably, this psalm dates from the postexilic period, since it contains expressions in Hebrew that come from that era. The appeal to God in 130:2 is in a form that appears elsewhere only in 2 Chronicles 6:40 ("Let . . . your ears [be] attentive to . . ."). The root behind the verb "attentive" is fairly common, but the adjective here (and another similar one in Neh. 1:6, 11) are clearly from late Hebrew. In addition, the word

---

20. There is insufficient evidence in the biblical text to determine how widely in Israel David's sin was regarded as incurring no penalty. It is possible that Ahithophel, David's counselor, was Bathsheba's grandfather (see 2 Sam. 11:3; 15:12; 23:34). If so, this would help explain why he deserted David and went over to Absalom, but no certainty can be reached on this.

for "forgiveness" in Psalm 130:4 occurs only here and in Daniel 9:9 and Nehemiah 9:17. It is significant that these three passages are all confessions of sin but have linked with them the assurance of God's pardoning mercy.

Psalm 130 starts with a cry for mercy, an appeal from a situation of deep distress. The phrase "out of the depths" in other Old Testament passages seems to refer to the depths of the sea (cf. 69:2, 14; Isa. 51:10; Ezek. 27:34), but here it relates to a deep consciousness of sin, since it is immediately followed by the words "If you, O LORD, should mark iniquities, O Lord, who could stand?" (Ps. 130:3). The Hebrew behind the verb "mark" (תִּשְׁמָר) may well have the somewhat stronger meaning of "record," as if sins were noted down in a book.[21] Behind this question lies the thought that it is impossible for a sinner to stand his ground before a holy God (see 24:3, "And who shall *stand* in his holy place?"). What gives the psalmist confidence is that "forgiveness" (סְלִיחָה) belongs to God—that is, it is his to dispense. God alone is able to forgive and remember sin no more (Isa. 43:25).

However, this psalm goes further, for after speaking of his own eager waiting for God's response and intervention in his need (Ps. 130:5–6), the psalmist issues a call to Israel: "O Israel, hope in the LORD! For with the LORD there is steadfast love, and with him is plentiful redemption. And he will redeem Israel from all his iniquities" (130:7–8). The link with God's covenant is made through the reference to the expression often used in connection with it: "steadfast love" (חֶסֶד). This is one of the terms that is intimately connected with the administration of God's covenant with Israel. The word used here for "redemption" (פְּדוּת) occurs only here and in Psalm 111:9, though it comes from a common root that is used in the final verse of the psalm. No adjective appears with "redemption," but "plentiful" is acceptable because "redemption" is governed by a verbal form meaning, "[he] *multiplies* redemption." While the Hebrew verb "redeem" is often used of deliverance or rescue from some distress, this is the only time it is employed with reference to redemption from sin. The extent of the removal of sin is stressed in the final statement of the psalm, where the verb from the same root, "redeem" (פָּדָה), occurs: "And he [the LORD] will redeem Israel from all his iniquities" (130:8). All the iniquities can be taken away, though it is only later in the New Testament that it is explained how this is effected (see 1 John 1:8–10). That forgiveness is an action of God is emphasized in the Hebrew text by the way the psalmist refers to iniquities being removed: "*He himself* will redeem Israel" (וְהוּא יִפְדֶּה).

Psalm 143

Psalm 143 is the last of Luther's "Pauline psalms" and also the last of the penitential psalms. Twice in his epistles (Rom. 3:20; Gal. 2:16), the apostle Paul quotes the second part of Psalm 143:2: "For no one living is righteous before you," and on both occasions

---

21. Clines, *Dictionary of Classical Hebrew*, 8:481, gives as the meaning here "give heed to, pay regard to, take note of," or perhaps "record." See also the comments of Mitchell Dahood, *Psalms III: 101–150: A New Translation with Introduction and Commentary*, AB 17A (Garden City, NY: Doubleday, 1970), 234.

he adds the words "not by works of the law" (ἐξ ἔργων νομου). This is an implication that Paul draws from the psalm.

Like other psalms (e.g., Psalm 86), the psalmist draws on a deep knowledge of other biblical passages in framing his petitions. There was clearly a great variety of language that could be used in prayer, which formed a reservoir of vocabulary and phrases suitable for individuals to employ in time of need. Throughout, this psalm contains some of the most beautiful language of faith and trust found anywhere in the Old Testament.

The first half of Psalm 143 consists of verses 1–6, which is marked off by the insertion of *selah* at the end of 143:6. In this section the psalmist describes his situation and makes his appeal to God. Once again, a psalmist makes his plea for mercy, asking God to listen to his prayer. The opening request is very similar to those in nearby psalms (see 140:6; 141:1), just as other words in this psalm (like "refuge") also have links with nearby poems (for "refuge," see 142:5). The appeal is for God to act according to his righteousness and to not enter into judgment with his servant. This is an acknowledgment that if the psalmist was put on trial, he could be judged and sentenced only according to his deserts. The reason behind the appeal is further emphasized in the declaration in 143:2: "For no one living is righteous before you." The implication is that the psalmist did not consider that anyone would achieve a righteous standing with God by performance of works of the law.

Other Psalter Passages

Luther seized on certain Psalter passages, probably because they were integral to his own spiritual experience. However, the so-called "Pauline psalms" are not the only Psalter passages that are relevant to the discussion of the doctrine of justification, and attention is now given to other passages.

The Penitential Psalms

From the time of the early church fathers, a group of psalms were referred to as the penitential psalms. Augustine (AD 354–430) knew them by this title, and Cassiodorus (ca. AD 485–ca. 585) was also familiar with them. Included were Psalms 6; 32; 38; 51; 102; 130; and 143. Four of these have already been discussed (Psalms 32; 51; 130; 143), and now the others must be given consideration. Psalms 6 and 38 have much in common, including the way they commence:

> O Lord, rebuke me not in your anger,
>   nor discipline me in your wrath. (6:1)

> O Lord, rebuke me not in your anger,
>   nor discipline me in your wrath. (38:1)[22]

---

22. There is some variation in the Hebrew, including different words for "wrath," but the essential meaning is identical in both psalms.

In Psalm 6, the psalmist goes on to ask for mercy to be shown to him in his distress, which brings him near to death (see 6:4–5). The latter part of the psalm (6:8–10) displays a completely different tone, which may indicate that a sacrifice had been made or a priestly word, like that given by Eli to Hannah (1 Sam. 1:17), had been spoken. Psalm 38 reveals a similar situation, with a combination of factors affecting the psalmist. On the one hand, he is distressed by bodily weakness and disease. On the other hand, he is also conscious of sin, saying, "I confess my iniquity; I am sorry for my sin" (38:18). He doesn't want to be forsaken by God but pleads for speedy help from the Lord, for his salvation (38:22).

Psalm 102 contains a very unusual title: "A Prayer of one afflicted, when he is faint and pours out his complaint before the Lord." No other psalm has a title like this, nor is there any indication of the historical circumstances behind it. The references to deserted Zion in 102:13, 16, and 21 are very similar to the description of Zion given in Lamentations 5:17–18 and hence most probably point to an exilic provenance. However, there is no direct confession of sin or indication that God is the one who removes guilt. The most that can be said is that individual weakness and national desolation are both matters that can be remedied only by divine intervention.

Psalm 49

Psalm 49 is a wisdom song, which the opening verses make plain (see the words "wisdom," "meditation," "proverb," and "riddle" in 49:3–4). Like other wisdom psalms, it notes that there are those who have false ideas about how they can achieve a reconciled relationship for themselves or others. The psalmist asserts, in opposition to these false ideas, that no man can possibly give a ransom price for another. One of the main verbs for "ransom" (פָּדָה) is used in 49:7, in a very strong assertion of the fact that no one can redeem a brother (אָח לֹא־פָדֹה יִפְדֶּה אִישׁ), almost as if the translation could be, "There's no way that a man can possibly ransom his brother."[23] In the parallel clause, "or give to God the price of his life," the term "price" (כֹּפֶר) is the common word for the "ransom" money given for the service of the sanctuary (Ex. 30:12). Another synonym follows in Psalm 49:8, where the psalmist refers to how costly ransom is. The word used, פִּדְיוֹן, is related to the verb פָּדָה in the previous verse. Two things are significant about the usage in Psalm 49. First, it illustrates the usage of two different Hebrew roots (פָּדָה and כָּפַר) in relation to redemption, and second, it declares plainly that redemption is not within man's province. No human can pay God to preserve life. Death is the inevitable end of all people, no matter how much wealth they might have accumulated during their lives.

Psalm 103

It is somewhat strange that Martin Luther did not link Psalm 103 with Psalms 32; 51; 130; and 143, since it sets out very clearly the Old Testament teaching regarding

---

23. Waltke, "Atonement in Psalm 51," 55–56.

forgiveness. This is done in a way that is almost comparable for clarity to the New Testament, for it is a proclamation of God's great love for his people, though the method of removing sin remained for later revelation. This song also has strong links with the idea of covenant, both through repeated mention of God's steadfast love (חֶסֶד, 103:4, 8, 17) and through the express reference to God's covenantal blessings (103:18), before the concluding call to all creation to bless the Lord (103:20–22). From various angles, this psalm is almost a creedal statement in itself. It commences with the triple call to bless the holy name of the Lord (103:1–2), which is matched by a quadruple call at the end of the psalm (103:20–22). After the opening call to himself ("my soul" here equals "I"),[24] the psalmist goes on to enumerate God's characteristics by means of a series of participles. These are followed by praise for divine revelation by word and deed (103:7), while setting the limits to God's righteous anger against sin. The psalmist declares that "he will not always chide" (103:9) and that he will not demand full payment according to our iniquities (103:10).

There is clear structure in the psalm, and in the section dealing with the mercy of God (103:8–19), the presentation is planned to highlight God's enduring character. First, negative statements set the scene for the statements that follow: "He will not always chide, nor will he keep his anger forever. He does not deal with us according to our sins, nor repay us according to our iniquities" (103:9–10). A time limit applies to God's judgment, and instead of strictly applying justice to sinners, he shows compassion in treating them differently from what they deserve. Following these negatives, the psalmist provides three illustrations to help in understanding how gracious God is. The first is that God's covenantal love is as great as the heavens are above the earth (103:11). Second, sin is so removed that just as it is impossible for east and west to come together, so it is impossible for our iniquity to return to us (103:12). Third, God shows fatherly compassion to his children, for he recognizes their frailty (103:15–16). They are human, dust of the earth, and to dust they will return (Gen. 3:19). Every time soil is tilled, it is a demonstration of both human origin and human destiny. The thought of frail humanity leads to the assertions in Psalm 103:17–19 that are similar to the thought of Psalm 90. Men appear on the earth but then vanish, whereas God's steadfast love and righteousness are eternal.

The psalmist notes God's characteristics by listing them, employing participles in Hebrew. The choice of this verbal form seems to have been deliberate in order to emphasize the ongoing activity of God.[25] This is the list, with each characteristic commencing with a participle yet without a relative pronoun, as is added in the ESV and in most English versions:[26]

---

24. Cf. the same usage in the Magnificat (Luke 1:46–55), where Mary's use of "my soul" and "my spirit" are just other expressions for "I."
25. The participle in Hebrew has no time designation built into it. Rather, it is timeless, taking its tense from the context. Participles "describe continuous action in the time of the context, which may be either past, present or future." Page H. Kelley, *Biblical Hebrew: An Introductory Grammar* (Grand Rapids, MI: Eerdmans, 1992), 200.
26. This quasi creed can be compared to the confession in 1 Tim. 3:16, where the phrases are not connected by pronouns or particles.

Forgives all your iniquity[27]
Heals all your diseases
Redeems your life from the pit
Crowns [better, *surrounds*] you with steadfast love and mercy
Satisfies you with good so that your youth is renewed like the eagle's

The word used for "forgive" (סָלַח) is used exclusively in the Old Testament of a gracious action of God in bypassing the transgressions of humans. It is never used of people forgiving one another. Its parallel is "heals" (רָפָא), which can be applied to the healing of spiritual diseases (see Ps. 147:3; Isa. 53:5), though here it is used of the literal healing of illnesses that have almost brought the psalmist down to the grave. The following phrase, "redeems your life from the pit," is used not of redemption from sin but of rescue from the grave.[28] While the translation "crowns you with steadfast love" is possible, the only unambiguous instance of the meaning "crowns" for this Hebrew term is Song of Songs 3:11. More feasible is the translation "surrounds," which gives the good idea that God's "steadfast love and mercy" totally encompasses the believer. The final participle in this list is "satisfies," which describes being invigorated with fresh strength so that the believer is like the mighty eagle (see the same imagery used in Isa. 40:31).

The longest section in the psalm is the second one (Ps. 103:6–19), with its historical references, a strong declaration of the reality of God's forgiveness, and a reassertion that the eternal God maintains his steadfast love for those who fear him. The introduction of Moses into the song is significant: "He made known his ways to Moses, his acts to the people of Israel" (103:7). After the sin of Israel at Sinai (Ex. 32:1–35), Moses interceded with God for the people. Among his petitions was this request: "Now therefore, if I have found favor in your sight, please show me now your ways, that I may know you in order to find favor in your sight" (33:13). What the psalm says is that God did make his "ways" known to Moses, using the same word for "ways" as in Exodus 33. The historical incident has to be when God passed by Moses, allowing him to see only his after-glory (33:17–34:9).

The link between Exodus 34 and Psalm 103 is confirmed by the quotation in the following verse of part of God's self-declaration of his own character: "The LORD is merciful and gracious, slow to anger and abounding in steadfast love" (103:8). These words are identical with those in Exodus 34, though lacking the final couplet, "and faithfulness." They form a definition of the manner in which God made his "ways" known to Moses. In the situation in which the people found themselves, God did not retain his anger forever, nor deal with them according to their sins, nor repay them according to their iniquities. Once more, the same triplet of terms for sin appears as that found in Psalms 32 and 51—"sin" (103:10), "iniquity" (103:3), "transgression" (103:12). The

---

[27]. The pronoun "your" refers back to "my soul" in Ps. 103:1–2. This means that it is equivalent to speaking about "my iniquities," "my diseases," "my life," and so forth.

[28]. The word for "redeem" here (גּוֹאֵל), while quite frequent in Exodus–Deuteronomy, is not the most common verb for "redeem," which is פָּדָה. The former verb comes from the realm of relationship, while the latter one is from commerce.

words that follow seem to be a commentary on what happened after God's declaration, for Moses's request that God forgive the people (Ex. 34:9) is immediately followed by the account of the restoration of the covenantal relationship (34:10–28). In recounting part of that history here, the psalmist emphasizes the free grace of God. The Lord acted contrary to what would have been expected ("according to our sins") and instead showed his "steadfast love" (Ps. 103:11, 17). This truth is reaffirmed in a different way in 103:13, where the psalmist speaks of God's "compassion," an echo from the declaration in Exodus 34:6. "Compassion" here is the verbal form of the same root that is used in an adjectival form in Exodus, translated "merciful" in the ESV. His fatherly interest in those who fear him manifests itself in merciful actions toward them.

The reality of divine forgiveness is brought out by the imagery of Psalm 103:12, which utilizes language other than the standard terms for forgiveness used earlier ("forgives," 103:3; "redeems," 103:4). Hebrew has no word for "infinity" but has to employ language like that here to express the concept. Sin is removed, says the psalmist, as far as the east is from the west. The idea is that the removal is so complete that there can be no thought of it ever being brought into reckoning again. This picture forms part of the imagery that the psalmists and prophets employ to designate the absoluteness of God's action in forgiving. Psalm 51 speaks of "blotting out" or "washing" to achieve spiritual cleanliness that is "whiter than snow" (51:1–2, 7, 9). Isaiah records God's call to his rebellious people to come to him and find that their sins can be made "as white as snow" (Isa. 1:18), and he proclaims God's promise that he will blot out sins for his own sake (43:25). Similar teaching is embodied in the language of Jeremiah when the Lord says, "I will forgive their iniquity, and I will remember their sin no more" (Jer. 31:34). Striking language occurs in Micah 7:19, where the Lord promises that he will renew his compassion and that the people's sins will be cast "into the depths of the sea." This is what Dale Ralph Davis identified as the "Egyptian treatment," since the language in Micah calls to mind the description in Exodus 15:4–5 and 10 of how the Egyptians went down under the waters, never to be seen again: "If Yahweh does that with his people's sin, then *their guilt can no longer haunt us.*"[29]

Comparison between the description of forgiveness in Psalm 103 and the procedure on the Day of Atonement is also warranted. On the one hand, Psalm 103 uses the language of infinity to spell out the severance between sinners and their sin. On the other hand, the Day of Atonement (Leviticus 16) provides pictorial language concerning the scapegoat that teaches to the same end. On the Day of Atonement, after the high priest made due preparations, one goat was offered as a burnt offering. This act symbolized the means by which forgiveness was effected, for without the shedding of blood there could be no expiation of sin. However, that left unstated the reality of forgiveness. Not only did the people need to appreciate how essential sacrifice was for sins, but they also needed reassurance of its effectiveness. That was obtained by the

---

29. Dale Ralph Davis, *Micah*, EP Study Commentary (Darlington, UK: Evangelical Press, 2010), 166; italics original.

use of the second goat, the scapegoat or "escape goat." After the priest had confessed the sins of the people on the goat, it was led away into the wilderness by a good man. It did not matter what happened to it there, for the picture was of the people's sins vanishing forever, never to be brought back into reckoning against them. Both Psalm 103 and Leviticus 16 teach the same truth. Sin, by means appointed by God, can be removed absolutely.

National or Collective Forgiveness

Another aspect that needs consideration relates to God's forgiveness of *Israel's sins*, looking at them in a collective fashion. God made several provisions whereby the historical facts of the exodus were continually brought before the people. The Passover, introduced at the time of the exodus, was in itself a teaching mechanism, intended to be used as a tool within the family circle for reminding everyone of what God had done. When the children asked, "What do you mean by this service?" this answer was to be given: "It is the sacrifice of the LORD's Passover, for he passed over the houses of the people of Israel in Egypt, when he struck the Egyptians but spared our houses" (Ex. 12:26–27). The Passover was an annual festival celebrating God's sparing mercy.

Song also played a prominent part in reminding Israel of how God had intervened in redeeming action for the people. Just prior to entry into the land of Canaan, God gave a special song to his people (Deut. 31:30–32:47). He delivered it to Moses (31:19), who wrote it down and taught it to the Israelites (31:22). Joshua joined Moses in this act (32:44), so the departing and incoming leaders of Israel were linked in giving this song.

The Song of Witness in Deuteronomy 32 has to be seen in a wider context, and this makes clear its connection with the historical psalms (e.g., Psalms 78; 105; 106; 135; 136). These songs are part of the response to the God of Israel, whether in private or public, whereby the people of Israel reaffirmed their commitment to the covenantal Lord. In these songs, the people not only magnified the deeds of the Lord but also made confession of their sin and covenant breaking. The inclusion of this particular song as "the song of Moses, the servant of God, and the song of the Lamb" in Revelation 15:3–4 testifies to its importance. It appears in Deuteronomy as part of a covenantal document and reflects certain strong resemblances to the covenantal pattern of the book itself.[30]

The historical psalms referred to above form a group of songs that enabled Israel to repeat her history again and again. They are poetical but narrate a story of the great deeds of the Lord, while also pointing to the waywardness of the people. Psalm 78 commences in a wisdom style (even using the word "parable," 78:2), encouraging parents to tell the deeds of the Lord to successive generations so that they, too, would come to trust him. Also, the point is emphasized that this passing on of the faith would ensure that they were not like their forefathers, "a stubborn and rebellious generation, a generation whose heart was not steadfast, whose spirit was not faithful to God" (78:8). Yet God,

---

30. I have discussed the covenantal implications of this song in Allan M. Harman, *Deuteronomy: The Commands of a Covenant God* (Fearn, Ross-shire, Scotland: Christian Focus, 2007), 271–73.

"being compassionate, atoned for their iniquity and did not destroy them; he restrained his anger often and did not stir up all his wrath" (78:38).

Psalms 105 and 106 together recount much of the history of Israel after leaving Egypt until the period after the occupation of the land of Canaan. There is a notable contrast drawn between the people's forgetfulness of God and his remembrance of them. Whereas he remembered his covenantal promises (105:8, 42), they forgot what he had done (106:7, 13, 21) and had to be urged to remember his wonders (105:5) and to seek his remembrance of them (106:4). These psalms testify that in spite of all their sins, God dealt in mercy with his people. Their sin was forgiven time and time again: "For their sake he remembered his covenant, and relented according to the abundance of his steadfast love" (106:45). The theme of enduring covenantal love carries over into Psalm 107, which opens with the words "Oh give thanks to the LORD, for he is good, for his steadfast love endures forever!" (107:1). It is clear that those words, which occur at the commencement of both Psalms 106 and 107, became a fixed part of the liturgy of Israel.

Psalms 135 and 136 form another pair of historical psalms placed in conjunction with one another. The authors of these psalms were very familiar with other parts of the Old Testament, especially with other psalms. There is a marked similarity between these two psalms, particularly in relation to the historical statements.[31] The opening call to praise the Lord sets the tone for Psalm 135, for it focuses on the character of God (in contrast to the inability of idols to help, 135:15–18), and his redemptive actions on behalf of Israel. God is not only "great," but he is also "good" (טוֹב, 135:3). This word "good" has strong covenantal connotations.[32] The opening of Psalm 136 repeats the liturgical statement of the first verse of both Psalms 106 and 107: "Give thanks to the LORD, for he is good, for *his steadfast love endures forever*." The combination of two specifically covenantal terms ("good" and "steadfast love") form a fixed pair in Hebrew, and it highlights the nature of the Lord's relationship to Israel.[33] He displayed his covenantal commitments to his people, redeeming them from slavery in Egypt "with a strong hand and outstretched arm" (136:12). This phrase is the echo of a frequent description of how Israel was brought out of slavery in Egypt, especially in the book of Deuteronomy (3:24; 4:34; 5:15; 6:21; 7:8, 19; 9:26; 11:2; 26:8).

What is unique in Psalm 136 is that the words "his steadfast love endures forever" form a refrain to every verse. The psalm itself continues the themes of God as Creator and Redeemer from the previous song. Redemption from Egypt and occupation of the land of promise are the central ideas of both psalms. The inability of Israel to save herself from bondage and dispossess the nations of Canaan is stressed by the

---

31. I have noted some of these parallels in Allan Harman, *Psalms*, Mentor Commentary (Fearn, Ross-shire, Scotland: Mentor, 2011), 2:941.

32. See the discussion by A. R. Millard, "For He Is Good," *TynBul* (1966): 115–17, and the literature he cites. For more on the covenantal significance of טוֹב (and its cognate טוֹבָה), see Paul Kalluveettil, *Declaration and Covenant: A Comprehensive Review of Covenant Formulae from the Old Testament and the Ancient Near East* (Rome: Biblical Institute Press, 1982), 42–47.

33. "Fixed pair" refers to two words in Hebrew that very frequently occur in combination, so that they almost represent a single idea.

terminology of Psalm 136 and also by the absence of any reference to the roles of Joshua and the Israelite army. Grace was shown to an undeserving people, and divine power accomplished all that forms the content of the psalm. From 136:4 to 136:25, every statement depends for its grammatical subject on the expressions in 136:1–3: "Lord," "the God of gods," and "the Lord of lords." No human agency could produce the outcome for Israel described here. The goodness and love of her covenantal Lord was the sole explanation of Israel's salvation and inheritance of Canaan.

So important was this affirmation of the enduring nature of God's covenantal mercy that it was used on numerous important occasions. It served to remind Israel of the character of her God and of his continued faithfulness to her. When David brought the ark of the covenant to Jerusalem, he sang a song of thanksgiving that combined parts of Psalms 96; 105; and 106, which included the words "Oh give thanks to the Lord, for he is good; for his steadfast love endures forever!" (1 Chron. 16:34). Similar significant religious events also called for such a declaration. On completion of the temple, the ark was brought into its place in the inner sanctuary. The musicians played, and the vocalists sang, "For he is good, for his steadfast love endures forever!" (2 Chron. 5:13). At the dedication of the temple, the same Psalter verse was sung by the assembled people of God (2 Chron. 7:3), while much later, Jehoshaphat, as he led his army into battle, appointed men to sing the same refrain (2 Chron. 20:21). Solemn liturgical occasions called for reaffirming central truths of the faith.

Justification in the Wisdom Books
The Nature of the Wisdom Books

A contrast between the Psalms and the Wisdom Books appears very quickly when comparing their treatments of the teaching concerning God's justifying grace, as we discuss in this section.

The Wisdom Literature is generally regarded as consisting of Job, Proverbs, and Ecclesiastes, with the Song of Songs added mainly because it features the name Solomon (Song 1:5; 3:7, 9, 11; 8:11–12) and because it is dealing with courtship and marriage. The grouping of these biblical books is due to the prevalence of the words "wisdom" (חָכְמָה) and "wise" (חָכָם) in them. Of 346 occurrences of the root חכם in the Old Testament, 189 are in Job, Proverbs, and Ecclesiastes, including 22 instances in which the Aramaic equivalents are used.[34] While passages in other books are very similar in style and content (as, for example, Psalms 37 and 73), they are not incorporated in this present discussion.

The Wisdom Literature is primarily concerned not with a forensic relationship but with the demonstration of godliness in practical life. The Hebrew word for "wisdom" refers to particular characteristics or special abilities of individuals. As Gerald Wilson puts it, "Wisdom is what we might call 'know-how'—practical skills and talents in areas

---

34. These statistics are taken from R. N. Whybray, *The Intellectual Tradition in the Old Testament*, BZAW 135 (New York: de Gruyter, 1974), 75n20.

as diverse as metal work, painting, agriculture, political scheming, and the like."[35] In the Wisdom Books we see displayed what a right relationship with God means in everyday life. Godliness, as portrayed in the Wisdom Literature, appears in working clothes. The writers reflect on human life from the standpoint of a right relationship with God, and they embody the distillation of practical wisdom.

In reviewing the Wisdom Literature in relation to justification, it should be apparent that no one should expect to find in them the explicit teaching on divine forgiveness contained in the Psalms, for their purpose is different. They contain teaching that is consonant with that of the Psalms and other Old Testament books, but they are not part of the canon aimed at expounding the means of reconciliation. They assume the Creator-creature distinction that is fundamental to Old Testament theology and recognize that deep dependence on God and his sovereign grace is essential for those who profess religious faith.

But it is surprising how often the concepts of "right" and "righteousness" do occur in the Wisdom Literature. In comparison to the sparse use of the Hebrew root צדק in Genesis (15x), Deuteronomy (18x), or Chronicles (6x), in Job, Proverbs, and Ecclesiastes, it occurs 140 times out of a total of 523 occurrences in the Hebrew Bible as a whole.[36] This means that in three Wisdom books are found just over a quarter of all occurrences of this root. Perhaps the reason for this lies in the fact that the wise men were deeply concerned with being right and acting rightly before God.

That relationship is tackled in another way too, which the prevalence of the concept of "the fear of the LORD" in these books demonstrates. Rather than being a concept foreign to the rest of Old Testament theology, "the fear of the LORD" may well be the unifying principle of the whole, "as one of the formal connectors between the wisdom writers and the theology of the *tora* and prophets."[37] This fear, which consists in a recognition of God's sovereignty and a response in awe and obedience, is called both "the beginning of knowledge" (Prov. 1:7) and "the beginning of wisdom" (Ps. 111:10; Prov. 9:10). Humility is a basic part of this fear, as humans, aware of the gap between a righteous God and themselves, bow before him and seek spiritual knowledge from him.

Job

Many questions relating to Job have to be set aside for this discussion, such as the date of the book, the significance of its structure, and textual difficulties. The last hundred or so years of the study of Job have not seen any radical change on dating, and a wide variety of dates are still proposed, from patriarchal to late postexilic. However, what is important is that Job is represented as living in the pre-Mosaic era. He is rich in cattle

---

35. Gerald H. Wilson, *Job*, Understanding the Bible Commentary Series (Grand Rapids, MI: Baker, 2007), 3.
36. These statistics are provided by David Reimer in *NIDOTTE*, 3:754.
37. Walter C. Kaiser Jr., "Integrating Wisdom Theology into Old Testament Theology: Ecclesiastes 3:10–15," in *A Tribute to Gleason Archer*, ed. Walter C. Kaiser Jr. and Ronald F. Youngblood (Chicago: Moody Press, 1986), 199. See also his earlier article "Wisdom Theology and the Centre of Old Testament Theology," *EvQ* 50 (1978): 132–46. One of the best discussions on the concept in its broadest sweep is Henri Blocher, "The Fear of the Lord as the 'Principle' of Wisdom," *TynBul* 28 (1977): 3–28.

and flocks, and as the head of the family, he is its priest, offering up sacrifices (Job 1:5; 42:8) just as the patriarchs did (Gen. 22:13; 31:54). Even the word for "sacrifices" (עֹלוֹת) is that for burnt offerings, not one of the more technical terms of the Mosaic law. Moreover, the words for God used by the speakers are associated with the patriarchal use (e.g., אֵל, אֱלוֹהַּ), though the distinctive covenantal name, יהוה (Yahweh), does appear in Job's final speeches.

The book of Job is structured around a core that consists of a series of long speeches by Job and his three friends. This is didactic poetry, which, while part of inspired revelation, contains fallacious arguments that are not specifically answered in the book. The introductory narrative in Job 1:1–2:13 sets the scene, while the divine speeches in chapters 38–41 provide God's response to Job's condition, to which Job replies in a short poetic speech admitting his inability to penetrate the mind of God (42:1–6). The final verses of the book form a concluding prose narrative matching the opening. They record how the three friends offered sacrifices, while Job prayed for them, and how in the end Job's prosperity was restored (42:7–17).[38]

While the problems of suffering and retribution are clearly part of the argument of Job, they cannot be regarded as the major theological issues since they are missing from the divine speeches at the end. Elihu finishes his speech by referring to the appearance of God in a whirlwind (37:14–24), and when the Lord speaks, he answers "out of the whirlwind" (38:1). The surprising thing is that the Lord does not address Elihu's arguments, for the introductory words of chapter 38 indicate that the Lord is answering not Elihu but Job (38:1). Nor does he explain the mystery of suffering.[39] Also, he does not enter into the arguments presented by the three friends. Rather, his response is grounded in the motifs of creation and providence, as he poses questions for Job that invite him to contemplate the majesty—and unfathomableness—of the created universe. From various angles the questions can be set alongside those presented in Isaiah 40:12–31, though in longer format.[40]

The questions presented to Job follow three distinct sequences.[41] The first deals with Job's nonparticipation in creation, his inability to understand it (Job 38:8). The second is about the management of the world, of God's providential ordering of it. Since Job has never commanded a new day to come forth, how can he possibly speak of the way in which the universe is governed (38:12, 31)? Third, the succession of questions about wild animals, not domesticated ones, stresses the many aspects about creation that are inscrutable to humans. The hippopotamus and the crocodile are part

---

38. For a good diagram of the structure of Job, see Elmer Smick, *Job*, in *1 Chronicles–Job*, vol. 4 of *The Expositor's Bible Commentary*, 2nd ed. (Grand Rapids, MI: Zondervan, 2010), 682.

39. This was seen long ago by William Henry Green in his book *The Argument of the Book of Job Unfolded* (New York: Robert Carter & Brothers, 1874), 286–87. He wrote, "The fact is, this discourse is not directed to an elucidation of that mystery [suffering] at all. It is not the design of God to offer a vindication of His dealings with men in general, or a justification of His providence towards Job."

40. In my commentary on Isaiah, I have commented on the comparison between Isa. 40:12–31 and Job 38–41, as well as noting parallels with other Old Testament passages. Allan Harman, *Isaiah: A Covenant to Be Kept for the Sake of the Church* (Fearn, Ross-shire, Scotland: Christian Focus, 2005), 307–12.

41. Here I am following the comments of David J. A. Clines, *Job 38–42*, Word Biblical Commentary 18B (Nashville: Thomas Nelson, 2006), xlv–xlvi.

of creation, but they represent all that is terrifying and all those creatures whose ways are not understood. David Clines observes, "God expects Job to realize, and Job is not slow at grasping the point, that the natural order—the principles on which the world was created—is analogous to the moral order—the principles according to which it is governed."[42] What all this means is that Job is compelled to acknowledge that God's ways are inscrutable to the human mind. What he had heard with his ears, he came to understand with his eyes (42:5). He knew, but he did not know, until God revealed things to him. We, too, must see God in his otherness, who, even though righteous, permits evil to exist. We have the sense that in this divine encounter, Job learns (as does the psalmist) that God is "not a God who delights in wickedness; evil may not dwell with [him]" (Ps. 5:4). Because God is at once holy and free, he cannot be called to account by humans, who lack sufficient understanding to judge (Job 42:1–3).[43]

Legal metaphors are prevalent in Job, with several different terms being used, almost exclusively in forensic contexts, to describe Job's relationships to God and to his community.[44] These include ones relating to worship ("pure," "clean") and others that have reference to a courtroom situation ("innocent," "free of legal claim" [free trans.]). Notable also is the use of רִיב, "to contend," but in Job there is the surprising application of it to a lawsuit between Job and God. Most of the legal metaphors do not directly help with understanding the way in which Job and his friends understood reconciliation between sinful man and a holy and righteous God. It has often been claimed that Job 19:23–27 is a clear indication of Job's belief in God as his Redeemer, a view popularized by George Frideric Handel's use and application of the passage in his oratorio *The Messiah*. However, it has to be recognized that these verses contain various difficulties of translation and interpretation. There is no problem with the introductory words in 19:23–24:

> Oh that my words were written!
> >Oh that they were inscribed in a book!
> Oh that with an iron pen and lead
> >they were engraved in the rock forever!

They are couched as a wish, signified by the opening "Oh" (מִי־יִתֵּן), which shows that what follows, far from being settled conviction, is a desire on Job's part. After these verses, uncertainty intrudes regarding various words and phrases: the meaning of גֹּאֵל ("redeemer"), the verb "lives," standing on the earth (or "dust"), destruction of the skin, being "in the flesh," and "seeing God." In view of the conflicting interpretations of this passage, it is best to leave it out of consideration as evidence of a redemptive

---
42. Clines, *Job 38–42*, xlvi.
43. Wilson, *Job*, 14. Wilson's "Introduction," 1–16, offers many perceptive comments on the book of Job.
44. See the excellent summary discussion, with good bibliographic references, in Gregory W. Parsons, "The Structure and Purpose of the Book of Job," in *Sitting with Job: Selected Studies on the Book of Job*, ed. Roy B. Zuck (Grand Rapids, MI: Baker, 1992), 26–33.

understanding by Job that would almost equal New Testament affirmations of Christ's role as Savior of sinners.[45]

Proverbs

It is clear that Proverbs cannot be divorced as easily from the rest of the Old Testament as is often claimed but rather stems from writers who were continuing the legacy of Mosaic teaching and the prophetic perspective of the Former Prophets. Only one reference to "covenant" occurs in the book: "the forbidden woman . . . who forsakes the companion of her youth and forgets *the covenant* of her God" (2:16–17). While it can be debated whether "the covenant of her God" is the Sinai covenant or the marriage bond stemming from God's laws, her sin is particularly heinous because she is acting against "*her* God."[46] Similarly, Agur's fear is that his sinful actions are to be condemned not only in themselves but also because they are a breach of loyalty against his God, whom he calls "*my* God" (30:9). The teaching of an individual sage can be referred to as his *torah*, but behind it stands *the Torah*, the forsaking of which means praising the wicked (28:4).

A discussion by Moshe Weinfeld has focused attention in a very helpful way on the parallels between Deuteronomy and the Wisdom Literature.[47] He points out numerous parallels between the two, including the appointment of judges (Deut. 1:9–18; 16:18–20), which appears elsewhere in the Old Testament only in Proverbs 24:23 and 28:21. This connection reinforces the idea that the covenantal framework is fundamental to the Wisdom Literature. Thus, Walter Kaiser Jr. can write that "wisdom was not cut off conceptually or theologically from materials which we have judged to be earlier than sapiential times."[48] Bruce Waltke has also expressed support for Weinfeld's argument, which he notes "shows a clear connection between wisdom and Deuteronomy both in specific legislation and in identical wordings (cf. Deut. 4:2; 13:1 and Prov. 30:5–6; Deut. 19:14 and Prov. 22:10; Deut. 25:13–16 and Prov. 20:23 [Deut. 6:1–9 and Prov. 3:1–10])."[49]

The link between the patriarchal narratives, the Mosaic covenant, and the Wisdom Literature is "the fear of the LORD." What was evident in Abraham's experience of God was displayed to a greater degree in the Mosaic era and was especially manifested in Deuteronomy. Israel was not to fear the Canaanites (Deut. 1:21, 29; 3:22; 7:18–19) or Og, king of Bashan (3:2). Rather, the object of the people's fear was to be the Lord their God (e.g., 6:2, 13, 24; 8:6; 10:12, 20; 13:4; 14:23). This concept is highlighted in

---

45. For representative viewpoints on the passage, and from different perspectives, see John E. Hartley, *The Book of Job*, NICOT (Grand Rapids, MI: Eerdmans, 1988), 290–97; David J. A. Clines, *Job 1–20*, WBC 17 (Dallas, TX: Word Books, 1989), 455–66; Smick, *Job*, 786–89.
46. This is pointed out by F. Derek Kidner, *Proverbs: An Introduction and Commentary*, TOTC (London: Tyndale Press, 1964), 34.
47. Moshe Weinfeld, "Wisdom Substrata in Deuteronomy and Deuteronomic Literature," in *Deuteronomy and the Deuteronomic School* (Oxford: Clarendon, 1972), 38–51.
48. Walter C. Kaiser Jr., *Toward an Old Testament Theology* (Grand Rapids, MI: Zondervan, 1978), 168. The same quotation can be found in his more recent book *The Promise-Plan of God: A Biblical Theology of the Old and New Testaments* (Grand Rapids, MI: Zondervan, 2008), 133.
49. Bruce K. Waltke, *The Book of Proverbs, Chapters 1–15* (Grand Rapids, MI: Eerdmans, 2004), 82n54.

Proverbs, and Proverbs 1:7 identifies it as the basic theme of the whole book. The form in which the expression occurs is also significant, for it is always "the fear of the LORD [יהוה]," using the distinctive covenantal name of God. This is another indication that, in continuity with the Pentateuch, covenant serves as the background of the instruction embodied in Proverbs. The expression occurs fourteen times in Proverbs, while the verbal forms of the root "to fear" appear another four times. The covenantal language comes to clearest expression in the father-son relationship stated in Proverbs 3:11–12: "My son, do not despise the LORD's discipline or be weary of his reproof, for the LORD reproves him whom he loves, as a father the son in whom he delights."

A final aspect that needs emphasis is the demarcation in Proverbs between sin and holiness, between being wise and being foolish. Many exhortations are given that direct one's obedience toward particular ends. The underlying implication is that humans deviate from God's paths and need correction. This is particularly so in the opening chapters, where the contrast is drawn repeatedly between living under the lordship of God or rejecting it by following crooked paths and thus coming under his curse. The path of the just is a shining light that increases more and more unto the perfect day (Prov. 4:18; cf. for the New Testament Phil. 1:6). There are even echoes of Genesis 2 in that four times the "tree of life" is mentioned (Prov. 3:18; 11:30; 13:12; 15:4). The way of the Lord is the way to life, and those who fear him display that in the application of divine wisdom to the realities of everyday life.

Ecclesiastes

If Job has seen a variety of interpreters, even more so has the book of Ecclesiastes. A great number of proposals have been made that relate to both the structure of the book and its essential meaning. The basic approaches can be narrowed down to three: a heterodox Qohelet, an orthodox Qohelet, and a struggling Qohelet.[50] The first of these proposals attempts to explain the book as a deviation from orthodox Old Testament teaching, the second holds that it agrees with Proverbs and that the positive elements in it outweigh the negative, and the third recognizes that the tensions expressed in the book remain unresolved. If the last viewpoint is taken along with a particular assessment of the structure of the book, we arrive at what seems to be the most acceptable approach. Qohelet's "autobiography" occupies most of the book (1:12–12:7), but it is framed by a short prologue (1:1–11) and a brief epilogue (12:8–14). It is the final call to revere God and live rightly (12:13) that both summarizes the book's message and links Ecclesiastes with the book of Proverbs.[51]

A problem facing all expositors of Ecclesiastes is the meaning of the refrain that occurs throughout the Hebrew text, הֶבֶל. It sounds like the bass pedal of the organ that has been left on right through a musical piece. It has often been rendered "vanity" or

---

50. For an excellent summary of these approaches, see Richard P. Belcher Jr., *A Study Commentary on Ecclesiastes* (Darlington, UK: EP Books, 2014), 29–40.
51. For discussion of this assessment, see Andrew G. Shead, "Ecclesiastes from the Outside In," *RTR* 55, no. 1 (1996): 24–37; Tremper Longman III, *The Book of Ecclesiastes*, NICOT (Grand Rapids, MI: Eerdmans, 1998), 15–24.

"emptiness," but other possible translations include words like "breath," "futility," and "enigma." Another suggestion seems nearer the mark: "transitoriness."⁵² This fits in well with the recurring reference to death throughout the book. Man is not immortal but has to accept the wages of sin (cf. Rom. 5:12; 6:23). Chapters 6–9 of Ecclesiastes especially highlight the universal occurrence of death for men and animals, so much so that we should write the Latin motto *memento mori* over them: "Remember that we must die."⁵³

But what is the final message of Ecclesiastes? The writer says in Hebrew, סוֹף דָּבָר הַכֹּל נִשְׁמָע (12:13). סוֹף, or "end," is well known because it is used in the expression סוֹף פָּסוּק, which refers to the punctuation mark at the end of a Hebrew sentence. דָּבָר means a "word" or "matter." This phrase is coupled with another expression that involves the Hebrew word כֹּל, which in the absolute form occurring in this verse means "everything," "the total," "the whole." The verbal form accompanying it, נִשְׁמָע, means "is heard." So the full saying is denoting the finality of that which has been expressed.⁵⁴ Immediately following this statement comes the summary of that teaching: "Fear God and keep his commandments." On the one hand, one must submit to God's claims and be wholeheartedly devoted to him. On the other hand, one must demonstrate this devotion by obeying his commandments.

Conclusion

The preceding discussion has indicated that the songs embodied in the Psalter display Israel's theology in poetic form. These enable us to see what was central in that theology and how it permeated the lives of the people over centuries. The holiness of God and the sinfulness of the human heart are set in contrast. Unable to attain to the standard of holiness that God requires by personal achievement, humans must be recipients of divine grace. Many of the psalms reveal how such grace was received and forgiveness appropriated. This theology is not, of course, unique to the Psalter, but in it the personal experience of individual believers is exemplified. It is not surprising that Old Testament believers wanted to sing of their confidence in a forgiving God.

The Wisdom Books, different in style from most of the psalms, contain a theology that is in agreement with the Psalms and the earlier covenantal theology of the Old Testament. Their practical orientation presents another focus, one that enables the reader to see how faith measures up in the rough and tumble of everyday life. Israel's faith was not just cerebral but was also a robust demonstration of loyalty to the sovereign Redeemer and one that was lived in his fear. Combined with the teaching of the Psalter, the books of Job, Proverbs, and Ecclesiastes give illustrations of how sinners lived by God's grace.

---

52. As suggested by Glenn Fobert, *Everything Is Mist: Ecclesiastes on Life in a Puzzling and Troubled Temporary World* (Belleville, Ontario: Guardian Books, 2003).

53. See the use of this motto in James Limburg, *Encountering Ecclesiastes: A Book for Our Time* (Grand Rapids, MI: Eerdmans, 2006), 103–11. He also quotes Karl Barth's words, "Some day a company of men will process out to a churchyard and lower a coffin and everyone will go home; but one will not come back, and that will be me" (*Dogmatics in Outline*, 117–18).

54. Limburg, *Encountering Ecclesiastes*, 132.

Recommended Resources

Psalms

Bullock, C. Hassell. *Encountering the Psalms: A Literary and Theological Introduction.* Grand Rapids, MI: Baker Academic, 2011.

Grogan, Geoffrey. *Prayer, Praise and Prophecy: A Theology of the Psalms.* Fearn, Ross-shire, Scotland: Christian Focus, 2001.

———. *Psalms.* Two Horizons Old Testament Commentary. Grand Rapids, MI: Eerdmans, 2008.

Harman, Allan. *Psalms.* 2 vols. Mentor Commentary. Fearn, Ross-shire, Scotland: Mentor, 2011.

VanGemeren, Willem A. *Psalms.* Vol. 5 of *The Expositor's Bible Commentary.* 2nd ed. Grand Rapids, MI: Zondervan, 2008.

Wilson, Gerald H. *Psalms.* Vol. 1. NIV Application Commentary. Grand Rapids, MI: Zondervan, 2002.

Wisdom Literature

Belcher, Richard P., Jr. *A Study Commentary on Ecclesiastes.* Darlington, UK: EP Books, 2014.

Hartley, John E. *The Book of Job.* New International Commentary on the Old Testament. Grand Rapids, MI: Eerdmans, 1988.

———. "Job: Theology of." In *New International Dictionary of Old Testament Theology and Exegesis*, edited by Willem A. VanGemeren, 4:780–96. Grand Rapids, MI: Zondervan, 1997.

Smick, Elmer. *Job.* In *1 Chronicles–Job.* Vol. 4 of *The Expositor's Bible Commentary*, 675–921. 2nd ed. Grand Rapids, MI: Zondervan, 2010.

Wilson, Gerald H. *Job.* Understanding the Bible Commentary Series. Grand Rapids, MI: Baker, 2007.

Zuck, Roy B., ed. *Reflecting with Solomon: Selected Studies on the Book of Ecclesiastes.* Grand Rapids, MI: Baker, 1994.

———, ed. *Sitting with Job: Selected Studies on the Book of Job.* Grand Rapids, MI: Baker, 1992.

3

Salvation Is the Lord's

Prophetic Perspectives

WILLEM A. VANGEMEREN

Jews and Protestants have the same Old Testament books but differ in their canonical divisions and ordering of the books. The Hebrew Bible has three divisions: the Torah (Pentateuch, or five books of Moses), the Nevi'im (Prophets), and the Ketubim (Writings). It is better known by the acronym TaNaK(h).[1] The books of the Nevi'im consist of two subdivisions: the Former Prophets, with four books (Joshua, Judges, the two books of Samuel, and the two books of Kings), and the Latter Prophets, also with four books (Isaiah, Jeremiah, Ezekiel, and the Twelve [i.e., the Minor Prophets]).[2] The Ketubim, or Writings, include the Poetical Books (Psalms, Job, Proverbs, Song of Songs, Ecclesiastes, Lamentations), Ruth, Esther, Daniel, Ezra, Nehemiah, and the two books of Chronicles. These three divisions of the Hebrew Old Testament may be thought of as three concentric circles. At the center of each is the triune God, who communicates himself in the three disparate canonical divisions: the revelation in Moses (Torah), in the Prophets, and in the Writings. Our focus is on the Prophets, particularly the Latter Prophets.

Moses (the Law) and the Prophetic Narratives

Moses
Moses clearly teaches that salvation is by grace and that justification is by faith. He witnesses to the frailty of the first humans, their disobedience, and the hope in God's

---
1. *Tanakh: The Holy Scriptures* (Philadelphia: Jewish Publication Society, 1988).
2. Daniel is not treated as a prophetic writing in Jewish circles. The Twelve count as one book in the Hebrew Bible. See Ron Haydon, "Seventy Sevens Are Decreed: A Canonical Approach to Daniel 9:24–27," JTISup 15 (Winona Lake, IN: Eisenbrauns, 2016), 150–52.

working out his purposes for humans in Jesus Christ. The patriarchs were instructed to place their hope in El Shaddai as they awaited the fulfillment of the divine promises. They were fully dependent on God, even though they made valiant strides to wing it on their own. In contrast, Moses, too, set out to deliver Israel in his own strength (Ex. 2:11–14). He had to learn to await God's manner and timing of so great a salvation. Moses was God's uniquely chosen "prophet," who served him faithfully for forty years. In this role, Moses was God's appointed agent in Israel's redemption from Egypt, teacher of Israel, mediator of the covenant, and founder of Israel's tabernacle worship. He also witnessed Israel's disobedience and rebelliousness and threatened Israel that they would not inherit God's rest.

The book of Deuteronomy is Moses's final testimony to Israel, in which he taught Israel to learn from the story of God's goodness and Israel's rebelliousness, of God's covenant and Israel's failure to maintain the covenant, of God's being a consuming fire but also remaining constant in his compassion for Israel, of God's covenantal curses but also his promise to spiritually transform Israel by a circumcision of the heart. God is the true source of life, blessing, and grace (Deut. 30:20). He called on Israel to love the Lord: "And now, Israel, what does the Lord your God ask of you but to fear the Lord your God, to walk in obedience to him, to love him, to serve the Lord your God with all your heart and with all your soul" (10:12; cf. 6:5).[3] After all, God is the source, giver, and sustainer of life:

> This day I call the heavens and the earth as witnesses against you that I have set before you life and death, blessings and curses. Now choose life, so that you and your children may live and that you may love the Lord your God, listen to his voice, and hold fast to him. For the Lord is your life, and he will give you many years in the land he swore to give to your fathers, Abraham, Isaac and Jacob. (30:19–20)

Moses prophetically forewarned Israel of her failure and of the exile but also promised God's ultimate compassion, forgiveness, and restoration (Deuteronomy 31–32).

Though Israel was permitted to enter the land, she could not enter the promise of rest (12:9–10; cf. Psalm 95). The Former Prophets develop the story of Israel's search for rest. These four books—Joshua, Judges, Samuel, and Kings—are also known as the Deuteronomistic Books, so called because of their close affinity to the book of Deuteronomy. These books are a prophetic narrative that develops the outworking of God's promises and curses (threats). The first of these books, Joshua, encouraged Israel to "serve" the Lord (Joshua 23–24) and trust in him for her future. Israel had not yet entered the rest. At the close of the prophetic narratives, we find Israel in exile and subjugated by the Babylonians and a remnant of Judah that was permitted to stay in the land (2 Kings 25). Out of fear of a Babylonian reprisal, some of those who were left in the land plotted against the good counsel of Gedaliah, who had encouraged the

---

3. Unless otherwise noted, Scripture quotations in this chapter are from the NIV.

remnant to submit themselves to Babylon (25:25). When the Judeans had to seek refuge in Egypt, the story of redemption had come full circle. Israel had been redeemed from Egypt under Moses only to find refuge in Egypt hundreds of years later. But even so, the Former Prophets end with a note of hope. Hope focused on Jehoiachin, one of the last kings of the Davidic dynasty. He was exalted by Nebuchadnezzar of Babylon (25:27-30). The light of Moses continued to flicker in the darkness of exile with the reassuring hope that God's justice is also compassionate.

Moses, the Prophetic Narratives, and the Latter Prophets

Moses and the Former Prophets form the background of the Latter Prophets. Readers cannot apprehend the depth of God's concern for humanity without a knowledge of the message of Moses and the Former Prophets. The preexilic Latter Prophets warned Israel of her impending doom and called on the people to return to the Lord, because he is compassionate, gracious, longsuffering, and forgiving. Their threats and promises of hope harked back to Moses and the (Former) Prophets. The prophets corrected and clarified Israel's understanding of the Mosaic hope. God was to be found in Israel's story of faithlessness, which nonetheless was guided by God's providence. The exile was not a historical accident. Israel's story of denouncement took the people from idolatry to an openness and longing for the living God. The prophets were God's messengers who perpetuated the legacy of Moses and the Former Prophets into and beyond the exile. They gave witness to a theological reality that opens believers to God's promises of a new world in Jesus Christ. God is just in his judgment and compassionate and forgiving. Micah affirms,

> Who is a God like you,
> > who pardons sin and forgives the transgression
> > of the remnant of his inheritance?
> You do not stay angry forever
> > but delight to show mercy.
> You will again have compassion on us;
> > you will tread our sins underfoot
> > and hurl all our iniquities into the depths of the sea.
> You will be faithful to Jacob,
> > and show love to Abraham,
> as you pledged on oath to our ancestors
> > in days long ago. (Mic. 7:18–20)

The prophetic witness is best understood by innerbiblical appropriations, images, and metaphors. The Latter Prophets connect with the prophetic vision, rooted in Moses, and project their vision to a postexilic world. They project God's compassion and forgiveness during and after Israel's history of rebelliousness. Hope lies in God alone. The late Dutch theologian Hendrikus Berkhof summarized the theological dimension of hope in the Old Testament in relation to God's fidelity thus: "Faithful Israel had access to the unknown future because it knew about past and present and believed in the faithfulness of its God. We may say that the eschatology of Israel is the confession of God's faithfulness projected on the screen of the future."[4]

The Message of the Latter Prophets

In this essay, we consider in greater detail the message of Isaiah and of Hosea since these two prophetical books are representative of the prophetic teaching on salvation. Isaiah is the first of the Latter Prophets, and Hosea is the first of the Twelve (i.e., the Minor Prophets). Isaiah ministered God's Word to Judah (ca. 740–ca. 685 BC) and overlapped with Hosea (750–725 BC) in time, but these two prophets probably did not know each other. Both addressed the impending fall of the northern kingdom (722 BC) and anticipated the desolation of Jerusalem (586 BC). Both hoped that Israel and Judah would learn from the catastrophic events that led to the exile of the North (722 BC). Both detail the sins of God's people and the necessity of divine judgment, forgiveness, and reconciliation. Both prophets have a grand view of God's holiness, righteousness, justice, compassion, and love. Both prophets open the future of Yahweh's renewal of the covenant and of his deeper involvement with a community renewed, justified, and sanctified by him. Yahweh is just in his wrath, but even in his wrath and judgment, he remains compassionate. His justice is compassionate, and his compassion is just. Justification is the work of the Holy One of Israel, who longs to dwell among his people (Isa. 12:6) and whose justice is compassionate. His wrath turns from justified anger to gracious comfort (12:1; 40:1; Hos. 11:8). God effects justification as he brings his children to himself and commits himself to them.

The ministries of Jeremiah and Ezekiel were some hundred years after Isaiah's. Like Isaiah, Jeremiah anticipated the fall of Jerusalem and the exile; unlike Isaiah, he also experienced it. He and his contemporary Ezekiel helped Judah understand the reasons for the catastrophic fall of Jerusalem (586 BC). Both envisioned a new community bound to Yahweh by a new covenant.

Jeremiah's vision of the new covenant (בְּרִית חֲדָשָׁה) reinforces Moses's projection of a new community transformed by Yahweh's will to be a spiritual community. The people had broken the terms of the covenant, and the curses of the covenant were overtaking their rebellious ways (Jeremiah 11; 34). Yet the Lord wills to continue the covenant / marriage relationship with Israel (וְאָנֹכִי בָּעַלְתִּי בָם, 31:32; cf. 3:14, 20). He monergistically internalizes his instruction from the inside out. They will have a heart for God and by God (נָתַתִּי אֶת־תּוֹרָתִי בְּקִרְבָּם). He forgives them and opens their hearts to "know" their loving God (כִּי־כוּלָּם יֵדְעוּ אוֹתִי לְמִקְטַנָּם וְעַד־גְּדוֹלָם, 31:34), because the new community is elevated by God to be his very own people/bride: "I will be their God, and they will be my people" (31:33). He will be found by his children who earnestly return to him:

---

4. Hendrikus Berkhof, *A Well-Founded Hope* (Richmond, VA: John Knox, 1969), 17–18.

"Then you will call on me and come and pray to me, and I will listen to you. You will seek me and find me when you seek me with all your heart. I will be found by you" (29:12–14). He will heal and restore his people: "'But I will restore you to health and heal your wounds,' declares the LORD, 'because you are called an outcast, Zion for whom no one cares'" (30:17). Salvation is God's alone (3:23).

Ezekiel portrays Yahweh's judgment of his people as the departure of his glory (11:23; see chaps. 1; 10; 11). Though the people have broken the covenant and the exile has become a reality, Yahweh promises to remember the people and to renew the covenant (16:8, 60, 62). He will provide an atonement to be reconciled to his rebellious people (16:63). This covenant of peace will transform everything (34:25), so that the people can again be called "my people" and "my sheep" (34:30–31). They are consecrated, and the Holy One of Israel will dwell with his people. The presence of God and the revelation of his transforming glory influence Ezekiel's vision of the new creation and humanity (chaps. 40–48). This central focus on hope gives shape to the eschatological vision of the prophet:

> I will make a covenant of peace with them; it will be an everlasting covenant [וְכָרַתִּי לָהֶם בְּרִית שָׁלוֹם בְּרִית עוֹלָם]. I will establish them and increase their numbers, and I will put my sanctuary among them forever [אֶת־מִקְדָּשִׁי בְּתוֹכָם לְעוֹלָם]. My dwelling place [מִשְׁכָּנִי] will be with them; I will be their God, and they will be my people. Then the nations will know that I the LORD make Israel holy, when my sanctuary [מִקְדָּשִׁי] is among them forever. (37:26–28; cf. 48:35)

He will favor his people and pour out his Spirit on them (39:29).

The Twelve (Hosea–Malachi), too, opened the doors to the future of God's grace and renewed covenantal commitment, the promise of the spiritual renewal of his people, forgiveness, and salvation. In brief, the Prophetic Books (the Major Prophets and the Twelve) reveal a thematic coherence:

1. God's declaration of guilt and complicity of Israel, Judah, and the nations
2. The character of God as being just and gracious, compassionate and forgiving, but also as being truthful and righteous in his judgment and salvation
3. God's zeal and wrath in the vindication of his glory and holiness
4. The good news of God's coming redemption—the great exchange from judgment to justification and from wrath to comfort
5. The invitation to return to the Lord, to come to know him through his mercy and forgiveness
6. The promise of an eschatological community—the kingdom of God, the messianic age, and the age of the Spirit of God

The Prophets hold out a vision of God's monergistic transformation of all things. He alone will bring about so great a salvation that gives life to humans by beholding the glory of the Lord who alone is full of grace and truth (cf. John 1:14).

The prophetic message, grounded in the Mosaic heritage, developed and appropriated Moses's central message to the prophets' own historical situations. The prophets embodied the "prophetic figure" of whom Moses spoke when he prophesied that the Lord would raise up a prophet like him (Deut. 18:15). The prophets also expected a prophet like and greater than Moses to whom God would speak "face to face" (Deut. 34:10).[5]

In this chapter we look at Isaiah as representative of the Latter Prophets and at Hosea as representative of the Minor Prophets. Instead of surveying all the prophets, I have chosen to lead readers into an experience with two significant prophets. Their message is representative as, on the one hand, they evidently connect with Moses, and, on the other hand, they contribute to the prophetic heritage. For example, the glory that God revealed to Moses holds the message of Moses and the Prophets together. Isaiah develops the glory of God's presence ("Immanuel") in salvation. Salvation is wholly God's, and the whole earth will see his glory (Isa. 40:5). Jeremiah calls on Israel to return to the Lord, so that the nations may see the glory of the Lord through the transformation of his people (Jer. 4:1–2). Ezekiel, the last of what we call the Major Prophets, testifies to the new reality of God's glorious presence in the wake of the fall of Jerusalem and of his renewed commitment to save his people (Ezekiel 40–48).

Hosea likens Israel's greedy practices to "prostitution," linking his message with that of Moses and the prophets (Isa. 1:21; Jer. 3:1; Ezek. 16:15–29; 20:5, 30). The reading of Isaiah and Hosea opens many perspectives and connections as they encourage the synoptic reading of Moses and the Prophets in preparation for God's revelation in one greater than Moses and the Prophets: his own Son.

The Message of Isaiah: Salvation Is of Yahweh Alone

Isaiah viewed himself as another Moses whom the Lord had called to teach Israel the way of justice. The opening words of the prophecy—"Hear me, you heavens! Listen, earth! For the LORD has spoken"—recall the words of Moses's Song of Witness (Isa. 1:2; cf. Deut. 32:1). The linkage with Deuteronomy sets the context for reading the book of Isaiah. Like Moses, Isaiah compared Israel to foolish and rebellious בָּנִים ("children," Isa. 1:2–3; cf. Deut. 32:5, 20), full of sin, guilt, evil, and corruption (Isa. 1:4; cf. Deut. 32:5), to Sodom and Gomorrah (Isa. 1:10; cf. Deut. 32:32), to harlotry (Isa. 1:21; cf. Deut. 31:16), and to a vineyard (Isa. 5:1–7; cf. Deut. 32:32).[6]

---

5. See Yoon-Hee Kim, "'The Prophet Like Moses': Deut 18:15–22 Reexamined within the Context of the Pentateuch and in Light of the Final Shape of the TaNaK" (PhD diss., Trinity Evangelical Divinity School, 1995).

6. Isaiah opened doors to a new world of righteousness and justice, if only God's people would return and listen to their true Father, lament their miserable state, and wait for his salvation (Isa. 63:7–64:12). He challenged the remnant (1:9; cf. 37:4, 31–32) that was left after the Assyrian invasion (701 BC) to hear the "word" of the Lord Almighty afresh (1:10). He likened them to Sodom and Gomorrah (1:10), a harlot (1:21), murderers (1:21), and thieves (1:23). God had expected faithfulness, justice, and righteousness (1:21), as well as compassion for the orphans and widows (1:17, 23), but God's children took advantage of the weak and vulnerable people. Their pious acts notwithstanding, they were guilty of bloodshed (1:11–15), defiled (1:16), and in need of forgiveness (1:18). They had to return to the Word of God and *learn* to practice compassionate justice (לִמְדוּ הֵיטֵב, 1:17; cf. 1:10). Jonathan Edwards comments, "I know of scarce any particular duty that is so much insisted upon, so pressed and urged upon us, both in the Old Testament and New, as this duty of charity to the poor." Edwards, "The Duty of Charity to the Poor," in *Sermons and Discourses, 1730–1733*, ed. Mark Valeri, vol. 17

The Prophetic Ministry

Charges against Israel and Judah

Isaiah was living in one of the best times under godly King Hezekiah and in one of the worst. He witnessed the exile of Israel (722 BC) and the near devastation of Judah under Sennacherib in 701 BC. It was a period of national and international intrigue and Realpolitik (Isaiah 7–11; esp. 8:12; 31). He railed against the self-reliance of the leaders, their concern with national destiny, and their plots to enrich themselves unjustly. The *central charge* is that they have abandoned (עָזְבוּ) and "spurned [נִאֲצוּ] the Holy One of Israel and turned their backs on him [נָזֹרוּ אָחוֹר]" (1:4).[7] The *central charge* is restated in terms of a rejection of Yahweh's *instruction* (cf. 1:10): "They have rejected the law of the LORD Almighty [מָאֲסוּ אֵת תּוֹרַת יְהוָה צְבָאוֹת] and spurned the word of the Holy One of Israel [וְאֵת אִמְרַת קְדוֹשׁ־יִשְׂרָאֵל נִאֵצוּ]" (5:24; cf. 1:4).[8] They had wronged God and people by their greed and opportunism. God's people had acculturated to the ways of the nations. While Moses had called on Israel to love and fear the Lord (Deut. 6:5; 10:12), they merely observed Mosaic rituals (Isa. 1:10–15) without knowing Yahweh. Because they did not know the Holy One of Israel, they did not understand the importance he attached to compassionate justice (58:6–7; 61:8; cf. Leviticus 19; Hos. 11:8).

Ministry of Hardening

Isaiah was called to harden[9] a callous people (Isa. 29:9–14, 18; 35:5; 43:8; 56:10; 59:10; 63:17; cf. Deut. 31:27), lest they comfort themselves with a false gospel (Isa. 6:10). The oracles of condemnation and judgment exposed the depth of Israel's corruption and sinfulness. Israel and Judah were under condemnation and would experience Yahweh's alienation and judgment. Yahweh had planned to abandon his people as the owner of an unproductive vineyard would rip out the vines and leave it fallow (5:1–7). They had

---

of *The Works of Jonathan Edwards* (New Haven, CT: Yale University Press, 1999), 375. Nicholas Wolterstorff calls the marginalized "the quartet of the vulnerable": "widows, orphans, resident aliens, and the poor." Wolterstorff, *Justice: Rights and Wrongs* (Princeton, NJ: Princeton University Press, 2008); Wolterstorff, *Justice in Love* (Grand Rapids, MI: Eerdmans, 2011), 75. The nature of Israel's injustice is further *specified* in the six woe oracles (cf. 1:4): opportunism and greed (5:8–10); hedonism and narcissism (5:11–17); deception, injustice, and sacrilege (5:18–19); perversion of justice and order (5:20); hubris and folly (5:21); and hedonism and injustice (5:22–23). (See also the six woes in chaps. 28–33 that contrast the hubris of Ephraim, Jerusalem, and Assyria [chaps. 28; 29; 33] and the Realpolitik of Judah [chaps. 30–31] with a just and righteous society [32:1–4] that is transformed by the Spirit of God [32:15–20].) People wronged God by improper worship, and they wronged their fellow humans simply by not caring for them. See also Wolterstorff, *Justice in Love*. The marginalized cried out for justice and righteousness, but cultural attitudes enforced prevailing customs and laws that choked out any possibility of compassionate justice (10:1–4; cf. 5:8). The civil religion of Judah combined a religious lifestyle with civil expectations that left no room for the Holy One of Israel (5:24; see also chaps. 28–33), who is exalted in justice (5:16). See Thomas L. Leclerc, *Yahweh Is Exalted in Justice: Solidarity and Conflict in Isaiah* (Minneapolis: Fortress, 2001); R. W. L. Moberly, "Whose Justice? Which Righteousness? The Interpretation of Isaiah V 16," *VT* 51, no. 1 (2001): 55–68.

7. In contrast, see the last use of "the Holy One of Israel" in Isa. 60:14, which witnesses to the radical and glorious transformation of Zion: "The children of your oppressors will come bowing before you; all who despise you will bow down at your feet and will call you the City of the LORD, Zion of the Holy One of Israel" (cf. 1:26).

8. The apposition of the names of God ("the LORD Almighty," "the Holy One of Israel," Isa. 1:4, 9; 5:24) and the mention of the "law" and the "word" (1:10; 5:24) suggest the close connection between chaps. 1 and 5.

9. Torsten Uhlig, *The Theme of Hardening in the Book of Isaiah: An Analysis of Communicative Action*, FAT 39 (Tübingen: Mohr Siebeck, 2009); Uhlig, "Too Hard to Understand? The Motif of Hardening in Isaiah," in *Interpreting Isaiah: Issues and Approaches*, ed. David G. Firth and H. G. M. Williamson (Downers Grove, IL: IVP Academic, 2009), 62–83.

experienced the desolations wrought by the Assyrians in Israel (722 BC) and in Judah (701 BC, 1:5–8; cf. chaps. 36–37) but were forewarned of an even greater desolation: the suspension of the Davidic dynasty, the destruction of Jerusalem and the temple, and the exile of Judah (64:10–12).

Ministry of Hope

Moses had forewarned Israel of their exile from the land and their being scattered among the nations (Deuteronomy 32). But Moses had also spoken of Yahweh's compassionate justice in which his wrath and judgment were exchanged for the gracious and free renewal of his love and his manifest presence with his people: land, progeny, spiritual transformation and restoration, and blessings (30:1–8). Yahweh committed himself to renew his commitments to an undeserving people. In his compassion he would forgive their guilt and sin and freely justify people so that they would come to know him, receive his instruction, and thus live as members of the new covenant community (Isa. 1:18; 2:5; cf. Num. 11:29; Deut. 10:16; 30:6; Isa. 5:24). Isaiah was a teacher of Israel who, like Moses, spoke in the name of Yahweh, the great "I am," and called Israel to leave a foreign country, to be servants of the Lord,[10] so that Yahweh might teach (מְלַמֶּדְךָ) and direct (מַדְרִיכְךָ) them "in the way[11] [they] should go [בְּדֶרֶךְ תֵּלֵךְ]" (48:17–20; cf. Ex. 6:2, 6, 8; Deut. 1:33). Yahweh promised to renew the covenant with all who would trust in him (48:18–20).

Ministry of Instruction

The love for God's instruction must lead to compassionate justice, because it begins with a lifestyle of learning to fear the Lord. Humility before God was the basis for parental *instruction* and modeling from generation to generation: "Assemble the people before me to hear my words so that they may learn to revere me [וְאַשְׁמִעֵם אֶת־דְּבָרָי אֲשֶׁר יִלְמְדוּן לְיִרְאָה] as long as they live in the land and may teach [יְלַמֵּדוּן] them to their children" (Deut. 4:10; cf. Gen. 18:19). Yahweh longed for such an eschatological community transformed by his *torah* of justice and compassion, "Oh, that their hearts would be inclined to fear me and keep all my commands always, so that it might go well with them and their children forever!" (Deut. 5:29). Instead, Isaiah had charged Israel with duplicity: "These people come near to me with their mouth and honor me with their lips, but their hearts are far from me. Their worship of me is based on merely human rules they have been taught" (Isa. 29:13).

Isaiah was God's appointed instructor (יוֹרֶה דֵעָה) but was ridiculed by his own people (28:9). Like Moses before him, he left a written record of the prophetic *torah* (תּוֹרָה,

---

[10]. See Gordon P. Hugenberger, "The Servant of the Lord in the 'Servant Songs' of Isaiah: A Second Moses Figure," in *The Lord's Anointed: Interpretation of Old Testament Messianic Texts*, ed. Philip E. Satterthwaite, Richard S. Hess, and Gordon J. Wenham (Grand Rapids, MI: Baker, 1995), 105–40.

[11]. See further Bo H. Lim, *The "Way of the Lord" in the Book of Isaiah*, LHBOTS 522 (London: T&T Clark, 2010).

8:16; cf. Deut. 17:18; 31:19; Isa. 29:11–12; 30:8–11).[12] He also had disciples (בְּלִמֻּדָי, 8:16) as witnesses to God's veracity. The transmission of his instruction (*torah*) through disciples was accompanied by Isaiah's consecration of Yahweh's name (8:13–14), by a life of *waiting* for the Lord and of *kenosis*, or suffering (8:17).[13]

Justice in Isaiah: Divine and Human

Isaiah was called to close the door of the old era of divine forbearance of a stiff-necked people and to open a door to a new era of Yahweh's redemption and transformation of a new "eschatological community" of Spirit-filled agents of justice and righteousness. These agents lament the people's inability to live up to God's high standards. The servants of the Lord suffer and wait for God's ultimate justice, while proclaiming the good news of Yahweh's kingdom of *compassionate and ecumenic justice* that brings together a remnant of Israel and of the nations.

God's Justice in Judgment and in Salvation

God's justice is *transcendent* and ultimate, while human justice is *proximate*. The experience and expression of human justice requires the endowment of *God's Spirit*, growth in wisdom (*sapiential justice*), and concern for and cultivation of *transcultural—or ecumenic or global—justice*.

God's justice is transcendent and ultimate. He loves justice (Isa. 61:8), and his justice is all-encompassing, ecumenic, and exalted (5:16; cf. 2:11, 12, 17).[14] Yahweh is the holy, glorious, and exalted King (chap. 6), whose justice is a manifestation of his holiness (5:14; 33:10). In his transcendence he reaches down to the earth to fill it with his glorious justice and righteousness (33:5). But who can stand his exalted justice?

On the one hand, Isaiah portrays God's coming in wrath:

> See, the Name of the LORD comes from afar,
>   with burning anger and dense clouds of smoke;
> his lips are full of wrath,
>   and his tongue is a consuming fire.
> His breath is like a rushing torrent,
>   rising up to the neck.
> He shakes the nations in the sieve of destruction;
>   he places in the jaws of the peoples
>   a bit that leads them astray. . . .
> The LORD will cause people to hear his majestic voice
>   and will make them see his arm coming down

---

12. Joseph Blenkinsopp suggests that *torah* be identified with a prophetic *torah*. *Isaiah 1–39: A New Translation with Introduction and Commentary*, AB 19 (New York: Doubleday, 2000), 243. It is evidently in opposition to the popular *torah* mentioned in Isa. 8:20.
13. The names of Isaiah and his children (Shear-Jashub and Maher-Shalal-Hash-Baz, Isa. 7:3; 8:1, 3) also left a record for Israel, as they were meant to be *signs* "from the LORD Almighty, who dwells on Mount Zion" (8:18).
14. See Thomas B. Song, "The Loftiness of God, the Humility of Man, and Restoration in Isaiah 57:14–21: A Text Linguistic Analysis of Their Convergence" (PhD diss., Trinity Evangelical Divinity School, 1997).

> with raging anger and consuming fire,
> > with cloudburst, thunderstorm and hail. (30:27–28, 30; cf. 66:15–16)

So dreadful is God's theophanic presence that the foundations of society and human civilization will crumble. Whatever is exalted will be brought down. People will flee, hide themselves, and be brought low (2:9–21). They will be terrified, because of the awesome presence of Yahweh (33:14).

Isaiah calls on people to fear God first. The fear of the Lord is the beginning of salvation:

> The LORD Almighty is the one you are to regard as holy,
> > he is the one you are to fear,
> > he is the one you are to dread.
> He will be a holy place;
> > for both Israel and Judah he will be
> a stone that causes people to stumble
> > and a rock that makes them fall.
> And for the people of Jerusalem he will be
> > a trap and a snare. (8:13–14)

Human accomplishments, righteousness, works, cultural achievements, and fortifications cannot insure people against God's dreadful presence (57:11–13a; cf. 2:9–21). But God does promise to be present with all who seek refuge in him: "But whoever takes refuge in me will inherit the land and possess my holy mountain" (57:13b; cf. 33:16).

On the other hand, the godly are filled with joy at his coming (30:29). They have been purified and sanctified by the presence of the Holy One of Israel. The ungodly ask, "Who of us can dwell with the consuming fire? Who of us can dwell with everlasting burning?" (33:14). But the godly have experienced the great transformation, because they have become citizens of Zion: "The LORD is exalted, for he dwells on high; he will fill Zion with his justice and righteousness" (33:5; see 33:15–16). They confess, "The LORD is our judge, the LORD is our lawgiver, the LORD is our king; it is he who will save us" (33:22). The people of God will be healed and forgiven (33:24).

God's awesome presence transforms curse into blessing, defeat into victory, and vulnerability into strength, because he is King (33:17, 20–24). He will establish a rule of justice and righteousness (28:17; 32:1–2). In these and many more oracles, Isaiah looks for the presence of the Holy One of Israel among his people (12:6). It will be like but greater than the experience of Israel in the wilderness, because the people will be washed, cleansed, consecrated, and glorified (4:2–6). God will establish his sovereignty over the earth, so as to protect, vindicate, give reasons for celebrations, and he will end all shame and death (25:1–8). Salvation is God's alone: "In that day they will say, 'Surely this is our God; we trusted in him, and he saved us. This is the LORD, we trusted in him; let us rejoice and be glad in his salvation'" (25:9). He is the refuge of the afflicted: "The LORD has established Zion, and in her his afflicted people will find refuge" (14:32; cf. 4:6).

Human Justice

God's expectations for his children remain high (Isa. 33:15), but they cannot live up to them. No human being can live up to God's standard of justice. His justice is ultimate, whereas every human act of justice is proximate. A redemptive lifestyle reaches out to the needy and oppressed (58:6–12; cf. 56:1). It requires a life of humility and suffering (*kenosis*), and an absolute fidelity to God may require unjust suffering and the laying down of one's life for others. It is a life of dependency on divine justice and vindication, while growing in proximate justice that includes sapiential and ecumenic perspectives.[15] It is a life of generous and gracious living under constant stress.

Divine justice (salvation) and human proximate justice are corollary but also paradoxical. Isaiah summarizes the paradox: "Maintain justice [מִשְׁפָּט] and do what is right [צְדָקָה], for my salvation [יְשׁוּעָתִי] is close at hand and my righteousness [וְצִדְקָתִי][16] will soon be revealed" (56:1; cf. Deut. 30:10–15; Isa. 48:17–20; 58:5–12).[17] But how can humans participate in such a way that God accepts proximate justice and rewards them with his salvation?

It is little wonder that God's people confess their inability to bring about justice and righteousness (59:1–15). They cry out for God's salvation, but it is far off:

> So justice [מִשְׁפָּט] is driven back,
>   and righteousness [וּצְדָקָה] stands at a distance;
> truth [אֱמֶת] has stumbled in the streets,
>   honesty [וּנְכֹחָה] cannot enter.
> Truth [הָאֱמֶת] is nowhere to be found,
>   and whoever shuns evil becomes a prey. (59:14–15)

They confess that all their righteous acts amount to nothing in God's eyes, asking, "How then can we be saved?" while confessing, "All of us have become like one who is unclean, and all our righteous acts are like filthy rags; we all shrivel up like a leaf, and like the wind our sins sweep us away" (64:5–6). The children of God pray that their Father[18] will save them, because evil is everywhere and they are subject to persecution (64:8; cf. 57:1). They wait for him (64:4) but experience his alienation (64:9).

But Yahweh's justice is beyond human comprehension. The servants of the Lord struggle with God's sovereignty and freedom, while waiting for his redemption (see esp.

---

15. Paul's definition of the kingdom of God is quite useful: "For the kingdom of God is not a matter of eating and drinking, but of righteousness, peace and joy in the Holy Spirit, because anyone who serves Christ in this way is pleasing to God and receives human approval. Let us therefore make every effort to do what leads to peace and to mutual edification" (Rom. 14:17–19). He defines compassionate justice in terms of the promotion of righteousness, peace, and joy in the Spirit. It is an example of sapiential justice, which by its very nature is proximate justice.
16. Note that the NIV sometimes translates the Hebrew word צְדָקָה as "right" and "salvation."
17. Rolf Rendtorff, "Isaiah 56:1 as a Key to the Formation of the Book of Isaiah," in Rendtorff, *Canon and Theology: Overtures to an Old Testament Theology*, trans. and ed. Margaret Kohl, OBT (Minneapolis: Fortress, 1993), 181–89.
18. See Willem A. VanGemeren, "'Abba' in the Old Testament?," *JETS* 31, no. 4 (1988): 385–98.

63:7–64:12).[19] They confess the guilt of the community,[20] wait for the Lord's salvation, and suffer. Yahweh responds to their confession of sin and frustration. His justice and righteousness are not within human reach,[21] because no human being can live up to his ultimate justice or stand his just wrath (57:17; 60:10; 63:3, 6; 64:9; 66:15). He reassures them and stresses that salvation is his alone. He promises to come through for them as the Divine Warrior (59:16–20; 63:1–6) and save his people without any human help. That salvation is wholly from the Lord is the foundation of Isaiah's vision of Zion, the proclamation of comfort,[22] the vision of a new community of God's servants, and the climactic hope of a new heaven and earth without evildoers (60:1–63:7; 65–66). Isaiah points to the messianic agent to bring in an era of justice and righteousness, of protection and peace, and of ultimate salvation (9:6–7; 11:1–9). He speaks of a servant wounded for our transgressions and bearing our sins (53:5, 10, 12). We have found this salvation in Jesus Christ, the God-man. He is the true image of God who in his humanity was perfected through suffering (Heb. 2:10). There is no other salvation than what is found in the Lord Jesus Christ.

God's Sovereignty and Freedom in Salvation

God is sovereign and free. His salvation is sovereign. He alone transforms whoring Zion into "the City of Righteousness, the Faithful City" (Isa. 1:26). He washes Zion's citizens, purifies them, forgives, consecrates, and glorifies them (1:18; 4:2–6; 60). He restores the messianic offspring as a true agent of justice, righteousness, and peace (chaps. 9; 11). He promises that he will be victorious over all enemies and evil (34; 45–48; 63:1–6; 65:25) and will establish Zion as a secure place for his redeemed people (chaps. 60; 65–66; cf. Revelation 21–22). He will rejoice in his people, and they in him (Isa. 65:18). He brings about a new state of shalom, justice, and righteousness. The zeal of the Lord Almighty will monergistically accomplish his sovereign purposes: a world of justice, righteousness, peace, glory, and joy (9:8; 26:11; 37:32; 42:13; 59:17; cf. 63:15). Rightly does Brevard Childs comment, "The description of the eschatological rule is not part of a human social program."[23]

His sovereignty in salvation implies his freedom.[24] He is free in the manner and timing of the execution of his justice. The God of justice patiently waits (יְחַכֶּה)[25] to manifest his compassion and grace to his children (30:18; cf. 65:2–3; 2 Pet. 3:9), while

---

19. Kim Ayun, my last doctoral student, is writing a dissertation on Isa. 63:7–64:11: "The Servants' Prayer of Lament: A Canonical Study of Isa. 63:7–64:11."
20. See Judith Gärtner, "'. . . Why Do You Let Us Stray from Your Paths . . .' (Isa 63:17): The Concept of Guilt in the Communal Lament Isa 63:7–64:11," in *Seeking the Favor of God*, vol. 1, *The Origins of Penitential Prayer in Second Temple Judaism*, ed. Mark J. Boda, Daniel K. Falk, and Rodney A. Werline, EJL 21 (Atlanta: Society of Biblical Literature, 2006), 145–63.
21. See Gregory J. Polan, *In the Ways of Justice toward Salvation: A Rhetorical Analysis of Isaiah 56–59* (New York: Peter Lang, 1986).
22. Yun-Gab Choi, "To Comfort All Who Mourn: The Theological and Hermeneutical Function of Isa 61–62 in the Book of Isaiah" (PhD diss., Trinity Evangelical Divinity School, 2017).
23. Brevard S. Childs, *Isaiah*, OTL (Louisville: Westminster John Knox, 2001), 31.
24. Willem A. VanGemeren, "Prophets, the Freedom of God, and Hermeneutics," *WTJ* 52, no. 1 (1990): 79–99.
25. The NIV's translation "longs to" removes the theological difficulty. In Isaiah the godly wait for the Lord, but here God waits for the people. His patient waiting is like that of a wise judge who intends to dispense gracious justice and patiently waits for the right occasion.

committing himself to those children who wait for his vindication. He guarantees his salvation for the sake of his own glory: "In that day the LORD Almighty will be a glorious crown, a beautiful wreath for the remnant of his people. He will be a spirit of justice to the one who sits in judgment, a source of strength to those who turn back the battle at the gate" (Isa. 28:5–6; cf. 58:8; 59:19; 60:1, 2, 13, 19; 66:18). The freedom of God comes to expression in the indeterminacy of "that day." He knows and cares, but in Jesus's words, "It is not for you to know the times or dates the Father has set by his own authority" (Acts 1:7).

God's children will see the true beauty of their Savior-King: "Your eyes will see the king in his beauty [בְּיָפְיוֹ]" (Isa. 33:17). The revelation of God's beauty is for Zion's sake. It is a place of security and peace (33:18–22) and of healing and forgiveness, because God's rule is redemptive: "For the LORD is our judge [שֹׁפְטֵנוּ], the LORD is our lawgiver [מְחֹקְקֵנוּ], the LORD is our king [מַלְכֵּנוּ]; it is he who will save us" (33:22).

No human can bring in a world of justice and righteousness, of salvation and victory. Only God can save, as the name Isaiah ("Salvation is of Yahweh [alone]") suggests. Yahweh is the Divine Warrior who brings an end to oppression and injustice and who brings in "an everlasting salvation" (45:17). Matthew highlights the ministry of Jesus with these words: "He will save his people from their sins" (Matt. 1:21). God is incarnate in Jesus Christ. He is the Savior who forgives and brings an everlasting righteousness and justice into his creation (Isa. 51:5–6; cf. Dan. 9:24). He is the hope of humanity and the answer to her injustice.

The Spirit of God

The motif of God's salvation witnesses to God's monergistic power and freedom in salvation. The Spirit of God is also engaged in the transformation of the world and of people. He creates a just and caring society (Isa. 32:1–5) and transforms the world into a place of righteousness, peace, justice, glory, and security (32:15–20; cf. 32:1–5).[26] The Spirit works in and through his agents: the messianic agent, the servants of the Lord, and his people will all be endowed with and transformed by the Spirit (11:1–2; 42:1; 44:1–5; 59:21; 61:1).

The Spirit of God and the Messianic Agent

The messianic agent will be empowered by the Holy Spirit to bring in a kingdom of wisdom, power, justice, and righteousness, so as to protect the oppressed. The resulting peace is only possible by the presence and endowment of the Spirit of God (Isa. 11:1–2). The messianic agent will successfully deal with injustice in the world. Isaiah focuses hope on a Davidic descendant to bring in a reign of justice and peace (9:7; cf. 16:5). The cryptic mention of the four throne names—"Wonderful Counselor, Mighty God,

---

26. See Willem A. VanGemeren, "The Spirit of Restoration," *WTJ* 50, no. 1 (1988): 81–102; Willem A. VanGemeren and Andrew Abernethy, "The Spirit of God and the Future: A Canonical Approach," in *Presence, Power, and Promise: The Role of the Spirit of God in the Old Testament*, ed. David G. Firth and Paul D. Wegner (Downers Grove, IL: IVP Academic, 2011), 321–45.

Everlasting Father, Prince of Peace" (9:6)—and the commentary about it in 11:1–9 suggest a weak pattern-fulfillment in Hezekiah (Isaiah 36–39) and an ultimate realization in Jesus Christ (Matt. 1:21).

The Spirit of God and the Servant(s) of the Lord

Though Isaiah 40–66 makes no overt mention of a Davidic king, the hope of a Davidic agent lingers in the background. Isaiah also depicts the servants of the Lord as agents who serve the Lord as his appointed leaders of and witnesses to the nations (55:3–5). The Spirit of the Lord is on the servants of the Lord (42:1; 44:2–5; 48:16b; 59:21; 61:1; cf. 11:1–2). They have a prophetic-priestly-royal mission as they proclaim and teach the good news of the kingdom of compassionate justice (41:1, 4; 49:2–9). They model humility, righteousness, justice, and faithfulness (42:2–4; cf. 11:1–5). They reach out to Israel and the nations (42:6–7; 49:6–9).

The model servant has been discipled by the Lord: "The Sovereign Lord has given me a well-instructed tongue [לְשׁוֹן לִמּוּדִים], to know the word that sustains the weary. He wakens me morning by morning, wakens my ear to listen like one being instructed [לִשְׁמֹעַ כַּלִּמּוּדִים]" (50:4; see 50:5–9). He suffers at the hand of unjust people and is an instrument of divine redemption (50:6–9; 52:13–53:12). The effect of his ministry is the transformation of Zion into a just community without any oppressors (54:11–17). The transformation also includes a multiplication of faithful servants, all of whom are instructed by the Lord: "All your children will be taught by the Lord [לִמּוּדֵי יְהוָה], and great will be their peace" (54:13; cf. 54:17; 59:21).

The Spirit of God and Proclamation

The Spirit of God attends the proclamation of the "good news." God saves, and humans participate by proclaiming and living the good news. The good news is beautiful news when it is God centered, empowered by the Spirit, redemptive in the broadest sense of the word, and transformative. This proclamation of comfort[27] envisions change at many levels so that people's experience of human dignity is raised to a wholly new level.[28] Theirs is a future with the Lord.

Isaiah speaks of the glory and beauty of God's mission. The good news is beautiful: "How beautiful [מַה־נָּאווּ] on the mountains are the feet of those who bring good news, who proclaim peace, who bring good tidings, who proclaim salvation, who say to Zion, 'Your God reigns!'" (Isa. 52:7). The servant is in awe of God's commitment to justice, righteousness, and faithfulness (61:8), which assures him of the heritage, covenantal relationship, rewards, and transformation.[29] In keeping with the message of the

---

27. See the thematic development of *comfort* in Rolf Rendtorff, "The Composition of the Book of Isaiah," in Rendtorff, *Canon and Theology*, 146–69.
28. Isaiah 61:1–2 is cited at the beginning of Jesus's ministry in Luke 4 and frames the ministry of Jesus (Luke) and of the apostles (Acts).
29. See Hee-Sung Lee, "The Inheritance of the Servants in Isaiah 40–66: A Textlinguistic Analysis" (PhD diss., Trinity Evangelical Divinity School, 2007).

whole book—salvation is of Yahweh alone—there are many participants on the way of justice, but no servant or participant actually forgives sin, makes covenant, empowers and transforms a new community, or brings about a world of justice. God alone is the Redeemer-Warrior-King: "So his own arm achieved salvation for him, and his own righteousness sustained him. He put on righteousness as his breastplate, and the helmet of salvation on his head; he put on the garments of vengeance and wrapped himself in zeal as in a cloak" (59:16–17; cf. 12:1–6; 28:5–6). Yahweh enlarges the community of servants (59:21; 60:22) and gloriously renews Zion (chap. 60). He sends forth the messengers of the good news in order to comfort and restore "the poor . . . the brokenhearted . . . the captives . . . the prisoners [LXX, 'the blind'] . . . all who mourn . . . those who grieve" (61:1–3; cf. 40:1), so that they may experience freedom, divine favor, beauty, gladness, and praise (61:1–3). The new righteous community is likened to a grove of oak trees (61:3) in fulfillment of God's promise of the "holy seed" (6:13; cf. 65:23).

In the New Testament, Luke structures the two books of Luke and Acts against the background of Isaiah. He unfolds what a compassionate and generous ministry looks like. The good news of Jesus Christ advances into a movement that takes the gospel from Jerusalem to the ends of the world. We are a part of this story as well.[30]

A Spirit-Filled Community

God wills for his servants to participate in compassionate justice, though it is only proximate. Their participation will involve suffering (*kenosis*), growth in wisdom,[31] waiting for God's ultimate justice, and a ministry of comfort, teaching, proclamation, and witness bearing. Sapiential justice is compassionate and shows understanding, patience, gentleness, and character growth. After all, wisdom is from the Almighty and is proximate in God's servants (Isa. 28:29; 31:2). Beginning with the fear of the Lord (transcendence), humans discover aspects of divine justice, righteousness, and wisdom (33:5).

Abraham as the father of sapiential justice. Abraham models sapiential and ecumenic justice. The Lord had commanded him to walk before him with integrity (Gen. 17:1), expecting that he would "direct [יְצַוֶּה] his children and his household after him to keep the way of the LORD by doing what is right and just [וְשָׁמְרוּ דֶּרֶךְ יְהוָה לַעֲשׂוֹת צְדָקָה וּמִשְׁפָּט]" (18:19). From God's relationship with Abraham, we learn that Abraham lived by faith and grew in wisdom and in character. The Lord tested him and found him to be a person of integrity (22:16). He feared the Lord, trusting in his ultimate veracity and transcendent justice. He interceded on behalf of Sodom and Gomorrah in order to find out the limits of God's compassionate justice (18:23–33). Abraham's pleading for these wicked cities illustrates how he pleased God and people by demonstrating his compassionate justice.

---

30. Bart J. Koet, "Isaiah in Luke-Acts," in *Isaiah in the New Testament*, ed. Steve Moyise and Maarten J. J. Menken (London: T&T Clark, 2005), 78–100.
31. See Hee-Suk Kim, "Proverbs 1–9: A Hermeneutical Introduction to the Book of Proverbs" (PhD diss., Trinity Evangelical Divinity School, 2010).

Abraham learned through suffering. He awaited the promise of a son, believing in God's promise. He was also promised that God's blessing would extend to his descendants and to the nations. Abraham was God's chosen agent to model justice and righteousness as he sojourned among the nations. Abraham's justice was proximate, because he learned to trust God while growing in character and in obedience. He experienced suffering (*kenosis*) while waiting for the fulfillment of God's promises. He was a blessing to the nations. For Isaiah the paradigm of Abraham suggests the triumph of God in a new and transcultural (ecumenic) community:

> Look to Abraham, your father,
>   and to Sarah, who gave you birth.
> When I called him he was only one man,
>   and I blessed him and made him many.
> The LORD will surely comfort Zion
>   and will look with compassion on all her ruins; . . .
> Instruction will go out from me;
>   my justice will become a light to the nations.
> My righteousness draws near speedily,
>   my salvation is on the way,
>   and my arm will bring justice to the nations.
> The islands will look to me
>   and wait in hope for my arm. (Isa. 51:2–5)

Inner renewal. Isaiah called on Israel to *learn* the way of compassionate justice: "Take your evil deeds out of my sight; stop doing wrong. Learn to do right; seek justice [לִמְדוּ הֵיטֵב דִּרְשׁוּ מִשְׁפָּט אַשְּׁרוּ]. Defend the oppressed" (Isa. 1:16–17). He well realized that some would "learn righteousness" (צֶדֶק לָמְדוּ) while others would receive grace upon grace yet "not learn righteousness" (בַּל־לָמַד צֶדֶק) nor see the God of glory (וּבַל־יִרְאֶה גֵּאוּת יְהוָה; 26:9–10). Compassionate justice is in response to the glory and holiness of God. It begins with the knowledge and imitation of God. It is intimately connected with the fear of the Lord—that is, the knowledge of the Holy One of Israel (1:3; 5:24; cf. Heb. 12:28–29). The combination of the knowledge of God and the renewal of the image of God gives shape to a new community of justice, compassion, patience, love, faithfulness, and forgiveness.[32]

Isaiah prophetically models the lifestyle of waiting and trusting among his disciples: "I will wait [וְחִכִּיתִי] for the LORD, who is hiding his face from the descendants of Jacob. I will put my trust in him [וְקִוֵּיתִי־לוֹ]" (Isa. 8:17; see 8:16). The voice of the new community and of the prophet come to expression in 26:8–9:

> Yes, LORD, walking in the way of your laws,
>   we wait for you [קִוִּינוּךָ];
> your name and renown

---

32. On the combination of justice and love, see Wolterstorff, *Justice in Love*.

are the desire of our hearts [תַּאֲוַת־נָפֶשׁ].
My soul yearns for you [נַפְשִׁי אִוִּיתִךָ] in the night;
  in the morning my spirit longs for you.
When your judgments come upon the earth,
  the people of the world learn righteousness [צֶדֶק לָמְדוּ].

God's beatitude rests on all who trust him, waiting for his salvation (אַשְׁרֵי כָּל־חוֹכֵי לוֹ, 30:18). The reversal of fortunes, described in 30:19–26, introduces unidentified "teachers" (אֶת־מוֹרֶיךָ) who will instruct the people to walk in the way of the Lord (30:20).[33] The transformed people walk obediently on the way, and the Lord miraculously removes their enemies (30:30; 27–33), provides for them, and heals their wounds (30:23–26), resulting in great joy (30:29; cf. 33:24).

The new community waits for Yahweh to strengthen them in their hope: "LORD, be gracious to us; we long [לְךָ קִוִּינוּ] for you. Be our strength every morning, our salvation in time of distress" (33:2; cf. 40:31; Rom. 5:3–5). As they wait for him (וְקֹוֵי יְהוָה), trusting in him, and longing for him to bring in the long-awaited justice, they will be renewed from the inside out (Isa. 40:31). And while hoping, they renew themselves in the sovereignty, power, providence, and wisdom of the incomparable God (40:25–26). They are called to proclaim the good news of his coming in glory and with salvation (40:3–5, 10–11). They become involved in his kingdom program that entails living justly, righteously, and faithfully. They receive his strength while waiting in hope for the Lord's redemption and while remaining faithful to their high calling.

Waiting for the Lord's justice involves hungering and thirsting for justice, suffering and persecution, exile and marginalization, becoming a disciple and student of the Almighty and Holy One of Israel, and witnessing to the reality of the good news. Isaiah expands the vision of the participants in God's plan of bringing righteousness to earth. They include a Davidic king (chaps. 9; 11; 36–39), a royal-priestly servant (42:1–4), a prophetic servant (48:16b; 61–62), a suffering servant (chaps. 49; 50; 52–53), and the servants of the Lord (chaps. 54–66). They subordinate their will to him, suffer *kenosis*, are obedient to him, are empowered by the Spirit of God, extend themselves to a lifestyle of justice and righteousness, and participate in God's mission to bear witness to Israel and to be a light[34] for the nations (42:1–4,[35] 7; 43:10, 12; 44:8; 49:6; 54:4; cf. 60:3, 19–20). It is a mission of comfort (chaps. 40; 49; 51; 61; 66), proclamation (chaps. 40; 43; 48; 52; 61–62; 66), and justice (chaps. 42; 51; 56; 58–59; 61–62).

The covenant of peace. The exile signifies divine abandonment. However, divine alienation does not imply divine rejection. It is a period of isolation to bring God's people

---

33. The teachers could be associated with Isaiah and his disciples, or possibly the plural form is a circumlocution for Yahweh or a singular teacher. Blenkinsopp suggests the image of a prophetic-like figure. *Isaiah 1–39*, 1:421.

34. See Kang-Ho Kil, "The Light and Darkness Motif in the Book of Isaiah: A Textlinguistic Analysis" (PhD diss., Trinity Evangelical Divinity School, 2005).

35. See Elizabeth R. Hayes, "The One Who Brings Justice: Conceptualizing the Role of 'The Servant' in Isaiah 42:1–4 and Matthew 12:15–21,' in *Let Us Go Up to Zion: Essays in Honour of H. G. M. Williamson on the Occasion of His Sixty-Fifth Birthday*, ed. Ian Provan and Mark J. Boda, VTSup 153 (Leiden: Brill, 2012), 143–51.

to their senses. After all, they had spurned the Holy One of Israel (Isa. 1:4; 5:24; 8:6; cf. 30:12). Hence, they were exiled from the land (49:21) but not ultimately (41:9). God promised to renew and improve the terms of the covenant. He promised to show his compassion in giving his people his peace and to transform their inability to maintain the relationship: "'Though the mountains be shaken and the hills be removed, yet my unfailing love for you will not be shaken nor my covenant of peace be removed,' says the LORD, who has compassion on you" (54:10). This covenant will bring about the glory, security, and benefits of Zion, the City of God. Isaiah waxes lyrical as he envisions the presence of God with his people (54:11–17; 60:20). The people of God, also known as the servants of the Lord, will be instructed by the Lord (54:13), enjoy the divine vindication (righteousness and peace), and experience the splendor of God's city (54:11–12).

The covenant is guaranteed by God:

> "As for me, this is my covenant with them," says the LORD. "My Spirit, who is on you, will not depart from you, and my words that I have put in your mouth will always be on your lips, on the lips of your children and on the lips of their descendants—from this time on and forever," says the LORD. (59:21)

The Spirit will work in the children of the Lord from generation to generation. Having been taught by the Lord, they will experience the working out of God's purposes for his people (chap. 60). They will experience the glory and light of the Lord, international recognition, pride, and joy (60:1–14), divine compassion (60:10), redemption and praise (60:16–18), and all God's people will be declared righteous (60:21–22). After all, Zion will be "the City of the LORD, Zion of the Holy One of Israel" (60:14). The Lord will be the light of his people, and sorrow will end (60:19–20; cf. 35:10; 51:11; Revelation 21). No longer will Zion be reckoned as a whore—defiled, abandoned, or associated with darkness. Instead, she will be like a bride—pure, the City of God, and full of light.

The inclusion of the nations. The inclusion of the nations in the patriarchal heritage shapes Isaiah's concern for a global, transcultural, ecumenic view of social justice.[36] The Lord had promised the patriarchs that the nations would also be blessed with covenantal benefits (Gen. 17:5, 16; 22:18; cf. Isa. 2:2–4; 56:2–7). Isaiah expands the vision: the nations will receive the light of Yahweh's instruction, walk in his way of justice (cf. 2:2–4; 51:1–3), participate in Israel's redemption (chaps. 60; 61; 66), and become full members of the covenantal community ("servants," 56:6–7; 57:13)—and they may even serve as priests and Levites (66:21). The qualities of the servants of the Lord are many. They love the Lord and fear him (50:10; 55:6; 56:6; 61:6), find refuge in their God (57:13), pursue justice and righteousness (51:1, 7; 55:1; 56:1–2; 58:6–10; 59:4, 15; 61:8–9), and commit themselves to faithfulness, contrition, and humility (56:2, 4; 57:15; 58:13–14; 59:14–15, 19, 20; 66:2). They proclaim comfort to Zion and long for the coming of God's kingdom (61–62; 66:7–15; cf. 52:7).

---

36. See Yongsub Lim, "The Nations in the Book of Isaiah: Inclusion of the Nations in Yahweh's Eschatological Salvation on Mount Zion" (PhD diss., Trinity Evangelical Divinity School, 2004).

They form a spiritual community committed to living by the Word (59:21; 66:2, 5). They live with great joy while anticipating and living out their newfound sense of transcendent justice and righteousness (56:7; 58:14; 65:14). The Lord will fully fulfill his promises in a new Jerusalem in a new heaven and earth (chaps. 65–66).[37]

Nations come to Zion to receive God's justification and instruction in the way of justice, because "the law will go out from Zion, the word of the LORD from Jerusalem" (2:3). When the God of justice (30:18) fills Zion with "justice and righteousness" (33:5; cf. 1:21) and instructs the nations in his *torah* of justice (2:3; 51:4–5), the world will finally be at rest. Throughout the prophecy Isaiah develops the theme of God's rule of international law resulting in a new world of righteousness, justice, and peace. He knows that a small remnant of evil can spoil the beautiful vision of God's kingdom. Israel and the nations share the same *torah*, the same Savior, and the same hope:

> Listen to me, my people;
>   hear me, my nation:
> Instruction [תּוֹרָה] will go out from me;
>   my justice [וּמִשְׁפָּטִי] will become a light to the nations [לְאוֹר עַמִּים].
> My righteousness draws near speedily,
>   my salvation is on the way,
>   and my arm will bring justice to the nations.
> The islands will look to me
>   and wait in hope for my arm. (51:4–5)

Today the situation is reversed. The church is largely a Gentile church. Is there still hope for the Jewish people to be included in God's purpose? An exegetically informed response looks for the inclusion of the Jews as well (Romans 9–11).[38] J. Ross Wagner concludes, "With Isaiah, Paul insists that God will at last rise up to redeem his people Israel and, in so doing, bring to completion his rectification of the entire cosmos."[39]

Isaiah projects the effective transformation of Zion as the revelation of God's beauty (glory), which transforms injustice into justice, weakness into strength, and shame into glory (28:5–6; 33:17–24; 35:1–10; 40:1–5; 60:1–22; 62:1–12). The servants of the Lord herald the coming glory of the Lord that will fill the whole earth (6:3; 40:5; cf. 11:9). Everything associated with God reveals his beauty. His instruction will be increasingly more glorious (יַגְדִּיל תּוֹרָה וְיַאְדִּיר; 42:21). The suffering servant of the Lord is beautiful in wisdom (52:13). The remnant will renew their hope in the beauty (לַעֲטֶרֶת צְבִי וְלִצְפִירַת תִּפְאָרָה) of his compassionate justice (וּלְרוּחַ מִשְׁפָּט; 28:5–6; cf. 4:2, 4).

---

37. The identity of the servant(s) awaits a grand unfolding of what Childs calls "an eschatological dimension to the servant." Childs, *Isaiah*, 442. See Willem A. VanGemeren, "Our Missional God: Redemptive-Historical Preaching and the Missio Dei," in *Living Waters from Ancient Springs: Essays in Honor of Cornelis Van Dam*, ed. Jason Van Vliet (Eugene, OR: Pickwick, 2011), 198–217.

38. Willem A. VanGemeren, "Israel as the Hermeneutical Crux in the Interpretation of Prophecy: Part 1," *WTJ* 45, no. 1 (1983): 132–45; VanGemeren, "Israel as the Hermeneutical Crux in the Interpretation of Prophecy: Part 2," *WTJ* 46, no. 2 (1984): 254–97.

39. J. Ross Wagner, "Isaiah in Romans and Galatians," in Moyise and Menken, *Isaiah in the New Testament*, 129.

Luke responds to the questions of his time by presenting Jesus in the light of Isaiah. Jesus is the servant of the Lord, and his disciples are the servants of the Lord. Koet comments, "Our survey of the Isaianic material makes clear that Luke uses the figure of the servant to depict Jesus, his mission, and that of his disciples."[40]

Conclusion on Isaiah

The book of Isaiah develops the multifaceted motif of salvation. Salvation is more than forgiveness and reconciliation. God offers human beings the privilege of participation and fellowship with him so that they may come to know the fullness (glory) of the Lord and enjoy the presence of the Holy One of Israel in their midst. The work of God involves the messianic agent, the Spirit of God, and the new community. The Lord exchanges wrath, vengeance, and alienation for comfort, vindication, and reconciliation. He welcomes his people from Israel and the nations to Zion, his holy hill. He justifies, cleanses, and sanctifies her citizens.

In the process of salvation, God's servants become servants of righteousness (Rom. 6:18), instead of slaves to sin (6:6, 16). Their lives are committed to the pursuit of justice and righteousness. But unlike God's justice, which is transcendent, they learn to appropriate justice and righteousness by following Jesus Christ. Social justice at the human level is analogical to divine justice when it is compassionate, Spirit filled, sapiential, and transcultural (ecumenic). But humans can never fulfill God's high expectations of justice. Their justice is proximate at best. However, in the Lord Jesus Christ, Christians are justified and present themselves as servants of righteousness (6:18). They participate in God's purposes by modeling Jesus Christ while being empowered by the Spirit of God. In relation to the persons of the Trinity, God may accept their feeble, proximate efforts, overlooking their blindsidedness and ethnocentric perspectives. They grow in a Christlike transcendence by the Spirit, in wisdom, and in a transcultural (ecumenic) perspective.

Jesus is the glorious *image* of God. He is the Creator, who came down to atone for sins and has ascended into glory (Heb. 1:3). Matthew presents Jesus as full of compassionate justice when he looked at people "harassed and helpless, like sheep without a shepherd" (Matt. 9:36, cf. Mark 6:34). In his compassion, Jesus healed the sick and fed the crowds (Matt. 14:14; 15:32). He touched the blind and healed them (20:34; cf. Mark 1:41). Paul exhorts the Colossians to "clothe (them)selves with compassion, kindness, humility, gentleness and patience" (Col. 3:12). He defines the "new self" as a life of renewal in the image of the Creator, without "anger, rage, malice, slander, and filthy language," without deception and discrimination (Col. 3:8–11).

In Philippians Paul constructs the paradigm of the incarnation for Christ's followers to imitate. They are in union with Christ, in fellowship "in the Spirit," and full of "comfort," "tenderness," and "compassion," being united by love, "one in spirit and of one mind." This is the life of *perichoresis* (fellowship with God). From the heights

---

40. Koet, "Isaiah in Luke-Acts," 98–99.

of *perichoresis*, they see others as having greater worth without "selfish ambition or vain conceit." This is the life of *kenosis* (Phil. 2:1–8). It is rooted in Trinitarian theism, flourishes in union with Jesus Christ and by the power of the Spirit, and is shaped by Scripture and by the world around God's people.

The Message of Hosea: Return to Your Husband and Father

The prophet Hosea is representative of the prophets' connection with Moses and with each other. By a careful study of Hosea, we enter into the metaphorical world of the prophets. The image of God as Husband and as Father heightens the paradox of God's presence and hiddenness. The Prophets present multifaceted images, and Hosea is rich in his use of figures and images. As we looked at Isaiah in greater detail and highlighted several developments in Jeremiah and Ezekiel, so we will observe more carefully the message of Hosea as representative of the message of Moses and the Prophets.

Hosea and the Twelve

The message of Hosea makes a distinct contribution to the prophetic corpus. He does not only charge Israel with covenantal or marital infidelity, he also confirms the promises of God by grounding the future in the very being of God. Hosea's metaphorical theology presents many aspects of the triune God. God is sovereign in justice and in compassion: he is the sovereign Judge, the gracious Redeemer, the loving Husband of an unfaithful wife, the hurt Father of a lost (prodigal) son, and the caring Physician. Hosea follows the footsteps of Moses and of the Prophets as he develops a metaphorical theology. In the depiction of Israel and Judah, we see ourselves in a mirror, and we also see the Father reaching out to us. It is Hosea's intent for us to turn to God when we see the ugliness, selfishness, and elusiveness of our idolatrous and greedy ways and to find true beauty and love in the living God. This kind of theology is reliable, because God alone is true and certain, as Martin Luther reminds us in his *Larger Commentary on Galatians*:

> And this is the reason why our theology is certain: it snatches us away from ourselves and places us outside ourselves, so that we do not depend on our own strength, conscience, experience, person, or works but depend on that which is outside ourselves, that is, on the promise and truth of God, which cannot deceive.[41]

In Luther's understanding of the doctrine of justification, God's Word and faith are correlative. As Oswald Bayer comments, "Word and faith are at the core of his (Luther's) theology."[42] The good news of the gospel must give expression to a renewed sense of freedom in Christian men and women who are renewed by God's grace and liberation.[43] Justification reconnects the justified sinner with God, the self, the church, and the world.

---

41. Cited in Oswald Bayer, "Luther as an Interpreter of Holy Scripture," in *The Cambridge Companion to Martin Luther*, ed. Donald K. McKim, CCR (Cambridge: Cambridge University Press, 2003), 77.
42. Bayer, "Luther as an Interpreter," 77.
43. Bayer, "Luther as an Interpreter," 77–79.

The message of the Twelve evidently reveals a great variety of themes, motifs, images, and canonical connections. These twelve books come to us from preexilic prophets to the northern kingdom (Hosea, Amos) and to the southern kingdom (Micah, Nahum, Habakkuk, Zephaniah). Obadiah spoke shortly after the exile of Judah. Haggai, Zechariah, and Malachi addressed the postexilic community. Joel and Jonah are hard to date, though I am not uncomfortable with a postexilic date for the final composition. There is little agreement on the canonical order (cf. Masoretic Text and Septuagint), structural connections, or formal characteristics.[44] The books were copied on a single scroll but remained divided by title.[45] It is not easy to determine the main message of the Twelve, but the motif of the day of the Lord is a favorite. It is a polyvalent designation for a time (καιρος) when God establishes his kingdom, vindicating the remnant and avenging himself on the wicked.

The promise is to be received and believed. The prophets prepare Israel for the coming fullness of the Word by calling her to return to and listen to God. The prophets charge Israel, Judah, and the nations with hubris, rebellion, and corruption. All are guilty and are condemned. But they also speak of divine salvation, compassion, justification, and reconciliation. Primarily they address their contemporaries, but their message always carries a surplus as the message to one generation remains the Word of God for another. Their message extends beyond the confines of space and time, ethnicity, gender, age, and social status.

Justification is God's monergistic and free grace bestowed on people who have offended his holiness, whether they be Jews or non-Jews. God freely shows his love and compassion to people and treats them as righteous. When they return to him, confess their waywardness, and look to him for forgiveness and salvation, God promises to love them freely: "I will heal their waywardness and love them freely, for my anger has turned away from them" (Hos. 14:4). Such people confess that they have no claim or merit to fall back on. Justification is a free act of God's grace in Jesus Christ. It is God's act of favor on behalf of sinners, who deserve his condemnation and judgment. Justification as an act of divine grace is the basic promise of the gospel.

The first three of the Twelve—Hosea, Joel, and Amos—appropriate and develop the concept of the day of the Lord as a heuristic device to imprint on the people the power of God in salvation and in judgment, in wrath and in compassion. *Hosea's* contribution will be further developed, but suffice it to say that the Prophets—both the "Major" and the "Minor"—contribute to the diverse aspects of God's judgment and salvation. They speak of human accountability in time and anticipate a final vindication of the righteous and a judgment of the wicked. What is surprising is the prophetic expectation of a godly remnant from all nations. This remnant is characterized by faith, trust, and seeking and calling on the name of the Lord. They await God's ultimate redemption. The prophets

---

44. See Daniel C. Timmer, "The Twelve," in *A Biblical-Theological Introduction to the Old Testament: The Gospel Promised*, ed. Miles V. Van Pelt (Wheaton, IL: Crossway, 2016), 321–39.
45. See Timmer, "The Twelve," 321–27.

apprehend that salvation belongs to the Lord, but they do not yet clearly see that this salvation is found in the God-man, Jesus Christ. The apostles appropriate the prophetic message and align it with the ministry of the Holy Spirit, who witnesses to the ultimate reality that Jesus Christ saves all who call on him in faith (1 Pet. 1:10–12).

Joel proclaims the salvation of the Lord amid judgment (the day of the Lord). God will sovereignly pour out his Spirit on all who call on him, that is, all who are called by the Lord (Joel 2:28–32). God's people are secure, because God is their protector: "The Lord will roar from Zion and thunder from Jerusalem; the earth and the heavens will tremble. But the Lord will be a refuge for his people, a stronghold for the people of Israel" (3:16). They are sanctified and participate in his holy presence: "Then you will know that I, the Lord your God, dwell in Zion, my holy hill. Jerusalem will be holy; never again will foreigners invade her" (3:17).

Amos also appropriates the dark reality of the day of the Lord for his age (Amos 5). God's people had worshiped the creature rather than the Creator:

> "Therefore this is what I will do to you, Israel, and because I will do this to you, Israel, prepare to meet your God." He who forms the mountains, who creates the wind, and who reveals his thoughts to mankind, who turns dawn to darkness, and treads on the heights of the earth—the Lord God Almighty is his name. (4:12–13)

Amos calls the people of God to seek Yahweh and live: "This is what the Lord says to Israel: 'Seek me and live'" (5:4). The search for the living God entails a radical change. Being justified by him, God's people must become servants of his justice and righteousness: "But let justice roll on like a river, righteousness like a never-failing stream!" (5:24). Their future is secure in him (9:13–15), the Davidic dynasty will undergo renewal (9:11–12), and a remnant from all nations will participate in God's salvation (see Acts 15:15–19).

The following six books—Obadiah, Jonah, Micah, Nahum, Habakkuk, and Zephaniah—show familiarity with the background of the imperial ambitions of Assyria and Babylon. Though not all books were written before the fall of Jerusalem, the prophetic authors appropriate their message to help God's people apprehend that God uses the destructive power of the nations. Through his servants the prophets, Yahweh prepares a faithful remnant.

Obadiah clarifies the evil of the Edomites at Jerusalem's fall and symbolically captures the evil of the kingdoms of this world. All humanity is under God's judgment. The desecration of Zion and her inhabitants will be overturned when the Lord delivers and consecrates his people: "But on Mount Zion will be deliverance; it will be holy, and Jacob will possess his inheritance" (Obad. 17).

Jonah extends God's compassion to the people of Nineveh. When they turned to him and away from their evil, the Lord had compassion on them: "When God saw what they did and how they turned from their evil ways, he relented and did not bring on them the destruction he had threatened" (Jonah 3:10).

Micah develops the awesome nature of God's wrath and the just judgment that brings an end to human structures and institutions: "Her leaders judge for a bribe, her priests teach for a price, and her prophets tell fortunes for money. Yet they look for the LORD's support and say, 'Is not the LORD among us? No disaster will come upon us'" (Mic. 3:11). Jerusalem (Zion) with her sacred temple will not escape God's judgment: "Therefore because of you, Zion will be plowed like a field, Jerusalem will become a heap of rubble, the temple hill a mound overgrown with thickets" (3:12). Even so, he promises to restore "his sacred temple": "In the last days the mountain of the LORD's temple will be established as the highest of the mountains; it will be exalted above the hills, and peoples will stream to it" (4:1). God's kingdom is secure, and so is the kingdom of David (chaps. 4–5). At the conclusion of his prophecy, Micah prays that God will remain true to his character and promises:

> Who is a God like you,
> > who pardons sin and forgives the transgression
> > of the remnant of his inheritance?
>
> You do not stay angry forever
> > but delight to show mercy.
>
> You will again have compassion on us;
> > you will tread our sins underfoot
> > and hurl all our iniquities into the depths of the sea.
>
> You will be faithful to Jacob,
> > and show love to Abraham,
>
> as you pledged on oath to our ancestors
> > in days long ago. (7:18–20)

Nahum assures God's people that Yahweh has seen the affliction of Israel and Judah at the hands of the Assyrians. The Assyrians will not escape Yahweh's wrath (Nah. 1:2–6). God promises to protect all who have faith in him: "The LORD is good, a refuge in times of trouble. He cares for those who trust in him" (1:7).

Habakkuk appropriates the day of the Lord in the context of the Babylonian rise to power. Though their evil is greater than that of the Judeans, God reveals to Habakkuk that he plans to use the Babylonians as instruments of the day of the Lord on Judah. The righteous will live by faith that is faithful (Hab. 2:4; see Rom. 1:17; Gal. 3:11; Heb. 10:38). The end result of God's judgment(s) is a new world in which righteousness dwells: "For the earth will be filled with the knowledge of the glory of the LORD, as the waters cover the sea" (Hab. 2:14). To this end, Habakkuk suffers, awaiting and praying for God's salvation to come to God's world: "Yet I will rejoice in the LORD, I will be joyful in God my Savior. The Sovereign LORD is my strength; he makes my feet like the feet of a deer, he enables me to tread on the heights" (3:18–19).

Zephaniah also applies the metaphor of the day of the Lord to the last days of Judah. Though he prophesies before Habakkuk, his ministry clarifies who may be saved, namely, all who call on God's name, including the nations: "Then I will purify the lips of the peoples, that all of them may call on the name of the Lord and serve him shoulder to shoulder" (Zeph. 3:9). The remnant of the peoples is known for its meekness and trust in the Lord: "But I will leave within you the meek and humble. The remnant of Israel will trust in the name of the Lord" (3:12). The Lord commits himself to all who rely on his power to save: "The Lord your God is with you, the Mighty Warrior who saves. He will take great delight in you; in his love he will no longer rebuke you, but will rejoice over you with singing" (3:17).

The last three prophetic books reflect postexilic developments. *Haggai* and *Zechariah* encourage the remnant that has returned from exile with assurances of God's presence and of the work of God's Spirit in renewing the relationship between God and his people (Hag. 1:12, 14; 2:2; Zech. 4:6). Zion will again symbolize God's presence with his people. Jerusalem will truly reflect God's character of truth and holiness: "I will return to Zion and dwell in Jerusalem. Then Jerusalem will be called the Faithful City, and the mountain of the Lord Almighty will be called the Holy Mountain" (8:3). But *Malachi* laments the direction of postexilic Judaism. The people have become jaded, sarcastic, and legalistic. They no longer serve and honor God. Only a small remnant fear the Lord: "Then those who feared the Lord talked with each other, and the Lord listened and heard. A scroll of remembrance was written in his presence concerning those who feared the Lord and honored his name" (Mal. 3:16). Though the ultimate distinction fades in the vagaries of life, the Lord knows who are his and will reward them: "And you will again see the distinction between the righteous and the wicked, between those who serve God and those who do not" (3:18).

The prophetic language and imagery is far from uniform, but their expectation is framed in Mosaic terms: return to Yahweh, fear him, and love him, because he is a forgiving and compassionate God. Some of the prophets also intimate the place of the messianic king in the grand scheme of things. The vista of Hosea, one of the earlier prophets, is the most distinct: "Afterward the Israelites will return and seek the Lord their God and David their king. They will come trembling to the Lord and to his blessings in the last days" (Hos. 3:5). In other words, the key to a future with God requires a return to the living God and to his messianic agent (Micah 4–5; Psalm 2; cf. Acts 2:36–38). Hosea does not integrate the messianic hope except to hint that the remnant must cultivate the worship of God that is inclusive of messianic expectations. Other prophets gradually shine light as they come to expect a Davidic king with divine qualities. They do not yet understand how the divine and the human will be united in the Lord Jesus Christ, because that remains a mystery until the incarnation of our Lord. The prophetic apprehension of God was always overcast by dark shadows. Their vision encouraged them to await more understanding (1 Pet. 1:10–12). The great light that brought together the message of Moses and the Prophets came in the incarnation and ministry of the Lord Jesus together with the outpouring of the Holy Spirit. Hosea's hope is not well defined, but he speaks of an eschatological era ("the last days") when Yahweh will do a great work, when his people will return to him and to David (Hos. 3:5).

Hosea among the Prophets

Hosea develops the motif of God's consistent and persistent care for his people, even in his wrath. He addresses the northern kingdom, Israel, from 750 to 725 BC, but also includes the southern kingdom, Judah. All have sinned against God, who is forbearing, compassionate, and forgiving (Hos. 1:7; 14:3–4). Though he is angry, condemns, and punishes, he promises to show compassion and save his people marvelously and graciously, because he is holy (11:9–11). Yahweh is King, Lord, Redeemer, Husband, Father, and Physician of all the twelve tribes. These images originate with Moses in the Pentateuch and shape the prophetic foundations and expectations.

Moses is the fountainhead of the prophets.[46] All prophets show their connections with the Mosaic foundations. Their message *accords* with that of Moses. The prophets provide a commentary, an appropriation, and a contextualization of the message of Moses. They prophesy but do not predict in the narrow sense. They speak of God's judgment (the day of the Lord) but are not specific in prophesying the date or the manner of God's judgments of Israel, Judah, and the nations. They charge people with covenantal breach yet promise God's monergistic renewal of the covenant that reveals both the justice and compassion of God.

The future is grounded in Yahweh's character and promises. The special relationship between God and his people is likened to a marriage (see Hosea 1–3) in which God (the Bridegroom/Husband) takes his people to himself. He is their King (Shepherd), and they are his people ("sheep"). Other frequent images include Father and son (child), Master and servant (not a slave but a personal and dignified representative of Yahweh). However, the special relationship between God and his people was not to be taken for granted. Yahweh intended for Israel to know him by his perfections, by his acts and word, and by the story of redemption and the providential outworking of his purposes. He had guaranteed to Moses that he is a God of compassion, grace, patience, love, faithfulness, and forgiveness but also a God of justice and righteousness (Ex. 34:6–7).

The law of Moses developed a system with the hope that Israel would come to know her God. It treated the Israelites as immature partners who had to be tested in their faith that they might grow to trust the Lord of the covenant and walk humbly with him. The goal proved to be lofty, if not too lofty, for Israel. All that God expected from them was to walk in the footsteps of Abraham: "Follow justice and justice alone" (Deut. 16:20). But the expectations were not too lofty (30:11–14; cf. Rom. 10:5–13), if only they had experienced a change of heart, also known as circumcision of the heart (Deut. 30:6; cf. 10:16).

---

46. Willem A. VanGemeren, *Interpreting the Prophetic Word* (Grand Rapids, MI: Zondervan, 1990).

The message of Hosea is rooted in Moses, or what may be called Deuteronomic theology, with its emphases on (1) God's historic commitment to his "bride," (2) the failure of Israel, (3) the certainty of retribution (judgment), and (4) the depth of Yahweh's compassion for his "children." Hosea develops Israel's story beyond Moses by the mention of post-Mosaic events: Achor (Hos. 2:15; cf. Josh. 15:7), David (Hos. 3:5), and the division of the kingdom into Israel and Judah (1:1, 11). The mention of the kings of Judah and of Israel (1:1) links the prophecy with the books of the Former Prophets, especially the books of Kings, which record the historical, political, social, and religious background of the book of Hosea. The prophecy of Hosea connects closely with the message of Moses and the Prophets.

Jesus highlighted the close connection between Moses and the Prophets as a hermeneutical tool. The Sadducees and other groups appealed to Moses (the Pentateuch) exclusively. The Pharisees had a broader canon but embraced the Torah more warmly than the Prophets. Jesus, however, was truly canonical, because he integrated the Prophets together with not only Moses but also the Writings. He appealed repeatedly to the unified message of "Moses and the Prophets." After his resurrection, he summarized the message of the whole Old Testament as framing his ministry: suffering, glory, and witness to the nations (Luke 24:27, 44; cf. Matt. 5:17; Luke 16:29, 31).

The Metaphorical World of Hosea

Hosea makes a significant contribution to the biblical corpus. He is the only prophet from Israel, the northern kingdom, whose writing is extant.[47] His style is laden with similes and imagery by which he invites his audience to enter his metaphorical world.[48] Through metaphors and imagery, the prophets encouraged their audience to see their world from a more transcendent perspective:

> When I found Israel,
>   it was like finding grapes in the desert;
> when I saw your ancestors,
>   it was like seeing the early fruit on the fig tree.
> But when they came to Baal Peor,
>   they consecrated themselves to that shameful idol
>   and became as vile as the thing they loved.
> Ephraim's glory will fly away like a bird—
>   no birth, no pregnancy, no conception.
> Even if they rear children,
>   I will bereave them of every one.
> Woe to them
>   when I turn away from them!

---

47. Jonah also hails from the North, but the book of Jonah is about Jonah, not the northern kingdom.
48. Göran Eidevall, *Grapes in the Desert: Metaphors, Models, and Themes in Hosea 4–14*, ConBOT 43 (Stockholm: Almqvist & Wiksell, 1996).

> I have seen Ephraim, like Tyre,
> > planted in a pleasant place.
> But Ephraim will bring out
> > their children to the slayer. (Hos. 9:10–13)

In this text the prophet surveys Israel's story from the wilderness wandering ("desert . . . Baal Peor," 9:10) to his time ("Ephraim") using vegetative imagery (grapes, figs, "planted [שתל] in a pleasant place," 9:10, 13; cf. 2:14; 10:1; 14:7) and ornithological imagery ("like a bird—no birth, no pregnancy, no conception," 9:11; cf. 11:11–12). He sketches with words and outlines the wretched history of Israel. The mention of Israel's idolatrous and lewd apostasy at Baal-Peor shortly before their entry into the land (Num. 25:1–18) reveals the true nature of Israel at an early stage. Idolatry and lewd living continued in his day. Hosea is fond of historical-geographical allusions, such as regions and countries (Assyria, Egypt, Ephraim, Gilead, Judah) and cities (Bethel, Gibeah, Gilgal). He speaks of Israel as Ephraim, playing on the popular etymology associating Ephraim with fertility (פרה, "be fruitful").[49] He delves into Israel's history: Jacob, exodus, conquest, kingship, idolatry.[50] The story of Israel is the story of Yahweh's growing resentment of Israel: "Because of all their wickedness in Gilgal, I hated them there. . . . I will no longer love them" (9:15). The verb "hate" (שׂנא) signifies alienation in an increasingly tense relationship and is the opposite of "love" (cf. Mal. 1:2–3).

Yahweh and His Unfaithful Wife (Hosea 1–3)

Hosea develops the metaphor of prostitution (זנה, 14x). The very first command of the Lord is for Hosea to marry a prostitute (אֵשֶׁת זְנוּנִים, 1:2, "a wife of whoredom," ESV; "an adulterous wife," NIV). The Lord had warned Israel not to defile themselves by following the culture of the Canaanites, whether through idolatry, syncretism, or illicit sexual relationships, because it would capture their hearts and estrange them from the covenant relationship. Acculturation to an idolatrous way of life had led God's people astray. Their wrongheaded commitments were like a slow-working addiction that had won the hearts of the people and had turned them against the God of the covenant.

The relationship between Yahweh and Israel is likened to a marriage.[51] Any competing commitment is nothing less than spiritual adultery (Luke 14:26). The prevalent image of prostitution in Hosea evidently originates with Moses. He had forewarned Israel of the links between human identity and idolatry.[52] Idolatry is not just false

---

49. Ephraim is Hosea's favorite designation for the northern kingdom in contrast to Judah. Ephraim's bellicose history was well known from the days of the judges (cf. Psalm 78). It had risen to dominant leadership among the northern tribes, evident also in the election of Jeroboam I as their first king.
50. Douglas Stuart observes that Gilgal is a synecdoche for Israel. *Hosea–Jonah*, WBC 31 (Waco, TX: Word Books, 1987), 154. Hosea mentions Gilgal in association with idolatry, sacrifices, and altars (Hos. 4:15; 9:15; 12:11 [12:12 MT]).
51. See Gordon P. Hugenberger, *Marriage as a Covenant: Biblical Law and Ethics as Developed from Malachi*, Biblical Studies Library (Grand Rapids, MI: Baker, 1994).
52. See Richard Lints, *Identity and Idolatry: The Image of God and Its Inversion*, NSBT 36 (Downers Grove, IL: InterVarsity Press, 2015).

worship. It changes one's identity by making people less than what God had planned for them to be. It brings about an inversion in human identity that hinders the relationship of people with their God and with each other. Moses had observed the changes in the heart commitment of Israel and had warned them of the correlation between idolatry (prostitution) and breach of covenant, on the one hand, and God's wrath, alienation, judgments, and exile, on the other:

> And the LORD said to Moses: "You are going to rest with your ancestors, and these people will soon *prostitute* themselves to the foreign gods of the land they are entering. They will forsake me and *break the covenant* I made with them. And in that day I will become *angry* with them and *forsake them*; I will hide my face from them, and they will be destroyed. *Many disasters and calamities* will come on them, and in that day they will ask, 'Have not these disasters come on us because our *God is not with us*?' And *I will certainly hide my face* in that day because of all their wickedness in turning to other gods. (Deut. 31:16–18)

Thus, Moses had forewarned Israel of the dangerous turn they had already taken.

The first chapter of Hosea invites the readers to focus on the consequences of prostitution by introducing the children. We learn little about Gomer's unfaithfulness before or after her marriage. *Her children and not her marriage* are the subject of the first two chapters. *The names of her children are symbolically significant*: Jezreel, Lo-Ruhamah ("not loved"), and Lo-Ammi ("not my people"). Not much is said about Gomer, except that she was the daughter of Diblaim, was a "woman of whoredom," and gave birth to "children of whoredom" (1:2; 2:4 ESV; "children of adultery," NIV).[53] The first chapter details the sequence and the symbolic significance of the children's names.

The text is unclear whether Gomer had prostituted herself before marriage or even whether she was a prostitute at all. Gomer's prostitution may have taken the form of the greed and reckless abandon that had also captured the heart of Israel. *The imagery of whoring is likely a metaphor for Israel's idolatry, self-fulfillment, and syncretism.*[54] *Israelite syncretism was the ability to worship Yahweh and forms of Baalism without experiencing any inner conflict.* But little did Israel realize the long-term impact of such openness to foreign influences. The prophet warned and threatened Israel of the consequences represented by the symbolic significance of his children's names. Israel was compromised and had not heeded the Mosaic warning. The names of the children symbolically apply Moses's words to the world of Hosea.

The Symbolic Names of Hosea's Children

The children born to Hosea and Gomer were to be known as "children of whoredom" (Hos. 1:2 ESV). The actual names are Jezreel, Lo-Ruhamah, and Lo-Ammi (1:4, 6, 9).

---

53. Raymond C. Ortlund Jr., *God's Unfaithful Wife: A Biblical-Theology of Spiritual Adultery*, NSBT 2 (Downers Grove, IL: InterVarsity Press, 2002).
54. Stuart, *Hosea–Jonah*, 26–27.

They symbolize the end of Yahweh's relationship with Israel and the resultant abandonment, guilt, punishment, and captivity.

Jezreel. The name given to the first child, Jezreel, is a play both on the town by that name in the fertile valley by Mount Gilboa and on the kingdom of Israel. The name Jezreel (יִזְרְעֶאל; "God sows/plants") is associated with sowing (זרע; "sow") and fecundity. The name is also a sardonic reminder of Israel's history of cruelty, oppression, and bloodshed. They had pursued emptiness: "They sow (זרע) the wind and reap the whirlwind" (Hos. 8:7). Hosea employs the agricultural image of act and consequences (planting, harvesting, and eating) to clarify their evil way of life: "But you have planted wickedness, you have reaped evil, you have eaten the fruit of deception" (10:13). Because of the inversion in relationships, Israel was deceived and considered herself righteous. If the people had only sought Yahweh, they would have grown in the goodly virtues of righteousness and faithfulness: "Sow [זרע] righteousness for yourselves, reap the fruit of unfailing love, and break up your unplowed ground; for it is time to seek the LORD, until he comes and showers his righteousness on you" (10:12). But they had not sought him, had not received a righteousness by faith, and had produced a righteousness based on the works of the law to their own condemnation (cf. Rom. 9:20–31).

Jezreel was associated with bloodshed and captivity. The reigning monarch of Israel, Jeroboam II (793–753 BC), was a descendant of the house of Jehu (842–753 BC), which had its origin in a bloody revolution (842 BC; see 2 Kings 10). Ephraim's history, too, was bloody.[55] The reasons for Israel's impending doom are sprinkled throughout the book. The Lord had been patient with his people, but throughout her history the people of Israel were faithless and deceptive. They did not know the Lord and cared little for their fellow humans (see Hos. 4:1–3; 5:1–15; 6:11–7:1; 9:7–17; 10:1–15; 11:12–12:14). Destitution, deprivation, and death were God's signs of what lay ahead for Israel in exile.

Lo-Ruhamah. Lo-Ruhamah (לֹא רֻחָמָה; "not the object of compassion," from רחם, "have compassion") signifies God's attitude to Israel's suffering. He will not show compassion when Israel finally calls on him. She will have to endure the separation, come to her senses, and await God's mercy and forgiveness. Yahweh is free to show compassion to whomever he gives it: "I will have compassion on whom I will have compassion [רחם]" (Ex. 33:19). He withheld it from Israel, which went into captivity in 722 BC, but he continued to be compassionate toward Judah (Hos. 1:7). Yahweh preserved Judah, while he hid his face from Israel. The distinction between God's attitude to Israel and to Judah is the subject of Isaiah 1–39 and is symbolized by the name Immanuel ("God is with us")—that is, he protected Judah (see Isa. 7:14; 8:8–10) in the aftermath of the Assyrian invasions and conquest of Israel under Shalmaneser V (r. 727–722 BC) and

---

55. See the lessons of wisdom to be derived from Psalm 78: Ephraim's bloody and rebellious history, God's judgments, and his election of the Davidic dynasty.

Sargon II (r. 722–705 BC) that resulted in the destruction of Samaria and the exile of Israel (722 BC). Israel was no longer to be reckoned as the people of God (Lo-Ammi).

Lo-Ammi. The central tenet of the Mosaic covenant assures Israel that Yahweh is her God and that Israel is his people. The naming of the third child Lo-Ammi signifies the end of the covenant relationship, the end of God's "marriage" to Israel. Hosea explains the name in these words: "For you are not my people [לֹא עַמִּי], and I am not your God" (Hos. 1:9). The designation "my people" connotes a close relationship between Yahweh and his "covenant partner." It was his intent for them to get to *know* him (2:20) by reflecting his purity and holiness. Instead, they went their own way and experienced estrangement and corruption, deceived themselves (4:6–12), and subjected themselves to God's wrath, retribution, and desolation. In his loving concern, Yahweh reached out to his people, but her sin was too exposed for him to ignore: "Whenever I would restore the fortunes of my people, whenever I would heal Israel, the sins of Ephraim are exposed and the crimes of Samaria revealed. They practice deceit, thieves break into houses, bandits rob in the streets" (6:11–7:1).

The Three Children Revisited

The promises regarding the reversal of names are in the form of two bookends (Hos. 1:10–11; 2:21–23). Both sections are connected by the names Jezreel (1:11; 2:22), (Lo-)Ammi (1:10; 2:1, 23) and (Lo-)Ruhamah, (2:1, 23). In between this framework, the readers receive insight into the relationship between Yahweh and Israel. Hosea speaks about the grand transformation as an eschatological era in which God promises to monergistically bring about a holistic transformation of creation, the nations, and his people. This era of transformation (καιρος) is known as the great "day of Jezreel" (1:11), the day of Israel's renewal and commitment to Yahweh (2:16), the day of Yahweh's renewal of creation (2:18), and the day of Yahweh's responsiveness to bless his people (2:19). This "day" reverses the dire effects of the day of the Lord's wrath, known as the "day of reckoning" (5:9) and as the "days of punishment" (9:7).

Table 3.1 is suggestive of the symbolic significance of the three children. The first column delineates the cause of God's displeasure (bloodshed) and the resulting cessation of the northern kingdom (Jezreel), God's withdrawal of his love (Lo-Ruhamah), and the effects of his hiddenness (Lo-Ammi). In the second column, Hosea develops the future of Ammi in close connection with "the day of Jezreel" (1:10–11) and lays out the aspects of the new eschatological era in five sets of monergistic promises (2:14–22) that culminate with the mention of Jezreel (2:22), which links up—by the verb זרע ("sow")—with the final mention of Ruhamah and Ammi (2:23). In other words, Ammi and Jezreel are closely associated at the beginning of the chapter (1:10–11), and Ruhamah and Ammi are interwoven with Jezreel at the end of the chapter (2:22–23). The transformation of Jezreel is the focus of the oracles of salvation, assured by two direct divine utterances ("declares the Lord," 2:16, 21; cf. 11:11) within a set of five monergistic promises (2:14–23).

Table 3.1 Symbolic Significance of Hosea's Children

Names: Days of Punishment	New Names: Eschatological Era
Jezreel Spirit of "prostitution": bloodshed, corruption, violence The end of the kingdom Subjugation *Lo-Ruhamah* No compassion for Israel Compassion for Judah: Marvelous Deliverance *Lo-Ammi* No covenantal relationship or protection Estrangement from God God's hiddenness Subject to curses	**1:10–11** **Bookend A** *Ammi* Population explosion "Children of the living God" Union of Israel and Judah under one leader Renewal "from the earth" The great day of *Jezreel* **2:1–13** *Ammi* and *Ruhamah* witness against their mother and explain parabolically what God will do to bring Israel back to her senses **2:14–15** God's tender speech Promise of restoration Transformation from trouble to hope The people's response to God **2:16–17** Divine utterance (נְאֻם־יְהוָה) Eschatological day Renewal of marriage Promise of inner transformation of the people **2:18** Eschatological day Promise of covenant with creation Promise of end of war Promise of security and protection **2:19–20** Promise of renewal of the everlasting marriage Divine qualities: Righteousness and justice, love and compassion, faithfulness Knowledge of the Lord **2:21–23** Divine utterance (נְאֻם־יְהוָה) Eschatological day Promise of God's response (ענה) affecting the response of heaven, earth, crops, resulting in the blessing of *Jezreel* (people) Promise of God's "sowing" (זרע) in the land **Change of names: Bookend B** *Ruhamah*: Promise of compassion *Ammi*: Promise of covenant relationship

Ammi and Jezreel (Hos. 1:10–11). Hosea reintroduces Ammi and Jezreel, in reverse order from Hosea 1, as symbols of the new eschatological age. It is called "the day of Jezreel," whose greatness will be celebrated (1:10–11). It is great because of the numerous descendants, "like the sand on the seashore, which cannot be measured or counted" (1:10; cf. Gen. 22:17), and because of the renewal of the covenant with Yahweh, signified by a new name given to Lo-Ammi, "children of the living God" (Hos. 1:10). Moreover, the people of Judah and of Israel will constitute one nation under one leader (ראש; 1:11). The union of Israel and Judah suggests that the division comes to an end when the exile is over. More than that, God's compassion will extend to the whole (cf. 1:6–7). Further, the new leader is known as the "head" (ראש; 1:11 ESV).[56] He will not carry the baggage associated with past leaders (kings, princes, rulers). Hosea stands critically opposed to kingship, because of its associations with oppression and with political and religious power plays. He details the excesses of leaders and people as well as the many forms of divine alienation they will experience. The exile forcibly removed the people from their land and their ancient markers of identity. But at God's appointed time, they will "come up out of the land [or earth]" (1:11). The meaning of this phrase may signify their marvelous redemption, like that promised in 13:14 (cf. 1 Cor. 15:54–55).[57] The nation will die but will rise again (cf. Rom. 11:15). The people are like germinating seeds, or possibly, they will experience the proverbial life from the dead.[58] Hosea envisions an eschatological community, characterized by population explosion and by unity under one leader (Hos. 1:10–11). It marks a return to the Deuteronomic ideal of the worship of God by the one people united under one leader[59] and blessed by God's presence and forgiveness. After a period of alienation (1:4–5), the people of the former northern kingdom will be incorporated into the New Israel, which includes a remnant from both North and South. They will constitute one nation under one leader (1:11).

Hosea will take up the transformation of the symbolic significance of the names (2:22–23) after explaining parabolically his plans for Israel's isolation and restoration (2:1–15). After five sets of monergistic promises (2:14–23), he picks up again the significance of the names.

Jezreel, Ruhamah, and Ammi (Hos. 2:22–23). The mention of Jezreel (Hos. 2:22) closes God's promise of renewed fertility (2:21–22) and in Janus-like fashion anticipates the development in 2:23: "I will plant [וּזְרַעְתִּיהָ, 'sow'] her for myself in the land." The act of sowing suggests the increase of the decimated population of Jezreel (see 1:10). The name Jezreel will come to signify blessing. It marks the end of the covenantal curses and the

---

56. Since the new leader is not specified to be a Davidide and receives the ambiguous designation "head" ("chief," "leader"), it is unclear whether the prophet speaks of a divine kingdom or a transformed human kingdom.
57. The interpretation of Hos. 13:14 is difficult. Is the word "compassion" to be understood as God's showing no compassion or as "relenting" in the sense of not showing remorse in having promised to redeem—so Thomas Edward McComiskey, *Hosea*, in *The Minor Prophets: An Exegetical and Expository Commentary*, ed. Thomas Edward McComiskey (Grand Rapids, MI: Baker Academic, 2009), 222? Hans Walter Wolff reads it as introducing 13:15: "Compassion is unknown to my eyes." *Hosea*, Hermeneia, trans. Gary Stansell, ed. Paul D. Hanson (Philadelphia: Fortress, 1974), 222.
58. See Ezek. 37:12–14. The expression may also signify the sprouting of seed. Wolff, *Hosea*, 28.
59. At this juncture, the text does not determine who the leader is. It may be God, a Davidic king, or a divinely approved leader, such as a Moses or Joshua.

beginning of the eschatological era (καιρος) of divine blessing when the people of God experience the reality of his promise to Abraham in a marvelous population explosion (1:10), undergo a spiritual transformation as "children of the living God" (1:10), and experience God's rich blessings (2:21–22).

The name Ruhamah (2:23) is variously translated as Pitied, Loved, Object of Compassion. The lexeme רחם signifies God's compassion for his people. He sustains the covenant relationship with his compassion, as promised to Moses: "The LORD, the LORD, the *compassionate* and gracious God, slow to anger, abounding in love and faithfulness, maintaining love to thousands, and forgiving wickedness, rebellion and sin" (Ex. 34:6–7). Even though Israel has broken the covenant, God's love covers a multitude of sins. Moses spoke of this glorious day in Deuteronomy:

> Then the LORD your God will restore your fortunes and *have compassion* on you and gather you again from all the nations where he scattered you. Even if you have been banished to the most distant land under the heavens, from there the LORD your God will gather you and bring you back. (Deut. 30:3–4)

Hosea appropriates and develops the importance of God's ancient promises to God's renewed acts of compassion for the sake of the remnant of Israel and Judah.

The change from Lo-Ammi ("not my people") to Ammi ("my people") similarly symbolizes the radical transformation of Israel (Hos. 2:23). God's monergistic declaration changes everything. Once they did not belong, but God's renaming signifies that they are still heirs of the promise made to Abraham. They will experience that Yahweh alone is the true source of life.[60] God calls them "'You are my people,' and they will say, 'You are my God'" (2:23). The new covenant relationship will make an impact on people, land, and creation, when God's people will enjoy the realization of his promises made to the patriarchs, but the renewal of the covenant and its associated blessings are God's alone. They will "live," because God alone is the source of renewal and life. The confession "You are my God" is singularly important, because it "expresses in its terseness complete trust in God's faithful relationship with his people."[61]

The New Testament Appropriation of Hosea's Children

In a strange twist of providence, Paul appropriates God's promises given to Israel for Gentile believers who have received God's righteousness by faith (Rom. 9:30), while he condemns his fellow Jews for pursuing righteousness by works of the law (9:31). Paul appropriates the change in the names of Hosea's children in explaining that Gentiles who were Lo-Ammi and Lo-Ruhamah have become "my people," "my loved one," and "children of the living God" (9:15–26; see Hos. 1:10; 2:23; cf. 1 Pet. 2:10). Yet he awaits a transformation of Israel when the fullness of the Gentiles brings about Israel's participation (Rom. 11:25–32). Though Israel is disobedient, a remnant is God's beloved

---

60. Wolff, *Hosea*, 27.
61. Wolff, *Hosea*, 55.

(11:28) who will be saved, incorporated into the covenant, and forgiven (11:26–28), "for God's gifts and his call are irrevocable" (11:29).

Likewise, Peter understands the place of Gentiles in the church in the light of Hosea. God's mercy is so rich that Gentiles, who had not obtained mercy, receive it in the gospel. D. A. Carson comments, "Peter's reference to Hosea is more than a type/anti-type set of assumptions . . . but it may be a meditation on God's great mercy to Jew and Gentile alike, once both are declared to be guilty 'Gentiles.'"[62]

The parable of the unfaithful wife and mother may be interpreted from many angles. The parable would help Israel understand her alienation from God once in exile. It has three conclusions, each introduced with "therefore" (לָכֵן):

1. God creates difficulties and adversities for Israel (Hos. 2:6).
2. God removes the benefits and support structures (2:9).
3. God allures Israel and speaks to her heart until she responds positively (2:14).

The experience of exile explains these three aspects.

The exile was Israel's lengthy period of separation giving her an opportunity to "seek the Lord." The search for God gives God's children time to reflect, to be quiet, and to wisely discern which way they should go. Hosea leads his audience on a quest for true wisdom. He is a sapiential prophet who in his marital life, imagery, and proverbs challenges people to seek true wisdom. The last verse of the book restates what the book is all about. The search for wisdom is the search for God: "Who is wise? Let them realize these things. Who is discerning? Let them understand. The ways of the LORD are right; the righteous walk in them, but the rebellious stumble in them" (14:9; cf. 4:5). The frequent call on Israel to "return" must inevitably lead to the shocking realization of the many wrong turns God's people take. The righteous will learn to walk, whereas the fools keep on stumbling.

Yahweh's Commitment to the Renewal of the Covenant/Marriage

The prophet appropriates the symbolism of his marriage for that of Yahweh and Israel.[63] Hosea calls on the transformed descendants[64] (Hos. 1:10) to witness to Israel that salvation is experienced only in the new relationship with Yahweh. The change in names symbolizes much more than a change in ecclesiology. God's grace is poured out on the new community that is reconstituted on the basis of faith in the living God. The members of this community receive a righteousness and holiness that is not their own doing. They will be called "children of the living God" (1:10), "my people" (Ammi), and "my loved one" (Ruhamah) (2:1).

---

62. D. A. Carson, "1 Peter," in *Commentary on the New Testament Use of the Old Testament*, ed. G. K. Beale and D. A. Carson (Grand Rapids, MI: Baker Academic, 2007), 1032.
63. See Seock-Tae Sohn, *YHWH, the Husband of Israel: The Metaphor of Marriage between YHWH and Israel* (Eugene, OR: Wipf and Stock, 2002).
64. Who are the "brothers" and "sisters" (Hos. 2:1)? Are they Gomer's other children (McComiskey, *Hosea*, 32) or future generations (Stuart, *Hosea–Jonah*, 40)?

Yahweh reflects on Israel's past and future. She is an unfaithful wife who must learn to be done with her silly things and come to her senses (2:2–13). Israel, like Gomer, must be exposed to alienation, shame, and vulnerability (2:2–6). It is hoped that the prodigals will return home and get tired of their search for provisions and shelter (2:7–13). Israel must come to the stark realization that they have forgotten Yahweh, the true source of life (2:13). Israel must come to the end of her road (the "desert," 2:3; the "wilderness," 2:14) and remember that Yahweh has been with her from the very beginning. God promises to love Israel as a lover, bestowing on her the bounty of his presence, speaking to her, and treating her as if the waywardness has not taken place (2:14–15). In God's presence, the wilderness will be transformed into vineyards and the Valley of Achor (= "trouble") into "a door of hope" (2:15).

Hosea details the nature of the eschatological day. Though Israel is guilty and must justly suffer on the day of judgment, Yahweh opens up a glorious "day" in a series of sovereign and monergistic promises.

First, Yahweh will restore her fortunes when Israel responds (ענה) to her lover (2:14–15). Yahweh promises to restore Israel's vineyards and remove her troubles by opening a new door, "a door of hope" (2:15). Observe the monergistic language: "*I am now going to allure* her; *I will lead her* into the wilderness and *[I will] speak tenderly* to her. *There I will give her back* her vineyards" (2:14–15).

Second, on the eschatological day (וְהָיָה בַיּוֹם־הַהוּא; 2:16), Yahweh will transform Israel's heart (2:16–17).[65] God commits himself to be with his people, just as he did when Israel left Egypt (2:15). Yahweh has not changed (13:4; cf. 12:9). He has been with Israel from her early beginnings, the days of Jacob (12:12) and Moses (12:13). He redeemed Israel out of Egypt (13:4). But Israel must change. This change is brought out by a play on the word for בַּעַל (*ba'al*, "husband"). Because of Israel's history of intoxication with Baal worship and the Canaanite culture, Hosea fights the cultural addictions. Truly, God is "the husband" (בַּעַל, or *ba'al*) of his people (cf. Jer. 31:32). But he is not to be identified with Baalism. So the people must distinguish between the false worship and the true worship of Yahweh. Hosea has them speak of Yahweh as "my man" (אִישִׁי; Hos. 2:16), rather than בַּעְלִי.[66] Thus, Yahweh will monergistically end Israel's commitment to Baalism: "*I will remove* the names of the Baals from her lips" (2:17).

Third, on the eschatological day (בַּיּוֹם הַהוּא), Yahweh will renew his covenant with creation (2:18). On this great eschatological day, Yahweh will create a new cosmos, a home for animals and his children. It is a world of true shalom (2:18). Yahweh's commitment ("covenant") extends to creation and particularly to his people. They will thrive when warfare ceases and when they live in the security of God's protection (2:18).

---

65. Benjamin Breckinridge Warfield explicates the importance of the heart in John Calvin's theology. He writes, "It is quite clear, then, that Calvin did not consciously address himself merely to the securing of an intellectual assent to his teaching, but sought to move men's hearts. His whole conception of religion turned, indeed, on this: religion, he explained, to be pleasing to God, must be a matter of the heart, and God requires in His worshippers precisely heart and affection. All the arguments in the world, he insists, if unaccompanied by the work of the Holy Spirit on the heart, will fail to produce the faith which piety requires." "Calvin's Doctrine of God," *Princeton Theological Review* 7, no. 3 (1909): 386–87.

66. Today, Israeli wives still call their husbands בַּעְלִי ("my husband").

Observe the monergistic promises: "In that day [בַּיּוֹם הַהוּא] *I will make a covenant* for them with the beasts of the field. . . . Bow and sword and battle *I will abolish* from the land, so *that I will settle them down* in safety" (my trans.; NIV, "so that all may lie down in safety," 2:18).

Fourth, Yahweh renews his commitment to his people. He promises to renew his relationship with a series of three monergistic promises:

> *I will betroth you* [וְאֵרַשְׂתִּיךְ] to me forever; *I will betroth* [וְאֵרַשְׂתִּיךְ] *you* in righteousness and justice, in love and compassion [לִי בְּצֶדֶק וּבְמִשְׁפָּט וּבְחֶסֶד וּבְרַחֲמִים]. I will *betroth* [וְאֵרַשְׂתִּיךְ] you in faithfulness [בֶּאֱמוּנָה], and you will acknowledge [וְיָדַעַתְּ][67] the Lord. (2:19–20)

His commitment is without any preconditions, except that they entrust themselves to him as the "door of hope" and return to him as their only God (2:15–16). He renews his vows with the strength of his character: righteousness, justice, love, compassion, and faithfulness. God's bride will come to *know* (ידע; 2:20) him iteratively as she absorbs the grace and compassion of her lover.

Fifth, on the eschatological day (בַּיּוֹם הַהוּא), Yahweh will "respond" (ענה) to his people by renewing creation and by transforming his people (2:21–23). The fifth set of monergistic promises closes the chapter with a symbolic change of names and connects with the opening oracle of salvation (1:10–2:1). The key word in the first and fifth set of promises is "respond" (ענה). The people "respond" to Yahweh (2:15) by turning to him, and God's response involves the renewal of creation (heaven, earth, crops [grain, wine, oil]), and thus all the needs of "Jezreel" will be taken care of (2:21–22). The intimacy of the relationship is brought out in the fivefold repetition of the verb "respond" (ענה): "'In that day *I will respond* [ענה],' declares the Lord—'*I will respond* [ענה] to the skies, and they will *respond* [ענה] to the earth; and the earth will *respond* [ענה] to the grain, the new wine and the olive oil, and they will *respond* [ענה] to Jezreel'" (2:21–22). Yahweh, the Maker of heaven and earth, sovereignly and graciously remakes his creation to bless his people. He is like a farmer who sows (זרע)[68] "her"[69] for himself! The people who were under curse are assured of God's rich and undeserved blessings. The monergistic emphasis is continued when the prophet details the change in names from Lo-Ruhamah ("not loved") and Lo-Ammi ("not my people") to Ruhamah ("loved") and Ammi ("my people").[70]

Hosea's Detailed Charges against Israel: The Spirit of Prostitution (Hosea 4–8)

Hosea could see himself in the mirror of God's anguish for unfaithful Israel. He was not only a hurt husband, he was God's prophet. He was commanded to bring formal charges against Israel, to prosecute her, and to detail the appropriate punishments.

---

67. "Know" (ידע), rather than the NIV "acknowledge."
68. NIV "plant." Jezreel is connected to this lexeme in the Hebrew text.
69. The referent of "her" is unclear. It could refer to Jezreel or anticipate Lo-Ruhamah. See further Wolff, *Hosea*, 47, 54.
70. Observe the reversal in order in Hos. 2:1 [2:3 MT]), from Lo-Ruhamah and Lo-Ammi to Ammi and Ruhamah (cf. 1:6–8).

Covenant Breach

The oracles in Hosea 4–14 charge Israel and Judah with arrogance and guilt. This lengthy section opens with an indictment that specifies the nature of Israel's covenantal infidelity. Israel is charged with covenant breach, because "there is no faithfulness, no love, no acknowledgment [Heb. 'knowledge'] of God in the land" (4:1). In the absence of the covenant relationship, signified by the words "faithfulness," "love," and "knowledge of God" (cf. 2:19–21), the people flippantly take oaths, deceive one another, and encourage corruption and violence through their complicity. They are too much taken with themselves to see that corruption will inevitably lead to divine discipline (4:3). Political leaders (king, princes, rulers: 7:3, 5, 7; 8:4; 13:10) and religious leaders (priests: 4:4, 6, 7, 9; 6:9; 10:5; prophets: 4:5) individually and corporately participate in the corruption of society (5:1). Judah is also guilty as charged (11:12).

Instead of relying on Yahweh, Israel involved herself in power plays, turning to Assyria and to Egypt in the face of the growing power of Assyria (5:13; 7:11; 8:9; 11:5; 12:1). The backdrop of Hosea's ministry is a crosscurrent of international diplomacy. With the ascendancy of Assyria under King Tiglath-pileser III (r. 745–728 BC), Israel and Aram (Syria) made an alliance that directly invited the Assyrians to crush the Syro-Ephraimite coalition. In 732, Tiglath-pileser successfully destroyed Damascus, deposed the Israelite king, Pekah, and installed a puppet king, Hoshea, the last king of Israel. Samaria was destroyed, and Israel was exiled under Shalmaneser V (r. 727–722 BC) and Sargon II (r. 722–705 BC).

Syncretism

Israel's worship was syncretistic. Baalism was easily mixed with Yahwism. Though Baal was the name of the Phoenician god, Israel's religious expressions probably had many local variations (Hos. 2:8, 13, 17; 11:2; 13:1). It is difficult to distinguish between religious and cultural Baalism. This explains Israel's readiness to call on the Egyptians and Assyrians for help (5:13; 7:11; 8:9; 11:5; 12:1). In all areas, whether in religion, commerce, or politics, Israel did not recognize boundaries.

Covenantal Yahwism had deteriorated to folk religions in the North, while Judah in the South was more conservative. But both kingdoms had departed from the Mosaic foundation. People did not distinguish between Yahweh and cultural adaptations of indigenous forms of religion. Hosea castigates these forms of piety as false attempts at seeking the Lord, but they cannot find him because "he has withdrawn himself from them" (5:6). They are "unfaithful," and their descendants are "strangers" to the covenant (NIV, "illegitimate children"; lit. "strange or foreign children"), who do not know God and who do not know what it means to walk with God (5:7). God will not accept their sacrifices even when they go "to seek the LORD," and when they seek him, he will not be found, because "he has withdrawn himself from them" (5:6; cf. John 16:16–22).

The judgment of desolation and exile must first take place (Hos. 5:9–12), and their attempts at political and military aid must be frustrated (5:13–14). In the end, their pursuit turns out empty-headed, because Yahweh will not let his people get their way (5:6–12). He will wound them like a lion and wait for them to turn to him and seek his face (5:14–15).

False Piety

God waits patiently until Israel is in deep pain and "will earnestly seek" him (Hos. 5:15). The penitential prayer (6:1–3) that follows includes pious words expressive of an easy and confident turning to the Lord. Israel is all too ready to adjust her way to accommodate God. Confession of guilt and a sense of complicity come relatively easy (6:1–3) but are rejected by God as a farce (6:4). Further, Yahweh rejects the people's cover of piety as morning mist: "What can I do with you, Ephraim? What can I do with you, Judah? Your love is like the morning mist, like the early dew that disappears" (6:4). In the past, his prophets had pointed out and explained the reasons for the catastrophes that "happened" in Israel (6:5; cf. Isa. 1:5–6) to redirect her path to what is vital to the true worship of God: faithfulness (NIV, "mercy") and the knowledge of God (Hos. 6:6). Israel's evil nature and deep-seated spirit of prostitution witness against them (6:6–11). The people have broken the covenant and have a long history of treachery as children of "Adam" (6:7).[71] The charges include thievery, murder, deception, defilement, and "prostitution" (6:7–11; cf. 4:1–4) and involve people from Israel and Judah, the Cisjordan (Gilead), and the Transjordan (Shechem, Ephraim). God's people do not differ from the nations; they, too, love intrigue and are confident of the success of their political schemes.

The oracle against Ephraim and Judah closes on a flicker of hope: "Whenever I would restore the fortunes of my people, whenever I would heal Israel . . ." (6:11–7:1). But the light is quickly cut off by the darkness of the people. Wolff comments, "Whenever Yahweh has mercy on his people, their pious outward appearances are not followed by appropriate deeds; rather there is theft and robbery within and without."[72]

No Search for God

Hosea singles out Ephraim's dependence on Assyria, corruption, weakness, stubbornness, desolation, and exile (Hos. 7:1–16). Yet they do not return to Yahweh (7:10), knowing that he could "redeem" (פדה) them (7:13). They lament their weakness and frailty but do not cry out to him (7:14), having forgotten that Yahweh had supported them (7:15; cf. 11:1–2). They keep relying on Egypt and Assyria (7:11). They fail to "return" to Yahweh (7:10, 13, 16), whom they claim to "know" (8:2; NIV, "acknowledge"), but as in their earlier confession of repentance (6:1–3), their claims are self-serving and duplicitous. Israel has broken the covenant (8:1). She was corrupt (8:5), idolatrous (8:4–6), full of schemes (8:7–10), and very religious (8:11–13), but she has

---

71. The reading "Adam" could also speak of a region in the Transjordan, which may be reminiscent of Israel's idolatry before their entrance into the Promised Land—so Wolff, *Hosea*, 121. For the allusion to Adam, the father of humanity, see McComiskey, *Hosea*, 95.
72. Wolff, *Hosea*, 124.

forgotten her "Maker" (8:14). Yahweh will hand his people over to the nations and treat them as Lo-Ruhamah ("no comfort") and as Lo-Ammi ("not my people"). The palaces and fortified cities of both kingdoms will be destroyed (8:14). And they were. By 722 BC Samaria was taken, and the population of Ephraim went into captivity. By 701 most of Judah was subjugated. Jerusalem alone was spared (1:7; cf. Isaiah 36–37).

Israel's Punishments: God's Justice and Wrath (Hosea 9–10)
The Day of Punishment

The people have defiled themselves by their prostituting ways of life (Hos. 6:7–11). They will be exiled by the Assyrians to Assyria, where they will have to eat defiled food (9:1–6). Hosea clarifies the metaphorical allusion of a return to Egypt (7:16; 8:13; 9:6); it signifies an end to the exodus and conquest tradition. The people will be subjugated and sent off to Assyria. The joy at harvest season will come to an end, because the land is not theirs anymore. Their food will be defiled, and they will be unable to enter into God's holy presence. Their offerings, sacrifices, and festivals will become distant memories of a time that had given them joy and meaning and will be associated with defilement and death in a foreign land (9:1, 4–6). They will have entered a new period with horrid memories of their national history: captivity, the absence of God, and the reversal of blessings to curses.[73] It is the period of punishment and reckoning: the day of the Lord (5:9; 9:7). The prophet had spoken as to their dark future, but the people had treated him as a fool and a madman in their hatred of his accusations (9:7–8; cf. 2 Kings 9:11). Hosea had brought to light the darkness of their hearts but also their fears.

A Historical Perspective: God's Patience

Little do the people recognize that God has shown his forbearance, mercy, and patience with Israel. The history of Israel was full of tokens of God's grace. For hundreds of years, Yahweh had put up with his people. The prophetic ministry was a token of God's presence in Israel. The prophet was God's "watchman" (Hos. 9:8;[74] cf. Jer. 6:17; Ezek. 3:17; 33:2, 6, 7), who gave his people a transcendent and historical perspective on their world. He spoke in the name of the Lord and helped people diagnose the long history of their apostasy and evil. The prophetic institution, though also corrupted (Hos. 4:5), was a bright light in a dark era. Hosea, then, reflects on the ministry of Moses (12:13) and God's word through the prophets to Israel in the past (9:7–8; 12:10). Proof of Israel's history of waywardness is traced by the geographical references. The mention of these place names charges Israel with a history of rebelliousness (Baal Peor, Bethel [i.e., Beth-Aven], Gibeah, Gilead, Gilgal, Mizpah, Tabor).[75]

---

73. For a list of the many types of curses in the Pentateuch, see Stuart, *Hosea–Jonah*, xxxii–xlii.
74. The text of Hos. 9:8 is notoriously difficult and could be interpreted as a question—"Is Ephraim a watchman?" (so Stuart, *Hosea–Jonah*, 139)—or as a statement about the prophet, who calls himself "the watchman of Ephraim."
75. (1) Baal Peor: There was a long history of corruption associated with Baal Peor (Hos. 9:9–10). At Baal Peor, Israel worshiped the Baal and prostituted herself with a sexual orgy (Numbers 25). (2) Bethel: Bethel ("house of God") was a well-known site at the time of the patriarchs, where God met with Jacob (Hos. 12:4; cf. Gen. 35:15). But it had become a cultic center for the worship of the golden calf. It was known for its wickedness (Hos. 10:5), hence the derogatory name

Hosea also reflects on the beautiful memories of God's finding his people precious like grapes in the desert, like early figs, and like a "spreading vine" (9:10; 10:1). But they committed themselves to Baal, also known in the Hebrew Bible as "shame" (לַבֹּשֶׁת; 9:10). The people will be ashamed when God allows everything to be destroyed and they find themselves without any help on the day of punishment. It is too late, for king and God will not come to their aid (10:1–3).

In the absence of the fear of God (10:3), the people became glib with their oaths, increasingly more unjust in their social fabric (10:4; cf. 4:2), and idolatrous (calves at Beth-Aven [i.e., Bethel]). Their confidence in royalty will soon come to a disappointing end: "So in my anger I gave you a king, and in my wrath I took him away" (13:11; cf. 5:10; 7:7, 16; 9:15; 10:3, 7, 15; 13:10).

The Severity of Yahweh's Punishment

When they are carried off to Assyria, shame will seize them (Hos. 10:5–6). Kingship will cease, the idolatrous places at Bethel will be destroyed, and the people will long for a quick death (10:7–8; cf. Luke 23:30; Rev. 6:16). Hosea looks beyond Bethel to Gibeah. She, too, will experience retribution for her injustices (Hos. 10:9–10).[76] God requires righteousness (צְדָקָה) and faithfulness (חֶסֶד): "Sow righteousness for yourselves, reap the fruit of unfailing love, and break up your unplowed ground" (10:12). But there can be no understanding of true righteousness and justice unless people undergo an internal transformation and are right with God. Hence, he declares that now it is "time to seek the LORD" (10:12). The future is in God's hands and cannot be averted by a change in religious affinity. Faith is first, and good works flow concomitantly from faith. After all, God's people learn righteousness and love/faithfulness from their marriage partner, who is none other than the triune God[77] (2:19–20). But the people have refused to engage themselves with the plowing and the sowing (זֶרַע) of righteousness and faithfulness and instead have increased wickedness, injustice, and lies (10:13). Instead of turning to Yahweh, they have trusted in their own strength (10:13). Consequently, the judgment stands. Their fortifications and power structures will fail them (10:13–15). Mothers and children will receive no pity from the warriors. Whatever people sow, they will harvest (10:13; cf. Gal. 6:7–8).

Beth-Aven ("house of wickedness"). It would be ruthlessly destroyed (5:8; 10:8). (3) Gibeah: The mention of Gibeah could be a reminder of the days of the judges when a great evil took place in Gibeah (Judges 19–21). The place was also associated with Saul's kingship as the city of his birth (1 Sam. 10:26). Its history of evil was proverbial (Hos. 9:9; 10:9) and, hence, its destruction. (4) Gilead: Gilead was a region in the Transjordan known for its evil and bloodshed (6:8; 12:11). (5) Gilgal: At Gilgal Saul was coronated (1 Sam. 11:14–15) and was disobedient to Yahweh (15:21–23). It was a cultic site as well, where people celebrated their religious festivals (Hos. 4:15; 12:11 [12:12 MT]). Yahweh began the separation between himself and Ephraim because of the spirit of Gilgal: "Because of all their wickedness in Gilgal, I hated them there. Because of their sinful deeds, I will drive them out of my house. I will no longer love them; all their leaders are rebellious" (9:15; cf. 4:15; 10:9). (6) Mizpah: Mizpah was a city associated with Saul's coronation (1 Sam. 10:17–27; cf. Hos. 5:1). (7) Tabor: Tabor was a mountain peak in Galilee, associated with the period of the judges (Judges 4–5; cf. Hos. 5:1).

76. The Masoretic Text is difficult; see the commentaries for proposals.

77. I heartily agree with John Calvin's Trinitarian understanding. As Trinitarian theists, we hold to God being triune from Genesis 1 to Revelation 22.

Israel's Future: Yahweh's Holiness and Compassion (Hosea 11–14)

Will Yahweh show any compassion? So far, the argument has been straightforward (Hosea 4–10). Yahweh has charged Israel (and Judah) with covenant infidelity, apostasy, the syncretistic pursuit of folk religion, stubbornness and pride, corruption, and political and religious opportunism (4:1–3, 7–10; 5:1–4, 5–7, 13–15; 6:7–11a; 6:11b–7:16; 10:1–12). Yahweh is *justified* in his charges, because Israel has "prostituted" herself and has a long history of alienation, rebelliousness, and arrogance (chap. 10). Her doom is sure. She will go into captivity as a just punishment and application of the covenantal curses (4:4–6; 5:8–12; 7:14–16; 8:1–14; 9:1–17; 10:13–15). But the promised reversal held out by the renewal of the covenant/marriage has not been further developed in chapters 4–10. Has not God promised to renew the marriage monergistically, so that the people may come to truly know him as their God, who is righteous, just, committed in his love, compassionate, and faithful (2:19–20)? Has not the change in names signified a reversal from curse to blessing (2:19, 22–23)? Instead, Hosea accuses and charges the people with crimes against Yahweh and humanity. God will show no compassion on any segment of the population: poor or rich, religious leaders or political leaders or warriors, and women, mothers, and children. The last verses of this unit sum up the threat:

> But you have planted wickedness,
>> you have reaped evil,
>> you have eaten the fruit of deception.
> Because you have depended on your own strength
>> and on your many warriors,
> the roar of battle will rise against your people,
>> so that all your fortresses will be devastated—
> as Shalman devastated Beth Arbel on the day of battle,
>> when mothers were dashed to the ground with their children.
> So will it happen to you, Bethel,
>> because your wickedness is great.
> When that day dawns,
>> the king of Israel will be completely destroyed. (10:13–15)

Yahweh Is a Just and Holy Father

Hosea restates his case using the metaphor of Israel as a child. In the Father-Son relationship, we find the reality of God's nature. Hosea affirms that Yahweh is just *and* compassionate, even as Moses had argued (Deut. 4:30–31; cf. 30:3). The affirmations in Hosea 11 and 14 hold out the hope that justice and compassion come together in God as Father: "How can I make you like Zeboyim? My heart is changed within me; all my compassion is aroused" (11:8); "for in you the fatherless find compassion" (14:3).

Yahweh's love for his people finds many expressions in Hosea: the metaphor of Yahweh as a hurt husband and gracious lover (chaps. 1–3), Yahweh's love for Israel in

Egypt and in the desert (2:14–15; 9:10; 10:1; 12:9, 13; 13:4–6), the metaphor of Yahweh as Father (chap. 11), and the final invitation to return to Yahweh as the lover of his people (chap. 14). It appears that the opening (chaps. 1–3) and the closing chapters (chaps. 11–14) frame the hope of God's ultimate salvation. His love and compassion open a new era of undeserved hope in which God justifies a sinful people. Justification is the affirmation not just that God is righteous but also that the people are treated as righteous, just, loving, compassionate, and faithful. The transformation from their pretense of knowing God to their actual practice of the knowledge of God lies at the heart of the book of Hosea. Hosea has given hope to prodigal sons and daughters who have looked for a way home. They sought God and found him to be a faithful, generous, gracious, and righteous Father who is compassionate, awaiting his prodigal children to come home and to get to know him anew.

The Father of Prodigal Children: Holiness and Compassion
Yahweh's commitment to Israel takes shape in the portrayal of Israel's early history. A prophet, Moses, led God's people out of Egypt (Hos. 12:13), and prophets, like Hosea, had instructed Israel to walk in the way of the Lord (6:5; 9:8; 12:10). Yahweh had adopted Israel to be his "son" when he called the nation out of Egypt (11:1; cf. Matt. 2:15). He patiently guided and trained his people to walk with him, but the people rebelled against him. He showed his loving care, but they attributed it all to other forces (Hos. 11:3). He loved them as a father loves his young children (11:4). The discipline of the prodigal child required separation, and that came in the form of captivity and the desolation of their cities (11:5–6). Now the people have a form of religion but do not know the nature of true transcendence (11:7). But the father of the prodigal child does not despair or force the child to come home. He reveals his inner anguish as he is filled with compassion. His justice is compassionate (11:8). After all, he is the Holy One of Israel, whose anger is not all-consuming. The Holy One of Israel himself opens the door to reconciliation. He will not destroy what still could be saved (11:9), because he fulfills his goal to bring his people back to himself (11:9; cf. Isa. 12:6). Hosea likens God's redemption to the roaring of a lion. Normally people flee from the lion, but the divine lion roars to lead his children home (Hos. 11:10–11).

Judah. Hosea turns again to the two separate kingdoms of Judah and of Israel. In contrast to Judah, he portrays Israel as deceptive, violent, and chasing after the wind as she pursues alliances with Assyria and Egypt (Hos. 11:12–12:1). In contrast, Judah was less unfaithful and would receive compassion (1:7). Isaiah, Hosea's contemporary, confirms God's promise to preserve Judah, having given a sign to King Ahaz, a Judean king. It was the sign of the Immanuel ("God is with us," Isa. 7:14; 8:8, 10) and the deliverance of Judah from the Assyrians (Isaiah 36–37). The captivity of the northern tribes was 140 years before the exile of Judah. By the time of Jeremiah, the situation had changed, because he called the remnant of Israel more pious than Judah (Jer. 3:11).

Nevertheless, Hosea charges Judah with deeds that require divine retribution (Hos. 12:2). He puts before Judah three historical images associated with their forefather Jacob: Jacob's attempts at supplanting Esau (Gen. 25:26), Jacob's wrestling at Peniel (32:22–32), and God's appearance to Jacob at Bethel (35:15). In his experiences, Jacob's character was tested, as he intensely sought the favor and assurance of "the LORD God Almighty," whose name is Yahweh (Hos. 12:3–5). Hosea appealed to the people of Judah to return in faith to their God, who was the God of Jacob, and to commit themselves to "wait for [their] God always" by living out their faith in their lives (12:6).

Ephraim. Hosea likens Ephraim to a merchant who uses deception and intimidation to enrich himself, while protesting his innocence when caught (Hos. 12:7–8). Ephraim will have to live in tents rather than in their richly furnished mansions, but God, who speaks of himself saying, "I have been the LORD your God," is still committed to his people (12:9). He has been present in Israel's history by the ministry of the prophets (12:10) and of Moses (12:13). Nevertheless, Israel is guilty of evil, false worship, and deception. Ephraim, too, is reminded of her forefather Jacob, who fled to and suffered disgrace in Aram (12:12, 14). Hosea still encourages Ephraim by the historical examples of Jacob and Moses. God preserved deceptive Israel through Moses. Marvelous are God's ways, his path beyond finding out.

Ephraim is addicted to power. Her people are numerous, her territory is vast, and she has access to the nations through a network of international roads. She is awe-inspiring (13:1), but so is her leadership in idolatry (13:2). She is very impressive, but from God's vantage point, Ephraim is like dew, the morning mist, chaff, and smoke (13:3; cf. 6:4). She has forgotten her Maker (13:4–8; cf. 8:14). He had brought Israel out of Egypt, had provided for his people in the wilderness, and had given her the land (13:4–6). But their protector has become their adversary. He will tear his people like a lion, a leopard, a mother bear, or a wild beast (13:7–8). The people had put their confidence in their leadership—kings, princes, and judges—but in vain (13:9–10). It was Yahweh who gave them leaders, and he will remove them to demonstrate that he alone is the true help (13:9, 11). The region of Ephraim, a play on the lexeme פרא ("be fruitful," 13:15; cf. Gen. 41:52), was proverbial for its verdancy and fruitfulness, but it will dry up, because of her rebelliousness. Children and pregnant women will perish (Hos. 13:16; cf. 10:14). The people are foolish, but Yahweh promises to deliver them even from the power of death (13:14). In his appropriation of Hosea's confidence in God's power over death, Paul assures the Christian community of the victory of Jesus at his resurrection (1 Cor. 15:54–55).

Final invitation: "Come home." Hosea has explicated the nature of Israel's and Judah's infidelity as well as their political and religious power plays (Hosea 4–14). He has detailed the nature of God's alienation from his own people. They have to go through the experiences of warfare, desolation, death, and exile. God's son, Israel, is beloved, though prodigal, deserving God's wrath and punishment. Yet God has promised not to destroy his children in a wrathful fit. He will bring his people home (11:8–11). He is a compassionate father, "for in [him] the fatherless find compassion"; as God says, "I will heal their waywardness and love them freely, for my anger has turned away from them" (14:3–4). He is also a lover of his people (14:4), suggested by the images that are found in love songs, which, "replete with rich and colorful metaphors, . . . attest to the efficacy of God's love."[78] The climactic ending (14:1–9) opens broad vistas of hope. The prophecy of Hosea is well worth reflecting on, regardless of the many accusations and threats of an impending captivity, when read in the light of the promise of God's love and compassion for his people. His fatherly heart aches for his children (11:8):

> When you are in distress and all these things have happened to you, then in later days you will return to the LORD your God and obey him. For the LORD your God is a merciful God; he will not abandon or destroy you or forget the covenant with your ancestors, which he confirmed to them by oath. (Deut. 4:30–31; cf. 30:3)

Isaiah, too, invites the people to return to Yahweh:

> Seek the LORD while he may be found;
>   call on him while he is near.
> Let the wicked forsake their ways
>   and the unrighteous their thoughts.
> Let them turn to the LORD, and he will have *mercy* on them,
>   and to our God, for he will freely pardon. (Isa. 55:6–7)

Also, the poets of Israel call on those who fear the Lord to find refuge and trust in him alone (Ps. 33:16–22; cf. Psalms 49; 146). The witness of the Old Testament accords with the expression of the psalmist, "It is better to take refuge in the LORD than to trust in princes" (118:9).

Yahweh's compassion opens the doors to heaven. He promises to be the healer, lover, Husband, and Father that humanity is looking for. He forgives, loves, gives vitality, beautifies, protects, and provides. He renews the lives of his people within a restored created order (Hos. 14:4–7; cf. 2:21–23). He will not remain angry forever (11:9; cf. 8:5; Isa. 12:1). He is the Holy One of Israel who freely loves his prodigal children who return home. He takes his children in, renews the covenant, prepares a banquet, answers prayers, and cares for his children freely and graciously (Hos. 14:7–8; cf. 2:12–23; Isa. 55:1–3). Jesus himself repeatedly invites people to return home to their Father in heaven, as he does, for example, in the story of the "prodigal" son (Luke 15:11–32; cf. Matt. 22:1–14; Luke 14:15–24; Rev. 22:17). But he opens the door because he is the healer, lover, and Husband.

Conclusions

God is a lover who opens his heart to the beloved (Hos. 14:1–9). He calls on Israel to return. The prophet restates the reasons for returning to the Lord. Unlike earlier (6:1–3;

---

78. Wolff, *Hosea*, 235.

8:2), true repentance does not ask God to change his mind but begins with a search for the Lord. The transformation of the people of Israel begins with the certain knowledge that God is the Lord, their God, and that no one else can satisfy their inner desire. God's love is efficacious in changing the affections of his people. Yet they must return to him, asking him for forgiveness of their infidelities and praying that he might accept their worship and sacrifices (6:6; cf. 8:13; 9:4). Such sacrifices represent a knowledge of who God is and a life committed to what Yahweh values: faithfulness, love, righteousness, and commitment (6:6). He alone can save (ישׁע) them. The prophet guides his people as to how to return to their Father (14:3). Hosea's words fully accord with the elemental covenantal expectations when the offending party petitions God for compassion. While God had declared not to show Israel compassion (Lo-Ruhamah), he shows compassion to all who seek him and call on him. He is the Father of the fatherless and needy (14:3; cf. Pss. 10:14–18; 68:5; 82:3).

The exilic experience in Assyria (Hos. 8:13; 9:3; 10:5–6; 11:5)[79] brings sense to a small remnant, when they become more aware of being defiled (9:3) and realize the futility of their idolatrous way of life. In the end, they must confess that Yahweh alone can save and heal (14:2–3). A remnant does return to Judea, a Persian province. The postexilic prophetic books Haggai, Zechariah, and Malachi provide significant insights into the transformation of the people, as do the books of Ezra and Nehemiah. Idolatry has come to an end, but a new kind of idolatry is not far off. It is called legalism, with its variant of human autonomy. This spirit is represented by the last of the Twelve, Malachi.

Read together, Hosea, the first of the Twelve, and Malachi, the last of the Twelve, insightfully address the failure of Israel to walk in the way of Yahweh. Three hundred years before Malachi, Hosea had charged Israel with the spirit of prostitution. Malachi charges Israel with observing the law of Moses but without apprehending the nature of the true worship of Yahweh. Malachi closes the door of the kingdom to priests and people alike (Malachi 1–3). Unless Israel serves the Lord as a son (1:6; 3:18), God will reach out to the nations and reveal his kingdom to them (1:11, 14).[80]

Less than five centuries after Malachi, the apostle Paul appropriates the message of the Twelve. He vindicates the Gentile believers as people who have received God's righteousness by faith (Rom. 9:30) and condemns his fellow Jews as pursuing a righteousness by the works of the law (9:31). Paul appropriates the change in the names of Hosea's children in explaining that Gentiles who were Lo-Ammi and Lo-Ruhamah have become "my people," "my loved one," and "children of the living God" (9:15–26; cf. Hos. 1:10; 2:23; 1 Pet. 2:10). Yet he anticipates that a transformation of Israel will bring about a fullness of God's people from the Gentiles as well as from Israel (Rom. 11:25–32). However, the apostle also strongly warns against the incipient forms of idolatry (prostitution) that Gentiles may bring into the new community: sexual immorality, impurity,

---

79. For rhetorical reasons, Hosea includes Egypt as a place of exile. It turns out that after the destruction of the temple in 587 BC, a group of Judeans (and Israelites) do leave for Egypt. Hosea, though, does not directly address the exile of Judah. The exile of Israel was restricted to Assyria.

80. See Hugenberger, *Marriage as a Covenant*.

greed, lust, and evil desires (Eph. 5:5; Col. 3:5). He argues that all who are in Christ, Gentiles and Jews, are renewed in him (3:10–12), being created in his image, and must be clothed with Christlike virtues: "Therefore, as God's chosen people, holy and dearly loved, clothe yourselves with compassion, kindness, humility, gentleness and patience" (3:12; cf. Eph. 5:3–17). Elsewhere, Paul clarifies that the new nature is also the work of the Holy Spirit: "But the fruit of the Spirit is love, joy, peace, forbearance, kindness, goodness, faithfulness, gentleness and self-control. Against such things there is no law" (Gal. 5:22–23).

We are justified by faith in the Lord Jesus Christ, but rampant desires, self-gratification, lies, hypocrisy, duplicity, and corrupt thoughts, practices, and words invert the truth of the gospel. Spiritual prostitution, autonomy, and acculturation are forms of idolatry that keep the light of Christ from shining in a dark world. Justification that connects the power of the Word of God with living faith in the Lord Jesus Christ cannot coexist with corruption, deception, and infidelity!

Recommended Resources

Abernethy, Andrew T. *The Book of Isaiah and God's Kingdom: A Thematic-Theological Approach*. New Studies in Biblical Theology 40. Downers Grove, IL: InterVarsity Press, 2016.

Eidevall, Göran. *Grapes in the Desert: Metaphors, Models, and Themes in Hosea 4–14*. ConBOT 43. Stockholm: Almqvist & Wiksell, 1996.

Hugenberger, Gordon P. *Marriage as a Covenant: Biblical Law and Ethics as Developed from Malachi*. Biblical Studies Library. Grand Rapids, MI: Baker, 1994.

Kakkanattu, Joy Philip. *God's Enduring Love in the Book of Hosea: A Synchronic and Diachronic Analysis of Hosea 11, 1–11*. Forschungen zum Alten Testament 2, no. 14. Tübingen: Mohr Siebeck, 2006.

McComiskey, Thomas Edward. *Hosea*. In *The Minor Prophets: An Exegetical and Expository Commentary*, edited by Thomas Edward McComiskey, 1–237. Grand Rapids, MI: Baker Academic, 2009.

Moyise, Steve, and Maarten J. J. Menken, eds. *Isaiah in the New Testament*. London: T&T Clark, 2005.

Ortlund, Raymond C., Jr. *God's Unfaithful Wife: A Biblical Theology of Spiritual Adultery*. New Studies in Biblical Theology 2. Downers Grove, IL: InterVarsity Press, 2002.

Sohn, Seock-Tae. *YHWH, the Husband of Israel: The Metaphor of Marriage between YHWH and Israel*. Eugene, OR: Wipf and Stock, 2002.

Uhlig, Torsten. *The Theme of Hardening in the Book of Isaiah: An Analysis of Communicative Action*. Forschungen zum Alten Testament 39. Tübingen: Mohr Siebeck, 2009.

VanGemeren, Willem A. *Interpreting the Prophetic Word*. Grand Rapids, MI: Zondervan, 1990.

———. "Our Missional God: Redemptive-Historical Preaching and the *Missio Dei*." In *Living Waters from Ancient Springs: Essays in Honor of Cornelis Van Dam*, edited by Jason Van Vliet, 198–217. Eugene, OR: Pickwick, 2011.

VanGemeren, Willem A., and Andrew Abernethy. "The Spirit of God and the Future: A Canonical Approach." In *Presence, Power, and Promise: The Role of the Spirit of God in the Old Testament*, edited by David G. Firth and Paul D. Wegner, 321–45. Downers Grove, IL: IVP Academic, 2011.

Wolterstorff, Nicholas. *Justice in Love*. Grand Rapids, MI: Eerdmans, 2011.

4

Setting the Record Straight

Second Temple Judaism and Works Righteousness

ROBERT J. CARA

In 1977, E. P. Sanders forcefully argued to New Testament scholars that Second Temple Judaism was *not* works-righteousness oriented.[1] Instead, Second Temple Judaism was *uniformly* grace based, and Sanders coined the term "covenantal nomism" to describe this.[2]

Although there were precursors to Sanders's view, his new perspective on the soteriology of Judaism laid the foundation for a reevaluation of Paul, especially as it relates to the doctrine of justification. Famously, the result of this reevaluation of Paul was termed the "New Perspective on Paul" (hereafter, NPP), which is especially associated with the names of James D. G. Dunn and N. T. Wright.[3] To reemphasize for purposes

---

1. Significant portions of this article are taken from Robert J. Cara, *Cracking the Foundation of the New Perspective on Paul: Covenantal Nomism versus Reformed Covenantal Theology*, REDS (Fearn, Ross-shire, Scotland: Mentor, 2017). Used by permission of Christian Focus.
2. E. P. Sanders, *Paul and Palestinian Judaism: A Comparison of Patterns of Religion* (Philadelphia: Fortress, 1977). According to Sanders, all Judaisms during the Second Temple period had a "pattern of religion" that included "getting in" the covenant by election and "staying in" by obedience to works of the law that the covenant required. The covenant also included means for the atonement of transgressions once one was in the covenant. To be clear, Sanders emphasizes that the "staying in" with its works was not merit based since the starting point, election, was clearly grace based. Sanders terms this pattern of religion "covenantal nomism." For Sanders's explanation of a "pattern of religion," see 12–18; for his fullest summary of "covenantal nomism," see 422–23.
3. So named by James D. G. Dunn in his famous article "The New Perspective on Paul," *BJRL* 65, no. 2 (1983): 95–122. For important works, see the following by N. T. Wright: "The Paul of History and the Apostle of Faith," *TynBul* 29 (1978): 61–88; *The Climax of the Covenant: Christ and the Law in Pauline Theology* (Minneapolis: Fortress, 1991); *What Saint Paul Really Said: Was Paul of Tarsus the Real Founder of Christianity?* (Grand Rapids, MI: Eerdmans, 1997); *Justification: God's Plan and Paul's Vision* (Downers Grove, IL: IVP Academic, 2009); *Paul and the Faithfulness of God*, COQG 4 (Minneapolis: Fortress, 2013); and see the following by James D. G. Dunn: *The Theology of Paul the Apostle* (Grand Rapids, MI: Eerdmans, 1998); *The New Perspective on Paul*, rev. ed. (Grand Rapids, MI: Eerdmans, 2008). Others also agree with Sanders but complain that the NPP did not go far enough with Paul. They conclude that there is little difference between Paul and Second Temple Judaism and that, in fact, Paul did not break with Judaism. This is termed the

of this essay, Sanders's new perspective on Judaism is the logical foundation of the New Perspective on Paul. This is readily acknowledged by NPP authors.[4]

Again, according to Sanders, Second Temple Judaism was not works-righteousness oriented, but instead, its soteriology was grace based. How does this relate to Paul and justification? NPP authors note that justification is discussed in contexts that include first-century non-Christian or Christian Jews (e.g., Romans 2; 9–11; Galatians 3–5; Philippians 3).[5] The traditional Reformational view sees Paul contrasting two soteriological schemes: the grace-based justification by faith against the works righteousness of justification by works. Therefore, the traditional view must be wrong according to those who follow Sanders. Why? Paul could not have been arguing against works righteousness because it did not exist during the first century AD! Further, if one has justification by works wrong, then its assumed opposite, justification by faith, must also be wrong.[6] N. T. Wright comments, "Judaism in Paul's day was not, as has regularly been supposed, a religion of legalistic works righteousness. If we imagine it was, and that Paul was attacking it as if it was, we will do great violence to it and him."[7]

As can be seen from above, the logical foundation of the NPP is the belief that the soteriology of Second Temple Judaism was not works-righteousness oriented but instead was uniformly characterized as grace-based covenantal nomism. For purposes of this chapter, I am *not* dealing directly with NPP or with many aspects of covenantal nomism,

---

"radical new perspective" or "Paul within Judaism." See Magnus Zetterholm, *Approaches to Paul: A Student's Guide to Recent Scholarship* (Minneapolis: Fortress, 2009), 231–40; Mark D. Nanos and Magnus Zetterholm, eds., *Paul within Judaism: Restoring the First-Century Context to the Apostle* (Minneapolis: Fortress, 2015). Finally, the "apocalyptic Paul" school is not as interested in Sanders. See, e.g., J. Louis Martyn, *Galatians: A New Translation with Introduction and Commentary*, AB 33A (New York: Doubleday, 1997), 146–47, 266–67; and N. T. Wright's complaint about this school, including Martyn, as to its neglect of Sanders in *Paul and His Recent Interpreters: Some Contemporary Debates* (Minneapolis: Fortress, 2015), 155–86, esp. 172.

4. James D. G. Dunn lists "four aspects" of the NPP. The first argues, "The new perspective on Paul arises from a new perspective on Judaism." "New Perspective View," in *Justification: Five Views*, ed. James K. Beilby and Paul Rhodes Eddy (Downers Grove, IL: IVP Academic, 2011), 176–201, esp. 193–95. Dunn also states, "For both of us [Dunn and Wright] Sanders is to be given credit for challenging and undermining the then dominant view that the Christian Paul regarded his native Judaism as entirely legalistic." "An Insider's Perspective on Wright's Version of the New Perspective on Paul," in *God and the Faithfulness of Paul: A Critical Examination of the Pauline Theology of N. T. Wright*, ed. Christoph Heilig, J. Thomas Hewitt, and Michael F. Bird (Minneapolis: Fortress, 2017), 347–58, esp. 348. Kent L. Yinger gives three "main lines" of the NPP. The first states, "First-century Judaisms were not legalistic, but were characterized by covenantal nomism—saved by God's grace and obligated to follow his ways." *The New Perspective on Paul: An Introduction* (Eugene, OR: Cascade Books, 2011), 30. See also Wright, *Paul and His Recent Interpreters*, 64–76, 88–89.

5. Fair enough. However, I would add that Paul also argues that some in Old Testament Israel misunderstood justification (Romans 9–11) and that some understood it (Romans 4); hence, Paul is not limited to first-century AD Jewish views. Anti-NPP authors with a high view of Scripture complain that many NPP authors tend to allow their Second Temple Judaism views to *control* their exegesis of Scripture, for example, Guy Prentiss Waters, *Justification and the New Perspectives on Paul: A Review and Response* (Phillipsburg, NJ: P&R, 2004), 154–55; S. M. Baugh, "The New Perspective, Mediation, Justification," in *Covenant, Justification, and Pastoral Ministry: Essays by the Faculty of Westminster Seminary California*, ed. R. Scott Clark (Phillipsburg, NJ: P&R, 2007), 137–63, esp. 145–47.

6. Some NPP authors, in their later works, have said that there is some level of compatibility between the traditional and NPP views of justification. For example, see Dunn, "The New Perspective on Paul: Whence, What, Whither?," in *The New Perspective on Paul*, 20–21; N. T. Wright, *Paul: In Fresh Perspective* (Minneapolis: Fortress, 2005), 116–17. For me, Dunn and Wright's compatibility statements are either too vague or simply do not give enough ground to get to an acceptable Reformational view. See my discussion in Cara, *Cracking the Foundation*, 177–82, 188–93.

7. Wright, *What Saint Paul Really Said*, 18–19. Similarly, Wright states, "[Paul's] polemic against 'works of the law' is not directed against those who attempted to *earn* covenant membership through keeping the Jewish law (*such people do not seem to have existed in the 1st century*)." "Justification," in *New Dictionary of Theology*, ed. Sinclair B. Ferguson and David F. Wright (Downers Grove, IL: InterVarsity Press, 1988), 359–61; first italics his, second mine. Pro-Sanders author George W. E. Nickelsburg notes, "If the church developed in the matrix of Judaism and the mother was very different from what we have imagined and described, then we must reconsider the nature of the child." *Ancient Judaism and Christian Origins: Diversity, Continuity, and Transformation* (Minneapolis: Fortress, 2003), 3.

since Timo Laato's chapter in this book addresses these topics head-on.[8] Instead, I present evidence that works righteousness did exist in Second Temple Judaism documents, which functionally eliminates a uniform covenantal nomism. Also for purposes of this essay, I am not considering evidence from the New Testament.[9]

To be clear: My view is *not* that every document or Jewish group was works-righteousness oriented. I am simply trying to show that some were. Once given this, then there is no need to deny that some of Paul's opponents held these views since this seems to be the straightforward way to take many of Paul's statements. Hence, my thesis is that *there are many examples of works righteousness (Pelagian and semi-Pelagian versions) in Second Temple Judaism literature, and therefore, Sanders's uniform covenantal nomism is mistaken*. In this essay, I present several representative examples. Also, since so much of scholarship seems to assume Sanders's conclusions, it is helpful to see Sanders's explanations for the documents that appear to include works righteousness, as he readily admits. Hence, I have added Sanders's various explanations for many of the examples below. I have the sense that much of New Testament scholarship is aware of his conclusions but not as aware of his various explanations for the conflicting data.

As a final point of introduction, from my perspective, the ultimate argument that vindicates the Reformational view of justification is made from the biblical texts themselves. Implications from noncanonical sources may be useful, but they are only fallible aids.[10] However, I do believe that my primary thesis considered from the standpoint of the NPP's authors' own presuppositions logically destroys their conclusions.[11]

Definition of Works Righteousness

When I use the term *works righteousness*, I am implying *legalistic* works righteousness. Others use synonyms, such as *self-righteousness* or *meritorious works righteousness*. Unfortunately, sometimes in the literature the term *works righteousness* is used somewhat loosely, so a clear definition is useful.[12]

I am using *legalistic* in the sense that it relates to laws and a law court. In general, legalistic works refer to works that are done to fulfill a law and that are declared righteous by a judge. More specifically in this context, a *works-righteousness theology means that one's works are, in part or the whole, the ground by which God the Judge declares one righteous (justification) and qualified to enter the afterlife.*

---

8. For my explanation and broad-brush critiques of covenantal nomism, see Cara, *Cracking the Foundation*, 59–75.
9. Various pro–covenantal nomism authors consider Matthew 23; Luke 18:9–14; and the deutero-Pauline texts Eph. 2:8–10; 2 Tim. 1:8–10; and Titus 3:4–7 as surface-level problems for their views, but these texts are written by "outsiders" and should not be considered actual Second Temple Judaism views. See my rebuttals in Cara, *Cracking the Foundation*, 72–74, 127–95.
10. As opposed to Scripture interpreting Scripture, which is an "infallible" aid (Westminster Confession of Faith 1.9).
11. Note N. T. Wright's view that it is wrong to see any works righteousness in Second Temple Judaism. He states, "Recent attempts to suggest a more variegated attitude to the Law than was allowed for by E. P. Sanders in *Paul and Palestinian Judaism* are undoubtedly right to stress variety, and undoubtedly wrong to try to use that as a way of smuggling back an anachronistic vision of a Pelagian (or semi-Pelagian) or medieval works-righteousness." *Paul: In Fresh Perspective*, 108–9.
12. Moisés Silva complains that "Sanders operates with an understanding of 'legalism' that is at times fuzzy and ambiguous, at other times quite misleading. More to the point, Sanders (along with biblical scholars more generally) has an inadequate understanding of historical Christian theology, and his view of the Reformational concern with legalism does not get to the heart of the question." "The Law and Christianity: Dunn's New Synthesis," *WTJ* 53, no. 2 (1991): 348.

Note that included in my definition of works righteousness is "in part or the whole." That is, whether one's theology combines aspects of grace and works righteousness together ("in part") or is a crass complete-human-merit theology ("the whole") for justification, both of these are works-righteousness theologies from a traditional Protestant perspective.[13]

To use anachronistic terms, if justification is based on a combination of grace from God and human works, then it is considered semi-Pelagianism. If based on works only, it is considered Pelagianism. Both are legalistic works righteousness.[14]

Examples of Works Righteousness in Second Temple Judaism Literature

4 Ezra[15]

Fourth Ezra includes chapters 3–14 of a longer work known as 2 Esdras.[16] The extant text is in Latin and several other languages, but scholars assume that the original Jewish document, 4 Ezra 3–14, was written in Hebrew or Aramaic near AD 100. Fourth Ezra is unusual as an apocryphal book in that it is an apocalypse.

Fourth Ezra includes seven visions given to Ezra while he is in Babylon during the exile. Ezra asks questions of God, and God sends an angel to answer Ezra. Most of Ezra's questions relate to sin, suffering, and God's justice in the purported context of Israel's destruction in 587 BC but are actually related to the temple's destruction in AD 70. The third vision, 4 Ezra 6:35–9:25, concerns the final judgment. My discussion and the selected quotations concentrate on the third vision and works righteousness:

> For God strictly commanded those who came into the world, when they came, what they should do to live, and what they should observe to avoid punishment. (7:21)

> For you have a treasury of works laid up with the Most High. (7:77)

> Now this is the order of those who have kept the ways of the Most High. . . . They laboriously served the Most High, and withstood danger every hour that they might keep the Law of the Lawgiver perfectly. (7:88–89)

> The day of judgment is decisive and displays to all the seal of truth. . . . For then everyone shall bear his own righteousness or unrighteousness. (7:104–5)

---

13. Of course, I would argue that the traditional Protestant perspective is Paul's perspective!

14. Pelagius was a British theologian in the late fourth to early fifth centuries. He clashed with Augustine over original sin and the place of works in salvation. Semi-Pelagianism is popularly used to designate theologies that combine grace and works. The Lutheran Formula of Concord condemns by name both of these ("Epitome," art. 2, neg. theses 2–3). See B. B. Warfield's brief summary of semi-Pelagianism, which he describes as an "elastic system of compromise" between Augustinianism/Calvinism and Pelagianism. "Calvinism," in *Selected Shorter Writings: Benjamin B. Warfield*, ed. John E. Meeter (Nutley, NJ: P&R, 1970–1973), 2:411–47, esp. 411–12; see also Warfield, *The Plan of Salvation* (1915; repr., Boonton, NJ: Simpson, 1989), 29–33.

15. English translations of 4 Ezra and Sirach are from *The Apocrypha of the Old Testament: Revised Standard Version: Expanded Edition Containing the Third and Fourth Books of the Maccabees and Psalm 151*, ed. Bruce M. Metzger (New York: Oxford University Press, 1977).

16. Second Esdras is sixteen chapters long, of which scholars see chaps. 1–2 and 15–16 as Christian interpolations into an original Jewish document consisting of chaps. 3–14.

For the righteous, who have many works, laid up with you, shall receive their reward in consequence of their own deeds. (8:77)

As can be seen from the above text, 4 Ezra has a clear works-righteousness view of salvation for individuals.[17] There is one text in 4 Ezra that is confusing and at first glance appears to offer both a salvation by works option and a salvation by faith option:

And it shall be that everyone who will be saved and will be able to escape on account of his works, or on account of the faith by which he has believed . . . (9:7, cf. 8:36)

As Michael Stone notes, this is not teaching two methods of salvation: "While not asserting that these two concepts, faith and works, are identical, we may say that they were not very clearly differentiated and are used interchangeably."[18]

Fourth Ezra is one of the few documents that Sanders agrees is a works-righteousness document.[19] However, he argues that the works righteousness of 4 Ezra is not representative because it is a polemical document produced by the pressures of the Roman oppression near AD 70.[20] I respond that if difficult times produced a works-righteousness document, could not one argue that other types of difficulties would also produce works-righteousness attitudes?

Sirach (Ecclesiasticus, Wisdom of Jesus the Son of Sirach)

As to genre, Sirach is similar to Proverbs. It includes a prologue by the author's grandson, who explains that while living in Egypt he translated his grandfather's original Hebrew into Greek.[21] The grandfather's name is Jesus the son of Sirach (Sir. 50:27). This is the only apocryphal book in which the author identifies himself. Following are quotations from Sirach that relate to the works-righteousness question:

For kindness to a father will not be forgotten, and against your sins it will be credited[22] to you. (3:14)

Water extinguishes a blazing fire: so almsgiving atones for sin. (3:30)[23]

---

17. Bruce W. Longenecker concludes a discussion of covenant according to the view of 4 Ezra's author as follows: "Confidence in God's justice and faithfulness is the mainstay of the author's covenantal perspective, but it is a perspective that seems to be characterized by two other factors: (1) a somewhat skeptical attitude towards the people's ability to keep the law with the kind of rigorous and exacting standards that are required, and (2) the virtual absence of a robust theology of grace." *2 Esdras* (Sheffield: Sheffield Academic Press, 1995), 100. In an earlier work, Longenecker states, "The author of 4 Ezra has advanced a new understanding of the character of Jewish existence without the temple: salvation is not a national privilege but an individual responsibility worked out with great effort by works of merit. Divine grace is, for all purposes, absent in his scheme, except as an eschatological reflex to those who have saved themselves anyway by their works." *Eschatology and the Covenant: A Comparison of 4 Ezra and Romans 1–11*, JSNTSup 57 (Sheffield: Sheffield Academic Press, 1991), 152.
18. Michael Edward Stone, *A Commentary on the Book of Fourth Ezra*, Hermeneia (Minneapolis: Fortress, 1990), 296. Similarly, see Simon J. Gathercole, *Where Is Boasting: Early Jewish Soteriology and Paul's Response in Romans 1–5* (Grand Rapids, MI: Eerdmans, 2002), 138–39.
19. Sanders, *Paul and Palestinian Judaism*, 409.
20. Sanders, *Paul and Palestinian Judaism*, 427.
21. Apparently, the Hebrew was written in approximately 180 BC in Palestine, the Greek translation with prologue, approximately 125 BC in Egypt.
22. The Greek is προσανοικοδομέω; "credited" could be more mechanically translated "built up."
23. Tobit 12:9 has a very similar statement: "For almsgiving delivers from death, and it will purge away every sin." Gathercole sees both Sirach and Tobit as having works-righteousness views that are for "this" world. *Where Is Boasting?*, 37–40.

> For it is easy in the sight of the Lord to regard a man on the day of death according to his conduct. (11:26)
>
> He will make room for every act of mercy; everyone will receive in accordance with his deeds. (16:14)
>
> Store up almsgiving in your treasury, and it will rescue you from all affliction. (29:12)
>
> Who has been tested by [love of gold] and been found perfect? Let it be for him a ground of boasting.... His prosperity will be established and the assembly will relate his acts of charity. (31:10–11)
>
> So if a man fasts for his sins, and goes again and does the same things, who will listen to his prayer? (34:26)
>
> Do your work before the appointed time, and in God's time he will give you your reward. (51:30, the final verse in the book)

Sanders argues that the author "believes that a man is rewarded in this life strictly according to his merits."[24] However, since the author does not believe in an afterlife, the question of works for final salvation is moot.[25] I am not convinced that Sirach does not believe in an afterlife (11:26); however, even if he did not, one reading Sirach who did believe in an afterlife would certainly understand it as advocating either a Pelagian or semi-Pelagian view of works righteousness. It is not a far step from works righteousness for this life to works righteousness as a basis for the afterlife.

2 Baruch[26]

Second Baruch consists of eighty-seven short chapters.[27] On the surface, 2 Baruch is written by Baruch, Jeremiah's scribe (Jer. 36:32), shortly after the destruction of Jerusalem in 587 BC. However, the real author is writing in approximately AD 100, after the AD 70 destruction of the Jerusalem temple.[28] The following are quotations from 2 Baruch that relate to the works-righteousness question:

> For the righteous justly have good hope for the end and go away from this habitation without fear because they possess with you a store of good works which is preserved in treasuries. (14:12)
>
> For behold, the days are coming, and the books will be opened in which are written the sins of all those who have sinned, and moreover, also the treasuries in which are

---

24. Sanders, *Paul and Palestinian Judaism*, 341.
25. Sanders, *Paul and Palestinian Judaism*, 420.
26. All English translations from the Old Testament Pseudepigrapha are from *The Old Testament Pseudepigrapha*, ed. James H. Charlesworth, 2 vols. (Garden City, NY: Doubleday, 1983–1985).
27. The extant primary text is in Syriac, and there are some extant partial Greek texts. It is assumed that the original was in Hebrew or Aramaic.
28. The epistle of Barnabas appears once to quote 2 Baruch (Barn. 11:9 // 2 Bar. 61:7).

brought together the righteousness of all those who have proven themselves to be righteous. (24:1)

For behold, I see many of your people who separated themselves from your statutes and who have cast away from them the yoke of your Law. . . . Their time will surely not be weighed exactly, and they will certainly not be judged as the scale indicates? (41:3, 6)

Behold, your Law is with us, and we know that we do not fall as long as we keep your statutes. (48:22)

Miracles, however, will appear at their own time to those who are saved because of their works and for whom the Law is now a hope. (51:7)

[Concerning the approaching Assyrian army and Hezekiah's request to God,] Hezekiah trusted upon his works, and hoped upon his righteousnesses. (63:3)

[Jewish forefathers] intervened for us with him [God] who has created us since they trusted in their works. And the Mighty One heard them and purged us from our sins. (85:2)

Second Baruch intends to give comfort to the reader. Even though Israel was punished (e.g., the Babylonian exile, the Roman destruction of Jerusalem) and not all Israelites will reach heaven, those who live by the law will. This is works righteousness. A. F. J. Klijn bluntly gives the author's view: "He who chooses to live according to the Law will receive eternal life."[29] Among other things, note the several references above to a treasury of works (14:12; 24:1) and scales (41:6). Gathercole comments, "The stores [treasury] of good works are the deeds done by these righteous in obedience to Torah, and these same works are an instrumental cause of their final salvation."[30]

Testament of Abraham

The Testament of Abraham is a fascinating story. Righteous Abraham is told by the angel Michael that God wants Abraham to give a testament and then to give up his soul (die) by following Michael to heaven. Abraham refuses (T. Ab. A 1–7) and offers a compromise. Abraham wishes to see all the inhabited world before he dies. God grants this request (A 8–9). Michael takes Abraham up into the clouds so he can see the whole world. Abraham now sees all the evil in the world and condemns it without mercy (A 10). God stops the tour and has Michael take Abraham to the entrance of heaven to see how God determines who gets in, which includes a balance of good and evil works (A 11–14). After this, Abraham still refuses to give up his soul (A 15). God now sends Death to get Abraham's soul. Through some trickery, Abraham finally dies, and his soul goes to heaven (A 16–20).

---

29. A. F. J. Klijn, "2 (Syriac Apocalypse of) Baruch: A New Translation and Introduction," in Charlesworth, *Old Testament Pseudepigrapha*, 1:619. He lists several proof texts: 2 Bar. 32:1; 38:1; 48:22; 51:3, 4–7; 54:15.
30. Gathercole, *Where Is Boasting?*, 140.

The Testament of Abraham is extant in multiple Greek manuscripts, and the current scholarly consensus is that the original language was Greek. Given that factor and the lack of specific Jewish ceremonial works in the book, the original provenance is assumed to be Egypt with a date range from AD 50 to 110. The work exists in two Greek recensions, the longer one labeled *A*, and the shorter, *B*. Most consider *A* as closer to the theoretical original.[31]

For our purposes, it is interesting to note that Abraham is considered perfectly righteous, but his method of judgment is improper—it has no mercy. More important, Testament of Abraham A 11–14 describes the judgment process that includes three gates being overseen by Adam. The first that leads to heaven is for those who are clearly righteous. The third that leads to destruction is for those who are clearly evil. The middle gate includes a balance held by an angel where one's good and evil deeds are weighed to see whether one goes to heaven or destruction. This middle gate is the one that Abraham was not considering. The following are quotes from Testament of Abraham A:

> [Michael says to God,] Master, Lord, let your might know that I cannot announce the mention of death to the righteous man [Abraham] because I have not seen upon earth a man like him—merciful, hospitable, righteous, truthful, God-fearing, refraining from every evil deed. (A 4:6)

> [God said to Michael,] For behold, Abraham has not sinned and he has no mercy on sinners. (A 10:14)[32]

> The two angels on the right and on the left recorded. The one on the right recorded righteous deeds, while the one on the left recorded sins. The one who was in front of the table, who was holding the balance, weighed the souls. (A 12:12–13)

> The Commander-in-chief said, "Hear, righteous Abraham: Since the judge found its sins and its righteous deeds to be equal, then he handed it over neither to judgment nor to be saved, until the judge of all should come. . . . If [one] could acquire one righteous deed more than one's sins, one would enter in to be saved." (A 14:2–4)

As Abraham is watching the balancing, the situation occurs where a person's sins and righteous deeds perfectly balance. Abraham says a prayer for the person, and this tips the scale in favor of that person going to heaven (A 14:1–8).

Clearly, the Testament of Abraham has a works-righteousness view. God allows the perfect to go to heaven, and in "mercy," God also allows those with more good deeds than sins to go to heaven. Both of these scenarios are presented in a Pelagian manner. Yes, the book teaches that one does not have to be perfect to go to heaven, but it still

---

31. See George W. E. Nickelsburg, *Jewish Literature between the Bible and the Mishnah: A Historical and Literary Introduction*, rev. ed. (Philadelphia: Fortress, 1987), 248–53; James R. Mueller, "Abraham, Testament of," in *Anchor Bible Dictionary*, ed. David Noel Freedman (New York: Doubleday, 1992), 1:43–44.

32. Confusingly, when talking to Michael, Abraham calls himself a "sinner" (T. Ab. A 9:3). Later, after seeing the method of balance, Abraham states that he has "sinned" (A 14:12).

teaches that one gets to heaven by performing works. As Chris VanLandingham notes, "The only criterion for this judgment relies on deeds—Gentiles are not damned because they are Gentiles, and neither are Jews saved because they are Jews."[33]

How does Sanders respond to this? He says nothing in *Paul and Palestinian Judaism*; however, he did write the article on the Testament of Abraham in the *Old Testament Pseudepigrapha*.[34] He states, "The judgment on the basis of deeds is standard, both in Jewish and Christian literature.... The efficacy of repentance and God's merciful inclination to delay the death of sinners until they repent are noteworthy."[35] Upon reading the article, I am not sure if Sanders sees the Testament of Abraham as teaching works righteousness or not. Gathercole assumes that he does and further assumes that since the provenance is Hellenistic, Sanders does not see it as pertinent.[36] Possibly Sanders does not admit to works righteousness here since repentance is a key theme for him.

In any event, the Testament of Abraham is a Second Temple Judaism document that clearly has a works-righteousness soteriology.

Psalms of Solomon

The Psalms of Solomon are a group of eighteen psalms related to the 63 BC Roman invasion of Jerusalem and desecration of the temple.[37] The author(s) delineates three groups: wicked Gentile invaders, wicked Jews, and righteous Jews. God's allowing the invasion is justified because it was due to the sins of the wicked Jews. The author also sees God vindicating the righteous by raising them to eternal life (Pss. Sol. 3:12) and eventually sending a special Messiah (chap. 17). The following are some pertinent quotations from the Psalms of Solomon related to the question of works righteousness:

> I considered in my heart that I was full of righteousness, for I had prospered and had many children. (1:3)

> He atones for (sins of) ignorance by fasting and humbling his soul, and the Lord will cleanse every devout person and his house. (3:8)

> May God remove from the devout those who live in hypocrisy; may his flesh decay and his life be impoverished. May God expose the deeds of those who try to impress people; (and expose) their deeds with ridicule and contempt. (4:6–7)

> Our works (are) in the choosing and power of our souls, to do right and wrong in the works of our hands, and in your righteousness you oversee human beings. The one who does what is right saves up life for himself with the Lord, and the one who does

---

33. Chris VanLandingham, *Judgment and Justification in Early Judaism and the Apostle Paul* (Peabody, MA: Hendrickson, 2006), 169. Nickelsburg notes, "Although the author ascribes to the patriarch some of the virtues traditionally attributed to him (righteousness, hospitality), he has glaringly omitted the most celebrated of these: Abraham's obedient faith." *Jewish Literature*, 251.
34. E. P. Sanders, "Testament of Abraham," in Charlesworth, *Old Testament Pseudepigrapha*, 1:871–902.
35. Sanders, "Testament of Abraham," 1:878.
36. Gathercole, *Where Is Boasting?*, 27–28.
37. The extant manuscripts are in Greek and Syriac, but most scholars assume that the original was written in Hebrew while the author was in Jerusalem. It is not clear why the author used Solomon's name, maybe because of Psalm 72.

what is wrong causes his own life to be destroyed; for the Lord's righteous judgments are according to the individual and the household. (9:4–5)

And whose sins will he forgive except those who have sinned? You bless the righteous, and do not accuse them for what they sinned. And your goodness is upon those that sin, when they repent. (9:7)

The Lord is faithful to those who truly love him, to those who endure his discipline, To those who live in the righteousness of his commandments, in the Law, which he has commanded for our life. The Lord's devout shall live by it forever; the Lord's paradise, the trees of life, are his devout ones. (14:1–3)

As the above quotations show, the Psalms of Solomon include statements with both mercy and works of righteousness required for eschatological salvation.

The clearest statements that deeds are required for eschatological salvation are Psalms of Solomon 9:1–5 and 14:2–3. As 9:5 states, "The one who does what is right saves up life for himself with the Lord." Psalms of Solomon 14:2–3 includes an apparent quotation from, or at least an allusion to, Leviticus 18:5.[38] Eschatological life is connected to the righteous deeds of the law.

Of course, some of these works statements could be taken in the sense of the Reformational third use of the law. However, since I do not see a clear and overwhelming grace pattern in the Psalms of Solomon, I consider this document semi-Pelagian. I agree with Gathercole's summary of the Psalms of Solomon: "The role of works in final vindication cannot be ruled out simply by asserting that the mercy of God is basic for life and salvation: both viewpoints are held simultaneously."[39]

Sanders has a long discussion on the Psalms of Solomon. He notes both the mercy passages and the works passages. However, he emphasizes the supposed covenant background and concludes that "God's covenant is the basis of salvation, and the elect remain in the covenant unless they sin in such a way as to be removed."[40] One of Sanders's standard rebuttals to possible works righteousness is that any time he sees mercy from God owing to repentance, he assumes the document has no works righteousness.[41] For me, Sanders's analysis overplays his assumed covenant background and ignores the category of semi-Pelagianism.[42]

---

38. For a detailed discussion of Lev. 18:5 and the Psalms of Solomon, see Preston M. Sprinkle, *Law and Life: The Interpretation of Leviticus 18:5 in Early Judaism and in Paul*, WUNT, 2nd ser., vol. 241 (Tübingen: Mohr Siebeck, 2008), 87–100. Paul uses Lev. 18:5 in two key works-righteousness passages: Rom. 10:5; Gal. 3:12.

39. Gathercole, *Where Is Boasting?*, 67. For a view between Sanders and me, see Daniel Falk, "Prayers and Psalms," in *Justification and Variegated Nomism*, vol. 1, *The Complexities of Second Temple Judaism*, ed. D. A. Carson, Peter T. O'Brien, and Mark A. Seifrid, WUNT, 2nd ser., vol. 140 (Grand Rapids, MI: Baker Academic, 2001), 35–51.

40. Sanders, *Paul and Palestinian Judaism*, 408. For the entire discussion, see 387–409.

41. Sanders, *Paul and Palestinian Judaism*, 46, 177.

42. Charles Lee Irons argues that "righteousness" language in the Psalms of Solomon includes both "ethical righteousness" and "God's judicial righteousness (*iustitia distributiva*)." In context, Irons is arguing against the Cremer/Dunn/Wright view of righteousness as the "the covenant faithfulness of God." More directly to our topic, Irons notes, "Yes, there is mercy for those who repent, but repentance is turning oneself back to the Law. It is a way of getting back onto the path of righteousness. In the final analysis, righteousness by Law-keeping is still the necessary means of obtaining eschatological life." *The Righteousness of God: A Lexical Examination of the Covenant-Faithfulness Interpretation*, WUNT, 2nd ser., vol. 386 (Tübingen: Mohr Siebeck, 2015), 222–25.

Psalms of Solomon 4 is a famous chapter denouncing hypocrisy. The author is condemning others who are acting as if they follow the law but are violating it in secret. Clearly, to condemn hypocrisy is not necessarily a works-righteousness act (Matt. 6:2; 23:13; Mark 7:6). However, the author is aware of others who are acting hypocritically. To act hypocritically need not be done out of works-righteousness motives, but oftentimes it is. And if it is, then we have another piece of evidence that works-righteousness views historically existed in Second Temple Judaism.

Rule of the Community (1QS)[43]

The Rule of the Community (1QS) and the Damascus Document (CD) are two major texts that give us an understanding of the Qumran community.[44] The Rule of the Community is written in Hebrew on a scroll that measures 6.5 feet long by 10 inches wide, with eleven columns of writing (each column appropriately equal in length to a biblical chapter). The estimated date of composition is 100–75 BC.[45]

A simple outline for 1QS might be as follows:

I–IV   Entrance into the community and two spirits
V–IX   Rules of the community per se
X–XI   Hymn to God

The Rule of the Community includes many directives about entering and staying in the group and ends with a long, psalm-like hymn praising the grace of God.[46] To enter the community is to enter the true "covenant of God."[47] Those not in the community are not destined for salvation (1QS V, 7–19). The Rule of the Community is probably the most important document for understanding the Qumran community. One's view of this writing colors much of one's view of the rest of the Dead Sea Scrolls.

The following are quotations from the Rule of the Community related to the question of works righteousness:

> He shall admit into the Covenant of Grace all those who have freely devoted themselves to the observance of God's precepts, that they may be joined to the counsel of God and may live perfectly before Him in accordance with all that has been revealed. (I, 7–8)

---

43. All English translations from the Dead Sea Scrolls are from Geza Vermes, trans. and ed., *The Complete Dead Sea Scrolls in English*, rev. ed. (New York: Penguin, 2004).
44. The Rule of the Community is sometimes called the Manual of Discipline. The "S" in 1QS stands for the Hebrew סרך ("rule"). In addition to 1QS, other recensions and fragments of this work include 4Q255; 4Q280, 286–87; 4Q502; and 5Q11, 13.
45. Nickelsburg, *Jewish Literature*, 132; J. Murphy-O'Connor, "Community, Rule of the (1QS)," in Freedman, *Anchor Bible Dictionary*, 1:1110–12.
46. Part of the hymn is as follows: "I will sing with knowledge and all my music shall be for the glory of God. . . . Before I move my hands and feet, I will bless His Name. . . . If I stumble, the mercies of God shall be my eternal salvation" (1QS X, 8, 15; XI, 12).
47. After evaluating "covenant" in the Dead Sea Scrolls, Craig A. Evans concludes, "Simply put, the distinctive feature of the understanding of Covenant at Qumran is the reduction of the number of elect." "Covenant in the Qumran Literature," in *The Concept of the Covenant in the Second Temple Period*, ed. Stanley E. Porter and Jacqueline C. R. de Roo; JSJSup 71 (Atlanta: Society of Biblical Literature, 2007), 80.

> They shall not depart from any command of God concerning their times; they shall be neither early nor late for any of their appointed times, they shall stray neither to the right nor to the left of any of His true precepts. . . . [They] shall enter into the Covenant before God to obey all His commandments. (I, 13–17)

> Let him then order his steps (to walk) perfectly in all the ways commanded by God concerning the times appointed for him, straying neither to the right nor to the left and transgressing none of His words, and he shall be accepted by virtue of a pleasing atonement before God and it shall be to him a Covenant of the everlasting Community. (III, 9–12)

> But when a man enters the Covenant to walk according to all these precepts that he may be joined to the Holy Congregation, they shall examine his spirit in community with respect to his understanding and practice of the Law. . . . And they shall examine their spirit and deeds yearly, so that each man may be advanced in accordance with his understanding and perfection of way, or moved down in accordance with his distortions. (V, 20–24)

> Whoever has deliberately deceived his companion by word or by deed shall do penance for six months. (VII, 5)

> [The Council of the Community] shall preserve the faith in the Land with steadfastness and meekness and shall atone for sin by the practice of justice and by suffering the sorrows of affliction. (VIII, 3–4)

> And no man among the members of the Covenant of the Community who deliberately, on any point whatever, turns aside from all that is commanded, shall touch the pure Meal of the men of holiness or know anything of their counsel until his deeds are purified from all injustice and he walks in perfection of way. (VIII, 17–18)

> [Members of the Community] shall atone for guilty rebellion and for sins of unfaithfulness, that they may obtain loving-kindness for the Land without the flesh of holocausts and the fat of sacrifice. And prayer rightly offered shall be as an acceptable fragrance of righteousness, and perfection of way as a delectable free-will offering. (IX, 4–6)

> I will declare His judgment concerning my sins, and my transgressions shall be before my eyes as an engraved Precept, I will say to God, "My Righteousness" and "Author of my Goodness" to the Most High. (X, 12–13)

> If I stagger because of the sin of flesh, my justification [משפטי][48] will be by the righteousness of God which endures for all time. (XI, 12)

As shown in Rule of the Community I, 7–8, there are strict requirements for Jews entering the community. On the surface, this argues against Sanders's view that all Jews are presumed to be in the covenant by election and that "getting in" is by grace.[49]

---

48. A better translation would be "my judgment."
49. Timo Eskola vigorously opposes Sanders here: "One cannot say that grace would have had anything to do with entering the [Qumran] community. The membership was not granted on the ground of nationality or circumcision. The

As can be seen from many of the above quotations, "staying in" the community requires strict adherence and penance for misdeeds. Although in principle this does not contradict Sanders's view of "staying in" by works (not works righteousness in his view), would one not agree that this strictness would tend in a works-righteousness direction even for one who was committed to Sanders's covenantal nomism?

In Rule of the Community III, 9–12, ritual atonement is connected to doing good deeds. The Qumran community did not participate in the existing temple sacrifices. Yes, this could be taken in a metaphorical third-use-of-the-law way, as the New Testament takes it (Heb. 13:15–16); however, the strictness of the community's rules and the lack of a clear avenue of actual atonement, such as Christ's death, argue against this.

Much is made of the psalm-like ending showing God's grace (1QS X–XI).[50] And it should be. However, this at best gives the document a semi-Pelagian view. Possibly the two parts of the Rule of the Community were separate; if so, the first part would indicate the presence of Pelagianism in the community.[51]

George Nickelsburg, a pro-covenantal-nomism author, says that "we should not presume that Judaism was characterized by a 'works righteousness' that excluded the grace integral to the structure of biblical covenantal theology." He goes on to quote from the ending psalm of the Rule of the Community. Nickelsburg further notes the "corresponding lists of good and evil deeds and their respective rewards and punishments" in the Rule of the Community. He concludes by saying, "In all these respects, these ancient documents defy the consistency of later philosophical speculation about free will and much Christian theology that derives from that speculation."[52] Nickelsburg's solution is to see the document as simply inconsistent.[53] I prefer to see it as semi-Pelagian.

Sanders admits that there "may appear to be a significant distinction between the legalistic works-righteousness of 1QS I–IX" and the ending psalm. But properly understood, he argues, it confirms his view of covenantal nomism in that *"the principal point of the punishment for deeds but reward for mercy theme is that, while man can forfeit salvation by transgression, he can never be sufficiently deserving to earn it by obedience."*[54] I beg to differ and simply note that the ending psalm proves that the Rule

---

covenant of God was a covenant of law. The sociological 'getting in' had only to do with law." "Paul, Predestination and 'Covenantal Nomism'—Re-assessing Paul and Palestinian Judaism," *JSJ* 28, no. 4 (1997): 405.

50. Preston M. Sprinkle agrees that 1QS X–XI is gracious to a significant degree, but he notes that the context is the final judgment of those who have demonstrated obedience. He further observes that Paul has a higher view of divine agency because he advocates for the *initial* justification of the *ungodly*. *Paul and Judaism Revisited: A Study of Divine and Human Agency in Salvation* (Downers Grove, IL: IVP Academic, 2013), 167–70.

51. Although not conclusive, supporting the two-separate-documents view is that the Damascus Document (CD) is very similar to the Rule of the Community, except for the psalm-like ending.

52. Nickelsburg, *Ancient Judaism and Christian Origins*, 50–51. VanLandingham argues that the psalm is not actually grace based at all. *Judgment and Justification*, 126–34. This is going too far for me. See Robert J. Cara, review of *Judgment and Justification in Early Judaism and the Apostle Paul*, by Chris VanLandingham, *WTJ* 70 (2008): 388–92.

53. Markus Bockmuehl similarly concludes that 1QS has an "unsystematic soteriology": "As it stands, salvation is on the one hand 'legalistic' both in its individualistic voluntarism and in its closely regimented corporate life; and yet it is the gift of divine grace alone, both objectively in regard to predestination and subjectively in the experience of the believer. The evidence itself now confirms that the intrinsically unsystematic soteriology of a central document like 1QS is due at least in some part to textual development over a considerable length of time." "1QS and Salvation at Qumran," in Carson, O'Brien, and Seifrid, *Justification and Variegated Nomism*, 1:413.

54. Sanders, *Paul and Palestinian Judaism*, 291, 293; italics original.

of the Community is not, at least as a total document, Pelagian. However, it appears to be clearly semi-Pelagian.[55]

Pesher Habakkuk (1QpHab)

The word *pesher* translates as "commentary." Hence, Pesher Habakkuk is a commentary on Habakkuk. In the Dead Sea Scrolls, there are approximately eleven different commentaries. This one is the most well known. It is the longest of the pesherim, the best preserved, and it provides useful information about the Teacher of Righteousness.[56]

Pesher Habakkuk expounds the biblical book of Habakkuk half verse by half verse from Habakkuk 1:1 through 2:20. The author reads contemporary events into the biblical book (e.g., the "Chaldeans" in Hab. 1:6 are the Romans ["Kittim"], 1QpHab I, 10). There are three prominent persons: (1) the Teacher of Righteousness, who is the leader of the Qumran community; (2) the Liar, who apparently used to follow the Teacher but has now rebelled; and (3) the Wicked Priest, who initially followed the truth but now is a horrible ruler who abuses the poor and desecrates the temple and who has "pursued the Teacher of Righteousness to the house of his exile" (1QpHab X, 5–6). There is a significant emphasis on the final age and judgment.

The following are quotations from Pesher Habakkuk related to the question of works righteousness:

> "If it tarries, wait for it, for it shall surely come and shall not be late" [Hab. 2:3b]. Interpreted, this concerns the men of truth who keep the Law, whose hands shall not slacken in the service of truth when the final age is prolonged. (1QpHab VII, 10–13)

> "Behold, [his soul] is puffed up and is not upright" [Hab. 2:4a]. Interpreted, this means that [the wicked] shall double their guilt upon themselves [and it shall not be forgiven] when they are judged. (1QpHab VII, 14–16)

> "But the righteous shall live by his faith" [Hab. 2:4b]. Interpreted, this concerns all those who observe the Law in the house of Judah, whom God will deliver from the House of Judgment because of their suffering and because of their faith in the Teacher of Righteousness. (1QpHab VIII, 1–3)

> [Interpreting Hab. 2:16:] For [the Wicked Priest] did not circumcise the foreskin of his heart, and he walked in the ways of drunkenness that he might quench his thirst. (1QpHab XI, 12)

---

55. Peter Stuhlmacher cites 1QS along with 4 Ezra, 1QpHab, 4QMMT, and 2 Baruch as examples throughout Second Temple Judaism of "two contrary principles . . . , a principle of election and a principle of retribution," within the same documents. *Revisiting Paul's Doctrine of Justification: A Challenge to the New Perspective* (Downers Grove, IL: InterVarsity Press, 2001), 41. Barry D. Smith, an anti-NPP author, evaluates the Qumran literature, including 1QS, and concludes that God is shown both as merciful and as a righteous judge. This produces a synergistic soteriology. See his *What Must I Do to Be Saved? Paul Parts Company with His Jewish Heritage*, New Testament Monographs 17 (Sheffield: Sheffield Phoenix, 2007), 22–34, 47–72.

56. The standard reference work on Pesher Habakkuk is William H. Brownlee, *The Midrash Pesher of Habakkuk*, SBLMS 24 (Missoula, MT: Scholars, 1979).

[Interpreting Hab. 2:17:] The "beasts" are the simple of Judah who keep the Law. (1QpHab XII, 4–5)

The text that receives the most attention is Pesher Habakkuk VIII, 1–3, since this is the interpretation of Habakkuk 2:4, "The righteous shall live by his faith," which Paul refers to in Romans 1:17 and Galatians 3:11 (also see Heb. 10:38). The author of Pesher Habakkuk inserts the observance of the law into this "faith alone" text. (He interprets "faith" as faith in the Teacher of Righteousness.) In several other places, the observance of the law is also inserted (1QpHab II, 14; VII, 10–13; XII, 4–5). Preston Sprinkle summarizes, "Faith and works of the law are seen as essential partners in humanity's justification and deliverance."[57] Although Sprinkle does not like the term semi-Pelagian, this is the substance of his conclusion.[58]

Larry Helyer goes further and concludes that Pesher Habakkuk is making the exact opposite point that Paul makes:

[In Pesher Habakkuk,] one gains God's grace and favor by a punctilious observance of all the law, in this case, of course, the halakic interpretation advocated by the Teacher of Righteousness. This pesher on Habakkuk is evidence that Paul's polemic against salvation by works is not a fabrication on his part.[59]

The author of Pesher Habakkuk multiple times inserts observance of the law into his interpretation of Habakkuk, which at that point has little to do with the law. This shows that the author is clearly not using the law in a Reformational "third use" way. He probably has a Pelagian understanding. Hence, I agree with Helyer.

Miqsat Ma'ase Ha-Torah (4QMMT)[60]

Miqsat Ma'ase Ha-Torah is an apparent letter that was found in six incomplete manuscripts with the composite text being about 120 lines long.[61] The manuscripts are numbered 4Q394–99, and the letter is separated by scholars into three major sections (4QMMT A, 4QMMT B, 4QMMT C). The title is the transliteration of the Hebrew phrase "some of the works of the Law," which is near the end of the letter (4QMMT C 27).

This letter has garnered much scholarly attention, including articles from both Dunn and Wright.[62] Two important expressions are similar to those in Paul. The

---

57. Sprinkle, *Paul and Judaism Revisited*, 167. Similarly, Francis Watson argues, "Right interpretation, practice, and belief belong together, ensuring that the righteous person will live—that is, be delivered from 'the house of judgment.'" *Paul and the Hermeneutics of Faith* (London: T&T Clark, 2004), 523; also see 119–26.
58. Sprinkle prefers to evaluate the relationship between "divine and human agency" and not use the terms typical of "Old or New Perspectives on Paul." *Paul and Judaism Revisited*, 25.
59. Larry R. Helyer, *Exploring Jewish Literature of the Second Temple Period: A Guide for New Testament Students* (Downers Grove, IL: InterVarsity Press, 2002), 232–33.
60. מקצת מעשי התורה.
61. For a good summary article of 4QMMT, see Elisha Qimron, "Miqcat Ma'ase Hatorah," in Freedman, *Anchor Bible Dictionary*, 4:843–45. Also see John Kampen and Moshe J. Bernstein, eds., *Reading 4QMMT: New Perspectives on Qumran Law and History*, SBLSS 2 (Atlanta: Scholars Press, 1996).
62. James D. G. Dunn, "4QMMT and Galatians," in *The New Perspective on Paul*, 339–45 (originally published in *NTS* 43, no. 1 [1997]: 147–53); N. T. Wright, "4QMMT and Paul: Justification, 'Works,' and Eschatology," in *History*

4QMMT C 27 wording "works of the law" matches Paul (e.g., Rom. 3:20; Gal. 2:16).[63] Also, "And it will be reckoned to you as righteousness" in 4QMMT C 31 is very similar to Genesis 15:6; Psalm 106:31; and various Pauline passages (e.g., Rom. 4:3; Gal. 3:6).[64] In addition, on the surface, 4QMMT appears to have a clear works-righteousness theology.

The opening and closing of the apparent letter is missing. The first section that is extant, 4QMMT A, is a 364-day calendar that primarily lists the dates for the Sabbath—for example, "On the twenty-eighth day of the [twelfth month], sabbath" (4QMMT A 19). The second section, 4QMMT B, lists twenty halakhot (rules) that mostly relate to temple ceremonies—for example, "Concerning the skin of the carcass of a clean animal, he who carries their carcass shall not touch the [sacred] purity" (4QMMT B 22–23). In the final extant section, 4QMMT C, the author notes that he and his group have separated themselves from the "mass of people," and he wants the addressee (singular "you") to follow the author's interpretation of Moses, the Prophets, and David as to the halakhot (4QMMT C 7–12). Following these halakhot will be beneficial for Israel (4QMMT C 27).

Although it is not explicitly stated, the author appears to be the leader of the Qumran community, and it is a reasonable guess that he is the Teacher of Righteousness. The addressee is some type of leader in Israel (4QMMT C 23–25) who has influence at the temple. There are also references to "they," which appears to refer to a group with competing views for proper temple ceremonies, maybe the Pharisees or Sadducees.

The following are quotations from the Miqsat Ma'ase Ha-Torah related to the question of works righteousness:

> These are some of our teachings which are the works which we think all of them concern the purity. (B 1–2)

> And he shall not sow his field and vineyard with two kinds. For they are holy and the sons of Aaron are most holy. And you know that some of the priests and the people mingle and they unite and defile the holy seed and also their seed with whores. (B 78–82)

> And you know that we have separated from the mass of people and from mingling with them in these matters and from being in contact with them in these matters. And you know that no treachery or lie or evil is found in our hands. (C 7–9)

> We recognize that some of the blessings and curses which are written in the Book of Moses have come. (C 20–21)

---

and Exegesis: New Testament Essays in Honor of Dr. E. Earle Ellis for His 80th Birthday, ed. Sand-Won Son (New York: T&T Clark, 2006), 104–32.

63. The Hebrew מעשי התורה includes the definite article before "law." Paul's expression ἐξ ἔργων νόμου does not. This can easily be explained: within a Greek prepositional phrase, the definite article is often dropped. For the general rule, see BDF §255; Daniel B. Wallace, *Greek Grammar beyond the Basics: An Exegetical Syntax of the New Testament* (Grand Rapids, MI: Zondervan, 1996), 247.

64. בהונחש לך לצדקה (4QMMT C 31); ויחשבה לך לצדקה (Gen. 15:6).

Remember the kings of Israel and understand their works that each of them who feared the Law was saved from troubles, and to those who were seekers of the Law, their iniquities were pardoned. Remember David, that he was a man of piety, and that he was saved from many troubles and pardoned. (C 23–26)

We have also written to you concerning some of the works[65] of the Law, which we think are beneficial to you and your people. For we have noticed that prudence and knowledge of the Law are with you. (C 26–28)

Understand all these matters and ask Him to straighten out your counsel and put you far away from thought so evil and the counsel of Belial. (C 28–29)

You will rejoice at the end of time when you discover that some of our sayings are true. And it will be reckoned for you as righteousness when you perform what is right and good before Him, for your own good and for that of Israel. (C 30–32)

In 4QMMT C 20–21 and 26–28, the benefits/blessings of a return to following the law relates to the current time. However, in 4QMMT C 30–32, the "reckoned to you for righteousness" is in an eschatological context. And in that context, it is the "works of the Law" from 4QMMT C 27 that are the basis for being reckoned righteous and receiving eschatological blessings. Is this not a straightforward works-righteousness view? One could argue that the author does believe that (prior?) sins may be pardoned, but the way to obtain that pardon is to do the law (4QMMT C 23–24). In 4QMMT C 28–29, the author does urge the addressee to ask God for "counsel" and for God to "put you far away from thoughts of evil." This is the only verse with divine agency in 4QMMT—even so, this would admit at best to a semi-Pelagian view of works righteousness.

How do Dunn and Wright respond? After citing Genesis 15:6 and Psalm 106:31, Dunn confusingly agrees that here justification, righteousness, and works of the law are all related. He notes that this is just another example in Second Temple Judaism of "covenant faithfulness."[66] I assume that by "covenant faithfulness" Dunn means Sanders's covenantal-nomism scheme. Apparently, it is this scheme that allows him to not term this teaching works righteousness.

Wright agrees that 4QMMT C 30–32 is ultimately eschatological, although he wants to stress that it is also covenantal.[67] Fair enough. Wright then sees these emphases as confirming that 4QMMT follows Sanders's scheme and is not works-righteousness theology. For him, "righteousness"/"justification" refers to one "staying in" and not "getting in" the community.[68] He argues that *"the language of C 31 is not about entry into the community, but about being demonstrated to be within*

---

65. Vermes translates this term as "observances."
66. Dunn, "4QMMT and Galatians," 343–44.
67. Wright, "4QMMT and Paul," 112. He goes on to argue that "Paul's doctrine has exactly the same *shape* as that of MMT." Wright, "4QMMT and Paul," 120; italics original.
68. Wright explicitly refers to Sanders's terms here. "4QMMT and Paul," 117.

it."⁶⁹ However, the context of the letter is implicitly asking the addressee and his followers to "get in" the community. Also, the final judgment is in view, which is more than "staying in." To prove his point about "staying in," Wright paraphrases 4QMMT C 30–32:

> If through prayer and the moral strength that God supplies (C 28–29) *you keep these precepts*, you will rejoice at the end of time, in finding that the advice given, this selection of commands, was on the right track. That is when (C 31) "*it will be reckoned to you as righteousness* when *you perform* what is right and good before him."⁷⁰

Based simply on the above paraphrase, Wright attributes a semi-Pelagian view to the author of 4QMMT.⁷¹ I appreciate his emphasis on works being done by the power of God, but the problem is that he attaches these works to justification. Whether one is referencing justification related to "getting in," "staying in," or the final judgment, if it involves works, it is works-righteousness theology.⁷²

Rabbinic Literature

Rabbinic Judaism is the name given to the religious party that is the continuation of the Pharisee party after the AD 70 fall of Jerusalem. Classic rabbinic literature begins with the Mishnah (AD 200) and ends with the Babylonian Talmud (AD 600).

Before AD 200, there are no extant written documents for rabbinic Judaism. Not all scholars want to use rabbinic literature to evaluate Second Temple Judaism. I believe that there certainly is some continuity between the Pharisees and the Mishnah and Tosefta. I have my doubts about later rabbinic literature, including the Talmuds.⁷³ Sanders bases much of his argument on traditional Tannaitic material (rabbis who lived from 50 BC to AD 200) in the rabbinic literature. This would include the Mishnah, major portions of the Tosefta, supposed Tannaitic portions of the Talmuds,⁷⁴ and even later midrashim such as the Midrash Rabbah.

Presented below are various texts that I believe show a works-righteousness soteriology. Sanders, of course, does not view these texts this way. I note here that not even all Jewish authors agree with Sanders. Some give an explicitly Pelagian view of the rabbis. For example, Isidore Epstein argues,

---

69. Wright, "4QMMT and Paul," 117; italics original. Elsewhere, Wright views the Pharisees as sharing the same "shape of how eschatology works in relation to election and thus to present justification" as does 4QMMT. *Paul and the Faithfulness of God*, 184.
70. Wright, "4QMMT and Paul," 116; italics added.
71. Sprinkle complains that Wright will not admit that "a return to the law in the eschatological age is a means of eliciting the covenant blessing, not merely a way to identify who the righteous really are." *Paul and Judaism Revisited*, 78.
72. M. G. Abegg Jr. disagrees with me and considers my view a "knee-jerk reaction": "The emphasis on the need for repentance and focus on God's grace in this and other Qumran writings should convince that a knee-jerk reaction that suggests that 4QMMT reflects a 'works-earn-righteousness' religion is hardly justified." He goes on to reference Sanders. See Abegg, "Miqcat Ma'aSey Ha-Torah (4QMMT)," in *Dictionary of New Testament Background*, ed. Craig A. Evans and Stanley E. Porter (Downers Grove, IL: InterVarsity Press, 2000), 710–11. Also see his article "4QMMT C 27, 31 and 'Works Righteousness,'" *DSD* 6, no. 2 (1999): 139–47.
73. For a defense of this view, see Cara, *Cracking the Foundation*, 212–14, 270–71.
74. When the Talmuds refer to earlier Tannaitic material that is not in the Mishnah or Tosefta, this is referred to as "baraitot."

[Talmudic] Judaism further denies the existence of original sin, needing a superhuman counterweight, and allows only the free choice to sin, an inevitable concomitant of free will. . . . Obedience or return to God after offending carries with it divine favour and reward. . . . Judaism makes salvation depend on right conduct.[75]

Jacob Neusner, while not explicitly Pelagian, argues that the rabbis' view of an eschatological resurrection and an eschatological judgment by God clearly requires that "deeds done in this world bear consequences for his situation in the world to come, and the merit attained through this-worldly deeds, for example, generosity, persists."[76]

Mishnah[77]

The Mishnah was completed in approximately AD 200 and is the foundational document for rabbinic Judaism. The Mishnah is a large book (about half the size of the Bible) arranged in six major divisions that separate sixty-three topics, or "tractates."

m. Abot

"Abot" translates as "Fathers." It is one of the few tractates that does not have an explicit parallel in the Tosefta or the two Talmuds. Of all the tractates in the Mishnah, this one has more theological comments per se and fewer halakhot.[78] Unrelated to works righteousness, this tractate is important in the Mishnah because it presents the view that the oral law, in addition to the written law, came from Moses (m. Abot 1:1–2). Also, it includes the concept that the oral law is a fence around the written law (1:1, 3:13). Related to works righteousness, m. Abot 3:15 is often quoted.

The following are quotations from m. Abot related to the question of works righteousness:

> Be meticulous in a small religious duty as in a large one, for you do not know what sort of reward is coming for any of the various religious duties. . . . And keep your eyes on three things, so you will not come into the clutches of transgression: Know what is above you: An eye which sees, an ear which hears, and all your actions are written down in a book. (2:1–2)

> Rabbi Eliezer says, "Let the respect owing to your fellow be as precious to you as the respect owing to you yourself. And don't be easy to anger. And repent one day before you die." (2:10)

> Rabbi Simeon says, "Be meticulous in the recitation of the *shema* and the Prayer. . . . But let it be a plea for mercy and supplication before the Omnipresent blessed be he." (2:13)

---

75. Isidore Epstein, *Judaism: A Historical Presentation* (1959; repr., New York: Penguin, 1990), 142–43.
76. Jacob Neusner, *Judaism When Christianity Began: A Survey of Belief and Practice* (Louisville: Westminster John Knox, 2002), 167.
77. All English translations from the Mishnah are from Jacob Neusner, *The Mishnah: A New Translation* (New Haven, CT: Yale University Press, 1988).
78. Some see this tractate as the latest of those in the Mishnah and added to the Mishnah in AD 250. So Jacob Neusner, *Rabbinic Literature: An Essential Guide* (Nashville: Abingdon, 2005), 8.

If you have learned much Torah, they will give you a good reward. And our employer can be depended upon to pay your wages for what you do. And know what sort of reward is going to be given to the righteous in the coming time. (2:16)

Rabbi Eleazar the Modite says, "He who treats Holy Things as secular, and he who defiles the appointed times, he who humiliates his fellow in public, he who removes the signs of the covenant of Abraham, our father, may he rest in peace, and he who exposes aspects of the Torah not in accord with the law, even though he has in hand learning in Torah and good deeds, will have no share in the world to come." (3:11)

Rabbi Aqiba says, . . . "Everything is foreseen and free choice is given. In goodness the world is judged. And all is in accord with the abundance of deeds." (3:15)

Rabbi Eliezer son of Jacob says, "He who does even a single religious duty gets himself a good advocate. He who does even a single transgression gets himself a prosecutor. Penitence and good deeds are like a shield against punishment." (4:11)

Despite your wishes [you are] going to give a full accounting before the King of kings, the Holy One, blessed be he. (4:22)

He who brings merit to the community never causes sin. . . . Moses attained merit and bestowed merit on the community. So the merit of the community is assigned to his credit. (5:18)

Ben He He says, "In accord with the effort is the reward." (5:23)

As can be seen from the above quotations, m. Abot emphasizes performing good deeds and warns that God will evaluate those deeds now and at the final judgment.[79] In addition to individual merit, there is some aspect of community merit (5:18). It appears that one did not have to perfectly fulfill the law to enter heaven since allowance is made for repentance, but it is still true that good deeds in conjunction with repentance are required (4:11). The somewhat well-known m. Abot 3:15 ("all is in accord with the abundance of deeds") implies that most of one's deeds need to be positive for eschatological life.

How does Sanders respond? First, Sanders admits that m. Abot 3:15, m. Abot 4:22, and t. Qiddushin (discussed below) at first reading "may be taken to support the view that weighing fulfillments against transgressions constitutes Rabbinic soteriology."[80] However, Sanders argues that elsewhere it is implied that by one good deed (m. Abot 2:10) one may get into the afterlife and that one evil deed (3:11) may prevent it. And if that is true, the weighing-of-good-and-evil-deeds statements must be considered against

---

79. See Philip S. Alexander's discussion of m. Abot specifically and the Tannaitic literature in general. He concludes that "Tannaitic Judaism can be seen as fundamentally a religion of works-righteousness, and it none the worse for that." He does, however, note that the scales of justice for the amount of good works required for entrance into heaven were weighted toward mercy. "Torah and Salvation in Tannaitic Literature," in Carson, O'Brien, and Seifrid, *Justification and Variegated Nomism*, 1:261–301, esp. 283–88, 298–301, quotation on 300.

80. Sanders, *Paul and Palestinian Judaism*, 128.

the one-deed statements. Hence, Sanders concludes that "it is apparent that the [m. Abot 3:15] saying intends to hold judgment by grace and by works in balance. Not being a systematic theologian, Rabbi Akiba did not explain how the two parts of the saying fit together."[81] Sanders also uses the argument that these works-oriented statements are merely "exhortative" and "the point is to encourage people to obey and not transgress."[82]

In response, I note that the one-good-deed argument is suspect in m. Abot. Sanders only cites m. Abot 2:10, "Repent one day before you die." It is hard to believe that this comment, which is among two other deeds, is to be taken with the sense that all life's previous sins are forgiven and only good deeds on the final day of life are required for heaven. (Admittedly, this view may be elsewhere in the Mishnah—for example, m. Sanhedrin 6:2, t. Qiddushin 1:16—but not here.) As to the one-evil-deed argument, it seems to me that m. Abot 3:11 proves the opposite of Sanders's intention. In m. Abot 3:11, Rabbi Eleazar lists five sins that prevent one from entering the afterlife despite having "learning in Torah and good deeds." That is, there are sins so heinous that positive deeds cannot overcome this. This, I conclude, implies that there is a scale of judgment on which good and evil deeds are weighed.

From my perspective, it is not necessary to prove that the rabbis had a scale of good versus evil deeds. Yes, maybe this is a broad metaphor. However, it is clear that works are involved in the final judgment to determine eschatological life, and overwhelmingly so. This is a works-righteousness soteriology.

As quoted above, Sanders even agrees that "grace and works are held in balance," but this is excused because Rabbi Aqiba is not a "systematic theologian." I assume, tongue in cheek, that Sanders means that if Rabbi Aqiba were a systematic theologian, he would have solved the grace and works tension by means of the covenantal-nomism scheme. In any case, Sanders's comment about grace and works is, at least on the surface of it, semi-Pelagian. Also, he excuses some of these works statements based on their being "exhortative." That is, the rabbis used a soteriological incentive for good works that violated their actual soteriology. On the one hand, even if that were true, one's incentive for good works *is* part of one's theology, whether it is consistent or not. On the other hand, I think it is better to say that the rabbis' exhortation was consistent with their view that final judgment is related to works.

m. Sotah

"Sotah" translates as a wife who has possibly "turned astray" and in context is a suspected adulterer.[83] The tractate m. Sotah is primarily related to Numbers 5:11–31, which is case law for a woman suspected of adultery. A key aspect of the Old Testament ceremony is the suspected woman's drinking of "bitter" water, whose effects will be physically evident if she is guilty of adultery (5:18, 26–27).

---

81. Sanders, *Paul and Palestinian Judaism*, 132; also see discussion on 138–39.
82. Sanders, *Paul and Palestinian Judaism*, 129.
83. "Sotah" is from the Hebrew root שטה, "to turn aside, go astray." In Num. 5:12, 19, 20, 29, it is used to refer to a wife who has "turned astray," that is, committed adultery.

Concerning the question of works righteousness, two texts are quoted below. The first concerns a woman who is guilty of adultery. She drinks the bitter water, but the curse's effects do not immediately show. The second is the final pericope in the tractate. It follows a somewhat sad section that recounts various losses to the Jewish people from the destruction of Jerusalem through the defeat of Bar Kochba (m. Sotah 9:10–14):

> There is the possibility that merit suspends the curse for one year, and there is the possibility that merit suspends the curse for two years, and there is the possibility that merit suspends the curse for three years.
>
> On this basis Ben Azzai says, "A man is required to teach Torah to his daughter. For if she should drink the water, she should know that [if nothing happens to her,] merit is what suspends [the curse from taking effect]."
>
> . . . Rabbi Simeon says, "Merit does not suspend the effects of the bitter water. And if you say, 'Merit does suspend the effects of the bitter water,' you will weaken the effect of the water for all the women who drink it who turned out to be pure." (3:4–5)

> Upon whom shall we depend? Upon our Father in heaven. Rabbi Pinhas son of Yair says, "Heedfulness leads to cleanliness, cleanliness leads to cleanness, cleanness leads to abstinence, abstinence leads to holiness, holiness leads to modesty, modesty leads to the fear of sin, and fear of sin leads to piety, piety leads to the Holy Spirit, the Holy Spirit leads to the resurrection of the dead, and the resurrection of the dead comes through Elijah, blessed be his memory, Amen." (9:15)

In m. Sotah 3:4–5, if a guilty woman does not immediately show the effects of the bitter water, it is because she has previously accrued "merit." Rabbi Simeon objects to this because it confuses the results of the ceremony for those who are pure.

Concerning our purposes related to works righteousness, how does the woman acquire merit? Commonly in rabbinic literature, studying the Torah is a good deed. Ben Azzai argues that this ceremony teaches that even daughters should learn the Torah because doing so acquires merit. This comment by Ben Azzai prompts a long discussion in the Babylonian Talmud (b. Sotah 20b–22b).[84] Part of the discussion relates to whether women should study the Torah and Mishnah with the answer being that women need to know about the Torah and Mishnah in order to encourage their sons to read them (b. Sotah 21a). Another part of the discussion is whether transgressions may cancel out merit. That is, does not the adultery cancel out any merit from good deeds? The rabbis answer that "while a transgression extinguishes the merit of a religious duty one has performed, it does not extinguish the merit of Torah one has studied" (b. Sotah 22a).[85] Although the above discussions in the Mishnah and Babylonian Talmud are referring to merit that is applied during this life (the woman does not show immediate effects of

---

84. The Tosefta skips m. Sotah 3:4–5 in its discussion; see t. Sotah 2:3–4.
85. All English translations of the Babylonian Talmud are from Jacob Neusner, *The Babylonian Talmud: A Translation and Commentary*, 22 vols. (Peabody, MA: Hendrickson, 2005).

the bitter water), this still shows a works-righteousness system as good and evil deeds are balanced against each other in this life, and presumably would be for eschatological life also (cf. m. Sotah 9:15).

Sanders, in an offhanded comment, concedes that m. Sotah 3:4 does teach that good deeds "may suspend the punishment of transgressions," but he will not concede that good deeds are used "to offset or compensate for transgressions at the judgment."[86]

Compared to most of the Mishnah, m. Sotah 9:15 is written in more of a poetical manner.[87] Various good habits lead to "piety," which in turn leads to the "Holy Spirit," which in turn leads to the "resurrection of the dead." The reference to the Holy Spirit is fairly rare in the Mishnah and is probably associated with the Ezekiel 37 resurrection. This is a clear eschatological context that includes "piety" as the rationale for the resurrection. The reference to the Holy Spirit aiding in the resurrection and the comment that one is to depend on the Father imply strongly that God would also aid in piety. If so, this would be a semi-Pelagian view of works righteousness.

Tosefta[88]

The Tosefta is very similar to and an expansion of the Mishnah. It is four times as large as the Mishnah, but it has the same six divisions and virtually the same tractate titles. The Tosefta was written in approximately AD 300, a century after the Mishnah. Two extra generations of rabbis are included, in addition to those quoted in the Mishnah.

t. Qiddushin

"Qiddushin" translates as "sanctification." The t. Qiddushin tractate primarily concerns betrothals of a woman to a man. The title relates to a woman becoming "sacred" (or "set apart") to a man upon their betrothal (t. Qiddushin 1:1).

Below is a fairly long passage related to the question of works righteousness. The passage is not discussing betrothals per se but laws to obey when in the Promised Land. This passage is often quoted because it includes a balance for weighing good and evil deeds:

> Whoever does a single commandment—they do well for him and lengthen his days and his years and he inherits the Land. And whoever commits a single transgression—they do ill to him and cut off his days, and he does not inherit the Land. And concerning such a person it is said, "One sinner destroys much good" [Eccl 9:18]. By a single sin this one destroys many good things. *A person should always see himself as if he is half meritorious and half guilty. If he did a single commandment, happy is he, for he has inclined the balance for himself to the side of merit. If he committed*

---

86. Sanders, *Paul and Palestinian Judaism*, 146. He goes on to say that "transgressions . . . are atoned for rather than balanced by a corresponding good deed."
87. These ending comments in m. Sotah 9:15 are not discussed in the Tosefta or the Babylonian Talmud.
88. All English translations are from Jacob Neusner, *The Tosefta: Translated from the Hebrew with a New Introduction* (Peabody, MA: Hendrickson, 2002).

a single transgression, woe is he, for he has inclined the balance to the side of guilt. Concerning this one it is said, One sinner destroys much good. By a single sin this one has destroyed many good things.

Rabbi Simeon son of Eleazar says in the name of Rabbi Meir, "*Because the individual is judged by his majority of deeds, the world is judged by its majority. And if one did one commandment, happy is he, for he has inclined the balance for himself and for the world to the side of merit.* If he has committed one transgression, woe is he, for he has inclined the balance for himself and for the world to the side of guilt. And concerning such a person it is said, One sinner destroys much good [Eccl 9:18]. By the single sin which this one committed, he destroyed for himself and for the world many good things."

Rabbi Simeon says, "If a man was righteous his entire life but at the end rebelled, he loses the whole, since it is said, 'The righteousness of the righteous shall not deliver him when he transgresses' [Ezek 33:12]. If a man was evil his entire life but at the end he repented, the Omnipresent accepts him. As it is said, 'And as for the wickedness of the wicked, he shall not fall by it when he turns from his wickedness' [Ezek 33:12]. Whoever occupies himself with all three of them, with Scripture, Mishnah, and good conduct, concerning such a person it is said, 'And a threefold cord is not quickly broken'" [Eccl 4:12]. (t. Qiddushin 1:13–16; italics added)[89]

In t. Qiddushin 1:13–16, three rabbinic views are presented that do not necessarily contradict each other, although they may. The first view, from the Tosefta editors, focuses on a single good or evil deed. Every deed is important and could be the one that either gets a person into the Promised Land or prevents a person from entering. This then prompts the recommendation that one should always see oneself on a balance with exactly half good and half evil deeds so that one presumably will have more incentive for the next deed to be good.

The second view is from Rabbi Meir, communicated by Rabbi Simeon son of Eleazar. Every deed is important because both the individual and the world will be judged by a majority of either their good or evil deeds.

The third view is from Rabbi Simeon and takes a different tack than the first two. Based on Ezekiel 33:12, it is the end of life just before one dies that counts. If one is righteous his whole life but then rebels at the end, he will not enter the world to come. If one is rebellious his whole life but repents at the end, he will have eschatological life. Rabbi Simeon then comments that the righteous life is filled with "Scripture, Mishnah, and good conduct."

The first and second views on the surface are very works-righteousness oriented because the balance of good and evil deeds shows. The third view, with its emphasis on end-of-life repentance, does not seem to set forth a works-righteousness soteriology. Repentance does not appear to be presented as a work, although the subsequent statement about "Scripture, Mishnah, and good conduct" may contradict this.

---

89. This is an expansion of m. Qiddushin 1:10.

Whether intentionally or not, the editors allowed both a clear works-righteousness soteriology and a possibly non-works-righteousness soteriology to stand side by side in the Tosefta.

In the Babylonian Talmud, the tension is seen between the first two views and the third view. The question is asked, "Why not regard the case of the righteous one who rebels at the end as one that is half transgression and half merit?" That is, could it really be true that if a person lives most of his life with merit but falls at the end, he would *not* receive eschatological life? Rabbi Simeon son of Laquish answers yes: "It is a case of his regretting his former good deeds" (b. Qiddushin 40b). That is, if one intentionally renounces all his good deeds, his balance would be negative, and that explains why he does receive eschatological life. The Babylonian Talmud turns the third view into works-righteousness theology. Thus, all three views exhibit works righteousness in the Babylonian Talmud.

Sanders's response to t. Qiddushin 1:13–16 is included with his response to m. Abot 3:15. He explicitly comments about t. Qiddushin 1:13 that the balance of good and evil deeds is a "non-systematic exhortation."[90] For Sanders, the rabbis' nonsystematic character and exhortative contexts militate against concluding that these passages teach a works-righteousness soteriology even though they appear on the surface to do so.[91] For more of his argument and my rebuttal, see my earlier discussion about m. Abot 3:15 (p. 165).[92]

t. Sanhedrin

A "sanhedrin" in rabbinic literature refers to a Jewish law court in any city. According to rabbinic literature, in Jerusalem there were two courts: the "great Sanhedrin" of seventy-one members and a lesser Sanhedrin of twenty-three members (m. Sanhedrin 1:6).[93] There is a large section of t. Sanhedrin that deals with capital punishment. The seven exegetical rules of Hillel the Elder, which in context are seven modes of arguing at court, are found in t. Sanhedrin 7:11.

In m. Sanhedrin 10 there is a discussion concerning who will "have share in the world to come" (m. Sanhedrin 10:1). According to Cohen, "Not a single tractate in the Mishnah is devoted to a theological topic," and m. Sanhedrin 10 is "the lone chapter of the Mishnah that treats theological topics."[94] Cohen is probably overstating the case as to the uniqueness of m. Sanhedrin 10, but it is certainly true that m. Sanhedrin 10 and its exposition in t. Sanhedrin 12:9–14:11 are important for our topic. Also, this section of the Tosefta has many more quotations of the Old Testament than is usual.

---

90. Sanders, *Paul and Palestinian Judaism*, 130.
91. Sanders, *Paul and Palestinian Judaism*, 141–47.
92. For Gathercole's response to Sanders's view of t. Qiddushin 1:14, see *Where Is Boasting?*, 153–56. Gathercole's view is similar to mine.
93. Many doubt the historical accuracy of much of rabbinic literature's comments about the great Sanhedrin. So Anthony J. Saldarini, "Sanhedrin," in Freedman, *Anchor Bible Dictionary*, 5:975–80.
94. Shaye J. D. Cohen, *From the Maccabees to the Mishnah*, 2nd ed. (Louisville: Westminster John Knox, 2006), 212.

As to the question of works righteousness, below are three passages from t. Sanhedrin. The first shows an aspect of the gracious character of a judge in an arbitration case. The second and third passages relate to the eschatological question of who will enter the world to come. The second deals with Manasseh, and the third argues that there are three groups to consider.

t. Sanhedrin 1:3–4. The first quotation, t. Sanhedrin 1:3–4, is about arbitration as opposed to a normal judicial ruling:[95]

> And so it says in the case of David, "And David acted with judgment and charity to all his people" [2 Sam. 8:15]. Now is it not so that in any case in which there is judgment, there is no charity, and in any case in which there is charity, there is no judgment? So what is the judgment in which there also is charity? You have to say, This is arbitration.
>
> If one has judged a case, declaring the guiltless to be guiltless, and imposing liability on the guilty party, if one then has imposed liability on a poor man, he takes the necessary funds out of his own pocket and gives it to him. That is how he turns out to do charity with this one and true justice with that one.
>
> Rabbi says, "If one has judged a case, declaring the guiltless to be guiltless and imposing liability on the guilty party, he turns out to do charity with the one who is liable, for he removes the stolen goods from his possession. And he does justice to the innocent party, for he restores to him what belongs to him."

Second Samuel 8:15 states that David "administered justice and equity." The Hebrew behind "equity" is צדקה and is often translated in English Bibles as "righteousness." However, the rabbis often interpret this as righteous acts, preeminently, alms to the poor—hence the translation above that "David acted with judgment and *charity*." This then prompts the question of how a judge could act with both "judgment and charity" in an arbitration case. Two conflicting answers are given, with the first one being more mercy oriented.

An example is given of a poor man who has stolen goods. The first answer is that the judge should declare the poor man guilty and require him to pay restitution but that then the judge should also give the poor man money out of his own pocket—hence a merciful way to combine "judgment and charity."

The second answer is to take the money from the poor guilty man and give it to the innocent man. Taking money from the poor man is considered true charity. It is implied that charity should not be defined as giving alms to thieves.

I have included t. Sanhedrin 1:3–5 because I am assuming that the rabbis viewed some sense of continuity between their judgments and God's eschatological judgments. I note that this section includes both a very interesting "mercy" solution and also a straightforward judgment solution for how to combine "judgment and charity."

---

95. This is not discussed in the m. Sanhedrin. This section of the Tosefta is quoted in the Babylonian Talmud, but there is no further discussion of it (b. Sanhedrin 6b).

t. Sanhedrin 12:11. The second quotation, t. Sanhedrin 12:11, concerns the case of Manasseh:

> Four kings, Jeroboam, Ahab, Ahaz, and Manasseh have no portion in the world to come.
> Rabbi Judah says, "Manasseh has a portion in the world to come since it is said, 'His prayer also, and how God was entreated of him, and all his sin and his trespass, and the place wherein he built high places and set up the asherim and the graven images, before he humbled himself, behold they are written in the book of Hozeh' [2 Chron. 33:19]. This teaches that God accepted his prayer and brought him into the life of the world to come."

The Old Testament presents Manasseh as a very evil king (2 Kings 21:1–18; 23:26; 24:3; 2 Chron. 33:1–20). However, 2 Chronicles 33:12–13, 18–19 records that he repented through prayer. As can be seen from the above quotation, some believed that Manasseh would not have eschatological life, while Rabbi Judah believed he would. Rabbi Judah's argument is based explicitly on Manasseh's prayer of repentance that qualified him for eschatological life.

In the Mishnah parallel, m. Sanhedrin 10:2, both views of Manasseh are also given. A significant difference is that Rabbi Judah quotes 2 Chronicles 33:13, as opposed to 2 Chronicles 33:19. Because in 2 Chronicles 33:13 God restores Manasseh's "kingdom," an explicit rationale is given as to why Manasseh will not have eschatological life—the restoration relates only to his earthly kingdom, not to the world to come.[96]

The Babylonian Talmud parallel also acknowledges that the Tannaitic authorities disagree on Manasseh's fate (b. Sanhedrin 102b–103b). Additional arguments are included to buttress both sides of the debate. One argument for Manasseh receiving eschatological life is that he did not repent just one time but did so for twenty-three years (b. Sanhedrin 103a). This argument is based on supposed Tannaitic authority.

Clearly, some of the rabbis do not accept that Manasseh's repentance made him fit for eschatological life. Possibly they saw repentance as a work and believed that Manasseh did not perform enough works to overcome his evil deeds. Either way, this appears to be a problem for Sanders.

One of Sanders's primary arguments that his covenantal nomism is grace based is the "staying in" aspect of repentance:

> Repentance was the sovereign means of atonement. . . . Repentance is not a "status-achieving" activity by which one initially courts and wins the mercy of God. It is a "status-maintaining" or "status-restoring" attitude which indicates that one intends to remain in the covenant. . . . Obedience is rewarded and disobedience punished. In case of failure to obey, however, man has recourse to divinely ordained means of atonement.[97]

What does Sanders do with these discussions in the Mishnah, Tosefta, and the Babylonian Talmud, in which at least some rabbis deny eschatological life to the repentant

---

96. Another difference is that the Mishnah parallel has only three kings; Ahaz is left out.
97. Sanders, *Paul and Palestinian Judaism*, 180, 178.

Manasseh? He cannot say that they are Amoraic rabbis (AD 225–500), because virtually all these sources refer to Tannaitic rabbis (50 BC–AD 200). Sanders simply admits that this is an "exception to the rule that repentance atones."[98] Given the importance of this tractate as one of the few that has a sustained discussion of who will be in the world to come, this response appears inadequate.

t. Sanhedrin 13:2–4. Now to the third quotation, t. Sanhedrin 13:2–4 (italics added):

> Rabbi Eliezer says, "None of the gentiles has a portion in the world to come, as it is said, 'The wicked shall return to Sheol, all the gentiles who forget God' [Ps. 9:17]. The wicked shall return to Sheol—these are the wicked Israelites" [implying that the "wicked" in Ps. 9:17 refers to Jews and that Gentiles in Ps. 9:17 are Gentiles].
>
> Said to him Rabbi Joshua, "If it had been written, 'The wicked shall return to Sheol—all the gentiles' [Ps. 9:17], and then said nothing further, I should have maintained as you do. Now that it is in fact written, 'All the gentiles who forget God' [Ps. 9:17], it indicates that there are also righteous people among the nations of the world, who do have a portion in the world to come."
>
> The House of Shammai says, *"There are three groups, one for eternal life, one 'for shame and everlasting contempt' [Dan. 12:2]—those who are completely evil. An intermediate group [evenly balanced][99] go down to Gehenna and scream and come up again and are healed. As it is said, I will bring the third part through fire and will refine them as silver is refined and will test them as gold is tested, and they shall call on my name and I will be their God* [Zech. 13:9]. *And concerning them did Hannah say, 'The Lord kills and brings to life, brings down to Sheol and brings up'"* [1 Sam. 2:6].
>
> And the House of Hillel say, "'Great in mercy' [Ex. 34:6]—He inclines the decision toward mercy, and concerning them David said, 'I am happy that the Lord has heard the sound of my prayer' [Ps. 116:1], and concerning them is said the entire passage."
>
> The Israelites who sinned with their bodies and gentiles who sinned with their bodies go down to Gehenna and are judged there for twelve months. And after twelve months their souls perish, their bodies are burned, Gehenna absorbs them, and they are turned to dirt.

This quotation concerns the eschatological judgment of the three groups.[100] To give some context, both the Mishnah and the Tosefta note many who will *not* have eschatological life. These include Gentiles, various evil Jewish kings, inhabitants of apostate towns, men of Sodom, Balaam, Doeg, Ahitophel, Gehazi, the flood generation, Epicureans, minors of wicked parents (only in the Tosefta), those who deny the resurrection of the dead, those who deny that the Torah is from heaven, those who pronounce the

---

98. Sanders, *Paul and Palestinian Judaism*, 180. Other exceptions that Sanders notes include m. Abot 5:8; p. Hagigah 77b; Sifre Numbers 136.
99. A more mechanical translation for "intermediate group" is "evenly balanced." Sanders agrees with this translation. *Paul and Palestinian Judaism*, 142.
100. The three groups are not discussed in m. Sanhedrin or b. Sanhedrin.

divine name as it is spelled out, and the ten tribes who did not return (m. Sanhedrin 10:1–4; t. Sanhedrin 12:9–14:3).

Before getting to the three groups, Rabbi Eliezer and Rabbi Joshua disagree. Rabbi Eliezer believes, based on Psalm 9:17, that no Gentiles will have eschatological life. Rabbi Joshua disagrees, because Psalm 9:17 mentions not simply Gentiles but "all the gentiles *who forget God*" (italics added). Therefore, there are some righteous Gentiles who did not forget God.

The house of Shammai argues for three groups related to eschatological judgment: (1) the one with "eternal life," (2) the one destined to "everlasting contempt," and (3) the intermediate one that is "evenly balanced." The intermediate, evenly balanced group goes "down" to Gehenna for a time to be "refine[d]" (Zech. 13:9). Then the Lord will "raise up" those in this group to the world to come (1 Sam. 2:6).

The house of Hillel notes that God "inclines the decision toward mercy." I assume that the house of Hillel is speaking of the evenly balanced group. They are "on the fence," but God decides toward eschatological life. Possibly, the difference with the house of Shammai is that this group does not have to go to Gehenna for a while and may go straight to eschatological life.

The quoted passage above ends by describing both Israelites and Gentiles who have "sinned with their bodies." They go to Gehenna for twelve months, and then after being burned, they are turned into dirt. These are obviously part of the "everlasting contempt" group.

The above quotation presents two problems for Sanders: (1) Gentiles receiving eschatological life and (2) the three groups. The first problem concerns Gentiles who receive eschatological life. They are not in the covenant. Hence, on what basis do they "get in," "stay in," and pass the final judgment? Apparently, it is their righteous deeds. On the surface of it, Sanders cannot assume that their "getting in" comes through a gracious election by means of the covenant. Sanders agrees that the righteous Gentiles are a problem for him, especially our passage in t. Sanhedrin.[101] For those rabbinic passages confirming that Gentiles may receive eschatological life, Sanders admits that it would be on the basis of them being "kind and charitable" and would be limited to those "who did not transgress any of the principal prohibitions of Judaism."[102] Since the covenantal nomism is so strong, it shows that the situation of righteous Gentiles "did not, however, lead to a fundamental re-thinking of the soteriology that applied to the members of the covenant, and the Gentiles are not systematically worked into Rabbinic" soteriology.[103] To solve his "Gentile problem," Sanders again reverts to his standard explanation that the rabbis were not systematic.

The second problem has to do with the logic of the three ways. For the house of Shammai and the house of Hillel, eschatological life for the intermediate, evenly balanced group is based on the weighing of their good and evil deeds. This produces no

---
101. Sanders, *Paul and Palestinian Judaism*, 206–12, esp. 209.
102. Sanders, *Paul and Palestinian Judaism*, 211.
103. Sanders, *Paul and Palestinian Judaism*, 212.

preponderance in either direction. But God does eventually refine them in Gehenna (house of Shammai option) and does give them eschatological life (both houses). This evenly balanced group is reminiscent of Testament of Abraham A 14:1–8 (see above discussion, p. 153). Once given that the intermediate group gains eschatological life by a weighing of good and evil deeds, it is then further implied that the good group also gains eschatological life by an overwhelming amount of good deeds. This discussion of the intermediate group in t. Sanhedrin is a clear example of works-righteousness soteriology.

Sanders directly addresses this problem also. He turns my argument on its head. He notes that those in the intermediate group do get eschatological life and that it is only the "whole-heartedly wicked" that do not. Hence, "the righteous are not the sinless, but those who confirm the covenant."[104] I might respond that the immediately preceding verses concern righteous Gentiles whom he admits do not have a covenant. Why bring the covenant in here? Also, how is the intermediate group distinguished from the good group? Is it not by the weighing of good and evil deeds?

From my perspective, t. Sanhedrin overall includes a variety of views. It certainly includes works-righteousness views. I have presented Sanders's three arguments:

1. Rabbis' not allowing for Manasseh's repentance was just an exception to the rule.
2. Righteous Gentiles who were not in the covenant is another example of non-systematic rabbinic thought.
3. The existence of an intermediate somewhat sinful group that receives eschatological life shows that rabbinic soteriology was gracious.

I am not convinced by these arguments.

However, I do find the possibility of some more gracious aspects set alongside works righteousness. The example of the judge who shows charity and the rabbis who accept Manasseh's repentance show more of the possibility of a grace system, although not clearly so. Having conflicting soteriological systems existing in rabbinic literature appears to fit the data better than Sanders's supposed one-size-fits-all grace system. Still, I must say, the eschatological sections in the Mishnah and Tosefta for tractate Sanhedrin are significantly oriented toward works righteousness.

Conclusion

Sanders argues that Second Temple Judaism was uniformly a grace soteriology; it was uniformly *not* works-righteousness oriented. His view began a reevaluation of Paul in New Testament scholarship that resulted in, among other things, the New Perspective on Paul and its denial of the Reformational view of justification.

Although not all Jews in the first century AD were works-righteousness oriented, I believe that many documents in Second Temple Judaism clearly show that a works-righteousness soteriology existed (either Pelagian or semi-Pelagian). Above, I have

---

104. Sanders, *Paul and Palestinian Judaism*, 142–43.

discussed two apocryphal works (4 Ezra and Sirach), three works from the Old Testament Pseudepigrapha (2 Baruch, Testament of Abraham, Psalms of Solomon), three documents from the Dead Sea Scrolls (Rule of the Community, Pesher Habakkuk, Miqsat Ma'ase Ha-Torah), and four rabbinic tractates (m. Abot, m. Sotah, t. Qiddushin, t. Sanhedrin). In several of these discussions, I have also given Sanders's explanations and my counterexplanations.

Given my conclusions, the soteriology in these works dovetails well with the Reformational view that Paul considers "works" and "works of the law" as terms designating a works-righteousness soteriology that existed in first-century Judaism and at various times throughout the history of Israel.

Recommended Resources

Bauckham, Richard. *The Jewish World around the New Testament*. Grand Rapids, MI: Baker Academic, 2010.

Cara, Robert J. *Cracking the Foundation of the New Perspective on Paul: Covenantal Nomism versus Reformed Covenantal Theology*. Reformed, Exegetical and Doctrinal Studies. Fearn, Ross-shire, Scotland: Mentor, 2017.

Carson, D. A., Peter T. O'Brien, and Mark A. Seifrid, eds. *Justification and Variegated Nomism*. Vol. 1, *The Complexities of Second Temple Judaism*. Wissenschaftliche Untersuchungen zum Neuen Testament, 2nd ser., vol. 140. Grand Rapids, MI: Baker Academic, 2001.

Chapman, David W., and Andreas J. Köstenberger. "Jewish Intertestamental and Early Rabbinic Literature: An Annotated Bibliographic Resource Updated (Part 1)." *JETS* 55, no. 2 (2012): 235–72.

———. "Jewish Intertestamental and Early Rabbinic Literature: An Annotated Bibliographic Resource Updated (Part 2)." *JETS* 55, no. 3 (2012): 457–88.

Cohen, Shaye J. D. *From the Maccabees to the Mishnah*. 2nd ed. Louisville: Westminster John Knox, 2006.

Collins, John J., and Daniel C. Harlow. *Early Judaism: A Comprehensive Overview*. Grand Rapids, MI: Eerdmans, 2012.

DeSilva, David A. *Introducing the Apocrypha: Message, Context, and Significance*. Grand Rapids, MI: Baker Academic, 2002.

Evans, Craig A. *Noncanonical Writings and New Testament Interpretation*. Peabody, MA: Hendrickson, 1992.

Gathercole, Simon J. *Where Is Boasting? Early Jewish Soteriology and Paul's Response in Romans 1–5*. Grand Rapids, MI: Eerdmans, 2002.

Helyer, Larry R. *Exploring Jewish Literature of the Second Temple Period: A Guide for New Testament Students*. Downers Grove, IL: InterVarsity Press, 2002.

Moore, George Foot. "Christian Writers on Judaism." *Harvard Theological Review* 14, no. 3 (1921): 197–254.

Neusner, Jacob. *Rabbinic Literature: An Essential Guide*. Nashville: Abingdon, 2005.

Nickelsburg, George W. E. *Ancient Judaism and Christian Origins: Diversity, Continuity, and Transformation.* Minneapolis: Fortress, 2003.

Sanders, E. P. *Paul and Palestinian Judaism: A Comparison of Patterns of Religion.* Minneapolis: Fortress, 1977.

Smith, Barry D. *What Must I Do to Be Saved? Paul Parts Company with His Jewish Heritage.* New Testament Monographs 17. Sheffield: Sheffield Phoenix, 2007.

Sprinkle, Preston. *Paul and Judaism Revisited: A Study of Divine and Human Agency in Salvation.* Downers Grove, IL: IVP Academic, 2013.

VanLandingham, Chris. *Judgment and Justification in Early Judaism and the Apostle Paul.* Peabody, MA: Hendrickson, 2006.

5

What Does Justification Have to Do with the Gospels?

BRIAN VICKERS

What do the Gospels have to do with justification? Based on the occurrences of the word "justification" in the Gospels, particularly in comparison to Paul, one might answer, "Not much." Counting words, however, doesn't always prove a great deal. For instance, one might conclude, as some scholars continue to do, that the kingdom of God is not a central theme in Paul, especially in comparison to the Gospels.[1] It is not the case, however, that the kingdom is less important or less central to Paul than to the Gospel writers. He just speaks of it differently. Besides the explicit occurrences of "kingdom" in Paul, there is the foundational idea that the risen Jesus ascended to the throne and now rules and reigns as king. For instance, when Paul speaks of Jesus as seated at God's right hand (Rom. 8:34; Eph. 1:20; Col. 3:1), of Jesus in relation to David (Rom. 1:3; 15:12; 2 Tim. 2:8), or of Jesus's rule and authority both now and as revealed fully in the future (1 Cor. 15:24; Eph. 1:21; Col. 2:10), he is speaking of the kingdom. Read together, the Gospels and Paul, not to mention the rest of the New Testament, expand and deepen our understanding of the kingdom. The same is true with justification. While the Gospel writers may not use the word "justification" often, the central salvation themes in their narratives of Jesus intersect justification at multiple points. Themes such as repentance, obedience, forgiveness, cleansing, abiding, and, of course, faith and believing permeate their narratives. In this chapter I don't wish to explore simply how the Gospel writers teach justification—though I will do that—but how the words and works of Jesus in the Gospels complement, broaden, and, most importantly, display the doctrine of justification by faith.

---

1. There are fourteen explicit occurrences of "kingdom" spread throughout most of Paul's letters (Rom. 14:17; 1 Cor. 4:20; 6:9, 10; 15:24, 50; Gal. 5:21; Eph. 5:5; Col. 1:13; 4:11; 1 Thess. 2:12; 2 Thess. 1:5; 2 Tim. 4:1, 18).

The Gospel of Matthew: A Greater Righteousness

Righteousness in the Sermon on the Mount

In Matthew, Jesus calls for a greater righteousness in contrast to the scribes and Pharisees. In the context, Jesus proclaims himself as the fulfillment of the Mosaic Law and the Prophets, the goal to which they pointed (Matt. 5:17). He follows that assertion by warning anyone who "relaxes one of the least of these commandments" and commending those who do and teach them (5:19). The commands here refer to Jesus's teaching in the Sermon on the Mount. He is refocusing obedience on himself, the fulfillment of the law, and his teaching. Rejecting Jesus's teaching results in being "the least in the kingdom," while embracing it results in becoming "great in the kingdom" (5:19). "Least" and "great" are not rankings in the kingdom. One is either in ("great") or out ("least"), and membership is based solely on allegiance to Jesus. In fulfilling the law—bringing it to its appointed end—Jesus isn't offering a new take on the Mosaic law but is bringing the underlying core emphasis—namely, heart obedience—fully to the surface. Obedience from the heart was the intention all along (Deut. 10:16; 30:6).[2] Against this backdrop, Jesus makes a statement that must have been even more jarring in that day than now: "For I tell you, unless your righteousness exceeds that of the scribes and the Pharisees, you will never enter the kingdom of heaven" (Matt. 5:20).

The righteousness in 5:20 cannot be measured on, say, a scale of one to ten, with ten being the greatest. So Jesus is not saying, "The righteousness of the scribes and Pharisees is a three but you need at least an eight or higher, and ideally a ten." The greater righteousness is not a matter of degree. Jesus does not command *more* righteousness but a different sort of righteousness. As R. T. France puts it, "Jesus is not talking about beating the scribes and Pharisees at their own game, but about a different level or concept of righteousness altogether."[3] The "righteousness" of the scribes and Pharisees, then, turns out to be no righteousness at all—it is false righteousness. This is precisely in keeping with "least in the kingdom of heaven" referring to exclusion from the kingdom rather than to just the lowliest members. It is righteousness based on a certain commitment to keep commandments and traditions, but it rejects the commands of Jesus and misses the true righteousness, the kind Jesus teaches, that flows from the heart (e.g., 5:21–22, 27–28).

What, then, is this exceeding righteousness? Answers are readily at hand in the sermon itself. It is the righteousness that comes from God, who fills those who "hunger and thirst" for it (5:6). It is God's righteousness, which, along with his kingdom, Jesus commands his disciples to seek (6:33). It is a righteousness founded on hearing and obeying Jesus's teaching, "like a wise man who built his house on the rock" (7:24). To

---

2. See the discussion on these texts as background for the Sermon on the Mount below.
3. R. T. France, *The Gospel of Matthew*, NICNT (Grand Rapids, MI: Eerdmans, 2007), 189. Charles Quarles, who also cites the comment from France, gives in insightful summary argument against the quantitative view held by Ulrich Luz and by W. D. Davies and D. C. Allison. Charles Quarles, *Sermon on the Mount: Restoring Christ's Message to the Modern Church*, NAC Studies in Bible and Theology (Nashville: B&H Academic, 2011), 102–3; Ulrich Luz, *Matthew: A Commentary*, Hermeneia (Minneapolis: Fortress, 2001), 1:221; W. D. Davies and D. C. Allison, *A Critical and Exegetical Commentary on the Gospel according to Saint Matthew*, ICC (London: T&T Clark, 2004), 1:500.

those things we can add that it's Christian obedience from the heart; it's what characterizes the true people of God who believe in and follow Jesus; it's the righteousness that the law pointed to but didn't provide—and any number of biblically and theologically sound statements about righteousness. Those statements, however much they *describe* righteousness in Matthew, still leave questions: What is the source of the greater righteousness? What is the righteousness that we must seek? The best, first reply is that those questions aren't Jesus's (or Matthew's) questions.[4] We shouldn't begin by seeking to harmonize Matthew to Paul, or vice versa, for doing so guarantees that we will skip over Matthew's authorial intention. At some point, however, after describing the ethical and moral heart righteousness of the Sermon on the Mount, after pointing out all the differences between the righteousness Jesus teaches and commands and that of the scribes and Pharisees, there is still a question of *how*. How do Jesus's followers act on Jesus's teaching? How do we attain that exceeding righteousness? Even if it's not Matthew's question, it is still a question that Bible readers and preachers can, and should, ask. Another way to ask this is, How do we read Matthew theologically in the larger New Testament context?

As nearly everyone speaking or writing about the Sermon on the Mount points out, the righteousness in view is not a forensic (legal) declaration of righteousness.[5] In other words, it is not a declared, legal status through faith in Christ as found in Paul's letters (e.g., Rom. 3:24; Gal. 2:15–16; Phil. 3:9; Titus 3:7); it is not righteousness imputed to us by faith (Rom. 4:3–5); it is not the righteousness we have in union with Christ, the sacrifice for our sins (2 Cor. 5:21); and it is not the righteousness grounded in the obedience of Christ, the second Adam (Rom. 5:18–19).[6] The term "righteousness" (δικαιοσυνη) appears seven times in Matthew (3:15; 5:6, 10, 20; 6:1, 33; 21:32) and refers to ethical behavior, doing what is right.[7] More specifically, righteousness is doing what is right in the eyes of God. When teaching and preaching from Matthew, it will not do simply to say that "the greater righteousness is the imputed righteousness of Christ" and ignore the context of righteousness in Matthew. At the same time, if we preach the Sermon on the Mount and never address the question of *how*, then we end up with a message that conflicts theologically with other parts of Scripture, or, perhaps worse, makes obeying God's commands all the more impossible, or creates an aberrant, new covenant version of the righteousness of the scribes and Pharisees.

---

4. As Carson rightly points out with regard to Matt. 5:20, "Verse 20 does not establish how the righteousness is to be gained, developed, or empowered; it simply lays out the demand." D. A. Carson, *Matthew*, in *Matthew, Mark, Luke*, vol. 8 of *The Expositors Bible Commentary*, ed. Frank E. Gaebelein (Grand Rapids, MI: Zondervan, 1984), 147.

5. Charles Lee Irons, *The Righteousness of God: A Lexical Examination of the Covenant-Faithfulness Interpretation*, WUNT, 2nd ser., vol. 386 (Tübingen: Mohr Siebeck, 2015), 266; Quarles, *Sermon on the Mount*, 101.

6. Obviously, these aspects of justification in Paul overlap and are interconnected. The point here is simply to distinguish the various emphases of these justification texts in contrast to the emphasis on ethical righteousness in Matthew.

7. See the helpful discussion of righteousness in the Sermon on the Mount in Jonathan T. Pennington, *The Sermon on the Mount and Human Flourishing: A Theological Commentary* (Grand Rapids, MI: Baker, 2017), 87–91. He defines "righteousness" in Matthew as "*whole-person behavior that accords with God's nature, will, and coming kingdom*. The 'righteous' person, according to Matthew, is one who follows Jesus in this way of being in the world. The righteous person is the *whole/telios* person (5:48) who does not only do the will of God externally but, most importantly, from the heart." Pennington, *Sermon on the Mount*, 91; italics original.

If it's not just a matter of outdoing the scribes and Pharisees, how can one hope to attain this sort of righteousness? I can well imagine listening to Jesus and thinking, "This sounds great, but how in the world am I going to do this? Even if I don't murder or commit adultery, what happens when I feel hatred or lust? And how am I going to love my enemies (5:44) and turn my cheek when someone hits me (5:39)?"[8] That's not a far-fetched way to take the sermon. Over the course of church history, readers have interpreted it in just that way—the sermon only amplifies, by its emphasis on the heart, our inability to obey God. Like the law but even more so, it will drive us to Jesus and the gospel. While there is something valid to that idea, it does not capture the full intent or character of the sermon, and even less the message of Matthew's Gospel generally. The answer lies in the sermon itself, for in it Jesus directs his hearers to trust in God (6:25–34) and to come before him simply, in childlike fashion, asking him for everything with the expectation that he will certainly provide (7:7–8). Hungering and thirsting for righteousness (5:6) connects to asking, seeking, and knocking. In other words, the greater righteousness is tied inextricably to faith. Those who believe will be filled with the exceeding righteousness (5:6). This filling, moreover, will show itself in obedience to Jesus's teaching—righteousness will be evident, is itself evidence, in the lives of those who follow him. As Jesus says, "Every healthy tree bears good fruit" (7:17).

Two Horizons

Concerning the question of justification, the two contexts of Matthew come into consideration. On the one hand, there is the original context—the life and ministry of Jesus. When Jesus sits down on the mountainside and begins the Beatitudes (Matt. 5:1–10), he is in the midst of inaugurating the kingdom, fulfilling the long-awaited promises of God; he's announcing the kingdom (4:17). In that context there is no question raised about how uncircumcised Gentiles can be part of God's people,[9] no discussion of who receives the Spirit, no occasion to declare God's justifying verdict on all who believe and trust in Jesus as Savior. The groundwork for what's to come later, however, is there. Faith in God, trust in his promises, true obedience from the heart, and righteousness as evidence of following Jesus are all in view. Historically speaking, Jesus's teaching in Matthew, as in all the Gospels, opens the way to the teaching of the apostles after the resurrection.

On the other hand, Matthew's Gospel appears in a much different setting than the life and ministry of Jesus. In order to read, teach, and preach Matthew faithfully, we must be mindful of that context.

---

8. As Carson notes, "Just as the beatitudes make poverty of spirit a necessary condition for entrance into the kingdom, so Matt 5:17–20 end up demanding a kind of righteousness which must have left Jesus' hearers gasping in dismay and conscious of their own spiritual bankruptcy." D. A. Carson, *The Sermon on the Mount: An Evangelical Exposition of Matthew 5–7* (Grand Rapids, MI: Baker, 1982), 39.

9. I am not implying that justification arose only because of the controversy over the inclusion of the Gentiles in the early church, but the controversy did give a sharper focus to the doctrine in an instrumental sense. See "A Gospel to the Gentiles: Connecting Luke and Acts," in my discussion of Luke (p. 201).

Reading in Matthew's Context

By the time Matthew writes, the controversy over the inclusion of the Gentiles was long-standing. The event that caused such an uproar in Acts—namely, Gentiles believing and receiving the Spirit (Acts 10–11) and the apostles responding agreeably (Acts 15)—already had a substantial history. Paul had already written to the Galatians and the Philippians dealing with the issue of justification by faith alone apart from circumcision, law keeping generally, and ethnicity. Matthew reflects this new context.[10]

We typically associate Matthew's Gospel with Jewish Christians as the primary audience. Matthew emphasizes Jesus as the Messiah, the fulfillment of God's promise to Abraham, but a major part of that message is that the Gentiles are part of God's people too. One of Matthew's central themes is *"the redefinition of the people of God as based on faith-response to Jesus rather than ethnicity."*[11] Right from the outset, Gentiles are included in Jesus's genealogy (Matt. 1:1–17), the Gentile wise men are contrasted with Jews in Jerusalem (2:1–12), and John the Baptist declares that God can make descendants of Abraham from stones quite apart from ethnic lineage (3:7–12). These texts provide a theological foundation for what's to come in Matthew. Later, in contrast to unbelief among most Jews, Jesus commends a Roman centurion for his faith and declares that Gentiles ("many . . . from east and west") will join the Jewish forefathers in the kingdom, even as unfaithful Jews will be condemned (8:10–12). The infamous Gentile sinners of Tyre, Sidon, and Sodom will have an easier time than those from Israelite towns who reject God's work in Jesus (11:20–24).[12] A believing Syrophoenician woman is set in contrast to unbelieving scribes and Pharisees (15:1–28). The capstone of this theme comes later in a warning that "the kingdom of God will be taken away from you and given to a people producing its fruits" (21:43).

Matthew, like Paul, is not making a case that the Gentiles are included just for being Gentiles. The point is that the people of God, regardless of ethnicity, are those who identify with Jesus, that is, believe in him. This emphasis is not created by Matthew for his own context, it began in the historical context of Jesus. Matthew does, however, spotlight this Gentile inclusion theme as a major part of his Gospel, and we can assume that it's more than just a report of history—it also fits his church context. As such, it fits right in with the emphasis so often repeated in Paul. The gospel is "to the Jew first and also to the Greek" (Rom. 1:16); God is not only the God of the Jews, but "of Gentiles also" (3:29); for the sake of his glory, God called both Jews and Gentiles (9:24–25). The shared church context that reflects these common themes is nowhere more evident than in Galatians 3:28–29: "There is neither Jew nor Greek, there is neither slave nor free, there is no male and female, for you are all one in Christ

---

10. Romans does too, but I think the occasion of Romans, though shaped by Paul's past experience with the controversy, is far broader than the inclusion issue.
11. Pennington, *Sermon on the Mount*, 95; italics original. Pennington provides a list of examples showing that the theme of the inclusion of the Gentiles permeates Matthew. The examples provided here are taken from his list.
12. By "easier time," I don't mean that the text implies they will be saved. The point is to compare these famously sinful pagan cities with the unfaithfulness among the Jews. The inhabitants of Chorazin, Bethsaida, and Capernaum will, as a result of their rejection of Jesus, face the same sort of judgment as the pagans. Their ethnicity and lineage will not save them.

Jesus. And if you are Christ's, then you are Abraham's offspring, heirs according to promise." Reading Matthew in his own context provides connections to the rest of the New Testament that are neither strained nor simply inferences drawn from particular strains of Protestant systematic theology.

New Covenant Righteousness

The heart righteousness Jesus calls for in Matthew is part and parcel of the new covenant. Of course, the original, historical context is vital, but we must remember that the only access we have to the historical event is through Matthew's writing. The Sermon on the Mount, in its literary context, is fully situated in the time and context of the fulfillment of the new covenant promises. There is, furthermore, a canonical consideration. Once the Gospel of Matthew is put together with the rest of the biblical canon (encompassing the Old and New Testaments), it has a new context that is as essential as the historical setting and as Matthew's own setting.

The Sermon on the Mount is, for anyone living beyond the life setting of Jesus, a sermon for the new covenant community. It is instruction for and explication of life in the new covenant. It is how the people of God, those who believe in Jesus Christ for the forgiveness of sins and who have received the Holy Spirit, should live. Not that it's a comprehensive guide for every circumstance or a *how-to manual* for Christian living, but rather, it shows the reality of living in the age of the fulfillment of God's promises in Christ. It is a sermon for people with the new covenant heart promised in Jeremiah 31:33. The new covenant will not be written externally on stone tablets: "For this is the covenant that I will make with the house of Israel after those days, declares the Lord: I will put my law within them, and I will write it on their hearts. And I will be their God, and they shall be my people."

The heart promised in the new covenant is inseparable from the promise of the Spirit, just as Ezekiel prophesied:

> I will sprinkle clean water on you, and you shall be clean from all your uncleannesses, and from all your idols I will cleanse you. And I will give you a new heart, and a new spirit I will put within you. And I will remove the heart of stone from your flesh and give you a heart of flesh. And I will put my Spirit within you, and cause you to walk in my statutes and be careful to obey my rules. (Ezek. 36:25–27)

Note in both places the new heart that leads to obedience to God's commands. The prophets pick up on the promise God made to Israel long before. In Deuteronomy 10, after recounting their sin and unfaithfulness, God tells the people what they need to do in order to obey him: "Circumcise therefore the foreskin of your heart, and be no longer stubborn" (Deut. 10:16). Circumcision all along pointed to something else, namely, a new heart.

How can they, given their track record of disobedience to God's law, attain the new heart God commands? Certainly not by simply doing a better job at keeping the law, just as a righteousness that exceeds that of the scribes and Pharisees is not attained by trying harder. The answer comes later in Deuteronomy: "And the Lord your God will circumcise your heart and the heart of your offspring, so that you will love the Lord your God with all your heart and with all your soul, that you may live" (Deut. 30:6). Just as in Jeremiah and Ezekiel (who have Deuteronomy as their foundation), the new heart is the source for obedience. God promises to provide the means, a new heart, for faithfulness and obedience. This is the biblical background for understanding how Jesus could demand a righteousness greater than the scribes and Pharisees and do so with the expectation that his followers could attain such righteousness. Such a reading fits well with the New Testament Epistles.

Righteousness as Evidence of the "Righteous"
Paul's teaching in Romans 6 is a counterpart to Matthew's idea of righteousness. There Paul turns to the issue of how the justified, those declared righteous by faith in Jesus, will *be* righteous. The verdict of justification creates people who do righteousness from the heart. Justification by faith (Rom. 3:21–31) follows Paul's presentation of God's case against both Gentiles and Jews (1:18–3:20). Justification by faith is not Paul's invention but was established with Abraham, whom God counted righteous apart from works (4:1–5). The foundation for the verdict of "righteous," the source of righteousness, is the obedience of Jesus, the true Adam (5:12–21). Heading off a possible misunderstanding of his teaching, Paul shows that justification by faith apart from works is the only foundation for doing righteousness. Having been justified, believers are now able to do the thing they could never do before—choose obedience over sin (6:12–13). In other words, it is justification by faith, being declared righteous by God, that is *the* foundation for doing righteousness. Those declared righteous will be righteous. Former slaves to sin, now justified by faith in Christ, "have become obedient from the heart to the standard of teaching to which you were committed" (6:17). Looking ahead to Romans 8, it is the Spirit who will enable this obedience, "in order that the righteous requirement of the law might be fulfilled in us, who walk not according to the flesh but according to the Spirit" (8:4).

The point here is not that Paul explains what's missing in Matthew or that he fills in the gaps Matthew missed. Reading them together does not diminish the necessary ethical righteousness of Matthew any more than Romans 3–5 diminishes Paul's teaching in Romans 6. When we read them together, taking their shared canonical context into consideration, we have a greater and God-given biblical and theological framework for preaching and teaching both Matthew and Paul.

God's Righteousness
God's righteousness in Matthew 6:33 is not synonymous with the "righteousness of God" found so often in Paul. For Paul, it is God's saving and judging righteousness in Christ that provides the foundation for the declaration of righteousness in Christ, that is, justification. Thus, seeking God's righteousness means embracing Jesus and

his teaching. He is, in that sense, God's righteousness. The point is that in Matthew, righteousness is not purely a matter of ethics, not simply doing, but is grounded in Jesus himself and his kingdom.[13] In Matthew, as in the rest of the Scripture, there is no righteousness apart from Christ, for "this righteousness is not possible without Jesus."[14]

Finally, we must read the Sermon on the Mount in light of the climax of Matthew's Gospel, namely, the death and resurrection of Jesus. In other words, the "righteousness" of Matthew 5:20 appears in the context of redemption.[15] If we practically separate the Sermon on the Mount from the passion narrative, we risk disconnecting ethics from the cross. In addition, though the context of Matthew has first priority for interpretation, the larger New Testament teaching must be considered. Matthew, like the rest of the New Testament, should also be interpreted within its canonical context. Doing so does not mean that we are bound inevitably to flatten out individual texts simply into broad theological themes. It is possible, after all, to take the broader New Testament teaching on righteousness and justification into consideration without neutering the very real warning that there is no entrance into the kingdom of heaven apart from the righteousness Jesus teaches in the Sermon on the Mount. The New Testament, indeed, upholds that very idea, for "the unrighteous will not inherit the kingdom of God" (1 Cor. 6:9; see also 6:10; Gal. 5:21; Eph. 5:5).

Mark: Faith in the King Who Forgives and Atones

In Mark 1:15, Jesus enters Galilee with a statement that is both programmatic of and a summary of his entire ministry: "The time is fulfilled, and the kingdom of God is at hand; repent and believe in the gospel." The kingdom of God is *the* controlling theme in Mark. Jesus not only proclaims and teaches the kingdom (4:1–32) but also shows the kingdom by healing the sick (1:34), casting out demons (1:32, 34), and calming a storm (4:39). In all these things, Jesus displays his dominion over everything.

One thing that is not, however, an explicit part of Jesus's kingdom ministry in Mark is justification by faith—especially if we look only for Pauline terms. As in the other Gospels (Luke 18 being the closest thing to an exception), Mark does not articulate the doctrine of justification by faith in Pauline fashion. That's hardly surprising given that Paul didn't write the Gospel of Mark. On the other hand, key elements of Jesus's kingdom ministry in Mark are not only compatible with but are central to justification, which is itself central to God's larger work of salvation. Mark tells his story of how Jesus the King brought God's promised salvation. Faith, forgiveness, and atonement—all major themes in New Testament soteriology and therefore themes connected to

---

13. This is what Roland Deines refers to as "Jesus-righteousness." Deines, "Not the Law but the Messiah: Law and Righteousness in the Gospel of Matthew—An Ongoing Debate," in *Built upon the Rock: Studies in the Gospel of Matthew*, ed. Daniel M. Gurtner and John Nolland (Grand Rapids, MI: Eerdmans, 2008), 81. I'm grateful to Mark A. Seifrid, who directed me to Deines's essay. The work most often cited by Matthew scholars is Deines's larger work on Matthew, *Die Gerechtigkeit der Tora im Reich des Messias: Mt 5,13–20 als Schlüsseltext der matthäischen Theologie*, WUNT 177 (Tübingen: Mohr Siebeck, 2004).
14. Deines, "Not the Law but the Messiah," 81.
15. The same can and should be said of all the Gospels. The passion narrative in each Gospel is the climactic event for all the Evangelists. Whatever their various emphases on Jesus's life and ministry, including righteousness in Matthew, they are already taking place in the larger context of redemption.

justification—are central to that story. In Mark, people with no hope come to Jesus for help and healing, and he accepts them. He heals and forgives them, regardless of their sinful past, their background, ethnicity, or their works of any kind. The weak and the sick, all those who cannot help themselves, are welcome in Jesus's kingdom. In his kingdom, those who are least in the eyes of the world and in their own estimation are the greatest. Full membership is based on one thing alone, faith in Jesus the King, who came specifically "to give his life as a ransom for many" (Mark 10:45).

Not the Righteous but Sinners

When they notice that Jesus makes a habit of eating with the wrong sorts of people, the scribes of the Pharisees ask his disciples, "Why does he eat with tax collectors and sinners?" (Mark 2:16). Jesus, not the disciples, has the answer: "Those who are well have no need of a physician, but those who are sick. I came not to call the righteous, but sinners" (2:17). The key to understanding that verse is to see first how Mark fills out the meaning through examples. Mark does not so much *say* who are the sinners and righteous, he *shows* them in his story.

Repentance

Forgiveness of sins is fundamental to the message of Mark.[16] The Gospel begins with John the Baptist "proclaiming a baptism of repentance for the forgiveness of sins" (Mark 1:4). Right after that, we read Mark's first recorded words of Jesus: "Repent and believe in the gospel" (1:15). The proclamation of the kingdom, which is the proclamation of the gospel, has repentance at its core. Jesus's call for repentance, like John's baptism, carries with it three easily understood implications. First, it is a call to sinners to turn from their sin. Only sinners need to repent. Apart from sin, there is no need for repentance. Second, repentance implies guilt, and guilt implies judgment. Third, the proclamation implicitly offers forgiveness to those who repent. The good news of the kingdom is that the King has come to fulfill God's kingdom promises, and saving his people from sin is top priority.

Wholeness and Forgiveness

Like the other Gospel writers, Mark firmly anchors John the Baptist's ministry in fulfillment of Isaiah 40:3: "Prepare the way of the Lord, make his paths straight" (Mark 1:3; cf. Matt. 3:3; Luke 3:4; John 1:23). It's not just the quote from Isaiah 40 but also the larger context in Isaiah that provides the backdrop for Mark.[17] Isaiah prophesies of a time when Yahweh will come to save his people. This salvation is linked not only to miraculous signs in the wilderness but also to healing:

---

16. As R. T. France puts it, "Jesus' mission, no less than John's baptism, is concerned with the ἄφεσις ἁμαρτιῶν. In the rest of the gospel this theme will not be explicit, but it has been laid down so clearly at the outset that the reader is expected to bear it in mind as the background against which to interpret the later statements of Jesus' purpose, in particular the λύτρον ἀντὶ πολλῶν of 10:45 and the words about the vicarious shedding of blood in 14:24." *The Gospel of Mark: A Commentary on the Greek Text*, NIGTC (Grand Rapids, MI: Eerdmans, 2014), 135.

17. For a comprehensive work on Isaiah as the background for Mark see, Rikki E. Watts, *Isaiah's New Exodus in Mark*, WUNT, 2nd ser., vol. 88 (Grand Rapids, MI: Baker, 1997).

> The wilderness and the dry land shall be glad;
> > the desert shall rejoice and blossom like the crocus;
> it shall blossom abundantly
> > and rejoice with joy and singing.
> The glory of Lebanon shall be given to it,
> > the majesty of Carmel and Sharon.
> They shall see the glory of the Lord,
> > the majesty of our God.
>
> Strengthen the weak hands,
> > and make firm the feeble knees.
> Say to those who have an anxious heart,
> > "Be strong; fear not!
> Behold, your God
> > will come with vengeance,
> with the recompense of God.
> > He will come and save you."
>
> Then the eyes of the blind shall be opened,
> > and the ears of the deaf unstopped;
> then shall the lame man leap like a deer,
> > and the tongue of the mute sing for joy.
> For waters break forth in the wilderness,
> > and streams in the desert. (Isa. 35:1–6)

Taking one more step back in the context of Isaiah, the prophet speaks of the sinners and the godless in Zion who will tremble in fear, in contrast to the one "who walks righteously and speaks uprightly" (33:14–15). They will see "the king in his beauty" (33:17), and there will be a restored, everlasting Jerusalem with the Lord as its center (33:20). Then Isaiah makes this pronouncement: "For the Lord is our judge, the Lord is our lawgiver, the Lord is our king; he will save us" (33:22). In the new city, in the presence of the Lord, "no inhabitant will say, 'I am sick;' the people who dwell there will be forgiven their iniquity" (33:24). The themes of judgment, restoration, and forgiveness are linked in Isaiah to the coming of the king. When God acts decisively on behalf of his people, they will be healed, and their sins will be forgiven.[18] This is the background to have in mind when reading Mark's story of Jesus healing and forgiving sin as he proclaims the good news of the kingdom of God.

Healing is a sign of God's coming salvation in Isaiah, and Mark weaves that theme throughout his Gospel from the beginning. Soon after the announcement in Mark 1:15, Jesus begins his work by casting out a demon (1:25) and healing Simon Peter's mother-in-law (1:30–31). Miraculous healing and exorcisms are staples in the rest of Jesus's

---

18. As Watts says, "The restoration of Israel's fortunes under Yahweh as rightful king is described in terms of the forgiveness of sins which is specifically linked with the absence of sickness." Watts, *Isaiah's New Exodus in Mark*, 174.

ministry. Though Mark does not call such works "signs," as in the Gospel of John (e.g., John 4:54), they function in much the same way to provide evidence of Jesus's authority and power.[19] Healings in Mark, however, do not serve simply as objective evidence for Jesus; they also show what it looks like to believe in him. The healing narratives that include detailed narration from Mark and dialogue between Jesus and those who come to him depict people in despair, with no hope in themselves.[20] Over the course of Mark's Gospel, moreover, the healings increasingly become examples of faith in Jesus over against those who reject him.

The Leper (Mark 1:40–45)

Mark 1:40–45 is the first healing narrative with dialogue. Suffering leprosy, this man is perpetually unclean and comes straight up to Jesus. Rather than recoiling in fear of becoming unclean or from disgust at the mere sight of the man, Jesus engages him, accepts him. Notice that the leper doesn't ask for healing—he asserts that Jesus *can* heal him if he is willing to do so. Mark does not offer a narrative comment or record Jesus's words about the man's disposition or motivation (as in the next examples); Jesus simply says, "I will; be clean" (1:41). Though there is no commentary, it is clear in this text that the man believed Jesus could heal him—his faith in Jesus made him whole.

The Paralytic (Mark 2:1–10)

The link between faith, forgiveness, and healing is explicit in the famous healing story in Mark 2. After the commotion caused by men digging a hole in the roof and then lowering down their paralytic friend, Mark says, "And when Jesus saw their faith, he said to the paralytic, 'Son, your sins are forgiven'" (2:5). I take "their faith" to mean that of the paralytic and his friends. Though "their" could refer only to the friends, there is no particular reason in the text or context to exclude the paralytic's faith. I suppose it's possible that they brought him to Jesus against his wishes (powerless as he was to stop them), but the context of Mark makes that unlikely. If the paralytic's faith is not included, then he is the only person in an extended healing narrative in Mark who is healed apart from either explicit or implicit faith. Moreover, the paralytic is a perfect example of faith alone. He cannot even bring himself to Jesus; he can only believe. What's most important here is the direct connection between faith, forgiveness, and healing.

Mark makes it clear that faith prompts both the declaration and the healing. What gets the attention of the scribes is the proclamation of forgiveness. Though they reject Jesus, they are right about one thing: only God can forgive sin (2:7). In response to the unbelief of the scribes, Jesus says (to paraphrase), "If you want to know how I have

---

19. John's "signs" are not limited to healing. John identifies the turning of water into wine at the wedding in Cana of Galilee as "the first of his signs" (John 2:11).
20. That is, healing narratives in which Mark focuses on specific individuals *and* includes something of their personal narrative.

authority to forgive sins, then watch this," and then proceeds to heal the paralytic (2:10–11). The irony is that the scribes, of all people, should have put forgiveness and healing together. Besides Isaiah, the Old Testament regularly joins sin and sickness, healing and forgiveness. For instance, Psalm 41:4 says, "Heal me, for I have sinned against you."[21]

In this story, it is not the highly educated scribes steeped in Mosaic law and traditions who come to Jesus but a man and his friends with nowhere else to turn. Jesus accepts the paralytic because of his faith—he heals and forgives him. This healing narrative sets the scene for the following examples of healing in Mark. From here on, faith in Jesus is explicitly instrumental in the healing stories. The tensions between Jesus and the religious leaders steadily increase from this point too. The story also provides the immediate background to Jesus's statement that he came for sinners rather than for the righteous.

Jairus and the Woman with the Hemorrhage (Mark 5:22–43)

The story about Jairus and his daughter includes the story of a woman with long-standing menstrual bleeding.[22] Jairus is an exception when it comes to the attitude of most Jewish leaders toward Jesus. A leader of a synagogue, he comes as a father in desperation to Jesus—his daughter is dying. Note Jairus's confidence that Jesus can heal his daughter: "Come and lay your hands on her, so that she may be made well and live" (Mark 5:23). He *believes* Jesus can help.

From the imploring of the ritually clean Jairus, the action moves to a huge crowd around Jesus, in the midst of which is a woman suffering from menstrual hemorrhaging for twelve years. In her condition, she is always unclean. Perhaps her awareness of this fact is what motivated her to sneak up unseen in the crowd (5:27). Mark tells his readers three more things about her:

1. She had "suffered" at the hands of many doctors.
2. She spent all her money looking for a cure.
3. In spite of all the doctors and money, she became only worse over time (5:26).

I suggest that Mark's intention is to show the woman's absolute helplessness and desperate need and the abject failure of all other avenues for healing. She has nothing to offer but can only receive. She is, moreover, so aware of her condition, so ashamed of her state, that she can't bear to come before Jesus face-to-face.[23] Mark lets us into the woman's thoughts and motivation: "She had heard the reports about Jesus and came

---

21. Cited by William L. Lane in *Commentary on the Gospel of Mark*, NICNT (Grand Rapids, MI: Eerdmans, 1974), 94. Lane cites several other texts that relate forgiveness and healing: 2 Chron. 7:14; Pss. 103:3; 147:3; Isa. 19:22; 38:17; 57:18; Jer. 3:22; Hos. 14:4.
22. The order reflects the events as they took place, and Mark's inclusion of the woman increases the tension and drama of the Jairus story. I will consider them as Mark presents them.
23. Without claiming a direct link, I see connections with the parable of the Pharisee and the tax collector in Luke 18 (see "The Pharisee and the Tax Collector" below, p. 202). The story of the woman reminds me of the attitude of the tax collector, who could only bow his head and plead for mercy. At the very least, both are story-examples showing what salvation by faith looks like.

up behind him in the crowd and touched his garment. For she said, 'If I touch even his garments, I will be made well'" (5:27–28). She touched him and received healing.

Jesus's reaction, "Who touched my garments?" (5:30), is not meant to launch readers into debates about Jesus's limitations and extent of knowledge.[24] In 2:8, Jesus knows what the scribes are thinking, but his question here is sincere. All Mark asserts is that Jesus knew, or sensed, that the healing took place because "power had gone out from him" (5:30). Mark's interest is in showing the encounter between the sick woman and Jesus—an encounter in which faith in Jesus led to complete healing. Jesus's question and the subsequent question of the disciples, which basically amounts to, "Are you really asking, in this crowd, who touched you? Virtually everyone is touching you" (cf. 5:31), draw the reader further into the story and highlight the exchange of sickness for wholeness through faith. As Jesus turns to look, the woman, overwhelmed by what's happened to her, falls before him and tells him the whole story (5:33). Jesus comforts her with words of acceptance and assurance: "Daughter, your faith has made you well; go in peace, and be healed of your disease" (5:34).

Meanwhile, there is still an anxious father waiting for Jesus to come to his dying daughter. He has to wait while Jesus attends to an unclean woman—hardly Jairus's social peer. Jesus is equally the friend to the outcast woman and the upstanding Jairus. Their opposite social standings are erased by their common experience of desperate need for Jesus and his love for them.

Just as Jesus is speaking to the woman, messengers come to tell Jairus the news: his daughter is dead; he doesn't need to bother Jesus any longer. Jesus, hearing the message, turns to Jairus and simply says, "Do not fear, only believe" (5:36). His genuine concern and love resonate in the words, calm in the midst of an emotional storm. The narrative focuses squarely on Jesus and quickly moves ahead to the scene at the house. Like the crowds surrounding Jesus when the woman touched him, the situation at Jairus's house is chaotic with people "weeping and wailing loudly" (5:38). From the perspective of the people at the house, who know a dead body when they see one, Jesus's question and statement are inconceivable: "Why are you making a commotion and weeping? The child is not dead but sleeping" (5:39). The reaction of those at the house increases the contrast in the story between belief and unbelief. One simple phrase from Jesus, "Little girl, I say to you, arise" (5:41), and she rises from the dead to the understandable shock and awe of everyone there.

The movement in the Jairus story, from his plea for help to the delay caused by healing the woman to the tragic news from the messengers, focuses the reader on faith in the midst of hopelessness and on Jesus's power to heal. One more story from Mark further solidifies this theme.

---

24. That's not to say that there is nothing further for us to discuss or consider. I'm simply pointing out that Mark is not engaged in a theological abstraction about the attributes of Jesus in the incarnation. Like the other Gospel writers, Mark freely includes instances in which Jesus, admittedly, doesn't have immediate knowledge of certain events (see Mark 13:32; cf. Matt. 24:36). The story leads readers into the mystery of the incarnation, where the Son of God becomes one of us.

Blind Bartimaeus (Mark 10:46–52)

If ever a character exemplified helplessness, it's Bartimaeus. Blind and begging for his livelihood, he is powerless to make himself, or any aspect of his life, better. In Mark, the scene is set by a series of teaching events with the disciples that begin with Peter's confession at Caesarea Philippi that Jesus is the Christ (Mark 8:29). Though Peter doesn't understand the depth of his confession (as is clear when he tries to stop Jesus from going to Jerusalem), he is right. From there Jesus teaches his disciples what it means for him to be the Christ, the Messiah, and what it means to follow him (8:31–9:1; 9:30–50; 10:32–45). That context, along with the kingdom background discussed earlier, is important for this story, because of how Bartimaeus addresses Jesus.

This is the first time the title "Son of David" appears in Mark. Whatever Bartimaeus knows when he uses the title—whether from divine insight or because he has heard stories and knows what will get attention—the use of it here in Mark further underscores Jesus's kingly identity.[25] Jesus is the King, the Messiah with power to heal. Bartimaeus does not only call Jesus the Son of David but also asks for mercy (10:47–48), two times. Jesus, in contrast to those who tell Bartimaeus to be quiet, and probably to their surprise, has mercy on him (10:49). Jesus knows what Bartimaeus wants—it's not hard to figure out a blind beggar's needs—but in order to draw out faith, Jesus asks him, "What do you want me to do for you?" (10:51). Bartimaeus, addressing Jesus as "Rabbi" (only the disciples address Jesus this way in Mark, e.g., 9:5; 11:21; 14:45[26]), wants his sight back. Similar to his reply to the woman in chapter 5, Jesus says, "Go your way, your faith has made you well," and Bartimaeus, who addresses Jesus like a disciple, receives his sight and follows Jesus (10:52). Once again, a person with nothing to commend himself and with no means of helping himself puts his faith in Jesus and is healed.

In two of the four preceding examples, Mark records Jesus saying that faith has brought about healing. To both the woman in chapter 5 and to Bartimaeus, Jesus says, "Your faith has made you well." With the paralytic in chapter 2, Jesus recognizes faith. In the case of the leper in 1:40, there is no explicit mention of faith, but given his certainty that Jesus can heal him and Jesus's willingness and power, faith is implied. The same goes for Jairus. Jesus tells him to believe, and when Jairus's daughter is brought to life, surely Mark is connecting faith to the event.

What, then, does the phrase "Your faith has made you well," whether faith is explicit or implicit, mean? Does it imply that the power rested in the people coming to Jesus and that they just needed to exercise enough faith to be healed? Certainly that is not the case. Otherwise, the source and power for healing is in those who are sick, and Jesus is essentially a life coach who helps people reach their full potential. Jesus—who says, "Your faith has made you well"—is the source of healing. These stories confront

---
25. France, *Mark*, 432.
26. France, *Mark*, 424.

us with the nature of faith itself. It is not simply "faith" conjured up by those in need that heals. While it is absolutely right to say, with Jesus, "Your faith has made you well," we must recognize from the narrative itself that faith is *in* Jesus and that it is he, not faith in itself, who heals. What does Jesus say to Bartimaeus? "What do you want *me* to do for you?" What does the leper say to Jesus? "If *you* will, *you* can make me clean." The woman hemorrhaging blood says to herself, "If I touch even *his* garments, I will be made well," and when she does, Jesus senses power—his power—going out to the woman. Jairus's faith does not raise his daughter from the dead; it is Jesus who enters, speaks, and raises the dead. Faith is indispensable (instrumental) in each of these stories, just as it is in every relationship to Jesus. Faith, however, is not in itself the power that heals or the power that saves. It is what connects the believer to the object of faith, Jesus himself. The miracles of healing do not happen apart from faith; they happen through faith in Jesus to heal—faith that knows he is who he says he is and will do what he says he will do.

There is an analogy here to justification, specifically, what we mean by "justified by faith." Paul, in Romans 4:3, cites Genesis 15:6, "Abraham believed God, and it was counted to him as righteousness," to show that his gospel of justification by faith alone is hardly a new thing. It was not, however, Abraham's faith by itself but specifically faith in God, who delivers the verdict of righteousness. In Romans 4, Paul shows that it is the ungodly, not those who work, whom God justifies through faith. God justifies sinners—those who are weak, ungodly, and have nothing with which they can commend themselves. Mark is not developing the theme of justification of the ungodly via Romans, but there is a pattern in these healing stories that goes hand in hand with the role of faith in justification. The helpless, those who have no hope in themselves, who look outside themselves to Jesus alone, find absolute healing and restoration through faith in him. These stories are not mirror images of justification, but they don't have to be for readers to see in them what it looks like for sinners—those for whom Jesus expressly came (Mark 2:16–17)—to turn to him in faith.

Contrasting Belief and Unbelief in Mark[27]

Mark gives nearly equal time to those who reject Jesus. Like all the Gospel writers, Mark shows clearly the opposition of the religious leaders to Jesus.

This Man Is Blaspheming (Mark 2:1–12)

The tension begins with the forgiving and healing of the paralytic in Mark 2. The scribes in the room take special offense at Jesus's pronouncement of forgiveness: "Why does this man speak like that? He is blaspheming! Who can forgive sins but

---

27. Virtually every commentary on Mark emphasizes the tension between Jesus and the scribes and Pharisees, with particular focus on Pharisaic law keeping and traditions, as these themes appear in specific texts. There are numerous articles on these and related themes, but for a concise and accessible treatment, see C. A. Evans, "Mark," in *New Dictionary of Biblical Theology*, ed. T. Desmond Alexander, Brian S. Rosner, D. A. Carson, and Graeme Goldsworthy (Downers Grove, IL: InterVarsity Press, 2000), 271.

God alone?" (2:7). What they miss is that this man from Galilee is fulfilling Isaiah's promise of healing and forgiveness in God's future dominion. The kingdom arrives in front of them, and they don't have the eyes to see it. Jesus connects the two things for them:

> And immediately Jesus, perceiving in his spirit that they thus questioned within themselves, said to them, "Why do you question these things in your hearts? Which is easier, to say to the paralytic, 'Your sins are forgiven,' or to say, 'Rise, take up your bed and walk'? But that you may know that the Son of Man has authority on earth to forgive sins"—he said to the paralytic—"I say to you, rise, pick up your bed, and go home." (2:8–11)

The healing is not an end in itself but a sign that the time is fulfilled and the kingdom of God is at hand. Jesus heals the man to show that he has the power to forgive. The scribes wrongly distinguish the two things when brought together in the person of Jesus. Contrast their reception of Jesus to that of the paralytic and his friends. They had faith that caused them to chip a hole in the roof to get to him, while the scribes, on the other hand, accuse him of blasphemy.

What about the Sabbath? (Mark 2:23–28)

On the heels of Jesus's new wineskins analogy for the reality of the new covenant, the Pharisees are upset over Jesus's disciples eating grain while walking through a field on the Sabbath. The issue is not that they are eating but that they are working, that is, they are plucking the grain off the wheat (Mark 2:23–24). It doesn't take the full revelation of the new covenant to see that the Pharisees are way off base. Jesus directs them back to David, who, with his men, ate the consecrated bread in the tabernacle (1:24–25; cf. 1 Sam. 21:1–6). This seems like an odd analogy since the example doesn't relate to the Sabbath. It almost sounds like Jesus is saying that everyone breaks commands from time to time, and if David did, then people should overlook the disciples' minor infraction. Of course, that's not what he means. For one, he points implicitly to his identity in Mark as the true Son of David and explicitly to his authority as "lord . . . of the Sabbath" (Mark 2:28).[28] He refocuses their perspective on the law and the intention of the law squarely on himself. It is he, not the Pharisees, who has authority. His other point is direct and simple and flows from the first: the Sabbath is God's gift to man. The Sabbath command was not simply a thing to keep, much less compound with add-on rules or microcosmic management, but a thing to enjoy. The Pharisees are more concerned with the command than with the intention of the command or the one who gave it. Now that the Lord of the Sabbath has arrived, their command-centric (rather than theocentric) type of law keeping is exposed. Everything, including the Sabbath, is now Christocentric.

---

28. See the excellent discussion in France, *Mark*, 145–46. As France also points out, the parallel in Matthew 12 provides solid support that Jesus is claiming "personal authority at least as great as that of David."

Choose Life (Mark 3:1–6)

By chapter 3, the leaders look for ways to kill Jesus. There is a man in the synagogue with a withered hand, and Jesus is there, "and they watched Jesus, to see whether he would heal him on the Sabbath, so that they might accuse him" (Mark 3:2). They know his reputation; they *know* what he'll do! Jesus is making people well, he's doing good to all and preaching God's kingdom, and they only see reasons to get rid of him. Their incredulous scheming alone is enough to condemn these law keepers.

Jesus knows what they are up to. He calls the man with the withered hand up front and puts them to the test. It's an easy question, and the answer is obvious, or should be: "Is it lawful on the Sabbath to do good or to do harm, to save life or to kill?" (3:4). The experts of tradition, the meticulous command keepers, have nothing to say. They *know* he has cornered them, and Jesus is angry at their obstinate rejection of the work of God. He answers his own question by showing them what it looks like when one understands God's intention in the law. Jesus chooses life. He has the power to heal, the man before him is in need of healing, and on the day God gave to Israel to commemorate all his works—works of goodness and grace—Jesus restores the man's hand.

The Pharisees don't need Jesus, his healing, or his teaching. They aren't sick; they are already "righteous"—at least in their own eyes. They show just how righteous they are by immediately meeting with some Herodians (hardly scrupulous law keepers and faithful covenant keepers) to plan how to get rid of Jesus once and for all. These particular Pharisees are law keepers who, with regard to righteousness under the law, see themselves as blameless (Phil. 3:6). What they miss is the God who gave the law and who now offers life through faith in Jesus of Nazareth.

Many Other Traditions (Mark 7:1–15)

The full expression of the fundamental conflict between Jesus and the religious leaders comes in Mark 7. This time the local Pharisees, along with some scribes from Jerusalem, pit themselves against Jesus over their traditions. As with the wheat grains (2:23–28), these Jewish leaders have a problem with Jesus's disciples—and so ultimately a problem with him. Jesus's disciples don't wash their hands before eating. They are, in the estimation of the scribes and Pharisees, defiled, unclean (7:2). Mark breaks into the story, speaking in his own voice, to explain Pharisaic customs to his readers. They are meticulously clean. They wash their hands constantly and refuse to eat unless they first wash. Mark identifies their sensibilities as "holding to the tradition of the elders." He also mentions their fondness for clean pots, pans, and tables, as part of "many other traditions that they observe" (7:3–4).

The scribes and Pharisee have a question: Why don't Jesus's disciples follow our traditions? It's clear what constitutes righteousness and sin in the eyes of the scribes and Pharisees. Jesus is swift to pronounce judgment—the same judgment the Lord pronounced through Isaiah against Israel's hypocritical unfaithfulness: "Well did Isaiah prophesy of you hypocrites, as it is written, 'This people honors me with their lips, but their heart is far from me; in vain do they worship me, teaching as doctrines the commandments of men'" (7:6–7; cf. Isa. 29:13). In pursuing their traditions, they turn from God's commandment. According to Jesus, they reject God's commandment so they can uphold their own traditions (Mark 7:9). In an effort to be "righteous," they choose themselves over God. Jesus has an example at hand.

When a man pledges "Corban" (an offering devoted to God), he promises to give his money, which otherwise would help support his parents, to be used for the temple or by the priests. The tradition gave a son a legal way to get around his duty to his parents. That rule is bad enough, but what's worse is that the pledge is forever binding. So if a son changes his mind or for whatever reason decides he must help his parents, he is not allowed to do so. It's not just the existence of such a pledge but the unscrupulous enforcement of it that Jesus condemns. The Pharisees allow the practical breaking of the fifth commandment in favor of their own tradition (7:9–13). Would they have described their traditions as contrary to the law? Never. Their traditions were extensions of their Torah keeping and reveal their fundamental misunderstanding of both the law and God.

In essence, they understand their relationship to God as primarily law based, which is no relationship with God at all. What makes them hypocritical? They claim to be the faithful followers of God and members of the covenant, the true descendants of Abraham, the fathers, and Moses. Then Jesus arrives in fulfillment of all the promises, and they reject him for their own brand of law keeping, status, and prestige—in short, their own righteousness. They claim to know and follow God and keep his commandments, but they are, in the words of Jesus, "hypocrites." They are the true descendants of their fathers who rejected Moses and all the true prophets of God.

Mark includes a parable that gets to the bottom of the issue. Faithfulness to God is not about what's merely done but rather about the heart, from which all actions flow—a heart devoted to God. Jesus says that it's not what goes in but what comes out that makes a person unclean (7:15). In the explanation that follows, readers get a firsthand look at Mark's own context. Mark says that through this teaching about true defilement, Jesus "declared all foods clean" (7:19). In other words, the apostolic teaching concerning the law did not begin with the apostles or with Peter's vision in Joppa (Acts 10:9–17) but with Jesus. The food laws were not an end in themselves—their old covenant function of identifying the people of God had come to an end. The people of God now identify only with Jesus. Things like food laws and circumcision had run their course. In his own context, Jesus anticipates what's to come and again draws attention to the heart. There is a heart problem that no amount of handwashing can ever remedy.

Mark gives concrete examples of what Jesus means by saying that he came to call not the righteous but sinners (Mark 2:17). The "righteous" are those who are righteous in their own sight, who have no perceived need of him. Thus, the religious leaders are the "righteous" of 2:17, because they reject God's work in Jesus, whom they regard as a blasphemer (2:7) and as in league with and at work through Beelzebul (3:22), and they ultimately hand him over to be crucified by the Romans. On the other hand, those who come to him in faith, knowing their helplessness and need, are the sinners whom Jesus calls and includes in his kingdom. Mark also describes the way Jesus secures their ultimate salvation. He gives his life in atonement for their sins.

Atoning Sacrifice (Mark 10:45)

Jesus's kingdom ministry reaches its climax in a way no one expected. True, many were awaiting the Messiah, the Son of David, to come and restore the nation as the Lord promised through the Old Testament prophets, but not in the way Jesus intends to fulfill that role. Teaching his disciples one more time about what he has come to do, Jesus grounds his teaching about greatness in the kingdom in his own ultimate purpose. Combining the suffering servant of Isaiah 53 with the royal figure of the Son of Man from Daniel 7, Jesus declares his own mission. Servanthood in the kingdom rests in the ultimate Servant-King: "For even the Son of Man came not to be served but to serve, and to give his life as a ransom for many" (Mark 10:45).

The word "ransom" (λυτρον) denotes a payment made to free captives, a price paid for release. Though the word appears with some frequency in the Septuagint, it does not appear in Isaiah 53, largely identified as the background for this text. France makes a convincing case that the lack of the word in Isaiah 53 poses little problem for understanding that text as the background for Mark 10:45.[29] Though ransom language is not used in Isaiah, the background is clear:

> Yet it was the will of the LORD to crush him;
>   he has put him to grief;
> when his soul makes an offering for guilt,
>   he shall see his offspring; he shall prolong his days;
>   the will of the LORD shall prosper in his hand.
> Out of the anguish of his soul he shall see and be satisfied;
> by his knowledge shall the righteous one, my servant,
>   make many to be accounted righteous,
>   and he shall bear their iniquities.
> Therefore I will divide him a portion with the many,
>   and he shall divide the spoil with the strong,
> because he poured out his soul to death
>   and was numbered with the transgressors;
> yet he bore the sin of many,
>   and makes intercession for the transgressors. (Isa. 53:10–12)

One of the many striking features that link Isaiah's text to Mark is the phrase translated in the ESV as "offering for guilt." In the Hebrew text of Isaiah, the word is אָשָׁם. This is the term used often in Exodus, Leviticus, and Numbers for the sin offering for

---

29. France, *Mark*, 420. Though there is not space here to show the details of his exegesis, France summarizes the main issues debated by scholars.

forgiveness, cleansing, and restoration in various situations.[30] Though not explicitly a "ransom," the sin offering is a sacrifice for the sin of the one who brings the offering. The offering bears the punishment for sin. It is a vicarious offering. In Mark 10:45, there is no mention of sin,[31] but in the context of Mark, and given the trajectory followed to the cross from this text, vicarious atonement for sin, so clear in Isaiah, is present in Jesus's "giving his life as a ransom for many."[32]

Jesus's substitutionary, atoning death is not simply *a* theme of the gospel; it lies at the very core of the gospel. Without it, there is no "gospel of Jesus Christ, the Son of God" (1:1). Without it, those who come to him in faith cannot be healed or forgiven. So while Mark's Gospel does not speak directly to justification by faith, Mark's central themes of forgiveness and faith, grounded in the atonement in Jesus's cross—core aspects of justification—provide for a richer understanding of justification by faith, particularly as we pursue and develop New Testament theology.

Luke: The Justification of Sinners

Of all the Gospel writers, Luke has the only explicit justification text. In his interpretation of the parable of the Pharisee and the tax collector, Jesus says that the tax collector, who humbled himself and pleaded for mercy, not the scrupulous and boasting Pharisee, "went down to his house justified" (Luke 18:14). Tax collectors, who worked for the Romans and added an extra fee to the top for their own profits, were not among the most popular Jews in Jesus's day. They weren't model covenant keepers either. The contrast with the Pharisees would have been immediately recognized by those listening to Jesus. For Gospel readers, however, barring a few exceptions (Nicodemus, Joseph of Arimathea, and a few others), the Pharisees are the constant antagonists in the story, always objecting to Jesus's way of teaching about and bringing the kingdom of God, always rejecting Jesus. One of the tragic ironies in all the Gospels is that the people who think they live according to Moses and try to maintain faithfulness to the covenant are the ones who completely miss the fulfillment of the promises for which they so eagerly waited.

Of course, we recognize the Pharisee as the bad guy in the story. Do we, however, stop and consider how often we more closely resemble the Pharisee rather than the

---

30. There are too many instances of the word to list here. For examples, see Ex. 29:14, 36; Lev. 4:3, 8, 14, 28; 5:8, 11, 12; 9:2, 7, 10; 16:3, 6, 9, 27; Num. 6:11, 16; 7:22, 34, 46; 8:8, 21.

31. Robert H. Gundry makes this observation: "Isaiah prophesies Yahweh's Servant as providing a vicarious atonement for sins. Isaiah's vocabulary is rich and repetitive in reference to them. Vicarious atonement may stand in the wings of Mark 10:45, but it does not come on stage. Sins go entirely unmentioned. To mention vicarious atonement for sins would go beyond what is needed to illustrate the motif of service in the Son of Man's giving his life as a ransom in substitution for many." *Mark: A Commentary on His Apology for the Cross* (Grand Rapids, MI: Eerdmans, 1993), 591. I understand the effort to avoid overreading Mark's text, but Mark *is* going beyond the motif of service in Jesus's sacrifice. No New Testament text, including this one, is fully dependent on, or limited by, Old Testament supporting texts for its meaning.

32. Hengel links Mark 10:45 to the Lord's Supper, in which Jesus says that the cup is his blood of the new covenant, "which is poured out for many" (14:24). In addition, he also links it to "the God-forsakenness which Jesus takes upon himself at Gethsemane vicariously for all and which ends with the Aramaic cry of prayer from the cross from Ps. 22:2 [MT; 22:1 Eng.]; the rending of the curtain of the temple which opens up the way to the 'holy of holies'; the confession exclaimed by the astonished pagan centurion ([Mark] 15.38f.); and the directions given by the angel at the empty tomb for the real highlights of the message of salvation narrated in the Gospel and at the same time proclaimed in the narrative." Martin Hengel, *The Four Gospels and the One Gospel of Jesus Christ: An Investigation of the Collection and Origin of the Canonical Gospels*, trans. John Bowden (Harrisburg, PA: Trinity Press International, 2000), 95.

tax collector, or the older brother in the parable of the prodigal son—a parable told by Jesus in direct condemnation of the Pharisees—rather than the sinners with whom Jesus associated? Certainly, we are not meant to see ourselves only in the heroes, the faithful, those who welcomed and believed in Jesus. The Pharisees are there not simply to show us the enemies of Jesus but also to expose our own hearts and lives. This parable is about justification, but it's not a theological abstraction about God's forensic (legal) declaration that sinners are justified by faith alone (nor are Paul's justification texts abstractions for that matter). The parable shows us what it looks like to be justified before God. We are the tax collectors who come to God with nothing to claim in and of ourselves, bowed down with guilt and knowing that we stand under his judgment and plead for mercy. Just as important, the parable shows us what it looks like to rely on ourselves and our own works even while believing we are faithful to the God we claim to love and serve. Just like the doctrine of justification by faith in Paul, the story of justification in the parable points both to the despairing and the boasting in God alone. The parable is not, however, the only connection to justification in Luke. I'll return to the parable shortly, but first, a brief survey of the sort of people featured in his Gospel.

Salvation for Outsiders and Outliers

Luke's Gospel is filled with people who are not, by any stretch of the imagination, natural-born heroes. They are, typically, the marginalized people who live on the outer rim of society. In these characters, we can see some distinct contours of justification. Whom does God justify? Sinners who, with no hope in themselves, come to him through faith in Christ alone.

Shepherds

God chose to announce the birth of the Savior to shepherds, living in a perpetually unclean state, necessary for the economy, but best left out in the fields, away from society (Luke 2:1–20). Shepherds don't play a role later in Jesus's ministry except in a parable or two, but it is they, not leaders, priests, or the religious elite, who see and hear the announcement that God has kept his promises in a baby lying in a manger. They also, in contrast to other characters later in the story, respond to and worship him.

Samaritans

After Jesus heals ten lepers, only a Samaritan returns to give thanks (Luke 17:15–16). The Samaritans, with their sketchy temple and priesthood up on Mount Gerizim, were the unwelcome and disliked half cousins of the Jews. Nevertheless, it is a Samaritan, not a priest or a Levite, who comes to the aid of a wounded man on the road to Jericho in one of Jesus's most famous parables (10:30–35). Luke doesn't sugarcoat the Samaritans, for he also includes a story of how a whole village of Samaritans refused Jesus (9:52–53). They aren't intrinsically faithful. If anything, that story makes their rather positive place in Luke all the more surprising.

Sinners and Tax Collectors

Clearly, sinners and tax collectors are not the most savory people among the descendants of Abraham, but Jesus welcomes them and makes himself at home among them (Luke 15:1). "Sinners" is a general category and includes any number of people who live outside the covenant, people known to live in sin, like prostitutes, for instance. In the Gospels, generally, the term refers to anyone who doesn't live up to the standards and ideals of the Pharisees. It is their description of Jesus's preferred dinner company. Besides the tax collector in the parable, Jesus calls a high-ranking tax collector down out of a tree and invites himself over to dinner (19:5). Finally, there is the most famous of all tax collectors, Matthew, called by Jesus as a disciple and included among his closest friends (Luke 6:15; cf. Matt. 9:9).

The Poor

As is so often the case in the Bible, the poor receive special notice from Luke. Jesus inaugurated his ministry by reading and commenting on Isaiah 61. Not only the poor but also the disenfranchised, the prisoners, and the oppressed are the recipients of the gospel in the age that dawns in Jesus: "The Spirit of the Lord is upon me, because he has anointed me to proclaim good news to the poor. He has sent me to proclaim liberty to the captives and recovering of sight to the blind, to set at liberty those who are oppressed, to proclaim the year of the Lord's favor" (Luke 4:18–19). In Luke's version of Jesus's most famous sermon, Jesus says, "Blessed are you who are poor" (6:20), instead of Matthew's "poor in spirit" (Matt. 5:3).[33] Later, when John the Baptist has his moment of doubt, Jesus replies with another word from Isaiah: "Go and tell John what you have seen and heard: the blind receive their sight, the lame walk, lepers are cleansed, and the deaf hear, the dead are raised up, the poor have good news preached to them" (Luke 7:22; cf., Isa. 29:18; 35:3).

Luke gives these groups special notice not because the poor, tax collectors, Samaritans, or shepherds are naturally virtuous or accepted by God simply on the basis of who they are—it's not a matter of the simple redistribution of spiritual wealth.[34] Luke's emphasis on the outsiders underscores the type of people for whom Jesus also came. These are not the cultural, civic, or religious leaders. These are the most unlikely characters in a story about a kingdom. In Jesus's kingdom, all are welcome, and worldly standards of greatness do not apply. In short, and in contrast to religious leaders like the Pharisees, the people Luke features are not the sort of people one would include when writing the script for who will play the standouts in the greatest, and ultimately only, kingdom.[35] Which people in Luke know themselves to be the least deserving of Jesus? The same people who

---

33. That is not to imply that the phrases mean radically different things. The difference is emphasis. In Luke, the poor are not blessed simply on the basis of poverty but are emblematic of those who have, and know themselves to have, the greatest need.

34. Lepers are another group that fits this list. As in the Gospels generally, Jesus has no qualms whatsoever about coming into contact with lepers—something the Pharisees and scribes would never do.

35. Jesus's disciples, including fishermen, a tax collector, and a Zealot, could be added to the list. Though they represent various social strata, they are a far cry from those whom we might expect a king to choose for his closest companions.

come to him in faith alone with nothing to offer and find themselves accepted and welcomed by him. They are living testimonies of those justified by faith apart from works.

A Gospel to the Gentiles: Connecting Luke and Acts

Luke gives particular attention to Gentiles. Not only are they the ultimate outsiders, but if we follow their trajectory into Acts, Luke's second volume, then we find a link to the New Testament doctrine of justification. In his own context, his Gentile emphasis would resonate with his contemporaries. The inclusion of the Gentiles was one of the major issues among Christians in the apostolic era. Luke's focus on the Gentiles in Acts begins in his Gospel. The other Evangelists share this theme, but Luke includes a couple of his own special examples.

The first such text is the story of the old man Simeon who takes the baby in his hands and, echoing Isaiah, proclaims the Christ child as "a light for revelation to the Gentiles, and for glory to your people Israel" (Luke 2:32; cf. Isa. 42:6; 49:6; 60:3). Like Matthew, Luke includes the story of the healing of the centurion's servant (Luke 7:1–10; cf. Matt. 8:5–10), as well as the story of the healing of the Gerasene demoniac (Luke 8:26–39; cf. Matt. 8:28–34; Mark 5:1–21). Though similar to Matthew's Great Commission (Matt. 28:18–20) in trajectory and intent, Luke alone includes these words from Jesus before his ascension: "Thus it is written, that the Christ should suffer and on the third day rise from the dead, and that repentance for the forgiveness of sins should be proclaimed in his name to all nations, beginning from Jerusalem" (Luke 24:46–47). Readers of Acts will hear the similarity between that text and Acts 1:8: "You will receive power when the Holy Spirit has come upon you, and you will be my witnesses in Jerusalem and in all Judea and Samaria, and to the end of the earth." As the apostles and others carry Jesus's message to the ends of the earth, the inclusion of the Gentiles by faith in Jesus alone, apart from circumcision, quickly becomes a central focus of their ministry and message. It's not simply the inclusion of Gentiles that causes such a stir but the free inclusion of them apart from the law.

The fulfillment of Jesus's commission necessarily brings about the church's earliest major controversy and subsequently influences the fuller developments and descriptions of the doctrine of justification by faith found in some of Paul's letters. Though justification by faith is not limited only to the Jew-Gentile controversy in the New Testament, it does surface with a sharper focus because of the inclusion of the Gentiles. In recent years, New Testament scholars tend to either overstate or underestimate the inclusion controversy in relation to justification. The controversy serves as a means for, though not the sole occasion for, the development of the New Testament doctrine of justification by faith alone. In Acts, when Gentiles believe and receive the Spirit, it becomes crystal clear that a right relationship with God is not on the basis of law, which was, according to Peter, a "yoke . . . that neither our fathers nor we have been able to bear" (Acts 15:10).[36] Later, taking up this same idea, Paul declares that God accepts and forgives

---

36. The doctrine of justification by faith was not *caused* by, much less devised as a result of, the Jew-Gentile controversy. Abraham was justified by faith long before Cornelius believed the gospel. That's precisely why Paul cites Abraham

all people who believe in Jesus, "and by him everyone who believes is *justified* from everything from which you were not able to be *justified* by the law of Moses" (Acts 13:39, my trans.).[37] In his Gospel, Luke shows that this new reality took shape in the ministry of Jesus, who commissioned the apostles to take his message to the Gentiles.

The Pharisee and the Tax Collector

The parable of the Pharisee and the tax collector shows polar opposite approaches to God, two men before the face of God with two different concepts of how they relate to him. That's really the point here, namely, What is the basis for how people relate to God? Luke gives his readers the interpretive key for understanding why Jesus told this parable: "He also told this parable to some who trusted in themselves that they were righteous, and treated others with contempt" (Luke 18:9). Don't miss the two-part reason: (1) self-righteousness and (2) contempt for others. Readers who are focused intently on the issue of justification have a tendency to put all the emphasis on the first thing but skip over, or give short shrift to, the second. Both ideas are vital for understanding the parable and justification.

"The Pharisee was standing and praying like this about himself" (18:11 CSB) is all that's really needed to understand the Pharisee.[38] His prayer isn't really a prayer but rather an announcement of his own accomplishments and personal distinctions. He does seem to begin in the right place: "God, I thank you." *Seem* is the operative word. Even if he's thanking God for his divine grace and election, and even if he's thanking God for the gift or empowerment to live what he considers a faithful life,[39] the words hardly ring of sincere appreciation and gratitude. Ultimately, there is no use talking about what the Pharisee thinks or what he intends personally one way or another. He doesn't actually think or intend anything at all—he's a character in a story. The only

---

in Romans 4 and Galatians 3—God was already justifying people by faith before the law was given. The Jew-Gentile controversy instrumentally heightened the prominence of justification. The doctrine is not just *occasional*; rather, the circumstances in the first century were the means by which this core doctrine of God's salvation was made clear. Justification as a doctrine would exist, absolutely, apart from the first-century controversy, but in the providence of God, the controversy provided the way for justification to receive its central focus. I plan to develop this view of the instrumental, or even providential, role of the controversy over the inclusion of the Gentiles in future research. The best treatment of this issue in regard to Romans, showing that Jewish particularity is *not* Paul's motivation in writing that letter is Mark A. Seifrid, "Particularity and Universalism in Romans," in *Spurensuche zur Einleitung in das Neue Testament: Eine Festschrift im Diaog mit Udo Schnelle*, ed. Michael Labahn, FRLANT 271 (Göttingen: Vandenhoeck & Ruprecht, 2017), 143–59. Seifrid's chapter is in English.

37. Here I translate δικαιόω as "justified," not "freed" (ESV, NASB), a translation with which I disagree. The NIV translates, "Through him everyone who believes is set free from every sin, a justification you were not able to obtain under the law of Moses."

38. If, as in the ESV, Luke 18:11 reads, "The Pharisee, standing by himself, prayed thus," then perhaps the implication is that the Pharisee stood apart so that he might be seen praying. That is not, in my opinion, the best reading of the Greek phrase πρὸς ἑαυτὸν. I think the better translation is "about [concerning] himself," as in the CSB. This reading takes the prepositional phrase as modifying the verb "prayed" rather than the participle "standing." The NIV is very similar: "The Pharisee stood by himself." While the ESV translation of 18:11 has a certain descriptive parallel with 18:13 (i.e., the Pharisee "standing by himself"; the tax collector "standing far off"), the Greek constructions are not the same. The distinction does not affect the interpretation all that much. If, as seems likely, the best translation is "about himself," it does further emphasize the self-centered nature of the prayer. If we take it like the ESV and NIV, the Pharisee's focus on himself is hardly lost.

39. However, such an interpretation sounds more like a reflection on soteriology in a larger theological sense. That is, the Pharisee is thanking God for what he's done in him. In a large part of the Reformation tradition, theologians have been careful to state that we are justified by grace through faith alone and not by our own works—including anything we have done or *currently do* or *will do*. That is, our justification is not based on works we did that made us acceptable to God (which is impossible), nor is it based on works we do as members of the new covenant through the Spirit.

intent here is Jesus's in telling it and Luke's in including it. Luke tells us *exactly* how to read the parable when he gives the reason Jesus told it.

The Pharisee's prayer does not reflect a relationship with God as described in the Bible, whether under the old or new covenant. No one in a covenantal relationship with God could link true gratitude to God directly to personal performance and unbridled disdain for others. The character in the parable does not depict a faithful covenant member, if, that is, membership in the covenant has anything do to with loving God and neighbor.

First, the Pharisee's basis for judgment is in comparison with others, specifically in comparing their sin to his personal righteousness. Obviously, there is something legitimate about being thankful to God that, in his providence, one is not a cheat or an adulterer. The idea here, however, is contempt and disdain. Just as Luke says, the parable was told to people who have contempt for others. That means that readers should hear contempt in the Pharisee's voice and read his "thanks" as disingenuous. His identity—or better, the identity of those about whom the parable is told—is wrapped up in a standard moral superiority to others. Before he even mentions fasting and tithing, this is already a works-based prayer. Why? Because, before God, *any* self-identification apart from God points to something we do (or don't do). "I am not like others" means "I don't do what they do. I do other, righteous things." Any attempt to read his thanks or the comparisons in a positive light is negated by the inclusion of "even like this tax collector." The contempt is clear. Here is a man standing before the God who commands, "Love your neighbor as yourself," and his only concern is how other people prove his own goodness. Their sin is a means of his personal boasting. This easily happens to us when we unthoughtfully use the phrase "*those* people." It's almost certain that however we finish that sentence, we will sound a lot like the Pharisee's prayer. Not only is there contempt and complete lack of love of neighbor, there is no acknowledgement of personal sin or confession in the Pharisee's prayer. He's not a sinner, like all those other sinners out there, including tax collectors. His self-justification is already complete.

Then comes the list of accomplishments, the "Look at me!" part of the prayer. He fasts twice a week. It was fine for him to fast twice a week. He could fast six days a week if he desired, but there is only one required Jewish fast a year: the annual fast associated with the Day of Atonement (e.g., Leviticus 16). There were other special fasts associated with various days, but fast once a year, and the legal requirement is fulfilled. This is as clear an example of works-based righteousness as there can be. If there is a law that says, "No drinking cow's milk," then all you have to do is avoid milk from a cow. You can't keep the law any better by, say, refusing to drink almond or soy milk or keeping out of the dairy aisle at the supermarket. Upping the ante on requirements does not in the least increase either innocence or standing before God. So the Pharisee could fast all he wanted, but fasting twice a week—which is clearly a distinction from others—and boasting about it focuses purely on righteousness by doing. It is works righteousness. And when righteousness is based on doing (or not doing), then the more one does, the better. Same for tithing. Presumably, he not only tithes on income but on everything. Whatever the case, his obedience is a feather in his cap.

The point is that the Pharisee relates to God on the basis of his own accomplishments and in distinction from others who fall short of his personal righteousness. His character is quite similar to that of the older brother in the parable of the prodigal son—another parable aimed at the Pharisees and scribes (Luke 15:11–32). There the older son basically relates to his father according to what he's done for him. When his younger brother returns home to a party in his behalf, the older brother refuses to come rejoice but rather becomes angry with his father and lashes out at him: "Look, these many years I have served you, and I never disobeyed your command, yet you never gave me a young goat, that I might celebrate with my friends. But when this son of yours came, who has devoured your property with prostitutes, you killed the fattened calf for him!" (15:29–30). Unlike his repentant brother, the older brother doesn't even address his father as "Father" (15:21) and instead of saying, "my brother," says, "this son of yours." It's not that the older brother was wrong to stay home and obey, but when his brother—a sinner—comes home, the older son reveals that his relationship to his father is based on simply doing and therefore getting what he deserves. Not only that, but he uses his brother's sin to prop up his own obedience. His anger shows a heart that in no way reflects the grace and mercy of his father. He doesn't know his father at all. If he did know him, he would show it by acting like his father. If the Pharisees and scribes were really loyal to God, they would show it by rejoicing in the mission of Jesus rather than scorning both him and those whom he came to save: "This man receives sinners and eats with them" (15:2).

Though the terms have fallen out of vogue since the late twentieth century, the Pharisee in the parable exemplifies *works righteousness* and, yes, *legalism*. Call it what you will, but any attempt to identify ourselves over against the practices of others and to distinguish ourselves on the basis of who we are, where we come from, or anything other than God's love and mercy is to rely on works righteousness, or as it is popularly called, legalism. We are free to do many things, follow various practices, engage in different activities, but the one thing we cannot do is turn our practices into distinguishing marks. Markers of all kinds, even boundary makers, are a way of establishing ourselves apart from how God himself identifies sinners as righteous through faith in Christ. That's works righteousness in any century. The way Paul put it was to say that whether you are circumcised or uncircumcised doesn't matter—you can go either way, but just don't believe for a second that either one will make something special before God (Gal. 5:6; 6:15).

Then there is the tax collector. With him there is no declaration, list of works, or comparing himself to others. He stands before God as a sinner in need of mercy.[40] There

---

40. As an aside, this parable reminds us that no matter how much community emphasis there is in regard to being members of God's covenant people, justification before God is the sinner, each sinner, standing before God and judged by God for his or her own sins but through faith in Christ receiving forgiveness and a positive verdict of "righteous" in God's eyes.

is an unmistakable sense of judgment with the tax collector. Why else does he bow down and beat his chest and confess that he is a sinner? Is it not because this is a depiction of a man who knowingly stands under God's judgment? Condemnation before God is what brings the tax collector to God for mercy. Without condemnation and judgment, there would be no need of confession, no need for mercy. Though not explicit, there is no mistaking that the tax collector comes in faith. Jesus does not say, "And the tax collector, by faith, stood," nor does Luke insert a comment about faith. Faith is looking outside oneself to God for rescue. This man doesn't hide his sin, much less make a show of his works, but owns his sin, brings it to God, confesses, and asks for mercy.

Notice that he identifies himself not simply as someone who commits sins (like the way the Pharisee identifies himself by his works) but as "a sinner." Committing sins is inseparable from being a sinner, but we should at least notice that one of the two men lists his accomplishments and the other describes his entire state of being. That's his identity, his status before God. The Pharisee is confident because of the acts he points to as evidence, but the tax collector is completely undone by the guilt and condemnation of knowing he's a sinner.

Jesus's interpretation of the parable is simple: The tax collector "went down to his house justified, rather than the other. For everyone who exalts himself will be humbled, but the one who humbles himself will be exalted" (Luke 18:14). Jesus's interpretation amounts to a verdict: "justified." And the follow-up commentary provides the principle. The one humbles himself as a sinner before God, knowing himself to be under God's judgment, and throws himself on God's mercy. Therefore, he is exalted.

The Greek word for "justified" is the same term so often associated with Paul's theology of justification. Is this a full-blown story form of the doctrine of justification in its entirety? Not exactly, but he is declared righteous, and what has he done? He has repented and thrown himself on God's mercy. Faith is implicit—he confesses he's a sinner and asks for mercy. Jesus, in his interpretation, says he was justified. It is, then, a depiction of a sinner who is declared to be justified. He was counted as something he was not. It is not at all a stretch to say that this parable is a picture of reckoned, or imputed, righteousness. The point may not be to establish the imputation of righteousness apart from works, but if we had to describe the parable and its interpretation together, what would be a better biblical analogy than Romans 4:1–8? A sinner, apart from his works, is declared to be righteous in contrast to one who counts on his works.

Again, the prodigal son provides a parallel. The prodigal, who reaches rock bottom and comes to his senses, can only return home hoping for mercy. Before he can even get his rehearsed speech out of his mouth, this father sees him, runs to him, and greets him with an embrace and a kiss. As for the son, he knows he has nothing to bring except a confession of guilt: "Father, I have sinned against heaven and before you. I am no longer worthy to be called your son" (Luke 15:21). His father, however, not only lets him back in but fully restores and exalts him (15:22–24). There is no pronouncement of mercy, grace, or justification for that matter, but certainly, the welcome-home party is a picture of pure mercy and grace. It would not be far off the mark to come to the end of the parable of the prodigal son, compare the two brothers in relation to their father, and say, "One of those brothers was justified—and it was the sinner."

Jesus's acceptance and welcoming of sinners, coupled with the exposing of the Pharisees' self-righteousness and the assertion that the tax collector in the parable was indeed justified, create clear thematic links to the larger doctrine of justification. I would go so far as to say that Luke, like Matthew and Mark, helps us to see justification even more clearly by giving us stories—both historical and imaginary (parables)—that show what it looks like when sinners, the outcasts, and the outliers of the world come to God by faith in Christ and find welcome and acceptance—that is, justification.

John: Faith in the Obedient Son

If a Bible reader decided to do a study on justification and started off with a lexicon, Bible dictionary, or concordance, only two verses in John would turn up. The word "righteousness" appears in John 16:8 and 10. During the Upper Room Discourse (John 14–16), Jesus says to the disciples, "And when he [the Spirit] comes, he will convict the world concerning sin and *righteousness* and judgment: concerning sin, because they do not believe in me; concerning *righteousness*, because I go to the Father, and you will see me no longer; concerning judgment, because the ruler of this world is judged" (16:8–11). In this text, sin is understood as not believing in Jesus, and judgment of the world is directly linked to the judgment of Satan. But righteousness is more difficult to understand. How will the world be convicted of righteousness *because* Jesus will return to the Father? What does it mean to be *convicted* of righteousness in the first place?[41]

While it may be theologically tempting to think that the text means that the Spirit will convict the world on the basis of Jesus's righteousness in life and death, such a reading doesn't fit well in context. A more nuanced reading takes the text to mean that the world will be convicted by the Spirit, proving the world was wrong to judge and condemn Jesus who was "really innocent and just."[42] The phrase "because I go to the Father," if taken to refer to Jesus's vindication in his resurrection and ascension, lends support to that interpretation. So the Spirit convicts the world for the sin of disbelieving Jesus and convicts the world with regard to righteousness—that is, "being wrong about justice."[43] The best suggestion, however, is to place the pronoun "its" in front of "righteousness."[44] The Spirit will convict the world of "*its* righteousness." This interpretation takes "righteousness" in an ironic sense—the world's false righteousness.[45] The strength of this reading comes

---

41. Not least of the challenges is grasping the idea of the Spirit acting as a prosecutor. That and the other exegetical details are beyond the scope of this chapter, but for interested readers, a good place to begin wading through the literature on this text is D. A. Carson's discussion in *The Farewell Discourse and Final Prayer of Jesus: An Evangelical Exposition of John 14–17* (Grand Rapids, MI: Baker, 1992), 138–48. Carson distills the text down to the essential points and questions raised within it.
42. Raymond E. Brown, *The Gospel according to John: A New Translation with Introduction and Commentary*, AB 29 (New York: Doubleday, 1970), 712.
43. Brown, *Gospel according to John*, 712.
44. D. A. Carson, *The Gospel according to John*, PNTC (Grand Rapids, MI: Eerdmans, 1991), 536–38.
45. As Edward W. Klink III puts it, "The term is not being used in a positive sense (i.e., a genuine, God-approved righteousness); it is the righteousness displayed by the (sinful) world." He also shows that a negative sense of the word, as in

from the context of John where the "righteousness" of the Pharisees and scribes is exposed continually, and at times through an ironic twist: "Jesus said, 'For judgment I came into this world, that those who do not see may see, and those who see may become blind'" (John 9:39).[46] It fits well, moreover, with the other Gospel writers who use the word ironically, "I came not to call the *righteous*" (Mark 2:17), and who use it to refer to the self-righteousness of the Pharisees, "He also told this parable to some who trusted in themselves that they were righteous, and treated others with contempt" (Luke 18:9). Such an idea is evident in Paul's letters too (e.g., Rom. 10:3; Phil. 3:6–9; Titus 3:5).[47] In this text, then, the conviction of the world for unbelief pairs with the conviction of the world's false righteousness. After the resurrection and ascension, the Holy Spirit will judge the world for its rejection of Jesus and for its own brand (however it manifests itself) of righteousness apart from Jesus—in other words, false righteousness.

There are a number of themes in John that connect to justification by faith, but I will focus briefly on two in particular. Faith is a common theme throughout the Synoptic Gospels, and John is no different. In John, however, there is something of a different emphasis, and that is faith as taking part in Christ, or in union with Christ. This idea is best exemplified in the well-known, and forever uncomfortable, language found in John 6—a turning point in the ministry of Jesus and in John's Gospel.

The second theme is obedience. That sounds common enough in the Gospels. After all, obedience to Jesus is directly linked to being his disciples. Discipleship and obedience are necessarily part of John's Gospel too. It would be next to impossible to write an accurate Gospel and not highlight discipleship. John, however, speaks explicitly of Jesus's obedience—namely, his obedience in life and in death to the Father's will. The most important thing about these two themes, faith in Jesus and Jesus as obedient Son, is that John ties them together. These two themes are, in turn, linked directly to eternal life for those who believe.

Faith for Life

Just a day after feeding five thousand people, all from a handful of bread and fish, Jesus loses a large number of followers. His own words are the reason (i.e., the immediate cause) that so many abandon him. Ironically, it all starts with people asking Jesus for a sign—he had just fed them the day before—and they quote Nehemiah's retelling of the exodus story and of God's provision of manna for the people (John 6:31; cf. Neh. 9:15).[48] The fact that Nehemiah told that story to postexilic Israelites to highlight unfaithfulness seems to have gone unnoticed by those citing it.

Isa. 64:6 and Dan. 9:18, comports with John's message. This negative sense of righteousness relates to the sin of unbelief. *John*, ZECNT 4 (Grand Rapids, MI: Zondervan, 2016), 680.

46. Carson lists and discusses texts in John that underscore the failings of the practices and behavior of the Pharisees (their "righteousness") in contrast to Jesus, e.g., 2:13–23; 7:19; 12:42–43. Carson, *Gospel according to John*, 537–38. See also Carson, *Farewell Discourse*, 141–42.

47. Carson, *Farewell Discourse*, 142.

48. Another layer of irony is that after Jesus fed them, they declared, "This is indeed the Prophet who is to come into the world," and they decided he should be king (John 6:14–15).

Jesus tells them that he is "the bread of life" (John 6:35, 48) and "the living bread that came down from heaven" (6:51). He then adds that he, the true bread, is the source of life: "If anyone eats of this bread, he will live forever. And the bread that I will give for the life of the world is my flesh" (6:51). Not surprisingly, they miss his meaning. He, in turn, makes things more difficult: "So Jesus said to them, "Truly, truly, I say to you, unless you eat the flesh of the Son of Man and drink his blood, you have no life in you. Whoever feeds on my flesh and drinks my blood has eternal life, and I will raise him up on the last day" (6:53–54)." A paraphrase will give his meaning: "You have to take part in me and my work—you have to believe in me—and if you do, you will live forever." The evidence that eating his flesh and drinking his blood refers to faith comes from Jesus himself. He says, "Whoever feeds on my flesh and drinks my blood abides in me" (6:56), and later when he's explaining his teaching to the disciples, he warns of unbelief even among their ranks (6:64). More proof comes at the end of the chapter when Peter, speaking for the Twelve in answer to Jesus's question about whether they will turn away from him like the crowds, says, "Lord, to whom shall we go? You have the words of eternal life, and we have believed, and have come to know, that you are the Holy One of God" (6:68–69). Besides those specific texts, the whole event makes it clear that the crisis over Jesus's teaching is a crisis of faith—whether people will believe he is who he says he is and that he has come to do what he says he'll do. Eternal life, as Jesus offers it, comes down to whether people believe in him.

Life through Obedience

Jesus offers both life and assurance of life to all who believe on the foundation of his obedience. No one who comes to him will ever hunger or thirst again, which Jesus explains as being raised on the last day and receiving eternal life. Moreover, those who come to him in faith are secure in him because he has come to do and will accomplish his Father's will. His Father's will is that he will keep all those who come to him (John 6:37–40). Jesus accomplishes his Father's will and secures life for those who come to him precisely by giving his flesh for them—that is, by dying for them (6:51). The obedience of Jesus the Son secures eternal life for believers.

John emphasizes Jesus's obedience in more than one place.[49] Before surveying those texts, a quick word about the obedience of Jesus in the doctrine of justification by faith. Jesus's obedience is the foundation for being constituted as righteous before God (Rom. 5:18–19). As the second Adam, Jesus attains the goal of life through his obedience—the goal Adam lost through disobedience, which subsequently led to death for him and all his descendants. Often, this obedience is broken down into two parts, traditionally identified as *active* and *passive* obedience. First, there is Christ's *active obedience*, which is his obedience in life, doing the will of his Father, obeying the law,

---

49. This section is adapted from Brian Vickers, *Justification by Grace through Faith: Finding Freedom from Legalism, Lawlessness, Pride, and Despair* (ISBN: 978-1-59638-050-9), Explorations in Biblical Theology (Phillipsburg, NJ: P&R, 2013), 42–44. Used by permission of P&R Publishing Co.

and so forth. Second is his so-called *passive obedience*, usually identified as his sacrificial death on the cross. Both aspects are necessary. The reason they are necessary is not because distinguishing them upholds a particular historical Protestant doctrine but because *every* act of obedience—whether Christ's or anyone else's—is both active and passive. Obedience is passive because it involves, in some way or another, submitting to some outside being or force (e.g., a law, parent, teacher, military commander, or God). But it is impossible to obey only passively, even if the command is to refrain from an action, as in "Do not murder" or "Do not exceed the speed limit." Even *not acting*, as directed in prohibitions, is active obedience. One must submit *and* actively follow the command—even if it means *not doing*. What this means is that if Jesus obeyed at all, he did so both actively and passively. It also means that his obedience cannot be portioned neatly between active obedience in life and passive obedience in death.[50] We can make a theological distinction without straining for a practical distinction. John's Gospel bears out this conclusion.

Besides the text cited above in John 6:38, "I have come . . . not to do my own will but the will of him who sent me," John records Jesus as saying, "My food is to do the will of him who sent me and to accomplish his work" (4:34). The "work" and the "will" Jesus came to do focus on his death, but the doing is no less active because of it. John also includes teaching from Jesus that, while emphasizing the forgiveness supplied through his death on the cross, includes all the work he accomplishes in obedience to the Father:

> So Jesus said to them, "When you have lifted up the Son of Man, then you will know that I am he, and that I do nothing on my own authority, but speak just as the Father taught me. And he who sent me is with me. He has not left me alone, for I always do the things that are pleasing to him." (8:28–29)

That text combines action and submission seamlessly, and even while Jesus is speaking, some believe in him.

John 10:17–18, perhaps more than any text in the New Testament, binds the two aspects of obedience together. As Jesus speaks of his sacrificial works—the Good Shepherd who gives his life for the sheep, done in the mutual knowledge of Father and Son (10:15)—he declares, "For this reason the Father loves me, because I lay down my life that I may take it up again. No one takes it from me, but I lay it down of my own accord. I have authority to lay it down, and I have authority to take it up again. This charge I have received from my Father" (10:17–18). Readers should note that in a text where Jesus puts special emphasis on his submission to the Father regarding his sacrificial death, he puts equal emphasis on his action: "I lay it down of my own accord." This

---

50. At its best, this is a theological (rather than a practical) distinction and quite an important distinction as well. The two sides of obedience account for the forgiveness required for sin and the status of righteousness needed to stand before God and receive the verdict "righteous." There is forgiveness and the imputation of Christ's obedience (righteousness) as the second Adam who secures God's goal for humanity, namely, life. These are, I realize, presuppositions about what constitutes justification. They are not, however, unsubstantiated. My exegetical and theological arguments are spelled out in *Jesus' Blood and Righteousness: Paul's Theology of Imputation* (Wheaton, IL: Crossway, 2006). Also see chap. 14, by Brandon Crowe, in this book.

time Jesus's teaching leads to a sharp difference of opinion. Some conclude that Jesus is possessed by a demon and insane, while others cannot dismiss Jesus's works, much less attribute them to demonic forces (10:20–21).

Jesus's teaching, including that which concerns his own work, is itself an act of obedience: "For I have not spoken on my own authority, but the Father who sent me has himself given me a commandment—what to say and what to speak. And I know that his commandment is eternal life. What I say, therefore, I say as the Father has told me" (12:49–50). The Father's commandment—here Jesus's teaching—is the way to eternal life. In the Upper Room Discourse, Jesus speaks openly of his death, and in terms of Satan's coming attack, he is confident that "the ruler of this world" can do him no harm, for "he has no claim on me, but I do as the Father has commanded me" (14:30–31). That text shows the cross to be the *ultimate act of obedience*, and it is not merely passive.

Finally, in the High Priestly Prayer (John 17), the unbreakable link between Jesus's obedience to the Father and the gift of eternal life to his followers—those united to him—is unmistakable. As I state elsewhere,

> On the night that he was betrayed, he prays to his Father and speaks of "having accomplished the work that you gave me to do" (17:4). The High Priestly Prayer in John 17 is filled with petitions based on the Son's accomplishment of the Father's will. More specifically, the accomplished work is the salvation of the people given to the Son by the Father. Jesus' obedience is the means to his being glorified as he was before the world began (v. 5) and to his followers' receiving eternal life (v. 2), being sanctified in the truth of God's word (v. 17), and entering into unity with the Son and the Father (vv. 21–23).[51]

The contexts, emphases, and purposes need not be identical for John's Gospel to be linked with Paul's teaching on justification. There is, moreover, no cause to show *how* John teaches justification. John neither set out to write Romans 5:12–21 nor intended one of his favorite words, "abiding," to be synonymous with the union language of Philippians 3:9, in which Paul speaks of his desire to be found "in him, not having a righteousness of [his] own." We could just as easily go to Paul and see how his "in Christ" metaphor is compatible with John's abiding. John makes his own unique contribution that deepens our understanding of God's salvation in his Son. He helps us see more clearly the necessity of Jesus's obedience as the foundation for eternal life, and he does this apart from referring to Christ as the second Adam.

Conclusion

The Gospel writers give us stories of salvation. Stories of faith, rejection, judgment, repentance, mercy, and obedience. Though they may not teach justification by faith directly, they show what it looks like for sinners to turn to Jesus in faith and to receive

---

51. Vickers, *Justification by Grace through Faith*, 43–44.

forgiveness and eternal life. We see Jesus as the atoning sacrifice for sin, the obedient Son of God who gave his life as a ransom for many. In other words, we don't have to see justification by faith behind every verse of the Gospels to gain a deeper understanding of God's justifying work in Christ. In fact, the less we try to find justification, the more we'll learn of it. We neither have to force it on their teaching nor apologize for their lack of explicit references. The themes and contours are there—they must be, because, like Paul, they teach salvation through faith in Jesus of Nazareth. We need the entire witness of the New Testament in order to fully grasp the importance and place of justification in relation to the whole story of the fulfillment of God's salvation in Christ. We don't need to make them all say the same thing—nor should we try. We must bow to God's authority and hear the Evangelists in their own voices. We need them as much as we need Paul. When it comes to the entire story of God's salvation found across the New Testament, we can apply what John says about the story of Jesus near the end of his Gospel. There are many other things that could be written to describe and illustrate salvation by faith in Christ, including justification, and if they were, "I suppose that the world itself could not contain the books that would be written" (John 21:25).

Recommended Resources

Bauckham, Richard. *The Gospels for All Christians: Rethinking the Gospel Audiences.* Grand Rapids, MI: Eerdmans, 1997.

Carson, D. A. *The Gospel according to John.* Pillar New Testament Commentary. Grand Rapids, MI: Eerdmans, 1991.

———. *The Sermon on the Mount: An Evangelical Exposition of Matthew 5–7.* Grand Rapids, MI: Baker, 1982.

Deines, Roland. "Not the Law but the Messiah: Law and Righteousness in the Gospel of Matthew—An Ongoing Debate." In *Built upon the Rock: Studies in the Gospel of Matthew*, edited by Daniel M. Gurtner and John Nolland, 53–84. Grand Rapids, MI: Eerdmans, 2008.

France, R. T. *The Gospel of Mark: A Commentary on the Greek Text.* New International Greek Testament Commentary. Grand Rapids, MI: Eerdmans, 2014.

———. *The Gospel of Matthew.* New International Commentary on the New Testament. Grand Rapids, MI: Eerdmans, 2007.

Garland, David E. *Luke.* Zondervan Exegetical Commentary on the New Testament 3. Grand Rapids, MI: Zondervan, 2011.

Green, Joel B., ed. *Dictionary of Jesus and the Gospels.* 2nd ed. Downers Grove, IL: IVP Academic, 2013.

Hengel, Martin. *The Four Gospels and the One Gospel of Jesus Christ: An Investigation of the Collection and Origin of the Canonical Gospels.* Translated by John Bowden. Harrisburg, PA: Trinity Press International, 2000.

Irons, Charles Lee. *The Righteousness of God: A Lexical Examination of the Covenant-Faithfulness Interpretation.* Wissenschaftliche Untersuchungen zum Neuen Testament, 2nd ser., vol. 386. Tübingen: Mohr Siebeck, 2015.

Keener, Craig S. *The Gospel of John: A Commentary*. 2 vols. Grand Rapids, MI: Baker Academic, 2010–2012.

Pennington, Jonathan T. *The Sermon on the Mount and Human Flourishing: A Theological Commentary*. Grand Rapids, MI: Baker, 2017.

Quarles, Charles. *Sermon on the Mount: Restoring Christ's Message to the Modern Church*. NAC Studies in Bible and Theology. Nashville: B&H Academic, 2011.

Schlatter, Adolf. *The History of the Christ: The Foundation of New Testament Theology*. Translated by Andreas Köstenberger. Grand Rapids, MI: Baker, 1997.

Strauss, Mark L. *Four Gospels, One Jesus: A Survey of Jesus and the Gospels*. Grand Rapids, MI: Zondervan, 2007.

6

The Righteous God Righteously Righteouses the Unrighteous

Justification according to Romans

ANDREW DAVID NASELLI

Paul's letter to the Romans is not terribly long.[1] It takes about sixty minutes to read aloud. Its God-breathed and life-giving words are worth investing thousands of hours of your life to memorize and meditate on. They explain and exult in and apply the greatest news we could hear. If we dare to speak of portions of Scripture as more important than others, I would argue that Romans is the single most important piece of literature in the history of the world.[2]

And at the heart of Romans is justification. That is what this chapter explores: *What does Romans say about justification?* This chapter answers that question by answering three others:

1. What is the theological message of Romans?
2. What does Paul mean in key texts on justification in Romans?
3. How does Romans contribute to a systematic theology of justification?

What Is the Theological Message of Romans?

If I presented this essay more inductively, I would swap parts 1 and 2—first exegete key texts, and then construct the letter's theological message. First the trees, then the

---

[1]. Thanks to friends who examined a draft of this essay and shared helpful feedback, especially Brent Aucoin, Andrew Cowan, Matt Klem, Jenni Naselli, Matt Perman, Tom Schreiner, Joe Tyrpak, Richard Winston, Jonathon Woodyard, and Bob Yarbrough.
[2]. See Benjamin L. Merkle, "Is Romans Really the Greatest Letter Ever Written?," *SBJT* 11, no. 3 (2007): 18–33.

forest. But I think it will help orient readers if I begin by flying a drone over the forest of Romans before examining the bark formations on particular trees.

This is the gist of what Paul argues in Romans—in five steps:[3]

1. We all need God's righteousness because we are all sinners (1:18–3:20).
2. Faith alone in Jesus is how God will justify us—that is, declare us righteous (3:21–4:25).
3. When we obtain God's righteousness, we experience several results: God reconciles us to himself (5:1–21), he liberates us from sin's dominating power (6:1–23), he frees us from the law (7:1–25), and he gives us assurance and security (8:1–39).
4. The relationship between the gospel and Israel calls the reliability of God's Word into question, so Paul vindicates God's righteousness (9:1–11:36).
5. The gospel transforms how we live and produces righteous living (12:1–15:13).

Here is what I think the theological message of Romans is in one sentence: *the gospel reveals how God is righteously righteousing (i.e., justifying) unrighteous individuals—both Jews and Gentiles—at this stage in the history of salvation.* That happens by faith in Christ apart from the law-covenant, and it happens ultimately for God's glory.

That briefly sketches how I understand Romans and specifically how justification fits into what Paul argues. My (much longer) answers to the next two questions attempt to support and apply the previous paragraph.

What Does Paul Mean in Key Texts on Justification in Romans?

The root δίκ occurs seventy-six times in Romans. Table 6.1 lists the words in the order in which they first appear in the letter.

Table 6.1 The Δίκ Word Group in Romans (76x)

Word	Gloss	Frequency	Passages
δικαιοσύνη	righteousness	33x	1:17; 3:5, 21, 22, 25, 26; 4:3, 5, 6, 9, 11 (2x), 13, 22; 5:17, 21; 6:13, 16, 18, 19, 20; 8:10; 9:30 (3x), 31; 10:3 (2x), 4, 5, 6, 10; 14:17
δίκαιος	righteous	7x	1:17; 2:13; 3:10, 26; 5:7, 19; 7:12
ἀδικία	unrighteousness	7x	1:18 (2x), 29; 2:8; 3:5; 6:13; 9:14
δικαίωμα	requirement, righteous deed	5x	1:32; 2:26; 5:16, 18; 8:4
δικαιοκρισία	righteous verdict	1x	2:5

---

3. This list condenses and updates Andrew David Naselli, *From Typology to Doxology: Paul's Use of Isaiah and Job in Romans 11:34–35* (Eugene, OR: Pickwick, 2012), 7–11.

Word	Gloss	Frequency	Passages
δικαιόω	declare righteous	15x	2:13; 3:4, 20, 24, 26, 28, 30; 4:2, 5; 5:1, 9; 6:7; 8:30 (2x), 33
ἄδικος	unrighteous	1x	3:5
ἔνδικος	just, righteous	1x	3:8
ὑπόδικος	accountable	1x	3:19
δικαίωσις	justification	2x	4:25; 5:18
ἐκδικέω	take revenge	1x	12:19
ἐκδίκησις	vengeance	1x	12:19
ἔκδικος	avenger	1x	13:4

The δίκ word group occurs most densely from 1:17 to 10:10—seventy-two of the seventy-six times (see fig. 6.1).

Figure 6.1 The Frequency of the Δίκ Word Group in Sections of Romans

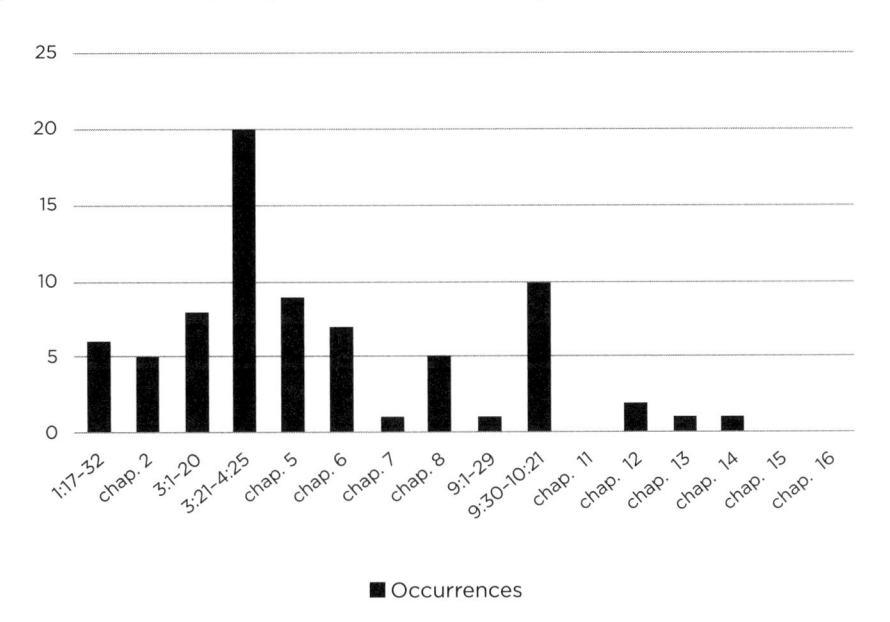

Table 6.1 and figure 6.1 help us identify the most significant passages for understanding what Romans teaches about justification. The following subsections exegete those passages. But first, three introductory notes:

1. My exegesis is concise. I focus on what each passage teaches about justification without being as comprehensive as are more detailed exegetical commentaries, monographs, and articles (e.g., journal articles that focus on just one aspect of one passage).

2. The best way I know how to concisely exegete a passage is to phrase it, so I have created a phrase diagram of each passage using Biblearc software, and these

diagrams are available online at the Biblearc website.⁴ These diagrams support my commentary below on what is significant about each passage regarding justification.⁵

3. The two best commentaries on Romans are by Douglas Moo and Thomas Schreiner, and my exegesis is largely consistent with theirs.⁶ Both Moo and Schreiner recently updated their commentaries for second editions, and they generously shared drafts of their manuscripts with me.⁷ Their second editions will probably release at about the same time that this book on justification is published. Since the first editions of their commentaries will be obsolete then and since they have significantly updated their commentaries,⁸ I interact below with their second editions and cite them not by page numbers but by referring to the passage they are commenting on (e.g., Moo, *Epistle to the Romans*, on 3:21).

Romans 1:16–17

Most commentators on Romans agree that 1:16–17 is central to the letter's theological message. (I include 1:18 in the phrase diagram online because it mentions "unrighteousness" twice.) The gospel reveals δικαιοσύνη θεοῦ—"the righteousness of God." But commentators disagree on how to precisely identify what "the righteousness of God" is (1:17; 3:5, 21, 22, 25, 26; 10:3 [2x]). There are three basic options (though exegetes combine these options in every way possible when they factor in what Paul says about justification elsewhere in Romans and his other letters):⁹

1. What God *is*—God's *attribute* of being righteous or just. As one of God's perfections, "God's righteousness means that God always acts in accordance with what is right and is himself the final standard of what is right."¹⁰ The opposite of "the righteousness of God" is the "ungodliness and unrighteousness of men" (1:18). God is righteous; humans are unrighteous.

---

4. Andrew David Naselli, "Justification according to Romans," July 17, 2018, https://biblearc.com/author/Andy_Naselli/Justification_according_to_Romans/.
5. A phrase diagram is a type of an argument diagram, which is a figure that graphically discerns and displays a text's logical flow of thought by dividing up the text into propositions and phrases and then noting logical relationships between them. A phrase diagram indents clauses and phrases above or below what they modify and adds labels that explain how the propositions and phrases logically relate. The phrase diagrams posted online (https://biblearc.com/author/Andy_Naselli/Justification_according_to_Romans/) that are related to my work in this chapter are in English, but I first phrased the Greek text and then mirrored that in the ESV as much as possible. For an introduction to phrasing, see chap. 5 in Andrew David Naselli, *How to Understand and Apply the New Testament: Twelve Steps from Exegesis to Theology* (Phillipsburg, NJ: P&R, 2017), 121–61. I prepared all the phrase diagrams related to my work in this chapter using Biblearc software; see www.Biblearc.com.
6. Douglas J. Moo, *The Epistle to the Romans*, 1st ed., NICNT (Grand Rapids, MI: Eerdmans, 1996); Thomas R. Schreiner, *Romans*, 1st ed., BECNT 6 (Grand Rapids, MI: Baker Academic, 1998).
7. Douglas J. Moo, *The Epistle to the Romans*, 2nd ed., NICNT (Grand Rapids, MI: Eerdmans, 2018); Thomas R. Schreiner, *Romans*, 2nd ed., BECNT 6 (Grand Rapids, MI: Baker Academic, 2018).
8. Two examples: (1) In Moo's first edition, he argues that on the "already–not yet" spectrum, justification is "already" only, but in his second edition, he argues that in some texts (most convincingly in Galatians), Paul thinks of justification also as a future verdict at the last judgment. (2) In Schreiner's first edition, he argues that righteousness is transformative. In a book published three years after his Romans commentary, Schreiner includes this footnote: "I am grateful to Bruce Ware and especially Don Carson for personal correspondence in which they responded to my section on righteousness. They persuaded me that righteousness is forensic rather than transformative, and hence what I have written here is an adjustment to the view I expressed in my book *Romans*." Thomas R. Schreiner, *Paul, Apostle of God's Glory in Christ: A Pauline Theology* (Downers Grove, IL: InterVarsity Press, 2001), 192n2.
9. Cf. Moo, *Epistle to the Romans*, on 1:17. For a historical survey, see Charles Lee Irons, *The Righteousness of God: A Lexical Examination of the Covenant-Faithfulness Interpretation*, WUNT, 2nd ser., vol. 386 (Tübingen: Mohr Siebeck, 2015), 9–60.
10. Wayne Grudem, *Systematic Theology: An Introduction to Biblical Doctrine* (Grand Rapids, MI: Zondervan, 1994), 203. See Moo, *Epistle to the Romans*, "Excursus: 'Righteousness' Language in Paul," after comments on 1:17.

2. What God *gives*—God's *gift* of a righteous status to sinful people.[11] The metaphor is from the law court (righteousness = judicial [e.g., see 8:33]); it is not about people living in a more righteous way (righteousness ≠ transformative). That is, this gift is God's legally *declaring* people to be righteous before him; it does not morally *make* them righteous by gradually infusing righteousness into them.[12]
3. What God *does*—God's *activity* of saving sinful people. He rights what is wrong. Some who hold this view define God's righteousness as his covenant faithfulness and define justification as what enables us to know who is part of the people of God, particularly by declaring that God has included Gentiles in his covenant community.[13]

It is too narrow to say that "the righteousness of God" refers to only one of the three options and not the other two. I agree with what John Stott says about these three options: "All three are true and have been held by different scholars, sometimes in relation to each other. For myself, I have never been able to see why we have to choose, and why all three should not be combined."[14]

In my view, *God's attribute of being righteous* (option 1) is the fundamental concept, and in the context of Romans, that entails both *God's gift of a righteous status* (option 2) and *God's activity of saving* (option 3—minus the "covenant faithfulness" definition).[15] Of the three options, *God's gift of a righteous status* (option 2) is most prominent in Romans. "The righteousness of God" refers primarily to God's positive attribute of being righteous, and when sinful people experience that aspect of God, God either (1) saves them by righteously giving them a righteous status or (2) condemns them. And while God will faithfully fulfill his promises because he is righteous, the essence of God's righteousness is not his covenant faithfulness.[16]

I joyfully affirm and celebrate the traditional Protestant view of justification. Before Martin Luther embraced justification by faith alone, he experienced terror and despair over "the righteousness of God" in Romans 1:17. He thought "the righteousness of God" in 1:17 refers to the *exacting justice* of God—that God would eternally damn all sinners. He hated God for that.

---

11. Cf. Charles Hodge, *A Commentary on the Epistle to the Romans* (Philadelphia: Perkins, 1836), 27–28; John Murray, *The Epistle to the Romans: The English Text with Introduction, Exposition and Notes*, NICNT (Grand Rapids, MI: Eerdmans, 1959–1965), 1:29–31; C. E. B. Cranfield, *A Critical and Exegetical Commentary on the Epistle to the Romans*, ICC (Edinburgh: T&T Clark, 1975–1979), 95–99; Irons, *Righteousness of God*, 311–36.

12. Thomas Schreiner, *Faith Alone: The Doctrine of Justification; What the Reformers Taught . . . and Why It Still Matters*, Five Solas Series (Grand Rapids, MI: Zondervan, 2015), 158–69, 175. Proverbs 17:15 illustrates that justification is judicial and not transformative: "He who justifies the wicked and he who condemns the righteous are both alike an abomination to the Lord." John MacArthur and Richard Mayhue argue, "If justification were transformative, how could it be said that making a wicked person righteous is an abomination? Transforming the character of a wicked person and infusing him with righteousness would be a righteous act! . . . To justify the wicked is not to make him righteous but to declare him righteous when he is not." John MacArthur and Richard Mayhue, gen. eds., *Biblical Doctrine: A Systematic Summary of Bible Truth* (Wheaton, IL: Crossway, 2017), 613.

13. E.g., N. T. Wright, *Justification: God's Plan and Paul's Vision* (Downers Grove, IL: IVP Academic, 2009), 59–79.

14. John R. W. Stott, *The Message of Romans: God's Good News for the World*, Bible Speaks Today (Downers Grove, IL: InterVarsity Press, 1994), 63. Similarly, David G. Peterson, *Commentary on Romans*, Biblical Theology for Christian Proclamation (Nashville: B&H, 2017), 105.

15. See the detailed arguments in Moo, *Epistle to the Romans*, on 1:17; Schreiner, *Romans*, on 1:17; Denny Burk, "The Righteousness of God (*Dikaiosunē Theou*) and Verbal Genitives: A Grammatical Clarification," *JSNT* 34, no. 4 (2012): 346–60. Cf. also Richard N. Longenecker, *The Epistle to the Romans: A Commentary on the Greek Text*, NIGTC (Grand Rapids, MI: Eerdmans, 2016), 168–76.

16. For the monograph that most decisively refutes the covenant-faithfulness view, see Irons, *Righteousness of God*. Cf. Thomas R. Schreiner's review of the book for the Gospel Coalition, September 2, 2015, https://www.thegospelcoalition.org/article/book-reviews-righteousness-of-god-lee-irons.

Luther's exegetical breakthrough came when he discovered the gospel as he studied the Psalms, Romans, Galatians, and Hebrews—especially Romans 1:17:

> I had indeed been captivated with an extraordinary ardor for understanding Paul in the Epistle to the Romans. But up till then it was not the cold blood about the heart, but a single word in Chapter 1, "In it the righteousness of God is revealed" [1:17], that had stood in my way. For I hated that word "righteousness of God," which, according to the use and custom of all the teachers, I had been taught to understand philosophically regarding the formal or active righteousness, as they called it, with which God is righteous and punishes the unrighteous sinner.
>
> Though I lived as a monk without reproach, I felt that I was a sinner before God with an extremely disturbed conscience. I could not believe that he was placated by my satisfaction. I did not love, yes, I hated the righteous God who punishes sinners, and secretly, if not blasphemously, certainly murmuring greatly, I was angry with God, and said, "As if, indeed, it is not enough, that miserable sinners, eternally lost through original sin, are crushed by every kind of calamity by the law of the decalogue, without having God add pain to pain by the gospel and also by the gospel threatening us with his righteousness and wrath!" Thus I raged with a fierce and troubled conscience. Nevertheless, I beat importunately upon Paul at that place, most ardently desiring to know what St. Paul wanted.
>
> At last, by the mercy of God, meditating day and night, I gave heed to the context of the words, namely, "In it the righteousness of God is revealed, as it is written, 'He who through faith is righteous shall live.'" There I began to understand that the righteousness of God is that by which the righteous lives by a gift of God, namely by faith. And this is the meaning: the righteousness of God is revealed by the gospel, namely, the passive righteousness with which merciful God justifies us by faith, as it is written, "He who through faith is righteous shall live." Here I felt that I was altogether born again and had entered paradise itself through open gates. . . .
>
> And I extolled my sweetest word with a love as great as the hatred with which I had before hated the word "righteousness of God." Thus that place in Paul was for me truly the gate to paradise. Later I read Augustine's *The Spirit and the Letter*, where contrary to hope I found that he, too, interpreted God's righteousness in a similar way, as the righteousness with which God clothes us when he justifies us. Although this was heretofore said imperfectly and he did not explain all things concerning imputation clearly, it nevertheless was pleasing that God's righteousness with which we are justified was taught.[17]

God not only *is* righteous but also *gives* righteousness. "This teaching," Timothy George notes, "became the guiding principle of Luther's thought and the cornerstone of Reformation theology."[18] As Stott puts it,

---

17. Martin Luther, "Preface to the Complete Edition of Luther's Latin Writings," *LW* 34:336–37.
18. Timothy George, "Luther, Martin," in *Biographical Dictionary of Evangelicals*, ed. Timothy T. Larsen (Downers Grove, IL: InterVarsity Press, 2003), 376.

"The righteousness of God" is God's just justification of the unjust, his righteous way of pronouncing the unrighteous righteous, in which he both demonstrates his righteousness and gives righteousness to us. He has done it through Christ, the righteous one, who died for the unrighteous, as Paul will explain later. And he does it by faith when we put our trust in him, and cry to him for mercy.[19]

The gospel reveals "God's righteous way of 'righteoussing' the unrighteous."[20] "The righteousness of God" refers not only to what God *is* when he justifies you but to what God *gives* you when he justifies you: God is both "just and the justifier of the one who has faith in Jesus" (3:26). God righteously "righteouses" the unrighteous.

Romans 2:5–16

In Romans 2:1–3:8, Paul indicts Jews for rejecting what God revealed to them. In 2:6–16,[21] he argues that God will impartially judge both Gentiles and Jews according to what they have done.[22] Jews (who have the Mosaic law) are not inherently more likely to receive eternal life than Gentiles (who do not have the Mosaic law) because *having* the law is not what matters—*obeying* it is (2:12–13). Further, there is a sense in which the Gentiles have the law (2:14–16).[23]

But as Paul indicts the Jews, he seems to teach that God justifies people based on what they do:

> He will render to each one according to his works: to those who by patience in well-doing seek for glory and honor and immortality, he will give eternal life. . . . [There will be] glory and honor and peace for everyone who does good, the Jew first and also the Greek. . . . [It is] *the doers of the law who will be justified*. (2:6–7, 10, 13)

There are two good options for identifying these do-gooders:

1. *People in general*. The condition for earning eternal life apart from Christ is to persevere in good works ("by patience in well-doing," 2:7), but apart from Christ no one can meet that condition (3:9–20).[24]
2. *Christians*. Because Christians are united to Christ, they are able to persevere in good works that serve as the necessary evidence for their faith on judgment day.[25]

---

19. Stott, *Romans*, 64.
20. Stott, *Romans*, 37.
21. Cf. Moo, *Epistle to the Romans*, on 2:1–16.
22. The chiasm in Rom. 2:6–11 is visible in the phrase diagram for this passage posted online at https://biblearc.com/author/Andy_Naselli/Justification_according_to_Romans/.
23. There are two good options for identifying the "Gentiles" in Rom. 2:14: (1) Non-Christian Gentiles do part of the law. See Moo, *Epistle to the Romans*, on 2:14. (2) Christian Gentiles fulfill the law because they are in Christ. See Schreiner, *Romans*, on 2:12–16 (Schreiner changed his view; his first edition argues for the previous option); Simon J. Gathercole, "A Law unto Themselves: The Gentiles in Romans 2.14–15 Revisited," *JSNT* 24, no. 3 (2002): 27–49; A. B. Caneday, "Judgment, Behavior, and Justification according to Paul's Gospel in Romans 2," *Journal for the Study of Paul and His Letters* 1 (2011): 153–92. I lean toward the first option, but both options agree that God does not justify people based on their works.
24. Moo, *Epistle to the Romans*, on 2:9–10.
25. Schreiner, *Romans*, on 2:6–11 and 2:25–29. For how Schreiner understands Romans 2 in light of the rest of the New Testament, see Thomas R. Schreiner, "Justification apart from and by Works: At the Final Judgment Works Will Confirm Justification," in *Four Views on the Role of Works at the Final Judgment*, ed. Alan P. Stanley, Counterpoints: Bible and Theology (Grand Rapids, MI: Zondervan, 2013), 71–98 (also 51–56, 148–54, 191–96).

The first option is better because of the passage's literary context, but both options are consistent with what the Bible teaches elsewhere. In order to understand justification in Romans, it is not crucial to choose one of those two views. It is more important to conclude from this passage that (1) God does not justify people *based on* their works and that (2) in 2:13 "Paul essentially defines δικαιόω as 'to declare one to be δίκαιος before God.'"[26]

Romans 3:9–20

It is not merely that all sorts of humans are sinful; all humans without exception are sinful. Paul uses absolute negative language to emphasize that human sinfulness is all-inclusive. Absolute negative language avoids misunderstanding and emphasizes universality without exception. For example, "Absalom has struck down *all* the king's sons, and *not one* of them is left" (2 Sam. 13:30).[27] So when Paul wants to emphasize that every single human without exception is sinful, he expresses it with absolute negatives: "*None* is righteous, *no, not one*. . . . *No one* does good, *not even one*" (Rom. 3:10, 12).[28]

No human being will be justified "by works of the law"—that is, by obeying the entire Mosaic law (3:20). "Works of the law" are a subset of "works" in general; no human being will be justified by works of any kind at all.[29] Contra proponents of the so-called New Perspective on Paul, "works of the law" do not refer primarily to laws that distinguish Jews from Gentiles—that is, Jewish boundary markers such as circumcision, the Sabbath, and food laws.[30]

Justification is not by works. That is, humans cannot earn justification. They cannot earn a right standing before God based on how they live. God does not declare humans to be righteous based on their good works.

Romans 3:21–4:25

The δίκ word group appears in Romans 3:21–4:25 twenty times—the densest cluster of references to righteousness in the entire letter (see fig. 6.1). And it begins with what is arguably the most important paragraph in the Bible.

Romans 3:21–26

In the margin of the Luther Bible, Martin Luther describes Romans 3:21–26 as "the chief point, and the very central place of the Epistle [to the Romans], and of the whole

---

26. Irons, *Righteousness of God*, 339.
27. One could find scores of examples like this by searching the Bible for the words "not one," "not even one," "no one," or "none" (e.g., Ex. 8:31; 9:6; 10:19; Num. 11:19; Josh. 10:8; 21:44; 23:14; Matt. 24:2; Luke 12:6; John 17:12; 18:9; Acts 4:32; Rom. 14:7).
28. Bryan Blazosky argues that the Mosaic law condemns and enslaves Gentile sinners and not just Jews. See Bryan Blazosky, "The Law's Universal Condemning and Enslaving Power: A Study of the Relationship of Gentiles to the Law in Paul, the Old Testament, and the Second Temple Jewish Literature" (PhD diss., Ridley College, Melbourne, 2016).
29. Paul later refers to works in general and not to works of the law in particular (Rom. 4:2, 6; 9:32; 11:6).
30. The literature on the phrase "works of the law" is massive. For helpful summaries and arguments, see Moo, *Epistle to the Romans*, on 3:20 and the subsequent excursus, "The 'New Perspective on Judaism' and the 'New Perspective on Paul'"; Schreiner, *Romans*, on 3:20; Schreiner, *Faith Alone*, 97–111, 239–52. See also chap. 9, by Timo Laato, in this book, which critiques the New Perspective on Paul.

Bible."³¹ Leon Morris calls it "possibly the most important single paragraph ever written."³²

Romans 3:21–26 breaks down into four major parts:³³

First, the righteousness of God has been revealed at this point in salvation history apart from the now obsolete law-covenant, and the Old Testament prophetically testifies to this shift (3:21).³⁴

Second, the righteousness of God is universally available without ethnic distinction (3:22–23). It is available only by trusting Jesus, and it is available for all who trust Jesus—whether Jews or Gentiles. "Through *faith* [πίστεως] in Jesus Christ for all who *believe* [πιστεύοντας]" (3:22) could read "through *trust* in Jesus Christ for all who *trust*."³⁵ I am not aware of any English translations that maintain that parallelism—that is, *trust* and *trust*. English translations obscure what is apparent in Greek. The noun *faith* and the verb *believe* sound totally different in English, but in Greek they are cognates. It would be like this in English: "through *faith* in Jesus Christ for all who *are faithing*." Paul repeats *all* to emphasize the universal scope, which connects this paragraph with 1:18–3:20: *all* are under sin; *all* are condemned; *all* need God's righteousness; and *all* are savable.

Third, the righteousness of God is free and expensive (3:24). God declares believers righteous (1) freely (i.e., as a gift—neither earned nor purchased), (2) by his grace (i.e., by his undeserved kindness—not because believers are inherently better than others), and (3) through the costly redemption Jesus purchased. Paul connects justification to union with Christ (ἐν Χριστῷ Ἰησοῦ, "in Christ Jesus"): "*In-Christ-redemption* is the instrument of grace to bring about justification. . . . Justification occurs through *in-Christ-redemption*, which is the instrument of grace."³⁶

Redemption is a metaphor drawn from the world of commerce and slavery. Redemption in both the Greco-Roman and Jewish contexts commonly referred to freedom from slavery after someone paid the price or ransom. In our case, we are enslaved to sin, and Jesus frees us from that slavery by paying the price—his death. D. A. Carson explains,

> The way it normally worked was like this: the redeemer paid the price money for the slave to a pagan temple plus a small cut for the temple priests (and how small a cut was variable!). Then the temple paid the price money to the owner of the slave, and

---

31. Martin Luther, *Luther Bible*, margin at Rom. 3:23ff., quoted in Moo, *Epistle to the Romans*, 1st ed., 218n1.
32. Leon Morris, *The Epistle to the Romans*, PNTC (Grand Rapids, MI: Eerdmans, 1988), 173.
33. On this passage, see Moo, *Epistle to the Romans*, on 3:21–26; Schreiner, *Romans*, on 3:21–26; D. A. Carson, "Atonement in Romans 3:21–26: God Presented Him as a Propitiation," in *The Glory of the Atonement: Biblical, Historical, and Practical Perspectives; Essays in Honor of Roger R. Nicole*, ed. Charles E. Hill and Frank A. James III (Downers Grove, IL: InterVarsity Press, 2004), 119–39.
34. Carson, "Atonement in Romans 3:21–26," 121–23.
35. It is much more likely that πίστεως Ἰησοῦ Χριστοῦ ["faith of Jesus Christ"] is an objective genitive (i.e., faith *in* Jesus Christ) rather than a subjective genitive (i.e., Jesus Christ is faithful, thus, the faithfulness of Jesus Christ). See Schreiner, *Romans*, on 3:22; Schreiner, *Faith Alone*, 124–32; Carson, "Atonement in Romans 3:21–26," 125–27; Kukwah Philemon Yong, "The Faith of Jesus Christ: An Analysis of Paul's Use of ΠΙΣΤΙΣ ΧΡΙΣΤΟΥ" (PhD diss., Southern Baptist Theological Seminary, 2003), 147–201.
36. Constantine R. Campbell, *Paul and Union with Christ: An Exegetical and Theological Study* (Grand Rapids, MI: Zondervan, 2012), 114. Campbell skillfully synthesizes justification and union with Christ; see 388–405.

the slave was then transferred to the ownership of this temple's god. Thus, the slave was redeemed from the slavery to the slave owner, in order to become a slave to the god. Of course, if you are a slave to a pagan god, that basically means that you are free and can do anything you want. It was in part a legal fiction in order to say that the person does not lose his slave status but nevertheless is freed from slavery in the human sphere because the price has been paid. The man has now been redeemed.

Paul picks up that language and says that Christians have been redeemed from slavery to sin, but as a result of this, they have become slaves of Jesus Christ (see Romans 6).[37]

Fourth, the righteous God presented Jesus as a propitiation (3:25–26). In 3:21–22, "the righteousness of God" is what God *gives*—God's *gift* of a righteous status to sinful people. In 3:25–26, it refers to what God *is*—God's *attribute* of being righteous or just.[38]

In the Greco-Roman world of Paul's day, pagans would offer sacrifices to their gods to make the gods *propitious* or favorable. Their sacrifices were propitiations. But that parallel breaks down when we apply it to Jesus's propitiation that made God the Father propitious because God the Father himself sends Jesus, God the Son, to make the propitiation. Propitiation is the only biblical term related to God's saving us for which God is both the subject and object. That is, God is the one who propitiates (he is the subject doing the propitiation), and God is the one who is propitiated (he is the object receiving the propitiation). God the Son is the propitia*tion*, and God the Father is the propitia*ted*. Jesus's sacrificial death propitiates the Father—that is, Jesus turns God's wrath against us into favor. According to Stott, "This is the righteous basis on which the righteous God can 'righteous' the unrighteous without compromising his righteousness."[39]

Propitiation is accessible to us through faith alone (3:25). God presented Jesus as a propitiation to demonstrate that he was and is righteous: (1) he was righteous for leaving the sins committed before the cross unpunished (3:25), and (2) he is righteous to declare that believing sinners are righteous (3:26).

First, God was righteous for leaving the sins committed before the cross unpunished (3:25). Modern readers may puzzle over 3:25: "This was to show God's righteousness, because in his divine forbearance he had passed over former sins." Paul's point is that Old Testament sacrifices were valid in God's mind based on Christ's future sacrifice. It is like how you buy an item on credit. When my vehicle needs more gas, I stop at a gas station and refuel. Rather than walking into the store to pay, I conveniently slide my credit card through the machine at the pump and fill up my gas tank. I do not pay any cash, but I still get the gas. How? I get the gas *on credit*. Within a month of filling up my tank, I receive a bill with the account payable to the credit card company. That is when I must pay for what I borrowed on credit. That illustrates how God saved Old

---

37. D. A. Carson, *Scandalous: The Cross and Resurrection of Jesus*, Re:Lit (Wheaton, IL: Crossway, 2010), 59.
38. Carson, "Atonement in Romans 3:21–26," 137–38.
39. Stott, *Romans*, 115. Contra C. H. Dodd, *The Epistle of Paul to the Romans*, MNTC (London: Collins, 1932), 54–55. Leon Morris soundly refutes Dodd in Morris, *The Apostolic Preaching of the Cross*, 3rd ed. (Grand Rapids, MI: Eerdmans, 1965), 144–213.

Testament believers on credit. Just like I slide my credit card through the machine, they offered sacrifices to God in faith. Just like I get the gas, they received genuine forgiveness of sin. Just like I receive a bill for the gas and pay it, Christ received their bill and paid their sin debt in full. Christ died publicly to demonstrate God's righteousness in saving Old Testament saints on credit.

Second, God is righteous to declare that believing sinners are righteous (3:26). I was recently talking to a relative who informed me that he no longer professed to be a Christian. One reason he gave for not embracing Christianity is that the doctrine of justification seems immoral. I asked him if this illustration was what he meant: *The gospel is like a judge who hears the case of a guilty person before him at the bar, and the judge pronounces the sentence. Then the judge steps back from the bench, takes off his robes, and goes down to take the guilty person's place in prison or pay the fine.* My relative said yes—that is the concept he finds problematic. Then I surprised him by explaining why I agree that the illustration is problematic. It's misleading.[40]

That illustration is not entirely wrong because it illustrates that Jesus substitutes for sinners. But it is misleading because in Western judicial systems, the judge must neutrally administer the law. The guilty person's offense is not against the judge. If the guilty person is guilty for harming the judge, then the judge must recuse himself from the case. Judges excuse themselves from a case because of a possible conflict of interest that makes it challenging for them to judge impartially. The judge is not supposed to be the offended party. Criminals offend the state or the law or the republic or the crown—not the neutral judge.

But not with God. God is both the judge and the most offended party when people sin. He never recuses himself, and he is always just. The reason he can justly pronounce believing sinners to be innocent is that Jesus propitiates his righteous wrath. Justice is served. Propitiation demonstrates that God is righteous when he declares that a believing sinner is righteous.

Romans 3:27–31

Paul draws three inferences about faith from Romans 3:21–26:

First, humans cannot boast because God justifies them by faith alone (3:27–28). Works earn, but faith only receives. Paul uses a play on words in 3:27 by using "law" metaphorically for a principle: "By what kind of law [i.e., principle]? By a law [i.e., principle] of works? No, but by the law [i.e., principle] of faith."

Second, God justifies both Jews and Gentiles by faith (3:29–30). He does not exclude Gentiles. Gentiles can access God the same way Jews can—by faith.[41] He justifies both groups by faith based on Jesus's sacrifice—not the Jewish distinctive of circumcision.

---

40. The rest of this section paraphrases Carson, *Scandalous*, 65–66.
41. "God is one" (Rom. 3:30) refers not only to Deut. 6:4 but also to Zech. 14:9: "And the Lord will be king over all the earth. On that day the Lord will be one and his name one." God is now the covenant Lord of both Jews and Gentiles. See Christopher R. Bruno, *"God Is One": The Function of* Eis Ho Theos *as a Ground for Gentile Inclusion in Paul's Letters*, LNTS 497 (London: T&T Clark, 2013), 114–61.

Third, God's people fulfill the law by this faith—they do not nullify it (3:31). Here Paul does not specify how, but he seems to later: for "those who are in Christ Jesus" (8:1), "the righteous requirement of the law might be fulfilled in us, who walk not according to the flesh but according to the Spirit" (8:4). Christ fulfilled what the law commanded, so believers fulfill the law because they are in Christ, who represents them and enables them to persevere in good works (see 13:8–10).[42]

Then, in chapter 4, Paul uses Abraham to illustrate those inferences about faith. The first two sections of chapter 4 correspond to the first two inferences: 4:1–8 illustrates 3:27–28, and 4:9–17 illustrates 3:29–30. Throughout chapter 4 Paul elaborates on Genesis 15:6: Abraham "believed the LORD, and he counted it to him as righteousness."[43]

Romans 4:1–8

Romans 4:1–8 elaborates on 3:27–28: the Jewish patriarch Abraham illustrates that humans cannot boast, because God justifies them by faith alone (see the section on 3:27–31 above). Abraham could boast if God justified him based on his works,[44] but then justification would be not a gift from God but something Abraham earned (4:2, 4). But justification is not based on works. Abraham's faith is counted to him as righteousness (4:3, 5). God did not justify Abraham *because* Abraham was godly. Abraham was ungodly (4:5; cf. Josh. 24:2–3). And God "justifies the ungodly" by faith alone (Rom. 4:5).

That is the same God who pronounced, "I will not acquit the wicked" (Ex. 23:7), and who condemns human judges who "justify" guilty people (Prov. 17:15; 24:24; Isa. 5:23). So how can God righteously acquit guilty people? What exactly is he imputing to them? Their own faith? To answer that question requires systematically correlating what Paul writes about imputation in three key texts (Rom. 4; 5:12–21; 2 Cor. 5:21) and three other related texts (Rom. 9:30–10:4; 1 Cor. 1:30; Phil. 3:9).[45]

In Romans 4, "Paul never links explicitly the imputation of righteousness with the righteousness of Christ. There is no explicit mention of Christ in any connection until verses 24 and 25. The content of the imputed righteousness is, however, already spelled out as the righteousness from God that is ours through Christ on the basis of Christ's work on our behalf (3:21ff)."[46] Carson explains Paul's logic in Romans 4:5:

> God's imputation of Abraham's faith to Abraham as righteousness *cannot* be grounded in the assumption that that faith is itself intrinsically righteous, so that God's "imputing" of it to Abraham is no more than a recognition of what it intrin-

---

42. Moo, *Epistle to the Romans*, on 3:31. (See the section on 8:1–4 below.)
43. See "Excursus: Genesis 15:6," after comments on Rom. 4:7–8, in Moo, *Epistle to the Romans*.
44. "Works" (Rom. 4:2) refers to obeying God, not to "works of the law," because the Mosaic law came 430 years after Abraham (Gal. 3:17).
45. That is exactly what the following book (persuasively) does: Brian Vickers, *Jesus' Blood and Righteousness: Paul's Theology of Imputation* (Wheaton, IL: Crossway, 2006). Vickers's thesis is that "the imputation of Christ's righteousness is a legitimate and necessary synthesis of Paul's teaching. While no single text contains or develops all the 'ingredients' of imputation, the doctrine stands as a component of Paul's soteriology" (18). See also J. V. Fesko, *Death in Adam, Life in Christ: The Doctrine of Imputation*, REDS (Fearn, Ross-shire, Scotland: Mentor, 2016), 197–223.
46. Vickers, *Jesus' Blood and Righteousness*, 109.

sically is. If God is counting faith to Abraham *as* righteousness, *he is counting him righteous*—not because Abraham is righteous in some inherent way (How can he be? He is ἀσεβής! ["ungodly"]), but simply because Abraham trusts God and his gracious promise. In that sense, then, we are dealing with what systematicians call an alien righteousness.[47]

Faith is not *what* God imputes but the *means* by which God imputes righteousness (cf. 4:11: "righteousness would be counted to them").[48] That "alien righteousness" must belong to Christ, "whom God put forward as a propitiation by his blood, to be received by faith" (3:25). God can righteously acquit guilty people who are in Christ. When God justifies a believing sinner, he counts (i.e., reckons or credits or imputes) Christ's righteousness to that sinner.[49]

God does that by means of faith alone—not the believer's good works. And the result is that believers are simultaneously justified and sinners. The Latin phrase Luther popularized is *simul iustus et peccator*—justified and at the same time sinners.

David's words in Psalm 32:1–2 support the idea that God counts a person righteous apart from works (Rom. 4:6–8). Being forgiven is a component of being justified. When God declares people righteous, he forgives their sins. God no longer counts their sins against them. That is why they are "blessed" (4:7).

Romans 4:9–17

Romans 4:9–17 elaborates on 3:29–30: the Jewish patriarch Abraham illustrates that God justifies both Jews and Gentiles by faith (see the section on 3:27–31 above). God justified Abraham by faith *before* Abraham was circumcised to make Abraham the spiritual father of both believing Jews and believing Gentiles; thus, circumcision is not necessary to be justified—faith is (4:9–13). Depending on keeping the law would nullify faith because "the law brings wrath" since humans cannot keep it (4:14–15). Therefore, all humans access the inheritance God graciously promised by faith—as Abraham did (4:16–17).

Romans 4:18–25

Abraham *believed* what God promised, even when circumstances seemed to indicate that what God promised would never happen (Rom. 4:18–21). Thus, God justified him by faith alone (4:22). And God justifies others by faith alone. The God "who gives life to the dead" (4:17) revived Abraham's body that "was as good as dead" (4:19), and he "raised from the dead Jesus our Lord," whom God delivered over to death to take care

---

47. D. A. Carson, "The Vindication of Imputation: On Fields of Discourse and Semantic Fields," in *Justification: What's at Stake in the Current Debates*, ed. Mark A. Husbands and Daniel J. Treier (Downers Grove, IL: InterVarsity Press, 2004), 60.
48. Carson, "Vindication of Imputation," 65.
49. Carson, "Vindication of Imputation," 68–78; Schreiner, *Faith Alone*, 179–90, 253–61; John Piper, *Counted Righteous in Christ: Should We Abandon the Imputation of Christ's Righteousness?*, in *The Collected Works of John Piper*, ed. David Mathis and Justin Taylor (Wheaton, IL: Crossway, 2017), 5:323–77.

of our trespasses and whom God raised to take care of our justification (4:23–25).⁵⁰ The clauses in 4:25 are parallel:

> Jesus was delivered up   *for* [διά] our trespasses.
> Jesus was raised   *for* [διά] our justification.

Instead of "for," a better way to translate the preposition διά here is "on account of" or "to take care of." Both Jesus's death and his resurrection identify him with believers. When he died for believers, he took care of their trespasses by removing them, and when he was resurrected for believers, he took care of their justification by confirming it.⁵¹ That is possible because believers are united with Jesus, whose resurrection justified, or vindicated, him.⁵²

Romans 5:1–11

The "therefore" (οὖν) that begins Romans 5 introduces an inference—namely, five results of 3:21–4:25:

1. We have peace with God (5:1).
2. We have obtained access through Jesus Christ by faith into this grace in which we stand (5:2).
3. We rejoice in the hope of the glory of God (5:2).
4. We rejoice in our sufferings (5:3–10).
5. We rejoice in God (5:11).

Those results flow from being justified by faith. Paul argues from the greater to the lesser in 5:9: because we have now been justified by Jesus's blood while we were still sinners (the greater work), Jesus will certainly save us from God's wrath in the future (the lesser work).

The phrases "we have been justified by faith" (5:1) and "we have now been justified by his blood" (5:9) raise a question: How do the "by" phrases differ? We are not justified "by faith" and "by his blood" in the same way. The instrumental phrases are not synonymous:

- "by [ἐκ] faith" (5:1): Faith is the *means* by which God justifies us. It is a human activity that God enables.
- "by [ἐν] his blood" (5:9): Jesus's sacrificial death in our place is the *basis* on which God justifies us.

---

50. Paul likely alludes to the suffering servant of Isaiah 53 (LXX), especially 53:10–12.
51. Colin G. Kruse cautions, "In 5:18 Paul says that it was Christ's 'righteous act,' that is, his death on the cross, that led to our justification. This should alert us to the fact that it was not Paul's intention in 4:25 to drive a wedge between the effects of Christ's death (securing forgiveness for our transgressions) and his resurrection (leading to our justification). Rather, it was the death and resurrection of Jesus as one great salvation event that secured both our forgiveness and our justification. While it is possible to speak separately about forgiveness and justification, they cannot be separated in fact. Those whose sins God forgives he also justifies." *Paul's Letter to the Romans*, PNTC (Grand Rapids, MI: Eerdmans, 2012), 223–24.
52. See G. K. Beale, *A New Testament Biblical Theology: The Unfolding of the Old Testament in the New* (Grand Rapids, MI: Baker Academic, 2011), 496–97.

Romans 5:15–21

Adam's sin resulted in God's judging sinners, but Christ's sacrificial death resulted in God's justifying believing sinners (Rom. 5:15–19). Adam represents all humans, and Jesus represents humans who receive the gift of a righteous status by faith.[53] Grace in Christ abounds more than our sins so that grace reigns "through righteousness," resulting in eternal life by means of Jesus (5:20–21). That righteousness (5:21) is "the free gift" (5:16–17) of a righteous status that God gives believing sinners when he justifies them: "As by the one man's disobedience the many were made [i.e., have the status of] sinners, so by the one man's obedience the many will be made [i.e., have the status of] righteous" (5:19).[54] Sinners can have the status of righteous because they are united to Christ as their representative—it is "a representative union."[55] Adam made a mess, and Christ not only cleaned up the mess but gives believing sinners the status of righteous.[56]

Romans 6:12–23

God's people must become what they are—that is, they must live in a way that is consistent with their legal status before God. Those whom God has declared to be righteous must live righteously. Everyone is a slave—either a slave to sin or a slave to God and righteousness. A Christian is not a slave to sin but a slave to God and righteousness.[57]

Romans 8:1–4

Condemnation is the opposite of justification (Rom. 5:18; 8:33–34). Those whom God has justified "are in Christ Jesus," so there is "no condemnation" for them (8:1). God condemned their sin by sending Jesus to die for their sin and thus to conquer its condemning power (8:3). God did that for a specific purpose: "in order that the righteous requirement of the law might be fulfilled in us, who walk not according to the flesh but according to the Spirit" (8:4). There are two viable ways to interpret how

---

53. See Joshua M. Philpot, "SBJT Forum: How Does Scripture Teach the Adam-Christ Typological Connection?," *SBJT* 21, no. 1 (2017): 145–52.

54. "Were made" and "will be made" translate forms of the verb καθίστημι. After surveying that word's semantic domain and use in the Septuagint, Vickers concludes, "We do not need to back away from the word *made* and make it a synonym for the word *reckon*. Paul's use of καθίστημι is itself the best argument against a transformative interpretation of this text. The confusion over 5:19 stems most likely from the meaning of the English word *made*, rather than to any ambiguity in the Greek text. The statements in Romans 5:19 refer to statuses. One is either a 'sinner' or one is 'righteous.' It is perhaps the most basic point made in all Scripture, and it is a profound point as well, because each individual person possesses his status because he was 'made' a sinner or 'made' righteous on the basis of another's action. Again Paul's word selection could hardly be more fitting since he is speaking about being legally placed into one category or the other. The focus in this text is not on the actions of the person receiving the status, nor is it on the instrumentality by which a person acquires the status, but on the status itself with particular emphasis on the actions that resulted in the status." *Jesus' Blood and Righteousness*, 122. Vickers clarifies in a later book, "The status with which we are appointed is due to the fact that we are counted to have sinned in Adam and counted to have obeyed in Christ. So while *made* does not mean *impute*, the two are inseparable actions. . . . Paul has already established righteousness through imputation in Romans 4, and that provides the backdrop for understanding what is at work when a person is 'made' righteous." *Justification by Grace through Faith: Finding Freedom from Legalism, Lawlessness, Pride, and Despair*, Explorations in Biblical Theology (Phillipsburg, NJ: P&R, 2013), 48. Cf. Micah John McCormick, "The Active Obedience of Christ" (PhD diss., Southern Baptist Theological Seminary, 2010), 253–62.

55. Vickers, *Jesus' Blood and Righteousness*, 195.

56. Cf. Thomas R. Schreiner, "Sermon: From Adam to Christ; The Grace That Conquers All Our Sin (Romans 5:12–19)," *SBJT* 15, no. 1 (2011): 80–90.

57. See Murray J. Harris, *Slave of Christ: A New Testament Metaphor for Total Devotion to Christ*, NSBT 8 (Downers Grove, IL: InterVarsity Press, 1999), esp. 81–84.

Christians fulfill "the righteous requirement of the law" (I lean toward the second): (1) by keeping it through the Spirit's enabling[58] or (2) by being in Christ, who perfectly fulfilled the law for them.[59]

Romans 8:28–30

God sovereignly works all things together for good for his people (Rom. 8:28–30). He does not lose one of his people. This chain of God's actions is unbreakable: foreknew → predestined → called → justified → glorified. Without exception, everyone is the object of either all or none of those actions. For example, it is impossible to be justified without finally being glorified.

Romans 8:31–39

Romans 8:31–39 is the climax of chapter 8 and an inference from everything Paul says in 5:1–8:30 about the glorious results of our justification. It is as if Paul takes a deep breath as he thinks back over 5:1–8:30 and then asks God's people, "What then shall we say to these things? If God is for us, who can be against us?" (8:31). That second question is rhetorical, so it has the force of a proposition: *since God is for us, nothing can be against us!* Paul then supports what he asserts with four proofs:

1. *God will graciously give us all things* (8:32). Paul argues from the greater to the lesser. If God gave us the greatest gift (i.e., he "did not spare his own Son but gave him up for us all"), then God will certainly give us everything else we need (i.e., he will also with Jesus "graciously give us all things").
2. *No one will bring a charge against us* (8:33). No one can take us to court before God and win a case against us because God himself is the one who has declared us to be righteous.
3. *No one will condemn us* (8:34). No one can condemn us to hell on judgment day, because Christ Jesus himself died for us, was raised for us, and is now at the right hand of God interceding for us. We are eternally secure in Christ.
4. *Nothing will separate us from the love of Christ* (8:35–39). Christ loves us, and no enemy or weapon or calamity can separate us from the love of God in Christ Jesus our Lord.

Romans 9:30–10:13

Paul contrasts the righteousness of believing Gentiles and of unbelieving Israel in Romans 9:30–10:6 (see table 6.2).

---

58. Schreiner, *Romans*, on 8:4; Kevin W. McFadden, "The Fulfillment of the Law's *Dikaiōma*: Another Look at Romans 8:1–4," *JETS* 52, no. 3 (2009): 483–97; John Piper, "Appendix 6: Twelve Theses on What It Means to Fulfill the Law; With Special Reference to Romans 8:4," in *The Future of Justification: A Response to N. T. Wright*, in Mathis and Taylor, *Collected Works of John Piper*, 7:221–31; Eckhard J. Schnabel, *Der Brief des Paulus an die Römer*, vol. 2, *Kapitel 6–16*, Historisch Theologische Auslegung (Witten, Germany: SCM R. Brockhaus, 2016), 204–5.

59. John Calvin, *Commentaries on the Epistle of Paul the Apostle to the Romans*, ed. and trans. John Owen (Grand Rapids, MI: Eerdmans, 1947), 283; Moo, *Epistle to the Romans*, on 8:4.

Table 6.2 Two Kinds of Righteousness in Romans 9:30–10:6

Righteousness of Believing Gentiles	Righteousness of Unbelieving Israelites
δικαιοσύνην . . . τὴν ἐκ πίστεως "a righteousness that is by faith" (9:30)	νόμον δικαιοσύνης "a law that would lead to righteousness" (9:31)
τὴν τοῦ θεοῦ δικαιοσύνην . . . τῇ δικαιοσύνῃ τοῦ θεοῦ "the righteousness of God . . . God's righteousness" (10:3)	τὴν ἰδίαν [δικαιοσύνην] "their own [righteousness]" (10:3)
ἡ . . . ἐκ πίστεως δικαιοσύνη "the righteousness based on faith" (10:6)	τὴν δικαιοσύνην τὴν ἐκ νόμου "the righteousness that is based on the law" (10:5)

The believing Gentiles did not attempt to establish their own righteousness but instead submitted to God's righteousness, "a righteousness [i.e., a right standing with God] that is by faith" (9:30). Unbelieving Israel sought "to establish their own" righteousness (10:3), not "by faith, but as if it were based on works" (9:32). Paul repeats his genuine desire for his fellow Israelites to be saved (10:1; cf. 9:1–4): they need to be saved because their religious zealotry is misinformed (10:2). Israel's plight is so tragic because they stumbled over Christ (9:32–33), who in the sweep of salvation history "is the end of the law for righteousness to everyone who believes" (10:4). Unbelieving Israel chose to try to earn "the righteousness that is based on the law" (10:5) and rejected "the righteousness based on faith" (10:6).

Righteousness based on the Mosaic law is impossible, but righteousness based on faith is accessible to everyone—both Gentiles and Jews (10:5–13). What is essential to attain that righteousness is faith in Jesus: "If you confess with your mouth that Jesus is Lord and *believe in your heart that God raised him from the dead, you will be saved*. For *with the heart one believes and is justified*, and with the mouth one confesses and is saved" (10:9–10).

The main idea of 9:30–10:13 is not that Israel is guilty for zealously maintaining its nationalistic boundary markers (circumcision, Sabbath, food laws). Rather, Israel failed to believe in Jesus and foolishly attempted the impossible—to merit "the righteousness that is based on the law" (10:5).[60]

In Philippians 3:2–9, Paul explains that his right standing with God is based not on his own righteousness but on God's—a righteousness that God gives to sinners. Paul's confidence, he clarifies, is "not having a righteousness of my own that comes from the law, but that which comes through faith in Christ, the righteousness from God that depends on faith" (Phil. 3:9). That is significant for confirming how we interpret Romans 9:30–10:13 because the righteousness in 10:1–5 is identical to the righteousness in Philippians 3:9. Those passages parallel each other in at least four ways:[61]

---

60. Dane C. Ortlund, *Zeal without Knowledge: The Concept of Zeal in Romans 10, Galatians 1, and Philippians 3*, LNTS 472 (London: T&T Clark, 2012), esp. 118–36; Richard Wellons Winston, "Misunderstanding, Nationalism, or Legalism: Identifying Israel's Chief Error with Reference to the Law in Romans 9:30–10:13" (PhD diss., Central Baptist Theological Seminary, 2015); Irons, *Righteousness of God*, 325–27.
61. See Schreiner, *Romans*, on 1:17 and 10:3. Cf. Irons, *Righteousness of God*, 334–36, who builds on Schreiner's analysis in the first edition of his *Romans* commentary.

1. They refer to God's righteousness (Rom. 10:3; Phil. 3:9).
2. They contrast righteousness by law and righteousness by faith.
3. They feature people trying to establish their own righteousness (Paul in Philippians and Israel in Romans).
4. They emphasize that it is futile to establish one's own righteousness based on "the law"—that is, for law keeping to be the basis for one's right standing before God (Rom. 10:3, 5; Phil. 3:6, 9).

Schreiner argues,

> We can go one step farther [than the parallel between Philippians 3 and Romans 10]. It is unlikely that the "righteousness of God" in Rom 1:17 and 3:21–22 has a different meaning from what we have found in Romans 10. In all three texts we have similar contexts and similar subject matter. In every case the phrase occurs in a soteriological context, and thus all three passages almost certainly teach that righteousness is a gift of God given to believers.[62]

How Does Romans Contribute to a Systematic Theology of Justification?

The above passages in Romans contribute to a systematic theology of justification in at least nineteen ways, which I group under eight headings—justification's meaning, need, basis, means, accessibility, results, future, and goal.

The Meaning of Justification

1. *Justification is judicial, not experiential.* Justification means to *declare* righteous, not to *make* righteous (in the sense of transforming one's character to be righteous). It is a metaphor from the law court, where a judge pronounces someone as either guilty or not guilty. Paul contrasts condemning (pronouncing guilty) and justifying (pronouncing not guilty but righteous) in Romans 8:33–34: "Who shall bring any charge against God's elect? It is God who justifies. Who is to condemn?" (cf. 5:18; 8:1). God "justifies the ungodly" (4:5) in that he legally declares ungodly people to be innocent and righteous—not in that he transforms ungodly people into godly people.[63]

2. *Justification includes forgiveness* (4:6–8). When God justifies believing sinners, he forgives those sinners' "lawless deeds" and covers their sins and no longer will count their sins against them.

3. *Justification includes imputation* (4:1–8; 5:15–19). Justification is a blessing because God imputes Christ's righteousness to the believing sinner. God does not merely cancel a sinner's guilt and declare that the sinner is *innocent* (neutral). God imputes Christ's righteousness to the believing sinner's account and declares that the sinner is

---
62. Schreiner, *Faith Alone*, 174.
63. Cf. Herman Bavinck, *Reformed Dogmatics*, ed. John Bolt, trans. John Vriend, vol. 4, *Holy Spirit, Church, and New Creation* (Grand Rapids, MI: Baker Academic, 2008), 204–9.

righteous (positive).⁶⁴ That is why "the one to whom God counts righteousness apart from works" experiences a "blessing" (4:6; cf. 4:7–9): "As by the one man's disobedience the many were made sinners, so by the one man's obedience the many will be made [i.e., have the status of] righteous" (5:19).

4. *Justification is vertical, not horizontal* (1:17; 3:21–26; 9:30–10:13; et al.). Contrary to the New Perspective on Paul, justification is fundamentally about how sinful humans relate to the righteous God, not to other humans. It is primarily about soteriology, not ecclesiology.⁶⁵

The Need for Justification

5. *Justification is necessary because all humans without exception are sinners under God's condemning wrath* (Rom. 1:18–3:20). "None is righteous, no, not one" (3:10). No one can stand before God as righteous on his or her own merits.

The Basis of Justification

6. *Justification is based on God's imputing Christ's righteousness to believing sinners* (Rom. 4:1–8; 5:15–19)—*which is possible because of propitiation* (3:25–26). (On forgiveness and imputation, see statements 2–3 above.) How can God be a just judge (i.e., a judge who is morally right and fair) if he declares that guilty people are not only innocent but righteous? Because justification depends on propitiation—that is, Jesus's sacrificial death propitiates God the Father. Jesus satisfies God's righteous wrath against us and turns it into favor. We are justified by Jesus's blood—that is, based on his sacrificial, substitutionary death (5:9). The righteous God *righteously* righteouses the unrighteous. Justification vindicates God in justifying the ungodly because of propitiation.

7. *Justification is based on God's imputing Christ's righteousness to believing sinners* (4:1–8; 5:15–19)—*which is possible because God raised Christ from the dead* (4:24–25). God raised Christ from the dead to publicly vindicate him and thus take care of or confirm our justification. Charles Hodge infers from 4:24–25 (and 1 Cor. 15:17), "The resurrection of Christ was necessary for our justification, inasmuch as it was the formal acceptance of his sufferings, as the expiation for our sins."⁶⁶ John Murray similarly infers, "The resurrection of Jesus is viewed as that which lays the basis for this justification."⁶⁷

---

64. Many Protestant theologians contrast forgiveness with the imputation of Christ's righteousness and then argue that forgiveness alone does not solve the plight of sinners (e.g., Grudem, *Systematic Theology*, 725–26). That is not wrong, but Vickers explains, "It is biblically sound to think of forgiveness itself as a positive standing before God. The sacrificial texts in the Pentateuch, for instance, consistently refer to a person being forgiven as a result of sacrifices offered.... The Old Testament does not have a sense of 'mere' forgiveness, but often speaks exclusively in terms of forgiveness to describe what people need from God, desire from God, and what God promises to give or warns that he will withhold. Forgiveness is presented as that which is needed for a restored relationship with God." Vickers qualifies, "There is a sense... in which we can speak legitimately of needing a 'positive standing,' and mean by that, something besides forgiveness when speaking of Christ's fulfilling the role of second Adam." *Jesus' Blood and Righteousness*, 108, 200.

65. Cf. Andrew Michael Hassler, "Justification and the Individual in the Wake of the New Perspective on Paul" (PhD diss., Southern Baptist Theological Seminary, 2011).

66. Hodge, *Romans*, 103.

67. Murray, *Romans*, 1:55–56.

8. *Justification is based on God's imputing Christ's righteousness to believing sinners* (Rom. 4:1–8; 5:15–19)—*which is possible because of union with Christ* (3:24; 5:12–21; 8:1). "Union with Christ," Marcus Johnson observes, "provides the basis for our justification."[68] This is related to the previous statements about propitiation and resurrection. Christ's propitiation and resurrection benefit believing sinners because they are united to Christ. Brian Vickers ends his careful study of imputation by agreeing with J. Gresham Machen that there is no hope without Christ's active obedience:

> Christ's fulfilling of all righteousness—his obedience to the Father's will and commands in his role as the second Adam, his sacrificial death, and his resurrection that vindicates the cross and ushers in a new eschatological era—becomes ours by faith *in union with him*. It is on this basis that a believer is reckoned righteous.[69]

The Means of Justification

9. *Justification is a gracious gift that sinful humans cannot earn* (Rom. 2:5–16; 3:9–20, 24, 27–28; 4:1–5; 5:16–17; 9:30–10:5). The means of justification is not our good works. We are justified δωρεὰν τῇ αὐτοῦ χάριτι—freely (i.e., as a gift, without payment) by his grace (3:24). Sinners cannot merit a right standing before God based on their works, so they cannot boast before God (4:2). Calvin infers a universal principle: "Whoever glories in himself, glories against God."[70] "In every age of human history," explain John MacArthur and Richard Mayhue, "religion has answered that we can get to heaven by being good people. The various religious systems of the world concoct lists of rituals and ceremonies that must be performed to achieve a measure of righteousness that might avail in the courtroom of God."[71] "A true view of justification," asserts Grudem, "is the dividing line between the biblical gospel of salvation by faith alone and all false gospels of salvation based on good works."[72]

10. *Justification is accessible by faith alone in Christ alone* (1:17; 3:22, 25; 4:3–5, 9–25; 5:1–2; 9:30–10:13). The means of justification is faith in Christ. Faith is instrumental. Being justified does not include works, and the object of faith does not include oneself or anyone else other than God in Christ: "To the one who does not work but believes in him who justifies the ungodly, his faith is counted as righteousness" (4:5). John Piper remarks, "Romans 4:5 is perhaps the most important verse on justification by faith alone in all the New Testament."[73]

---

68. Marcus Peter Johnson, *One with Christ: An Evangelical Theology of Salvation* (Wheaton, IL: Crossway, 2013), 90. Johnson defends that thesis on 90–114.
69. Vickers, *Jesus' Blood and Righteousness*, 237; italics added. Cf. Richard B. Gaffin Jr., *By Faith, Not by Sight: Paul and the Order of Salvation*, 2nd ed. (Phillipsburg, NJ: P&R, 2013), 56–59. See also chap. 15, by David VanDrunen, in this book.
70. John Calvin, *Institutes of the Christian Religion*, ed. John T. McNeill, trans. Ford Lewis Battles, LCC 20–21 (Philadelphia: Westminster, 1960), 765.
71. MacArthur and Mayhue, *Biblical Doctrine*, 609.
72. Grudem, *Systematic Theology*, 722. One qualification: some world religions have aspects to them that are similar in some ways to *sola fide* and *sola gratia*. For a nuanced answer to the question "Is 'salvation by grace through faith' unique to Christianity?" see Timothy C. Tennent, *Theology in the Context of World Christianity: How the Global Church Is Influencing the Way We Think about and Discuss Theology* (Grand Rapids, MI: Zondervan, 2007), 135–61.
73. John Piper, *Brothers, We Are Not Professionals: A Plea to Pastors for Radical Ministry*, in Mathis and Taylor, *Collected Works of John Piper*, 3:181.

11. *Justification occurs through redemption* (3:24). We are justified "through the redemption that is in Christ Jesus" (3:24). The human means of justification is faith; the divine means is redemption.

The Accessibility of Justification

12. *Justification is accessible to everyone without ethnic distinction* (Rom. 3:22–23, 29–30; 4:9–17; 10:11–13). "There is no distinction between Jew and Greek. . . . 'Everyone who calls on the name of the Lord will be saved'" (10:12–13).

The Results of Justification

13. *Justification is now inseparably connected to freedom from the law* (Rom. 3:19–21; 7:1–25; 9:30–10:13). God's people are now under the new covenant and not the Mosaic law-covenant.[74] Justification now fulfills the law (3:21, 31; 8:4). The Old Testament prophetically testifies to the salvation-historical shift that occurred with Christ's death that made the Mosaic law-covenant obsolete. Now God's people uphold the law "by this faith" (3:31).

14. *Justification is inseparably connected to peace with God* (5:1). While the justification metaphor is judicial, the reconciliation metaphor is relational. Before being justified, a sinner is God's enemy and is under God's wrath. After being justified, a sinner is God's friend and has peace with God.

15. *Justification is inseparably connected to the most deeply rooted and satisfying rejoicing* (5:2–11). Those who are justified rejoice in the hope of the glory of God (5:2), in their sufferings (5:3–10), and in God himself (5:11). Justification is good news not primarily because God forgives our sins and we escape God's wrath. Justification is good news primarily because it enables us to enjoy God himself. Piper explains:

> Justification is not an end in itself. Neither is the forgiveness of sins or the imputation of righteousness. Neither is escape from hell or entrance into heaven or freedom from disease or liberation from bondage or eternal life or justice or mercy or the beauties of a pain-free world. None of these facets of the gospel-diamond is the chief good or highest goal of the gospel. Only one thing is: seeing and savoring God himself, being changed into the image of his Son so that more and more we delight in and display God's infinite beauty and worth.[75]

16. *Justification is inseparably connected to progressive sanctification* (6:1–23). For Roman Catholics, "faith + works → justification," and for Protestants, "faith → justification + works" (where "→" means *results in* or *leads to*).[76] But even some

---

74. Douglas Moo, "The Law of Christ as the Fulfillment of the Law of Moses: A Modified Lutheran View," in *Five Views on Law and Gospel*, ed. Wayne G. Strickland, Counterpoints (Grand Rapids, MI: Zondervan, 1996), 319–76 (also 83–90, 165–73, 218–25, 309–15); Thomas R. Schreiner, *40 Questions about Christians and Biblical Law*, 40 Questions (Grand Rapids, MI: Kregel, 2010); Jason S. DeRouchie, *How to Understand and Apply the Old Testament: Twelve Steps from Exegesis to Theology* (Phillipsburg, NJ: P&R, 2017), 427–59.

75. John Piper, *God Is the Gospel: Meditations on God's Love as the Gift of Himself*, in Mathis and Taylor, *Collected Works of John Piper*, 6:291.

76. John Gerstner, quoted in R. C. Sproul, *Faith Alone: The Evangelical Doctrine of Justification* (Grand Rapids, MI: Baker, 1995), 155. For explanations and evangelical critiques of how Roman Catholicism understands

Protestants—especially advocates of higher life theology—separate justification from transformation.[77] "The whole point of Romans 6," though, is this: "God not only frees us from sin's penalty (justification), but He frees us from sin's tyranny as well (sanctification)."[78] "A major flaw" with how higher life theology interprets Romans 6 is that "Paul is not telling believers *how* a justified person can lead a holy life, but *why he must* lead a holy life."[79]

Progressive sanctification is distinct yet inseparable from justification (see table 6.3). Faith alone justifies, but the faith that justifies is never alone. God's grace through the power of his Spirit ensures that the same faith that justifies a Christian also progressively sanctifies a Christian. As Jonathan Pratt states, "Fruit-bearing necessarily and inevitably flows from justification."[80]

Table 6.3 Contrasts between Justification and Progressive Sanctification[81]

	Justification	**Progressive Sanctification**
Quality	Instantly declared righteous	Gradually made righteous
	Objective, judicial (nonexperiential): legal, forensic position	Subjective, experiential: daily experience
	External: outside the believer	Internal: inside the believer
	Christ's righteousness imputed, received judicially	Christ's righteousness imparted, worked out experientially
	Instantly removes sin's guilt and penalty	Gradually removes sin's pollution and power
	Does not change character	Gradually transforms character
Quantity	All Christians share the same legal standing	Christians are at different stages of growth
Duration	A single, instantaneous completed act: once for all time, never repeated	A continuing process: gradual, maturing, lifelong

17. *Justification is inseparably connected to assurance that God will finish what he planned, accomplished, and applied* (8:28–39). God *planned* to save his people—he foreknew and predestined them. God *accomplished* his plan through Christ's life, death, and resurrection. He *applied* his plan—he effectually called and justified his

---

justification, see R. C. Sproul, *Are We Together? A Protestant Analyzes Roman Catholicism* (Orlando, FL: Reformation Trust, 2012), 29–50; J. V. Fesko, *Justification: Understanding the Classic Reformed Doctrine* (Phillipsburg, NJ: P&R, 2008), 349–87; Gregg R. Allison, *Roman Catholic Theology and Practice: An Evangelical Assessment* (Wheaton, IL: Crossway, 2014), 431–45; Schreiner, *Faith Alone*, 209–38. See also chap. 23, by Leonardo De Chirico, in this book.

77. On higher life theology, see Andrew David Naselli, *No Quick Fix: Where Higher Life Theology Came From, What It Is, and Why It's Harmful* (Bellingham, WA: Lexham, 2017).

78. John MacArthur, *Faith Works: The Gospel according to the Apostles* (Dallas: Word, 1993), 121.

79. William W. Combs, "The Disjunction between Justification and Sanctification in Contemporary Evangelical Theology," *DBSJ* 6 (2001): 34.

80. That is the (persuasive) thesis of Jonathan R. Pratt, "The Relationship between Justification and Spiritual Fruit in Romans 5–8," *Them* 34, no. 2 (2009): 162–78.

81. Reproduced from Naselli, *No Quick Fix* (Lexham, 2017), 51. Used by permission of Lexham Press.

people. And God will finish what he started—he will glorify them.[82] Since God is for us, absolutely nothing can be against us (8:31)!

The Future of Justification

18. *Justification is definitive and will be final when God publicly vindicates believers.* When God initially justifies a believer, that justification is definitive and once for all time. But it is private. When God resurrects believers in the future, he will *publicly* vindicate them at the last judgment. This is clearer in Galatians than in Romans,[83] but some passages in Romans could refer to that final justification (2:13; 5:18; 8:30, 32–34).[84]

The Goal of Justification

19. *Justification ultimately glorifies God.* A goal of justification is to enable guilty sinners to stand before the righteous God as righteous. But that is not its ultimate goal. Justification occurs ultimately to glorify God. That is why Romans 1–8 ends by praising God for the results of justification—namely, that since God is for us, nothing can be against us (8:31–39). That is why Romans 9–11 ends by praising God for his deep riches, wisdom, and knowledge regarding how he saves his people throughout history (11:33–36). That is why the letter ends by praising God for his righteousness that is now manifested apart from the law-covenant and to which the Law and the Prophets testify (3:21):

> According to the revelation of the mystery that was kept secret for long ages but has now been disclosed and through the prophetic writings has been made known to all nations, according to the command of the eternal God, to bring about the obedience of faith—to the only wise God be glory forevermore through Jesus Christ! Amen. (16:25–27)

In short, "From him and through him and to him are all things"—especially our justification. "To him be glory forever. Amen" (11:36).

Conclusion

The righteous God righteously righteouses the unrighteous. That summarizes what Paul teaches about justification in Romans.

For the last several years, I have woken up each morning to my alarm clock playing the chorus of the song "Jesus, Thank You" (by Pat Sczebel), which highlights three themes connected to justification:

> Your blood has washed away my sins [i.e., forgiveness].
> Jesus, thank you.

---

82. See John Murray, *Redemption Accomplished and Applied* (Grand Rapids, MI: Eerdmans, 1955). The title of that excellent book could be even better by adding the verb *planned*—that is, *Redemption Planned, Accomplished, and Applied*.
83. See Douglas J. Moo, *Galatians*, BECNT (Grand Rapids, MI: Baker Academic, 2013), 60–62.
84. See Beale, *New Testament Biblical Theology*, 469–526, esp. 498–504; Schreiner, *Faith Alone*, 153–57.

> The Father's wrath completely satisfied [i.e., propitiation].
> Jesus, thank you.
> Once your enemy, now seated at your table [i.e., reconciliation].
> Jesus, thank you.[85]

So many blessings Christians enjoy are connected to justification.

On the day before J. Gresham Machen died, he sent a famous message about imputation to his fellow New Testament theologian John Murray: "I'm so thankful for the active obedience of Christ; no hope without it."[86] We can say the same thing for justification more broadly: Praise God for justification; no hope without it. Raymond Ortlund puts it well:

> You do not forgive me by overlooking your law. Instead, the cross liberates your love by enforcing your law. Your justice has been satisfied. You have taken my guilt and put it onto Christ at the cross, where he suffered in my place the penalty my guilt deserved. And you have taken his righteousness and credited it to me, paying my moral debt in full forever. This mysterious exchange, my sin for his merit, is the wonder of free justification at the cross.[87]

Recommended Resources

Burk, Denny. "The Righteousness of God (*Dikaiosunē Theou*) and Verbal Genitives: A Grammatical Clarification." *Journal for the Study of the New Testament* 34, no. 4 (2012): 346–60.

Carson, D. A. "Atonement in Romans 3:21–26: God Presented Him as a Propitiation." In *The Glory of the Atonement: Biblical, Historical, and Practical Perspectives; Essays in Honor of Roger R. Nicole*, edited by Charles E. Hill and Frank A. James III, 119–39. Downers Grove, IL: InterVarsity Press, 2004.

———. "The Vindication of Imputation: On Fields of Discourse and Semantic Fields." In *Justification: What's at Stake in the Current Debates*, edited by Mark A. Husbands and Daniel J. Treier, 46–78. Downers Grove, IL: InterVarsity Press, 2004.

Irons, Charles Lee. *The Righteousness of God: A Lexical Examination of the Covenant-Faithfulness Interpretation*. Wissenschaftliche Untersuchungen zum Neuen Testament, 2nd ser., vol. 386. Tübingen: Mohr Siebeck, 2015.

Moo, Douglas J. *The Epistle to the Romans*. 2nd ed. New International Commentary on the New Testament. Grand Rapids, MI: Eerdmans, 2018.

Naselli, Andrew David. "Justification according to Romans." https://biblearc.com/author/Andy_Naselli/Justification_according_to_Romans/. Phrase diagrams created using Biblearc software.

---

85. "Jesus, Thank You," music and words by Pat Sczebel. © 2003 Integrity's Hosanna! Music (ASCAP) / Sovereign Grace Worship (ASCAP). Sovereign Grace Music, a division of Sovereign Grace Churches, www.SovereignGraceMusic.org. All rights reserved. Used by permission. Administrated worldwide at www.CapitolCMGPublishing.com, excluding the UK, which is administrated by Integrity Music, part of the David C. Cook family.

86. Quoted in Ned B. Stonehouse, *J. Gresham Machen: A Biographical Memoir*, 50th anniversary ed. (Willow Grove, PA: Committee for the Historian of the Orthodox Presbyterian Church, 2004), 252.

87. Raymond C. Ortlund Jr., *A Passion for God: Prayers and Meditations on the Book of Romans* (Wheaton, IL: Crossway, 1994), 63. Ortlund is reflecting on Romans 3:21–26.

Piper, John. *Counted Righteous in Christ: Should We Abandon the Imputation of Christ's Righteousness?* In *The Collected Works of John Piper*, edited by David Mathis and Justin Taylor, 5:323–77. Wheaton, IL: Crossway, 2017.

Schreiner, Thomas R. *Faith Alone: The Doctrine of Justification; What the Reformers Taught . . . and Why It Still Matters*. Five Solas Series. Grand Rapids, MI: Zondervan, 2015.

———. *Romans*. 2nd ed. Baker Exegetical Commentary on the New Testament 6. Grand Rapids, MI: Baker Academic, 2018.

Stott, John R. W. *The Message of Romans: God's Good News for the World*. Bible Speaks Today. Downers Grove, IL: InterVarsity Press, 1994.

Vickers, Brian. *Jesus' Blood and Righteousness: Paul's Theology of Imputation*. Wheaton, IL: Crossway, 2006.

7

"By Grace You Have Been Saved through Faith"

Justification in the Pauline Epistles

BRANDON CROWE

No biblical author is more important for the doctrine of justification than the apostle Paul. This is different from saying that justification is the center of Paul's theology. Instead, it is better to consider justification to be an important aspect of Paul's soteriology, which may be subsumed under the organizing rubric of union with Christ.[1] Yet as justification is a significant aspect of Pauline thought, it is appropriate for us to consider it at length. Indeed, debates surrounding justification are largely debates about Paul's letters. Probably no single letter is as important for understanding Paul's doctrine of justification as is Romans (and it fittingly receives a dedicated chapter in this volume—see chap. 6). But we dare not miss the importance of Paul's other letters as well, since his doctrine of justification appears in a variety of contexts throughout the Pauline corpus.

But to propose that we need to look at the Pauline corpus immediately raises a question: What letters in the Pauline corpus should we consider when investigating *Paul's* doctrine of justification? Traditionally, Paul has been understood to be the author of all thirteen letters found in the New Testament that bear his name.[2] In the past two hundred

---

1. See, e.g., John Murray, *Redemption Accomplished and Applied* (Grand Rapids, MI: Eerdmans, 1955), 161–73; Herman N. Ridderbos, *Paul: An Outline of His Theology*, trans. John Richard de Witt (Grand Rapids, MI: Eerdmans, 1975), 57–64; cf. John Calvin, *Institutes of the Christian Religion*, ed. John T. McNeill, trans. Ford Lewis Battles, LCC 20–21 (Louisville: Westminster John Knox, 1960), 3.1.1; Francis Turretin, *Institutes of Elenctic Theology*, trans. George Musgrave Giger, ed. James T. Dennison Jr. (Phillipsburg, NJ: P&R, 1992–1997), 16.3.5.
2. Many historically have also understood Paul to be the author of Hebrews, but this is exceptionally unlikely (cf. Heb. 2:3).

years, however, this ages-long consensus has been challenged. Today scholars often agree that Paul wrote seven letters of the Pauline corpus (Romans, 1–2 Corinthians, Galatians, Philippians, 1 Thessalonians, and Philemon), and possibly a couple of others as well (2 Thessalonians and Colossians). This leaves Ephesians, 1–2 Timothy, and Titus (and possibly 2 Thessalonians and Colossians) as letters that many Pauline scholars consistently question as authentic (or simply conclude to be inauthentic as a matter of course).[3] The upshot of this is that discussions of Paul's doctrine of justification tend to focus on Romans and Galatians in particular, while often ignoring significant statements in other texts that are viewed by many in the guild of New Testament scholarship as inauthentic.[4]

This issue has come to a head particularly in the past forty years or so of Pauline scholarship with the so-called New Perspective on Paul (NPP).[5] Stated simply, the NPP argues that justification is more about who constitutes the true people of God than about how individuals are made right before God.[6] Yet the NPP is difficult to summarize because NPP scholars hold to a variety of views that are not always consistent with one another, and they do not even always agree on the meaning of justification. What becomes clear in these debates is that most reformulations of the Pauline doctrine of justification typically deal only with a limited selection of the traditional Pauline corpus. Texts like Colossians and Ephesians—much less the Pastoral Epistles—are rarely engaged at length.[7] This means that one's view of authorship (and thus the legitimacy or illegitimacy of canonical, pseudepigraphal apostolic letters) is the engine that remains out of sight but drives much of the conversation. This point is not always stated explicitly, but we do well to linger over it—the doctrine of justification has often been reformulated based on a limited subset of Pauline texts. The result is that many pro-NPP interpreters are dealing with a "stacked deck" that presents a truncated picture of the Pauline evidence, which can lead to a skewed doctrine of justification. Put starkly, it is much easier to argue for a recalibration of the Pauline doctrine of justification along NPP lines when one excludes the witness of texts like Ephesians and Titus. It is therefore important to recognize this phenomenon and in turn to be sure we include the entire Pauline corpus in discussions of justification.

I am well aware that many would object to the notion that an undisputed letter such as Galatians and a disputed letter such as Titus are "equally Pauline," but this essay is

---

3. Two examples of recent books on Pauline theology that focus only on the seven undisputed letters of Paul are Michael Wolter, *Paul: An Outline of His Theology*, trans. Robert L. Brawley (Waco, TX: Baylor University Press, 2015), 6; E. P. Sanders, *Paul: The Apostle's Life, Letters, and Thought* (Minneapolis: Fortress, 2015), xxii–xxiii.

4. A recent work addressing this tendency is Robert J. Cara, *Cracking the Foundation of the New Perspective on Paul: Covenantal Nomism versus Reformed Covenantal Theology*, REDS (Fearn, Ross-shire, Scotland: Mentor, 2017), esp. 127–95.

5. This terminology can be traced back to James D. G. Dunn, "The New Perspective on Paul," *BJRL* 65, no. 2 (1983): 95–122. Thus, the term *New Perspective on Paul* is not pejorative but is used by the proponents themselves. Perhaps the two most notable in this regard to date have been Dunn and N. T. Wright.

6. See, e.g., N. T. Wright, *What Saint Paul Really Said: Was Paul of Tarsus the Real Founder of Christianity?* (Grand Rapids, MI: Eerdmans, 1997), 119: "In standard theological language, [justification] wasn't so much about soteriology as about ecclesiology; not so much about salvation as about the church."

7. Likewise, the Pauline passages from Acts are not, by and large, part of the conversation, though Paul's sermon at Pisidian Antioch in Acts 13:16–41 would add another dimension to the conversation in ways that do not support the NPP (i.e., relating justification to the forgiveness of sins in contrast to the law of Moses in 13:38–39). See also John Piper, *The Future of Justification: A Response to N. T. Wright* (Wheaton, IL: Crossway, 2007), 83–85.

simply not the venue to attempt to reverse the strong current of much New Testament scholarship that distinguishes between authentic and inauthentic Pauline letters. At the same time, it is crucial that we consider all the Pauline evidence, since on this point I am concerned that too much scholarship has become an echo chamber for looking only at seven (or so) Pauline letters. Given the constraints of this essay, I am not able to argue *for* Pauline authorship of the entire Pauline corpus; I must assume it. However, I can say in passing that objective measures taken to test for quantifiable differences between the authentic and disputed Paulines do not provide much support for positing different authors for these letters.[8] We also know that anytime a purported apostolic writing was found to be spurious in the early church, it was rejected.[9] The strongest arguments for non-Pauline authorship of some letters of the Pauline corpus are the apparent differences in content and tone between the so-called undisputed and disputed Pauline letters. But even here, the conclusions seem to rest mostly in the eye of the beholder. Indeed, even though he shies away from basing his arguments on the disputed Pauline letters, N. T. Wright has warned that we may be cutting the legs out from authentic Pauline letters by seeing irreconcilable conflicts between letters where there are none.[10] Even those who deny Pauline authorship of the disputed Pauline letters must at least admit that they are early letters that demonstrate an exceptionally early reception history of Pauline theology.[11] (And in the context of the broad scope of interpretive history, the current trend among Pauline scholars to consider only a subset of the Pauline evidence is quite anomalous.)

Another curious phenomenon one may encounter is that Paul's doctrine of justification is often discussed in relation to Jewish texts such as 4QMMT *to a greater extent* than—and sometimes *rather* than—traditional Pauline texts like Ephesians. We should not protest when Jewish documents are considered part of the historical and cultural context surrounding the New Testament; indeed, such approaches are necessary. But we should protest if more attention is given to the Qumran sectarians than to the witness of the traditional Pauline corpus.

Those who do accept the perspective that Paul wrote all thirteen letters—or at least believe that we must read the letters as a corpus in the context of the canon—should recognize the approach to the primary sources taken by the authors they are reading: Which Pauline letters do the authors use to construct a Pauline theology?

---

8. As N. T. Wright has observed, "Those who have done computer analyses of Paul's style come up with more 'conservative' results than we might have expected." *Paul and the Faithfulness of God*, COQG 4 (Minneapolis: Fortress, 2013), 1:60.

9. See, e.g., the response of Serapion of Antioch to the so-called Gospel of Peter (Eusebius, *Historia ecclesiastica* 6.12) and the discussion of Tertullian about the Asian church leader who wrote the Acts of Paul and Thecla (Tertullian, *De baptismo* 17). See further C. E. Hill, "The New Testament Canon: *Deconstructio ad absurdum?*," *JETS* 52, no. 1 (2009): 101–19; Bruce M. Metzger, *The Canon of the New Testament: Its Origin, Development, and Significance* (Oxford: Clarendon, 1987), 174–75; F. F. Bruce, *The Canon of Scripture* (Grand Rapids, MI: InterVarsity Press, 1988), 261; D. A. Carson and Douglas J. Moo, *An Introduction to the New Testament*, 2nd ed. (Grand Rapids, MI: Zondervan, 2005), 337–50.

10. See N. T. Wright, *Paul: In Fresh Perspective* (Minneapolis: Fortress, 2005), 18–19; Wright, *Paul and the Faithfulness of God*, 1:56–63.

11. For example, Ephesians is likely cited as Scripture already by Polycarp of Smyrna (*Epistle to the Philippians* 12.1), and the Pastorals (at least 1–2 Timothy) were likely known by Ignatius of Antioch—so Michael W. Holmes, ed., *The Apostolic Fathers: Greek Texts and English Translations*, 3rd ed. (Grand Rapids, MI: Baker Academic, 2007), 175.

My aim, however, is not primarily deconstructive but constructive: What do the twelve letters of the Pauline corpus (aside from Romans)[12] say about justification? This is an important question given the dearth of attention often given in contemporary discussions to the disputed Pauline letters on the matter of justification. I begin with what may well be the most consequential of these twelve letters, and the letter that has been most widely discussed in relation to justification: Galatians. From there, I consider 1–2 Corinthians and 1–2 Thessalonians, then the Prison Epistles (Ephesians, Philippians, Colossians, Philemon), followed by the Pastoral Epistles (1–2 Timothy, Titus). I argue that Paul understands justification to be primarily about how individuals are made right before a holy God based on faith alone, apart from any moral works. Though there are clearly social implications of justification, these are not what justification is primarily about. But such a claim must be demonstrated by exegesis, which is the task to which we now turn.

Justification in Galatians

Probably no letter apart from Romans has generated as much discussion on justification as Galatians. Surely one reason is that all agree that Galatians is an authentic Pauline letter. But even more significant, justification by faith is at the heart of Galatians. I therefore give extended attention to what Galatians has to say about justification. This discussion also serves as the foundation on which I build when looking at other Pauline texts in this chapter.

Galatians 1–2

Early in his letter Paul identifies the Lord Jesus Christ as the one "who gave himself for our sins [τοῦ δόντος ἑαυτὸν ὑπὲρ τῶν ἁμαρτιῶν ἡμῶν] to deliver us from the present evil age" (Gal. 1:4).[13] Though not using the terminology of justification per se, it is clear that Paul has in view the salvific work of Christ. He builds on this theme in his discussions of justification throughout the letter.

Historical Context

It is helpful to consider briefly (if not decisively) the likely recipients of the letter. Who were the churches of Galatia (Gal. 1:2) to whom Paul wrote? Two major theories have been set forth. The North Galatian theory argues that Paul was writing to the regions of North Galatia, where one might more naturally think of ethnic Galatians residing.[14] One drawback to this view is that it is unclear when or whether Paul engaged in an extensive ministry there.[15] Thus, in recent decades the South Galatian theory has gained momentum, and this is the view I find to be most likely.

---

12. I will refer to Romans where necessary, but for a more extensive treatment of Romans, see chap. 6, by Andrew David Naselli, in this volume.
13. Unless otherwise indicated, all Scripture quotations in this chapter are my own translations.
14. See F. F. Bruce, *The Epistle to the Galatians*, NIGTC (Grand Rapids, MI: Eerdmans, 1982), 3–18; Douglas J. Moo, *Galatians*, BECNT (Grand Rapids, MI: Baker Academic, 2013), 3–8; Thomas R. Schreiner, *Galatians*, ZECNT 9 (Grand Rapids, MI: Zondervan, 2010), 22–31.
15. So Moo, *Galatians*, 8.

The South Galatian theory states that Paul wrote to churches in the cities he visited on his first missionary journey (i.e., Pisidian Antioch, Iconium, Lystra, Derbe; cf. Acts 13:14–14:23). This view is typically (though not always) tethered to an earlier date for Galatians. Indeed, it is quite plausible to place the writing of Galatians in the latter part of the AD 40s—before the so-called Jerusalem Council of Acts 15. This is significant because in Galatians Paul is addressing not only justification by faith but also the related issue of how the Mosaic law functions in a community composed of both Jews and Gentiles. This is precisely the issue addressed by the Jerusalem Council. It is therefore most likely that the Jerusalem Council took place *after* Paul wrote Galatians, which explains why Paul never mentions the council's decree in Galatians.[16]

A South Galatian destination also means that it would be imprudent to ignore Paul's speeches in Acts addressing justification, some of which recount Paul's ministry in South Galatia during his first missionary journey. Though many have doubted the truly "Pauline" nature of the Pauline speech material in Acts, such objections are overblown. Luke, who by all accounts wrote Acts, is firmly established in the New Testament and early Christian tradition (and in Acts itself) as an associate and traveling companion of the apostle Paul.[17] Therefore, the burden of proof should be on those who would dismiss Luke's claims to represent Paul accurately, not the other way around. Thankfully, many today recognize that the Paul of Acts is indeed the Paul of the letters[18] (though that is not to say that Luke necessarily used Paul's letters). This means that Paul's sermons in Acts that speak to the issue of justification—especially on his first missionary journey in South Galatia—are important texts to consider.[19]

The Gospel and Justification

Paul's discussion of justification ramps up in Galatians 2. In his survey of his conversion and previous activity, Paul has much to say about the "gospel" (εὐαγγέλιον). The term "gospel," we can assume, summarizes the content of Paul's message in Galatians. It has to do with "the grace of Christ" (χάριτι Χριστοῦ, 1:6)[20] and with belief (1:8–11; cf. 1 Cor. 15:1–2). But the gospel also relates to Paul's doctrine of justification;

---

16. This would place Galatians around AD 48 and the Jerusalem Council in AD 48 or 49. See F. F. Bruce, *The Acts of the Apostles: The Greek Text with Introduction and Commentary*, 2nd ed. (Grand Rapids, MI: Eerdmans, 1952), 55; cf. 289; Carson and Moo, *Introduction*, 369, 464.

17. Cf. Brandon D. Crowe, "The Sources for Luke and Acts: Where Did Luke Get His Material (and Why Does It Matter)?," in *Issues in Luke-Acts: Selected Essays*, ed. Sean A. Adams and Michael W. Pahl, GH 26 (Piscataway, NJ: Gorgias, 2012), 90–91.

18. See, e.g., Craig S. Keener, *Acts: An Exegetical Commentary* (Grand Rapids, MI: Baker Academic, 2012-15), 1:221–57; Martin Hengel, *Acts and the History of Earliest Christianity*, trans. John Bowden (London: SCM, 1979); Stanley E. Porter, *The Paul of Acts: Essays in Literary Criticism, Rhetoric, and Theology*, WUNT 115 (Tübingen: Mohr Siebeck, 1999); Eckhard J. Schnabel, *Acts*, ZECNT 5 (Grand Rapids, MI: Zondervan, 2012), 38–41.

19. The longest Pauline sermon in Acts, and thus the longest sermon of Paul's first missionary journey, is the synagogue speech at Pisidian Antioch, in South Galatia. (For the relationship of "Pisidian Antioch" to Galatia, see Bruce, *Galatians*, 3–18, esp. 6n17; Schnabel, *Acts*, 573; Keener, *Acts*, 2:2032–33.) There can be no doubt that this is a programmatic speech for Paul's ministry and is indicative of the sort of sermon he would have delivered elsewhere in Galatia. Thus, Paul's Pisidian Antioch sermon is important evidence. For more on this speech, see John Eifion Morgan-Wynne, *Paul's Pisidian Antioch Speech (Acts 13)* (Eugene, OR: Pickwick, 2014).

20. There is some question whether the text includes Χριστοῦ. However, one's textual choice here makes little difference for the present point.

justification explicates the content and logic of the gospel message that he refers to on several occasions.

This brings us to one of the most important justification passages in the letter: Galatians 2:16. The context recalls Paul's opposition to Peter face-to-face in (Syrian) Antioch for not living in accord with the truth of the gospel when Peter removed himself from eating with Gentiles (2:11–14).[21] Peter's lack of conformity to the gospel manifested a lack of understanding of justification, which leads to Paul's statement in 2:16: "But[22] we know that a person is not justified by works of the law but only[23] through faith in Jesus Christ, and indeed[24] we have believed in Christ, in order that we might be justified by faith in Christ and not by works of the law, for by works of the law no flesh will be justified." Several aspects of Paul's language here merit comment.

Justification and faith in Christ. First, as my translation indicates, justification necessitates faith *in Christ*. That justification is tied to faith is not in doubt. However, in many renderings of this passage, the language of *through/by faith in [Jesus] Christ* (διὰ πίστεως Ἰησοῦ Χριστοῦ; ἐκ πίστεως Χριστοῦ) is instead rendered *through/by the faithfulness of Jesus Christ*,[25] thus taking the genitive construction as a subjective genitive (the one who lived faithfully or believed is Christ himself) rather than an objective genitive (the object of one's belief is Jesus).[26] In favor of the subjective genitive rendering, one could argue that Paul would be auspiciously tautological to say the same thing in three ways in the same verse: a person believes in Christ for justification / we have believed in Christ / we have been justified by believing in Christ. Instead, it would be more poetic for Paul to state that we are saved by the faithfulness of Jesus Christ and that we have indeed believed in him.[27]

---

21. Reconstructing the details of this so-called "Antioch incident" has proved to be one of the elusive conundrums of New Testament scholarship. Who were the people from James? Why and on whose authority did they come? Why did Peter remove himself from the Gentiles if he indeed was the key agent through whom the gospel first came to the Gentiles (cf. Acts 10)? Such questions are beyond the purview of this essay. For a brief discussion, see Hengel, *Acts*, 96–97.

22. The δέ may very possibly be omitted here, but it does not affect my argument. I am following the text of Nestle-Aland, 28th edition, at this point. If included, it would be, as Moo puts it, "mildly adversative." *Galatians*, 173.

23. An adversative translation of ἐὰν μή is also preferred by Schreiner, *Galatians*, 163; Bruce, *Galatians*, 138; Moo, *Galatians*, 162–63; Ernest De Witt Burton, *A Critical and Exegetical Commentary on the Epistle to the Galatians*, ICC (Edinburgh: T&T Clark, 1921), 120–21 (who also translates the phrase "but only"); R. Barry Matlock, "The Rhetoric of πίστις in Paul: Galatians 2.16, 3.22, Romans 3.22, and Philippians 3.9," *JSNT* 30, no. 2 (2007): 197–98n25. See also BDF §376; "ἐάν," 1.c.β, BDAG 267–68; A. T. Robertson, *A Grammar of the Greek New Testament in the Light of Historical Research*, 4th ed. (New York: George H. Doran, 1923), 1024–25.

24. I take this as an ascensive use of καί, which might also be rendered "even." See Daniel B. Wallace, *Greek Grammar beyond the Basics: An Exegetical Syntax of the New Testament* (Grand Rapids, MI: Zondervan, 1996), 670–71; BDF §442(12); cf. "καί," 2.b, BDAG 495–96. For similar views, see Bruce, *Galatians*, 139; Moo, *Galatians*, 163; Burton, *Galatians*, 123.

25. So, e.g., Richard B. Hays, *The Faith of Jesus Christ: The Narrative Substructure of Galatians 3:1–4:11*, 2nd ed., BRS (Grand Rapids, MI: Eerdmans, 2002), 161–62; Wright, *Paul and the Faithfulness of God*, 2:856–57.

26. See Moisés Silva, "Faith versus Works of the Law in Galatians," in *Justification and Variegated Nomism*, vol. 2, *The Paradoxes of Paul*, ed. D. A. Carson, Peter T. O'Brien, and Mark A. Seifrid, WUNT, 2nd ser., vol. 181 (Grand Rapids, MI: Baker Academic, 2004), 227–34; James D. G. Dunn, *The Theology of Paul the Apostle* (London: T&T Clark, 1998), 379–85 (§14.8); Dunn, "Once More, ΠΙΣΤΙΣ ΧΡΙΣΤΟΥ," in Hays, *Faith of Jesus Christ*, 249–71; Schreiner, *Galatians*, 163–66; Moo, *Galatians*, 160–61; John Murray, *The Epistle to the Romans: The English Text with Introduction, Exposition and Notes*, NICNT (Grand Rapids, MI: Eerdmans, 1959), 1:363–74.

27. That ἡμεῖς εἰς Χριστὸν Ἰησοῦν ἐπιστεύσαμεν refers to faith *in* Christ is not in doubt, given the preposition εἰς and the verb πιστεύω. Cf. Bruce, *Galatians*, 139; Schreiner, *Galatians*, 166; Moo, *Galatians*, 163; Silva, "Faith versus Works," 232; Richard B. Hays, "The Letter to the Galatians," in *The New Interpreter's Bible*, vol. 11 (Nashville: Abingdon, 2000), 237; Hays, *Faith of Jesus Christ*, 123; Wright, *Paul and the Faithfulness of God*, 2:857, 857n237.

Yet as theologically accurate as it would be to say that Jesus was the perfectly faithful one, it is unlikely that subjective genitive constructions are in view in Galatians 2:16. Rather than being tautological, it appears that Paul is emphasizing faith in Christ by stating the matter in a variety of ways.[28] Additionally, it is noteworthy that from what we know of the Greek church fathers, it does not appear that any of them (who spoke Greek natively) read this genitive construction as a *subjective* genitive.[29] To show the logic of Paul's thought as it pertains to faith in Christ, I suggest the following structure:[30]

    a A person is not **justified** by works of the law,
        b but [**is justified**][31] only through *faith in Jesus Christ*,
            c and indeed we have *believed in Christ Jesus*,
        b' in order that we might be **justified** by *faith in Christ* and not by works of the law,
    a' for by works of the law no flesh will be **justified**.

    a οὐ **δικαιοῦται** ἄνθρωπος ἐξ ἔργων νόμου
        b ἐὰν μὴ [**δικαιοῦται**] διὰ *πίστεως Ἰησοῦ Χριστοῦ*
            c καὶ ἡμεῖς *εἰς Χριστὸν Ἰησοῦν ἐπιστεύσαμεν*
        b' ἵνα **δικαιωθῶμεν** ἐκ *πίστεως Χριστοῦ* καὶ οὐκ ἐξ ἔργων νόμου
    a' ὅτι ἐξ ἔργων νόμου οὐ **δικαιωθήσεται** πᾶσα σάρξ[32]

The phrases *faith in [Jesus] Christ* and *believing in Christ Jesus* are thus mutually reinforcing. Paul does not repeat himself verbatim but speaks variously of justification *through* faith in Christ and *by* faith in Christ, and he asserts explicitly via the verb ἐπιστεύσαμεν that he (Paul) and Peter had themselves placed their faith in Christ.[33] It is thus best to understand the genitive constructions ἐκ/διὰ πίστεως [Ἰησοῦ] Χριστοῦ to be objective genitives. Although one's reading of the genitive constructions is not decisive for one's view of justification in Paul, it is an important factor and will again be significant for the discussion of Galatians 3 below.

Justification, "works of the law," and forgiveness of sins. We must also read Galatians 2:16 in light of the Antioch incident recounted in 2:11–14. Here the question arises, What does Peter eating with Gentiles have to do with justification? In recent years

---

28. On redundancy in this passage, see John M. G. Barclay, *Paul and the Gift* (Grand Rapids, MI: Eerdmans, 2015), 381. See also Rom. 3:22.
29. See Silva, "Faith versus Works," 228–30.
30. The following structure reflects my own assessment of the text. Others have suggested some similar possibilities; see Matlock, "Rhetoric," 193–99 (which is apparently followed by Barclay, *Paul and the Gift*, 372n55). Matlock surveys several structural options, including some chiastic possibilities, though my proposal does not match precisely any of the options he gives.
31. This is implied.
32. I have included the first and last phrase of 2:16 to show principles that Paul begins with and returns to. One might also choose to leave off the final ὅτι clause and find the chiastic arrangement concluding with οὐκ ἐξ ἔργων νόμου. This is done by Michael Theobald, whose structure is otherwise quite similar to my own. "Der Kanon von der Rechtfertigung (Gal. 2,16; Röm. 3,28)—Eigentum des Paulus oder Gemeingut der Kirche?," in *Worum geht es in der Rechtfertigungslehre? Das biblische Fundament der "Gemeinsamen Erklärung" von katholischer Kirche und lutherischem Weltbund*, ed. Thomas Söding, QD 180 (Freiburg: Herder, 1999), 137–38, noted by Matlock, "Rhetoric," 196.
33. So Schreiner, *Galatians*, 166.

many—especially those associated with the NPP—have underscored the social dimensions of justification in large measure because of Galatians 2 and other texts that seem to view justification largely in *horizontal* terms. On this view, justification addresses how Jews and Gentiles relate in the new covenant community.[34] Justification is thus said to concern who constitutes the people of God.[35] In contrast to more traditional readings that understand "works of the law" to be the works of the Mosaic law broadly conceived (as a microcosm of a larger reality to adhere to a path of works more generally),[36] this newer perspective on justification often understands "works of the law" to be a specific subset of works of the Mosaic law that summarily define the people of God in the first century: Sabbath observance, dietary laws, and circumcision.[37] Works of the law on this construal are not works that one does to render oneself acceptable before God, but rather, they identify those who belong to the people of God. This would seem to fit with the context of Galatians 2, where eating—along with circumcision, which pervades the letter—is the point of contention.[38]

A fuller discussion of works of the law must take into account other texts in Galatians. But what can be said about works of the law at this point? Does Paul mainly refer to social distinctions between Jews and Gentiles? If so, would that mean that the contrast between works of the law and justification is primarily about defining the people of God? Despite the popularity of this view, I am unconvinced that this approach to works of the law is superior for several reasons.

First, it is simply not clear that works of the law should be *limited* to a few specific works of the Mosaic law that differentiate Jews from Gentiles.[39] As I argue below, Paul's use of Deuteronomy 27:26 in Galatians 3:10 to highlight the entirety of the law should give one pause at this point.

Second, such a delimitation is not clear in extant, early Jewish sources. The partially extant Jewish text from Qumran known as 4QMMT, which is often compared to Galatians, speaks of works of the law more broadly than circumcision, dietary laws, and Sabbath.[40] As Simon Gathercole rightly concludes, the notion that works of the

---

34. Cf. Tom Wright, *Justification: God's Plan and Paul's Vision* (London: SPCK, 2009), 95–98; Dunn, *Theology of Paul*, 359–60 (§14.5).
35. See especially Wright, *What Saint Paul Really Said*, 120–22. But see the clarification in Wright, *Justification*, 124.
36. Cf. Bruce, *Galatians*, 137–38.
37. So James D. G. Dunn, "Works of the Law and the Curse of the Law (Galatians 3:10–14)," NTS 31 (1985): 523–42. Though see more recently Dunn, *Beginning from Jerusalem*, vol. 2 of *Christianity in the Making* (Grand Rapids, MI: Eerdmans, 2009), 488; cf. Thomas Schreiner, *Faith Alone: The Doctrine of Justification; What the Reformers Taught . . . and Why It Still Matters*, Five Solas Series (Grand Rapids, MI; Zondervan, 2015), 100n5.
38. A likely reference to Sabbath is found in Gal. 4:10. Cf. Schreiner, *Galatians*, 279; Moo, *Galatians*, 278; G. K. Beale, *A New Testament Biblical Theology: The Unfolding of the Old Testament in the New* (Grand Rapids, MI: Baker Academic, 2011), 791–95.
39. See also Barclay, *Paul and the Gift*, 374.
40. See the various discussions in Wright, *Paul and the Faithfulness of God*, 1:184–86; Simon J. Gathercole, *Where Is Boasting? Early Jewish Soteriology and Paul's Response in Romans 1–5* (Grand Rapids, MI: Eerdmans, 2002), 93–95; Moo, *Galatians*, 175–76; Barclay, *Paul and the Gift*, 375n64; Cara, *Cracking the Foundation*, 99. Dunn sees the sectarian nature of the Qumran community reflected in the works of the law in view in 4QMMT. *Theology of Paul*, 357–58 (§14.4). Further discussion and interaction with Dunn are found in Scott J. Hafemann, "Paul and the Exile of Israel in Galatians 3–4," in *Exile: Old Testament, Jewish, and Christian Conceptions*, ed. James M. Scott, JSJSup 56 (Leiden: Brill, 1997), 342–44nn33–34. Indeed, though we do find an eschatological focus at the end of 4QMMT, the earlier sections sound more like the Mishnah. A relation to the Mishnah is also noted by Martin Hengel and Roland Deines, "E. P. Sanders' 'Common Judaism,' Jesus, and the Pharisees," JTS 46, no. 1 (1995): 8.

law should be taken as boundary markers in Paul does not correspond to 4QMMT, which speaks of eschatological life in connection with one's adherence to works of the law.[41] Indeed, 4QMMT may be most valuable as a contrast to Paul's doctrine of justification by faith as *opposed to* works of the law; Paul does not use "works of the law" positively in Galatians (or anywhere else).[42] In distinction from 4QMMT, Paul writes with the conviction that the Messiah has already come, and this eschatology affects his understanding of the law's role in the era of "faith" (cf. Gal. 3:23). I have more to say about this below.

Third, even if one did delimit works of the law to refer to boundary markers, this would not negate the reality that adhering to such works could have led to boasting.[43] Any work(s) can become grounds for boasting, which Paul will have no part of (cf. 6:14).

Fourth, does Paul actually speak of justification in tandem with the *forgiveness* of sins in Galatians? One may be reminded here of Krister Stendahl's watershed article—a forerunner of the NPP—in which he argued that Paul was not concerned with how to soothe a seared conscience from the torments of sin in the presence of a holy God.[44] Justification, it is sometimes argued, is not about forgiveness of sins, which provides further reason to conclude that the doctrine is largely about how both Jew and Gentile constitute the people of God.[45] This view, however, is not persuasive. We could note, for example, the collocation of *justification* language in Galatians 2 with the *gospel* that Paul preached (cf. 2:14, 16). We must ask the question, What makes justification good news?[46] The answer is that it enables all who are sinners—both Jew and Gentile—to be accepted before a holy God (now!), and this by faith alone. Moreover, in what follows Paul denies that the justification of sinners by faith somehow makes Christ a minister of sin (2:17–18).[47] He then contrasts dying to the law (because of sin) to living in Christ (2:19, 21). New life in Christ is possible because Paul has been crucified with Christ (2:19 [2:20 Eng. versions]).

A number of questions arise in these latter verses of Galatians 2, and I am not able to address all of them. It appears, for example, that Paul may be responding to accusations against him in 2:17.[48] However, I want to highlight that Paul relates *justification* and *life* with *sin* and *death*. In 2:19, Paul speaks of dying to the law that he might live to God. On the one hand, this might sound like a way for Paul to speak simply of the redemptive-historical shift in respect to the law with the coming of Christ (cf. 2:18)—

---

41. Gathercole, *Where Is Boasting?*, 94–95.
42. Silva, "Faith versus Works," 219.
43. See Gathercole, *Where Is Boasting?*, esp. 37–111.
44. Krister Stendahl, "The Apostle Paul and the Introverted Conscience of the West," *HTR* 56 (1963): 199–215; cf. Stephen Westerholm, *Justification Reconsidered: Rethinking a Pauline Theme* (Grand Rapids, MI: Eerdmans, 2013), 5.
45. See Wright, *What Saint Paul Really Said*, 119. See also Wright, *Paul and the Faithfulness of God*, 2:856–60. Wright clearly sees justification as an eschatological doctrine—e.g., *Paul and the Faithfulness of God*, 2:1167–68; Wright, *Justification*, 79–81, 124.
46. This question is commonly posed; cf. Westerholm, *Justification Reconsidered*, 6, 21, 96.
47. These are difficult verses. For discussions of options, see Schreiner, *Galatians*, 167–69; Bruce, *Galatians*, 140–41; Moo, *Galatians*, 163–67.
48. So Moo, *Galatians*, 165; Bruce, *Galatians*, 140.

Paul is no longer defined by the law's "badges" of membership. But the stakes here are higher than that, for Paul is discussing the reasons for Christ's actual death (2:21). Justification is necessary because of sin, which warrants death; Christ died to bring justification that we might live. Paul's discussion of justification is thus not simply about works of the law as boundary markers; it is rather about the death that results from sin and the sacrificial death of Christ that provides justification unto life.

The testimony of Acts must also be included. I noted earlier the importance of Paul's sermon at Pisidian Antioch (Acts 13:16–41) not only in the context of Acts but also as the epitome of the sort of preaching that was characteristic of Paul on his first missionary journey—including his time with the residents of (South) Galatia. Significantly, Acts 13:38–39 speaks of forgiveness in conjunction with being justified from the law of Moses[49]—elements that proponents of the NPP are loath to see in Galatians.[50] We also see beyond Galatians that Paul does indeed tie justification explicitly to the language of forgiveness. Moreover, the conceptual framework of justification and forgiveness is often present even where the language of justification may not appear[51] (cf., e.g., 1 Cor. 6:11; Eph. 1:7, 13; 4:32; Col. 1:14; 2:13; 3:13).[52] Although Paul may not explicitly use the language of forgiveness of sins in relation to justification in Galatians 2, the broader picture reveals that Paul does indeed relate justification to the forgiveness of individuals' sins before a holy God.

Summary: Galatians 2:16 and Justification

I can now summarize the significance of Galatians 2:16 for justification in Paul. First, the gospel entails faith in Christ. Second, this faith in Christ is good news because it speaks to the way that we can be delivered from our sins through the self-offering of Jesus for us (cf. 1:4). Justification by faith is therefore good news for sinners in need of deliverance. Key here is the correlation between the gospel, sins, and justification that we see not only in Galatians but even more clearly in light of the broader Pauline corpus. Third, Paul contrasts faith in Christ—that is, in Christ's work for us—and works of the law. And to understand more fully the contours of works of the law in Galatians, it is necessary to turn to Galatians 3, where we find more discussion about Christ's curse-bearing death for us.

Galatians 3

Galatians 3:1–9

One of the most debated passages about justification in Galatians, and perhaps in all Scripture, is Galatians 3. This is especially true for Galatians 3:10–14, a passage known for its exegetical difficulties. To wrestle with this passage, we must broaden the context

---

49. Many translations opt for the language of *freed* from the law of Moses rather than *justified* from the law of Moses (cf. ESV, NIV, NRSV). But the language of *justification* is to be preferred (cf. CSB, KJV). See also Rom. 6:7.

50. Yet even if one opted for the North Galatian theory, Paul's preaching in Acts is still relevant for understanding Paul's epistles.

51. It is important to remember the dangers of overreliance on word searches. The word-concept distinction posits that a specific word need not be present for the concept to be present.

52. Justification is also explicitly tied to forgiveness of sins in Rom. 4:4–8.

to consider what comes just before it.[53] In 3:2, works of the law are again contrasted with faith: Paul asks if the Galatians had received the Spirit by works of the law (ἐξ ἔργων νόμου) or by the hearing of faith (ἐξ ἀκοῆς πίστεως). Likewise, in 3:5, Paul asks if the miracles done among them came by works of the law or by the hearing of faith. This provides Paul the opportunity to discuss Abraham's belief by which it was counted to him as righteousness in 3:6 (Ἀβραὰμ ἐπίστευσεν τῷ θεῷ, καὶ ἐλογίσθη αὐτῷ εἰς δικαιοσύνην; cf. Gen. 15:6). Abraham is thus set forth as a model of the righteousness of faith apart from works of the law.[54]

Galatians 3:10

Paul's introduction of Abraham in Galatians 3:1–9 provides necessary context for interpreting 3:10–14. The difficulties begin at the outset of 3:10—Who are the cursed people who are characterized by works of the law (ὅσοι γὰρ ἐξ ἔργων νόμου εἰσίν)? This phrase has been variously translated and vigorously debated. One's reading of this phrase will likely determine the way one reads the rest of the passage.[55] The phrase has traditionally been rendered, "For all *who rely on* works of the law."[56] Such people—those who rely on a legalistic standing before God based on their works—are under a curse.[57] The reason for this interpretation is largely because of Paul's appeal to Deuteronomy 27:26 in the same verse: "Cursed is everyone who does not abide in all the words in the book of the law, to do them." This apparently all-encompassing statement assumes that it is necessary for a person to keep the *entire* law to avoid the curse of God. The logic of this so-called implied-premise view would thus go as follows:[58]

1. All who rely on works of the law for justification are under a curse.
2. [Implied:] No one (whether Jew or Gentile) is able to obey the law perfectly.
3. Therefore, every person stands under a curse before God.

This is the view of Luther and of Calvin.[59] As Calvin observes, "All who have transgressed any part of the law are cursed."[60] The curse is therefore not simply a curse on the Jewish people (read *exile*) but rather applies universally to both Jew and Gentile. Perhaps the most glaring drawback to this view, however, is the ambiguity of the Greek phrasing. The text does not explicitly say that "all people" are under a curse; this conclusion must be inferred.

---

53. See Moisés Silva, "Abraham, Faith, and Works: Paul's Use of Scripture in Galatians 3:6–14," *WTJ* 63, no. 2 (2001): 251–67.
54. Indeed, Abraham came before the Mosaic law was given, as Paul makes clear in Gal. 3:17.
55. So also Silva, "Abraham, Faith, and Works," 358; cf. Silva, "Faith versus Works," 222.
56. See the renderings of CSB, ESV, NET, NIV, NRSV.
57. See, e.g., Burton, *Galatians*, 164; Bruce, *Galatians*, 158.
58. For a listing of some options, see N. T. Wright, *The Climax of the Covenant: Christ and the Law in Pauline Theology* (Minneapolis: Fortress, 1992), 144–45.
59. Martin Luther, *Lectures on Galatians*, in *LW* 26:248–68.
60. John Calvin, *The Epistles of Paul to the Galatians and Ephesians*, trans. William Pringle, in *Calvin's Commentaries*, vol. 21 (Grand Rapids, MI: Baker, 2003), 89. Luther and Calvin are just the tip of the iceberg of the proponents of this view. See further Burton, *Galatians*, 163–65; Bruce, *Galatians*, 157–59; Schreiner, *Galatians*, 203–7; Moo, *Galatians*, 201–5; Ronald Y. K. Fung, *The Epistle to the Galatians*, NICNT (Grand Rapids, MI: Eerdmans, 1988), 142; Richard N. Longenecker, *Galatians*, WBC 41 (Nashville: Thomas Nelson, 1990), 116–18.

Thus, despite the popularity of this implied-premise position, it has been reevaluated and challenged in recent years. Of particular importance is the notion that the specific and preeminent curse in view in Deuteronomy 27 (and consequently Galatians) is the covenantal curse of exile.[61] We might call this view of the curse in Galatians 3:10 the corporate-exilic position. All those who are ἐξ ἔργων νόμου are therefore all those who are defined by works of Torah—especially Sabbath, dietary laws, and circumcision.[62] This view understands Paul's references to cursing, in light of Deuteronomy 27:26, to be the curse of exile experienced by God's people. The Jewish people are defined by Torah and are thus specifically under a curse. This position seeks to pay careful attention to the Old Testament context of Deuteronomy 27:26—part of the so-called Shechemite Dodecalogue, which addressed the blessings and curses of the Mosaic covenant. It must be admitted that this corporate-exilic interpretation has a compelling logic to it. We must indeed take seriously the original contexts of Old Testament quotations, and we must be tethered tightly to the text itself and not adhere to traditional readings simply for the sake of tradition.

However, despite strong arguments in favor of the corporate-exilic position of Galatians 3:10, the traditional reading best captures Paul's logic for several reasons. First, the contrast between faith and works in this passage is absolute, corresponding to Abraham's model of faith in 3:6–9. This makes it unlikely that Paul uses the language of "curse" in 3:10 to refer to true believers among God's people who underwent the curse of exile. Instead, the curse is for those characterized by works of the law (however one defines them) in contrast to faith. Understanding Abraham and his offspring as people of faith best accords with Paul's pervasive contrast between faith and works.[63] Moisés Silva has captured the crux of the issue: "It is implausible that Paul would indiscriminately describe his fellow-Jews as people not characterized by faith."[64] This conclusion necessitates reading 3:10 closely in tandem with 3:6–9.[65] The true offspring of Abraham have always been those of faith (3:7), and such people are not best understood as remaining under a curse.[66] On the other hand, *all people*—whether Jews or Gentiles—who are characterized not by faith (but by works of the law) are under a curse.[67]

Second—and another helpful point made by Silva—Paul often leaves his logic unstated in Galatians. Therefore, the implied-premise reading is consistent with Paul's elliptical logic elsewhere in Galatians 3.[68]

---

61. See Wright, *Climax*, 140, 146.
62. See also, e.g., Dunn, "Works of the Law," 533–34, 538; Dunn, *Theology of Paul*, 361 (§14.5); Norman H. Young, "Who's Cursed—and Why? (Galatians 3:10–14)," *JBL* 117, no. 1 (1998): 80; Terence L. Donaldson, "The 'Curse of the Law' and the Inclusion of the Gentiles: Galatians 3:13–14," *NTS* 32, no. 1 (1986): 97.
63. So Silva, "Abraham, Faith, and Works," 260; cf. Ridderbos, *Paul*, 154.
64. Silva, "Abraham, Faith, and Works," 260.
65. A point emphasized by Silva, "Abraham, Faith, and Works," 260. While in Nestle-Aland, 28th edition, Gal. 3:10 begins a new paragraph, in the *Greek New Testament, Produced at Tyndale House Cambridge*, ed. Dirk Jongkind and Peter J. Williams (Wheaton, IL: Crossway, 2017), Gal. 3:10–12 is included in the same paragraph as 3:5–9.
66. This also assumes a strong sense of continuity with Abraham's children across the Testaments.
67. See Silva, "Abraham, Faith, and Works," 260. As my several references to Silva indicate, his contribution to debates surrounding Gal. 3:10–14 are among the most trenchant.
68. Silva, "Abraham, Faith, and Works," 253–54. One example given by Silva is the implied premise necessary to relate 3:5 and 3:6: it must be true that God supplies the Spirit by the hearing of faith.

Third, it is not only the implied-premise position that fills in gaps in Paul's logic; any reading of the curse in Galatians 3:10 that makes much of the exile is also filling in perceived gaps in Paul's logic—Paul does not mention the exile explicitly.[69] To be sure, one can rightly conclude that the exile does provide an important background for understanding many texts in the New Testament, and discussions of blessings and curses are particularly to be read in relation to the exile as covenant curse. Yet the wider context of Galatians should give one pause before isolating the curse of 3:10 to the exile experienced by the Jewish people. For if the curse falls on those who are characterized by works of the law, and if that curse fell even on the true sons of Abraham, then it would follow that Abraham and his offspring must also be characterized by the works of the law. In contrast, I have argued that true believers are rather characterized as people of faith and that Paul contrasts those characterized by works of the law with true believers. Elsewhere in his letters Paul clearly views all humanity as being under the law (Rom. 2:12–16; 6:12–14[70]), and all are sinners, subject to death and the wrath of God (cf. Rom. 3:5, 9, 23; 5:12–13; Gal. 3:22).[71] This universal emphasis, which includes both Jew and Gentile, best accords with the scope of the curse in Galatians 3:10.

Fourth, the implied-premise position, which entails that all people who are not characterized by faith are under a curse, is not an invention of the Reformation—this interpretation goes back at least to the days of Justin Martyr (mid-second century AD). Justin clearly states that *all* humanity is under a curse (*Dialogus cum Tryphone* 95).[72]

In sum, the curse on those who are characterized by works of the law in Galatians 3:10 is best taken as a reference to any person (whether Jew or Gentile) who is not characterized by the faith of Abraham and who is therefore not justified before God by faith.

Galatians 3:11–14

One's interpretation of Galatians 3:10 thus sets the stage for interpreting the rest of the passage. In 3:11, justification is mentioned explicitly: no one is justified (οὐδεὶς δικαιοῦται) before God by means of the law. Here again those who seek to be justified by the law (earlier noted as *works* of the law) are contrasted with those who live by faith. As in 2:16, in 3:11 we encounter the genitive construction ἐκ πίστεως, this time in a quotation of Habakkuk 2:4. Traditionally, this quotation ("the righteous one will live by faith") has been taken as a reference to the faith of the believer. However, in recent years many have understood Habakkuk 2:4 to refer to the faithfulness of Jesus himself.[73] While this is an intriguing possibility, it remains unlikely for similar reasons covered above in relation to Galatians 2:16. Moreover, in the Old Testament itself we encounter verbal parallels between Habakkuk 2:4 and the faith of Abraham in Genesis

---

69. Silva, "Abraham, Faith, and Works," 257, 261–62.
70. The example of Romans 6 comes from Moo, *Galatians*, 267.
71. Cf. Guy Waters, *The End of Deuteronomy in the Epistles of Paul*, WUNT, 2nd ser., vol. 221 (Tübingen: Mohr Siebeck, 2006), 102–3.
72. See also C. Kavin Rowe, *One True Life: The Stoics and Early Christians as Rival Traditions* (New Haven, CT: Yale University Press, 2016), 153; also noted in Silva, "Abraham, Faith, and Works," 266.
73. See especially Hays, *Faith of Jesus Christ*, 132–56.

15:6 (especially אמן and צדק), which encourage us to read Paul's citation of Habakkuk 2:4 as a reference to the faith of believers, which has its model in Abraham.[74] Instead of finding a reference to Christ in Habakkuk 2:4, it is better to find Christ brought into the discussion in Galatians 3:13, where he is identified as the curse bearer.[75] Paul's point is thus again the contrast between those who seek to be justified (δικαιοῦται) by the law (which is not possible) and those who are righteous (δίκαιος) by faith.

The exegetical difficulties continue in 3:12. What does Paul mean when he says that the law is not of (ἐκ) faith? And why does he apparently cite Leviticus 18:5 ("He who does them [i.e., the commandments] will live by them") negatively? Galatians 3:12 is the second half of a contrast between two ways of living (ζήσεται). One way of living, which we saw in 3:11 by means of the citation of Habakkuk 2:4, is living by faith (like Abraham). The second way of living is illustrated by Leviticus 18:5: by works of the law. Paul therefore continues the contrast between faith and works that has occupied him throughout Galatians 3.

But if Paul is continuing this contrast, at least one important question remains: Why does he use Leviticus 18:5 negatively? We need to remember that what now concerns us—and indeed, the question that Paul was addressing in Galatians 3:10–14—is how one is justified before God. Paul's clear answer is that justification comes by faith, not by the law (cf. 3:11). In this light Paul leans on Leviticus 18:5 to demonstrate the fundamental principle of living by works of the law: *full* obedience. When combined with the all-encompassing description of doing *all* the things written in the book of the law (Deut. 27:26 in Gal. 3:10; cf. 5:3),[76] Paul highlights the incessant *doing* that must be characteristic of anyone who seeks eternal life by keeping the law (cf. Luke 10:25).[77] Paul's use of Leviticus 18:5, in other words, assumes that *perfect* obedience is necessary to live by works of the law.[78]

This interpretation, however, is contested and thus requires much more comment. Indeed, the question whether the law requires perfect obedience is one of the key debates surrounding Galatians 3:10–14, and therefore is one of the debates about the nature of justification itself. The traditional answer[79] holds that Paul does indeed see the law as requiring perfect obedience, as I have shown above with the correlation especially of Deuteronomy 27:26 and Leviticus 18:5 in Galatians 3.[80] This is relevant for justification because, as I argue in chapter 14 of this volume, the foundation of justification is the perfect obedience of Jesus Christ. This is necessary because God has tethered eternal

---

74. Moisés Silva, *Interpreting Galatians: Explorations in Exegetical Method*, 2nd ed. (Grand Rapids, MI: Baker Academic, 2001), 166.
75. Contrast C. E. B. Cranfield, *A Critical and Exegetical Commentary on the Epistle to the Romans*, 2 vols., ICC (Edinburgh: T&T Clark, 1975–1979), 2:522n2. On asyndeton and the shift in topic in 3:13, see Norman Bonneau, "The Logic of Paul's Argument on the Curse of the Law in Galatians 3:10–14," *NovT* 39, no. 1 (1997): 72.
76. The citations of Deut. 27:26 and Lev. 18:5 both include ποιέω and αὐτά.
77. Cf. Gathercole, *Where Is Boasting?*, 121–23.
78. See also Brandon D. Crowe, *The Last Adam: A Theology of the Obedient Life of Jesus in the Gospels* (Grand Rapids, MI: Baker Academic, 2017), 178–82; John Murray, *The Epistle to the Romans: The English Text with Introduction, Exposition and Notes*, NICNT (Grand Rapids, MI: Eerdmans, 1965), 2:249–51.
79. I speak from the perspective of traditional Reformed theology, without claiming that this is a consensus for all traditions.
80. Cf. also Peter C. Craigie, *The Book of Deuteronomy*, NICOT (Grand Rapids, MI: Eerdmans, 1976), 334.

life to perfect obedience. To be justified before God requires meeting God's covenantal requirement of perfect obedience. This is the light in which to read Paul's contrast between the two ways of living. To walk the path of works for justification would require that path to be walked perfectly, something manifestly impossible. To walk by faith means to trust in the one who has borne the curse for us (3:13), which assumes that Christ himself is the one who walked the path of obedience perfectly (see also 4:4–5). Justification by faith in Christ means trusting in the perfection of Christ himself and not in our own, imperfect works.

This view, however, has been routinely questioned in recent years as being out of accord with Paul's thought and anachronistic in a first-century setting.[81] I do not have the space to discuss first-century Judaism at length, but the reading I am proposing is not so out of place as it has sometimes been made out to be. For example, it is true that the Mosaic law was never about working one's way to God.[82] Yet this is precisely the point that Paul has to make clear to his readers, for it seems that many were—if not in explicit word, at least in deed—holding that one could be acceptable to God based on what one had done. But such a view runs counter to the need for faith that was characteristic of Abraham and his true children. Abraham—the model of faith—could not have been righteous based on works of the Mosaic law, since the law came 430 years later (3:17). Abraham was justified before God on the basis of faith (cf. 3:6–9). Abraham's model of faith demonstrates that adherence to the law is not what finally makes one acceptable to God. The Mosaic law was given to a redeemed people, and was God's beneficent condescension to his people. But sinful people have a decided ability to twist gifts of God for improper ends, and this appears to be what was happening in Galatia.

The Mosaic law, given to a redeemed people, did not require *perfect* obedience for one to be a faithful covenant member.[83] But that is not all that needs to be said, nor does it answer all the questions about Paul's use of Leviticus 18:5. In Galatians 3:12, Paul invokes a principle that is on full display in the law of Moses: perfect obedience is necessary for eschatological life. The problem in Galatia was the erroneous teaching that it was possible to realize eschatological life by keeping the law of Moses.

Such a view—life by law adherence—misses not only the inability of sinful humanity to keep the law perfectly but also the role of the law in redemptive history. The law was given as a covenant administration until the promised seed would come (3:19). As such, it was a temporary administration, which exacerbated the problem of sin (cf. 3:22–24). Thus, the false teachers in Galatia had a defective eschatological understanding of the coming of Christ in relation to the Mosaic law.[84] They had misunderstood its provisional character, even as they underestimated the degree of obedience necessary for someone to rely on law keeping as a means of acceptance before God. The conclusion that *perfect*

---

81. See, e.g., Michael Cranford, "The Possibility of Perfect Obedience: Paul and an Implied Premise in Galatians 3:10 and 5:3," *NovT* 36, no. 3 (1994): 242–58; Hays, "Galatians," 257.
82. See, e.g., Wright, *Justification*, 204–5.
83. For more on this discussion, see chap. 14, my other essay in this volume. The Mosaic law is best understood under the rubric of the covenant of grace.
84. See especially Ridderbos, *Paul*, 161–66, 170–74.

law keeping is ultimately necessary for true justification makes sense of all Paul's statements that we have seen thus far in 3:10–12. Furthermore, when Paul says that the law is not of faith, he is saying (as he does in 3:23) that the law belongs to the era of anticipation, whereas Christ is the fullness of the content of our faith that has come in these last days.[85] To be ἐξ ἔργων νόμου would be to belong to the old order of things and thus to be deficient vis-à-vis the object of our faith.

In 3:13, we at last come to Christ himself in the passage at hand: Christ redeemed us from the curse of the law by becoming a curse for us. Two key questions emerge here. First, who are the "us" who are redeemed? The "us" here must be the same group of people in view in 3:10, who are subject to a curse. I have argued that the curse in 3:10 applies to everyone characterized by works as opposed to those characterized by faith (i.e., everyone apart from Christ). The "us" in 3:13 is therefore a reference not simply to *Jewish* believers[86] but to *all* true believers (whether Jew or Gentile),[87] for whom Christ bore the curse as a substitutionary representative.[88] This also makes the best sense of the unity that Paul sees among Jew and Gentile in Galatians (cf. 3:28–29).

The second (and related) question is the nature of the curse in view. Is this the curse of exile, or is the curse of God's wrath on all people because of sin? One reason for the former interpretation is the logic of 3:14, where two ἵνα ("in order that") clauses are used to explain the benefits of Christ's redemption from the curse: the first ἵνα clause refers to the blessing of Abraham coming to the Gentiles, whereas the second ἵνα clause indicates that "we" might receive the promise of the Spirit by faith. Given the mention of Gentiles in 3:14a and the apparent distinction from the "we" that receive the Spirit by faith in 3:14b, there is a strong argument to be made for this view. However, on balance the structure of the ἵνα clauses is not decisive; the two phrases need not necessitate a distinction between two groups throughout 3:10–13. If both Jews and Gentiles are subject to the curse, both are presented as being in need of redemption. This must mean that the two ἵνα clauses in 3:14 refer not to two distinct outcomes of the work of Christ for two different groups of people but instead to two benefits of the work of Christ—with the reception of the Spirit by faith applying to both Jew and Gentile. We might therefore paraphrase 3:14 as follows: "Christ redeemed [all true believers] from the curse in order that the blessing of Abraham might come to the Gentiles, in order that we [all, together,] might receive the promise of the Spirit by faith."[89] This reading also makes sense of the Gentiles being included in the faith of Abraham—the paradigmatic man of faith.

Thus, if the "us" includes both Jewish and Gentile Christians in 3:13–14, then this confirms that the curse in 3:10 and 13 is best taken more inclusively to refer to the wrath of God on sin. This further makes sense of the substitutionary language used for Jesus's

---

85. See, e.g., Schreiner, *Galatians*, 245–46; Moo, *Galatians*, 241; Silva, "Abraham, Faith, and Works," 265; Silva, "Faith versus Works," 243–44.
86. See, e.g., Wright, *Climax*, 151–53; Donaldson, "'Curse of the Law,'" 97.
87. So, e.g., Fung, *Galatians*, 149; Bruce, *Galatians*, 167; Moo, *Galatians*, 213.
88. Thus note the preposition ὑπέρ.
89. Cf. Bruce, *Galatians*, 167–68; Schreiner, *Galatians*, 218–19.

death in 3:13,⁹⁰ which is consistent with Pauline language for Jesus giving himself up on behalf of (ὑπέρ) the sins of his people (cf. Rom. 5:8; 1 Cor. 15:3; 2 Cor. 5:21; Gal. 1:4). We also should revisit Acts 13, where Deuteronomy 21:23—which is quoted in Galatians 3:13—is likely alluded to in Acts 13:29.⁹¹ If so, then this verbal link may provide further reason to relate Galatians with Paul's preaching (in South Galatia) in Acts 13, which would add further weight to the close, logical relationship between justification and forgiveness of sins—in contrast to works (so Acts 13:38–39).

One's reading of Galatians 3:10–14 must therefore take into consideration the role of Abraham as a man of faith in 3:6–9, and is largely dependent on one's rendering of those characterized by works of the law in 3:10. The best reading is that Paul demonstrates that justification is by faith for all who believe, apart from any human works (including those focused on the law of Moses).

Galatians 4–6

I will say less about the rest of Galatians because much of the framework for understanding justification in the rest of Galatians is provided by Galatians 2:16 and 3:6–14. Another dimension to justification, which builds on 3:10–14, is found in 4:4–5. Here we read again of the redeeming work of Christ for those who were under the law. This is the same "redeem" (ἐξαγοράζω) language used of Christ's redeeming work in 3:13, and one's interpretation there will likely be indicative of one's understanding of Galatians 4:4–5. The curse of the law is not mentioned explicitly in 4:4–5, but being "under the law" (ὑπὸ νόμον) most likely implies being under the curse of the law (ὑπὸ κατάραν), as in 3:10.⁹² In answer to the question, Who are the people under the law? one possibility is the Jewish people,⁹³ to whom the Mosaic law was given.⁹⁴ But a more likely option is that Paul is making a point here about all Christians—both Jews and Gentiles—who are redeemed from the curse of the law. As noted earlier, elsewhere in Paul's letters all people are under God's law, are sinners, and are subject to God's wrath.⁹⁵ Likewise, the result of this redemption is that "we" might receive adoption as sons (4:5), which parallels the statement in 3:14 that Christ redeemed us so that we might receive the Spirit by faith. In both cases, both Jewish and Gentile Christians are in view.

If Paul makes much of justification in Galatians, he also makes much of freedom. In 3:22, Scripture (perhaps especially with a view to law⁹⁶) shut up (συνέκλεισεν) everything under sin, so that we might receive the promise and thus be free by faith in Christ (cf. 5:1, 13). Similarly, in 3:23, the law held people captive until faith (that is, salvation

---

90. Cf. Murray J. Harris, *Prepositions and Theology in the Greek New Testament: An Essential Reference Resource for Exegesis* (Grand Rapids, MI: Zondervan, 2012), esp. 214–16.
91. In both Deut. 21:23 and Acts 13:29, the term for cross is ξύλον rather than the more common σταυρός.
92. See Bruce, *Galatians*, 156. Thus, in Gal. 3:10, we read of being "under the law" and in 3:13, being "under the curse of the law." The language of 3:13 is therefore fuller and makes clear that being under the law and being under the curse speak of the same reality.
93. In Wright's view, they are seen as representatives for Adamic humanity. *Climax*, 208.
94. See Moo, *Galatians*, 267.
95. See the discussion of Gal. 3:10 above (p. 249).
96. See, e.g., Moo, *Galatians*, 239; Bruce, *Galatians*, 180.

in Christ) was revealed.[97] The law is not designed to be a means of seeking righteousness apart from faith, but it has often been misused for this purpose.[98] Justification by faith in Christ, therefore, also means freedom from the bondage of living under the law.

Paul further speaks about freedom from the law in the example of Hagar and Sarah in 4:21–31. Those who seek to live under the law, Paul argues, should listen to what the law says about freedom and bondage in relation to Abraham's two sons (4:21). Hagar and Sarah point to two contrasting ways of living: one by faith unto freedom (Sarah) and one by works unto bondage (4:25–26). This is further seen in the way the women represent two covenants, the one Sinai (= Hagar), the other the Jerusalem above (= Sarah). To view Sinai as a means of living—apart from the eschatological promise—is to live in bondage. Instead, we should learn from Sinai that the promised son of Abraham was coming. He is greater even than Isaac and is the one to whom Sinai looked. Thus, a distinction exists even in the law itself between children of promise (i.e., sons of Abraham that come through faith, just as Isaac was a child of promise) and children of the flesh (i.e., children of works, much like Ishmael, who represents works apart from faith).[99] The children of the two women continue to Paul's own day: those of faith are like Isaac—free (4:26). The children of the flesh, those who do not have faith in the promised seed of Abraham (cf. 3:19), are in bondage (4:25). Though much more could be said about this passage, Paul highlights a contrast in the law itself between those who live by faith and those who live by works. Paul fittingly concludes his discussion with the observation that Christ *freed* us for the purpose of *freedom* (5:1; cf. 5:13). This entails freedom not only from the curse of sin but also from the bondage of seeking to be justified by works apart from faith.

Paul then moves to circumcision to drive his point home further. To require the work of circumcision for justification would be not only to revert to the Mosaic law as the norm for living but also to embrace a way of being that is "by works" in contrast to faith (5:2)—the point that has occupied Paul throughout much of Galatians. In this case, circumcision is not simply a Jewish boundary marker but serves metonymically for the "way of works" that, if embraced, would lead again to bondage, since no one is able to keep the whole law (5:3–4; cf. 6:12–14).[100] The point is that keeping the whole law, as we saw in 3:12 with the citation of Leviticus 18:5, assumes that justification by law keeping can come only by perfect law keeping—a manifest impossibility.[101]

Galatians: Conclusion

Galatians presents us with two options: justification by works of the law or justification by faith. If one were to be justified by the law, then perfect obedience would be

---

97. Cf. Ridderbos, *Paul*, 162.
98. See, e.g., Bruce, *Galatians*, 180.
99. Ishmael may also represent the persecution of God's people. See Schreiner, *Galatians*, 295, 305.
100. See similarly Moo, *Galatians*, 322.
101. See also Peter's speech at the Jerusalem Council in Acts 15:6–11. Consistent with Galatians, Peter concludes that circumcision is unnecessary for Gentiles. To think otherwise would be to place the yoke of the Mosaic law around the Gentiles' neck, which not even the Jewish people had been able to bear. Instead, salvation comes to all through the grace of the Lord Jesus (15:11).

necessary. The attempts by the religious adversaries to require circumcision for salvation fall into the trap of requiring salvation by works of the law. Such an approach, however, can lead only to bondage. True freedom and salvation come through faith in Christ—who redeemed us from the curse of works of the law.

Justification in the Corinthian and Thessalonian Correspondence

1 Corinthians

We begin in 1 Corinthians by noting the centrality of the cross early in the letter (1:17–2:5), which speaks to the issue of justification by faith. As in Galatians, there are two ways of living according to Paul: by works or by faith. To live by works is to put confidence in one's own efforts and is antithetical to living by faith in Christ. In Galatians Paul's boast is not in his own works but in the cross of Christ by which he has been crucified (Gal. 2:19 [2:20 Eng. versions]; 6:14; cf. 1 Cor. 1:18–19, 29, 31). Likewise, in 1 Corinthians Paul's boast is in the cross of Christ, which is an affront to the world (and to the Corinthian culture). The cross disallows the possibility of any human effort garnering God's favor, since the cross demonstrates with graphic emphasis that the death of God's own Son is necessary to deal with the profound depths of our sin. The cross is therefore a stumbling block to those who look for respectable and impressive ideas (1 Cor. 1:22–23). Yet the cross is the power of God for justification (1:18, 24; cf. Rom. 1:16) because it shifts the focus from our own works to the work outside us—the self-giving sacrificial death of Christ.

A few verses later, in 1 Corinthians 1:30–31, we come to a debated passage in many discussions of justification: In what sense did Christ Jesus become wisdom, righteousness, sanctification, and redemption? Some find here support for imputation—the crediting of the righteousness of Christ to believers by faith for justification.[102] Others object to such a reading because, for example, we do not speak of the imputation of Christ's wisdom, which is also mentioned in this passage, and because it is difficult to understand how Christ was "redeemed."[103] Nevertheless, the sense of imputation here is apparent in the way that righteousness is found *in Christ*. Righteousness, then, is not an inherent possession of the individual but is found in identification with Christ.[104] Yet even if one were to demur at this particular text, Paul's collective teaching on justification necessitates the imputation of Christ's righteousness (cf. Rom. 4:4–8). Imputation is the means by which the requirement of *perfect* obedience, which is necessary for eternal life, is met in those whose obedience falls profoundly short of perfection.[105] I cover additional texts on this matter below.

---

102. See Beale, *New Testament Biblical Theology*, 473–77; Herman Bavinck, *Reformed Dogmatics*, ed. John Bolt, trans. John Vriend, vol. 4, *Holy Spirit, Church, and New Creation* (Grand Rapids, MI: Baker Academic, 2008), 185, 210–11, 257; Turretin, *Institutes*, 16.3.17.

103. See Wright, *Justification*, 132–34. For the relation of Christ's "redemption" to his resurrection, see Beale, *New Testament Biblical Theology*, 474.

104. See David E. Garland, *1 Corinthians*, BECNT (Grand Rapids, MI: Baker Academic, 2003), 79; Beale, *New Testament Biblical Theology*, 473–74. Garland further argues that righteousness, sanctification, and redemption are not coordinate with wisdom. *1 Corinthians*, 79.

105. Cf. Bavinck, *Reformed Dogmatics*, 4:209.

The next text to consider is 1 Corinthians 4. Though it is not always obvious in English translations, Paul uses justification language in 4:4 (though see the CSB). Discussing his role as a servant of Christ and steward (οἰκονόμος) of the mysteries of God (4:1), Paul denies that he is therefore justified by discharging his task faithfully (4:4): "For I do not know of anything against myself, but I have not been justified [δεδικαίωμαι] by this; he who judges me is the Lord." If we indeed translate δεδικαίωμαι as *justified*,[106] then Paul is saying that not even his faithfulness to his task as an apostle merits justification.[107]

Another important passage to consider is 1 Corinthians 6:9–11. In 6:9a, Paul states a principle: the unrighteous (ἄδικοι) will not inherit the kingdom of God. Whatever else Paul says about justification by faith alone—and he moves quickly to justification in 6:11—we must not allow the truth of 6:9a to be dismissed or treated as somehow hypothetical or irrelevant if we believe in justification by faith. The Scriptures consistently teach that the unrighteous will not inherit the kingdom of God (Rom. 1:18–32; Gal. 5:19–21; Eph. 5:3–7; Col. 3:5–8; 1 Thess. 4:3–8; Titus 3:3–7; Rev. 21:8; 22:14–15; cf. 1 Tim. 1:8–10; 2 Tim. 3:1–9; 1 Pet. 4:1–5). In 1 Corinthians 6:9b–10, Paul illustrates the type of unrighteousness he has in view in 6:9a, before reminding the Corinthians of the effects of the gospel among them in 6:11: "But you were washed, but you were sanctified, but you were justified [ἐδικαιώθητε] in the name of the Lord Jesus Christ and by the Spirit of our God." In 6:11, Paul speaks of the transition of the Corinthians from darkness to light: they were washed from their sins (cf. Eph. 5:26; Titus 3:5); they were justified and freed from condemnation; they were sanctified and set apart as holy. This sanctification is best taken as a once-for-all sanctification, sometimes called "definitive sanctification."[108] Yet definitive sanctification does not negate the need for progressive sanctification—or growth in holiness—as the vice list in 6:9–10 warns.

In 1 Corinthians 6, we see in short scope two corresponding realities. On the one hand, by being washed, justified, and (definitively) sanctified, the Corinthian Christians were cleansed from past sins like the list in 6:9b–10. At the same time, if anyone—even among confessing Christians—were to live in accord with the vice list of 6:9b–10, then he or she would be disqualified from inheriting the kingdom of God (cf. 2 Pet. 1:5–9). Yet this warning does not undermine the freedom granted in justification, nor does it contradict justification by faith alone apart from works. Neither does it mean that one could be truly justified and then lose that justification. It does mean, however, that those who are justified by faith must manifest the truth and vitality of their faith by walking in a manner pleasing to and submissive to God.[109] It also means that one's profession of faith in Christ must be accompanied by growth in holiness. Though we may not be able to understand exactly how these two statements dwell together in harmony, we

---

106. So also Garland, *1 Corinthians*, 128.
107. See also Beale, *New Testament Biblical Theology*, 511.
108. See John Murray, "Definitive Sanctification," in *The Collected Writings of John Murray*, vol. 2, *Select Lectures in Systematic Theology* (Edinburgh: Banner of Truth, 1977), 277–84.
109. See, e.g., Turretin, *Institutes*, 4.18.25; Westminster Confession of Faith 13.1; 16.2.

must allow the apostle to speak. Both are true: those who live unrighteously will not inherit the kingdom of God, and God justifies sinners by faith alone apart from any works they could do.

Paul returns to the cross in 1 Corinthians 15:1–4, where he discusses more fully the nature of the gospel message. The gospel is that which we receive (15:1) and by which we are saved (15:2), provided we hold fast to it. He goes on to note that "Christ died for our sins" (Χριστός ἀπέθανεν ὑπὲρ τῶν ἁμαρτιῶν ἡμῶν). Significantly, Paul also emphasizes the resurrection of Christ (15:4), which is no less in accord with the Scriptures than the death of Christ. Later in 1 Corinthians 15, Paul expounds the resurrection and its implications in great detail (15:12–28, 42–58). Though he does not say much about the resurrection and *justification* in 1 Corinthians 15, Paul does link both the death and resurrection to the gospel message by which we are saved, and elsewhere he states explicitly that we are justified by the resurrection of Christ (Rom. 4:25; cf. Acts 13:36–39). Just as Christ was vindicated, or *justified*, from his unjust death by means of his resurrection (1 Tim. 3:16), so will the resurrection of all those in Christ be their justification from death (Rom. 4:25).[110] Had Christ not been raised, then we would still be in our sins (1 Cor. 15:13–14, 17). But because Christ has been raised—*justified*—from the dead, we can be justified in him.

2 Corinthians

Second Corinthians is another important letter for understanding Paul's doctrine of justification. We begin in 5:10, where Paul says that we must all stand before the judgment seat of Christ in order to receive according to what each one has done in the body. If this were all we knew of Paul's theology, perhaps we would conclude that Paul believed in something like acceptance before God on the final day *on the basis of* our works. But surely that is an unsound conclusion in light of what Paul says elsewhere, and indeed, what he says later in the chapter. In light of Paul's teaching on justification, it is better to say that this final judgment is *according to works* (κατὰ τὰ ἔργα; cf. Rom. 2:6) and not *because of* (διά) nor *on the basis of* (ἐκ) *works*.[111] In other words, our works (even regenerate works) do not serve as the foundation of our acceptance before God. Instead, Christ's perfect obedience is the basis of our justification, while our good works are necessary corollaries of justification.[112]

Paul then proclaims that all those in Christ are participants in new creation (2 Cor. 5:17), and this through God who reconciled (καταλλάξαντος) us to himself (5:18) and does not count our sins against us (5:19). This points to the initiative of God to forgive our sins and accept us as righteous in his sight, which is tantamount to saying that we

---

110. See especially Richard B. Gaffin Jr., *Resurrection and Redemption: A Study in Paul's Soteriology* (Phillipsburg, NJ: Presbyterian and Reformed, 1987), 119–24; Gaffin, *By Faith, Not by Sight: Paul and the Order of Salvation* (Waynesboro, GA: Paternoster, 2006), 84–86.
111. See Gaffin, *By Faith, Not by Sight*, 98–99; Ridderbos, *Paul*, 178–81. Wright misses this distinction when he uses "on the basis of" and "according to" interchangeably; compare *Justification*, 130 with 230n11. Paul's reticence to boast or commend himself or his ministry in the following verses (esp. 5:12–15, which speaks of the death of Christ) is likely to be understood in light of his persuasion that his boast is ultimately in the cross of Christ (cf. 1 Cor. 1:18–31).
112. See Westminster Confession of Faith 11.1–2; 16.2, 5–6; 33.1; Bavinck, *Reformed Dogmatics*, 4:209.

are justified by faith. This sets us up to consider the much-discussed 5:21: "The one who did not know sin [i.e., Christ] was made sin on our behalf, in order that we might become [γενώμεθα] the righteousness of God [δικαιοσύνη θεοῦ] in him." One question that arises from this text is, What does it mean for Christ to have been "made sin"? Here a likely answer is that Christ was made a sin *offering* on our behalf, given the way that sin offerings are often referred to metonymically as "sin" in the Septuagint (e.g., Ex. 29:14; Lev. 4:8, 20–21, 24, 29, 34, et al.).[113]

A second question is, What does it mean for us to become the righteousness of God? This statement has often been understood as referring to the imputation of Christ's righteousness in justification.[114] Others object. Wright, for example, argues that the context of 2 Corinthians 5 focuses not on the need for the Corinthians to be reconciled but on Paul's apostolic ministry of reconciliation (cf. 5:20).[115] In this construal, the "righteousness of God" that we "become" is not something like "God's own character" but is instead better taken as becoming ministers of God's covenant faithfulness.[116] Wright also observes that it is God's own righteousness in view, which further discourages us from understanding 5:21 to refer to the righteousness of Christ.[117] However, it is better to take "righteousness of God" to refer not strictly to God's covenant faithfulness but to his character by which he "judges justly" and "acquits those who have faith in Jesus."[118] Thus, this justice of God does manifest itself in faithfulness to his covenant and issues forth in salvation. But we also retain the notion of God's just judgment.[119] And it is not a problem for imputation that the righteousness *of God* is mentioned, since Paul clarifies that this is the righteousness of God *in Christ*.[120] The "we" of 5:21, therefore, likely refers not to the ministry of apostles,[121] but to all God's people who are counted righteous in Christ,[122] which further elucidates the nature of reconciliation emphasized in the immediate context (cf. 5:18–19). In short, becoming the righteousness of God means that when we are reconciled, we are considered righteous in God's sight in the context of our union with Christ.[123]

1–2 Thessalonians

By all accounts 1 Thessalonians is one of the first Pauline letters. At first glance, it may not seem like justification is an important topic in this letter. However, as Stephen

---

113. See Beale, *New Testament Biblical Theology*, 472n8; compare Murray J. Harris, *The Second Epistle to the Corinthians: A Commentary on the Greek Text*, NIGTC (Grand Rapids, MI: Eerdmans, 2005), 452–54; David E. Garland, *2 Corinthians*, NAC 29 (Nashville: Broadman, 1999), 300–301.
114. See, e.g., Beale, *New Testament Biblical Theology*, 472–73; Harris, *Second Epistle to the Corinthians*, 454–55 (though see his hesitation at 455–56n207); Schreiner, *Faith Alone*, 186–88; Ridderbos, *Paul*, 174–75; Turretin, *Institutes*, 16.3.
115. On this issue in 2 Cor. 5, see Wright, *Justification*, 135–44.
116. For Wright's understanding of δικαιοσύνη θεοῦ as "God's covenant faithfulness," see *Justification*, 45–52, 141; Wright, *Paul and the Faithfulness of God*, 795–804.
117. Cf. Wright, *Justification*, 140–42.
118. Bavinck, *Reformed Dogmatics*, 4:185; cf. Ridderbos, *Paul*, 163–66; John Murray, *O Death, Where Is Thy Sting? Collected Sermons* (Philadelphia: Westminster Seminary Press, 2017), 9–12, 30–32. A helpful contemporary survey is found in Schreiner, *Faith Alone*, 144–78.
119. So also Schreiner, *Faith Alone*, 148–52.
120. Beale, *New Testament Biblical Theology*, 472.
121. For this view, see Wright, *Justification*, 140.
122. See Schreiner, *Faith Alone*, 187; Harris, *Second Epistle to the Corinthians*, 455–56n207.
123. See also Garland, *2 Corinthians*, 302.

Westerholm has recently observed, Paul's fervent desire that the Thessalonians be delivered from the wrath of God (cf. 1 Thess. 1:9–10; 2:16; 4:6; 5:1–11; 2 Thess. 1:8–9) underscores the need for what justification has traditionally been understood to be about: How can unrighteous people escape the wrath of God and be acceptable to a holy God?[124] Though Paul does not use the language of justification in 1 Thessalonians, his discussion does manifest the need for sinners to be acceptable in the sight of a holy God. The answer to escaping the wrath of God is justification by faith in God's action in Christ on our behalf.

Texts relating explicitly to justification in 2 Thessalonians are also sparse, though given the tenor of the letter, we may conclude that the need to be delivered from God's wrath was again a central Pauline assumption (2 Thess. 1:5–10; 2:10, 12). In 2:13–15, Paul speaks of being saved by sanctification of the Spirit (ἐν ἁγιασμῷ πνεύματος, 2:13). The language of sanctification may refer to the *means* by which we attain final salvation—that is, growth in holiness—or it could refer to the once-for-all sanctification of renewal.[125] In neither case are we saved by our works, for God chose us to salvation in the first place (2:13). Indeed, the traditions by which we are saved (2:15) must be the same traditions that Paul outlines in his encapsulation of the gospel in 1 Corinthians 15:1–4[126] (cf. 1 Cor. 11:2): those traditions pertain to the work of Christ on our behalf for salvation, which benefit us by faith (1 Cor. 15:2; 2 Thess. 2:13).

Justification in Paul's Prison Epistles

Ephesians

Ephesians is an epitome of Pauline theology.[127] It is therefore no surprise that we find much material relevant for our discussion of justification. We begin with Ephesians 1:3–14, in which we are given a glimpse into the majestic depths of the mystery of God's sovereignty in salvation. God has chosen his beloved people in Christ before the foundation of the world (1:4) and predestined them for adoption as sons (1:5). Here adoption is closely related to justification.[128] Paul goes on to note that we have redemption (ἀπολύτρωσις) through the blood of Jesus (1:7). Though the terminology of justification is not used, the forgiveness of sins is a key component of justification. A few verses later Paul emphasizes the importance of faith in Jesus (τὴν καθ' ὑμᾶς πίστιν ἐν τῷ κυρίῳ, 1:15), entailing the conclusion that this faith is the means by which the blessings outlined in 1:3–14 are experienced.

---

124. See Westerholm, *Justification Reconsidered*, 4–8.
125. See variously F. F. Bruce, *1 and 2 Thessalonians*, WBC 45 (Nashville: Thomas Nelson, 1982), 190; Gene L. Green, *The Letters to the Thessalonians*, PNTC (Grand Rapids, MI: Eerdmans, 2002), 326–27; Richard D. Phillips, *1 and 2 Thessalonians*, REC (Phillipsburg, NJ: P&R, 2015), 363; Beale, *New Testament Biblical Theology*, 864.
126. Note the similar terminology present in 1 Cor. 15:1–4 and 2 Thess. 2:13–15: "gospel" (εὐαγγέλιον), "to stand" (ἵστημι), "salvation" / "to save" (σωτηρία/σῴζω), "traditions" / "to hand down" (παράδοσις/παραδίδωμι), "belief" / "faith" / "to believe" (πίστις/πιστεύω).
127. See Markus Barth, *Ephesians 1–3: A New Translation with Introduction and Commentary*, AB 34 (New York: Doubleday, 1974), 3–4, 12. The term *epitome* is my own, but it is possible I have gleaned it from someone else over the years.
128. See, e.g., Westminster Confession of Faith 12; David B. Garner, *Sons in the Son: The Riches and Reach of Adoption in Christ* (Phillipsburg, NJ: P&R, 2016).

Further insight into justification comes in Ephesians 2. In 2:1–9, Paul extols the mercy and grace of God (2:4–5, 8–9), who made us alive with Christ even when we were spiritually dead in our trespasses and sins (2:1, 5). Indeed, he saved us even when we were by nature under the wrath of God (2:3). As we have seen in both Galatians and 1 Thessalonians, justification is necessary to be delivered from the wrath of God. Paul provides one of the most striking and succinct statements of justification by faith alone in Ephesians 2:8–9: "For by grace you have been saved through faith. And this is not your own doing; it is the gift of God, not a result of works so that no one may boast" (ESV). Paul thus emphasizes the vivifying grace of God in contrast to our deadness and inability, which are due to our own sin. The more general emphasis on "works" (ἔργα) here is instructive. As we have seen, proponents of the NPP often reduce works to those works of the law that distinguish Jews from non-Jews (Sabbath, dietary laws, circumcision). Ephesians 2, however, provides further reason to reject this truncated perspective. Paul does not mention works *of the law* but has in view any sort of works.[129] Moreover, Paul excludes the possibility of boasting in any work unto salvation, consistent with Galatians. Indeed, even if one wanted to reduce works here to "works of the law" narrowly defined, the danger of boasting would still be something Paul would have to counter. Our standing before God is not due in any part to anything we could do. Thus, Ephesians 2:1–9 is about justification—being made spiritually alive and delivered from God's wrath—by faith alone. The term *justification* does not appear here, but the term does not have to be used for the doctrine to be present. We are justified by grace through faith, not by any work done by us.

Those who are by nature children of wrath are not capable of saving themselves by any good works. Ephesians 2:8–9 makes this point abundantly clear. And yet we must not overlook the teaching of 2:10, which says that although we are not saved *by* good works, we are saved *for* good works (cf. 1:4). Only after being renewed and saved by grace can we truly embark on a path of good works. Good works are therefore imperative for the Christian (see especially Ephesians 4–6), though sinners are entirely incapable of meriting eternal life on the basis of those good works. They are instead the evidences of true, justifying faith. This manifests the indicative-imperative structure of Pauline thought.[130] The indicative refers to what God has done for us in Christ and can be correlated to justification by faith alone. This is a unilateral act of God.[131] The imperative refers to the call to true Christian discipleship in light of the indicative and can be correlated to sanctification. Sanctification is progressive growth in grace; in this, believers have a role to play.[132] These two issues are seen in brief scope in 2:8–10.

If 2:1–10 (especially 2:1–9) has primarily in view our *vertical* relationship to God (which is the concern of justification), then 2:11–22 has primarily in view the *horizontal*

---

129. See Thomas R. Schreiner, *New Testament Theology: Magnifying God in Christ* (Grand Rapids, MI: Baker Academic, 2008), 527.
130. See Ridderbos, *Paul*, 253–58; Gaffin, *By Faith, Not by Sight*, 68–75.
131. See Westminster Shorter Catechism 33.
132. See Westminster Shorter Catechism 35.

implications of justification—that is, how we relate to one another in the church. In this regard we can observe the way that Paul uses peace (εἰρήνη) in Ephesians 2. In 2:13–14, Paul teaches that those in Christ have been brought near by Christ's blood which provides peace with God. In light of this, we are to live at peace with one another—regardless of each other's heritage (2:15–17).

Most of Paul's theology of the indicative in Ephesians comes in the first three chapters, but we also find indications of Paul's view on justification in Ephesians 4–6. In 4:32, the pattern for our tenderness and forgiveness toward one another is founded on the kindness of God, who forgave us in Christ. Likewise, in 5:26–27, Christ cleanses his church that she might be holy. These passages are relevant for discussions on justification because Paul correlates forgiveness of sins to justification.

As I argued earlier, if Ephesians were a more prominent source for one's articulation of justification, then perhaps NPP readings of Paul would be deemed less persuasive. Indeed, John Barclay recently concluded that "works" in Ephesians 2 (and 2 Tim. 1:9; Titus 3:5) go beyond boundary markers and must be works of any kind.[133] It is better to find agreement in the usage of "works" in Ephesians and "works of the law" in Galatians, both of which point to the futility of clinging to any human works to merit eternal life or forgiveness of sins.

Philippians

The most important passage in Philippians that bears on the doctrine of justification is Philippians 3. Here we again find Paul boasting not in himself but in Jesus Christ (3:3). As I argued earlier, this boasting in Christ derives from the theological truth that we are saved not by any works we could do before God but only on the basis of Christ's work for us (cf. 1 Cor. 1:18; Gal. 6:14). Paul does not place any confidence in works of the flesh. Two key questions in this passage are these:

1. What were the works and righteousness in which Paul did not place his trust?
2. In what sense was Paul blameless with respect to the righteousness of the law?

We begin with the first question: What were the works in which Paul did not place his trust? On the one hand, in Philippians 3:4–6, Paul clearly has in view his life under the Jewish law: Paul was circumcised the right way (i.e., on the eighth day), he lived in accord with the Pharisaic approach to the law, and he was zealous to the point of persecuting the church for perceived blasphemy. One could therefore make a strong argument that the works in view are those quintessential Jewish works that marked out Jews from non-Jews. Indeed, circumcision appears to be (as in Galatians) an important issue here (Phil. 3:2–3, 5). It is therefore not surprising that in some renderings these particular works of the law have become the defining issue, since Paul could view himself as "blameless" according to the law (3:6).[134] On the other hand, I have argued that such a

---
133. Barclay, *Paul and the Gift*, 571. However, Barclay considers these writings to be deutero-Pauline.
134. Compare Dunn, *Theology of Paul*, 369–71 (§14.6).

view of Jewish works does not do justice to the sweeping claims made by Paul regarding the inability of the law to save. Justification is more than just about who constitutes the people of God; it is about how all people can be made right before a holy God. Thus, whereas Paul may have counted his actions under the law to his advantage apart from Christ (3:7), he rejects the notion that any of his works could benefit him before God in the end (3:7–8). Indeed, the language of "confidence" (πεποίθησις, 3:3–4) makes more sense in the context of trusting one's acceptance before God than in that of trusting who is and is not a member of the people of God (cf. 2 Cor. 3:4; Eph. 3:12).

This brings us to the debated phrase "righteousness of God" (τὴν ἐκ θεοῦ δικαιοσύνην) in Philippians 3:9, which is set in contrast to the "righteousness from the law" (δικαιοσύνην τὴν ἐκ νόμου).[135] Paul contrasts a righteousness that God grants us (thus, a righteousness "from God,"[136] consistent with his own character of judging justly) with a righteousness that we seek to establish by our own efforts. Only the righteousness that comes from God is able to stand before God,[137] and this comes by faith in Christ (διὰ πίστεως Χριστοῦ, 3:9).[138] As in Galatians 2:16, it is not unnecessarily redundant for Paul to mention our faith twice in Philippians 3:9 (διὰ πίστεως Χριστοῦ . . . ἐπὶ τῇ πίστει). Thus, it is unlikely that διὰ πίστεως Χριστοῦ should be translated "through the faithfulness of Christ." Instead, Paul emphasizes faith *in* Christ while also emphasizing that the righteousness granted by God depends on faith, not on any work we can do.

This leads us to the second question: In what sense was Paul blameless with respect to the righteousness of the law? Given the discussion above, this cannot mean that he was accepted before God on the basis of any works of the Mosaic law. As I argued from Galatians, to live under the Mosaic administration of the law would be insufficient in light of the coming of Christ—Christ is the end of the law for righteousness (Rom. 10:4). Moreover, to live according to works of the law stands contrary to the life of faith in Christ (Phil. 3:9). Philippians 3:9 assumes that one's only hope before God is the righteousness that comes by faith in Christ—the perfectly obedient one who has been raised, who now has all authority, and to whom every person will one day bow (2:6–11). This again speaks to imputation: Paul counts his own works rubbish in order to gain Christ (ἵνα Χριστὸν κερδήσω, 3:8) and to be found in him (εὑρεθῶ ἐν αὐτῷ, 3:9), which most likely entails Christ's righteousness as well.[139]

Finally, an eschatological goal is in view (3:12)—attaining the resurrection of the dead (3:11). As I argue in chapter 14 in this volume, resurrection life requires perfect adherence to the law of God. This is not always appreciated in discussions of justification and Philippians 3.[140] If Paul is indeed to meet the covenantal requirements for

---

135. Wright, *Justification*, 128.
136. See Moisés Silva, *Philippians*, 2nd ed., BECNT 11 (Grand Rapids, MI: Baker Academic, 2005), 159–62; Bavinck, *Reformed Dogmatics*, 4:185.
137. See Ridderbos, *Paul*, 163–64. Ridderbos also rightly notes that righteousness is a forensic category, a view held also by Schreiner, *Faith Alone*, 158–69.
138. On the objective genitive, see the discussion on Gal. 2:16 above, under "The Gospel and Justification" (p. 243).
139. Beale, *New Testament Biblical Theology*, 473.
140. Though see Beale, *New Testament Biblical Theology*, 472–73.

resurrection life, then he must trust in the perfect obedience of Christ, which leads to Christ's resurrection (cf. 2:6–11).[141] Attaining the resurrection of the dead can thus be realized only in the context of union with Christ. On the one hand, Paul recognizes his need to press forward to strive to attain this resurrection—he looks forward to what lies ahead (3:13).[142] At the same time, Paul's effort is not antithetical to God's work of grace in him. Instead, Paul strives forward by faith—working out his salvation with fear and trembling (cf. 2:12–13)—while also recognizing that God grants righteousness by faith.

Colossians

Early in Colossians we read of a common Pauline emphasis: faith *in* Jesus Christ. In the case of 1:4, the wording leaves little doubt as to the best translation (τὴν πίστιν ὑμῶν ἐν Χριστῷ Ἰησοῦ). Later, Paul speaks of the deliverance God has wrought for us through Christ from the authority of darkness to the kingdom of Christ (1:13). As in Ephesians, Paul speaks of this redemption in Christ entailing the forgiveness of sins (Col. 1:14; cf. Eph. 1:7). This statement further recalls Galatians 1, where Paul speaks of being delivered from this present evil age by Christ, who gave himself for our sins (Gal. 1:4). Colossians 1:13–14 uses the language of redemption to speak of being transferred from death to life and having our sins blotted out—all of which could be subsumed under the theological term *justification*.[143]

Though Paul does not say much about justification explicitly in Colossians, several other statements support a traditional understanding of justification. For example, Colossians 2:13–14 speaks of new life in Christ through the forgiveness of our sins. Moreover, in 2:14, we find a likely reference to the legal debt that lies on all those who do not walk by faith. As in Philippians 3, regardless of how well we may think we keep the law, the reality is a burden of debts piled up against us that must be addressed by the cross of Christ (cf. Eph. 2:15).[144] Likewise, in Colossians 3:13, we are reminded to bear with and forgive one another because we have freely been forgiven in Christ (cf. Eph. 4:32). Clearly, forgiveness is important in Colossians, which is necessary for acceptance before God. Thus, in Colossians 3:5–7, we see the need to be delivered from God's wrath, which correlates to the forgiveness of sins and the putting off of the old, sinful way of living.[145] This deliverance from wrath can come only if our sinful debts can be canceled. In this way, Paul teaches the need for justification (and indeed, sanctification), even if these terms are not used in Colossians.

Philemon

There is little explicit in Philemon that speaks to the issue of justification by faith, but at least two aspects of Philemon bear mentioning. First, Philemon provides additional

---

141. See my discussion of the logic of resurrection in Philippians 2 in chap. 14, my other essay in this volume.
142. See Bavinck, *Reformed Dogmatics*, 4:235.
143. See also Bavinck, *Reformed Dogmatics*, vol. 3, *Sin and Salvation in Christ* (2006), 340; 4:43.
144. Compare Bavinck, *Reformed Dogmatics*, 3:224, 340, 451; 4:450; Douglas J. Moo, *The Letters to the Colossians and to Philemon*, PNTC (Grand Rapids, MI: Eerdmans, 2008), 210–11; C. F. D. Moule, *The Epistles of Paul to the Colossians and to Philemon: An Introduction and Commentary*, CGTC (Cambridge: Cambridge University Press, 1957), 98–99.
145. See Bavinck, *Reformed Dogmatics*, 3:451.

warrant for understanding Paul's potentially ambiguous Greek references to either *faith in Christ* or *the faithfulness of Christ* as objective genitives: *faith in Christ*. In Philemon 5, Paul speaks explicitly of the faith that Philemon has "toward the Lord Jesus" (πρὸς τὸν κύριον Ἰησοῦν).[146] Second, Paul's view of Onesimus as a full brother in the Lord further suggests that faith in Jesus leads to a new status. Paul now views Onesimus as a child in the faith (10). What then ensues is likely a play on words: formerly Onesimus was useless (ἄχρηστος, 11) and, we can conclude, apart from Christ (ἄχριστος), whereas now (νυνί) Onesimus is useful (εὔχρηστος) and, we can conclude, "in Christ" (ἐν Χριστῷ; cf. 8, 20, 23). This is most likely a play on words between *useful/useless* and Onesimus's relationship to *Christ* (cf. Rom. 2:4; 1 Pet. 2:3). This transition in Onesimus's status is best taken to indicate one who previously did not have faith toward Christ but now (like Philemon) does. In light of this, Paul exhorts Philemon to receive Onesimus back as a brother in the Lord (Philem. 16). Such is the grace of our Lord Jesus Christ (3, 23).

Justification in the Pastoral Epistles

Though the Pauline corpus contains *thirteen* Pauline letters, a great many Pauline studies rely on only *seven* (or so) Pauline letters in any significant way. This has created a situation in which the fullness of Paul's biblical voice goes unheard. Bifurcating between authentic and inauthentic Pauline letters may have a precedent in (recent) academic study of the Bible, but it does not reflect the sentiment of the church through the ages, nor does it do justice to the Pauline *corpus*. Indeed, it behooves the modern exegete to take seriously Pauline attributions of authorship, for if they are authentic, then the Pastorals should be no less authoritative for understanding Paul's theology than Romans or Galatians or any other "undisputed" Pauline letter. Yet even if one were to argue that Paul did not write the Pastoral Epistles, it would remain artificial to exclude them as part of the canonical Pauline witness. It is important, therefore, to consider the contribution of the Pastoral Epistles to justification.

1 Timothy

In 1 Timothy 1:15, Paul provides a striking picture of his own sinfulness in the sight of God: "The saying is trustworthy and deserving of full acceptance, that Christ Jesus came into the world to save sinners, of whom I am the foremost" (ESV). This follows Paul's litany of offenses that he committed, including being a blasphemer and persecutor of the church. This is the same Paul who claims in Philippians 3 that he was blameless with respect to the righteousness that comes by the law (3:6). How could the same Paul say in 1 Timothy that he was a worse sinner than anyone else? We need not posit a different author for 1 Timothy to reconcile these two writings. As I argued previously from Philippians 3, though Paul may have been blameless with regard to the righteousness

---

146. So also ESV.

that comes by the law, this would still be insufficient for justification. What we have in 1 Timothy is consistent with what Paul says in Philippians 3—Paul's righteous standing before God could not be based on anything that Paul himself could do or had done, but he could be justified only by faith in Christ. Likewise, the issue in view in 1 Timothy 1:6–11 is the proper understanding of the law. Doubtless there were those who accused Paul of antinomianism since he did not espouse righteousness on the basis of the law[147] (though as we see here and elsewhere, he does emphasize the need for godly living; e.g., 1:5; 2:2; 4:7–8; 6:3, 6, 11). But Paul's more fundamental point is that the law must be used rightly (1:8) and not (perhaps) as a means to acceptance before God.[148] Instead, we must recognize that Christ Jesus came to save sinners, which applies even to Paul himself. Indeed, Paul may wish to show here that even someone who could outwardly adhere flawlessly to the law may nevertheless be quite far from the heart of the law, which has always been about faith (cf. Rom. 9:32).

First Timothy, then, provides a theological assessment of how Paul—and all humanity—needs a mediator between God and man (cf. 2:5). This reveals the magnificent mercy of God—even to Paul, who was a persecutor and murderer of Christians. As such, Paul is an encouragement and example for those who would believe in Christ unto eternal life (1:16). Explicit mention of Christ as Mediator comes in 2:5. The uniqueness of Christ is on brilliant display in this passage: Jesus is the only Mediator between God and humanity, and he is indeed a man himself. How does this mediatorial role of Christ relate to justification? Both Jesus's divine nature and human nature are necessary for our justification. As fully God, he is able to provide eternal life.[149] As fully man, he has fully obeyed the law and suffered the consequences resulting from humanity's sin.[150] Only Jesus can save us from sin. In debates about justification, we must not lose sight of the uniqueness of our Mediator: fully God and fully man. The necessity of a mediator is at the heart of Paul's doctrine of justification.

This leads us to a remarkable statement about Jesus in 1 Timothy 3:16. Indeed, it is a statement about the *justification* of Jesus. In what may well be an early liturgical snippet, Paul identifies the mystery of godliness to include Jesus's manifestation in the flesh, justification by the Spirit (ἐδικαιώθη ἐν πνεύματι), appearance to angels, being preached among the nations, being believed in the world, and ascension in glory. Key for our discussion is the phrase ἐδικαιώθη ἐν πνεύματι. Two questions of translation must be dealt with here. First, how should one translate the aorist form of δικαιόω? One option is "vindicated," which is indeed a fitting translation. But perhaps it is better to translate the term as "justified." I will explain why in a moment. Second, how does one take ἐν πνεύματι? The two best options are "in [the realm of] the Spirit" or "by the Spirit." Either way, the Holy Spirit must be in view, given the eschatological-soteriological matrix

---

147. See, e.g., William D. Mounce, *Pastoral Epistles*, WBC 46 (Nashville: Thomas Nelson, 2000), 31–32.
148. Cf. Mounce, *Pastoral Epistles*, 32.
149. Louis Berkhof, *Systematic Theology*, 4th ed. (Grand Rapids, MI: Eerdmans, 1941), 319; cf. Bavinck, *Reformed Dogmatics*, 3:214, 223; Geerhardus Vos, *Reformed Dogmatics*, trans. and ed. Richard B. Gaffin Jr., vol. 3. *Christology* (Bellingham, WA: Lexham, 2014), 46.
150. Berkhof, *Systematic Theology*, 319.

of ideas. In terms of ἐν + the dative, it may be best to take this as a reference to the agency of the Holy Spirit.[151] Either way, Jesus's justification[152]—from the dead—points to his perfect obedience. Jesus was therefore not paying the penalty for his own sins (μὴ γένοιτο!) but for the sins of others. His resurrection thus demonstrated that sin had no claim on Jesus. As Richard Gaffin argues, "The eradication of death in [Jesus's] resurrection is nothing less than the removal of the verdict of condemnation and the effective affirmation of his (adamic) righteousness. His resurrected state is the reward and seal which testifies perpetually to his perfect obedience."[153] The translation "justified" for ἐδικαιώθη is preferable because it underscores the solidarity between Jesus's experience in being raised from the dead and our own experience of justification.[154] Our justification is founded on the full obedience of Christ. The testimony of 1 Timothy deserves a larger place in present discussions of justification.

2 Timothy

Second Timothy 1:8–14 also deserves a larger place in discussions of justification.[155] In 1:9, we read that God saved us and called us, apart from any works. Again, human works are contrasted with our acceptance before God on the basis of Christ's work. Further, it is unlikely that the works in view here are simply select works of the Jewish law. Rather, the contrast is between the grace of God in Christ and any work that we could do, which manifests the Pauline doctrine of justification by faith alone.[156] Also, Jesus is identified as our glorious Lord and Savior, who has abolished death and brought light and immortality (1:10). As in 1 Timothy 3:16, Jesus's abolition of death points to his own perfect obedience (cf. 1 Cor. 15:21), which benefits all who believe in him.

Titus

The final Pauline text to consider is Titus 3:4–7—an important text that contrasts the grace of God toward us in Christ with any work we could do. In 3:5, God saved us not because of works we had done in righteousness but because of his mercy. Thus again Paul contrasts our works—any righteous works—with the mercy of God. Furthermore, the washing of regeneration and renewal by the Holy Spirit (3:5) includes the washing away of our sins and our rebirth to new life in Christ (cf. John 3:3). Paul then explicitly relates this to justification by grace (Titus 3:7); the aorist participle δικαιωθέντες ("having been justified") in 3:7 is best taken adverbially to refer back to the saving work of God outlined in the previous verses.

---

151. So ESV, NIV 2011. Even if it refers to the *realm* of the Spirit, the Spirit is constitutive of the new age. Cf. Gaffin, *Resurrection and Redemption*, 120–21.
152. This point stands even if one translates δικαιόω in terms of "vindication."
153. Gaffin, *Resurrection and Redemption*, 121–22.
154. Gaffin states, "Nothing warrants a different sense for the verb than its virtually uniform meaning elsewhere in Paul." *Resurrection and Redemption*, 121.
155. By way of example, in Wright's *Justification*, there are no references in the index to 2 Timothy (or to Titus).
156. See also Schreiner, *Faith Alone*, 111; Cara, *Cracking the Foundation*, 167.

Thus, Titus 3:4–7 includes at least two aspects of justification that proponents of the NPP sometimes argue are not part of the Pauline equation. First, works in 3:5 are not delimited to "works of the law" that some might argue refer to the three pillar works of Judaism. Second is our need both to have our sins washed away and to experience new life. If justification is merely about social markers for the people of God, then the need for new life is not acute. However, if, as we see in Titus 3, justification has to do with the need for new life in Christ, then justification must address how ungodly sinners can be accepted before a holy God. A robust and well-rounded view of justification must include the contribution of Titus 3.

Conclusion

In light of the exegesis provided above, I highlight a few points by way of conclusion.

First, if we want to understand accurately Paul's doctrine of justification we cannot leave six (or so) of the Pauline letters out of the equation. To look only at Romans, 1–2 Corinthians, Galatians, Philippians, 1 Thessalonians, and Philemon (and possibly a few others) will necessarily lead to a truncated, and likely distorted, view of Paul's doctrine of justification. In this case the tail that threatens to wag the dog is the widespread acceptance of pseudepigraphy in our canonical Pauline corpus. *If* Paul really did write the Pastoral Epistles—as the letters themselves claim (1 Tim. 1:1; 2 Tim. 1:1; Titus 1:1)—then we should allow his mature reflections on justification in books like Titus to make a contribution to the discussion. As it stands, those who use only the undisputed Pauline epistles do not take sufficiently into account the full range of evidence. Those who may be moved to reconsider the Reformational teachings on justification may therefore benefit from asking if newer readings have dealt adequately with texts such as Ephesians, Titus, and Acts.

Second, one must wrestle with whether the law of God ultimately requires perfect obedience for eternal life. This is different from asking whether the Mosaic administration of the law required perfection on a day-to-day basis for covenant members. The view that does the most justice to the most Pauline texts understands justification to entail not only forgiveness of sins but also the imputation of the perfect obedience of Christ for eternal life. To demonstrate this, one must go beyond Moses to Adam.

Third, one cannot fudge on the historical Adam. Though in this essay I have not tackled the question of Adam directly,[157] the question whether God requires perfect obedience for eternal life is tied to whether this was the covenantal arrangement given to a particular, representative man who stands at the beginning of creation. To address justification, one must take an exegetical-theological stand on the historical Adam. If one denies the reality of Adam, then one's understanding of justification is necessarily affected as well. It may sound like hyperbole to say that one's understanding of justification is tethered to one's understanding of Adam, but logically, this is indeed the case.[158]

---

157. I address this issue a bit more in chap. 14, my other essay in this volume.
158. For fuller discussions of the interrelationship of the historical Adam and Paul's teaching on justification, see the concise study of Richard B. Gaffin Jr., *No Adam, No Gospel: Adam and the History of Redemption* (Phillipsburg, NJ: P&R, 2015).

Fourth, interpreters of Paul must take account of both biblical and systematic theology. Good systematic theology helps us think about the implications of texts along with the full range of evidence from across the biblical canon. Indeed, sometimes it is surprising to find how relevant the exegetical discussions in systematic works hundreds of years old are for contemporary exegesis. I therefore advocate not only making the entire Pauline corpus part of the conversation on Paul's doctrine of justification but also including a wider range of exegetical sources. This will also provide a healthy context to current debates in the history of exegesis that can be lost if we read Pauline studies from only the past forty—or even two hundred—years. Though the old, of course, is not always better,[159] I have often found that some of the best contemporary exegesis finds fecund support in our exegetical-theological predecessors. The Reformed tradition, in particular, has a great deal of potential for contemporary discussions, with its rich and nuanced understanding of the relationship between justification and sanctification and its nuanced distinctions concerning covenantal administrations (e.g., between Adam, Moses, and Christ). The long history of exegesis also includes voices from the earlier days of the church, such as the Epistle to Diognetus, which must be considered as well.[160]

In the end, justification is not a theoretical doctrine for Paul; it is good news for sinners. There is much more to Pauline theology than justification, but one will struggle to understand Paul's theology without a rich appreciation for justification.[161]

Recommended Resources

Bavinck, Herman. *Reformed Dogmatics*. Edited by John Bolt. Translated by John Vriend. 4 vols. Grand Rapids, MI: Baker Academic, 2003–2008.

Beale, G. K. *A New Testament Biblical Theology: The Unfolding of the Old Testament in the New*. Grand Rapids, MI: Baker Academic, 2011.

Calvin, John. *Institutes of the Christian Religion*. Edited by John T. McNeill. Translated by Ford Lewis Battles. 2 vols. Library of Christian Classics 20–21. Louisville: Westminster John Knox, 1960.

Gaffin, Richard B., Jr. *By Faith, Not by Sight: Paul and the Order of Salvation*. Waynesboro, GA: Paternoster, 2006.

Gathercole, Simon J. *Where Is Boasting? Early Jewish Soteriology and Paul's Response in Romans 1–5*. Grand Rapids, MI: Eerdmans, 2002.

Murray, John. *Redemption Accomplished and Applied*. Grand Rapids, MI: Eerdmans, 1955.

Ridderbos, Herman N. *Paul: An Outline of His Theology*. Translated by John Richard de Witt. Grand Rapids, MI: Eerdmans, 1975.

---

159. Indeed, it is sometimes necessary to disagree with those who have come before us on matters of exegesis. For example, despite what some Reformed theologians have held through the ages, Rom. 1:3–4 is not about the human and divine natures of Christ but about two modes of existence. See Gaffin, *Resurrection and Redemption*, 98–113.

160. See, e.g., Epistle to Diognetus 9.5 and the discussion in Brandon D. Crowe, "Oh Sweet Exchange! The Soteriological Significance of the Incarnation in the *Epistle to Diognetus*," ZNW 102, no. 1 (2011): 96–109; cf. Schreiner, *Faith Alone*, 187.

161. Thanks to David Barry for his comments on an earlier draft of this essay.

Schreiner, Thomas. *Faith Alone: The Doctrine of Justification; What the Reformers Taught . . . and Why It Still Matters*, Five Solas Series. Grand Rapids, MI: Zondervan, 2015.

Silva, Moisés. "Abraham, Faith, and Works: Paul's Use of Scripture in Galatians 3:6–14." *Westminster Theological Journal* 63, no. 2 (2001): 251–67.

Turretin, Francis. *Institutes of Elenctic Theology*. Translated by George Musgrave Giger. Edited by James T. Dennison Jr. 3 vols. Phillipsburg, NJ: P&R, 1992–1997.

Westminster Confession of Faith. Agreed on by the Assembly of Divines at Westminster. London, 1646–1647.

8

An Epistle of Straw?

Reconciling James and Paul

DAN MCCARTNEY

The epistle of James has long been appreciated by ordinary believers for its practical orientation.[1] Its interest in true, godly wisdom and consistent Christian behavior and its large supply of memorable phrases and aphorisms encapsulate many aspects of practical Christian life. James has not, however, had a great deal of influence on the development of the church's theology and has proved nettlesome in its apparent conflict with Paul's teaching on justification. This, along with the less developed Christology of James, led Martin Luther to question its validity as an expression of the gospel of Jesus. Luther even went so far as to call it "an epistle of straw."[2] Most of the Reformers, however, including Luther's protégé Philipp Melanchthon, along with most of the church throughout its history, took a more tempered view and argued that, when more carefully analyzed, James is not really in conflict with Paul.[3] In fact, Luther's own theology is closer to James than he perhaps realized. In Luther's preface to Romans, he declares that real faith is

> a living, busy, active, mighty thing, this faith. . . . It is impossible for it not to be doing good works incessantly. It never asks whether good works are to be done; it

---

1. Parts of this chapter are adapted from Dan G. McCartney, *James*, BECNT (Grand Rapids, MI: Baker Academic, 2009). Used by permission of Baker Academic, a division of Baker Publishing Group.
2. These famous words appear in the 1522 edition of Luther's German Bible. *D. Martin Luthers Werke, Kritische Gesamtausgabe* (Weimarer Ausgabe), part 3, *Die deutsche Bibel*, vol. 7, *Episteln und Offenbarung*. An English translation is available in Martin Luther, *Word and Sacrament I*, in *LW* 35:362. Luther did not, however, exclude James from his New Testament. He grouped it along with Hebrews(!), Jude, and Revelation as less important Scripture.
3. Philipp Melanchthon, *Loci Communes* 9.5.12.

has done them before the question can be asked, and is always doing them. Whoever does not do such works is an unbeliever.... Thus it is impossible to separate works from faith, quite as impossible as to separate heat and light from fire.[4]

Yet like Luther, many readers still find James's comments on justification in James 2 to present a jarring challenge to Paul's doctrine of justification apart from works, especially as Paul expresses it in Romans 3–5 and Galatians 2–3. The problem can be seen most starkly by directly comparing Romans 3:28 with James 2:24:

Paul: For we hold that one is justified by faith apart from works of the law.
James: You see that a person is justified by works and not by faith alone.

The contrast appears so blatant that it is easy to conclude that Paul and James are simply at loggerheads. The problem is exacerbated when we see both Paul and James using the example of Abraham and specifically referring to Genesis 15:6 ("[Abraham] believed the LORD, and he counted it to him as righteousness") to prove their points, though in contrasting ways. Paul highlights the fact that Abraham was justified when he believed, before he had done anything; James points to Abraham's obedience (offering of Isaac) as that which fulfilled the verse in question.

This different use of the same verse in Genesis proves to be one of the keys to resolving the apparent contradiction. Further, a close examination of Paul's use of the terms "faith," "works," and "justified" in comparison with James 2 shows that they are using these words quite differently and are addressing very different problems. We will look more closely at this and other exegetical matters, but it may be helpful first to consider the question of James's relationship to Paul's letters.

The Literary Relationship between James and the Letters of Paul

The first question to resolve is, Was James even responding to Paul, or was he simply addressing the broad problem of hypocrisy? In general there are four approaches to understanding the interaction of Paul and James:[5]

1. James and Paul were reacting not to each other but rather to entirely different situations, and the verbal similarities of their letters are due to a shared Jewish background.
2. Paul was reacting critically to James (this, of course, assumes James was written prior to Galatians).
3. James was reacting critically to Paul (which assumes James had read Paul).
4. James was reacting to a garbled version of Paul's doctrine.

---

4. Luther, *Word and Sacrament I*, in LW 35:370–71.
5. Dale C. Allison Jr. articulates six discrete views on the relationship between the letter of James and the letters of Paul, but it appears to me that these can be collapsed into the four that follow here. Allison, "Jas 2:14–26: Polemic against Paul, Apology for James," in *Ancient Perspectives on Paul (1)*, ed. Tobias Niklas, Andreas Merkt, and Joseph Verheyden, NTOA/SUNT 102 (Göttingen: Vandenhoeck & Ruprecht, 2013), 123–25.

First, a few scholars argue that, despite the fact that James and Paul are using the same terms and examples, they are doing so quite independently, as well as differently.[6] The similarity of the cluster of terms ("justify," "faith," "works"), the common reference to Abraham, and the shared citation of Genesis 15:6 are not because one is attacking the other or even because one misunderstands the other. Rather, James and Paul share a Hellenistic Jewish environment, and those terms, examples, and Scripture texts arise from a common heritage. The differences in the meaning of the terms employed (especially "works" and "faith" but possibly also "justify") suggest a radical difference in the problems they are addressing. Further, James makes no mention at all of the precipitating issues in Galatians and Romans—namely, circumcision and separation of Jews from Gentiles—and he seems unaware of Paul's comments about the law "killing." Paul, on the other hand, though he does criticize "certain men from James" in Galatians (2:12 NASB), does not attack anything actually stated in the letter of James. It seems unlikely, then, that James actually read Paul's letters,[7] or vice versa. They are arguing not with each other but with entirely different opponents on behalf of different audiences. The language resemblance is superficial only.

There are other considerations that may support the independence view. While external attestation for James is weak until the late second century,[8] some internal evidence suggests the possibility of a very early date for James, perhaps even prior to Paul's letter to the Galatians.[9] The church situation seen in James is one where (Jewish) Christians are apparently still meeting together with non-Christian Jews in their synagogues (2:2–7), which suggests that James might have been written quite early. Further, James evinces a Christology that is very basic and therefore might reflect a church situation where the implications of Jesus's person and work have not yet been extensively worked out.

The main drawback to this view is that the justification and faith language of James 2 and Romans 3–4 and Galatians is *so* similar (as discussed in the third view below) that it is difficult to suppose that there is no relationship between them.[10] James is clearly attacking *someone's* position in James 2. If James's target was not Paul or a misconstrual of Paul, then that means someone *else* in the early church, prior to Paul, was speaking

---

6. Most notably, J. B. Lightfoot, *St. Paul's Epistle to the Galatians*, rev. ed. (London: Macmillan, 1890), 164, 370; Hubert Frankemölle, *Der Brief des Jakobus*, ÖTKNT 17, nos. 1–2 (Würzburg: Echter, 1994), 469, 473. Even if one does not adopt this view, we certainly ought to listen to what James says on his own terms rather than simply treat the letter as a reaction to Paul. Cf. Luke Timothy Johnson, *The Letter of James: A New Translation with Introduction and Commentary*, AB 37A (New York: Doubleday, 1995), 247.
7. Cf. Peter H. Davids, *The Epistle of James: A Commentary on the Greek Text*, NIGTC (Grand Rapids, MI: Eerdmans, 1982), 130–31. Davids does not consider the letters entirely independent but does note that James does not seem to have firsthand knowledge of Paul's letters.
8. It is not, however, entirely absent. The many parallels to the Mandates of the Shepherd of Hermas and a few in 1 Clement suggest that James was known to the author of the Shepherd (written probably in the first half of the second century) and probably to Clement (late first or early second century). Cf. McCartney, *James*, 20–26.
9. J. B. Mayor, who dates James in the AD 40s, dedicates the whole of chap. 7 of his introduction to the dating question. *The Epistle of St. James: The Greek Text with Introduction, Notes, and Comments*, 2nd ed. (New York: Macmillan, 1897); cf. esp. cxxi–cxxiii. Douglas J. Moo also argues for a very early date for James, before Paul clarified his teaching at the Jerusalem Council. *The Letter of James*, PNTC (Grand Rapids, MI: Eerdmans, 2000), 25–27. Cf. McCartney, *James*, 14–32.
10. Allison sets out the case sharply. He argues that there is no evidence in Judaism or elsewhere that anyone *except* Paul and those who follow him used language of "justification by faith apart from works." "Jas 2:14–26," 125–26. It seems incredible that James would attack a position no one was yet advocating, using the exact same terms, the same example (Abraham), and the same text (Gen. 15:6) that Paul himself used.

of some kind of "justification by faith without works." That seems very unlikely. Most scholars, therefore, have worked on the assumption there must be *some* connection between them.

Second, the view that Paul in Galatians was responding to the letter of James is also not commonly held,[11] but it, too, is not impossible. While the letter of James does not actually refer to Paul by name, in Galatians 2:12 Paul does refer to James (or rather "men from James," NASB), mentioned specifically as the precipitating cause of Peter's separating himself from table fellowship with Gentile Christians. Perhaps an early garbled rumor of Paul's teaching on justification had gotten back to James, who wrote to attack it, precipitating Paul's counterattack in Galatians. Things were then perhaps resolved at the Jerusalem Council in AD 49 (Acts 15), once Paul and James were able to speak directly.[12]

Assuming that the shared use of Genesis 15:6 and the language of justification indicate a dependency one way or the other, it is, according to this view, easier to read Paul as correcting James (or an abuse of him by "Judaizers") than to suppose that James is correcting Paul.[13] However, if Paul is in fact responding to the *letter* of James, it seems odd that he instead mentions only "men from James" and not James himself. Additionally, the social situation implied in James appears to be radically different from that evoked by Galatians, and thus Paul's attack on the "men from James" does not link up very well with the actual content of the letter of James. Further, this view, like the first, must suppose that someone earlier than Paul had argued for a justification by faith apart from works.

Third, that the letter of James was specifically written to contradict Paul's doctrine was, of course, implicitly Luther's view, and it has frequently been adopted by recent scholars, most notably Martin Hengel and Dale Allison.[14] On first reading, this might seem to be the apparently obvious interpretation, for the following reasons:

1. The use of "justification by faith apart from works" is unheard of prior to Paul,[15] and even in Paul not before the Galatians controversy, so Paul is the only known candidate for someone to whom James might be replying. Why would James attack a view no one had propounded?
2. Both James and Paul refer to Abraham as exemplars of (true) faith and justification.
3. Paul refers to Genesis 15:6 to support his view, and James also refers to it but argues that it must be understood in relation to its "fulfillment" in Abraham's

---

11. The best-known proponents of this view are probably Theodor Zahn, *Introduction to the New Testament* (Edinburgh: T&T Clark, 1909), 1:124–28, Mayor, *Epistle of St. James*, xci–xcviii; J. A. T. Robinson, *Redating the New Testament* (Philadelphia: Westminster, 1976), 126–28. However, all these see Paul as reacting not to the letter of James as such but to an abuse of James in a way radically dissonant with James's intent.
12. Moo, *James*, 25–27.
13. Mayor, *Epistle of St. James*, xcviii.
14. Allison, "Jas 2:14–26"; Martin Hengel, "Der Jakobusbrief als Antipaulinische Polemik," in *Tradition and Interpretation in the New Testament*, ed. Gerald F. Hawthorne and Otto Betz (Grand Rapids, MI: Eerdmans, 1987), 248–78. Cf. Gerd Lüdemann, *Opposition to Paul in Jewish Christianity*, trans. M. Eugene Boring (Minneapolis: Fortress, 1989), 144–49.
15. Allison, "Jas 2:14–26," 126–28.

obedience, as is seen in the Genesis 22 story of the offering of Isaac (often called the Aqedah, Hebrew for "binding"). Genesis 15:6 by itself does not directly support James's point, making it difficult to see why James would have referred to it except to correct what he saw as a misinterpretation of the verse.

4. We know from Galatians 2:12 that there was a controversy over justification between Paul and "men from James" (NASB), which may have continued beyond that time.[16]

On the other hand, as I hope to demonstrate below, a closer study of what Paul and James are actually saying makes it clear that the "faith without works" condemned as useless by James bears little resemblance to Paul's faith apart from works that yields justification. Paul's justifying faith is an obedient and active faith, not an idle one. If James had actually read Paul's letters directly, then he seriously misunderstood Paul. It is much more likely, if we assume James is reacting to Paul at all, that he is attacking a truncated perversion of Paul's theology.[17] And this brings us to the final view.

The fourth view is that the letter of James is attacking a misunderstanding or abuse of Paul's doctrine of justification by faith apart from works.[18] It is usually considered unlikely that the similarity of language, the mention of Abraham, and the reference to Genesis 15 are explainable apart from dependency. It is also deemed unlikely that James was written prior to Paul's teaching on justification. The conclusion is that James probably heard some version of Paul's doctrine and is reacting to it. But it is also clear that what James attacks is not at all what Paul is actually teaching; Paul does not advocate a faith that has no consequences in ethical life. So James is reacting not to Paul but to a misappropriation of Paul that turned "justification apart from works" into "justification without obedience."

Though most who hold this view date James later than Paul's major letters, the misunderstanding may have occurred very early, possibly before Paul's meeting with James at the Jerusalem Council of AD 49 (recorded in Acts 15), at a time when James may have heard only distorted rumors of Paul's teaching.[19] Certainly, distorted versions of Paul's doctrine had been around a long time. Paul himself encountered perversions of his teaching. In Romans 3:8, he asks, "And why not do evil that good may come?—as some people slanderously charge us with saying." This is not quite the same, since here Paul

---

16. Of course, this would mean that the book of Acts is artificially glossing over the friction between Paul and James. Those inclined to doubt the historical reliability of Acts may find this view attractive, but since Acts does not gloss over other early church frictions, it is unlikely that it would do so here. On the reliability of Acts, see Colin J. Hemer, *The Book of Acts in the Setting of Hellenistic History* (Winona Lake, IN: Eisenbrauns, 1990); Craig S. Keener, *Acts: An Exegetical Commentary* (Grand Rapids, MI: Baker Academic, 2012), 1:166–220.

17. Allison has argued that the literary parallels between James and several of Paul's letters (in particular Romans and 1 Corinthians) indicate a high probability that James had read Paul's letters and was therefore replying directly to Paul. "Jas 2:14–26," 135–40. However, if this is so, then James seems to have picked up on isolated phrases while entirely ignoring the content of the letters themselves.

18. E.g., R. V. G. Tasker, *The General Epistle of James: An Introduction and Commentary*, TNTC 16 (Grand Rapids, MI: Eerdmans, 1957), 28–32; Franz Mussner, *Der Jakobusbrief: Auslegung*, 2nd ed., HTKNT 13, no. 1 (Freiburg: Herder, 1967), 18–22; Timo Laato, "Justification according to James: A Comparison with Paul," trans. Mark A. Seifrid, *TJ*, n.s., 18, no. 1 (1997): 43–84.

19. Moo, *James*, 19.

indicates that some ill-minded people are alleging that *he* advocates lawlessness, not that *they* are advocating it. It is, however, clear that some people were already misreading Paul. Also, given the care Paul takes throughout Romans (and elsewhere) both to maintain the link between faith and obedience and to uphold the law, it seems he was aware that someone might take his teaching in an antinomian direction and therefore tried to forestall it. Unfortunately, the misunderstanding continued into the second century and beyond with Marcion and the gnostics.

No position is without difficulty, but scholars on every side of the issue are increasingly aware that James's attacks, even if they were intended as direct criticism of Paul, are not against what Paul actually teaches on justification. Let us look now at what James and Paul actually say about faith and works.

Faith according to James

With the exception of chapter 2, the book of James (like the rest of the New Testament) treats faith not as a bare acknowledgment of facts about God but as trust and fidelity (see 1:5–6; 5:15), specifically, fidelity to Jesus Christ as the Lord of glory (2:1).[20] Genuine faith, for James, stems from the implanted word (1:21), which is the word of truth (1:18; cf. Col. 1:5). This word of truth when planted (received) yields salvation. This stands in contrast to the deceitful temptation that when planted brings forth sin and death (James 1:14–15). For James as much as for Paul, the receiving of God's word (i.e., *believing* the gospel of Christ) is the means whereby people obtain life. Faith is therefore just as important to James as to Paul.[21]

Commensurately, the opposite of faith for James, namely, "doubt" (1:6–8), is a *lack* of fidelity and commitment. The person who doubts is double-minded (James may have actually coined the word δίψυχος, literally, "two-souled"). Just as in James real faith is not a mere intellectual acknowledgment of propositions but a full-bodied commitment rooted in covenantal relationship, so doubt is not a matter of thinking critically about the intellectual content of one's belief (as though self-examination were bad), nor is it the capacity to question. Doubt means "sitting on the fence," a reluctance to commit. The English word "waffling" would be a good equivalent. This is why the doubter is compared to a wave in the sea; there is no solidity to the doubter's convictions. The doubter just "goes with the flow," the result being that the one who doubts is inconstant and unreliable. Unlike the person of faith, the doubter cannot stand up to the pressures of testings or temptations, because he has no grounded commitment; his "faith" is superficial and transient.

This kind of doubt is what results in a pretense of faith (hypocrisy), for which the designation "two-souled" would also be appropriate. Although James does not use the word

---

20. The phrase in Greek is ἔχετε τὴν πίστιν τοῦ κυρίου. The construction ἔχετε τὴν πίστιν + the genitive occurs elsewhere in the New Testament only in Mark 11:22, where it cannot mean anything other than "to put faith in," "to trust in" (God). Cf. McCartney, *James*, 135–36.
21. In my commentary on James, I suggest that virtually the entirety of James is addressing the problem of behavior inconsistent with faith. James 1:3 may then be seen as setting forth the theme of the letter: how faith is tested. McCartney, *James*, 56–57, 66–67.

"hypocrite" (ὑποκριτής) or "hypocrisy" (ὑπόκρισις), the pretense of faith is certainly a major concern for him. It is all too easy to deceive oneself and be a hearer of the word only (1:22). If one is not a doer of the word, that shows that the word never actually took root.

The Practical Problem in James 2 (James 2:1–13)

Chapter 2 is where James focuses attention on the practical problem of a faith that is not genuine. *Claiming* to have faith yet showing favoritism to the rich and disrespecting the poor is a travesty of faith. This is quite in keeping with Paul (as well as the Old Testament). Partiality is contrary to God's character (2 Chron. 19:7; Acts 10:34; Rom. 2:11; Gal. 2:6; Eph. 6:9; Col. 3:25), and therefore, his people must also be impartial (Deut. 16:19; 1 Tim. 5:21). Those who do show partiality are wicked (Mal. 2:9; Jude 16). Favoritism is therefore a radical departure from faith.

That people were claiming to have faith in Christ (James 2:1) but were nevertheless showing favoritism is what leads James into attacking the notion of a faith that does not do deeds in accordance with faith (2:14–25).

"Faith" without Faith Deeds Is Not Faith (James 2:14–17)

Notice first that James does not say, "If someone has faith but does not have works...," but "If someone *says* he has faith but does not have works..." (James 2:14).[22] The claim to have faith is not the same as actually possessing faith. James is referring to the "faith" of the person who claims to believe in God but does not live accordingly. So when James asks, "Can *that* faith save him?" (2:14),[23] he is not rejecting the notion of "saving faith" (cf. 5:15) but only the notion that a faith without faith deeds can save.[24]

In 2:15–16, James points to the care of needy fellow believers (brothers or sisters) as a basic faith deed. The main point is to draw an analogy. Just saying "go in peace" to a desperate brother or sister without doing anything to meet his or her need is a meaningless blessing. It does neither the needy person nor the well-wisher any good. Likewise, faith that does no deed is meaningless faith. But the very nature of the analogy also points to a tragic manifestation of deedless "faith": the neglect of fellow believers in need. Such "faith" is worthless. A profession of faith that is not followed by works does not and cannot benefit from inactive faith. James is saying, "If your 'faith' doesn't benefit others, it won't benefit you either."[25]

---

22. C. E. B. Cranfield points out that only for the sake of argument is James conceding the use of the term "faith" to this pale imitation of it. An inactive faith is as much a contradiction in terms as a living corpse. "The Message of James," *SJT* 18, no. 2 (1965): 185.

23. The article before the second occurrence of "faith" is probably an article of previous reference. It cannot mean "Can *the* faith [i.e., Christianity] save him?" Nor is it likely to be an abstraction: "Can faith abstractly considered save him?" Hence, as the ESV reads, "Can that faith save him?"

24. The "saving" in view here, as in James 1:21 and 5:20, refers to the deliverance from eschatological judgment, as Martin Dibelius observes, and hence to deliverance from death and the reception of the "crown of life" (1:12) from God. Dibelius, *James: A Commentary on the Epistle to James*, rev. Heinrich Greeven, trans. Michael A. Williams, ed. Helmut Koester, Hermeneia (Philadelphia: Fortress, 1975), 152. Without "faith-ful" behavior, the claim to have faith will not result in deliverance from judgment, because it is an invalid claim.

25. There is an echo here of Jesus's words in Matt. 25:31–46, where Jesus's future verdict to the nations is based on their response to the nakedness, hunger, and imprisonment of Jesus's "little ones," that is, Jesus's followers.

So, too, *that* kind of faith (2:17),[26] the kind that is unaccompanied by appropriate deeds (a faith that is "by itself"), shows itself to be *dead*. Its inaction is a mute but powerful testimony to its deadness (dead bodies do nothing) and shows itself to be a false and worthless faith by the way it responds to the needy brother. Indeed, such a faith is worse than worthless; it is repulsive. James pulls no punches here: this faith devoid of deeds is not just sick or in danger of dying; it is νεκρά, dead, a corpse (an evaluation repeated in 2:26). Religious Jews, for whom contact with a dead body imparted ceremonial pollution, would have considered such an image especially repugnant.

Affirming Doctrine by Itself Is Not Faith (James 2:18–20)

In the short paragraph of James 2:18–20, James deals with two misconceptions about faith, or two dimensions of the fake faith that he is attacking. First, he assails the notion that somehow faith can be valid without works, that "works" and "faith" are two equally valid but differentiable ways of approaching God; second, he repudiates the notion that faith consists in only affirming certain doctrines.

The paragraph begins with a hypothetical dialogue between James and what he thinks his opponent might say. The overall point is that the indicator of genuine faith is works, so in contrast to the wisdom from above (3:17), a so-called faith that does not do the things faith does is a foolish "faith."

The passage is notoriously obscure. One would expect James to have said, "But someone will say, 'You have works and I have faith,'" instead of the other way around. Although it is an interesting exegetical conundrum, its resolution is not necessary to understand what James is intending to say in the passage as a whole. The best way to understand it is to take it as a general comment: "Some say they have faith, others say they have works, but actually faith and works must always go together."[27]

James 2:19 introduces another way of regarding this workless faith, as simply believing *that* certain doctrinal statements are true. James says that even demons believe *that* God is one. The most basic doctrine of Judaism was that there is only one God, given expression in the Shema of Deuteronomy 6:4. James remarks that demons know fully well that there is only one God, but so what? Believing *that* there is one God is good as far as it goes, but it is far from the kind of faith that has any value.

Hence (James 2:20), that kind of faith is ἀργή ("useless," "ineffective"),[28] and anyone who places confidence in such "faith" is downright foolish, an ἄνθρωπος κενός ("empty, vain, shallow person").

True Faith Is Completed by Works (James 2:21–26)

The verses in James 2:21–26 are often troubling for Protestants. Verse 21 asks the rhetorical question, "Was not Abraham our father justified by works?" (expecting a

---

26. As in James 2:14, the article in 2:17 is an article of previous reference.
27. For a discussion of proposed solutions, see McCartney, *James*, 157–60.
28. Possibly James is making a word play, since ἀργή is derived from α + ἔργα ("not working"). As Moo puts it, "A faith that doesn't work, doesn't work." *James*, 132.

positive answer), and verse 22 draws the practical conclusion from Abraham's justification: "You see that his faith and his actions were working together, and his faith was made complete by what he did" (NIV). His faith "cooperated," or "worked together" (συνήργει), with his works, and his faith was "completed" (ἐτελειώθη) by works, just as sin is completed by death in 1:15 (cf. Rom. 6:16). Later we address the question of what exactly James means by "justified." Here we simply note that James is not talking about how one obtains a relationship with God or how a sinner may hope to receive a verdict of "not guilty" in the final judgment but how faith will *necessarily* result in works. Thus, the "synergism" in view is far from the notion that humans cooperate with God in their salvation. James is rather speaking about a person's faith operating in synergy with his or her works as an unfolding of the righteous life.

A key to understanding James's understanding of the relationship of faith and works lies in his observation that Genesis 15:6 (God's declaration of Abraham's righteousness) was "fulfilled" in Abraham's obedience (James 2:23). The term "fulfill" literally means "to fill fully," but when applied to texts, it means "to complete," "to bring to its intended result." Thus, when an Old Testament passage is said in the New Testament to be fulfilled by some event, the point is not always that the Old Testament passage was *predicting* the event that fulfilled it (though that is certainly true in some cases, e.g., with the "it will come to pass . . ." prophecies). Rather, sometimes such language means that the event has brought to completion the ultimate purpose of that Old Testament passage. The use of the word "fulfilled" here underscores that for James, justification does not simply deliver from judgment but also results in the confirmation of right-ness, which is obedience to God. If obedience is never forthcoming, that indicates that the alleged "faith" is void. So the work (obedience) of Abraham brings to practical completion what God earlier had declared, that Abraham was righteous. In that sense Abraham was indeed "justified by his works." He was not justified by some kind of faith that was devoid of obedience. Whatever James means by "justify" (discussed below), this linking of obedience, righteousness, and fulfilling of Scripture is quite in harmony with Paul, who in Romans 8:2–4 says that believers "walk" (i.e., behave) according to the Spirit, thus "fulfill[ing]" the righteous requirement of the law.

Further, note the nature of Abraham's obedience: it was not a "good deed" considered abstractly but the action of faith, a faith deed. He believed God's promise in Genesis 15, but then he also believed it when he was put to the test in Genesis 22.[29] Hebrews 11 points out that Abraham effectively believed in resurrection, since he both accepted the promise of many descendants through Isaac and at the same time accepted the command to offer Isaac. His obedient response *completed* his faith; faith propelled Abraham to act.

---

29. The suggestion of R. B. Ward that both Abraham's and Rahab's "good deed" was hospitality is rather a stretch. "The Works of Abraham: James 2:14–26," *HTR* 61, no. 2 (1968): 283–90. While Rahab's sheltering of the spies might possibly be seen as hospitality, the only work that James mentions of Abraham is the offering of Isaac. Furthermore, it misses James's point, which certainly is not that "hospitality" is *the* ticket to justification but that genuine faith results in commensurate behavior. Abraham's and Rahab's actions of obedience were uniquely *faith* actions; they were deeds that an unbelieving person simply would never have done.

It is in this context that James states that Abraham was justified by works and not by faith alone.³⁰ Later we more closely examine the meaning of "justified," but here we note that Abraham's work (the Aqedah) was a *faith deed*, not a "work of the law" in Paul's sense.

The nature of a faith deed by which someone is justified is even more evident in James's second example, Rahab. James specifically identifies her as "Rahab the prostitute" (James 2:25), which should signal that it was not Rahab's previously righteous life that led to her justification. Rather, it was her *belief deed*. She was not obeying some command; she sheltered the Israelite scouts (James calls them ἄγγελοι—"messengers") because, as the text of Joshua says (Josh. 2:9–13), she *feared* God. She was convinced that God really would bless Israel and destroy Jericho, and she *acted* on that belief.

James closes his diatribe against false faith by again likening it to a corpse (James 2:26). Just as a body without breath is dead, so faith without works is dead. Luther took some umbrage at this analogy, because in his view it was faith, not works, that should be identified as the "spirit" that gives a body life.³¹ Good works do not make faith alive; rather, living faith produces good works. But James is asking a different question; he is interested not in the problem of how a Christian gets life but in the problem of how to distinguish true faith from pretense. Also, James's analogies should not be pressed to develop theological formulations; they serve simply as illustrations of particular points.³² James is asking, "What is the difference between real and fake faith?" His answer: works. The way to tell if a body is alive or not is by noticing whether there is breath. Likewise, the mark of living faith is works. As Jesus said, "You will recognize them by their fruits" (Matt. 7:16, 20).

We have looked with some detail at what James means by "faith," noting especially what kind of "faith" James regards as inadequate in James 2. Now let us briefly examine Paul's use of the term.

Faith according to Paul

Paul claims that faith in Christ is the sole vehicle of justification. What is the nature of faith for Paul? Does Paul regard justifying faith as simply believing something to be true?

We begin by noting that the Greek words for "faith" and "believe" virtually never mean *simply* an intellectual acquiescence to a proposition. A quick consultation of Greek lexicons and dictionaries easily proves the point.³³ The Greek words for "faith" and "believe" are much more closely related to trust, commitment, reliance, loyalty, and fidelity.³⁴ This contrasts starkly with our anemic modern idea of faith as thinking that a

---

30. It is worth observing that Paul never actually speaks of justification by faith *alone*. He does argue for justification by faith *apart from works* [of the law] but never suggests that faith can be somehow isolated from obedience.
31. Martin Luther, *Table Talk*, in *LW* 54:425.
32. This is true of many of James's vivid illustrations. Pressing James's analogies beyond their simple illustrative purpose can get a reader tied up in theological knots.
33. In addition to BDAG and LSJ, cf. the more extensive discussions in *TDNT* 6:174–228; *NIDNTT* 3:759–71.
34. In a recent book about faith and salvation, Matthew Bates argues that "allegiance" better captures the semantic content of the Greek word for "faith" and shows its difference from the modern notion of "faith" or "belief." *Salvation by Allegiance Alone: Rethinking Faith, Works, and the Gospel of Jesus the King* (Grand Rapids, MI: Baker Academic,

propositional statement is true. Sadly, the question, "Do you believe in God?" put to a typical Westerner is typically understood to mean, "Do you think there is a god," not, "Do you put your life in God's hands?" But that etiolated notion of belief is not Paul's, or that of any New Testament author.

The noun πίστις in the New Testament refers to a trust relationship, either to the *act* of trusting (putting faith in someone; e.g., 1 Pet. 1:21) or to the *attribute* of trustworthiness (faithfulness; e.g., Rom. 3:3, which speaks of God's πίστις). In both cases faith is personal and relational, not abstract. It is sometimes difficult to parse out whether trust (act) or fidelity (attribute) is to the fore because one implies the other. Trust entails commitment, and vice versa. The link to trust and commitment becomes even stronger when one considers the Hebrew covenantal background, but even in Greek literature the πίστις/πιστεύω word group has a connection to agreements and bonds.[35] In covenantal relationships, πίστις means being *faithful* to the terms of the covenant and thus also *trusting* the other party to fulfill the promises made therein.

Even when faith does have some focus on acceptance of a truth (as is more often the case with the verb πιστεύω than with the noun πίστις), this is more a function of accepting the *reliability* or trustworthiness of a statement or claim than an intellectual concurrence with a statement considered abstractly from personal connection. Hence, when Paul and the Gospels speak of believing the gospel, it means acknowledgment of its truth claims *and* a concomitant loyalty to the person of Jesus Christ, whose gospel it is.[36] Faith in Christ is thus a *life orientation*, a disposition of the heart toward faithfulness to him, a loyalty to his covenant that includes commitment to its ethical obligations.[37] Faith therefore entails *conversion*, or *turning* from a wrong orientation to a right one. Jesus himself, when he calls people to *believe* the gospel (e.g., Mark 1:15), insists that this believing is necessarily accompanied by repentance (a *turning* away from sin and turning to obedience) and that faith is exercised by discipleship (Mark 8:34 par.; John 10:26–27). The life of faith is a life of *following* Jesus, walking in his footsteps in accord with the life-pattern that he himself set forth and lived (1 Pet. 2:21).

Likewise for Paul, faith is something that yields obedience (Rom. 1:5; 16:26) and works (1 Thess. 1:3; 2 Thess. 1:11), especially love (Gal. 5:6). It is this robust kind of

---

2017). Bates's work may overaccentuate this difference (there *is* after all significant cognitive content to faith), but it does bring to the fore the distinction between Paul's robust notion of faith and the intellectualized kind of "faith" so current in many churches today. See the critique by Thomas Schreiner, "Saved by 'Allegiance' Alone? On a New Attempt to Revise the Reformation," The Gospel Coalition, March 3, 2017, https://www.thegospelcoalition.org/reviews/salvation-by-allegiance-alone/.

35. *NIDNTT* 3:760.

36. This is particularly true in the Gospel of John, where the construction πιστεύω εἰς ("believe into," "to place trust on") predominates. (By my count, πιστεύω εἰς occurs thirty-four times in the Gospel of John but only three or four times elsewhere in the New Testament.) The normal Greek construction is πιστεύω + the dative, which means accepting someone's testimony or evidence, equivalent to the English "I believe [you]" or "I trust [you] in this matter." Both expressions exhibit the aspect of personal trust, not abstract acceptance of a proposition, as in accord with a fact impersonally considered, though John's construction certainly accentuates the commitment.

37. Perhaps one of the best definitions of faith is provided by Anthony C. Thiselton: "Believing [is] a *disposition to respond* to situations both by expressing and by 'standing behind' belief-utterances in *situations that challenge belief*, or that demand *action appropriate to belief*. . . . Belief, then, is *action-oriented, situation-related* and embedded in the *particularities and contingencies* of everyday living." *Hermeneutics of Doctrine* (Grand Rapids, MI: Eerdmans, 2007), 21; italics original.

faith that Paul regards as the sole vehicle for one's justification before God. It is, in other words, the trust relationship, not thinking something is true, that is critical.

"Works of the Law" in Paul

In Romans and Galatians, Paul contrasts justification by faith with the futile search for justification by "works of the law." He also speaks of the law "killing" a person and aggravating sin (Rom. 7:7–13). However, Paul makes clear that the problem is not the law in itself, which is good, because it is God's law (7:12). The law becomes a problem when one thinks to gain life on the ground of one's obedience to it rather than in looking to God for mercy and trusting him.[38] The law also provides sin with a weapon to whisper rebellion in the heart (cf. 1 Cor. 15:56).

Thus, seeking one's righteousness by means of law observance is a futile venture for several reasons:

1. The law must be kept in its entirety (Gal. 5:3), and an infringement of one part is an infringement of the whole (a sentiment that James also articulates in James 2:10–11).
2. The law not only does not enable one to keep it but often does just the opposite by providing focus for one's proclivity to sin (Rom. 7:8–11).
3. The law provides occasion for those who think they are assiduously keeping it to wrongly regard themselves as superior to those who cannot do so (cf. Luke 18:9), or worse, to think they are achieving righteousness before God by doing so (Rom. 9:31–33; 10:3).

When attempted by those who claim to know Christ, law righteousness becomes an effective denial of the gospel (Galatians 2–3), a reversion to acting as though Christ had not died and risen. It effectively places oneself back into bondage instead of embracing the freedom that Christ has brought (4:1–9). This is the attitude Paul refers to as seeking justification by "works of the law."[39] He roundly condemns it because when people think to establish their own righteousness (Rom. 10:3; Phil. 3:9), it leads to "boasting." It can result in putting up fences, in partitioning the "godly law keepers" from the *hoi polloi* who know themselves to be sinners, or in separating the pious and ritually clean Jews from the "uncircumcised" Gentiles (Galatians 2), even though in Christ those walls have been torn down (Eph. 2:14).

---

38. Herman N. Ridderbos, *Paul: An Outline of His Theology*, trans. John Richard de Witt (Grand Rapids, MI: Eerdmans, 1975), 139.

39. Some recent works on Paul have argued that Paul's "works of the law" focus primarily on the "boundary markers" of the people of God, such as circumcision, food laws, and Sabbath observance, and that the "justification" in question is a matter of being in God's family. This is not the place to delve into this matter (see chaps. 4, 7, and 9 in this volume), but even if this be so, James breathes not a word about circumcision, food laws, Sabbath keeping, or any other "boundary marker," so the distinction between James's "works" and what Paul means by the term is even sharper. It is more likely, however, that with regard to the first point, Paul is not thinking *only* of cultic boundary markers but also of all "observing" the law without the substance of relational connection to God and a commensurate trust in him for that relationship, especially when such use of the law becomes a source of boasting (Rom. 4:2–4). And with regard to justification, it seems to me that the declaration of being in God's family cannot be sharply distinguished from his granting of a favorable verdict on a person. At the very least, adoption and justification are inseparable, as Romans 8 surely shows.

In short, no sinner is justified by works of the law. Rather, a sinner is justified through faith in Christ alone.

Works of Faith in Paul

On the other side, Paul as well as James advocates genuine works, that is, works of faith. Paul, like James, thinks good works must flow from faith. Paul never uses the word "faith" in the empty sense condemned by James. Paul's faith is one that works: "Neither circumcision nor uncircumcision counts for anything, but only faith *working* through love" (Gal. 5:6). For Paul as well as James, God's grace eventuates in good works, especially in concern for the poor:

> And God is able to make all grace abound to you, so that having all sufficiency in all things at all times, you may abound in every good work. As it is written,
>
> "He has distributed freely, he has given to the poor;
>   his righteousness endures forever." (2 Cor. 9:8–9)

When Paul addresses the broad issues of law and righteousness, he is completely in agreement with James: in Romans 2:13, it is not the hearers but the *doers* of the law who will be justified, a statement fully congruent with James 1:22–25. Even if Romans 2 should be regarded as purely hypothetical,[40] the underlying principle remains: professing to be a child of God without a commensurate life of obedience is of no value and will not result in justification.

Finally, we may note that Paul shares James's concern regarding a claimed faith that does not behave accordingly. First Corinthians 13:2 declares that someone who has faith without love, even if it be so strong as to move mountains, is "nothing." That is, his faith is empty. Titus 1:16 warns of people who "profess to know God" but "deny him by their *works*." And 2 Timothy 3:5 cautions against "having the appearance of godliness, but denying its power." This surely refers to people who claim to have some kind of faith in God but do not have the changed life that results from true faith. In Galatians and 1 Corinthians, Paul speaks of evil works that are so contrary to faith that those who do them have no share in the kingdom of God (1 Cor. 6:9–10; Gal. 5:21). It should not be too surprising, then, that prior to the specific controversy over "works of the law," Paul commends the Thessalonians for their *work*, specifically their "work of faith" (1 Thess. 1:3; cf. 2 Thess. 1:11). For Paul it is not *works* versus faith but *law works* versus *working faith*.

The Law in James and in Paul

But do not Paul and James disagree on the *nature* of the law? Does James not consider the law "liberating," whereas Paul sees it as enslaving? Once again, a careful look at

---

40. Since in Rom. 2:15 Paul refers to those who have the law written on the heart (echoing the new covenant language of Jeremiah 31), it is best taken as an actual statement about Christians, who, because they are in Christ, are actually doers of the law and will therefore be regarded as righteous, even if they are uncircumcised. Cf. Ridderbos, *Paul*, 178–81.

the whole of Paul's corpus shows that he and James are, on a deeper level, quite in agreement.

James refers to the law fairly often (9x) and always in a positive light. The law is perfect (James 1:25), a law of liberty (1:25, 2:12), and a "royal law" (2:8). It is a perfect law of liberty because it informs the reader of God's character and because obeying it yields blessing (1:25). Conversely, showing favoritism (2:9), backbiting (4:1–4), slandering (4:11–12), failing to pay employees on time (5:4–6)—such things are both contrary to the law and inconsonant with faith.

This wholly positive approach to the law may seem at first to be in contrast to Paul's teaching that the law enslaves and kills (Rom. 7:1–13). Of course, James has nothing corresponding to Paul's language of the law awakening sin or the law's impotence due to the "flesh."

However, Paul also not infrequently speaks of the law of God in a positive sense. Even in contexts where his concern with the "killing" or "enslaving" aspects is to the fore, he reminds readers that the law itself is good, holy, and righteous (7:12). If the law is seen not as a potential way to obtain a relationship with God but as a revelation of the goodness of God perceived by one who has faith in Christ, then the law is viewed positively. Hence, Paul claims that faith, far from overthrowing the law, rather upholds it (3:31). And when he exhorts his readers to live godly lives, he does so by quoting or alluding to the law (e.g., Ephesians 5–6; Colossians 3–4). Even when arguing against justification by works of the law (Romans 4; Galatians 3–4), he backs up his case by referring to and quoting from the law.

Furthermore, note that Paul's comments on the negative function of the law are found only in contexts dealing with self-righteousness, with the search for self-justification by law, or with drawing ethnic boundaries (the counterpart to the condemnation of economic partiality in James 2). In other places, references to the law are always straightforward applications of the law to life, to Christian character, and to godly obedience. He uses the Jeremiah language of new covenant (2 Corinthians 3)—which involves writing none other than the law, not on stony tablets but on the heart—to describe this new relation of the Christian to the law. Since it is in relation to Christ that the believer has this new and positive relation to the law, Paul can refer to it as the "law of Christ," or "Christ law" (1 Cor. 9:21). That new relation to the law "in Christ" liberates from the tyranny of the law considered apart from Christ.[41]

But freedom from the curse of the law and being no longer "under" law does not mean that obedience is no longer relevant. Quite the contrary, not being under law

---

41. There is debate over exactly what Paul means by "in the law of Christ" (ἔννομος Χριστοῦ). In the context of 1 Corinthians 9, Paul explains that, even though "to those outside the law [he] became as one outside the law" to win them, he nevertheless is not actually "outside the law of God but *within* [not under] the law of Christ [ἔννομος Χριστοῦ]" (9:21, my trans.). So being ἔννομος Χριστοῦ is a different way of being in God's law. This νόμος Χριστοῦ cannot be too remote from the "law of the Spirit of life," which likewise liberates from the law of sin and death (Rom. 8:2) and which also results in "the righteous requirement of the law" being "fulfilled in us, who walk not according to the flesh but according to the Spirit" (8:4). Note that the law remains the revelation of God's character. The law is "fulfilled" by "walk[ing]" (i.e., living, behaving) according to the Spirit and not according to the "flesh" (the sinful proclivity of fallen humanity). This is quite in harmony with James, who says that Abraham's obedience (his *walking* according to God's direction) "fulfilled" (brought to completion) his faith (James 2:20).

means freedom from sin, freedom to obey God truly, not freedom from obedience. Paul explains this idea in Romans 6:15–22:

> What then? Are we to sin because we are not under law but under grace? By no means! Do you not know that if you present yourselves to anyone as obedient slaves, you are slaves of the one whom you obey, either of sin, which leads to death, or of obedience, which leads to righteousness? But thanks be to God, that you who were once slaves of sin have become obedient from the heart to the standard of teaching to which you were committed, and, having been set free from sin, have become slaves of righteousness. I am speaking in human terms, because of your natural limitations. For just as you once presented your members as slaves to impurity and to lawlessness leading to more lawlessness, so now present your members as slaves to righteousness leading to sanctification.
>
> For when you were slaves of sin, you were free in regard to righteousness. But what fruit were you getting at that time from the things of which you are now ashamed? For the end of those things is death. But now that you have been set free from sin and have become slaves of God, the fruit you get leads to sanctification and its end, eternal life.

Note Paul's emphasis on *results* and *fruit*. Being slaves to sin leads to more and more *law*lessness (ἀνομία), and its fruit is shame and death (very similar to James 1:15). Being slaves to righteousness, on the other hand, leads to sanctification, and the end of sanctification is eternal life. Paul was horrified that anyone would understand his teaching as promoting lawlessness (Rom. 3:8). Freedom is not freedom to ignore God's law but freedom to serve God, freedom to manifest his character and righteousness in life. And since a person's slavery is to the one he or she obeys, if one yields oneself to committing sin, he or she is a slave of sin, and that person's end is death. In other words, any presumed "faith" that does not do righteousness will eventuate only in death.

James's concern with the law is likewise always related to the character issue: he is never interested in the cultic aspects such as circumcision, food laws, or ritual cleanness. Rather, he focuses on matters such as how the one who shows favoritism is convicted by the law or how speaking evil of a brother is the opposite of submitting to the law (James 4:11), points with which Paul concurs (2 Cor. 6:8; 12:20; Eph. 4:31; Col. 3:8).

Another commonality between James and Paul with regard to the law is visible in James's reference to the "royal" law (James 2:8). This could be just an acknowledgment of the kingship of the one whose law it is (God), but since James then cites Leviticus 19:18, it is more likely that the term "royal" draws on the fact that the love command was the one held central by Jesus, the King (Matt. 5:43; 22:39; par.). Paul also cites Leviticus 19:18 in both Romans (13:9–10) and in Galatians (5:14), both times in a positive sense, showing that obeying this law of love is a sign of a believer's life of faith and that doing so even "fulfill[s] the law" (Rom. 13:10)! James's "royal law" is what Paul commends as the "law of Christ" (Gal. 6:2).

We noted already that faith for Paul also must be "*working* through love" (Gal. 5:6). This is very interesting because "faith working through love" (which matters) is set over against "circumcision or uncircumcision" (which does not matter), a construction repeated in Galatians 6:15–16, where what matters is "new creation," that is, the eschatological reality in which believers in Christ participate and by which they are transformed. And again in 1 Corinthians 7:19, what matters is not circumcision or uncircumcision but "*keeping the commandments of God.*" Paul as much as James acknowledges that life *in Christ* is one of joyful obedience, not a dismissal of God's law.

Again, when one closely examines the quite different problems that James and Paul were facing with regard to the law, we find Paul in agreement with James in seeing the law, considered in Christ, a boon and help, a liberating revelation of what God sees as good.[42] It is true that Paul speaks of "law works" in a negative way, as things done *apart from* faith in Christ, while James would no doubt think of "law works" positively, as works done *because of* faith in Christ, but as we have seen, it is the particular problems Paul was confronting that gave rise to the phrase "works of the law" being contrary to faith.

The Meaning of the Word "Justify"

We have seen that what James ridicules as a worthless faith is not at all the kind of faith Paul sees as the sole route to justification. Likewise, the works James considers indispensible for justification are unrelated to the "works of the law" that Paul warns against as not only inadequate but effectively a denial of the gospel.

However, even if "works" be regarded as genuine faith works, the fact that James advocates *justification* by works (James 2:21) is still jarring. This discomfort is generated by reading James as though he were using terms in the same way as Paul. Just as James (in James 2) and Paul (in Romans and Galatians) use the words "faith" and "works" differently, so there is some distinction between the kind of "justification" James has in view vis-à-vis Paul.

Of the five possible meanings of the word δικαιόω ("justify") in biblical literature, only two are possible here in James 2:[43]

1. To *declare* someone righteous (generally) or in the right (on a specific issue); to *render a verdict* of "innocent"; to *acquit* (thus the opposite of condemn; see, e.g., Matt. 12:37; Rom. 8:33–34). This *forensic* meaning is the most common biblical usage, both in the Greek Old Testament and in the New Testament. In Scripture it often refers to the verdict given to "the righteous" on judgment day. It can also

---

42. For more on Paul's positive use of the law, see Ridderbos, *Paul*, 278–88.
43. For a complete discussion, see McCartney, *James*, 162–68. The other meanings of δικαιόω—"provide justice for," "clear a debt," and the very rare meaning "make righteous" (found only once in biblical literature [Ps. 72:13 LXX // 73:13 Eng.])—are not relevant here.

be more general, referring simply to acceptance or approval (especially by God, as, for example, in Luke 18:14—the tax collector, as opposed to the Pharisee, obtains God's approval[44]).

2. The second general meaning of justification is to *prove* or manifest that someone is righteous or in the right. For example, when Jesus says, "Wisdom is justified by her deeds" (Matt. 11:19), it means that wisdom is *shown to be right* by the deeds that proceed from her (cf. Jer. 3:11 LXX; Rom. 3:4; 1 Tim. 3:16).[45] This is clearly the meaning when it is God who is justified (e.g., Ps. 50:6 LXX [= 51:6 MT; 51:4 Eng.]). Proving or showing someone to be righteous or in the right is not unrelated to the forensic meaning, of course, because giving a verdict of "righteous" in court, or even simply vindication in a general sense, entails the demonstration or proof of a party being righteous (or in the right).

Justification in Paul

Paul's use of the word clearly falls into the forensic category (meaning 1). His interest in Romans is in how a person may have a legal standing of "righteous" before the eschatological tribunal of God.[46] He is particularly concerned with how God can rightly give a verdict of "righteous" for a sinner (3:26; 4:5). The answer Paul develops in Romans 4–5 is that the one who trusts in Christ is united to him by faith, and as a result, God's eschatological verdict of "righteous," which for Jesus was declared by his resurrection (4:25), is reckoned also to that believer, both at the final judgment and in the present life of the believer.[47] Thus can one who is a sinner, under sentence of eternal death, have instead the positive verdict God gave to Jesus reckoned or imputed to his or her account.[48]

This cannot happen through the futile efforts of an individual apart from Christ's obedience ("works of the law"); it can happen only through covenantal connection to Christ. And that connection is a personal faith connection, not one acquired by the performance of certain duties. Justification is thus by faith alone, not by "works of the law."

---

44. The perfect passive participle in the parable cannot refer to the future judgment day. It means the tax collector was in a condition of having been accepted or approved by God.
45. This meaning could be further subdivided into "proving righteous" and "proving to be in the right" (i.e., correct or wise), the former being moral and the latter epistemic, but the key distinctive of this meaning is "proof" or "demonstration," and a biblical line between moral righteousness and wisdom is difficult to draw.
46. According to the New Perspective on Paul, justification concerns how one may be included in the covenant people. Certainly, inclusion in the covenant people is an aspect of justification, and that may even have been the precipitating issue in Galatians, but the word itself and its use in Romans suggest that broader issues are at stake for Paul, namely, one's standing before God and the impending eschatological verdict.
47. For an exposition of Paul's theme of justification and other benefits of Christ's resurrection being reckoned to those united to him by faith, see Richard B. Gaffin, *The Centrality of the Resurrection: A Study in Pauline Soteriology* (Grand Rapids, MI: Baker, 1978; reissued as *Resurrection and Redemption: A Study in Paul's Soteriology* [Phillipsburg, NJ: Presbyterian and Reformed, 1987]), esp. 119–24. Cf. also Ridderbos, *Paul*, 166–69.
48. Paul links faith in Christ to a reckoning (i.e., imputation) of righteousness on believers, which is not inherent in them but is acceded to them by virtue of their covenantal union with Christ (Gal. 2:17; etc.). Though the language of imputation has recently been questioned in some quarters, it should surely be clear that for Paul the possibility of sinners being reckoned righteous is predicated on what Christ has done, not on what they on their own have done (Rom. 3:22–25; 4:5; etc.). This is because Paul is dealing with the issue of how any person, Jew or Gentile, may hope for a favorable verdict from a holy God who will by no means clear the guilty. But this issue is not the issue James is dealing with, and James ought not to be read with these questions in mind.

Hence, justification in Paul's sense can be regarded as both the securing of a favorable final verdict through Christ's death and resurrection and *also* God's acceptance and approval in effect at the beginning and during the Christian life, for it is an already-experienced union with Christ by faith that both initiates and maintains the relationship.[49]

Justification in James

Many scholars since John Calvin have seen the word "justified" in James 2 as meaning "demonstrated," "manifested," or "proved" (meaning 2). This is clearly different from the forensic justification Paul says is by faith and not works. Calvin argues,

> We must take notice of the two-fold meaning of the word *justified*. Paul means by it the gratuitous imputation of righteousness before the tribunal of God; and James, the manifestation of righteousness by the conduct, and that before men, as we may gather from the preceding words, "Shew to me thy faith," &c. In this sense we fully allow that man is justified by works, as when anyone says that a man is enriched by the purchase of a large and valuable estate, because his riches, before hid, shut up in a chest, were thus made known.[50]

So Abraham's obedience recounted in Genesis 22 *demonstrated* his righteousness. It thus brought to fruition God's earlier declaration of Abraham's righteousness. Since Genesis 15 recounts an event several years before the offering of Isaac, the offering of Isaac could not be the *basis* for his righteousness. Rather, it was (as is indicated by James's use of the word "fulfill") the necessary and proper outworking and manifestation of Abraham's righteousness. So Abraham's faith and his works together resulted in a genuinely righteous life. But it is the *works*, especially the obedience in offering Isaac, not a bare claim to faith, that "justified" Abraham—that is, *showed* him to be righteous. In Calvin's words, "Man is not justified by faith alone, that is, by a bare and empty knowledge of God; he is justified by works, that is, his righteousness is known and proved by its fruits."[51]

Similarly, in the case of Rahab, her sheltering of the spies was *probative evidence* that she really believed that the God of Israel would enable Israel to conquer her Canaanite city (Josh. 2:1–11). She was "justified" by her outward act of giving succor to the

---

49. An ongoing debate as to whether (and to what extent) Paul's forensic meaning of justification relates specifically to judgment-day justification or more generally to God's acceptance and approval already experienced is difficult, and we need not solve it here. If Paul regards present justification and future justification as aspects of the same thing, so that his primary meaning is the eschatological justification applied to the believer in advance, that application is by virtue of the believer's union with Christ and is experienced already by the believer as God's acceptance and liberation from sin. Justification, therefore, can be regarded as one being (already) in right standing with God. Conversely, if Paul is *differentiating* the believer's experience of justification from final justification, it is nevertheless not an entirely separate justification, because both the status of being justified and the present experience of justification are ultimately founded on the future eternal vindication, already given by Christ's resurrection. In both cases, Paul's interest is in how a sinner may rightly expect to receive God's positive verdict or approval, both now and in the future.

50. John Calvin, *Commentaries on the Catholic Epistles*, trans. and ed. John Owen (1855; repr., Grand Rapids, MI: Baker, 1979), 315.

51. Calvin, *Catholic Epistles*, 316.

people of God and later by doing as she had been instructed (6:21–25), because those acts evidenced her righteousness.

Nevertheless, many scholars still see justification in the forensic sense (meaning 1) operative here in James. They point not only to the predominance of the forensic meaning ("acquit," "declare righteous," or "accept as righteous") in the biblical literature generally but also to the fact that James begins this diatribe in James 2:14 with the question, "Can that [workless] faith *save* him?" The "saving" in question is deliverance from eschatological judgment (1:21, 5:20) and reception of the "crown of life" (1:12). Hence, it could be that James has in mind the future judgment verdict of "righteous," given for Abraham and Rahab.[52] This view faces some difficulty in that James uses an aorist passive (ἐδικαιώθη) in 2:21 and 2:25 rather than the future tense.[53] More likely, "justified" refers to God's approval of Abraham, stated in Genesis 15:6 and reaffirmed in his being called "friend of God" (James 2:23), and of Rahab, evidenced by her being rescued from Jericho's fate.

If one adopts this forensic understanding of "justify" in James, whether future or general, it still differs from Paul's specific use, however, in that James's interest is not in the question of how one obtains or maintains covenantal relationship with God,[54] how God can righteously pronounce a verdict of "righteous" to sinners, or how "right standing" with God is possible for sinners and Gentiles. James's question is simply, *What marks the life God approves?* The term "justified" in James's sense is applicable to those who have that kind of life, who do not just claim to have faith but act like it.

Thus, whichever of the two meanings of "justification" James had in mind, "to declare righteous" or "to prove righteous," he is not contradicting Paul, because he is addressing an entirely different problem.

Conclusion

Though James's teaching on faith and works appears at first glance to be a direct contradiction to Paul's statement in Romans 3:28 ("One is justified by faith apart from works of the law"), the different contexts of their statements and the difference in meaning of the terms "faith" and "works," along with the different focus of the word "justify," mean that the contradiction is only on the surface. Alfred E. Garvie put it trenchantly over a century ago: "The faith Paul commends is not the same as the faith James condemns, and the works James commends have no likeness to the works Paul condemns."[55]

The upshot of all this is that even though we are justified (in Paul's sense) not by our obedience but by faith through our union with Christ, there is no justification of any

---

52. Moo, *James*, 135, 141.
53. Just a couple of verses later (James 3:1), where James makes an unambiguous reference to future judgment, he uses the expected future tense (λημψόμεθα).
54. If there is any hint in James of how one's relationship to God is initiated and maintained, it would seem to lie in receiving "the implanted word, which is able to save your souls" (James 1:21).
55. Alfred E. Garvie, *Romans*, New Century Bible (New York: Frowde, 1901), 24.

kind without a resultant obedience, because no obedience means no faith. We ought never to suppose that the life of faith is easy. Jesus tells his disciples that they must "strive" to enter by the narrow gate (Luke 13:24; cf. Heb. 4:14). When he said that, he did not *really* mean "don't strive." Whether James was reacting to a misinterpretation of Paul or simply to hypocrisy generally, it should be clear that for him the Christian life has no place for complacency.[56] People of faith do "faith-ful" things. Those who claim to be "justified by faith" but are not living faith-fully have only a false hope. They have deceived themselves (James 1:22). Good works, the fruit of faith, are not optional.

As Calvin wrote, "We, indeed, allow that *good works are required for righteousness*; we only take away from them the power of conferring righteousness, because they cannot stand before the tribunal of God."[57] Calvin's point, like that of James, is that *without the believer's good works, there is no justification*. In a day when people often confuse justification by faith with justification by *profession* of faith, we do well to hear James's concern.

Recommended Resources

Allison, Dale C., Jr. "Jas 2:14–26: Polemic against Paul, Apology for James." In *Ancient Perspectives on Paul (1)*, edited by Tobias Niklas, Andreas Merkt, and Joseph Verheyden, 123–49. NTOA/SUNT 102. Göttingen: Vandenhoeck & Ruprecht, 2013.

Bates, Matthew. *Salvation by Allegiance Alone: Rethinking Faith, Works, and the Gospel of Jesus the King*. Grand Rapids, MI: Baker Academic, 2017.

Bauckham, Richard. *James: Wisdom of James, Disciple of Jesus the Sage*. New Testament Readings. London: Routledge, 1999.

Calvin, John. *Commentaries on the Catholic Epistles*. Translated and edited by John Owen. 1855. Reprint, Grand Rapids, MI: Baker, 1979.

Cranfield, C. E. B. "The Message of James." *Scottish Journal of Theology* 18, nos. 2–3 (1965): 182–93, 338–45.

Fung, Ronald Y. K. "Justification in the Epistle of James." In *Right with God: Justification in the Bible and the World*, edited by D. A. Carson, 146–62. Carlisle, UK: Paternoster, 1992.

Hengel, Martin. "Der Jakobusbrief als Antipaulinische Polemik." In *Tradition and Interpretation in the New Testament*, edited by Gerald F. Hawthorne and Otto Betz, 248–78. Grand Rapids, MI: Eerdmans, 1987.

Jeremias, Joachim. "Paul and James." *Expository Times* 66, no. 12 (1955): 368–71.

Laato, Timo. "Justification according to James: A Comparison with Paul." Translated by Mark A. Seifrid. *Trinity Journal*, n.s., 18, no. 1 (1997): 43–84.

---

56. It is therefore regrettable that our modern notion of faith has lost the component of fear. To truly believe in God entails fearing him (as both Testaments repeatedly aver), not because one cannot have assurance that God is our loving Father but because that loving Father is also a completely holy God in whose presence nothing evil can stand. It is part of what keeps believers faith-ful.

57. Calvin, *Catholic Epistles*, 317; italics added. The translation by A. W. Morrison in the Torrance edition misleadingly renders the italicized phrase "good works are required *of* righteousness," which is also a true statement but cannot properly translate Calvin's Latin: "Fatemur quidem requiri *ad* iustitiam bona opera." *Calvin's New Testament Commentaries*, vol. 3, *Matthew, Mark and Luke and the Epistles of James and Jude*, ed. David W. Torrance and Thomas F. Torrance (Grand Rapids, MI: Eerdmans, 1960).

Mayor, J. B. *The Epistle of St. James: The Greek Text with Introduction, Notes, and Comments*. 2nd ed. New York: Macmillan, 1897.

McCartney, Dan G. *James*. Baker Exegetical Commentary on the New Testament. Grand Rapids, MI: Baker Academic, 2009.

Ridderbos, Herman N. *Paul: An Outline of His Theology*. Translated by John Richard de Witt. Grand Rapids, MI: Eerdmans, 1975.

Stein, Robert H. "'Saved by Faith [Alone]' in Paul versus 'Not Saved by Faith Alone' in James." *Southern Baptist Journal of Theology* 4, no. 3 (2000): 4–19.

9

The New Quest for Paul

A Critique of the New Perspective on Paul

TIMO LAATO

In New Testament scholarship, Pauline research continues to triumph.[1] The debate about the New Perspective on Paul broadens and gains depth, yet it also becomes more difficult and complicated with time. Interpretations diverge strongly. For the moment, they mostly exhibit diversity.[2]

The present debate was launched in 1977 with the publishing of E. P. Sanders's broad work *Paul and Palestinian Judaism*.[3] Since then, we have been overwhelmed with thousands of articles and essays, studies and investigations, volumes, monographs, and dissertations. Among the large number of scholars, two especially stand out: James D. G. Dunn and N. T. Wright.[4] They stand—so to speak—"a head taller than any of the others" (1 Sam. 9:2).[5] Additionally, in recent times J. M. G. Barclay has made his mark on the state of research and distinguished himself from his equals. He has presented fresh insights into some stagnating problems and imparted a very welcome disturbance in the current debate.[6]

---

1. This essay is dedicated to Professor Mark A. Seifrid on his sixty-fifth birthday, in appreciation of his scholarship and friendship.
2. The New Perspective advocates are a large number of scholars who do not often find any consensus in their interpretations. Still, they do have something in common; otherwise, it would not make sense to speak of a fresh wave of research. Writing an overall research history seems next to impossible. In a brief article it is necessary to limit not only one's subject but also the number of scholars to include in one's notes. Who could demand more? No need to settle for less. On the research history, see Stephen Westerholm, "The 'New Perspective' at Twenty-Five," in *Justification and Variegated Nomism*, vol. 2, *The Paradoxes of Paul*, ed. D. A. Carson, Peter T. O'Brien, and Mark A. Seifrid, WUNT, 2nd ser., vol. 181 (Grand Rapids, MI: Baker Academic, 2004), 1–38.
3. E. P. Sanders, *Paul and Palestinian Judaism: A Comparison of Patterns of Religion* (Philadelphia: Fortress, 1977).
4. Cf. Douglas J. Moo: "Israel and the Law in Romans 5–11: Interaction with the New Perspective," in Carson, O'Brien, and Seifrid, *Justification and Variegated Nomism*, 2:185: "These two scholars [J. Dunn and N. T. Wright] are the best representatives of the 'new perspective.' [. . .] They will serve therefore as my major 'sparring partners.'"
5. Unless otherwise noted, Scripture quotations in this chapter are my own translations (often in reliance on the NIV).
6. See his major work: John M. G. Barclay, *Paul and the Gift* (Grand Rapids, MI: Eerdmans, 2015).

My task is to critically analyze the turning point in Pauline research that took place through Sanders and was later developed by Dunn and Wright. Last, but not least, the recent progress, initiated by Barclay, deserves attention. It goes without saying that not every detail in their overall views can be scrutinized. One must be selective, while at the same time recognizing that all involved, the present author included, attempt to contribute through their own unique work. Therefore, certain crucial themes are picked up and reflected on in more depth. Clearly, they are distinct from case to case: Those prominent scholars have their marked centers of gravity. To be sure, I hope that my selective use of their writings adequately embodies what they really want to say. The discussion, if needed, has to be continued on a wider scale in the future. Self-evidently, the view of Sanders is first in line, then those of Dunn, Wright, and Barclay.

E. P. Sanders

Covenantal Nomism in Judaism

Interestingly, the New Perspective on Paul basically arises from the new perspective on Judaism. If the old perspective on Judaism as a religion of gaining merits and earning salvation is no longer valid, it is no more possible to stand up for the old perspective on Paul as preaching against the legalistic understanding of God's grace. As a result, we have to reconsider the reasons for his break with his former beliefs.

Sanders dubbed the common Jewish "pattern of religion" *covenantal nomism*. He helpfully summarizes the position as follows:

> God has (1) chosen Israel and (2) given the law, which implies both (3) God's promise to maintain the covenant and (4) the requirement of obedience. (5) God rewards obedience and punishes disobedience. (6) The law ordains means of expiation and (7) the expiation restores the broken covenant. (8) All who through obedience, expiation and God's grace remain in the covenant will be saved.[7]

In other words, one gets in the covenant through acceptance of the law and remains in it through fulfillment of the law. Both the election (point 1) and the salvation of Israel (point 8) depend on God's grace, not on human merit. Succinctly, obedience as such earns neither election nor salvation. It effects the remaining within the covenant.[8]

Over the years, the sketch of covenantal nomism as the common denominator of the Jewish religion has caused much debate. It has been defended; it has been rejected; it has been modified; it has been amplified.[9] Still, Sanders has absolutely shown that Judaism should not be identified with a religion of complete self-salvation ("eine Religion

---

7. Sanders, *Paul and Palestinian Judaism*, 422. Surprisingly, the depiction of covenantal nomism includes no answer to the question of how one gets into the covenant. See Timo Laato, *Paulus und das Judentum: Anthropologische Erwägungen* (Åbo: Åbo Academy Press, 1991), 73–74. Also available in English: Timo Laato, *Paul and Judaism: An Anthropological Approach*, trans. T. McElwain, SFSHJ 115 (Atlanta: Scholars Press, 1995), 58–59.
8. Sanders, *Paul and Palestinian Judaism*, 419–22.
9. Cf., e.g., the discussion in James D. G. Dunn, "The New Perspective: Whence, What, Whither?," in *The New Perspective on Paul: Collected Essays* (Tübingen: Mohr Siebeck, 2005), 55–63. See previously Laato, *Paulus und das Judentum*, 38–82; Laato, *Paul and Judaism*, 31–66.

völliger Selbsterlösung").¹⁰ He rightly affirms God's grace as the basis of fulfilling the law. In other words, covenant is the origin of nomism. Therefore, the concept of covenantal nomism as an interrelationship between gracious election and required obedience clarifies the main lines well enough.¹¹

To say this, however, is not to say that the concept of covenantal nomism achieves precision and clarity. It leaves, indeed, a great deal to be desired.

First, Sanders never explains in the most fundamental way why Jewish *texts* frequently fall short of such constitutive elements as covenant and election. He asserts, for example, that "rabbinic discussions are often at the third remove from central questions of religious importance."¹² However, he immediately rushes forward paying no attention whatsoever to his observation. Further, how does Sanders know that the rabbinic discussions about different halakic matters are merely "at the third remove from central questions"? If they are unimportant for him and his academic research, they still may be crucial for the original authors who wrote about them. No one would produce thousands of large sheets (e.g., Mishnah and Talmud) if he did not greatly appreciate his literary work.¹³

Second, the concept of covenantal nomism implies the question of human action and capacity in salvation. Sanders, however, mostly ignores anthropological emphases or premises. Only in passing does he acknowledge that the Jews should obey the law in their own strength.¹⁴ In this respect his line of reasoning needs to be completed. As Sanders specifically investigates how a religion functions, the definition of his task begs the question of what an adherent of that religion can and cannot do on behalf of his or her salvation. Where does one receive the power to move step-by-step to the final goal?¹⁵ Even though the notion of God's grace permeates covenantal nomism, the whole process of redemption from beginning to end is not necessarily by God's grace alone.¹⁶

I have pointed out elsewhere that the idea of human free will amounts to *opinio communis* in Judaism. (One exception confirms the rule: the Qumran community seems to represent an absolute fatalism.¹⁷) Consequently, in covenantal nomism the Jews are

---

10. Contra Paul Billerbeck in Hermann L. Strack und Paul Billerbeck, *Exkurse zu einzelnen Stellen des Neuen Testaments: Abhandlungen zur neutestamentlichen Theologie und Archäologie*, KNTTM 4 (München: C. H. Beck, 1928), 6. See Laato, *Paulus und das Judentum*, 11–12, 32–37; Laato, *Paul and Judaism*, 9–10, 26–30.

11. Dunn, "New Perspective," 62. Evidently, his conclusion reiterates the outcome of the fiery academic debate between Sanders and Jacob Neusner already in the 1980s. The latter asserts what the former, based on his (confusing) definition of the task, should have compared. On the other hand, the former affirms what he in fact did compare. Still, they both concede the existence of covenantal nomism in the rabbinical texts. For the whole discussion, see Laato, *Paulus und das Judentum*, 67–72; Laato, *Paul and Judaism*, 54–58.

12. Sanders, *Paul and Palestinian Judaism*, 71.

13. Laato, *Paulus und das Judentum*, 71–72; Laato, *Paul and Judaism*, 56–58. Sanders admits that he has not sufficiently taken into account the special features of the various forms of Judaism. Rather, he has focused on one common thread (i.e., covenantal nomism) running through his main sources. See Laato, *Paulus und das Judentum*, 68–69; Laato, *Paul and Judaism*, 54–55.

14. Sanders, *Paul and Palestinian Judaism*, 114–15, 261–70.

15. Laato, *Paulus und das Judentum*, 58–63; Laato, *Paul and Judaism*, 47–50.

16. Laato, *Paulus und das Judentum*, 73–78; Laato, *Paul and Judaism*, 58–62; these sections also include a similar discussion of Pauline soteriology.

17. Laato, *Paulus und das Judentum*, 83–94; Laato, *Paul and Judaism*, 67–75. Later, Stephen Westerholm, "Paul's Anthropological 'Pessimism' in Its Jewish Context," in *Divine and Human Agency in Paul and His Cultural Environment*, ed. John M. G. Barclay and Simon J. Gathercole, LNTS 335 (London: T&T Clark, 2008), 71–98.

supposed to contribute to their attaining of eternal life by doing their very best. They can and should do their best in their own strength but not to the exclusion of divine grace altogether. The issue at stake is cooperation. Covenantal nomism is a synergistic soteriology.[18]

Third, as Sanders delineates the main lines in covenantal nomism, he frequently causes confusion by using the word *salvation* in a narrow sense. It denotes either (1) the salvation-historical action of God (the establishing of the covenant at Sinai) or (2) the present state of salvation (belonging to the covenant) but not (3) the final salvation (eternal life). Thus, it remains unclear who in the end will be saved. The Jews must, after salvation is gained, carry on and exert themselves to achieve the future salvation, or else they might forfeit it. In other words, all's well that ends well (but not before the end arrives).[19]

From that point of view, fulfilling the Mosaic law is the *conditio sine qua non* for final salvation in covenantal nomism. The Jews have to be obedient and carry out their good deeds in order to ensure their entrance into the world to come. Their contributions through human free will make the difference. Covenantal nomism is not a "pure" religion of grace without synergistic tendencies.[20]

Barclay has summed up the shortcomings in Sanders's overall portrayal of Judaism cogently:

> Sanders's analysis of the structure and content of Judaism emphasized primarily the *priority* of grace, the divine initiative that founded the people of Israel and contextualizes their observance of the Torah. He succeeded in demonstrating that, understood in these terms, grace is everywhere in Second Temple Judaism.[21]

Later he states,

> Sanders leaves unclear to what extent Jewish texts from this period do, or do not, *also* perfect the incongruity of grace. . . . Finding grace everywhere, he gave the impression that grace is everywhere the same, and that one perfection (priority) necessarily entails another (incongruity).[22]

Therefore, a comprehensive anthropological analysis bears heavily on the new perspective on Judaism. A reading along those lines has come to stay (without the prospect of any backtracking). By now, it has largely been acknowledged as an indispensable outcome and a turning point in the present state of research.[23]

---

18. Laato, *Paulus und das Judentum*, 185–211; Laato, *Paul and Judaism*, 147–68.
19. Laato, *Paulus und das Judentum*, 196–98; Laato, *Paul and Judaism*, 156–57.
20. Laato, *Paulus und das Judentum*, 195–99; Laato, *Paul and Judaism*, 155–58.
21. Barclay, *Paul and the Gift*, 152; italics original.
22. Barclay, *Paul and the Gift*, 158; italics original; see also 191–92.
23. Stephen Westerholm, "Finnish Contributions to the Debate on Paul and the Law," in *The Nordic Paul: Finnish Approaches to Pauline Theology*, ed. Lars Aejmelaeus and Antti Mustakallio, LNTS 374 (London: T&T Clark, 2008), 14. For other references to secondary literature, see Timo Laato, "'God's Righteousness'—Once Again," in Aejmelaeus and Mustakallio, *Nordic Paul*, 41–44. See also Preston M. Sprinkle, *Paul and Judaism Revisited: A Study of Divine and Human Agency in Salvation* (Downers Grove, IL: IVP Academic, 2013). Sprinkle writes that "a full-scale treatment of the anthropology was lacking until Timo Laato published his dissertation, *Paul and Judaism: An Anthropological Approach*." Then, he insists that many opponents of the New Perspective "have taken Laato's conclusion at face value." As a result,

Participatory Eschatology in Pauline Theology

Following Albert Schweitzer, Sanders brings to the fore "participatory" categories in place of "juristic" ones. In other words, he promotes the idea of Christians being in Christ (in the Spirit) or participating in Christ (in the Spirit) rather than the message of justification through faith. Salvation is to be incorporated into Christ, to be united with his death and resurrection. The new life begins, persists, and reaches its completion in him.[24] The doctrine of justification is seen as one attempt to argue why Gentiles are admitted into the people of God without fulfilling the Mosaic law.[25]

Consequently, Paul thinks "backward." He proceeds "from solution to plight." Insofar as Christ exercises his lordship over those who believe in him, it follows inevitably that sin exercises its lordship over those who do not believe in him. As evidence Paul refers to the irrefutable experience that we all sin. Thus, he deduces from his soteriology his anthropology. He starts from the axiom *Christ is the Savior* and then derives his anthropological premise: *everyone needs a Savior.*[26]

On the whole, Sanders calls the Pauline way of reasoning "participatory eschatology." He describes it as follows:

> 1. God sent Christ in order that all (Jews and Gentiles) might be saved. 2. One is saved when he is united to Christ, that is, dies and is resurrected with him. 3. Only on the Day of Judgment will the Christian be fully incorporated into Christ. 4. Already in this time the behavior of Christians should be an expression of their new existence in Christ. 5. Since Christ died for all, all must have been under the dominion of sin. They have lived "in the flesh" and not "in the spirit."[27]

In the wake of the initial contribution of Sanders, the discussion has advanced to a great extent in close connection with his innovative arguments. It has been shown that a sharp polarization of participatory and juristic categories is in fact more or less artificial. They rather support and explain each other. Often they even appear side by side in the same verse. To illustrate this, I have presented participatory expressions in **bold** and juristic expressions in *italic* as follows:[28]

---

they have "assumed that Laato's study ended the discussion, hammering the proverbial nail in the coffin" and that "Laato's study is proof enough" (126–27). Next, Sprinkle asks if my work is "the final word on anthropology" and concludes rightly that "there is much more to be said" (127). He refers to Stephen Westerholm's important studies. To be sure, "Westerholm arrives at a conclusion similar to Laato's" (127). Therefore, Sprinkle sets before himself the laudable task of examining "the soteriological structure of Paul and Judaism" more closely. However, in the end he examines the soteriological structure of Paul and the Dead Sea Scrolls (28). He concludes that the anthropological view is more pessimistic in Qumran than in Judaism in general (125–44). All in all, his conclusion is in full agreement with the outcomes of Westerholm's studies and mine. They simply give expression to well-known facts that are generally recognized—now also by Sprinkle himself. Cf. Laato, *Paul and Judaism*, 72; Laato, *Paulus und das Judentum*, 91: "In summary: it appears that free will in the domain of soteriology among the Jews from Sirach until the Babylonian Talmud was *opinio communis*. A single (important) exception confirms the rule: the Qumran community seems to represent an absolute fatalism." (A question of much more weight concerns the consequences of anthropology in the soteriological context, discussed further below.)

24. Sanders, *Paul and Palestinian Judaism*, esp. 463–68; see also 434–41, 491–95, 502–3.
25. Sanders, *Paul and Palestinian Judaism*, 497. See also E. P. Sanders, *Paul, the Law, and the Jewish People* (Philadelphia: Fortress, 1983), 47–48 and passim.
26. Sanders, *Paul and Palestinian Judaism*, 442–47, 474–75, 499.
27. Sanders, *Paul and Palestinian Judaism*, 549.
28. Laato, "'God's Righteousness,'" 63. See also Timo Laato, "Paul's Anthropological Considerations: Two Problems," in Carson, O'Brien, and Seifrid, *Justification and Variegated Nomism*, 2:348–49.

> Of him you are **in Christ Jesus**, who has become for us wisdom, *righteousness*, holiness, and redemption from God. (1 Cor. 1:30)
>
> God made him who had no sin to be sin for us, so that **in him** we might become the *righteousness* of God. (2 Cor. 5:21)
>
> If, while we seek to be *justified* **in Christ**, it becomes evident that we ourselves are sinners, does that mean that Christ promotes sin? Absolutely not! (Gal. 2:17)
>
> ... and be found **in him**, not having a *righteousness* of my own that comes from the law, but that which is through faith in Christ—the *righteousness* that comes from God and is by faith. (Phil. 3:9)

Compare further these similar passages:

> ... and are *justified* by his grace as a gift, through the redemption that is **in Christ Jesus**, whom God put forward as a propitiation by his blood [Gk. **in his blood**], to be received by faith. This was to show God's *righteousness*. (Rom. 3:24–25)
>
> Therefore, there is now no *condemnation* for those who are **in Christ Jesus**. (Rom. 8:1)
>
> But you were washed, you were sanctified, you were *justified* **in the name of the Lord Jesus Christ and by the Spirit of our God**. (1 Cor. 6:11) [God's name (as known) is frequently identified with God himself in the Old Testament.]
>
> So the law was put in charge [παιδαγωγός] to lead us to Christ that we might be *justified* by faith. ... You are all sons of God through faith **in Christ Jesus**. (Gal. 3:24, 26).

Under such circumstances, it is no longer worth inquiring whether participatory or juristic terminology expresses the center of Paul's theology better or more accurately. He makes no (theological) distinction between them. Rather, he integrates them together. From different perspectives they both illustrate his soteriology. They are like two sides of one coin. One does not exist without the other.[29]

Still, in connection with his soteriology, Paul emphasizes the Christian's being in Christ but not, strictly speaking, Christ's being in the Christian. Accordingly, he always preserves the objectivity of the salvific event. It does not fade into a merely subjective experience. Justification happens outside the believer. He is counted righteous in Christ.[30]

---

29. Peter Stuhlmacher states, "Führende Vertreter der New Perspective propagieren aufs neue die uralte Zweiteilung der paulinischen Soteriologie in einen juridischen und einen partizipatorischen Teil. ... Diese Aufteilung wird überflüssig, wenn man den von Paulus selbst klar herausgestellten Zusammenhang von Rechtfertigung, Sühne und Versöhnung beachtet und bedenkt, dass der Christus Jesus für den Judenchristen Paulus immer auch eine korporative Repräsentationsfigur ist." "Zum Thema Rechtfertigung," in *Biblische Theologie und Evangelium: Gesammelte Aufsätze*, WUNT 146 (Tübingen: Mohr Siebeck, 2002), 54. Dunn also states, "It is important at this point to avoid the polarisation of 'justification' and 'participation' encouraged by the well known assertion of A. Schweitzer." "New Perspective," 83–84n354. Yet in the same context, Dunn does not recognize the need to distinguish between soteriological and ethical aspects. According to him, justification and sanctification blend together, and thus salvation is reduced to "*a process of transformation* of the believer." "New Perspective," 84.

30. Paul applies participatory and juristic categories also in the area of ethics. They are then not to be mixed up with his teaching of justification (cf., e.g., Romans 1–4; 6). This is where Dunn makes a cardinal error! See "New Perspective," 80–86.

Linked to the previous point, there is a kind of "instrumentalism" or "sacramentalism" to justification. The participation in Christ and in his righteousness is completed explicitly in the proclaimed and written gospel, in baptism (see Rom. 6:1–11; 1 Cor. 6:11; Gal. 3:24–27), and in Holy Communion (1 Cor. 10:16–17; 11:23–29). It does not depend on internal persuasion, though it surely has a connection to it.[31]

Although Sanders lays great weight on the participatory categories, he does not sufficiently take them into consideration in his further appraisal of Pauline theology or soteriology. Granted that anyone not incorporated into or united with Christ stands under the dominion of sin, it definitely follows that he is not free and not even able to free himself from his bondage. Surely, he needs help. More than that: he needs to become "a new creature" (2 Cor. 5:17) through God's creative word (4:6). He cannot rely on his own strength at some stage in his conversion. Neither at some stage after his conversion can he trust in his own power. On the contrary, he lives if and since Christ lives in him (Gal. 2:20). Alternatively, he fulfills the law if and since the Spirit produces fruit in him (5:22).[32]

Thus, in contrast to synergistic tendencies in covenantal nomism, Paul unambiguously represents a monergistic soteriology.[33] He maintains that salvation depends only on God's grace. As a consequence, he asserts that justification by the same token is by faith, not by any other means. On the whole, an obvious correlation exists between anthropology and soteriology. The idea of the total depravity of the human race implies the notion of the absolute superiority of divine mercy.[34]

Finally, the theory of Paul's thinking "from solution to plight" (and not vice versa) holds true as a *historical* description of his conversion: the shocking encounter with Christ on the road to Damascus started a far-reaching process in him and led him to rethink his theology, including anthropological premises. Yet the *theological* reflection runs the other way around, "from plight to solution" (and not vice versa): the anthropological analysis of human existence under the lordship of sin in Romans 1–3 points to the necessity of Christ's salvific death on the cross. Precisely in this respect Paul does not think "backward" but "forward" (as Rudolf Bultmann has stated).[35]

Paul's Break with Judaism

Since Sanders insists that covenantal nomism is not at all based on self-righteousness, merit, and boasting, he concludes that Paul did not discard Jewish religion because of its assumed legalistic soteriology. No, not in the slightest! The main reason was first and foremost Christological. Paul stands for a very exclusive Christology. He affirms that no other can save but Christ. Sanders argues that Paul did not consent to the Jewish

---

31. Laato, "'God's Righteousness,'" 63–65. See also Laato, "Paul's Anthropological Considerations," 348–49.
32. Laato, *Paulus und das Judentum*, 190–94, 199–204, 207–9; Laato, *Paul and Judaism*, 150–54, 158–62, 164–66.
33. See Matthew Barrett, *Salvation by Grace: The Case for Effectual Calling and Regeneration* (Phillipsburg, NJ: P&R, 2013).
34. Laato, *Paulus und das Judentum*, 210–11; Laato, *Paul and Judaism*, 167–68.
35. See Laato, "Paul's Anthropological Considerations," 343–53.

soteriology simply (and this is somewhat simplified) because it was not *Christ*ianity: "In short, *this is what Paul finds wrong in Judaism: it is not Christianity.*"[36]

Later Sanders clarifies his position as follows: "What is wrong with the law, and thus with Judaism, is that it does not provide for God's ultimate purpose, that of saving the entire world through faith in Christ, and without the privilege accorded to Jews through the promises, the covenants, and the law."[37]

Thus, the Christological argument is accompanied by emphasizing that salvation is meant for all and everyone, Gentiles as well as Jews. Accordingly, as the apostle to the Gentiles, Paul could no longer stay inside the narrow boundaries of the Mosaic law. In his thinking, particularism had to give way to universalism. The old covenant was replaced by the new.

However, neither a Christocentric nor an ethnocentric reading of Pauline theology—important as they are in themselves—should replace an anthropocentric perspective. Without a doubt, covenantal nomism amounts to a synergistic soteriology. Sanders himself admits that "to be righteous" in Judaism means staying within the covenant through fulfilling the law.[38] As a result, the final salvation depends on human efforts. Covenantal nomism involves the thought of cooperation that is based on an optimistic anthropology (the notion of free will). Indeed, it does not promote anything like God's grace alone.[39] Saying this does not mean that we should return to different, distorted pictures of Judaism(s).[40]

On the whole, it follows that Paul has reason to criticize the self-righteousness and boasting arising from covenantal nomism. His critical remarks go back to his highly pessimistic (or realistic) anthropology.[41]

James D. G. Dunn

The Question of Synergism

Initially, the New Perspective on Paul was so dubbed by James D. G. Dunn. He also emphasizes that it in fact flows from the new perspective on Judaism (as has already been pointed out above).[42] Thus, he principally shares the overall delineation of covenantal nomism.[43]

Yet Dunn argues that "it may well be the case, no doubt is the case, that some of Sanders' statements are imbalanced in that they overstate the covenant side of the inter-relationship."[44] Despite this, "there was an inter-relationship between given election

---

36. Sanders, *Paul and Palestinian Judaism*, 552.
37. Sanders, *Paul, the Law, and the Jewish People*, 47.
38. Sanders, *Paul and Palestinian Judaism*, 544–45 and passim. See also above.
39. Laato, *Paulus und das Judentum*, esp. 263–65; Laato, *Paul and Judaism*, esp. 209–10. See also above.
40. Laato, *Paulus und das Judentum*, 32–37; Laato, *Paul and Judaism*, 26–30.
41. Laato, *Paulus und das Judentum*, 263–65 and passim; Laato, *Paul and Judaism*, 209–10 and passim.
42. Dunn states that the New Perspective on Paul "builds on Sanders' new perspective on Second Temple Judaism, and Sanders' reassertion of the basic graciousness expressed in Judaism's understanding and practice of covenantal nomism." "New Perspective," 15.
43. Dunn, "New Perspective," 55–63.
44. Dunn, "New Perspective," 56.

and required obedience in the soteriology of Second Temple Judaism," an inner linkage "which prior to Sanders was not sufficiently recognized, and which can now be fairly and effectively characterized in the phrase 'covenantal nomism.'"[45] Accordingly, Dunn also nicely consents to the outcome of the previous analysis.

In addition, Dunn even acknowledges a clear-cut synergism in Judaism.[46] Therefore, he actually admits that Judaism does teach salvation by human cooperation but based on God's amazing grace (covenant). Once again, his conclusion seems obvious (for the very reasons stated earlier).

Then, Dunn goes one step further and suggests that Paul himself allows for synergistic tendencies to permeate his soteriology. Dunn specifically refers to judgment according to works.[47] He makes his readers wonder whether they have to face the theological dispute from the past relating to Pelagius and his heretical teachings. Was it that we discuss the *New* Perspective on Paul? Frankly speaking, one must wonder whether we are here involved in *Pauline* theology at all.

At long last, Dunn fervently denies that "Paul's understanding of salvation was synergistic." Rather, his concern was "to question whether the charge of synergism should be laid so confidently at the door of Judaism when some of Paul's language seems vulnerable to the same charge" and "to take more seriously and with due seriousness the other Pauline teaching" (predominantly on judgment according to works).[48] By and large, Dunn's back-and-forth rhetoric is aimed at downplaying the notion of human cooperation. Ultimately, he would be willing to drop the verdict against legalism in Pauline soteriology, provided that the charge of synergism in Judaism is not taken at face value!

Dunn's overall thinking becomes even more bewildering as he on another occasion writes as follows: "In all these cases [i.e., Rom. 4:4–5; 10:2–4; Phil. 3:7–9], therefore, it is difficult to sustain the claim that Paul was polemicizing against 'self-achieved righteousness.' *Of course the texts just reviewed can be read that way*."[49] In reality, Dunn admits here that his own reading of the Pauline texts is *not* the only one. Indeed, it is possible to understand Paul polemicizing against self-achieved righteousness (which goes back to the synergistic trends in Judaism).[50] That is exactly what "the later Paul"

---

45. Dunn, "New Perspective," 62.
46. Dunn, "New Perspective," 54–80, esp. 69–72, 80.
47. Dunn, "New Perspective," 72–79.
48. Dunn, "New Perspective," 80.
49. James D. G. Dunn, *The Theology of Paul the Apostle* (Grand Rapids, MI: Eerdmans, 1998), 370; italics added. Cf. Dunn, "New Perspective," 41: "Here again I do not question the fundamental statement of principle which Paul enunciates in these passages [Rom. 3:20; 4:4–5; 9:11–12]. But again I wonder if the conclusion that Paul is attacking a works-righteousness attitude, an attitude embraced by Jews of his time, is *quite so soundly* based as most think, and whether Paul's attack is again *somewhat broader*" (italics added). Contra Dunn, cf. further Robert W. Yarbrough, "Paul and Salvation History," in Carson, O'Brien, and Seifrid, *Justification and Variegated Nomism*, 2:308.
50. Cf. some remarkable passages in James D. G. Dunn, *Romans 1–8* (Dallas: Word Books, 1988): "What is attacked, therefore, is the self-confidence of the synagogue attender who faithfully hears the law being read Sabbath by Sabbath and who in consequence counts himself as one of the righteous, one of the chosen people (an equation encouraged not least once again by the Wisdom of Solomon and *Psalms of Solomon*), that is, one who is already assured of a favorable final verdict because as a member of the covenant people he has remained within the covenant, loyal to the covenant" (104–5). Or later: "In any case we must assume that Paul, in looking back on his life as a Pharisee, had long ago concluded that the law, far from binding individuals closer to God in truthful obedience, actually separated them from God and prevented them from accepting God's grace in its complete gratuitousness" (352). Or later: "With insight born of his conversion

(the one who wrote Ephesians)⁵¹ does. Dunn suggests, "That [the disapproval of self-achieved righteousness] may have happened already in Eph. 2:8–9, where the issue does seem to have moved from one of works of law to one of human effort."⁵²

Later, in another context, he writes,

> Here [in Eph. 2:8–9] the thought seems to have broadened out to refer to human effort in general as inadequate to the demands of salvation; salvation could be accomplished only by grace alone through faith alone. At the very least that implies that the Reformation understanding of Paul's theology of justification was already shared by the first Christian commentator on that theology.⁵³

All in all, Dunn seems to saw off the branch on which he is sitting. He acknowledges that

1. Judaism was synergistic,
2. some crucial Pauline texts can be read as polemicizing against self-achieved righteousness, and
3. "the later Paul" does exactly that as he disapproves every kind of legalism.

So the question naturally arises: Why not interpret the theology of Paul and his break with Judaism along these lines? Is there any compelling or convincing need for the New Perspective? Truly, it looks as if there is none. Rather, one should simply say that the Judaism of what Sanders christened as covenantal nomism was synergistic. As a result, Paul has every reason for criticism.

"Works of the Law" as Jewish Identity Markers

In his concise summary of the New Perspective on Paul, Dunn does not simply build on Sanders's new perspective on Second Temple Judaism. He also observes and emphasizes "a social function of the law" as an integral feature of covenantal nomism. To put it in a well-defined dictum, the Mosaic law serves to mark off Israel from all the other nations.⁵⁴ Accordingly, Dunn argues as follows:

> When Paul said in effect, "All are justified by faith and not by works," he meant *not* "Every individual must cease from his own efforts and simply trust in God's acceptance," however legitimate and important an interpretation of his words that is. What he meant was, "Justification is not confined to Jews as marked out by their distinctive works; it is open to all, to Gentile as well as Jew, through faith."⁵⁵

Paul sees that attitude to have been motivated (subconsciously) in large part by fear—a fear of failing to match up to a standard of exact obedience, a fear in other words not so much of God as of what his fellow Pharisees might think or say of his failure to conform. Paul thus, in all probability, extrapolates his own experience to that of his readers, confident that his Jewish and God-worshipping audiences have found in Christianity the same liberation as he had himself (v 2)" (460).

51. Dunn, "New Perspective," 51. The later Paul is the one who also wrote the Pastorals. "New Perspective," 53–54.
52. Dunn, *Theology of Paul*, 371.
53. Dunn, "New Perspective," 52. That kind of reasoning continues also in Dunn's treatment of the Pastorals. "New Perspective," 53–54.
54. Dunn, "New Perspective," 15.
55. James D. G. Dunn, "The Justice of God: A Renewed Perspective on Justification by Faith," in Dunn, *New Perspective on Paul*, 199.

Consequently, Dunn contends that "works of the law" in the Pauline Epistles serve as "Jewish identity markers." They especially indicate circumcision, food, and Sabbath laws, even if they should not be narrowed to boundary issues only. By focusing particularly on those regulations, the Judaizers in Galatia put to the test the willingness of the Gentiles to enter into covenant membership and their readiness to remain faithful to the whole of Old Testament traditions and customs.[56]

The explicit emphasis on national separation or division by Dunn has caused much turbulence in the ongoing discussion. In the first place, Mark Seifrid raises objections. He regards it as "highly questionable" that Jewish identity markers symbolize "*mere national identity.*"[57] Rather, he contends that circumcision (for instance, in Josephus's account of the circumcision of King Izates) symbolizes "not merely separation from other nations, but an ethically superior monotheism."[58]

On balance, Dunn seems not to have turned a deaf ear to a call to revise his position. Later he writes as follows:

> I have no doubt that "works of the law" refer to what the law requires, the conduct prescribed by the Torah; whatever the law requires to be done can be described as "doing" the law, as a work of the law. . . . The phrase "works of the law" is a way of describing the law observance required of all covenant members, and could be regarded as an appropriate way of filling out the second half of the Sanders' formula—"covenantal *nomism.*"[59]

Taken at face value, the quotation shows undeniably that "works of the law" point not simply to distinctive *ethnic* features but also to diverse *ethical* features.[60] In that case, Paul renouncing "works of the law" excludes not merely Jewish national priority but human arrogant superiority as well. I am in full agreement with Seifrid: "All these observations give us reasons for thinking that in rejecting ἔργα νόμου as a guarantee of salvation, Paul rejects a moral superiority gained by obedience, notwithstanding that Jews who adopted such a stance would have attributed their progress to God's gracious covenant with Israel."[61]

Astoundingly, Dunn himself applauds these words as "a basis for a richer synthesis,"[62] even though they actually overturn his New Perspective on Paul! Rejecting "a moral superiority gained by obedience," the apostle to the Gentiles at the same time abrogates every kind of synergism in Jewish soteriology. In the end, this is what he finds wrong with covenantal nomism.

---

56. Dunn, "New Perspective," 22–26.
57. Mark A. Seifrid, "Blind Alleys in the Controversy over the Paul of History," *TynBul* 45, no. 1 (1994): 77.
58. Seifrid, "Blind Alleys," 79. Later Seifrid adds that it is "impossible to sustain the claim that Jewish 'boundary markers' signalled exclusivism or national identity alone. I must confess considerable puzzlement that both Dunn and Wright, who recognise that some Jews could regard other Jews as outside the community of the elect on the basis of halakhah, regard distinctive practices as simply 'exclusivistic,' borders without interior meaning." "Blind Alleys," 80–81.
59. Dunn, "New Perspective," 22–23.
60. Cf. R. Barry Matlock, "Sins of the Flesh and Suspicious Minds: Dunn's New Theology of Paul," *JSNT* 21, no. 72 (1999): 78–80.
61. Seifrid, "Blind Alleys," 85.
62. Dunn, "New Perspective," 26n107. In addition, Dunn affirms that Seifrid "is much more nuanced than the others."

The Request for Consistency

By and large, reading Dunn (and above all, his copious commentary on Romans) is puzzling. He indicates that he has reconsidered his position. Despite his apparent reassessment, it seems that he still tries to hold on to his original understanding of works of the law as "Jewish identity markers." To quote him, "I confess to being a little surprized by the difficulty apparently experienced by some respondents in recognizing how ἔργα νόμου can denote what the law requires, but with special reference to such crucial issues [as Jewish identity markers]."[63]

Without doubt, Dunn was obliged to reassess his previous position to avoid the morbid criticism that it caused. However, the extension of "works of the law" to "what the law requires" with special reference to Jewish identity markers is not the same as the notion of "works of the law" as solely Jewish identity markers. All that the law requires (notwithstanding the special reference to the Jewish identity markers) comprises not only *ethnic* but also *ethical* dimensions. This is completely at odds with what Dunn suggests. In this case, we are talking not just about Jewish national priority; at stake is arrogant human superiority combined with strong synergistic tendencies.

Elsewhere, I have emphasized that Dunn has modified his former stance considerably.[64] It is not surprising at all that he fervently denies such a conclusion.[65] He maintains to have adjusted his "initial formulation" only,[66] a claim of which I am strongly suspicious. The discussion above runs completely counter to any denial. The fact remains that Dunn has fundamentally altered the content of "works of the law." Besides, he admits that Judaism is pervaded by human cooperation (synergism). As a result, what will be left of his New Perspective? On the whole, it seems to me that his overall interpretation has really collapsed under its own weight.

N. T. Wright

Preliminary Remarks

By and large, N. T. Wright (like Dunn) makes his case for the new perspective on Judaism. He wholeheartedly hails Sanders for bringing to light that "Judaism, so far from being a religion of works, is based on a clear understanding of grace, the grace that chose Israel in the first place to be a special people. Good works are simply gratitude, and demonstrate that one is faithful to the covenant."[67] In addition, Wright also (like Dunn) especially understands circumcision "as a badge of national identity"[68] and acknowledges it as defining boundaries between Jews and Gentiles.[69] Therefore,

---

63. See James D. G. Dunn, "Yet Once More—'The Works of the Law': A Response," in Dunn, *New Perspective on Paul*, 208. *Pace* Dunn, see Francis Watson, *Paul and the Hermeneutics of Faith* (London: T&T Clark, 2004), 334–35n41; Matlock, "Sins of the Flesh," 78–80.
64. Laato, "Paul's Anthropological Considerations," 356n71.
65. Dunn, "New Perspective," 22n94.
66. Dunn, "New Perspective," 22.
67. N. T. Wright, "The Paul of History and the Apostle of Faith," *TynBul* 29 (1978): 80 and later passim.
68. Wright, "Paul of History," 65.
69. N. T. Wright, *The Climax of the Covenant: Christ and the Law in Pauline Theology* (Minneapolis: Fortress, 1993), 240–44. See also Dunn, "New Perspective," 25n106.

there is no need to prolong the discussion on those aspects beyond what has been confirmed so far.

Yet it might be added that even Wright (like Dunn) ultimately shows the necessity for an extension of "works of the law" from "Jewish boundary markers" to all that the law requires. He maintains that Israel still lives in exile. Though she came back from Babylon, the divine promise of a glorious future remained unfulfilled. Thus, Wright asks what Israel should be doing in the present to hasten the time when God would act on her behalf.[70] Accordingly, he indicates that she, "sheltered behind the religious boundary-markers," should do her very best to "keep the covenant" with all her might.[71] In that case, the Jews (as expected) are indeed to obey the *whole* law, possibly concentrating on those aspects that isolate themselves from the Gentiles but not to the exclusion of other aspects in their Torah. For that reason, Jewish badges of covenant membership imply a wider reference to covenantal nomism, the entire body of Israel's sacred traditions.

Saying this is not tantamount to approving the thought of ongoing exile. Wright suggests that Israel (despite her strong emphasis on nomism in reliance on human freedom as a vital feature of covenant membership) is guilty not of any legalistic works righteousness but of "national righteousness." The law functions "as a charter of national privilege."[72] The future return from exile would amount to the fulfillment of distinct *Jewish* longing. Then God will rescue his own people and do this by his grace. At that moment he brings the good old times (or even better times) back again. What is more, Gentiles were also supposed to be flocking into Zion to acknowledge him as their Lord. Their imminent coming occurs according to the Old Testament expectations.[73]

On the other hand, Wright suggests that on the road to Damascus, Paul was brought to realize the astonishing accomplishment of his former national hopes. Surprisingly, the exile has already ended! Israel has truly been delivered from her oppression and oppressors. There is no need to yearn for her redemption any more. The Messiah has come. He has exhausted the curse of sin and death.[74] Besides, the gospel involves an extensive redefinition of Israel. She "is transformed from being an ethnic people into a worldwide family," including Gentiles.[75] Hence, what counts is grace, not race.[76] To put it simply, "The one true God had done for Jesus of Nazareth in the middle of time, what Saul had thought he was going to do for Israel at the end of time."[77]

Obviously, a short summary cannot do full justice to the overall picture of Wright's analysis. He has much more to say on Jewish and Pauline theology. Even so, his specific theory of Israel in exile is to be examined more closely next.

---

70. N. T. Wright, *The New Testament and the People of God* (Minneapolis: Fortress, 1992), 268–69.
71. Wright, *People of God*, 271–72.
72. Wright, "Paul of History," 65, 71.
73. Wright, *People of God*, 268–79.
74. Wright, *Climax*, 141–55.
75. Wright, *Climax*, 240.
76. Wright, *Climax*, 168, 194, 238.
77. N. T. Wright, *What Saint Paul Really Said: Was Paul of Tarsus the Real Founder of Christianity?* (Grand Rapids, MI: Eerdmans, 1997), 36.

Israel Still in Exile?

Old Testament

On the whole, Wright regards the so-called Deuteronomic view of history as "constitutive of the underlying narrative framework" in the Old Testament as well as in later writings.[78] He maintains that "a great many second-Temple Jews interpreted *that part of the continuing narrative in which they were living* in terms of the so-called Deuteronomic scheme of sin—exile—restoration, with themselves still somewhere in the middle stage, that of 'exile'" (especially Deuteronomy 27–30).[79] A similar sequence of events culminating in a continuing exile and an ultimate return emerges in Leviticus 26.[80] Both Ezra (Ezra 9:6–9) and Nehemiah (Neh. 9:32–37), in their great prayers, speak of a constant calamity, which amounts to a hapless exile.[81] Also, the prophet Daniel in Daniel 9 "poured out his heart and soul in prayer, insisting that it must be time for the exile to end" (because Jeremiah predicted that it would last for seventy years).[82] But he is informed by the angel that "the exile will not last for seventy years, but for *seventy times seven*." He ought not run ahead of reality. There will be an extension of the time schedule. Until then, the hoped-for restoration falls short.[83]

Despite some strong tendencies in the current academic debate, it has not been substantiated that Wright is correct in his analysis of the biblical data.[84] Here, for obvious reasons, a full-scale evaluation of his arguments would go too far. Still, a number of germane aspects, not always taken at their face value, are needed.

The most common word for "exile" in the Old Testament is גולה (גלות). It stems from the verb גלה, which literally means "to uncover" and is used in various contexts. The phrase "to uncover the ear"—with either man or God as its subject—means "to show" or "to reveal." Though not a technical term for "divine revelation," it conveys that meaning too. In Leviticus 18 and 20, the verb גלה occurs in the expression "to uncover the shame," which denotes sexual intercourse in proscribed circumstances, usually incest. It occurs also in the prophetic complaint that Israel has "uncovered her nakedness," a metaphor implying that she has thrown off her loyalty to the Lord. As a rough punishment, her land will be "uncovered" as the people go into exile (e.g., Ezek. 16:36; Hos. 2:10).[85] Here the idea of "uncovering" is associated with the conditions of a ruined land[86] and probably with the humiliation of the prisoners of war being led

---

78. N. T. Wright, *Paul and the Faithfulness of God* (London: SPCK, 2013), 162. See also 139–40, 142–43, 149–50.
79. Wright, *Paul and the Faithfulness of God*, 140.
80. Wright, *Paul and the Faithfulness of God*, 149–50.
81. Wright, *Paul and the Faithfulness of God*, 151.
82. Wright, *Paul and the Faithfulness of God*, 142.
83. Wright, *Paul and the Faithfulness of God*, 142. See also 140, 143–46, 151, 160–62.
84. Cf. Wright's own evaluation in *Paul and the Faithfulness of God*, 139n263. He refers to James M. Scott, who suggests that the notion of the ongoing exile is now widely recognized and speaks of a growing consensus. That is—Wright reasonably fears—"over-optimistic."
85. See especially Bruce K. Waltke, "גלה," in *Theological Wordbook of the Old Testament*, ed. R. Laird Harris, Gleason L. Archer, and Bruce K. Waltke (Chicago: Moody Press, 1980), 160–61. He regards it as "an open question whether we are dealing with one or two roots" and therefore discusses the verb גלה under two main meanings: "to uncover" and "to depart, to go into exile." However, the two main meanings are connected because "the land is uncovered when people are removed." See Allen P. Ross, "Exile," in *NIDOTTE*, 4:595.
86. Ross, "Exile," 4:595.

naked into captivity.[87] During the time of Israel's "scattering" among the nations, her whole holy terrain "will rest and enjoy its Sabbaths," a rest it did not have the entire time she lived in it (Lev. 26:33–34).

The Lord's judgment of leading all the Israelites out of the land into captivity functions as an appropriate contrast to his fulfilling the promises to lead them into the land at the beginning of their history. Accordingly, his repeated warnings through the prophets to lead them out of the land correspond exactly to his recurring promises to the fathers to lead their descendants into the land.[88] Thus, as God remembers his covenant with Abraham, Isaac, and Jacob, he certainly remembers also the land at the same time (see Lev. 26:42). Both aspects are very closely intertwined. Indeed, the thought of an ongoing exile would be awkward in Old Testament theology. It does not make any more sense if the Lord would bring back his people into the Promised Land but then nevertheless leave them in a state of ongoing exile. He is a trustworthy God, not an arbitrary one.

Additionally, the notion of exile is both lexically and theologically linked with "nakedness." In other words, it is associated with heinous sins, such as idolatry (Israel uncovering her nakedness), forbidden sexual relationships (Israelites uncovering the shame of their relatives or neighbors), and constant violation of Sabbath rules. Those really loathsome connotations are included in the language of the Old Testament. Therefore, the theory of ongoing exile suggests that Israel is still involved in grievous transgressions in one way or another. I strongly suspect that it properly renders the common Jewish thinking after the rebuilding of the temple (see below).

To be precise, the Deuteronomic view of history does not amount to the scheme of sin—exile—restoration but rather to the scheme of sin—punishments—restoration (in which the exile is the climax of the punishments). In Deuteronomy 28, the exile arises recurrently during the whole chapter as the harshest chastisement (e.g., 28:21, 25, 32, 36–37, 41, 49–52, 63–68). The repetition aims to underline the seriousness and severity of the divine retribution. Transgressing the law ushers in a catastrophe. In Leviticus 26, the whole long story ends with the retribution of the exile (26:32–39). The line of thought is more linear, leading finally to the return and restoration of Israel (26:40–45).

The factual composition in Deuteronomy 28 and Leviticus 26 indicates, as Steven Bryan suggests, that the exile would take place "as the ultimate punishment invoked only when the other curses had at last failed to bring Israel out of its recurrent recalcitrance."[89] The long list of punishments reaches the culmination there, with the last one being the absolute worst. Cogently, if the exile is going on, at least most other

---

87. M. G. Klingbeil, "Exile," in *Dictionary of the Old Testament: Pentateuch*, ed. T. Desmond Alexander and David W. Baker (Downers Grove, IL: InterVarsity Press, 2003), 246.
88. Waltke, "גלה," 161.
89. Steven M. Bryan, *Jesus and Israel's Traditions of Judgement and Restoration*, SNTSMS 117 (Cambridge: Cambridge University Press, 2002), 17. Bryan examines the book of Jubilees, and in contrast to seeing the exile as "the ultimate punishment," an "obvious way of reading the curses of Deuteronomy 32," in *Jubilees* 23 the significance of the exile has been reduced. . . . Captivity is simply one of a litany of curses." In the Old Testament the significance of the exile has not been downgraded but upgraded as the worst curse. See my arguments below.

chastisements (but not necessarily all and all the time) are likewise in force. In that case, Israel suffers as well from serious diseases, insanity, extreme drought and other environmental calamities, unceasing hunger and thirst, dire poverty, the burdens of huge debts, brutal robbery, constant oppression, the desire to be married to a woman but someone else ravishing her, building a house but not living in it, ploughing and sowing but not reaping the harvest, planting a vineyard but not enjoying its fruit, slaughtering an ox but not eating any beef, the curse of eating one's own children. To be sure, the Jews would not have been thinking about living in ongoing exile and on the whole suffering from this kind of chaos and anarchy after having returned from Babylonia back to the Promised Land. Without a doubt, life was hard in ancient times and circumstances, but it was scarcely *too* tough, especially if you were released from your captivity among foreign nations (see also below).

The books of Ezra and Nehemiah shed more light on the crucial aspects included in the concept of exile. The rest of Israel has returned from Babylon to the Promised Land. As a result, they have started to rebuild the temple and, soon after, the tumbled walls of Jerusalem. In the meantime, it is important to learn from the mistakes of the past, repenting of them and definitely not repeating them. Otherwise, the people run the risk of a new exile, in which they will be punished because of their inward stubbornness.

It is no coincidence that the books of Ezra and Nehemiah strictly forbid those sins that especially brought about the exile, in other words, offenses that are closely associated with "nakedness." Thus, Israel is not to "uncover her nakedness," showing disloyalty to God by failing to complete the rebuilding of the temple or the fallen walls of Jerusalem (Ezra 4:1–6:22; Neh. 3:17–6:19). Neither is Israel to "uncover the shame of others" by marrying foreigners (Ezra 9–10; Neh. 13:1–6, 23–31). Neither should Israel reject the Sabbath and cause the land to turn into "naked" (or desolate) conditions to enjoy its Sabbatical rest that it was not allowed to have under the Israeli regime (Neh. 13:15–22).

Further, it should also be borne in mind that the punishment for the sins associated with "nakedness" is nothing less than the exile. If Israel forsakes God, he, in turn, will forsake her as well as the land where she lives (as already shown in Deuteronomy 28). Likewise, prohibited sexual relationships result in captivity. In fact, there are, strictly speaking, no offerings that bring reconciliation in that case. If Israel defiles the land, it will simply vomit her out (see Lev. 18:24–28, cf. 20:22–24; 26:31). Similarly, if Israel does not keep the Sabbath laws, she will be driven out from her land, and the land will be laid waste. Then it will have the rest it needs (26:34–35).

The seriousness of the situation makes it more understandable why both Ezra and Nehemiah are ready to use or threaten violence in order to avoid intermarriage or prevent the recurring violation of Sabbath rules (Ezra 10:8; Neh. 13:15–22). Sins like those have resulted in exile, a fact that they both explicitly refer to (Ezra 9:10–15; Neh. 13:17–18). Thus, there is definitely no room for slackness and vagueness. Restricted violence is better than the whole hell of savagery and bloodshed, prompted by furious enemies who—if worse comes to worst—will take Israel into captivity once again.

Also, 4 Baruch (dated to the first half of the second century AD) shows much later the same line of thought. It announces the end of the exile. However, those who do not separate from their foreign wives have to return to Babylon. They go back but are not allowed to resettle there anymore. Therefore, they must come back and build a city (i.e., Samaria) for themselves (8:1–11). Here, a certain sin is closely connected with the punishment of the exile as in the Old Testament. This is to say nothing of the Gospels, where the Pharisees really do their utmost to especially keep the Sabbath rules and purity laws (not least those concerning sexuality). Without a doubt, their devout practice maintains to a large extent substantial continuity with the national revival of Ezra and Nehemiah.[90]

In addition, it is worth mentioning that the Deuteronomic scheme of sin—punishments—restoration (in which the exile is the ultimate punishment) is taken at face value in Haggai as well. Yet now the curses are made to function in reverse (or, so to speak, "backward"). They do not disappear all at once but rather in the long run. To be sure, the exile is over. The rebuilding of the temple has begun without being finished. Therefore, the prophet urges his kinsmen to complete it. If God's own house remains a ruin, there are no abundant blessings. So far, "the heavens have withheld their dew and the earth its crops" (Hag. 1:10). As soon as the work on the temple is making real progress and coming to an end, a fabulous change takes place. The Lord says, "From this day on I will bless you" (2:19). It denotes—as expected—the rich blessings of the heavens and the earth. To sum up, not long ago Israel has returned from Babylon to the Promised Land. In a little while she will live in abundance in the land flowing with milk and honey.

The future will be even much brighter. Notwithstanding the fact that the new temple seems "like nothing" in comparison with the old one (2:3), the Lord promises that he will fill it with glory (2:7). In the end, the glory of the new temple will be greater than the glory of the old one (2:9). The divine prophecy was fulfilled at least in two different ways: first, through the insane construction projects of Herod the Great as he enlarged the temple and made it one of the most astounding buildings in its own time; second, through the entering of the Messiah (Jesus) into that temple.[91]

All this shows that the full restoration of Israel does not occur at once. It takes time—much more time than originally thought. Yet it would be wrong to argue on that basis alone that the exile is still going on.

Daniel 9 infers nothing like the theory of the ongoing exile (whether at present or in the remote future). On the contrary, it "explicitly and positively recalls Jeremiah's prediction of seventy years, suggesting that the author regarded Jeremiah's prophecy not as

---

90. For the Pharisees before AD 70, see particularly Jacob Neusner, *The Rabbinic Traditions about the Pharisees before 70*, 3 vols. (Leiden: Brill, 1971).

91. Strictly speaking, the temple that Herod the Great enlarged was still the second one (not the third one), since the sacrificial cult was not interrupted during the long construction work. Thus, the prophecies in Haggai 2 were fulfilled in the long run.

incorrect."⁹² By the same token, it assertively envisions the hope for the final atonement and everlasting righteousness (Dan. 9:24). In short, the exile will soon be over, but the full restoration will take time to be completed.

Largely, Wright's theory of Israel still in exile is backed up by no noteworthy biblical data. For sure, the next issue concerns whether it could be traced to other Jewish texts.

Other Jewish Texts

On the whole, Wright has to deal with the fact that Jewish writings "in which exile language occurs are rare." Therefore, much of the evidence for his case is drawn from a more wide-ranging perspective.⁹³ Accordingly, Wright expands the textual basis for his theory of ongoing exile. To support it, he quotes texts

1. reflecting on the Diaspora,
2. bemoaning the bondage of Israel (such as already seen in Ezra 9:8–9; Neh. 9:36–37), and
3. underlying the nonrestoration (or incomplete restoration) of Israel.⁹⁴

Yet equating the Diaspora, the bondage of Israel, and the nonrestoration of Israel with exile displays a serious methodological problem:

1. Accurately, the Diaspora and exile are not synonymous. In the latter case, prisoners of war are not allowed to return from the land(s) of their captivity. In the former case, they have become accustomed to living outside their home country and by their own choice reside where they are. They could go back where they (originally) are from, but at present—for one reason or another—they do not.
2. Similarly, living in bondage is not exactly tantamount to exile. In Old Testament times, Israel has been living in bondage in her own land every so often without living in exile (which denotes the obligation to live in a foreign country).
3. To be precise, the nonrestoration of Israel does not absolutely suggest that exile still continues. For certain, there was plenty of room for future revelations and end-time perfection after the return of Israel from Babylonia as well. The end of Babylonian captivity was not the end of all eschatology in the proclamation of the prophets.

Despite the indisputable fact that Jewish writings "in which exile language occurs are rare," Wright remarkably assumes that "we can no doubt go on *fine-tuning the details of what kind of exile* people thought they were living in."⁹⁵ There are at least geographical, political, cultural, and theological adjustments to exile.⁹⁶ Yet "the sense of living within the middle term of the Deuteronomic scheme [of sin—exile—restoration]" is applied on all levels. This remains true, Wright argues,

---

92. Bryan, *Jesus and Israel's Traditions*, 18.
93. Bryan, *Jesus and Israel's Traditions*, 13, 19.
94. Wright, *Paul and the Faithfulness of God*, 139–63.
95. Wright, *Paul and the Faithfulness of God*, 140; italics added.
96. Wright, *Paul and the Faithfulness of God*, 139–40.

1. whether, for those concerned, "exile" was still in fact a geographical reality, as it was for many in the Diaspora;
2. whether they were aware of the continuing theological and cultural oppression of foreign nations as indicating that Daniel 9 had not yet been fulfilled; or
3. whether they believed that in some sense they themselves were the advance guard of the "real return from exile," indicating that it had been going on right up to their time and still was for everyone except themselves (as in Qumran).[97]

Wright's efforts to fine-tune the details of what kind of exile we ultimately are talking about run into grievous methodological shortcomings. He equates here again exile with the Diaspora (point 1) and with the nonrestoration of Israel (point 2). To that extent, his conclusions are unwarranted—as already shown above. In addition, Wright argues from the sectarian viewpoint of Qumran that all other Israelites live in exile, as if the exclusive indoctrination of a religious minority correctly expressed the common Jewish desperation felt by the majority (point 3). Rather, one could understand the whole state of affairs very much to the contrary: while a rigorous sect like that in Qumran is not ashamed of asserting that all the others of their kinsmen still live in exile, this suggests that the Israelites themselves in general did *not* think along those lines (see below).

Overall, Wright fails to convince. His methodological fallacies call into question his conclusions. The "fine-tuning" of the details in the notion of exile remains a flop. A meticulous exegetical analysis of data is missing. Wright has not shown that his way of reading varied Jewish texts is possible—much less that it is even plausible. The proof of evidence lies on him.

Astonishingly, Wright himself admits that there are a number of remarkable exceptions from his theory of ongoing exile. As already stated, he considers the vast literature of the tiny sect in Qumran one of them. Additionally, he also mentions the books of Sirach and Judith.[98] All these examples draw attention to the fact that Israel has already returned from her exile to the Promised Land.

In the case of Tobit,[99] 1 Enoch,[100] and, as it seems, Jubilees,[101] Wright focuses on "a double return from exile." Certainly, the first return has already taken place. A number of Israelites have come back to the Promised Land. God has shown "mercy on them" (Tob. 14:5). Still, the second return will take place sometime in the future.

That said, Wright explains the double return from exile by downplaying the first one. He writes, "Yes, there had been a 'return from exile'—of sorts: but it had not been the real thing." Hence, Israelites have "experienced a kind of 'return,'" but are "still awaiting the *true* 'return.'"[102] On balance, the first return from exile does not override the second one. In fact, the exile has not ended but at the present goes on as ever.

---

97. Wright, *Paul and the Faithfulness of God*, 140.
98. Wright, *Paul and the Faithfulness of God*, 157–58.
99. Wright, *Paul and the Faithfulness of God*, 154–55.
100. Wright, *Paul and the Faithfulness of God*, 155.
101. Wright, *Paul and the Faithfulness of God*, 156. After having acknowledged "a double return from exile" in Tobit and 1 Enoch, Wright continues: "So too with *Jubilees*."
102. Wright, *Paul and the Faithfulness of God*, 155.

Frankly, Wright's devaluation of the first return seems unwarranted. The most natural interpretation of the double return from exile denotes the gathering of *all* Jews: at the outset merely the *southern* tribes of Judah from Babylon, then also and especially the *northern* tribes of Israel (including the rest of the other Jews as well) from different countries. Since the northern tribes never came back, their future gathering was an end-time dream. That vision will come true at long last—not before:

> God will again have mercy on them [i.e., the Israelites], and God will bring them back into the land of Israel; and they will rebuild the temple of God, but not like the first until the period when the times of fulfilment shall come. After this they *all* will return from their exile and will rebuild Jerusalem in splendour. (Tob. 14:5)[103]

As a result, the whole of Israel (all her tribes) will be saved.

The fulfillment of the traditional hope as to the redemption and restoration of all Israel in the end is the content of the double return from exile. It does not indicate that the first return is not essentially a "true" one. Neither does it suggest that the Jews at year zero in general regarded themselves as being in exile and estranged from God. Wright is not right. He does not even discuss other alternatives but only his own previously established and closed position, which assumes that no critical remark should be thought through.

On the contrary, Wright is correct that the view of an ongoing exile does occur in the book of Baruch. The alleged author is pseudonymous. He is portrayed as Jeremiah's secretary. Thus, the book has a fictive setting in the Babylonian exile, though it is usually dated to the second century BC.[104] In Baruch, there are indeed passages that state that Israel will return from her exile in the future. Jerusalem is admonished to rejoice since her children are coming from everywhere (4:37). She should take off her garments of mourning and instead wear the marvelous clothes of divine glory at that moment (5:1).

Even so, the reader of Baruch is naturally supposed to understand that the "today of the exile" is simply a literary setting.[105] The long-promised foretelling as to the end of exile has already come true. Israel has returned from her captivity. What has been told to Baruch was verified long ago. Accordingly, he has been confirmed as a trustworthy man, sent from God. To be sure, the book of Baruch was not written to show that it for the most part has completely failed (conveying that Israel should return when in fact she did not)! In that case, it is not to be used as evidence for the theory of ongoing exile.[106]

Neither do the books of the Maccabees say what Wright thinks. Referring to "such exalted language about the results of Simon's rule,"[107] Wright, as expected, recognizes

---

103. The quotation according to Wright, *Paul and the Faithfulness of God*, 154.
104. Wright, *Paul and the Faithfulness of God*, 151–52.
105. Seifrid, "Blind Alleys," 88.
106. Pace J. M. Scott, "Restoration of Israel," in *Dictionary of Paul and His Letters*, ed. Gerald F. Hawthorne, Ralph P. Martin, and Daniel G. Reid (Leicester: InterVarsity Press, 1993), 796–99. Scott repetitively quotes the book of Baruch as evidence for an ongoing exile. A better understanding of the literary setting of the writing would have resulted in another conclusion.
107. Wright, *Paul and the Faithfulness of God*, 159.

the difficulty "to imagine that in the heady days of Hasmonean success," the Jews generally "perceived themselves to be in exile."[108] However, he also now speaks of the "double return," asserting that God has already rescued Israel and will soon gather all Israelites everywhere.[109] On that basis, he then suggests that "the promised time of full blessing" has not arrived. Accordingly, he concludes that the curse of being in exile prevails.[110]

Once again, Wright rushes into his vague methodological point of departure and simply overemphasizes the eschatological language of Israel's complete restoration. As pointed out, his line of reasoning falls short on account of (1) the equating of incomplete restoration with exile and (2) the devaluing of the first return while recurring to the idea of the double return from the exile. Both methodological fallacies cause Wright to misinterpret the obvious meaning and sense of the books of the Maccabees.

In the case of Josephus, Wright asserts that "the period of life under Rome was a time of *douleia*, 'slavery,' and it was all Israel's own fault."[111] Therefore, he concludes that because of that enslavement, Israel still lives in exile. But this is simply a blatant *non sequitur*. The equating of bondage (or slavery) with exile is another methodological fault that leads astray (as shown above).

What is more, Wright must know well that Josephus "regards the beginning of Jewish slavery as having occurred because of the Jewish civil strife leading to Pompey's entrance."[112] Thus, as Steven Bryan observes, "Inasmuch as Josephus regards the enslavement that began under Pompey as the end of a preceding period of liberty, it is difficult to see how or why he would have connected this new situation of bondage with exile."[113] Astonishingly, the more detailed facts like these are hidden in a footnote and hastily forgotten.[114] Why? It is obvious that as a consequence the view of an ongoing exile completely collapses. To put it bluntly, Wright distorts the plain meaning of the original text by his tendentious interpretation. He forces his sources to say what he likes.[115]

All in all, the theory of an ongoing exile lacks evidence. It does not do justice to the Jewish texts and their apparent message. On the contrary, a more comprehensive inquiry into the data shows that a number of Israelites have indeed returned to the Promised Land. The end of exile was generally perceived and recognized. Not even the notion of a double return entails that the first return is not a "true" one.[116]

---

108. Wright, *Paul and the Faithfulness of God*, 160, in reference to Bryan, *Jesus and Israel's Traditions*, 15.
109. Wright, *Paul and the Faithfulness of God*, 159.
110. Wright, *Paul and the Faithfulness of God*, 159–60.
111. Wright, *Paul and the Faithfulness of God*, 159.
112. Bryan, *Jesus and Israel's Traditions*, 15.
113. Bryan, *Jesus and Israel's Traditions*, 15. Wright is acquainted with the arguments here; see *Paul and the Faithfulness of God*, 160–62.
114. Wright, *Paul and the Faithfulness of God*, 159n332.
115. Texts like 4 Ezra (see Wright, *Paul and the Faithfulness of God*, 156) are not discussed here since they are written after the devastation of the temple in AD 70. As a result, a new age of exile was launched.
116. Cf. Seifrid, "Blind Alleys," 87. He writes with more caution: "More precisely stated: the early Jewish tradition of an extended period of exile for Israel is more complicated than recent advocates of this perspective often have taken into account. Dissatisfaction with the condition of Jerusalem and the Temple is not precisely the same as the theme of a continuing exile. And to view the exile as in some sense continuing is not the same as regarding 'all' of Israel as being in exile or estranged from God."

Paul and His Pharisaic Past

All things considered, the theory of an ongoing exile is not to be assumed as Jewish background for the interpretation of the New Testament. As it happens, the Gospel of Matthew begins with the genealogy of Jesus, where the author makes a clear distinction between the age before and after the exile to Babylon (1:11–12, 17), a kind of prelude that acts as a fitting introduction to the other canonical books. That is an important lesson to be learned from it!

Once, Paul, as a devout Pharisee, did not think of himself as living in exile because of his own fault or as a result of the guilt of all Israel. He returned from the Diaspora to Jerusalem in his youth. In addition, he regarded his former practice of the law as "blameless" (Phil. 3:6). There is no hint that he felt culpable. Paul was one of the best and advanced in self-righteousness, beyond many others (Gal. 1:14). Further, his declaration of "the earthly Jerusalem being enslaved with her children" does not derive from the ongoing Roman occupation but rather is a consequence of Israel's failure to believe the gospel (Gal. 4:25). In Romans 9–11, it rather seems that a new exile has begun (or shortly will begin) in Israel's unbelief![117] It is well known that this prediction was fulfilled in concrete history through the fall of Jerusalem in AD 66–70 (cf. also the later revolt in AD 132–135).

There is no reason to dwell further on details in the Pauline letters. To state the obvious: the idea of Israel still living in exile fails to carry conviction. Accordingly, it is not to be taken for granted in the reading of the New Testament on the whole. A more comprehensive exegesis of certain features, particularly in Galatians and Romans, confirms that such is the case.

Concluding Remarks on Wright

As usual among the proponents of the New Perspective, Wright rejects the notion of the "introspective conscience" in Pauline thinking. Paul did not struggle with an anguished mind and spirit before his conversion. Rather, he and all Israel have lamented their corporate failures. This is what the theory of the ongoing exile implies. Conversely, the proclaiming of the gospel is the difference; it insists that the end of the exile has already arrived in Jesus's cross and resurrection.[118]

In truth, to shift from speaking of the burden of personal guilt to that of the nation is a mere variation on an older theme. It represents no real movement away from psychologism. "The Paul of the introspective conscience is ushered out the door," whereas "the Paul of the social conscience is welcomed in." Oddly, "an early twentieth-century existentialist Paul is replaced by a late twentieth-century Paul disturbed by the malaise of the world."[119]

---

117. Mark A. Seifrid, *Christ, Our Righteousness: Paul's Theology of Justification*, NSBT 9 (Downers Grove, IL: InterVarsity Press, 2000), 21–25.
118. Wright, *People of God*, 268–79. See the well-known article by Krister Stendahl, "The Apostle Paul and the Introspective Conscience of the West," *HTR* 56, no. 3 (1963): 199–215.
119. Seifrid, "Blind Alleys," 90–91. See also Seifrid, *Christ, Our Righteousness*, 22.

Even worse, the compulsive need to explain the majority of the Jewish texts through the category of the ongoing exile characterizes the kind of interpretation that is to a great extent artificial, as if practically the whole Jewish religion simply was an abject fiasco and in dire need of the reparation kit of the arising Christianity. Wright pushes through his theory whenever he thinks it feasible. When not, then he speaks of *exceptions*. Alternatively, he speaks of a double return from exile, underlining that the first one is not a *true* one. In addition, he confuses the idea of exile with that of the Diaspora, the bondage of Israel, and the nonrestoration of Israel. Finally, he asserts that he has confirmed his main thesis as much as possible: since Israel lives in exile, she has failed.

Surprisingly, Wright's new perspective is increasingly coming to resemble the outdated old perspective. The common denominator is the exaggerated proclivity to represent the Jewish religion as a failure that paves the way for the definite triumph of Christianity. Previously, the focus was laid on works righteousness (with basically no sense for God's grace). This time, the emphasis is placed on the life in exile (with principally no sense for any relief). In both cases, a flagrant distortion of the facts follows.[120]

It is no longer possible to discuss Wright's interpretation of the Pauline doctrine of justification. In part, it seems to be determined by his theory of Israel still being in exile. At least some anomalies in his overall thinking are easier to overcome on that basis. For instance, he affirms that justification first and foremost is a declaration of status ("you are already in") but not ultimately a declaration of entrance ("welcome in"), as if the question concerns living in the Promised Land or outside it.[121] Likewise, Wright asserts that justification is twofold and presupposes "the work of the Spirit," as if he is thinking of the new life in the Promised Land, including the readiness to accomplish basic obligations in various conditions and circumstances therein. Moreover, Wright speaks of future justification and maintains that it is on account of the entire life, as if he is imagining a continued existence in the Promised Land.[122]

In any case, the cornerstone of Wright's theological position is his well-known theory of the ongoing exile. The floundering of his main thesis together with the critical remarks against his interpretation of "works of the law" as "badges of identity" and his

---

120. Wright refers frequently to Odil Hannes Steck, *Israel und das gewaltsame Geschick der Propheten: Untersuchungen zur Überlieferung des deuteronomistischen Geschichtsbildes im Alten Testament, Spätjudentum und Urchristentum*, WMANT 23 (Neukirchen-Vluyn: Neukirchener Verlag 1967). Wright notes, "The fundamental study for this remains that of O. H. Steck, and I suspect from some of the reactions to further presentations of the theme that his work has remained unread." *Paul and the Faithfulness of God*, 139. But does Steck's notion of an ongoing exile in the end represent the *old* perspective on Judaism, something that Wright uncritically has adopted? Steck writes in his book, "Die Gegenwart ist bestimmt von der Andauer des Gerichts, von der Andauer der Schuld des Volkes und von Umkehr und Gesetzesgehorsam als dem einzig möglichen Weg zu Jahwe"; (203) and, "Muss es darum auch immer Verkündigung gegeben haben, die sich auf das vorfindliche Israel im ganzen richtete, es zur Umkehr aufrief, zum Gehorsam mahnte und darüber belehrte, was der Gebotswille Gottes ist. Entsprechend sind wir [. . .] immer wieder auf den Vorgang solcher Umkehrpredigt und Gesetzesbelehrung im Volk gestossen." *Israel und das gewaltsame Geschick der Propheten*, 203, 215–16. Similar passages are to be found also elsewhere. They outline the central thesis of the whole book (cf. 64–80). See also Odil Hannes Steck, "Das Problem theologischer Strömungen in nachexilischer Zeit," *EvT* 28, no. 9 (1968): 445–58.
121. Wright, *What Saint Paul Really Said*, 139, 157.
122. Wright, *What Saint Paul Really Said*, 128–30, 159–79. See also Wright, *Justification: God's Plan and God's Vision* (London: SPCK, 2009), 122–24, 158–68. It is in this light that I understand what Seifrid wrote to me in an email dated April 24, 2017: "I do think that there is a subtle connection between 'return from exile' and Wright's conception of justification—and his eschatology: it pictures redemption in terms of the transformation of the present world and opens the door to the minimizing of the final judgment that appears in Wright's thought."

neglect of synergistic propensities in Judaism—all this calls into question the credibility of his overall view.

John M. G. Barclay
Diverse Graces—Different Meanings

Recently, John M. G. Barclay has made an important contribution to the present-day debate. He has studied the occurrence and meaning of the different words for *gift* in the sociopolitical context of the Greco-Roman and Jewish frames of reference. Within that wider perspective, he then situates the Pauline teaching on grace. His thorough exegetical analyses provide the basis for a taxonomy of theologies of God's mercy.[123]

Barclay suggests that *gift* can be "perfected" (or drawn out into some essential or ultimate form) in a number of ways. He enumerates six perfections:

1. superabundance: the extravagance and overwhelming scale of the gift
2. singularity: the attitude of the giver as marked solely and purely by benevolence and including no punishment for evil
3. priority: the timing of the gift always before the recipient's initiative
4. incongruity: the bestowal of the gift without any regard to the worth of the recipient
5. efficacy: the impact of the gift on the nature or agency of the recipient
6. noncircularity: no expected return for the gift, no cycle of reciprocity[124]

As a result, *gift* is a polyvalent symbol. One does not necessarily have all six definitions in mind when using the word.[125] Definitely, there may be more perfections of gift. Still, no single one of them should be regarded as *conditio sine qua non*. Each has its own worth. Hence, it need not be completed by other meanings.[126] Nor is it the case that the more perfections various ancient texts have, the better off they are.[127]

Further, Barclay claims that scholars often talk past each other by sharpening and perfecting gift or grace in one way but not making any allowance for another way of sharpening and perfecting gift or grace. He does his best to avoid that kind of dichotomy, which derails academic debate from the outset. Thus, he provides a stable foundation for moving forward to an in-depth analysis of the ancient texts.[128]

In view of his methodology, Barclay's treatment has strengths and weaknesses. As a specialist in New Testament theology and a professional scholar in the academic world, he is certainly a competent judge for his case. Yet he follows a procedure that has turned out to be problematic at least since the publication of Gerhard Kittel's standard dictionary, *Theologisches Wörterbuch zum Neuen Testament*. First, the entries appeal to the

---

123. See Barclay, *Paul and the Gift*.
124. Barclay, *Paul and the Gift*, 70–75, 185–86; for the concept of "perfection," see 67–68.
125. Barclay, *Paul and the Gift*, 75–76.
126. Barclay, *Paul and the Gift*, 68–70, 76–77.
127. Barclay, *Paul and the Gift*, 69–70.
128. Barclay, *Paul and the Gift*, 67–70.

secular Greek literature, then the Old Testament as well as other Jewish sources, and finally relevant New Testament writings. This kind of reading runs the obvious risk of imposing an external model on the analysis of target texts (the canonical books), which should instead be interpreted in relation to their own defining characteristics.[129]

In the case of Barclay, he starts with some insights into cultural anthropology. Then he proceeds to the ancient Greco-Roman literature and analyzes most of it with discernment. Next, he surveys selected Jewish writings. In his inquiries, he principally concentrates on the concept of *gift* while examining the Pauline teaching on grace. Barclay works as if he is making a long entry in Kittel's *Theologisches Wörterbuch*. He paints with a broad brush and creates a canvas moving from the distant past to New Testament times, and even explores the contours of church history.[130] Yet it is questionable whether the content is rendered as accurately as possible.

The Pauline Teaching on Grace

As to the Pauline teaching on grace, Barclay particularly emphasizes the concept of incongruity but also the subjects of superabundance, priority, and efficacy.[131] His argument appears predominantly sound, so there is no need to go into the details. However, it seems that none of his six perfections of *gift* in truth depicts the Pauline notion of *grace*. Barclay himself properly delineates the exceptional understanding of God's mercy primarily in Romans and Galatians. His exegetical analysis is helpful in its basic outline. He affirms that "grace effects a new reality." It is "no ordinary existence, but the product of an impossibility, the resurrection of Christ." Hence, it is "a life whose source lies outside of themselves [Christians], the life of the risen Christ." In other words, it "is not some reformation of the self, or some newly discovered technique in self-mastery." On the contrary, it is rather an "eccentric" phenomenon or an "extrinsic" incident.[132] Further, it "is permanently at odds with the natural (post-Adamic) condition of the human being," no matter how much some Christians "may (and should) grow in holiness." Their inner "capacity depends on a transformation of the self or, better, a *new* self, derived from the risen Christ."[133] They do not achieve "a series of 'graces' won by increases in sanctification." Neither do they acquire a set of "competencies added to their previous capacities, nor an enhancement of their previous selves." What is given to them "is a death and the emergence from that death of a new self."[134]

In view of the Pauline definition and interpretation of God's amazing grace, all other perfections of gifts outside the new reality, present in the risen Christ alone, fall short since they actually do not alter the human conditions and circumstances radically and completely but only improve them more or less. In such cases, nothing has been changed

---

129. See *Theologisches Wörterbuch zum Neuen Testament I–X/2*, ed. Gerhard Kittel (Stuttgart: Kohlhammer, 1933–1979).
130. Cf. Barclay's definition of his task in *Paul and the Gift*, 77–78.
131. Barclay, *Paul and the Gift*, 569.
132. Barclay, *Paul and the Gift*, 500–501.
133. Barclay, *Paul and the Gift*, 503.
134. Barclay, *Paul and the Gift*, 518.

ultimately, even though there are improvements of different kinds. No real transformation has taken place. The old life and the old being are still the same in the midst of religious reformation agendas and programs. Thus, a general divine benevolence, discovered in the many-faceted forms of gifts, does not make any difference. It does not amount precisely to the special divine grace as substantiated in Pauline theology. This general divine benevolence and special divine grace are not strictly on a par with each other. The soteriological focus moves from the reparation of the old self in the former case to the rebirth of the new self in the latter case. For that reason, the gift in Greco-Roman culture can never replace God's grace in Pauline theology, which alone brings forth a totally new existence in contrast to the conventional old way of being and living.

The transformation of reality is centered on the "Christ event" (his death and resurrection), not elsewhere, irrespective of how much talk there is about a general divine benevolence. Once again in line with Barclay, it is apparently neither about "a narrative progression in human history" nor "an additional chapter in a developing human story." It is "no process of maturation," nor any series of "preceding epochs of human history," but more accurately "the *reversal* of previous human conditions." It "represents not continuity, but interruption," even "miracle," indeed, "a new creation in the midst of the present evil age."[135] In brief, it is an "impossibility"[136] that surprisingly turns into a possibility and reality. Hence, it is "not a goal yet to be attained or a favor yet to be gained from God."[137] It already exists in the risen Lord.

On the whole, after having dusted down the fundamentals and distinctive understanding of grace in Pauline theology, Barclay astonishingly concludes as follows:

> It would be a mistake to regard the incongruity of grace as ubiquitous in Judaism, but equally wrong to consider this notion uniquely Pauline. Paul's is one Jewish voice in a chorus of divergent opinions, distinctive in certain respects, but not qualitatively or quantitatively *more distinct* than the voices of other Jews. Paul stands *among* fellow Jews in his discussion of divine grace, not *apart from* them in a unique or antithetical position.[138]

This quotation shows a blatant non sequitur compared with what Barclay in his exegetical analysis has brought forward. Here the nonbiblical taxonomy of *gift* is imposed on the understanding of *grace* in Pauline theology, and the meaning of grace is reduced to one sense of gift, namely, that of incongruity. The conclusion is neither justified nor substantiated in any way. The evidence points in another direction: none of the six perfections of gift encompasses the Pauline definition of grace. This absolutely ruins the entire taxonomy used by Barclay in his investigation. But he still remains stuck in his own categories, without perceiving that they do not work in the soteriological matrix of Romans and Galatians. The methodological flaw like that in Kittel's *Theologisches*

---
135. Barclay, *Paul and the Gift*, 412–13.
136. Barclay, *Paul and the Gift*, 421.
137. Barclay, *Paul and the Gift*, 446.
138. Barclay, *Paul and the Gift*, 565.

Wörterbuch has caught up with him. To repeat, not even the incongruous perfection of the gift as recognized in the sociopolitical context of the Greco-Roman and Jewish frames of reference does justice to the Pauline concept of grace, which assumes a totally new reality extrinsic to special human efforts and general divine benevolences.

By and large, the necessity of a totally new reality in the risen Christ makes all the definitions or perfections of gifts to depend on human cooperation, notwithstanding many-faceted divine benevolences. Therefore, the Pauline understanding of grace really makes the difference. It does not fit into a straitjacket of modern exegetical taxonomy taken from the sociopolitical context of the Greco-Roman and Jewish culture. Barclay admits that the idea of "pure gift" is a late interpretation. He does not find any traces of it in his ancient texts.[139] That may be right. (I have to leave it to the experts to resolve.) But at least the notion of "pure *grace*" does occur as an essential element in Pauline theology. It takes the form of a new creation, an extrinsic existence in the risen Christ. As such, it is absolutely independent of any human efforts, even though a response certainly is expected or intended in return.

Oddly, it seems that Barclay's taxonomy of perfections of gifts does not have any sense for synergism in a soteriological setting. At the very least, he intentionally circumvents that kind of speech.[140] Instead, everything is labeled as a perfection of God's grace. The obvious methodological tendency of Barclay sticks out especially in the question of the Pelagian controversy. He asserts that both Augustine and Pelagius (and those in favor of his position) agree "in their emphasis on the priority of grace."[141] The latter "clearly believed in the *priority* and *superabundance* of grace."[142] However, the former insisted on the *priority*, *incongruity*, and *efficacy* of grace.[143] Thus, the controversy between them was in fact about different perfections of grace. The traditional question of synergism is conspicuous by its absence. Moreover, there is no clear-cut explanation for the shift of the focus.[144] To be sure, old theological disputes are open to modern and fresh interpretations. That in itself is a good thing. But how can it be that Pelagius and his spiritual followers, who were declared heretics (by the First Council of Ephesus in 431) on account of their synergism, are unexpectedly the ones who have "perfected" God's grace in their own way? Why condemn them at all, then? It seems, at the least, that Barclay owes a clarification to his readers. He does not pursue his investigation through to the end.

Even so, Barclay's clear statement of the impossibility of the "pure gift" is evidence for the synergistic thinking that permeates Greco-Roman and Jewish theology, something that he repeatedly shows in his analysis. In this respect, he fully agrees with the other main proponents of the New Perspective, particularly with Sanders, Dunn, and

---

139. Barclay, *Paul and the Gift*, 59–63, 66.
140. Quite strangely, it seems that Barclay only addresses the issue of synergism by criticizing me and others for making use of "the terminology of the Reformation tradition." Barclay, *Paul and the Gift*, 168–69.
141. Barclay, *Paul and the Gift*, 92.
142. Barclay, *Paul and the Gift*, 93.
143. Barclay, *Paul and the Gift*, 97.
144. Barclay, *Paul and the Gift*, 92–97.

Wright. Despite all the differences in their overall positions, they share at least one common denominator: they take for granted that the Jewish soteriology without a doubt indicates a strong synergistic feature. On the other hand, the Pauline understanding of divine grace radically differs from that kind of tendency. It is not based on human efforts or cooperation (as already recurrently recognized above). Salvation is found in the risen Lord, in a reality called into being through the gospel, in an existence extrinsic to oneself. In brief, it is an impossible possibility, an exceptional life, where truly "I no longer live, but Christ lives in me" (Gal. 2:20). As a result, it necessarily ushers in a breakdown of the Jewish soteriology.[145]

Beyond the New Perspective?

In his conclusions, Barclay regards his special contribution as going beyond the New Perspective, in other words, as "a reconfiguration of 'the new perspective,' placing its best historical and exegetical insights within the frame of Paul's theology of grace."[146] His analysis of "works of the law," a central issue in Pauline theology and absolutely decisive for the overall view of Dunn and Wright, as already shown above, serves particularly well as a test case for his self-evaluation.

Right from the outset, Barclay emphasizes that works of the law refer to the practice of the Jewish law. The expression is, for certain, Pauline shorthand. It echoes the scriptural commands to "do" the Torah.[147] But even so, "what is significant is not the bare fact of practices (and thus not 'works' as such) but that they derive from, and are oriented to, the Torah." Palpably, the Gentile mission threw some works into special relief (e.g., circumcision and dietary regulations). Yet "there is no reason to restrict the referent of ἔργα νόμου" principally to "those rules that created boundaries between Jews and Gentiles (*pace* Dunn)." Rather, "the issue is the validity of the Torah" in defining and establishing righteousness. Then, "it becomes clear" that the real question is about "the practice of the Torah as though it were the authoritative cultural frame of the good news."[148]

Despite his stout criticism of works as mere "identity markers," Barclay still shares Dunn's conviction that the major shift in the interpretation of ἔργα νόμου "may be traced in the deutero-Pauline letters, where works are refocused as moral achievements" (Eph. 2:8–10; 2 Tim. 1:9; Titus 3:5).[149] Neither does boasting indicate "the

---

145. To be sure, "Paul does not have to play the agency of the believer off against the agency of Christ / the Spirit," and "God's grace does not exclude, deny, or displace believing agents; they are not reduced to passivity or pure receptivity." Barclay, *Paul and the Gift*, 518, 519; cf. 503n17. Nevertheless, it is true that Paul lives only because Christ lives in him (Gal. 2:20) or that he lives together with Christ only after having been put to death together with him (Rom. 6:4). In this sense, the real agent is indeed Christ (*pace* Barclay). See Laato, *Paulus und das Judentum*, 199–204; Laato, *Paul and Judaism*, 158–62.
146. Barclay, *Paul and the Gift*, 573. On the other hand, Barclay regards his special input "as a re-contextualization of the Augustinian-Lutheran tradition, returning the dynamic of the incongruity of grace to its original environment where it accompanied the formation of new communities." *Paul and the Gift*, 573.
147. Barclay, *Paul and the Gift*, 373–74.
148. Barclay, *Paul and the Gift*, 374; see also 444, 567–68.
149. Barclay, *Paul and the Gift*, 571. Earlier, Barclay makes the following clarification: "What changes is not that a specific Pauline rule ('works of the Law') becomes generalized as 'works,' but that Paul's critique of the *criteria* of worth being applied in the formation of the community becomes a critique of the *achievement* of worth whose criteria, in an established Christian tradition, are themselves unproblematic." *Paul and the Gift*, 546n57.

cultural confidence of the Jew in the Torah (or of the Greek in wisdom), but pride in achievement" (Eph. 2:9).[150] Concisely, the previous apostolic missionary theology is now "turned inwards."[151]

Principally, Barclay's critique of the practice of the Torah as "the authoritative cultural frame of the good news" derives from his downplaying of synergism in the Jewish soteriology. *Therefore*, he has to find out some other reasons for the apostolic disapproval of works of the law. Despite the fact that he explains his reading of the Pauline texts at length, the exact meaning of his interpretation remains vague. It leaves the impression of unnecessary hairsplitting. In the end, how precisely does Barclay come to his conclusion that works of the law express "the authoritative cultural frame of the good news" and should be discarded for that very reason? Elsewhere, I have argued that Paul in Galatians raises the requirement of not only a quantitatively but even a qualitatively impeccable law observance.[152] Thus, he "maintains that those who rely on works of the law fail to do the works of the law!"[153] The question is simply about works as such. Accordingly, the severe denunciation is leveled against synergism in so-called covenantal nomism.[154]

Evidently, there is no alteration of the interpretation in the allegedly deutero-Pauline letters. The line of thought is similar everywhere in *corpus Paulinum*. For instance, Ephesians 2:8–10 summarizes the theological substance in Romans and Galatians. It remains unmistakable that works of the law stand for every kind of human striving and yearning in a soteriological context. It follows that Barclay's analysis here fails to carry conviction.

Summary

All in all, considering soteriological issues, the most popular advocates of the New Perspective to a large extent ignore the principal importance of anthropology in that context. To be sure, they do agree and admit that Judaism is synergistic. Yet they try to downplay that observation one way or another. This is true in the cases of E. P. Sanders, James D. G. Dunn, N. T. Wright, and John M. G. Barclay.

It seems that strong synergistic facets in Judaism are regarded as problematic because they easily explain why Paul disregarded his former Pharisaic past. As a result, many alternative ways of expounding his conversion, advocated by the representatives of the New Perspective, fail to carry conviction or else fall short as an overall account of it. Dunn especially raises the question of synergistic inclinations in Pauline theology but wisely rejects them in the end. Those outdated and old-fashioned (in the deepest sense, heretical) accusations hardly fit the image of the *New* Perspective.

---

150. Barclay, *Paul and the Gift*, 571.
151. Barclay, *Paul and the Gift*, 571.
152. Laato, "Paul's Anthropological Considerations," 353–59.
153. Laato, "Paul's Anthropological Considerations," 357.
154. Laato, "Paul's Anthropological Considerations," 359.

It follows that an anthropological approach is surpassed neither by a Christocentric nor by an ethnocentric reading of Pauline theology—important as these are in themselves. Works of the law are not eradicated simply for the reason that they are not based on Christ (*pace* Sanders) or that they are based on ethnic privileges (*pace*, in the first place, Dunn and Wright). On the contrary, they are abandoned because they are human efforts (for certain, not to the exclusion of divine grace) to guarantee one's own salvation. Therefore, different anthropological presuppositions lead to different soteriological conclusions. A correlation exists between them both. Paul emphasizes the necessity of becoming an entirely new creature. He promotes a life outside oneself, attained in the risen Christ alone. In view of that, all various definitions of gifts in the sociopolitical context of the Greco-Roman and Jewish culture and all divine benevolences perfected in them do not prevail. They do not actually do justice to the meaning of pure grace in Pauline theology, which stands out as a unique masterpiece in the midst of the ancient religious world (*pace* Barclay). Besides, the theory of Israel's ongoing exile as the black background of the New Testament proclamation of salvation in the risen Lord is to be rejected (*pace* Wright).

Thus, this chapter as a whole ushers in a conclusion that is stressed elsewhere but that I inevitably want to make my own:

> That Luther, to this extent at least, gets Paul "right" is part of what I intended when I once suggested, somewhat epigrammatically, that Pauline scholars can learn from the Reformer. . . . Still, one has only to read a few passages of his writings (most any will do) to realize that, in crucial respects, he inhabits the same world, and breathes the same air, as the apostle. . . . Such kindredness of spirit gives Luther an inestimable advantage over many readers of Paul in "capturing" the essence of the apostle's writings. On numerous points of detail, Luther may be the last to illumine. For those, however, who would see forest as well as trees, I am still inclined to propose a trip to the dustbins of recent Pauline scholarship—to retrieve and try out, on a reading of the epistles, the disregarded spectacles of the Reformer.[155]

Long ago, Ernst Käsemann published an article that initiated a new quest for Jesus. The old by itself was not bad in his eyes. Actually, he went forward by going backward. Hence, he found the historical Jesus all over again. In the Reformation Jubilee year 2017, the New Perspective on Paul was forty years on (after Sanders published his book *Paul and Palestinian Judaism* in 1977). During all those years, many scholars have pointed out faults and flaws in its basic structure. What is left now? When all is said and done, the fact remains that the Jewish soteriology was synergistic despite divine benevolences and compassion in the covenantal context. To be sure, the most acknowledged advocates of the New Perspective admit it, although not showing a lot of enthusiasm for the result. Nevertheless, the breakthrough draws closer: obviously, the strong synergism of Jewish soteriology launched the morbid reproach especially in

---

155. Westerholm, "'New Perspective' at Twenty-Five," 37–38.

Romans and Galatians (the denunciation of works of the law). If so much is agreed on, then, the longed-for new quest for Paul is about to begin.

Recommended Resources

Barclay, John M. G. *Paul and the Gift*. Grand Rapids, MI: Eerdmans, 2015.

Dunn, James D. G. "The New Perspective: Whence, What, Whither?" In *The New Perspective on Paul: Collected Essays*, 1–88. Tübingen: Mohr Siebeck, 2005.

Laato, Timo. "'God's Righteousness'—Once Again." In *The Nordic Paul: Finnish Approaches to Pauline Theology*, edited by Lars Aejmelaeus and Antti Mustakallio, 40–73. Library of New Testament Studies 374. London: T&T Clark, 2008.

———. *Paul and Judaism: An Anthropological Approach*. Translated by T. McElwain. South Florida Studies in the History of Judaism 115. Atlanta: Scholars Press, 1995.

———. "Paul's Anthropological Considerations: Two Problems." In *Justification and Variegated Nomism*. Vol. 2, *The Paradoxes of Paul*, edited by D. A. Carson, Peter T. O'Brien, and Mark A. Seifrid, 343–59. Wissenschaftliche Untersuchungen zum Neuen Testament, 2nd ser., vol. 181. Grand Rapids, MI: Baker Academic, 2004.

Sanders, E. P. *Paul and Palestinian Judaism: A Comparison of Patterns of Religion*. Minneapolis: Fortress, 1977.

———. *Paul, the Law, and the Jewish People*. Philadelphia: Fortress, 1983.

Seifrid, Mark A. "Blind Alleys in the Controversy over the Paul of History." *Tyndale Bulletin* 45, no. 1 (1994): 73–95.

———. *Christ, Our Righteousness: Paul's Theology of Justification*. New Studies in Biblical Theology 9. Downers Grove, IL: InterVarsity Press, 2000.

Westerholm, Stephen. "Finnish Contributions to the Debate on Paul and the Law." In *The Nordic Paul: Finnish Approaches to Pauline Theology*, edited by Lars Aejmelaeus and Antti Mustakallio, 3–15. Library of New Testament Studies 374. London: T&T Clark, 2008.

———. "Paul's Anthropological 'Pessimism' in Its Jewish Context." In *Divine and Human Agency in Paul and His Cultural Environment*, edited by John M. G. Barclay and Simon J. Gathercole, 71–98. London: T&T Clark, 2008.

Wright, N. T. *Paul and the Faithfulness of God*. London: SPCK, 2013.

10

What's Next?

Justification after the New Perspective

DAVID A. SHAW

In many respects, the study of Paul's theology over the past century consists of a series of footnotes to Albert Schweitzer and his *Mysticism of the Apostle Paul*.[1] The family tree that develops beneath this patriarch is diverse, and the Schweitzer family likeness emerges in different ways through different family lines, but all his children have learned from him a certain way of framing key questions about Paul's theology and justification's place within it. As a consequence, the best way to understand justification in the present is to study the past. To begin, we consider Schweitzer's critique of the traditional reading of justification. We can then briefly see how the New Perspective develops as one offspring of that critique before focusing our attention on a rival sibling to the New Perspective—what's known as the *apocalyptic* reading of Paul.[2]

Schweitzer's Account of Justification

One of Albert Schweitzer's enduring legacies is his insistence that Paul be interpreted against a Jewish background—more specifically, against the backdrop of Jewish eschatology. For Schweitzer, as for William Wrede before him, this has a significant impact on Paul's account of the human plight: "The natural world is, in the eschatological view, characterised not only by its transience, but by the fact that demons and angels

---

1. Albert Schweitzer, *The Mysticism of Paul the Apostle*, trans. William Montgomery (London: A&C Black, 1931).
2. The New Perspective is addressed in chap. 9, by Timo Laato, of this volume. Hence, our discussion will be brief, but the interaction between Schweitzer's offspring is significant and illuminating.

exercise power in it."[3] As to the solution, at its most general level, eschatological redemption consists in the Messiah putting an end to the dominion of angels by a future act of judgment. Although Paul has inherited this expectation and expresses it in various places, Schweitzer argues that this is not his preferred mode of speaking about redemption. Rather than look at the solution from the outside (evil powers are now defeated), Paul prefers to look at it from within (the elect are now in mystical union with Christ).

One of the attractions of this approach for Schweitzer's Paul is that it solves the puzzle of why, contrary to the eschatological worldview, the new age has not visibly dawned, even though a resurrection has occurred. The answer is not to reject the eschatological premise: "If Jesus has risen, that means, for those who dare to think consistently, that it is now already the supernatural age."[4] But how can that be when to all appearances the world is unchanged? The answer is that as a theater's stage scenery is transformed behind a curtain, so now "behind the apparently immobile outward show of the natural world, its transformation into the supernatural was in progress."[5]

For the believer, by virtue of being in Christ, there is liberation from those powers and an experience of the age to come. Schweitzer produces Galatians as a witness to this view:

> In the Epistle to the Galatians . . . it is not a question of an atonement made to God through Christ, but a most skilfully planned foray made by Christ against the Angel-powers, by means of which He frees those who are languishing under the Law (Gal 4:5) and so brings about "the Coming of faith" (Gal 3:25).[6]

Romans sits less comfortably in Schweitzer's scheme, however, for Romans 2:11–4:25 dispenses with "all speculations about the Law and the dominion of the Angel-powers" and derives a plight solely from "the nature of Law and in the nature of man."[7] The result is an account of salvation that is regrettably *individualistich* ("individualistic") and *unkosmisch* ("uncosmic").[8] More remarkably still, though, Schweitzer is not simply pitting Galatians against Romans:

> In the Epistle to the Romans an amazing thing happens, that, after the new righteousness has been presented at length as coming from faith in Christ's atoning sacrifice (Rom 3:1–5:21), it is explained a second time, without any reference whatever to the previous exposition, as founded on the mystical dying and rising again with Christ (Rom 6:1–8:1). To the presence of these two independent expositions of the same

---

3. Schweitzer, *Mysticism of Paul the Apostle*, 57. Cf. William Wrede, who traces two aspects to the human plight. First, "men are here under the domination of dark and evil powers. The chief of these are the 'flesh,' sin, the Law, and death." But second, "the picture is supplemented by a view taken from a particular standpoint. Paul believes that mankind is under the sway of mighty spirits, demons, and angelic powers." *Paul*, trans. Edward Lummis (London: P. Green, 1907), 92, 95.
4. Schweitzer, *Mysticism of Paul the Apostle*, 98.
5. Schweitzer, *Mysticism of Paul the Apostle*, 99.
6. Schweitzer, *Mysticism of Paul the Apostle*, 212.
7. Schweitzer, *Mysticism of Paul the Apostle*, 212.
8. Schweitzer, *Mysticism of Paul the Apostle*, 219.

question is due the confusing impression which the Epistle to the Romans always makes upon the reader.[9]

What motivates Schweitzer to insist that Romans 1–5 is incommensurate with 6–8? In part, he has a methodological taste for antitheses: "Progress always consists in taking one or other of two alternatives, in abandoning the attempt to combine them."[10] Additionally, Schweitzer is determined to make Paul seem strange. He is rightly unimpressed by accounts of Paul that recreate him in the image of the Enlightenment, and a dark and demonic eschatological backdrop will certainly alienate Paul from his latter-day champions. But Schweitzer also intends to develop a critique of the traditional reading of justification that still reverberates today.

First, as noted above, he complains that it is individualistic rather than cosmic in its scope. Here Schweitzer reflects a growing criticism of the Reformation's legacy, wherein "the soul-strivings of Luther have stood as model for the portrait of Paul."[11]

Second, Schweitzer would have us note that Paul's account of justification in the early chapters of Romans is designed to argue for the freedom of his Gentile converts from the law. At the very least, that seems to imply that the doctrine has quite a specific purview and is limited to only a few sections of Paul's letters, where the legitimacy or safety of his Gentile churches is at stake. Additionally, Schweitzer argues that Paul's defense of those churches reflects this polemical and occasional character. Paul's argument cannot proceed "by straightforward logic" and so requires some creative handling of Old Testament texts and generates a number of self-contradictions and problems.

Third, one of the chief problems Paul generates for himself relates to ethics: "Paul arrives at the idea of a faith that rejects not only the works of the Law, but works in general. He thus closes the pathway to a theory of ethics."[12] This is one of the chief proofs for Schweitzer that the doctrine of justification by faith is occasional. He himself is not troubled by that, of course, because he sees the heart of Paul's theology elsewhere, in his mysticism.

Taken together, then, these are grounds on which Schweitzer famously declares that "the doctrine of righteousness by faith is . . . a subsidiary crater, which has formed within the rim of the main crater—the mystical doctrine of redemption through the being-in-Christ."[13]

---

9. Schweitzer, *Mysticism of Paul the Apostle*, 226. Within the late nineteenth- and early twentieth-century setting, Schweitzer is not alone in discerning competing soteriological models in Paul and refusing to attempt a synthesis. See also Eduard Reuss, *Histoire de la Théologie Chrétienne au Siècle Apostolique*, vol. 2, 3rd ed. (Paris: Treuttel et Wurtz, 1864); Hermann Lüdemann, *Die Anthropologie des Apostels Paulus und ihre Stellung innerhalb seiner Heilslehre: Nach den vier Hauptbriefen* (Kiel: Universitäts-Buchhandlung, 1872).
10. Albert Schweitzer, *The Quest of the Historical Jesus*, ed. John Bowden (London: SCM, 2000), 198.
11. Wrede, *Paul*, 146.
12. Schweitzer, *Mysticism of Paul the Apostle*, 225.
13. Schweitzer, *Mysticism of Paul the Apostle*, 225. Cf. Wrede's dismissal of justification by faith: "The Reformation has accustomed us to look upon this as the central point of Pauline doctrine; but it is not so. In fact the whole Pauline religion can be expounded without a word being said about this doctrine, unless it be the part devoted to the Law. It would be extraordinary if what was intended to be the chief doctrine were referred to only in a minority of the epistles. That is the case with this doctrine: it only appears where Paul is dealing with the strife against Judaism. And this fact indicates the real significance of the doctrine. It is the *polemical doctrine* of Paul, is only made intelligible by the struggle of his life, his controversy with Judaism and Jewish Christianity, and is only intended for this." *Paul*, 122–23.

The New Perspective

Our survey of Schweitzer demonstrates that in some respects the New Perspective was never all that new. When E. P. Sanders discussed Paul's own theology, he arrived at very similar conclusions:

> "Righteousness by faith" is the heuristic category employed by Paul against the notion that obedience to the Law is necessary. We should repeat here the observation that "righteousness by faith" receives very little positive working out by Paul. It does not lead to ethics.[14]

Likewise, he thought that Romans 1–4 represented an ad hoc and self-contradictory rationalization for a law-free gospel mission and found the heart of Paul's theology elsewhere, in "eschatological participation" (Sanders's more helpful gloss of Schweitzer's "mysticism"). Sanders, therefore, was happy to leave justification languishing on the periphery of Paul's thought. It is polemical and therefore peripheral. It was James D. G. Dunn and N. T. Wright, however, who innovated, arguing that justification by faith is polemical and therefore central. Paul, after all, is the apostle to the Gentiles, and so his argument concerning the means by which Gentiles take their place with the people of God might well be close to the heart of his mission-minded theology.

The stage was set, therefore, for justification to make its return, but two factors would deny it access in its traditional form. First, Schweitzer's critique of the individualism associated with the Reformation reading still stood and had been influentially developed by Krister Stendahl's famous essay "The Apostle Paul and the Introspective Conscience of the West."[15] Second, Sanders's analysis of Second Temple Judaism was adopted by Dunn and Wright, such that Paul's polemic could not be read in opposition to a view of salvation by works. In light of these two pressures, justification underwent some significant changes. It became the doctrine that urges unity between Jew and Gentile on the basis that faith, rather than other badges, marks out God's people. For Wright especially, δικαιοσύνη speaks of God's *covenant faithfulness*; used in relation to humans, it means *covenant membership*—something now marked out by faith in Jesus as Lord. Thus, justification became primarily corporate and ecclesiological rather than individualistic and soteriological.[16] Justification also took a certain ethical and ecumenical flavor—addressing a late twentieth-century context with its concern for inclusivity across ethnic, social, and denominational divides.

To sum up, then, we have just described the way in which a traditional reading of justification has been pushed to the edge of Paul's theology. For as long as it retains its

---

14. E. P. Sanders, *Paul and Palestinian Judaism: A Comparison of Patterns of Religion* (London: SCM, 1977), 492. Sanders was also reacting against an increasingly individualistic and existential reading of Paul, which better deserves the strictures that Wrede and Schweitzer address to the Reformed tradition in general. It cannot be underestimated how much the New Perspective was a reaction against the ahistorical existentialism (and anti-Semitic trajectories) of Rudolph Bultmann and his pupils.
15. Krister Stendahl, "The Apostle Paul and the Introspective Conscience of the West," *HTR* 56, no. 3 (1963): 199–215.
16. I use the word *primarily* with care. Early expressions of the New Perspective were more antithetical (justification as ecclesiological *and not* soteriological). More recently, ecclesiology is taken to be the dominant but not exclusive note.

traditional meaning, it must remain there, but we have seen that by allowing itself to undergo some redefinition, it can find its way back to the center. That has been its experience under the New Perspective, and it is a pattern repeated in another line that descends from Schweitzer, the *apocalyptic* reading of Paul. This approach builds on Schweitzer's reading of Paul (and his critique of justification) and allows only a very drastically redefined version of justification back in (reframed as *rectification* or *deliverance*).

Justification after the New Perspective: An Apocalyptic Either/Or

A powerful argument can be made that the most important movement in twentieth-century New Testament theology was what Klaus Koch called "the recovery of apocalyptic." This rediscovery of apocalyptic theology in our time is in the process of reshaping our understanding of the cross.[17]

The apocalyptic reading of Paul, much like the New Perspective, is no one thing. The thought that Paul is an apocalyptic theologian really emerges in the work of Ernst Käsemann and for a number of reasons. In part, he was engaged in a history-of-religions quest for the background of Paul's ideas. The notion that a gnostic Redeemer myth lay behind Paul's Christology had been discredited, and so Schweitzer's argument that Jewish eschatology was the proper context in which to understand Paul was reprised.[18] In that sense, as Käsemann famously declared, "Apocalyptic was the mother of all Christian theology."[19] At the same time, Käsemann embraced the language of apocalyptic to put some distance between himself and his mentor Rudolf Bultmann. Profoundly shaped by his experience of Nazi Germany, Käsemann was determined to undermine a form of German Christian pietism that had chosen not to speak out against Hitler. For that reason, he commandeered apocalyptic to describe a future hope that ought to shake people free from the grip of the world and also a cosmic horizon that confronts the world with its Creator and his claim on their lives. Hence, with reference to the latter, the apocalyptic question is "To whom does the sovereignty of the world belong?"[20]

For all that, Käsemann remains true to his Lutheran roots in important ways. He conceives of the cosmological drama as one in which Creator and creature are locked in conflict: "The Judge always comes upon the scene in conflict with human illusion. Illusion is any state which attacks the lordship of the Creator by forgetting one's creatureliness."[21]

---

17. Fleming Rutledge, *The Crucifixion: Understanding the Death of Jesus Christ* (Grand Rapids, MI: Eerdmans, 2015), 139.
18. In light of this connection, Martinus C. de Boer argues that "the understanding of Paul as an apocalyptic thinker owes most to Albert Schweitzer." "Paul and Apocalyptic Eschatology," in *The Encyclopedia of Apocalypticism*, vol. 1, *The Origins of Apocalypticism in Judaism and Christianity* (London: Continuum, 2000), 347.
19. Ernst Käsemann, *New Testament Questions of Today*, trans. W. J. Montague (London: SCM, 1969), 102.
20. Käsemann, *New Testament Questions*, 135.
21. Ernst Käsemann, *Commentary on Romans*, trans. Geoffrey W. Bromiley (Grand Rapids, MI: Eerdmans, 1980), 58. Compare Bultmann on this point, who defines sin as "man's self-powered striving to undergird his own existence in forgetfulness of his creaturely existence." *Theology of the New Testament*, trans. Kendrick Grobel (London: SCM, 1952), 1:264. One can detect the existential influence here. The way in which Käsemann and Bultmann attacked the abstract *homo religiosus* justified some of the New Perspective's protest regarding ahistorical readings of Paul, and their identification of the Jew as *homo religiosus in excelsis* was also rightly challenged.

The bursting of those creaturely illusions constitutes "the inalienable spearhead of justification because it attacks the religious person and only in so doing preserves the sense of the justification of the ungodly."[22] Therefore, justification by faith is the answer to Käsemann's apocalyptic question. To whom does the world belong? Answer: Not you, mere creature!

There are quirks here, to be sure, but there is not yet a sense in which justification and apocalyptic are in conflict. That changes, however, with J. Louis Martyn, who takes up the term *apocalyptic*, self-consciously assuming Käsemann's mantle as he does so and yet setting an apocalyptic reading against justification by faith.

Martyn's Apocalyptic Paul

> Paul's view of wrong and right is thoroughly apocalyptic, in the sense that on the landscape of wrong and right there are, in addition to God and human beings, powerful actors that stand opposed to God and that enslave human beings. Setting right what is wrong proves, then, to be a drama that involves not only human beings and God, but also those enslaving powers. And since humans are fundamentally slaves, the drama in which wrong is set right does not begin with action on their part. It begins with God's militant action against all the powers that hold human beings in bondage.[23]

As one can readily tell, Schweitzer's mantle would be a better fit here, with the reference to powerful enslaving actors against which God must act for our liberation. There are also hints here of how a traditional account of justification will be thrust onto the periphery of Paul's thought. Indeed, Martyn will go further and essentially identify a traditional reading (or at least a caricature of it) with Paul's opponents. To see how that is accomplished, it is helpful to outline an argument on which Martyn depends. His doctoral student, Martinus de Boer, has argued that Jewish apocalyptic literature falls into two streams. In what de Boer calls "forensic Jewish apocalyptic eschatology,"

> things have gone wrong because human beings have wilfully rejected God, thereby bringing about death and the corruption and perversion of the world. Given this self-caused plight, God has graciously given the cursing and blessing Law as a remedy, thus placing before humanity the Two Ways, the way of death and the way of life. Human beings are accountable before the bar of the Judge. But, by one's own decision, one can accept God's Law, repent of one's sins, receive nomistic forgiveness, and be assured of eternal life.... This kind of apocalyptic eschatology is fundamental to the message of the Teachers who invaded Paul's Galatian churches.

In what de Boer calls "cosmological Jewish apocalyptic eschatology,"

> anti-God powers have managed to commence their own rule over the world, leading human beings into idolatry and thus into slavery, producing a wrong situation that

---

22. Käsemann, *Romans*, 102.
23. J. Louis Martyn, *Theological Issues in the Letters of Paul* (Edinburgh: T&T Clark, 1997), 87.

was not intended by God and that will not be long tolerated by him. For in his own time, God will inaugurate a victorious and liberating apocalyptic war against these evil powers, delivering his elect from their grasp and thus making right that which has gone wrong because of the powers' malignant machinations. This kind of apocalyptic eschatology is fundamental to Paul's letters.[24]

We ought to notice several things here. First, the either/or is constructed in such a way that a forensic account of the human plight is entwined with a Pelagian soteriology, in which humans are capable of initiating salvation. Our only other option is a liberative, nonforensic account of salvation that stresses divine initiative.[25] A more Augustinian anthropology coupled with a forensic atonement for sin initiated by God is not on the menu.[26]

Second, Paul is aligned with the latter cosmological outlook. His eschatology is cosmological and not forensic. How then does Martyn account for the forensic language that appears in his letters? In part, he exhibits a Schweitzerian preference for Galatians, where the language of redemption, slavery, and so on is frequently found. Other references to forensic language are to be explained by the realization that Paul is seeking to move his churches from forensic Jewish apocalyptic eschatology to cosmological Jewish apocalyptic eschatology. Chiefly, Martyn sees this at work in Galatians 1:4. When we read that Christ "gave himself for our sins to deliver us from the present evil age," we should detect a traditional formula in the first half, which Paul quotes "in order affirmatively to correct it by means of an additional clause," which Martyn glosses as "that he might snatch us out of the grasp of the present evil age."[27]

By such means, "justification," and the cluster of terms that traditionally attends it ("forgiveness," "atonement," "condemnation," etc.) are placed in the mouths of Jewish Christians against whom Paul sets himself. Like the New Perspective, however, Martyn is unwilling to dispense completely with Paul's language of "righteousness." And like the New Perspective, Martyn is willing to readmit it to somewhere near the center of Paul's theology but only once it has undergone some significant redefinition. For

---

24. Martyn, *Theological Issues*, 298. Note that these two quotations are Martyn's summary of de Boer's work. De Boer himself is careful to say that these are heuristic categories and that elements of both can be found in Paul. The nuance disappears in Martyn, however. The significance of de Boer's work is that he has attempted to ground the adjective *apocalyptic* in the corpus of Jewish apocalypses. The absence of that engagement has been a longstanding critique of the apocalyptic reading, but de Boer's typology has not satisfied many. See, e.g., N. T. Wright, *Paul and His Recent Interpreters: Some Contemporary Debates* (London: SPCK, 2015), 155–66.
25. Cf. de Boer: "Whereas track 1 underscores the human need for God's help and action, track 2 underscores human accountability to God for sin and its terrible consequences." "Paul and Jewish Apocalyptic Eschatology," in *Apocalyptic and the New Testament: Essays in Honor of J. Louis Martyn*, ed. Joel Marcus and Marion L. Soards, JSNTSup 24 (Sheffield: Sheffield Academic, 1989), 181.
26. This arrangement of the data becomes even more tendentious when de Boer argues that the Käsemann/Bultmann debate represents the same clash of cosmological Jewish apocalyptic eschatology and forensic Jewish apocalyptic eschatology that we find in the Pauline letters and that that mid-twentieth-century German debate is itself a template for contemporary apocalyptic readers' attempts to redress the forensic excesses of popular American evangelicalism.
27. J. Louis Martyn, *Galatians: A New Translation with Introduction and Commentary*, AB 33A (New York: Doubleday, 1997), 90. The widespread but frankly bizarre notion endures that if an author can be shown to quote traditional material, then in all likelihood he doesn't approve or endorse the sentiment as fully as he might if he had expressed it in his own words.

Martyn, that redefinition is best captured in a retranslation of δικαιοσύνη as "rectification," that is, God putting right what is wrong.[28] As we have seen, for Martyn, behind that language lies a very different account of the human plight.

Martyn's Legacy

This approach to Paul is in the ascendancy, and Martyn has inspired a number of other scholars (often known as the Union school, given Martyn's post at Union Theological Seminary in New York).[29] One of their significant developments of Martyn's work has been the effort to read Romans in similarly apocalyptic terms. All of them take inspiration from Martyn's model of reading Galatians 1:4—that is, to detect traditional language of atonement and forgiveness and argue that Paul speaks in those terms only to transcend or subvert them.

For Beverly Gaventa, Paul writes to Rome in order to evangelize them with his apocalyptic gospel, presenting the human situation from the outset as one of captivity to the powers of sin and death.[30] We are under the power of sin (Rom. 3:9). We have been handed over "to anti-god powers, chief among them Sin and Death."[31] This handing over thereby becomes "an event in God's conflict with the anti-god powers,"[32] which is the central conflict resolved by the gospel, rather than the propitiation of God's wrath toward sinful human beings. Thus, when we get to Romans 3:21–26, the significant term for Gaventa is "redemption":

> The nuance at work here is not that of ransom (i.e., the payment of a price), but of liberation, as in liberation from slavery. This view is reinforced when we observe that v. 25 refers to the passing over or "release" (almost certainly not "forgiveness") from former sins.[33]

---

28. The language of *rectification* is also adopted by Leander Keck and Richard K. Moore.
29. We focus on Beverly Gaventa, Martinus de Boer, and Douglas Campbell. For recent publications on and around this movement, see Douglas A. Campbell, *The Deliverance of God: An Apocalyptic Rereading of Justification in Paul* (Grand Rapids, MI: Eerdmans, 2009); Beverly Roberts Gaventa, ed., *Apocalyptic Paul: Cosmos and Anthropos in Romans 5–8* (Waco, TX: Baylor University Press, 2013); Joshua B. Davis and Douglas Harink, eds., *Apocalyptic and the Future of Theology: With and beyond J. Louis Martyn* (Eugene, OR: Cascade Books, 2012); David A. Shaw, "'Then I Proceeded to Where Things Were Chaotic' (1 Enoch 21:1): Mapping the Apocalyptic Landscape," in *Paul and the Apocalyptic Imagination*, ed. Ben C. Blackwell, John K. Goodrich, and Jason Maston (Minneapolis: Fortress, 2016), 23–41.
30. The capitalization of *sin* and *death* is a feature of apocalyptic readings of Paul. As to its significance, the picture is not at all clear. Several apocalyptic readers of Paul want to resist the thought that Paul's personification of sin and death (a prominent feature of Romans 5–8) is metaphorical, usually on the inadequate basis that metaphor equates to mere literary flourish. No one, however, wants to describe them as having existence as actual demonic beings. They appear to occupy a convenient middle ground—real enough to be the true object of God's hostility but flexible enough to refer to evil at a corporate or cosmic level without committing apocalyptic readers to comment on the actual existence of the demonic. This is one notable departure from Schweitzer, who drew unflinching attention to the spiritual world in Paul.
31. This reading is based on the use of the term παραδίδωμι in some contexts to mean "to turn someone or something over into the custody of another or to surrender in a military context." Contextually, however, there are no indications that the primary conflict is between God and the hostile powers. Humanity is handed over to inward corruption, not outside forces, and they are handed over as a punishment, expressing the wrath of God in the present (Rom. 1:18) and anticipating the punishment of death to come (1:32).
32. Beverly Roberts Gaventa, "God Handed Them Over: Reading Romans 1:18–32 Apocalyptically," *ABR* 53 (2005): 47–48.
33. Beverly Roberts Gaventa, "Interpreting the Death of Jesus Apocalyptically: Reconsidering Romans 8:32," in *Jesus and Paul Reconnected: Fresh Pathways into an Old Debate*, ed. Todd D. Still (Grand Rapids, MI: Eerdmans, 2007), 137. Here Gaventa relies on Douglas A. Campbell, *The Rhetoric of Righteousness in Romans 3:21–26*, JSNTSup 65 (Sheffield: JSOT Press, 1992).

Even if the opening chapters of Romans also include some reference to God's condemnation of sinful actions, Gaventa argues that Romans 5–8 enters into a deeper and truer account of the human situation, in which sin and death strut onto the cosmic stage, threatening to separate humanity from God's love, but are ultimately defeated by God, who accomplishes the universal salvation of humanity.

By contrast, and with some justification, Martinus de Boer's approach to Romans struggles to find such apocalyptic themes in Romans 1–4. For that reason, he argues that Paul is accommodating to the more traditional expectations of his audience before transitioning from forensic to cosmological categories in 5:12 and onward:

> While texts such as 8:1 and 8:33–34 indicate that forensic categories have hardly been given up or left behind, the structure and progression of Paul's argument in Romans 1–8 suggest that cosmological categories and motifs circumscribe and, to a large extent, overtake forensic categories and motifs.[34]

Most well known, however, is Douglas Campbell's work *The Deliverance of God: An Apocalyptic Rereading of Justification in Paul*. The first part of the title represents Campbell's preferred gloss for δικαιοσύνη θεοῦ—Paul's gospel announces the liberative saving work of God that delivers humanity from an Adamic condition in which sin has taken up residence. Perhaps, too, it refers to Campbell's aim: the deliverance of God from the shackles of what Campbell calls "Justification Theory."[35] The second half of the title is something of a misnomer, for the vast majority of this enormous book is devoted to an attack on the traditional reading of Paul rather than to offering a constructive and thoroughgoing rereading.[36] A lengthy quote from an earlier work captures what Campbell understands Justification Theory to involve:

> Since the Reformation and its immediate aftermath, the centre of Paul's thought has consistently been presented in terms of "justification by faith." . . . This model relies heavily on Romans, particularly the first four chapters. At the heart of this model is a transfer from one state to another, a transfer that we activate.
>
> The first state is "legalism," within which people try to work their way to heaven. It presupposes a judgment according to works and desert. But a sensitive

---

34. De Boer, "Paul and Apocalyptic Eschatology," 365. For his work on Romans, see Martinus C. de Boer, *The Defeat of Death: Apocalyptic Eschatology in 1 Corinthians 15 and Romans 5*, JSNTSup 22 (Sheffield: JSOT Press, 1988); "Paul's Mythologizing Program in Romans 5–8," in Gaventa, *Apocalyptic Paul*, 1–20. He has also continued to develop Martyn's reading of Galatians in de Boer, *Galatians: A Commentary* (Louisville: John Knox, 2011).

35. Initially, Campbell proposed three possible centers of Pauline theology: Justification by Faith (based on Romans 1–4); a form of Sanders's participatory eschatology, expanded to Pneumatologically Participatory Martyrological Eschatology (based on Romans 5–8); and Salvation History (based on Romans 9–11). Justification by Faith subsequently became Justification Theory in light of Campbell's hopes to resurrect Paul's language of justification by faith to speak of deliverance by means of Christ's faithfulness. This shift occurs between Campbell's *The Quest for Paul's Gospel: A Suggested Strategy* (London: T&T Clark, 2005) and *The Deliverance of God* (2009). To further clarify the true target of his critique, however, Justification Theory has become Forward Theory, for reasons that will become apparent. For this change and its rationale, see Douglas A. Campbell, "An Attempt to Be Understood: A Response to the Concerns of Matlock and Macaskill with the Deliverance of God," *JSNT* 34, no. 2 (2011): 162–208.

36. Strikingly, this is to the frustration of Beverly Gaventa: "Campbell's version of Paul's apocalyptic theology becomes just a little tepid. He insists on God's unilateral rescue of humanity but from what? By obsessing over the bathwater, Campbell has forgotten the baby." Gaventa, "Rescue Mission: Review of *The Deliverance of God* by Douglas A. Campbell," *The Christian Century*, May 17, 2010, http://www.christiancentury.org/reviews/2010-05/rescue-mission.

conscience soon realizes that this scheme is hopeless and that, far from obtaining salvation, it only ensures one of a certain eventual fate of eternal damnation. Repeated transgressions make one liable to the just wrath of God, which will be experienced in full on the Day of Judgment. A state of anxiety and guilt therefore ensues. But this is a good thing because this phase is essentially preparatory and is not an end in itself. At this point, the proclamation of the gospel must be greeted by great delight. If one only believes in the gospel then one is forgiven all one's various sins and is transferred to a new state of salvation. One cannot but be interested, especially in view of one's experience of the previous unsaved state, which resulted in guilt, anxiety and even terror. The transfer is effected on God's part, by a cunning piece of dual-entry accounting. The sinner's transgressions are credited or imputed to Christ on the cross, and so dealt with there. And Christ's perfect righteousness is credited to the sinner, clothing him/her with perfection (although some suggest that this second action is not strictly necessary). So God's justice is satisfied but the human transgressor is not condemned and destroyed during the process. All that is needed for the transaction to take place is faith on the part of the individual. Faith is therefore the trigger or catalyst for appropriation of salvation by the individual.[37]

As with Schweitzer and Stendahl, there is a concern over the Reformation's introspective turn and an undue emphasis on Romans 1–4. As with Martyn, de Boer, and Gaventa, there is a strong emphasis on divine initiative, over against the thought that humans can activate their salvation. If the quote above gives the impression that Campbell has declared war on a straw man, the specific charges he lays at Justification Theory's feet confirm the impression:

- In the area of theology proper, "in Justification theory the critical attribute of God is retributive justice, and this dictates in turn that any wrongdoing be appropriately punished."[38]
- In addition, Justification Theory "has no role for the Spirit, and so is not recognizably Trinitarian."[39]
- In its anthropology, "Justification theory assumes that people are rational, self-interested, ethical individuals."[40]
- In epistemological terms, Justification Theory is rationalist and inconsistent, relying first on truths revealed in natural law and then switching to special revelation. The gospel is presented to human beings who are able both to discern their plight from general revelation and to respond appropriately.
- Regarding the moral life, "Justification theory famously struggles with ethics" since it begins by launching "a scathing attack on ethical behavior."[41]

---

37. Campbell, *Quest for Paul's Gospel*, 34.
38. Campbell, *Deliverance of God*, 75.
39. Campbell, *Deliverance of God*, 184.
40. Campbell, *Deliverance of God*, 75.
41. Campbell, *Deliverance of God*, 81.

By contrast, the God of Pneumatologically Participatory Martyrological Eschatology "is inherently benevolent."[42] Human beings are in the grip of sin to the extent that they are "incapable of any such reasoning or activity."[43] It is only when believers' epistemological and ethical faculties are reconstituted by God that they can, in *a posteriori* fashion, perceive their past plight. The notable effect is that Campbell can lay claim to a more radical account of human sin and yet downplay human accountability. While commenting on Ephesians 2, Campbell argues that humanity is "not held fully (i.e., 'strongly') accountable (although neither is humanity without accountability)."[44] As Campbell acknowledges elsewhere, the mind of the flesh is hostile to God (Rom. 8:7), but that is to say that humanity "is profoundly mistaken and disoriented."[45]

Furthermore, since the soteriology of Pneumatologically Participatory Martyrological Eschatology is not limited by a person's willingness to exercise faith and is initiated by a fundamentally benevolent God, there are good reasons to believe that "God's decisive act on behalf of humanity in Christ is not likely to be qualified, limited, or inadequate."[46] This salvation, therefore, is universal.[47]

Responses to Campbell's caricatured account of Justification Theory fill the reviews of *The Deliverance of God*, so we need not delay here.[48] Likewise, Campbell's attempt to reread Romans 1:18–3:20 as Paul's satirical deconstruction of Justification Theory as proclaimed by a false teacher supposedly en route to Rome has persuaded no one, as far as I can tell.[49]

There are, however, a number of reflections on Campbell and the wider apocalyptic movement that allow us to explore the theological atmosphere in which we seek to give

---

42. Campbell, *Deliverance of God*, 75.
43. Campbell, *Deliverance of God*, 75.
44. Campbell, *Deliverance of God*, 930. The fact that this discussion comes at the very end of the book, in a section titled "Loose Ends," of which "God's wrath" is the last, seems to imply a judgment. But it also includes a significant admission: Campbell grants a secondary place for God's wrath—"directed against any situation that is evil" and "comprehensible as God's reaction against a sinful situation." Campbell, *Deliverance of God*, 929–30. We surely aren't far from Rom. 1:18–21 at this point.
45. Campbell, *Deliverance of God*, 65. In this way, the apocalyptic reading takes its place alongside the New Perspective as an attempt to exegete Paul responsibly in a post-Holocaust context. But whereas the New Perspective sought to remove the negative stereotype of Jews, the apocalyptic reading places them, along with everyone else, in a state of disorientation and therefore of diminished responsibility.
46. Douglas A. Campbell, "Christ and the Church in Paul: A 'Post–New Perspective' Account," in *Four Views on the Apostle Paul*, ed. Michael F. Bird, Counterpoints: Bible and Theology (Grand Rapids, MI: Zondervan, 2012), 20.
47. Universalism is widely held among apocalyptic readers of Paul. See, e.g., de Boer, "Paul and Apocalyptic Eschatology," 371–74; Beverly Roberts Gaventa, *Our Mother Saint Paul* (Louisville: Westminster John Knox, 2007), 152–53. For his part, Schweitzer rejected Wrede's universalism, arguing that "in Paul, salvation has no reference to mankind as a whole, but only to the elect." Schweitzer, *Paul and His Interpreters: A Critical History*, trans. William Montgomery (London: A&C Black, 1912), 169–70.
48. Pride of place goes to R. Barry Matlock, "Zeal for Paul but Not according to Knowledge: Douglas Campbell's War on 'Justification Theory,'" *JSNT* 34, no. 2 (2011): 115–49. But see also Douglas J. Moo, "Review Article: *The Deliverance of God: An Apocalyptic Rereading of Justification in Paul* by Douglas A. Campbell," *JETS* 53, no. 1 (2010): 143–50; Grant Macaskill, "Review Article: *The Deliverance of God*," *JSNT* 34, no. 2 (2011): 150–61. R. Michael Allen also defends the Reformation tradition against several of Campbell's charges; see Allen, *Justification and the Gospel: Understanding the Contexts and Controversies* (Grand Rapids, MI: Baker Academic, 2013), 42n29.
49. Campbell describes Romans 1–4 as the "citadel" of Justification Theory, "the only text in Paul where the apostle arguably sets out a theological program that is overtly prospective and foundationalist, and in a discussion that is extensive enough to launch Justification Theory." *Deliverance of God*, 528. For engagement with this proposal, see especially Robin Griffith-Jones, "Beyond Reasonable Hope of Recognition? *Prosōpopoeia* in Romans 1:18–3:8," in *Beyond Old and New Perspectives on Paul: Reflections on the Work of Douglas Campbell*, ed. Chris Tilling (Eugene, OR: Cascade Books, 2014), 161–74; Bruce Clark, "Review Article: *The Deliverance of God: An Apocalyptic Rereading of Justification in Paul* by Douglas A. Campbell," *TynBul* 64, no. 1 (2013): 55–88.

an account of justification and to explore how that might best be done. We consider a number of theological issues, but to begin, we must highlight a key methodological point, and that is to be ready to reject the premise of the question put to us.[50]

As noted above, the New Perspective was an energetic reaction against a Bultmannian reading of Paul. Much of its rhetorical momentum, however, was gained by projecting Bultmann's views back onto the whole Reformed tradition.[51] R. Michael Allen rightly chastises Campbell's apocalyptic reading of Paul on the same grounds: "One cannot read his tome without assessing that he has confused Rudolph Bultmann and classical Reformational theology."[52]

To advance the debate, then, it is vital not to accept the Schweitzerian premise of the question. We are frequently presented with an either/or choice, in which the traditional reading is caricatured, while the apocalyptic reading combines some theological strengths, chiefly raided from the Reformed tradition's cupboard, and some seriously erroneous arguments about the character of God and the nature of salvation.

Reflections

Theology Proper

In John Barclay's helpful taxonomy, Campbell insists on the *singularity* of divine grace—"the giver's sole and exclusive mode of operation is benevolence or goodness."[53] As Barclay rightly argues, this emphasis in Campbell tends toward Marcionism and is protected only by that grudging acknowledgement that God's wrath can be a response to evil. This emphasis on God's benevolence is crucial to maintain and develop, lest we live up to a caricature that sets divine attributes in tension or rank.[54] On a theological level, an appreciation of divine simplicity helps here, for it teaches us to speak of God as his attributes, rather than partaking in qualities outside himself or as composed of parts that might be played off against one another.[55] Exegetically, it is noteworthy that many of Paul's greatest appreciations of divine love come precisely in contexts of propitiation and forgiveness (Gal. 2:20; 1 Tim. 1:15; cf. Rom. 5:6–8). Put simply, a diminished view of God's wrath diminishes his love in equal measure, and to anticipate my later argument, it also cuts the nerve to ethics, for it is those who have been forgiven much who love much (a point to which we shall return). There is also a final, apologetic point to make here, since there are serious questions of theodicy involved in presenting a God of pure benevolence in a world so filled with malevolence and injustice. The promise of perfect retribution for wrongdoing, though humbling, is also deeply hopeful.

---

50. With thanks to Leo McGarry for his help on this point.
51. Endearingly, James Dunn has acknowledged fault here. See, e.g., James D. G. Dunn, "A New Perspective on the New Perspective on Paul," *EC* 4, no. 2 (2013): 157–82.
52. Allen, *Justification and the Gospel*, 43n29.
53. John M. G. Barclay, *Paul and the Gift* (Grand Rapids, MI: Eerdmans, 2015), 71.
54. Even if Campbell and Wright struggle to cite any major theologians who fall into the error of constructing a violently angry God, the caricature gains traction from somewhere.
55. See chap. 12, by Matthew Barrett, in this volume.

The Doctrine of Sin

Second is our account of sin. There is pressure from several directions here. The apocalyptic reading insists that Paul is more concerned with *sin* as an enslaving power than *sins* as specific infractions of the divine will. And as we have seen, Martyn sharply distinguishes between a two-actor drama (God and a culpable humanity) and a three-actor drama (God, enslaved humanity, and the culpable "powers").[56]

Paul's alleged preference for *sin* as opposed to *sins* is debatable, and the statistics need interrogating here. Should the citation of traditional formulae (if formulae they are) be marked down for unoriginality (e.g., 1 Cor. 15:1–3; Gal. 1:4)? What is the significance of singular and plural forms of ἁμαρτία?[57] Are disputed Pauline letters being included? Crucially, is δίκαιος language treated? As we have seen, the apocalyptic reading discounts it as traditional forensic language that Paul is stepping away from. Meanwhile, Wright has argued for some time that it is not moral but forensic and covenantal language. Clarity is desperately needed here. Given the ways in which the adjective δίκαιος and the noun δικαιοσύνη (along with their antonyms ἄδικος and ἀδικία) are deployed by Paul and set alongside terms such as ἀσέβεια, they clearly address moral behavior. To have righteousness, in this ordinary sense, is to be righteous, to do good (Rom. 3:12). To be unrighteous is to be ungodly (1:18).[58]

This is significant for both New Perspective and apocalyptic debates. Contrary to the former, questions of righteousness in Romans 1–4 should be seen to relate primarily to the reconciliation of God and humanity rather than to that of Jew and Gentile.[59] Contrary to the latter, Paul's description of humanity as unrighteous suggests that Paul's emphasis lies not on the *singularity* of grace but on its *incongruity*.[60] What makes God's benevolence so striking is the unworthiness of its object. This is Paul's consistent theme—God's love sparkles against the dark background of human idolatry, sin, and rebellion (Rom. 5:6–11; Eph. 2:1–10). To describe humanity as the victim of sin, or as merely disoriented, is actually to obscure the love and grace of God.

The challenge, then, is to retain a "thick" account of the human plight. We insist on human captivity *and* culpability. As Richard Hays writes,

---

56. In at least one place, Martyn describes this threefold *dramatis personae* as the hallmark of apocalyptic. J. Louis Martyn, "Epilogue: An Essay in Pauline Meta-Ethics," in *Divine and Human Agency in Paul and His Cultural Environment*, ed. John M. G. Barclay and Simon J. Gathercole, LNTS 335 (London: T&T Clark, 2006), 178n12.

57. A helpful discussion of these first two questions can be found in Simon J. Gathercole, *Defending Substitution: An Essay on Atonement in Paul*, ASBT (Grand Rapids, MI: Baker Academic, 2015), 48–53.

58. To be sure, δίκαιος and δικαιοσύνη can be used in covenantal contexts (where faithfulness to one's commitments constitutes righteousness), but these nuances cannot be imported back into every use. The verb δικαιόω ought to be treated separately, for it is more exclusively a legal term; in Paul's usage (following the Septuagint), it signifies acquittal, the opposite of κατάκριμα, "condemnation." On these points, Stephen Westerholm remains a helpful guide. See Westerholm, *Perspectives Old and New on Paul: The "Lutheran" Paul and His Critics* (Grand Rapids, MI: Eerdmans, 2004); Westerholm, *Justification Reconsidered: Rethinking a Pauline Theme* (Grand Rapids, MI: Eerdmans, 2013); Westerholm, "Righteousness, Cosmic and Microcosmic," in Gaventa, *Apocalyptic Paul*, 21–38.

59. Of course, throughout Romans 1–4, Paul has an eye on applying justification to the Jew-Gentile question and its instantiation in a church threatened by boasting and judgmentalism.

60. For this term, see Barclay, *Paul and the Gift*, 72–73. Here, the gift is given "without regard to the worth of the recipient," that is, without any inherent preceding merit. In Paul this is present in a special sense; the incongruity of God's gift is accented by its reception among universally *unworthy* people. For an extension of this thesis into Jesus's ministry, see John M. G. Barclay, "'Offensive and Uncanny': Jesus and Paul on the Caustic Grace of God," in Still, *Jesus and Paul Reconnected*, 1–18; on the same theme, a superb little treatment is F. F. Bruce, *Paul and Jesus* (London: SPCK, 1977), 51–57.

The Bible's sober anthropology rejects the apparently commonsense assumption that only freely chosen acts are morally culpable. Quite the reverse: the very nature of sin is that it is not freely chosen. That is what it means to live "in the flesh" in a fallen creation. We are in bondage to sin but still accountable to God's righteous judgment of our actions.[61]

Indeed, we must also push beyond that understanding to integrate Schweitzer's emphasis on the demonic, as Paul does in 2 Corinthians 4:1–6 and Ephesians 2:1–3. Yet even here what is notable is the compatibility of this perspective with an equal emphasis on human complicity. Indeed, Paul embeds that compatibility within the very phrases he uses to communicate this reality: the prince of this world has blinded the minds of "unbelievers," and he is at work in the sons of "disobedience." It is a both/and.[62]

The Nature of Human-Divine Relationships

An overarching emphasis on divine initiative and human incapacity is often spoken of as a hallmark of the apocalyptic reading. For Campbell, "the term 'apocalyptic' emphasizes the dramatic, reconstitutive and fundamentally unconditional nature of the acts of which these narratives speak—and in a permanent protest against their reduction to a merely human level."[63] The alternative is styled as a contractual account of salvation in which faith plays a meritorious role. Campbell derives the language of contract (and much of his understanding of the Protestant tradition) from an article by James B. Torrance that charts a decline from covenantal understandings of the divine-human relationship, such as one finds in the magisterial Reformers, to the contractual, or more subtly, the introduction of contractual language when defining the nature of a covenant.[64] For Torrance, the result is the regrettable superstructure of a covenant of works and "conditional grace,"[65] and with them "the whole focus of attention moves

---

61. Richard B. Hays, *The Moral Vision of the New Testament: Community, Cross, New Creation; A Contemporary Introduction to New Testament Ethics* (Edinburgh: T&T Clark, 1996), 390.
62. Relatedly, N. T. Wright's recent argument that sin primarily addresses a "human failure of vocation" and falls into idolatry rather than disobedience to a command could easily degenerate into an either/or, even though Wright is careful to avoid that. *The Day the Revolution Began: Reconsidering the Meaning of Jesus's Crucifixion* (San Francisco: HarperOne, 2016), 84; for the whole discussion, see 84–87, 97–106.
63. Campbell, *Deliverance of God*, 756. Cf. Beverly Roberts Gaventa, "The God Who Will Not Be Taken for Granted: Reflections on Paul's Letter to the Romans," in *The Ending of Mark and the Ends of God: Essays in Memory of Donald Harrisville Juel*, ed. Beverly Roberts Gaventa and Patrick D. Miller (Louisville: Westminster John Knox, 2005).
64. James B. Torrance, "Covenant or Contract: A Study of the Theological Background of Worship in Seventeenth-Century Scotland," *SJT* 23, no. 1 (1970): 51–76. It is worth noticing here that Torrance's concerns have also surfaced in one of N. T. Wright's recent works. For all his trenchant criticism of the apocalyptic approach, Wright has also recently opposed an understanding of Eden in terms of a covenant of works, preferring to speak of Adam and Eve's covenantal vocation. *Day the Revolution Began*, 74–77. As a corollary of the covenant of works, Wright takes aim at the popular preaching/perception that God is "a bloodthirsty tyrant," citing the lyric "And on that cross as Jesus died / The wrath of God was satisfied" (from Keith Getty and Stuart Townend's "In Christ Alone," © 2002 ThankYou Music [PRS], administered worldwide at CapitolCMGPublishing.com, excluding Europe, which is administered by IntegrityMusic.com) and spelling out the underlying logic as follows: "a. All humans sinned, causing God to be angry and to want to kill them, to burn them forever in 'hell.' b. Jesus somehow got in the way and took the punishment instead (it helped, it seems, that he was innocent—oh, and that he was God's own son too.) c. We are in the clear after all, heading for 'heaven' instead (provided, of course, we believe it)." Wright, *Day the Revolution Began*, 38. For his sustained and very helpful critique of the apocalyptic reading, see Wright, *Paul and His Recent Interpreters*, 135–218.
65. Torrance, "Covenant or Contract," 56.

away from what Christ has done for us and for all men, to what we have to do IF we would be (or know that we are) in covenant with God."⁶⁶

In effect, then, the apocalyptic reading essentially treats divine and human agency as a zero-sum game. Either God takes the initiative, or human faith activates salvation. Thus, in Campbell's eyes, for grace to be grace, it must refer to "unconditional actions by God that deliver salvation to a given constituency with no strings attached, as pure gift."⁶⁷ In Barclay's terms, we are now speaking of the "noncircularity" of grace.⁶⁸

It is this stress that accounts for the importance attached to treating the much-debated πίστις Χριστοῦ as a reference to Christ's own faith(fulness) rather than to human faith in Christ.⁶⁹ For Martyn,

> The difference between these readings [i.e., Martyn's own readings of key passages] and the traditional ones is monumental. That is to say, in our effort to understand Gal 2:15–16a and 3:2, the apparently pedestrian task of translating the Greek text proves to be what Paul would call a matter of life and death.⁷⁰

Martyn seems only a hair's breadth from declaring the objective genitive anathema, but instead of leaping to its defense, it is wiser for us to reject yet another premise. For Martyn, you either choose his way or accept that God's actions merely open up the possibility of a self-willed human decision.⁷¹

In many ways one could wish that the Reformed cupboard had been raided a little more, for it is perfectly possible to affirm divine initiative and be enthusiastic about an instrumental role for human faith. Without that, we find ourselves screening out every summons to repent and believe, and we end up, among other things, with a diminished account of Abraham as Paul's great model of Christian faith:

- The one who reckons with his own situation and finds only death in his body and that of his wife (Rom. 4:19)
- The one whose own efforts at securing the promise by the flesh end in slavery (Genesis 16; Gal. 4:21–31)

---

66. Torrance, "Covenant or Contract," 69; emphasis original.
67. Campbell, *Deliverance of God*, 100.
68. The term is introduced in Barclay, *Paul and the Gift*, 74–75, and is discussed with reference to Campbell on 171.
69. As with several debates, one learns to ask *why* others hold a view and what they think is at stake before knowing how best to respond, for the prominence of Christ's faith can serve all sorts of different programs. When arguments in favor of the subjective genitive first emerged, they were frequently embraced within a wider concern to emphasize the narrative and Christological qualities of Paul's theology—Christ has been faithful where Israel failed. For this approach, see Richard B. Hays, *The Faith of Jesus Christ: The Narrative Substructure of Galatians 3:1–4:11* (Grand Rapids, MI: Eerdmans, 2002); N. T. Wright, *Paul and the Faithfulness of God*, book 2, Parts 3 and 4, COQG 4 (London: SPCK, 2013), 836–51. There is much to affirm here (even if I remain unpersuaded about the subjective reading), but significantly, it was never connected with a theological objection to the concept of human faith. In apocalyptic readings, however, part of the impetus for the πίστις Χριστοῦ reading is that it deletes a good number of what might be taken as references to human faith and so serves that wider project. Strikingly, however, Michael Allen has also been arguing that a reference to Christ's faithful obedience is both compatible with Nicene Christology and makes a key contribution to the defense of double imputation (a delightful exercise in theological jujitsu). Allen, *The Christ's Faith: A Dogmatic Account*, T&T Clark Studies in Systematic Theology (London: T&T Clark, 2009); Allen, *Justification and the Gospel*, part 2.
70. J. Louis Martyn, "The Apocalyptic Gospel in Galatians," *Int* 54, no. 3 (2000): 250.
71. Ironically, Martyn ends up sounding like the forensically minded false teacher he describes as Paul's opponent, "placing before humanity the Two Ways, the way of death and the way of life."

- The one who then reckons with God's great power and trustworthiness and so embraces his promises in faith and by doing so makes a response that gives glory to God, in contrast to the unbelieving Gentile world that knows of God's power and divine nature but refuses to glorify him (Rom. 4:20; cf. 1:20–21)

The significance of that last point should not be lost. An instrumental role for human faith does not claw back some moral or epistemological agency for humanity; rather, it ascribes glory to God since he is the worthy object of our faith. *Sola fide* paves the way to *soli Deo gloria*.

The Theological Location of Justification

If Schweitzer wanted to exile justification to the periphery of Paul's thought, the current apocalyptic reading wants at least to match that and in some cases to go further and thrust it into the darkness. If there are good reasons to resist such an impulse, there remains the question of justification's proper place. If it ought to be restored, then restored to where?

Inevitably, given the shape of the debate, we are also forced to think about justification in relation to its putative rival as the theological apple of Paul's eye, namely, participation in Christ. This question receives extensive treatment elsewhere in this volume, but some brief comments are worthwhile here.[72]

First, the notion that there must be one distinct theological concept at the heart of Paul's theology is often assumed rather than proved. Candidates for that post are often so broad as to be relatively meaningless ("God," for example) or too narrow to justify subordinating other major concepts under them.

Second, there is peculiar temptation to expand the meaning of justification in order to preserve its place at the center or to accomplish ecumenical ends. In this train of thought, if there are two opposing views of justification, one forensic, the other transformative, then perhaps they are both right, and thus, justification has that dual aspect. To some extent, this is what happens in Käsemann's view of justification as gift and power.[73] It is also what seems to be happening in Michael Gorman's recent treatment of justification as he seeks to navigate a way forward beyond Campbell. Gorman describes his own discomfort with the notion of a center but nonetheless argues that "theosis is the center of Paul's theology."[74] Justification, by contrast, is disqualified by virtue of the fact that it is "a bit too narrow to indicate the heartbeat of Pauline soteriology."[75] Curiously, however,

---

72. See chap. 15, by David VanDrunen, and chap. 16, by R. Lucas Stamps, in this volume.
73. Käsemann also finds the gift/power character of righteousness useful in prodding his frequent opponents: the pietistic cannot receive the gift without also coming under the lordship of Christ; legalists need to hear the emphasis on gift; enthusiasts (those tempted to rely on their own resources) need to hear of *God's* power. The appeal of this expanded definition (although exegetically questionable) was clearly irresistible.
74. Michael J. Gorman, *Inhabiting the Cruciform God: Kenosis, Justification, and Theosis in Paul's Narrative Soteriology* (Grand Rapids, MI: Eerdmans, 2009), 171. Gorman's account of theosis emphasizes that the goal of salvation is to become like God, but more specifically, to become like God as he has revealed himself in Jesus, and more specifically still, to become like him in his suffering. The goal of theosis is thus, even more specifically, Christlikeness, and the nature of Christlikeness is cruciformity. Gorman nonetheless retains the term *theosis*, in part to bring the Eastern church fathers into the picture.
75. Gorman, *Cruciform God*, 171.

in the body of the work, justification expands in its meaning to incorporate Eastern as well as Western categories, and Catholic as well as Protestant definitions of justification:

> Holiness is not a supplement to justification but the actualisation of justification.[76]

> Justification has . . . *substantive content*, which includes reconciliation, participation, and transformation.[77]

> We see transformation as innate to reconciliation/justification according to 2 Cor 5:14–21.[78]

> The realities narrated in these chapters (Romans 5–8) are constitutive of, not consequences of, justification.[79]

Perhaps most striking of all: "Justification is itself theosis."[80] This, to be sure, is a way of preserving the centrality of justification, but in the process, the doctrine has become a bloated signifier of the whole salvific process.

Third, to correlate justification and participation, we must recognize that the latter is used in at least two separate senses. On the one hand, it can be used as a synonym for *mysticism*, or "in Christ" language. If that is in view, then it is important to hold justification and participation together. Much mischief is made by arguing that they are mutually exclusive options when Paul clearly states that he has an alien righteousness by virtue of being found "in Christ" (Phil. 3:9). The righteousness is not his own (hence alien), but he is not alienated from Christ such that righteousness needs to be transferred across a space that divides them. In John Calvin's words, "We do not, therefore, contemplate him outside ourselves, from afar in order that his righteousness may be imputed to us but because we put on Christ and are engrafted into his body—in short, because he deigns to make us one with him."[81]

On the other hand, participation can be used to speak of the goal of salvation or as the cruciform pattern for the Christian life. In these senses, justification and participation ought to be carefully distinguished. Where Gorman fails in this respect, Allen succeeds. In his account, "while participation in God is the goal of the gospel, justification is the ground of that sanctifying fellowship."[82] This is a nice way of capturing the distinctive contribution of justification and its relation to a more expansive account of the Christian life. In rare fashion, baby and bathwater are both present and correct.[83]

---

76. Gorman, *Cruciform God*, 2.
77. Gorman, *Cruciform God*, 56–57; italics original.
78. Gorman, *Cruciform God*, 56.
79. Gorman, *Cruciform God*, 73.
80. Gorman, *Cruciform God*, 2.
81. John Calvin *Institutes of the Christian Religion*, ed. John T. McNeill, trans. Ford Lewis Battles, LCC 20–21 (1960; repr., Louisville: Westminster John Knox, 2006), 3.11.10. Thus, Michael F. Bird's language of "incorporated righteousness" is helpful to ward off that particular caricature. See Bird, *The Saving Righteousness of God: Studies on Paul, Justification, and the New Perspective*, PBM (Milton Keynes, UK: Paternoster, 2007), 60–87.
82. Allen, *Justification and the Gospel*, 37.
83. If there is a weakness to this proposal, it might be that justification's own basis in union with Christ can be obscured if justification is principally described as the grounds of participation in Christ/God.

One clear implication of this is that we ought not to attempt making a strictly forensic view of justification *the* theological center of Paul or our own theological systems. There is a reason that justification language falls away after Romans 5:1 in the argument of the letter, even if it is not, contra the apocalyptic reading, because Paul is silently taking leave of the theology of Romans 1–4. The discussion of how it is that any sinful human being, whether Jew or Gentile, is put in the right with God is settled by 5:1. Paul is not thereafter continuing to define it, contra Gorman, as 5:1 makes abundantly clear.[84] Rather, Paul is now expressly developing its implications. Justification and its circumstances ("while we were still sinners" and "enemies," 5:8, 10) are the foundation on which Paul can then develop the themes of hope, freedom from the grip of sin, and life in the Spirit.

That said, careful attention to Paul's arguments reveals several senses in which justification has a privileged role.[85] There is, first, a general (though not universal) pattern in which Paul speaks of justification as the past event that guarantees future salvation. Second, justification language—specifically, the antithesis of faith versus works of the law / works / anything good or bad—allows Paul to accent the sense in which salvation is a gift, and it provides a criterion by which to identify and condemn false gospels. That no *flesh* will be justified before God (Paul's citation of Ps. 143:2 in Rom. 3:20 and Gal. 2:16) also reflects the way in which justification language is closely tied to Pauline anthropology. Third, in light of Genesis 15:6 and Habakkuk 2:4 and the references to the promised δικαιοσύνη θεοῦ in Isaiah, justification terminology allows Paul to demonstrate that his gospel truly is in accordance with the Law and the Prophets, as he is frequently at pains to emphasize (Rom. 1:2; 16:25–26; 1 Cor. 15:3–4).[86] Finally, and despite frequent claims to the contrary, it can be seen that Paul found justification by faith to be enormously fruitful in the ethical formation of the early Christian communities. Developing that point will be the substance of our last reflection.

The Ethics of Justification

Let us first review the charges:

> Paul arrives at the idea of a faith that rejects not only the works of the Law, but works in general. He thus closes the pathway to a theory of ethics.[87]

> "Righteousness by faith" receives very little positive working out by Paul. It does not lead to ethics.[88]

> Justification theory famously struggles with ethics.[89]

---

84. The same shape is evident in Gal. 1:4, despite the apocalyptic reading's attempt to find a rejection of forensic categories therein. Rather, we find that forensic categories are necessary and fundamental to liberative language: "The Lord Jesus Christ *gave himself for our sins to* [ἵνα] *rescue us from the present evil age.*"
85. The following list was conceived apart from but intersects in various ways with D. A. Carson, "Reflections on Salvation and Justification in the New Testament," *JETS* 40, no. 4 (1997): 581–608; Allen, *Justification and the Gospel*, 3–31.
86. To be sure, other soteriological concepts have clear Old Testament backgrounds, but the presence of justification language and the confluence of δικ- terms with πίστις especially support Paul's arguments.
87. Schweitzer, *Mysticism of Paul the Apostle*, 225.
88. Sanders, *Paul and Palestinian Judaism*, 492.
89. Campbell, *Deliverance of God*, 80.

The first claim is palpably false, of course. Paul does not reject works in general but speaks highly of them (1 Cor. 15:58; 2 Cor. 9:8; Eph. 2:10; Col. 1:10). The second and third claims oppose the thought that justification is central to Paul on the grounds that it does not lead to ethics. Happily, the previous section relieves the pressure to prove that it does. If justification is not the center but the entry point into the grace in which we now stand and the life of the Spirit, then it does not itself need to lead directly to ethics. Paul can say that we are freed from sin's penalty in the terms of justification and then develop our freedom from sin's power and our motivations to live thus in other language.

So, as it happens, can the Heidelberg Catechism, in question 86:

Q. Since we have been delivered
from our misery
by grace through Christ
without any merit of our own,
why then should we do good works?

A. Because Christ, having redeemed us by his blood,
is also restoring us by his Spirit into his image,
so that with our whole lives
we may show that we are thankful to God
for his benefits,
so that he may be praised through us,
so that we may be assured of our faith by its fruits,
and so that by our godly living
our neighbors may be won over to Christ.[90]

Justification does not have to do all the heavy lifting, therefore. On the other hand, we should not underestimate how transformative it can be to reflect on the character of our justification.

We could illustrate this point from the flow of Paul's argument in Romans. Indeed, one of the best arguments for the integrity of Paul's letter to the Romans (in the face of those who could excise Romans 1–4) is the way that Paul can be seen to be laying a foundation for his ethical and evangelistic exhortations in those opening chapters with their emphasis on judgmentalism and boasting.[91] But instead, we might finish with Jesus. One of the most revealing aspects of Jesus's parables and his interactions with the Pharisees and scribes is to see the judgmentalism, harshness, violence, vanity, and miserliness of self-righteousness; the ways in which people are commodified, either as those to whom I can favorably compare myself or those who might glorify and honor

---

90. Heidelberg Catechism, Reformed Church in America, accessed September 6, 2018, https://www.rca.org/resources/heidelberg-catechism-gratitude.
91. On this point, see David A. Shaw, "A Sketch of the Justified Life," *Primer* 4 (2016): 60–73; Simon J. Gathercole, "Romans 1–5 and the 'Weak' and the 'Strong': Pauline Theology, Pastoral Rhetoric, and the Purpose of Romans," *RevExp* 100, no. 1 (2003): 35–51.

me; the ways in which that sense of identity, when challenged by Jesus, produces hostility and murderous intent. Neither love for neighbor nor love for God: the ethics of self-righteousness. And then compare that to the tax collector at the temple who goes home justified, the unnamed woman at Simon the Pharisee's house, Zacchaeus—these display humility, generosity, joy. Love for neighbor and love for God: the ethics of justification.

Conclusion

In the course of the last one hundred years or so, the traditional Reformed view of justification has been challenged and attacked in diverse ways. Where there have been lessons to learn and nuance to add, we ought to be grateful. To some extent, the dust is settling on the New Perspective, and those lessons have been learned.[92] By contrast, the apocalyptic reading of Paul likely represents the next major wave of critique. It must be weighed up carefully, and in some respects it ought to be found seriously wanting.

In all we have surveyed, it seems clear that justification by faith has been ill served both by those who caricature it and by those who, seeking to defend it, either live up to that caricature or expand justification's purview beyond the scriptural account. Justification is not the sum of the Christian life, nor is it the only way by which to speak of the significance of the atonement. And yet by paying careful attention to the content and the application of apostolic teaching on justification, we discover that it peerlessly reveals the grace, justice, and love of God in ways that ground other spiritual blessings, and it generates an ethical posture of humility and charity that has the potential to transform love for God and neighbor. In light of that, and mindful of the deadly fruits of self-righteousness, perhaps the greatest need is that those who take the clarion call of "Here I stand" to their lips also take to heart that they stand in grace (Rom. 5:2). Thanks be to God for his indescribable gift!

Recommended Resources

Allen, R. Michael. *Justification and the Gospel: Understanding the Contexts and Controversies*. Grand Rapids, MI: Baker Academic, 2013.

Anderson, Garwood P. *Paul's New Perspective: Charting a Soteriological Journey*. Downers Grove, IL: IVP Academic, 2016.

Barclay, John M. G. *Paul and the Gift*. Grand Rapids, MI: Eerdmans, 2015.

Campbell, Douglas A. "Christ and the Church in Paul: A 'Post–New Perspective' Account." In *Four Views on the Apostle Paul*, edited by Michael F. Bird, 113–43. Counterpoints: Bible and Theology. Grand Rapids, MI: Zondervan, 2012.

---

92. For some mature reflection on the debate, see James D. G. Dunn, "What's Right about the Old Perspective on Paul?," in *Studies in the Pauline Epistles: Essays in Honor of Douglas J. Moo*, ed. Matthew S. Harmon and Jay E. Smith (Grand Rapids, MI: Zondervan, 2014), 214–29; Stephen Westerholm, "What's Right about the New Perspective on Paul?," in Harmon and Smith, *Studies in the Pauline Epistles*, 230–42; Garwood P. Anderson, *Paul's New Perspective: Charting a Soteriological Journey* (Downers Grove, IL: IVP Academic, 2016).

———. *The Deliverance of God: An Apocalyptic Rereading of Justification in Paul*. Grand Rapids, MI: Eerdmans, 2009.

———. *The Quest for Paul's Gospel: A Suggested Strategy*. London: T&T Clark, 2005.

Davis, Joshua B., and Douglas Harink, eds. *Apocalyptic and the Future of Theology: With and beyond J. Louis Martyn*. Eugene, OR: Cascade Books, 2012.

de Boer, Martinus C. *The Defeat of Death: Apocalyptic Eschatology in 1 Corinthians 15 and Romans 5*. Journal for the Study of the New Testament Supplement Series 22. Sheffield: JSOT Press, 1988.

———. *Galatians: A Commentary*. Louisville: John Knox, 2011.

———. "Paul and Apocalyptic Eschatology." In *The Encyclopedia of Apocalypticism*. Vol. 1, *The Origins of Apocalypticism in Judaism and Christianity*, edited by John J. Collins, 345–83. London: Continuum, 2000.

Gaventa, Beverly Roberts, ed. *Apocalyptic Paul: Cosmos and Anthropos in Romans 5–8*. Waco, TX: Baylor University Press, 2013.

———. *Our Mother Saint Paul*. Louisville: Westminster John Knox, 2007.

Gorman, Michael J. *Inhabiting the Cruciform God: Kenosis, Justification, and Theosis in Paul's Narrative Soteriology*. Grand Rapids, MI: Eerdmans, 2009.

Martyn, J. Louis. "The Apocalyptic Gospel in Galatians." *Interpretation* 54, no. 3 (2000): 246–66.

———. "Epilogue: An Essay in Pauline Meta-Ethics." In *Divine and Human Agency in Paul and His Cultural Environment*, edited by John M. G. Barclay and Simon J. Gathercole, 173–83. Library of New Testament Studies 335. London: T&T Clark, 2006.

———. *Galatians: A New Translation with Introduction and Commentary*. Anchor Bible 33A. New York: Doubleday, 1997.

———. *Theological Issues in the Letters of Paul*. Edinburgh: T&T Clark, 1997.

Schweitzer, Albert. *The Mysticism of Paul the Apostle*. Translated by William Montgomery. London: A&C Black, 1931.

Shaw, David A. "'Then I Proceeded to Where Things Were Chaotic' (1 Enoch 21:1): Mapping the Apocalyptic Landscape." In *Paul and the Apocalyptic Imagination*, edited by Ben C. Blackwell, John K. Goodrich, and Jason Maston, 23–41. Minneapolis: Fortress, 2016.

Stendahl, Krister. "The Apostle Paul and the Introspective Conscience of the West." *Harvard Theological Review* 56, no. 3 (1963): 199–215.

Westerholm, Stephen. *Justification Reconsidered: Rethinking a Pauline Theme*. Grand Rapids, MI: Eerdmans, 2013.

Wrede, William. *Paul*. Translated by Edward Lummis. London: P. Green, 1907.

Wright, N. T. *Paul and His Recent Interpreters: Some Contemporary Debates*. London: SPCK, 2015.

———. *Paul and the Faithfulness of God*. Book 2, *Parts 3 and 4*. Christian Origins and the Question of God 4. London: SPCK, 2013.

PART TWO

JUSTIFICATION IN THEOLOGICAL PERSPECTIVE

11

"Behold, the Lamb of God"

Theology Proper and the Inseparability of Penal-Substitutionary Atonement from Forensic Justification and Imputation

STEPHEN J. WELLUM

In church history people have disagreed as to what justification is, and the purpose of this chapter is not to restate all the data for the Reformation's view of justification as the biblical view.[1] Numerous books have argued this case, along with other chapters in this book.[2] Instead, I assume that the Reformation's view of justification is the biblical view, and in this section I summarize the overall view only to set the stage for my argument that the Reformation's view of justification and penal substitution are inseparably related.

What Is Justification in Scripture and Reformation Theology?

Justification is a word/concept from the law court denoting, primarily, that action whereby a judge upholds the case of one party in dispute before him. Having heard the

---

1. On the history of the doctrine of justification, see Alister E. McGrath, *Iustitia Dei: A History of the Christian Doctrine of Justification*, 2nd ed. (Cambridge: Cambridge University Press, 1998); cf. James K. Beilby and Paul Rhodes Eddy, eds., *Justification: Five Views*, Spectrum Multiview Books (Downers Grove, IL: IVP Academic, 2011).
2. For example, see John Owen, *A Dissertation on Divine Justice*, in *The Works of John Owen*, ed. William H. Goold, vol. 10, *The Death of Christ* (London: Banner of Truth, 1967), 481–624; Thomas Schreiner, *Faith Alone: The Doctrine of Justification; What the Reformers Taught . . . and Why It Still Matters*, Five Solas Series (Grand Rapids, MI: Zondervan, 2015); Brian Vickers, *Justification by Grace through Faith: Finding Freedom from Legalism, Lawlessness, Pride, and Despair*, Explorations in Biblical Theology (Phillipsburg, NJ: P&R, 2013); James R. White, *The God Who Justifies: The Doctrine of Justification* (Minneapolis: Bethany, 2001); Bruce Demarest, *The Cross and Salvation: The Doctrine of Salvation*, Foundations of Evangelical Theology (Wheaton, IL: Crossway, 1997), 345–82; Anthony A. Hoekema, *Saved by Grace* (Grand Rapids, MI: Eerdmans, 1989), 152–91; John Murray, *Redemption Accomplished and Applied* (Grand Rapids, MI: Eerdmans, 1955), 117–31.

case, the judge reaches a verdict in favor of the person and thereby "justifies" him; this action has the force of "acquittal." The judge's declaration entails that the person is not penally liable and thus is "entitled to all the privileges due to those who have kept the law. Justification settles the legal status of the person justified and thus it is a forensic term (Deut. 25:1; Prov. 17:15; Rom. 8:33–34)."[3] As a forensic concept, a person who is justified is "just," "righteous"—not as a description of his or her moral character but as a statement of his or her *status* or *position* before the court. Thus, "to justify" does *not* mean to *make* righteous—that is, to change a person's character[4]—but rather to *constitute* righteous by declaration.[5] In the case of God as the Judge of the world, when he justifies us, he declares us to be just and righteous *before him* and not first to be in the covenant community.[6]

In the New Testament, especially in Paul's letters, it is always God as our Creator, Lord, and Judge who "justifies," and it is always humans who are justified.[7] For Paul, justification is always *forensic* and *before* God (Rom. 2:13; 3:20). It is by grace through faith in Christ (Rom. 3:28, 30; 5:1; Gal. 2:16; 3:8, 24), and it is not by "works" (Rom. 4:2; Eph. 2:8–10) or by the "works of the law"—that is, by obedience to the law's demands (Rom. 3:20, 28; Gal. 2:16).[8] Evidence for its *forensic* meaning is found in Romans 8:1, 33–34, where "to justify" is contrasted with "to condemn" (κατακρίνω), and in the synonyms of "justification"—"to vindicate" and "to acquit"—which convey the meaning "to declare righteous." In fact, "to condemn" is not to *make* someone sinful

---

3. J. I. Packer and R. M. Allen, "Justification," in *Evangelical Dictionary of Theology*, ed. Daniel J. Treier and Walter A. Elwell, 3rd ed. (Grand Rapids, MI: Baker Academic, 2017), 455.
4. See Packer and Allen, "Justification," 456. For the forensic use of "made righteous" (καθίστημι) in Rom. 5:19, see Vickers, *Justification by Grace through Faith*, 47–49.
5. "Justification" and "righteousness" language is rooted in the δικ- root, especially the verb δικαιόω and the noun δικαιοσύνη. In the Septuagint, δικαιόω normally translates two Hebrew words of the צדק word group. In the *qal* form of the verb, it means " to be just" or "to be righteous" (Gen. 38:26; Job 9:15; Ezek. 16:52), and in the *hiphil* form of the verb, it means "to declare righteous" (Ex. 23:7; Deut. 25:1). In the Old Testament, the verb is used in a *judicial, forensic* sense. Sometimes the judge who pronounces righteous or acquits is human (Deut. 25:1; Isa. 5:23), and at other times he is God (Ex. 23:7; 1 Kings 8:32; 2 Chron. 6:23; Ps. 82:3; Isa. 50:8). As Douglas Moo notes, "Even when the term is not used with explicit reference to the law court, the forensic connotations remain (cf. Gen. 38:26; 44:16; Jer. 3:11; Ezek. 16:51–52)." *The Epistle to the Romans*, NICNT (Grand Rapids, MI: Eerdmans, 1996), 80. Also see Schreiner, *Faith Alone*, 144–78; David G. Peterson, *Commentary on Romans*, BTCP (Nashville: B&H, 2017), 61–66.
6. To say that justification is God's declaration that in Christ we stand righteous *before* God is contrary to the "New Perspective(s) on Paul." For example, N. T. Wright argues that justification is God's declaration (hence, forensic and not transformative) that we belong to God's covenant community, *not* first that we stand right *before* God. Wright states it this way: "Justification is not how someone *becomes* a Christian. It is the declaration that they *have become* a Christian." *What Saint Paul Really Said: Was Paul of Tarsus the Real Founder of Christianity?* (Grand Rapids, MI: Eerdmans, 1997), 129; cf. Wright, *Justification: God's Plan and Paul's Vision* (Downers Grove, IL: IVP Academic, 2009). To be a member of the covenant is a *result* of justification, but justification is our right standing before God. It is not enough to say that "God's righteousness," by which we are declared righteous before him, fulfills his covenant promises and thus is God's "covenant faithfulness." "Justification/righteousness" is *not* first God fulfilling or keeping his covenant promises but rather God's vindication of himself and his people (see Rom. 3:21–26). Justification is God's *declaration* that his people are *righteous* before him; this is no legal fiction, because of our union with Christ, which results in *Christ's* righteousness being imputed to us. For a critique of Wright's view, see Cornelis P. Venema, "What Did Saint Paul Really Say? N. T. Wright and the New Perspective(s) on Paul," in *By Faith Alone: Answering the Challenges to the Doctrine of Justification*, ed. Gary L. W. Johnson and Guy P. Waters (Wheaton, IL: Crossway, 2006), 33–59.
7. The one exception is 1 Tim. 3:16, where Christ is "justified" in his resurrection, which is better translated "vindicated."
8. Unless otherwise noted, Scripture quotations in this chapter are from the NIV. On the meaning of "works of the law" in contrast to the New Perspective, which interprets this phrase to refer to boundary markers that divide Jews and Gentiles, see Schreiner, *Faith Alone*, 249–52. For a critique of the New Perspective, see Robert J. Cara, *Cracking the Foundation of the New Perspective on Paul: Covenantal Nomism versus Reformed Covenantal Theology*, REDS (Fearn, Ross-shire, Scotland: Mentor, 2017); Guy P. Waters, *Justification and the New Perspectives on Paul: A Review and Response* (Phillipsburg, NJ: P&R, 2004); Stephen Westerholm, *Perspectives Old and New on Paul: The "Lutheran" Paul and His Critics* (Grand Rapids, MI: Eerdmans, 2004), 297–340.

or to infuse sin or rebellion into someone; rather, it is to *find* someone guilty. When God justifies us, he, as the Judge, declares us "not guilty."[9] The forensic meaning of δικαιόω is emphasized in Romans 4:5: "And to the one who does not work but believes in him who justifies [δικαιοῦντα] the ungodly, his faith is counted as righteousness" (ESV). The word translated "counted" or "credited" (λογίζεται) is a legal term thus underscoring the fact that God "justifies" the wicked not by "making" us righteous by transformation but by "declaring" us righteous because of our faith in Christ's finished work.[10] As Anthony Hoekema summarizes, "By *dikaioō* Paul means the legal imputation of the righteousness of Christ to the believing sinner."[11]

In the New Testament, however, in contrast to the Old Testament perspective, our justification does not take place only on the "last day," when we stand before God on "the day of the Lord" (Isa. 2:10–22; 13:6–11; Jer. 46:10; Amos 5:19–20; Obad. 15; Zeph. 1:14–2:3). Instead, justification is God's end-time verdict that by faith in Christ, we *now* are justified and stand righteous before God (Rom. 4:2; 5:1; 8:1); God's final judgment verdict has been brought into the present even though we still remain sinners and await our full transformation and glorification.[12] This entails that the "justifying sentence, once passed, is irrevocable. God's wrath will not touch the justified (Rom 5:9). Those accepted now are secure forever."[13]

How is this possible? How can God, who is holy and just, declare sinners *now* justified? (Rom. 4:5; 8:1). God is able to do so by grace, not because he has overlooked our sin, nor because we are righteous in ourselves, but because God's declaration views us in relation to the person and work of our covenant Mediator, who stands in our place, bears our sin, and satisfies all God's righteous demands against us. In Christ, we receive the gift of righteousness, which is now ours by faith in him. In union with his people, Christ, our new covenant head, obeys in our place, dies our death, and satisfies divine justice, evidenced by his resurrection from the dead. As a result, by faith alone and in Christ alone, his righteousness is ours, now and forever (2 Cor. 5:21; Gal. 3:13). In him, we stand complete: justified before God by the forgiveness of our sins and clothed in Christ's righteousness.

Justification and Imputation

Justification, then, goes beyond the forgiveness of our sins. In fact, it has two sides to it. First, "it means the pardon, remission, and nonimputation of all sins, reconciliation to God, and the end of his enmity and wrath (Acts 13:39; Rom. 4:6–7; 5:9–21; 2 Cor.

---

9. See Schreiner, *Faith Alone*, 158–69.
10. This does not entail that we are not transformed "in Christ" by the Spirit's regenerative and sanctifying work. As 1 Cor. 1:30 teaches, in Christ, no one is justified who is also not made alive by the Spirit and sanctified. In the application of Christ's work to us, justification and sanctification are inseparably related but distinct blessings. On this point, see Hoekema, *Saved by Grace*, 152–233; Murray, *Redemption Accomplished and Applied*, 117–73.
11. Hoekema, *Saved by Grace*, 154.
12. See George E. Ladd, *A Theology of the New Testament*, ed. Donald A. Hagner, 2nd ed. (Grand Rapids, MI: Eerdmans, 1993), 482–84. Cf. J. V. Fesko, *Justification: Understanding the Classic Reformed Doctrine* (Phillipsburg, NJ: P&R, 2008), 93–106.
13. Packer and Allen, "Justification," 456.

5:19)."[14] The ground for this is Christ's cross work in our place as our substitute who pays for our sins in full by satisfying God's righteous demands against us. Second, justification "means the bestowal of a righteous status and a title to all the blessings promised to the just—a thought that Paul amplifies by linking justification with the adoption of believers as God's children and heirs (Rom. 8:14–39; Gal. 4:4–7)"[15]—along with the gift of the Spirit (Eph. 1:13) and all the salvation blessings that are ours in Christ Jesus. The ground for this is Christ's active obedience for us as our covenant head, representative, and Mediator who perfectly obeys all God's righteous demands in his humanity. And thus, for those in Christ, his righteousness "is imputed to our account and we are accordingly accepted as righteous in God's sight."[16]

In biblical thought, it is not enough to have our sins forgiven, as wonderful as that is. God, as our Creator–covenant Lord, rightly demands from us perfect obedience—wholehearted devotion—so that we also need a positive standing before him. As Michael Horton reminds us, "Without the latter [positive standing of righteousness], the goal of the covenant as well as its conditions are left unfulfilled."[17] Indeed, as Horton continues,

> Apart from the positive imputation of righteousness, based on Christ's active obedience (fulfilling the law in our place), justification truly is a "legal fiction," as its critics allege. On the other hand, because the obedience of Christ is actually imputed or credited to us, we are just/righteous before God.[18]

Both sides of justification are taught in Romans 5:1–2: we have peace with God because our sins are fully forgiven, and we stand before God as righteous because Christ's righteousness is imputed to us (cf. 4:4–6; 5:12–21; 2 Cor. 5:21; Phil. 3:1–9).[19]

The Westminster Confession of Faith's statement on justification nicely encapsulates the Reformation's view. What is justification? It is the following:

> 1. Those whom God effectually calleth he also freely justifieth: not by infusing righteousness into them, but by pardoning their sins, and by accounting and accepting their persons as righteous: not for anything wrought in them, or done by them, but for Christ's sake alone; not by imputing faith itself, the act of believing, or any other evangelical obedience, to them as their righteousness; but by imputing the obedience and satisfaction of Christ unto them, they receiving and resting on him and his righteousness by faith: which faith they have not of themselves; it is the gift of God.

---

14. Packer and Allen, "Justification," 456.
15. Packer and Allen, "Justification," 456. See Schreiner, *Faith Alone*, 179–90.
16. Murray, *Redemption Accomplished and Applied*, 124. The work of Christ as the *incarnate* Son and last Adam, and thus our Mediator, is described throughout the New Testament in terms of his covenantal obedience. In Christ's obedience as our new covenant head and substitute, he achieves our justification (e.g., Rom. 5:19; Phil. 2:8; Heb. 5:8–9).
17. Michael Horton, "Traditional Reformed View," in Beilby and Eddy, *Justification: Five Views*, 101.
18. Horton, "Traditional Reformed View," 101.
19. For a current discussion and defense of the imputation of Christ's righteousness, see D. A. Carson, "The Vindication of Imputation: On Fields of Discourse and Semantic Fields," in *Justification: What's at Stake in the Current Debates*, ed. Mark A. Husbands and Daniel J. Treier (Downers Grove, IL: InterVarsity Press, 2004), 46–78; cf. J. V. Fesko, *Death in Adam, Life in Christ: The Doctrine of Imputation*, REDS (Fearn, Ross-shire, Scotland: Mentor, 2016); K. Scott Oliphint, ed., *Justified in Christ: God's Plan for Us in Justification* (Fearn, Ross-shire, Scotland: Mentor, 2007).

2. Faith, thus receiving and resting on Christ and his righteousness, is the sole instrument of justification; yet it is not alone in the person justified, but is ever accompanied with all other saving graces, and is no dead faith, but worketh by love.[20]

How Does the Doctrine of God Undergird Justification?

Justification, as taught in Scripture and the Reformation, has two aspects to it. First, for God to declare sinners just (Rom. 4:5), there must be the full forgiveness of our sin, which is secured by Christ's cross work. In other words, there is no justification apart from Christ's mediatorial work for us and our receiving it by faith (3:21–26; 5:1). Since our justification is the revelation of *God's* justice/righteousness, this also assumes that the claims of God's law have been fully met and satisfied in Christ and his work. In our justification, God does not forgive us without atonement, nor does he alter his law or suspend it. Instead, he forgives us of our sins because Christ fully pays for our sins in his substitutionary death, and as a result, there is no longer any outstanding debt against us.

Second, justification also insists that for sinners to stand righteous before God, we, now and forever, require a perfect, righteous standing before God—a righteousness not of our own. This assumes that God demands from his image bearers a perfect obedience, which, since Adam's fall, we do not render but Jesus, as the last Adam, does for us. God the Son becomes incarnate to represent us as our covenant head, and in his humanity, he perfectly obeys God's righteous demands for us (Matt. 3:15; Gal. 4:4–7). For this reason, Christ's obedience in life and death is the ground of our justification and eternal salvation (cf. Phil. 2:8; Heb. 5:8–9; 10:1–18). Because Jesus as our covenant head obeys for us and because we are in union with him, his righteousness is now ours by imputation; God declares us righteous in his sight.

But what theology, or more precisely, what *theology proper*, accounts for this view of justification? To answer this question fully, much needs to be said about God's goodness, grace, mercy, and love. However, to make sense of forensic justification and imputation, a specific view of God as the triune Creator, Lord, *and Judge* is also required. After all, justification is a law court image that speaks of the Creator–covenant God, who as the Judge of all the earth always does what is right (Gen. 18:25). The Reformation's view of justification assumes that God's justice has a strong retributive sense because it is *essential* to him, and as such, *God* is the moral standard of the universe.[21] God is *not* like a human judge, who adjudicates a law external to him; instead, the triune God *is* the law.[22] When God judges, he remains true to his own perfect, moral demands, which

---

20. G. I. Williamson, ed., *The Westminster Confession of Faith* (Philadelphia: Presbyterian & Reformed, 1964), 103 (9.1–2).
21. God's justice/righteousness is more than retributive, but it is certainly not less. For a discussion of God's justice, see Herman Bavinck, *Reformed Dogmatics*, ed. John Bolt, trans. John Vriend, vol. 2, *God and Creation* (Grand Rapids, MI: Baker Academic, 2004), 216–28; John M. Frame, *The Doctrine of God*, Theology of Lordship (Phillipsburg, NJ: P&R, 2002), 446–68; Schreiner, *Faith Alone*, 170–78; Edmund P. Clowney, "The Biblical Doctrine of Justification by Faith," in *Right with God: Justification in the Bible and the World*, ed. D. A. Carson (Grand Rapids, MI: Baker, 1992), 17–50.
22. Post-Reformation theologians such as Francis Turretin and John Owen strongly emphasized this point. See Richard A. Muller, *Post-Reformation Reformed Dogmatics: The Rise and Development of Reformed Orthodoxy, ca. 1520 to ca. 1725*, vol. 3, *The Divine Essence and Attributes* (Grand Rapids, MI: Baker Academic, 2003), 476–97. Also see James

means that he remains true to himself.²³ Sin, then, is not against an abstract principle or impersonal law; instead, sin is against the personal God who is holy and just, which entails that for sinners to be declared just, our justification before God requires that our sin is fully paid and that we have a perfect righteousness by imputation.

Scripture and theology best capture the view that God is the law by grounding God's justice in divine aseity. *Aseity* is from the Latin *a se*, which means "from or by himself,"²⁴ and it is linked to the ideas of God's independence and personal self-sufficiency. Yet aseity is more than a metaphysical attribute that stresses God's self-existence; it equally applies to the epistemological and moral realms. As John Frame notes,

> God is not only self-existent, but also self-attesting and self-justifying. He not only exists without receiving existence from something else, but also gains his knowledge only from himself (his nature and his plan) and serves as his own criterion of truth. And his righteousness is self-justifying, based on the righteousness of his own nature and on his status as the ultimate criterion of rightness.²⁵

In Scripture, divine aseity is also closely associated with God's holiness. God is the Creator–covenant Lord who is holy (Ex. 3:5–6; 15:11; 19:23–25; Lev. 11:44; 19:1; 1 Sam. 2:2; Ps. 99:3, 5, 9; Isa. 6:1–5; 57:15; Ezekiel 1–3; Heb. 12:28; 1 Pet. 1:15–16; 1 John 1:5; Revelation 4). In previous generations, theologians viewed God's holiness as central to all the divine attributes.²⁶ One must exercise care in elevating one divine attribute over others, yet there is a sense in which holiness defines the very nature of God. In fact, whenever we combine God's holiness with love, justice, and goodness, we always say that it is holy love, holy justice, and holy goodness. The meaning of the Hebrew noun "holiness" (קֹדֶשׁ) and its related adjective (קָדוֹשׁ) is difficult to determine etymologically. The most common suggestion is "to set apart," but holiness conveys more than merely God's transcendence.²⁷ Rather, God's holiness is uniquely associated with his aseity, sovereignty, majesty, and complete devotion to himself.²⁸ As the Lord over all, he is the Creator who is exalted, self-sufficient, and unique. The "gods" of the nations do not compare to him; God alone is holy. Also, inseparably tied to God's metaphysical holiness is his personal-moral perfection. He is "too pure to behold evil" and unable to tolerate wrong (Hab. 1:12–13; cf. Isa. 1:4–20; 35:8). The God who is holy in himself *must* act with holy justice when his people sin, thus first glorifying himself as the highest good (*summum bonum*). As the righteous God, God upholds his own holiness

---

Buchanan, *The Doctrine of Justification* (1867; repr., Carlisle, PA: Banner of Truth, 2016), 249–70; Geerhardus Vos, *Reformed Dogmatics*, trans. and ed. Richard B. Gaffin Jr., vol. 1, *Theology Proper* (Bellingham, WA: Lexham, 2012), 26–35.

23. Oliver D. Crisp describes the key theological assumptions undergirding penal substitution and by extension the Reformation's doctrine of justification. First, divine justice is retributive, tied to God's nature. Second, given our sin before God and his justice, for God to declare us just, there must be a full payment of our sin. Crisp, "The Logic of Penal Substitution Revisited," in *The Atonement Debate: Papers from the London Symposium on the Theology of the Atonement*, ed. Derek Tidball, David Hilborn, and Justin Thacker (Grand Rapids, MI: Zondervan, 2008), 209–12.

24. See Frame, *Doctrine of God*, 600.

25. Frame, *Doctrine of God*, 602.

26. For a helpful discussion of this point, see Muller, *Post-Reformation Reformed Dogmatics*, 3:497–503.

27. See Jackie A. Naudé, "קדשׁ," in *NIDOTTE*, 3:877–87.

28. See Muller, *Post-Reformation Reformed Dogmatics*, 3:497–503; Bavinck, *Reformed Dogmatics*, 2:216–21.

and acts against every violation of it. Yet in love, the triune covenant God chooses to show his good pleasure to what lies outside him as the God of "covenant faithfulness" (חֶסֶד) who loves his people with a holy love (Hos. 11:9).

In thinking about God's holiness, it is best to think about its primary and secondary senses. Primarily, it refers to God's lordship: transcendent self-sufficiency. It is associated with such biblical language as "high and lifted up," "above," and "greatness and majesty," and it is organically linked to God's name—"the Holy One."[29] In this sense, it refers to what the triune God is internally or intrinsically. Secondarily, it entails a moral-ethical sense and presents God as the standard of moral perfection, the one who is pure, good, righteous, and just, and thus utterly separate from sin.[30] For this reason, Scripture stresses that God's holiness and our sin are incompatible. His eyes are too pure to look on evil; he cannot tolerate wrong (Ex. 34:7; Rom. 1:32; 2:8–16). Our sins separate us from him, so that his face is hidden from us (Isa. 59:1–2). And closely related to God's holiness is his wrath, that is, his holy reaction to evil (Rom. 1:18–32; John 3:36). The wrath of God, unlike his holiness, is not an *internal* perfection; rather, it is a function of his holiness against sin. Where there is no sin, there is no wrath, but there is always holiness. But where the holy God confronts his creatures in their rebellion, there *must* be wrath; otherwise, God is not the holy God he claims to be. Ultimately, the price of diluting God's wrath is to diminish his holiness and aseity along with the exercise of his holiness in justice and righteousness.[31]

Alongside God's holiness is also God's love, and Scripture never pits one of these against the other. Divine holiness and love are taught in the Old Testament, but in a greater way, the New Testament reveals how God's holiness and love are united in Christ's cross and our justification. John, for example, does not think of God's love as mere sentimentality or an overlooking of our sin; rather, he views divine love as that which loves the unlovely and undeserving. In fact, the supreme display of God's love is found in the Father giving his own Son as our propitiation, which turns back his own holy anger against us and satisfies the demands of justice on our behalf (1 John 2:1–2; 4:8–10). Thus, in Christ's cross, we see the greatest demonstration of the holiness *and* love of God, where God remains just *and* the justifier of those who have faith in Christ Jesus (Rom. 3:21–26).[32]

Combining these truths, Scripture presents the triune, self-sufficient God of holy love *as the law*, that is, the moral standard of the universe, who always acts consistently with who he is. This is why the collision of our sin with his righteousness *necessarily* results. Given who *he* is, God *cannot* tolerate sin; he *must* act in holy justice. Yet since divine holiness and love are not pitted against each other, a *tension* results in the Bible's

---

29. See, e.g., Deut. 26:15; 1 Chron. 16:10, 35; 29:16; Pss. 3:4; 11:4; 20:6; 22:3; 28:2; 48:1; 65:4; Isa. 6:1; 40:12–26; 45:11; 47:4; 48:17; 52:10; 54:5; 55:5; 57:13–15; 63:10; Jer. 25:30; Ezek. 28:14; Joel 2:1; Amos 2:7; Zech. 2:13.
30. See, e.g., Lev. 19:2; 20:3, 26; Josh. 24:19; 1 Sam. 6:20; Pss. 24:3; 60:6; 89:35; 145:17; Isa. 5:16; Jer. 23:9; Ezek. 22:8, 26; 36:22; 39:7; Hos. 11:9; Amos 4:2; Mal. 2:11; Heb. 7:26; 12:10; 1 Pet. 1:15–16; Rev. 15:4.
31. See D. A. Carson, *The Gagging of God: Christianity Confronts Pluralism* (Grand Rapids, MI: Zondervan, 1996), 232–34.
32. See D. A. Carson, *The Difficult Doctrine of the Love of God* (Wheaton, IL: Crossway, 1999).

storyline of how God will demonstrate his holy justice *and* covenant love, given his free choice to redeem us. This tension is rooted in *who* God is vis-à-vis sin, and it is at the heart of the Bible's view of justification and the cross. Since God is the law, he *cannot* justify us without the full satisfaction of his holy and righteous demands. God cannot overlook our sin, nor can he relax the retributive demands of his justice. To justify the ungodly (Rom. 4:5), God must take the initiative to provide a Redeemer who can pay for our sin and act in perfect obedience for us. Theologically, *this* view of God makes sense of forensic justification and imputation. In fact, differing views of justification and the atonement are best explained by differences in theology proper.

For this reason, because *this* conception of God is being recast in various ways today, it is not surprising that there are also diverse views of justification and the nature of the atonement. For example, a mantra against retributive justice is that it is too influenced by Western culture. In its place, "justice" and "righteousness" are defined as God's "covenant faithfulness" or "God making all things right."[33] No doubt, "God's righteousness" does refer to his saving activity (Pss. 31:1; 36:10; 71:2; Isa. 45:8; 46:13; 51:4–8), yet first and foremost, it refers to who God is in himself as the holy and just one. God is true to his covenant promises and acts righteously *ad extra*, but in so doing, he does what is right and remains true to who he is *ad intra*. The Old Testament insists that God is "righteous in all his ways" (Ps. 145:17), a "God who does no wrong" (Deut. 32:4), because *he* is the standard of what is right. This is why his law is "holy, righteous and good" (Rom. 7:12), since it reflects his own holy nature. As the righteous Judge, God punishes sin and holds people accountable for their actions (Ex. 34:6–7; Pss. 9:5–6, 15–20; 94:7–9; Prov. 24:12; Amos 1:3–3:2; Rom. 1:18–3:20). Ultimately, final judgment is a reality because God, thankfully, does not allow sin to go unpunished, since it is against *him* (Revelation 19–20).

Most fundamentally, the problem with the "new" view is that it fails to tie God's righteousness to his own nature and inner life. Garry Williams rightly contends that rejecting retributive justice results in some form of "moral naturalism"—that is, "God has created the world in such a way that sin has its punishment as a natural consequence,"[34] a kind of justice or righteousness that upholds the moral governing of the universe but does not view sin as a personal affront against the holy God who will not let sin go unpunished.[35] But this "natural" consequence occurs without any judicial act on the

---

33. For example, see Fleming Rutledge, *The Crucifixion: Understanding the Death of Jesus Christ* (Grand Rapids, MI: Eerdmans, 2015), 106–45; N. T. Wright, *The Day the Revolution Began: Reconsidering the Meaning of Jesus's Crucifixion* (San Francisco: HarperOne, 2016), 81–87, 263–351; Wright, *What Saint Paul Really Said*, 96, 103; Wright, *Justification*, 164–65; Darrin W. Snyder Belousek, *Atonement, Justice, and Peace: The Message of the Cross and the Mission of the Church* (Grand Rapids, MI: Eerdmans, 2012), 369–80; Joel B. Green and Mark D. Baker, *Recovering the Scandal of the Cross: Atonement in the New Testament and Contemporary Contexts*, 2nd ed. (Downers Grove, IL: InterVarsity Press, 2011), 68–70; Joel B. Green, "Theologies of the Atonement in the New Testament," in *T&T Clark Companion to Atonement*, ed. Adam J. Johnson (New York: Bloomsbury T&T Clark, 2017), 126–29.
34. Garry Williams, "The Cross and the Punishment of Sin," in *Where Wrath and Mercy Meet: Proclaiming the Atonement Today*, ed. David Peterson (Carlisle, UK: Paternoster, 2001), 95–96.
35. For a famous example of this view, see C. H. Dodd, *The Bible and the Greeks* (London: Hodder & Stoughton, 1935). In response to Dodd's view, see John R. W. Stott, *The Cross of Christ* (Downers Grove, IL: InterVarsity Press, 2006), 166–73; Roger R. Nicole, "C. H. Dodd and the Doctrine of Propitiation," *WTJ* 17, no. 2 (1955): 117–57.

part of God after the sin has been committed—hence the dismissal or downplaying of a retributive sense of justice or the notion that God's wrath is directed against people. In this view, Williams observes, "For sin to receive its punishment, God has to do nothing other than sustain the existence of the world which he has created."[36] This new view, however, loses the linkage of God's justice to his own inner life and loses the idea that God in justice will fully punish sin as the Judge who always does what is right (Gen. 18:25).[37] This view also has the unfortunate consequence of undercutting the warrant for objective morality grounded in God's own nature, which will inevitably require a redefinition of the doctrines of justification and atonement, a point to which we now turn.

What Theology of Atonement Best Grounds Justification?[38]

My argument is that penal substitution best grounds forensic justification and imputation; in fact, the two are inseparably related. Why? Because penal substitution best accounts for the theological assumption underneath the doctrine of justification, namely, the biblical conception of God, who is the Creator–covenant Lord and the Judge of all the earth. As noted above, Scripture presents the triune God as the God of holy love, who *is the law* and who always acts in perfect justice. Since sin is primarily against *him*, God *cannot* justify us without the full satisfaction of his holy and righteous demands. God cannot overlook our sin, nor can he relax the retributive demands of *his* justice. For sinners to be justified, *God* must act in grace and provide a Redeemer, who can pay for our sin *and* perfectly obey God's law for us, which is precisely how penal substitution expounds Christ's work.

What Is Penal Substitution?

Penal substitution may be explained by unpacking the words *penal* and *substitution*. *Penal* is shorthand for the larger issue of the nature of the human problem before God. Scripture describes our fallen condition as one in which, "in Adam," we stand under God's judgment, namely, the penalty of death, which includes all the diverse consequences of sin on the human race. Sin is viewed as lawbreaking but is certainly much more.[39] Scripture also contends that one cannot make sense of the human problem of sin and its solution in Christ apart from a historical Adam, who in the biblical storyline is the covenant head and representative of humanity. Since Adam as our covenant head disobeyed God, his sin is now our sin by nature, imputation, and choice (Rom. 5:12–21), and as a result, we are all under the

---

36. Williams, "Cross and the Punishment of Sin," 96.
37. See Paul Wells, *Cross Words: The Biblical Doctrine of the Atonement* (Fearn, Ross-shire, Scotland: Christian Focus, 2006), 55–80.
38. This section adapts some material from Stephen J. Wellum, *Christ Alone: The Uniqueness of Jesus as Savior; What the Reformers Taught . . . and Why It Still Matters* (Grand Rapids, MI: Zondervan, 2017), 165–92. Used by permission of Zondervan.
39. Contra Stephen R. Holmes, "Penal Substitution," in Johnson, *T&T Clark Companion to the Atonement*, 295–314. Holmes casts penal substitution solely within the "logic of the law court" and argues that sin "is understood as lawbreaking" (295), giving the impression that the view overemphasizes the forensic and is thus reductionistic. No doubt, penal substitution is forensic, but it is much more. At its heart, it wrestles with the God-law-sin relationship, and it is set within the Bible's covenantal storyline, which is not reducible to the "law court."

penalty, power, and guilt of sin and death (3:23; 6:23; cf. Eph. 2:1–4).[40] Due to our sin, we are alienated from the triune God, who created us to know and love him, and because he is personal, holy, and righteous, God stands opposed to us in his wrath (Rom. 1:18–32).

Substitution is shorthand for who our Redeemer is and what the nature of his work is. Central to Christ's work is substitution since he dies in our place and on our behalf. The term also captures a major truth of the Bible's storyline as unfolded through the covenants, namely, that our triune God has chosen to redeem a people for himself by the provision of a substitute for us. As our new covenant head, Jesus, the *incarnate* Son—the last Adam—by virtue of his obedient life, acts as our representative by perfectly fulfilling God's righteous demands for us.[41] By his perfect obedience to his Father, Jesus becomes the perfect covenant keeper for us. In his obedient death, Jesus, as the *divine* Son, stands in our place and fully satisfies all *God's* righteous demands against us. As a result of Christ's penal substitution for us and through our faith union with him, the Father declares us just—imputing Christ's righteousness to us and forgiving us of our sin. In Christ, sin and all its consequences are defeated, which frees us from sin's power and the tyranny of Satan, who once held the verdict of death and condemnation over us (2 Cor. 5:21; see Rom. 8:32; Gal. 3:13; Col. 2:13–15; Heb. 2:5–18; 9:28; 1 Pet. 3:18).

Penal substitution is the theological account of the atonement that best makes sense of forensic justification and imputation. It speaks of the triune God in all his love, holiness, and justice. It reminds us that it is against *God* that we have sinned yet that it is also God who has chosen in sovereign grace to redeem us. Penal substitution reminds us that the human race is in a hopeless state before God because we are guilty, corrupted, and under God's death sentence with all its entailments. Yet penal substitution also reminds us of our glorious Savior—the substitute—whose cross work accomplished everything for us, precisely because of *who* he is and *what* he did. Because he is *God the Son*, he is able to meet God's own—indeed, *his* own—holy, righteous demands by bearing the penalty we deserve. Because he is the *incarnate* Son, he perfectly fulfills the purpose of humanity, namely, to love and obey God and others in perfect obedience. Because Christ, in his mediatorial office, acts as our covenant head, for those of us in union with him, his perfect obedience and righteousness are ours by imputation, and the debt of our sin is fully paid in his death and resurrection, thus grounding our justification.

Historical Development of Penal Substitution

In the Reformation era, penal substitution as a full atonement theology came into its own, although there were precursors to it in church history. In the Patristic era, no single atonement theology dominated, yet penal-substitutionary elements existed. Eusebius

---

40. See Fesko, *Death in Adam*; Hans Madueme and Michael Reeves, eds., *Adam, the Fall, and Original Sin: Theological, Biblical, and Scientific Perspectives* (Grand Rapids, MI: Baker Academic, 2014).
41. See Brandon D. Crowe, *The Last Adam: A Theology of the Obedient Life of Jesus in the Gospels* (Grand Rapids, MI: Baker Academic, 2017).

of Caesarea insisted that Christ's substitutionary death was penal.[42] Athanasius, who viewed the cross in terms of recapitulation, also insisted that Christ's death paid the debt of our sin.[43] Chrysostom taught that "God was about to punish them [humans], but He forbore to do it. They were about to perish, but in their stead He gave His own Son, and sent us as heralds to proclaim the Cross."[44] Tertullian and Augustine said something similar when they described Christ's death as a priestly sacrifice and offering for sin.[45] Augustine spoke of Christ's death as a sacrifice for sin: "We came to death through sin; [Christ came to it] through righteousness; and, therefore, as our death is the punishment of sin, so his death was made a sacrifice for sin."[46] The best example of penal substitution in the Patristic era is the Epistle to Diognetus, with its emphasis on Christ, the holy and righteous one, who covers our sins with his righteousness and secures our justification by substitution: "O sweet exchange! O unsearchable operation! O benefits surpassing all expectation! That the wickedness of many should be hid in a single righteous One, and that the righteousness of One should justify many transgressors!"[47]

In the medieval era, Anselm's *Why God Became Man*[48] advanced our understanding of the cross by gaining conceptual clarity regarding God as the proper object of the cross, a point further developed in penal substitution. Anselm's view is often criticized for being too culturally influenced by the feudal system and its emphasis on legal relationships.[49] As the story goes, Anselm elevated the concept of *honor* into a legal framework that required exact satisfaction to restore a person's dishonored name. For Anselm, Christ's death provided the exact satisfaction or payment for our sin. Although there is a modicum of truth in this critique, Anselm's view was not *merely* indebted to feudalism. For Anselm, sin is not against an abstract law but against *God*. The Reformers later fortified Anselm's view by stressing God's holiness, righteousness, and justice, but Anselm rightly insisted that the true object of the cross is God, given *who* God is and that sin is against *him*. Anselm, along with the Reformers, correctly grasped the idea that central to one's view of the cross, including one's view of justification, is one's doctrine of God.[50]

This does not mean that the Reformers did not see problems with Anselm's view. For example, Anselm overstressed God's honor instead of accenting God's holiness and justice. Anselm did not fully stress that Christ underwent vicarious punishment to meet the demands of God's holiness and his personal wrath against sin, which would

---

42. Eusebius of Caesarea, *Proof of the Gospel* 10.1.
43. See Athanasius, *On the Incarnation of the Word* 20, in *NPNF2*, 4:343.
44. John Chrysostom, *Homilies of St. John Chrysostom: Homilies on 1 Timothy*, hom. 7, in *NPNF1*, 13:431.
45. See Tertullian, *On Flight in Persecution* 12, in *ANF*, 4:123; Augustine, *The City of God* 10.20, in *NPNF1*, 2:193; Augustine, *On the Trinity* 4.14.19, in *NPNF1*, 3:79.
46. Augustine, *On the Trinity* 4.12.15, in *NPNF1*, 3:77.
47. Epistle to Diognetus 9.2–5, in *ANF*, 1:28.
48. Anselm, *Why God Became Man*, in *Anselm of Canterbury: The Major Works*, ed. Brian Davies and G. R. Evans, Oxford World's Classics (Oxford: Oxford University Press, 1998), 260–356.
49. See Katherine Sonderegger, "Anselmian Atonement," in Johnson, *T&T Clark Companion to Atonement*, 175–93. For an example of this criticism, see Green and Baker, *Recovering the Scandal of the Cross*, 151–61.
50. See Adonis Vidu, *Atonement, Law, and Justice: The Cross in Historical and Cultural Contexts* (Grand Rapids, MI: Baker Academic, 2014).

have required Anselm to connect the cross's necessity more directly to God's nature. In addition, Anselm did not stress enough God's love,[51] nor did he "connect" Christ to his people by covenantal union.[52] Anselm failed to sufficiently locate Christ's work within its biblical, covenantal context and thus de-emphasized Christ's covenantal representation and substitution. By not working with the Bible's own covenantal categories, Anselm did not unite the life *and* death of Christ as the obedient incarnate Son to his people and thus did not sufficiently stress the vicarious obedience of Christ as the ground of our justification before God. By neglecting Christ's obedience as our new covenant head, Anselm failed to properly capture the biblical warrant for our justification and to adequately explain both how Christ's righteousness becomes ours and how his death fully satisfies God's righteous demands. The Reformers and their heirs improved on Anselm by better connecting Christ's cross to our justification via our covenantal union in Christ.

Nevertheless, probably the central reason why penal substitution came into its own with the Reformers and their heirs was due to the key theological insight they gave to the church, namely, greater clarity regarding the God-law-sin relationship—a relationship also foundational to the doctrine of justification.[53] The Reformers and especially their heirs (e.g., Francis Turretin, John Owen) argued that the triune God *is the law* and not merely the adjudicator of laws external to him. In relation to sin, this is why, given who God is, our sin necessarily clashes with his righteous character. God *cannot* tolerate iniquity; he *must* act with holy justice against it. Yet God is also the God of grace and love who promises to redeem us. If we are to be justified, then the triune God must act in grace *and* provision, and in a way that is consistent with himself. As creatures *and* sinners, we can offer God nothing. In our sin, we deserve only its penalty—spiritual and physical death (Gen. 2:16–17; Rom. 6:23). Yet our triune God, prompted solely by his grace, planned our salvation in his eternal wisdom. As Donald Macleod writes, "The triune God resolve[d] to save the world, and to accept the good offices of a Mediator who shall act for mankind as their representative and suffer for them as their substitute: so accommodating is the divine will, and so predisposed to forgive our transgressions."[54] Yet in choosing to redeem us, God cannot deny himself; our salvation must be consistent with who he is in his holy justice. For our part, we offer nothing to God for our salvation, but for God's part, *he* alone must save us. God will provide the perfect substitute, and given that our sin is against *him*, that substitute must be God himself.[55] In God's eternal plan, the divine Son becomes our Mediator, and by virtue of his incarnation, he

---

51. See H. D. McDonald, *The Atonement of the Death of Christ: In Faith, Revelation, and History* (Grand Rapids, MI: Baker, 1985), 171–72.
52. See McDonald, *Atonement of the Death of Christ*, 172–73.
53. See Vidu, *Atonement, Law, and Justice*, 92–97; cf. Herman Bavinck, *Reformed Dogmatics*, vol. 3, *Sin and Salvation in Christ* (2006), 345.
54. Donald Macleod, *Christ Crucified: Understanding the Atonement* (Downers Grove, IL: IVP Academic, 2014), 177.
55. Stott reminds us that in the drama of the cross, we see not three actors but two: God and ourselves. Not "God as he is in himself (the Father), but God nevertheless, God made-man-in-Christ (the Son). Hence the importance of those New Testament passages which speak of the death of Christ as the death of God's Son. . . . For in giving his Son he was giving himself. This being so, it is the Judge himself who in holy love assumed the role of the innocent victim, for in and through the person of the Son he himself bore the penalty which he himself inflicted." *Cross of Christ*, 158.

is able to represent us as our covenant head. In his obedient life, Christ renders perfect human obedience for us—the true covenant keeper—and in his death, he bears the penalty of our sin. His work is fully sufficient to ground our justification.

Penal Substitution's Link to Justification

The Reformers' (and especially their heirs') grasp of the God-law-sin relationship is crucial not only in explaining penal substitution but also in explaining why penal substitution is linked inseparably to justification. Of all the diverse atonement theologies, penal substitution best captures the God-centered nature of the cross and how God simultaneously remains just and the justifier of the ungodly (Rom. 3:24–26; 4:5). Other atonement theologies make the object of the cross either to be sin (e.g., forms of the recapitulation view), Satan (e.g., the ransom theory), or the powers (e.g., forms of *Christus Victor*), or they cast the cross as the means by which God upholds the moral governing of the world (e.g., the governmental view).[56] No doubt, these views capture many biblical truths, but they also unite in downplaying or denying the biblical understanding of the God-law-sin relationship. By contrast, penal substitution, while vociferously insisting that there are numerous entailments of the cross, contends that the "internal mechanism" of the cross is best explained by the God-law-sin relationship.[57] Thus, the ultimate object of the cross is not sin, Satan, or the powers but God. Given God's choice to justify us, he cannot do so by denying himself. God must meet his own righteous demands, and the only way he can do so is in God the Son incarnate. By grasping the God-law-sin relationship, the Reformers and their heirs grounded the gospel of sovereign grace in God himself and explained why Christ's penal-substitutionary work is the basis for our justification.

For example, John Calvin captured this point by explaining that because Jesus acted in our place, "we have in his death the complete fulfillment of salvation, for through it we are reconciled to God, his righteous judgment is satisfied, the curse is removed, and the penalty paid in full."[58] Martin Luther taught that through Christ alone our sin, guilt, and punishment were atoned for and that by "putting on your sinful person, he [Christ] bore your sin, death, and curse. He became a sacrifice and a curse for you, in order thus to set you free from the curse of the law."[59] The Heidelberg Catechism (1563)

---

56. Among theologians in the Patristic era, a recapitulation view is often identified with Irenaeus and Athanasius, while a ransom-to-Satan view is associated with Origen and Gregory of Nyssa. *Christus Victor* is a form of the ransom-to-Satan view, yet in modern theology, it is associated with Gustaf Aulén and various current theologians from a wide theological spectrum ranging from Gregory Boyd to N. T. Wright. The governmental view is often identified with Arminian theology (e.g., Hugo Grotius, John Miley), although Jacobus Arminius himself held to penal substitution. For a discussion of these views in church history, see Ben Pugh, *Atonement Theories: A Way through the Maze* (Eugene, OR: Cascade Books, 2014); cf. McDonald, *Atonement of the Death of Christ*, 115–341.

57. For a description of "means" and "internal mechanism," see Jeremy R. Treat, *The Crucified King: Atonement and Kingdom in Biblical and Systematic Theology* (Grand Rapids, MI: Zondervan, 2014), 45–50, 225n123. Cf. D. A. Carson, "Atonement in Romans 3:21–26: 'God Presented Him as a Propitiation,'" in *The Glory of the Atonement: Biblical, Historical, and Practical Perspectives; Essays in Honor of Roger R. Nicole*, ed. Charles E. Hill and Frank A. James III (Downers Grove, IL: InterVarsity Press, 1998), 136–39.

58. John Calvin, *Institutes of the Christian Religion*, ed. John T. McNeill, trans. Ford Lewis Battles, LCC 20–21 (Philadelphia: Westminster, 1960), 2.16.13.

59. Martin Luther, *Lectures on Galatians*, in *LW* 26:288. Timothy George nicely illustrates how Luther viewed the God-law-sin relationship in the cross. George argues that Luther did not completely accept Anselm's *either punishment or*

captured the God-centered nature of the cross in question 40: "Why did Christ have to suffer death?" Answer: "Because God's justice and truth require it: nothing else could pay for our sins except the death of the Son of God."[60]

One last important observation: to establish the inseparable link between penal substitution and the doctrine of justification, the Reformers and their heirs also placed the entire discussion of the cross and justification within the Bible's storyline, which provides the theological content and framework to make sense of both doctrines. For example, Calvin places Christ's work within the Bible's own covenantal structures and then develops Christ's threefold office of prophet, priest, and king. Similar to the recapitulation theme of the Patristic era, Calvin also speaks of the cross's achievement by tracing the Adam–last Adam typological relationship with a specific focus on Christ's active and passive obedience as our new covenant head. Also, Calvin thinks of the cross in *Christus Victor* terms while noting that the "internal mechanism" of the cross is penal substitution, given our sin before God.[61] All this was necessary to make clear the inseparable and systemic connection between the human problem and its solution in Christ and his work.

Alternative Atonement Theologies

What about other atonement theologies? Can they ground the doctrine of justification in the same way as penal substitution? My answer is no. Why? Because *all* non-penal-substitution views, as varied as they are, unite in viewing the God-law-sin relationship differently, which correspondingly requires a recasting of the doctrine of justification. Although there are multiple views of the cross, a spectrum emerges in relation to the theology proper sketched above. On the one end is penal substitution, which insists that God cannot justify us apart from a perfect obedience imputed to us and the full payment of our sin. On the opposite end is the view that God *can* justify us apart from an atonement and the full satisfaction of God's righteous demands—what I label the Socinian-classic, liberal-postmodern view. Between these two views is some version of the governmental view—a kind of *via media*. It insists that God *cannot* justify us unless "some kind" of satisfaction of God's justice is achieved, yet it denies that our justification is only possible if Christ perfectly obeys for us *and* satisfies the full retributive demands of God's justice in his death. But what is important to observe is that the governmental view necessarily redefines the nature of Christ's cross *and* the doctrine of justification. Before we turn to this point, let us outline these alternatives to penal

---

satisfaction alternative since "the satisfaction Christ offered to the Father on the cross was not in lieu of the penalty owed because of sin. No, it was precisely the penalty (*poena*) itself due to us from God the Judge because of our transgression of his holiness, justice and goodness." See George, "The Atonement in Martin Luther's Theology," in Hill and James, *Glory of the Atonement*, 274.

60. "Heidelberg Catechism," Christian Reformed Church, accessed February 24, 2018, https://www.crcna.org/welcome/beliefs/confessions/heidelberg-catechism.

61. See Robert A. Peterson, *Calvin and the Atonement: What the Renowned Pastor and Teacher Said about the Cross of Christ* (Fearn, Ross-shire, Scotland: Mentor, 1999).

substitution and think a bit more about how they reconceive of the God-law-sin relationship, which is foundational to penal substitution *and* the doctrine of justification.

The Socinian-Classic, Liberal-Postmodern View of the Atonement

Socinianism represents a nonorthodox rejection of penal substitution and redefinition of justification. Broadly conceived, Socinianism continues today within the liberal theological tradition. Faustus Socinus (1539–1604), a founder of the movement, rejected historic Christianity, specifically, the doctrines of the Bible's authority, the Trinity, Christ's deity, original sin, and not surprisingly, penal substitution and forensic justification.[62] Although Socinianism is contrary to historic Christianity, in its view of the God-law relationship, it represents a stream of thought that continues to our present day.

What was the Socinian view in its original expression? Similar to earlier forms of divine voluntarism that viewed God's acts solely in terms of his will,[63] Socinianism viewed the law as a function of God's will and *not* of his will *and nature*. God, then, may decide to exercise retributive justice, but there is no necessity to do so. For this reason, God can forgive sin without atonement. For Socinianism, then, penal substitution is *unnecessary*; *unjust*, because Christ as the innocent person suffers while the guilty go free; and *unloving*, because it portrays a God who delights in innocent suffering. God can justify us on the basis of our life and works and apart from Christ's cross. Richard Muller captures this point: "The Socinian argument was that God's punitive justice was the result of the free will of God, much like the creation of the world. Just as God was free to will or not will the existence of the world, so is he free to will or not will the enactment of justice and the punishment of sin."[64] As Muller explains, "By extension and intent, the [Socinian] argument undermined the satisfaction theory of atonement: if the Socinian view were correct, salvation could be grounded in something other than a satisfaction of the divine justice."[65]

Why the cross? The Socinian answer was a variation of the moral-influence view, which had its roots in the theology of Peter Abelard (1079–1142) but with some major modifications owing to its nonorthodoxy.[66] Given the Socinian view that God's love is more fundamental than God's justice and that divine justice is a function of God's will, Christ's death is not necessary to satisfy divine justice. Because Christ is the model man, his death serves as the best example of God's love and mercy.[67] Christ's true significance lies not in his death but in his exemplary life.

The Socinian view, unfortunately, is not a historical aberration; it continues to dominate theological liberalism.[68] In nineteenth-century "classic" liberal theology and in

---

62. For a discussion of Socinianism, see Bavinck, *Reformed Dogmatics*, 3:347–51.
63. See Vidu, *Atonement, Law, and Justice*, 79–88.
64. Muller, *Post-Reformation Reformed Dogmatics*, 3:491. Cf. Alan W. Gomes, "Socinus," in Johnson, *T&T Clark Companion to the Atonement*, 753–57.
65. Muller, *Post-Reformation Reformed Dogmatics*, 3:491.
66. See Gregg R. Allison, *Historical Theology: An Introduction to Christian Doctrine* (Grand Rapids, MI: Zondervan, 2011), 397–98.
67. See Allison, *Historical Theology*, 402.
68. For example, see Horace Bushnell, *God in Christ* (repr., New York: AMS Press, 1972); L. Harold DeWolf, *The Case for Theology in Liberal Perspective* (Philadelphia: Westminster, 1959). For a critique of liberalism, see J. Gresham Machen, *Christianity and Liberalism*, new ed. (Grand Rapids, MI: Eerdmans, 2009).

today's "neoliberal, postmodern" theology, the God-law-sin view of Socinianism continues albeit with different emphases.[69] But despite differences, liberal theology unites in separating God's law from God's nature, thus making the exercise of divine justice a voluntary exercise of God's will while stressing the priority of divine love. God, to justify us, does *not* demand full payment for our sin or the imputation of Christ's righteousness to us. This kind of theology, whether old or new, rejects historic Christianity because it adopts a different view of God—his triune nature, holiness, justice, and love—and correspondingly, a different view of sin, salvation, and Christ.

The Governmental View of the Atonement

The governmental view emerges from within orthodoxy, unlike the previous view, and it takes on a number of formulations. In the post-Reformation era, the view served as a *via media* between Socinianism and penal substitution and is identified with Hugo Grotius, John Miley, and many in the Arminian tradition.[70] Yet it is not limited to this specific formulation. For example, today, people who reject penal substitution adopt the basic understanding of the God-law-sin relationship within the governmental view and then combine it with versions of recapitulation, *Christus Victor*, vicarious repentance, or a "many metaphors" approach, thus embracing substitution but not *penal* substitution. These views may be diverse, yet they unite by insisting that penal substitution is *not* the best explanation of the "internal mechanism" of the cross.[71]

Description of the Governmental View

The governmental view insists that Christ's person and work are necessary for our salvation but only in a "hypothetical" sense, since God could have redeemed us apart from Christ's death if he had so chosen. Yet God has chosen that Christ and his work are the means by which we are justified; Christ alone is Savior, and apart from his

---

69. For the classical-liberal tradition, see Friedrich Schleiermacher and Albrecht Ritschl in McDonald, *Atonement of the Death of Christ*, 208–15. For a discussion of postmodern-pluralistic thought, see Kevin J. Vanhoozer, "The Atonement in Postmodernity: Guilt, Goats, and Gifts," in Hill and James, *Glory of the Atonement*, 367–404.

70. Representing a minority view, Garry Williams questions whether Hugo Grotius held to the governmental view. Garry Williams, "A Critical Exposition of Hugo Grotius's Doctrine of the Atonement in *De Satisfactione Christi*" (DPhil diss., Oxford University, 1999). For a traditional interpretation of Grotius, see Gert van den Brink, "Hugo Grotius," in Johnson, *T&T Clark Companion to the Atonement*, 523–25. Roger Olson also argues that Arminius and John Wesley embraced penal substitution and not the governmental view. Roger E. Olson, *Arminian Theology: Myths and Realities* (Downers Grove, IL: IVP Academic, 2006), 200–241. Also see Stephen M. Ashby, "A Reformed Arminian View," in *Four Views on Eternal Security*, ed. J. Matthew Pinson (Grand Rapids, MI: Zondervan, 2002), 137–87. Ashby is Arminian yet holds to penal substitution and the imputation of Christ's righteousness. Yet within Arminianism there is a strong embrace of the governmental view *and* a corresponding denial of the doctrine of imputation, for example, John Miley, Philip Limborch, Charles Finney, H. Orton Wiley, R. Larry Shelton—hence Arminianism's identification with the view. For a survey of Wesleyan-Arminian theology on the atonement, see Thomas H. McCall, "Wesleyan Theologies," in Johnson, *T&T Clark Companion to the Atonement*, 797–800.

71. For example, see Rutledge, *Crucifixion*; Wright, *Day the Revolution Began*; Belousek, *Atonement, Justice, and Peace*; Green and Baker, *Recovering the Scandal of the Cross*; Scot McKnight, *A Community Called Atonement* (Nashville: Abingdon, 2007); Colin E. Gunton, *The Actuality of Atonement: A Study of Metaphor, Rationality, and the Christian Tradition* (London: T&T Clark, 1988); Hans Boersma, *Violence, Hospitality, and the Cross: Reappropriating the Atonement Tradition* (Grand Rapids, MI: Baker Academic, 2004); John McLeod Campbell, *The Nature of the Atonement*, 2nd ed. (1867; repr., Edinburgh: Handsel Press, 1996); Gregory A. Boyd, "Christus Victor View," in *The Nature of the Atonement: Four Views*, ed. James Beilby and Paul Eddy (Downers Grove, IL: IVP Academic, 2006), 23–49; Joel B. Green, "Kaleidoscopic View," in Beilby and Eddy, *Nature of the Atonement*, 157–85.

work, there is no salvation.[72] However, the governmental view revises the God-law-sin relationship of penal substitution. It insists that God *can* justify us without requiring the full payment of our sin *and* a perfect obedience before him—hence the rejection of Christ's imputed righteousness.

Why does the governmental view revise the God-law-sin relationship? John Miley tells us. Miley denies that God's justice *necessitates* the full payment of our sin. He acknowledges that God's punishment of sin is just and righteous "but not in itself an obligation. The intrinsic evil of sin renders its penal retribution just, but not a requirement of judicial rectitude."[73] God, as the moral governor, can choose to relax the requirements of divine retributive justice without requiring full satisfaction, thus forgiving sinners by his mercy alone. Divine forgiveness and our justification do *not* demand a penal substitute to obey for us and fully pay for our sin.[74]

But how can God relax the requirements of divine retributive justice and still remain just? If God can forgive us because of his mercy, why not embrace Socinianism and argue that the cross is not necessary for our salvation? Two further points are required to account for the overall view.

First, as Oliver Crisp explains, one must grasp that the governmental view decouples divine *rectoral* justice (i.e., God's governance of the world according to his moral law) from divine *retributive* justice (i.e., God's demands that his law is perfectly obeyed and that any violation of it results in eternal death) for the purposes of our salvation. Crisp clarifies:

> Whereas the former [rectoral justice] must be satisfied in some sense, there may be a relaxation of the requirements of divine retributive justice so that Christ may act in a manner consistent with rectoral justice . . . but without acting so as to satisfy divine retribution as a penal substitute.[75]

For the governmental view,

> rectoral justice *must* be satisfied, whereas retributive justice *may* be satisfied. God may waive the satisfaction of retributive justice and remain perfectly just in so acting because this aspect of God's distributive justice may be relaxed. The same cannot be said of rectoral justice, which is dependent on the divine moral law, and therefore may not be relaxed without vitiating God's just and moral rule of the created order.[76]

---

72. See Oliver D. Crisp, "Penal Non-Substitution," *JTS*, n.s., 59, no. 1 (2008): 140–53.
73. John Miley, *Systematic Theology* (New York: Eaton & Mains, 1894), 2:162.
74. Various streams of Calvinism also embrace the governmental view, sometimes dubbed the "Edwardian theory." See E. A. Park, "Introductory Essay," in *The Atonement: Discourses and Treatises by Edwards, Smalley, Macxy, Emmons, Griffin, Burge, and Weeks*, ed. Edwards Amasa Park (Boston: Congregational Board of Publications, 1859), ix–lxxx. Park captures the Edwardian theory in nine propositions. On many points, even though the Edwardian theory differs from Arminianism, they both agree that Christ "satisfied the general justice of God, but did not satisfy his distributive justice," or that Christ suffered an "equivalent in meaning to the punishment threatened in the moral law, and thus they satisfied Him who is determined to maintain the honor of this law, but they did not satisfy the demands of the law itself of our punishment," or that Christ honors the distributive justice of God but God does not "eternally demand the punishment of every one who has sinned" (x).
75. Crisp, "Penal Non-Substitution," 148–49.
76. Crisp, "Penal Non-Substitution," 149.

Why is this point significant? It explains why the governmental view argues that Christ's death is required in satisfying rectoral justice but *not* retributive justice, hence its rejection of penal substitution as necessary. Since God is the moral governor, he governs his world by upholding the moral order. God's law is for the ordering of society, and that ordering is secured only as the moral law is upheld. Contrary to Socinianism, if God does not satisfy rectoral justice but merely demonstrates his mercy by forgiving sinful people, he undermines himself as the governor and does not act in the best interests of the governed. Christ's death, then, satisfies rectoral justice and reveals what God thinks of sin, but it does not satisfy the full demands of God's retributive justice.

How, then, are sinners justified before God? By a combination of Christ's satisfying God's rectoral justice and our expressing faith and repentance. But Christ does *not* bear the penalty of divine retributive justice for us, nor is our guilt imputed to him and his righteousness to us. In fact, none of this is necessary for God to justify us since God is able to relax the retributive demands of the law. Since God does *not* demand perfect obedience from us, Christ does *not* have to obey the law perfectly or pay the full penalty of our sin. Instead, Christ's atoning death functions as a suitable equivalent that upholds God's moral governance and reveals the awful nature of our sin. Objectively, Christ's death upholds the moral governance of the world, while the demands of God's retributive justice are relaxed. Subjectively, the punishment inflicted on Christ is *exemplary*: it reveals God's hatred of sin and motivates us to repent and to follow Christ. Yet we must still ask, How can God relax the demands of his retributive justice and still remain just? This question leads to the second point required to account fully for the governmental view.

Second, most governmental advocates think that God can relax the demands of his retributive justice because they view the moral law as a function of God's will, similar to divine voluntarism and contrary to penal substitution.[77] In other words, many advocates of the view insist that the "moral law" is a function of God's will and thus "outside" him. Because the law is *not* intrinsic or essential to God's nature, he is free to relax its full retributive demands. Unlike post-Reformation theology, which maintains that God *cannot* forgive sin without its full satisfaction,[78] the governmental view argues that God is free to justify us without the full payment of our sin by Christ and his perfect righteousness imputed to us.[79]

---

77. Divine voluntarism is associated with Duns Scotus and William of Ockham. It argues that God's moral law is a function of God's will, which is not grounded in God's essential nature—something Reformation theology rejected. See Richard A. Muller, *Dictionary of Latin and Greek Theological Terms: Drawn Principally from Protestant Scholastic Theology* (Grand Rapids, MI: Baker, 1985), 330–33.

78. See Carl R. Trueman, "John Owen's *Dissertation on Divine Justice*: An Exercise in Christocentric Scholasticism," *CTJ* 33 (1988): 87–103.

79. Crisp notes that most advocates of the governmental view argue for a "legal voluntarism"—that is, the moral law is established by an act of the divine will. Crisp proposes that it is possible to argue that God *is the law*, to reject penal substitution, and to uphold the governmental view. He suggests that "it might still be the case, given this non-voluntaristic account of the generation of the moral law, that more than one means of salvation is available to God, consistent with his moral law." "Penal Non-Substitution," 153–57, quotation on 156. But what is it? Elsewhere, Crisp suggests that another possible means of satisfying God's justice is the vicarious penitence of Christ as a suitable equivalent, yet there are problems with this view. First, God's law, tied to his nature, demands more than perfect penitence; it demands that the *penalty* of our sin be satisfied in death (Rom. 6:23). Why *must* Christ *die*? Because apart from Christ's death as our *penal* substitute, God's own moral demand is not satisfied. Second, God demands from his image bearers perfect obedience, which we do not render but which Christ must render for us in his humanity. A perfect vicarious repentance does not meet this demand.

Given these two points of clarification, we are better able to compare and contrast the governmental view with penal substitution and to set the stage for how each view thinks of the doctrine of justification. For penal substitution, since God *is* the law, given his free choice to redeem us, he *cannot* justify sinners apart from the full payment of our sin *and* the imputation of Christ's perfect obedience to us. Given the God-law-sin relationship and the demands of the covenant, Christ's obedient life and death as our covenant representative and penal substitute are necessary for our justification before God. God himself *must* meet his own righteous demands against us in order to forgive us, since our sin is first against *him*. In addition, we need a human to represent us and to obey the full demands of God's law for us. However, for the governmental view that elevates rectoral justice over retributive justice[80] and, in most cases, decouples the moral law from God's nature, it "dismisse[s] the atonement of Christ as an exact payment of the penalty demanded by the [retributive] justice of God and expressed in his law. Christ suffered and died, not as a satisfaction for the exact penalty, but as a token of God's concern to uphold his moral law."[81] For God to justify sinners, Christ's work is required but not as a *penal* substitute who fully pays for our sin *and* whose perfect obedience is imputed to us. Instead, justification is God's declaration that we are forgiven of our sin by God's relaxing the full penalty of the law against us and receiving our repentance toward God and faith in Christ.

Critique of the Governmental View

Why is the governmental view important? Within orthodox theology, it functions as the main alternative to penal substitution. Unless one adopts the Socinian-liberal view that God can simply justify us without atonement (which Scripture and historic Christianity deny), then some form of the God-law-sin relationship of the governmental theory must be embraced. But if one walks this path, it is crucial to note that a redefinition of justification will also occur, a point I will return to below. Today, some within evangelical theology embrace the governmental view, though often combining it with other themes, such as recapitulation or *Christus Victor*.[82] Given that this view is the main alternative to penal substitution, a brief word of critique is necessary.

In contrast to the Socinian-liberal view, the governmental view better explains why Christ and his work are necessary for our salvation. God cannot simply justify sinners without a suitably equivalent act of atonement. Christ's death is required as God's chosen means to satisfy the demands of rectoral justice, thus demonstrating God's just governance.

Third, how is vicarious penitence an act of atonement? How are the *penal* consequences of sin actually atoned for? Crisp admits that most governmental advocates assume a different view of divine justice (although he tries to escape this conclusion). He states, "Specifically, [the view] must allow that, under certain conditions, and for certain acts, God may forgive sin without the penal consequences for that sin having been atoned for. God can accept Christ's vicarious humanity and penitence as sufficient without additional satisfaction for the penal consequences of human sin. This means amending the strong version of divine retributive justice with which we began [what we have called the Reformed view]. The defender of non-penal substitution might just opt for the weaker view instead, which stipulates only that divine justice does not require forgiveness." "Non-Penal Substitution," *IJST* 9, no. 4 (2007): 415–33, quotation on 432.
80. See Crisp, "Penal Non-Substitution," 149.
81. Allison, *Historical Theology*, 404.
82. For examples, see the literature in note 71.

However, negatively, the central problem of the view is its inadequate theology proper. In its standard form, it insists that the moral law is only a function of God's will and thus "outside" God. The law is *not* viewed as an expression of God's will *and* nature.[83] Because God is *not* the law, he can relax the demands of retributive justice and justify sinners without a full payment of their sin. Yet the governmental view of the God-law-sin relationship is highly questionable biblically and theologically. The triune God does not adjudicate the law as does a human judge. Rather, God *is the law*, and in our justification, God *cannot* forgive us apart from the full payment of our sin *and* his demand of a perfect obedience from his covenant creatures. Moreover, the decoupling of God's law from his nature leads to at least two further problems.

First, as Robert Letham argues, the governmental view severs "the connection between sin and punishment,"[84] which explains why it denies the need for Christ to act as our penal substitute for the satisfaction of divine justice. Oliver Crisp disagrees, arguing that Letham overlooks the prioritizing of rectoral justice over retributive justice.[85] Yet Letham assumes that divine justice is essential to God's nature, and since sin is against *him*, God cannot deny himself by relaxing his own righteous demands. For God to justify sinners, sin *must* be fully paid. Scripture also speaks of Christ *bearing* our sins on the cross, of the Father placing our iniquity on Christ, and of Christ dying specifically for our sins (Rom. 8:3; 1 Cor. 15:3; Gal. 1:4; 3:13; 1 Pet. 2:24; cf. Isa. 53:5–6, 8). This data is difficult to reconcile with a governmental view.

Second, the governmental view does not view Christ's obedient life and death as fully satisfying God's retributive justice since the guilt of sin is forgiven by God's gracious action in relaxing its punishment. Christ dies as a sacrifice to satisfy rectoral justice, but he does not die in *my* place or bear *my* sin. The penalty of sin is left unsatisfied and unpaid, which has direct implications for one's view of justification, a point to which we now turn.

Non-Penal-Substitution Atonement Theologies and the Doctrine of Justification

My overall argument is that there is an inseparable relationship between penal substitution and forensic justification and imputation. One cannot have one without the other.[86] Another way of illustrating this point is to think about how departures from penal substitution require a revision of one's doctrine of justification. Consider the spectrum of atonement theologies discussed above.

The Socinian-Classic, Liberal-Postmodern View

Socinianism and other views that adopt its interpretation of the God-law-sin relationship illustrate the inseparable relationship between one's view of atonement and justification. The Socinian view emphasizes God's love, mercy, and grace over against his

---

83. What Park labeled the "Edwardian theory" is an exception to this. See Park, "Introductory Essay," ix–lxxx.
84. Robert Letham, *The Work of Christ*, CCT (Downers Grove, IL: InterVarsity Press, 1993), 168.
85. Crisp, "Penal Non-Substitution," 160.
86. Letham illustrates this point by appealing to Rom. 4:25. *Work of Christ*, 177–94.

justice. It asserts that God *can* forgive our sin and justify us apart from atonement or the satisfaction of divine justice. In justifying us, God does not exact the full demands of his law. He is a loving Father who seeks the rehabilitation of his prodigal children. Also, given the Socinian view of divine justice, God does *not* demand perfect obedience from his creatures. For this reason, the view argues as follows: "That Christ by his death has *merited* salvation for us and has *made satisfaction* freely for our sins . . . is fallacious and erroneous and wholly pernicious."[87] Penal substitution is simply *unnecessary* for God to forgive us of our sins and to justify us.

Why, then, did Jesus die? He died for a variety of reasons but primarily as a moral example. Justification has more to do with God's acceptance of us as we progress morally, following Christ's example and walking in his steps. Justification is not the legal imputation of Christ's righteousness to sinners. When we repent of our sins and live moral lives, God regards us as righteous people. Bruce Demarest captures this view well: "God forgives and raises to immortality all who repent, who follow the precepts and example of Christ (a human prophet whose death was the supreme display of obedience), and who strive to live virtuously."[88]

In the nineteenth and early twentieth centuries, classic liberalism affirmed a similar view.[89] Albrecht Ritschl (1822–1889) is a good example of the view as represented by his work *The Christian Doctrine of Justification and Reconciliation*. For Ritschl, similar to the Socinians, the context of justification is not divine justice but divine love: "The conception of love is the only adequate conception of God."[90] God can forgive our sins apart from an atoning sacrifice and restore us to relationship with him. But in our sin (defined more in terms of ignorance and human weakness), we have wrong views of God, and in salvation, God corrects our false views in Christ. Jesus is the founder of God's kingdom, and in his life and teaching, he reveals to us that God is love, eager to forgive, and wanting us to live ethical lives. For Ritschl and much of classic liberal theology, justification is not God's declaration that we stand right before God because Christ Jesus has paid for our sins and perfectly obeyed for us,[91] but justification is God accepting us, the removal of our false sense of guilt, and our restoration to a proper trust of God. Those who experience justification and reconciliation will live moral lives and help usher in God's kingdom.

More examples could be multiplied, but the point is this: the Socinian-classic, liberal-postmodern view demonstrates that there is an inseparable relationship between one's doctrine of God, Christ, and the nature of his atonement and one's understanding of the meaning of justification.

---

87. "The Racovian Catechism (1605)," 5.8, in *The Polish Brethren: Documentation of the History and Thought of Unitarianism in the Polish-Lithuanian Commonwealth and in the Diaspora, 1601–1685*, ed. and trans. G. H. Williams (Missoula, MT: Scholars Press, 1980), 1:222.
88. Demarest, *Cross and Salvation*, 348.
89. For an extensive survey of the liberal position, see chap. 24, by Bruce P. Baugus, in this volume.
90. Albrecht Ritschl, *The Christian Doctrine of Justification and Reconciliation: The Positive Development of the Doctrine*, ed. H. R. Mackintosh and A. B. Macaulay (Clifton, NJ: Reference Book Publishers, 1966), 274.
91. Ritschl called forensic justification and imputation "altogether false." Ritschl, *Christian Doctrine*, 70.

The Governmental View and Its Varieties

It is not surprising that the governmental view also redefines the Reformation's view of justification. For example, for those within the Arminian tradition who accept the governmental view, Christ's cross is seen as suitably meeting the demands of divine rectoral justice but not retributive justice. As such, by Christ's death, God relaxes the full penal demands of the law, which results in our justification as we repent and believe in Christ.

A number of Arminian authors make this precise point. For example, John Miley writes, "God may and does wish that he may save. . . . And real as the divine displeasure is against sin and against sinners, atonement is made, not in its satisfaction, but in fulfillment of the rectoral office of justice."[92] Christ's suffering atones for our sins but not in the full retributive justice sense. Or as H. Orton Wiley states, "The atonement was not a satisfaction to any internal principle of the divine nature, but to the necessities of government."[93] Or R. Larry Shelton says it this way: "The governmental interpretation of the atoning sufferings of Christ is not that they substitute Christ for the sinner in receiving the penalty of retributive justice, but the Atonement is provisory in that it renders people salvable but does not of necessity save them."[94] J. Kenneth Grider insists on something similar. In our justification there is the nonexecution of the full penalty of our sin, since Christ's death upholds God's rectoral justice, which allows for God to forgive us while remaining consistent with that justice. Christ suffers for all without exception (universal) as a provisional substitute for a relaxed penalty, and God forgives all those who repent and believe while maintaining his moral governance.[95]

Theological Implications of the Governmental View

At least two theological conclusions follow from the governmental view of the cross. First, given proponents' view of the God-law-sin relationship, for God to forgive our sins, he does not require the full payment of our sin. All that is required is a general, provisional satisfaction for sin that upholds divine rectoral justice, which then allows God to relax the law's full demand. Second, in relaxing the law's full demand, God does not require from us a perfect obedience. This is why a good portion of Arminian theology consistently denies the imputation of Christ's active and passive obedience.[96] Both of these conclusions result in a redefined view of justification.

---

92. Miley, *Systematic Theology*, 2:186. Also see Charles Finney, *Finney's Systematic Theology*, ed. J. H. Fairchild (Minneapolis: Bethany, 1976). Finney argues that Christ's death upholds the moral governing of the world but that it does not satisfy the demands of retributive justice (322). Finney denies both the imputation of Adam's sin and Christ's righteousness (333). In terms of justification, God pardons sinners who reform their lives by following Christ, and the conditions of justification are a combination of Christ's sacrifice, our repentance, faith in Christ, and our present sanctification. As Demarest summarizes Finney's view, "Finney believed that God declares righteous persons who actually *are so*." *Cross and Salvation*, 354.

93. H. Orton Wiley, *Christian Theology* (Kansas City, MO: Beacon Hill, 1952), 2:252.

94. R. Larry Shelton, "Initial Salvation: The Redemptive Grace of God in Christ," in *A Contemporary Wesleyan Theology: Biblical, Systematic, and Practical*, ed. Charles W. Carter (Grand Rapids, MI: Francis Asbury Press, 1983), 504. Also see Shelton, *Cross and Covenant: Interpreting the Atonement for 21st Century Mission* (Tyrone, GA: Paternoster, 2006), 171–225.

95. See J. Kenneth Grider, "Atonement," in *Beacon Dictionary of Theology*, ed. Richard S. Taylor (Kansas City, MO: Beacon Hill Press, 1983), 54–55.

96. Richard Watson (1781–1833) denies the imputation of Christ's righteousness. Watson was a Wesleyan theologian who argued that justification is God's forgiveness of our sins and an act of God's grace received by faith. By justification we

Willard Taylor captures the Arminian view in these words: "Calvin taught that imputation in the strict sense means that the obedience of Christ is accepted for us as if it were our own. This is fictional."[97] Taylor goes on to argue that justification is "both a declaration and a renovation" whereby God forgives a person of sin and "accepts him as righteous and makes him a new creature with initial righteousness, on the basis of the sinner's trustful and obedient response to the redeeming work of Christ on the Cross."[98] R. Larry Shelton says something similar: "On the basis of God's justifying action in the death and resurrection of Christ, the sinner has been acquitted and enjoys in actuality the righteousness of a new relationship with God."[99] But in our justification, there is no imputation of Christ's righteousness. Shelton goes on to say, "God pronounces believers righteous and justifies them when they fulfill by faith-obedience the requirements of the covenant relationship. This faith-obedience is based on Christ's work. . . . This is righteousness, not a quality to be imputed or imparted."[100] Shelton speaks of our righteousness in terms of a covenant relationship, but he does not stress God's covenant demand for perfect obedience. Justification is about being "rightwised" with God, not about the imputation of Christ's righteousness.[101] For many within the Arminian tradition, this also entails that we can forfeit our justification by willful sin so that the certainty of our final justification is impossible. But this view of justification is quite different from the Reformation view. What has drastically changed is what it means to be *now* justified in Christ on the basis of his finished work and imputed righteousness to us.

What results from this redefinition of justification? Theologically and practically, this redefined view of justification entails that before God our sin is not fully paid and that we have no positive or imputed righteousness, which is hard to square with Scripture. In addition, this view of justification also does not meet the need of a sinner's heart and conscience. Given this version of Arminian theology, because God can relax the law, as Donald Macleod points out, Arminians argue that God no longer requires "legal obedience," "that is, compliance with the whole moral law."[102] Instead, "he [God] now require[s] only 'evangelical obedience'; in other words, faith and repentance," which entails that "the righteousness of Christ [has] to be supplemented by something of our own. Justification [is] no longer *through* faith (*per fidem*); it [is] *on account of* faith (*propter fidem*)."[103] This may look like a distinction with no practical difference. Ultimately, however, this subtle shift entails a different view of what Christ achieved on

---

are no longer guilty for our sins. Also, God counts us righteous but on account of faith and not the imputation of Christ's righteousness. He regarded the latter as "fictitious." "For this notion, that the righteousness of Christ is so imputed as to be accounted our own," he argued, "there is no warrant in the word of God." Or, "Justification, being the pardon of sin by judicial sentence of the offended Majesty of heaven . . . the term affords no ground for the notion, that it imports the imputation or accounting to us the active and passive righteousness of Christ, so as to make us both relatively and positively righteous." *Theological Institutes: Or, a View of the Evidences, Doctrines, Morals, and Institutions of Christianity* (New York: B. Waugh and T. Mason, 1834), 2:216, 226, 215.

97. Willard H. Taylor, "Justification," in Taylor, *Beacon Dictionary of Theology*, 298.
98. Taylor, "Justification," 298.
99. Shelton, "Initial Salvation," 493.
100. Shelton, "Initial Salvation," 494.
101. See Shelton, *Cross and Covenant*, 223.
102. Macleod, *Christ Crucified*, 180.
103. Macleod, *Christ Crucified*, 180–81.

the cross and what our justification is before God. Instead of placing our faith in Christ alone, who in his perfect obedience fully satisfied God's righteous demands, our focus shifts to Christ *and* our faith as a condition for our justification.[104] The problem with this view, however, is this: our faith and repentance are never enough. Our only hope in life and in death is that Jesus paid it all and that by faith union we are complete in him.

Macleod drives this point home by recounting the dying words of J. Gresham Machen, the founder of Westminster Theological Seminary. As Machen lay dying in a North Dakota hospital in December 1936, he wrote to his young colleague, John Murray, these words: "I am so thankful for the active obedience of Christ. No hope without it."[105] Why? Because unless Christ, as my covenant representative and substitute, fulfills *all* righteousness, obeys God's righteous demands perfectly for me, and fully pays for my sin, *my* sin before God is not fully atoned for. Consequently, I do not have a righteous standing before the Judge of the universe.

Variations of the Governmental View

What can we say about the governmental view when it is combined with other themes and emphases? Do these versions of the view also lead to a redefinition of justification given their adoption of a similar God-law-sin relationship? The answer is yes.

For example, think of some of the current formulations of the so-called New Perspective(s) on Paul. Due to the influence of the New Perspective, it is quite common to define justice/righteousness apart from God's own internal, moral nature.[106] This approach undercuts the concept that God is the law who remains true to himself and who *must* punish sin according to his own righteous demands—a concept central to retributive justice. Instead, "God's righteousness" (δικαιοσύνη θεοῦ) is defined in relation to God's moral governance, namely, *rectoral* justice. Or as Fleming Rutledge argues, we ought to view God's righteousness not as a noun but as a verb.[107] Thus, as Rutledge and others insist, "When we read in the Old Testament that God is just and righteous, this doesn't refer to a threatening abstract quality that God has over against us. It is much more like a verb than a noun, because it refers *to the power of God to make right what has been wrong.*"[108] Rutledge proposes that we translate "justification" as "rectification" because God, the righteous one, governs his universe in such a way as to make things right, which entails for us that justification is more restorative and transformative than forensic.[109] God's righteousness "is not retributive but restorative,"[110] and ultimately, it means "not so much that God *is* righteous but he *does* righteousness."[111] Or as N. T. Wright insists, God's righteousness is not first an attribute tied to God's own

---

104. See Jeffrey K. Jue, "The Active Obedience of Christ and the Theology of the Westminster Standards: A Historical Investigation," in Oliphint, *Justified in Christ*, 106–9.
105. Quoted in Jue, "Active Obedience," 181.
106. See Fesko, *Death in Adam*, 155–58.
107. See Rutledge, *Crucifixion*, 133–37.
108. Rutledge, *Crucifixion*, 134; italics original; cf. 325–30.
109. Rutledge, *Crucifixion*, 556–58.
110. Rutledge, *Crucifixion*, 136.
111. Rutledge, *Crucifixion*, 137; italics original.

holy self-sufficient nature; rather, it is his "covenant faithfulness."[112] God's righteousness, then, is more of a relational concept based on the covenant "than an absolute ethical norm,"[113] so that in Christ's cross, God defeats the powers and upholds the moral governing of his universe by "making right what is wrong in the world."[114]

Given this combination of the governmental view with *Christus Victor* and its embrace of the governmental privileging of rectoral over retributive justice, it is not surprising that a redefinition of justification occurs. For N. T. Wright, justification has nothing to do with Christ's imputed righteousness to us or Christ's acting as our penal substitute. Wright strongly rejects the doctrine of imputation. He famously states, "It makes no sense that the judge imputes, imparts, bequeaths, conveys or otherwise transfers his righteousness to either the plaintiff or the defendant. Righteousness is not an object, a substance or gas that can be passed across the courtroom."[115] Instead, justification is God's declaration that we belong to God's covenant community, *not* first that we stand right *before* God because our covenant head, representative, and substitute has fully satisfied God's righteous demands for us. In addition, Wright argues that our future justification is grounded not in Christ's righteousness alone but "on the basis of performance, not possession,"[116] which is viewed in terms of "the totality of the life lived."[117] Two assumptions here depart significantly from the Reformation's view of justification:

1. The assumption that there is no need for the full payment of our sin since justice/righteousness is about God rectifying things more in a rectoral sense than in a retributive sense
2. The assumption that in our justification God does not demand from us perfect obedience—hence the rejection of the need for Christ's imputed righteousness

What, then, is Christ achieving on the cross? In this view, he is not dying as our penal substitute who acts for us to satisfy God's righteous moral demands that we have violated.[118] In fact, Wright argues that the traditional interpretation of Romans 3:21–26 is mistaken. He insists that in this text "there is no mention here of such a punishment then exhausting divine wrath."[119] Instead, Paul says that "God has chosen to overlook the 'former sins,'" meaning that "he has pushed the 'former sins' to one side,"[120] which he interprets to mean that the "whole point of *anochē* ['passing over'] is that sins are *not* punished."[121] This entails that in Christ's cross, God is not satisfying

---

112. N. T. Wright, "Romans and the Theology of Paul," in *Pauline Theology*, vol. 3, *Romans*, ed. David M. Hay and E. Elizabeth Johnson (Minneapolis: Fortress, 1995), 38–39; Wright, *Paul and the Faithfulness of God* (Minneapolis: Fortress, 2013), 774–1042; Wright, *Day the Revolution Began*, 321–24. Cf. Rutledge, *Crucifixion*, 133.
113. Rutledge, *Crucifixion*, 327.
114. Rutledge, *Crucifixion*, 328.
115. Wright, *What Saint Paul Really Said*, 98.
116. N. T. Wright, *Romans*, in *The New Interpreter's Bible*, vol. 10 (Nashville: Abingdon, 2002), 440.
117. N. T. Wright, "The Law in Romans 2," in *Paul and the Mosaic Law*, ed. James D. G. Dunn (Grand Rapids, MI: Eerdmans, 2001), 144.
118. Wright, *Day the Revolution Began*, 331.
119. Wright, *Day the Revolution Began*, 331.
120. Wright, *Day the Revolution Began*, 331.
121. Wright, *Day the Revolution Began*, 330.

his own righteous demands against us. Instead, in the cross, Christ takes "upon himself the *consequence* of Israel's idolatry, sin, and exile, which itself brought into focus the idolatry, sin, and exile of the whole human race."[122] Through Christ's faithfulness in life and death, he has won victory over the powers and freed us from our sin and idolatry by restoring us to what God created us to be in the first place. Christ died "so that our sins could be forgiven"[123] but more in terms of a defeat of the powers, a proper demonstration that God is faithful to his covenant promises and that in the end, he makes all things right.[124]

What these departures from penal substitution illustrate is a corresponding revision of the doctrine of justification. This is another way of demonstrating an inseparable and systemic relationship between one's atonement theology and one's view of justification. If one affirms a non-penal-substitutionary view of the cross, one inevitably undercuts the basis for forensic justification and imputation, since penal substitution serves as its ground.

Biblical-Theological Truths Warranting the Reformation View[125]

So far, I have sought to demonstrate the inseparable bond between penal substitution and forensic justification and imputation, and correspondingly, to show that departures from either will inevitably lead to a redefinition of both. But why hold to the Reformation's view of the cross and justification? For Christians the only answer is that it is biblical, not only according to specific texts but also according to the Bible's entire storyline. To defend such an assertion would require much more space than I have here, so I will only outline four significant biblical truths, or building blocks, that are essential in warranting the Reformation's view of atonement and justification.

God as Triune Creator–Covenant Lord

Underneath my argument is the belief that atonement and justification debates are fundamentally theology-proper debates, especially if viewed through the prism of the God-law-sin relationship. Also, the way Scripture presents the God-law-sin bond is the same way that penal substitution and justification understand it. Let us reflect on this point, which will help establish the first crucial truth that provides biblical warrant for the Reformation view.

Who is the God of Scripture? *He* is the triune Creator–covenant Lord.[126] From the opening verses of Scripture, God is presented as the uncreated, independent, self-existent,

---

122. Wright, *Day the Revolution Began*, 330.
123. Wright, *Day the Revolution Began*, 358.
124. Rutledge argues for a similar view of the cross. In Christ, God is making all things right by destroying the powers, transforming people, and absorbing all the sin and injustices of this world. In her view, sin is not fully paid and Christ's righteousness is not imputed to us. Instead, in Christ's cross, sin is obliterated, its power is broken, and "God's righteousness"—that is, God's rectification of all things—is displayed. In the end, God upholds the moral governing of the world and removes every memory of the awful effects of sin. *Crucifixion*, 462–612.
125. This section adapts some material from Wellum, *Christ Alone*, 36–53. Used by permission of Zondervan.
126. For God as the "covenant Lord," see Frame, *Doctrine of God*, 1–115.

self-sufficient, all-powerful Lord who created the universe and governs it by his word (Genesis 1–2; Pss. 50:12–14; 93:2; Acts 17:24–25). This is why the most fundamental distinction central to all Christian theology is the Creator-creature distinction. God alone is God; all else in creation depends on God for its existence. But the transcendent lordship of God (Pss. 7:17; 9:2; 21:7; 97:9; 1 Kings 8:27; Isa. 6:1; Rev. 4:3) does not entail a remote deity or a God uninvolved in human history. God is transcendent *and* immanent, one who is fully present in his world and involved with his creatures: he freely, sovereignly, and purposefully sustains and governs all things to his desired end (Ps. 139:1–10; Acts 17:28; Eph. 1:11; 4:6).

As Creator and covenant Lord, God also sovereignly rules over his creation personally. He rules with perfect power, knowledge, and justice (Ps. 139:1–4, 16; Isa. 46:9–11; Rom. 11:33–36) as the only being who is truly independent and self-sufficient. God loves, commands, comforts, punishes, and rewards, according to the personal, covenant relationships that he establishes. As we progress through time, God discloses himself as tripersonal, a unity of three persons: Father, Son, and Spirit (Matt. 28:18–20; John 1:1–4; 1 Cor. 8:5–6; 2 Cor. 13:14). As the triune Lord, God acts in, with, and through his creatures to accomplish all he desires in the way he desires.

Scripture also presents this one Creator–covenant Lord as the Holy One over all his creation (Gen. 2:1–3; Lev. 11:44; Isa. 6:1–3). As noted above, holiness conveys much more than God's transcendence; it is uniquely associated with his aseity. In the moral realm, God's aseity entails that he *is* the law. This is why, in light of sin, God *must* remain true to himself and act in holy justice. Yet he loves his people with a holy love (Hos. 11:9). Within God there are no tensions, but because of sin and his choice to redeem us, a question emerges: How will God demonstrate his holy justice *and* covenant love? This question is only truly answered in Christ, his cross, and our justification (Rom. 3:21–26).

This brief description of God's identity undergirds the theology proper that warrants penal substitution and the doctrine of justification. Let us consider three examples to make this point. First, the *triunity of God* is minimally required to make sense of Christ's identity and cross. Jesus views himself as the eternal Son who even after adding to himself a human nature continues to relate to the Father and Spirit (John 1:1, 14). As the eternal Son, Jesus has an exclusive identity that explains why he has universal significance for all humanity and creation. Moreover, Jesus's work also unpacks Trinitarian relations. It is the Son and not the Father or the Spirit who becomes flesh. The Father sends the Son, the Spirit attends his union with human nature, and the Son bears our sin and the Father's wrath as a man in the power of the Spirit. And yet, as God the Son, Jesus lived and died in unbroken unity with the Father and Spirit because they share the same identical divine nature. Christ is not some third party acting independently of the other two divine persons. At the cross we see not three parties but only two: the triune God and humanity. The cross is a demonstration of the Father's love (John 3:16) by the gift of his Son.[127] Penal substitution is nonsensical apart from the doctrine of the Trinity.

Second, the triune God as the *covenant* God is also crucial in establishing the work of Christ. I am thinking not first about the biblical covenants in history but about the *pactum salutis*, or the "covenant of redemption."[128] Scripture teaches that God has an eternal plan of salvation (Ps. 139:16; Eph. 1:4, 11; 1 Pet. 1:20). In that plan, the divine Son, in relation to the Father and Spirit, is appointed the Mediator of his people. And the Son gladly and voluntarily accepts this appointment with its covenant stipulations and promises, which are enacted in his incarnation, life, and cross work. This eternal plan establishes Christ as Mediator, defines the nature of his mediation, and assigns specific roles to each person of the Godhead. In our redemption, all three persons act inseparably according to their personal relations. Finally, the *pactum salutis* provides for our covenantal union with Christ as our Mediator and representative substitute, which grounds the application of Christ's work to us in our justification.

Third, the *lordship* of the triune covenant God establishes a specific God-law relationship that is foundational to penal substitution and justification. When God's lordship is applied to the moral realm, it establishes why God's will *and* nature constitute the moral standard of the universe. God's righteousness is based "on the righteousness of his own nature and on his status as the ultimate criterion of rightness."[129] This point is vital in grasping why the New Perspective is flawed. Being reductionistic, it links righteousness and justice to covenant faithfulness—that is, God is righteous in that he keeps his promises to save. No doubt, this is true, but it is insufficient. God will keep his promises to his people, and he will execute justice for them and act to save them. Yet this approach fails to see first that righteousness, justice, and holiness are tied to God's nature, which entails that God's righteousness also means that he will punish sin. This latter truth is what grounds divine retributive justice and its forensic nature, and it is wrong to dismiss it as merely a Western construct. Scripture insists that God's justice is essential to him and thus explains why God *must* punish sin *and* why our justification requires a full atonement.

Adam and God's Demand for Covenantal Obedience

To establish God's demand for perfect obedience from us, it is crucial to place Adam properly in relation to the triune God, who sets the conditions of the covenant and rightly demands from his image bearers total trust and love. It is also vital to ground the truth of Christ's active and passive obedience, which are essential to penal substitution and our justification. To grasp the nature of the cross and the doctrine of justification, we must start with the creation covenant between God and humanity and see how the link between the command and curse of the first Adam leads to the coming obedience and death of the last Adam.

---

127. See Macleod, *Christ Crucified*, 90–100; Stott, *Cross of Christ*, 133–62.
128. See Macleod, *Christ Crucified*, 90–100; J. V. Fesko, *The Trinity and the Covenant of Redemption* (Fearn, Ross-shire, Scotland: Mentor, 2016).
129. Frame, *Doctrine of God*, 602.

God's demand from us for perfect covenantal obedience is established in creation, specifically, with the historical Adam.[130] Scripture divides the human race under two representative heads: Adam and Christ. In the beginning of time, God created the first Adam from the earth; in the fullness of time, God sent his Son from heaven to become the first man of the new creation (Rom. 5:14). God covenanted with the first Adam as the head of the human race to spread the image of God in humanity over the whole earth.[131] Adam's headship had a deeper privilege than ordinary fatherhood. It also had the dignity of defining what it means to be human: a son of God and his true image bearer. Yet Adam failed in his headship over humanity, thereby creating the necessity for the last Adam not to fail in his headship over a new humanity.

Central to the covenant is God's demand for obedience (Gen. 2:15–17). This demand flows from God's own identity and is apparent in his command to Adam and in his curse after Adam's disobedience. As the Creator–covenant Lord, God requires perfect trust and obedience as the only proper and permissible way to live in covenant with him. Also, the Lord created and covenanted with Adam for the purpose of bearing God's image in human dominion over creation. Adam was called to rule over creation under the rule of God in obedience to his commands and ways of righteousness, yet Adam disobeyed and ruined the entire human race.

The two trees of Eden demonstrate the nature of this requirement for covenantal obedience. When God placed Adam in Eden, he gave him two trees to guide him into the joy of covenant relationship. The first tree held forth the conditional promise of eternal life.[132] The promise is not explicit, but it is implied when God exiles Adam from Eden *so that* he could not "take also from the tree of life and eat, and live forever" (Gen. 3:22). The tree of life was placed before Adam as a sign of his reward for obedience under God's blessing to fill the earth with God's image. But Adam rejected the reward of the first tree by eating from the second tree. The tree of the knowledge of good and evil came with a clear prohibition against eating its fruit under penalty of death. This tree of death was placed before Adam as a test of his loving obedience to his Creator. But with ruinous effect, Adam disobeyed God and committed an act of treason against God.

Starting with the creation covenant shows us how God's demand of perfect obedience shapes the Bible's storyline, and it sets the backdrop to Christ's work. The historical drama of Adam's command and curse demonstrates that obedience is central to the covenant relationship. Where Adam disobeyed, the last Adam must obey for us. Moreover, the covenant places Christ and his work within a representative, legal, and substitutionary framework (Rom. 5:12–21). To undo, reverse, and pay for Adam's sin,

---

130. Today many dismiss the historicity of Adam and the fall, but this completely undercuts the Bible's storyline and renders nonsensical the link between Adam and Christ, the nature of sin, and its solution in the cross. Those who deny the historicity of Adam inevitably deny the imputation of Adam's sin and Christ's righteousness and redefine the nature of the cross and justification. On this point, see Fesko, *Death in Adam*, 235–38.

131. For a defense of a creation covenant, see Peter J. Gentry and Stephen J. Wellum, *Kingdom through Covenant: A Biblical-Theological Understanding of the Covenants*, 2nd ed. (Wheaton, IL: Crossway, 2018), 179–258, 647–712.

132. See G. K. Beale, *A New Testament Biblical Theology: The Unfolding of the Old Testament in the New* (Grand Rapids, MI: Baker Academic, 2011), 29–87.

the last Adam must come from the human race (Gen. 3:15) and render the required covenantal obedience demonstrating what we are supposed to be. Yet the reversal of Adam's sin will require more than a demonstration of true humanity; it will require a representative substitute who will pay the penalty for our sin and give us his righteousness, thus securing our justification before God.

Human Sin, Divine Justice, and Divine Forgiveness

In the Bible's storyline, Adam's sin changes everything. From Genesis 3 onward, Adam's disobedience results in living under God's wrath and in humanity's corruption.[133] Genesis 1:31 says that "God saw all that he had made, and it was very good." But Genesis 3 records that Adam disobeyed God (3:6), which resulted in the opposite of good: Adam and Eve were exiled from Eden (3:21–24). By Genesis 6:5, we hear that "the Lord saw how great the wickedness of the human race had become on the earth, and that every inclination of the thoughts of the human heart was only evil all the time." Through his disobedience, Adam, our covenant head, filled the earth with a corrupt image of God, with wickedness instead of righteousness, so that Paul would later say, "There is no one righteous, not even one. . . . For all have sinned and fall short of the glory of God" (Rom. 3:10, 23). In truth, Adam's covenant disobedience turned the created order upside down so that "in Adam" we all die (5:12–21) because of the penalty for sin (6:23). The only way we can explain Adam's sin being charged to us is by legal imputation, given that Adam is our covenant head.[134] The result of such imputation is that humanity now stands guilty and condemned before God—something only God can remedy and reverse.

But how? If God chooses to redeem us, then how does he do so and still remain true to himself given *who* God is? God *must* punish sin because he *is* holy and personal; God cannot overlook our sin or relax the retributive demands of his justice. To be justified, we must have our sin fully atoned for.[135] But God also created and covenanted with man to glorify himself in the righteous rule of humanity over creation, not in his destruction. How, then, can God punish our sin, satisfy his own righteous demands, *and* justify sinners?

As we fast-forward to the New Testament, we discover that God does both in the gracious provision of Christ and his work. In Christ's incarnation and obedient human life, he, as the Mediator of the new covenant and our legal representative, obeys for us. And in his obedient death, the divine Son satisfies his own righteous demands against us by bearing the penalty for our sin as our substitute (Rom. 5:18–19; Phil. 2:6–11; Heb. 5:1–10). God then declares sinners just. Through our faith union with Christ, his perfect obedience is imputed to us, and the debt of our sin is fully atoned for (Rom. 4:1–8; 5:1–2, 9–11), which is precisely how the New Testament grounds our justification. Romans

---

133. See Moo, *Romans*, 315; cf. Gentry and Wellum, *Kingdom through Covenant*, 666–85.
134. For a defense of the imputation of Adam's sin to the human race, see Fesko, *Death in Adam*, 175–273; Madueme and Reeves, *Adam, the Fall, and Original Sin*.
135. See Stott, *Cross of Christ*, 124–32.

3:21–26 explicitly explains *why* Christ and his cross are necessary for our justification—an explanation that centers on the question of how a holy God can truly justify the ungodly without denying himself. Three points from the text will substantiate this point.

First, Romans 3:21–26 must be placed in the larger context of Paul's argument.[136] Starting in 1:18–3:20, Paul establishes that apart from Christ, all humans (Jews and Gentiles) are under divine wrath and stand condemned before God,[137] which he ultimately traces back to the sin of Adam as our covenant head (5:12–21). By citing a litany of Old Testament texts in 3:9–20, Paul concludes that apart from God's gracious initiative to redeem, we all stand guilty and condemned before God.

Second, in Romans 3:21, Paul shifts to the good news centered on God's grace and provision of Christ and his cross. Paul highlights the redemptive-historical shift that has occurred in Christ's coming ("But now . . .")—a shift that introduces a contrast between the old and new covenants and a shift that explains *why* the cross is necessary in our justification before God.[138] In Christ's cross, the righteousness of God (δικαιοσύνη θεοῦ)—that is, God's justifying activity[139]—is now revealed, a righteousness rooted in his covenant promises that results in *justification* for all who believe in Christ.[140]

Third, the revelation of God's righteousness in Christ is the fulfillment of the Old Testament (3:21) *and* is necessary to demonstrate that God is truly just (3:25–26). Why? Under the old covenant, God justified people without a full atonement. Under the old covenant, God entered into relationship with his people, and through the Levitical priesthood and sacrificial system, God granted forgiveness to them as they believed God's promises (Gen. 15:6; see Romans 4). Yet Scripture is clear: God never intended for the old covenant ultimately to redeem us. Built within the old covenant were God-given limitations—for example, no adequate substitute; the repetitious nature of the system, which revealed its inability to forgive sin; and no provision for high-handed sins.[141] But in a number of ways, the old covenant and the prophets prophesied the dawning of a new covenant, a greater priest, and a better sacrifice. In this way, the Old Testament revealed that God's righteousness was to come "apart from the law" (3:21). Yet the law-covenant also anticipated a complete salvation that has *now* come in Christ and his cross.[142]

But given that the Old Testament covenants did not fully pay for sins, how could God declare Old Testament believers justified if sin remained unpunished (e.g., Gen.

---

136. On Rom. 3:21–26, see Carson, "Atonement in Romans 3:21–26," 119–39.
137. On God's wrath in the Old and New Testaments, see Leon Morris, *The Apostolic Preaching of the Cross*, 3rd ed. (Grand Rapids, MI: Eerdmans, 1965), 147–54, 179–84.
138. See Carson, "Atonement in Romans 3:21–26," 121–23; Thomas R. Schreiner, *Romans*, BECNT 6 (Grand Rapids, MI: Baker Academic, 1998), 178–81.
139. See Moo, *Romans*, 79–89, 222. Moo argues that the "righteousness of God" is "the justifying activity of God." From God's side, this includes his active, miraculous intervention to vindicate and deliver his people, in fulfillment of his covenant promises (see Isa. 46:13; 50:5–8; Mic. 7:9)—that is, his saving work and activity. From the human side, to those who receive God's "righteousness," it also includes the aspect of *gift* or *status* of acquittal acquired by the person declared just.
140. On this point, see Moo, *Romans*, 79–89, 227–30; Carson, "Atonement in Romans 3:21–26," 124–25.
141. See Bruce K. Waltke, "Atonement in Psalm 51: My Sacrifice, O God, Is a Broken Spirit," in Hill and James, *Glory of the Atonement*, 57–58.
142. See Carson, "Atonement in Romans 3:21–26," 122–25.

15:6; Ps. 32:1–2)? Within the Old Testament, this is a major problem. In fact, it is due to *this* problem that Paul explains *why* the cross is necessary. The Father has publicly set forth his Son as a propitiation (ἱλαστήριον).[143] In him, *God* demonstrates that he is just because although in God's forbearance, "[God] had left the sins committed beforehand unpunished" (Rom. 3:25), in Christ, they are now fully paid.[144] As Douglas Moo explains,

> This does not mean that God failed to punish or "overlooked" sins committed before Christ; nor does it mean that God did not really "forgive" sins under the Old Covenant. Paul's meaning is rather that God "postponed" the full penalty due sins in the Old Covenant, allowing sinners to stand before him without their having provided an adequate "satisfaction" of the demands of his holy justice (cf. Heb. 10:4).[145]

One can make sense of this line of thought only if one assumes the God-law-sin relationship of penal substitution, forensic justification, and imputation. Paul assumes that unpaid sin is something God cannot indefinitely postpone—hence the rationale for Christ and his cross. Furthermore, he assumes that for God truly to justify sinners, our sin must be paid in full, and we need a perfect righteousness not our own. Apart from this, for God to justify us would ultimately question his own integrity, justice, and moral character. That is why the prophets promised the coming of a new covenant, secured by the work of a greater priest-king (Psalm 110; Isaiah 53) who would achieve the full forgiveness of our sin (Jer. 31:34). Romans 3:21–26 confirms what the Bible's storyline teaches: for God truly to justify sinners, a full atonement must be rendered that satisfies *God's* righteous demands, and this atonement has now come in Christ. Thus, our justification results not because God has overlooked our sin or relaxed his own retributive demands but because Jesus, our covenant head, has acted as our representative–penal substitute.

God Himself Saves through His Obedient Son

The last truth that warrants the inseparable link between Christ's work and our justification is the Bible's covenantal storyline, which underscores the twin truths that God alone must save us *and* that he must do so through a perfectly obedient Son.

Just as human sin before God creates a tension in the biblical storyline, so its resolution raises the question of *who* can save us and establish God's saving rule on earth. The answer is given through the biblical covenants. God's initial promise of redemption (Gen. 3:15) is given greater clarity over time. Instead of God swiftly bringing full judgment on us, he acts in sovereign grace, choosing to save a people for himself and to

---

143. On the debate regarding ἱλαστήριον, see Carson, "Atonement in Romans 3:21–26," 129–35.
144. John Ziesler and Stephen Travis argue that "passing over" (πάρεσις) refers to God's forgiveness, *not* his forbearance or postponing of the full requirement for the payment of our sin. This interpretation sees no tension between God's righteous demands against sin and his "passing over" our sins. But as Carson argues, πάρεσις means *not* "forgiveness" but "postponement," which warrants the traditional view that there is a tension between God's righteous demands against us and his declaration of justification in the Old Testament and his "leaving sin unpunished." See Carson, "Atonement in Romans 3:21–26," 136–38.
145. Moo, *Romans*, 240.

reverse the manifold effects of sin. His choice to redeem is evident in the *protevangelium* given immediately after the fall. This promise anticipates a coming Redeemer, the "seed of the woman," who though wounded himself in conflict will destroy the works of Satan and restore goodness to this world. This promise creates the expectation that when it is finally fulfilled, sin and death will be defeated, and the fullness of God's saving reign will come to this world as its inhabitants acknowledge and embrace God's rightful rule. As God's plan unfolds, we discover *how* God will save us by this "seed," which ultimately is fulfilled in Christ's obedient life and death. Three steps will develop this last point.

First, God's plan unfolds across time as God enters into covenant relations with Noah, Abraham, Israel, and David. By his mighty acts and words, God prepares his people to anticipate the coming of the "seed of the woman," the Messiah, who will *fulfill* all God's promises by ushering in God's saving rule to this world.[146] This point is vital for establishing *who* the Redeemer will be. Scripture teaches that the fulfillment of God's promises will be accomplished *through a man*, whose identity is developed through various typological persons and groups, such as Adam, Noah, Moses, Israel, and David. But Scripture also teaches that this Messiah is more than a mere man since he is *identified with God*. How so? By fulfilling God's promises, he literally inaugurates *God's* saving rule and shares God's throne—something no mere human can do.

Second, how does God's kingdom come in its *redemptive–new creation* sense? As the Old Testament unfolds, God's saving kingdom is revealed and comes to this world, at least in anticipatory form, through the covenants and their representatives—Adam, Noah, Abraham, Israel, and most significantly, David and his sons. Yet the Old Testament teaches that all the covenant sons fail to fulfill God's promises, something specifically evident in the Davidic kings, who are "sons" to Yahweh, the representatives of Israel, but who do not fully obey. It is only when a true, obedient son comes, a son whom God himself will provide, that God's rule will finally be established and all his promises fulfilled. In Old Testament expectation, the arrival of God's kingdom is organically linked to the dawning of the new covenant.

Jeremiah 31 is probably the most famous new covenant text in the Old Testament, although teaching on the new covenant pervades the Prophets. New covenant teaching is also found in the language of "everlasting covenant" and the prophetic prediction of the coming of the new creation, the Spirit, and God's saving work among the nations. Among the postexilic prophets, there is an expectation that the new covenant will have a purpose similar to the Mosaic covenant, namely, to bring the blessing of the Abrahamic covenant back into the present experience of Israel and the nations. Yet, significantly, there is also the expectation that the new covenant will result in the full forgiveness of sin (Jer. 31:34). In the Old Testament, forgiveness of sin is normally granted through the sacrificial system. Yet the Old Testament believer, if spiritually perceptive, knew that this was never enough, as evidenced by the repetitive nature of the system. And now

---

146. See Gentry and Wellum, *Kingdom through Covenant*, 647–712. Cf. Stephen Dempster, *Dominion and Dynasty: A Biblical Theology of the Hebrew Bible*, NSBT 15 (Downers Grove, IL: InterVarsity Press, 2003).

Jeremiah reinforces this truth by announcing that in the new covenant, God "will remember their sins no more" (31:34),[147] which entails that sin will finally be paid in full, precisely what Paul teaches in Romans 3:21–26. The Old Testament, then, anticipates the dawning of a new covenant that will result in a perfect, unfettered fellowship of God's people with the Lord, a harmony restored between creation and God—a new creation and a new Jerusalem—where the dwelling of God is with men (see Ezek. 37:1–23; cf. Isa. 25:6–9; Dan. 12:2; Rev. 21:3–4), precisely because sin is finally removed along with its penalty of death.

Third, the Bible's basic covenantal storyline establishes not only who Christ is but also the nature of his work and our justification. In regard to *who* Christ is, the answer is that he is the divine Son, given that he alone is able to fulfill all *God's* promises, inaugurate *God's* saving rule, and do what only *God* can do, namely, forgive all our sins (Col. 1:13–14; 2:13–15). However, through the biblical covenants, we also learn that alongside *God himself* redeeming us, the Old Testament stresses that Yahweh will do so *through* another David, a human son but one who is closely identified with Yahweh. Isaiah teaches this point. This coming king will sit on David's throne (Isa. 9:7), and he will bear the titles/names of God (9:6). This king, though another David (11:1), is also David's Lord, who shares in the divine rule (Ps. 110:1; cf. Matt. 22:41–46). He will be the mediator of a new covenant; he will perfectly obey and act like the Lord (Isa. 11:1–5), yet he will suffer for our sin in order to justify many (53:11). It is through him that forgiveness will come, for he is "the LORD our righteousness" (Jer. 23:5–6). In other words, the coming Messiah will be fully human and fully God, who in his life perfectly obeys the covenant obligations for us and who in his death meets God's own righteous requirements for us, thus securing our forgiveness of sin in a new and better covenant.

"Behold, the Lamb of God": Concluding Reflection

In Scripture and theology, there is an organic relationship between the nature of the human problem and its solution in Christ. The Bible's overall storyline establishes the inseparable bond between penal substitution and forensic justification and imputation. Not only does it establish that Jesus is the divine Son of the Father who is able to fulfill all God's promises and achieve the full forgiveness of our sin in his cross, but it also establishes the need for him to be *human* and obey for us, which grounds forensic justification and imputation. In Jesus's obedient life, death, and resurrection, our Mediator acts as our covenant representative, perfectly obeying for us, and as our penal substitute, fully paying for our sin. Apart from *who* he is as God the Son incarnate and *what* he does in his covenantal obedience for us, we have no justification before the triune God. But in Jesus all our needs are perfectly met. What a glorious Savior is our Lord Jesus Christ. In Christ alone do we see

---

147. The concept of "remembering" in the Old Testament is not simple recall (cf. Gen. 8:1; 1 Sam. 1:19). For God not to remember (Jer. 31:34) means that under the new covenant, a full and complete forgiveness of sin will result. See William J. Dumbrell, *Covenant and Creation: A Theology of the Old Testament Covenants*, 2nd ed. (Milton Keynes, UK: Paternoster, 2002), 181–85.

the resolution of God to take on himself our guilt and sin in order to reverse the disastrous effects of the fall and to satisfy his own righteous demands, to make this world right, and to bring about a just and righteous justification.

Recommended Resources

Anselm. *Why God Became Man*. In *Anselm of Canterbury: The Major Works*, edited by Brian Davies and G. R. Evans, 260–356. Oxford World's Classics. Oxford: Oxford University Press, 1998.

Bavinck, Herman. *Reformed Dogmatics*. Vol. 3, *Sin and Salvation in Christ*. Edited by John Bolt. Translated by John Vriend. Grand Rapids, MI: Baker Academic, 2006.

Beilby, James K., and Paul R. Eddy, eds. *Justification: Five Views*. Spectrum Multiview Books. Downers Grove, IL: IVP Academic, 2011.

———, eds. *The Nature of the Atonement: Four Views*. Downers Grove, IL: IVP Academic, 2006.

Buchanan, James. *The Doctrine of Justification*. 1867. Reprint, Carlisle, PA: Banner of Truth, 2016.

Calvin, John. *Institutes of the Christian Religion*. Edited by John T. McNeill. Translated by Ford Lewis Battles. Philadelphia: Westminster, 1960.

Crowe, Brandon D. *The Last Adam: A Theology of the Obedient Life of Jesus in the Gospels*. Grand Rapids, MI: Baker Academic, 2017.

Fesko, J. V. *Death in Adam, Life in Christ: The Doctrine of Imputation*. Reformed, Exegetical and Doctrinal Studies, edited by Matthew Barrett and J. V. Fesko. Fearn, Ross-shire, Scotland: Mentor, 2016.

Hill, Charles E., and Frank A. James III, eds. *The Glory of the Atonement: Biblical, Historical, and Practical Perspectives; Essays in Honor of Roger R. Nicole*. Downers Grove, IL: InterVarsity Press, 1998.

Husbands, Mark A., and Daniel J. Treier, eds. *Justification: What's at Stake in the Current Debates*. Downers Grove, IL: InterVarsity Press, 2004.

Jeffery, Steve, Michael Ovey, and Andrew Sach. *Pierced for Our Transgressions: Rediscovering the Glory of Penal Substitution*. Wheaton, IL: Crossway, 2007.

Johnson, Adam J., ed. *T&T Clark Companion to Atonement*. New York: Bloomsbury T&T Clark, 2017.

Macleod, Donald. *Christ Crucified: Understanding the Atonement*. Downers Grove, IL: IVP Academic, 2014.

McGrath, Alister E. *Iustitia Dei: A History of the Christian Doctrine of Justification*. 2nd ed. Cambridge: Cambridge University Press, 1998.

Morris, Leon. *The Apostolic Preaching of the Cross*. 3rd ed. Grand Rapids, MI: Eerdmans, 1965.

Owen, John. *A Dissertation on Divine Justice*. In *The Works of John Owen*. Edited by William H. Goold. Vol. 10, *The Death of Christ*, 481–624. London: Banner of Truth, 1967.

Rutledge, Fleming. *The Crucifixion: Understanding the Death of Jesus Christ*. Grand Rapids, MI: Eerdmans, 2015.

Schreiner, Thomas. *Faith Alone: The Doctrine of Justification; What the Reformers Taught . . . and Why It Still Matters*. Five Solas Series. Grand Rapids, MI: Zondervan, 2015.

Stott, John R. W. *The Cross of Christ*. Downers Grove, IL: InterVarsity Press, 2006.

Tidball, Derek, David Hilborn, and Justin Thacker, eds. *The Atonement Debate: Papers from the London Symposium on the Theology of the Atonement*. Grand Rapids, MI: Zondervan, 2008.

Treat, Jeremy R. *The Crucified King: Atonement and Kingdom in Biblical and Systematic Theology*. Grand Rapids, MI: Zondervan, 2014.

Vidu, Adonis. *Atonement, Law, and Justice: The Cross in Historical and Cultural Contexts*. Grand Rapids, MI: Baker Academic, 2014.

Wells, Paul. *Cross Words: The Biblical Doctrine of the Atonement*. Fearn, Ross-shire, Scotland: Christian Focus, 2006.

Wright, N. T. *The Day the Revolution Began: Reconsidering the Meaning of Jesus's Crucifixion*. San Francisco: HarperOne, 2016.

———. *Justification: God's Plan and Paul's Vision*. Downers Grove, IL: IVP Academic, 2009.

12

Raised for Our Justification

The Christological, Covenantal, Forensic, and Eschatological Contours of an Ambiguous Relationship

MATTHEW BARRETT

In the conceptual world of the evangelical mind, there are two roads that rarely intersect: resurrection and justification. In most publications on the doctrine of justification, the resurrection of Jesus Christ is quietly absent. Rarely do evangelical theologians consider how the empty tomb should influence their dogmatic formulation of justification *sola fide* and the forensic nature of imputation. The closest encounter between these doctrinal domains occurs when the Christological basis for justification is thrown into question and necessitates clarification. Even then, the doctrinal spotlight is placed entirely on the cross as the objective, legal basis for the application of Christ's redemptive work at the moment of faith.

Similarly, when the resurrection is addressed, few consider its import for the jurisdictive status of the ungodly. Resurrection language is segregated to apologetics, or it becomes the property of biblical studies, that is, the narrative climax to a variety of canonical themes—exile, kingdom, victory—present in the Old Testament but finding their fulfillment in the New Testament, particularly in the ministry of Christ. When the resurrection does appear in systematics, it is handled more or less as an appendix to the work of Christ, a prelude to Pentecost and pneumatology. As long as these two roads—resurrection and justification—run parallel but not perpendicular to one another, theology itself remains a short-circuited enterprise.

Indiscrete as theology may be, theological method is where the misstep has occurred. The task of the theologian is to ask not only how any doctrine is substantiated by the biblical text itself but also how every doctrine is to be read in view of every other doctrinal domain. To proof-text doctrinal conclusions only to set them aside in order to move on to an altogether separate doctrinal domain is to leave the theological task incomplete. Needed today, especially in evangelicalism, are more theologians capable of transitioning from mere theology to dogmatics. Theologians of past centuries may be a model in this regard, for they saw value in ushering doctrines into the hallway of dogmatics to begin dialogue. The Reformed tradition, for instance, offers a rich storehouse of resources in this regard. Rarely can one read Herman Bavinck's *Reformed Dogmatics* without pausing to consider the multifaceted ways this Dutch dogmatician connects doctrinal threads one to another.[1] Puritans like John Owen did the same centuries prior to Bavinck.[2] To confront the contours of soteriology never meant emptying one's theological framework—a type of dogmatic kenosis. Far from renunciation, the theologian operated with all doctrinal hands on deck, reading soteriology with the presuppositions of theology proper and Christology in full view.

How odd it is, then, that so few contemporary discussions of justification find a pathway to resurrection, and vice versa.[3] As biblical theologians readily observe, that neglect would not sit well with the New Testament authors, especially the apostle Paul in his epistle to the Romans.[4] This chapter is meant to fill that puzzling lacuna, no longer permitting these two doctrinal domains to remain segregated or ambiguous. Both doctrines are invited into the hallway of dogmatics and given permission to speak to one another. This is not, as some might fear, an exercise in theological speculation. Rather, it is built on the firm (Pauline) conviction that such doctrinal overlap was never foreign to the mind-set of the first-century church. In fact, to those who stared at the empty tomb and watched their Messiah ascend into the heavens, it would have appeared ahistorical to imagine a world in which resurrection was anything but directly and explicitly integrated into a Christian understanding of justification, the former validating, securing, and vindicating the latter.

More specifically, our method escorts us to the Pauline conclusion that not only is the resurrection of Christ, properly interpreted, necessary to make sense of justification, but its very nature demands a theory of justification that is forensically grounded in the imputed righteousness of Christ. That "nature" consists in Christological, covenantal, forensic, and eschatological contours, each of which is critical to establishing

---

1. Herman Bavinck, *Reformed Dogmatics*, ed. John Bolt, trans. John Vriend, 4 vols. (Grand Rapids, MI: Baker Academic, 2003–2008).
2. John Owen, *The Doctrine of Justification by Faith*, in *The Works of John Owen*, ed. William H. Goold, vol. 5, *Faith and Its Evidences* (Edinburgh: Banner of Truth, 1965), 7–41.
3. The exception in our own day is Richard B. Gaffin Jr., who has stressed throughout his career the implications of resurrection for an entire soteriology. See *Resurrection and Redemption: A Study in Paul's Soteriology* (Phillipsburg, NJ: Presbyterian and Reformed, 1987). Also see the festschrift in his honor, Lane G. Tipton and Jeffrey C. Waddington, eds., *Resurrection and Eschatology: Theology in Service of the Church; Essays in Honor of Richard B. Gaffin Jr.* (Phillipsburg, NJ: P&R, 2008). At a more popular level is Adrian Warnock, *Raised with Christ: How the Resurrection Changes Everything* (Wheaton, IL: Crossway, 2010). Also, although it is but a small section, see Paul D. Molnar, "The Theology of Justification in Dogmatic Context," in *Justification: What's at Stake in the Current Debates*, ed. Mark A. Husbands and Daniel J. Treier (Downers Grove, IL: InterVarsity Press, 2004), 241–47.
4. See Geerhardus Vos, *The Pauline Eschatology* (Phillipsburg, NJ: Presbyterian and Reformed, 1979); Vos, *Biblical Theology: Old and New Testaments* (Grand Rapids, MI: Eerdmans, 1959).

an evangelical, Reformed doctrine of justification. Therefore, we move back and forth between the *historia salutis* and the *ordo salutis*, between redemption accomplished and redemption applied, until the intrinsic tie between resurrection and justification is no longer perceived to be awkwardly ambiguous but lucid and essential to our formulation of the material principle.

Justifying the Righteous Judge

Romans 1–3 represents a vertical movement in Paul's thought, vertical because Paul's momentum is upward, ascending from death to life. Romans 1:18 announces God's wrath against "all ungodliness and unrighteousness of men, who by their unrighteousness suppress the truth." Chronicling the variegated manifestations of ungodliness (1:26–32), all of which presuppose the exchange of "the glory of the immortal God for images resembling mortal man" (1:23), Paul reaches a verdict: "God gave them up . . ." (1:24) a phrase that conveys the hopeless condemnation of those worshiping the creature rather than the Creator (1:25).

Paul's aim, in part, is to leave the ungodly without recourse to excuse (2:1), which is why his emphasis lands on divine justice: "We know that the judgment of God rightly falls on those who practice such things" (2:2). No one characterized by the idolatry in 1:24–25 or by the long list of iniquities in 1:26–32 will escape his judgment (2:3). Those who "presume on the riches of his kindness and forbearance and patience"—meant to lead the ungodly to repentance (2:4)—will discover that their "hard and impenitent heart" is only "storing up wrath," which will be unleashed "on the day of wrath when God's righteous judgment will be revealed" (2:5).

The emphasis on retributive justice is key to Paul's argument. God sees every wicked deed, and "he will render to each one according to his works" (2:6). On the one hand, nothing but "wrath and fury" await the unrighteous (2:8). On the other hand, those who do good, regardless of whether they are Jew or Greek, will be rewarded with glory, honor, and peace. That Paul views God as Judge is conspicuous in his concluding statement: "For God shows no partiality" (2:11). The Creator is Judge, and his judgment is righteous through and through.

The scales of justice color the way Paul pictures the history of the world since Adam. The judicial lens of Paul's logic matures only when he introduces the law. A detailed explanation of the law, as presented in Romans 2:12–29, is unnecessary for the purposes of this chapter. Nevertheless, at the very least, it should be noted how the law frames the destiny and eternal status of humanity. Forensic notions pervade Paul's use of the law through and through (e.g., "For it is not the hearers of the law who are righteous before God, but the doers of the law who will be justified," 2:13).

By the end of Romans 2, it is clear that a standard is in place, one that measures up to the character of its Creator, the righteous God. That standard, as expressed in the law, holds sinners accountable for their ungodliness. To sin "under the law" is to invite the full weight of the law's judgment (they "will be judged by the law," 2:12).

Not even Gentiles, who do not have the law, escape, for even they have the law "written on their hearts" (2:15). If chapter 1 declares the presence of God's wrath now, chapter 2 takes that reality a step further, confirming that a future day awaits all who have sinned, and on that day God will judge "the secrets of men by Christ Jesus" (2:16). Eschatology is inherently contingent on divine retribution against the wicked. The sobering reality of Romans 3 is that no one can dismiss the judgment of the eschaton as irrelevant to one's personal standing. Paul explodes that myth in his extended quotations from the Psalms.

Before we explore the universal nature of depravity, Romans 3:1–8 should not be overlooked. Without delving into the Jew-Gentile issues surrounding this text, the heart of the objection is pertinent for our purposes. Paul intends his reader to notice how the condemnation of man's unrighteousness serves to magnify God's own righteous perfection. That observation instigates an objection: "But if our unrighteousness serves to show the righteousness of God, what shall we say? That God is unrighteous to inflict wrath on us?" (3:5). And again, "But if through my lie God's truth abounds to his glory, why am I still being condemned as a sinner? And why not do evil that good may come?" (3:7–8). Paul, no doubt frustrated with the caricature, reveals that this is what "some people slanderously charge us with saying" (3:8). Paul need not argue that this objection is a miscalculation of divine justice—though he does so in 3:6 ("By no means! For then how could God judge the world?")—since the presentation of the objection itself is portrayed in the most negative light. One will never be excused from eschatological judgment by justifying his own unrighteousness because it serves to showcase God's just character. A lie is not excusable because by contrast it displays divine truth. That logic is as irrational as the reasoning of those who say that we should go on sinning that grace may abound (6:1). Despite one's best efforts to excuse unrighteousness, it is unavoidable that all stand under judgment.

The notion that condemnation is universal, applicable to the Jew as much as to the Greek (3:9–10), is plain in Paul's appeal to the Psalms (14:1–3; 53:1–3; 5:9; 140:3; 36:1). The pervasiveness of wickedness within the human heart is striking ("There is no fear of God before their eyes," Rom. 3:18), and Paul allows an exception for no one ("None is righteous, no, not one," 3:10). Paul's perception of mankind's status is reminiscent of the time before the flood: "The LORD saw that the wickedness of man was great in the earth, and that every intention of the thoughts of his heart was only evil continually" (Gen. 6:5). Yet with the full weight and visibility of the law in view, Paul accents the psalmist's anthropology because it shuts the mouths of Jews and Gentiles alike in their attempt to escape the eyesight of the omniscient Judge of the earth. In Paul's words, "every mouth" is to be "stopped," and the "whole world" is to be "held accountable to God" (Rom. 3:19). Despite the attempt of the New Perspective on Paul to remove soteriological notions from Paul's judicial flow of thought, Paul most definitely has such categories in view when he concludes, "For by works of the law no human being will be justified in his sight, since through the law comes knowledge of sin" (3:20).

The dejection that characterizes Romans 1:18–3:20—namely, all history this side of Genesis 3—leads the reader to ask the question, What hope is there, then, for humanity under the wrath and retribution of the Creator-Judge? Appeal cannot be made to the law, for the law exposes one's inability and failure to keep it. Works performed under its tutelage add not to one's justification but to one's condemnation, revealing just how far a person falls short. The guilt accrued from lawbreaking has resulted in the justification of the Judge, not the justification of the sinner—unless, of course, there is another way, a path external to the lawbreaker yet internal to the Lawgiver.

Theology Proper and the Justification Dilemma

Romans 3 presents a dilemma for theology proper. Paul shows his hand even prior to exposing mankind's reprobation: "For I am not ashamed of the gospel, for it is the power of God for salvation to everyone who believes, to the Jew first and also to the Greek. For in it the righteousness of God is revealed from faith for faith, as it is written, 'The righteous shall live by faith'" (1:16–17).

With universal degradation in view—over the span of three chapters—that opening jubilee seems, at first glance, premature. As long as divine justice governs, and with it the law's sentencing verdict, a gospel grounded in the righteousness of God only entertains futility—that is, with one exception: the Judge himself provides a way forward by means of his own righteousness, as Romans 1:17 assumes. Otherwise, as long as the Creator-Judge is to remain righteous, he cannot overlook the unrighteousness of his image bearers. Nor can he justify his image bearers on the basis of a righteousness that does not perfectly reflect his own perfect standard of righteousness exhibited in the law's commands. For God to relax the law is to relax his own moral perfection, which is why Paul never severs the law's inherent justness from God's own character. For that reason, the grounding of justification must be external to the sinner, though not external to the nature of God himself or, thus, to his law and its legal demands.

The resolution of these tensions arrives in Romans 3:21–26. The good news of 1:16–17 is legitimate—rather than a bypass of divine justice—precisely because the righteousness of God is a gift. It is true that "all have sinned and fall short of the glory of God" (3:23), but the condemned can be justified because their justification is no longer according to their own works of the law (3:20). That type of justification is impossible with a fallen humanity. Instead, the ungodly are "justified by his grace as a gift, through the redemption that is in Christ Jesus" (3:24). The redemption Paul has in mind is one of propitiation. In correlation to the forensic context of chapters 1–3, that is unsurprising.

Of course, the propitiation must be penal; anything else cannot solve the condemnation of humanity and the transgression of God's law. Justification can occur only through a mediator whose blood has propitiating power (the one whom "God put forward as a propitiation by his blood," 3:25). Unless Christ takes on himself the penalty for sin, drinking the cup of wrath on behalf of the unrighteous, and unless Christ bears such wrath in full, spilling his own blood in accordance with the atonement system inherent to the covenant (e.g., Leviticus 16), man's condemnation remains. Guilt is absolved only if the blood of the incarnate Son appeases the wrath that was ours.

Notice, however, that the justification Christ secures by propitiation is not won by circumventing the law's demands (and with it God's justice). When Paul says in Romans 3:21 that the righteousness of God "has been manifested apart from the law," he means to reiterate 3:20: "For by works of the law no human being will be justified." Far from circumventing the requirements of the law, 3:25–26 demonstrates that the offer of propitiation actually fulfills the law's requirements, which Paul says "the Law and the Prophets" foreshadowed (3:21). Otherwise, propitiation seems irrelevant to the problem at hand, the problem being the impossibility of a righteous God justifying the unrighteous. Propitiation is the solution because the penalty deserved for breaking the law is met in the suffering servant. With that penalty paid, anyone whose faith is in the propitiator is forgiven; the debt has been paid.

Golgotha, therefore, cannot be a way around the justice of the Lawgiver but rather is considered *the way* the Lawgiver remains righteous (justified) in the justification of the unrighteous: "This was to show God's righteousness, because in his divine forbearance he had passed over former sins. It was to show his righteousness at the present time, so that he might be just and the justifier of the one who has faith in Jesus" (3:25–26). Passing over former sins is Paul's way of conveying the necessity of judgment, the divine obligation to return wickedness with its deserved retribution. If God does not exercise his justice in the condemnation of the wicked, then his own righteousness is thrown entirely into question (which explains why Paul begins by saying, "This was to show God's righteousness"). The solution is genius in that it guards God himself from injustice while simultaneously providing a way for the ungodly to be justified in his sight. Paul's wording is stronger still: justification is not *despite* divine righteousness but *because of* it, grounded in its establishment and fulfillment at the cross. Justifying the ungodly does not merely maintain God as just but magnifies the glory of his just character because the Son of God himself has borne the penalty of injustice in his own body on the tree; on that basis, the one with faith has guilt no more. Propitiation not only results in the justification of the ungodly by fulfilling the law's demands but also magnifies the righteousness of God himself. The glory of God radiates in his impeccable holiness.

Although Paul does not describe the imputed righteousness of Christ in so many words, the indivisible connection he makes between the "righteousness of God" (3:21, 26) and the means of such righteousness being given to the sinner as a gift (3:24) at the very least alludes to the fact that the righteousness that justifies the ungodly is the righteousness *given to* the ungodly. But where is this alien, imputed righteousness to be found? Commentators are divided as to whether Romans 3:21–26 identifies the source of this righteousness in Christ. A strong case can be made in the affirmative.[5]

---

5. E.g., John Murray, *The Epistle to the Romans: The English Text with Introduction, Exposition and Notes*, NICNT (Grand Rapids, MI: Eerdmans, 1968), 108–21.

Nevertheless, even many commentators who do not believe imputation is specified in 3:21–26 still believe that the rest of Romans, especially chapter 5, points in that direction, identifying Christ as the representative of the justified, whose obedience, both in life and in death, fulfilled the law. Once a person exercises faith, Christ's perfect record of obedience is reckoned to the believer's account, granting him or her a new status in Christ. As Brandon Crowe demonstrates in chapter 14 of this volume, forgiveness stems from the *suffering* of Christ (suffering the penalty for breaking the law), yet the righteous status needed for justification (i.e., not guilty but righteous) stems from the *obedience* of Christ, the righteous one. His mission was to obey the law in the place of those who did not. He is righteous for the unrighteous.

Both aspects—passive and active—are essential, a point we shall return to again. Neither should be divorced from one another, nor segregated strictly to the life or death of Christ. For apart from Christ's active obedience transferred to the sinner's account, the believer is left incomplete, forensically naked before the heavenly courtroom, without a positive righteousness to speak of before the presence of the Holy One. The sinner may have escaped death, but he must be qualified to enter life—otherwise, Paul cannot legitimately say that Christ's "one act of righteousness leads to justification and life" (5:18) and that through his "obedience the many will be made righteous" (5:19).[6] The negative (passive) and positive (active) aspects of Christ's whole work counteract the penalty and righteousness of the law, as emphasized by Paul when he concludes, "Now the law came in to increase the trespass, but where sin increased, grace abounded all the more, so that, as sin reigned in death, grace also might reign through righteousness leading to eternal life through Jesus Christ our Lord" (5:20–21).

As we will see, apart from the resurrection, sin's penalty may be paid by Christ's suffering, but his righteousness remains defeated and unacceptable. Yet if he is raised by the Father, then righteousness has been raised with him, restored, revived, and renewed.[7] It is only because Christ fulfilled the law by his obedience that he was "declared to be the Son of God in power according to the Spirit of holiness by his resurrection from the dead" (Rom. 1:4).

Resurrection as the Covenantal Inauguration of the New Age

Romans 4 substantiates Paul's claim in 3:20 and 22 that one is justified not by works but only through faith, as exemplified in the justifying faith of Abraham while he was still uncircumcised. For our purposes, our discussion of Romans 3 has significant implications for how Paul concludes Romans 4. Recounting Genesis 15, Paul targets the justifying nature of Abraham's faith but not to advocate (as some have thought) that faith is righteousness itself (an interpretive move out of line with everything Paul has said thus

---

6. Also see Brandon D. Crowe, *The Last Adam: A Theology of the Obedient Life of Jesus in the Gospels* (Grand Rapids, MI: Baker Academic, 2017).
7. John Calvin, *Institutes of the Christian Religion*, ed. John T. McNeill, trans. Ford Lewis Battles, LCC 20–21 (Philadelphia: Westminster, 1960), 2.16.13.

far and one that would turn faith itself into a work of the law).[8] Rather, Paul pinpoints that phrase—"his faith was 'counted to him as righteousness'" (Rom. 4:22)—because faith, as Brian Vickers explains, "is what unites us to God's righteousness, so when Paul says that Abraham's faith was counted as righteousness, he means specifically that his faith *in God* was counted as righteousness."[9]

That issue aside, Paul is eager to draw the connection between Abraham's justification by grace alone through faith alone and that of the new covenant believer: "The words 'it was counted to him' were not written for his sake alone, but for ours also" (4:23–24). How so? "It will be counted to us who believe in him who raised from the dead Jesus our Lord, who was delivered up for our trespasses and raised for our justification" (4:24–25). *Sola fide* was instrumental in the justification of Abraham, the means through which Abraham not only became the covenant recipient of Yahweh's promises but also acquired a new status, namely, a righteous one.[10] Being "counted" righteous is a theme pervasive in Paul's corpus, one that solidifies justification not as a moral transformation or sanative renewal (ontological in nature) but instead as a forensic change in legal status, namely, from condemnation to justification.[11] In the shadow of Christ's finished work, Paul is adamant that anyone whose faith is placed in Christ will also receive, like Abraham, a new, righteous standing before God.

What is surprising, at least in light of the emphasis given to the cross throughout the Pauline corpus and New Testament canon, is that Paul does not merely make such a forensic point by turning to the cross but by forging ahead with his eyes set most emphatically on the resurrection of Christ. On the one hand, Paul does say that this new reality—being "counted" righteous like Abraham—is due to him who was "delivered up for our trespasses." Faith must reside in what occurred at Calvary. As we discovered in Romans 3, if Christ is not our propitiation, our condemnation remains, and we still need to make payment for our transgressions against God's law. The object of faith is Christ and him crucified. But twice Paul says that the faith that leads to justification must be a faith in the resurrected Christ. One is only "counted" righteous if one places faith in "him who raised from the dead Jesus our Lord."

That turn in emphasis may appear odd given other Pauline texts on justification that restrict themselves to the cross (e.g., Gal. 6:14; Eph. 2:16). However, it is my argument that Paul's emphasis on the empty tomb is central to the justified standing he celebrates throughout Romans. The reason why is to be found in the covenantal nature of the resurrection itself.

---

8. J. I. Packer explains that many Arminians have historically argued that faith itself is counted for righteousness because "it is in itself actual personal righteousness, being obedience to the gospel viewed as God's new law." Therefore, the Reformed "argument against both Romans and Arminians was that by finding the ground of justification in the believer himself they ministered to human pride on the one hand, and on the other hand robbed the Son of God of the glory which was his due." J. I. Packer, *A Quest for Godliness: The Puritan Vision of the Christian Life* (Wheaton, IL: Crossway, 1990), 153.

9. Brian Vickers, *Justification by Grace through Faith: Finding Freedom from Legalism, Lawlessness, Pride, and Despair*, Explorations in Biblical Theology (Phillipsburg, NJ: P&R, 2013), 77.

10. For a treatment of *sola fide*, see Vickers, *Justification by Grace through Faith*.

11. To further explore the forensic and transformative, see R. Michael Allen, *Justification and the Gospel: Understanding the Contexts and Controversies* (Grand Rapids, MI: Baker Academic, 2013), 33–72, 127–52.

First, Paul believes that the resurrection is the fulfillment of God's covenant promises to Abraham. Paul's attention in Romans 4 to the nature of justifying faith in Abraham is anything but ahistorical. Set within the context of redemptive history—specifically, the covenantal nature of that history—Abraham's trust in God is not just another example of faith but rather the beginning of an age that will reach its fulfillment only with the coming of the Messiah. Paul hints at this future fulfillment with his global emphasis. Seemingly an insignificant detail, that Abraham's faith precedes his circumcision proves critical: "He received the sign of circumcision as a seal of the righteousness that he had by faith while he was still uncircumcised" (4:11). That order not only precludes justification by works of the law or by Jewish ritual but also sets the pattern for how all people, Jew and Gentile alike, are reconciled to God.

The promises of Abraham come not by Jewish requirements of the law but by faith alone, for Abraham himself was justified before circumcision had taken place:

> The purpose was to make him the father of all who believe without being circumcised, so that righteousness would be counted to them as well, and to make him the father of the circumcised who are not merely circumcised but who also walk in the footsteps of the faith that our father Abraham had before he was circumcised. (4:11–12)

Then comes Paul's unashamedly global emphasis: "For the promise to Abraham and his offspring that he would be heir of the world did not come through the law but through the righteousness of faith" (4:13). Abraham's becoming heir of the world, Paul goes on to explain, could find fulfillment in a soteriological structure based on nothing but *sola fide*:

> For if it is the adherents of the law who are to be the heirs, faith is null and the promise is void. . . . That is why it depends on faith, in order that the promise may rest on grace and be guaranteed to all his offspring—not only to the adherent of the law but also to the one who shares the faith of Abraham, who is the father of us all. (4:14, 16)

Notice that not only does Abraham himself depend on a gracious soteriology, but so, too, do his heirs, heirs who will come from all nations. The moment of justifying faith in Abraham's experience is not merely monumental for his own right standing with God; whether he knows it or not, it sets the pattern for anyone and everyone who will claim to be a child of Abraham. If his children must adhere to the law, then the promises to Abraham (and the nations he represents) are emptied of their power. Israel's history demonstrates that the people cannot keep the law, thereby forfeiting the promises. Instead, the covenant promises must stem from a father whose status depends on "the righteousness of faith" (4:13). For if by faith, then anyone, of any nation, can become a child of Abraham simply by trusting in those same covenant promises. Faith, not works of the law, is the only program that can guarantee that the promises of the covenant will one day become a reality; it is the only guarantee that Abraham will be the father of many nations.

Yet the question everyone after Abraham wanted answered, including Jesus's own disciples, was this: When will the covenant promises of Abraham be fulfilled? And perhaps more personally, When will we know? Eschatologically, questions like these could be framed this way: When will the new era arrive? And how will we know it has come? As Abraham stared into the starry skies, he must have wondered when all this would come about, and his wonder tested his faith at times because the age of Sarah seemed to bring into question the validity of such promises. Nevertheless, Paul says,

> In hope he believed against hope, that he should become the father of many nations, as he had been told, "So shall your offspring be." He did not weaken in faith when he considered his own body, which was as good as dead . . . , or when he considered the barrenness of Sarah's womb. No unbelief made him waver concerning the promise of God, but he grew strong in his faith as he gave glory to God, fully convinced that God was able to do what he had promised. That is why his faith was "counted to him as righteousness." (4:18–22)

For Paul, here is the precise point at which God's power over the material realm must be considered. Although Abraham's and Sarah's bodies looked as good as dead, the promises they trusted in rested ultimately in one who has power to give life where there only seems to be death. Abraham was "fully convinced" that God could breathe life into Sarah's dead womb and aged body because the God of the covenant is Creator and Lord.

The implications for the resurrection of Christ and the fulfillment of God's covenant promises are manifold. The resurrection of Jesus from the dead is the most physical signal that God "was able to do what he had promised" to Abraham. Raising an heir out of the grave of Sarah's womb was but the first indication that Abraham's faith was not in vain, for this same God would one day fulfill his promises to the patriarch by raising his own Son to life, thereby inaugurating the new era that Abraham could not yet see. By raising his crucified Son from the dead, the Father announced to the world that he had finally and definitively fulfilled his covenantal word to Abraham, and its fruit would now be manifested as the good news of this resurrected heir was embraced by the nations. As Thomas Schreiner says,

> The resurrection of Jesus in history signaled the fulfillment of God's covenant promises to his people, indicating that the new age had commenced. There is a direct link, then, between the promises of Abraham and Christ's resurrection, for the resurrection . . . inaugurates the new world promised to Abraham.[12]

Ever since Jesus's inauguration of this new world, the way into it has not changed. It is still by faith alone. There lies the beauty of soteriology across redemptive history. Although Abraham waited for God to fulfill his covenant promises and commence

---

12. Thomas Schreiner, *Romans*, BECNT 6 (Grand Rapids, MI: Baker Academic, 1998), 242.

this new age, the way Abraham became a recipient of those covenantal blessings was through faith and faith alone. And the same is true for his heirs this side of Calvary. They, too, become recipients, true heirs of the Abrahamic covenant by faith in the covenant's promises. The difference is that at this stage in redemptive history, those who believe have the advantage of knowing *who* has brought those covenant promises to completion and *how* he has done so. To trust in the promises of God to Abraham no longer involves looking ahead knowing that God will provide a way but looking back knowing that the way has been ratified in the person and work of Jesus Christ. Over against Hendrikus Boers, Schreiner contests,

> Nowhere does Paul say that Abraham believed in the resurrection of Jesus. The element of continuity is that both believed in the God who resurrects the dead and in a God who would fulfill his promises. For Christians such faith necessarily involves belief in the resurrection of Jesus in history, while Abraham could not have such a specific faith because he lived before the time of fulfillment. Boers . . . fails to grasp the importance of this salvation-historical shift, and thus mistakenly concludes that Jews in Paul's day who did not believe in Jesus can be counted as believers. Surely those who lived before the cross and resurrection were righteous if they had faith in a resurrecting and sovereign God who fulfills his saving promises. But now that the Messiah has come this faith must be specifically placed in Jesus of Nazareth, and one must believe that he died for our sins and was raised for our justification.[13]

By trusting in the person and work of Jesus, the sinner is justified, counted righteous, because he has believed in him who raised Abraham's true heir and true son from the grave. Hence, when Paul says that Christ was raised for our justification, he assumes the inauguration of a new covenantal order, yet one in which the same faith that justified Abraham—who believed God would come through on his promises, although his body was as good as dead—also justifies those who believe in him who has raised his own Son from the dead. Both his death and his resurrection, then, form the basis on which the ungodly are justified and the means by which Abraham becomes father to the nations.

Causal Parallelism

Thus far, we have focused on the fabric of redemptive history, following its covenantal threads from Abraham to Christ. To stop there, however, would fail to tease out the full theological import of Romans 4:25. It is necessary to move from biblical theology to systematic theology, though always operating on the sure footing of the former.

We begin with a question: When Paul says that Christ was raised for our justification, does he assume a forensic framework? The answer must be in the affirmative, since, as we've seen so far, the context (Romans 1–4) is ingrained with forensic contrasts (faith versus law, condemnation versus justification, guilt versus righteousness, language of "counted righteous," etc.). Furthermore, Romans 4:25 does not sever resurrection

---
13. Schreiner, *Romans*, 243.

from atonement. Our focus may be on the mutual dependency of resurrection and justification, but we cannot pretend that resurrection is isolated from the cross. Christ was, says Paul, "delivered up for our trespasses," and "trespasses" is forensic terminology. It is safe to conclude that if, as we've seen, the context of 4:25 oscillates between themes such as condemnation, righteousness, judgment, and the law, it is irresponsible to sidestep the forensic nature of Paul's resurrection theology.

It remains to be discovered, nevertheless, what the forensic nature of this relationship between resurrection and justification looks like. It encompasses a whole range of theological implications. The first stems from Paul's own confession, which ties resurrection to an atonement penal in character. To say, as Paul does, that Jesus "was delivered up for our trespasses" is to introduce the legal infrastructure of the cross. We need not regurgitate Romans 3:25 and Paul's choice wording ("propitiation"). It does deserve observing, however, that 4:25 makes sense only if 3:25 is interpreted correctly. To be delivered up for our trespasses conveys not only the substitutionary nature of the cross but its penal ramifications as well. Being handed over for trespasses is an allusion to Isaiah 53:12, where the guilt of lawbreaking and the penalty it deserves are placed on the shoulders of the suffering servant.[14] Only by Christ bearing that penalty is forgiveness able to be freely granted to those possessing Abraham-like faith.

Resurrection is not without relation to Christ being "delivered up for our trespasses" either. There is a causal link in the text itself, as conveyed by the use of the Greek preposition διά. It is appropriate to interpret the first use of διά as causal. To say that Jesus was "delivered up for our trespasses" is to say that he was delivered up *because of* our trespasses.[15] However, interpreting the second διά as causal feels awkward. One might object: Why would Christ be raised *because of* our justification? Nevertheless, commentators like Schreiner believe that the "parallelism of the two clauses favors such a rendering," despite the fact that many others "resist the idea that the resurrection would depend on justification." Those who reject a causal parallelism interpret the second διά to mean that Jesus "was raised with a view to our justification." That reading is less than satisfying for exegetical, contextual, and theological reasons. As Schreiner observes, "To say that Jesus was raised because of our justification is to say that his resurrection authenticates and confirms that our justification has been secured. . . . The resurrection of Christ constitutes evidence that his work on our behalf has been completed."[16]

The causal parallelism, therefore, not only makes best sense of Paul's wording, which sees no breach between atonement and resurrection, but also does justice to his logic up to this point. Abraham-like faith can be substantiated only if the covenant promises are secured by an heir who can remove our transgressions. Apart from the resurrection, no confirmation exists that the atoning work of Christ has effectively purchased a forgiven

---

14. Schreiner, *Romans*, 243.
15. Schreiner, *Romans*, 244.
16. Schreiner, *Romans*, 244.

status. Understood in Pauline vocabulary, only a causal parallelism can explain why the believer's new status is contingent on a resurrected Messiah. If we are right, then we would expect Paul to say in another letter, "If Christ has not been raised, your faith is futile and you are still in your sins" (1 Cor. 15:17). Futile faith is a death sentence to the covenant promises made to Abraham. But if the resurrection validates the cross as an atonement for sins, then faith in a crucified Christ is defensible.

The *Pactum Salutis* and the Resurrection as Christological, Covenantal Vindication

The causal parallelism between resurrection and justification in Romans 4:25, a parallelism substantiated by 1 Corinthians 15:17, is full of theological significance. Primarily, the parallelism supports what Reformed dogmatics has called the *vindication* of resurrection, following Paul, who, describing the "mystery of godliness," says of Christ,

> He was manifested in the flesh,
>   vindicated by the Spirit,
>   seen by angels,
> proclaimed among the nations,
>   believed on in the world,
>   taken up in glory (1 Tim. 3:16).

Justification as a divine forensic declaration cannot be separated from vindication. Usually, vindication is considered anthropologically—that is, it has the vindication of the ungodly in view. Those with the imputed guilt of Adam face condemnation unless they are vindicated by a God who can provide a penal substitute. In Christ Jesus, the wrath of condemnation is paid, and the debt of original guilt is met, so that upon Abraham-like faith in that priestly substitute, the ungodly receive the status of righteous in God's sight.

If that change of status is to occur, however, the object of faith, namely, Christ, must undergo a vindication of his own. His vindication is a priority to man's vindication not only chronologically but also causally. For unless his obedience and suffering is validated, authenticated, and vindicated by the Father in the resurrection, there can be no assurance that the ungodly can be justified. Since vindication is Christological, it must find its source in the Father's own satisfaction with the work of his Son. Vindication does not have an anthropological genesis, nor is Christological vindication an end in and of itself, but ultimately it is to be traced back to the domain of theology proper, situated within the life of the triune God.

The Trinitarian nature of this vindication is not foreign to Scripture. Both in Christ's active obedience in fulfillment of the law and in his passive obedience undergoing suffering, the success of the Son's mission in the incarnation as the second Adam depends on whether he will fulfill the mission *given to him by his Father*. That Trinitarian structure means that the mission is not accidental or ad hoc but precedes Christ born in a manger, reaching back into eternity. As the Reformed tradition has not been shy to stress, we must not limit the road to vindication to the cross and resurrection but must trace its origins to the eternal *pactum salutis*, also labeled *the covenant of redemption*. The covenant of redemption, says Richard Muller, is the "pretemporal, intratrinitarian agreement of the Father and the Son concerning the covenant of grace and its ratification in and through the work of the Son incarnate."[17] It is, observes J. V. Fesko, "the eternal intra-trinitarian covenant to appoint the Son as covenant surety of the elect and to redeem them in the temporal execution of the covenant of grace."[18] Or to quote John Owen, the covenant of redemption is that "compact, covenant, convention, or agreement, that was between the Father and the Son, for the accomplishment of the work of our redemption by the mediation of Christ, to the praise of the glorious grace of God."[19] Vindication and justification depend on the Father appointing the Son to be the "head, husband, deliver[er], and redeemer of his elect, his church, his people, whom he did foreknow," and on the Son "freely undertaking that work and all that was required thereunto."[20]

A range of proof texts could be explored in support (Pss. 2:7; 110; Zech. 6:13; Ephesians 1; 2 Tim. 1:9–10; etc.), but as I have said elsewhere,

> One should note (1) how the covenant of redemption is assumed in the language Scripture uses to speak of God's eternal decree (Eph. 1:4–12; 3:11; 2 Thess. 2:13; 2 Tim. 1:9; James 2:5; 1 Peter 1:2), and (2) how Jesus refers back to his preincarnate existence and the mission the Father gave to him, as well as the appointment he has received (Luke 22:29; John 5:30, 43; 6:38–40; 17:4–12).[21]

The consequences of this *pactum* are anything but minor. "If there had been no eternal counsel of peace [i.e., covenant of redemption] between the Father and the Son," writes Louis Berkhof, "there could have been no agreement between the triune God and sinful men."[22] Berkhof's point is that without the *pactum salutis*, the *ordo salutis* is ineffectual. Yet it is not merely the *ordo salutis* that is compromised but the *historia salutis* as well,

---

17. "The Son covenants with the Father, in the unity of the Godhead, to be the temporal sponsor of the Father's *testamentum* (q.v.) in and through the work of the Mediator. In that work, the Son fulfils his *sponsio* (q.v.) or *fideiussio* (q.v.), that is, his guarantee of payment of the debt of sin in ratification of the Father's *testamentum*." Richard A. Muller, *Dictionary of Latin and Greek Theological Terms: Drawn Principally from Protestant Scholastic Theology* (Grand Rapids, MI: Baker, 2004), s.v.

18. J. V. Fesko, *The Covenant of Redemption: Origins, Development, and Reception*, RHT 35 (Göttingen: Vandenhoeck & Ruprecht, 2015), 15. Cf. J. V. Fesko, *The Trinity and the Covenant of Redemption* (Fearn, Ross-Shire, Scotland: Mentor, 2016).

19. John Owen, *The Mystery of the Gospel Vindicated*, in Goold, *Works*, vol. 12, *The Gospel Defended*, 497; cf. Owen, *An Exposition of the Epistle to the Hebrews*, in Goold, *Works*, 18:87–88. Owen clarifies, however, that there is but one will in God, corresponding to the one nature in God who is triune in person.

20. Owen, *Mystery of the Gospel*, in *Works*, 12:497. Owen argues that biblical support is found in Heb. 10:7 and Ps. 40:7–8. He also appeals to Isa. 49:6–12 in *The Death of Death in the Death of Christ*, in Goold, *Works*, vol. 10, *The Death of Christ*, 170.

21. Matthew Barrett, *40 Questions about Salvation* (Grand Rapids, MI: Kregel Academic, 2018), 69; cf. Louis Berkhof, *Systematic Theology* (Edinburgh: Banner of Truth, 1996), 266.

22. Berkhof states, "The counsel of redemption is the eternal prototype of the historical covenant of grace. . . . The former is eternal, that is, from eternity, and the latter, temporal in the sense that it is realized in time. The former is a compact between the Father and the Son as the Surety and Head of the elect, while the latter is a compact between the triune God and the elect sinner in the Surety." *Systematic Theology*, 270.

which, of course, includes the resurrection of Christ. The *pactum salutis* is the eternal source and, in Christ, the necessary impetus by which redemption is not only *applied* but also *accomplished*.

With that Christological, covenantal presupposition in place, the agreement reached in eternity must be met by the Son in his active and passive obedience. If it is not—if the unthinkable occurs, namely, that Christ fails in his mission—no vindication will follow. In plain language, the tomb will not be found empty. Christ must not only suffer the penalty for lawbreaking but also obey the law without imperfection. His obedience, to clarify, is not to a law removed from the character of God. The law itself is grounded in the righteousness of God's essence.[23] Christ's obedience to the law is not to be detached from fulfilling the mission his Father entrusted to his care, which is why Christ can speak so regularly of his ministry in paternal categories. Every teaching, every miracle, every act of obedience and suffering is intentionally related to the Father. As Jesus says in John 5:19, "Truly, truly, I say to you, the Son can do nothing of his own accord, but only what he sees the Father doing. For whatever the Father does, that the Son does likewise." Here we see a glimpse of the economic Trinity in the redemptive, incarnational mission of the Son. He is not just another prophet, like John the Baptizer, but bears a greater testimony, one whose origin is from the Father: "For the works that the Father has given me to accomplish, the very works that I am doing, bear witness about me that the Father has sent me" (5:36).

If this Trinitarian *pactum* is to work, however, it cannot but be based on the whole life lived. Unless both active and passive obedience are present, justification is incomplete. Sins may be forgiven, but no alien righteousness speaks on behalf of the ungodly before the heavenly courtroom. Moreover, one must not parcel out active and passive, as if the former speaks of Christ's ministry and the latter of his cross work. If we are right, that the *historia salutis* stems from the *pactum salutis*, then Christ goes to the cross to fulfill the mission handed to him by the Father. As much as crucifixion is about propitiation, that propitiation itself is a type of economic obedience when looked at through Christological and Trinitarian lenses. The other side of this coin matters as well. Suffering is not to be delegated to the final chapter of Christ's mission. As much as the cross itself is an atonement for sin, the whole life of suffering preceding sacrifice takes on a substitutionary dynamic. All that to say, vindication in resurrection must be considered holistically, encompassing the economy of the gospel in all its Christological facets.

Within this Trinitarian and Christological context, the resurrection is a type of vindication. As the Son signs his name, so to speak, to the *pactum salutis* and then fulfills the conditions of that *pactum* in his whole life of obedience and suffering, the Father then honors his Son's accomplishment of redemption in the *historia salutis* by raising his Son from the grave. Yet it is not mere honor that is his due but the type of honor that validates the effectiveness of Christ's work. Raising his Son is not merely paying homage to the example

---

23. See chap. 11, by Stephen Wellum, in this volume.

his Son has set but *ratifying* his substitutionary work. The Father's stamp of approval is not mere recognition but vindication, apart from which the work itself would prove ineffective—hence the forensic nature of this vindication, a point we will return to shortly. Believers with Abraham-like faith receive no justified status unless the Father's satisfaction with the Son is expressed by declaration. "For if Christ were not risen," says Jonathan Edwards, "it would be evidence that God was not yet satisfied for [our] sins. Now the resurrection is God declaring his satisfaction; he thereby declared that it was enough; Christ was thereby released from his work; Christ, as he was Mediator, is thereby justified."[24]

The Father's vindication of his Son in resurrection, therefore, is a justification of the Son himself. This justification differs from that of the ungodly; Christ is not justified for the forgiveness of his sins, but instead, his payment for the forgiveness of sins is met with approval. While the ungodly are not justified by works of the law (says Paul in Rom. 3:20), Christ's works in fulfillment of the law on behalf of the ungodly certainly are justified by the Father. That distinction is not to shift Pelagianism from the *ordo salutis* to the *historia salutis*, as some have claimed. Rather, it is to recognize that the one who is sinless and in no need of justification became incarnate to substitute himself on behalf of those who are sinful and do need justification. Christ's obedience is to merit eternal life not for himself but for the unrighteous, equipping them with the righteous status they need to enter into eternal life. His suffering for sin's penalty serves not himself but those condemned, as he is condemned for them.

The resurrection, then, is the final verdict that Christ's righteousness and condemnation, on behalf of others, satisfy the requirements of God's law. That explains Paul's conclusion to his contrast of the first Adam and second Adam:

> Therefore, as one trespass led to condemnation for all men, so one act of righteousness leads to justification and life for all men. For as by the one man's disobedience the many were made sinners, so by the one man's obedience the many will be made righteous. Now the law came in to increase the trespass, but where sin increased, grace abounded all the more, so that, as sin reigned in death, grace also might reign through righteousness leading to eternal life through Jesus Christ our Lord. (Rom. 5:18–21)

It is "the resurrection of Christ that inaugurates the eschatological age," that is, the age of the second and last Adam, who became "a life-giving Spirit" (1 Cor. 15:45).[25]

If Christ is the second Adam, the covenantal representative and federal head of all those who believe, then the doctrinal thread from resurrection to forensic imputation is legitimate. Imputation—the perfect righteous status of Christ reckoned to the account of those in Christ—is typically grounded in the life and death of Christ.[26] However, we've

---

24. Jonathan Edwards, *The "Miscellanies": Entry Nos. a–z, aa–zz, 1–500*, ed. Thomas A. Schafer, vol. 13 of *The Works of Jonathan Edwards* (New Haven, CT: Yale University Press, 1994), 227.
25. J. V. Fesko, *Justification: Understanding the Classic Reformed Doctrine* (Phillipsburg, NJ: P&R, 2008), 209.
26. For a defense of imputation, see John Piper, *Counted Righteous in Christ: Should We Abandon the Imputation of Christ's Righteousness?* (Wheaton, IL: Crossway, 2002); Brian Vickers, *Jesus' Blood and Righteousness: Paul's Theology of Imputation* (Wheaton, IL: Crossway, 2006); Michael S. Horton, "Traditional Reformed View," in *Justification: Five Views*, ed. James K. Beilby and Paul Rhodes Eddy, Spectrum Multiview Books (Downers Grove, IL: IVP Academic, 2011), 83–111.

seen that Christ's vindication and justification are the vindication and justification of the ungodly as well. If Christ truly acts as head of the covenant, the federal representative of covenant recipients, which Romans 5 seems to teach in a variety of ways, then when the Father declares his satisfaction with Christ, he is *equally and essentially* declaring his satisfaction with those in Christ.

It will not do, then, to limit the Father's declarative, judicial approval of his Son *to his Son's work*. That forensic favor, expressed in the Father's stance toward his Son, is the believer's, for when the Son stands risen before his Father, he does so on behalf of all those he represents. As Hebrews repeatedly reiterates, Christ is the High Priest, not only mediating between God and man but representing man before God in his own offering for man's transgressions (Hebrews 4–10). That federal priestly role, however, is incomplete if Christ remains crucified and lifeless. Only after he is resurrected are his priestly duties brought to finality, for only then does the Father declare his Son righteous and the covenant children righteous in his Son. Federal headship, for this reason, must not be restricted to the cross but should continue with the resurrection; otherwise, the life and death of Christ—and the active and passive elements of his work—have no forensic power in the imputation event itself.[27]

No Mere Vindication: Resurrection as Prophetic, Forensic, Soteriological Guarantee and Pledge

If the resurrection of Christ is a Christological vindication, it cannot be denied that it reaches not only backward—justifying the work of Christ—but forward as well, announcing the security of justification for all those who believe. And if it reaches forward, the resurrection cannot be described as *mere* vindication, as if it only authenticates what Christ *has* done. True as that may be, if the resurrection has a causal parallelism with justification, as we've seen, it must reach forward, securing, guaranteeing, and pledging that which is to come in the *ordo salutis*. In the words of Geerhardus Vos, "Christ's resurrection was the *de facto* declaration of God in regard to his being just. His quickening bears in itself the testimony of his justification." Yet the Godward, vertical focus of resurrection (God's own justification in Christ) has horizontal ramifications: "God, through suspending the forces of death operating on Him, declared that the ultimate, the supreme consequence of sin had reached its termination. In other words, resurrection had annulled the sentence of condemnation."[28]

The prophetic nature of resurrection was hinted at earlier in the words of Schreiner: "To say that Jesus was raised because of our justification is to say that his resurrection authenticates and confirms that our justification has been secured."[29] The declaration in resurrection points forward as much as backward; it is prospective, not merely retrospective. Christ is justified, but in his justification, so is the believer justified upon

---

27. For a defense of federal headship, see John Murray, *The Imputation of Adam's Sin*, in *Justified in Christ: God's Plan for Us in Justification*, ed. K. Scott Oliphint (Fearn, Ross-shire, Scotland: Mentor, 2007), 205–94.
28. Vos, *Pauline Eschatology*, 151.
29. Schreiner, *Romans*, 244.

exercising faith in that risen Christ. The law has been obeyed by the last Adam, and sin's penalty has been paid by the spotless Lamb of God; therefore, the resurrection is the Father's declaration that his Son's life and death have secured right standing for all who believe.

The word "secured" (Schreiner) may be the closest to capturing the prophetic nature of justification. Typically, debates over the extent of the atonement have moved the Reformed tradition to stress the effective or effectual nature of Christ's work for the elect. The same vocabulary could be applied to the resurrection. The resurrection not only justifies what Christ has done (confirming, authenticating, vindicating) but also secures and effects the justification of the believer. "As the rising of the sun removes the darkness," said Charles Spurgeon, "so the rising of Christ has removed our sin. The power of the resurrection of Christ is seen in the justifying of every believer; for the justification of the Representative is the virtual justification of all whom he represents."[30] That last phrase says it all and deserves repeating: "The justification of the Representative is the virtual justification of all whom he represents."

For that reason, representation (the type Paul teaches in Romans 5) is fundamental to the prophetic nature of justification. Otherwise, a resurrected Christ is merely a Christ who *hopes and wishes* that his own justification would result in the justification of others. But if his resurrection is not merely provisional and conditional (i.e., redemption has been made a *possibility*, its success conditioned on man's choice) but effective and unconditional (i.e., redemption has been successfully secured and guaranteed for God's elect, conditioned only on God's gracious purpose), then the resurrection itself has forensic, prophetic power. The empty tomb does not merely signal God's goodwill if only someone would believe. Rather, it announces that redemption is a certain reality. Those who trust in Christ need not wonder if his work is sufficient and effective; the King has risen. That is all the assurance they need. As Vos says,

> By raising Christ from death, God as the supreme Judge set his seal to the absolute perfection and completeness of his atoning work. The resurrection is a public announcement to the world that the penalty of death has been borne by Christ to its bitter end and that in consequence the dominion of guilt has been broken, the curse annihilated forevermore.[31]

Therefore, as critical as it is to describe the resurrection as vindication, mere vindication is insufficient. If Jesus is truly vindicated in his resurrection, then such vindication secures the status of the believer. The *historia salutis* guarantees the *ordo salutis*. That is Paul's point in 1 Corinthians 15:17, where he conveys, with great seriousness, that unless Christ is raised, condemnation ensues; faith is futile. Yet it is also a principle he assumes throughout his epistles, and not only with justification but with sanctification as well.

---

30. Charles Spurgeon, "The Power of His Resurrection," delivered on April 21, 1889, at the Metropolitan Tabernacle, Newington, in *Metropolitan Tabernacle Pulpit* (London: Passmore and Alabaster, 1889), 35:211.

31. Geerhardus Vos, *Grace and Glory: Sermons Preached in the Chapel of Princeton Theological Seminary* (1992; repr., Edinburgh: Banner of Truth, 1994), 161.

Bearing fruit (Rom. 7:4), Christ's ongoing intercession (8:34), walking as those no longer under the dominion of sin but as those alive in Christ (6:5–12), setting one's mind on things above (Col. 3:1–4)—these sanctifying realities, and more, are all secured in Christ's resurrection and caused by Christ's ascent from the dead. We should conclude, then, that the causal link between resurrection and justification, or more broadly between the *historia salutis* and the *ordo salutis*, is not foreign to Scripture itself. In "more than several places," observes J. V. Fesko, "Paul makes the resurrection of Christ the power of soteriological realities."[32]

If the resurrection takes on this prophetic power, then it is legitimate to say, as we've hinted at already, that the resurrection itself has forensic force for such soteriological realities. As mentioned at the start, in evangelical literature at large, most attention on the resurrection is aimed at proving that Jesus is who he says he is. Metaphysics (demonstrating Christ rose *bodily*) is the way to Christological verification (Jesus is the Son of God). That is a worthy focus, and a necessary one. Contrary to Protestant liberalism, Christ's resurrection is not merely spiritual; contrary to atheism, Christ's resurrection is not the invention of those who feel a longing to be religious.

Yet has that healthy focus led evangelicals to overlook the *theological* consequences of the resurrection, *forensic* consequences included, identifying that causal, Pauline link between resurrection and soteriology? Remember, it is the ontological and transformative nature of the resurrection that leads Paul to draw forensic conclusions not only for theology proper (God is victorious; the Trinity is redeemed in the fulfillment of the *pactum*) and Christology (Christ is vindicated) but also, and perhaps most especially, for soteriology (those whom Christ represented are justified). Fully alive, his body proclaimed to the world not only the Father's satisfaction with the work of his Son but the new status anyone (Jew and Gentile) now has if he or she is found in Christ. While we dare not mesh forensic and transformative, legal and sanative, in our doctrinal formulations of the *ordo salutis* (justification and sanctification are not synonymous, contra Rome), if it were not for both of these dimensions in a resurrection, not only transformative but also forensic, such distinctions would be impossible to make in the soteriological domain at all.

Resurrection as the Ground of Justification and the Object and Source of Saving Faith

The previous point about imputation implies that the *object* of saving faith—that is, Christ—must be positioned far more systemically. When the unbeliever hears the gospel, he or she is then urged to trust in Christ, but too often the assumption is that the believer's faith is to rest merely on the atoning work of Christ. Gospel presentations follow this mold: to share Christ is to point unbelievers to his cross. On the one hand, that is a right impulse and a necessary one. The object of saving faith can be

---

32. Fesko, *Justification*, 207.

nothing less; otherwise, salvation is no longer *in Christ* and him crucified. However, it certainly must be much more; otherwise, the good news has been short-circuited. If, as we saw already, imputation depends on the forensic declaration of the Father in the resurrection, announcing not only the justification of the federal Head but all the covenant recipients he represents, then the object of saving faith must include that resurrection itself. To believe in Christ for the forgiveness of sins and the imputation of righteousness is to believe not only in his perfect obedience and his sacrificial death but also in his victorious resurrection.

Is this not the biblical model—that "if you confess with your mouth that Jesus is Lord and believe in your heart *that God raised him from the dead*, you will be saved" (Rom. 10:9)? Faith is the instrumental cause of justification; therefore, it must be tied to the resurrection as its objective ground. Paul assumes this much when he then says, "For with the heart one believes and is justified, and with the mouth one confesses and is saved" (10:10).

In the book of Acts, it is this model that Peter follows. With Jesus risen and ascended, the Spirit descends on the apostles. As onlookers wonder what this Pentecost could mean, Peter gives a gospel presentation, one that capitalizes on the resurrection. Peter appeals to the fulfillment of Old Testament prophecy (e.g., Joel 2) in the "mighty works and wonders" God did in and through his Son (Acts 2:22). He also appeals to the crucifixion not merely as the outcome of wicked schemes by lawless men but ultimately as the "definite plan" of God (2:23). Yet Peter's climactic proof is the resurrection itself: "God raised him up, loosing the pangs of death, because it was not possible for him to be held by it" (2:24). Believing the resurrection to be foreshadowed by David in Psalm 16:8–11—especially 16:10, "For you will not abandon my soul to Sheol, or let your holy one see corruption"—Peter concludes that such a psalm reaches beyond David, for he "died and was buried, and his tomb is with us to this day" (Acts 2:29). David himself understood a greater fulfillment was in the works:

> Being therefore a prophet, and knowing that God had sworn with an oath to him that he would set one of his descendants on his throne, he foresaw and spoke about the resurrection of the Christ, that he was not abandoned to Hades, nor did his flesh see corruption. This Jesus God raised up, and of that we all are witnesses. Being therefore exalted at the right hand of God, and having received from the Father the promise of the Holy Spirit, he has poured out this that you yourselves are seeing and hearing. For David did not ascend into the heavens, but he himself says,
>
> "The Lord said to my Lord,
> 'Sit at my right hand,
>   until I make your enemies your footstool.'" (Acts 2:30–35; cf. Ps. 110:1)

Peter is persuaded that David "foresaw and spoke about the resurrection of the Christ," which explains why Peter labels David "a prophet." In saying so, Peter's purpose is not only redemptive-historical but historically evangelistic: "Let all the house of Israel therefore know for certain that God has made him both Lord and Christ, this Jesus whom you crucified" (2:36).

With such gospel certainty proclaimed, Peter's listeners are "cut to the heart" (2:37) and respond, asking what they must then do to be saved. Peter answers, "Repent and be baptized every one of you in the name of Jesus Christ for the forgiveness of your sins, and you will receive the gift of the Holy Spirit" (2:38). Lucid and unambiguous, Peter stresses that salvation depends on faith, but it is faith *in Christ,* which for Peter entails not only Christ crucified but also Christ justified, as his typological transition from David to Jesus demonstrates.

The pattern Peter exemplifies continues in Acts as Luke's narrative transitions to Paul and Barnabas at Pisidian Antioch. In Acts 13, Paul addresses the rulers of the synagogue after a reading from the Law and the Prophets. Beginning with Israel's fathers, Paul paints the story of Israel's liberation from Egypt to the rise of King David. David is pivotal for Paul's biblical theology: "Of this man's offspring God has brought to Israel a Savior, Jesus, as he promised" (13:23). Paul then addresses these rulers as recipients of this messianic heritage ("Brothers, sons of the family of Abraham . . . ," 13:26) to announce that "to us has been sent the message of this salvation" (13:26). Such a salvation was accomplished when Jesus was put to death by God's own covenant people: "For those who live in Jerusalem and their rulers, because they did not recognize him nor understand the utterances of the prophets, which are read every Sabbath, fulfilled them by condemning him" (13:27). Paul cannot stress enough how their wickedness only served to fulfill God's plan and promise declared beforehand in the Scriptures: "And when they had carried out all that was written of him, they took him down from the tree and laid him in a tomb" (13:29).

Like Peter, however, Paul does not end at the cross; if he did, then the "message of this salvation" would be incomplete and invalid. Paul moves quickly from death to resurrection: "But God raised him from the dead" (13:30). Having chronicled Jesus's appearances (13:31), Paul is now in a position to announce salvation: "And we bring you the good news that what God promised to the fathers, this he has fulfilled to us their children by raising Jesus" (13:32–33). Paul quotes not only from Psalm 2:7 ("You are my Son, today I have begotten you") to demonstrate that such good news was promised to Israel's forefathers but from Isaiah 55:3 and Psalm 16:10 as well. In Paul's mind, these passages speak of the incorruptible Christ. Having been raised from the dead, Christ is "no more to return to corruption" (13:34), says Paul. David, now asleep with his fathers (13:36), saw corruption, but "he whom God raised up did not see corruption" (13:37).

Yet one would be mistaken to think that Paul's emphasis on incorruption somehow precludes forensic consequences. It is because of his incorruptibility that sinners receive mercy: "Let it be known to you therefore, brothers, that through this man forgiveness of sins is proclaimed to you, and by him everyone who believes is freed from everything from which you could not be freed by the law of Moses" (13:38–39). As it was for Peter, so for Paul it is not only the death of Christ but also his resurrection that judicially liberates those under the law, so that anyone who believes in Christ has his or her sins pardoned. The resurrection does not merely accompany the announcement of the gospel but is the very basis on which good news can be proclaimed to anyone at all.

Whether in narrative (Acts 2; 13) or didactic literature (Rom. 10:9), the New Testament authors do not believe that justification and conversion depend on a *historia salutis* that finalizes at the cross. Apart from the resurrection, the objective ground of saving faith is insecure and incomplete, its efficacy invalid. Or in Paul's language, "If Christ has not been raised, your faith is futile" (1 Cor. 15:17). The resurrection is no mere capstone to the cross, legitimizing faith; it is the forensic ground on which faith itself proves instrumental to a new status in Christ. Although N. T. Wright and I disagree in our understanding of justification's eschatological nature (see my next section, "Resurrection and Reconciliation"), as well as our understanding of the doctrine of imputation, Wright helpfully stresses resurrection as the ground for justification when he writes,

> For Paul, the resurrection of Jesus of Nazareth is the heart of the gospel (not to the exclusion of the cross, of course, but not least as the event which gives the cross its meaning). It is the object of faith, the ground of justification, the basis for obedient Christian living, the motivation for unity, and, not least, the challenge to the principalities and powers. It is the event that declares that there is "another king," and summons human beings to allegiance, and thereby to a different way of life, in fulfillment of the Jewish Scriptures and in expectation of the final new world which began at Easter and which will be completed when the night is finally gone and the day has fully dawned.[33]

Along with the cross, the resurrection is not only the *ground* of justification and the *object* of saving faith but also the *source* of faith. Wright's comment turns our attention to faith throughout the Christian life, a point we will emphasize shortly. Nevertheless, what Wright fails to give attention to is the resurrection as the source and fountain of initial, converting, justifying faith. John Calvin explains,

> For since only weakness appears in the cross, death, and burial of Christ, faith must leap over all these things to attain its full strength. We have in his death the complete fulfillment of salvation, for through it we are reconciled to God, his righteous judgment is satisfied, the curse is removed, and the penalty paid in full. Nevertheless, we are said to "have been born anew to a living hope" not through his death but "through his resurrection" [1 Peter 1:3 p.]. For as he, in rising again, came forth victor over death, so the victory of our faith over death lies in his resurrection alone. Paul's words better express its nature: "He was put to death for our sins, and raised for our justification" [Rom. 4:25]. This is as if he had said: "Sin was taken away by his death; righteousness was revived and restored by his resurrection." For how

---

33. N. T. Wright, *The Resurrection of the Son of God* (London: SPCK, 2003), 266.

could he by dying have freed us from death if he had himself succumbed to death? How could he have acquired victory for us if he had failed in the struggle? Therefore, we divide the substance of our salvation between Christ's death and resurrection as follows: through his death, sin was wiped out and death extinguished; through his resurrection, righteousness was restored and life raised up, so that—thanks to his resurrection—his death manifested its power and efficacy in us. Therefore, Paul states that "Christ was declared the Son of God . . . in the resurrection itself" [Rom. 1:4 p.], because then at last he displayed his heavenly power, which is both the clear mirror of his divinity and the firm support of our faith.[34]

Calvin concludes by turning our attention to Peter, who says that God "raised him from the dead and gave him glory, *so that your faith and hope are in God*" (1 Pet. 1:21). Calvin does not mean to undermine the significance of the cross; he is simply determined to convey that the resurrection is instrumental, the source even, of faith in the resurrected King. "Not that faith, supported by his death, should waver," Calvin notes, "but that the power of God, which guards us under faith, is especially revealed in the resurrection itself."[35] As Paul says to the Colossians, we have been "buried with him in baptism" and "raised with him through faith in the powerful working of God, who raised him from the dead" (Col. 2:12).

A resurrected Christ is one who has not only mediated on behalf of the ungodly on the cross—which is fitting since he is, as Hebrews says repeatedly, our Great High Priest—but who also continues to mediate on behalf of those who have believed by interceding for them at the right hand of his Father (Hebrews 7–10). Those with faith in Christ no longer stand condemned because "Christ Jesus is the one who died—more than that, who was raised—who is at the right hand of God, who indeed is interceding for us" (Rom. 8:34). The intersection of resurrection and ascension is not to be disregarded. That intersection not only substantiates the continual priestly mediation of Christ but is also the wellspring from which our faith arises. As Peter and the apostles told those who prohibited them from sharing the good news of the crucified and risen Christ, "The God of our fathers raised Jesus, whom you killed by hanging him on a tree. God exalted him at his right hand as Leader and Savior, to give repentance to Israel and forgiveness of sins" (Acts 5:30–31). Repentance and forgiveness are gifts; so is the faith that leads to repentance and is rewarded with forgiveness (13:48–50; Eph. 2:8–10; Phil. 1:29–30; 2 Pet. 1:1). But the faith that brings repentance and forgiveness is bestowed only if the object of faith itself—namely, Christ—is risen. If Christ is risen, then faith has its assurance and conviction (Heb. 11:1).

The Christological focus of faith, as grounded in the resurrection itself, should guard us from the danger of self-justification as well. If Christ and his resurrection are the object and the source of faith, then justification itself cannot come by anything but by faith *alone*. That may appear obvious to evangelicals, but pragmatically it is not so

---

34. Calvin, *Institutes*, 2.16.13.
35. Calvin, *Institutes*, 2.16.13.

easily adhered to, especially for evangelicalism, a movement that is known for its emphasis on spiritual experience. To see this point more objectively, perhaps it is best to consider a test case external to evangelicalism itself. Comparing Karl Rahner and Karl Barth brings this point into sharper focus. Paul Molnar observes,

> Whereas Rahner appeals to our experiences of hope and of faith to understand the meaning of the resurrection and the incarnation and then explains that meaning in terms of our *a priori* subjective transcendental horizon, Barth insists that the meaning of Christian hope and faith is determined by Jesus himself who rose from the dead and who alone is therefore capable of enabling faith and hope through the Holy Spirit even today. That is why Barth insists that our justification cannot be found within our experience but must be sought and found in Jesus Christ himself as he lived the transition from death to life for us and as we participate in that new life in faith and hope.... Barth and Rahner are separated here by the fact that Rahner refuses to begin his thinking about the resurrection and thus about faith and hope with the risen Lord himself. Instead he begins with our transcendental experiences or what he calls our common human experience. And his conclusions create uncertainty where there should be certainty. Rahner argues that the resurrection would have no objective meaning without the disciples' faith and without ours and that in his humanity Jesus is the supreme instance of human existence and so becomes the Word of God. By contrast Barth stresses that the resurrection and the incarnation have an objective meaning with or without both the faith of the disciples and ours. The risen Lord calls for and enables faith and hope but one could never say that faith and the resurrection or Christology and anthropology were mutually conditioning factors unless one had somehow confused the power of the resurrection with the faith of the disciples and our own faith once again.... In an actual encounter with the risen Lord the disciples were enabled by Christ to believe in him; today the same risen and ascended Christ, through the Holy Spirit, enables us to believe in him. But the movement is from unbelief to belief in Jesus Christ himself and not from belief in our experiences or ideas to Christian faith and hope. The former view reflects Barth's application of the doctrine of justification by faith while the latter view represents another form of self-justification.[36]

One need not agree with Barth's view of justification to see that he is protecting the doctrine from a dangerous threat. Rahner had so subjectivized the resurrection that its objectivity was dependent on man's religious-faith experience. The resurrection was removed from the domain of Christology only to be swallowed whole by anthropology. The Christ of faith took priority over the Jesus of history. With human religious experience at the center, the resurrection could no longer be the object and source of faith, but faith was now the object and source of the resurrection. The movement from the *historia salutis* to the *ordo salutis* had been flipped on its head.

---

36. Molnar, "Theology of Justification," 246–47. Molnar has in view Karl Barth, *Church Dogmatics*, ed. G. W. Bromiley and T. F. Torrance, trans. G. T. Thomson et al. (Edinburgh: T&T Clark, 1936–1977), vol. 3, pt. 2, 449; vol. 4, pt. 1, 557.

While we may want to debate the consistency of Barth's own position,[37] nevertheless, Barth recognizes the inversion that Rahner and company created. Barth is attempting to reverse the pattern, making Christ the center once more. To do so, faith's power lies not in its own ability to justify but rather in the object it adores. It is faith *in Christ* as opposed to faith in *my experience of Christ* that preserves not only the objectivity and power of the resurrection but the graciousness of justification itself.

The Rahner-Barth contrasts should be a lesson for evangelicals as well. For all our stress on genuine faith and the authenticity of a faith encounter with Christ, we must be careful lest we, ironically, find ourselves operating with the same *telos* as Protestant liberalism. Is it faith itself—that is, the religious experience of faith—that grounds justification? Or is faith, as argued already, instrumental, a gift from above that is not meant to be the focus but merely the tool that the Spirit uses to point us to the empty tomb? As critical as faith is to justification, the *sola* in *sola fide* is preserved—and self-justification detained—only if that faith has as its object and source the crucified and risen Christ. Our faith does not validate his resurrection; his bodily resurrection—which is historical in every sense of the word—validates our faith. The subjective does not ground the objective but the objective the subjective.

Resurrection and Reconciliation

If, as we've argued, the resurrection is no mere vindication but the prophetic, forensic, and soteriological guarantee of justification and imputation, then we would expect Scripture to ground reconciliation in the resurrection as well. Reconciliation would be the necessary outcome if Christ's resurrection is forensically effective in establishing the sinner's right standing with God.

That outcome is evidenced immediately after Romans 4:25. Having demonstrated that both the cross and the resurrection are "for our justification," Paul's very next sentence, which begins with "therefore," turns our attention to the reconciliation that follows: "Therefore, since we have been justified by faith, we have peace with God through our Lord Jesus Christ. Through him we have also obtained access by faith into this grace in which we stand, and we rejoice in hope of the glory of God" (5:1–2).

That Paul is grounding reconciliation not only in Christ's atonement but also in his resurrection becomes increasingly apparent in Romans 5:6 and following. Paul first explains the logic of the cross. God's love comes first; because of our depravity, his love is prevenient: "For while we were still weak, at the right time Christ died for the ungodly. . . . God shows his love for us in that while we were still sinners, Christ died for us" (5:6, 8). Having identified the motivating factor (divine love) and the priority it has if redemption is to be *sola gratia*, Paul then draws out the eschatological consequences if Christ's death has truly effected justification for the ungodly: "Since, therefore, we have now been justified by his blood, much more shall we be saved by him from the wrath of

---

37. See chap. 24, by Bruce P. Baugus, in this volume.

God" (5:9). The judgment to come, which Paul warned about at the start of his letter, is terrible news to those outside Christ. They may suppress the truth now, indulging in "all manner of unrighteousness" (1:29), but the righteous judgment of the righteous Judge awaits them. "He will render to each one according to his works" (2:6), which cannot be good news for those who have only their works to show for themselves on the last day: "But because of your hard and impenitent heart you are storing up wrath for yourself on the day of wrath when God's righteous judgment will be revealed" (2:5).

However, for those united to Christ, there is no wrath to come. As Paul reminds the Thessalonians, they "turned to God from idols to serve the living and true God," and they are "to wait for his Son from heaven, *whom he raised from the dead, Jesus who delivers us from the wrath to come*" (1 Thess. 1:9–10). The wrath that was theirs was placed on the substitute, the one who was the propitiation (Rom. 3:25). And because that substitute not only bore that wrath unto death but rose as victor, all those waiting for him need not fear the wrath he brings. That explains why Paul can say in Romans 5:9 that the blood of Christ *justifies*, and if it justifies, it liberates from the wrath at the eschaton. Yet Paul does not limit himself to the death of Christ; Christ's resurrection life is absolutely central to reconciliation and the salvation it brings: "For if while we were enemies we were reconciled to God by the death of his Son, much more, now that we are reconciled, shall we be saved by his life. More than that, we also rejoice in God through our Lord Jesus Christ, through whom we have now received reconciliation" (5:10–11).

Several observations are in order. First, it is because the sinner is justified not on the basis of his works but on the basis of Christ's death and resurrection that he enjoys a new relationship with God, no longer his enemy but his friend. The forensic grounds the relational. Whether one can enjoy all the familial benefits that come with reconciliation depends on whether guilt and wrath have been legally resolved and whether a new righteous status has been granted and received.

Second, the soteriological benefits Paul has in mind are not limited to reconciliation. Reconciliation is the door to a whole new world—indeed, a whole new life. But that new life is intrinsically reliant on a Savior who has risen. This much is apparent when Paul says, "For if while we were enemies we were reconciled to God by the death of his Son, much more, now that we are reconciled, shall we be saved by his life" (5:10). "Life" (ζωῇ) refers to the resurrection of Christ. Paul's lesser-to-greater argument builds from one soteriological benefit (reconciliation) to its eschatological finality, as his "much more" language conveys. Paul is communicating that if there is reconciliation by Christ's death, then salvation in all its fullness is ours, thanks to Christ's resurrection life. "Saved" here is not limited to initiation but is used broadly to encompass the whole of the Christian life and its climax in glorification. Not only justification and reconciliation but adoption, sanctification, and final glory result from an empty tomb. By "saved," Paul may more acutely have in mind, especially in light of the eschatological context, salvation from the wrath to come. Christ's resurrection means that life, not death, awaits those united to him.

This eschatological focus in 5:10, even if only hinted at by Paul, does bring us to the precipice of the relationship between justification and eschatology, to which we now turn.

Resurrection, Justification, and Eschatology

It deserves emphasizing that the prophetic, forensic nature of the resurrection, its causal link to justification, means resurrection and justification are inherently eschatological in nature. When the eschatological nature of resurrection is referenced, it is the future, bodily resurrection of the believer that is immediately relevant. As Paul counters a culture suspicious of the bodily resurrection of the dead, he appeals to Christ's bodily resurrection to confirm not only the believer's future, bodily resurrection but also the hope that every Christian has in the risen Christ. Resurrected and ascended, Christ is the "firstborn from the dead" (Col. 1:18; cf. Rev. 1:5) and the firstfruits of the great harvest to come (1 Cor. 15:20). Although the future, bodily resurrection of Christ's bride is the "not yet" of eschatology, it is guaranteed by a Savior who has risen and reigns. "The resurrection of Christ," asserts J. Christiaan Beker, "is therefore not so much an event *in the midst of* history as an event that inaugurates *the end of* history."[38]

Equally important, however, is the way eschatology is an "already" reality, as seen in the soteriological spoils that the victor brings to God's elect when he rises from the grave. Before we too quickly move from the third day to the final day, we should bear in mind that everything in between (the *ordo salutis*) stems from and is caused by resurrection Sunday. Those in Christ may await that final day and the glorification it brings, but eschatology has already been inaugurated now wherever there is a faith union with the risen Christ. While our attention has been on resurrection and justification, we have acknowledged that the causal link between the *historia salutis* and the *ordo salutis* is not restricted to justification but continues with all the soteriological benefits that flow out of union with Christ (adoption, sanctification, preservation). Those soteriological benefits, already experienced by the believer, are indicators that the last days have arrived. Yes, saints await future glory, but that glory is secure, and its glory is seen already in the new life, new status, and new walk that the believer experiences.

Unfortunately, some have created a bifurcation that will, if followed, cause the eschatological force of this new reality to implode. The New Perspective on Paul has rightly stressed the eschatological nature of justification but has done so at the expense of justification's soteriological identity. Justification is no longer about *how one gets in* but *who is in* the new covenant. The issue is not soteriology but ecclesiology. Justification, says Wright, "in the first century was not about how someone might establish a relationship with God. It was about God's eschatological definition, both future and present, of who was, in fact, a member of his people." Following Sanders at this point, Wright concludes, "It was not so much about 'getting in.' In standard Christian

---

38. J. Christiaan Beker, *The Triumph of God: The Essence of Paul's Thought*, trans. Loren T. Stuckenbruck (Minneapolis: Fortress, 1990), 73.

theological language, it wasn't so much about soteriology as about ecclesiology; not so much about salvation as about the church."[39]

Many notable responses have been given to Wright's theses, so that a reaction is unnecessary here.[40] For our purposes, it should simply be observed how contrary Wright's thesis is to Paul's logic in Romans 4:25 and 1 Corinthians 15:17. Certainly, justification is eschatological but not in the way Wright thinks. For Paul not only believes justification is soteriological—as his extended appeal to Abraham reveals—but Paul is convinced that the eschatological nature of the resurrection itself is soteriologically driven. To say, "If Christ has not been raised, your faith is futile and you are still in your sins," is as strong a soteriological statement as it is an eschatological one. More precisely still, it is an eschatological statement only *because* it is a soteriological one. If Paul's resurrection theology is not inherently soteriological, then it cannot be eschatological. To say that Christ was "delivered up for our trespasses and raised for our justification" (Rom. 4:25)—a justification entirely connected to the one who, like Abraham, has his faith "counted to him as righteousness" (4:22)—is to say that the eschaton is already at hand in the new status of those united to a resurrected Christ. Believers do not await a future day in the uncertain hope that they will then be justified; they *have been* justified already, as soon as they exercised faith in the crucified and risen Christ. A righteous status is not potential but actual. For those who are justified in Christ, the eschaton has broken into the present. Their eternal status was settled once they exercised faith in the Savior, who no longer resides in the tomb but in the clouds. Yes, they await their Savior's return but not without assurance of their right standing before the heavenly throne. Therefore, although the believer will not be *publicly* recognized as justified until that final day of judgment, his or her eschatological status is already secure in the risen Christ, clothed in his righteousness and declared right in the eyes of God (5:1). Schreiner notes,

> The end-time declaration has been pronounced in advance by the death and resurrection of Jesus Christ. This means that every text that speaks of past justification is also an eschatological text, for justification belongs to believers inasmuch as they are united to Jesus Christ as the crucified and risen Lord. The future is revealed and announced in the present. . . . Still, they look forward to the day when the declaration will be announced *publicly* and to the entire world. In this sense, . . . justification is an already but not yet reality.[41]

That said, Richard Gaffin's observation is far more Pauline than Wright's: "All soteric experience derives from solidarity in Christ's resurrection and involves existence in the new creation age, inaugurated by his resurrection."[42] Or as Fesko stresses, "All soteriology, including justification, is eschatological because of its connection to the

---

39. N. T. Wright, *What Saint Paul Really Said: Was Paul of Tarsus the Real Founder of Christianity?* (Grand Rapids, MI: Eerdmans, 1997), 119.
40. E.g., Thomas Schreiner, *Faith Alone: The Doctrine of Justification; What the Reformers Taught . . . and Why It Still Matters*, Five Solas Series (Grand Rapids, MI: Zondervan, 2015), 239–61.
41. Schreiner, *Faith Alone*, 156.
42. Gaffin, *Resurrection and Redemption*, 138.

resurrection of Christ, the in-breaking eschaton."[43] Fesko goes on to argue that while Wright believes resurrection is primarily connected to ecclesiology (not how one gets in but who is in), such a connection is foreign to Paul. In texts like 1 Corinthians 15:17, "Paul connects the resurrection to soteriology" and to "the conquest of sin and death."[44]

Consider a concluding question: What is it that breaks the power of the old era and ushers in the conquest of the new era? The answer to that eschatological question is *the resurrection*. But how can this be? Answer: the resurrection spells the death of death and with it sin. Notice, eschatology is only as effective as resurrection, and the justification it effects is soteric. No final wedge can be driven through this causal relationship lest we do harm to the biblical understanding of eschatology and the justification it objectifies through a resurrected Christ.[45]

Newness of Life

Finally, the resurrection, along with its relation to justification, is a major factor in the type of life the believer is said to participate in as one who is no longer dead but alive to God. As we've seen, Paul believes the new Adam's obedience and righteousness has led to "justification and life for all men" (Rom. 5:18; cf. 5:19). Although the law increased trespasses, grace abounded and reigned "through righteousness leading to eternal life through Jesus Christ our Lord" (5:20–21).

With this new status in Christ, as well as the eternal life promised through Christ, those redeemed by Christ's cross and resurrection life can no longer give themselves over to sin. That would be the spiritual equivalent of schizophrenia. The life of a believer is to be consistent with his or her identity *in Christ*. "How can we who died to sin still live in it?" (6:2), Paul asks rhetorically. "Do you not know that all of us who have been baptized into Christ Jesus were baptized into his death?" (6:3). The Christian's identity in Christ is not merely traced back to the cross, for living the Christian life involves not only mortification but also vivification. Walking the vivified life presupposes resurrection: "We were buried therefore with him by baptism into death, in order that, just as Christ was raised from the dead by the glory of the Father, we too might walk in newness of life" (6:4). Newness of life for the Christian is viable only if Christ is risen. Regeneration, or being "made alive together with him" (Col. 2:13), as well as mortification and vivification (3:1–2), not to mention future bodily resurrection (3:4)—all these stem from the one who has been made alive bodily.

---

43. Fesko, *Justification*, 238.
44. Fesko, *Justification*, 238.
45. This is not a point limited to Protestantism but is highlighted by some Roman Catholics as well. For example, consider Thomas Weinandy: "Because Jesus suffered our condemnation, having put to death our sinful nature, and because he equally offered his holy life as a loving sacrifice to the Father, the Father has raised him gloriously from the dead. Being the risen Lord, he is now empowered to send forth the new life of the Holy Spirit. In the person of the resurrected Jesus himself the *eschaton* is now fully present and actualized, and so, in him, the end is beginning to be made available to all. It is here in the resurrected Jesus that the new eschatological life of the Spirit, a life that will be entirely free from suffering, because it is entirely free from sin, finds its beginning and its end. . . . Through his death and resurrection Jesus established a whole new salvific order." *Does God Suffer?* (Notre Dame, IN: University of Notre Dame Press, 2000), 234.

To be hidden with Christ and to be found in Christ, therefore, must rest on a risen Savior, for only a risen Savior can fortify the type of walk that should characterize the believer from justification to glory. As Paul says to the Colossians,

> If then you have been raised with Christ, seek the things that are above, where Christ is, seated at the right hand of God. Set your minds on things that are above, not on things that are on earth. For you have died, and your life is hidden with Christ in God. When Christ who is your life appears, then you also will appear with him in glory. (3:1–4)

Or as Paul says to the Corinthians, "For the love of Christ controls us, because we have concluded this: that one has died for all, therefore all have died; and he died for all, that those who live might no longer live for themselves but for him who for their sake died and was raised" (2 Cor. 5:14–15).

Any doubt that Paul sees Christ's resurrection as the source not only of believers' new status but also of the newness of life that is to characterize their "walk" is removed by Paul's appeal to union with Christ itself: "For if we have been united with him in a death like his, we shall certainly be united with him in a resurrection like his" (Rom. 6:5). While "union with Christ" language is typically oriented toward the *ordo salutis*, Paul's statement clarifies that it can never be defined apart from the objective reality of the *historia salutis*. Union with Christ is an unbreakable chain between the *ordo salutis* and the *historia salutis*, or redemption accomplished and redemption applied. And the implications for the justified life of the believer are life changing:

> We know that our old self was crucified with him in order that the body of sin might be brought to nothing, so that we would no longer be enslaved to sin. For one who has died has been set free from sin. Now if we have died with Christ, we believe that we will also live with him. We know that Christ, being raised from the dead, will never die again; death no longer has dominion over him. For the death he died he died to sin, once for all, but the life he lives he lives to God. So you also must consider yourselves dead to sin and alive to God in Christ Jesus. (Rom. 6:6–11)

Paul's admonition has inestimable significance for the Christian mind. The most basic reason why the believer cannot live comfortably with sin present is because he is "dead to sin and alive to God in Christ Jesus," and that new life is contingent on an objective reality, providing the believer with fortified assurance (6:11). What is that objective reality? "We know that Christ, being raised from the dead, will never die again" (6:9). Just as death no longer has dominion over him, it no longer has dominion over the believer. In Christ's death he died to sin, and in Christ's resurrection he is alive to God.

If union with Christ is that unbreakable chain between the *historia salutis* and the *ordo salutis*, then Paul's next move is understandably didactic:

> Let not sin therefore reign in your mortal body, to make you obey its passions. Do not present your members to sin as instruments for unrighteousness, but present your-

selves to God as those who have been brought from death to life, and your members to God as instruments for righteousness. For sin will have no dominion over you, since you are not under law but under grace. (Rom. 6:12–14)

With Christ risen, he alone is King, and he reigns supreme. Sin can no longer have dominion for those "alive to God in Christ Jesus."

Conclusion

Few will deny that Christ was raised for our justification. Yet the common inability to ground justification in resurrection can only mean that Christians today struggle with what Paul intends, as though the relationship between resurrection and justification is awkwardly ambiguous. That ambiguity is without warrant, foreign to the mind-set of the biblical authors, especially the apostle Paul. It also threatens to bypass the Christological, covenantal, forensic, and eschatological contours of the resurrection itself, which would do untold harm to the imputed righteousness of Christ and the justified status it brings. It is not an overstatement to conclude that a neglect of the former (Christological, covenantal, forensic, and eschatological facets) is disastrous for the latter (imputation). Paul agreed: if Christ has not been raised for our justification, then our faith is futile and we are still in our sins.

Recommended Resources

Allen, R. Michael. *Justification and the Gospel: Understanding the Contexts and Controversies*. Grand Rapids, MI: Baker Academic, 2013.

Barrett, Matthew. *40 Questions about Salvation*. Grand Rapids, MI: Kregel, 2018.

Calvin, John. *Institutes of the Christian Religion*. Edited by John T. McNeill. Translated by Ford Lewis Battles. Library of Christian Classics 20–21. Philadelphia: Westminster, 1960.

Crowe, Brandon D. *The Last Adam: A Theology of the Obedient Life of Jesus in the Gospels*. Grand Rapids, MI: Baker Academic, 2017.

Fesko, J. V. *The Covenant of Redemption: Origins, Development, and Reception*. Reformed Historical Theology 35. Göttingen: Vandenhoeck & Ruprecht, 2015.

———. *Justification: Understanding the Classic Reformed Doctrine*. Phillipsburg, NJ: P&R, 2008.

———. *The Trinity and the Covenant of Redemption*. Fearn, Ross-Shire, Scotland: Mentor, 2016.

Gaffin, Richard B., Jr. *Resurrection and Redemption: A Study in Paul's Soteriology*. Phillipsburg, NJ: Presbyterian and Reformed, 1987.

Horton, Michael S. "Traditional Reformed View." In *Justification: Five Views*, edited by James K. Beilby and Paul Rhodes Eddy, 83–111. Spectrum Multiview Books. Downers Grove, IL: IVP Academic, 2011.

Köstenberger, Andreas J., and Scott R. Swain. *Father, Son, and Spirit: The Trinity and John's Gospel*. NSBT 24. Downers Grove, IL: InterVarsity Press, 2008.

Molnar, Paul D. "The Theology of Justification in Dogmatic Context." In *Justification: What's at Stake in the Current Debates*, edited by Mark A. Husbands and Daniel J. Treier, 241–47. Downers Grove, IL: InterVarsity Press, 2004.

Murray, John. *The Epistle to the Romans*. NICNT. Grand Rapids, MI: Eerdmans, 1968.

———. *The Imputation of Adam's Sin*. In *Justified in Christ: God's Plan for Us in Justification*, edited by K. Scott Oliphint, 205–94. Fearn, Ross-shire, Scotland: Mentor, 2007.

Piper, John. *Counted Righteous in Christ: Should We Abandon the Imputation of Christ's Righteousness?* Wheaton, IL: Crossway, 2002.

Owen, John. *The Doctrine of Justification by Faith*. In *The Works of John Owen*. Edited by William H. Goold. Vol. 5, *Faith and Its Evidences*, 1–400. Edinburgh: Banner of Truth, 1965.

———. *The Mystery of the Gospel Vindicated*. In *The Works of John Owen*. Edited by William H. Goold. Vol. 12, *The Gospel Defended*, 85–617. Edinburgh: Banner of Truth, 1991.

Schreiner, Thomas. *Faith Alone: The Doctrine of Justification; What the Reformers Taught . . . and Why It Still Matters*. Five Solas Series. Grand Rapids, MI: Zondervan, 2015.

———. *Romans*. Baker Exegetical Commentary on the New Testament 6. Grand Rapids, MI: Baker Academic, 1998.

Tipton, Lane G., and Jeffrey C. Waddington, eds. *Resurrection and Eschatology: Theology in Service of the Church; Essays in Honor of Richard B. Gaffin Jr.* Phillipsburg, NJ: P&R, 2008.

Vickers, Brian. *Jesus' Blood and Righteousness: Paul's Theology of Imputation*. Wheaton, IL: Crossway, 2006.

———. *Justification by Grace through Faith: Finding Freedom from Legalism, Lawlessness, Pride, and Despair*. Explorations in Biblical Theology. Phillipsburg, NJ: P&R, 2013.

Vos, Geerhardus. *Biblical Theology: Old and New Testaments*. Grand Rapids, MI: Eerdmans, 1959.

———. *The Pauline Eschatology*. Phillipsburg, NJ: Presbyterian and Reformed, 1979.

Wright, N. T. *The Resurrection of the Son of God*. London: SPCK, 2003.

13

The Theology of Justification by Faith

The Theological Case for *Sola Fide*

MARK THOMPSON

The deep ground of the doctrine of justification only by faith is the person, character, and purpose of the triune God, and its focus is the death of Jesus Christ for sinners. In the body of Christian teaching, this doctrine has a special place, guarding and securing the priority of grace and the entire sufficiency of the atonement effected by Christ. In shorthand, justification is only by faith because salvation is only by Christ, and salvation only by Christ is the outworking of God's eternal gracious purpose anchored in the immeasurable depth of his triune life. That is why Martin Luther spoke of this doctrine as the article by which the church stands or falls.[1] If the Christian confession fails at this point, it compromises our utter dependence on Christ and the sheer gratuity of grace, and as a result, the Christian life, corporately as well as individually, begins to unravel. Ultimately, the doctrine of God begins to be redrawn to accommodate notions of human merit and divine obligation. Luther's fierce determination to concede nothing when it comes to this doctrine finds its true explanation here rather than in his personal psychology or polemical context: he understood just what was at stake.[2]

The rich tapestry that makes up this doctrine, into which is woven the person, character, and purpose of God, the profundity of human sin and its impact on every human faculty, and the glorious sufficiency of Christ's propitiatory sacrifice find concentrated

---

1. Martin Luther, commenting on Psalm 130:4, stated, "When it stands by this article, the church stands, when [this article] falls the church falls." *In XV Psalmos graduum* (1532), in WA 40.3:352.1–3.
2. In Luther's words, "On this article rests all that we teach and practice against the pope, the devil and the world." Martin Luther, "The Schmalkaldic Articles" (1537), 1.5, in *WA* 50:199.22–200.5; or William R. Russell, *Luther's Theological Testament: The Schmalkald Articles* (Minneapolis: Fortress, 1995), 122.

expression in the words of the apostle Paul, in the midst of what Leon Morris once described as "the most important single paragraph ever written":[3]

> For there is no distinction: for all have sinned and fall short of the glory of God, and are justified by his grace as a gift, through the redemption that is in Christ Jesus, whom God put forward as a propitiation by his blood, to be received by faith. This was to show God's righteousness, because in his divine forbearance he had passed over former sins. It was to show his righteousness at the present time, so that he might be just and the justifier of the one who has faith in Jesus. (Rom. 3:22–26)

These critical sentences occur within the integrated argument of Paul's epistle to the Romans, in which he expounds the gospel of God (1:1), which is first and foremost the gospel concerning his Son (1:3), and as a consequence, the power of God for salvation (1:16). Taking that movement seriously is at least part of the antidote to an anthropocentric construal of salvation, which theologians such as John Webster have warned against.[4] The proper starting point is God, not the human predicament. A clear focus on the person and work of Christ rather than the instrument of faith also helps us avoid distorting our account of the doctrine. Just as critical is the distinction between the justifying act of God and the consequences of that act in the life of the believer or the believing community. Peace with God and the removal of barriers to table fellowship between believing Jews and believing Gentiles follow necessarily from the reality this doctrine speaks of, but the righteousness of God, the ineradicable forensic element in the human condition postfall, and the essentially object-focused character of faith—each have a more basic and determinative role in the exposition of the doctrine itself.

"That He Might Be Just and the Justifier"

We start with God. This may at first seem counterintuitive, since justification only by faith is also described as the justification of the ungodly. Isn't the doctrine first and foremost about how sinful human creatures are put in the right with God? Isn't it a soteriological doctrine, teaching about what is involved in our salvation, rather than part of theology proper? Such questions are no doubt legitimate, and they alert us to the contemporary danger of allowing biblical teaching about salvation to be swallowed up by accounts of the Trinity that are extended in a universalist direction. Nevertheless, in both Romans 3—"so that *he* might be just and the justifier of the one who has faith in Jesus" (3:26)—and even in Romans 4—where Abraham is a pattern for "the one who does not work but believes in *him* who justifies the ungodly" (4:5)—our attention is drawn back to God, the one who justifies. There is a sense in which the doctrine is first and foremost a doctrine about God and how he acts in a perfect expression of his being and character when he provides the grounds and

---

[3]. Leon Morris, *The Epistle to the Romans* (Grand Rapids, MI: Eerdmans, 1988), 173.
[4]. John Webster, "*Rector et iudex super omnia genera doctrinarum?* The Place of the Doctrine of Justification," in *What Is Justification About? Reformed Contributions to an Ecumenical Theme*, ed. Michael Weinrich and John P. Burgess (Grand Rapids, MI: Eerdmans, 2009), 39.

means by which sinners are justified. Salvation has this larger context: it "occurs as part of the divine self-exposition; its final end is the reiteration of God's majesty and the glorification of God by all creatures."[5] So how God acts in the economy of creation and redemption is entirely consistent with God's eternal being and character. In technical terms, the divine missions arise appropriately from the divine processions. Or as Jonathan Edwards put it, "'Tis fit that the order of the acting of the persons of the Trinity should be agreeable to the order of their subsisting."[6] Christian soteriology is enclosed and undergirded by the Christian doctrine of God while not being simply another element of that doctrine.

Karl Barth recognized this when he began his treatment of the doctrine of justification with a remarkable series of questions that he believed illustrate "the problem of the doctrine of justification":

> To what extent does God act and speak and prove and show Himself in the justification of man . . . as God the Father, Son and Holy Spirit, in whom there is no contradiction or caprice or disorder, no paradox or obscurity, but only light? To what extent does He demonstrate and maintain in this remarkable justification His righteousness as the Creator confronting the creature and as the Lord of His covenant with man? . . . How in this justification can God be effectively true to Himself and therefore to man—to man and therefore primarily to Himself?[7]

Barth was, of course, not the first to notice the importance of the strictly *theological* dimension of the doctrine. Thomas Aquinas, fully seven centuries earlier, insisted that "all things are dealt with in sacred doctrine in terms of God, either because they are God himself or because they are relative to God as their origin and end."[8] Whatever the precise topic being considered, theology rightly understood traces the lines of connection to the person, character, and purpose of God. Aquinas specifically applied this thinking to the doctrines of salvation, concluding that "knowledge of the divine persons was necessary for us . . . chiefly, that we may think rightly of the salvation of the human race, accomplished by the incarnate Son and by the gift of the Holy Spirit."[9] Almost equidistant in time between Aquinas and Barth, John Owen concluded that "the greatness, the majesty, the holiness, and the sovereign authority of God, are always to be present with us in a due sense of them, when we inquire how we may be justified before him."[10] Such a connection is critical not simply for a right ordering of our doctrine of

---

5. John Webster, "'It Was the Will of the Lord to Bruise Him': Soteriology and the Doctrine of God," in *God without Measure: Working Papers in Christian Theology*, vol. 1, *God and the Works of God* (London: Bloomsbury T&T Clark, 2016), 148.
6. Jonathan Edwards, "Economy of the Trinity and Covenant of Redemption" (1730) ["Miscellanies" entry no. 1062], in *The Works of Jonathan Edwards*, vol. 20, *The "Miscellanies": Entry Nos. 833–1152*, ed. Amy Plantinga Pauw (New Haven, CT: Yale University Press, 2002), 431.
7. Karl Barth, *Church Dogmatics*, vol. 4, bk. 1, *The Doctrine of Reconciliation, Part 1* (1953), ed. T. F. Torrance, trans. G. W. Bromiley (Edinburgh: T&T Clark, 1956), 517.
8. Thomas Aquinas, *Summa Theologiae* 1a.1.7, in Blackfriars ed. (London: Eyre and Spottiswoode, 1963), 1:27.
9. Aquinas, *Summa Theologiae* 1a.32.1 (my trans.; cf. Blackfriars trans., 6:109).
10. John Owen, *The Doctrine of Justification by Faith, through the Imputation of the Righteousness of Christ, Explained, Confirmed, and Vindicated* (1677), in *The Works of John Owen*, ed. William H. Goold, vol. 5, *Faith and Its Evidences* (repr., London: Banner of Truth, 1967), 13.

salvation in Christ but also for its right application in terms of assurance and comfort. John Webster pointed in this direction when he remarked, "Salvation is secure because the works of the redeemer and the sanctifier can be traced to the inner life of God, behind which there lies nothing."[11] In summary, if theology is an account of God and therefore of all things in relation to God, it should not be surprising that a theological exposition of the doctrine of justification begins at this point too.

The triune God who acts in justification is free and unconditioned by anything outside himself. This is critical. Not only is God full and complete in his own being—that is, he does not need anything outside himself to somehow supplement the eternal relation of Father, Son, and Spirit—but also God's work is not directed or required by anyone or anything outside himself. How could that be since he is the uncreated Creator of all things? His immanent relations and his external work are entirely unconstrained and are therefore able to give perfect expression to his being and character. His work for us is, then, entirely *for us*. It is not necessary for his own life or required by some external power or code. We, his creatures, have no claim on him. As John Chrysostom put it, "He desires nothing from us except our salvation. He does not need our service or anything else but does everything for this end."[12]

The sheer graciousness of God's provision of justification is anchored in who God is and how God is. It is not responsive in the sense of acknowledging a creaturely need, disposition, or action as the proper source or cause of grace. So Wilhelmus à Brakel, a theologian of the Dutch *Nadere Reformatie*, spoke of "God himself" as the cause of justification,

> that is, Father, Son and Holy Spirit each in their own role in the economy of the covenant. This is a work of God, for God is the only Lawgiver (James 4:12), the only Judge of all the earth (Gen. 18:25), and the righteous Judge (Psa. 7:11). He, being righteous, can by no means clear the guilty (Ex. 34:7), His judgment is according to truth (Rom. 2:2), and His judgment is a righteous judgment (Rom. 2:5). Righteously He condemns the ungodly, and righteously He justifies believers. As I stated before, this is the work of God.[13]

This language of causation is not without its problems, particularly when Aristotle's classification of causes shapes the discussion of the doctrine and one feels pressured to identify the formal cause, material cause, instrumental cause, final cause, and so forth. Such a scheme can have the effect of "muddying the waters," placing God's being, character, and work as merely one among many causes of the justification of human beings, as this scheme most certainly had done in the medieval period.[14] Yet à Brakel's

---

11. Webster, "'It Was the Will of the Lord,'" 154.
12. John Chrysostom, "Homilies on Ephesians," 1.1.6, extracted in *Ancient Christian Commentary on Scripture: New Testament*, vol. 8, *Galatians, Ephesians, Philippians*, ed. Mark J. Edwards (Downers Grove, IL: InterVarsity Press, 1999), 113.
13. Wilhelmus à Brakel, *The Christian's Reasonable Service*, vol. 2, *The Church and Salvation*, trans. Bartel Elshout, ed. Joel R. Beeke (Grand Rapids, MI: Reformation Heritage Books, 1993), 349.
14. This is not the case with Calvin, who neatly anchored each element in God: "The mercy of God is the efficient cause, Christ with His blood the material cause, faith conceived by the Word the formal or instrumental cause, and the glory of both the divine justice and goodness the final cause." John Calvin, *The Epistles of Paul the Apostle to the Romans and*

concern to identify justification as entirely a *work of God* and to anchor this work of God in his character and eternal being is reflective of the New Testament exposition of the doctrine, not least in Romans 3.

God acts in perfect freedom and grace when he justifies "the one who has faith in Jesus." Such a one is always justified "by his grace, as a gift." Just as critical, though, is the truth that God's freedom perfectly coheres with his righteousness or justice. "God is sovereign, but not arbitrary," writes Eberhard Jüngel, "and his sovereignty shows itself in the fact that, far from being arbitrary, he remains faithful to himself."[15] This is, after all, the burden of Paul's words to the Romans that have been framing our discussion—"God's righteousness," "his righteousness," "so that he might be just." Jüngel again: the task of the doctrine of justification "is to demonstrate that God in his freedom remains faithful to himself, in that he remains faithful to human beings, whom he created *good*."[16] The one who does not need us but chooses not to be without us is, in Abraham's words, "the Judge of all the earth" who cannot but act justly if he is to be true to himself (Gen. 18:25). Calvin, commenting on Romans 3, wrote, "God is just, not indeed as one among many, but as one who contains in Himself alone all the fulness of righteousness."[17] God's freedom and grace are not in conflict with his justice and righteousness. Each finds perfect expression in the other since both arise from the depth of God's own eternal life and being.

Even more basically, God is not made up of parts, as if grace and righteousness exist as distinct (even if inseparable) principles within the Godhead. His justice is gracious, and his grace is just. This is demonstrated time and again in the history of redemption, Old Testament and New. In the destruction of Sodom and Gomorrah, to which we have already alluded, God acts justly and graciously. The outcry from the victims did not go unanswered, and yet in grace Lot and his daughters were spared. The exodus, the overthrow of Egypt and its pantheon, and the rescue of the Hebrews in the midst of it again demonstrate a grace that does not overturn justice and a justice that does not forget grace. So, too, do the election of David, the preservation of a remnant in and through the entirely just judgment of the exile, and, preeminently, the cross of Christ, where human sin is met with an act of supreme justice and grace. Human sin and its penalty are not

---

to the *Thessalonians*, trans. Ross Mackenzie, ed. David W. Torrance and Thomas F. Torrance (Grand Rapids, MI: Eerdmans, 1960), 75. Compare Calvin to the formulation of the Council of Trent: "The final cause indeed is the glory of God and of Jesus Christ and life everlasting; while the efficient cause is a merciful God who washes and sanctifies gratuitously, signing, and anointing with the holy Spirit of promise, who is the pledge of our inheritance; but the meritorious cause is his most beloved only-begotten, our Lord Jesus Christ, who, when we were enemies, for the exceeding charity wherewith he loved us, merited Justification for us by his most holy Passion on the wood of the cross, and made satisfaction for us unto God the Father; the instrumental cause is the sacrament of baptism, which is the sacrament of faith, without which [faith] no man was ever justified; lastly, the alone formal cause is the justice of God, not that whereby he himself is just, but that whereby he maketh us just." "The Canons and Decrees of the Council of Trent," session 6, chap. 7, in *The Creeds of Christendom: With a History and Critical Notes*, ed. Philip Schaff and David S. Schaff, 6th ed. (Grand Rapids, MI: Baker, 1983), 2:94–95. Aquinas had written of four necessary elements of justification: "the infusion of grace; a movement of free choice directed towards God [*in Deum*] by faith; a movement of free choice directed towards sin [*in peccatum*]; and the forgiveness of sins." Aquinas, *Summa Theologiae* 1a2ae.113.6, in Blackfriars ed., 30:181.

15. Eberhard Jüngel, *Justification: The Heart of the Christian Faith*, trans. Jeffrey F. Cayzer (Edinburgh: T&T Clark, 2001), 39.
16. Jüngel, *Justification*, 40; italics original.
17. Calvin, *Romans*, 77.

ignored but borne in full. In one and the same act, grace is extended to human sinners. There is no struggle within God as he acts in created time and space to accomplish his eternal purpose. He freely acts in perfect accord with who and how he is. From beginning to end, he is gracious precisely as he is just, and he is just precisely as he is gracious. There is more than mere coherence here. God is always true to himself. He always does what is right. He always acts with grace. More than that, he does not only act justly, he *is* just. He does not only act with grace, he *is* grace.[18] When God's perfect self-expression dwells among us, he is "full of grace and truth" (John 1:14). Karl Barth put it this way: "God is altogether everything that He is. In everything that He is, He is Himself. And everything that He Himself is, He is in unsurpassable, unchallengeable perfection. But He is so in His own perfection, not in one which is arbitrarily determined."[19]

This being so, God's grace and freedom are described as just not by appeal to an abstract moral principle of rectitude, as was attempted by some in the Enlightenment.[20] Such an attempt relies on our capacity to trace the scope and content of that principle. It also runs the risk of pursuing the same illusory ideal as that promised in the garden: the independent knowledge of good and evil—independent, that is, of God (Gen. 3:5). Rather, the justice of God is properly seen only in God himself, in Jesus Christ who has exegeted the Father for us (John 1:18). Jesus is repeatedly described as "the Righteous One" (Acts 7:52; 22:14), echoing Old Testament descriptions of God (Isa. 24:16) and the servant (Isa. 53:11). More particularly, the righteousness or justice of God is revealed in the gospel concerning his Son (Rom. 1:3, 17). What exactly is it, then, that we see demonstrated in the gospel? Jüngel suggests that the answer lies, not least, in God's own self-consistency:

> This is the righteousness of God: that God is the eternal and almighty *Father* and is *at the same time* the *Son* who came as a man in poverty into the world, perishing in and by the world, that is, *Jesus Christ*, crucified in weakness (2 Cor. 13:4). God is righteous in the lack of internal contradiction in this extreme tension between the almighty Father—the origin of all life and being—and the Son who suffered death. This is where the *foundations* lie for the fact that the ungodly are justified.... In Jesus Christ crucified, God is *consistent with, in concord with himself* by the fact that he himself brings people who are in con*flict* with him into con*cord* with him. In Jesus Christ, God's being and our becoming coincide.[21]

---

18. Here we must be wary of the modern danger of collapsing the immanent life of God into the economic activity of God without remainder. Bruce McCormack's development of Barth is problematic: "There is a triune being of God—only in the covenant of grace." Bruce L. McCormack, "Election and Trinity: Theses in Response to George Hunsinger," *SJT* 63, no. 2 (2010): 215. In contrast, Owen explains, "The justice of God, *absolutely* considered, is the universal *rectitude and perfection* of the divine nature; for such is the divine nature antecedent to all acts of his will and suppositions of objects towards which it might operate." John Owen, *A Dissertation on Divine Justice* (1653), in Goold, *Works of John Owen*, vol. 10, *The Death of Christ*, 498.

19. Barth, *Church Dogmatics*, vol. 2, bk. 1, *The Doctrine of God, Part 1*, ed. G. W. Bromiley and T. F. Torrance, trans. T. H. L. Parker et al. (1940; repr., Edinburgh: T&T Clark, 1957), 376.

20. For example, John Balguy stated, "I have proposed to reconcile the Doctrine of *Redemption* with the principle of *Rectitude*." *An Essay on Redemption*, 2nd ed. (Winchester: Lockyer & Davis, 1785), 5; italics original.

21. Jüngel, *Justification*, 79–80 (slightly amended trans.). See also Webster, "*Rector et iudex*," 50: "His righteousness is the unbroken and fully realized harmony of God's life and his will, in the eternal moments of paternity, filiation, and spiration that constitute his being."

Once again, Jüngel suggests that this is not simply a consistency of action, or even a consistency between God's action and his eternal being, but it goes deeper to the nature of this eternal being himself:

> God exists in relation to himself in such a way that he exists as Father, Son and Holy Spirit. He so relates to himself in this threefold personal existence that Father, Son and Holy Spirit mutually affirm each other in their respective *otherness*. When we talk of God's righteousness this is the decisive point of view: that God is not a lone being, but that in God himself, *otherness* has been and is being affirmed: not the otherness of three distinct beings, but the otherness of distinct ways of being or persons of one and the same being. . . . The righteousness of God is the epitome of a well-ordered system of relationships which God does not reserve for his own benefit in some fit of divine selfishness; no, he gives his people a part in it by making them partners in the covenant. . . . God's righteousness is no divine attribute reserved for God alone. It is one which he shares with others.[22]

God's own life and his activity in the world he created define righteousness for us. In the gospel of the incarnate, crucified, and risen Savior, we are shown God acting freely and fully in perfect accord with his nature: he keeps the promises he has made; he is covenantally faithful; he gives himself in genuine other-centered concern for the welfare of those he calls to himself; he treats the horrific contradiction of sin with the utmost seriousness, ignoring neither its repudiation of his gift of every breath and heartbeat nor the injury it causes to fellow creatures in its blind self-centeredness; he pours out his love and compassion on those who are lost and in danger, who are "like sheep without a shepherd" (Matt. 9:36). Benedict Pictet, a late seventeenth-century successor of Calvin in the Academy at Geneva, began his treatment of the justice of God by suggesting that the word *justice* can be understood, at least in some of its occurrences in Scripture, as "that most sacred union of divine qualities, shining forth in the words and actions of God."[23] It can, therefore, find expression in both God's proper condemnation and punishment of sin—that element of righteousness that so struck fear into the heart of the young Luther—and his gift of salvation to sinners in and through Christ—the insight that conducted Luther through "the gates of paradise."[24]

It is possible to see each of these, God's perfect freedom, grace, and righteousness—together with his goodness and mercy—as more basically "attributes of God's love," to use Wolfhart Pannenberg's phrase.[25] The "propitiation by his blood," which Paul declares was to show God's righteousness (Rom. 3:25), is just as much, according to the apostle John, a demonstration of his love: "In this is love, not that we have loved God but that he loved us and sent his Son to be the propitiation for our sins" (1 John

---

22. Jüngel, *Justification*, 82–83, 86.
23. Benedict Pictet, *Christian Theology*, trans. Frederick Reyroux (1696; repr., Weston Green, UK: Seeley & Sons, 1834), 89.
24. Martin Luther, "Preface to the Complete Edition of Luther's Latin Writings" (1545), in *LW* 34:337.
25. Wolfhart Pannenberg, *Systematic Theology*, trans. G. W. Bromiley (Edinburgh: T&T Clark, 1991), 1:432–33.

4:10). The point is that we must take care not to isolate justice and love. Barth insisted that "according to the witness of the Old and New Testaments, the love and grace and mercy of God, Jesus Christ, are the demonstration and exercise of the righteousness of God. And it is only in this way that the divine love and grace and mercy can be truly recognised and felt and appropriated."[26] This is certainly true. Yet so, too, is the obverse. His righteousness is an expression of his unshakable determination to seek the welfare of the "other," his love for his creatures, which is an overflow of the perfect, abundant love of the triune persons. God is love:

> The Father loves the Son and has given all things into his hand. (John 3:35; cf. 5:20)

> God so loved the world, that he gave his only Son, that whoever believes in him should not perish but have eternal life. (John 3:16)

The justification of the ungodly, on the basis of the propitiation provided by God himself in and through the person of the Son, is equally an expression of his righteousness and his love. It is a wide-open window into the character and being of the triune God. If justification were not by faith only, we would have to recast our understanding not only of God's promises and purposes but also of God's being and character. God has acted in perfect freedom, grace, righteousness, and love because this is what he is like through and through.

"All Have Sinned and Fall Short of the Glory of God"

While the ground of justification only by faith is the being, character, and purpose of the triune God, its necessary context is the devastating and universal sin of his creatures. The universality of sin is the argument in Romans that sets the immediate backdrop for the paragraph on justification: "None is righteous, no not one; no one understands; no one seeks for God. All have turned aside; together they have become worthless; no one does good, not even one. . . . All have sinned and fall short of the glory of God" (Rom. 3:10–12, 23). None are excluded from this predicament save the one who came to "save his people from their sins" (Matt. 1:21), who came "in the likeness of sinful flesh and for sin" in order to "[condemn] sin in the flesh" (Rom. 8:3)—the "man . . . from heaven" (1 Cor. 15:47). Every mouth is stopped and "the whole world [is] held accountable to God" (Rom. 3:19), because with or without the law of God, the primal decision for autonomy and self-determination is repeated by each one of us except, again, the one who always did his Father's will (John 5:36; 8:29) and spoke the words given to him by the Father (15:15; 17:8, 14).

Sin is complex. It is a disposition, a decision, and an action. Its consequences are guilt, corruption, and enslavement. Nevertheless, there are a number of simple constants. From the very beginning, sin has set human beings before the judgment of God. It has this unavoidable forensic consequence. The man and the woman (and the serpent!)

---

26. Barth, *Church Dogmatics*, 2.1.384.

were called to account before God: "What is this that you have done?" (Gen. 3:13). They might have sought to establish themselves as arbiters of good and evil, right and wrong, but it was ultimately beyond them. So, ironically, one of the first consequences of this grasp for moral autonomy was unavoidable accountability. They had to answer for what they had done and bear the penalty associated with the choice they had made. They had been created to live in fellowship with their Creator and to receive from him words of life and purpose, but they had doubted those words—and ultimately, the one who spoke them—and listened to the words of another. And the consequences were nothing short of catastrophic for themselves and all who came after them.

Sin is associated from the beginning with death: "For in the day that you eat of it you shall surely die," God had warned them (Gen. 2:17). From the moment they ate, death shadowed them. To turn from the one who gives life is to face death. So further on in Romans, Paul writes, "Sin came into the world through one man, and death through sin, and so death spread to all men because all sinned" (Rom. 5:12), and most starkly of all, "The wages of sin is death" (6:23). Death is not natural and cannot be domesticated. Nor can it be contained. It is a massively interruptive force indicating that something is now profoundly wrong in the world created good and created "by," "through," and "for" the Son (Col. 1:16), "the Author of life" (Acts 3:15). The scope of the destructive impact of sin is the entire creation.

Also, from the beginning, sin has involved a repudiation of the word God has spoken, not least his word about the nature and seriousness of sin itself. In the garden, Adam and Eve's refusal to accept their life as creatures—"you will be like God" (Gen. 3:5)—was recast in positive terms: "good for food," "a delight to the eyes," "to be desired to make one wise" (3:6). What they had been told would inevitably lead to death became in their eyes something not only to embrace but to celebrate. This conflict between the good word God has given and the determined pursuit of self-determination in one form or another became a feature of human history. Its climax came when the Word become flesh was nailed to a cross.

"You have not yet considered how heavy the weight of sin is," Anselm protested to Boso.[27] Though the consequence of death in and of itself should have pressed on the human race the seriousness of sin (leaving aside for the moment the way in which the cross of Christ makes this point with considerable force), human beings habitually have downplayed the gravity of the situation. This is itself part of the noetic impact of sin, that blindness or futility of thinking to which God hands over those who refuse to honor him or give thanks to him (Rom. 1:21).[28]

Michael Ovey draws attention to the critical inadequacy of some medieval pictures of the impact of sin, such as those used by Gabriel Biel in his sermon "The Circumcision of the Lord" (1460). Biel spoke of the salvation effected by Christ in medical terms: "In

---

27. Anselm, *Why God Became Man* (1098), 1.21, in *Anselm of Canterbury: The Major Works*, ed. Brian Davies and G. R. Evans, Oxford World's Classics (Oxford: Oxford University Press, 1998), 305.
28. One of very few explorations of the noetic impact of the fall is Stephen K. Moroney, *The Noetic Effects of Sin: A Historical and Contemporary Exploration of How Sin Affects Our Thinking* (Lanham, MD: Lexington Books, 2000).

truth He has *already saved* His people by preparing medicine. He *continues to save* them daily by driving out disease. He *will save* them ultimately by giving them perfect health and preserving them from every ill."[29] A little further in the sermon, Biel quoted Duns Scotus approvingly: "Grace is an enrichment of nature that is pleasing to God's will."[30] Finally, he illustrated how grace elevates human power beyond itself using the metaphor of "a bird that has a stone tied to it so that it could scarcely fly away. Now if this bird's wings were strengthened, then we would say that the impediment to flight had been lessened, although the weight of the stone had not been lessened."[31] At each point, and in the parable of the king and the rings with which he concluded the sermon, Biel underestimated the impact of sin on the creature. As Ovey puts it, picking up the bird image in particular, "In this image the bird is fundamentally intact. All that is wrong with the bird is the stones."[32] The bird retains the ability to fly, and an enrichment of this natural ability will see it fly again. Similarly, Biel's medical image suggests that there is still life and hope, while the apostle Paul reminds the Ephesians that they were "dead in [their] trespasses and sins" (Eph. 2:1, 5). What is necessary is not just medicine but resurrection—he "raised us up with him" (2:6).

The starkest of contrasts with the medieval way of viewing the impact of sin is found in Luther's *Heidelberg Disputation* (1518). Luther understood that an appreciation of the depth of human sin is critical for a proper grasp of the gospel truth of justification. We will not flee to Christ and call on him to save us while there is the slightest hope that we can save ourselves. We will not stop trying to save ourselves, to establish our own righteousness, until we have been brought this low. As he put it, "It is certain that man must utterly despair of his own ability before he is prepared to receive the grace of Christ."[33]

The depth of our problem is exposed when we realize that *even at our best*, our behavior is shaped and colored by sin. Luther turned to Ecclesiastes 7:20: "Surely there is not a righteous man on earth who does good and never sins"—and then he argued, "Since there is no righteous person on earth who in doing good does not sin, the unrighteous person sins that much more when he does good."[34] The judgment of Isaiah needs to be taken seriously: "We have all become like one who is unclean, and all our righteous deeds are like a polluted garment" (Isa. 64:6). A favorite illustration of Luther's at this point appears to have been "a rusty and rough hatchet." No matter how hard you swing such an implement, and no matter how skilled a craftsman you are, it will not cut cleanly. It leaves "bad, jagged, and ugly gashes."[35] In fact, the harder

---

29. Gabriel Biel, "The Circumcision of the Lord" (1460), in *Forerunners of the Reformation: The Shape of Late Medieval Thought, Illustrated by Key Documents*, ed. Heiko A. Oberman, trans. Paul L. Nyhus, LEH (London: Lutterworth, 1967), 166.
30. Biel, "Circumcision of the Lord," 168, apparently citing J. Duns Scotus, *Commentary on the Sentences*, 3.17.1.
31. Biel, "Circumcision of the Lord," 171–72.
32. Michael J. Ovey, "Justification by Faith Alone," in *Celebrating the Reformation: Its Legacy and Continuing Relevance*, ed. Mark D. Thompson, Colin Bale and Edward Loane (London: Apollos, 2017), 206. For more detailed treatments of Biel, see chap. 19, by Nick Needham, and chap. 20, by Matthew Barrett, in this volume.
33. Martin Luther, *Heidelberg Disputation* (1518), in *LW* 31:40.
34. Luther, *Heidelberg Disputation*, in *LW* 31:59.
35. Luther, *Heidelberg Disputation*, in *LW* 31:60.

you swing, the more damage you could do. Sin is so deceptive, and yet its impact so profound, that our only hope is a salvation from outside us.

This was an insight that fueled the common Reformation insistence that justification can only be by faith. So Calvin said,

> For we will never have enough confidence in him unless we become deeply distrustful of ourselves; we will never lift up our hearts enough in him unless they be previously cast down in us; we will never have consolation enough in him unless we have already experienced desolation in ourselves. . . . For to the extent that a man rests satisfied with himself, he impedes the beneficence of God.[36]

Thomas Cranmer added this confronting clause to a general confession in the 1552 Book of Common Prayer: "and there is no health in us."[37] We cannot rely on anything within us to contribute even the most minute amount to our salvation. Critically, Cranmer saw this as a prayer to be said *by Christians*. Our good works after conversion, even the very best of them, are useless in this connection. We never stand beyond the need of that justification that can come to us only from Christ.

Such insight also fueled the Reformers' critique of the statements on justification by the Council of Trent. "The principal cause of obscurity," wrote Calvin, "is that we are with the greatest difficulty induced to leave the glory of righteousness entire to God alone. For we always desire to be somewhat, and such is our folly, we even think we are."[38] Later in his *Canons and Decrees of the Council of Trent with the Antidote*, Calvin wrote, "It is, indeed, a gross and impious delusion, not to acknowledge that every work which proceeds from us has only one way of obtaining acceptance, viz., when all that was vicious in it is pardoned by paternal indulgence."[39] Martin Chemnitz put it this way:

> And for the doctrine of justification solely through the grace, or mercy, of God, on account of the obedience of the one Mediator Christ, it is necessary that it be removed and taken away completely from all the things which are, or inhere, in man, whether he be Jew or Gentile, regenerate or unregenerate.[40]

"Whom God Put Forward as a Propitiation by His Blood"

In the teaching of Jesus and in the teaching of Paul, a close connection is forged between the justification of the sinner and a propitiation provided by God himself. In the parable of the Pharisee and the tax collector, Jesus speaks of the man who, standing at a distance from the proud Pharisee and despairing of his own worthiness, can only cry,

---

36. John Calvin, *Institutes of the Christian Religion* (1559), 3.12.8, ed. John T. McNeill, trans. Ford Lewis Battles, LCC 20–21 (Philadelphia: Westminster, 1960), 762.
37. "Morning Prayer," in *The First and Second Prayer Books of Edward VI* (London: Dent, 1910), 348.
38. John Calvin, *Canons and Decrees of the Council of Trent, with the Antidote* (1547), in *Tracts and Letters*, vol. 3, *Tracts, Part 3*, ed. and trans. Henry Beveridge (1851; repr., Edinburgh: Banner of Truth, 2009), 108.
39. Calvin, *Antidote*, 146.
40. Martin Chemnitz, *Examination of the Council of Trent: Part 1* (1565), trans. Fred Kramer (Saint Louis, MO: Concordia, 1971), 492.

"God, propitiate me, the sinner" (Luke 18:13).⁴¹ He is not attempting to propitiate God with what he says or something he has done. He apparently knows he cannot do that, no matter how many times he beats his breast and conscientiously adopts the posture of a penitent. How he knows that and on what basis he makes his plea are not germane to the purpose of the parable, which is, after all, to challenge those "who trusted in themselves that they were righteous, and treated others with contempt" (18:9). Yet it is clear that the tax collector abandons all pretense of human capacity and calls on God to do what only God can do. The picture is emphatically of one devoid of all resources. And remarkably, it is the man who cries out, "God propitiate me, the sinner," who went home justified, rather than the man who draws attention to his religious devotion and his scrupulous observance of the law. Here is the narrative counterpart to Paul's "justified by faith apart from works of the law" (Rom. 3:28).

The connection between justification and propitiation in this parable is astonishing because it is so singular—the word "propitiate" (ἱλάσκομαι) is found on Jesus's lips only here—and because it is made prior to and without any immediate reference to Jesus's death. When similar prayers are addressed to Jesus throughout the Synoptic Gospels, the word used is "have mercy" (ἐλεέω). While the meanings of these two words most certainly overlap, "propitiate" has specific overtones: something must be interposed between the sinner and the wrath and condemnation of God.⁴² Once again, the point is that the man in this parable, actually both men in this parable, were not in any position to do that. In contrast to the illusory righteousness of those against whom the parable was told in the first place, a right standing before God (righteousness, the state of being justified) is something that is given as the result of a propitiation effected entirely by God.

Romans 3:21–26 fills out the details that are left implicit in the parable of the Pharisee and the tax collector. The context, the argument of 1:18–3:20, gives an important place to the realities of the wrath of God and judicial condemnation in its description of the human predicament. If the gospel is to be an answer to that predicament in full, then these two realities must be addressed. The wrath of God referred to in 1:18 and elsewhere in the New Testament is to be understood as "not some irrational passion bursting forth uncontrollably, but a burning zeal for the right coupled with a perfect hatred for everything that is evil."⁴³ In Emil Brunner's words, "It has nothing whatever to do with primitiveness, with naive anthropomorphism. On the contrary, it is the necessary expression of God, taking himself and us seriously."⁴⁴ "Condemnation" stands as the opposite of "justification" repeatedly in the New Testament, not least in Romans 8:33–34: "Who shall bring any charge against God's elect? It is God who justifies. Who is to condemn?" Human sin is universal, devastating in its impact on who we are as

---

41. My translation of ὁ θεός, ἱλάσθητί μοι τῷ ἁμαρτωλῷ.
42. The best treatment of the vocabulary of "propitiation" is still Leon Morris, *The Apostolic Preaching of the Cross*, 3rd ed. (Grand Rapids, MI: Eerdmans, 1965), 144–213.
43. Morris, *Apostolic Preaching*, 209.
44. Emil Brunner, *The Scandal of Christianity* (London: SCM, 1951), 77.

well as what we do, and it is intractable. It places us all on a collision course with the right and holy wrath of God and the most searching judgment of all, a judgment that reaches further than words and deeds to the mind and the heart. A final confrontation is unavoidable: "so that every mouth may be stopped, and the whole world may be held accountable to God" (3:19). What, then, can be interposed between the sinner and the wrath and condemnation of God? How can those who deserve to be condemned be declared righteous? The critical verses we have been examining point to "the redemption that is in Christ Jesus" and "a propitiation by his blood" (3:24–25). This is the key to being "justified by his grace as a gift."

The justification of the sinner is possible only because of the cross of Christ. The substitutionary death of the incarnate Son is the centerpiece of the doctrine: "Christ died *for our sins* [ὑπὲρ τῶν ἁμαρτιῶν] in accordance with the Scriptures" (1 Cor. 15:3). The Son of Man gave himself "as a ransom *in the place of many* [ἀντὶ πολλῶν]" (Mark 10:45, my trans.). His life of perfect obedience had its great culmination at this point. Indeed, it was indispensable to the logic of the substitution. He could die for the sins of others, and the shedding of his blood could be that propitiation that is critical to justification only because he had no sin of his own for which to atone and had perfectly fulfilled the will of the Father. Here the writer to the Hebrews helps us to understand the uniqueness of Jesus's sacrifice and why he can be spoken of as our Great High Priest (Hebrews 9–10). It is precisely because it is inextricable from this precious shedding of blood (Heb. 12:24; cf. 1 Pet. 1:18–19), that the justification of sinners is a demonstration of the righteousness of God (Rom. 3:25–26).

Once again, it was Luther, the great expounder of the doctrine of justification only by faith, who saw its relation to the substitutionary atonement flowing out of the "wonderful exchange":

> This is that mystery which is rich in divine grace to sinners: wherein by a wonderful exchange our sins are no longer ours but Christ's: and the righteousness of Christ is not Christ's but ours. He has emptied himself of his righteousness that he might clothe us with it, and fill us with it: and he has taken our evils upon himself that he might deliver us from them, so that the righteousness of Christ might already be ours, not [only] in an objective way but formally, just as our sins are Christ's not only objectively but formally. In the same manner as he grieved and suffered in our sins, and was confounded, we rejoice and glory in his righteousness, and he suffers really and formally in these, as we see here.[45]

The violent death of Christ, a death that involves the shedding of his innocent blood,[46] stands between the sinner and the outpouring of the wrath of God. Such is the value of the death of "the Righteous One" (Acts 7:52) that all claims against those covered by it can no longer be pressed. It is this perfect, holy propitiation that keeps the declaration

---

45. Martin Luther, *Operationes in Psalmos* (1519–1521), in *WA* 5:608.6–14 (commenting on Ps. 22:2).
46. Alan M. Stibbs, *The Meaning of the Word "Blood" in Scripture* (London: Tyndale Press, 1962).

of justification from being merely a legal nicety, a fiction without ground in reality. No claim can be admitted because this propitiation has been put forward—and put forward by none other than the Judge himself. The just penalty has not so much been absorbed but exhausted in the person and work of Christ. As Heinrich Bullinger put it,

> One obtains forgiveness of sins, true righteousness, and eternal life only through him, his passion, and his death and not through any other means. That is to say, he is the only mediator, priest, intercessor, comforter, the one and only righteousness, satisfaction, redemption and sanctification and the one and only eternal sacrifice, pledge of grace and salvation.[47]

So the doctrine of justification only by faith ultimately draws attention to the death of Christ for sinners. Its focus is, perhaps surprisingly, on the cross rather than the divine courtroom. Indeed, justification only by faith guards this focus on Christ's death, inseparable as it is from his resurrection: "[He] was delivered up for our trespasses and raised for our justification" (Rom. 4:25). Here is its only ground, and nothing, not even the appropriate response of faith, can stand beside it at this point. Justification is only by faith because salvation is only by Christ.

"To Be Received by Faith"

What, then, is the role of faith? In the letters of Paul, faith is contrasted with works. It is the correlate of grace and excludes any notion of human performance or merit. The great exposition of this teaching is Romans 4, where Paul insists that justification, or the reckoning of righteousness, belongs to "the one who does not work but believes in him who justifies the ungodly" (4:5). Paul goes to some lengths to insist that what Abraham received in justification was not in any way earned and that the significance of faith in his case was that it was directed toward the promise of God and ultimately the trustworthiness of the one who had made the promise. "It depends on faith," Paul says, "in order that the promise may rest on grace" (4:16). Abraham was "fully convinced that *God* was able to do what he had promised" (4:21).

Faith must not, then, be treated as itself a work, a substitute or additional ground for justification. That ground can only ever be the person and work of Jesus Christ, in whom all the promises of God find their fulfillment (2 Cor. 1:20). Nor is faith joined to works of love or obedience, as if, while insufficient in itself, it is able, when joined to these, to provide a better foundation for God's act of justification. Aquinas insists that "the movement of faith is only perfect if it is informed by charity; and so, in the justification of the unrighteous, there is also a movement of charity together with the movement of faith."[48] This thinking arises from an attenuated view of faith that fails to see that its critical element is trust. Karl Barth rightly countered, echoing "Older Protestantism," that

---

47. Heinrich Bullinger, *The Old Faith* (1537), D.iv.; translation in Joe Mock, "Bullinger's *The Old Faith* (1537) as a Theological Tract," *Unio cum Christo* 3, no. 2 (2017): 147.
48. Aquinas, *Summa Theologiae* 1a2ae.113.4, in Blackfriars ed., 30:175.

"faith becomes faith only when it is *fiducia* [trust, 'reliance on God's reliability']. *Notitia* [knowledge] and *assensus* [assent] alone would not be faith."[49] Precisely because it has this character of trust, faith is essentially "outward referring": it gains its character and efficacy from its object. This is reflected in the Westminster Larger Catechism's answer to the question of how faith justifies, which is helpfully summarized as follows: "Faith is not efficacious in itself nor for its accompanying graces, but only inasmuch as it is an instrument for the reception and application of Christ's person and righteousness."[50]

At the point of justification, faith stands alone. The letter of James, on the other hand, stresses that such faith is not an abstract notion, nor a merely intellectual one. It is a reorientation that necessarily finds expression in the concrete, everyday life of the believer. It does not exist in isolation but in the closest possible relation to all that the Spirit works in us. To consider faith distinct or separate from a transformed life is folly: "For as the body apart from the spirit is dead, so also faith apart from works is dead" (James 2:26). This is the sense in which James argues "that a person is justified by works and not by faith alone" (James 2:24, the only time the precise expression "faith alone" is found in the New Testament). The idea of a faith that does not manifest itself in a transformed life is a grotesque distortion of the New Testament teaching. So, far from contradicting each other, Paul and James complement one another when the question being explored at each point is identified. Paul is addressing the nature of justification; James is addressing the true nature of faith. Paul's concern that faith justifies apart from works of the law (his way of putting it in Rom. 3:28) is filled out by James's concern that the faith we are talking about is the genuine article and not some anemic counterfeit that has no visible impact on how we now live. Calvin, once again in his *Canons and Decrees of the Council of Trent with the Antidote*, brought these two perspectives together in a wonderfully memorable way: "It is therefore faith alone which justifies, and yet the faith which justifies is not alone: just as it is the heat alone of the sun which warms the earth, and yet in the sun it is not alone, because it is constantly conjoined with light."[51] Paul made the same point, with a remarkable conjunction in his letter to the Ephesians:

> For by grace you have been saved through faith. And this is not your own doing; it is the gift of God, *not a result of works*, so that no one may boast. For we are his workmanship, *created* in Christ Jesus *for good works*, which God prepared beforehand, that we should walk in them. (Eph. 2:8–10)

In both Paul and James, faith goes beyond knowledge and assent to include personal trust. It is a matter of the mind, the will, and the heart which cannot but be expressed in

---

49. Karl Barth, *Church Dogmatics*, vol. 1, bk. 1, *The Doctrine of the Word of God, Part 1*, ed. G. W. Bromiley and T. F. Torrance, trans. G. T. Thomson (1932; repr., Edinburgh: T&T Clark, 1975), 235. Zacharias Ursinus, in his commentary on the Heidelberg Catechism, insisted that "the *property*, or peculiar character of this faith, is trust and delight in God." *The Commentary of Dr. Zacharias Ursinus on the Heidelberg Catechism*, trans by G. W. Williard (repr., Phillipsburg, NJ: P&R, n.d.), 110.

50. R. Michael Allen, *Justification and the Gospel: Understanding the Contexts and Controversies* (Grand Rapids, MI: Baker Academic, 2013), 116.

51. Calvin, *Antidote*, 152.

words and action. Most significantly, as we have already noted, it takes its character and strength from its object rather than its subject. After all, faith in an unreliable promise or in one who is either unable or unwilling to effect what was promised, would be useless, no matter how much effort is exerted by the believer. The power of saving faith lies in the reliability, the power, and the benevolence of Christ and his promise. Thus Calvin's famous definition of faith: "Now we shall possess a right definition of faith if we call it a firm and certain knowledge of God's benevolence toward us, founded upon the truth of the freely given promise in Christ, both revealed to our minds and sealed upon our hearts through the Holy Spirit."[52]

Such faith is a gift. That much is clear from the words of Ephesians quoted above.[53] It is not a natural human capacity, nor is it the result of human effort. It is simply "not in the power of sinner and rebels to have this faith for themselves."[54] "It has been granted to you that for the sake of Christ you should not only believe in him but also suffer for his sake," Paul told the Philippians (Phil. 1:29). Augustine reflected on the Ephesians passage repeatedly. In his *On the Grace of Christ and on Original Sin*, he wrote,

> And yet further, lest it should be imagined that faith itself is to be attributed to men independently of the grace of God, the apostle says: "And that not of yourselves; for it is the gift of God." It follows, therefore, that we receive, without any merit of our own, that from which everything which, according to them, we obtain because of our merit, has its beginning—that is, faith itself.[55]

In his *On the Predestination of the Saints*, written about ten years later, Augustine quoted from Paul's prayer for his fellow Jews in Romans 10:1 and then continued,

> He prays for those who do not believe,—for what, except that they may believe? For in no other way do they obtain salvation.... When, therefore, the gospel is preached, some believe, some believe not; but they who believe at the voice of the preacher from without, hear of the Father from within, and learn; while they who do not believe, hear outwardly, but inwardly do not hear nor learn;—that is to say, to the former it is given to believe; to the latter it is not given.... Therefore, to be drawn to Christ by the Father, and to hear and learn of the Father in order to come to Christ, is nothing else than to receive from the Father the gift by which to believe in Christ.[56]

So the means by which we receive what is given to us in justification is itself a gift. That is why it cannot be spoken of as meritorious. The most profound and enduring metaphor of faith is that of an empty hand, which brings nothing but receives everything

---

52. Calvin, *Institutes*, 3.2.7, in Battles, 551.
53. Abraham Kuyper once observed that "nearly all the church fathers and almost all the theologians eminent for Greek scholarship judged that the words 'it is the gift of God' refer to faith." *The Work of the Holy Spirit*; trans. Henri De Vries (1888; repr., Grand Rapids, MI: Eerdmans, 1946), 407.
54. D. Broughton Knox, *Justification by Faith* (London: Church Book Room Press, 1959), 10, reprinted in *D. Broughton Knox: Selected Works*, vol. 3, *The Christian Life*, ed. Tony Payne and Karen Beilharz (Kingsford, NSW: Matthias Media, 2006), 73.
55. Augustine, *On the Grace of Christ and on Original Sin* (418), in NPNF1, 5:230.
56. Augustine, *On the Predestination of the Saints* (428/429), in NPNF1, 5:506.

from another. Toplady's lyric "Nothing in my hand I bring, simply to thy cross I cling" comes to mind.[57] The image of an empty, open hand reinforces the instrumental role of faith. Martin Chemnitz put it this way: "For faith is the means, or *organon* ('instrument'), through which we seek, apprehend, receive, and apply to ourselves from the Word of the Gospel the mercy of God, who remits sins and accepts us to life eternal for the sake of his Son, the Mediator."[58] Faith is the God-given way in which his provision for the justification of the sinner is received. This is not an arbitrary mechanism chosen by God despite its critical disproportion and natural unseemliness. It is not as if faith is the awkward stand-in for the perfect obedience we should but cannot provide. Rather, it is an entirely appropriate instrument since God's saving provision and the justification bound up with it are offered to us in the form of promises. As the Australian theologian Broughton Knox put it,

> The justification which the love of God has provided in Christ is offered to men in the form of promises to be taken hold of by faith. The Scriptures abound with many promises of forgiveness, mercy, acceptance, justification. God's provision is made known to us in these promises, and is made ours by God when we respond to the promises.

Such a response is itself the gift of God.[59]

"In Him Who Justifies the Ungodly"

One final critical element of the doctrine of justification only by faith is developed not in the paragraph from Romans 3 but in the next chapter of Paul's epistle, the chapter in which God is provocatively described as one "who justifies the ungodly" (4:5). That expression itself powerfully draws attention to the extrinsic character of the righteousness that is gifted to the believer in justification. God does not justify on account of Christ those who are already righteous people. Rather, he justifies the ungodly, those without a righteousness of their own who must rely entirely on a righteousness that is outside them, the righteousness of another. Paul wrote to the Philippians of his desire to gain Christ and be found in him, "not having a righteousness of my own that comes from the law, but that which comes through faith in Christ, the righteousness *from God* that depends on faith" (Phil. 3:8–9). It is something *given* to a person rather than something *found in* a person. Luther described it as an "alien righteousness, that is, the righteousness of another."[60] "Through faith in Christ," he wrote, "Christ's righteousness becomes our righteousness and all that he has becomes ours; rather, he himself becomes ours."[61]

---

57. August M. Toplady, "Rock of Ages" (1763), one of the grandest pieces of Reformed hymnody. See also Chemnitz, *Examination*, 577.
58. Chemnitz, *Examination*, 565.
59. Knox, *Justification*, 8, in Payne and Beilharz, *Selected Works*, 3:70.
60. Martin Luther, "Two Kinds of Righteousness" (1519), in *LW* 31:297.
61. Luther, "Two Kinds of Righteousness," in *LW* 31:298. See also Calvin: "For Scripture everywhere proclaims that God finds nothing in man to arouse him to do good to him but that he comes first to man in his free generosity." *Institutes*, 3.14.5, in Battles, 771.

But how does it become ours? Paul's consistent answer, like that of Luther, is not by God imparting this alien righteousness to us so that we cease to be sinners in need of grace and so that righteousness becomes now something we naturally possess. Rather, God "*counts* righteousness apart from works" (Rom. 4:6). It is a matter of counting, reckoning, or imputing. God makes a judicial declaration—the opposite of the condemnation we deserve—based on Christ and his work and received by faith. It is not an *imparting* of righteousness but an *imputing* of righteousness. God's act of justification is *forensic* in character rather than *factitive*. So as Luther famously taught, Christians, though rightly described as saints, are nevertheless sinners and righteous at one and the same time:

> The saints are always sinners in their own sight, and therefore always justified outwardly. But the hypocrites are always righteous in their own sight, and thus always sinners outwardly. I use the term "inwardly" to show how we are in ourselves, in our own eyes, in our own estimation; and the term "outwardly" to indicate how we are before God and in His reckoning. Therefore, we are righteous outwardly when we are righteous solely by the imputation of God and not of ourselves or of our own works. For his imputation is not ours by reason of anything in us or in our own power.[62]

Luther is more pointed just a few pages on in his *Lectures on Romans*:

> But the "righteousness" of Scripture depends upon the imputation of God more than on the essence of a thing itself. For he does not have righteousness who only has a quality, indeed, he is altogether a sinner and an unrighteous man; but he alone has righteousness whom God mercifully regards as righteous.[63]

This leads, wonderfully, to Luther's most famous passage on this subject, from his exposition of Romans 7:

> Now notice what I said above, that the saints at the same time as they are righteous are also sinners; righteous because they believe Christ, whose righteousness covers them and is imputed to them, but sinners because they do not fulfil the Law, are not without concupiscence, and are like sick men under the care of a physician; they are sick in fact but healthy in hope and in the fact that they are beginning to be healthy, that is, they are "being healed." They are people for whom the worst possible thing is the presumption that they are healthy, because they suffer a worse relapse.[64]

An important corollary of this teaching is that justification is a declaration, an act rather than a process. In Romans 5:1, Paul writes of how, having been "justified by faith, we have peace with God." He could remind the Corinthians that they "were justified" (1 Cor. 6:11). In this respect, justification is distinguished from the accompanying grace

---

62. Martin Luther, *Lectures on Romans* (1515–1516), in *LW* 25:257.
63. Luther, *Lectures on Romans*, in *LW* 25:274.
64. Luther, *Lectures on Romans*, in *LW* 25:336.

of sanctification (though sanctification has a definitive aspect as well, and that is what is picked up in the very same verse of 1 Corinthians 6). We are being sanctified, declares the writer to the Hebrews (Heb. 10:14); we are being transformed "from one degree of glory to another" (2 Cor. 3:18); and God's great purpose, the good he has for us, is that we are being "conformed to the image of his Son" (Rom. 8:29). The Christian life is one of growing in maturity in the fellowship of his people (Eph. 4:13). Luther recognized that "the gifts and the Spirit increase in us every day." Yet he insisted that God's "grace is not divided or parcelled out, as are the gifts, but takes us completely into favor for the sake of Christ our Intercessor and Mediator."[65] God does not justify us in pieces but as a whole. Our justification does not need to be augmented or perfected, since it is the eschatological verdict of God (Acts 17:31), brought into the present because its basis is already secure and because the instrument by which it is received is faith. This truth and anchor of Christian assurance is obscured when, as so often has happened, the distinction between justification and the other elements of our salvation is blurred, and justification becomes both act and process. One important remedy to that confusion is to acknowledge that justification, while a critical element in God's saving work, is not the entirety of God's saving work. Those who are justified are also adopted, cleansed, sanctified, and glorified.

The righteousness of Christ that is imputed to the believer is focused on the cross of Christ, the "propitiation by his blood" (Rom. 3:25). Yet the blood that was shed for us was not only the blood of the innocent one; it was the blood of the righteous one (Acts 7:52; 22:14). Christ was not only blameless in the sense of being "without sin" (Heb. 4:15; cf. 2 Cor. 5:21); he was just as importantly the one who was fully and entirely righteous. He kept his Father's commandments and remained in his love (John 15:10). He became "obedient to the point of death, even death on a cross" (Phil. 2:8). The propitiation came through his death but precisely because it was *his* death. As the person and the work of Christ cannot be separated, so what has been known through the centuries as Christ's active obedience (his perfect fulfillment of the law) is inseparable from his passive obedience (his perfect sacrifice of himself). He always did what was pleasing to the Father (John 8:29). His bearing of the sin of the world and laying down his life was the final act of that obedience, as he had prayed, "Not as I will, but as you will" (Matt. 26:39; cf. 26:42).

For this reason, the imputation of Christ's righteousness is centrally the forgiveness of sins but also the reckoning of righteousness.[66] We are brought not just back to ground zero, as if we had never sinned; rather, we are brought all the way to

---

65. Martin Luther, "Preface to the Epistle of Paul to the Romans" (1546), in *LW* 35:370.

66. The best contemporary treatment of the history of the doctrine of the imputation of Christ's righteousness is found in J. V. Fesko, *Death in Adam, Life in Christ: The Doctrine of Imputation*, REDS (Fearn, Ross-shire, Scotland: Mentor, 2016). The best exegetical defense is D. A. Carson, "The Vindication of Imputation: On Fields of Discourse and Semantic Fields," in *Justification: What's at Stake in the Current Debates*, ed. Mark A. Husbands and Daniel J. Treier (Downers Grove, IL: InterVarsity Press, 2004), 46–78. An intriguing recent study of the debates surrounding Johannes Piscator's objection to the use of Christ's active obedience in defining the righteousness that is imputed to the sinner is Heber Carlos de Campos, *Doctrine in Development: Johannes Piscator and Debates over Christ's Active Obedience*, RHTS (Grand Rapids, MI: Reformation Heritage Books, 2017).

righteousness, as if we had fulfilled all that God has asked of us. It is Calvin who best explains what this means:

> Justified by faith is he who, excluded from the righteousness of works, grasps the righteousness of Christ through faith, and clothed in it, appears in God's sight not as a sinner but as a righteous man. Therefore, we explain justification simply as the acceptance with which God receives us into his favor as righteous men. And we say that it consists in the remission of sins *and* the imputation of Christ's righteousness.[67]

For Calvin, these two elements, "the remission of sins" and "the imputation of Christ's righteousness," are each unimaginable without the other, just as the earthly obedience of Christ to the express will of his Father and his "laying down of his life for the sheep" are each unimaginable without the other. Yet they do not simply collapse into each other either. The Second Helvetic Confession, of which the chief author was Heinrich Bullinger, put it this way:

> Therefore, solely on account of Christ's suffering and resurrection God is propitious with respect to our sins and does not impute them to us, but imputes Christ's righteousness to us as our own, so that now we are not only cleansed and purged from sins or are holy, but also, granted the righteousness of Christ, and so absolved from sin, death and condemnation, are at last righteous and heirs of eternal life.[68]

The doctrine of justification only by faith must be traced back to its source in the person, character, and purpose of the triune God. It is first and foremost about what God has done, in perfect holiness, justice, and compassion, to deal with the forensic element of our predicament as sinners: we all must appear before the judgment seat of Christ (2 Cor. 5:10). It has its sharpest focus in the person of Christ and particularly in his blood shed as a propitiation for our sins, which grounds the imputation of Christ's righteousness and its reception by faith. God's act of justification takes place within the larger context of a full-orbed and complete salvation that addresses not only the forensic aspects of the human condition but every other aspect as well. More fully, God's redemptive work fits within the entirety of his work *ad extra*. Yet what matters most is that it is entirely, from beginning to end, a work of God, as Thomas Cranmer explained in the third of his homilies, *A Sermon of the Salvation of Mankind by Only Christ Our Saviour from Sin and Death Everlasting*:

> Justification is not the office of man, but of God. For man cannot make himself righteous by his own works, neither in part, nor in the whole; for that were the greatest arrogancy and presumption of man that Antichrist could set up against God, to affirm that a man might by his own works take away and purge his own sins, and so

---

67. Calvin, *Institutes*, 3.11.2, in Battles, 726–27; italics added.
68. Second Helvetic Confession (1566), 15.3, trans. and cited in Fesko, *Death in Adam*, 87.

justify himself. But justification is the office of God only; and is not a thing which we render unto him, but which we receive of him; not which we give to him, but which we take of him, by his free mercy, and by the only merits of his most dearly beloved Son, our only Redeemer, Saviour, and Justifier, Jesus Christ.[69]

Recommended Resources

Allen, R. Michael. *Justification and the Gospel: Understanding the Contexts and Controversies*. Grand Rapids, MI: Baker Academic, 2013.

Aquinas, Thomas. *Summa Theologiae* (1261–1263). 60 vols. in Blackfriars ed. London: Eyre and Spottiswoode, 1963.

Augustine. *On the Grace of Christ and on Original Sin* (418). In *Nicene and Post-Nicene Fathers of the Christian Church*, 1st ser., edited by Philip Schaff, 5:217–55. Grand Rapids, MI: Eerdmans, 1971.

———. *On the Predestination of the Saints* (428/429). In *Nicene and Post-Nicene Fathers of the Christian Church*, 1st ser., edited by Philip Schaff, 5:497–519. Grand Rapids, MI: Eerdmans, 1971.

Barth, Karl. *Church Dogmatics*. Vol. 4, bk. 1, *The Doctrine of Reconciliation* (1953). Edited by T. F. Torrance. Translated by G. W. Bromiley. Edinburgh: T&T Clark, 1956.

Biel, Gabriel. "The Circumcision of the Lord" (1460). In *Forerunners of the Reformation: The Shape of Late Medieval Thought Illustrated by Key Documents*, edited by Heiko A. Oberman, translated by Paul L. Nyhus, 165–74. London: Lutterworth, 1967.

Calvin, John. *Acts of the Council of Trent with the Antidote* (1547). In *Tracts and Letters*. Vol. 3, *Tracts, Part 3*, edited and translated by Henry Beveridge, 17–188. 1851. Reprint, Edinburgh: Banner of Truth, 2009.

———. *Institutes of the Christian Religion* (1559). Edited by John T. McNeill. Translated by Ford Lewis Battles. 2 vols. Library of Christian Classics 20–21. Philadelphia: Westminster, 1960.

Carson, D. A. "The Vindication of Imputation: On Fields of Discourse and Semantic Fields." In *Justification: What's at Stake in the Current Debates*, edited by Mark A. Husbands and Daniel J. Treier, 46–78. Downers Grove, IL: InterVarsity Press, 2004.

de Campos, Heber Carlos. *Doctrine in Development: Johannes Piscator and Debates over Christ's Active Obedience*. Reformed Historical-Theological Studies. Grand Rapids, MI: Reformation Heritage Books, 2017.

Fesko, J. V. *Death in Adam, Life in Christ: The Doctrine of Imputation*. Reformed, Exegetical and Doctrinal Studies. Fearn, Ross-shire, Scotland: Mentor, 2016.

Jüngel, Eberhard. *Justification: The Heart of the Christian Faith*. Translated by Jeffrey F. Cayzer. Edinburgh: T&T Clark, 2001.

Luther, Martin. *D. Martin Luthers Werke, Kritische Gesamtausgabe*. 73 vols. Weimar: Hermann Böhlaus Nachfolger, 1883–2009 (herein WA).

———. *Heidelberg Disputation* (1518). In *LW* 31:39–70.

———. *In XV Psalmos graduum* (1532). In *WA*, vol. 40, pt. 3, 9–475.

---

69. *Certain Sermons or Homilies Appointed to Be Read in Churches* (1673; repr., London: SPCK, 1864), 26.

———. *Lectures on Romans* (1515–16). In *LW* 25.

———. *Luther's Works*. Edited by Jaroslav Pelikan and Helmut T. Lehmann. American ed. 82 vols. (projected). Philadelphia: Fortress; Saint Louis, MO: Concordia, 1955– (herein *LW*).

———. *Operationes in Psalmos* (1519–1521). In WA 5.

———. "Preface to the Complete Edition of Luther's Latin Writings" (1545). In *LW* 34:327–38.

———. "Preface to the Epistle of Paul to the Romans" (1546). In *LW* 35:365–80.

———. "The Schmalkaldic Articles" (1537). In WA 50:192–254.

———. "Two Kinds of Righteousness" (1519). In *LW* 31:297–306.

Morris, Leon. *The Apostolic Preaching of the Cross*. 3rd ed. Grand Rapids, MI: Eerdmans, 1965.

Ovey, Michael J. "Justification by Faith Alone." In *Celebrating the Reformation: Its Legacy and Continuing Relevance*, edited by Mark D. Thompson, Colin Bale, and Edward Loane, 201–18. London: Apollos, 2017.

Owen, John. *A Dissertation on Divine Justice* (1653). In *The Works of John Owen*. Edited by William H. Goold. Vol. 10, *The Death of Christ*, 481–624. Reprint, London: Banner of Truth, 1967.

———. *The Doctrine of Justification by Faith, through the Imputation of the Righteousness of Christ, Explained, Confirmed, and Vindicated* (1677). In *The Works of John Owen*. Edited by William H. Goold. Vol. 5, *Faith and Its Evidences*, 1–400. Reprint. London: Banner of Truth, 1967.

Webster, John. "'It Was the Will of the Lord to Bruise Him': Soteriology and the Doctrine of God." In *God without Measure: Working Papers in Christian Theology*. Vol. 1, *God and the Works of God*, 143–57. London: Bloomsbury T&T Clark, 2016.

———. "*Rector et iudex super omnia genera doctrinarum*? The Place of the Doctrine of Justification." In *What Is Justification About? Reformed Contributions to an Ecumenical Theme*, edited by Michael Weinrich and John P. Burgess, 35–56. Grand Rapids, MI: Eerdmans, 2009.

14

The Passive *and* Active Obedience of Christ

Retrieving a Biblical Distinction

BRANDON CROWE

What is the ground, or basis, of justification? Stated succinctly, justification is based on the perfect obedience of Christ.[1] In that light, a key question worthy of our attention is, How do we define or delimit the obedience of Christ? On the one hand, Scripture often emphasizes the death of Christ in relation to justification (e.g., Rom. 4:25; 5:9–10). It is therefore not surprising that, as we will see, some have argued that we are saved by the death (and resurrection) of Christ *simpliciter*. Indeed, this is a common way of reading Paul's statement in Romans 5:18, that Jesus's (one) act[2] of righteousness leads to justification and life for all. If Romans 5:18 teaches that justification comes by one act, then it seems logical to conclude that the one act is Jesus's death (in conjunction

---

1. I write this essay from a Reformed perspective. The language I use echoes Westminster Confession of Faith 11.1, which states that God justifies "by imputing the obedience and satisfaction of Christ . . . receiving and resting on him and his righteousness, by faith." In Westminster Confession of Faith 11.2, the ground on which our justification rests is "Christ and his righteousness." Likewise, Westminster Larger Catechism 70 speaks of the "perfect obedience and full satisfaction of Christ," and Westminster Shorter Catechism 33 speaks concisely of the imputation of Christ's righteousness. For this essay I am using *The Westminster Confession of Faith and Catechisms as Adopted by the Presbyterian Church in America: With Proof Texts* (Lawrenceville, GA: Christian Education & Publications Committee of the Presbyterian Church in America, 2007). Cf. Francis Turretin, *Institutes of Elenctic Theology*, trans. George Musgrave Giger, ed. James T. Dennison Jr. (Phillipsburg, NJ: P&R, 1992–1997), 16.3; Herman Bavinck, *Reformed Dogmatics*, ed. John Bolt, trans. John Vriend, vol. 4, *Holy Spirit, Church, and New Creation* (Grand Rapids, MI: Baker Academic, 2008), 214; Charles Hodge, *Systematic Theology* (repr., Peabody, MA: Hendrickson, 2008), 3:147; Louis Berkhof, *Systematic Theology*, 4th ed. (Grand Rapids, MI: Eerdmans, 1941), 523; Richard B. Gaffin Jr., *By Faith, Not by Sight: Paul and the Order of Salvation* (Waynesboro, GA: Paternoster, 2006), 51.
2. As we see below, it is a matter of debate whether Rom. 5:18 speaks of *one act of righteousness* or the *righteous act of one man*.

with his resurrection). Such a reading seems to be consistent with other Pauline statements that speak of the centrality of the cross in relation to salvation (e.g., 1 Cor. 1:18; 2:2; Gal. 2:20; 6:14; Eph. 2:16; Phil. 2:8; cf. Rom. 1:16). For Paul, the cross of Christ is clearly central.

And yet historically, many have held that the obedience of Christ beyond the cross, inclusive of his whole life, is necessary for justification. Readers may already be familiar with the terms often used in this discussion: the passive obedience of Christ and the active obedience of Christ. It is imperative that we understand these terms properly. Some have argued that the passive obedience of Christ refers to Jesus's death, whereas his active obedience refers to his life.[3] However, such a view is insufficient both theologically and exegetically. Indeed, it seems likely that a misunderstanding of these terms has led to undue confusion not only about the obedience of Christ but also about justification and the related doctrine of imputation.

I argue that justification rests on the entire righteousness, or perhaps better, the entire *obedience*, of Jesus Christ—passive and active. We are not justified only on the foundation of the death of Christ, nor are we justified only on the basis of the passive obedience of Christ (which is not simply coterminous with his death). Certainly, the cross is central, and by no means should we belittle its importance. However, we must take care to guard the unity of and appreciate the totality of Christ's obedience for justification. I proceed in three parts. In the first part, I turn to a definition of terms, which may help clear up confusion. This also provides an opportunity to explain the context for the argument in the second and third parts, where I seek to demonstrate that the logical distinction between the passive and active obedience of Christ is biblical and necessary and that the entire obedience of Jesus provides the ground for justification.

Part 1: Definitions and History of Interpretation

Definition of Terms

Before we look more closely at the biblical texts themselves, it is prudent to begin with a definition of terms and a brief sketch of the ways that the passive and active aspects of the obedience of Christ have been understood historically, especially in relation to justification. In the realm of New Testament scholarship, the terms *passive obedience* and *active obedience* have not infrequently been met with either resistance or misunderstanding. It is therefore crucial to explain these terms correctly. Indeed, many aversions to these concepts may be assuaged by a right understanding of the terminology.

Simply put, *passive* obedience and *active* obedience refer to two aspects of Jesus's unified obedience to the law as Mediator. *Passive obedience* refers to the penal effects of sin that Jesus bore *throughout his life* as Mediator. *Active obedience* refers to Jesus's perfect, posi-

---

3. See, for example, Richard N. Longenecker, "The Obedience of Christ in the Theology of the Early Church," in *Reconciliation and Hope: New Testament Essays on Atonement and Eschatology Presented to L. L. Morris on His 60th Birthday*, ed. Robert Banks (Grand Rapids, MI: Eerdmans, 1974), 142–52. Though Longenecker upholds the unity of Christ's obedience in both its passive and active aspects, he nevertheless equates the passive obedience of Christ with Jesus's death and the active obedience with Jesus's life (e.g., 143–45, 148).

tive accomplishment of all that God's law requires of humanity.[4] Crucially, these are *logical* and not *temporal* distinctions. We cannot ascribe passive obedience to one stage or one act of Jesus's life, nor can we ascribe the active obedience to one stage or one act of Jesus's life. The two always coincide in the lifelong, integrated, vicarious obedience of Jesus.[5] Yet it is important to make a logical distinction between the two. They are distinct but inseparable.

Moreover, *passive obedience* does not mean *passivity*. Instead, the term *passive* derives from the Latin *patior*, meaning "to suffer."[6] Jesus's suffering was an *active* suffering.[7] Indeed, as John Murray notes, to say Jesus was entirely *passive* "would contradict the very notion of *obedience*."[8] Jesus's passive obedience therefore refers to obediently suffering the penalty due to sin accorded by the law throughout his life.

Similarly, the *active obedience* of Christ is also about Jesus's entire obedience, including his death. Thus, it would be a mistake to think of the death of Jesus as somehow *not* constituting his active obedience.[9] For indeed, it is in the death of Christ that we most starkly see the voluntary submission of the Son to his Father in the economy of redemption. Additionally, Jesus's role as the Lamb of God who takes away the sin of the world (e.g., John 1:29; 1 Cor. 5:7) necessitates his entire sinlessness. For Jesus to be a spotless sacrifice, he was required to do (positively) *all* that God requires.[10] What is more, in the New Testament we find that the moral law is much more demanding than many in Jesus's day thought (cf. Matt. 5:17–20; 7:12). For not only must we not steal, but we must also use our hands to work so that we might help those in need (Eph. 4:28). Not only must we not commit adultery, but we must also not even entertain a lustful thought (Matt. 5:28). The law requires that we positively love God and neighbor (Matt. 22:37–38 parr.; cf. Lev. 19:18; Deut. 6:5). Or as Matthew states twice in his Gospel, the Lord requires both mercy (or steadfast love [Heb. חֶסֶד]) and sacrifice (Matt. 9:13; 12:7; cf. Hos. 6:6). Simply put, were Jesus to have failed to complete all that God requires—by way of shorthand, fully loving God and neighbor—then he would not have been sinless and therefore would not have been qualified to serve as a perfect sacrifice. Justification rests on our Savior's entire, perfect obedience.

Two Benefits of Justification

The two aspects of Jesus's unified obedience—the passive and active aspects—are both necessary for justification. This logical distinction speaks to two benefits of justification

---

4. See, e.g., John Murray, *Redemption Accomplished and Applied* (Grand Rapids, MI: Eerdmans, 1955), 20–21; Geerhardus Vos, *Reformed Dogmatics*, trans. and ed. Richard B. Gaffin Jr., vol. 3, *Christology* (Bellingham, WA: Lexham, 2014), 112, 127–31; Vos, *Reformed Dogmatics*, vol. 4, *Soteriology* (2015), 154–55; Herman Bavinck, *Reformed Dogmatics*, vol. 3, *Sin and Salvation in Christ* (2006), 394–95; Turretin, *Institutes*, 14.13.
5. Bavinck, *Reformed Dogmatics*, 3:394–95; Vos, *Reformed Dogmatics*, 3:129; Robert Letham, *The Work of Christ*, CCT (Downers Grove, IL: InterVarsity Press, 1993), 130; Donald Macleod, *Christ Crucified: Understanding the Atonement* (Downers Grove, IL: IVP Academic, 2014), 180–81.
6. Note also the Greek πάσχω; cf. Letham, *Work of Christ*, 130.
7. Vos, *Reformed Dogmatics*, 3:128.
8. Murray, *Redemption Accomplished and Applied*, 20; italics original.
9. Cf. Bavinck, *Reformed Dogmatics*, 3:378.
10. According to rabbinic tradition, of the 613 commands in the Torah, 248 were positive commands. See b. Makkot 23b–24a.

as historically understood, namely, the forgiveness of sins and the right to eternal life.[11] On the one hand, the law requires punishment for sin. Sin cannot simply be swept aside and forgotten without recompense. Sin brings a penalty, leading to death, for every person born naturally since Adam. That penalty must be paid.[12] This aspect of Jesus's obedience is not that controversial for the many today who recognize the need for forgiveness of sins through the death of Christ. However, a right understanding of passive obedience also tells us that Jesus bore the wrath of God throughout the whole course of his lifelong obedience. This means that, as Geerhardus Vos has argued, the blood Jesus shed in his circumcision is no less atoning than the blood he shed at Calvary.[13] This lifelong suffering is memorably captured in the Heidelberg Catechism, question and answer 37:

> Q. What do you understand by the word: "suffered"?
>
> A. That all the time [Christ] lived on earth, but especially at the end of His life, He bore, in body and soul, the wrath of God against the sin of the whole human race; in order that by His passion, as the only atoning sacrifice, He might redeem our body and soul from everlasting damnation, and obtain for us the grace of God, righteousness and eternal life.[14]

Jesus's passive obedience thus speaks to the penalty he paid throughout his life, which corresponds to the forgiveness of our sins in justification.

Yet justification consists in more than the forgiveness of sins. For if we are "only" forgiven for our sins, we still have not realized the requirements for eternal life, as laid out in God's law. Attaining eternal life requires perfect obedience.[15] Here we must consider Adam, who was promised eternal life on condition of personal, entire, exact, and perpetual obedience.[16] Adam, as we know, failed to exhibit the obedience necessary to realize this prospect of glorious, everlasting life. However, we should not think that with Adam's failure, the requirement of perfect obedience for eternal life is somehow swept away, as if with a wave of the hand. Instead, perfect obedience continued to be the requirement for the inheritance of eternal life. To be clear, this obedience must be *perfect obedience* and not the obedience of believers in sanctification. As Herman Bavinck cogently argues,

> The works accomplished after justification by faith cannot be considered for justification . . . because those good works are still always imperfect and polluted by sin,

---

11. Turretin, *Institutes*, 16.4; Bavinck, *Reformed Dogmatics*, 3:394; Vos, *Reformed Dogmatics*, 4:152; Berkhof, *Systematic Theology*, 381; cf. Hodge, *Systematic Theology*, 3:161–62. Sometimes adoption is also considered here as a benefit of the active obedience of Christ. See Turretin, *Institutes*, 16.6; Berkhof, *Systematic Theology*, 515–16.
12. See Bavinck, *Reformed Dogmatics*, 3:226.
13. Vos, *Reformed Dogmatics*, 3:192.
14. Taken from *Heidelberg Catechism: German and English; Revised according to the Originals* (Green Bay, WI: Reliance, 1950), 96–97. "By his passion" [*mit seinem Leiden*] can also be translated "by his suffering," as it is in many English editions.
15. Cf. Norval Geldenhuys, *Commentary on the Gospel of Luke*, NICNT (Grand Rapids, MI: Eerdmans, 1951), 312.
16. Westminster Confession of Faith 19.1.

and not in keeping with the full requirement of the divine law (Matt. 22:37; Gal. 3:10; James 2:10). God, being faithful and true, cannot view as perfect that which is not perfect. As the righteous and holy One, God cannot give up the demands of the law nor content himself with a semirighteousness, which is basically no righteousness at all.[17]

For Bavinck, as with Reformed theology more broadly, eternal life requires perfect obedience to God's law.[18] As I argue later, appreciating the perfection of obedience required for eternal life is a foundational element to understanding the nature of justification in the New Testament, and that is helpful to keep in mind when interacting with advocates of other views. For in the Old Testament, it is only with Adam in his sinless, created estate that the possibility of eternal life on condition of perfect obedience is possible. Once sin enters the world, original sin affects all those born naturally after Adam. As we will see, this is because Adam is a covenant (or representative) head of humanity. Although the Mosaic law later comes to Israel in the Old Testament, this law is given within the context of the covenant of grace. The Israelites were never in a position to gain eternal life by their law keeping, since grace preceded the giving of the Mosaic law and since the Mosaic law was never intended as the means to secure eternal life. Only *perfect* obedience can meet the demands of eternal life; imperfect obedience simply cannot suffice.

Jesus's obedience can therefore be understood to have passive and active dimensions, which correspond to the two benefits of justification. Forgiveness of sins corresponds to Christ's passive obedience, and the securing of eternal life corresponds to Christ's active obedience.[19] And just as we must not artificially divide the passive and active obedience of Christ, so we must not divide the benefits of Christ's unified obedience, as if one could possess one without the other. It is not just "this" or "that" part of Jesus's obedience that provides the ground for justification; it is the *entire* obedience of Jesus that saves.[20] As Calvin succinctly states, "How has Christ abolished sin, banished the separation between us and God, and acquired righteousness to render God favorable and kindly toward us? . . . He has achieved this by the whole course of his obedience."[21]

When we ask how the obedience of Christ can be reckoned to us, the best answer is by means of *imputation*.[22] In brief, imputation means that in justification the obedience (or righteousness) of Christ—including both passive and active dimensions—is forensically,

---

17. Bavinck, *Reformed Dogmatics*, 4:209; cf. Macleod, *Christ Crucified*, 180–81.
18. E.g., Herman Bavinck, *Reformed Dogmatics*, vol. 2, *God and Creation* (2004), 564–65; 3:226; 4:223; Turretin, *Institutes*, 8.3; 16.2; Vos, *Reformed Dogmatics*, vol. 2, *Anthropology* (2013), 41; 4:170; Berkhof, *Systematic Theology*, 216; Heidelberg Catechism 62; Westminster Confession of Faith 19.
19. Turretin, *Institutes*, 14:13; 16.4; Bavinck, *Reformed Dogmatics*, 3:394; 4:223–24; Vos, *Reformed Dogmatics*, 4:152.
20. See Bavinck, *Reformed Dogmatics*, 4:263; Turretin, *Institutes*, 16.4; Berkhof, *Systematic Theology*, 379–81.
21. Calvin, *Institutes*, 2.16.5; translation from *Institutes of the Christian Religion*, ed. John T. McNeill, trans. Ford Lewis Battles, LCC 20 (Louisville: Westminster John Knox, 1960), 1:507.
22. Bavinck, *Reformed Dogmatics*, 4:223–26, 263, 635; Turretin, *Institutes*, 16.3–4; Berkhof, *Systematic Theology*, 523; Gaffin, *By Faith, Not by Sight*, 51–52; Herman Ridderbos, *Paul: An Outline of his Theology*, trans. John Richard de Witt (Grand Rapids, MI: Eerdmans, 1975), 174–78; Thomas Schreiner, *Faith Alone: The Doctrine of Justification; What the Reformers Taught . . . and Why It Still Matters*, Five Solas Series (Grand Rapids, MI: Zondervan, 2015), 179–90.

or legally, credited to believers by faith alone.[23] Key here is the recognition that the righteousness is the righteousness of another.[24] Put differently, the righteousness that is imputed is the entire obedience of Jesus.[25] This is necessary because Adam's sin, given his role as covenantal and representative head of humanity, has been imputed to all humanity.[26] However, as the last Adam born of a virgin, Jesus similarly stands at the head of a new humanity, and he is not affected by the guilt and corruption of sin. Thus, the remedy to the imputation of Adam's sin comes by means of the righteousness of the last Adam, whose obedience is imputed to all who believe in him. It is important to understand that Adam not only transgressed the command of God but also failed positively to exhibit perfect obedience to the stipulations of the covenant. Therefore, the work of the last Adam involves not only forgiving sin but also realizing the perfect obedience that the first Adam never achieved in order to secure eternal life.[27]

A Contested Concept

Readers, no doubt, will have noticed that to this point I have said relatively little about the biblical texts—which may be surprising given the subtitle of this chapter. The question ought to arise, Is the preceding construal consistent with the way that Paul and other New Testament authors speak? Earlier I noted the emphasis that Paul places on the cross. How, then, does the argument that justification rests on the passive and active obedience of Christ derive from the texts themselves?

Perhaps it is not surprising that many have disagreed with the notion that Christ's righteousness is imputed to believers. On the one hand, it is rather uncontroversial to say that Christ's death (including his resurrection) is imputed or somehow reckoned to believers. And yet discussions of the *active* obedience of Christ often meet with more reservations. It has been necessary to lay out what the terms mean and sketch the Reformed view before discussing the texts since a lack of clarity often characterizes sources that express reservations about the imputation of Christ's active obedience.[28] Often the critiques of the imputation of Jesus's obedience are of straw men and bear little resemblance to the careful, biblical expressions in the best of Reformed theology.[29] Now that the doctrines have been sketched, albeit briefly, we turn our attention to some key texts.

---

23. E.g., Bavinck, *Reformed Dogmatics*, 3:102; 4:212.
24. Imputed righteousness is often contrasted with *infused* righteousness, in which the believer's righteousness somehow becomes part of the ground for justification (see Turretin, *Institutes*, 16.2; Bavinck, *Reformed Dogmatics*, 4:209–12, 222–24; Berkhof, *Systematic Theology*, 523). Imputed righteousness means that an *alien* righteousness serves as the ground for justification; this righteousness is thus not the obedience of the believer.
25. Bavinck, *Reformed Dogmatics*, 4:224; Murray, *Redemption Accomplished and Applied*, 123–24.
26. See the important work of John Murray, *The Imputation of Adam's Sin* (Grand Rapids, MI: Eerdmans, 1959).
27. As I argue later, in his created state Adam was bound to the whole moral law; he was not bound only to one, isolated act. See Bavinck, *Reformed Dogmatics*, 2:574; Turretin, *Institutes*, 8.3–4; 9.4; Berkhof, *Systematic Theology*, 216–17.
28. See, e.g., Longenecker, "Obedience of Christ," 143–45, 148; Tom Wright, *Justification: God's Plan and Paul's Vision* (London: SPCK, 2009), 204–5; though see with perhaps more nuance Wright, *Letter to the Romans*, in vol. 10 of *The New Interpreter's Bible* (Nashville: Abingdon, 2002), 529.
29. For example, Douglas A. Campbell mistakenly argues that though the Calvinist tradition does underscore the representative obedience of Christ, any notion of active obedience plays little role in what he labels "Justification Theory." *The Deliverance of God: An Apocalyptic Rereading of Justification in Paul* (Grand Rapids, MI: Eerdmans, 2009), 211–12, 987n86. Instead, he claims that Jesus's perfect life is typically taken to safeguard Jesus from sin so that he can serve as sinless sacrifice (cf. 76). His puzzlement regarding the "active" nature of Christ's righteousness among those who hold to such

Part 2: The Passive and Active Obedience of Christ in the New Testament Epistles

We turn now to some of the most explicit texts that speak of the obedience of Christ in the Pauline and other New Testament Epistles. There can be no doubt that the cross is the climactic act of Jesus's obedience and is central for Paul's understanding of justification. And yet I suggest that a careful reading of Paul, not least in the way he relates the work of Christ to Adam, helps us see that the cross is not to be viewed as an isolated act of obedience but is an integral aspect of Jesus's entire obedience.

Romans 5: Adam, Christ, and Justification unto Life

The Argument of Romans 5

One of the most important passages for our present purposes is the Adam-Christ comparison that Paul makes in Romans 5:12–21. There is a great deal of theology packed into this passage, and we do well to parse it out carefully. In sum, we see in this passage that the sin of one man, Adam, led to death and condemnation for all (5:12, 18). In contrast, the obedience of one man (Jesus Christ) leads to justification and life for all (5:18). Through the disobedience of Adam, "the many were constituted [κατεστάθησαν] sinners"; through the obedience of Jesus Christ, "the many will be constituted [κατασταθήσονται] righteous" (5:19).[30] Paul's primary point in this text moves from 5:12 to 5:18, with 5:13–17 providing two clarifying points for the tricky statement made in 5:12 (especially ἐφ' ᾧ πάντες ἥμαρτον).[31] This means that, although 5:13–17 includes crucially important verses pertaining to salvation history, Paul is primarily concerned in 5:12–21 to explain parallels between Adam and Christ. Adam's one sin led to death for all people because, in some sense, "all sinned" (5:12).[32] Indeed, the passage starts with, and sustains, an emphasis on the tragedy of the sin of Adam that led to the reign of death over all. Paul makes this point, explicitly or implicitly, no less than eight times in these ten verses. Likewise, no less than six times Paul explicitly or implicitly relates righteousness or justification to life. For example, on the one hand, in 5:12, Paul states that sin entered the world through one man and death through sin. On the other hand, in the conclusion of this section, Paul proclaims that whereas sin reigned in death, grace reigns in

---

things is also curious—he maintains that theories of Jesus's imputed righteousness remain primarily about Jesus's sacrificial death (987n86; cf. 949n18). Elsewhere, he states that Justification Theory has no place for the resurrection of Jesus and that for Justification Theory, Jesus's death "accomplishes all things necessary for salvation, perhaps assisted by his perfect righteousness" (395). These statements do not hold up well to scrutiny, as the survey of classic Reformed theology above and the following discussion (including a discussion of the resurrection) should demonstrate.

30. Unless otherwise noted, Scripture quotations in this chapter are my own translations. The term καθίστημι can be difficult to translate. I have chosen "constitute," following Murray, *Imputation*, 64–95; cf. Murray, *The Epistle to the Romans: The English Text with Introduction, Exposition and Notes*, NICNT (Grand Rapids, MI: Eerdmans, 1959), 1:203–6; Ridderbos, *Paul*, 98. Many others opt for "made." See also Thomas R. Schreiner, *Romans*, BECNT (Grand Rapids, MI: Baker, 1998), 287–88; "καθίστημι/καθιστάνω," BDAG 493. On possible legal uses of this term, see F. W. Danker, "Under Contract: A Form-Critical Study of Linguistic Adaptation in Romans," in *Festschrift to Honor F. Wilbur Gingrich: Lexicographer, Scholar, Teacher, and Committed Christian Layman*, ed. Eugene Howard Barth and Ronald Edwin Cocroft (Leiden: Brill, 1972), 106–7.

31. See especially Murray, *Imputation*, 7; cf. C. E. B. Cranfield, *A Critical and Exegetical Commentary on the Epistle to the Romans* (Edinburgh: T&T Clark, 1975), 1:288–89.

32. In addition to Murray, *Imputation*, see S. Lewis Johnson, "Romans 5:12—An Exercise in Exegesis and Theology," in *New Dimensions in New Testament Study*, ed. Richard N. Longenecker and Merrill C. Tenney (Grand Rapids, MI: Zondervan, 1974), 298–316; cf. Turretin, *Institutes*, 9.9.

righteousness unto eternal life (εἰς ζωὴν αἰώνιον). Indeed, in 5:18, we should likely take the phrase δικαίωσιν ζωῆς to refer either to justification that consists in life or, perhaps better, to justification that results in life.³³

Of central importance in this passage are the actions of two representative men: Adam and Christ. Paul does not simply provide a fictional illustration. Instead, Paul explains the origin and universality of sin and death and the only means by which these can be overcome. Adam's sin brought the tragic reality of condemnation and death to all because he was acting in a representative capacity. Though it is debated whether the Adamic administration is best identified as a covenant, this is the best view. It makes sense not only of the representative role Adam occupies but also of the promise accorded to him on condition of perfect obedience.³⁴ The answer to Adam's sin is the obedience of a second representative man, Jesus Christ, which leads to righteousness and life. The key figures in world history concerning condemnation and justification are Adam, the progenitor of death, and Christ, the progenitor of life.

Romans 5 and the Integrated Obedience of Jesus

How, then, does Paul's overarching point relate to the present discussion of the passive and active obedience of Christ as it connects with justification? I mention here three points by way of overview, after which I interact in more detail with some possible objections.

First, the obedience of Christ in view in Romans 5:18–19 is most likely Jesus's *entire* obedience and is not limited only to the cross. Here our attention focuses on the terms Paul uses to describe the obedience of Christ in 5:18–19, which is contrasted with the disobedience of Adam. In 5:18, Adam's trespass (παραπτώματος) is set in parallel to the righteous act of Christ (δικαιώματος). This latter term is used in a slightly different way in 5:16, where it is often translated "justification." However, there is no need to drive a sharp wedge between the usage of δικαίωμα in 5:16 and its use for Christ's work in 5:18. For what is likely in view in 5:18 is Christ's obedience in meeting the requirements for our justification, which is perfect obedience. In 5:19, it is through the disobedience of one man (Adam) that the many were made sinners, which is set in parallel to the way the many will be made righteous—through the obedience of one man (Jesus Christ). However, in 5:18–19, the righteous act (5:18) and obedience of Christ (5:19)

---

33. See BDF §166 (noted in Cranfield, *Romans*, 1:289); Ridderbos, *Paul*, 181n64; cf. Murray, *Romans*, 1:202; Schreiner, *Romans*, 287; Douglas J. Moo, *The Epistle to the Romans*, NICNT (Grand Rapids, MI: Eerdmans, 1996), 341; Richard. B. Gaffin Jr., "The Work of Christ Applied," in *Christian Dogmatics: Reformed Theology for the Church Catholic*, ed. Michael Allen and Scott R. Swain (Grand Rapids, MI: Baker Academic, 2016), 275. Note that there is no verb in Rom. 5:18.

34. Though not explicitly stated, it has long been recognized that the prospect of life in the garden is seen in the tree of life and in the curse of death that stands in contrast to it. Cf. Turretin, *Institutes*, 8.3; Berkhof, *Systematic Theology*, 213, 216. Additionally, Hos. 6:7 likely refers to a covenant with Adam. For a recent defense of this view and for other texts that bespeak an Adamic covenant, see Brandon D. Crowe, *The Last Adam: A Theology of the Obedient Life of Jesus in the Gospels* (Grand Rapids, MI: Baker Academic, 2017), 56–61; see also G. K. Beale, *A New Testament Biblical Theology: The Unfolding of the Old Testament in the New* (Grand Rapids, MI: Baker Academic, 2011), 32–46; Thomas R. Schreiner, *Covenant and God's Purpose for the World*, SSBT (Wheaton, IL: Crossway, 2017), 19–29.

are singular nouns.³⁵ From this, many have concluded that the one act of righteousness and the one act of obedience of Christ in 5:18–19 refer to Jesus's obedience in death.³⁶ To be sure, the cross is central to Paul, and he even speaks a few verses earlier of being saved by Jesus's death (5:10). Yet Paul not only speaks of reconciliation by the death of Christ in 5:10—which is consistent with the way Paul often speaks of reconciliation³⁷—but he also speaks in 5:10 of being saved by Jesus's (resurrection) life. Similarly, in 4:25, Paul speaks of Jesus being handed over for our trespasses (παραπτώματα) and raised for our justification. Again, the death *and* resurrection of Christ are in view. This is significant because the resurrection of Christ is the de facto vindication of Jesus's complete obedience³⁸ and therefore assumes his perfect obedience throughout his life.³⁹ It is therefore best not to try to divide the obedience or righteous acts of Christ into parts.⁴⁰ Instead, the singular righteous act (5:18) more likely refers to the *entire* obedience of Jesus (cf. 5:19), which culminates in his death. Put another way, even if Paul does have Jesus's death primarily in view, his overall argument necessitates that Jesus's death incorporates, sums up, and completes the obedience of Jesus's entire substitutionary life.⁴¹ Likewise, the resurrection of Christ that Paul often invokes is the vindication of Christ's entire, lifelong obedience—it is not *only* the vindication of his death.

Second, in light of the preceding discussion, perfect obedience is necessary to inherit eternal life. Therefore, justification must somehow meet this demand. When we read about the obedience of Jesus that brings justification and secures eternal life (5:18–19, 21), we therefore must correlate this to the realization, in light of the entire teaching of Scripture, that justification and the right to eternal life can be a reality only where the covenantal requirements of perfect obedience have been met.⁴² Adam was presented with the prospect of the curse of death if he chose the path of disobedience (Gen. 2:17; cf. Rom. 6:23), but the other side of this administration was the prospect of eschatological life that was held out to Adam if he obeyed.⁴³ This reality is underscored in 5:12–21 by the link between sin, condemnation, and death that came through Adam on the one hand, and righteousness, justification, and (eternal) life that come through Christ on the other hand. As argued above, sin involves any transgression of the law of

---

35. This is true whether one takes ἑνός in Rom. 5:18 adjectivally as a neuter ("one trespass . . . one act of righteousness") or substantivally as a masculine ("the trespass of one man . . . the righteous act of one man"). Even if the substantival masculine reading of ἑνός is preferred, a singular act is mentioned. I discuss this in more detail in the next section ("Possible Objections"). There I argue that it is slightly more likely that Paul has in view here ἑνός substantivally as a masculine, referring to "one man" in each case.
36. See, e.g., James D. G. Dunn, *Romans 1–8*, WBC 38A (Nashville: Thomas Nelson, 1988), 284; Schreiner, *Romans*, 287; Moo, *Romans*, 344; Colin G. Kruse, *Paul's Letter to the Romans*, PNTC (Grand Rapids, MI: Eerdmans, 2012), 251–52.
37. So Murray, *Romans*, 1:174.
38. See Geerhardus Vos, *The Pauline Eschatology* (Grand Rapids, MI: Eerdmans, 1961), 151, noted by Richard B. Gaffin Jr., *The Centrality of the Resurrection: A Study in Paul's Soteriology*, BBM (Grand Rapids, MI: Baker, 1978), 122. The resurrection is also the de jure vindication of Jesus's complete obedience.
39. See Acts 2:24–28; Bavinck, *Reformed Dogmatics*, 3:430–42; Vos, *Reformed Dogmatics*, 3:220–23; Gaffin, "Work of Christ Applied," 275; Beale, *New Testament Biblical Theology*, 472, 496.
40. See Bavinck, *Reformed Dogmatics*, 3:378; cf. Calvin, *Institutes*, 2.16.5.
41. Though not a precise quote, this is the language of Bavinck, *Reformed Dogmatics*, 3:378.
42. See John Calvin, *Commentaries on the Epistle of Paul the Apostle to the Romans*, trans. and ed. John Owen (1849; repr., Grand Rapids, MI: Baker, 2003), 212–13.
43. See, e.g., Turretin, *Institutes*, 8.5–6; Bavinck, *Reformed Dogmatics*, 2:564–65.

God, whether by deeds of commission or omission (cf. James 2:10).[44] And as Paul states earlier in Romans, not only have all sinned (3:12–18, 23), but there is no one who is righteous, does good, or seeks God (3:10–12). Later, Paul states that the wages of sin is death (6:23), but he also draws attention to the positive side—the principle that life comes by keeping the commands—when he quotes Leviticus 18:5 ("He who does them [i.e., the commandments] shall live by them") in Romans 10:5.[45] Justification must account for both aspects of sinfulness (i.e., sins of commission and omission). Therefore, the obedience of Christ that provides the answer to the sin, condemnation, and death of Adam is a full-orbed justification that rests on the perfect, unified obedience of Jesus.[46] Anything less than perfect obedience would not lead to justification and eternal life.

Given the present focus on the unity of Jesus's obedience in Romans 5, it is also significant that Adam was not merely tasked with one, arbitrary command in the garden. Instead, Adam's probationary test (i.e., not to eat of the tree of the knowledge of good and evil) was a summary command that encapsulated Adam's duty to the entire moral law of God.[47] In other words, the problem is not simply that Adam sinned by an isolated act but that Adam failed to love and obey God fully, as the law required already in his state of innocence. Ever since Adam sinned, no one born naturally after him can ever meet the requirements of perfection required by the law, since all are constituted sinners in Adam (5:12, 19). Therefore, only Jesus, the last Adam, who was not born by ordinary generation and not represented by Adam, is able to meet the demands of eternal life.[48]

Third, as noted above, Jesus is the representative last Adam whose obedience leads to a better result than Adam's trespass. The gift of justification that is based on the perfect obedience of Christ is possible because all humanity stands in relation to either Adam or Christ—just as Adam is the representative for all humanity leading to death, all those who would be saved must identify with Christ as their obedient representative. Adam's trespass led to death; Christ's obedience leads to justification. Again, it is important to underscore that the obedience of Christ must meet the divinely ordained requirement for eternal life, which is perfect obedience. This is one way that the gift is better than the trespass (5:15–16). For by only one transgression eternal life is forfeited (6:23; cf. James 2:10), whereas eternal life is not gained simply by doing one righteous deed.[49] To be viewed as righteous, we must meet the demands of the law entirely and perfectly. The

---

44. See also Turretin, *Institutes*, 9.13.3.
45. Thus, I believe Paul invokes Lev. 18:5 in Rom. 10:5 and Gal. 3:12 to invoke the principle that life comes in conjunction with God's covenantal requirement of perfect obedience. This is true even though Leviticus 18 is found in the context of the Mosaic law, which was given to a redeemed people and was part of the covenant of grace. I say more about Lev. 18:5 in my discussion of Galatians 3 in chap. 7, my other essay in this volume. See also Turretin, *Institutes*, 8.3, 6; Bavinck, *Reformed Dogmatics*, 2:565; 3:174, 183–84, 226; 4:601; John Murray, *The Epistle to the Romans: The English Text with Introduction, Exposition and Notes*, NICNT (Grand Rapids, MI: Eerdmans, 1965), 2:249–51; Ridderbos, *Paul*, 156; Crowe, *Last Adam*, 178–82.
46. So Bavinck, *Reformed Dogmatics*, 4:263.
47. See, e.g., Turretin, *Institutes*, 8.3; 9.6.1; 9.8.7; Bavinck, *Reformed Dogmatics*, 2:574; Vos, *Reformed Dogmatics*, 2:48–49; Berkhof, *Systematic Theology*, 216–17.
48. Though Paul does not explicitly mention the virginal conception of Jesus in his letters, he may allude to it in Gal. 4:4–5, and his logic in Rom. 5:12–21 necessitates that the birth of Jesus was not according to ordinary generation. Cf. J. Gresham Machen, *The Virgin Birth of Christ* (Grand Rapids, MI: Baker, 1930), 259–63.
49. Turretin, *Institutes*, 1.4.

logic of imputation is built on this two-Adam structure: just as Adam's sin is imputed or reckoned legally to all humanity, so can the obedience of Christ be reckoned to all who are united to Christ by faith.[50] As Thomas Goodwin memorably states, "[Paul] speaks of [Adam and Christ] as if there had never been any more men in the world . . . because these two between them had all the rest of the sons of men hanging at their girdle."[51]

Possible Objections

Thus far, I have argued that Romans teaches not just that Christ's death leads to justification and life but that justification depends on Jesus's entire, integrated obedience. However, a number of objections could be raised at this point. I mention three here.

Objection 1: Christ's death is the one act of obedience. First, if the parallel between Adam and Christ were to be made most starkly, perhaps Paul has focused on *one* act of each man: Adam's eating the forbidden fruit and Christ's death on the cross.[52] Indeed, in early Christian tradition, the sin of Adam in relation to the tree is sometimes contrasted with Christ's obedience on a tree. As Irenaeus explained in the second century, "So, by means of the obedience by which He obeyed unto death, hanging upon the tree, He undid the old disobedience occasioned by the tree."[53] Such an understanding would seem to fit with Paul's proclivity to emphasize the cross and with the singular significance of Adam's sin. This would be particularly fitting if Paul speaks of "one trespass" (ἑνὸς παραπτώματος) and "one act of obedience" (ἑνὸς δικαιώματος) in Romans 5:18.

Several points, however, can be offered in response. To begin, it is not entirely clear that "one" (ἑνός) should be taken adjectivally as neuter to modify παραπτώματος and δικαιώματος, respectively. Instead, it is probably better to take ἑνός substantivally as masculine, with ἑνός referring to one *man* in each case.[54] Further, even if Paul does have the death of Christ largely in view in 5:18–19 (and it is quite possible that he does), it still remains that his logic necessitates that more than *only* the death of Christ must be in view.[55] In this light, even if we take ἑνός adjectivally for one trespass and one act of righteousness in 5:18, this one act of righteousness could be construed as the *entire* obedience (singular!) of Jesus.[56] Speaking summarily of *one* act of righteousness befits Christ's unified obedience. Additionally, Paul speaks in 5:18 of righteousness unto life, and I have argued that the righteousness that leads to life cannot be attained by one isolated act of obedience. Instead, eternal life requires the fullness of perfect obedience.

---

50. See, e.g., Murray, *Imputation*.
51. Thomas Goodwin, *Christ Set Forth*, in vol. 4 of *The Works of Thomas Goodwin* (Edinburgh: James Nichol, 1862), 31; cf. F. F. Bruce, *The Epistle of Paul to the Romans: An Introduction and Commentary*, 2nd ed., TNTC (Grand Rapids, MI: Eerdmans, 1985), 120. See also Bavinck, *Reformed Dogmatics*, 2:565, 578–79; 3:83–85, 103–6, 225–28, 378–79; Vos, *Reformed Dogmatics*, 2:31–36.
52. For example, John H. Walton speaks of the punctiliar act of fall and the punctiliar act of redemption. *The Lost World of Adam and Eve: Genesis 2–3 and the Human Origins Debate* (Downers Grove, IL: IVP Academic, 2015), 103.
53. Irenaeus, *On the Apostolic Preaching*, trans. John Behr, PPS (Crestwood, NY: Saint Vladimir's Seminary Press, 1997), 62. See also Irenaeus, *Against Heresies* 5.16.3.
54. So, e.g., Schreiner, *Romans*, 286n8; Moo, *Romans*, 341n125; Cranfield, *Romans*, 1:289. On this reading the double usage of ἑνός in 5:19 (where it clearly refers first to Adam and then to Christ) clarifies the use of ἑνός in 5:18.
55. See the helpful comments in Letham, *Work of Christ*, 131–32; cf. Turretin, *Institutes*, 9.9.39.
56. So Murray, *Romans*, 201, 205.

Christ's obedience is better than Adam's disobedience because it was not simply one isolated act of obedience but was a lifelong obedience that overcame the curse of sin and therefore leads to life everlasting. Thus, even *if* Paul speaks of *one act* of righteousness, the righteous act of Christ and his obedience in 5:18–19 refer to Jesus's obedience as a "compact unity."[57] Indeed, although Irenaeus does compare Jesus's obedience on the tree to Adam's disobedience centering on a tree, Irenaeus has a much more comprehensive schema (i.e., *recapitulation*) in which Jesus's *lifelong* obedience is necessary to overcome the sin of Adam.[58] So it is with Romans 5:18–19: inasmuch as the death of Christ may be in view, this act of obedience cannot be separated from Jesus's unified, lifelong obedience.

One final word is necessary in relation to this first objection: even if one were to limit the obedience of Christ in Romans 5 to his death, this would not be the same as saying that Romans 5 has only the *passive* obedience of Christ in view. For, as I argued above, the passive obedience of Christ describes his lifelong obedience. Likewise, the active obedience of Christ extends throughout his life (and culminates in his death). Thus, even if the focus in Romans 5 is on Christ's death, it would therefore necessarily still be on *both* the passive obedience and the active obedience of Christ; these are logical (rather than temporal) distinctions of a unified obedience. Put starkly, the death of Christ on the cross is integral to his active obedience (cf., e.g., Matt. 26:39; Mark 14:36; Luke 22:42; John 4:34). As it pertains to justification, I have argued that we can correlate forgiveness of sins (and certainly the problem of sin is in view in Rom. 5:12–21, and also in 5:8–11) to the passive obedience of Christ, and the right to eternal life (which is explicitly emphasized in 5:17–21) flows from the active obedience of Christ. Inasmuch as both forgiveness of sins and the right to eternal life are in view in a passage that explicates the obedience of Jesus as a representative figure, we are on firm ground to conclude that the dual aspects of Christ's obedience must be in view in Romans 5:12–21.

Objection 2: Perfect obedience is unnecessary. Second, some object (particularly in relation to Pauline theology) that the law does not require perfect obedience for salvation.[59] Such objections typically assume the question whether the *Mosaic law*, as a covenant administration, requires perfection. But to address the level of obedience required by the law, we must begin with an awareness of the manifold ways that the term "law" (Gk. νόμος) is used in Scripture, not least in Paul.[60] On this point, we must define our

---

57. Murray, *Romans*, 201.
58. See, e.g., Irenaeus, *Against Heresies* 3.18.1, 6–7; 3.21.10; 3.23.1; 4.4.2; 4.8.2; 5.1.2; 5.21.1.
59. See variously Michael Cranford, "The Possibility of Perfect Obedience: Paul and an Implied Premise in Galatians 3:10 and 5:3," *NovT* 36, no. 3 (1994): 242–58; Norman H. Young, "Who's Cursed—and Why? (Galatians 3:10–14)," *JBL* 117, no. 1 (1998): 83; James D. G. Dunn, *The Theology of Paul the Apostle* (London: T&T Clark, 1998), 361 (§14.5); James M. Scott, "'For as Many as Are of Works of the Law Are under a Curse' (Galatians 3:10)," in *Paul and the Scriptures of Israel*, ed. Craig A. Evans and James A. Sanders, JSNTSup 83 (Sheffield: Sheffield Academic Press, 1993), 195–96. See also the arguments of Wright, *Justification*, 204–5; Wright, *The Climax of the Covenant: Christ and the Law in Pauline Theology* (Minneapolis: Fortress, 1992), 145–46; Wright in Walton, *Lost World*, 172. However, Schreiner concludes that Wright does view perfect obedience to be necessary for a right standing before God (cf. Wright, *Justification*, 97), yet Schreiner doubts that Wright emphasizes this point sufficiently. Schreiner, *Faith Alone*, 242.
60. This point is commonly recognized. For example, Turretin argues that "law" in Scripture can refer to the whole Word of God, to the entire Old Testament, to the Mosaic books alone, to the Mosaic dispensation, to the covenant of

terms clearly. Often in Pauline discussions, it is taken for granted that "law" refers to the Mosaic law. Of course, this is indeed often the case. Yet Paul also uses νόμος to refer to the moral law of God in a way that transcends the Mosaic administration of the law. This is arguably the case in Galatians 3:10–14. In 3:10, Paul says (citing Deut. 27:26), "Cursed is everyone who does not abide in all the things written in the book of the law, to do them." In this case, Paul's quotation clearly comes from the end of Deuteronomy and the so-called Shechemite Dodecalogue. It is not surprising, therefore, that many conclude that Paul speaks in Galatians 3:10–14 simply of the Mosaic law.[61]

Yet Paul's logic discourages a facile conclusion on the matter, since he goes on to quote another part of the Mosaic law (Lev. 18:5) in Galatians 3:12 in a way that has long proved curious to interpreters: "The one who does them [i.e., the commandments] will live by them" (cf. Rom. 10:5), apparently in contrast to living by faith (cf. Hab. 2:4). As I argue in chapter 7 of this volume, it is best to understand Paul contrasting two ways of living in this passage: one way by faith in Christ and another by adhering to the Mosaic law. Paul warns that if one adheres to the Mosaic law as the ultimate standard in light of the coming of Christ, then Christ is of no value (cf. Gal. 5:2). Such people would be turning their backs on God's appointed means of justification (which is faith; see 3:11) and instead would be resigned to live by the principle of life-by-works that is attested to in the Mosaic law.

Thus, on the one hand, the Mosaic law in its redemptive-historical administration did not require perfect obedience for covenant members to walk in faithfulness before the Lord. Indeed, it was not possible for them to be perfectly obedient since they were born naturally after Adam. On the other hand, when Paul looked at the Mosaic law, he found a built-in principle that accords with the reality that fullness of life necessarily goes hand in hand with perfect and entire obedience. On that basis, the Mosaic law as a covenant administration (i.e., as part of the covenant of grace) did not require nor expect perfect obedience of a redeemed people for them to live as faithful covenant members. At the same time, the moral law of God more fundamentally does require perfect obedience for inheritance of salvation (and thus for justification), and this is attested to in the Mosaic covenant.[62] Faithful Israelites under the Mosaic economy were to walk by faith and obedience, though their obedience was always imperfect. Yet perfect obedience was ultimately required for them to inherit eternal life. Therefore,

---

works, or to the rule of things to be done and avoided. *Institutes*, 11.1.3. See also Thomas R. Schreiner, *The Law and Its Fulfillment: A Pauline Theology of Law* (Grand Rapids, MI: Baker, 1993), 34–36; Douglas J. Moo, "'Law,' 'Works of the Law,' and Legalism in Paul," *WTJ* 45, no. 1 (1983): 73–100. For an alternative view on νόμος in Paul, see N. T. Wright, *Paul and the Faithfulness of God*, COQG 4 (Minneapolis: Fortress, 2013), 1034n736; Wright, *Paul and His Recent Interpreters: Some Contemporary Debates* (Minneapolis: Fortress, 2015), 94–95.

61. Galatians 3:10–14 is a particularly thorny passage, entailing any number of debated issues. I am not able to engage them here, but I discuss this passage more fully in chap. 7 in this volume.

62. See Bavinck, *Reformed Dogmatics*, 3:226; cf. Ridderbos, *Paul*, 135–36. The Mosaic law has often been understood as having moral, ceremonial, and civic distinctions. See, e.g., Westminster Confession of Faith 19.3; Beale, *New Testament Biblical Theology*, 872–73. While a sharp line cannot always be drawn between these distinctions, in general they are helpful. Indeed, already in the Old Testament, a distinction is understood between ritual and true obedience. Thus the prophets often lament the hollow offering of sacrifices from offerers whose hearts are far from God (e.g., 1 Sam. 15:22; Ps. 40:6–8; Isa. 1:11; Jer. 4:4, 14; 7:1–34; Hos. 6:6). In contrast, when Jesus comes, we find the unity of mercy and sacrifice—the offerer is himself the perfectly sanctified one (cf. Heb. 10:5–7).

their justification must be based on the perfect obedience of Jesus, just as is the case for believers living after the coming of Christ.[63]

This is why it is so important to consider Romans 5 carefully and (following Paul's lead) to include Adam in conversations pertaining to justification. If eternal life is contingent on perfect obedience, according to God's covenantal requirements, then two men should dominate the conversation: Adam in the first place and Jesus (the last Adam) in the second. For many who deny that the law requires perfection, the discussion focuses on the Mosaic law, and the discussion starts with Abraham or Israel. However, to start with either Israel or Abraham is to miss the necessary protological foundation given in Genesis 1–3, which lays the groundwork for Paul's soteriology. When we start with Adam—as Paul does in Romans 5—it becomes clearer that the Mosaic law is not the first law in Scripture, and we can see with greater clarity why so many in the history of interpretation have maintained that perfect obedience is necessary for eternal life. If, to paraphrase Thomas Goodwin, all other men are hanging from the belt of Adam and Christ, this must include Abraham, Moses, and all Israelites.

Given the popularity of N. T. Wright's writings, not least his commentary on Romans in the *New Interpreter's Bible*, a brief interaction specifically with his reading of Romans 5 is warranted. Wright is by all accounts an engaging exegete who manifests a keen interest in biblical theology. I have often been informed, stimulated, and challenged by his writings, and he is often on the right side of debates in the world of New Testament scholarship.[64] However, when it comes specifically to the matter of justification, I remain unconvinced that his proposed recalibration is superior to the traditional Reformed understanding. Nor am I persuaded by all that he says on Romans 5. For Wright, the obedience that Paul has in view in Romans 5 is not the passive or active obedience of Christ but rather the obedience of Christ to the work of the Isaianic servant—that is, obedience to the "saving purpose of YHWH, the plan marked out for Israel from the beginning but that, through Israel's disobedience, only the servant, as an individual, can now accomplish."[65] For Wright, God has been true to the covenant with Abraham through the death of the Messiah, which deals with the sin of Adam and its consequences.[66] However, though the obedience to the Isaianic servant's task

---

63. See Westminster Confession of Faith 11.
64. For example, Wright's understanding of Jesus as the suffering servant (*Jesus and the Victory of God*, COQG 2 [Minneapolis: Fortress, 1996], 588–91); his affirmation of penal substitution (*Paul and His Recent Interpreters*, 210; *Justification*, ix, 178, et al.); his Trinitarian focus in Paul (*Justification*, 85, 115, 164); the importance of the bodily resurrection of Jesus (*The Resurrection of the Son of God*, COQG 3 [Minneapolis: Fortress, 2003]); the abiding normativity of Paul's sexual ethics consistent with God's created order (*Paul and the Faithfulness of God*, 1117–18, 1448, 1508; *Paul and His Recent Interpreters*, 93, 299–301); the importance of Daniel 7 as background to Jesus's Son of Man sayings (*The New Testament and the People of God*, COQG 1 [Minneapolis: Fortress, 1992], 291–97). See also his approbation for the work of Richard Gaffin and John Murray ("two of the most venerable Reformed thinkers") along with his rather positive assessment of Herman Ridderbos in *Paul and His Recent Interpreters*, 119 and 60–62, 60n113, respectively.
65. Wright, *Romans*, 529. See also Wright, *Justification*, 201.
66. Wright in Walton, *Lost World*, 172–73; cf. Wright, *Paul and the Faithfulness of God*, 787. Curiously, Wright states that Paul is primarily focused not on traditional soteriology but on the kingdom of God. In Walton, *Lost World*, 173. I am not entirely sure what "traditional soteriology" means for Wright (perhaps he means the atonement specifically; see Wright, *Paul and the Faithfulness of God*, 886), but soteriology is most certainly in view (to be fair, Wright does clarify elsewhere that Romans 5 is speaking about salvation; see Wright, *Paul and the Faithfulness of God*, 888). Additionally, it is unnecessary to separate soteriology from the kingdom of God, which is granted as a benefit of justification (e.g., the right to eternal life).

is understandable in broad strokes in Wright's construal, it remains nebulous how the Messiah's obedience would secure the eternal life that Paul has in view in Romans 5. Admittedly, Wright does relate this servant-shaped obedience to the role of the Torah given to Israel to be the means of overcoming the sin of Adam.[67] However, such a calling for Israel, epitomized in the servant, to be the means of accomplishing salvation is clear neither in the Old Testament nor in Paul.[68] In light of Paul's argument in Romans 5, Israel was never able to save anyone, nor was it called to. For the justification of eternal life to be realized, *perfect* obedience was necessary. As I have argued, God's saving answer therefore had to come by means of one who could keep the law perfectly, since this was the covenantal stipulation for eternal life. There should be no objection to identifying the saving, obedient work of Christ as the obedience of the Isaianic servant, even obedience of the servant unto death. But for this obedience to be a saving obedience resulting in eternal life, it must be *perfect* obedience to the law of God.[69]

Additionally, I can agree with Wright that the Mosaic law was not given as a ladder of good works that one would climb to earn righteousness, salvation, eternal life, and the like.[70] Though perhaps there are some who hold to such a view, it is not the view of classic Reformed theology. Reformed theologians consistently reject the notion that a person can "climb" a ladder of good works.[71] Indeed, the Mosaic law is best understood as part of the covenant of grace.[72] The Reformed doctrine of the covenant of works does not mean in any way that Adam could autonomously earn eternal life, as if man's obedience would put God in thrall to humanity. Indeed, even perfect obedience from created beings could never merit eternal life; even if we were to keep the law perfectly, we would still be only unworthy servants (cf. Luke 17:10).[73] What is more, the entire framework for man's interaction with God depends on God's covenantal condescension, without which there could be no fellowship between God and man.[74] God's covenant with Adam did entail the promise to bestow the gift of eschatological life to Adam on the condition of personal, entire, exact,

---

67. See also Wright, *Romans*, 530; Wright, *Paul and the Faithfulness of God*, 889–90.
68. However, the Israelites were intended to serve a missional role to those around them; cf. Christopher J. H. Wright, *Deuteronomy*, NIBC 5 (Peabody, MA: Hendrickson, 1996), 11–13.
69. Compare Wright, *Romans*, 529.
70. See, e.g., Wright, *Justification*, 204–5.
71. Wright himself seems to acknowledge this in *Paul and His Recent Interpreters*, 73 (cf. the positive assessments of the Mosaic law among Reformed theologians in Wright, *Justification*, 53; Wright, *Paul and His Recent Interpreters*, 29, where he also appreciates Calvin's doctrine of union with Christ). I am unsure which Reformed theologians Wright has in mind in his critique of legalism in *Justification*, where he views Reformed theology as having "lost its nerve" when it views Jesus as "the ultimate legalist" (see *Justification*, 205; cf. 134, 204), but elsewhere he expresses dissatisfaction with the tendency of Reformed theology (including the Westminster Confession of Faith) to detach its understanding of law from the Torah of Moses (see Wright, *Paul and His Recent Interpreters*, 95; cf. 116). I have argued above that νόμος in Paul does not always refer to the Mosaic law; Wright would likely disagree (Wright, *Paul and the Faithfulness of God*, 1034n736; Wright, *Paul and His Recent Interpreters*, 94–95). To give a sufficient account of justification, one must address the law of God given already to Adam and the necessity of perfect obedience—thus considering more than only the Mosaic administration of the law. This is what makes Romans 5 and the two-Adam structure of Paul's thought so important.
72. See Westminster Confession of Faith 7.3–5; 11.1; 19.6.
73. See Bavinck, *Reformed Dogmatics*, 2:570.
74. Bavinck, *Reformed Dogmatics*, 2:569–70. Westminster Confession of Faith 7.1 puts it concisely: "The distance between God and the creature is so great, that although reasonable creatures do owe obedience unto him as their Creator, yet they could never have any fruition of him as their blessedness and reward, but by some voluntary condescension on God's part, which he hath been pleased to express by way of covenant."

and perpetual obedience (cf. Gen. 2:17; 3:22), yet even this promise was in no way proportional to Adam's works.[75] Put differently, God is not intrinsically obligated to reward creaturely obedience with eternal life. Yet where the condition of obedience is met, eternal life is granted according to God's covenantal design.[76] This logic appears to underlie Romans 5.

Objection 3: Adam is an illustration, not a historical figure. Third, and more briefly, it may be objected that Paul's point in Romans 5:12–21 need not rely on a historical person called Adam to be theologically valid.[77] Therefore, we should be cautious about making too strict a historical connection between Christ's obedience and Adam's disobedience. Though there is no room for a full defense of the historicity of Adam in this essay, according to Scripture Adam must have really been the first person. To posit that Adam was not historical is for Paul's entire case—and here he is explaining the reality of death extending to all people as well as the way eternal life is secured—to come unhinged.[78] For Paul, Adam was undoubtedly a real person, as we see further in the discussion of 1 Corinthians 15 below. Paul's view is consistent with the reality of Adam's existence as taught throughout Scripture.[79] If Adam is not the progenitor of the human race, Paul's explanation for the unity of the entire human race's sinfulness and the universality of death is wrong. Likewise, if Adam is not the first man, then Paul's explanation of the nature of Christ's work as the head of the new humanity does not stand. Adam's real existence as the first human being must be a nonnegotiable for those who hold fast to Paul's exposition of the gospel.[80] Indeed, in two key texts in which Paul explains the saving work of Christ (Romans 5; 1 Corinthians 15), he explains the reality of Christ's work in relation to the reality of Adam.

In sum, I have argued that Romans 5 teaches that the entire obedience of Jesus—in both its passive and active dimensions—is necessary for the securing of eternal life. This is consistent with the covenantal conditions originally given to Adam. If we *only* receive forgiveness of sins, then we would not meet the requirements of eternal life, and the justification in view in 5:17–21 would not be full justification. Instead, Paul's glorious doctrine of justification is built on Jesus's *entire* obedience as its necessary foundation.

---

75. See further Bavinck, *Reformed Dogmatics*, 2:543–44, 568–76; Turretin, *Institutes*, 17.5 (cf. 8.6); Berkhof, *Systematic Theology*, 215–16; Vos, *Reformed Dogmatics*, 3:6–9, 21–24; 4:214–15; A. A. Hodge, *Outlines of Theology: Rewritten and Enlarged* (New York: Hodder & Stoughton, 1878), 527; cf. Richard A. Muller, *Dictionary of Latin and Greek Theological Terms: Drawn Principally from Protestant Scholastic Theology* (Grand Rapids, MI: Baker, 1985), 108–9, 190–92.

76. Of course, much more could be said here. For example, it is also important to relate the perfect obedience of Christ as fully man to his divine nature. See Vos, *Reformed Dogmatics*, 3:23–24.

77. In the next section, on 1 Corinthians 15, I will address the objection that Adam was historical but was not the first human.

78. See the short but insightful study by Richard B. Gaffin Jr., *No Adam, No Gospel: Adam and the History of Redemption* (Phillipsburg, NJ: P&R, 2015).

79. See, among others, Genesis 1–5; 1 Chron. 1:1; Hos. 6:7 (likely); Matt. 19:4; Mark 10:6; Luke 3:38; 1 Cor. 15:22, 45; 1 Tim. 2:13; Jude 14. It is insufficient to say, with Wright, that what matters is not Adam's existence but his vocation. Wright in Walton, *Lost World*, 170–72.

80. See again Gaffin, *No Adam*.

Francis Turretin on the Obedience of Christ in Romans 5

As we conclude this section on Romans 5, it may be helpful to consider the contribution found in Francis Turretin's *Institutes of Elenctic Theology*.[81] Turretin's treatment of Romans 5, though over three hundred years old, remains remarkably pertinent today. However, I do not recall seeing his argument engaged by any New Testament scholar who believes only one isolated act of Christ's obedience is in view in Romans 5:18–19.[82] Turretin provides several arguments why it is insufficient to say that the death of Christ is the only act of obedience in view in 5:19. As he discusses the mediatorial office of Christ and the nature of Christ's satisfaction, he explains that the obedience of the Mediator includes both passive and active dimensions. Turretin then defends the notion that Christ's satisfaction entails the obedience of his life (and not just his death) from various texts.

He begins with Romans 5:19, and his argument features several spokes. First, in 5:19, Paul treats the whole obedience of Christ without limitation, which means that it must refer to the obedience of Christ from the beginning to the end of his life, and this must not in any way be incomplete or imperfect. Second, the obedience of 5:19 has in view obedience not only to the sanction of punishment but principally to the keeping of the law's commandments. Third, the gift of righteousness that Paul speaks of here cannot be predicated of the sufferings of Christ. Fourth, Paul has in view that which is opposed to the disobedience of Adam. Since Adam was required to obey the whole law, the obedience in view must be the obedience to the whole law. Fifth, Paul addresses here what was due from us, regarding both punishment and precept. In other words, the righteousness in view in 5:19 is not only one act of righteousness but must be the righteousness that arises from a fullness of obedience.[83] Turretin concludes, "If by one sin guilt came upon all, righteousness does not pass from one act upon all because evil is from any kind of defect, but good requires a perfect cause."[84] Turretin later adds that the righteousness of Christ is not divided. Thus, even if Scripture ascribes redemption to Jesus's blood and death, this cannot be to the exclusion of the obedience of his life of humiliation.[85] In Turretin's words,

> If our salvation and redemption are ascribed to the blood and death of Christ, this is not done to the exclusion of the obedience of his life because nowhere is such a restriction found. Elsewhere . . . it is extended to the whole obedience and righteousness of Christ. Rather it must be understood by a synecdoche by which what belongs to the whole is ascribed to the better part because it was the last degree of

---

81. Here I am following Turretin, *Institutes*, 14.13.17, and am closely following the translation of George Musgrave Giger in vol. 2 of the P&R edition. I provide page numbers below where I include verbatim quotations.
82. Happily, Schreiner does include a brief discussion of Turretin on justification, though not on the issue of Rom. 5:18–19 per se. *Faith Alone*, 77–79. Schreiner leans toward understanding the singular act of obedience in 5:18 to refer to Jesus's death, though he does hold out the possibility that Jesus's entire obedience is in view. See Schreiner, *Romans*, 287.
83. Turretin apparently takes Rom. 5:18 to speak of "one act of righteousness" rather than "the righteous act of one man." Even so, he denies that it has less than the entire life of Christ in view. Turretin, *Institutes*, 14.13.17. See also Bavinck, *Reformed Dogmatics*, 3:377–78.
84. Turretin, *Institutes*, 14.13.17 (2:450).
85. Turretin, *Institutes*, 14.13.23.

his humiliation, the crown and completion of his obedience (which supposes all the other parts and without which they would have been useless).[86]

Thus, the *entire* obedience of Jesus is necessary for eternal life, and therefore, the entire obedience of Jesus must be in view in Romans 5.

1 Corinthians 15: Adam, Christ, and the Resurrection

Similar to Romans 5, in 1 Corinthians 15 Paul relates the work of Christ to the person and work of Adam. In particular, Paul's focus on the resurrection of Christ underscores the necessity for Jesus's entire obedience for justification. Of first importance for Paul is not only the death of Christ (15:3) but also that Christ was raised from the dead (15:4–8). Paul then proceeds to explain the significance of Christ's resurrection as the answer to the problem of death introduced by Adam's sin. In 15:21, Paul states the matter succinctly: since by man comes death, by man comes the resurrection of the dead. Consistent with the argument of Romans 5, one man's sin led to death for all humanity, whereas life comes through the second man. Indeed, Paul again makes it clear that he is working with a two-Adam structure to understand both world history and redemptive history. In 15:45, Paul contrasts the first man, Adam (ὁ πρῶτος ἄνθρωπος Ἀδάμ; also 15:46) with the last Adam (ὁ ἔσχατος Ἀδάμ), whom Paul also identifies as the second man (ὁ δεύτερος ἄνθρωπος, 15:47). Again, there are two representative men whose actions have implications for all humanity.[87]

Paul's argument in 1 Corinthians 15 necessitates that Jesus was resurrected as the fully obedient last Adam. The resurrection was a vindication of his perfect, entire obedience, not *only* the vindication of his unjust death (though it certainly entailed that). The sin that entered the world through Adam was the result of his failure to keep the entire law of God. Christ's resurrection, in contrast, was the result of his doing all that Adam should have done. If Adam's sin consisted in his lack of doing all that was required (personal, entire, exact, and perpetual obedience), Jesus's obedience in his state of humiliation was personal, entire, exact, and perpetual. By this obedience Jesus destroyed the sting of death (15:54–57) and has indeed, in principle, eradicated death itself (15:25–27). The resurrection victory and authority of Christ is inextricably tied to his perfect obedience to do what Adam should have done, as illustrated in the collocation of Psalms 8 and 110 (1 Cor. 15:25–27), which explain the resurrection authority of Christ in Adamic terms.[88] When Adam sinned, death reigned; when Christ as last Adam obeyed, death was overcome through the resurrection.

---

86. Turretin, *Institutes*, 14.13.23 (2:452).
87. See Murray, *Imputation*, 39. Some may object that Adam was a *real* person but not necessarily the *first* person. However, the polarity of options Paul sets forth in this text allows for no person who is not made in either the image of the first man or the image of the second man. All who are not in the second man are necessarily in the first man, and all those in the second man are naturally in the first man. Such a view also fails to account for the tragedy of death, which is not natural but only entered because of the sin of Adam. See further Gaffin, *No Adam*, 12.
88. See also the Adamic imagery in Eph. 1:10, which, for example, Irenaeus leans on for his theology of recapitulation, whereby the obedience of Christ as second Adam recapitulates and overcomes the sin of the first Adam. See, e.g., *Against Heresies* 1.10.1; 3.16.1; 5.20.2.

How does this Pauline theological structure relate to justification? First, we must understand that the resurrection of Christ was the vindication—or indeed, *justification*—of Christ's perfect obedience (passive and active). As Richard Gaffin has trenchantly argued, "The eradication of death in [Christ's] resurrection is nothing less than the removal of the verdict of condemnation and the effective affirmation of his (adamic) righteousness."[89] This is evident from Paul's argument not only in 1 Corinthians 15 (esp. 15:17) but also in Romans 4:25, in the declaration of Christ as the Son of God in power in Romans 1:3–4, and in Christ's vindication in/by the Spirit in 1 Timothy 3:16. As Gaffin further argues,

> The enlivening of Christ is judicially declarative not only . . . in connection with his messianic status as son, his adoption, but also with respect to his (adamic) status as righteous. The constitutive, transforming action of resurrection is specifically forensic in character. It is Christ's justification.[90]

Second, Christ's justification in his resurrection, which vindicates his entire obedience, is crucially important for the justification of those who place their faith in Christ. Simply put, Christ bore our sin in his death—and throughout his life—as a substitute.[91] As the last Adam, Christ's role was a representative one, and his obedience, manifested in his resurrection from the dead, benefits believers. Whereas sin brings death, the answer to death comes through being united by faith to the resurrected Christ, whose resurrection is the firstfruits of a fuller resurrection harvest (1 Cor. 15:20). Christ's resurrection, which is the seal of his perfect obedience, benefits believers no less than Christ's death benefits believers (cf. 15:17).[92] Because Christ's resurrection is the judicial verdict that his obedience was perfect, our justification is as certain as Christ's resurrection from the dead.

Philippians 2: Obedience unto Death

A third Pauline text that speaks of the obedience of Jesus is found in Philippians 2:8.[93] As is well known, the amount of material written on the so-called Christ hymn in 2:6–11 knows no bounds. However, for the present purposes, our focus is more narrowly on the obedience of Jesus in view in 2:8: "[Christ] humbled himself by becoming obedient to the point of death, even death on the cross." Thus, one can say without hesitation that the obedience of Christ in view in 2:8 must refer to his death. But does it refer *only* to Jesus's death?[94] Could we instead say that the obedience in view must also have in

---

89. Gaffin, *Centrality of the Resurrection*, 122. Here Gaffin is discussing the role of the resurrection particularly in Rom. 1:4, but the point holds true for 1 Corinthians 15 as well.
90. Gaffin, *Centrality of the Resurrection*, 124.
91. On substitution in 1 Corinthians 15, see Simon Gathercole, *Defending Substitution: An Essay on Atonement in Paul*, ASBT (Grand Rapids, MI: Baker Academic, 2015). Tellingly, the two texts Gathercole considers are Romans 5 and 1 Corinthians 15—two texts that explain the gospel in Adamic terms in reference to Christ's entire obedience for justification.
92. Cf. Gaffin, "Work of Christ Applied," 268–90.
93. Among those who recognize similarities to Romans 5 in Philippians 2, see Moisés Silva, *Philippians*, BECNT, 2nd ed. (Grand Rapids, MI: Baker Academic, 2005), 107; Wright, *Climax*, 57–59; Wright, *Paul and the Faithfulness of God*, 686–87.
94. This is a common view. See Gordon D. Fee, *Paul's Letter to the Philippians*, NICNT (Grand Rapids, MI: Eerdmans, 1995), 216n10; Wright, *Climax*, 39; Wright, *Paul and the Faithfulness of God*, 890, 989.

view Jesus's entire life of obedience?[95] To this question, I would answer in the affirmative. I provide here, briefly, four reasons.

First, not only is the death of Christ in view in this context (2:8), but so is the resurrection/ascension of Christ (2:9).[96] The resurrection is, as we have seen, the judicial declaration of Jesus's perfect obedience throughout his life. Combined with explicit mention of his obedience in 2:8, we are on firm ground to understand the obedience of Christ in Philippians 2 to encompass the entirety of Christ's obedience.[97]

Second, the broader context of Paul's argument in Philippians strongly suggests that we should think of the obedience of Christ in Philippians 2:8 in the broadest possible way. This so-called Christ hymn serves to support Paul's exhortation to the Philippians to live with one another in love and humility. To illustrate this most starkly, Paul points to the humility of Christ in his state of humiliation (2:5), which led to his exaltation. This mind-set is to be reflected among the Philippians, who are to consider others better than themselves (2:3) and are to look after the interests of others (2:4). A few verses later Paul encourages the Philippians—in light of the full-orbed obedience of Christ—to do *all things* without complaining or disputing (2:14), so that they may be blameless as children of God (2:15). In light of this call for the Philippians to be obedient in all things, surely it is not a stretch to say that Jesus's obedient humiliation in his incarnation was not limited to one or even a few acts, but he was constantly and in every way humbly obedient.

Third, if Jesus's entire obedience is in view, this means that Jesus's obedience "unto death" (μέχρι θανάτου) in 2:8 is likely not limited *exclusively* to his death[98] but is *inclusive* of Jesus's entire, lifelong obedience, which includes most climactically his death.[99] Support for this may be found in the flexibility of μέχρι ("unto") in Paul's writings, which often appears to be used inclusively rather than exclusively. For example, we again encounter the phrase μέχρι θανάτου in Philippians 2:30, there in reference to Epaphroditus's willingness to minister even to the point of death. To be sure, Paul seems to emphasize here the terminus of the extent to which Epaphroditus was willing to go—he was willing to serve *even to the point of death*. At the same time, however, Epaphroditus did not actually die in the service that Paul describes. Thus, Epaphroditus's ministry included his willingness to sacrifice his own life, but μέχρι θανάτου must include all he did to serve the Philippians, *short of* his own death. Epaphroditus's willingness to sacrifice his own life can surely be

---

95. See, e.g., Markus Bockmuehl, *The Epistle to the Philippians*, BNTC (Peabody, MA: Hendrickson, 1998), 138–40.
96. Bavinck puts it well: "The preposition διο (therefore) in Philippians 2:9 refers not to the order and logic but specifically to the meritorious cause of the exaltation. *Because* Christ humbled himself so deeply, *therefore* God has so highly exalted him." *Reformed Dogmatics*, 3:434; italics original. See further Bavinck, *Reformed Dogmatics*, 3:418–19, 423–24, 435. Though they are separate events, the resurrection and ascension can be placed together under the rubric of Christ's estate of exaltation; cf. Bavinck, *Reformed Dogmatics*, 3:339; Westminster Larger Catechism 51. (Additionally, at times Scripture can even speak of the death of Christ as his glorification; cf. John 12:32; Bavinck, *Reformed Dogmatics*, 3:423.)
97. If Philippians 2 is indeed to be taken as Adamic Christology, it would be another text where Paul speaks of Jesus's perfect obedience in relation to his resurrection authority.
98. This would typically mean that μέχρι is taken as a "marker of degree or measure," so "μέχρι," §3, BDAG 644. This is a standard view among commentators—e.g., Fee, *Philippians*, 216; G. Walter Hansen, *The Letter to the Philippians*, PNTC (Grand Rapids, MI: Eerdmans, 2009), 156. BDAG includes Phil. 2:8 under this heading.
99. This would not negate the *degree* of Jesus's obedience but may correspond to taking μέχρι with more of a temporal nuance. See "μέχρι," §2, BDAG 644: "marker of continuance in time up to a point." See also Turretin, *Institutes*, 14.13.18; Beale, *New Testament Biblical Theology*, 473.

seen as following the pattern of Christ, yet the same could be said of his entire ministry of service and suffering. If so, it is likely that Paul's earlier statement about Christ's obedience in 2:8 should likewise be taken to refer to Jesus's life of service as well.[100] Thus, γενόμενος ὑπήκοος μέχρι θανάτου in 2:8 probably includes more than *only* the obedience of Jesus in his death (though 2:8b confirms that Jesus's death on a cross is indeed squarely in view).

Again, we are reminded that the death of Christ incorporates, sums up, and completes the obedience of his entire life.[101] Jesus persevered in obedience throughout his life—he never grumbled, never selfishly disputed, and always considered others better than himself. In the death of Christ, we see most clearly what is always true of Jesus's obedience: the passive and the active are inextricably bound together.[102] Other Pauline uses of μέχρι seem to corroborate this view.[103] In 1 Timothy 6:14, Timothy is called to keep "the commandment" until (μέχρι) the appearing of the Lord Jesus Christ. Again, the point is for Timothy to keep the commandment not only to a certain degree or at the terminus point itself (i.e., Jesus's appearing) but also in the interim leading up to that day. Other inclusive uses of μέχρι in Paul (in various ways) include Romans 5:14; 15:19; Galatians 4:19; Ephesians 4:13; and possibly 2 Timothy 2:9. In light of all these texts, on balance it seems that μέχρι in Philippians 2:8 most likely has in view Jesus's life as well as the terminus point of his death.[104] Yet even if one argued that μέχρι focuses only on Jesus's death, the context of Philippians 2 seems to necessitate that Jesus's death would still serve synecdochically for Jesus's entire, unified obedience.[105]

Fourth, Paul's discussion of the righteousness of God that comes through faith in Philippians 3 supports the argument that Christ's entire obedience is in view in Philippians 2. I have already argued that the righteousness of Christ for justification is the righteousness of his entire obedience.[106] In light of this, the righteousness of God that comes through faith must be a Christological righteousness that benefits those who believe in Christ. The contrast, in other words, is between Paul's own understanding of righteousness, and the salvific righteousness of Christ that comes on the basis of faith. Such a reading is consistent with the view that the active and passive obedience of Christ is in view in Philippians 2:8. Again, we see that it is this entire obedience of Jesus that provides the ground for justification.

Conclusion to the Pauline Epistles

Many more Pauline texts could be invoked to support the argument that Paul views the obedience of Christ, in its entirety, to be necessary for justification. For example, other

---

100. See also Bockmuehl, *Philippians*, 138–39.
101. Again, this concept reflects the language of Bavinck, *Reformed Dogmatics*, 3:378; cf. 3:385, 407–8. See also Turretin, *Institutes*, 14.13.18.
102. So Macleod, *Christ Crucified*, 180.
103. Unfortunately, some of the following texts are not generally considered part of the conversation because they are not part of the "undisputed Pauline" letters. I engage this debate a bit more in chap. 7, my other essay in this volume.
104. See also ἄχρι θανάτου in Rev. 2:10; 12:11, which have faithfulness in one's life in view (and not only faithfulness in one's death). See further G. K. Beale, *The Book of Revelation: A Commentary on the Greek Text*, NIGTC (Grand Rapids, MI: Eerdmans, 1999), 665.
105. See again Bavinck, *Reformed Dogmatics*, 3:378.
106. This point is made by Murray, *Redemption Accomplished and Applied*, 123–24.

texts that most likely speak of imputation include 1 Corinthians 1:30 and 2 Corinthians 5:21.[107] For Paul, justification consists in both forgiveness of sins and the right to eternal life, as we have seen in brief scope in Romans 5:12–21. Elsewhere, Paul contrasts justification in Christ with deeds done in righteousness (Titus 3:5–7), and in Ephesians Paul's Adamic Christology (cf. 1:10, 20–22) is tied to his theology of salvation, whereby the work of Christ alone saves (2:8–9). In Galatians the cross is clearly important (Gal. 2:19–20; 3:10–14), though elsewhere Paul seems to have in view a more thoroughgoing obedience beyond only the cross (3:22–4:5).[108] For Paul, it is the entire, perfect obedience of Christ that provides the ground for justification.

Hebrews 10:5–7: Obedience and Sacrifice

Before we turn to the Gospels and Acts, two other texts are worthy of discussion. First is Hebrews 10:5–7. By quoting Psalm 40:6–8,[109] the author of Hebrews draws attention to the entire incarnate obedience of Jesus Christ. Hebrews 10:5–7, quoting Psalm 40, reads,

> Consequently, when Christ came into the world, he said,
>
> "Sacrifices and offerings you have not desired,
>   but a body have you prepared for me;
> in burnt offerings and sin offerings
>   you have taken no pleasure.
> Then I said, 'Behold, I have come to do your will, O God,
>   as it is written of me in the scroll of the book.'" (ESV)

The use of Psalm 40 in Hebrews 10 raises many fascinating questions,[110] but in sum this citation explains that the entire obedience of Christ in the incarnation overcomes the problematic dichotomy between sacrifice and obedience that was historically a problem for God's people.[111] Intriguingly, David (the author of the psalm)[112] seems to speak about himself to some degree in Psalm 40 as the one who came to do what was written of him in the book. This book likely refers first of all to the laws for the king in Deuteronomy 17. But the author of Hebrews clearly uses this psalm messianically (cf. Heb. 10:5), and he has in view a more thoroughgoing obedience than was realized by David himself. Indeed, in Psalm 40, David is not the agent of final deliverance because

---

107. See further Beale, *New Testament Biblical Theology*, 471–77.
108. So Longenecker, "Obedience of Christ," 145–46, 146n1. Many interpret the phrases διὰ/ἐκ πίστεως ['Ἰησοῦ] Χριστοῦ (and related constructions) in Galatians and other Pauline letters as subjective genitives ("the faithfulness of [Jesus] Christ"; cf., e.g., Longenecker, "Obedience of Christ," 146–47), which would therefore be understood as references to the obedience or faithfulness of Jesus. Such renderings are, of course, possible, but I am persuaded that these constructions are better taken as objective genitives denoting "faith in [Jesus] Christ," as I argue elsewhere in this volume.
109. This is Ps. 40:7–9 in the Masoretic Text. In the following discussion, I will refer to the English versification.
110. For example, do we have here a reference to the *pactum salutis*? See Vos, *Reformed Dogmatics*, 2:85; cf. Vos, *Reformed Dogmatics*, vol. 1, *Theology Proper* (2012), 75.
111. See the similar language of William L. Lane, *Hebrews 1–8*, WBC 47A (Nashville: Thomas Nelson, 1991), cxxxiv; Lane, *Hebrews 9–13*, WBC 47B (Dallas: Word, 1991), 266. Notably, Hebrews also relates an Adamic Christology to Jesus's obedience in the incarnation. See especially Hebrews 2 and the citation of Psalm 8.
112. Psalm 40 includes a Davidic superscription, which I take as authentic.

David looks ahead to future deliverance (see 40:13–17). What is more, David laments his own iniquities (40:12). The obedience of Christ in Hebrews 10:5–7, therefore, is a greater obedience than that exhibited by David and indeed brings the deliverance anticipated by David in Psalm 40. Christ brings this deliverance by offering himself as the final sacrifice. This was something that no other person had ever been able to do, since all other priests had first to offer sacrifices for themselves (Heb. 7:27). Yet even the blood of goats and bulls were insufficient ultimately to take away sin (10:4). Therefore, Christ is the better (heavenly) High Priest (cf. 8:1–2); his final sacrifice is perfect and effectual (9:14; 10:14). To be the perfect sacrifice without blemish, Jesus had to be fully devoted to God in every way. This was indeed the case, for in the body that was prepared for Jesus (10:5), he never sinned (which necessarily means he was free from both sins of commission and sins of omission), though he was tempted in every way (4:15).[113] Therefore, because he was fully obedient in his body (i.e., in the incarnation), Jesus was able to offer his body as the final sacrifice (10:10).[114]

A key point for the present focus on the passive and active dimensions of Christ's obedience is that by offering himself as the perfect sacrifice, Jesus finally and definitively overcame the problematic dichotomy between sacrifice and loving obedience that had all too often plagued God's covenant people. God desired his people to offer sacrifice in conjunction with love and obedience, not bare, ritualistic sacrifice (cf. 1 Sam. 15:22; Prov. 21:3; Isa. 29:13; Hos. 6:6; Amos 5:21–24). Indeed, this dichotomy is problematic for Jeremiah (cf. Jer. 6:21–24; 7:1–34), who prophesies the need for a *new covenant* (31:31–34; cf. Heb. 8:7), which is the focus of this section of Hebrews. In Jeremiah's new covenant, the dichotomy between internal and external religion would be overcome, because God's law would be written on his people's hearts (Jer. 31:31–34; cf. 4:4; 9:25), which is preeminently true of Christ (cf. Ps. 40:8).[115] The new covenant is instituted on the basis of Jesus's full obedience, whereby he has "eradicated the disparity between sacrifice and obedience presupposed by Ps 40:6–8."[116] Christ always delighted to do the will of God in every way (cf. 40:8). This unity of obedience and sacrifice in Hebrews lends additional warrant for understanding the unified obedience of Christ as having both passive and active dimensions.

2 Peter 1:1: Obedience and Righteousness Attained

A second non-Pauline epistolary text to consider briefly is 2 Peter 1:1. I include this passage as part of the conversation of Jesus's obedience, even though this text is rarely discussed in relation to the active and passive obedience of Christ. Nevertheless, it may

---

113. Harold Attridge also focuses on the obedience/faithfulness of Jesus in Hebrews. See Attridge, "The Psalms in Hebrews," in *The Psalms in the New Testament*, ed. Steve Moyise and Maarten J. J. Menken, NTSI (London: T&T Clark, 2004), 197–212, esp. 210–11. See also Simon J. Kistemaker, *The Psalm Citations in the Epistle to the Hebrews* (Amsterdam: Wed. G. van Soest, 1961), 126–28.
114. Cf. Bavinck, *Reformed Dogmatics*, 3:377, 387–89.
115. So Bavinck, *Reformed Dogmatics*, 3:394; Turretin, *Institutes*, 11.24.30; 14.13.18.
116. Lane, *Hebrews 1–8*, cxxxiv; Lane, *Hebrews 9–13*, 266. In Hebrews this new covenant has been inaugurated but has not yet been consummated, as the warnings make clear (cf. Heb. 10:26–31).

have something to contribute—though I would hasten to add that my argument does not rely on this text. Second Peter 1:1 speaks of the faith of equal standing that believers have obtained by the righteousness of our God and Savior Jesus Christ (τοῖς ἰσότιμον ἡμῖν λαχοῦσιν πίστιν ἐν δικαιοσύνῃ τοῦ θεοῦ ἡμῶν καὶ σωτῆρος Ἰησοῦ Χριστοῦ). The righteousness in view in 1:1, though closely related to the ethical righteousness emphasized in 2 Peter (cf. 2:5–8, 21; 3:13),[117] most likely refers to the saving righteousness of God that comes through (ἐν) Christ.[118] If we probe further and ask, "How does God's righteousness save us in Christ?" then the best answer is, "Through the righteousness of Jesus's *entire* obedience." Admittedly, this is not developed in 2 Peter. But if we ask how anyone can reach the goal of eternal life that 2 Peter clearly has in view as the outcome of our faith (1:11; 3:13; cf. Jude 21), the answer must be perfect obedience that corresponds to God's covenantal stipulations for eternal life.[119]

Part 3: The Passive and Active Obedience of Christ in the Gospels and Acts

We turn now to the passive and active obedience of Christ in the Gospels and Acts. In what follows, I summarize some of the argument from my recent extended study of this topic.[120] Readers wanting more discussion, defense, and bibliography should consult the book-length treatment. Here I simply provide a selective overview, with an emphasis on the necessary obedience of Christ throughout his life, which corresponds to the traditional categories of Christ's passive and active obedience. Here we look at five aspects of the Gospels that underscore the wide-ranging obedience of Jesus as the foundation for salvation.

First, we turn to Mark's Gospel, where the obedience of Jesus in the temptation corresponds to his binding of the strong man, which is part of the way the kingdom is established. In Mark 1:12–13, Jesus overcomes temptation in the wilderness, where he is with the wild animals. Quite significantly, this is Adamic Christology in Mark, since Christ proves to be the obedient one with dominion over the creatures, thus overcoming the sin of Adam and the resulting chaos.[121] This propels Jesus forward toward his ministry, as he begins to take on the kingdom of Satan by preaching, healing, and exorcising demons. Five conflicts follow the temptation account, and after the fifth conflict comes the explanation that Jesus is victorious over all opposition (3:22–30). Here Jesus explains the spiritual dimensions of the conflict and his concomitant spiritual authority. Additionally, this passage forms a literary frame with the temptation account, where we find that the key players are Jesus, the Holy Spirit, and Satan.[122] In Mark 3,

---

117. See the discussion in Richard Bauckham, *Jude–2 Peter*, WBC 50 (Nashville: Thomas Nelson, 1996), 168.
118. See Thomas R. Schreiner, *1, 2 Peter, Jude*, NAC 37 (Nashville: Broadman, 2003), 286; Douglas J. Moo, *2 Peter and Jude*, NIVAC (Grand Rapids, MI: Zondervan, 1996), 35; John Calvin, *Commentaries on the Catholic Epistles*, trans. and ed. John Owen (repr., Grand Rapids, MI: Baker, 2003), 366–67.
119. Cf. Bavinck, *Reformed Dogmatics*, 4:107, 184–86. Calvin relates 2 Pet. 1:1 to Rom. 3:22 and the righteousness that is imputed to believers. *Romans*, 138.
120. Crowe, *Last Adam*.
121. See, e.g., Joel Marcus, *Mark 1–8: A New Translation with Introduction and Commentary*, AB 27 (New York: Doubleday, 2000), 170–71; cf. Apoc. Mos. 39:1–3; Crowe, *Last Adam*, 23–28.
122. See Elizabeth E. Shively, *Apocalyptic Imagination in the Gospel of Mark: The Literary and Theological Role of Mark 3:22–30*, BZNW 189 (Berlin: de Gruyter, 2012), 43; Crowe, *Last Adam*, 154–57.

Jesus explains that the visible kingdom conflict (i.e., the plundering of the strong man's house) is proof that the strong man has already, in one sense, been bound. When did this happen? The literary structure of Mark strongly suggests that the initial binding of the strong man occurred in the temptation episode, where Jesus remained obedient to his Father despite the onslaughts of the devil.[123] In other words, Mark 3 points us to the humble obedience of Jesus as the means by which the strong man is bound and the kingdom is established. Additionally, the temptation account underscores the unity of Jesus's passive and active obedience, for in the temptation Jesus actively resists the devil and submits to his Father, even as he suffers lack in the wilderness. We thus see in Mark 1 that Jesus's obedience consists in actively obeying his Father and in enduring suffering.[124]

Second, Jesus's lifelong obedience fulfills Scripture. We see this in Matthew's ten fulfillment-formula quotations, which show how Jesus corresponds to Israel's prophetic expectations and how Jesus's obedience is the answer to Israel's perennial recalcitrance.[125] In Matthew Jesus's name means that he will save his people from their sins (Matt. 1:21), which corresponds to his wide-ranging obedience. Indeed, one Old Testament text that serves as a fulfillment-formula quotation comes from Isaiah 53:4 in Matthew 8:17: "He took our illnesses and bore our diseases" (ESV). Readers familiar with the Old Testament will no doubt recognize that Isaiah 53:4 is part of the well-known suffering-servant song in Isaiah 52–53. We rightly understand the crucified Christ as the suffering servant. And yet Matthew 8 invokes Isaiah 53 not for the crucifixion but to speak of Jesus's ministry of healing. This does not reveal a "free and wild" use of the Old Testament but indicates that Matthew understood Jesus's curse bearing to have extended beyond the cross, even to earlier parts of his ministry. Sickness and disease are effects of sin no less than death. Jesus's work of redemption does not just operate in a supposed "spiritual" realm, but he works to reclaim all that has been affected by sin.[126] As the suffering servant, Jesus bears the curse of sin even in the midst of his ministry as our priest.[127] This curse bearing corresponds to Jesus's *passive obedience*, even though it is not focused on the cross per se.

Additionally, the need for Jesus to conform to Scripture and to prove obedient in every way (including, but not only, in the temptation episode) underscores the active aspect of Jesus's obedience. For Jesus to save his people from their sins, he must himself be sinless. This is evident in John the Baptist's objection to baptizing Jesus into a baptism of repentance for the forgiveness of sins (Matt. 3:13–14). Jesus's response is telling, for he states that it was fitting for John to baptize Jesus in order to "fulfill all righteousness" (3:15). On the one hand, Jesus's baptism represents his entering vicariously into the

---

123. Ernest Best, *The Temptation and the Passion: The Markan Soteriology*, 2nd ed., SNTSMS 2 (Cambridge: Cambridge University Press, 1990), 12.
124. Indeed, the wilderness itself (Mark 1:12) recalls the effects of Adam's sin.
125. See Brandon D. Crowe, "Fulfillment in Matthew as Eschatological Reversal," *WTJ* 75, no. 1 (2013): 111–27; cf. Crowe, *Last Adam*, 84–85.
126. This point is emphasized throughout Bavinck's *Reformed Dogmatics*. See, e.g., vol. 1, *Prolegomena* (2003), 112, 362; 4:92, 435–36.
127. See also Irenaeus, *Against Heresies* 4.8.2; Beale, *New Testament Biblical Theology*, 906; Bavinck, *Reformed Dogmatics*, 3:366, 404, 408; 4:427–28.

estate of sin and bearing the curse as a representative, which Luke's Gospel in particular seems to underscore. For later in Luke's Gospel, after the baptism, Jesus speaks of a fire he has come to cast and a baptism he must undergo (12:49–50). As Richard Gaffin has argued, Luke 12:49–50 "warrants viewing the entirety of Jesus' ministry, from the Jordan to the cross, as a kind of baptism, one large submission to the baptism-ordeal of God's judicial wrath."[128] Thus, Jesus's statement in Matthew 3:15 speaks to the passive obedience of Christ. On the other hand, "fulfilling all righteousness" in Matthew 3:15 not only highlights Jesus's obedience to bear the wrath of God but also indicates his positive fulfillment of all the righteous requirements of God.[129] "Fulfilling all righteousness," in other words, also confirms the active aspect of Jesus's integrated obedience.

Third, Luke's "it is necessary" (δεῖ) statements point to the unity of Jesus's passive and active obedience, because these statements underscore the necessity of Jesus's incarnate works for the accomplishment of eschatological salvation beyond only the climactic events in Jerusalem.[130] To be sure, the death and resurrection of Jesus are important components of Luke's δεῖ statements (cf. 9:22; 13:33; 17:25; 22:37; 24:7, 26, 44–47). However, other Lukan δεῖ texts speak about events beyond the cross that were necessary for Jesus to fulfill. For example, in the first words that Jesus speaks in Luke, as a child in Jerusalem, Jesus states that it is necessary to be about the business of his father (2:49).[131] Additionally, two passages in Luke 13 (13:10–17, 31–35) testify to the necessity of Jesus's incarnate actions. In the one case, it is to heal and free the woman in bondage to Satan (13:16); in the other case, it is to complete his work "today and tomorrow" before finishing his course "on the third day" (13:32–33). The point for the present purposes is simply that Luke knows of no sharp division between the work of the cross and the work of Jesus throughout his ministry; both aspects are necessary for the realization of eschatological salvation. Again, we are cautioned not to divide the work of Christ into some parts that are more necessary than others.

Fourth, much as we saw in the discussion of Hebrews 10, Matthew shows us how love and obedience—or mercy and sacrifice—are perfectly coterminous in Jesus. A key text here is Hosea 6:6—"I desire mercy, not a sacrifice"—which is the only Old Testament text quoted more than once by Matthew (Matt. 9:13; 12:7). These quotations are found in Jesus's first two conflicts with the Pharisees, whose lips honored God but whose hearts were far from him (15:8; cf. Isa. 29:13). In contrast to the Pharisees, who neglected to keep the weightier matters of the law (Matt. 23:23), Jesus fulfilled the two great commandments of loving God and loving one's neighbor (22:37–39). Indeed, the term in Hosea 6:6 translated "mercy" (Gk. ἔλεος) may be better translated "covenant

---

128. Richard B. Gaffin Jr., "Justification in Luke-Acts," in *Right with God: Justification in the Bible and the World*, ed. D. A. Carson (Grand Rapids, MI: Baker, 1992), 111; cf. Crowe, *Last Adam*, 68–74, 100–102.
129. I lack sufficient space to defend this reading here. For a fuller discussion, see Crowe, *Last Adam*, 86–89.
130. On the Lukan nuance of δεῖ, see Joseph A. Fitzmyer, *The Gospel according to Luke (I–IX): A New Translation with Introduction and Commentary*, AB 28 (Garden City, NY: Doubleday, 1981), 179–81; Herman N. Ridderbos, *The Coming of the Kingdom*, trans. H. de Jongste, ed. Raymond O. Zorn (Philadelphia: Presbyterian & Reformed, 1962), 158–59; Crowe, *Last Adam*, 103–7.
131. The phrase ἐν τοῖς τοῦ πατρός μου in Luke 2:49 is debated, but it is best to take it in an active sense since Jesus is most likely speaking about what it is necessary for him to do to accomplish salvation. Cf. Crowe, *Last Adam*, 95n40, 104.

love" (Heb. חֶסֶד). Hosea 6:6 is about the need to love God and neighbor rather than simply offering (hollow) sacrifices. In light of what God requires, it is striking that Jesus embodied the mercy (or *love*) that God requires. In Jesus, there is no dichotomy of mercy and sacrifice, since the one who sacrificed his own life for the inauguration of the new covenant (cf. Matt. 26:28) is also the one who loved God most fully. Both aspects are integrated in the obedient life of Jesus.

Fifth, the resurrection accounts in the Gospels (and the resurrection emphasis in Acts) serve as the judicial, divine approbation of Jesus's perfect obedience. Given the centrality of the Passion week in the Gospels and the excitement of Jesus's ministry, one could incline to think of the resurrection accounts as mere addenda to the main events of Jesus's ministry and Passion. However, this would be a grave mistake. For if there were no resurrection accounts in the Gospels, then the Gospel narratives would be unresolved, and the enemies of Jesus would seem to emerge victorious in the spiritual conflict.[132] The resurrection accounts vindicate the innocence of Jesus, who was raised from the dead as the Holy One of God after being wrongfully condemned. This is Peter's point in Acts 2:27 (cf. Ps. 16:10) and Acts 3:14–15. Because Jesus is the Holy One of God, who was free from all sin, his body did not see decay. Put simply, as we saw with Paul's epistles, the resurrection of Jesus in the Gospels and Acts is built on the presupposition of his entire obedience and is the vindication that he had done all that was necessary to meet the conditions of everlasting life—perfect obedience throughout his life. From this perspective, the obedience of Christ yields not only forgiveness of sins but also the right to eternal life, which we have seen are two benefits of justification. Geerhardus Vos has captured it well:

> Had something been lacking in the suffering of Christ [i.e., in his passive obedience], then it would have been impossible that the violence of death had ceased even for a moment. Had there been something imperfect in the active obedience of the Mediator, then in no way could an enlivening have taken place in his soul and body. The resurrection must be viewed as God's *de facto* declaration of the perfection of Christ's work in both respects.[133]

Summary and Conclusion: The Unified, Perfect Obedience of the Crucified and Resurrected Last Adam

In this chapter I have argued for the unity of Jesus's obedience, which can be viewed as having both passive and active dimensions. Jesus's passive obedience corresponds to the forgiveness of sins in justification, and Jesus's active obedience corresponds to the right to eternal life. Key in this regard is the two-Adam structure of biblical theology, whereby Jesus as the last Adam realizes the perfect obedience that the first Adam

---

132. See Crowe, *Last Adam*, 192–97. Three of the four Gospels clearly end with the resurrected Christ appearing to his disciples. Mark's Gospel, however, most likely ends at 16:8 and therefore would not include an appearance of the risen Christ to his disciples. Nevertheless, the resurrection is clear in Mark in light of Jesus's three resurrection predictions (8:31; 9:31; 10:34) and the (angelic) pronouncement in 16:6–7.
133. Vos, *Reformed Dogmatics*, 3:221.

failed to achieve. It is the unified obedience of Jesus that provides the ground for justification. It is, therefore, unnecessary and indeed impossible to divide the obedience of Jesus into some aspects that are more necessary than others for salvation. For the death of Christ is not isolated from the rest of his life but is the crowning achievement of his entire incarnate obedience. This is good news, because if only the death of Christ were applied to us in justification, we would not have met the covenantal requirements for eternal life. But thanks be to God that we are justified on the basis of the entire—perfect—obedience of Jesus Christ, that grace might reign through righteousness unto eternal life (Rom. 5:21).[134]

Recommended Resources

Bavinck, Herman. *Reformed Dogmatics*. Edited by John Bolt. Translated by John Vriend. 4 vols. Grand Rapids, MI: Baker Academic, 2003–2008.

Calvin, John. *Institutes of the Christian Religion*. Edited by John T. McNeill. Translated by Ford Lewis Battles. 2 vols. Library of Christian Classics 20–21. Philadelphia: Westminster, 1960.

Crowe, Brandon D. *The Last Adam: A Theology of the Obedient Life of Jesus in the Gospels*. Grand Rapids, MI: Baker Academic, 2017.

Gaffin, Richard B., Jr. *The Centrality of the Resurrection: A Study in Paul's Soteriology*. Baker Biblical Monograph. Grand Rapids, MI: Baker, 1978.

Irenaeus. *Against Heresies*. In *The Ante-Nicene Fathers*, edited by Alexander Roberts and James Donaldson, 1:315–567. 1885–1887. Reprint, Peabody, MA: Hendrickson, 1994.

———. *On the Apostolic Preaching*. Translated by John Behr. Popular Patristics Series. Crestwood, NY: Saint Vladimir's Seminary Press, 1997.

Letham, Robert. *The Work of Christ*. Contours of Christian Theology. Downers Grove, IL: InterVarsity Press, 1993.

Murray, John. *The Imputation of Adam's Sin*. Grand Rapids, MI: Eerdmans, 1959.

———. *Redemption Accomplished and Applied*. Grand Rapids, MI: Eerdmans, 1955.

Turretin, Francis. *Institutes of Elenctic Theology*. Translated by George Musgrave Giger. Edited by James T. Dennison Jr. 3 vols. Phillipsburg, NJ: P&R, 1992–1997.

Vos, Geerhardus. *Reformed Dogmatics*. Translated and edited by Richard B. Gaffin Jr. 5 vols. Bellingham, WA: Lexham, 2012–2016.

---

134. Thanks to David Barry and Jonathan Gibson for their comments on earlier drafts of this essay.

15

A Contested Union

Union with Christ and the Justification Debate

DAVID VANDRUNEN

In recent years, theologians have paid considerable attention to the relationship between justification and union with Christ in historical, systematic, and biblical (especially Pauline) theology. They can hardly be accused of focusing on minor issues. Even a cursory look at the New Testament indicates that both ideas are very important and thus that any thorough biblical treatment of salvation ought to account for both.

My basic claim in this chapter is rather simple, although if true, it implies that many recent treatments of the subject have distorted biblical teaching to a greater or lesser degree. The claim is this: a faithful biblical soteriology should have robust doctrines of both union with Christ and justification (justification understood along traditional Reformed lines), but neither union with Christ nor justification should be subordinated to the other, for they are mutually determining and illuminating. That is, our theology should not attempt to define one of them independently of the other and then allow the former to control the meaning of the latter. Rather, each must be defined partly in relation to the other. If you ask me about my justification, I have to talk about my union with Christ; if you ask me about my union with Christ, I have to talk about my justification. To put it another way, union with Christ is a bond with the Lord Jesus consisting of a host of blessings, among which is justification, and justification takes place in union with Christ.[1]

---

1. In my own analysis, I am not using the language of *mystical* union often found in Reformed literature. The contemporary connotations of *mystical* do not make it a helpful adjective for communicating to the present generation, in my judgment. It is also not clear to me that Reformed theologians themselves have used the term consistently. For example,

The substance of my claim reflects standard, mainstream Reformed opinion. I understand myself to be appropriating and elaborating traditional Reformed sentiment in a way geared toward engaging contemporary debates. A variety of theologians have gone in a different direction recently, some drastically and others more slightly, elevating union with Christ as the central soteriological idea in the New Testament, or at least in Paul. To one degree or another, they allow union to determine justification's meaning or function, and in so doing, they reject one or more dimensions of biblical, Reformed soteriology.

Some writers accuse certain theologians of falling into the opposite error, that is, of subordinating union with Christ to justification.[2] Perhaps these charges are true. If so, my case implies criticism of these theologians as well. But I do not address this side of the issue here. Since it is fashionable today to subordinate justification to union, I focus my attention on that problem.

I begin with a brief explanation and basic defense of my claim and present some evidence that it has, in essence, been standard opinion among Reformed theologians. Then I address three ways in which contemporary theologians have gone in a different direction by subordinating justification to union with Christ. I move from more radical to less radical examples of such a move. Thus, my disagreement with the theologians I discuss becomes narrower as the chapter progresses. I consider, first, those who use union with Christ to jettison the substitutionary atonement as the ground of justification, as represented by Daniel Powers; second, those who use union to jettison the solely forensic character of justification, as represented by Michael Gorman; and third, those who use union to jettison or at least enervate the imputed active obedience of Christ as an aspect of justification, as represented by N. T. Wright and Michael Bird. Then, in the final section, I consider those who uphold all the elements of the Reformed doctrine of justification itself and would concur with most of the basic concerns of this chapter but who have used union to challenge the idea of an *ordo salutis* (order of salvation) in which justification is one of several soteriological blessings that unfold in a non-interchangeable relationship to one another, as represented by Richard Gaffin.

The Claim and Its Reformed Precedent

Before I interact with these modern-day theologians, some introductory discussion is necessary. In the first part of this section, I explain my claim in a bit more detail and offer a preliminary biblical case for it. I call it preliminary because I try to expand and enrich my biblical case in the course of evaluating other theologians in later sections. Here I focus mostly on the idea *that* union and justification are mutually illuminating,

---

Geerhardus Vos suggests that union with Christ is mystical in the sense of being subconscious, while John Murray describes it as reflecting the Pauline idea of once-hidden mysteries that are now revealed. See Geerhardus Vos, *Reformed Dogmatics*, trans. and ed. Richard B. Gaffin Jr., vol. 4, *Soteriology* (Bellingham, WA: Lexham, 2015), 21; John Murray, *Redemption Accomplished and Applied* (Grand Rapids, MI: Eerdmans, 1955), 206–7.

2. For example, Lane G. Tipton makes this sort of charge against Lutheran soteriology, and Marcus Peter Johnson makes a similar charge against Reformed theologian Louis Berkhof. Tipton, "Union with Christ and Justification," in *Justified in Christ: God's Plan for Us in Justification*, ed. K. Scott Oliphint (Fearn, Ross-shire, Scotland: Mentor, 2007), 42–43; Johnson, *One with Christ: An Evangelical Theology of Salvation* (Wheaton, IL: Crossway, 2013), 96–98.

and later I reflect on *how* they are. In the second part of this section, I discuss the Reformed precedent for my basic claim.

A Brief Explanation and Preliminary Defense

Scripture clearly says that Christians are united to Christ, but it is not intuitively obvious what this means. *Union with Christ* is a vague term. *How* is one united to Christ? The answers differ. Protestants, Roman Catholics, and Eastern Orthodox alike profess union with Christ while embracing soteriologies quite different from one another. And over the past century, prominent theologians have developed a variety of models to explain the nature of the union.[3]

When we examine Scripture, we find no discussion of union with Christ in the abstract. Instead, we learn what it means to be united to Christ as we read in Scripture about a range of events and blessings, such as Christ's death, burial, and resurrection (e.g., Rom. 6:3–5; Col. 2:11–12); baptism and the Lord's Supper (e.g., Rom. 6:3–4; 1 Cor. 10:16–17); the new covenant (e.g., Gal. 3:25–29); the outpouring of the Spirit (e.g., 1 Cor. 6:15–19); or calling (e.g., Phil. 3:14), justification (e.g., Rom. 8:1; Gal. 2:17), adoption (e.g., Rom. 8:15–17), and sanctification (e.g., Rom. 6:4; 1 Cor. 1:4–5). This observation helps to explain why different theological traditions can affirm union with Christ while attaching different meanings to it: since they have different theologies of the atonement, the sacraments, and the application of salvation, their theologies of union take on diverse hues.

Already, therefore, we confront a compelling reason to be cautious about making union with Christ a controlling concept. It is impossible to know what it means in the abstract. A bundle of other important biblical concepts give union with Christ its substantive meaning. One of these concepts is justification. Thus, a proper doctrine of justification (although obviously not *only* the doctrine of justification) helps us understand what it means to be united to Christ.

At the same time, it is also implausible to think that we can fully understand the doctrine of justification independently of union with Christ. Granted, it is probably easier to develop a biblical doctrine of justification than to develop a doctrine of union, since *justification* is considerably more concrete and specific than the rather vague *union with Christ*, and since a couple of places in Scripture, especially Romans 3–5, devote extended discussion to unpacking explicitly what justification is, which no extended text does for union. Nevertheless, a biblical doctrine of justification depends on union just as a biblical doctrine of union depends on justification. The most obvious reason why is that Paul, in the midst of the very texts we most associate with his doctrine of justification, says that justification occurs "in Christ" or "in him" (Rom. 3:24; 8:1; 2 Cor. 5:21; Gal. 2:17; Phil. 3:9). Evidently, a good doctrine of union provides necessary insight for understanding how God justifies us.

---

3. For a summary of five such models, see Constantine R. Campbell, *Paul and Union with Christ: An Exegetical and Theological Study* (Grand Rapids, MI: Zondervan, 2012), 60–61.

These initial considerations provide excellent reason to believe that neither union nor justification is fully self-explanatory but that the meaning of each depends on the other. And if so, our theology should not allow either one to control the other but should seek to understand them as mutually determining and illuminating. Many other areas of theology add weight to this preliminary case. I mention three in particular.

The first concerns Christ's resurrection. Scripture tells us that Christ was justified in his resurrection (e.g., 1 Tim. 3:16), that we have been raised with Christ (e.g., Eph. 2:6; Col. 3:1), and that Christ was raised for our justification (e.g., Rom. 4:25). This interconnected set of ideas implies that to understand our justification, we need to understand Christ's resurrection and our union with him; to understand Christ's resurrection, we need to understand his justification and our justification; and to understand our union with Christ, we need to understand his resurrection and our justification. This way of putting things may sound confusing, but it highlights an important point: the rich truths associated with Christ's resurrection indicate that justification and union with Christ are mutually illuminating.

Second, both union with Christ and justification are covenantal,[4] as demonstrated by Galatians 3, for example. This means that exploring the relationship of union and justification is to reflect on the covenant of grace, and explaining the covenant of grace is to reflect on union and justification. In Scripture, covenant is relational, since it binds two parties together in an oath-secured bond. But covenant in Scripture is also legal, since covenants involve mutual obligations that ought to be enforced. To recognize that the relational bond that constitutes biblical covenants has a legal dimension gives further reason to believe that justification and union with Christ need not be alternatives or competitors but are in fact mutually illuminating.

Third, a biblical doctrine of the Holy Spirit points to the same conclusion.[5] The Holy Spirit is the bond of our union with Christ (e.g., Rom. 8:9–10; 1 Cor. 6:15–19); the Spirit raised Christ from the dead (e.g., Rom. 1:4; 1 Pet. 3:18); in this resurrection, Christ was justified by the Spirit (e.g., 1 Tim. 3:16); and the Spirit creates the faith by which believers are justified (e.g., 1 Thess. 1:3–5). From this theological angle as well, therefore, justification and union with Christ illuminate one another.

Reformed Precedent

My purpose here is not to attempt a thorough survey of Reformed thought on these issues. I simply look briefly at a number of prominent Reformed theologians from the Reformation through the twentieth century, using works available in English that readers can consult for themselves. Although these theologians worked in theological climates different from our own and did not put things in exactly the terms I am using (such as "mutually illuminating"), they affirmed the importance and richness of union

---

4. This is an important theme in Michael S. Horton, *Covenant and Salvation: Union with Christ* (Louisville: Westminster John Knox, 2007); Grant Macaskill, *Union with Christ in the New Testament* (Oxford: Oxford University Press, 2013).

5. The role of the Spirit in union with Christ is another important theme in Macaskill, *Union with Christ*; see also Murray, *Redemption Accomplished and Applied*, 205–6.

with Christ and saw no conflict between that doctrine and the traditional Reformed doctrine of justification—the latter understood as grounded in Christ's substitutionary atonement, as solely forensic, as involving the imputation of Christ's active obedience, and as an aspect of an *ordo salutis* in which it precedes sanctification. The following theologians did not agree on every soteriological detail, but all held these basic convictions. Thus, this part of the chapter indicates that there is no major shift in perspective about union and justification in the Reformed tradition after John Calvin.[6]

I begin out of chronological order by first considering the Westminster Confession of Faith and the Larger and Shorter Catechisms. I do so because these documents have a special normative status for the Reformed tradition that no single theologian enjoys. They were the consensus product of over one hundred leading English Reformed theologians, and these theologians received counsel from several prominent Scottish Reformed theologians and communicated with Reformed churches throughout continental Europe. And Presbyterian churches around the world have adopted these documents as confessional standards ever since.[7] Following discussion of the Westminster Standards, I consider the theology of John Calvin, Francis Turretin, Wilhelmus à Brakel, John Brown of Haddington, Charles Hodge, Herman Bavinck, Geerhardus Vos, and John Murray.

The Westminster Confession and Catechisms (1646–1647)

Although not absent in the Westminster Shorter Catechism (WSC) and Westminster Confession of Faith (WCF), union with Christ receives special attention in the Westminster Larger Catechism (WLC). The Larger Catechism states that "union and communion with him in grace and glory" are "special benefits" of the invisible church (WLC 65). In what sounds like a basic definition, the Larger Catechism initially describes union in rather vague terms: believers are "spiritually and mystically, yet really and inseparably, joined to Christ as their head and husband." This answer does proceed to say, however, that union is accomplished "in their effectual calling," thereby explaining union in connection with other concrete soteriological blessings (WLC 66). Later questions deal with the communion in glory (WLC 82–83).

The Larger Catechism also has rich material on justification (see also WCF 11; WSC 33). Justification is grounded in the substitutionary atonement, Christ's "proper, real, and full satisfaction to God's justice" (WLC 71). Justification is also forensic, consisting in the pardon of sin and the accepting and accounting of believers as righteous (WLC 70). Furthermore, this declaration of righteousness is not a legal fiction but rests on

---

6. For more thorough arguments for this claim, see Richard A. Muller, *Calvin and the Reformed Tradition: On the Work of Christ and the Order of Salvation* (Grand Rapids, MI: Baker Academic, 2012), chaps. 6–7; J. V. Fesko, *Beyond Calvin: Union with Christ and Justification in Early Modern Reformed Theology (1517–1700)*, RHT 20 (Göttingen: Vandenhoeck & Ruprecht, 2012); J. Todd Billings, "The Contemporary Reception of Luther and Calvin's Doctrine of Union with Christ: Mapping a Biblical, Catholic, and Reformational Motif," in *Calvin and Luther: The Continuing Relationship*, ed. R. Ward Holder, RAS 12 (Göttingen: Vandenhoeck & Ruprecht, 2013), 165–82. Among those pressing a different historical interpretation, whom Muller, Fesko, and Billings critique, see Charles Partee, *The Theology of John Calvin* (Louisville: Westminster John Knox, 2008).

7. For recent work on the context and theology of the Westminster Assembly, see Chad Van Dixhoorn, ed., *The Minutes and Papers of the Westminster Assembly, 1643–1652*, 5 vols. (Oxford: Oxford University Press, 2012); J. V. Fesko, *The Theology of the Westminster Standards: Historical Context and Theological Insights* (Wheaton, IL: Crossway, 2014).

the "perfect obedience" of Christ, which is "imputed to them" (WLC 70). The Westminster Confession and Catechisms also portray justification as one of a series of great soteriological benefits, always discussing it after effectual calling and before adoption and sanctification (WLC 68–78; WCF 10–13; WSC 31–35).

Westminster Larger Catechism 69 provides the clearest explanation of the relationship between union and justification. It describes "communion in grace" as believers' partaking of the virtue of Christ's mediation "in their justification, adoption, sanctification, and whatever else, in this life, manifests their union with him." This reflects mutual determination and illumination. Union with Christ *is* partaking of Christ's work in justification (among other things). That is, justification is part of the definition of union. Ask someone what her union with Christ is, and justification is one of the first things she should talk about. But Larger Catechism 69 also says that justification "manifests" union with Christ. Thus, ask someone to describe what justification does, and he ought to mention union. By expressing this mutuality, the Westminster Standards implicitly reject attempts to subordinate either union or justification to the other.[8]

John Calvin (1509–1564)

Frenchman John Calvin, one of the Reformers of Geneva, wrote eloquently about union with Christ. For us to enjoy Christ's blessings, Calvin claims, "he must become ours and dwell in us," and we must "become one with him."[9] Calvin assigns this union "the highest rank." Christ makes us "partners with him in the gifts with which he was endued," and hence "we have put him on, and been ingrafted into his body" as he "deigns to make us one with himself."[10]

Calvin, of course, also explains justification in Reformed terms. He understands justification as grounded in Christ's substitutionary atonement:

> Our acquittal is this—that the guilt which made us liable to punishment was transferred to the head of the Son of God (Is. liii.12). We must specially remember this substitution in order that we may not be all our lives in trepidation and anxiety, as if the just vengeance, which the Son of God transferred to himself, were still impending over us.[11]

For Calvin, justification is also forensic, occurring when a person is acquitted "from the charge of guilt" and "in the judgment of God . . . deemed righteous."[12] This decree involves the "imputation of the righteousness of Christ."[13] Furthermore, justification is interconnected with other soteriological blessings. With respect to justification and sanctification, Calvin deems them "distinct" but "not separated"; they constitute a

---

8. For related comments, see Robert Letham, *Union with Christ: In Scripture, History, and Theology* (Phillipsburg, NJ: P&R, 2011), 76–77.
9. John Calvin, *Institutes of the Christian Religion*, trans. Henry Beveridge (Grand Rapids, MI: Eerdmans, 1953), 3.1.1.
10. Calvin, *Institutes*, 3.11.10; 3.11.3.
11. Calvin, *Institutes*, 2.16.5; see also 2.16.6–7 for further discussion of substitutionary atonement.
12. Calvin, *Institutes*, 3.11.2–3.
13. Calvin, *Institutes*, 3.11.2; see also 3.11.3, 23.

"twofold benefit" attained by faith and through union with Christ.[14] And although he discusses sanctification before justification in the *Institutes*, he viewed them as having an ordered relationship in which justification is foundational for sanctification. Unless one first understands what his "position is before God, and what the judgment which he passes upon" him is (that is, unless one understands his justification), that person has no foundation "on which piety towards God can be reared."[15] And without knowledge of the doctrine of Christian liberty, "a proper appendix to Justification," a person's "conscience can scarcely attempt anything without hesitation, in many must demur and fluctuate, and in all proceed with fickleness and trepidation."[16]

Finally, Calvin depicts justification and union in mutual relationship. Through "the imputation of righteousness," believers "are deemed righteous in Christ."[17] The only way we attain this righteousness is "by being made partakers with Christ," in whom "we possess all riches."[18]

Francis Turretin (1623–1687)

Our next theologian takes us more than a century forward but leaves us in Geneva. Francis Turretin's great work, the *Institutes of Elenctic Theology*, does not discuss union with Christ extensively, but it is clear that Turretin adheres to the concept and understands it in relation to justification. He writes, "As long as Christ is outside of us and we are out of Christ, we can receive no fruit from another's righteousness." But by the mystical union, Christ becomes surety and head of his people and "can communicate to us his righteousness and all his benefits."[19]

Turretin discusses all the main points of the Reformed doctrine of justification that I have been addressing. He presents the atonement along substitutionary lines, for Christ "died for us substitutively (i.e., in our place, that by being substituted in our place, he suffered the punishment due to us)."[20] This atonement is the ground of justification, for through it, Christ "meritoriously obtains the liberation of the guilty on the ground of justice."[21] Turretin also makes an extended defense of justification's forensic nature and of the imputation of Christ's active obedience.[22] Elsewhere, he describes an ordered relationship between justification and sanctification. The two blessings are distinct but inseparable.[23] Justification has priority but not in the sense that justification is more important. Rather, justification is foundational for sanctification, and sanctification is

---

14. Calvin, *Institutes*, 3.11.1, 11; 3.16.1. Calvin uses the term "regeneration," but he means by this the lifelong transformative work that later Reformed theologians ordinarily call "sanctification," rather than simply the initial renewing grace that enables a person dead in sin to believe the gospel.
15. Calvin, *Institutes*, 3.11.1.
16. Calvin, *Institutes*, 3.19.1.
17. Calvin, *Institutes*, 3.11.3.
18. Calvin, *Institutes*, 3.11.23.
19. Francis Turretin, *Institutes of Elenctic Theology*, trans. George Musgrave Giger, ed. James T. Dennison Jr. (Phillipsburg, NJ: P&R, 1992–1997), 2:647.
20. Turretin, *Institutes*, 2:427.
21. Turretin, *Institutes*, 2:426.
22. See Turretin, *Institutes*, 2:633–36 and 2:646–56, respectively (see 2:445–55 for additional discussion of active obedience).
23. Turretin, *Institutes*, 2:690–93.

a consequence or result of justification. For example, Turretin writes that "God justifies us" and that "on this account we are renewed because we derive the Spirit from our head, Christ."[24] In perhaps his most succinct explanation, he states, "Justification stands related to sanctification as the means to the end." God "does not take away guilt by justification except to renew his own image in us by sanctification because holiness is the end of the covenant and of all its blessings." Thus, justification "ought to enkindle the desire of piety and the practice of holiness."[25]

Wilhelmus à Brakel (1635–1711)

A look at Wilhelmus à Brakel takes us several decades ahead and to the Netherlands. À Brakel's magnum opus has a rich and warm summary of the nature of believers' union.[26] The Dutch theologian follows this by discussing the benefits that believers enjoy "due to being united with Christ." Among them, Christ's "satisfaction of the justice of God is their satisfaction," and "His perfect obedience and accomplishment of the law is their holiness, and this renders them perfect before God . . . and the righteousness of God in Him."[27] It is thus apparent that à Brakel views justification and union as standing in the closest of relationships.

This does not compromise à Brakel's Reformed treatment of justification. God is a "righteous judge" and thus only justifies the person who has "a perfect righteousness." Because of sin, believers can be justified only as "a partaker of the righteousness of Jesus Christ," who,

> as Surety, has paid for the sins of His elect, and has merited eternal felicity for them. . . . This righteousness God imputes to them by reason of His suretyship, and they partake of this righteousness by faith. . . . Adorned with this righteousness they come unto God and are justified by a perfect righteousness.[28]

In this statement, we see not only the basis of justification in Christ's substitutionary atonement but also à Brakel's commitment to the imputation of Christ's active obedience.[29] À Brakel defends the forensic character of justification at some length as well.[30] The ordered relationship of justification and sanctification is also of particular interest to him. À Brakel calls justification "the fountain of sanctification," such that "true holiness flows forth out of faith and justification."[31] Being justified makes the heart joyful, motivates perseverance, and fills the heart and mouth with worship.[32] He explains that

---

24. Turretin, *Institutes*, 2:647.
25. Turretin, *Institutes*, 2:692–93.
26. Wilhelmus à Brakel, *The Christian's Reasonable Service*, vol. 2, *The Church and Salvation*, trans. Bartel Elshout, ed. Joel R. Beeke (Grand Rapids, MI: Reformation Heritage Books, 1993), 89–90.
27. À Brakel, *Christian's Reasonable Service*, 2:91–92.
28. À Brakel, *Christian's Reasonable Service*, 2:349–50.
29. For extended discussion of Christ's imputed active obedience, see à Brakel, *Christian's Reasonable Service*, 2:350–56.
30. See à Brakel, *Christian's Reasonable Service*, 2:344–47.
31. À Brakel, *Christian's Reasonable Service*, 2:405, 615.
32. À Brakel, *Christian's Reasonable Service*, 2:404–5.

the person "who endeavors to attain to sanctification upon another foundation [than justification] has gone astray, and will never attain to it, and will never make progress in it.... Sanctification must necessarily proceed from justification."[33]

John Brown of Haddington (1722–1787)

John Brown of Haddington moves us about a half century later and to Scotland. His *Systematic Theology* displays great interest in union with Christ and affirms the traditional Reformed doctrine of justification. In fact, some of his explanation of union connects directly to matters of justification and substitutionary atonement and intertwines participatory, substitutionary, and forensic themes. He first identifies a legal union that believers have with Christ, which God established in eternity through election. In this union, Christ serves as surety, and all sins are reckoned to "Christ's account, that his satisfaction for them might be placed to ours in law-reckoning." Brown also identifies a spiritual or mystical union formed at believers' regeneration, in which Christ becomes their life and they become "partakers of him."[34] For Brown, therefore, the latter union is necessary for believers to enjoy the justification Christ purchased for them. As he explains, while bringing the themes of union, substitution, and justification together,

> In consequence of Jesus's fulfilling all righteousness for us, he, as our legal Head and Husband, received a full justification for us, which lies ready for us in the promises of the gospel; but till we be united to him, as our Head of influence, in whom all the promises are YEA and AMEN, we have no actual share in his righteousness and grace.[35]

In expounding justification in later pages, Brown defends its forensic nature and the imputed righteousness of Christ.[36] He also follows familiar Reformed paths in distinguishing justification and sanctification but also in affirming their interrelation. Brown explains that justification precedes sanctification, not in the chronological sense of one stage following another but in the "order of nature," an older Reformed term that addresses the same conceptual issues as the later phrase *ordo salutis*: "The justifying sentence which removes that curse, which is the strength of sin, must in order of nature, not of time, precede our implanted holiness, which is the beginning of that real eternal life, to which we are adjudged in justification."[37] Along similar lines, he says, "Through justification our person is delivered from the dominion and slavery of spiritual enemies, and their prevailing power gradually decreases."[38] For Brown, then, justification "precedes" sanctification and is its "source and foundation," and sanctification "manifests" justification and "follows" it "as its fruit and evidence, Rom. vi. 14. vii. 4, 6."[39] On

---

33. À Brakel, *Christian's Reasonable Service*, 2:405–6.
34. John Brown of Haddington, *Systematic Theology* (Grand Rapids, MI: Reformation Heritage Books, 2002), 337.
35. Brown, *Systematic Theology*, 339.
36. See Brown, *Systematic Theology*, 358–59 and 388–91, respectively.
37. Brown, *Systematic Theology*, 374.
38. Brown, *Systematic Theology*, 371.
39. Brown, *Systematic Theology*, 389–90, 400–401.

some occasions, Brown roots sanctification in both justification and union, evidently seeing no need to choose one route or the other.[40]

Charles Hodge (1797–1878)

We move now to the nineteenth century and across the Atlantic to Princeton Seminary. Charles Hodge, probably the greatest Reformed theologian of his day, saw the closest of relationships between justification and union with Christ. Hodge describes union as "mystical, supernatural, representative, and vital," and after a series of other rich statements about it, he declares,

> The Protestant doctrine of justification harmonizes with all these representations. If we are so united to Christ as to be made partakers of his life, we are also partakers of his righteousness. . . . One essential element of his redeeming work was to satisfy the demands of justice in their behalf, so that in Him and for his sake they are entitled to pardon and eternal life.[41]

Thus, among the "consequences of this union," Christians have with Christ the imputation of his perfect righteousness, whereby they are justified.[42]

While viewing justification as a blessing of union, Hodge affirms all the common elements of the Reformed doctrine of justification we have seen in his forebears. In the atonement, Christ was a "substitute," made "satisfaction," and became "a curse for us."[43] The atonement serves as the ground of justification since Christ "answered all the demands of God's law and justice against the sinner."[44] Justification itself is forensic in nature and involves the imputation of Christ's righteousness.[45] Hodge also distinguishes justification as "an act" from sanctification as "a continued and progressive work."[46] But mirroring other Reformed theologians, Hodge relates justification and sanctification in terms of "the order of nature," in which soteriological blessings "stand in a certain logical, and even causal relation to each other."[47] "If we are justified, we are sanctified," for the imputation of Christ's righteousness "secures the indwelling of the Holy Spirit" and thus "all the fruits of holy living."[48] Later he explains that those who are "under the law" are "under the curse" and "bring forth fruit unto death." But when "delivered from the law by the body or death of Christ, and united to him," believers "bring forth fruit unto God (Rom. vi. 8; vii. 4–6)." "Deliverance from the law," he concludes, "is the necessary condition of deliverance from sin."[49] Thus, as in Brown's exposition, Hodge roots sanctification in both justification and union.

---

40. See Brown, *Systematic Theology*, 399, 432.
41. Charles Hodge, *Systematic Theology* (Grand Rapids, MI: Eerdmans, 1995), 3:127.
42. Hodge, *Systematic Theology*, 3:227.
43. Hodge, *Systematic Theology*, 2:482, 497, 516–17.
44. Hodge, *Systematic Theology*, 2:482.
45. See Hodge, *Systematic Theology*, 3:118–34 and 3:144–61, respectively.
46. Hodge, *Systematic Theology*, 3:117. For a summary of their differences, see 3:231.
47. Hodge, *Systematic Theology*, 3:173.
48. Hodge, *Systematic Theology*, 3:171–72.
49. Hodge, *Systematic Theology*, 3:227.

Herman Bavinck (1854–1921)

With Herman Bavinck, we return to Europe and observe the rejuvenation of the Dutch Reformed tradition around the turn of the twentieth century. Bavinck travels in what is familiar territory by now. One important thing to note for present purposes is how Bavinck ties together ideas of union, substitutionary atonement, and the application of salvation in blessings such as justification. Channeling Calvin, he affirms that "there is no participation in the benefits of Christ other than by communion with his person." He describes an eternal union between Christ the Mediator and those his Father gave him, as well as a mystical union in which "substitution occurred" and "the whole church, comprehended in him as its head, has objectively been crucified, has died, been resurrected, and glorified with him." Bavinck finds "actively present in Christ" "atonement, forgiveness, justification, the mystical union, sanctification, glorification, and so on."[50]

Within the framework of this rich union with Christ, Bavinck defends the Reformed doctrine of justification along common lines. Justification is forensic, and through it God imputes Christ's active obedience.[51] The various saving benefits "are not an accidental aggregate but organically interconnected," for "the Holy Spirit distributed them in a certain order." After the initial benefits of calling, faith, and repentance, Bavinck identifies three groups of "following benefits": the restoration of right relation to God, renewal after God's image, and preservation for heaven. Bavinck summarizes this "order of salvation" as "calling (with regeneration in a restricted sense, faith, and repentance); justification; sanctification; and glorification."[52] Thus, while justification and sanctification are "equally necessary," "logically justification comes first."[53] Bavinck believed this had practical implications and was not merely a theoretical construct: "Certainly there can be no peace of mind and conscience, no joy in one's heart, no buoyant moral activity, or a blessed life and death, before the guilt of sin is removed."[54]

Geerhardus Vos (1862–1949)

Our final two Reformed theologians were born in Europe but spent their teaching careers in the United States. They provide evidence that the basic ideas defended by previous figures continued in Reformed thought deep into the twentieth century.

Geerhardus Vos, a native Dutchman, joined the ideas of union with Christ and of Christ's atoning work as Mediator and surety, and thus did not separate relational from judicial aspects of salvation. Vos explains that Christ, as Mediator, is "head" of his "glorious body" and "joined personally with those for whom He has become their surety."[55]

---

50. Herman Bavinck, *Reformed Dogmatics*, ed. John Bolt, trans. John Vriend, vol. 3, *Sin and Salvation in Christ* (Grand Rapids, MI: Baker Academic, 2006), 523.
51. See Bavinck, *Reformed Dogmatics*, vol. 4, *Holy Spirit, Church, and New Creation* (2008), 204–14.
52. Bavinck, *Reformed Dogmatics*, 3:593–95.
53. Bavinck, *Reformed Dogmatics*, 4:249.
54. Bavinck, *Reformed Dogmatics*, 4:179.
55. Vos, *Reformed Dogmatics*, 4:21. I deal with Vos after Bavinck since Vos was younger, even though the work of Vos I cite here was produced before the publication of Bavinck's *Dogmatics* cited above.

The way Vos describes the relationship between justification and union suggests that they are mutually defining. In one direction, believers' mystical union with Christ is a gift that extends to them from their justification. In the other direction, "all that the sinner receives flows from the living Christ. . . . He is regenerated, justified, sanctified, glorified, but all this is in the closest bond with the Mediator."[56]

Vos joins his fellow Reformed theologians in understanding justification as forensic and defending the imputed active obedience of Christ.[57] Although Vos ties justification and union together, he warns against the "great misconception" of concluding that "the bond with the Mediator is the legal basis on which God permits His merits to benefit the individual sinner." This "falsifies the fundamental element of the Christian doctrine of salvation: the element of justification by free imputation." Justification is never based on "an actually existing condition of our being righteous, but on the basis of a gracious imputation of God that is contradicted by our condition."[58] Consistent with this claim, Vos expounds the differences between justification and sanctification and defends justification's priority to sanctification in the *ordo salutis*.[59] In the *ordo salutis*, "there are a multiplicity of relationships and conditions to which all the operations of grace have a certain connection." Thus, there is "order and regularity in the application of salvation," and "the acts and operations each have their own fixed place" and "are connected to each other from what follows and from what precedes; they have their basis and their result."[60] In distinction from Roman Catholics, Protestants hold "that all improvement and conversion must have acquittal in God's tribunal as its starting point, and so . . . makes works a consequence of justification." No one can properly preach sanctification without justification, for "a Christian loves much after much has been forgiven him, not the reverse."[61] In short, "justification precedes" sanctification, and "the legal ground for sanctification lies in justification."[62]

John Murray (1898–1975)

Our final theologian, John Murray, was a Scotsman who also spent his career teaching in the United States. He, too, took great interest in union with Christ. Union, he writes, "is not simply a step in the application of redemption" but "underlies every step of the application of redemption." Murray even calls it "the central truth of the whole doctrine of salvation."[63] We see below that emphasis on the *centrality* of union has had problematic implications in the work of many contemporary theologians, but Murray did not use the idea to rework the basic elements of his Reformed predecessors' doctrine of justification. With respect to the specific relation between union and

---

56. Vos, *Reformed Dogmatics*, 4:22–23.
57. See Vos, *Reformed Dogmatics*, 4:137–38 and 4:152–53, respectively.
58. Vos, *Reformed Dogmatics*, 4:21–22. This "misconception" continues to arise, even in evangelical thought. Marcus Peter Johnson, for example, makes union with Christ itself the ground of justification; e.g., see *One with Christ*, 72, 75.
59. On their differences, see Vos, *Reformed Dogmatics*, 4:138–40.
60. Vos, *Reformed Dogmatics*, 4:1–2.
61. Vos, *Reformed Dogmatics*, 4:8–9.
62. Vos, *Reformed Dogmatics*, 4:193.
63. Murray, *Redemption Accomplished and Applied*, 201.

justification, Murray claims that believers are justified "in Christ" and "by union with Christ."[64]

Like his forebears, Murray believed that justification was founded on the substitutionary atonement. The "once-for-all redemptive accomplishment of Christ" must be at "the centre of attention when we are thinking of justification."[65] Murray also defended the forensic nature of justification and the imputation of Christ's active obedience.[66] With respect to justification and the other soteriological blessings, Murray writes that the application of redemption "comprises a series of acts and processes," all of which are distinct and have their own function and purpose and which "take place in a certain order."[67] In this *ordo salutis*, justification precedes sanctification. Sanctification "finds its basis in justification" and thus "presupposes" it.[68] But like other Reformed theologians studied above, Murray grounds sanctification in justification and union alike. Sanctification is not only based on justification but also "derives its energizing grace from" union with Christ.[69] Elsewhere, he writes that "it is easy to see . . . that justification lays the foundation upon which alone we may do that which is well-pleasing to God" and that "justification is the basis of sanctification, for it lays the foundation upon which a life of holiness can rest and develop," but then he also proceeds to stress the importance of union with Christ for godly living.[70]

In this survey of Reformed theologians from the sixteenth through twentieth centuries, we have seen a broad consensus on several points important to the present chapter. Reformed theologians have professed and defended the reality of believers' union with Jesus Christ and understood it in close relationship to justification. In doing so, they have not subordinated one to the other so as to allow one to control the other's meaning. They have acknowledged a broad biblical witness to justification as grounded in the substitutionary atonement, as forensic, as involving the imputation of Christ's active obedience, and as part of an *ordo salutis* in which it precedes sanctification. Justification takes place in union with Christ and gives insight into its meaning. In my own terms, they have generally viewed union and justification as mutually defining and illuminating. It is now time to consider how contemporary theologians have gone in a different direction. By interacting with these writers, I try to fortify and enrich the traditional Reformed understanding.

Union, Justification, and Substitutionary Atonement

The rest of this chapter discusses a number of recent studies that explore the relationship of justification and union with Christ. Most of the authors under consideration

---

64. Murray, *Redemption Accomplished and Applied*, 156.
65. Murray, *Redemption Accomplished and Applied*, 157; for his general defense of substitutionary atonement, see 30–35, 51–54.
66. Murray, *Redemption Accomplished and Applied*, 149–58.
67. Murray, *Redemption Accomplished and Applied*, 97–98.
68. Murray, *Redemption Accomplished and Applied*, 104–5, 177.
69. Murray, *Redemption Accomplished and Applied*, 104–5.
70. See John Murray, *Principles of Conduct: Aspects of Biblical Ethics* (Grand Rapids, MI: Eerdmans, 1957), 202–3, 206–7.

posit that union is in some way central to believers' salvation. For Reformed readers, this may not sound like a particularly remarkable move, and indeed, if centrality is defined in certain ways, it probably has an element of truth. But for the following first three groups of writers (most of whom would not claim to be Reformed), the centrality of union implies that the doctrine of union should control the doctrine of justification to one degree or another, in such a way that jettisons or enervates one of the standard Reformed elements of justification. I discuss these writers by moving from those who assign union a more controlling function to those who assign it a less controlling function. Thus, the degree of my differences with the writers under consideration diminishes as the chapter progresses. The final group of writers I consider share my Reformed understanding of justification itself but have used union to question the idea of an *ordo salutis* in which justification is foundational for sanctification. I begin by considering issues of union with Christ and the substitutionary atonement.

The Challenge
It seems fair to say that of all the major characteristics of the Reformed doctrine of justification highlighted in the theologians above, the idea that justification is grounded in Christ's substitutionary atonement is most fundamental.[71] Without Christ's substitution, none of the other aspects of the doctrine makes much sense. Thus, to view union with Christ as central to salvation in such a way that it eliminates the idea of substitution would be, I believe, the most thorough challenge to traditional Reformed ideas we could face. And this is what we find in Daniel Powers's work *Salvation through Participation*, which focuses on the notion of union with Christ in early Christianity, especially in Paul.

The centrality of union emerges early in Powers's book. "The center of Paul's theology," he writes, "revolves essentially around the notion of the turn of the old age to the new age," which coincides with "the death and resurrection of Jesus." And "many of the earliest Christians' notions concerning the salvifically beneficial effect of the death and resurrection of Jesus . . . are intrinsically based upon the notion of corporate unity between Christ and believers."[72] Powers often states that justification occurs through this participation in Christ. For example, "Justification is the result of the believer's participation in Jesus' resurrection."[73] Such statements about Christians' "corporate unity" or "participation" with Christ and about the close relationship of justification to union may sound similar to the teaching of the Reformed theologians discussed above, but Powers's reasoning moves only in one direction—from union to justification—rather than in both directions. This does seem consistent, however, with his view that participating in Christ's death and resurrection was central to early Christian belief.

What I wish to highlight is Powers's conviction that the reality of believers' *corporate unity* with Christ excludes the idea that Christ was a *substitute* or offered himself in

---
71. See chap. 11, by Stephen Wellum, in this book.
72. Daniel G. Powers, *Salvation through Participation: An Examination of the Notion of the Believer's Corporate Unity with Christ in Early Christian Soteriology*, CBET 29 (Leuven: Peeters, 2001), 12.
73. Powers, *Salvation through Participation*, 125. See also 134, 141, 189–90, 231.

a *vicarious* exchange. As Powers works his way through many Pauline texts, such as those teaching that Christ died "for us," "for our sins," or the like, he claims that they communicate notions of "solidarity," "unity," "close relationship," "participation," or "representation," but not of vicariousness or substitution.[74] He offers a stark alternative. We can interpret Christ's death *for* his people either as meaning "on behalf of" (representational) or as meaning "in the place of" or "instead of" (vicarious).[75] Rejecting the latter, with its legal implications, he favors a vision of salvation in which God's grace to Jesus "spills over" or "flows over" to believers by virtue of their solidarity with him.[76]

Part of Powers's case against substitution rests in showing that the notion itself leads to ridiculous conclusions. For example, in 1 Thessalonians 5:10, Paul could not have meant that Christ died vicariously for us, for we still die physically.[77] Or Paul could not have intended to teach substitution in 2 Corinthians 5:21, which would imply that "Christ became sin *instead of* us so that we might become the righteousness of God *instead of* Christ."[78]

But Powers's rejection of substitution seems to rest on something even more fundamental, a thread running through his analysis: he assumes that if corporate unity or participation marks the relationship between Christ and believers, then notions of substitution and vicarious exchange are necessarily ruled out. Only one or the other can be true. In Galatians 2:20, for example, "Christ's death for us involves us in dying with him," and "as a result it is rather obvious" that "on behalf of me" in this text "cannot be substitutional."[79] Elsewhere (concerning 2 Cor. 5:21), he sees a "line of demarcation" between ideas of "representation" and "substitution," and if one embraces the latter, then "Christ does not really participate in the sin of the sinner, nor does the sinner really participate in the righteousness of God." If one takes "the place of another," then he "foregoes participation." The question is this, he suggests: "Is Paul thinking here more in terms of exchange or in terms of interchange (that is, participation)?"[80] To take one other example, Powers claims that "on behalf of" in 2 Corinthians 5:14 is "controlled by the idea of representation or participation," and thus Paul could not have meant that "Christ died 'instead of' or 'in place of' all."[81]

The Case for Substitutionary Atonement

The last quotation may reveal something important about Powers's analysis: he gives the idea of participation a *controlling* function in interpreting early Christian soteriology. This accords with his initial claim about the centrality of believers' corporate unity with

---

74. E.g., see Powers, *Salvation through Participation*, 45, 55, 64, 79–84, 106, 117–18, 122, 134, 233. He does admit, however, that "on behalf of" has substitutionary nuance in several New Testament texts that he regards as later than Paul, such as Mark 10:45; Eph. 5:2; 1 Tim. 2:6; Titus 2:14.
75. Powers, *Salvation through Participation*, 106.
76. Powers, *Salvation through Participation*, 108, 186–87, 233.
77. Powers, *Salvation through Participation*, 43.
78. Powers, *Salvation through Participation*, 81.
79. Powers, *Salvation through Participation*, 122.
80. Powers, *Salvation through Participation*, 79–81.
81. Powers, *Salvation through Participation*, 64.

Christ in his death and resurrection. That Paul and other New Testament writers affirmed a union, participation, or corporate unity between Christ and believers is hardly controversial. But was this idea *central* for them, or more precisely, was this idea central so as to be *controlling*? Should the idea of union compel us to interpret substitutionary-sounding texts in a nonsubstitutionary way?

If there is considerable evidence that Scripture teaches a substitutionary atonement, then such an approach seems dubious. If Scripture presents much evidence for *both* union with Christ *and* substitutionary atonement, a much better approach is to interpret the two as mutually illuminating. Thus, I now offer some basic reasons to conclude that Scripture does indeed teach a substitutionary atonement, and then I reflect on how this doctrine and the doctrine of union illuminate one another.

A general theological concern relevant to substitutionary atonement is the terrible sinfulness of humanity and the profound justice and holiness of God. God declares that he will not justify (i.e., declare righteous) the one who is guilty (Ex. 23:7). Justifying the guilty and condemning the innocent are both abominable in his sight (Prov. 17:15). He shows no partiality and takes no bribes (Deut. 10:17). Yet guilty is precisely what every human being is. No one is righteous or does what is good (Rom. 3:10–12), by nature being dead in sin and children of wrath (Eph. 2:1–3). God may love us and desire to save us, but he cannot wink at sin. He is the Judge of all the earth who must do right (Gen. 18:25). The Lord is a God of recompense and retribution, and he will repay (Ps. 58:10–11; Jer. 51:56).

The substitutionary atonement is precisely how God rescues his people from judgment without compromising his justice along the way. Through Christ's work, God is both just and the justifier of those with faith in Jesus (Rom. 3:24–26).

The Old Testament sacrificial system showed God's way of dealing with his people's sin: by way of vicarious punishment. In the burnt offering, for example, the offerer was told to "lay his hand on the head of the burnt offering, and it shall be accepted for him to make atonement for him" (Lev. 1:4). Likewise, God commanded the one presenting a sin offering to "lay his hand on the head of the bull and kill the bull before the LORD" (4:4). On the Day of Atonement, Aaron was to "lay both his hands on the head of the live goat, and confess over it all the iniquities of the people of Israel, and all their transgressions, all their sins," and he was to "put them on the head of the goat" (16:21). These rituals were but a shadow of better things to come (Heb. 10:1). Thus, the Old Testament prophets portrayed the coming Messiah as one who would bear his people's sins in a definitive way. "He has borne our griefs and carried our sorrows"; he was "pierced for our transgressions; he was crushed for our iniquities; upon him was the chastisement that brought us peace, and with his wounds we are healed," for "the LORD has laid on him the iniquity of us all" (Isa. 53:4–6). Jesus accomplished this: "He himself bore our sins in his body on the tree," and thus, "by his wounds you have been healed" (1 Pet. 2:24). The New Testament describes this vicarious atonement in a number of other ways too. Paul and Hebrews, for example, speak of Christ dying "for us" and "for our sins" (e.g., Rom. 4:25; 5:8;

Heb. 7:27; 10:12). Paul says that Christ died "for us" (e.g., Eph. 5:2; Titus 2:14). Various texts also describe Christ's death as a "ransom" for his people (e.g., Mark 10:45; 1 Tim. 2:6).

I have been focusing here merely on what Reformed theology calls Christ's *passive obedience* (his suffering, punishment-bearing obedience). Later I also consider his *active obedience* (his fulfilling all the commands of God's law), which also has a substitutionary character. But our limited focus for now is sufficient for assessing Powers's claims. Weighty theological concerns and extensive biblical evidence suggest that Powers's stark contrast between union/participation and substitution/exchange is an attempt to make one biblical theme override another. To be faithful to Scripture's teaching holistically, we should seek a mutually illuminating interpretation of union with Christ, on the one hand, and substitutionary atonement as the ground of justification, on the other.

Union with Christ and Substitutionary Atonement: Mutually Illuminating

We first consider how substitutionary atonement might illuminate our understanding of union with Christ, and then we reflect on how the latter might illuminate the former.[82] First, the truth of substitutionary atonement indicates that union with Christ is a union with one who took our place as the condemned. That is not all our union with him is, but it is one important aspect of it. Romans 6:1–7:6 is helpful on this front. The one who has died with Christ—that is, been united with him in his death and burial—has been justified from sin (6:7), set free from slavery (6:16–22), liberated from the law that bound us as our spouse (7:1–3), and released us from the law that held us captive (7:6). Each of these statements has a clear forensic dimension: dying with Christ effects a dramatic legal change in the life of believers.[83] We who stood condemned under a merciless law have been released from it through participation in Christ's death "for us" (5:8) and "for our trespasses" (4:25). Our union with Christ binds us to him in a substitutionary, vicarious relationship.[84]

Second, the reality of union with Christ confirms that substitutionary atonement is not a mere commercial transaction but an exchange in relationship.[85] That is, substitutionary atonement is not like a stranger giving an anonymous gift or like a credit-card transaction in which cardholder, merchant, and bank remain unknown to each other and may never deal with one another again. Rather, Christ's substitution for his people resembles the love of husband and wife, in which the loving sacrifice of one for the other builds an enduring relationship (see Eph. 5:25–33). Far from substitution implying no participation, as Powers suggests, Christ's atonement draws his people to himself and secures their unbreakable relationship for ages everlasting.

---

82. For other discussions relevant to this issue, see also Letham, *Union with Christ*, 62–63; Macaskill, *Union with Christ*, 299.
83. See also Campbell, *Paul and Union with Christ*, 337.
84. For a related critique of Powers, see Campbell, *Paul and Union with Christ*, 351–52.
85. See also Cornelis van der Kooi and Gijsbert van den Brink, *Christian Dogmatics: An Introduction*, trans. Reinder Bruinsma with James D. Bratt (Grand Rapids, MI: Eerdmans, 2017), 683.

Union with Christ and Forensic Justification

When we move from the ground of justification in the substitutionary atonement to the doctrine of justification itself, the question of justification's basic nature has always been of prime importance for Reformed theologians. Over against the Roman Catholic understanding, Reformed and other Protestant theologians have insisted that justification is solely forensic in character and not at all transformative. In justification, God declares people righteous as a matter of law but does not renew people's hearts to make them subjectively righteous. How does the doctrine of union with Christ relate to this classic debate? In this section, I consider the work of another contemporary theologian who understands union with Christ to be central to Paul. Although a Protestant himself (albeit one who teaches at a Roman Catholic university and draws on common Eastern Orthodox themes), Michael Gorman argues from Paul's doctrine of union to the conclusion that justification is not solely forensic but also includes moral transformation. After explaining some of Gorman's relevant claims below, I argue in response that theology should not allow the doctrine of union to expunge the solely forensic character of justification but that the two ideas ought to be mutually illuminating.

Gorman's book *Inhabiting the Cruciform God* focuses on the idea of *theosis*, a term Eastern Orthodox theology often uses to describe the human calling to ever-greater communion with the life of the triune God. Gorman understands theosis to be the "transformative participation in the kenotic, cruciform character of God through Spirit-enabled conformity to the incarnate, crucified, and resurrected/glorified Christ."[86] By understanding it as "participation," Gorman obviously considers theosis to be a way of speaking about union with Christ. According to Gorman, his book drives at the conclusion that *"theosis is the center of Paul's theology."*[87] Thus, like Powers, Gorman embraces the centrality of union. Let us see what the implications are for justification.

Gorman sets out to show that justification *is* theosis and also that theosis is holiness. Thus, "holiness is not a supplement to justification but the actualization of justification, and may be more appropriately termed theosis."[88] This indicates early on that Gorman views justification through the lens of union and in so doing makes it an all-embracing concept that is both forensic and transformative. He confirms this initial impression as he works out the details. He explains that Paul thinks of justification as "an experience of participating in Christ's resurrection life that is effected by co-crucifixion with him." This perspective results in "a much more robust, participatory, and costly understanding of justification than one often finds attributed to Paul." Gorman insists that justification is by divine grace and thus not a self-justification by works but also that there should be no "rift" between justification and sanctification.[89] Although parts of the Christian church

---

86. Michael J. Gorman, *Inhabiting the Cruciform God: Kenosis, Justification, and Theosis in Paul's Narrative Soteriology* (Grand Rapids, MI: Eerdmans, 2009), 7.
87. Gorman, *Cruciform God*, 171. He says he is somewhat uncomfortable speaking about a center of Paul's thought, but he does so because that is how scholarly discussion has been framed.
88. Gorman, *Cruciform God*, 2.
89. Gorman, *Cruciform God*, 40.

"have become enamored with cheap justification," he is heartened by recent shifts in Reformation soteriology "from declaration and legal fiction to real participation and even 'divinization.'"[90] Readers need not doubt that Gorman means to be as critical of a strictly forensic view of justification as this sounds, for later he states explicitly, "The traditional Protestant distinction between justification and sanctification is, in some very essential way, deeply problematic."[91]

Gorman makes similar points elsewhere. He offers this definition of justification: "*the establishment or restoration of right covenantal relations—fidelity to God and love for neighbor—with the certain hope of acquittal/vindication on the day of judgment.*" Thus, again, he makes justification a rather all-embracing experience. To see justification as "juridical or judicial—the image of a divine judge pronouncing pardon or acquittal"—is indeed part of what justification is, "but only part." This judicial imagery "must be understood within a wider covenantal, relational, participatory, and transformative framework."[92] Gorman finds proof that moral transformation is "innate to reconciliation/justification" in 2 Corinthians 5:14–21, through its reference to new creation.[93] He also appeals to Romans 5–8. These chapters do not set out a linear *ordo salutis*, he holds, but present "several perspectives on the same reality." In Romans 6 in particular, Paul does not describe the "effects or consequences" of justification but "*defines* justification by faith."[94]

Gorman offers his proposal as the way to avoid certain problematic ideas. For example, he is keen to deny that "Paul works with two soteriological models or that participation is an experience 'added onto' justification."[95] Elsewhere, he insists that we should not separate faith from love and action, and this means that we cannot share in Christ's death except by "covenantal fidelity."[96] As the previous survey of Reformed theologians shows, traditional Reformed soteriology has not advocated competing soteriological models, made union an "add-on" to justification, or separated faith from love. But Gorman evidently believes that subsuming justification under a controlling and comprehensive notion of union with Christ is necessary for avoiding these errors.

The Case for Forensic Justification

When we step back and consider Gorman's argumentation, it seems clear that subsuming justification under union with Christ and thereby making union controlling is key to his case. In none of the texts he discusses can he show that Paul describes justification *itself* as transformative. These texts do relate justification and union with Christ, as well as justification and sanctification, but the presence of multiple ideas in a particular text does not in itself demonstrate that the ideas are basically identical or are different ways

---

90. Gorman, *Cruciform God*, 41–42.
91. Gorman, *Cruciform God*, 93.
92. Gorman, *Cruciform God*, 53–54.
93. Gorman, *Cruciform God*, 56.
94. Gorman, *Cruciform God*, 73–74.
95. Gorman, *Cruciform God*, 73.
96. Gorman, *Cruciform God*, 81.

of speaking about the same reality, as Gorman believes. In fact, there is overwhelming evidence in Scripture that justification is merely forensic. God does transform his people subjectively, but this is not what justification is. If this is true, we must conclude that Gorman has used one biblical theme (believers' union with, or participation in, Christ) to override another biblical theme (forensic justification). Thus, I now briefly survey the biblical case for the forensic nature of justification and then reflect on how forensic justification and union with Christ are mutually illuminating.

A simple but important argument for the solely forensic character of justification is that the Greek words Scripture uses to describe justification are forensic in meaning and do not communicate moral renovation. In Koine and classical Greek, "to justify" (δικαιουν) means "to declare righteous"—or sometimes "to show that one is righteous in a demonstrative sense"—but not "to make someone righteous."[97] It is possible that Paul and other biblical authors invented a new meaning for these common words, but the burden of proof lies on those advancing such a claim. In fact, Scripture's use of these words is completely consistent with the ordinary expectations of the Greek language.

The Greek Old Testament provides helpful background for New Testament discussion of "justification" language. In Exodus 23:7, God proclaims that he will not justify the wicked. God would never deny that he renovates the hearts of wicked people, but God will not declare righteous the one who is not righteous. The fact that God says this in the context of a lawsuit (23:6) confirms this forensic sense of "justify." Furthermore, human judges ought to follow the divine pattern. Deuteronomy 25:1 commands them to justify the righteous and to condemn the wicked. It counterposes "justify" and "condemn" because they are both forensic. "Justify" can hardly mean "make righteous," since no one needs to make righteous those who already are. Even more striking is Proverbs 17:15, which says that God finds it abominable when people justify the wicked and condemn the righteous. God would in no way think helping a sinner along the road to moral improvement is abominable. What he abhors is judging people in ways that are untrue and unjust. Or we might consider Isaiah 50:8, in which the servant of the Lord asserts that the one who justifies him draws near. Who, then, he asks rhetorically, can bring a charge against him? That makes sense as a forensic matter: if God has rendered a verdict of righteous, no one else can successfully press charges.

The word the New Testament uses for "justify" is the same word the Septuagint uses in all the preceding examples except Proverbs 17:15, and it continues to communicate a forensic declaration and not moral renovation. For example, Luke 7:29 comments that the people and tax collectors justified *God*. They obviously were not making God morally righteous, but they were perfectly capable of declaring God to be righteous. Perhaps it is most helpful to trace Paul's use of the term in Romans, however, since that is where he lays out his doctrine of justification in most detail.

---

97. E.g., see BDAG 249.

Paul uses "justify" at least once in a demonstrative sense in Romans, when he speaks of God being justified in his words (3:4); that is, his words show forth that he is righteous. But this also is clearly not transformative in meaning.[98] Throughout the rest of the epistle, Paul's use of the term is consistently forensic. We see this in 2:13, where he states that the doers of the law will be justified. It makes little sense to say that those who do the law will be made righteous, since those who do the law are already righteous. Instead, Paul makes this claim in the forensic context of God's judging people according to the law (2:12), of the conscience accusing or excusing (2:15), and of God judging the world on the last day (2:16). In the next chapter, Paul concludes that no one actually can be a doer of the law so as to receive the justification held out in 2:13.[99] There is no one righteous who does what is good (3:10–18), and thus through the *law*, every mouth is silenced and the whole world held *accountable* to God, so that no one will be *justified* in his sight (3:19–20). This holistic sinfulness and accountability to divine judgment does not entail that moral renovation is impossible, but it does preclude the forensic declaration of righteousness—unless, that is, there is some good news from God that makes the seemingly impossible possible, which is precisely Paul's claim in the following chapters. Through Jesus Christ comes a gift that brings justification, which overturns the judgment through Adam that brings condemnation (5:16). As expected, a forensic *condemnation* requires a forensic *justification*. And in 8:33–34, Paul picks up the rhetorical question of Isaiah 50:8: Who will bring a charge against those God has chosen? No one, Paul implies, for since God is the one who *justifies*, who can *condemn*?

In summary, the Greek words for justification are ordinarily forensic in meaning and simply do not communicate moral renovation. Scripture uses these terms in the ordinary way, and this is especially evident in Paul. Thus, Gorman has erred in making justification renovative as well as forensic. It seems correct to conclude that he has allowed a conception of union to determine and control his understanding of justification and thereby has jettisoned one biblical truth for the sake of another. Instead, we ought to affirm both the reality of union with Christ and forensic justification.

Union with Christ and Forensic Justification: Mutually Illuminating

In contrast to Gorman's approach, we may wonder again whether union with Christ and justification are mutually illuminating. In this case, does the forensic character of justification in part explain what union with Christ is, and does union with Christ in part explain what forensic justification is? Yes, I believe both are true.

---

98. Other demonstrative uses of "justify" include Matt. 11:19 and Luke 7:35—and probably James 2:21, 24. In these examples, too, justification cannot refer to moral transformation.

99. I interpret Rom. 2:13 as a statement of how things work under the law, as people are judged according to their own works, and hence as a description of affairs that will never be actualized (for anyone but Christ), given Paul's larger argument in this section (1:18–3:20). For defense of such a view, see Douglas J. Moo, *The Epistle to the Romans*, NICNT (Grand Rapids, MI: Eerdmans, 1996), 125–57; David VanDrunen, *Divine Covenants and Moral Order: A Biblical Theology of Natural Law*, EUSLR (Grand Rapids, MI: Eerdmans, 2014), 233–51. But even if 2:13 describes the final judgment as Christians will actually experience it, as many interpreters think, it does not change the main point I make here concerning the forensic nature of "justify."

First, the forensic character of justification implies that our union with Christ is, in part, forensic in nature. If justification indeed transpires in union with Christ (as indicated at least by Rom. 3:24; 8:1; 2 Cor. 5:21; Gal. 2:17; Phil. 3:9), and if justification is indeed a forensic act, then union is a legal union—whatever else it may also be.[100] In the previous section, we saw that union with Christ is such that it brings us into a substitutionary bond with Christ in his atoning work. It is no surprise, then, that such a union would bring forensic benefits to Christ's people. As indicated above, many Reformed theologians have affirmed just this conclusion.

Second, the reality of union with Christ illuminates forensic justification. A justification that occurs "in Christ" cannot refer to a judicial decree that has arrived on a piece of paper in our mailbox and that results in an abstract, theoretical change of judicial status. Even in our experience with human judicial affairs, we understand that forensic judgments are hardly just abstract and theoretical. To have a guilty sentence overturned in court means a person no longer belongs to the world of prison, the work camp, death row, or whatever—the world that lies under a sentence of condemnation. Instead, such a person belongs to the world of ordinary life, that of home, neighborhood, workplace, civil society—the community of those free from judicial guilt. Something analogous happens in forensic justification thanks to our union with Christ. Christ himself entered this present evil age (Gal. 1:4), bearing the likeness of sinful flesh (Rom. 8:3), and went to the cross where he bore the just curse lying on this age (Gal. 3:13). But in his resurrection, God lifted that curse and justified him (1 Tim. 3:16). In other words, God's declaration of Christ's righteousness transferred him from the present age that lies under condemnation to the age of resurrection, the age to come that exists free from any divine condemnation, a new creation of perfect peace. Believers' justification in union with Christ, therefore, means that the verdict we have received effects the same transfer. The implications of Christ's justification are the implications of our justification (cf. Isa. 50:8; Rom. 8:33–34). Thus, through our declaration of righteousness in Christ, we no longer belong to the present age of condemnation but to the new-creation age of justification. This accomplishes nothing morally transformative per se, but the mutually determining relationship of union and justification entails that justification is forensic in this rich and thick way. This insight will pay dividends again below.

Union with Christ and the Imputation of Christ's Active Obedience

In this section, we turn to the imputation of Christ's active obedience, another standard feature of traditional Reformed soteriology. According to Reformed theologians, Christ not only bore the penalty for believers' sins in his suffering unto death but also obeyed God's law holistically for them throughout all his life. As believers' sins were imputed to Christ, so also his active obedience has been imputed to believers. Thus, in

---

100. For similar conclusions, see Letham, *Union with Christ*, 57; Michael F. Bird, *The Saving Righteousness of God: Studies on Paul, Justification, and the New Perspective*, PBM (Milton Keynes, UK: Paternoster, 2007), 82.

justification, God both forgives believers' sins and reckons them as keepers of his law. From this perspective, justification truly is a declaration of righteousness and not simply a declaration of innocence.

I now consider the claims of two contemporary theologians who have critically engaged the idea of the imputation of Christ's active obedience, N. T. Wright and Michael Bird. While Bird leaves open a place for the doctrine in systematic theology, both Bird and Wright deny that Paul or other New Testament writers teach it, and both claim that union with Christ provides whatever benefit imputed righteousness allegedly brings to believers.

The Challenge

In his book *Justification: God's Plan and Paul's Vision*, Wright defends the forensic nature of justification and thus does not follow Gorman's analysis considered above.[101] One of Wright's chief burdens in this work is to set Paul's doctrine of justification in the context of many other important Pauline themes—especially Jesus as Israel's Messiah, the Abrahamic covenant, the divine law court, and eschatology[102]—and to critique advocates of the "old perspective" on Paul who downplay or ignore the relevance of these themes for justification. There are many things to appreciate in Wright's exegesis and in his attempt to relate justification to other important biblical-theological themes, as well as reasons to doubt the success of several aspects of this project. But I focus here only on his critique of the doctrine of Christ's imputed righteousness, a prevalent motif in the book.

Wright argues that "the righteousness of God," the key theme Paul announces in Romans 1:17, refers to God's faithfulness to the covenant—toward Israel and the whole creation—or as he puts it elsewhere, God's faithfulness to his single redemptive plan initiated in Abraham.[103] With respect to believers being declared righteous in their justification, Wright claims that this is courtroom language and that "righteousness" refers to the status of the vindicated person. "Righteousness" is thus not a moral quality but the status of having "membership in God's true family."[104] This means that "righteousness" cannot be Christ's moral perfection that is reckoned to those who believe in him. On some occasions, Wright speaks in rather caustic tones about this notion of imputed righteousness. For example, he thinks it depends on theological convictions that betray a "proto-Pelagianism" or "self-help moralism" and make Jesus "the ultimate legalist."[105]

On other occasions, however, he acknowledges that the doctrine has a certain insight, but he claims that union with Christ can provide what allegedly comes only through imputed righteousness. "The theological point" of imputed righteousness, he

---

101. E.g., N. T. Wright, *Justification: God's Plan and Paul's Vision* (Downers Grove, IL: IVP Academic, 2009), 12.
102. Wright, *Justification*, 11–12.
103. Wright, *Justification*, 178, 201.
104. Wright, *Justification*, 92, 121.
105. Wright, *Justification*, 230, 232.

comments, is "already taken care of 'in Christ.'"[106] We can now observe how Wright works this out with respect to several texts to which advocates of Christ's imputed righteousness often appeal.

One such text is Philippians 3:9. Wright says that both the structure and content of Philippians indicate that, for Paul, justification occurs "in the Messiah": "The status the Christian possesses is possessed because of that belongingness, that incorporation. This is the great truth to which the sub-Pauline idea of 'the imputation of Christ's righteousness' is truly pointing."[107] Thus, in 3:9, Paul refers to a righteousness *from* God rather than God's own righteousness or Christ's righteousness reckoned to believers. "Incorporation" is the means by which believers enjoy the blessings of justification.[108]

Wright thinks Romans points in the same direction. He finds in 3:25

> the truth to which, at its best, the doctrine of "imputed righteousness" can function as a kind of signpost. God has "put forth" Jesus so that, through his faithful death, all those who belong to him can be regarded as having died. God raised him up so that, through his vindication, all those who belong to him can be regarded as being themselves vindicated.[109]

Along similar lines, he comments from Romans 6 that "it is not the 'righteousness' of Jesus Christ which is 'reckoned' to the believer. It is his death and resurrection. . . . All that the supposed doctrine of the 'imputed righteousness of Christ' has to offer is available instead by Paul under this rubric."[110]

Bird voices many concerns similar to Wright's, although he purports to stake out a mediating position between Wright and traditional Reformed views.[111] He strongly defends the solely forensic character of justification, and he argues that union with Christ has a forensic dimension, since believers are justified through union with the justified Christ.[112] Bird asserts that "the righteousness of God should not be equated with . . . the imputation of righteousness" but refers to God's saving action revealed in the gospel.[113] No New Testament text teaches that Christ's obedience is imputed to believers.[114] Where many have seen imputation of Christ's righteousness, Bird sees union with Christ. In Romans 4, for example, Paul's references to imputation do not inform readers of the "mechanism of *how justification occurs*" but rather *that* justification occurs. Paul does not mention Christ's righteousness here but identifies the ground of justification as Christ's death and resurrection (4:25). God "justifies believers (credits righteousness) because of their union with Christ (raised for our justification)."[115] Likewise, in Romans

---

106. Wright, *Justification*, 217.
107. Wright, *Justification*, 141–42.
108. Wright, *Justification*, 150–51.
109. Wright, *Justification*, 206.
110. Wright, *Justification*, 232–33.
111. Bird, *Saving Righteousness of God*, 1.
112. Bird, *Saving Righteousness of God*, 4, 17, 58.
113. Bird, *Saving Righteousness of God*, 15–16.
114. Bird, *Saving Righteousness of God*, 2–3.
115. Bird, *Saving Righteousness of God*, 76–77.

5:18–19, Paul does not teach or deny imputation but describes "how this righteousness is applied to believers" in terms of "representation and participation."[116] Also, in 2 Corinthians 5:21, says Bird, "becoming God's righteousness is tied to union with Christ, not imputation." To be "in Christ" entails identification with Christ's death and resurrection, and this union is the "sphere or realm of justification."[117]

Bird obviously thinks union with Christ is Paul's way of describing how and why God declares believers righteous. Justification occurs because "believers are *incorporated into the righteousness of Christ*."[118] Through this incorporation, "what God declares true of Jesus is also true of them."[119] He thus understandably wonders "what further role exists for notions of imputation" if indeed "justification can be conceived of through union with the justified Messiah."[120] His ultimate answer is that it is best to speak in terms of incorporated righteousness on the "*exegetical level*" while reserving a place for imputation in systematic theology.[121] In the latter field, theologians may legitimately speak of imputation as implicit in Pauline teaching about Adam and Christ as representatives and about justification by an alien righteousness.[122]

The Case for the Imputation of Christ's Active Obedience

It would not be fair to accuse Wright and Bird of making union with Christ central for soteriology in the way we saw Powers and Gorman doing above. Neither specifically embraces the quest for a center, and Wright explicitly renounces it.[123] Yet Bird does call for making union "the matrix for understanding justification," perhaps suggesting a kind of controlling function for the former. In any case, both of them ask union with Christ to do much of the heavy lifting for the doctrine of justification that Reformation theology has traditionally assigned to the imputation of Christ's righteousness. It is now time, therefore, to consider briefly the exegetical case for the imputation of active obedience and then to ponder whether this may help us develop further the idea of mutual illumination.[124]

We could examine many texts, but in a short survey there may again be no better place to turn than Romans. At the beginning of the first main section of Romans (1:18–3:20), Paul identifies the fundamental problem: the ungodliness and *unrighteousness* of humanity, against which God's wrath has been revealed (1:18). In context, this

---

116. Bird, *Saving Righteousness of God*, 79.
117. Bird, *Saving Righteousness of God*, 84.
118. Bird, *Saving Righteousness of God*, 70.
119. Bird, *Saving Righteousness of God*, 8–9.
120. Bird, *Saving Righteousness of God*, 59.
121. Bird, *Saving Righteousness of God*, 3, 85.
122. Bird, *Saving Righteousness of God*, 70.
123. See Wright, *Justification*, 229.
124. The argument that follows counters the arguments not only of Wright and Bird but also of Marcus Peter Johnson. Johnson argues strongly that union is "the primary, central, and fundamental reality of salvation." *One with Christ*, 29. And as mentioned earlier, Johnson claims that *union itself* is the ground or basis of justification. See *One with Christ*, 72, 75. He does not deny the imputation of Christ's righteousness but speaks of this imputation as a consequence of already being declared righteous on the basis of union: "God declares us righteous because *Christ's* righteousness has become ours, and therefore he imputes it to us as such." *One with Christ*, 72. My argument that follows seeks to show that Christ's righteousness itself is the basis or ground of justification and that the imputation of Christ's righteousness is what accomplishes the justification. Scripture speaks of believers being justified *in* or *through* union but not on the basis of the union.

unrighteousness must be moral impurity, not a lack of proper status, for Paul proceeds to lay out the evidence for his claim by mentioning idolatry, sexual immorality, envy, murder, arrogance, and "all manner of unrighteousness" (1:21–32). This initial salvo implies that *righteousness* must be what humanity lacks and needs—righteousness consisting in moral purity. Paul confirms this suggestion in the next chapter by stating that one must *do the law* in order to be justified (2:13). To be declared righteous, one's moral record needs to match the law's standard.[125] And Paul confirms it again when he concludes this larger section with the verdict that no one will be justified before God by his or her works (3:20), since no one is *righteous* (3:10)—that is, everyone falls into all sorts of moral degradation (3:11–18) and thus stands accountable to God (3:19).

In 3:21, Paul begins to explain the good news in answer to this profound problem. The key problem is *unrighteousness* (1:18), and the key solution, appropriately, is *righteousness*, namely, the righteousness of God (3:21). Since the problem is *moral* unrighteousness, we expect the solution to be moral righteousness—not just a moral innocence but a real righteousness that accomplishes the requirements of the law (2:13). This is indeed where Paul takes us.

Paul first addresses the problem of unrighteousness and the wrath of God it provokes: God has put forward Christ as a "propitiation by his blood" (3:25). If God's *wrath* stands against his people (1:18), then *propitiation* is exactly what they need. Christ's blood evidently cleansed the guilt of their moral unrighteousness and quenched God's wrath. But purging the guilt of impurity, as crucial as it is, does not explain how God can actually declare sinful people morally *righteous*. Thus, it is no surprise that Paul promptly extends the discussion. In chapter 4, he turns to Abraham. Although his Jewish compatriots viewed Abraham as the great righteous man, Paul calls him "ungodly" and shows that he also needed to be justified by faith (4:1–5). Paul explains that when a person works for something, he receives a reward as his due, not as a matter of grace (4:4). We know this is true in ordinary life, and it also sounds like what Paul said in 2:13. But Abraham did not receive his reward in this way; rather, he was justified as an ungodly man (4:5). This makes no sense initially, for God hates the idea of justifying the wicked (Ex. 23:7; Prov. 17:15). So how could God do such a seemingly outrageous thing? The next verse tells us: God *imputes righteousness* apart from works (Rom. 4:6). Thus, as we would expect, God not only removes the guilt of moral unrighteousness but also imputes moral righteousness, which provides the just ground for him to justify sinners, that is, to declare them not merely innocent but righteous.[126]

---

125. See note 99 for comments on this interpretation of Rom. 2:13.
126. A number of writers have objected to reading Paul's statement about the imputation of righteousness in the straightforward way I do here. An important reason why, for some of them, is the fact that Paul uses the same terminology of "impute" in the same context but in these instances speaks of *faith* being imputed *unto righteousness* (Rom. 4:5, 9; see Gen. 15:6). E.g., see Robert H. Gundry, "The Nonimputation of Christ's Righteousness," in *Justification: What's at Stake in the Current Debates*, ed. Mark A. Husbands and Daniel J. Treier (Downers Grove, IL: InterVarsity Press, 2004), 17–45. The presence of these two ways of speaking in the same text does create challenging questions that any exegesis of Romans 4 needs to address. But it seems to me that there is a fairly simple solution. Paul uses these two ways of speaking about imputation elsewhere in Romans, and they evidently mean rather different things. On the one hand, as Paul writes of God imputing righteousness (4:6) or righteousness being imputed (4:11), so also he writes of God *imputing sin* (4:8) and of *wages being imputed* (4:4). This is evidently a straightforward or literal way of speaking. Sin is the kind of thing that

Yet there is still an element missing in Paul's argument thus far. Paul has said that God imputes righteousness to the believer but has not explained what or whose righteousness this is—although it must have something to do with Christ (3:21–22). The following chapter answers this lingering question. While Paul's covenant theology takes us back to Abraham in chapter 4, it takes us back even further in chapter 5, to the first man, Adam.[127] Here Paul works out an extended comparison of Adam and Christ as two great representative figures. He tells readers that in Jesus we receive a gift by grace (5:15) and that this gift brings justification (5:16)—this reminds us of 4:4–5: those who are justified by faith receive it by grace rather than as their due.

But what is this gift? The next verse explains that it is a gift *of righteousness*, which comes through Christ unto eschatological life (5:17).[128] This, too, reminds us of chapter 4, where Paul said that justification by grace involves the imputation of righteousness (4:6). Thus, this gift of righteousness in 5:17 must be the righteousness that Paul said was imputed in 4:6. But 5:18 makes the picture even clearer: the gift of righteousness through Christ refers to an "act of righteousness," that is, something that Christ has accomplished (rather than his eternal divine attribute of righteousness). And then 5:19 makes it more specific still: Christ's "obedience" has made the many righteous. Unlike the rest of us, Christ was a doer of the law, the obedient one, the one who performed moral righteousness. The righteousness imputed to believers (4:6) must refer to Christ's righteous obedience. The moral righteousness we lacked has been provided by Christ. The "righteousness of God" for our justification is the gift of Christ's righteousness imputed to us.[129]

Union with Christ and the Imputation of Christ's Righteousness: Mutually Illuminating

What Bird and especially Wright have done is allow union with Christ to swallow up at least one important aspect of the biblical doctrine of justification: the imputation of

---

is literally accounted to a moral ledger, and wages are the kind of thing that is literally accounted to a financial ledger. So, too, righteousness is the kind of thing literally accounted to a moral ledger. But on the other hand, Paul uses the expression "X is imputed unto Y" in a rather different way. He says that uncircumcision is imputed unto circumcision (2:26) and that the children of promise are imputed unto offspring/seed (9:8). By these expressions, Paul seems to mean that God sees one thing (one kind of people) and regards them as something else: God sees the uncircumcised person who keeps the law and regards him as circumcised, and God sees the children of promise and regards them as the true seed of Abraham. In light of this, when Paul says that faith is imputed unto righteousness (4:5, 9), he evidently means that God sees people of faith and regards them as righteous. But there is no reason to think that this expression nullifies the straightforward statements about the imputation of righteousness. Both ways that Paul speaks express an important truth, and they are perfectly harmonious. God imputes righteousness, and he also sees believers and regards them as righteous. For a response to Gundry's article cited above that defends the imputation of Christ's righteousness but from a different angle, see D. A. Carson, "The Vindication of Imputation: On Fields of Discourse and Semantic Fields," in Husbands and Treier, *Justification: What's at Stake*, 46–78.

127. While I agree with Wright's contention that Paul's covenant theology is important for his conception of justification, I believe Wright does not press his insight far enough. His analysis treats the Abrahamic covenant as foundational rather than seeing covenant theology as ultimately rooted in God's prelapsarian covenant with Adam. For Wright's views on the foundational character of the Abrahamic covenant, see, e.g., *Justification*, 216–17, 250–51. I also note that, in his treatment of Rom. 5:15–21, Wright says nothing about Adam, even though Adam is so important to this text; see *Justification*, 227–29.

128. The author of Hebrews seems to have something similar in mind in referring to righteousness as something *inherited* according to faith (11:7). An inheritance is a gift, not self-achieved.

129. For a recent, thorough argument in favor of this conclusion, and against Wright's conception of the "righteousness of God" as his covenant faithfulness, see Charles Lee Irons, *The Righteousness of God: A Lexical Examination of the Covenant-Faithfulness Interpretation*, WUNT, 2nd ser., vol. 386 (Tübingen: Mohr Siebeck, 2015), chap. 6.

Christ's active obedience. In some texts, Paul speaks about believers becoming righteous "in Christ" without mentioning imputation explicitly (e.g., 2 Cor. 5:21; Phil. 3:9). In other texts, Paul speaks of God imputing righteousness to believers without using language of union or participation (Rom. 4:6, 11). Rather than ignoring one set of texts or allowing one set to control the other, let us now reflect on how these two ideas—union with Christ and Christ's imputed righteousness—may be mutually defining and illuminating.

On the one hand, the doctrine of Christ's imputed righteousness indicates that union with Christ is in part an imputative union. Previous discussion has already suggested that our union is in part legal, and now we can further specify: through this union, God imputes the active obedience of his Son to believers that they, too, may be reckoned righteous. When thinkers such as Bird or Wright claim that union with Christ explains why believers are declared righteous, they are correct—texts such as 2 Corinthians 5:21 and Philippians 3:9 say exactly this. But to make this claim is to beg the next question: How does it work? What kind of a bond with Christ explains how *his* righteousness can be the basis for *our* justification? Scripture's answer is that a legal, imputative union is the kind of bond that does this. God imputes righteousness to believers (Rom. 4:6), which is a gift of Christ's righteous obedience (5:15–19), such that there is now no condemnation for those who are "in Christ Jesus" (8:1).

On the other hand, the fact that imputation occurs through union with Christ indicates that the righteousness imputed is not abstract or impersonal but a personal righteousness that guarantees God's justice when he justifies. If one hundred dollars is credited to my checking account, I do not care at all which collection of one hundred dollars that is. It makes no difference which pieces of green paper from the United States Treasury stand behind it, what mint printed them, or which people owned them previously. That one-hundred-dollar credit to my account is entirely abstract and impersonal. But that is not how the imputation of Christ's righteousness works. God imputes righteousness to believers, a righteousness that consists in perfect obedience to his law. Yet believers can never be indifferent as to what righteousness that is in particular. God credits to them a specific righteousness, the personal obedience of his Son, the God-man. It is not just any righteousness but the "righteousness of God." Believers are personally united to the one whose righteousness appears in their account. This is no accounting trick. There is no fiat money or debased currency involved. This is a real righteousness that believers claim as their own through an everlasting union with the one who was obedient unto death. Allegations of a legal fiction are thus preposterous.

Union with Christ, Justification, and the *Ordo Salutis*

As we reach the last main section of the chapter, I have now addressed the challenges, presented in the name of union with Christ, to the biblical doctrine of justification itself. But one final issue remains, the relation of union with Christ to the *ordo salutis*. As described above, Reformed theologians have understood justification to be one of a number of soteriological blessings that stand in established relations to one another. One of the relations in which these theologians were most interested is that between justification and sanctification. They not only distinguished (without separating) these two blessings but also insisted that justification precedes sanctification. They often noted that this precedence was not so much chronological in nature as theological. Justification is foundational for sanctification, while the opposite is not true. Justification is in some sense a cause of sanctification, but sanctification is in no way a cause of justification.

In this section, I discuss challenges to this *ordo salutis* prosecuted in the name of union with Christ. The theologians with whom I interact here affirm all the aspects of the traditional Reformed doctrine of justification itself. The issues are still important, however, because they and I wish to understand the foundation of the sanctified Christian life as Scripture teaches it and also wish to be able to answer as accurately as possible the perennial complaint that the Reformed doctrine of justification promotes indifference to holiness.

The Challenge

Richard Gaffin and those who seek to follow and extend his analysis believe there is no tension between the forensic and participatory aspects of salvation. They regard union with Christ as having a legal dimension and regard justification and other forensic benefits as coming in union with Christ.[130] Therefore, they would surely concur with my main claims thus far. But Gaffin also affirms a notion of which I have been critical in previous pages, namely, the notion that there is a *central* idea in the soteriology of Paul or Scripture in general. Gaffin finds such a center in Paul's doctrine of the believer's union with the exalted Christ. Although he warns against pressing the idea of centrality "rigidly or too narrowly," he finds it "difficult to deny" that there is a center, found in Christ's death and resurrection.[131] Elsewhere, he refers to union with the exalted Christ variously as having the "controlling place" and as "the central truth," "the key . . . reality," "the nub," and "the essence" of Paul's soteriology.[132] Gaffin's view of union does not jettison the doctrines of substitutionary atonement, forensic justification, or the imputation of Christ's active obedience. But he has treated union as a starting point for reflection in such a way that challenges the traditional Reformed doctrine of the *ordo salutis*, in which justification stands in established relationship to a number of other soteriological blessings. In a couple of recent essays, Gaffin does speak in a more positive way about the *ordo salutis*, suggesting agreement with many of my concerns here but without affirming everything I am saying.[133] Whatever the best

---

130. For example, see Richard B. Gaffin Jr., *Resurrection and Redemption: A Study in Paul's Soteriology* (Phillipsburg, NJ: Presbyterian and Reformed, 1987), 40; Gaffin, *By Faith, Not by Sight: Paul and the Order of Salvation* (Waynesboro, GA: Paternoster, 2006), 41; Tipton, "Union with Christ," 38.

131. Gaffin, *By Faith, Not by Sight*, 21.

132. Richard B. Gaffin Jr., "The Work of Christ Applied," in *Christian Dogmatics: Reformed Theology for the Church Catholic*, ed. Michael Allen and Scott R. Swain (Grand Rapids, MI: Baker Academic, 2016), 286; Gaffin, *By Faith, Not by Sight*, 24, 36, 43. See also Gaffin, *Resurrection and Redemption*, 135.

133. When Gaffin offered his most critical assessment of the Reformed *ordo salutis*, he stressed that his analysis was "partial and provisional"; see *Resurrection and Redemption*, 136. In his most lengthy revisiting of these issues, several decades later, he speaks positively of the *ordo salutis*, but he uses the term simply as a synonym for the application of salvation generally and not in the more technical sense that he critiqued earlier; see *By Faith, Not by Sight*, 18–19. I will

way to harmonize his various statements, his work has provoked debates within the Reformed community about the meaning and viability of the *ordo salutis* in light of union with Christ. I briefly describe some of the pertinent evidence from his writings but leave it open as to just how much disagreement there is between his views and mine—less rather than more, I hope.

Gaffin has written that the traditional Reformed *ordo salutis* is distinguished by its insistence that justification, adoption, and sanctification "are separate acts." But Paul, he continues, viewed them "not as distinct acts but as distinct aspects of a single act," that is, union with the resurrected Christ. He identifies two "significant" differences between the two conceptions. One is that the allegedly Pauline view avoids "the problem that faces the traditional *ordo salutis*" in needing "to establish the pattern of priorities (temporal? logical? causal?) which obtains among these acts."[134] It is not clear to me why needing to establish the pattern of priorities is a problem in need of solution, since earlier Reformed theologians seemed to think that establishing the pattern of priorities is a necessary task for Reformed soteriology and that the need to do so was precisely the point of developing the *ordo salutis* idea in the first place. In any case, the second difference between the two conceptions Gaffin identifies is "even more basic and crucial," thus expressing the heart of his concern: the *ordo salutis* idea "is confronted with the insoluble difficulty of trying to explain how these acts are related to the act of being joined *existentially* to Christ." Here Gaffin's understanding of union with Christ drives his critique of the *ordo salutis*:

> If at the point of inception this union is prior (and therefore involves the possession in the inner man of all that Christ is as resurrected), what need is there for other acts? Conversely, if the other acts are in some sense prior, is not union improperly subordinated and its biblical significance severely attenuated, to say the least?

By definition, then, the reality of union with Christ eliminates the viability of the traditional *ordo salutis*. Gaffin states, "The first and, in the final analysis, the only question for the Pauline *ordo* concerns the point at which and the conditions under which incorporation with the life-giving Spirit takes place."[135]

With respect to justification and sanctification specifically, Gaffin writes that they are "indissolubly linked as different facets of the single act of being raised (incorporated) with Christ."[136] Other writers following Gaffin's analysis seem to express the same idea through the notion of *simultaneity*.[137] Elsewhere, embracing Calvin's view (as he

---

consider below a couple of more recent examples in which he affirms an *ordo salutis* in the more technical sense. Professor Gaffin has told me in personal correspondence that he regards these more recent comments as clarifying but also as in complete continuity with his earlier writings.

134. Gaffin, *Resurrection and Redemption*, 138.
135. Gaffin, *Resurrection and Redemption*, 138–39.
136. Gaffin, *Resurrection and Redemption*, 131.
137. Lane Tipton, for example, sees union with Christ as furnishing "the organizing structure in terms of which the Spirit applies to believers all of the realized redemptive benefits in Christ distinctly, inseparably, simultaneously, and eschatologically." With approval, Tipton says Calvin regarded justification and sanctification as "distinct-yet-inseparable realities, which are received simultaneously in the believer's union with Christ." Tipton contrasts this view with Lutheran theology, which makes sanctification follow justification as its effect. See "Union with Christ," 24, 40, 42–43.

understands it), Gaffin writes that "the relative 'ordo' or priority of justification and sanctification is indifferent theologically."[138]

More recently, Gaffin has apologized for lack of clarity in statements such as this expressing the theological indifference of the order or priority of justification and sanctification, and he affirms that "justification is prior to sanctification in the sense that the latter, as a life-long and imperfect process, follows the former as complete and perfect from the inception of the Christian life."[139] In another more recent essay, Gaffin briefly describes the *ordo salutis* as he sees it: it begins with the effectual calling that unites to Christ, upon which a person believes, and by this faith a person experiences justification, adoption, and "definitive" sanctification simultaneously, and from there sanctification and perseverance continue on toward glorification.[140]

The Case for an Ordered Relationship between Justification and Sanctification

The point at issue here is obviously not whether justification and other soteriological blessings transpire in Christ. Nor does the "simultaneous" terminology quite get at it either, since there is an indisputable sense in which God bestows justification and sanctification together rather than as chronologically distinct stages of Christian experience. The question is whether justification and sanctification stand in an established relationship in which the former is foundational for the latter in some important way. Or does a sound theology of union with Christ make such a notion problematic? Gaffin affirms that justification precedes sanctification in the important sense that the former is a once-for-all act that is perfect and complete upon the first act of faith, while the latter is an ongoing experience proceeding from there, but he does not seem to affirm that justification is a cause of sanctification in any sense, as many of the Reformed theologians considered above thought. I now argue that there is such an established relationship and that justification is foundational for sanctification in the sense that sanctification is a result, purpose, and evidence for justification—whereas sanctification is in no sense foundational for justification. Then I conclude by reflecting on how union with Christ and the *ordo salutis* are mutually illuminating.

To begin, the fact that sanctification is not foundational for justification is clear. Scripture often teaches that people are not justified on the basis of their own works or virtues. God's renovative work, in other words, is not the ground for his justifying verdict. Perhaps no single biblical statement makes this as clear as Romans 4:5: God justifies "the ungodly." Believers are not justified as the sanctified. Sanctification can have no soteriological precedence to justification.

But justification does have soteriological precedence to sanctification in Scripture. As I have focused on Romans above, I continue to do so here. Following his extended

---

138. Richard B. Gaffin Jr., "Biblical Theology and the Westminster Standards," *WTJ* 65, no. 2 (2003): 177.
139. Richard B. Gaffin Jr., "A Response to John Fesko's Review," *Ordained Servant* 18 (2009): 105–7. Gaffin explains that his statement about theological indifference was meant to apply only to the order of teaching and not to the actual order of the application of salvation.
140. Gaffin, "Work of Christ Applied," 286.

explanation of justification in 3:21–5:21, Paul raises the obvious question whether his doctrine permits or even encourages people to continue in sin, and he emphatically denies it (6:1). Crucial to Paul's response in this new section of the epistle is the fact that believers have died, been buried, and risen with Christ: because of this, we have died to sin and walk in newness of life (6:2–4). Sanctification thus comes in union with Christ. But as his argument proceeds, Paul makes clear that sanctification also comes as a result of justification. It is worth noting what a powerful answer Paul provides to the hypothetical objection with which Romans 6 begins. It is not just that justification by faith is compatible with sanctification (which would be a genuine, though thin, answer to the objection) but that justification by faith is absolutely necessary for sanctification and even guarantees its presence.[141]

In Romans 6:14, for example, Paul states, "Sin will have no dominion over you, since you are not under law but under grace." Paul implies that sanctification is a *result* of justification. Why is it, Paul imagines someone saying, that sin has no dominion over us, that is, that we now walk in holiness as the sanctified? He responds: because you are not under the law. That is, it is because you are justified, for a person becomes no longer under the law when he is justified in Christ, by faith, through grace, not by works (3:19–24; see Gal. 3:10–14). Thus, the reality of justification provides proof that sanctification is present. This claim suggests that justification necessarily results in sanctification. One might object that Paul's point still holds even if justification and sanctification are simply simultaneous realities with no relationship of cause or foundation. But another statement shortly thereafter shows that this cannot be what Paul had in mind. In Romans 7:6, he writes, "But now we are released from the law, having died to that which held us captive, so that we serve in the new way of the Spirit and not in the old way of the written code." In short, believers are released from the law, "with the result that" (ὥστε) they serve in the newness of the Spirit. Release from the law is what happens in justification, and serving in the Spirit is the experience of sanctification. Justification thus *results in* sanctification. And if sanctification is a result of justification, justification must be in some sense a cause of sanctification.

And sanctification is not just a result of justification but also its *purpose*. Two verses earlier Paul wrote, "You also have died to the law through the body of Christ, so that you may belong to another, to him who has been raised from the dead, in order that we

---

141. Thus, I believe Tipton is incorrect to say that "Romans 6 is not about justification." "Union with Christ," 47. Romans 6–7 is not *only* about justification, but justification remains crucial for Paul's discussion of the sanctified life in these chapters. Tipton here says that Romans 6 is about "definitive sanctification" rather than justification, picking up on John Murray's terminology. In a more detailed interaction with Gaffin and Tipton, I would have to treat definitive sanctification at some length. I am not convinced that the category of definitive sanctification is necessary, either to account for Paul's discussion in Romans 6–7 or for Reformed soteriology in general. Gaffin and Tipton seem to treat definitive sanctification as transformative; e.g., see Gaffin, "Work of Christ Applied," 286; Tipton, "Union with Christ," 47. I am not entirely sure how to understand everything Murray writes on the topic, but he gives the believer's death to sin in Romans 6 an explicitly forensic meaning in his commentary on Romans; see *The Epistle to the Romans: The English Text with Introduction, Exposition and Notes*, NICNT (Grand Rapids, MI: Eerdmans, 1968), 1:222. He also speaks of definitive sanctification as a breach with the realm in which sin reigns, which also sounds forensic rather than transformative; see "Definitive Sanctification," in *The Collected Writings of John Murray*, vol. 2, *Select Lectures in Systematic Theology* (Edinburgh: Banner of Truth, 1977), 279. I believe Murray is correct to suggest that Paul teaches a definitive, forensic breach with the realm in which sin reigns, but I have argued above that this is something that happens in justification itself—as many of the Reformed theologians surveyed above also affirmed. Thus, I suspect that "definitive sanctification" is an unnecessary category and that it adds more confusion than clarity to Reformed soteriology.

may bear fruit for God" (7:4). To die to the law is justification, and to bear fruit for God occurs in sanctification. But this means that one of the very purposes of justification—"in order that" (ἵνα)—is that believers may live the sanctified life.[142] Other texts indicate that sanctification is also the *evidence* or *manifestation* of justification. In Luke 7:47, for example, Christ says of the sinful woman, "I tell you, her sins, which are many, are forgiven—for she loved much. But he who is forgiven little, loves little." In context, Jesus's explanatory statement, "for she loved much," is providing not the reason *why* she was forgiven but evidence *that* she was forgiven. In the preceding parable, Jesus had explained that the debtor who has a great sum forgiven will love his creditor more than the one who has a small sum forgiven (7:41–43). Thus also, this woman had her great debt of sin freely forgiven, and her great love for Christ made that manifest. Her sanctification, in other words, gave evidence of her justification.[143]

One might wonder how all this can be true when justification is forensic rather than transformative. To put it starkly, how can justification necessarily result in sanctification and be one of its causes if justification is purely legal?[144] The previous discussion of how union with Christ illuminates the character of forensic justification likely provides an important part of the answer. There we saw that the person justified in union with Christ receives not a bare, theoretical judicial verdict but a verdict that transfers her from this present evil age (an age lying under condemnation) to the new-creation age to come (an age of justification, in which all stands right before God). And those who belong to the new creation have a right to the benefits of heavenly citizenship. Among the greatest benefits is the indwelling Spirit, the Spirit of holiness who puts to death the old man and brings to life the new. This explains Paul's claim that the one who is released from the law serves in the newness of the Spirit *as a result*.[145] A more thorough examination of this topic would also require discussion of how Sin (personified) makes use of the law as its special tool to beat down those who are under the law, that is, those who are not justified. "The power of sin is the law" (1 Cor. 15:56). In fact, Paul turns to this theme in Romans 7 immediately after the verses we just considered (7:8–11). When a person is justified and thus released from the law's condemnation, Sin loses its access to this choice weapon, and the way of sanctification lies newly open.

Union with Christ and the *Ordo Salutis*: Mutually Illuminating

In Romans 6–7 and elsewhere in Scripture, justification and sanctification stand in an established relationship within the *ordo salutis* in which justification is foundational

---

142. Similar reasoning seems to be at work also in Rom. 8:3–4; Gal. 3:13–14; 5:13.
143. In James 2:14–26, a person's sanctification also gives evidence of his justification by faith.
144. Johnson thinks it "strange" that Reformed theologians would speak of sanctification as an "effect" of justification or of justification as a "ground" of sanctification. He suggests that this is the same as saying that justification "includes" sanctification, and thus it blurs the lines between Protestant and Roman Catholic understandings of justification. *One with Christ*, 112–13. As the survey above shows, however, Reformed theologians have been doing this "strange" thing throughout the history of Reformed Christianity, and it is difficult to believe that so many would have failed to understand their own justification doctrine. This section provides just one example of how justification can be foundational for sanctification without making the former transformative.
145. As mentioned above, for similar comments, see Turretin, *Institutes*, 2:647; Brown, *Systematic Theology*, 371, 432; Hodge, *Systematic Theology*, 3:171.

for sanctification. Rather than allowing a conception of union with Christ to call this into question, we should seek again to understand union and justification as mutually determining and illuminating.

First, the reality of an *ordo salutis* sheds light on the nature of union with Christ. What is union? In part, it is a bond in which multiple soteriological blessings flow to believers *in relation to each other*. The believer is justified and sanctified in union with Christ, in such a way that sanctification is a result, purpose, and evidence of justification.[146] The believer is justified and sanctified in union with Christ, in such a way that the forensic aspects of union precede the sanctifying aspect.[147] Union with Christ is an orderly union.

Second, the reality of union with Christ indicates that the *ordo salutis* describes a collection of gifts that bind us to their giver. The benefits of the *ordo salutis* do not unfold in a mechanical way. It is no deistic process in which God knocks over the first domino (effectual calling?) and the rest of the soteriological blessings tumble over in turn. Instead, each and every one is a blessing of Christ by his Spirit. Each draws believers into fellowship with their Lord. Furthermore, union with Christ illuminates the *ordo salutis* by demonstrating the ultimate unity of all its blessings. While the concept of the *ordo salutis* emphasizes the distinctions among the blessings and their interrelationships, union with Christ points to the single source and abiding power of them all.

Conclusion

Reformed theologians have long embraced a rich doctrine of union with Christ alongside their traditional doctrine of justification. Although Reformed theologians of previous generations did not use terminology such as "mutually determining and illuminating," their basic approach to soteriology seems to reflect such a dynamic. They made neither union with Christ nor justification a central doctrine so as to control or determine the nature of the other. They affirmed union with Christ even as they taught the substitutionary atonement, forensic justification, the imputation of Christ's active obedience, and an *ordo salutis* in which justification is foundational for sanctification. Despite a trend in contemporary theology to allow union to determine justification's meaning or function so as to reject one or more dimensions of biblical, Reformed soteriology, we have good biblical and theological reason to avoid such a move. We need a rich doctrine of union with Christ to do justice to Scripture's doctrine of justification. But the reverse is also true.

---

146. Thus, I question the helpfulness of saying that all soteriological blessings come to believers "immediately" in Christ; e.g., see Sinclair B. Ferguson, *The Holy Spirit*, CCT (Downers Grove, IL: InterVarsity Press, 1996), 102. Ferguson is trying to communicate the truth that all soteriological blessings are from Christ and bind us to him. But in an important sense, Christ by his Spirit sanctifies believers through the mediation of his (own!) work of justification and adoption.

147. This point needs some elaboration and qualification. Adoption, a forensic act, also precedes sanctification in the *ordo salutis* (e.g., see Rom. 8:14–15). However, regeneration (like sanctification) is a transformative act that precedes faith (and hence justification), and thus, not all the Spirit's transformative work follows justification and adoption.

Recommended Resources

Bird, Michael F. *The Saving Righteousness of God: Studies on Paul, Justification, and the New Perspective*. Paternoster Biblical Monographs. Milton Keynes, UK: Paternoster, 2007.

Campbell, Constantine R. *Paul and Union with Christ: An Exegetical and Theological Study*. Grand Rapids, MI: Zondervan, 2012.

Fesko, J. V. *Beyond Calvin: Union with Christ and Justification in Early Modern Reformed Theology (1517–1700)*. Reformed Historical Theology 20. Göttingen: Vandenhoeck & Ruprecht, 2012.

Gaffin, Richard B., Jr. *Resurrection and Redemption: A Study in Paul's Soteriology*. Phillipsburg, NJ: Presbyterian and Reformed, 1987.

Gorman, Michael J. *Inhabiting the Cruciform God: Kenosis, Justification, and Theosis in Paul's Narrative Soteriology*. Grand Rapids, MI: Eerdmans, 2009.

Husbands, Mark A., and Daniel J. Treier, eds. *Justification: What's at Stake in the Current Debates*. Downers Grove, IL: InterVarsity Press, 2004.

Irons, Charles Lee. *The Righteousness of God: A Lexical Examination of the Covenant-Faithfulness Interpretation*. Wissenschaftliche Untersuchungen zum Neuen Testament, 2nd ser., vol. 386. Tübingen: Mohr Siebeck, 2015.

Johnson, Marcus Peter. *One with Christ: An Evangelical Theology of Salvation*. Wheaton, IL: Crossway, 2013.

Letham, Robert. *Union with Christ: In Scripture, History, and Theology*. Phillipsburg, NJ: P&R, 2011.

Macaskil, Grant. *Union with Christ in the New Testament*. Oxford: Oxford University Press, 2013.

Powers, Daniel G. *Salvation through Participation: An Examination of the Notion of the Believer's Corporate Unity with Christ in Early Christian Soteriology*. Contributions to Biblical Exegesis and Theology 29. Leuven: Peeters, 2001.

Wright, N. T. *Justification: God's Plan and Paul's Vision*. Downers Grove, IL: IVP Academic, 2009.

16

Faith Works

Properly Understanding the Relationship between Justification and Sanctification

R. LUCAS STAMPS

The relationship between justification and sanctification is not an afterthought to the Reformation-era debates over the *articulus stantis et cadentis ecclesiae* ("the article on which the church stands or falls"). To introduce the doctrine of *sanctification* is not to change the subject from the material principle of the Reformation, the doctrine of *justification*. Nor is it merely an exploration of the practical or pastoral implications of a logically separate theological judgment concerning the doctrine of justification itself. Instead, there is a sense in which the relationship between these two doctrines constitutes the central distinction that must be grasped in order to understand the very heart of Reformation soteriology. In his classic work on the history of the doctrine of justification, Alister McGrath makes this precise point: "The essential feature of the Reformation doctrine of justification is that a deliberate and systematic distinction is made between *justification* and *regeneration*."[1] McGrath is using the term *regeneration* here in its Reformation-era sense, which included the whole work of God in renewing fallen humanity and which tracks closely with what came to be known in Reformed dogmatics as *sanctification*.[2] The failure to distinguish God's forensic declaration in

---

1. Alister E. McGrath, *Iustitia Dei: A History of the Christian Doctrine of Justification*, 2nd ed. (Cambridge: Cambridge University Press, 1998), 186.
2. The term *regeneration* later became narrowed in Reformed dogmatics to denote only the initial renewing work of God, by which he brings about the conversion of a sinner, and *sanctification* was preserved for the ongoing renewal of the believer's life and conduct by God's Word and Spirit. For a standard Reformed treatment of these doctrines, see John Murray, *Redemption Accomplished and Applied* (Grand Rapids, MI: Eerdmans, 1955).

justification, based on the alien righteousness of Christ, and God's transformative work in sanctification, which produces actual righteousness in the lives of believers, was the fundamental soteriological problem targeted by the great sixteenth-century Reformers.

In John Calvin's coinage, these two doctrines—justification and sanctification—constitute the *duplex gratia*, the "double grace" of union with Christ. They must be distinguished but never separated. To belong by faith to Christ—the God-man and Mediator in whom divinity and humanity are hypostatically united—is to receive Christ himself and all his benefits. No one is justified who will not also be sanctified. Christ alone is the basis of justification, and perseverance in good works is the necessary and evidentiary fruit of belonging to Christ. At the same time, the assurance of justification is not held in suspense until this sanctification is fully accomplished, because the judicial declaration of justification is based entirely on the imputed righteousness of Christ. This imputed righteousness ever remains, as Martin Luther stressed, *alien* to the believer—it is not intrinsically our own but can be found only (as regards justification) outside ourselves in Christ, with whom we are covenantally united by faith. Thus, properly relating justification and sanctification was one of the chief tasks of Reformation theology, with soteriological, Christological, and pastoral implications.

This chapter seeks to explore the relationship between justification and sanctification from the perspective of Scripture, in dialogue with historical and contemporary perspectives, and with a view to contemporary theological construction. The argument set forth here is that justification and sanctification are properly related not only when they are connected to the integrative theme of union with Christ but also when they are explicitly related to one another. To anticipate the theological conclusion, it is argued that even within the category of union with Christ, the decretal and forensic (legal) principles have logical priority over the transformative (mystical) principle. Therefore, justification can be said to have a kind of priority over sanctification even as both are inseparable benefits that accrue to believers by virtue of their faith union with Christ.[3] In order to defend this thesis, the chapter proceeds in three steps. First, we begin with some preliminary biblical and theological definitions of the principal terms in the discussion: *justification*, *sanctification*, and *union with Christ*. Second, we explore three broad trends in the historical and contemporary literature on this issue: theologies that tend to conflate justification and sanctification, theologies that tend to separate justification and sanctification, and theologies that seek to integrate justification and sanctification. Even within the last category, there are differing approaches when it comes to the question of prioritization. So the final section of the chapter seeks to defend an extended proposition (in the form of five theological axioms) that harvests the principal tenets of Reformation soteriology, with special attention given to the thought of John Calvin.

---

3. This thesis is hardly groundbreaking, and yet it wades into controverted territory among Reformed dogmaticians. As we will see in the contemporary literature, Michael Horton, J. V. Fesko, and Todd Billings (among others) have made the case for the priority of the forensic within union with Christ, while Richard Gaffin and Mark Garcia (among others) have argued against prioritization within union.

Preliminary Terminological Clarifications

There is a sense in which any initial attempt to define the terms of this debate involves a degree of question begging. For example, to define justification in exclusively forensic terms is already to take a position on a key dispute during the Reformation era. But in the interest of full disclosure, the following preliminary definitions are offered as a way of introducing the theological landscape that must be traversed in determining the relationship between these crucial doctrines. While several soteriological doctrines are implicated in this discussion (including election, regeneration, effectual calling, and adoption), we focus our attention on three primary terms: *justification*, *sanctification*, and *union with Christ*.

In both Lutheran and Reformed dogmatics, justification is defined as a legal declaration of God whereby he forgives sinners and reckons them to be righteous solely for the sake of Christ's righteousness, which is imputed to them by faith alone, apart from any works of righteousness on their part. Consider, for example, the definitions of justification provided by two of the most revered confessions of the post-Reformation era, the Lutheran Formula of Concord and the Reformed Westminster Confession of Faith, respectively:

> Accordingly, we believe, teach, and confess that our righteousness before God is (this very thing), that God forgives us our sins out of pure grace, without any work, merit, or worthiness of ours preceding, present, or following, that He presents and imputes to us the righteousness of Christ's obedience, on account of which righteousness we are received into grace by God, and regarded as righteous.[4]

> Those whom God effectually calleth, he also freely justifieth: not by infusing righteousness into them, but by pardoning their sins, and by accounting and accepting their persons as righteous; not for anything wrought in them, or done by them, but for Christ's sake alone; nor by imputing faith itself, the act of believing, or any other evangelical obedience to them, as their righteousness; but by imputing the obedience and satisfaction of Christ unto them, they receiving and resting on him and his righteousness, by faith; which faith they have not of themselves, it is the gift of God.[5]

Note that both confessional symbols define justification as (1) the forgiveness of sins and (2) the imputation of Christ's righteousness. Thus, justification means to *declare* righteous, not to *make* righteous. Calvin's view is in fundamental agreement with these later formulations.[6] He defines justification "simply as the acceptance with which God

---

4. Formula of Concord, 3.4, "Formula of Concord," The Book of Concord: The Confessions of the Lutheran Church, accessed September 6, 2018, http://bookofconcord.org/fc-ep.php.
5. Westminster Confession of Faith, 11.1, "Confession of Faith," Orthodox Presbyterian Church, accessed September 6, 2018, https://www.opc.org/wcf.html.
6. Adjudicating the "Calvin vs. the Calvinists" and the "Luther vs. the Lutherans" debates lies beyond the scope of this essay. The literature on these issues is voluminous. For starters, on the Calvinist side, see Paul Helm, *Calvin and the Calvinists*, 2nd ed. (Carlisle, PA: Banner of Truth, 1998); Richard A. Muller, *Calvin and the Reformed Tradition: On the Work of Christ and the Order of Salvation* (Grand Rapids, MI: Baker Academic, 2012). See also Muller's magisterial work expositing the theological tradition of Reformed orthodoxy: *Post-Reformation Reformed Dogmatics: The Rise and Development of Reformed Orthodoxy, ca. 1520 to ca. 1725*, 2nd ed., 4 vols. (Grand Rapids, MI: Baker Academic, 2003).

receives us into his favor as righteous men," which "consists in the remission of sins and the imputation of Christ's righteousness."[7] Luther's mature theology also reflected this exclusively forensic understanding of justification. In his *Lectures on Isaiah*, Luther asserts that "our righteousness is nothing other than the imputation of God."[8]

When Calvin seeks to defend this understanding from Scripture, he points to instances of "justification" that could not possibly mean something transformative. Clearly, when God himself is justified (Luke 7:29) or when wisdom is justified by her children (7:35), the notion is not one of conferring righteousness on the object of justification but of acknowledging and declaring the object to be in the right. Calvin then takes up the soteriological use of justification language and demonstrates that its character is exclusively forensic rather than transformative. For Paul, justification is set in contrast to accusation and condemnation (Rom. 8:33–34). Justification is a free gift bestowed through faith apart from works (3:26; 4:4–5) and is equated with the forgiveness of transgressions (4:5–8). Its meaning and character are entirely legal. When Paul appeals to Psalm 32:1 ("Blessed is the one whose transgression is forgiven"), "he is obviously discussing not a part of justification but the whole of it."[9]

Sanctification, on the other hand, is the transformative category in Reformation soteriology. As many have noted, sanctification language (the ἅγιος/ἁγιάζω word group) is often used in the New Testament to refer to the decisive setting apart of believers in Christ at the point of their conversion.[10] Some have referred to this concept as "definitive sanctification," an act of God that marks the decisive end to sin's power in the lives of the converted.[11] But the New Testament also uses the language of sanctification to refer to the believer's experiential growth in holiness. This "progressive sanctification" involves the process of moral transformation in the life of the believer by the inner work of the Holy Spirit in cooperation with the believer's own efforts (e.g., 1 Thess. 5:23). As Anthony Hoekema puts it, "Sanctification is a supernatural work of God in which the believer is active."[12]

As noted above, in the Reformation era, *regeneration* was often the preferred term for this transformative work of God in renewing God's people. Calvin himself uses regeneration and sanctification in roughly synonymous ways to speak of the transformative

---

7. John Calvin, *Institutes of the Christian Religion*, ed. John T. McNeill, trans. Ford Lewis Battles, LCC 20–21 (Louisville: Westminster John Knox, 1960), 3.11.2.

8. Martin Luther, *Lectures on Isaiah*, WA 31:439, cited in Korey D. Maas, "Justification by Faith Alone," in *Reformation Theology: A Systematic Summary*, ed. Matthew Barrett (Wheaton, IL: Crossway, 2017), 522. Maas recounts the ways in which Luther's mature theology of justification was influenced by Philipp Melanchthon, including evidence that Luther affirmed Melanchthon's view that justification is used in exclusively judicial terms. See Maas, "Justification by Faith Alone," 520–24.

9. Calvin, *Institutes*, 3.11.3.

10. See John Murray, "Definitive Sanctification," in *The Collected Writings of John Murray*, vol. 2, *Select Lectures in Systematic Theology* (Carlisle, PA: Banner of Truth, 1976), 277; Anthony A. Hoekema, *Saved by Grace* (Grand Rapids, MI: Eerdmans, 1989), 202–4; David Peterson, *Possessed by God: A New Testament Theology of Sanctification and Holiness*, NSBT 1 (Downers Grove, IL: InterVarsity Press, 1995). Peterson is particularly concerned to show that sanctification language is "primarily" and "regularly" used not to refer to the process of spiritual growth but to the decisive consecration of believers in Christ. *Possessed by God*, 27. But *sanctification* is sometimes used in the former sense, and given the New Testament emphasis on growth in holiness, it is a fitting term to refer to this transformational concept.

11. Murray, "Definitive Sanctification," 279.

12. Something similar takes place when theologians speak of the immaterial part of human nature as the "soul," even though the biblical terms that are translated "soul" (e.g., נֶפֶשׁ) have broader meanings.

aspect of redemption.[13] Thus, sanctification is set in contrast to justification precisely by its transformative and renewing character. In justification, God remits sin and counts the believer righteous in Christ by faith alone. In sanctification, God renews the believer progressively in concert with the believer's Spirit-enabled cooperation. The Westminster Confession of Faith defines sanctification as follows:

> They, who are once effectually called, and regenerated, having a new heart, and a new spirit created in them, are further sanctified, really and personally, through the virtue of Christ's death and resurrection, by His Word and Spirit dwelling in them: the dominion of the whole body of sin is destroyed, and the several lusts thereof are more and more weakened and mortified; and they more and more quickened and strengthened in all saving graces, to the practice of true holiness, without which no man shall see the Lord.[14]

What the confession denied of justification is here affirmed of sanctification. Justification is accomplished "not for any thing wrought in [believers] or done by them." Sanctification, on the other hand, is defined precisely in these terms: it is an internal work that envelops within it the participation of the believer. The confession cites as scriptural evidence for this view passages that speak of "sanctification" itself not only in terms of God's cleansing and renewing work within believers (e.g., John 17:17; Eph. 5:26; 2 Thess. 2:13) but also in terms of the believer's grace-enabled efforts at putting sin to death and putting holiness into practice.[15] Thus, the confession defines sanctification in terms of mortification (putting sin to death) and quickening, or vivification (being renewed in virtue). As McGrath points out, distinguishing this internal, transformative, and participatory righteousness from the alien and forensic righteousness of justification was the "essential feature" of Reformation soteriology.[16]

Union with Christ is the doctrine that integrates these two gifts of redemption, as Calvin explains in the opening chapter to book 3 of his *Institutes*, "The Way in Which We Receive the Grace of Christ":

> We must now examine the question. How do we receive those benefits which the Father bestowed on his only-begotten Son—not for Christ's own private use, but that he might enrich poor and needy men? First, we must understand that as long as Christ remains outside of us, and we are separated from him, all that he has suffered and done for the salvation of the human race remains useless and of no value to us. Therefore, to share with us what he has received from the Father, he had to become ours and to dwell within us. For this reason, he is called "our Head" (Eph. 4.15), and "the first-born among many brethren" (Rom. 8.29). We also, in turn, are said to be

---

13. Calvin, *Institutes*, 3.11.1.
14. Westminster Confession of Faith 13.1.
15. One classic work on the believer's experience of sanctification can be found in John Owen, *On the Mortification of Sin in Believers*, in *The Works of John Owen*, ed. William H. Goold, vol. 6, *Temptation and Sin* (Carlisle, PA: Banner of Truth, 1995).
16. McGrath, *Iustitia Dei*, 186.

"engrafted into him" (Rom. 11.17), and to "put on Christ" (Gal. 3.27); for, as I have said, all that he possesses is nothing to us until we grow into one body with him.[17]

So while the benefits of redemption are fully accomplished in the historical work of Christ ("all that he has suffered and done for the salvation of the human race"), the actual enjoyment of those benefits is contingent on the believer's union with Christ. As Calvin notes, the New Testament teaching on union is twofold; it involves a kind of mutual indwelling—Christ in the believer and the believer in Christ. And as Calvin makes clear, this union is wrought by the Holy Spirit. Thus, Calvin frames the whole of his soteriology in book 3 of the *Institutes* in terms of pneumatology. It is without exaggeration that B. B. Warfield can claim Calvin as "the theologian of the Holy Spirit."[18]

One could argue that the *locus classicus* on union with Christ is Ephesians 1:3–14, which locates all the spiritual blessings of redemption "in Christ." Some variation on the phrase "in Christ," "in him," or "through him" is used no less than eleven times in the space of these twelve verses.[19] From their election and predestination through their experience of redemption and the indwelling Holy Spirit all the way to the final, eschatological "possession" of their inheritance (1:14), believers enjoy the blessings of salvation always and ever "in Christ." Later refinements to the doctrine of union with Christ would describe the multifaceted nature of union's benefits in terms of three aspects: *decretal* union with Christ in election, *forensic* (or legal) union with Christ accomplished by his work as covenant representative, and *mystical* (or vital) union with Christ, which believers enjoy existentially, that is, in their own life and experience with Jesus.[20] As argued below, because of the multifaceted nature of union with Christ, grounding both justification and sanctification in union does not preclude the possibility of prioritization within the *ordo salutis*, or "order of salvation."

Mapping the Terrain: Historical and Contemporary Perspectives

With these preliminary definitions in place, we now proceed to survey how these doctrines have been related in the Western theological traditions since the time of the Reformation.[21] At the risk of oversimplification, we explore three broad trends when it comes to relating justification and sanctification: conflating the two, separating the two, and integrating the two.

---

17. Calvin, *Institutes*, 3.1.1.
18. B. B. Warfield, *Calvin and Augustine*, ed. Samuel G. Craig (Philadelphia: Presbyterian and Reformed, 1956), 484–85.
19. For a recent exegetical treatment of these Pauline themes, see Constantine R. Campbell, *Paul and Union with Christ: An Exegetical and Theological Study* (Grand Rapids, MI: Zondervan, 2012).
20. One version of the threefold aspect can be found in Hermann Witsius, although, for him, the three aspects are to be found in the eternal decree of God, the eternal covenant of redemption (*pactum salutis*), and the "true and real" union that takes place in regeneration and conversion. For a discussion of Witsius's theology of union, see J. V. Fesko, *The Covenant of Redemption: Origins, Development, and Reception*, RHT 35 (Göttingen: Vandenhoeck & Ruprecht, 2015), 105. Other versions of union speak of two aspects, forensic and mystical, and treat decretal union and the *pactum salutis* more explicitly under the doctrine of election. See Louis Berkhof, *Systematic Theology*, rev. ed. (Grand Rapids, MI: Eerdmans, 1996), 452.
21. Limiting ourselves to the Western traditions does not mean that Eastern Christianity will be completely ignored. As we see here, some of the recent Protestant attempts to rethink the doctrine of justification have been cast in explicitly ecumenical terms, with Eastern dialogue partners clearly in view.

Conflating Justification and Sanctification

Some theologies have tended to collapse the distinction between justification and sanctification, such that the former necessarily includes the latter, not merely as a necessary entailment or result but as a constitutive part. We briefly examine two Reformation-era examples of this tendency, followed by two more recent examples.

Roman Catholicism

As we have seen, drawing a notional distinction between justification and sanctification is a hallmark—perhaps the distinguishing characteristic—of Reformation soteriology. As such, the protest the Reformers were registering was set in contrast to what they perceived to be the unbiblical confusion of justification and sanctification in the Roman Catholic Church of the late medieval and early modern eras. Following Augustine, medieval Roman Catholic teachers maintained that humans are justified by means of infused grace, which brings about an inner transformation in concert with human cooperation (Lat. *liberum arbitrium*, "free will") and which in turn yields the remission of sins.[22] Thus, justification was explicated in a *sanative* (healing, transformative) sense. By contrast, the Reformers maintained that justification is to be conceived of simply in terms of the remission of sins and the imputation of Christ's righteousness. It is a strictly forensic, legal declaration. It necessarily entails the subsequent moral renewal of the believer, but it is notionally distinct from that renewal.

This Reformation critique of the Augustinian tradition on justification drew a sharp (and anathematizing) rebuke from the Council of Trent.[23] The Tridentine understanding of justification is explicitly sanative and not merely forensic. Justification is the "translation from that state in which man is born a child of the first Adam, to the state of grace and of the adoption of the sons of God through the second Adam, Jesus Christ our Saviour." This movement from sinful nature to grace "cannot, since the promulgation of the Gospel, be effected except through the laver of regeneration or its desire."[24] Thus, justification is defined in terms of cleansing and renewal. After a discussion of the necessity of preparation for justification, the council provides a fuller definition of justification:

> This disposition or preparation is followed by justification itself, which is not only a remission of sins but also the sanctification and renewal of the inward man through the voluntary reception of the grace and gifts whereby an unjust man becomes just and from being an enemy becomes a friend.[25]

The conflation of justification and sanctification is here made explicit. The Reformers had defined justification simply as remission and imputation. Trent includes sanctification and renewal, again not merely as necessary entailments or results of justification

---

22. For a helpful summary of late medieval soteriology, see Gerald Bray, "Late-Medieval Theology," in Barrett, *Reformation Theology*, 67–93.
23. For a more thorough treatment of Trent's response, see chap. 21, by Korey Maas, in this volume.
24. *The Canons and Decrees of the Council of Trent*, trans. H. J. Schroeder (Charlotte, NC: TAN Books, 1978), 31.
25. *Canons and Decrees*, 33.

(which the Reformers themselves affirmed) but as constitutive parts of justification. The council's canons on justification drive the point home even further:

> If anyone says that men are justified either by the sole imputation of the justice of Christ or by the sole remission of sins, to the exclusion of the grace and "the charity which is poured forth in their hearts by the Holy Ghost," and remains in them, or also that the grace by which we are justified is only the good will of God, let him be anathema.[26]

The Osiander Controversy

The Reformers also faced challenges to their sharp distinction between the two doctrines within their own emerging movement. The debate turned on the provocative proposal of Andreas Osiander, professor of theology at the University of Konigsberg. J. V. Fesko summarizes the nub of the debate: "Unlike Luther and [Philipp] Melanchthon, Osiander denied that justification was a forensic declaration and instead claimed that it required divine indwelling so that believers would share in Christ's personal and essential righteousness."[27] Luther and Melanchthon were prepared to admit the central place of union with Christ for justification, but for these Reformers, it was a union with Christ's person and the attendant imputation of his alien righteousness. For Osiander, union was effected between the believer and the divine nature of Christ and involved the actual renewal of the sinner. Justification was thus mediated by God's mystical, indwelling presence. Melanchthon rightly discerned the similarity of Osiander's view to the Roman view: "Thus in reality he is saying what the papists say: 'We are righteous by our renewal,' except that he mentions the cause where the papists mention the effect. We are just when God renews us."[28]

Calvin's involvement in the controversy was prompted by accusations that the Genevan Reformer himself had tendencies similar to Osiander. Certainly, Calvin, like Luther and Melanchthon, made Christ's indwelling presence central to his understanding of justification. But Calvin adamantly disavowed the notion that justification is to be founded in any internal work of God in the life of the believer. The basis of justification is the alien and imputed righteousness of Christ alone. Calvin spends several chapters in his treatment of justification in the *Institutes* refuting the errors of Osiander on this point. For Calvin, Osiander missed the mark because he fundamentally misunderstood what union with Christ entails: it is a union not with Christ's divinity but with the person of the Mediator and to his vicarious humanity. But with regard to justification itself, Osiander's central error was the confusion of justification and sanctification:

> For since God, for the preservation of righteousness, renews those whom he freely reckons as righteous, Osiander mixes that gift of regeneration [i.e., sanctification]

---

26. *Canons and Decrees*, 43–44.
27. J. V. Fesko, "Union with Christ," in Barrett, *Reformation Theology*, 430–31.
28. Philipp Melanchthon, "Confutation of Osiander," quoted in Fesko, "Union with Christ," 431–32.

with this free acceptance [i.e., justification] and contends that they are one and the same. Yet Scripture, even though it joins them, still lists them separately in order that God's manifold grace may better appear to us.[29]

Thus, against both the Roman Catholics without and certain aberrations within Protestantism, the Reformers asserted the notional distinction (but inseparability) of forensic justification and the elements of internal renewal (regeneration, sanctification, etc.).

The New Finnish Interpretation of Luther

The school of Luther interpretation that has grown up around Tuomo Mannermaa (1937–2015) at the University of Helsinki constitutes a more recent example of a theology that tends to conflate justification and sanctification.[30] As Mannermaa explains, the new approach to Luther studies emerged out of ecumenical dialogue with Eastern Christianity, especially around the important theme of *theosis*, or deification. According to Mannermaa and the so-called New Finnish school, Luther taught a more participatory understanding of justification that stands in contrast to the later, more exclusively forensic understanding of Lutheranism. A dominant theme in the New Finnish Interpretation is Luther's emphasis that "Christ is present in faith itself" (Lat. *in ipsa fide Christus adest*). New Finnish interpreters understand Luther's teaching here to imply a "real participation in God," on the basis of which Christ himself and his righteousness truly belong to the one who has faith.[31] Mannermaa grounds this interpretation in Luther's "classical realist epistemology," which posits a real unity of the intellect and its object.[32] This way of framing Luther's understanding of justification yields a very different result from that yielded by the forensic and imputational account of justification found in the Formula of Concord and later Lutheran thought. Justification is not merely a forensic declaration on the basis of Christ's imputed righteousness, but it includes within it the renewal of the believer, who by faith enjoys a real "participation in God's essence in Christ."[33] Thus, the line between the forensic and the transformative is blurred to the point of disappearance.

Whatever ecumenical utility the New Finnish Interpretation of Luther may possess, there is good reason to question its historical accuracy in describing Luther's theology of justification, especially in its mature form. As Korey Maas has pointed out, "Luther did often explain justification in terms of a mystical or ontological union with Christ and the inherent righteousness resulting; such explanations, however, are largely concentrated

---

29. Calvin, *Institutes*, 3.11.6.
30. See Tuomo Mannermaa, *Christ Present in Faith: Luther's View of Justification*, ed. Kirsi I. Stjerna (Minneapolis: Fortress, 2005). The German edition of this groundbreaking book first appeared in 1989. For an English language introduction to the New Finnish school, see Carl E. Braaten and Robert W. Jenson, eds., *Union with Christ: The New Finnish Interpretation of Luther* (Grand Rapids, MI: Eerdmans, 1998), especially the essays by Mannermaa himself. For a critique of the New Finnish Interpretation from a Reformed Luther scholar, see Carl R. Trueman, "Is the Finnish Line a New Beginning? A Critical Assessment of the Reading of Luther Offered by the Helsinki Circle," *WTJ* 65, no. 2 (2003): 231–44.
31. Tuomo Mannermaa, "Why Is Luther So Fascinating?," in Braaten and Jenson, *Union with Christ*, 2.
32. Mannermaa, "Why Is Luther So Fascinating?," 5, 6.
33. Mannermaa, *Christ Present in Faith*, 17.

in his earliest publications."[34] Under the influence of his friend and colleague Melanchthon, Luther came to describe justification in exclusively forensic terms and on the basis of Christ's imputed righteousness alone. Luther did not jettison his belief in the central role of union with Christ, but he did come to frame it more explicitly in the context of the imputation of an alien righteousness.[35] At any rate, the New Finnish school has recovered a sometimes-neglected theme in Luther's earlier writings. It is perhaps best, then, to consider the Finnish interpretation a constructive proposal rather than a purely exegetical one, but it seems clear that one of its hallmarks is the tendency to blur the lines between forensic and transformative/participatory categories.

The New Perspective on Paul

The so-called New Perspective on Paul constitutes another recent proposal that tends to conflate justification and sanctification. The literature on the New Perspective is voluminous, and a discussion of it is further problematized by the diversity to be found among its proponents. Any treatment of the New Perspective here must of necessity be brief and perhaps overly simplistic.

The New Perspective, grounded in the works of Krister Stendahl and E. P. Sanders and expressed brilliantly in the works of N. T. Wright and James D. G. Dunn, among others, sets itself in contrast to the "old perspective" to be found in the Reformation and post-Reformation theologians and exegetes.[36] Foundational to the New Perspective is a reappraisal of first-century Judaism, to which Paul was responding. According to Wright, Paul's polemic was less about combating a "proto-Pelagian" works righteousness and more about critiquing the ethnocentric Jewish identity markers (especially circumcision and the food laws) that stood in the way of the full inclusion of the Gentiles. In this context, as Wright puts it, Paul's doctrine of justification is "not so much about salvation as it is about the church."[37] Standard in New Perspective approaches is a denial of the Reformation doctrine of the imputation of Christ's righteousness, which Wright sees as "a straightforward category mistake." According to Wright, it "is not the 'righteousness' of Jesus Christ which is 'reckoned' to the believer. It is his death and resurrection."[38] Faith itself is also reconceived by Wright and other New Perspective proponents to mean something closer to "faithfulness to God."[39] So the composite understanding of justification in the New Perspective runs something like this: believers are justified, that is, declared to be true members of the new covenant community,

---

34. Maas, "Justification by Faith Alone," 541.
35. For a defense of this thesis, see Maas, "Justification by Faith Alone," 520–24. Trueman also faults the Finnish interpretation for failing to account for this historical development. "Is the Finnish Line a New Beginning?," 233.
36. See Krister Stendahl, "The Apostle Paul and the Introspective Conscience of the West," *HTR* 56, no. 3 (1963): 199–215; E. P. Sanders, *Paul and Palestinian Judaism: A Comparison of Patterns of Religion* (Philadelphia: Fortress, 1977); N. T. Wright, *What Saint Paul Really Said: Was Paul of Tarsus the Real Founder of Christianity?* (Grand Rapids, MI: Eerdmans, 1997); James D. G. Dunn, *The New Perspective on Paul: Collected Essays*, rev. ed. (Tübingen: Mohr Siebeck, 2008).
37. Wright, *What Saint Paul Really Said*, 119.
38. N. T. Wright, *Justification: God's Plan and Paul's Vision* (Downers Grove, IL: IVP Academic, 2009), 232.
39. So Wright: "Faith and obedience are not antithetical. They belong exactly together. Indeed, very often the word 'faith' itself could properly be translated as 'faithfulness,' which makes the point just as well." Wright, *What Saint Paul Really Said*, 160.

by faithfulness to the one true God as he is revealed in the faithfulness of Jesus Christ and his death and resurrection. As such, the New Perspective, similar to the New Finnish school, has blurred the lines between the forensic and the transformative, and thus between justification and sanctification.[40]

Separating Justification and Sanctification

Another trend in the history of these doctrines has been one of separation, rather than conflation. This tendency is seen especially in theologies that fall under the rubric of *antinomianism*. As its name suggests, antinomianism is a view that is, either in theory or in practice, antilaw ("law" in Greek is νόμος [*nomos*]). More specifically, antinomianism is a tendency to reject any positive use of the law as a moral guide to believers—what Calvin referred to as the law's "principal" use.[41] The law may be seen as a necessary tool to reveal sin, condemn self-righteousness, and lead one to the grace of God in Christ (the law's "first," or pedagogical, use), but it has no further role to play in the lives of those set free from its oppressive burdens. Antinomian controversies arose in the Reformation era and had expressions in all three major branches of the Reformation: Lutheran, Reformed, and Anabaptist. Sinclair Ferguson has also recently highlighted a fascinating and illuminating debate over antinomianism in the so-called "Marrow Controversy" of eighteenth-century Scotland.[42]

Antinomianism was also a common trait of certain forms of "high Calvinism" in Puritan-era England, with John Saltmarsh, John Eaton, Tobias Crisp, and Robert Lancaster among its principal proponents. Peter Toon describes the theology of such antinomians as follows:

> They explained the free grace of God to the elect in such a way as to neglect the Biblical teaching that a Christian has certain responsibilities to God such as daily humbling for sin, daily prayer, continual trust in God and continual love to men. One of their favorite doctrines was eternal justification, by which they meant that God not only elected the Church to salvation but actually justified the elect before they were born. As a development of this they taught that justification in time was merely the realisation that eternal justification was theirs already.[43]

This belief in eternal justification rendered moot any demand for sanctification in the lives of the elect. Thus, the fissure between justification and sanctification became a yawning chasm.

---

40. To be fair to Wright, he does distinguish between justification and sanctification, with the former seen as a "status" and the latter as a "process." See Wright, *Justification*, 156. The point being made here is not a total collapse of any conceptual distinctions but a blurring of the lines, especially between faith and obedience. For a critique of the New Perspective, see Stephen Westerholm, *Perspectives Old and New on Paul: The "Lutheran" Paul and His Critics* (Grand Rapids, MI: Eerdmans, 2004). See also Aaron T. O'Kelley, *Did the Reformers Misread Paul? A Historical-Theological Critique of the New Perspective*, SCHT (Milton Keynes, UK: Paternoster, 2014).
41. Calvin, *Institutes*, 2.7.12.
42. Sinclair B. Ferguson, *The Whole Christ: Legalism, Antinomianism, and Gospel Assurance—Why the Marrow Controversy Still Matters* (Wheaton, IL: Crossway, 2016).
43. Peter Toon, *The Emergence of Hyper-Calvinism in English Nonconformity, 1689–1765* (Eugene, OR: Wipf & Stock, 2011), 28.

But antinomianism is not always expressed in such theoretical and academic terms; it often manifests itself in more practical and popular ways as well. More recently, the so-called free-grace-theology movement associated with Zane Hodges, Charles Ryrie, and others has also developed a soteriology with antinomian tendencies. According to this teaching, eternal life is secured by faith alone, conceived in a truncated and absolute sense: simple belief in Jesus as Savior, without any reference to repentance or submission to Christ's lordship.[44] In this view, accepting Jesus as Savior is abstracted from following Jesus as Lord. Free-grace proponents do not so much reject the importance of sanctification as they deny its necessity for true saving faith and thus the reception of eternal life. What, then, becomes of those who make a profession of belief but do not persevere in obedience and good works? In some versions of free-grace theology, this contingency is explained in terms of "spiritual Christians" versus "carnal Christians."[45] It is possible to be a true Christian but to live carnally, that is, to live a life characterized by the flesh, not the Spirit. It is even possible for a Christian to lose his or her faith entirely and yet not lose eternal salvation. Hodges explains, "Nowhere does the Word of God guarantee that the believer's faith inevitably will endure.... The believer's basic relationship to God is unaffected by the overthrow of one's faith."[46] In this understanding, sanctification, it would seem, is more like an optional add-on to salvation—perhaps necessary for certain heavenly rewards but not an inseparable component of Christ's holistic work of salvation in the lives of believers. Saving faith is conceived of as simple belief (*notitia*) and assent (*assensus*), divorced from the Reformation emphasis on trust (*fiducia*).[47]

Some versions of the doctrine of "eternal security" can also fall into the trap of making perseverance in good works unnecessary for final salvation. While the locution "the eternal security of the believer" can express one important component of the Reformed doctrine of the perseverance of the saints, it can also be distorted into something closer to the free-grace position. In one popular defense of this perspective, we find such startling lines as this: "Even if a believer for all practical purposes becomes an unbeliever, his salvation is not in jeopardy. Christ will remain faithful."[48] In this rendering, as in all forms of antinomianism, the life of sanctification is divorced from God's verdict in justification, and the two doctrines are not only distinguished but severed from one another.

Integrating Justification and Sanctification

As we saw in our preliminary definitions and as we see in the constructive section below, the Reformers and the theological traditions that came in their wake sought to avoid

---

44. See, e.g., Zane Hodges, *Absolutely Free! A Biblical Reply to Lordship Salvation*, 2nd ed. (Corinth, TX: Grace Evangelical Society, 2014), 23–32.
45. Hodges, *Absolutely Free!*, 188–89.
46. Hodges, *Absolutely Free!*, 100.
47. For a critique of free-grace theology, see Michael S. Horton, ed., *Christ the Lord: The Reformation and Lordship Salvation* (Grand Rapids, MI: Baker, 1992). See also John MacArthur, *The Gospel according to Jesus: What Is Authentic Faith?*, rev. ed. (Grand Rapids, MI: Zondervan, 2008).
48. Charles Stanley, *Eternal Security: Can You Be Sure?* (Nashville: Thomas Nelson, 1990), 93.

both the conflation and the separation of justification and sanctification. Mainstream Reformation thought seeks an integration of these two crucial doctrines. Calvin summarized the Reformation position well in his response to Osiander: "Yet we must bear in mind what I have already said, that the grace of justification is not separated from regeneration, although they are things distinct."[49] Luther maintained the same dynamic in his discussion of "alien" and "proper" righteousness: "The second kind of righteousness is our proper righteousness, not because we alone work it, but because we work with that first and alien righteousness. This is that manner of life spent profitably in good works."[50] The two kinds of righteousness are notionally distinct but inseparable. They are also clearly ordered, with alien righteousness taking the "first" position and proper, or actual, righteousness being placed "second" and derivative of the first. Calvin also argued for the priority of justification: "For unless you first of all grasp what your relationship to God is and the nature of his judgment concerning you, you have neither a foundation on which to establish your salvation nor one on which to build piety toward God."[51] Thus, sanctification (the life of piety) is founded on justification (knowing the nature of God's judgment concerning you).

But the question of priority in the justification-sanctification relationship is sometimes debated among Reformed authors.[52] The debate often hinges on certain disputed passages in Calvin's corpus. At the risk of oversimplification, we may speak of two distinct camps of Calvin interpretation: those who believe that Calvin, in continuity with Philipp Melanchthon and Lutheran orthodoxy, argued for the priority of justification and those who believe that Calvin integrated both justification and sanctification to the logically prior category of union with Christ without any causal priority. Reformed theologians in the first camp argue for what we might call the *prioritization thesis*. Those in the latter camp maintain that the integrative theme of union with Christ renders any internal priority between justification and sanctification exegetically and theologically unnecessary.

Consider, for example, the interpretation of Calvin offered by Mark Garcia:

> In Calvin's framework . . . the life of obedience or sanctification by the Spirit does not flow from the imputation of Christ's righteousness but from Christ himself with whom the Spirit has united believers. In other words, for Calvin sanctification does not flow from justification. They are not related as cause and effect. Rather, together they are "effects" or, better, aspects of union with Christ.[53]

Garcia is concerned that the prioritization thesis risks the marginalization of sanctification in the experience of the believer:

---

49. Calvin, *Institutes*, 3.11.11.
50. Martin Luther, "Sermon on Two Kinds of Righteousness, 1519," in *The Annotated Luther*, vol. 2, *Word and Faith*, ed. Kirsi I. Stjerna (Minneapolis: Fortress, 2015), 16.
51. Calvin, *Institutes*, 3.11.1.
52. For a more extensive treatment of this issue, see chap. 15, by David VanDrunen, in this volume.
53. Mark A. Garcia, *Life in Christ: Union with Christ and Twofold Grace in Calvin's Theology*, SCHT (Eugene, OR: Wipf & Stock, 2008), 146.

Within Calvin's soteriological model, to make sanctification follow justification as an effect is to concede the theological possibility that one may be truly justified but not yet sanctified, with the result that the legal fiction charge, to which Calvin was always sensitive, would be validated.[54]

So for Garcia, union with Christ is primary, and the twin fruits of justification and sanctification are ordered toward it, without any relationship of priority.

In contrast, consider the opinion of Cornelis Venema in defense of the prioritization thesis with regard to the *duplex gratia*:

> According to Calvin, justification through faith is the "first" of these benefits or ways in which Christ lives in those who are engrafted into him. Whereas sanctification or repentance is the "second" of these gifts (*quae secunda est gratia*), justification or reconciliation is the "main hinge on which religion turns" (*praecipuus esse sustinendae religionis cardo*). When Calvin treats the benefits of our reception of God's grace in Christ, he clearly grants a kind of priority to justification as the "first" aspect of the "twofold grace of God." The preeminence of this benefit is affirmed in various passages in his writings, which speak of justification as the principal aspect of the "twofold grace of God."[55]

A complete adjudication of this intramural debate over Calvin's theology of the double grace lies beyond the scope of this chapter. But in what follows, a version of the prioritization thesis is defended on exegetical and theological grounds and with reference to some key passages in Calvin's writings.

Harvesting Reformation Soteriology: A Proposition

Given this long history of debate over the precise relationship between justification and sanctification, what can we say by way of a constructive theological argument? I remain convinced by the evidence—most fundamentally in Scripture but also acknowledged in Calvin and the subsequent Reformed tradition—that justification and sanctification should be seen as distinct but inseparable gifts that flow from union with Christ *and* that justification has a certain priority over sanctification even within this integrative motif of union with Christ. This argument assumes the abiding validity of the *ordo salutis* as a useful rubric for speaking about the relationships between certain aspects of redemption. While a full-orbed biblical soteriology should be thoroughly grounded in the *historia salutis*—the economy of salvation played out on the stage of redemptive history—this historical context does not preclude the possibility that Scripture also teaches a certain ordering within the work of Christ and its application to believers by the Holy Spirit.[56]

---

54. Garcia, *Life in Christ*, 264.
55. Cornelis P. Venema, *Accepted and Renewed in Christ: The "Twofold Grace of God" and the Interpretation of Calvin's Theology*, RHT 2 (Göttingen: Vandenhoeck & Ruprecht, 2007), 96–97.
56. For a helpful cataloging of critics of the *ordo*, see J. V. Fesko, *Beyond Calvin: Union with Christ and Justification in Early Modern Reformed Theology (1517–1700)*, RHT 20 (Göttingen: Vandenhoeck & Ruprecht, 2012), 53–71.

With these comments in place, I proceed to offer an extended proposition regarding Reformed soteriology, in the form of five theological statements, each of which is treated in turn:

(1) Justification and sanctification are inseparable gifts of redemption because they flow from the unified work of the triune God and his electing, redeeming, and renewing mercy. (2) Despite their inseparability, justification and sanctification are notionally distinct gifts that signify the forensic and the transformative aspects of redemption, respectively. (3) Even within the integrative category of union with Christ, there are distinct aspects, namely, the decretal, forensic, and mystical. (4) Therefore, framing all redemption in terms of union with Christ does not preclude the possibility of an ordering within the unified work of redemption. (5) Hence, justification has logical priority over sanctification as its objective ground and subjective motivational wellspring.

Inseparable Gifts

Justification and sanctification are inseparable gifts of redemption because they flow from the unified work of the triune God and his electing, redeeming, and renewing mercy.

Justification and sanctification, like all the benefits of redemption, are gifts of God's gratuitous mercy. Even sanctification, which enlists the cooperation of human effort, remains a gift of mercy. The fact that the New Testament uses the same term to describe the decisive consecration of believers at their conversion (definitive sanctification; e.g., 1 Cor. 6:11) and their ongoing growth in holiness (progressive sanctification; e.g., 1 Thess. 5:23) should clue us in to this reality. While sanctification is in some sense synergistic, encompassing the work of the sanctifying God and the works of the sanctified human agent, the priority of grace remains. We could even speak of sanctification, no less than justification, as a gift believers receive by grace alone through faith alone in Christ alone, at least in terms of the definitive cause of holiness in the lives of the elect.

Justification and sanctification remain inseparable because of their unity in the saving intention of God. The benefits of redemption are not like a buffet of options, piled into a compartmentalized cafeteria tray. They are more like a well-sourced and carefully crafted four-course meal prepared by a master chef and properly integrated so that each course leads irresistibly to the next. The Reformed tradition has rightly discerned in Scripture the permanence and invincibility of God's saving work in the lives of the elect—what has sometimes been referred to as the eternal security of the believer. But as we saw above, that particular locution is open to misrepresentation and abuse. The preferred historical term has been "the perseverance of the saints," which highlights not only God's work of *preserving* the elect but also their grace-enabled but no less necessary *perseverance* in the faith. As Calvin put it in his *Antidote to the Council of Trent*,

"It is therefore faith alone which justifies, and yet the faith which justifies is not alone. . . . Wherefore do not separate the whole grace of regeneration from faith."[57]

Furthermore, the scriptural teaching on a final judgment according to works precludes any kind of antinomian indifference to the actual righteousness of believers (e.g., 2 Cor. 5:10; 1 Pet. 1:17). Believers are justified *by* faith alone, but they will experience a final judgment *according to* works, where their good works are brought forth not as the legal ground of their vindication but as the necessary evidence of their faith union with Christ.[58] As one Baptist confession puts it, "All true believers endure to the end. . . . They shall be kept by the power of God through faith unto salvation."[59] Being kept (preservation) and enduring to the end (perseverance) belong together. This foregrounding of the believer's perseverance hardly counts as a slide into a nomistic understanding of "staying in" a state of grace (how could it, given the radical nature of grace expressed in the larger Reformed soteriological scheme?). Instead, it merely seeks to hold together the unified work of God in the lives of the elect: a work of both pardon and deliverance, both justification and sanctification. It is this holistic work of God that prompts the believer to say, in the words of the old hymn by Augustus Toplady,

> Rock of Ages, cleft for me,
> let me hide myself in thee;
> let the water and the blood,
> from thy wounded side which flowed,
> be of sin the double cure;
> save from wrath and make me pure.

The healing work of Christ produces a "double cure": the legal deliverance from sin's consequences and the transformative deliverance from sin's corrupting influence.

This unified work of salvation issues forth not from some generic divine benevolence but from the triune God, who is Father, Son, and Holy Spirit. The inseparability of justification and sanctification is grounded in the inseparability of Trinitarian operations. According to the doctrine of appropriation, we may speak of the electing Father, the redeeming Son, and the regenerating Holy Spirit, but in each of these works of divine mercy, it is the undivided Godhead who is working inseparably to bring about the salvation of the elect. God is one and acts as one. The benefits of redemption are inseparable because they flow from the unified work of the triune God. We can further spell out this first theological statement in several additional Trinitarian propositions.

Justification and sanctification are inseparable gifts of redemption because they are grounded in the Father's free and electing mercy. The Father's intention in election is to reckon sinners to be "in Christ" for the purpose of holiness and blamelessness (Eph. 1:4). His predestinating mercy has as its penultimate goal the adoption of the elect as

---

57. John Calvin, *Selections from His Writings*, ed. John Dillenberger (Atlanta: Scholars Press, 1975), 198.
58. For a discussion of the diverse views on the role of good works in salvation, see Alan P. Stanley, ed., *Four Views on the Role of Works at the Final Judgment*, Counterpoints: Bible and Theology (Grand Rapids, MI: Zondervan, 2013).
59. Baptist Faith and Message, 5.

sons of God through his beloved firstborn Son, Jesus Christ (1:5). It has as its ultimate goal the "praise of his glorious grace" (1:6) through the exaltation of Christ as the elder brother of the company of the redeemed, the renewed family of God (Rom. 8:29).

Justification and sanctification are inseparable gifts of redemption because they were secured in and by the person of Christ, in whom divinity and humanity are hypostatically united. As we saw above, union with Christ has sometimes been parsed in terms of decretal union, forensic union, and mystical union. We can also speak of this union with Christ in terms of three "moments": the eternal moment of election in Christ; the redemptive-historical moment of the believer's identification with Christ in his incarnation, life, death, burial, and resurrection (Rom. 6:1–4; Gal. 2:20); and the existential moment when the believer is brought by faith into a personal, organic union with Christ. The center category is secured in Christ himself. Union with Christ means most fundamentally union with his person, and in his person Christ is constituted as the believer's wisdom, righteousness, sanctification, and redemption (1 Cor. 1:30). Calvin makes use of an incarnational analogy in order to demonstrate the inseparability of justification and sanctification: "As Christ cannot be torn into parts, so these two which we perceive in him together and conjointly are inseparable—namely, righteousness and sanctification. Whomever, therefore, God receives into grace, on them he at the same time bestows the spirit of adoption (Rom. 8:15)."[60] Justification and sanctification can no more be separated in the lives of believers than they can be in the person of Christ himself.[61]

Justification and sanctification are inseparable gifts of redemption because they were accomplished by the "whole course" of Christ's obedience, not merely one aspect of his work abstracted from the others. The integral relationship between justification and sanctification is grounded not only in Christ's person but also in his mediatorial work. And while many evangelicals tend to truncate Christ's work of atonement to comprise only his work on the cross (and then only in terms of its forensic aspect), the New Testament places the climactic scene at Golgotha within the broader drama of Christ's holistic work—what Calvin referred to as "the whole course of Christ's obedience."[62] Christ accomplishes redemption not only through his wrath-bearing, Serpent-crushing death but also through his righteousness-fulfilling life (Matt. 3:15; Gal. 4:4), his justification-securing resurrection (Rom. 4:25), his glorious ascension to and session at the Father's right hand, his gracious gift of the Holy Spirit, his ongoing priestly intercession, and his final return in power and glory.[63] The application of redemption is holistic and unified because its accomplishment in Christ is holistic and unified.

Justification and sanctification are inseparable gifts of redemption because they are applied to the elect by the Holy Spirit, who unites them to Christ by faith. The

---

60. Calvin, *Institutes*, 3.11.6.
61. For a fuller treatment of the active obedience of Christ, see chap. 14, by Brandon Crowe, in this volume.
62. Calvin, *Institutes*, 2.16.5. Perhaps no one in contemporary theology has made more profound use of this Calvinian theme than Thomas F. Torrance. See, e.g., Torrance, *Incarnation: The Person and Life of Christ* (Downers Grove, IL: IVP Academic, 2008).
63. For a biblical overview of each aspect of Christ's work, see Robert A. Peterson, *Salvation Accomplished by the Son: The Work of Christ* (Wheaton, IL: Crossway, 2012).

work accomplished by Christ is applied to the elect by Christ's Spirit. The Spirit gives birth to faith, which alone is the instrument of justification. Salvation comes not by good works but by the regenerating and renewing work of the Spirit (Titus 3:5). But the Spirit who unites the elect by faith to the justifying verdict in Christ also consecrates them in Christ for a life of holiness and growth toward perfection (Gal. 3:3). It is with good reason that the Reformed tradition, stemming from Calvin himself, has grounded both justification and sanctification in the Spirit's work of uniting believers to Christ. As Calvin writes, "To sum up, the Holy Spirit is the bond by which Christ effectually unites us to himself."[64] The faith that unites believers to Christ forensically in justification and sustains them organically in an ongoing relationship to Christ is the result of the Spirit's work. "But faith is the principal work of the Holy Spirit," Calvin states; "by faith alone he leads us into the light of the gospel."[65]

So in sum, justification and sanctification are inseparable in the experience of the elect because they are inseparable in the saving intention of the triune God. They can no more be divided than can the persons of the Trinity or the two natures of Christ. Thus, to make sanctification some optional add-on to the settled verdict rendered in justification is to make a mistake of grave proportions. Justification is a settled verdict, founded on the righteousness of Christ alone and received by faith alone, but it always and inevitably brings about the sanctification of those justified. Therefore, all forms of antinomianism are excluded by the unified saving intentionality of the triune God.

Notionally Distinct Gifts

Despite their inseparability, justification and sanctification are notionally distinct gifts that signify the forensic and the transformative aspects of redemption, respectively.

As we have seen, for Calvin, one of the chief problems with Osiander's proposal was its conflation of justification and sanctification:

> For since God, for the preservation of righteousness, renews those whom he freely reckons as righteous, Osiander mixes that gift of regeneration [i.e., sanctification] with this free acceptance [i.e., justification] and contends that they are one and the same. Yet Scripture, even though it joins them, still lists them separately in order that God's manifold grace may better appear to us.[66]

A bit later Calvin reiterates the point: "Yet we must bear in mind what I have already said, that the grace of justification is not separated from regeneration, although they are things distinct."[67] Joined but listed separately, distinct but inseparable—these are the terms that summarize the Reformation view of the relationship between justification

---

64. Calvin, *Institutes*, 3.1.1.
65. Calvin, *Institutes*, 3.1.4.
66. Calvin, *Institutes*, 3.11.6.
67. Calvin, *Institutes*, 3.11.11.

and sanctification. Before Calvin, Luther had already made this crucial distinction. It was present in his 1519 sermon that outlined "two kinds of righteousness": the alien righteousness of Christ and the proper (or actual) righteousness in the lives of believers that flows from this alien righteousness.[68] The notional distinction between the two doctrines is also present in Luther's 1520 *Freedom of a Christian*, and is even more pronounced by the time we come to his 1535 commentary on Galatians.[69]

For both Calvin and Luther, these two doctrines are to be distinguished in large part because of the durative difference between them. Justification is punctiliar and complete; sanctification in this life is always gradual and partial:

> For God always begins this second point [sanctification] in his elect, and progresses in it gradually, and sometimes slowly, throughout life, that they are always liable to the judgment of death before his tribunal. But he does not justify in part but liberally, so that they may appear in heaven as if endowed with the purity of Christ.[70]

Sanctification, because of its partial and progressive nature, can never serve as the ground for the believer's certainty before the divine judgment. Justification alone is sufficient for this task because it alone is founded in the purity of Christ himself.

In the New Testament, Paul's sharp contrast between faith and works as opposing principles of justification underlines this distinction (Rom. 3:20–30; 4:1–5; 10:3–4; Gal. 2:16). The New Perspective on Paul, despite providing some helpful clarifications about the nature of first-century Judaism and the social and ecclesial context of Paul's doctrine of justification, has not succeeded in erasing this fundamental Reformation insight. For Paul, the "works of the law" may have Jewish identity markers (circumcision, food laws, Sabbath, etc.) partially or even primarily in view, but these attempts at justification by law are wrongheaded not only because they are ethnocentric but more fundamentally because they are opposed to the doctrine of grace.[71] Grace and works are mutually exclusive principles of acceptance before God; "otherwise grace would no longer be grace" (Rom. 11:6). This emphatically does not mean that works have no place in Paul's theology. Indeed, he sees good works as the intended result of God's gracious work of salvation: "For by grace you have been saved through faith. And this is not your own doing; it is the gift of God, not a result of works, so that no one may boast. For we are his workmanship, created in Christ Jesus for good works, which God prepared beforehand, that we should walk in them" (Eph. 2:8–10). Justification and sanctification, though indivisible, remain notionally distinct gifts of God's manifold grace.

---

68. Martin Luther, "Two Kinds of Righteousness."
69. See J. Todd Billings, "Union with Christ and the Double Grace: Calvin's Theology and Its Early Reception," in *Calvin's Theology and Its Reception: Disputes, Developments, and New Possibilities*, ed. J. Todd Billings and I. John Hesselink (Louisville: Westminster John Knox, 2012), 51; Carl Trueman, "*Simul peccator et justus*: Martin Luther and Justification," in *Justification in Perspective: Historical Developments and Contemporary Challenges*, ed. Bruce L. McCormack (Grand Rapids, MI: Baker Academic, 2006), 75–92.
70. Calvin, *Institutes*, 3.11.11.
71. Thomas R. Schreiner, "Another Look at the New Perspective," *SBJT* 14, no. 3 (2010): 6–10.

Distinct Aspects of Union with Christ

Even within the integrative category of union with Christ, there are distinct aspects, namely, the decretal, forensic, and mystical.

As argued above, justification and sanctification are benefits that accrue to believers by virtue of their Spirit-wrought union with Christ. Some have seen this emphasis on the centrality of union as a distinctive mark of Reformed soteriology, sometimes using it to displace the centrality of forensic justification and to distinguish the Reformed view from the Lutheran view.[72] But these neat lines of demarcation are not always borne out by the evidence. A strong case can be made that when it comes to the essential question of humanity's salvation before God, forensic justification is no less central for Calvin than it is for Luther. For Calvin, justification is the "main hinge on which religion turns" and the fount of all assurance and growth in piety.[73] Similarly, for Luther, union with Christ (especially the marital metaphor that he often employs) is an overarching theme.[74] To be sure, there are differences in emphasis between the two great Reformers and the traditions that follow in their wake, but they are not to be found in a sharp contrast between union with Christ and forensic justification as central motifs.[75]

Furthermore, even if we grant that union with Christ is an integrating motif both for Paul and for Calvin and the Reformed tradition, the appeal to union with Christ is multifaceted, not simple. Union with Christ is not so much a discrete "moment" in the order of salvation as it is an undergirding soteriological principle with distinct features.[76] As we have already seen, Reformed thinkers came to speak of union in terms of three distinct aspects: decretal union in election, forensic union in the work accomplished by Christ and applied in justification, and mystical union realized in the transformed experience of believers. Sometimes the typology has been reduced to two, forensic and mystical union (without, of course, leaving behind the content of decretal union in election). In his classic text on systematic theology, Reformed theologian Louis Berkhof employs this twofold distinction in order to highlight the priority of the forensic (judicial) element:

> The mystical union in the sense in which we are now speaking of it is not the judicial ground, on the basis of which we become partakers of the riches that are in Christ. It is sometimes said that the merits of Christ cannot be imputed to us as long as we are not in Christ, since it is only on the basis of our oneness with Him that such an imputation could be reasonable. But this view fails to distinguish between our legal unity with Christ and our spiritual oneness with Him, and is a falsification of the fundamental element in the doctrine of redemption, namely, of the doctrine of justification.[77]

---

72. Michael Horton takes on this charge in "Calvin's Theology of Union with Christ and the Double Grace: Modern Reception and Contemporary Possibilities," in Billings and Hesselink, *Calvin's Theology and Its Reception*, 72–94.
73. Calvin, *Institutes*, 3.11.1.
74. For more evidence along these lines, see Horton, "Union with Christ," 83–88.
75. Horton identifies Calvin's emphasis on "the reality of the new life" and the scope of his appeal to union with Christ as examples of his distinctive contribution. See Horton, "Union with Christ," 87–88.
76. Horton, "Union with Christ," 90.
77. Berkhof, *Systematic Theology*, 452.

For Berkhof, to argue that justification is somehow subordinated to mystical union with Christ, is problematic for two reasons. First, it fails to make a necessary distinction within the category of union itself. Union is twofold in Berkhof's accounting: "legal unity" and "spiritual oneness." If justification is grounded in union, then surely it is the former element that undergirds the imputation of Christ's merits to the elect. Second, grounding imputation in mystical union also threatens to undermine the doctrine of justification itself. God's declaration in justification is received by faith, to be sure, but it is not for that reason causally dependent on our spiritual faith union with Christ. Faith is simply the instrumental means by which God's elect "receive and rest upon Christ," who alone is the legal ground of their acceptance before God.[78] Distinguishing between elements or aspects of union, then, is not some kind of scholastic nitpicking; it is necessary in order to provide a proper ground for the believer's assurance. The old Osiandrian mistake of grounding justification in our spiritual transformation must be avoided at all costs.

Ordering within Redemption

Therefore, framing all redemption in terms of union with Christ does not preclude the possibility of an ordering within the unified work of redemption.

The point can now be pressed home explicitly. Because union with Christ is multifaceted, simple appeal to union as an integrative motif does not settle the most pressing issues. The logical priorities we see in the *ordo salutis* mirror, in some ways, the priority of the legal aspect within the category of union itself. As the Reformed biblical theologian Geerhardus Vos has argued, "In our opinion Paul consciously and consistently subordinated the mystical aspect of the relation to Christ to the forensic one. . . . The mystical is based on the forensic, not the forensic on the mystical."[79] The whole work of salvation flows from the free mercy of God in election. The legal barriers to God's salvific benefits are removed by the obedience of the incarnate Christ. Any transformative or personal effects that salvation has in the lives of the redeemed cannot serve as the ground of this eternal decision or this redemptive-historical accomplishment. Nor can our spiritual union with him provide the necessary precondition for these decretal and forensic benefits (though it does, no doubt, serve as the instrument of our personal reception of them). The work of redemption is an integrated whole, but it is composed of carefully arranged components.

Logical Priority of Justification

Hence, justification has logical priority over sanctification as its objective ground and subjective motivational wellspring.

Because legal union has priority over mystical union (inasmuch as election and the obedience of Christ have priority over our existential reception of their benefits), we

---

78. Westminster Shorter Catechism 86.
79. Geerhardus Vos, "The Alleged Legalism in Paul's Doctrine of Justification," in *Redemptive History and Biblical Interpretation: The Shorter Writings of Geerhardus Vos*, ed. Richard B. Gaffin Jr. (Phillipsburg, NJ: P&R, 1980), 384.

can also say that justification has priority over sanctification. But does this necessarily follow? And how can it be so, given that at least one part of our transformation, namely, regeneration, *does* seem to precede justification logically? We tackle each of these queries in turn.

First, does it necessarily follow that because there are distinct aspects of union, the downstream effects of those aspects must be ordered in an analogous way? Is it not enough to argue that justification is grounded in the legal aspect of union and that sanctification is grounded in the mystical aspect? Or perhaps we could even say that sanctification is in some sense grounded in the forensic aspect of union, but does it necessarily follow that sanctification is grounded in justification? Is it not better to preserve union as the overarching soteriological category, even with its multifaceted nature, and to maintain that justification and sanctification are sort of the twin progeny of this union? As we have seen, some Reformed theologians make this very case.

Is there any biblical data that can help guide a determination on this point? Are justification and sanctification ever explicitly ordered in Scripture? The epistle to the Romans would seem to be a fruitful resource for exploration. In Romans 5, for example, Paul makes the argument that justification is the fount from which further salvific blessings flow. Consider the logic of Paul's argument in the opening verses of the chapter:

> Therefore, since we have been justified by faith, we have peace with God through our Lord Jesus Christ. Through him we have also obtained access by faith into this grace in which we stand, and we rejoice in hope of the glory of God. Not only that, but we rejoice in our sufferings, knowing that suffering produces endurance, and endurance produces character, and character produces hope, and hope does not put us to shame, because God's love has been poured into our hearts through the Holy Spirit who has been given to us. (5:1–5)

After expositing humanity's universal condemnation and the failure of the law to secure God's justifying verdict (Romans 1–3) as well as the free gift of justification in Christ, received by faith alone apart from works (Romans 3–4), Paul now shifts his attention to the blessings that follow upon this free justification. Principal among these blessings is the peace that believers enjoy with God as a result of justification.[80] Justification is spoken of as an access point (προσαγωγή)—an entrée into the gracious presence of God—through which the blessings of the transformed life are secured. The blessing of perseverance is especially highlighted as Paul builds a logical chain from suffering through endurance and character all the way to the blessed hope granted by the Spirit-infused love of God. The language of sanctification is not employed here, but surely this life of perseverance—the grace in which believers stand—is conceptually one with the doctrine of sanctification.

---

80. There is a textual variant here, with some manuscripts containing the subjunctive form ἔχωμεν instead of the indicative ἔχομεν—"let us have" rather than "we have" peace with God. The internal evidence favors the latter, which is reflected in most translations. See Bruce M. Metzger, *A Textual Commentary on the Greek New Testament*, 3rd ed. (New York: United Bible Societies, 1971), 452.

Paul next engages in an extended *a maiore ad minus* argument—from the greater hurdle of the justification of enemies to the seemingly lesser obstacle of ensuring the final salvation of reconciled friends (5:6–11): "Since, therefore, we have now been justified by his blood, much more shall we be saved by him from the wrath of God. For if while we were enemies we were reconciled to God by the death of his Son, much more, now that we are reconciled, shall we be saved by his life" (5:9–10). Again, the ἁγιάζω/ ἅγιος word group is not employed here, but surely the concept of sanctification (culminating in glorification—final salvation from the wrath of God) is in view. We could look to Paul's argument in Galatians for similar logic: "Let me ask you only this: Did you receive the Spirit by works of the law or by hearing with faith? Are you so foolish? Having begun by the Spirit, are you now being perfected by the flesh?" (Gal. 3:2–3). Justification signals the beginning of the life of grace-enabled faith, which is extended in sanctification. "Perfection" is accomplished by the selfsame reliance on the Spirit, not the works of the law. Justification and sanctification are ordered by a relationship of origin and completion.

As we turn our attention back to Romans 5, Paul then extends his argument with a reflection on the Adam-Christ typology (5:12–21). Just as all sinned in Adam, the federal representative of all humanity, so also all who trust in Christ are accounted righteous in him. The transformative effects of Adam's sin follow logically upon the guilt that all humanity inherits in him. Likewise, the transformative effects of Christ's obedience follow upon the declaration of believers' righteousness in him.[81] Romans 6 and 8 evince the same basic pattern. Union with Christ in his atoning death is purposive: it yields the renewed life in union with Christ's resurrection (6:1–11). Similarly, in Romans 8, our condemnation in Christ produces the Spirit-empowered life that fulfills the law of God (8:1–7). Todd Billings points to Calvin's commentary on Romans 6 as especially illuminating on this point:

> While Calvin emphasizes that justification and sanctification are inseparable in his reflections on Romans 6, he also suggests a logical (but not temporal) ordering of being "justified" for the purpose that "afterwards" the life of holiness lived would not be focused on acquiring righteousness before God, but serving God in eager gratitude.[82]

Thus, the transformed life of sanctification is predicated on the logically antecedent forensic declaration of justification. Justification has priority over sanctification as its objective ground. Only those who are reckoned righteous in Christ can receive the extended blessing of Spirit-enabled moral transformation.

But Calvin also points to a kind of subjective priority that justification bears over sanctification. In his opening chapter on justification in the *Institutes*, Calvin speaks of justification and sanctification as a "double grace" that flows from union with Christ.

---

81. For an exegetical defense of the Reformed view of the imputation of Adam's guilt, see John Murray, *The Imputation of Adam's Sin* (Grand Rapids, MI: Eerdmans, 1959).
82. Billings, "Union with Christ," 55.

But for Calvin, these blessings are not symmetrically ordered: "For unless you first of all grasp what your relationship to God is and the nature of his judgment concerning you, you have neither a foundation on which to establish your salvation nor one on which to build piety toward God."[83] It is clear from this passage that justification ("the nature of his judgment concerning you") is foundational for sanctification (the life of "piety"). But what is interesting is the way in which Calvin highlights our "grasp[ing]" of this saving reality. An acknowledgment of our security in the justifying verdict of God serves as the motivational wellspring from which the life of holiness flows.[84] Calvin later speaks about justification freeing Christians from the "perpetual dread" they experienced under the law. The psychological benefits of justification vis-à-vis sanctification were already forcefully asserted by Luther in his classic treatise *The Freedom of a Christian*. It is only when the Christian is confident of God's gratuitous mercy in Christ that he is freed to love and serve his neighbor, not as a means of securing justification but as the overflow of the assurance of faith: "Here is the truly Christian life; here is faith really working by love; when a man applies himself with joy and love to the works of that freest servitude, in which he serves others voluntarily and for nought; himself abundantly satisfied in the fulness and riches of his own faith."[85] In sum, justification is foundational for sanctification not only because it removes the *objective* legal obstacle to God's sanctifying mercies but also because it effects a *subjective*, fundamental change within the person justified: from the slavery of the law to the freedom of the gospel.

One theological dilemma remains for the position that justification serves as the ground of sanctification: the problem of regeneration. Can we argue for the consistent priority of the forensic over the transformational when one aspect of our transformation, namely, our new birth by the Spirit, precedes conversion and thus precedes justification in the traditional Reformed *ordo salutis*? Here we might appeal to the insightful thesis of Michael Horton, adapted from Bruce McCormack, that justification serves as the "Word-constituting" source not only of sanctification but also of regeneration.[86] For McCormack, God's declaration in justification "creates the reality it declares."[87] This belief is based on McCormack's conviction that the gospel entails its own ontology that is ordered toward the eschaton: "The divine imputation is a verdict whose final meaning can only be grasped when it is seen in the framework of a teleologically-oriented covenant of grace."[88] Regeneration "flows from justification as its consequence" because it is grounded in a divine declaration that is constitutive of

---

83. Calvin, *Institutes*, 3.11.1.
84. We might even see parallels here to Calvin's double knowledge: the knowledge of the self in the knowledge of God and vice versa. Calvin, *Institutes*, 1.1.
85. Martin Luther, *The Freedom of a Christian*, in *Three Treatises*, 2nd ed. (Minneapolis: Fortress, 1970), 302.
86. Michael S. Horton, *Covenant and Salvation: Union with Christ* (Louisville: Westminster John Knox, 2007), 201. We have already seen this same logic in Billings's treatment of Calvin: justification is logically (but not temporally) antecedent to sanctification. Billings, "Union with Christ," 55.
87. Bruce L. McCormack, "What's at Stake in Current Debates over Justification? The Crisis of Protestantism in the West," in *Justification: What's at Stake in the Current Debates*, ed. Mark A. Husbands and Daniel J. Treier (Downers Grove, IL: InterVarsity Press, 2004), 107.
88. McCormack, "What's at Stake," 109.

the whole of redemption—from election to glorification—and which is secured in the "saving efficacy" of Christ's vicarious obedience.[89]

Horton extends McCormack's insight by means of a creative use of speech-act theory. Justification is the verdict that "does what it says."[90] The external call of the gospel—God justifies the ungodly—is a speech act that accomplishes what it pronounces when it is brought to bear on the elect internally.[91] As Hoekema explains, "The Word that is spoken in effectual calling is not only a discourse *about* justification, but *is* God's announcement of the justification of the sinner, received by faith."[92] The New Testament teaching that regeneration is mediated by the Word of God (1 Pet. 1:23, "You have been born again . . . through the living and abiding word of God") would seem to bear out this relationship between the outer and inner call of the gospel. Thus, a thoroughgoing "forensicism" ("rightly understood," as McCormack notes) is made possible without surrendering any of the transformative effects of the gospel.[93] In sum, regeneration itself is a transformative reality and, viewed from one perspective, has a kind of priority over justification, since regeneration elicits faith, which in turn is the means of receiving justification. But viewed from another perspective, since the judicial summons of the gospel call comes first, justification (God's forensic declaration) can be said to have a kind of logical priority over regeneration as the Word that "does what it says" in bringing about the renewal of the elect.

The logical priority of justification over sanctification can also be cashed out in terms of the Reformed distinction between "objective" and "subjective" justification, or "active" and "passive" justification. According to this distinction, the proclamation of Christ's person and righteousness logically precedes the exercise of faith and therefore the subjective appropriation of justification's benefits. Consider the opinion of Herman Bavinck:

> Now the distinction between active and passive justification served to escape this nomistic pattern. Active justification already in a sense occurred in the proclamation of the gospel, in the external calling, but it occurs especially in the internal calling when God by his word and Spirit effectually calls sinners, convicts them of sin, drives them out toward Christ, and prompts them to find forgiveness and life in him. Logically this active justification precedes faith. It is, as it were, the effectual proclamation of God's Spirit that one's sins are forgiven, so that persons are persuaded in their hearts, believingly accept—dare to accept and are able to accept—that word of God and receive Christ along with all his benefits. And when these persons, after first, as it were, going out to Christ (the direct act of faith), then (by a reflex act of faith) return to themselves and acknowledge with childlike gratitude that their sins too have been personally forgiven, then, in that moment, the passive justification occurs by which God acquits

---

89. McCormack, "What's at Stake," 109.
90. Horton, *Covenant and Salvation*, 217, 243.
91. I take it that regeneration (in the sense of the initial transformative work of the Holy Spirit by which he causes the new birth) and effectual calling are essentially synonymous. They are different metaphors (new life and verbal summons, respectively) that describe the same reality. See Hoekema, *Saved by Grace*, 106.
92. Hoekema, *Saved by Grace*, 203.
93. McCormack, "What's at Stake," 106.

believers in their conscience and by his Spirit bears witness with their own spirits that they are children of God and heirs of eternal life [cf. Rom. 8:15–17]. While there is here a priority of order, it is coupled with simultaneity of time.... Certainly one must take account of the fact that the above distinction, though it has logical import, has no temporal significance. While there is here a priority of order, it is coupled with simultaneity in time. Concretely the two coincide and always go together.[94]

Thus, the priority is logical, not temporal: "Active and passive justification, accordingly, cannot be separated even for a second."[95] As such, this prioritization of "active" justification should not be confused with the antinomian belief in an eternal justification, nor even in a belief that would locate justification itself in the historical accomplishment of salvation in Christ's life, death, and resurrection. But the priority remains important because it safeguards against the notion that faith itself brings about the judicial declaration of God in justification or that the legal aspect of redemption is somehow mediated through the transformative. The similarities between Bavinck's perspective and Horton's proposal are striking. Justification in its objective or active sense is located in the declaration of God himself in the gospel—externally proclaimed and internally realized—which then elicits faith in the elect and yields the subjective or passive experience of justification.[96]

Conclusion

How do we properly relate justification and sanctification? Certainly, all Christians committed to the great principles of the Reformation will answer with one voice, "In the person and work of Jesus Christ our Mediator." It will not do either to confuse or to separate these crucial doctrines because they are integrated in the holistic work of the singular person of the God-man. Union with Christ by the Holy Spirit is the integrative motif that holds these doctrines together, but even this soteriological category must be carefully parsed in terms of its various aspects. Justification and sanctification are distinct but inseparable, and thus all forms of antinomianism are ruled out. But justification and sanctification are also ordered toward one another in a specific manner. Justification has logical priority in the relationship because it serves as the legal ground and the subjective motivation for the life of holiness. Even if not all Reformational Christians can agree with this last statement, certainly all can celebrate the glorious work of our Christ, "who became to us wisdom from God, righteousness and sanctification and redemption" (1 Cor. 1:30).

Recommended Reading

Allen, Michael. *Sanctification*. New Studies in Dogmatics. Grand Rapids, MI: Zondervan, 2017.
Bavinck, Herman. *Reformed Dogmatics*. Edited by John Bolt. Translated by John Vriend. Vol. 4, *Holy Spirit, Church, and New Creation*. Grand Rapids, MI: Baker Academic, 2008.

---

94. Herman Bavinck, *Reformed Dogmatics*, ed. John Bolt, trans. John Vriend, vol. 4, *Holy Spirit, Church, and New Creation* (Grand Rapids, MI: Baker Academic, 2008), 219.
95. Bavinck, *Reformed Dogmatics*, 4:220.
96. For a discussion of active and passive justification in Witsius, see Fesko, *Covenant of Redemption*, 105–6.

Billings, J. Todd. "Union with Christ and the Double Grace: Calvin's Theology and Its Early Reception." In *Calvin's Theology and Its Reception: Disputes, Developments, and New Possibilities*, edited by J. Todd Billings and I. John Hesselink, 49–71. Louisville: Westminster John Knox, 2012.

Braaten, Carl E., and Robert W. Jenson, eds. *Union with Christ: The New Finnish Interpretation of Luther*. Grand Rapids, MI: Eerdmans, 1998.

Calvin, John. *Institutes of the Christian Religion*. Edited by John T. McNeill. Translated by Ford Lewis Battles. 2 vols. Library of Christian Classics 20–21. Philadelphia: Westminster, 1960.

The Canons and Decrees of the Council of Trent. Translated by H. J. Schroeder. Charlotte, NC: TAN Books, 1978.

Fesko, J. V. *The Covenant of Redemption: Origins, Development, and Reception*. Reformed Historical Theology 35. Göttingen: Vandenhoeck & Ruprecht, 2015.

———. "Union with Christ." In *Reformation Theology: A Systematic Summary*, edited by Matthew Barrett, 423–50. Wheaton, IL: Crossway, 2017.

Garcia, Mark A. *Life in Christ: Union with Christ and Twofold Grace in Calvin's Theology*. Studies in Christian History and Thought. Eugene, OR: Wipf & Stock, 2008.

Hoekema, Anthony A. *Saved by Grace*. Grand Rapids, MI: Eerdmans, 1989.

Horton, Michael S. "Calvin's Theology of Union with Christ and the Double Grace: Modern Reception and Contemporary Possibilities." In *Calvin's Theology and Its Reception: Disputes, Developments, and New Possibilities*, edited by J. Todd Billings and I. John Hesselink, 72–94. Louisville: Westminster John Knox, 2012.

———. *Covenant and Salvation: Union with Christ*. Louisville: Westminster John Knox, 2007.

Luther, Martin. *The Freedom of a Christian*. In *Three Treatises*, 261–316. 2nd ed. Minneapolis: Fortress, 1970.

———. "Sermon on Two Kinds of Righteousness, 1519." In *The Annotated Luther*. Vol. 2, *Word and Faith*, edited by Kirsi I. Stjerna, 9–24. Minneapolis: Fortress, 2015.

Maas, Korey D. "Justification by Faith Alone." In *Reformation Theology: A Systematic Summary*, edited by Matthew Barrett, 511–47. Wheaton, IL: Crossway, 2017.

Mannermaa, Tuomo. *Christ Present in Faith: Luther's View of Justification*. Edited by Kirsi I. Stjerna. Minneapolis: Fortress, 2005.

McGrath, Alister E. *Iustitia Dei: A History of the Christian Doctrine of Justification*. 2nd ed. Cambridge: Cambridge University Press, 1998.

Muller, Richard A. *Calvin and the Reformed Tradition: On the Work of Christ and the Order of Salvation*. Grand Rapids, MI: Baker Academic, 2012.

Murray, John. *Redemption Accomplished and Applied*. Grand Rapids, MI: Eerdmans, 1955.

Peterson, David. *Possessed by God: A New Testament Theology of Sanctification and Holiness*. New Studies in Biblical Theology 1. Downers Grove, IL: InterVarsity Press, 1995.

Stanley, Alan P., ed. *Four Views on the Role of Works at the Final Judgment*. Counterpoints: Bible and Theology. Grand Rapids, MI: Zondervan, 2013.

Trueman, Carl R. "Is the Finnish Line a New Beginning? A Critical Assessment of the Reading of Luther Offered by the Helsinki Circle." *Westminster Theological Journal* 65, no. 2 (2003): 231–44.

———. "*Simul peccator et justus*: Martin Luther and Justification." In *Justification in Perspective: Historical Developments and Contemporary Challenges*, edited by Bruce L. McCormack, 75–92. Grand Rapids, MI: Baker Academic, 2006.

Venema, Cornelis P. *Accepted and Renewed in Christ: The "Twofold Grace of God" and the Interpretation of Calvin's Theology*. Göttingen: Vandenhoeck & Ruprecht, 2007.

Vos, Geerhardus. "The Alleged Legalism in Paul's Doctrine of Justification." In *Redemptive History and Biblical Interpretation: The Shorter Writings of Geerhardus Vos*, edited by Richard B. Gaffin Jr., 383–99. Phillipsburg, NJ: P&R, 1980.

17

Justification, the Law, and the New Covenant

JASON MEYER

Books on justification can unintentionally diminish the doctrine of justification. How? Isolating the doctrine of justification can distort the doctrine by relegating it to a place of solitary confinement. In that place of isolation and segregation from other doctrines, people can fail to see the full scope of the unity and beauty of God's plan of salvation.

I applaud the work of other authors who tie together the doctrine of justification with the doctrine of union with Christ.[1] These organic connections avoid the confusion that grows in the greenhouse of isolation. But other connections exist that cause the doctrine of justification to shine with even greater glory. This essay argues that there are compelling connections between the doctrine of justification and the new covenant.

What does the reader gain from viewing justification in the light of the new covenant? The link between justification and the new covenant provides a framework that can distinguish between justification as an *event* and justification as a *gateway*. My thesis is that the act of justification provides a gateway to glories that are grander than justification by itself. One can see the event as a gateway only if justification is released from its solitary confinement. The blood-bought blessings of the new covenant and justification are distinguishable as doctrines but inseparable through union with Christ.

Outline

We will set this doctrine free from its solitary confinement in seven stages:

1. Connect justification to the new covenant
2. Connect the law to the old covenant

---

1. E.g., D. Martyn Lloyd-Jones, *Romans: Exposition of Chapter 5; Assurance* (Carlisle, PA: Banner of Truth, 1971), 54.

3. Show that Paul's gospel-law contrast concerning justification is a covenantal contrast
4. Trace the transition from the old covenant to the new covenant
5. Reflect on the role of the law for new covenant Christians
6. Highlight the way that the new covenant addresses both justification and sanctification
7. Show that justification and sanctification are distinguishable yet inseparable

Justification and the New Covenant

The glory of justification is grander when one grasps the intricate connection between justification and the new covenant. My dissertation, published as *The End of the Law*, was something of a minicrusade against the word-equals-concept fallacy when it comes to covenant in Paul's thought.[2] The word-equals-concept fallacy is a flawed approach that says certain concepts appear only where certain words explicitly occur. Those who commit this fallacy with respect to "covenant" restrict the covenant concept in Paul to the specific places where the word "covenant" (διαθήκη) shows up in Paul (Rom. 9:4; 11:27; 1 Cor. 11:25; 2 Cor. 3:6, 14; Gal. 3:15, 17; 4:24; Eph. 2:12). Therefore, some Pauline interpreters make the case that covenant was an afterthought in Paul's theology because the word "covenant" occurs only a few times.[3]

A better approach would recognize that certain words are so tied to the broader concept of covenant that they should be called *covenant terminology*. Stanley E. Porter has authored one of the most linguistically informed essays on this topic.[4] Porter prefers a study based on the semantic domain of διαθήκη through the use of the Louw-Nida lexicon and "contexts where other covenant terminology may be suggested by immediate usage."[5] This analysis leads him to assert that there is a semantic relationship between "covenant" (διαθήκη) and "righteousness" (δικ-) words based on semantic domain.[6]

The semantic relationship between "righteousness" and "covenant" has a profound effect on our understanding of the importance of the new covenant in Paul. The new covenant becomes a much more massive theme in Paul when one connects it to the concept of justifying righteousness. Porter agrees that the link between covenant and

---

2. Jason C. Meyer, *The End of the Law: Mosaic Covenant in Pauline Theology*, NACSBT 6 (Nashville: B&H Academic, 2009).
3. James D. G. Dunn, "Did Paul Have a Covenant Theology? Reflections on Romans 9.4 and 11.27," in *The Concept of the Covenant in the Second Temple Period*, ed. Stanley E. Porter and Jacqueline C. R. de Roo, JSJSup 71 (Leiden: Brill, 1993), 287–307. Dunn argues that covenant was an unimportant concept in Paul's thought and that he uses the terminology only in response to his opponents' use of the term.
4. Stanley E. Porter, "The Concept of Covenant in Paul," in Porter and de Roo, *Concept of the Covenant*, 269–85. Porter notes that even though many biblical scholars buy into James Barr's classic criticism of the word-equals-concept fallacy in *The Theological Dictionary of the New Testament*, some still unwittingly dredge it back up in their own writings. Porter says that Barr's work has become "one of those artifacts that is often acknowledged yet widely misunderstood, with the result that much lexicographical study of the Greek of the New Testament continues as before." The irony of Porter's essay preceding Dunn's contribution is that Dunn's work effectively becomes an example of what Porter stringently labels as "fundamentally flawed." Porter, "Concept of Covenant in Paul," 272, 273.
5. J. P. Louw and E. A. Nida, *Greek-English Lexicon of the New Testament Based on Semantic Domains*, 2 vols. (New York: United Bible Societies, 1988). See Porter, "Concept of Covenant in Paul," 282–83.
6. Louw and Nida, *Greek-English Lexicon*, 282–83.

righteousness would mean that covenant would become a major category in Paul. He gives Romans as an example. If the terms "covenant" and "righteousness" are linked, then the concept of covenant would not make its first appearance in Romans 9–11 but would occur as early as the theme verse (1:17). Habakkuk 2:4 would also be interpreted as a reference to the concept of the new covenant (Rom. 1:17; cf. Gal. 3:11).

Second Corinthians 3:9 may be the clearest textual connection between justification and the new covenant. Paul's contrast between the old covenant and the new covenant is framed as a contrast between an old covenant ministry of "condemnation" (κατάκρισις) and a new covenant ministry of "righteousness" (δικαιοσύνη). The fact that Paul contrasts righteousness with condemnation shows that Paul speaks of righteousness in the sense of justifying righteousness, because it represents the other side of the coin in a judicial verdict: condemnation. The new covenant is a ministry of justification; the old covenant is a ministry of condemnation.[7]

Paul speaks of the new covenant and justification in other parallel ways as well. Paul's discussion of the new covenant in 2 Corinthians is a good case in point. The apostle connects the service of his ministry to the new covenant (3:6). His epistles reveal that he regards himself as a "servant" (διάκονος) of "the new covenant" (καινῆς διαθήκης) and as a "servant" (διάκονος) of "the gospel" (εὐαγγελίου).[8] Further evidence emerges in 4:3–4, where the new covenant is parallel to "gospel" (εὐαγγέλιον), especially in light of the repetition of previous themes like "glory" and "veiled."[9]

Further, the tight correlation between justification and the blood of Christ constitutes additional evidence for the intricate connection between justification and the new covenant. Justification cannot be separated from the blood of Christ because Paul declares that we are "justified by his blood" (Rom. 5:9). In the same way, the new covenant is inseparable from the blood of Christ because the new covenant is "the new covenant in my blood" (1 Cor. 11:25).[10]

My dissertation took Porter's essay-length discussion and further developed it into a book-length treatment. My work established a more detailed case for viewing "righteousness" and "promise" language as covenant terminology.[11] I also expanded the parameters of covenant terminology to include other words and concepts as well. One

---

7. Recall that Porter asserts that "righteousness" (δικ-) words and "covenant" (διαθήκη) share a semantic relationship because they share the same semantic domain. Porter, "Concept of Covenant in Paul," 282–83. Petrus J. Gräbe follows Porter as well. Gräbe, *New Covenant, New Community: The Significance of Biblical and Patristic Covenant Theology for Contemporary Understanding* (Waynesboro, GA: Paternoster, 2006), 115–16.

8. See Eph. 3:6–7 and Col. 1:23 for references to Paul as a servant of the gospel. Other places in Paul's writings show that Paul serves in the work of the gospel (Phil. 1:22), has been set apart for the gospel (Rom. 1:1, 9) and proclaims the gospel of God as a minister of Christ (15:16).

9. Paul R. Williamson takes the same position: "Paul identifies the 'new covenant' as the gospel of Jesus Christ (2 Cor. 4:3–6), and the Christian community as those in whom the blessings of the new covenant have been realized (2 Cor. 3:3; cf. Jer. 31:32–33; Ezek. 11:19; 36:26–27)." Williamson, *Sealed with an Oath: Covenant in God's Unfolding Purpose*, NSBT 23 (Downers Grove, IL: InterVarsity Press, 2007), 192.

10. Kim Huat Tan makes the same case that the new covenant is connected with the cross. He demonstrates that the new covenant can be put into effect only by Christ's sacrificial blood. He also links covenant and cross with Jesus's preaching of the kingdom. Tan, "Community, Kingdom, and Cross: Jesus' View of Covenant," in *The God of Covenant: Biblical, Theological, and Contemporary Perspectives*, ed. Jamie A. Grant and Alistair I. Wilson (Downers Grove, IL: InterVarsity Press, 2005), 145–55.

11. See Meyer, *End of the Law*.

of the most far-reaching expansions was the recognition that just as "justification" is new covenant terminology, "law" is old covenant terminology.

The Mosaic Law and the Old Covenant

The old covenant plays a much greater role in Paul than a mere word count would suggest. The Mosaic covenant is a broad and overarching entity that incorporates many other elements. One obvious example is the Mosaic law. How could anyone categorically separate the Mosaic law from the Mosaic covenant? The historical connection between covenant and law authorizes a connection between the terms "covenant" (διαθήκη) and "law" (νόμος) when the context specifies a Mosaic referent. The fact that Paul gives parallel assessments of the old covenant and the law (i.e., both condemn and kill, and neither can secure righteousness and life) further confirms the connection between them.

There are other broad themes that belong to covenant terminology as well. Frank Thielman argues for the validity of understanding themes in their wider covenantal context: "The Mosaic covenant contains certain broad themes, such as the election of God's people and the importance of their sanctity, which reappear in Paul's letters in more subtle ways than a study only of Paul's explicit statements about the Mosaic covenant would detect."[12] N. T. Wright adds further weight to this claim with characteristic clarity:

> At this point at least I am fully on the side of E. P. Sanders when he argues that the covenant is the hidden presupposition of Jewish literature even when the word hardly occurs. Exegesis needs the concordance, but it cannot be ruled by it. It is no argument against calling Paul a covenantal theologian to point out the scarcity of *diathēkē* in his writings. We have to learn to recognize still more important things, such as implicit narratives and allusions to large biblical themes. Just because we cannot so easily look them up in a reference book that does not make them irrelevant.[13]

Paul R. Williamson shares this perspective in his work on covenant. He says that one must "recognize that the concept might sometimes be assumed even where the terminology is lacking."[14] He makes the case that words must not merely be counted but also weighed: "Thus, given the weight Paul attaches to the concept where it is mentioned, covenant—particularly the new covenant and its implications for the place of the law—is undoubtedly more foundational and pervasive in Pauline theology than a mere word study might suggest."[15] Many other scholars are starting to stress the importance of the covenant concept in Paul as well.[16]

---

12. Frank Thielman, *Paul and the Law: A Contextual Approach* (Downers Grove, IL: InterVarsity Press, 1994), 12.
13. N. T. Wright, *Paul: In Fresh Perspective* (Minneapolis: Fortress, 2005), 26.
14. Williamson, *Sealed with an Oath*, 186.
15. Williamson, *Sealed with an Oath*, 186. Williamson, however, still surveys the new covenant in Paul by studying the canonical occurrences of διαθήκη.
16. Herman N. Ridderbos, *Paul: An Outline of His Theology*, trans. John Richard de Witt (Grand Rapids, MI: Eerdmans, 1975), 333–41; R. David Kaylor, *Paul's Covenant Community: Jew and Gentile in Romans* (Atlanta: John Knox,

This essay has argued thus far for a connection between the new covenant and the language of "justification" on the one hand and the old covenant and the language of "the Mosaic law" on the other hand. If both of these points stand, then it leads to the third aspect of the argument. One must read the contrast between law and gospel in Paul as a covenantal contrast between the old covenant and the new covenant.

Paul's Law-Gospel Contrast as Covenantal

These semantic-domain studies provide important clues for concluding that the law-gospel contrast in Paul is a covenantal contrast.[17] Semantic studies, however, are necessary but insufficient. Conceptual connections must be established by careful exegesis of texts within their respective contexts. Are there extended exegetical arguments that justify reading the law-gospel contrast as a covenantal contrast?

One could begin in the Old Testament Prophetic Literature. Breaking the stipulations of the old covenant brings the curses of the covenant and death, but the promises of the new covenant provide great comfort and hope that God will bring life on the other side of death and judgment. For example, scholars frequently call Jeremiah 30–33 the "Book of Consolation," because it describes the salvation of the covenant people after the judgment and curse of exile in Jeremiah 1–25. The Old Testament prophets are covenant-lawsuit preachers who charge the people with breaking the terms and stipulations of the Mosaic covenant. Once judgment, curse, and condemnation come on the people, the note of comfort bursts forth into prominence, based on the promises of a new covenant. The old covenant brought death; the new covenant brings life.

This same dynamic appears in Paul many times. For example, the argument of 2 Corinthians 3:7–11 is that the new covenant, which brings justification, has come with much more glory than the old covenant, which could only bring not justification but its opposite: condemnation as a ministry of death.[18] Spatial restraints prevent us from examining a multitude of texts in a rigorous exegetical manner. I have chosen to highlight Paul's argument in Galatians 3:10–20 because it is a key text on justification and because it uniquely brings together two vital themes concerning the law: (1) the law could not bring justification and life, and (2) it was never designed to do so.

The Law Could Not Bring Justification and Life (Gal. 3:10–12)

Paul's law-gospel contrast is an antithesis between two opposing ways to attain life: a faith path and a works path. This contrast between the paths of faith and works remains constant throughout Galatians 3:1–14 (see table 17.1).

1988); N. T. Wright, *The Climax of the Covenant: Christ and the Law in Pauline Theology* (Minneapolis: Fortress, 1992); Bruce W. Longenecker, "Contours of Covenant Theology in the Post-Conversion Paul," in *The Road from Damascus: The Impact of Paul's Conversion on His Life, Thought, and Ministry*, ed. Richard N. Longenecker (Grand Rapids, MI: Eerdmans, 1997), 125–46; Gräbe, *New Covenant*.

17. This section on Galatians 3:10–20 borrows heavily from my earlier work on Galatians 3:10–20 in Jason C. Meyer, *The End of the Law: Mosaic Covenant in Pauline Theology* (Nashville: B&H Academic, 2009), 137–76. Used by permission of B&H.

18. See Meyer, *End of the Law*, 62–114.

Table 17.1 Faith Path and Works Path in Galatians 3

Faith Path	Works Path
"by hearing with faith" (3:2)	"by works of the law" (3:2)
"by hearing with faith" (3:5)	"by works of the law" (3:5)
"those of faith" (3:7)	"all who rely on works of the law" (3:10)
"live by faith" (3:11)	"live by them [God's statutes]" (3:12)

Paul uses parallel expressions for the attempt to attain life by the law: "justified before God by the law" (3:11; cf. 5:4), "live by them" (3:12), "inheritance comes by the law" (3:18), and "righteousness . . . by the law" (3:21). Paul constructs a chiasm in 3:11–12 that puts these two paths into sharp contrast:

a It is evident that no one will be justified "by the law" (ἐν νόμῳ) (3:11a)
  b because the righteous will live "by faith" (ἐκ πίστεως) (3:11b)
    b' However the law is not "by faith" (ἐκ πίστεως) (3:12a)
a' Rather the one who does them will live "by them" (ἐν αὐτοῖς) (3:12b).

The parallelism in this chiastic structure makes an important point in the current debates over justification language in Paul. Paul forms a parallel between "justify" (δικαιόω) in 3:11 and "live" (ζάω) in 3:12. This parallel stands opposed to the New Perspective's understanding of justification. Paul's doctrine of justification directly addresses the issue of eternal life (ζάω), not primarily nationalism.[19]

The law-gospel contrast in Galatians 3:10–14 is thoroughly covenantal. Paul explicitly states that the curse of the law comes on those who do not abide by all the things written in the law (3:10). The Mosaic covenant brought condemnation in the form of the curse of the law. The term "curse" (κατάρα) appears twice in this section (3:10, 13). The full phrase "the curse of the law" (τῆς κατάρας τοῦ νόμου) in 3:13 leaves no doubt as to what curse Paul has in mind. Paul refers to the curse of the law that was part of the Mosaic covenant. This relationship between the curse and the Mosaic covenant is so interwoven into the fabric of the Old Testament that one reads of the "curses of the covenant" in Deuteronomy 29:21.

Paul argues that the path laid out in the law cannot lead to life (Lev. 18:5) but will lead to curse (Gal. 3:10). This reading of Leviticus 18:5 coheres with this covenantal frame of reference. The wider context of Leviticus 18 features the covenantal consequences of reward and punishment. The chapter opens with a section that warns against living like the Canaanites (18:3) and ends with the same warning (18:28). Obey or the land will "vomit" Israel out like the Canaanites before them. Therefore, prolonged life in the land as the reward for obedience stands opposed to expulsion from the land as the punishment for disobedience.[20] This threat applies to the nation as well as to the individual (18:29).[21]

---

19. Paul certainly addresses Jewish exclusivism, but this emphasis is secondary and derivative, not primary.
20. Douglas J. Moo makes a similar point. See Moo, *The Epistle to the Romans*, NICNT (Grand Rapids, MI: Eerdmans, 1996), 648n13.
21. The immediate context of Lev. 18:5 does not contain any explicit indicators of a focus on the gracious elements of the law. In fact, Lev. 18:1–5 introduces the reader to a series of sexual laws that, when broken, require expulsion from

Therefore, Paul clearly contends that the law cannot bring justification, but he also just as clearly shows that it was never supposed to do so. One should not conclude from this discussion that God designed the Mosaic covenant to function as a competing way of salvation that is directly opposed to the faith path to life. The next section of Galatians makes this point in a multitude of ways.

The Law Was Not Designed to Bring Justification and Life (Gal. 3:15–20)

Before we continue tracing the argument of Galatians, the reader should pause and note the way that Galatians 3:15–20 provides further proof that the entire debate over justification and the law was a covenantal discussion. The term "covenant" (διαθήκη) occurs in 3:15 and 3:17 as part of Paul's contrast between the Mosaic law and the earlier Abrahamic promise. The logic leading up to this connection between the Abrahamic covenant and the law is clear. Paul begins with a human analogy and shows that people do not change or nullify the original stipulations of the agreement. Paul argues in 3:17 that the "covenant" of promise that God made with Abraham cannot be added to or invalidated by the law in such a way as to make the promise null and void. Consider the illustration from 3:15: If it is true "even" in a man-made arrangement that the terms cannot be set aside or supplemented, how much more is that so in a divine covenant?

Some scholars question the importance of the covenant concept at this point by arguing that "covenant" is an inconsequential term.[22] This approach is not convincing because the term "promise" (ἐπαγγελία) here should be read as covenant terminology. There are several lines of evidence for this connection. First, Porter argues that examining contexts in which the term "covenant" (διαθήκη) appears suggests a close relationship between words for "covenant" (διαθήκη) and "promise" (ἐπαγγελ-).[23] Parallel Pauline texts link the terms "covenant" (διαθήκη) and "promise" (ἐπαγγελία) together (Rom. 9:4; Eph. 2:12). Second, Paul establishes a grammatical link between the two terms in Galatians 3:17. Paul argues that the law cannot invalidate the Abrahamic covenant. The connection between covenant and promise comes in the purpose clause. If the Abrahamic "covenant" (διαθήκη) is invalidated, then the Abrahamic "promise" (ἐπαγγελία) would be rendered null and void. Paul clearly sees the two operating together. Third, the connection between promise and covenant enjoys Old Testament precedent in that it fits the common understanding of covenants as promises that are confirmed by an oath through a covenantal ceremony. This appears to be what Paul means when he calls them the "covenants of promise" (Eph. 2:12).[24]

---

the people (cf. 18:28–29) and even death (20:9–21). Furthermore, no sacrifice for sins exists for those who violate these things (18:29).

22. Dunn, "Did Paul Have a Covenant Theology?," 291–92. Dunn calls the conclusion that Paul is referring to the Abrahamic covenant "perverse," because Paul does not refer to covenants at all (whether Mosaic or Abrahamic). Dunn argues that the wordplay between "testament" and "covenant" in 3:15 further weakens a reference to "covenant" elsewhere. He sees further significance in the fact that Paul's parallel discussion in Rom. 4:13–21 does not once mention the term "covenant."

23. Porter, "Concept of Covenant in Paul," 283.

24. "Promises are given without their being covenants. Some promises are subsequently confirmed by an oath and then are called covenants. Hence a covenant is basically an oath-bound promissory relation." Fred H. Klooster, "The Biblical Method of Salvation: A Case for Continuity," in *Continuity and Discontinuity: Perspectives on the Relationship between*

The term "mediator" (μεσίτης) in Galatians 3:19–20 is also covenant terminology (mediator of the covenant). Paul stresses the unmediated way in which Abraham received the promise directly from God, whereas the Israelites received the law through the double delivery of the angels and Moses. Otto Becker also supports treating these two words together.[25] Paul calls Moses[26] the mediator between the Israelites and God, and the Judaism of Paul's day also referred to Moses as the mediator of the covenant.[27]

Now that the linguistic and conceptual details are in view, it is time to examine the way Paul argues that the Mosaic law was not designed to lead to justification or life. The structural similarities between Galatians 2:21; 3:18; and 3:21 make this point repeatedly (see table 17.2, where the phrasing of the three verses is slightly rearranged to show the parallels).

Table 17.2 Law Not Made to Justify

Galatians 2:21	Galatians 3:17-18	Galatians 3:21
I do not nullify the grace of God,	The law . . . does not annul a covenant previously ratified by God, so as to make the promise void.	Is the law then contrary to the promises of God? Certainly not!
for [γὰρ] . . . Christ died for no purpose	For [γὰρ] . . . it no longer comes by promise	For [γὰρ] . . . righteousness would indeed be by the law
if righteousness were through the law [*but that is false*].	if the inheritance comes by the law [*but that is false*].	if a law had been given that could give life [*but that is false*].

Therefore, all three main clauses make a claim. God did not design the law-covenant as an alternative to the saving grace found in the death of Christ. He did not give the Mosaic covenant to set up a contrast between the covenant with Abraham and the covenant with the people of Israel. The law-covenant should not be understood in a way that would effectively abolish God's promise to Abraham.[28] When understood correctly, the law does not oppose the promises of God.

Though Paul's argument appears to place the covenant of law and the covenant of promise in conflict, he states that God did not create that scenario.[29] If God did not

---

the Old and New Testaments; Essays in Honor of S. Lewis Johnson Jr., ed. John S. Feinberg (Wheaton, IL: Crossway, 1988), 149.

25. Otto Becker's treatment joins three Greek terms together (διαθήκη, ἔγγυος, and μεσίτης). See Becker, "Covenant," in *The New International Dictionary of New Testament Theology*, ed. Colin Brown (Grand Rapids, MI: Zondervan, 1975), 1:365–76. See also the close connection between διαθήκη and μεσίτης in Heb. 8:6; 9:15; 12:24.

26. Porter's otherwise excellent work errs at this point and does not consider "mediator" as a possible link with covenant because of mistakenly thinking that the "mediator" in Gal. 3:19–20 refers to the angels, not to Moses. He says, "The mediator is said here to be the angels who brought the law to Moses." See Porter, "Concept of Covenant in Paul," 281. Most scholars hold that the mediator in 3:19 is Moses, while Paul speaks of a mediator in general terms in 3:20. This reading affirms the divine origin of the law. Richard N. Longenecker, *Galatians*, WBC 41 (Dallas: Word, 1990), 140–41.

27. See As. Mos. 1:14 (ὁ δε μεσιτης της διαθηκης).

28. Paul's gospel teaches that God (θέος) graciously gave (χαρίζομαι) the inheritance to Abraham on the basis of promise, not law (Gal. 3:18). Galatians 2:21 also states that Paul's gospel does not set aside the grace (χάρις) of God (θεοῦ) because righteousness is not based on law.

29. Moisés Silva makes four points that cohere with this reading: (1) the phrase "as many as are of the works of the law" refers to Paul's opponents who seek to live (be justified) by works; (2) Paul's argument in Galatians 3 is eschatological

create the conflict, then who did? The obvious answer is Paul's opponents.[30] Only a wrongheaded reading of the Mosaic covenant could create an active opposition between God's promise and God's law. When read rightly, the promises and the law of God come together in a unified way within the united plan and purposes of God. Therefore, the only way to oppose the law and the promises is to pervert the plan and purposes of God by misreading redemptive history.[31]

Paul preserves the purity of the gospel by demonstrating the unity of God's plan of salvation. The opponents are guilty of Scripture twisting. They have created a false gospel by constructing a faulty condition. Righteousness and the inheritance are not based on law (and therefore, one should not attempt to make them so). Righteousness would be based on law only if God gave a law that was able to create life, but he did not.[32] Protecting the purity of the gospel and the unity of God's plan requires Paul to refute the false claims of his opponents' "gospel."

Galatians 3:18 in particular provides a helpful exposition concerning why adding the law to the promise with regard to the inheritance results in the nullification of the promise. Law keeping and promise cannot both serve as the basis of the inheritance.[33] Paul's position on this question betrays his "all or nothing" stance with regard to the promise and the law. In Paul's thought, there can be only one basis: either inheritance by law or inheritance by promise. Paul denies that the inheritance is based on law with the next statement: "But God gave it to Abraham by a promise" (3:18). Specifically, Paul rejects any notion of inheritance by law with the use of the verb "gave" (χαρίζομαι),[34] which

---

in character; (3) the Sinaitic law preceded the time of fulfillment, so its role in soteriology was preparatory and temporary; and (4) the Judaizing claim that the law could give life confuses these eschatological epochs and introduces an improper opposition between law and inheritance/promise, sets aside the grace of God, and makes Christ's death of no account. See Silva, "Faith versus Works of Law in Galatians," in *Justification and Variegated Nomism*, vol. 2, *The Paradoxes of Paul*, ed. D. A. Carson, Peter T. O'Brien, and Mark A. Seifrid, WUNT, 2nd ser., vol. 181 (Grand Rapids, MI: Baker Academic, 2004), 217–48.

30. Some read Gal. 3:18 as a corollary of Paul's own position. In other words, Paul's reading of the radical contrast between promise and law forced him to answer this burning question. See Meredith G. Kline, *By Oath Consigned: A Reinterpretation of the Covenant Signs of Circumcision and Baptism* (Grand Rapids, MI: Eerdmans, 1968), 22. But a crucial question should take center stage: Who is in danger of invalidating the original covenant so as to nullify the promise? Paul is certainly not in danger of invalidating the promise with his exposition, because he highlights the *superiority of the promise* over law. The answer is that the view of Paul's opponents results in the nullification of the promise.

31. The reader should not assume that Paul's opponents would share his assessment of their views. They would not say that their goal is to "nullify" the promise. All evidence in Galatians points to the contrary. They were not urging the Galatians to recant their faith in Christ. They would agree with Paul that faith in Christ is necessary for salvation. However, their case seems to consist of the additional claim that only those who are circumcised and obey the law will receive salvation, justification, life, and blessing. They may have pointed to passages from the Old Testament itself to support this statement. Thus, the Gentiles will have no part in Abraham's family unless they are circumcised and obey the law like Abraham. Far from advocating severing the Abrahamic covenant from the law, they are emphasizing the exact opposite: they need to be kept together.

32. Note that Paul's argument in the protasis incorporates both functional and ontological categories. The law and the promises are not (functionally) contrary or opposed to each other. Two points confirm this conclusion: (1) the law is *not able* (ontology) to impart life, and (2) the law *was not given* (function) to impart life. These principles from the protasis confirm the truth of the apodosis: righteousness is not based on law. Paul proclaims that the law and the promises would be on opposing teams only if they were competing ways of salvation (life, righteousness, the inheritance). But he denies this state of affairs and in so doing announces that the law and the promises are functionally complementary. In fact, Gal. 3:22–24 shows that the law and the promises are on the same team. The imprisoning power of the law reinforces the need for the freeing power of the promise, which is based on faith (3:22, 24).

33. The preposition ἐκ here denotes the "source" or the "basis" of something. Specifically, the expression ἐκ νομοῦ is contrasted with ἐξ ἐπαγγελίας. The contrast clearly shows that Paul is dealing with inheritance by law or inheritance by promise.

34. Daniel B. Wallace calls this verb a "perfect of allegory." Wallace, *Greek Grammar beyond the Basics: An Exegetical Syntax of the New Testament* (Grand Rapids, MI: Zondervan, 1996), 582. The verb denotes the gracious character

means "given according to grace, not according to what is due," and of the prepositional phrase "through the promise" (δι' επαγγελίας).

Paul's "all or nothing" logic is clear from a few different texts in Galatians. For example, the apostle states that trying to gain righteousness from the law actually sets aside the grace of God and makes the death of Christ unnecessary (2:21). This same perspective and terminology emerge again in 5:2–4.[35] Attempting to be justified by law equals being "fallen away from grace" and "severed from Christ" (5:4). Paul draws a clear dividing line: Christ and grace *or* law and works. While Paul does not deny that the death of Christ is sufficient for atonement, it is "self-evident" that Paul rejects the *claim* that one belongs to Christ because of one's reliance on the law for justification. Turning to the law at this point in redemptive history translates into turning away from Christ. Paul argues that people must turn away from the law so that they can turn back to Christ and his grace (i.e., escape the state of being "fallen away from grace" and "severed from Christ").[36]

These indictments make sense only if the gracious elements of the law-covenant are no longer in force. If the law-covenant has come to an end, then the sacrificial part of the covenant is also no longer in force. Consequentially, one reverts to a law stripped of all its atoning provisions.[37] The promise of life can now come only from the works of the law because the law principle now stands alone.

Andrew Das also contends that the gracious framework of Judaism has completely collapsed in Paul's theology. Paul does not grant any salvific capacity to the Mosaic covenant, Israel's election, or the sacrificial system.[38] Das points to positions taken in 4 Ezra; 2 Baruch; 3 Baruch; 2 Enoch; Testament of Abraham (i.e., post–AD 70 literature), which "independently bear witness to what happens when the framework collapses and the balance shifts toward a judgment according to works."[39]

Therefore, Paul likely responds to a mistaken notion of continuity. The promises and the law cannot be joined in a mathematical unity (promise + law keeping = inheritance). Rather, Paul argues for a teleological unity between the promise and the law. He labors to make a temporal distinction between the promise and the law (the law came centuries later) in order to make a functional point (the law does not nullify the promise). If the opponents respond by saying that they are not teaching the nullification of the promise,

---

of the promise. God "freely or graciously" gave the promise to Abraham. If the law is allowed to add conditions to this original promise, the free grace that characterizes the promise will be nullified. And if the free grace of the promise is nullified, the promise itself will follow suit.

35. Galatians 5:1–4 states that submission to circumcision imposes an impossible burden: the obligation to obey the *whole* law. The phrase "seeking to be justified by law" is a shorthand for this obligation to obey the whole law in order to attain life or salvation. Confirmation for this interpretation comes from Paul's analysis of the spiritual state of those submitting to circumcision in 5:4. If one seeks to be justified by the law, then one has "fallen away from grace" and is "severed from Christ."

36. Galatians 4:1–9 can say that reverting to the law at this stage in redemptive history is tantamount to returning to paganism. God has put an end to the old order, so those who seek him there find themselves engaged in pagan religion, that is, a religion devoid of grace. The law now belongs to the elements of the (old) world, which hold both Jews and Gentiles in bondage.

37. See also Thomas R. Schreiner, *The Law and Its Fulfillment: A Pauline Theology of Law* (Grand Rapids, MI: Baker, 1993), 44.

38. A. Andrew Das, *Paul, the Law, and the Covenant* (Peabody, MA: Hendrickson, 2001), 8, 214.

39. Das, *Paul, the Law, and the Covenant*, 214n76.

Paul counters by declaring that the promise is made null and void when additional stipulations are tacked on to it. The opponents are certainly guilty on this score.[40]

Now that the new covenant has brought a ministry of justification, what will happen to the old covenant? It comes to an end. In the next section, we trace the transition from the old covenant to the new covenant in the argument of Galatians 3–4.

The Transition from Old Covenant to New Covenant

The Law Had a Beginning

Galatians 3:17 stresses that the law had a beginning: 430 years after the promise. Paul's exposition of the temporary nature of the law stands out even more in light of the interpretation of Sirach 44:19–20:

> Abraham was the great father of a multitude of nations, and no one has been found like him in glory; He kept the Law of the most high, and was taken into covenant with him; he established the covenant in his flesh, and when he was tested he was found faithful.

By way of contrast, Paul does not emphasize the preexistence and eternality of the law that is implied in Sirach 44. Paul asserts the exact opposite. The law came into existence 430 years after the promise.

The Law Had an Ending

Paul also emphasizes that the law had a point of termination.[41] The law reached its divinely appointed end at the coming of the "offspring" (Gal. 3:19), who is Christ.

Galatians 3:23–26 and 4:1–7 demonstrate that the "seed" in 3:19 refers to Jesus of Nazareth. In 3:23–26, the law is compared to a "guardian" (παιδαγωγός). This "guardian" is given authority over a child for a specific duration of time (usually until adulthood).[42] The key event for Paul is the coming of "faith" (πίστις) (3:25). The dawning of this age brings the age of the guardian to an end: "But now that faith has come, we are no longer under a guardian" (3:25). The word "faith" clearly refers to a salvation-historical turning point, not a human response. If no one exercised faith until after the coming of Christ, then Abraham also did not exercise faith. And if Abraham did not exercise faith, then Paul's whole argument in 3:6–9 comes crashing down.

Therefore, the coming of faith (3:25) refers to the coming of the new era of fulfillment ushered in by the coming of Christ. Now that Christ has come, the era of the law

---

40. Paul maintains the integrity of the purposes for both the promise and the law by keeping them distinct. Notice the structure of Gal. 3:22 and 24: (1) Imprisonment under the Scripture (3:22) or law (3:24) takes place for (2) the purpose (ἵνα [3:22, 24]) of the promise of faith being given to those who believe (3:22) or are being justified by faith (3:24). Verse 24 should be translated, "Therefore the law has become our guardian until Christ, so that we may be justified by faith." The preposition εἰς functions in a temporal sense ("until Christ") not a telic sense ("unto Christ").

41. This section is adapted from Jason S. DeRouchie and Jason C. Meyer, "Christ or Family as the 'Seed' of Promise? An Evaluation of N. T. Wright on Galatians 3:16," *SBJT* 14, no. 3 (2010): 36–48. Used by permission of *Southern Baptist Journal of Theology*.

42. See the full discussion in Richard N. Longenecker, "The Pedagogical Nature of the Law in Galatians 3:19–4:7," *JETS* 25, no. 1 (1982): 53–62.

as the "guardian" (παιδαγωγός) has ended, so that believers are no longer under the law. Thus, the establishment of the new covenant and the reception of the promised Spirit (3:14) introduce an age when the distinguishing mark of God's people becomes faith in the Messiah, who has come and made himself known as Jesus.

The same structure of thought reoccurs in 4:1–7. An heir is "under guardians and managers" for a specific period of time ("until the date set by his father," 4:2). Once the date "set by his father" arrives, the "guardians and managers" no longer have authority over the heir. Paul spells out the significance of this analogy in 4:3–4. While children, "we" were held under the "elemental things of the world." But now the date "set by his father" has arrived in the coming of God's Son: "But when the fullness of the time had come, God sent forth his Son" (4:4). The parallel structure of thought contained in these passages is evident:

3:19	When the "offspring" comes, the authority of the law comes to an end.
3:23–24	When the "faith" era comes, the authority of the guardian[43] comes to an end.
4:1–2	When the time set by the Father comes, the authority of the guardians and managers comes to an end.
4:3–4	When the "Son" comes, the authority of the elemental things comes to an end.[44]

While under the age of law, one remains in the age of immaturity and under the status of illegitimacy with regard to the inheritance. If the individual is to establish a rightful claim to the inheritance, he or she must pass from the status of minor to the status of heir. However, adoption is the only way the individual can gain the status of heir. And for Paul, one must first be "redeemed" from the authority of the law before one can receive "adoption as sons" (4:5).

Therefore, if the law has come to an end, how do new covenant believers relate to the old covenant law today?

The Role of the Law in the Christian Life

We begin with an analysis of what Paul means by his claim that new covenant believers are no longer "under law."[45] Once that claim is clearly understood, we can discuss two ways that new covenant believers approach the old covenant law: (1) a new mode of engagement and (2) a new lens of love.

What does Paul mean when he consistently claims that Christians are no longer "under law" (Rom. 6:14–15; Gal. 5:18) or are "released from the law" (Rom. 7:6)? Some inter-

---

43. A babysitter is an imperfect, yet helpful, modern example of a child under the authority of another for a limited duration. Our modern notion of living under the rules of a parent until the "legal" age of eighteen is another example. The phrase "as long as you live under my roof, you will live under my rules" is a modern illustration.

44. A consideration of the occurrences of the verb ἔρχομαι in Galatians also adds further support to the above analysis. A very distinct pattern emerges: ἔρχομαι refers to spatial comings in Galatians 1 and 2, while it refers to salvation-historical comings in Galatians 3 and 4. Furthermore, the occurrences in Galatians 3 and 4 all function as references to the same event, the coming of Jesus the Messiah.

45. This section borrows heavily from Jason C. Meyer, "The Mosaic Law, Theological Systems, and the Glory of Christ," in *Progressive Covenantalism: Charting a Course between Dispensational and Covenant Theologies*, ed. Steven J. Wellum and Brent E. Parker (Nashville: B&H Academic, 2016). Used by permission of B&H Academic.

preters want to nuance these declarations so that they are not as far reaching as they may first appear. These theologians make a crucial distinction between the condemning function of the law and the guiding function of the law. They use this distinction to argue that the believer is no longer under the law of Moses in its *condemning* function but that the believer is under the law in its *guiding* function.[46] Richard B. Gaffin says that the law in its "*specific codification*" at Sinai "has been terminated in its entirety by Christ in his coming," but the moral core of the Mosaic law "specifies imperatives that transcend the Mosaic economy."[47] Gaffin clarifies: "In its central commands, the law given at Sinai, notably the Decalogue, reveals God's will as that which is inherent in his person and therefore incumbent on his image-bearing creatures as such, regardless of time and place, whether Jew or non-Jew."[48]

The problem with this view is not what it affirms but what it denies. Release from the law surely means that the believer is set free from the penalty of condemnation that the law brings to bear on us in terms of its capacity to curse and condemn. But it is not a fair reading of Paul to force Paul's statement about freedom from the law to apply narrowly and exclusively to the condemning function of the law alone. Why does that restricted reading not work? The context of these phrases must determine the meaning of these phrases. The context provides the greatest argument for reading Paul's claim in a way that includes both the condemning and guiding function of the law. Paul's treatment of these phrases is not narrow; his discussion in context is much more far reaching.

The context of Galatians 5:18 ("But if you are led by the Spirit, you are not under the law") includes a discussion on the fruit of the Spirit (5:22–23) and the call to keep in step with the Spirit (5:25). The Spirit's work within the Christian will produce behavioral qualities that are acceptable in the sight of God apart from adding the direct binding force of the Mosaic law code. Paul does not restrict his focus to the Mosaic law code; he argues that no law code in existence would speak against the fruits of the Spirit: "against such things there is no law" (5:23). In other words, the Mosaic law code is not a prerequisite for lawful conduct. The Spirit-empowered fruit of Christian obedience will accord with any law code of conduct, not just with the Mosaic law (5:23).

Paul's approach to behavioral fruit bearing in Romans 7 is similar to Galatians 5. The believer bears fruit for God *only after* being released from the law. The law is powerless to produce fruit for God; it can produce fruit only for death (Rom. 7:5). Release from the law enables the believer to escape the oldness of the letter and serve in the new way of the Spirit (7:6). Romans 7:6 bears witness to this shift with a clear redemptive-historical turning point: "But now . . ." This new way of the Spirit produces fruit for God—something the old way of the letter could never do. "Ironically and paradoxically, those who live under the law bear fruit resulting in sinful passions, transgression of the law, and death, while those who have died to the law bear fruit that amounts to the law's fulfillment."[49] Paul

---

46. Ridderbos, *Paul*, 282–83.
47. Richard B. Gaffin Jr., *By Faith, Not by Sight: Paul and the Order of Salvation*, 2nd ed. (Phillipsburg, NJ: P&R, 2013), 36; italics original.
48. Gaffin, *By Faith, Not by Sight*, 36.
49. Meyer, *End of the Law*, 283.

emphasizes that Christians "fulfill" the law (8:4; 13:8, 10; Gal. 5:14), while at the same time stressing that they are no longer "under the law" (Gal. 5:18; cf. Rom. 6:14–15).[50]

I find myself in hearty agreement with Douglas Moo's wise assessment of these texts. He says that the contexts of these texts (Romans 6–7; Galatians 5) cannot be restricted to the "*penalty* of sin" through the law, because Paul stresses freedom from the "*power* of sin" through the law.[51] He then reaches a judicious and compelling conclusion: "It is difficult to avoid the conclusion, then, that life in the Spirit is put forward by Paul as the ground of Christian ethics, *in contrast to* life 'under law.'"[52]

The simple fact is that these contexts do not stress the law's guiding function and its resulting fruitfulness for sanctification. Therefore, it seems illegitimate to introduce into the discussion distinctions that Paul did not make. He seems to speak of the law as a whole. Rather than distinguish between the condemning function and guiding function, Paul is speaking in all-inclusive terms: the new covenant Christian is no longer under the old covenant and its legal codification in the Mosaic law. Christians are under the law of Christ.

A New Mode: Indirect vs. Direct

The promises of the new covenant focus on the life-changing operation of the Holy Spirit. God intervenes in the new covenant with an internal heart change that empowers an external life change. The question is, How does that new work recalibrate our relationship to the old covenant law? Paul constructs a contrast between life in the Spirit and life under the law. One could say that life in the Spirit under the new covenant administration replaces life under the law in the old covenant administration.

The best way to summarize the evidence thus far is to say that the Mosaic law as an economy has come to an end *as a whole* and that the Mosaic law *as a whole* continues to serve as a helpful yet indirect guide. Paul relates to the law in terms of the entirety of its guiding wisdom, not as a direct and binding legal code. This approach is preferable because one can interact with the entirety of the Mosaic system, rather than trying to neatly distinguish between moral, civil, and ceremonial.

Moo is right that the law of Moses is "indirectly applicable to us through the 'fulfillment' of that law in Christ and his law."[53] What does "indirect" mean? One must distinguish between the law of Moses as Scripture and the law of Moses as a law code. The best way to frame the distinction is to say that the law of Moses has direct authority as *Scripture* and indirect authority as *law*. The fact that it has indirect authority as law today means that it has an *indirect application* to our lives today. In other words, the mode in which the law of Moses operates today makes all the difference in this discussion. Mode matters.

---

50. This dynamic is perhaps best spelled out by Stephen Westerholm, *Perspectives Old and New on Paul: The "Lutheran" Paul and His Critics* (Grand Rapids, MI: Eerdmans, 2004), 431–39.
51. Douglas J. Moo, "The Law of Moses or the Law of Christ," in Feinberg, *Continuity and Discontinuity*, 211.
52. Moo, "Law of Moses," 215; italics original.
53. Moo, "Law of Moses," 215.

The new covenant Christian meets the law of Moses in a distinctly different mode of existence than the old covenant Israelite. Under the old covenant, the law of Moses had direct authority as a complete legal code. It no longer functions in that way under the new covenant. It is completely authoritative as revelation, but it now serves as an indirect guide because we are no longer under the Mosaic code in its entirety.[54] We are directly dependent on Christ and his apostles for guidance in how to approach all past revelation (including the law of Moses).

Another contrast comes in the form that God's commands take in the old covenant documents and the new covenant letters. The old covenant law code is very detailed. It contains numerous case studies that prescribe specific ways of living and specific punishments if those ways are not followed. The New Testament takes a very different approach. It offers few detailed case studies on what to do and what the punishment should be if one transgresses a command. Paul certainly prescribes Christian behavior in his letters, but it is striking how little he prescribes behavior *with reference to the Mosaic law*. There are specific commands about divorce, immorality, greed, and many other topics, but he rarely appeals to the Mosaic law in a prescriptive way despite how often the Mosaic law addresses those topics. In discussions of the Mosaic law, Paul normally *describes* the "fruit" of Christian obedience with a retroactive reference to the way that it conforms to the law and thus amounts to its "fulfillment." This distinction should not be pressed too far so that it is overstated. It is true that one can find exceptions to this general rule. For example, Paul seems to prescribe direct obedience to Exodus 20:12 in Ephesians 6:1–3.[55] But the point is that one is struck by how little Paul takes this approach given how expansive the Mosaic law is in the old covenant.

This point raises a related question. If the Mosaic law has continuing relevance as an *indirect* guide, then what is the primary lens through which a Christian should read the old covenant law? Is there a consistent theme that one should look for in the commands of the Mosaic economy that puts the spotlight on its primary relevance today? The answer is love.

A New Lens: Christ's Love vs. Self-Love

The greatest guidance the law gives is in the area of love. The principle or standard of love found in the Mosaic law says, "Love your neighbor as yourself" (Lev. 19:18). The new principle or standard found in the law of Christ says, "Just as I have loved you, you also are to love one another" (John 13:34).

---

54. Brian S. Rosner rightly argues that we relate to the specific commandments in the law not as binding because they belong to the Mosaic system but as wisdom for believers living in the new covenant age. Believers "do not read the law *as law-covenant*, but rather *as prophecy* and *as wisdom*." See Rosner, *Paul and the Law: Keeping the Commandments of God*, NSBT 31 (Downers Grove, IL: InterVarsity Press, 2013), 218. D. A. Carson distinguishes between the law as law-covenant and the law as prophecy. See Carson, "Atonement in Romans 3:21–26: 'God Presented Him as a Propitiation,'" in *The Glory of the Atonement: Biblical, Historical, and Practical Perspectives; Essays in Honor of Roger R. Nicole*, ed. Charles E. Hill and Frank A. James III (Downers Grove, IL: InterVarsity Press, 2004), 139.

55. Rosner does not see this text as an exception. He would deny the prescriptive nature of Paul's appeal. Rather, he thinks that Paul appeals to the commandment of the Mosaic law "not as law (Eph. 6:1–2), but as advice concerning how to walk in wisdom (cf. Eph. 5:15)." *Paul and the Law*, 208. This distinction is difficult to maintain. I prefer to see it as an exception to Paul's general pattern.

Paul manifestly views the Old Testament law through the lens of love. He teaches that "the one who loves another has fulfilled the law" (Rom. 13:8). He proves that all the commandments are summed up in the command "You shall love your neighbor as yourself" (Lev. 19:18 as quoted in Rom. 13:9). He clearly states that "love does no wrong to a neighbor; therefore love is the fulfilling of the law" (13:10). Galatians 5:14 is equally unambiguous: "For the whole law is fulfilled in one word: 'You shall love your neighbor as yourself.'"

Therefore, the varied commands in the law of Moses give Christians a concrete expression of what love looked like in one specific cultural setting. We have to take the principle of love found in the command and apply it to our current cultural setting. New covenant Christians must ask, How does this command guide us in love for neighbor? The difference in cultural context between an Old Testament Israelite and a New Testament Christian will often preclude a direct transfer.

My colleague Jason DeRouchie gives a great example about how the law speaks of love for neighbor.[56] Moses commands the people to have a parapet or railing around their roof: "If you build a new house, make a railing around your roof, so that you don't bring bloodguilt on your house if someone falls from it" (Deut. 22:8 CSB). It would be wrong to approach this law by asking what parts of it are moral, civil, or ceremonial. It serves as an indirect guide for us today in terms of how we love our neighbor. In those days, the roof was flat, and it was a place where one would entertain guests. In Minnesota, where I live, there is no way that we are going to host gatherings on my roof. However, I have a deck where people come and sit with us. This text says that love for neighbors means that I will care about their safety and will put a protective railing around my deck. We could extend it further. If a family brings over a small child who could fall down a flight of stairs, then I should put up a protective gate. This law of love could also be extended to argue that love for neighbor includes purchasing insurance that would provide financial help if someone gets hurt at my home.

The Mosaic law also serves as a guide when it comes to the content of love. The word *love* is too often a squishy, sentimental word that lacks specific moral content in our culture. The law of Moses fills up the word *love* with God-breathed content. One can see the relevance of the Mosaic law when talking about breaking the covenant of marital love. Jesus addresses the issue of divorce in cases when "sexual immorality" is present (Matt. 5:32). But what specific acts are included? The word for "sexual immorality" (πορνεία) is a general term that does not specify the types of acts that are in view. The Mosaic law gives the most helpful interpretive backdrop that can provide needed specificity. Therefore, the New Testament's silence on "bestiality" does not imply that it has suddenly become morally acceptable. This example shows that it does not work to say that whatever is not explicitly reaffirmed in the New Testament is no longer binding for believers.

---

56. See Jason S. DeRouchie, *How to Understand and Apply the Old Testament: Twelve Steps from Exegesis to Theology* (Phillipsburg, NJ: P&R, 2017), 443–44.

The law of Moses is an authoritative expression of what love for neighbor looked like for old covenant Israel. It also provides new covenant Christians with a useful yet indirect guide of what love for neighbor can look like today. We receive the most direct and authoritative guidance for love in the law of Christ because the new standard for love in the new covenant is the cross of Christ.

The law of Christ is a progressive advancement over the law of Moses in that the law of Christ more directly and explicitly ties the believer to the cross of Christ. The law of Christ has a greater gospel shape than the law of Moses. The law of Moses was a grace from God and a law of love, but its standard of love falls short of the heights of love found in the sacrifice of Christ.

The best approach to understanding this phrase is to see the direct connection between the law of Christ and the cross of Christ. The place where the law of Christ is defined most directly is in Galatians 6:2: "Bear one another's burdens, and so fulfill the law of Christ." Here Paul draws a direct line between the cross of Christ (Christ carried our sins on the cross) and the law of Christ that calls us to carry one another's burdens. The law of Christ cannot be reduced to love in a way that empties it of other commands from Christ and his apostles. But its emphasis on the love of Christ gives it a greater gospel shape than the law of Moses because the cross is the new standard of love. There are other examples of this same dynamic, but we will focus on only two more: the love command and the idea of tithing today.

First, the new commandment is one of the best examples of how Christ recalibrates the whole law of Moses. Jesus refers to obedience to his own commandments as a measure of covenantal love; he does not appeal to the law of Moses: "If you love me, you will keep *my commandments*" (John 14:15). Jesus labels the love commandment a "new" commandment, even though the command to love is not "new" in the sense that it is unheard of in the Old Testament. The love command is new in one specific sense, in that it is tied to Jesus: "as I have loved you" (13:34).

John further expounds on the uniqueness of this love in his letters. In 1 John 3:24, he urges believers to keep God's commandments. When John unpacks his meaning, he stresses a singular commandment in two parts: believe in the gospel and love one another. Why don't these two things form a plural instead of a singular commandment? The love of Christ and the love command are so intertwined that John does not separate them. John's first letter offers a sterling example of how our love for others can no longer be separated from Christ's love for us. Christ's love is the new standard or definition of love: "By this we know love, that he laid down his life for us, and we ought to lay down our lives for the brothers" (3:16).

Putting up a railing to keep your neighbor safe is good and loving, but sacrificial love goes much further: "Greater love has no one than this, that someone lay down his life for his friends" (John 15:13). Love that acts to keep others safe is good; love that sacrifices for the good of others is greater. Soaking in the sacrifice of Christ becomes a prerequisite for loving like Christ.

Second, despite popular ideas of stewardship today, no New Testament text commands believers to give 10 percent of their income to the church. The tithe commandment comes from a paradigm relating to the twelve tribes of Israel. The Levites did not own land like the rest of the eleven tribes, and thus the tithe was an essential part of ensuring that they could continue to survive and minister. Nehemiah 13:10–12 highlights an example of how much the Levites depended on the tithe. The Christian lives under a new paradigm. Paul addresses financial themes frequently, but he never specifies an amount or percentage. He calls the Corinthians to set something aside to give "as he may prosper" (1 Cor. 16:2). But Paul does not make reference here to a new paradigm. What is the standard of giving? The most sustained exposition of stewardship in the New Testament (2 Corinthians 8–9) says that the grace of Christ's sacrifice is the new point of reference.

The Macedonians went well beyond a tithe. They gave sacrificially ("beyond their means," 2 Cor. 8:3) and willingly ("of their own accord," 8:3), despite "extreme poverty" and "a severe test of affliction" (8:2). Paul declares that "grace" (8:1) came down and produced "abundance of joy" in the Macedonians (8:2). God's grace comes first, and then joy springs up in the heart and overflows in "a wealth of generosity" (8:2). Seven verses later Paul comments further on this "grace." Sacrificial giving is grounded in the "grace" of Christ's sacrifice, which is spelled out in financial imagery: "For you know the grace of our Lord Jesus Christ, that though he was rich, yet for your sake he became poor, so that you by his poverty might become rich" (8:9). As noted earlier, Paul can look back at the priests as a reference point that supports why Christian ministers should get their living from the gospel (1 Cor. 9:13–14). But that example does not become the central reference point or the paradigm for all giving. All giving is recalibrated around the new paradigm of Christ's sacrifice.

This essay has covered a lot of conceptual ground. Let us review the flow of the argument thus far. This essay argues that understanding the relationship between the new covenant and justification can help set the doctrine of justification free from its solitary confinement. I am attempting to demonstrate that point in seven stages.

The first three stages tear down the conceptual wall that often separates justification and the new covenant. This wall prevents people from seeing how the apostle Paul ties justification and the new covenant together in his covenantal contrast between the gospel and the law.

Those first three stages also raise an important question: If obedience to the old covenant law does not justify, then what part should the law play in the life of a believer? Stages four and five answer that question by providing a summary sketch of the role that the old covenant law plays in the life of a new covenant believer.

Now it is time to move to stages six and seven in the attempt to release justification from its conceptual isolation from other doctrines. Stages six and seven demonstrate that understanding the new covenant is crucial for clarifying the inseparable connection that exists between justification and sanctification.

The New Covenant Incorporates Heart Change, Conversion, Justification, and Sanctification

Justification is an event that provides a gateway into greater glories.[57] The glories of the new covenant do not end with justification; they begin with justification. The new covenant incorporates both the justification of the ungodly and the transformation of the ungodly. Think through the wide range of blood-bought gifts contained in the new covenant: new heart and spirit (Ezek. 36:26), the gift of the Holy Spirit (36:27), divine enablement to walk in God's commands (36:27), the law written on the heart (Jer. 31:33), forgiveness of sins (31:34), and the internalization of the fear of the Lord (32:40).

Paul's exposition of the new covenant (2 Corinthians 3) includes a full range of blood-bought benefits in Paul's discussion: conversion, justification, and progressive sanctification. The first part of Paul's exposition highlights the heart change that comes from the new covenant (3:3–6). The second part puts the focus on justification (3:7–11). And the third part focuses on conversion and sanctification (3:12–18). Since I have already addressed the connection between justification and the new covenant earlier in the essay, in what follows I will unpack Paul's treatment of heart change and of conversion and sanctification.

Heart Change

First, Paul's argument in 2 Corinthians 3:1–6 brings together the new covenant promises from both Jeremiah and Ezekiel regarding a heart change. Paul contrasts the old and new covenants from the standpoint of the different ways God acts under both covenants. Paul stresses these different actions by highlighting the *different objects* on which God inscribes something.[58]

Seeing the web of allusions from the Old Testament in these verses helps the reader catch a fuller picture of the contrast between the covenants here. Carol Stockhausen[59] has convincingly argued for an extensive lexical web linking the Septuagint texts of Exodus 34:1–4 ("stone," "write"), Jeremiah 38 ("write," "covenant," "heart"), Jeremiah 39 ("covenant," "heart"), Ezekiel 11 ("stone," "covenant," "heart"), and Ezekiel 36 ("stone," "covenant," "heart").[60] Notice that the contrast remains constant between "stone" in the Sinai covenant and "heart" in the new covenant.

One can begin with the allusion to Jeremiah. Paul's contrast in 2 Corinthians 3:3 between writing on stone tablets and writing on the heart reflects the Old Testament

---

57. This section adapts material from Jason C. Meyer, *The End of the Law: Mosaic Covenant in Pauline Theology* (Nashville: B&H Academic, 2009), 102–3. Used by permission of B&H.
58. Paul's point may also contain an argument against his opponents. Steven L. McKenzie rightfully states that Paul addresses Moses "not to demean him or his work, but to point out that the 'ministry' under him, though necessary for its era, was imperfect and that blindly following him makes no sense in light of the availability of something far superior." McKenzie, *Covenant*, Understanding Biblical Themes (Saint Louis, MO: Chalice, 2000), 103.
59. Carol Kern Stockhausen, *Moses' Veil and the Glory of the New Covenant: The Exegetical Substructure of II Cor. 3,1–4,6*, AnBib 116 (Rome: Editrice Pontificio Istituto Biblico, 1989), 57.
60. Exodus 24:12; Deut. 5:22; 9:10 also contain the terms "stone" and "write," while Deut. 9:9, 11 has the terms "stone" and "covenant"; Deut. 4:13 has all three terms: "stone," "covenant," and "write."

contrast between the Sinai covenant and the new covenant of Jeremiah. This correspondence supports an allusion in 2 Corinthians 3 to the new covenant of Jeremiah 31 (see table 17.3).[61]

Table 17.3 Correlation of Old and New Covenants

Text	Deuteronomy 4:13	Jeremiah 31:33
Subject	God	God
Verb	wrote	will write
Direct object	them = ten words	them = my law
Prepositional phrase	on two stone tablets	on their hearts

God granted a great gift to Israel when he intervened in human history and provided a written expression of his will. However, this gracious gift remained external to Israel because they never internalized it. God grants a greater gift under the new covenant because God provides an internal intervention. God's will becomes internalized in the new covenant because he overcomes the resistance emerging from the inner core of the covenantal member. Francis Watson agrees with this description: "For Paul, the old and the new are characterized by two different accounts of divine agency."[62]

Therefore, the contrast in God's inscribing actions is between prescription and creation. Inscribing the ten words on tablets of stone produces prescription: what man must do. The new covenant account of divine agency centers on creation: what God will do.[63] God gives spiritual life (2 Cor. 3:6) and creates spiritual light (4:6) under the new covenant.

The "flesh-heart tablets" in 3:3 (my trans.) are the objects on which Christ wrote, and "the Spirit" is the instrument with which Christ wrote. Both the object and the instrument come from Ezekiel's new covenant promise. Some translations obscure Paul's textual strategy with the rendering "tablets of human hearts" (e.g., NIV). Paul uses the seemingly awkward adjective "flesh" for heart because he alludes to Ezekiel's description of the new heart as one of "flesh." One can call this reality an eschatological intervention because Ezekiel 11:19 and 36:26 announce a coming day (eschatology) when God will arrive on the scene (intervene) and effect an inner transformation.

The "flesh heart" is significant because it presupposes a prior inward intervention. The giving of the "flesh heart" can come only after God removes the "stone heart" (τὴν καρδίαν τὴν λιθίνην, 36:26 LXX).[64] Christ's act of writing on "flesh-heart tablets" with the Spirit assumes God's prior work of removing the stone heart. Now he proclaims the

---

61. Jan Lambrecht, *Second Corinthians*, SP 8 (Collegeville, MN: Liturgical Press, 1999), 46–47.
62. Francis Watson, *Paul and the Hermeneutics of Faith* (Edinburgh: T&T Clark, 2004), 312.
63. Watson, *Paul and the Hermeneutics of Faith*, 312.
64. Ezekiel's pairing of the "flesh heart" and the "stone heart" does not directly denigrate the "stone tablets" of the Sinai covenant. Readers cannot hold the "stone tablets" responsible for Israel's rebellion; Ezekiel pinpoints her "stone heart" as the problem. Paul makes a similar point in 2 Corinthians 3. The stone tablets did not cause the problem; they only confounded the problem that already existed, because the stone tablets could not conquer the stone heart of Israel.

indispensability of God's Spirit as part and parcel of this change in the next verse: "and I will put my Spirit within you" (36:27).

The letter-Spirit contrast in 2 Corinthians 3:6 highlights the constituent elements of the covenants along with their corresponding effects on their covenantal members. Therefore, the new covenant is the covenant of eschatological intervention because the life-giving power of the Spirit changes the person at the core of his or her existence (i.e., the heart).

Paul says the new covenant consists "not of the letter but of the Spirit" (3:6). This same contrast occurs in Romans 2:29. "Letter" and "Spirit" there qualify circumcision and clearly distinguish between a physical circumcision (external, visible) and a spiritual one (internal, visible only to God). Paul proclaims that the mere possession of the law in its written form (i.e., γράμμα) or circumcision in its physical form does not have salvific value and does not guarantee the fulfillment of the law's demands. The Spirit engenders this obedience through circumcising the heart.

Romans 7:6 complements this contrast between old and new because Paul stresses the difference between serving in oldness of the letter and newness of the Spirit and the corresponding results. This contrast is especially important for the present study because Paul correlates oldness with "letter" (παλαιότητι γράμματος) and newness with "Spirit" (καινότητι πνεύματος). This same pairing explicitly appears again with the "new covenant . . . of the Spirit" (καινῆς διαθήκης . . . πνεύματος) in 2 Corinthians 3:6. The contrast between old and new covenants in this contrast argues for the corresponding link between "old covenant" and "letter." Therefore, the pairing of "old" with "letter" and "new" with "Spirit" is completely consistent in these passages.[65]

Thus, Victor Paul Furnish correctly claims that the letter-Spirit contrast fundamentally concerns a distinction between two different powers and their corresponding effects.[66] The present author would only alter his summary by bringing out the eschatological overtones: two different powers *that represent two different ages or epochs*.[67]

The letter (or writing) kills not because it is inherently evil but precisely the opposite—because it is inherently good. God's good standards do not and cannot square with Israel's hardened condition. Death and condemnation result from this clash between a good law and an evil heart. Therefore, Richard Hays is correct to state that the primary problem with the old covenant as "script" or letter is that it "is (only) written, lacking the power to effect the obedience that it demands. Since it has no power to transform the readers, it can only stand as a witness to their condemnation."[68]

---

65. So also Moo, *Romans*, 421. He asserts that the contrast is between "the Old Covenant and the New, the old age and the new." See also Ridderbos, *Paul*, 215–19.

66. Victor Paul Furnish, *II Corinthians: A New Translation with Introduction and Commentary*, AB 32A (New Haven, CT: Yale University Press, 2010), 199.

67. James D. G. Dunn correctly captures the epochal force of this contrast. The "Spirit/letter contrast is between epochs and the experiences characteristic of these epochs," not a "spiritual" versus "literal" meaning of Scripture. See Dunn, *The Theology of Paul the Apostle* (Grand Rapids, MI: Eerdmans, 1998), 149n115.

68. Richard B. Hays, *Echoes of Scripture in the Letters of Paul* (New Haven, CT: Yale University Press, 1989), 131.

Paul correlates the nature of each covenant with its effects. In other words, the intrinsic character of each covenant produces results that flow from it. This reading would effectively militate against strictly separating the ontological and the functional categories with respect to the covenants. This recognition argues that the covenant consisting of letter will inevitably produce death, because the letter kills; the covenant consisting of the Spirit will inevitably produce life, because the Spirit creates life.

Rudolf Bultmann is thus fully justified in relating the two concepts "new covenant of the Spirit" and the life-giving aspect of the Spirit so that "the new covenant is a covenant of life."[69] Murray J. Harris also reads the contrast between old and new covenants as a contrast that focuses on their dominant characteristic (letter or Spirit) and inevitable outcome (death or life).[70]

Paul's correlation between the new covenant, the Spirit, and life faithfully echoes the eschatological intervention in Ezekiel once again. The life-giving (ζωοποιέω) power of the Spirit (2 Cor. 3:6) harks back to Ezekiel 37:3, where the question concerns whether the dead bones can "live" (ζήσεται, LXX). God announces that he will put his Spirit in them, which will result in life (ζήσεσθε, 37:6 LXX).

Conversion and Sanctification

Paul's discussion of the removal of the veil in 2 Corinthians 3:12–18 begins with conversion and culminates with progressive sanctification. Paul connects the experience of conversion with the removal of the veil. The "veil is removed" should be read as a divine passive.[71] God removes the veil whenever one turns to the Lord in conversion.

The removal of the veil must imply a heart change because Paul states that the veil covers the hearts of the Israelites. This heart change is probably another allusion to the promise of the new covenant. In this regard, it is instructive to see that Israel's hardened mind (3:14) and veiled heart (3:15) are the antithesis of the law written on the mind and heart of the Israel of Jeremiah's new covenant. In other words, the Septuagint version of Jeremiah 38:33 focuses on the "mind" (διάνοιαν) and "heart" (καρδίας) of Israel as the *loci* of God's eschatological intervention. God's new covenant eschatological intervention will produce a change with respect to the mind and heart. If God does not intervene, the mind and heart will remain hardened and veiled, as in the case of Israel from the time of Moses to the time of Paul. The experience of entering the new covenant corresponds to the experience of conversion and the removal of the veil.

This removal of the veil in conversion results in "freedom" (3:17). The term "freedom" should not be limited to the veil because the Spirit of the Lord brings freedom "from" the veil, which results in a freedom "for" gazing on the glory of God. "Freedom" is thus an expansive term that also refers to freedom of access into the presence

---

69. "Der neue Bund ist ein Bund des Lebens." Rudolf Bultmann, *Der zweite Brief an die Korinther*, KEK 6 (Göttingen: Vandenhoeck & Ruprecht, 1976), 81.
70. Murray J. Harris, *Second Corinthians*, NIGTC (Grand Rapids, MI: Eerdmans, 2005), 271.
71. Scott J. Hafemann, *Paul, Moses, and the History of Israel: The Letter/Spirit Contrast and the Argument from Scripture in 2 Corinthians 3*, WUNT 81 (Tübingen: Mohr Siebeck, 1995), 393.

of God. The veil prevented Israel from gazing on the glory of the face of Moses, while God's work in the heart of believers removes the veil and enables them to gaze on the glory of the Lord (2 Cor. 3:18), which they see in the face of Christ (4:6).

Most recognize that the "we all" of 3:18 broadens the referent from "we apostles" to "we Christians," so that Paul asserts that all Christians experience conversion and the removal of the veil. The gift of the Spirit in the new covenant results in a freedom to gaze on the glory of Christ; the letter's work of death results in an inability to gaze on the glory of Christ. Notice the connection between the pneumatological and Christological dimensions of the new covenant. The removal of the veil is thoroughly Christological because it is removed "only through Christ" (3:14). Furthermore, the Spirit's life-giving work (pneumatological) enables the believer to gaze freely on the glory of Christ (Christological).

The newness of the new covenant also includes bearing fruit for God instead of bearing fruit for death. The believer bears fruit for God as a result of experiencing the force of the verb "release" (καταργέω, Rom. 7:6) in relation to the law. Release from the law for the believer means that the believer no longer serves in "oldness of the letter" but now serves in "newness of the Spirit" (7:6, my trans.). The release from the law and its oldness means a release from sin ("sinful passions, aroused by the law," 7:5) and death ("bore fruit for death," 7:5). Entrance into the new existence means bearing fruit for God.

Romans 7:5 describes the opposite scenario. The law cannot result in fruit bearing for God; all it can produce is fruit unto death. Thus, 7:5 signifies why humanity needs freedom from the law. The law under the sway of the flesh could only incite humanity to further acts of sinful rebellion, the result of which is "fruit for death." Paul introduces a redemptive-historical turning point in 7:6. "But now" means that a dramatic shift has taken place in God's economy of salvation that frees humanity from the vise grip of the law, with the result that they can serve in the newness that comes from the Spirit, as opposed to the oldness that proceeds from the letter.

The "so that" (ὥστε) clause of 7:4 and the "but now" (νυνὶ δὲ) contrast with 7:5 help fill out the features of 7:6. Romans 7:6 expands on the result clause of 7:4 in a *negative way* by *negating* the ability of the law (i.e., highlighting the inability of the law) to produce the desired results of 7:4. On the contrary, it becomes the instrument that actually "produces" (ἐνεργέω) the negative outcome of 7:5: "fruit for death." The law cannot gain the upper hand over our flesh with its sinful passions.[72]

Romans 7:6 then acts to give an explanation and expansion of the result clause in 7:4 in a *positive way*. Bearing fruit for God means serving in the newness of the Spirit. That is, the Spirit gives birth to newness and fuels further new life. Therefore, the genitive of origin best fits the context because the "oldness" originates from the "letter" and because "newness" stems from the Spirit, as seen in the relationship between letter and Spirit and the results that flow from them (bearing fruit unto death

---

72. The genitival phrase τα παθήματα τῶν ἁμαρτιῶν (Rom. 7:5) probably represents an attributive genitive (i.e., "sinful passions").

vs. bearing fruit for God). The correlation of newness with Spirit and of oldness with letter in 7:6 forms a key piece of evidence in understanding the "new" covenant's correlation with the Spirit and not the letter ("newness of the Spirit and not oldness of the letter," my trans.).

The presence of the Spirit points to the new age in which the promise of the new covenant becomes a reality in terms spoken beforehand in Ezekiel 36:27.[73] The Spirit producing newness also fits well with the cause-and-effect relationship between the giving of the Spirit and the "caus[ing of] you to walk in my statutes" of 36:27. This approach fits the contrast with "oldness of the letter" in Romans 7:6 because the oldness is both derived from the letter (genitive of source) and produced by the letter (genitive of producer). Sinful passions were produced (ἐνεργέω) through the instrumentality of the law (διὰ τοῦ νόμου, 7:5).

However, these observations do not completely pinpoint the underlying rationale for old and new because they explain only the result clause of 7:4. One also has to account for the redemptive-historical nature of the "but now" that begins 7:6 and functions as support for the main point found in 7:4. If we omit the result clause, 7:4 states that believers "have died to the law through the body of Christ, so that you may belong to another, to him who has been raised from the dead." The concepts of union with Christ ("belong to another") and death ("have died") through the body of Christ and resurrection of Christ ("him who has been raised from the dead") all come together to explain the release from the law and the old age.

The question arises in response to these six stages, How would someone hold these truths together in a unified way that maintains essential emphases and distinctions? I believe that Martyn Lloyd-Jones is a great example of someone who preached these truths with passion and power and refused to separate them.

Justification and Sanctification Are Distinguishable yet Inseparable

Segregating justification and sanctification hinders readers of Scripture from seeing the holistic beauty of the whole counsel of God. This point landed on me in a fresh way through a recent writing project on the theology of the Welsh preacher D. Martyn Lloyd-Jones.[74] Lloyd-Jones believed that preaching justification in its purity will invariably open preachers up to the charge of antinomianism. He says that if "our preaching does not expose us to that charge and to that misunderstanding, it is because we are not really preaching the gospel."[75] Lloyd-Jones forcefully contends that no one raises that charge against the Roman Catholic Church, but it was frequently brought against

---

73. F. F. Bruce, *The Epistle of Paul to the Romans: An Introduction and Commentary*, 2nd ed., TNTC (Grand Rapids, MI: Eerdmans, 2000), 139. See also Thielman, *Paul and the Law*, 198. He shows that "newness of Spirit" points to the "arrival of the eschatological era predicted by the prophets in which God would restore his people by placing his Spirit among them."
74. Jason C. Meyer, *Lloyd-Jones on the Christian Life: Doctrine and Life as Fuel and Fire* (Wheaton, IL: Crossway, 2018).
75. D. Martyn Lloyd-Jones, *Romans: Exposition of Chapter 6; The New Man* (Carlisle, PA: Banner of Truth, 1972), 8.

Martin Luther.[76] Therefore, the charge of antinomianism can sometimes be the best test as to whether one is preaching justification in its Pauline purity.[77] Paul's portrayal of justification in terms of pure grace apart from works (Romans 3–5) causes the objection in Romans 6:1 to rise so forcefully: "Are we to continue in sin that grace may abound?" The rest of Romans 6 shows Paul's answer to the objection. Union with Christ, not a redefinition of justification, is the answer.

Lloyd-Jones was zealous to distinguish the doctrines without separating them. The Doctor (as he was often called) gave a series of lectures on biblical doctrines on Friday nights at Westminster Chapel in London from 1952 to 1955. These lectures were later published as the book *Great Doctrines of the Bible*. When he came to the doctrine of justification, Lloyd-Jones denounced the Roman Catholic error of confusing justification and sanctification.[78] He argued that we can further guard ourselves from confusing these two doctrines by distinguishing them while also refusing to separate them:

> Now it is right to distinguish them, but there is all the difference in the world between distinguishing between things and separating them. For the purposes of thought, and, indeed, in accordance with the Scripture, we must distinguish justification from sanctification. But that is a very different thing from separating them.[79]

The Doctor emphasized that doctrines belong together as a package. They form a singular whole with a "vital connection between them all." They are not "disjointed, dismembered teachings."[80] In particular, both justification and sanctification belong to the wider doctrine of union with Christ:

> If you are in Christ you are in Christ; and if Christ "has been made of God unto you wisdom, even righteousness and sanctification" (1 Cor. 1:30) He must be glorification to you also. You cannot divide Him and "take" justification only, or sanctification only. It is "all or nothing." You must not divide these things. It is unscriptural, indeed it is impossible. It is the Person of Christ that matters. He is indivisible. We have all these in Christ.[81]

Romans 6–8 functions as the greatest biblical warrant, Lloyd-Jones believed, for the inseparable nature of justification and sanctification. The thought of splitting these doctrines apart should lead to shock and horror:

> Indeed, we could say that the theme of Romans 6, 7 and 8 is to denounce, with horror, the tendency of people to separate justification from sanctification; to say that if you think you can stop at justification, you are doing something which the Apostle

---

76. Lloyd-Jones, *Romans: Exposition of Chapter 6*, 9.
77. Lloyd-Jones, *Romans: Exposition of Chapter 6*, 8.
78. D. Martyn Lloyd-Jones, *God the Holy Spirit*, vol. 2 of *Great Doctrines of the Bible* (Wheaton, IL: Crossway, 1997), 168.
79. Lloyd-Jones, *God the Holy Spirit*, 201.
80. Lloyd-Jones, *God the Holy Spirit*, 201.
81. Lloyd-Jones, *Romans: Exposition of Chapter 5*, 54.

believes is so terrible that he can say nothing about it but, "God forbid" that anybody should think such a thing or ever draw such a deduction.[82]

Lloyd-Jones enlists the economic Trinity and the division of labor in the Godhead for the doctrines of justification and sanctification. Justification is an act of the Father, while sanctification is essentially the work of the Spirit. God the Father makes the declaration of justification, while God the Holy Spirit sanctifies.[83] Perhaps we should go further and say that justification is an act of the Father based on *the work of the Son*. Sanctification is the work of the Spirit to conform us to *the image of the Son*.

The Welsh minister further distinguishes between justification and sanctification in five ways:

1. Justification means declared righteous; sanctification means made righteous.
2. Justification involves imputed righteousness; sanctification involves imparted righteousness.
3. Justification is instantaneous; sanctification is continuous.
4. Justification addresses the condemning power of sin; sanctification addresses the corrupting power of sin.
5. Justification involves no human works; sanctification does involve human works.[84]

Lloyd-Jones stresses that separating justification and sanctification robs the gospel of one of its greatest glories: the capture of the whole person. The gospel captivates and satisfies the whole person (mind, heart, and will). This complete capture is "one of the greatest glories of the gospel."[85] If we segregate justification and sanctification, we could give the impression that Christ's death produces only "lop-sided Christians":

> The Christian position is three-fold; it is the three together, and the three at the same time, and the three always. A great gospel like this takes up the whole man, and if the whole man is not taken up, think again as to where you stand. "You have obeyed from the heart the form of doctrine delivered unto you." What a gospel! What a glorious message! It can satisfy man's mind completely, it can move his heart entirely, and it can lead to wholehearted obedience in the realm of the will. That is the gospel. Christ has died that we might be complete men, not merely that parts of us may be saved; not that we might be lop-sided Christians, but that there may be a balanced finality about us.[86]

---

82. Lloyd-Jones, *God the Holy Spirit*, 223. Lloyd-Jones also distinguishes justification from regeneration in terms of the logical order of salvation. He stresses that the logical order in our minds must be justification before regeneration. We are not justified "because we are regenerate" or "have a new nature." The Doctor describes the teaching that regeneration precedes justification as "the Roman Catholic error and heresy." Paul makes it crystal clear that we are justified while we are "ungodly," "sinful," and "without any change in our nature." Lloyd-Jones, *God the Holy Spirit*, 206.
83. Lloyd-Jones, *God the Holy Spirit*, 175.
84. Lloyd-Jones, *God the Holy Spirit*, 169–78.
85. D. Martyn Lloyd-Jones, *Spiritual Depression: Its Causes and Its Cure* (Grand Rapids, MI: Eerdmans, 1965), 56.
86. Lloyd-Jones, *Spiritual Depression*, 60.

Conclusion

The act of situating the doctrine of justification within the framework of the new covenant opens up a new vista from which one can see that justification is both an *event* and a *gateway*. Justification is an event that provides a gateway to glories that are grander than justification by itself.

The doctrine of justification demands to be heralded, not merely studied. Preaching justification in its purity should cause some antinomian objections to rise up, but the biblical ammunition of (1) union with Christ and (2) the blood-bought blessings of the new covenant should together shoot down those objections. For example, justification does not nullify a passion for a holy life; it makes that passion possible. Justification does not make the sight of my own sin unnecessary or undesirable; it makes the sight welcome and the pursuit of purity possible. The heart cry of every justified believer is not "How far do I dare get from God?" but "How close can I get to God?" We must not isolate justification from the nature of the new life of regeneration. Regeneration in new covenant terms is God taking out the heart of stone and replacing it with a heart of flesh. One of the blessings of the new covenant is the God-wrought miracle that takes out the self-exalting heart and puts in the Christ-exalting heart that hungers and thirsts for righteousness.

Perhaps an analogy will help. No one instinctively wants to hear about everything that is wrong with him or her. Imagine going to an auto repair shop and the mechanic comes and tells you everything that is wrong with your car. That could be seen as unwelcome news. But change the context, and bring your father into the picture. Imagine that you are a young driver and that this is your first car. Your father has asked you to take this car to the mechanic because he wants you to drive a safe and reliable car. He has told you that he has already promised to pay the bill for any repair that is needed. Suddenly, you want to see all that is wrong because you want a car that will be reliable.

Justification is the note from the Father that all the bills are paid in full by Jesus. Sanctification flows from the new heart that now says, "Show me all that is broken and needs repaired." The redeemed heart says, "Show me all my sin. I want to walk in your light. I want everything that Jesus purchased for me in the new covenant with his own blood."

Recommended Resources

Carson, D. A., Peter T. O'Brien, and Mark A. Seifrid, eds. *Justification and Variegated Nomism*. Vol. 2, *The Paradoxes of Paul*. Wissenschaftliche Untersuchungen zum Neuen Testament, 2nd ser., vol. 181. Grand Rapids, MI: Baker Academic, 2004.

Das, A. Andrew. *Paul, the Law, and the Covenant*. Peabody, MA: Hendrickson, 2001.

Lloyd-Jones, D. Martyn. *Great Doctrines of the Bible*. Vol. 1, *God the Father, God the Son*. Wheaton, IL: Crossway, 1996.

———. *Great Doctrines of the Bible*. Vol. 2, *God the Holy Spirit*. Wheaton, IL: Crossway, 1997.

Meyer, Jason C. *The End of the Law: Mosaic Covenant in Pauline Theology*. NAC Studies in Bible and Theology 6. Nashville: B&H Academic, 2009.

———. "The Mosaic Law, Theological Systems, and the Glory of Christ." In *Progressive Covenantalism: Charting a Course between Dispensational and Covenant Theologies*, edited by Steven J. Wellum and Brent E. Parker, 69–99. Nashville: B&H Academic, 2016.

Rosner, Brian S. *Paul and the Law: Keeping the Commandments of God*. New Studies in Biblical Theology 31. Downers Grove, IL: InterVarsity Press, 2013.

Schreiner, Thomas R. *40 Questions about Christians and Biblical Law*. 40 Questions. Grand Rapids, MI: Kregel, 2010.

Westerholm, Stephen. *Perspectives Old and New on Paul: The "Lutheran" Paul and His Critics*. Grand Rapids, MI: Eerdmans, 2004.

Williamson, Paul R. *Sealed with an Oath: Covenant in God's Unfolding Purpose*. New Studies in Biblical Theology 23. Downers Grove, IL: InterVarsity Press, 2007.

PART THREE

JUSTIFICATION IN HISTORICAL PERSPECTIVE

18

Reformation Invention or Historic Orthodoxy?

Justification in the Fathers

GERALD BRAY

It is a commonplace of theology that the doctrine of justification by faith alone was a product of the sixteenth-century Protestant Reformation. Had justification been clear and agreed on before that time, there would presumably not have been a major debate about it that proved capable of splitting the church in two. What does this tell us about the doctrine that many Protestants would insist is the "article of a standing or falling church"? Why is it that nobody seems to have heard of it before Martin Luther (1483–1546) came along and made it the centerpiece of his theology? And what does that tell us about Luther—did he make it up or "discover" something that was not really there? Could 1,500 years of church history have been that mistaken about what was supposed to be one of its most fundamental doctrines?

It is obviously impossible to go back to men like Irenaeus, Tertullian, and Origen, all of whom were writing in the years around AD 200, and ask them what they would have thought about the theology of sixteenth-century Lutherans and Calvinists. The church fathers lived in a different world and had other challenges to face. The vast inheritance of medieval scholastic theology, which underlay so much of the Reformers' thinking, was completely unknown to them. They knew about "justification by faith," and even by faith "alone," but the subtler points of the Reformation argument, conditioned by centuries of detailed analysis about what that really meant, would probably have passed them by. Perhaps that is too pessimistic a judgment—operating from the same biblical texts as the Reformers did, they might have been able to offer an opinion about their interpretation, but we may legitimately ask whether they would have preferred to have the question rephrased and answered according to a different frame of reference.

The fathers were preoccupied with other theological questions—the goodness of creation, for example, and the deity of Christ—which the men of the sixteenth century were able to take for granted. It is hardly surprising if justification took something of a back seat in ancient times, but even so, it seems reasonable to suggest that many modern Western theologians have been too negative in their assessment of the use (or nonuse) of Paul's teaching about justification by faith in the pre-Augustinian theology of the church. For example, Krister Stendahl has written,

> It has always been a puzzling fact that Paul meant so relatively little for the thinking of the church during the first 350 years of its history. To be sure, he is honoured and quoted, but—in the theological perspective of the West—it seems that Paul's great insight into justification by faith was forgotten.[1]

Stendahl's view, which by its nature lacked any evidence to confirm it, was picked up and repeated by Alister McGrath in his monumental history of the doctrine of justification. McGrath states,

> It is . . . evident that the early Christian writers did not choose to express their soteriological convictions in terms of the concept of justification. This is not to say that the fathers avoid the term "justification"; their interest in the concept is, however, minimal, and the term generally occurs in their writings as a direct citation from, or a recognisable allusion to, the epistles of Paul, usually employed for some purpose other than a discussion of the concept of justification itself.[2]

It is significant, however, that McGrath makes no mention of Origen's great commentary on Romans, whose very existence is a refutation of this statement. In fact, as I hope to demonstrate, there is ample evidence from the early fathers that they were well aware of Paul's teaching about justification and made good use of it when the occasion arose.[3] That their views do not always dovetail with those of the early Protestants (or their papal opponents, for that matter) is hardly their fault, since they were completely unaware of that debate and did not tailor their observations to suit it, but that is no reason to minimize their contribution to our understanding of the doctrine of justification or deny its importance.

When we turn to the Reformers, it is obvious that they did have access to the writings of the early church fathers. Not only that, they were also concerned to make sure that their teaching coincided with what the church had always taught, even if they came to

---

1. Krister Stendahl, *Paul among Jews and Gentiles* (Philadelphia: Fortress, 1976), 83.
2. Alister E. McGrath, *Iustitia Dei: A History of the Christian Doctrine of Justification*, 3rd ed. (Cambridge: Cambridge University Press, 2005), 33.
3. For a recent study of the evidence, see Andrew Daunton-Fear, *Were They Preaching "Another Gospel"? Justification by Faith in the Second Century*, Latimer Studies 80 (London: Latimer Trust, 2015).

believe that the fathers (or some of them, at least) had been wrong on certain things, in particular on their understanding of the relationship between faith and works. There has long been a current of Protestant opinion that says that the pure gospel was lost after the close of the New Testament period, to be rediscovered only by Luther and his colleagues a millennium and a half later. Although some radical groups still hold this view, few serious scholars nowadays would accept that rather sweeping analysis of the church's history. The Reformers themselves certainly would have rejected it—they were convinced that what they were saying had always been the doctrine of the church but that that doctrine had been twisted and obscured by the casuistry of the medieval schoolmen who had turned it into something else. In their minds, an honest investigation of the ancient sources would have shown that they were right—more precise in their formulation of the principles perhaps, because of the misunderstandings that had crept in over the centuries, but essentially the same as what the fathers had said.

That the Reformers developed the doctrine of justification by faith alone in a way that had not been known in the church before their time is certainly true—they would not have become so closely associated with it had they been doing nothing but revive a long-forgotten teaching. But was that doctrine a deviation from what had gone before, an innovation or even a heresy, as their opponents claimed, or did it represent a fresh expression of the ancient truth in circumstances that required a more detailed exposition of the question than had previously been necessary? That is what we must try to find out.

The Faith of Abraham

It is appropriate to begin with a consideration of what the fathers had to say about Abraham, whom both Christians and Jews claim as their spiritual ancestor. In a well-known argument for justification by faith alone, the apostle Paul reminded the Roman Christians that Abraham had received circumcision as a sign of his faith. He was justified in God's sight not because he had been circumcised, as the law of Moses would later dictate, but because he believed in the promises that God had made to him. Writing to the Corinthian church a generation later, Clement of Rome had this to say about it:

> Why was our father Abraham blessed? Was it not because he attained righteousness and truth through faith? Isaac with confidence, knowing the future, was willingly led to sacrifice. Jacob with humility departed from his land . . . and the twelve tribes of Israel were given to him. . . . All therefore were glorified and magnified, not through themselves or their own works or the righteous actions which they did, but through his [God's] will. And so we, having been called through his will in Christ Jesus, are not justified through ourselves or through our own wisdom or understanding or piety or works which we have done in holiness of heart, but through faith, by which the Almighty God has justified all who have existed from the beginning, to whom be the glory for ever and ever. Amen.[4]

---

4. 1 Clement 31–32, trans. J. B. Lightfoot and J. R. Harmer, ed. and rev. Michael W. Holmes, *The Apostolic Fathers*, 2nd ed. (Grand Rapids, MI: Baker, 1989), 45–46. See also 1 Clement 10 (Holmes ed., 33–34). See also *ANF*, 1:13. Many

This passage could hardly be more explicit in its affirmation of justification by faith. Clement talked not only about Abraham but about all three of the patriarchs, whom he linked together as men blessed and justified by their faith. Moreover, he stated quite clearly that this faith was independent of any works or intellectual effort on their part. He even recognized that while it is possible to do good works in a spirit of holiness, these do not count toward our justification any more than works done before we have received the knowledge of salvation.

Later writers were less effusive on the subject, but they did not hesitate to appeal to the same basic principles. Justin Martyr (ca. 100–158), for example, in his account of a dialogue he supposedly had with the Jewish rabbi Trypho (Tarphon?), never mentioned Paul by name but made several references to Abraham that clearly echo the apostle's teaching in Romans. For example, he described the new covenant prophesied by Jeremiah as follows:

> We have been led to God through this crucified Christ, and we are the true spiritual Israel, and the descendants of Judah, Jacob, Isaac and Abraham, who, though uncircumcised, was approved and blessed by God because of his faith.[5]

Later on, he was even more explicit:

> When Abraham himself was still uncircumcised, he was justified and blessed by God because of his faith in him, as the Scriptures tell us. Furthermore, the Scriptures and the facts of the case force us to admit that Abraham received circumcision for a sign, not for justification itself.[6]

So important was this to him that he repeated it a third time, reminding Trypho that "Abraham was declared by God to be righteous, not on account of circumcision, but on account of faith."[7] Justin then went on to quote Genesis 15:6 ("[Abraham] believed the LORD, and he counted it to him as righteousness") and applied its lesson directly to Christians:

> We therefore, in the uncircumcision of our flesh, believing God through Christ, and having that circumcision which is of advantage to us who have acquired it—namely, that of the heart—we hope to appear righteous before and well-pleasing to God.[8]

And as if unable to let the subject drop, Justin returned to Abraham one more time and applied his example directly to us:

---

of the relevant references in *ANF* have been indexed and sometimes slightly condensed or modernized in David Bercot, *A Dictionary of Early Christian Beliefs: A Reference Guide to More Than 700 Topics Discussed by the Early Church Fathers* (Peabody, MA: Hendrickson, 1998), 574–79.

5. Justin Martyr, *Dialogue with Trypho* 11, in *ANF*, 1:200. See Jer. 31:31–32. Trypho is usually identified with Rabbi Tarphon, a leading Jewish scholar of his time, but whether Justin actually debated him or simply wrote using him as a literary interlocutor is unknown.

6. Justin Martyr, *Dialogue with Trypho* 23, in *ANF*, 1:206.

7. Justin Martyr, *Dialogue with Trypho* 92, in *ANF*, 1:245.

8. Justin Martyr, *Dialogue with Trypho* 92, in *ANF*, 1:245.

We shall inherit the holy land together with Abraham, receiving our inheritance for all eternity, because by our similar faith we have become children of Abraham. For, just as he believed the voice of God and was justified thereby, so we have believed the voice of God . . . and have renounced even to death all worldly things.[9]

A generation after Justin's time, we find the same appeal to Abraham's faith in Irenaeus of Lyons (ca. 130–ca. 200), who connected it with the faith of the apostles and of the Christians of his own day. In all three cases, it was their faith that justified them—there is no mention of works at all.[10] Exactly the same sentiment appears a few years later in the writings of Clement of Alexandria (ca. 150–215), who applied the example of Abraham to Christians and in no uncertain terms rejected any notion of the saving value of human works: "Abraham was not justified by works but by faith. It is therefore of no advantage to persons after the end of life, even if they do good works now, if they do not have faith."[11]

Remarkably, Clement then went to explain that the Old Testament was translated into Greek so that the pagan philosophers (against whom he was contending) would not be ignorant of the truth about justification. As he put it, knowledge of the truth is one thing, but the faith to believe and act on it is another. The first can be taught and learned, but the second is a gift of grace. The implication is that it is possible to imitate Abraham by doing good works, but even if that is right and good in itself, it cannot lead to salvation, which God bestows by grace through faith. Clement of Alexandria was more subtle than his namesake of Rome was a century earlier, but the message was still the same.[12]

A few years later still, Origen (ca. 185–ca. 254), who had been a pupil of Clement in Alexandria and had absorbed his teaching, clarified this idea as follows:

Before God, no living being will be justified. This shows that in comparison with God, and the righteousness that is in him, no one (not even the most perfect of saints) will be justified. We might take a different illustration and say that no candle can give light before the sun. We do not mean that the candle will not give out light, but that it will not be seen when the sun outshines it.[13]

In this particular passage, Origen does not mention Abraham, but the principle is the same—only by the grace of God can a person be justified in his sight. It was a teaching that Origen later expounded at length in his commentary on Paul's epistle to the Romans, and then in direct relation to Abraham. In commenting on Romans 4:2 ("If Abraham was justified by works, he has something to boast about, but not before God"), he had this to say:

---

9. Justin Martyr, *Dialogue with Trypho* 119, in ANF, 1:259.
10. Irenaeus of Lyons, *Against All Heresies* 4.5.3–5, in ANF, 1:467.
11. Clement of Alexandria, *Stromateis* 1.7, in ANF, 2:308.
12. See Peter Ensor, who demonstrates that Clement even believed in penal substitution, though he did not make it central to his thought. Ensor, "Clement of Alexandria and Penal Substitutionary Atonement," *EvQ* 85, no. 1 (2013): 19–35.
13. Origen, *Commentary on John* 2.11, in ANF, 9:333.

> This is a rhetorical argument, which goes like this: Someone who is justified by works has nothing to boast of before God. But Abraham did have something to glory in before God. Therefore he was justified by faith and not by works. . . .
>
> In this whole passage it seems that the apostle wants to show that there are two justifications, one by works and the other by faith. He says that justification by works has its glory but only in and of itself, not before God. Justification by faith, on the other hand, has glory before God, who sees our hearts. . . . The one who looks for justification by works may expect honour mainly from other persons who see and approve of them.
>
> Let no one think that someone who has faith enough to be justified and to have glory before God can at the same time have unrighteousness dwelling in him as well. For faith cannot coexist with unbelief, nor can righteousness with wickedness, just as light and darkness cannot live together.[14]

It is clear from this quotation that Origen recognized that justification by works, even if such a thing can be said to exist in a way, is still totally inadequate to earn favor with God. At the same time, he also understood that someone who has been justified by faith cannot go on living as if nothing has changed—a person who has experienced the power and presence of God in his life must demonstrate that by living accordingly.

Origen, it should be said, was well aware that when Paul spoke about "works," he was talking about the ritual observances of the law of Moses, and not about living the Christian life. It was an important difference. Keeping the Mosaic law was an attempt to obtain justification, whereas the imitation of Christ was a manifestation of a righteousness already received by God's grace. This is what he said when commenting on Romans 11:6:

> One should know that the works that Paul repudiates and frequently criticizes are not the works of righteousness that are commanded in the law, but those in which those who keep the law according to the flesh boast; i.e., the circumcision of the flesh, the sacrificial rituals, the observance of Sabbaths or new moon festivals. These, then, and works of this nature are the ones on the basis of which he says no one can be saved, and concerning which he says in the present passage, "not on the basis of works; otherwise, grace would no longer be grace." For if anyone is justified through these, he is not justified *gratis*. But these works are by no means sought from the one who is justified through grace; but this one should take care that the grace he has received should not be in him "in vain," as Paul also says: "For his grace in me was not in vain but I worked harder than any of them." And again he adds, as one mindful of grace: "Not I, but the grace of God with me" [1 Cor. 15:10]. So then, one does not make grace become in vain who joins works to it that are worthy and who does not show himself ungrateful for the grace of God.[15]

It is to that central question of grace that we must now turn.

---

14. Origen, *Commentary on Romans* 4.1.2–3, extracted in *Ancient Christian Commentary on Scripture: New Testament*, vol. 6, *Romans*, ed. Gerald L. Bray (Downers Grove, IL: InterVarsity Press, 1998), 105–6. See also Origen, *Commentary on the Epistle to the Romans*, trans. Thomas P. Scheck (Washington, DC: Catholic University of America Press, 2001–2002), 1:237–38.

15. Origen, *Commentary on Romans* 8.8.6, in Scheck, *Romans*, 2:162.

The Grace of God

Faith, Not Works, Justifies

When speaking of salvation, the fathers of the church almost always described it as an act of God's grace, freely bestowed on the undeserving. That was not an explicit denial of justification by works, but it amounted to the same thing in practice. As Ignatius of Antioch (d. ca. 118) wrote to the Magnesian church, "Let us not be ungrateful for God's kindness. For if he were to reward us according to our works, we would cease to be."[16] Ignatius was not concerned to distinguish good works from bad—from his view, *all* human works, whether good or bad, were useless in trying to gain a reward from God. Elsewhere, in a letter to the church at Philadelphia, he made his position clear:

> I heard some people say, "If I do not find it in the archives [Old Testament], I do not believe it in the Gospel." ... But for me, the archives are Jesus Christ ... his cross and death and his resurrection and the faith which comes through him; by these things I want, through your prayers, to be justified.[17]

It is true that Ignatius was writing while on his way to Rome, where he expected to meet a martyr's death. He regarded that as the fulfillment of his Christian discipleship, and this has often been taken to imply that he did not believe in justification by faith alone.[18] But the two things are not the same. Discipleship involves the imitation of Christ, which may extend to suffering a death like the one he suffered, and if we are Christians, then we are called to walk in his footsteps—the apostle Paul said as much on more than one occasion. Justification, however, is something else. Ignatius had no intention or desire to claim that he would have earned his place in heaven by being willing to suffer and die for Christ, as if some less sacrificial kind of death might have produced a different result. He knew that even if he were to be lost at sea, which was by no means impossible, he would still be justified by the blood of Christ! To be chosen to die a martyr's death (in imitation of Jesus's own death on the cross) was a privilege, but it was not the ground of his salvation, which was always and could only be what Jesus had done on his behalf.

In a similar vein, the anonymous Epistle to Diognetus, written sometime in the second century, says,

> Being convinced at that time of our unworthiness of attaining life through our own works, it is now, through the kindness of God, graciously given to us. Accordingly, it is clear that in ourselves we were unable to enter into the kingdom of God. However, through the power of God, we can be made able.[19]

---

16. Ignatius of Antioch, *Epistle to the Magnesians* 10, in *ANF*, 1:63. Unfortunately, the force of this is blunted by the Lightfoot/Harmer translation, which says: "Let us not be unaware of his goodness. For if he were to imitate the way we act, we are lost." Cf. Holmes, *Apostolic Fathers*, 96.
17. Ignatius of Antioch, *Epistle to the Philadelphians* 8, in *ANF*, 1:84, following Holmes, *Apostolic Fathers*, 108–9.
18. Daunton-Fear tends to agree with this assessment. *"Another Gospel"?*, 11–13.
19. Epistle to Diognetus 9, in *ANF*, 1:28. Here the Lightfoot/Harmer translation is somewhat better than in the case of Ignatius, though it is still rather weak. Cf. Holmes, *Apostolic Fathers*, 302.

Writing at about the same time, Polycarp of Smyrna (ca. 70–156), quoting Paul in his letter to the Ephesians, said, "You know that 'by grace you have been saved, not by works' [Eph. 2:8–9], but by the will of God through Jesus Christ."[20] This is not as clear a statement of justification by faith alone as we might wish, but it is consonant with that doctrine and has to be read in its historical context, where a quotation from Paul on the subject would undoubtedly have been understood in the same way.

A very similar statement can be found in Irenaeus of Lyons, a disciple of Polycarp and like him also originally from Smyrna, who wrote, "No one . . . has power to procure for himself the means of salvation. So the more we receive his grace, the more we should love him."[21] He expressed the same idea more clearly when he said,

> Christ redeems us righteously by his own blood. As regards those of us who have been redeemed, [he does this] by grace. For we have given nothing to him previously. Nor does he desire anything from us, as if he stood in need of it.[22]

Irenaeus was a great proponent of the hermeneutical method of reading Scripture known as *recapitulation*, a term that he seems to have retrieved from Ephesians 1:10.[23] According to this theory, the history of the world from Adam to Christ was one of a continuous fall into ever deeper sin. When things had gotten as bad as they could, God sent his Son to redeem the world by going over (recapitulating) each step that had led to the catastrophe and putting it right. Just as the original fall had been the work of one man and not a cooperative effort, so redemption from sin was also the work of one man:

> For as by the disobedience of the one man who was originally moulded from virgin soil, the many were made sinners, and forfeited life; so it was necessary that, by the obedience of one man, who was originally born from a virgin, many should be justified and receive salvation. . . . God recapitulated in himself the ancient formation of man, that he might kill sin, deprive death of its power, and vivify man; and therefore his works are true.[24]

Irenaeus's point was that just as the fall of man had been accomplished by a single individual, with no assistance from anyone else, so our rescue from the consequences of that fall was also the work of one person acting alone. This was the principle of recapitulation at work—sin and salvation parallel each other but move in opposite directions.

---

20. Polycarp of Smyrna, *Epistle to the Philippians* 1, in *ANF*, 1:33. Cf. Holmes, *Apostolic Fathers*, 123.
21. Irenaeus of Lyons, *Against All Heresies* 4.13.3, in *ANF*, 1:478.
22. Irenaeus of Lyons, *Against All Heresies* 5.2.1, in *ANF*, 1:523.
23. Quoted by him in *Against All Heresies* 1.10.1, in *ANF*, 1:330. English translations of the verse typically obscure this meaning by translating the Greek word "recapitulate" as "unite" or something similar. Even so, there is no reason to suppose that Paul subscribed to the same hermeneutic as Irenaeus.
24. Irenaeus of Lyons, *Against All Heresies* 3.18.7, in *ANF*, 1:448. Cf. 3.16.9, in *ANF*, 1:444, where Irenaeus quotes Rom. 5:9, making it plain that we have been justified by the shed blood of Christ.

That good works, however pious they might be and however much they were performed in honor of Jesus, could not save anyone was confirmed by Tertullian. When he was discussing the case of the sinful woman recorded in Luke 7:36–50, who received forgiveness not by her works but by her faith, he said,

> The behaviour of the woman who was a sinner, when she covered the Lord's feet with her kisses, bathed them with her tears, wiped them with the hairs of her head, anointed them with ointment, produced evidence that she deserved forgiveness according to the mind of the Creator, who is accustomed to prefer mercy to sacrifice. But even if the stimulus for her repentance proceeded from her faith, she heard her justification by faith pronounced through her repentance, in the words: "Your faith has saved you," by him who had declared by Habakkuk: "The just shall live by his faith" [Hab. 2:4; cf. Rom. 1:17].[25]

In the next generation, Cyprian of Carthage (ca. 200–258), who was an admirer if not a disciple of Tertullian, made it perfectly clear that nobody can earn God's favor:

> It is not necessary to pay a price either in the way of bribery or of labour—such that man's elevation or dignity or power would be begotten in him with elaborate effort. Rather, it is a gratuitous gift from God and is accessible to all.[26]

Of course, all these fathers of the church believed that once a person was justified by faith, he or she must then continue in it by working out his or her salvation in fear and trembling, as Paul told the Philippians (Phil. 2:12). There could be no question of what today would be called "easy believism." A man or woman who claimed to have the faith of Christ was required to demonstrate the truth of that claim by a life of godly behavior, which would naturally include good works, though it was not limited to (or defined by) them.

It is here that we can begin to see how the occasion for later confusion about the place of works arose. The Reformers' belief in justification by faith alone has been misunderstood by both Roman Catholics and some Protestants to mean that there is no place for good works in the Christian life, which is not what Martin Luther, John Calvin, or anyone else of significance in the Protestant Reformation actually said. Like the fathers, the Reformers believed that a justified person would be expected to live in a way that reflected that change, and they commended good works to believers as a sign of their faith. As evidence of this conviction, we may cite what Calvin (1509–1564) said in his commentary on James 2:21–26, which states both that Abraham was "justified" by works and that faith without works is dead:

> The sophists leap on the word "justification" and sing out in triumphant chorus that part of justification depends on works. A sober exegesis must be sought from

---

25. Tertullian, *Adversus Marcionem* 4.18, in *ANF*, 3:376. See also Tertullian, *Adversus Marcionem*, ed. and trans. Ernest Evans (Oxford: Clarendon, 1972), 2:356–57.
26. Cyprian of Carthage, *Epistle* 1.14, in *ANF*, 5:279.

the circumstances of the present passage. We have said that James is not here dealing with the source or the manner of man's attainment of righteousness (as is evident to all), but is stressing the single point, that good works are invariably tied to faith: so when he states that Abraham was justified by works his words are in confirmation of the justification. So when the sophists set James against Paul, they are deceived by the double meaning of the term "justification." When Paul says we are justified by faith, he means precisely that we have won a verdict of righteousness in the sight of God. James has quite another intention, that the man who professes himself to be faithful should demonstrate the truth of his fidelity by works. James did not mean to teach us where the confidence of our salvation should rest—which is the very point on which Paul does insist. So let us avoid the false reasoning which has trapped the sophists, by taking note of the double meaning: to Paul, the word denotes our free imputation of righteousness before the judgment seat of God, to James, the demonstration of righteousness from its effects, in the sight of men. . . . In this latter sense, we may admit without controversy that man is justified by works.[27]

Calvin's exegesis of James 2:21–26 tallies with that of the early fathers of the church, the main difference being that the latter did not speak in terms of Paul *versus* James, though Origen, at least, did distinguish two different meanings of the word *justification*. In his eyes there was a justification by faith, which makes the believer righteous in the sight of God, and there was a justification by works, which are meant to impress other people. The two overlap in the sense that a person who has been justified by faith in God will then be expected to behave in a way that will win the approval of his fellow men, but that is coincidental. Salvation depends entirely on the former and not at all on the latter.[28] For Origen, God justifies sinners on the basis of faith; what other people think about them is neither here nor there. If other people noticed a change for the better and approved of it, that was fine, but if they disapproved of it and made martyrs of believers, that was fine too—in fact, from one point of view, it was even better! Normally, however, the fathers did not analyze their salvation in this way. Instead, they combined the two aspects of justification into one, regarding justification proper as the fruit of faith and the works of the believer as its necessary consequence.[29]

This can be seen from the remarks Origen made in his commentary on Romans 3:28, where Paul specifically states that a man is justified by faith, apart from works. Origen's concern was to explain the meaning of this verse in the context of Paul's total teaching about the Christian life. In his words,

---

27. John Calvin, *A Harmony of the Gospels Matthew, Mark, and Luke, Volume 3, and the Epistles of James and Jude*, trans. A. W. Morrison, ed. David W. Torrance and Thomas F. Torrance (Edinburgh: Saint Andrew's Press, 1972), 285–86.
28. Origen, *Commentary on Romans* 4.1.3, in Scheck, *Romans*, 1:238.
29. This confusion is demonstrated by Thomas P. Scheck, *Origen and the History of Justification: The Legacy of Origen's Commentary on Romans* (Notre Dame, IN: University of Notre Dame Press, 2008), whose lengthy account is marred by precisely this misinterpretation of Origen's theology. It is true that the Reformers did not like Origen, but contrary to what Scheck claims, they were turned against him by Jerome's criticism of his allegorical exegesis more than by what he said about justification by faith.

A man is justified by faith. The works of the law can make no contribution to this. Where there is no faith which might justify the believer, even if there are works of the law, these are not based on the foundation of faith. Even if they are good in themselves they cannot justify the one who does them, because faith is lacking, and faith is the mark of those who are justified by God.[30]

The importance of justification by faith, and by faith alone, is brought out clearly by the case of the thief on the cross who believed in Jesus and was told that he would be in paradise that same day (Luke 23:43). He had no opportunity to do good works, and if they had been necessary for him to go to heaven, he would not have gone there. As Origen put it,

> In the Gospels, nothing is recorded about his good works, but for the sake of this faith alone Jesus said to him: "Truly I say to you: Today you will be with me in paradise. . . ." Through faith this thief was justified without works of the law, since the Lord did not require in addition to this that he should first accomplish works, nor did he wait for him to perform some works when he had believed. By his confession alone, Jesus, who was about to begin his journey to paradise, received the thief as a justified travelling companion with himself.[31]

The believing thief was admittedly an exceptional case, but Origen used it to underline the significance of faith (and faith alone) for justification. There is no indication that he received an inferior reward because of his lack of works; he was going to be in paradise with Jesus along with every other believer.

The idea that the works of the believer are somehow "meritorious" in the sense of earning salvation, or at least a higher position in heaven, is nowhere to be found in the fathers. It is sometimes claimed that Tertullian, who introduced the word "merit" into theology from the terminology of Roman law, held to the view that God was obliged to reward good deeds because they merited it.[32] But what Tertullian actually said was this:

> For God, never giving his sanction to the reprobation of good deeds, inasmuch as they are his own (of which, being the author, he must necessarily be the defender too), is in like manner the acceptor of them, and if the acceptor, likewise the rewarder. Let, then, the ingratitude of men see to it, if it attaches repentance even to good works; let their gratitude see to it too, if the desire of earning it be the incentive to well-doing . . . a good deed has God as its debtor, just as an evil has too; for a judge is rewarder of every cause.[33]

---

30. Origen, *Commentary on Romans* 3.9.5, in Bray, *Romans*, 100; Scheck, *Romans*, 1:228.
31. Origen, *Commentary on Romans* 3.9.3, in Scheck, *Romans*, 1:227.
32. Tertullian's use of Roman legal terms like "merit" and "satisfaction" has been the subject of much discussion. See Alexander Beck, *Römisches Recht bei Tertullian und Cyprian: Eine Studie zur frühen Kirchenrechtsgeschichte* (Halle: Niemeyer, 1930); Paolo Vitton, *I concetti giuridici nelle opere di Tertulliano* (Rome: Bretschneider, 1972), 50–54.
33. Tertullian, *On Repentance* 2, in ANF, 3:658.

In other words, if a man does good works, they are God's works in him, and for them he will not be punished. There is no suggestion that he will be rewarded for his own efforts. This is made perfectly clear by Origen, who is also often cited as being the ultimate source of the so-called "merit" theology of later times:

> It seems possible that rational natures, from whom the faculty of free will is never taken away, may be again subjected to movements of some kind, through the special act of the Lord himself. Otherwise, if they were always to occupy a condition that was unchangeable, they might not know that it is by the grace of God—and not by their own merit—that they have been placed in that final state of happiness.[34]

And again,

> It is advantageous for everyone to perceive his own particular nature and the grace of God. For he who does not perceive his own weakness and the divine favour . . . will imagine that the benefit conferred upon him by the grace of heaven is his own doing.[35]

Origen's attitude is summed up in his argument against the pagan philosopher Celsus: "The strength of our will is not sufficient to procure the perfectly pure heart. For we need God to create it."[36] One of the problems with so much of what Origen wrote is that we no longer possess the original Greek and so have to guess what words he might have used. Most probably the word that Rufinus translated as "merit" was ἄξια, with ἄξιος for "meritorious," but although these Greek words could have that meaning in a legal context, it was neither the natural nor the most common way of understanding them in Origen's day. To be ἄξιος was to be "worthy," a looser term than "meritorious," because it did not imply that the person's worth had been derived from his own effort or activity.[37] But time and again in the fathers, we read that the believer's "worth" in the sight of God depended not on anything he had done but entirely on the work of Christ on his behalf. Consider these words of Cyprian:

> Saving mercy is given from the divine goodness to the believer. . . . Christ bestows this grace. This gift of his mercy he confers upon us—by overcoming death in the trophy of the cross, by redeeming the believer with the price of his blood, by reconciling man to God the Father, and by giving life to our mortal nature by a heavenly regeneration.[38]

Then add these words, which Cyprian also wrote: "We must boast in nothing, since nothing is our own. In the Gospel of John: 'No one can receive anything unless it has been given to him from heaven' [John 3:27]."[39] Neither our faith nor our justification is self-generated!

---

34. Origen, *On First Principles* 2.3.3, in *ANF*, 4:272. Only the Latin translation of Rufinus survives.
35. Origen, *On First Principles* 3.1.12, in *ANF*, 4:313.
36. Origen, *Against Celsus* 7.33, in *ANF*, 4:624. See also Origen, *Contra Celsum*, ed. Henry Chadwick (Cambridge: Cambridge University Press, 1953), 421.
37. A better Latin translation for this would be *dignus*.
38. Cyprian of Carthage, *Treatise* 5.25, in *ANF*, 5:465.
39. Cyprian of Carthage, *Treatise* 12.3.4, in *ANF*, 5:533.

Imputed or Imparted Righteousness?

The evidence that the fathers, and Origen in particular, believed that justifying faith was a righteousness given to the believer by God and unobtainable otherwise is overwhelming, but a question about it still remains, and the answer to it is central to understanding the Reformation debates. Granted that justification is a gift, is it imputed to the believer or imparted to him? To put it another way, does the believer possess justification in some sense, or is he merely indebted to Christ's saving work, which remains what the Reformers would call an "alien righteousness"? It has always been the view of the Roman Catholic Church that saving grace is imparted to believers and that this interpretation is the correct understanding of both the fathers and the New Testament. On this point, if on no other, the Catholic view is that Luther went astray by denying that the justified believer is inherently righteous, and it is here, more than anywhere else, that the great traditions of Western Christianity part company. Which side would the early fathers have taken in this debate?

The medieval schoolmen—the theologians who composed the definition of *justificatio* approved by the Council of Trent and modern Catholic apologists—agreed that when Origen spoke about justification by faith, he was using a kind of shorthand to describe a process that involved the reception of divine grace and the performance of good works. It is therefore wrong, in their view, to isolate justification by faith alone as if nothing else matters.

In rhetorical terms, this shorthand is called *synecdoche*, a word that was in common use in the sixteenth-century debates but is apparently absent from Origen's own writings.[40] In debating with the Catholics of his time, the Lutheran Philipp Melanchthon (1497–1560) accepted this (by then) traditional interpretation and criticized Origen accordingly.[41] In his study of the question, written to defend the traditional Catholic position, Thomas Scheck has upheld this view:

> This synecdochal understanding helps to explain why Origen can say that not merely faith but also all the other virtues can be reputed for righteousness. For Origen justification is more than a nonimputation of past sins. It is an effectual and progressive sanctification in which sin is expelled and grace (sc. Christ), in all its aspects, is established in the believer's soul.[42]

He goes on to quote the contemporary Catholic theologian Prosper Grech, who has described Origen's position like this:

> Christian righteousness . . . consists in serving Christ in the Holy Spirit. Paul himself, who received the grace of the Spirit served wisdom, justice and all the

---
40. It is hard to be sure about this because so much of Origen's Greek corpus has been lost, but there is no sign of the word (or of the concept) in his surviving works.
41. Philipp Melanchthon, *Commentary on Romans (1540)*, trans. F. Kramer (Saint Louis, MO: Concordia, 1992), 253–54. The original text can be found in *Corpus Reformatorum*, ed. C. G. Bretschneider and H. E. Bindseil, 101 vols. (Halle: C. A. Schwetschke und Sohn, 1834–1963), 15:749; and Philipp Melanchthon, *Werke in Auswahl: Studeienausgabe*, ed. R. Stupperich (Gütersloh: C. Bertelsmann, 1951), 1:346.
42. Scheck, *Origen and the History of Justification*, 52.

other virtues which Christ is said to be. Christ certainly does save, but so does the Holy Spirit.[43]

Perhaps without fully realizing it, Grech has put his finger on the key factor that must determine how we interpret what Origen and the other fathers had to say about good works in the Christian life. The good works that we do are not ours but are works of the Holy Spirit, who has been given to us as believers. Origen stated this thinking quite clearly when he explained that the love of God that Paul mentions in Romans 5:5 is "the highest and greatest gift of the Holy Spirit so that, just as the gift was first received from God, we are able to love God himself."[44]

As for human effort, Origen explained how pointless and ineffectual it is:

> It is the wisdom of God to know God and to understand his mercy and his judgment and righteousness which he practises upon the earth, wherefore whoever boasts in these things should boast in the Lord. Human wisdom, however, cannot know and understand God nor can it understand his judgments and mercy and his righteousness which he practises on the earth. It is therefore an indifferent matter and is neutral.[45]

Origen admitted that someone who is well-trained in human wisdom may for that reason be readier to receive divine wisdom than someone who is not, but there is no guarantee of that actually happening. As he put it,

> If those neutral things are converted into virtues of the spirit and to the fruit of good works, they become worthy of boasting, just as, on the other hand, if they should be changed into evil works, . . . they are no longer neutral but are reckoned as evils. This is why they are called indifferent and neutral according to their own nature because, when attached to evil works, they can be called evil, and, when joined to good works, they can be designated as good. But people who call things good without tending toward either of these two must be believed to be unskilled and ignorant of rational definitions and classifications. . . . It is in an improper sense that we call a builder "wise" and designate a sea captain, architect and weaving woman as "wise."[46]

In other words, the wisdom of this world can go either way—it can be used for good, but it can be used for evil also, so that mere possession of it, while potentially an advantage, cannot be regarded as meritorious in itself.

Origen was also aware that a person's standing before God is not determined by his behavior. In a fascinating commentary on Romans 5:19, he pointed out that there are many examples in Scripture of righteous men who sin, just as there are of sinners who perform good deeds. In the former case, he acknowledges that people whom God reckons as righteous are still sinners, but they do not lose their salvation because of that.

---

43. Prosper Grech, "Justification by Faith in Origen's Commentary on Romans," *Augustinianum* 36, no. 2 (1996): 337–59, quotation on 350.
44. Origen, *Commentary on Romans* 4.9.12, in Scheck, *Romans*, 1:292.
45. Origen, *Commentary on Romans* 4.9.6, in Scheck, *Romans*, 1:288.
46. Origen, *Commentary on Romans* 4.9.6, in Scheck, *Romans*, 1:289.

Likewise, it is possible for sinners to do good things from time to time, but those good deeds can do nothing to justify them in the sight of God.[47] Origen made a distinction between a "righteous man" and a "sinner" that would probably have led him to reject Luther's famous *simul iustus et peccator* formula, but this is a matter of terminology, not of substance. Had Luther said *simul iustus et peccans* ("both righteous and sinning"), he would have been doing no more than paraphrasing Origen.

Abstracting the two men's formulations from their historical context, we might say that the difference between them is the difference between an anomaly and a paradox. In Origen's case we are (apparently) talking about a good person who sins, which in principle would be out of character for him. In Luther's case, we are talking about a bad man who has been made righteous in spite of himself. For that man to go on sinning is only to be expected—it is not out of character at all. But far from giving him a license to sin, this change makes Luther's *iustus peccator* more deeply dependent on the grace of God and the "alien righteousness" of Christ, without which he could literally achieve nothing at all.

How far apart are these two positions? In the sixteenth century, Luther's opponents could use Origen's terminology (and by extension, that of most of the fathers) to defend the Catholic view. A Christian is therefore essentially a good person who has relapses from time to time because of his inherent weaknesses and who therefore needs the medicinal grace of the sacraments in order to recover his spiritual health. In actual fact, most people fail to overcome this difficulty in this life, so when they die, they must go to purgatory, an imaginary place that the medieval church invented for the purpose of working off the remaining unpaid debts of sin.[48] Had Origen shared this medieval view, we would have expected him, or at least one of his followers, to have come up with a similar idea, but none of the fathers ever did. The complete absence of any notion of purgatory in ancient times speaks against any kind of merit theology.

The truth seems to be that both Origen and Luther believed that whatever good a justified man does is the work of the Holy Spirit in him and that left to his own devices, he would go on sinning. Whether this was because of a lingering weakness of the flesh that is practically incurable, as Origen thought, or because there has been no objective change in the believer's nature, as Luther insisted, this becomes more a matter of perspective and terminology than of substantive difference. It seems more than likely that if Origen had been obliged to think this matter through in the face of claims that a believer could somehow earn merit with God by his own efforts, he would have objected and come down on the side of Luther, especially as otherwise virtually nobody would ever be able to go to heaven. Luther defined the condition of fallen man more precisely than Origen did, but since Luther had the benefit of 1,300 years of theological reflection to draw on, that should not surprise us! In the language of the sixteenth century, it is

---

47. Origen, *Commentary on Romans* 5.6.6–8, in Scheck, *Romans*, 1:348–49.
48. On this subject, see Jacques Le Goff, *The Birth of Purgatory* (Chicago: University of Chicago Press, 1984), trans. Arthur Goldhammer from the original French edition, *La naissance du purgatoire* (Paris: Gallimard, 1981).

therefore fair to say that Origen almost certainly believed that justification was imputed to sinners as a gift of the Holy Spirit, not imparted to them by sacramental grace in the sense that Luther's adversaries understood such language.

Faith, Hope, and Love

One further point that must be considered is the relationship between faith, hope, and love, which Origen regarded as the foundation of the Christian life (1 Cor. 13:13). In his words:

> I consider faith to be the first beginnings and the very foundations of salvation; hope is certainly the progress and increase of the building; however, love is the perfection and culmination of the entire work. That is why love is said to be greater than everything else.[49]

In his analysis of Origen's thought, Scheck quotes this notion approvingly and adds the following:

> He views faith as the beginning step (*initium*) and foundation (*fundamentum*) of the process that is nourished by hope and culminates in love. In other words we attain to justification by stages and progressively. The gift of divine grace within us can increase, and it can also perish.[50]

This is a clear case of reading too much into what the early church father actually said. Undoubtedly, Origen did think of the Christian life in terms of a progression from faith to hope to love, but to claim that all three are part of a process of justification that is initiated but not completed by faith is to reflect the Roman Catholic theology of a later time and is not what Origen himself believed. In particular, the Catholic assumption that the divine grace within us can be regarded as a thing that can increase, decrease, or even disappear is entirely mistaken and reflects the objectification of "grace" that the Reformers so rightly protested against. Grace is not a thing but the indwelling presence of the Holy Spirit in the heart of the believer. The Spirit can be quenched, and there are plenty of warnings in the New Testament about the danger and consequences of apostasy (Matt. 13:18–23; 1 Thess. 5:9; Heb. 6:4–8), but that is different from justification, which is always and only by faith in Christ. The true apostate is not someone who has failed in love or abandoned hope but someone who has lost his faith. As the Reformers understood only too well, no Christian can attain the perfection of love, and some fall into despair, but as long as they cling to Christ in faith, they will be saved. Origen never seems to have gone that far in his analysis of the human condition, but that justification is by faith alone he had no doubt.

It is true that Origen went out on a limb somewhat by suggesting that love, along with other virtues besides faith, might be counted as a form of righteousness, but he

---

49. Origen, *Commentary on Romans* 4.6.3, in Scheck, *Romans*, 1:268.
50. Scheck, *Origen and the History of Justification*, 47.

was quite clear when he said that this was speculation on his part and not the actual teaching of Scripture. After quoting Paul's paean of praise to love in 1 Corinthians 13, Origen said,

> If someone should possess these things, it seems right to me to say that he has all love, a love which doubtless consists of those individual aspects enumerated by the Apostle. . . . Likewise it can be said about mercy and piety and the other virtues as well, in my opinion. And perhaps it is possible to be said in each instance, just as it was said about faith, that "faith was reckoned as righteousness" [Rom. 4:9, 22], so also of love, that love was reckoned to him as righteousness, or the same of piety or mercy.[51]

Earlier in his commentary, Origen had raised the same question but failed to answer it. Instead, he concentrated on what he saw as different degrees of faith, which were not counted as righteousness, because in Origen's opinion they were inadequate:

> [Is it] possible to say about all the other virtues the same thing that was said about faith, i.e., that it was reckoned to him as righteousness? For instance, could someone's mercy be reckoned for righteousness, or wisdom or knowledge or gentleness or humility? Or would faith be reckoned to every believer as righteousness? When I have recourse to the Scriptures, I do not find that faith is reckoned to every believer as righteousness. After all, it is written of the sons of Israel: 'They believed in God and in his servant Moses" [Ex. 14:31]; however it is not added that it was reckoned to them as righteousness, as was written about Abraham. This leads me to believe that in their case they did not possess the perfection of faith . . . which deserved to be reckoned as righteousness, as was taught to be the case for Abraham.[52]

A modern reader may be puzzled or irritated by what appears to be Origen's unwarranted speculation about these different degrees of faith, but at least it is clear that he did not teach that the other virtues could also produce righteousness in the sight of God. On the contrary, they would have been just as susceptible to failure in this respect as faith was, because if it is viewed as a human work, "faith" is no more pleasing to God than anything else is.

What Augustine Inherited

By the middle of the third century, what might be described as the "classical" pre-Augustinian view of justification by faith had been fully articulated, especially by Origen, whose authority for subsequent generations in antiquity was as decisive as Augustine's would later be for medieval and Reformation thought.[53] It had been expressed mainly in

---
51. Origen, *Commentary on Romans* 4.6.5, in Scheck, *Romans*, 1:270.
52. Origen, *Commentary on Romans* 4.1.12, in Scheck, *Romans*, 1:242.
53. Origen would be condemned for heresy at the Second Council of Constantinople in 553, but that was three centuries after his death, by which time his views had left an indelible mark, not only on the Greek-speaking world (where they were constantly recycled without acknowledgment) but also among Latin speakers, as the survival of Rufinus's translation of his commentary on Romans reminds us.

the course of debates with Jews over the significance of the law of Moses, an approach that clearly reflects that of the New Testament and especially of the apostle Paul. How serious the threat from Judaism actually was is hard to say because ancient writers had a tendency to develop stock themes, whether they were of immediate concern or not. But as long as Christianity remained a proscribed religion in the Roman Empire, which Judaism was not, we must assume that the contest between them was a real one that demanded attention from Christian writers.[54]

The main outline of the fathers' argument is abundantly clear from the evidence and corresponds with what Paul taught: Abraham was justified by his faith, not by anything that he had done to deserve it. The law of Moses was a system of ritual "works" that could not produce righteousness, and those who believed otherwise were guilty of spurning the grace of God. Christians are justified by their faith, just as Abraham was, and so there is no need for them to perform the works of the Jewish law. The practical result of justification by faith in Christ is that God has now sent his Holy Spirit into the hearts of believers, giving them new and eternal life. That life must be manifested in changed behavior, which inevitably includes "works" of love. Anyone whose life does not demonstrate this change is lying about his or her so-called faith and is not accepted as a true believer. If such a person were to claim to be justified by "faith alone," his or her claim would be rejected, because of lack of evidence for it in his or her life. Christians must take care not to find themselves in that position and must remember that their justification is a gift of divine grace, not something that they can boast of having achieved by their own efforts.

That, in a nutshell, is what Christians generally taught and believed, and it does not seem to have provoked any great controversy within the church. From at least the second century, it was clear to everyone that Christians were not Jews and that they denied that the Mosaic law had any power to save them from God's righteous judgment. Christ had set them free from that legal requirement by justifying them through his blood shed on the cross. By the power of the indwelling Holy Spirit, they were able to live a new life that was the fruit of their justification by faith.

This settled and widely shared conviction may help explain the relative dearth of references to the subject between the death of Origen (around 254) and the outbreak of the Pelagian controversy in 411.[55] It is never safe to argue from silence, and for all we know, justification by faith may have been a frequent topic of conversation and of preaching in the church during this time. But we do know that there were other controversies, particularly those concerning the person of Jesus Christ, that occupied people's attention, and it would not be surprising if they thought that justification by faith was

---

54. The classic study of this topic is Marcel Simon, *Verus Israel: A Study of the Relations between Christians and Jews in the Roman Empire, AD 135–425*, trans. H. McKeating (Oxford: Oxford University Press, 1986). The original French edition was published in 1948 by Éditions E. de Bocard, Paris.

55. Pelagius had been teaching long before that, of course, but it was only when refugees fleeing the sack of Rome in 410 reached North Africa that Augustine heard from some of them who had been Pelagius's disciples what he had been saying and concluded that it could not be accepted as the right understanding of the gospel message. The controversy followed on naturally from that.

something that Christians generally agreed on and that did not need the same kind of detailed exposition they gave to the deity of Christ. After all, if Jesus were not fully God and fully man, he could not have been our Savior, and if that were the case, what would faith in him have even meant?

But if it seems clear that justification by faith did not receive the same degree of attention that was reserved for Christology, the evidence that does exist tallies with what we already know from the earlier period. For example, Marius Victorinus (fl. fourth century), who lived a generation before Augustine and whose conversion to Christianity made a great impression on Augustine, was quite clear that our justification is by faith and not by works. Commenting on Ephesians 2:9, Victorinus said,

> The fact that you Ephesians are saved is not something that comes from yourselves. It is the gift of God. It is not from your works, but it is God's grace as God's gift, not from anything you have deserved. Our works are one thing, what we deserve another. . . . Remember that there are faithful works that ought to be displayed daily in services to the poor and other good deeds.[56]

A generation later, preaching on the same passage, John Chrysostom (ca. 349–407) told his congregation,

> God's mission was not to save people in order that they may remain barren or inert. For Scripture says that faith has saved us. Put better: since God has willed it, faith has saved us. Now in what case, tell me, does faith save without itself doing anything at all? Faith's workings themselves are a gift of God, lest anyone should boast. What then is Paul saying? Not that God has forbidden works but that he has forbidden us to be justified by works. No one, Paul says, is justified by works, precisely in order that the grace and benevolence of God may become apparent![57]

In both of these writers, the first from the Latin- and the second from the Greek-speaking world, we find exactly the same thing: justification is by faith alone and is followed by the good works that naturally result from the indwelling presence of the Holy Spirit in a Christian's life.

Sometime in the later fourth century, there appeared a commentary on Paul's epistles that was written by a now anonymous author and preserved for centuries as the work of Ambrose of Milan (ca. 339–397). This man, known to us now as "Ambrosiaster," a nickname given to him by his seventeenth-century editors, was a skilled interpreter of the New Testament, and Augustine was aware of his work. In working his way through Romans, Ambrosiaster frequently said that justification is through faith alone and not by works of the law. He also made it clear that the righteousness of the Christian is the righteousness of God, which appears to us as his mercy:

---

56. Marius Victorinus, *Commentary on Ephesians* 1.2.9, extracted in *Ancient Christian Commentary on Scripture: New Testament*, vol. 8, *Galatians, Ephesians, Philippians*, ed. Mark J. Edwards (Downers Grove, IL: InterVarsity Press, 1999), 134.
57. John Chrysostom, "Homily on Ephesians" 4.2.9, extracted in Edwards, *Galatians, Ephesians, Philippians*, 134.

What is called the righteousness of God appears to be mercy, because it has its origin in the promise, and when God's promise is fulfilled, it is called the righteousness of God. For it is righteousness when what is promised has been delivered. And when God accepts those who flee to him for refuge, this is called righteousness, because wickedness would not accept such people.[58]

Shortly afterward, Ambrosiaster had this to say about Romans 4:2–3:

Abraham does indeed have glory before God, but this is only because of the faith by which he was justified, since nobody is justified by the works of the law in a way which would give him glory before God. . . . Paul revealed that Abraham had glory before God not because he was circumcised, nor because he abstained from evil, but because he believed in God.[59]

Everything that Ambrosiaster said in his remarks on this passage from Romans tells the same story. At one point, indeed, he seemed to go even further than his predecessors—and in a way that anticipated what the Reformers would say more than a thousand years later:

If the death of the Saviour benefitted us while we were still ungodly, how much more will his life do for us who are justified when he raises us from the dead? For just as his death freed us from the devil, so his life will deliver us from the day of judgment. Paul teaches us that we should thank God, not only for the salvation and assurance which we have received, but that we should also rejoice in God through our Lord Jesus Christ, because through his Son the Mediator, God has been pleased to call us his friends.[60]

The key term here is "assurance," which would become a major subject of Reformation soteriology but which is seldom expressly mentioned in ancient texts. Yet at the same time, there are other passages in Ambrosiaster that appear to strike a somewhat different note. For instance, when contrasting the law with faith, Ambrosiaster remarked that nobody can claim any merit for keeping the law because that is an obligation imposed on him, and the person who fulfills it is merely doing his duty. But

on the other hand, to believe or not to believe is a matter of choice. No one can be obliged to believe something which is not obvious, but he is invited—he is not forced, but persuaded. Therefore he obtains merit, for like Abraham he believes what he does not see, but hopes for.[61]

And in a similar vein, Ambrosiaster remarked on the suffering that produces endurance as follows:

---

58. Ambrosiaster, *Commentaries on Romans and 1–2 Corinthians*, trans. Gerald L. Bray, ACT (Downers Grove, IL: InterVarsity Press, 2009), 28, commenting on Rom. 3:21.
59. Ambrosiaster, *Commentaries*, 31.
60. Ambrosiaster, *Commentaries*, 39–40, commenting on Rom. 5:10–11.
61. Ambrosiaster, *Commentaries*, 31, commenting on Rom. 4:4.

> To despise present sufferings and hindrances and not to give in to pressure, because of hope for the future, has great merit with God. Therefore a person should rejoice in suffering, believing that he will be all the more acceptable to God, as he sees himself made stronger in the face of tribulation.[62]

And in explaining the meaning of Ephesians 2:8–10, Ambrosiaster had this to say:

> It is true that we must render all thanks to God who has given us his grace to recall sinners to life even when they are not looking for the true way. Therefore there is no reason for us to glory in ourselves, but rather in God, who has regenerated us to a heavenly birth through the faith of Christ, so that tested by the good works which God has appointed for those who are already born again, we may deserve to receive the things promised.[63]

What are we to make of passages like these? Ambrosiaster is clearly speaking about works performed after justification, and to that extent, he is in line with the tradition he inherited. At the same time, he appears to be suggesting that there is merit in obeying God. Earlier writers said that works after justification were expected of the believer and were therefore "necessary" in order to show that one's faith was sincere. It was generally believed that with the help of the indwelling Holy Spirit, a believer would be able to please God in word and deed. In the normal course of events, that is what ought to happen, though an exception would obviously have to be made for special cases like that of the thief on the cross or of an infant who dies before being able to say or do anything. But here the suggestion is not only that God is happy with the works that believers perform but that there is some "merit" in them as well. Ambrosiaster did not specify what that might mean, but the fact that he suggested it at all opens the door to the idea that our works can earn favor with God and help promote our salvation. Perhaps Ambrosiaster would have reacted negatively if the matter had been put to him in those terms, but it is certain that the sixteenth-century Reformers would have avoided using this kind of language. They might have conceded that Ambrosiaster was speaking incautiously (at best), but in the heated atmosphere of the time, it is more likely that they would have seen statements like these as a betrayal of the gospel of grace—and that their opponents would have seized on them as proof that their view of the meritorious character of good works was right after all.

What is certain is that had he been living in the sixteenth century, Ambrosiaster could not have escaped with this sort of ambiguity; he would have had to declare his hand one way or the other. The weight of the tradition he inherited suggests that he would have avoided any suggestion that justification by works was possible and would have found less contentious ways of expressing his belief in the importance of good works in the Christian life. On the other hand, the weight of subsequent tradition would point

---

62. Ambrosiaster, *Commentaries*, 37–38, commenting on Rom. 5:3.
63. Ambrosiaster, *Commentaries on Galatians–Philemon*, trans. Gerald L. Bray, ACT (Downers Grove, IL: InterVarsity Press, 2009), 40, commenting on Eph. 2:8–10.

in the opposite direction, making him a forerunner, if not an advocate, of late medieval Catholic theology a millennium before it came into existence. That Protestants today generally incline toward the former interpretation and Roman Catholics toward the latter reminds us that here (as elsewhere) the fathers left loose ends that would later have to be tied up and incorporated into a fuller and more obviously consistent system.

This, then, is the theology that Augustine inherited. How much of it he had really absorbed before the Pelagian controversy began is hard to say. He certainly knew the writings of Tertullian, Cyprian, Marius Victorinus, and Ambrosiaster, but he may not have paid much attention to their comments on justification, particularly since they were neither contentious nor central to their concerns. Whether he had any direct knowledge of Origen is doubtful. Rufinus of Aquileia (ca. 340–410) completed his translation of the commentary on Romans in about 406, so it would have been available to Augustine in the latter part of his life and even at the time when the Pelagian controversy broke out, but there is no indication that he engaged with it, and we must assume that it was unknown to him. Nevertheless, what Origen believed was not so distinctive that Augustine would have found it odd or unacceptable. We must therefore conclude that he would have shared in the consensus of his time, on which Origen's opinions had a formative, if not a decisive, influence.

Conclusion

When we turn to the sixteenth-century Reformation, it is obviously more difficult to decide to what extent Luther and Calvin were natural successors to the fathers of the early church. Luther developed his ideas not by reading the fathers but by examining the New Testament directly, and it was from there that his preaching and teaching derived. Of course, the fathers did the same, but viewed from the perspective of Luther's time, they were almost bound to seem unsatisfactory. For them, justification was not a central topic of theology, and what they had to say about it was at least susceptible to a different interpretation—the one that Luther's opponents claimed was the true legacy of the ancient tradition and that Roman Catholic apologists continue to defend to this day. A close examination of the available evidence shows that those Catholic claims are exaggerated, though they are not entirely without foundation. On balance, the fathers were closer to the mind of the apostle Paul than most Catholic apologists have been willing to acknowledge, and their thought is therefore less alien to that of the Protestant Reformers than they have maintained. As I have tried to demonstrate, it is perfectly possible to read the ancient texts in a way that is consonant with standard Protestant teaching, and it is my contention that on the whole, that teaching is closer than any available alternative to the spirit of the fathers.

At the same time, it is clear from hindsight that the fathers left unfinished business regarding justification. The subsequent controversies, both in the time of Augustine and in the sixteenth century, were the inevitable consequence of that gap. We cannot now go back beyond them to that simpler time, when the great matters at stake in the Reformation were as yet insufficiently articulated. But there can be no doubt that the Reformers were not inventing something new in their doctrine of justification by faith alone. For the most part, they were restating historic orthodoxy in a way that would meet the questions and challenges of their own time. More than that we have no right to expect.

Recommended Resources

Sources

Ambrosiaster. *Commentaries on Galatians–Philemon*. Translated by Gerald L. Bray. Ancient Christian Texts. Downers Grove, IL: InterVarsity Press, 2009.

———. *Commentaries on Romans and 1–2 Corinthians*. Translated by Gerald L. Bray. Ancient Christian Texts. Downers Grove, IL: InterVarsity Press, 2009.

Ancient Christian Commentary on Scripture: New Testament. Vol. 6, *Romans*. Edited by Gerald L. Bray. Downers Grove, IL: InterVarsity Press, 1998.

Ancient Christian Commentary on Scripture: New Testament. Vol. 8, *Galatians, Ephesians, Philippians*. Edited by Mark J. Edwards. Downers Grove, IL: InterVarsity Press, 1999.

Ante-Nicene Fathers. Edited by Alexander Roberts and James Donaldson. 10 vols. 1885–1896. Reprint, Peabody, MA: Hendrickson, 1994.

The Apostolic Fathers. Translated by J. B. Lightfoot and J. R. Harmer. Edited and revised by Michael W. Holmes. 2nd ed. Grand Rapids, MI: Baker, 1989.

Calvin, John. *A Harmony of the Gospels Matthew, Mark, and Luke, Volume 3, and the Epistles of James and Jude*. Translated by A. W. Morrison. Edited by David W. Torrance and Thomas F. Torrance. Edinburgh: Saint Andrew's Press, 1972.

Origen. *Commentary on the Epistle to the Romans*. Translated by Thomas P. Scheck. 2 vols. Washington, DC: Catholic University of America Press, 2001–2002.

———. *Contra Celsum*. Edited by Henry Chadwick. Cambridge: Cambridge University Press, 1953.

Tertullian. *Adversus Marcionem*. Edited and translated by Ernest Evans. 2 vols. Oxford: Clarendon, 1972.

Studies

Beck, Alexander. *Römisches Recht bei Tertullian und Cyprian: Eine Studie zur frühen Kirchenrechtsgeschichte*. Halle: Niemeyer, 1930.

Daunton-Fear, Andrew. *Were They Preaching "Another Gospel"? Justification by Faith in the Second Century*. Latimer Studies 80. London: Latimer Trust, 2015.

Ensor, Peter. "Clement of Alexandria and Penal Substitutionary Atonement." *Evangelical Quarterly* 85, no. 1 (2013): 19–35.

Grech, Prosper. "Justification by Faith in Origen's Commentary on Romans." *Augustinianum* 36, no. 2 (1996): 337–59.

McGrath, Alister E. *Iustitia Dei: A History of the Christian Doctrine of Justification*. 3rd ed. Cambridge: Cambridge University Press, 2005.

Melanchthon, Philipp. *Commentary on Romans (1540)*. Translated by F. Kramer, Saint Louis, MO: Concordia, 1992.

Scheck, Thomas P. *Origen and the History of Justification: The Legacy of Origen's Commentary on Romans.* Notre Dame, IN: University of Notre Dame Press, 2008.

Simon, Marcel. *Verus Israel: A Study of the Relations between Christians and Jews in the Roman Empire, AD 135–425.* Translated by H. McKeating. Oxford: Oxford University Press, 1986.

Stendahl, Krister. *Paul among Jews and Gentiles.* Philadelphia: Fortress, 1976.

Vitton, Paolo. *I concetti giuridici nelle opere de Tertulliano.* Rome, Bretschneider, 1972.

19

The Evolution of Justification

Justification in the Medieval Traditions

NICK NEEDHAM

In this chapter, the spotlight falls on Augustine of Hippo, Anselm of Canterbury, Bernard of Clairvaux, Peter Lombard, Thomas Aquinas, Gabriel Biel, and Theophylact of Ochrid. From the time frame involved, the alert reader will instantly see that the chapter endeavors to cover one thousand years of theological reflection. He who would survey the entire medieval understanding of the doctrine of justification, including Augustine of Hippo as the wellspring of that understanding in the Latin-speaking West, in the space of a single chapter within this book, might perhaps be accused of a foolhardy enterprise.

To take the edge off that potential accusation, let me define and thereby narrow the parameters of what I am attempting to do here. First, I indeed pay considerable attention to Augustine. There is a sense in which a survey of Augustine tells us in advance what the Western medieval tradition is going to say about justification—as about virtually everything else, so commanding was the bishop of Hippo's influence. Second, I thereafter limit myself to looking at a relatively small selection of medieval theologians, mostly those who have generally occupied the "limelight" in the West's own theological self-consciousness and who cover a reasonably wide period. I thus consider the teaching of Anselm of Canterbury, Bernard of Clairvaux, Peter Lombard, Thomas Aquinas, and Gabriel Biel, as representing the Western medieval tradition of biblical exegesis, and lastly, Theophylact of Ochrid, as representing the Eastern medieval tradition of biblical exegesis. This delimitation of the purpose and contents of this chapter should—arguably, at least—give it some sense of coherence and value, despite its many omissions.

One further point: the best, fullest, and most scholarly treatment of the history of the Augustinian and medieval doctrine of justification remains the relevant chapters within Alister McGrath's magisterial *Iustitia Dei*.[1] Yet McGrath's treatment is structured in such a way that when we pass from the medieval period to the era of the Protestant Reformation in the sixteenth century, the Protestant doctrine of justification as a forensic declaration (in effect, a sharing by the believer in the Father's verdict of "righteous" passed on the Son in the resurrection) is presented as a pure theological innovation. This Protestant understanding had no roots in the Augustinian or medieval tradition, according to McGrath.[2] In McGrath's words, "The Reformation understanding of the *nature* of justification—as opposed to its mode—must . . . be regarded as a genuine theological *novum*."[3]

Since McGrath holds to a Newmanian understanding of the ongoing development of Christian doctrine through the ages,[4] the perceived novelty of the Reformation's view of justification does not trouble him. It was a *positive* development. Indeed, elsewhere McGrath explicitly appraises this novelty as constructively expressing the "creative genius" of Reformation theology: "The creative genius of Protestantism lies at least in part in its new understanding of the nature of justification which has such profound consequences for Protestant spirituality."[5]

McGrath's presentation of profound organic discontinuity between the Augustinian and medieval traditions and Protestant theology concerning the heart of the latter's soteriology (forensic justification through faith alone)[6] has influenced many. It is therefore a matter of legitimate concern for the present chapter to pay some attention to this issue. In our own survey of Augustinian and medieval understandings of justification, we find reasons to be more circumspect than McGrath in his ascriptions of pure novelty and

---

1. Alister E. McGrath, *Iustitia Dei: A History of the Christian Doctrine of Justification*, 3rd ed. (Cambridge: Cambridge University Press, 2005).
2. Nor indeed did it have roots in the Patristic tradition, in McGrath's view, but this lies outside the scope of the present chapter. See chap. 18, by Gerald Bray, in this volume.
3. McGrath, *Iustitia Dei*, 217; italics original. The "mode" of justification is divine grace (which in the Augustinian tradition is conceived of as residing ultimately in God's free, eternal election), as mediated through the church's gospel and sacraments.
4. This is the idea that the original apostolic deposit of the faith can be likened to an acorn that, over lengthy periods of time, grows and develops into a mature theological tree, as sanctified reason works to elucidate the legitimate consequences of the original deposit. An acorn does not look much like an oak tree, and mature theological developments may look rather unlike the unsophisticated apostolic acorn. Applied in a Protestant fashion to soteriology, this enables a Protestant theologian to hold that there is nothing very like the sixteenth-century doctrine of justification in previous eras of church history yet to see this doctrine as a warrantable development within the dogmatic corpus. The essence of this concept of development, expressed in a Roman Catholic direction, was pioneered by John Henry Newman in his 1845 treatise *An Essay on the Development of Christian Doctrine*.
5. Alister E. McGrath, "Forerunners of the Reformation? A Critical Examination of the Evidence for Precursors of the Reformation Doctrines of Justification," *HTR* 75, no. 2 (1982): 241.
6. Martin Luther famously affirmed that forensic justification through faith alone was the article of a standing or falling church: "If the article of justification be once lost, then is all true doctrine lost." Luther, *A Commentary on St. Paul's Epistle to the Galatians*, trans. Erasmus Middleton (Grand Rapids, MI: Zondervan, 1979), xvi. John Calvin echoed this verdict in his treatment of justification within his *Institutes of the Christian Religion*: "The theme of justification was therefore more lightly touched upon because it was more to the point to understand first how little devoid of good works is the faith, through which alone we obtain free righteousness by the mercy of God; and what is the nature of the good works of the saints, with which part of this question is concerned. Therefore we must now discuss these matters thoroughly. And we must so discuss them as to bear in mind that this is the main hinge on which religion turns, so that we devote the greater attention and care to it. For unless you first of all grasp what your relationship to God is, and the nature of his judgment concerning you, you have neither a foundation on which to establish your salvation nor one on which to build piety toward God." Calvin, *Institutes of the Christian Religion*, ed. John T. McNeill, trans. Ford Lewis Battles, LCC 20–21 (Philadelphia: Westminster, 1960), 3:11:1. Perhaps surprisingly, then, justification (not predestination) is for Calvin "the main hinge on which religion turns."

"creative genius" to Protestant soteriology. There were deeper elements of continuity with Augustinian and medieval theology than the Oxford scholar seems to allow for. I hope to highlight these as a corrective, suggesting that McGrath's otherwise masterly tome must be used with some caution on this point.[7]

Augustine of Hippo (354-430)

The fountainhead of all Western medieval theologizing about the doctrine of justification was Augustine and the Augustinian corpus of writings. Whether one thinks of Augustine as shedding light or casting a shadow, his influence over all subsequent theology in the Latin West was surely vast and indisputable. Alfred North Whitehead famously called all post-Plato Western philosophy "a series of footnotes to Plato"; much the same might be said of Augustine and post-Augustine Western theology. For example, whenever Thomas Aquinas, prince of the schoolmen, referred simply and without qualification in his writings to "the theologian," he meant Augustine. The animated verdict of Augustine's contemporary French disciple, Prosper of Aquitaine, spoken without any apparent sense of exaggeration at the close of his master's life, continued to reverberate down through the Middle Ages:

> Augustine, at the time the first and foremost among the bishops of the Lord. . . . Among many other divine gifts showered on him by the Spirit of Truth, he excelled particularly in the gifts of knowledge and wisdom flowing from his love of God, which enabled him to slay with the invincible sword of the Word not only the Pelagian heresy, still alive now in some of its offshoots, but also many other previous heresies, . . . this doctor [i.e., teacher], resplendent with the glory of so many palms and so many crowns which he gained for the exaltation of the Church and the glory of Christ, . . . Augustine, the greatest man in the Church today.[8]

Whether, therefore, we consider Christian epistemology, a Christian understanding of history, the Trinity, anthropology, soteriology, ecclesiology, or various other issues, we find Augustine living and breathing in the thoughts and attitudes of his successors in the West. It is to Augustine of Hippo we must turn, then, in order to orient ourselves in exploring the Western medieval doctrine (or doctrines) of justification.

Sovereign Grace and Eternal Election

The backdrop of Augustine's understanding of justification is his belief in the sovereignty of grace, whose fountain is eternal election. We might even say that the two are

---

7. Other historians of doctrine have effectively sounded this or a similar note of caution. See, e.g., Anthony N. S. Lane, *Justification by Faith in Catholic-Protestant Dialogue: An Evangelical Assessment* (New York: T&T Clark, 2006), 139–40; Lane, "Ten Theses on Justification and Sanctification," in *Mission and Meaning: Essays Presented to Peter Cotterell*, ed. Antony Billington, Tony Lane, and Max Turner (Carlisle, UK: Paternoster, 1995), 197. See also Bradley G. Green's chapter on Augustine in *Shapers of Christian Orthodoxy: Engaging with Early and Medieval Theologians*, ed. Bradley G. Green (Downers Grove, IL: IVP Academic, 2010); M. Eugene Osterhaven, *The Faith of the Church: A Reformed Perspective on Its Historical Development* (Grand Rapids, MI: Eerdmans, 1982); Nathan Busenitz, *Long before Luther: Tracing the Heart of the Gospel from Christ to the Reformation* (Chicago: Moody Publishers, 2017).

8. Prosper, *Letter to Rufinus*, sec. 3, 18, in Prosper of Aquitaine, *Defense of St Augustine*, trans. P. de Letter, ACW 32 (New York: Newman, 1963).

conceptual twins, in that, for the bishop of Hippo, election is God's free grace in eternity, and justification is his free grace in time. The eternal dimension of grace—God's sovereign election—finds frequent expression in the Augustinian corpus. Here is an eloquent example from *On the Predestination of the Saints*:

> God chose us in Christ before the creation of the world and predestined us to be adopted as his children. He did this, not because we were going to be holy and blameless by our own will, but rather he chose and predestined us that we might *become* holy and blameless. Moreover, he did this according to the good pleasure of *his* will, so that nobody might glory in his own will but in God's will toward himself. He also did this according to the riches of his grace, according to his good will, which he purposed in his beloved Son. In him we have obtained an inheritance, being predestined according to the purpose (his, not ours) of the one who works all things to such an extent that he works even in our wills. Moreover, he works according to the counsel of his will, so that we may be for the praise of his glory.
>
> This is the reason why we cry that no one should glory in anything human, and thus not in himself; but whoever glories, let him glory in the Lord, that he may be for the praise of the Lord's glory. For he himself works according to his purpose that we may be for the praise of his glory, and, of course, holy and blameless, for which purpose he called us, having predestined us before the creation of the world [Eph. 1:3–6]. In all this, his purpose is the special calling of the elect for whom he works all things together for good, because they are called according to his purpose [Rom. 8:28]; and "the gifts and calling of God are without repentance" [Rom. 11:29].[9]

The later theologians of the Protestant Reformation would find this eternal dimension of God's free grace such a congenial element in Augustine's thinking that they might not have taken seriously the fact that Augustine's understanding of justification did not exactly, or not always, correspond with their own. There were indeed ardent Augustinians in the sixteenth and seventeenth centuries who were not Protestants at all and who rejected the Lutheran-Reformed understanding of justification in the very context of embracing Augustine's conception of God's eternal electing grace. One has only to think of the influential Jansenist movement within the Roman Catholic Church as one example.[10]

If, then, we turn from the eternal backdrop of Augustine's soteriology to its execution in time, we confront an immediate challenge. Although Augustine's theology of justification was the wellspring of later Western medieval thinking on the topic, we are somewhat embarrassed to find that the man regarded as "the theologian" by Western medieval thinkers never actually wrote a treatise on justification, nor even

---

9. Augustine, *On the Predestination of the Saints* 37, my rendering of the Latin. All subsequent Latin passages rendered into English are my own translations unless stated otherwise.
10. For a (hopefully) accessible modern treatment of Jansenism, see Nick R. Needham, *2000 Years of Christ's Power*, vol. 4, *The Age of Religious Conflict* (Fearn, Ross-shire, Scotland: Christian Focus, 2016), chap. 6.

subjected the doctrine to any focused consideration in any of the multitudinous treatises that poured from his pen.[11] This anomaly doubtless rests on the simple fact that there was no "justification controversy" in the Patristic period. (The church would have to wait until the sixteenth century for that.) The student of historical theology is thus compelled to trawl through Augustine's writings to distill an understanding of justification as it existed in unsystematic form in the mind of Augustine himself. Mostly, but not exclusively, the relevant passages occur in the bishop of Hippo's anti-Pelagian treatises.

Moral Transformation

From what Augustine said, it seems that his fundamental understanding of the New Testament term "justify" and its cognates included both the initial event and the ongoing process of salvation in sinners. He therefore embraced within this understanding both the forgiveness of sins and the moral transformation of the sinner (regeneration and sanctification). A key passage illustrating this thinking is found in his *Unfinished Work against Julian* (i.e., Julian of Eclanum, an Italian Pelagian bishop, Augustine's chief opponent in the final decade of the Pelagian controversy):

> Justification is given not through forgiveness of sins alone. . . . God justifies ungodly people, not only by forgiving their evil deeds, but also by infusing love into them, so that they might turn away from the evil and do the good through the Holy Spirit.[12]

Often, however, Augustine concentrated his attention on the morally transformative aspect of justification, so that a less-than-careful reading of his writings could easily convey the impression that by *justification* Augustine meant solely what Protestant theology would call *regeneration* and *sanctification*. In the words of David Wright, "There is general agreement that he [Augustine] took it [justification] to mean 'to make righteous' and held to this throughout his writing career."[13] This "general agreement" has been set forth most fully and cogently by McGrath in his aforementioned *Iustitia Dei*:

> Augustine understands the term *iustificare* to mean "to make righteous," an understanding of the term which he appears to have held throughout his working life. . . . Augustine's basic definition of justification may be set out in a little detail, so that its full significance can be appreciated.
>
> > What does "justified" mean other than "made righteous," just as "he justifies the ungodly" means "he makes a righteous person out of an ungodly person"?

---

11. As David F. Wright puts it, Augustine "nowhere systematized his position, which explains why his interpreters have not always agreed about him." "Justification in Augustine," in *Justification in Perspective: Historical Developments and Contemporary Challenges*, ed. Bruce L. McCormack (Grand Rapids, MI: Baker Academic, 2006), 55.
12. Augustine, *Unfinished Work against Julian* 2.165 (PL 45:1212). "Love" here is "charity" (*caritas*).
13. Wright, "Justification in Augustine," 56.

> (*Quid est enim aliud, quam iusti facti, ad illo scilicet qui iustificat impium, ut ex impio fiat iustus?*)

There is no hint in Augustine of any notion of justification purely in terms of "reputing as righteous" or "treating as righteous," as if this state of affairs could come into being without the moral or spiritual transformation of humanity through grace. The pervasive trajectory of Augustine's thought is unambiguous: justification is a causative process, by which an ungodly person is made righteous. It is about the transformation of the *impius* to *iustus*.[14]

Certainly, Augustine did very often present justification, and the associated concept of the righteousness of God (cf. Rom. 1:17), in this way. He saw God's righteousness as self-communicative and salvific (so we should rejoice that God is righteous), but he generally presented this divine saving righteousness in transformative terms. For example, in commenting on Psalm 3 in his *On the Spirit and the Letter*, he said, "This then is the righteousness of God, the righteousness which He not only teaches through the instruction of the law, but also actually confers through the gift of the Spirit."[15]

One can find this morally transformative sense of justification and the gift of God's righteousness almost at random in Augustine's soteriology:

> Those who consider the issue in a clear-headed and honest way can perceive here an evident manifestation of the power of God's free grace and realize that they are justified from their sins by the same grace that made the human nature of Christ Jesus free from the possibility of sin.[16]

> Nor is it because they are upright in heart, but that they may become so, that he grants them his righteousness by which he justifies the ungodly.[17]

> Whatever righteousness a person has, he must not presume that he has it from himself, but from the grace of God, who justifies him. He must still go on hungering and thirsting for righteousness from him who is the living bread and with whom is the fountain of life.[18]

> Since therefore the will is either good or bad, and since of course we do not derive the bad will from God, it remains that we derive from God a good will. Otherwise, since our justification proceeds from a good will, I do not know what other gift of

---

14. McGrath, *Iustitia Dei*, 46–47. McGrath effectively marginalizes or ignores any nuance in Augustine's understanding of justification that might take it outside the scope of a morally transformative definition.
15. Augustine, *On the Spirit and the Letter* 32.56.
16. Augustine, *Enchiridion* 36. In other words, grace cleansed and made perfect the assumed human nature of Christ at the moment of the virgin conception, and the same grace "justifies" sinners, that is, cleanses the ungodly from the corruption of sin. On Augustine's doctrine of the cleansing of Christ's human nature, see also *On Forgiveness and Baptism* 2.38: "Christ either sanctified that nature in order to take it, or else he sanctified it in the very act of taking it." Although this may conceivably sound strange to modern ears, it is in fact the standard understanding of the sinlessness of Christ's humanity throughout that "orthodox" stream of Christology that takes its cue from Patristic thinking.
17. Augustine, *On the Spirit and the Letter* 11.
18. Augustine, *On the Spirit and the Letter* 65.

God we ought to rejoice in. That, I suppose, is why it is written, "The will is prepared by the Lord" (Prov. 8:35, Septuagint).[19]

The reason why Augustine was able with such ease to expound justification in this morally transformative sense was his reliance on the then-current Latin translation(s) of the Bible,[20] which rendered the key Pauline Greek term δικαιόω by the Latin *iustifico*. The form of the Latin verb with its *-fic* ending (from *facere*, "to make") was very plausibly understood by Augustine as meaning "to make righteous"—that is, moral transformation. Although Augustine knew Greek at an elementary level, he does not seem to have been sufficiently adept to have appreciated that in Pauline usage, δικαιόω has a forensic sense—the declaratory verdict of a law court rather than the moral transformation of character. The bishop of Hippo's predominantly Latin mind, language, and Bible translations, therefore, largely account for his general understanding of justification in a morally transformative sense, rooted in his interpretation of *iustifico* as "to make righteous."[21] This set the tone for later medieval Latin understandings of justification.

A Fuller Picture

True though this description of Augustine is, a careful reading of his works shows that it is not the whole truth about his doctrine of justification. Despite the main drift of his teaching clearly leaning toward a morally transformative interpretation, it was not the only thing the bishop of Hippo had to say on the subject. There are, so to speak, minor currents flowing within the main drift that point in other directions. Augustine was not quite so purely monolithic as has sometimes been made out.[22]

First of all, there is that element in Augustine's understanding of justification that foregrounds the forgiveness of sins. Sometimes, indeed, he virtually defines justification as forgiveness:

> And certainly it is in harmony with justice that we, whom the devil held as debtors, should be dismissed free by believing in him whom the devil put to death without any debt. In this way, we are said to be justified in the blood of Christ; in this way, his innocent blood was shed for the forgiveness of our sins. . . . But here is the true reason why it is by the blood of Christ that we are justified, when we are rescued from the devil's power through the forgiveness of sins.[23]

---

19. Augustine, *On the Merits and Forgiveness of Sins* 2.30. There are many other such references.
20. A number of "Old Latin Bibles" preceded Jerome's Vulgate, although the Vulgate itself perpetuated the tradition of translating δικαιόω by *iustifico*.
21. For this background, see McGrath, *Iustitia Dei*, 45–49. Some have sought to mitigate this view of the origin of medieval transformative accounts of justification by arguing that medieval interpreters were perfectly capable of deriving a transformative sense of Paul's justification language from a close study of Paul's letters themselves, without any preconceived notion of the Vulgate's *iustificare* as transformative in meaning. There may be substantial truth in this. Yet at the same time, one cannot help remembering that these interpreters were reflecting on the Latin text of Paul, which precluded them from any primary consideration of the sense of Paul's justification language in the actual Greek of the New Testament. It seems more than a naked coincidence that a forensic understanding of δικαιόω is found in the medieval Greek exegete Theophylact of Ochrid (discussed below) and in Western Renaissance (and later Protestant) scholarship, which took the original Greek as their locus of exegetical and theological reflection.
22. For an accessible modern treatment, see Busenitz, *Long before Luther*, chaps. 7–8 passim.
23. Augustine, *On the Trinity* 13.18.

> God foresaw also that by his grace a people would be called to adoption and that they, being justified by the forgiveness of their sins, would be united by the Holy Spirit to the holy angels in eternal peace.[24]

> We are all justified in Christ, receiving pardon from him not only for original sin but also for all those other sins we have ourselves added to it.[25]

If we were to collect statements of this sort from the bishop of Hippo's writings, we would arrive at a conception of justification in nontransformative terms as the divine remission of the guilt of sin (both original and personal).

In other places, Augustine approached far closer to a fully Pauline and Lutheran-Reformed understanding of justification as a reckoning or imputation of righteousness to the believer. In his treatise *On Grace and Free Will*, commenting on Romans 2:13 ("For it is not the hearers of the law who are righteous before God, but the doers of the law who will be justified"), Augustine said,

> On the other hand, Scripture uses the phrase "They will be justified" to mean "They will be counted or reckoned as righteous," just as the Gospel says about a particular man, "But he, desiring to justify himself" [Luke 10:29]. That is to say, he wanted to be considered and reckoned as a righteous man. In the same way, we must understand the words "God sanctifies his saints" to mean one thing but the words "Sanctified be your name" to mean something quite different. In the first phrase, we understand the words to mean that God makes people into holy people who were not previously holy; in the second phrase, we understand that the prayer requires human beings to consider as holy what is always holy in itself.[26]

In *On the Merits and Forgiveness of Sins*, Augustine said,

> Now if it lay within the power of any human being to assert confidently, "I justify you," then the unavoidable consequence would be that such a person could also say, "Believe in me." However, it has never lain within the power of any of God's holy people to say such a thing. This belongs exclusively to the Holy One of holy ones, who said, "You believe in God, believe also in me." Because he is the one who justifies the ungodly, therefore, with respect to anyone who believes in him as justifying the ungodly, that person's faith is imputed for righteousness.[27]

In *On the Deeds of the Pelagians*, Augustine similarly stated,

> The evident explanation for why the apostle so often declares that righteousness is imputed to us, not from our works but from our faith, while on the other hand faith itself works through love, is to keep anyone from thinking that he arrives at faith itself

---

24. Augustine, *City of God* 12.22.
25. Augustine, *On the Merits and Forgiveness of Sins* 1.16.
26. Augustine, *On Grace and Free Will* 45.
27. Augustine, *On the Merits and Forgiveness of Sins* 1.18.

through the merit of his works. Quite the opposite! Faith is the wellspring from which good works originally flow, since whatever does not proceed from faith is sin.[28]

Augustine also used an imputational notion of justification in his commentary on the Psalms:

> In order that, believing in him who justifies an ungodly soul, their faith may be counted for righteousness.[29]

> There seems to me to be an implied faith that goes before works; for the ungodly person is justified through faith without the merits of good works, even as the apostle declared, "To the one who believes in him who justifies the ungodly, his faith is counted for righteousness," so that subsequently faith may itself begin to work through love.[30]

> And when I am righteous, it will be your own righteousness that I have; for I shall be righteous by a righteousness given to me by you; and it shall be my righteousness in such a way that it will be yours, that is, given to me by you. For I believe in him who justifies an ungodly person, so that my faith is reckoned for righteousness.[31]

It is also interesting that at times Augustine could employ clothing imagery for the righteousness that justifies (we think ahead to the common Reformation trope of the "robe" of Christ's imputed righteousness). For example, he stated, "The righteousness of God is not that by which he himself is righteous but that with which he clothes a person when he justifies the ungodly."[32] Augustine was also capable of describing the believer's righteousness as residing not in the believer himself but in Christ—prefiguring, perhaps, the "alien righteousness" of Christ as the believer's justification in Reformation soteriology: "Christ was made sin, even as we are made righteous—our righteousness not being our own but God's, and not in ourselves but in Christ."[33]

Finally, Augustine was perfectly capable of consciously distinguishing between grace as forgiveness of sins and grace as moral transformation. Although they went together, they were nonetheless distinct. Augustine called this distinct-yet-allied gift "the double assistance of grace":

> "He will spare the helpless and needy man" (Ps. 72:13). In other words, God will forgive the sins of the person who is humble. Such is the person who doesn't trust in his own virtues and doesn't hope for salvation because of his own moral excellence but instead knows that he needs the grace of his Savior. However, when the psalmist then added, "and he will save the souls of the poor" (Ps. 72:13), he was trying to

---

28. Augustine, *On the Deeds of the Pelagians* 14.34.
29. Augustine, *Expositions on the Psalms*, on Ps. 51:13.
30. Augustine, *Expositions on the Psalms*, on Ps. 68:32.
31. Augustine, *Expositions on the Psalms*, on Ps. 71:2.
32. Augustine, *On the Spirit and the Letter* 15.
33. Augustine, *Enchiridion* 41.

thrust upon our awareness the double assistance of grace. For first, on the one hand, when the psalmist says, "He will spare the helpless and needy man," we have here the assistance that brings us forgiveness of our sins. On the other hand, second, when he adds, "He will save the souls of the poor," we have here the assistance that takes the shape of implanting righteousness within us.[34]

If, then, we allow these subcurrents within the mainstream of Augustine's thinking to bear their due significance, we will most probably be compelled to echo the considered verdict of David Wright:

> We should not lose sight of the genuine affinity between Augustine and the sixteenth-century Reformers on justification. It is well possible—and I have experienced this—to pass from reading extensively in Augustine's writings of his anti-Pelagian years (which encompass the whole latter half of his theological life as a churchman) to Calvin, Bucer, Cranmer, Martyr, and Knox without immediately being aware that they functioned with a different understanding of *iustificatio*.[35]

Augustine said enough outside the specific context of his use of *iustificare* for us to say that he foreshadowed (at the very least) the Reformation understanding of justification.

Anselm of Canterbury (1033-1109)

The Italian churchman Anselm is often regarded as standing at the fountainhead of the West's tradition of scholastic theology, and certainly his philosophical, theological, and devotional writings had a strong and enduring impact on those who came after him. In a sense, Western thought has never ceased to gnaw away at his famous, or infamous, "ontological proof" for the existence of God—savaged by Thomas Aquinas, revived by Descartes, destroyed by Kant, reinvigorated by Hegel (and so it goes). Our concern here, however, is with Anselm's equally provocative soteriology.

Anselm the Augustinian

Anselm was a committed theological and philosophical disciple of Augustine.[36] The theology of the medieval archbishop therefore shared the bishop of Hippo's "backdrop of grace" in God's free, merciful election of all who are to be saved. However, Anselm gave it a less overtly biblical and more philosophical turn than Augustine had ever done in his *Compatibility of God's Foreknowledge, Predestination, and Grace with Human Freedom* (in Latin, *De Concordia*). In his more renowned *Cur Deus Homo* (discussed below), Anselm taught that divine predestinating grace assigns the number of the elect

---

34. Augustine, *Sermon on Psalm 72:15*. Here we see Augustine making, in effect, a notional, or conceptual, distinction within grace between forgiveness and regeneration/sanctification while holding them together in the concrete experience of salvation. This conceptual distinction would later be emphasized by Duns Scotus. See Lane, *Justification by Faith in Catholic-Protestant Dialogue*, 139–40.
35. Wright, "Justification in Augustine," 71.
36. Anselm acquired two contemporary nicknames, "the Second Augustine" and "the Tongue of Augustine," which reveal the emphatic degree to which he was regarded in his own time as a follower of Augustine. See Philip Schaff, *History of the Christian Church* (Grand Rapids, MI: Eerdmans, 1994), 5:475.

from among the sinful mass of humankind to make up the number of angels lost from the celestial city by the fall of Lucifer.[37]

When we look at Anselm's conception of the temporal execution of this eternal electing grace, in the salvific event of justification, we find little or nothing to differentiate Anselm from the morally transformative view of the word that dominated Augustine.[38] The Italian archbishop taught that justification flows indeed from divine grace alone but that to be justified means becoming just (which he defined as possessing "uprightness of will"). In *De Concordia* he stated,

> Let us consider whether those who do not possess uprightness of will can achieve it by their own effort in some way. They can surely achieve it by their own effort only by willing it or not willing it. Yet no one who lacks uprightness of will is capable of achieving it himself by an act of will. And it is foolish to think that those lacking uprightness of will can achieve it by their own effort by *not* willing it! There is therefore no way in which a created being can have uprightness of will by himself. Nor can one created being give it to another. Created beings cannot save other created beings; nor can they give other created beings the means needed for salvation. It follows therefore that a created being possesses the uprightness of will I have termed rectitude of will only by God's grace. . . . And even though God does not give grace to all, since "he has mercy on whomever he will, and whom he will he hardens" [Rom. 9:18], he nonetheless does not give grace to anyone as a recompense for any preceding merit, since "who has first of all given to God, that it shall be recompensed to him again?" [Rom. 11:35].[39]

For Anselm, when he read in his Latin New Testament that sinners were justified, he took this to mean regenerated and sanctified. No comfort here, then, for Reformation Protestants. As with Augustine himself, we are driven to look elsewhere than Anselm's verbal understanding of *iustificare* to see whether the archbishop believed, in other terms, in a more biblically aligned notion of God's free forgiveness in Christ for those who have faith in him.

Justification in Anselm's *Cur Deus Homo*

Let us turn first to Anselm's doctrine of the atoning death of Christ. In his major treatise on the subject, the celebrated *Cur Deus Homo*, this was a doctrine that Anselm construed differently than the Reformers did, and indeed, than Augustine did, in that Anselm did not understand the cross in terms of penal-substitutionary atonement.[40] In

---

37. Anselm, *Cur Deus Homo* 1.16–18. The idea is itself Augustinian: see Augustine's *Enchiridion* 29.
38. On this point, see rightly McGrath, *Iustitia Dei*, 57–81, 98.
39. Anselm, *De Concordia* 3.3.
40. For Augustine on penal-substitutionary atonement, see, e.g., his *Reply to Faustus the Manichee*: "'Cursed is everyone who hangs on a tree' [Gal. 3:13]. Not just this or that particular person but everyone without exception. Even the Son of God? Yes, indeed. You take offense at precisely this; you are so desperate to dodge precisely this. You will not admit that Christ was cursed for us, because you will not admit that he died for us. Being spared Adam's curse would mean being spared Adam's death; but Christ underwent death as a human being and on humanity's behalf. So also, though he was the Son of God—eternally living in his own righteousness but dying for our sins—he submitted as a human being and on humanity's behalf to bear the curse that goes along with death. In bearing our punishment, he died in the flesh he took; so likewise, while eternally blessed in his own righteousness, he was cursed for our sins, in the death he underwent when

Cur Deus Homo, Anselm saw punishment and satisfaction as alternative ways of repairing the injury done by human sin to God's honor or dignity.[41] "Satisfaction" is the restoration to God of the honor lost to him by the commission of sin. Unless his honor is restored, punishment must follow. The way God pursues our salvation, according to Anselm, is the way not of vicarious punishment but of vicarious satisfaction, whereby the incarnate Son, rather than suffer our penalty, gives to the Father a gift so transcendent in value that it outweighs the infinite dishonor done by human sin. That gift is Christ's perfect life offered freely in death. In consequence of this vicarious satisfaction of God's honor, sinners are spared the punishment they deserve.

One might have thought so different a conceptual framework for the atonement would prevent Anselm from thinking of any imputation of righteousness or merit from the dying Christ to believing sinners. Yet even within the Anselmic framework, the basic problem of sinful humanity is an unpaid debt owed to God, even if this is conceptualized as a debt of honor; what Christ does is pay that debt on sinners' behalf.[42] Here, therefore, albeit without the language, is the core idea of imputation. Sinners are in debt to God; they cannot repay their debt, since nothing *they* might give would outweigh the infinite dishonor done by sin. But Christ the God-man, on sinners' behalf, pays their debt by giving to the Father an infinitely valuable gift, his own self. In other words, the merit of Christ is put to the credit of sinners. I can see no essential difference between this and the imputation to sinners of Christ's righteousness (albeit perhaps his passive righteousness specifically). Anselm has achieved within his framework of the doctrine of atonement what the Reformers would achieve in theirs: the vicarious payment of debt. Here is underlying if veiled continuity between the soteriology of the medieval archbishop and that of the Reformation.[43]

Justification in Anselm's Devotional Writings

When we turn to Anselm's various written prayers and meditations, we find that he often set forth the sinner's sole hope and trust as lying in God's free, unmerited mercy (a mercy

---

enduring our punishment.... Whoever believes in the true teaching of the gospel will understand that Moses doesn't slander Christ when he speaks of him as being 'cursed' [Deut. 21:23]—cursed, that is, not in his glory as God but when hanging on the tree as humanity's substitute, enduring our punishment. This is no insult to Christ, any more than the Manichees glorify him when they deny he had a mortal body or experienced genuine death. In the curse pronounced by the prophet, there is glorification of Christ's humility; in the pretended esteem of the heretics, there is an accusation of pretense. If, then, you deny that Christ was cursed, you must deny that he died; and then you have to take up the argument not with Moses but with the apostles. Acknowledge that Christ died, and you can also acknowledge that he, without accepting our sin, accepted its punishment." Augustine, *Reply to Faustus the Manichee* 14.6–7. There are many other references in the Augustinian corpus to penal-substitutionary atonement.

41. The alternative—either satisfaction or punishment—is set out by Anselm thus: "It is not fitting for God to permit anything disorderly in his kingdom.... Therefore either the honor that was taken away from him must be paid back, or else punishment must follow.... Every sin is necessarily followed either by satisfaction or by punishment." *Cur Deus Homo* 1:11–13, 15.

42. I am summarizing the argument of *Cur Deus Homo*. Specific references to the text are difficult to pick out since the whole argument is sustained throughout the text. A good summary of the whole argument is found in Robert S. Franks, *A History of the Doctrine of the Work of Christ in Its Ecclesiastical Development* (London: Hodder and Stoughton, 1930), 1:164ff. A readable modern translation by Janet Fairweather may be found in *Anselm of Canterbury: The Major Works*, ed. Brian Davies and G. R. Evans, Oxford World's Classics (New York: Oxford University Press, 1998).

43. Others have recognized such a veiled continuity. See especially the stimulating chapter on the doctrine of justification by faith in James Orr, *The Progress of Dogma, Being the Elliot Lectures, Delivered at Western Theological Seminary* (London: Hodder and Stoughton, 1901), lecture 8.

often conceived as concretized in the atoning work of Christ), without using the terminology of *iustificare*. This is especially vivid and graphic in Anselm's "Second Prayer":

> I beseech that you will free me from the fetters of my sins by your only Son, who is eternal with you. My ill deserts put me in jeopardy with the verdict of death; reinstate me in life, placated by the intercession of your supremely precious Son, who is seated at your right hand. I do not know of any other intercessor on my behalf that I might set before you, other than the one who is himself the propitiation for our sins, seated at your right hand, making intercession for us.[44]

It seems clear that Anselm's personal hope of salvation lay in the effective intercession of Christ on his behalf. The archbishop placed no confidence in any merits of his own; indeed, he spoke only of his demerits. This is what James Orr would later describe as the piety of justification by faith without its technical language.[45]

Once again, in the same vein, Anselm prayed,

> I have placed all my hope in you. As my advocate, I have set before you your beloved Son; as a Mediator, I have placed between you and me your glorious Offspring. Up to you, I say, in prayer I have sent him as Intercessor through whom I trust you for pardon. With my words of prayer I have sent up the Word whom I have acknowledged was sent down for my deeds. I have paid to you the death of your all-holy Child, a death I believe he underwent for my sake. I believe that Deity, sent by you, took my humanity, in which he submitted to suffer binding, beatings, spitting, mockery, indeed, the very cross and its nails. This humanity of his, in which he first clothed himself with the cries of an infant, was then wrapped in the lowly garments of a child, fraught with toils, emaciated through fasts, exhausted through vigils, fatigued with travels, then lashed with whips, marred with abuse, counted among the dead, but then endowed with the splendor of the resurrection! Thus he has taken his humanity into the joys of heaven, setting it exalted on your right hand. Behold, this atones for me; this atones you![46]

Also in the "Second Prayer," there is another passage that has been compared with the "wonderful exchange" that meant so much to the Protestant Reformers, in which the sinless Christ takes on himself our sin and its consequences, while we receive his obedience unto death and its consequences:

> O wondrous covenant of judgment! O pact of indescribable mystery! He who is unjust sins, and the Just One is punished! He who is guilty goes astray, and the

---

44. Anselm, "Second Prayer." A good older translation of the meditations and prayers, easily accessible on the internet, was done by E. B. Pusey, *Meditations and Prayers to the Holy Trinity and Our Lord Jesus Christ* (Oxford: John Henry Parker, 1856), available online at https://ia902708.us.archive.org/19/items/meditationsandp00ansegoog/meditationsandp00ansegoog.pdf, accessed June 10, 2017. For a modern selection, including Anselm's prayers to the saints (another area in which the Italian archbishop is characteristically un-Protestant), see Benedicta Ward, trans., *The Prayers and Meditations of Saint Anselm* (Harmondsworth, Middlesex, UK: Penguin, 1973).
45. See Orr, *Progress of Dogma*, 250–54.
46. Anselm, "Second Prayer."

Innocent One is chastised! The ungodly one transgresses, and the Godly One is condemned! The Good One endures what the evil one deserves! The Lord pays the penalty for the crime committed by the slave.... For I have behaved wickedly, and you undergo the penalty; I have sinned, and the vengeance falls on you; I have perpetrated crimes, and you are made subject to suffering; I have been guilty of pride, and you have been humiliated; I have been arrogantly inflated, and you are emaciated; I have plainly disobeyed, and you pay the penalty of my disobedience through your own obedience to the Father.[47]

Here Anselm employed the older Augustinian language of penal substitution, in contrast with his "either satisfaction or punishment" alternative in *Cur Deus Homo*, in which the God-man offers the first to save us from the second.

Within the Anselmic corpus there is an influential manual of practical piety titled *Exhortation to a Dying Man, Greatly Alarmed on Account of His Sins*. Modern scholarship denies its attribution to Anselm, but for our purposes this is virtually irrelevant; in terms of its reception by medieval readers—and indeed, Reformation readers—it was regarded as Anselm's (and known as the *Admonitio Sancti Anselmi*).[48] We may therefore usefully include it here. In the manual, the dying man is to be exhorted not to despair as he trembles on the verge of meeting God his Judge but rather to place his trust in Jesus Christ and his atoning death as sufficient to enable him to face God in a state of peace:

> Q. Do you acknowledge that you have lived a sinful life, so that everlasting punishment is what you have deserved?
> A. I acknowledge it.
>
> Q. Do you repent of your sinful life?
> A. I repent.
>
> Q. Had you the time, would you be willing to change your life for the better?
> A. I would.
>
> Q. Do you believe that the Lord Jesus Christ died for you?
> A. I believe it.
>
> Q. Are you grateful to him?
> A. I am.
>
> Q. Do you believe that his death alone can save you?
> A. I believe it.
>
> Come then! While you still have life, put your complete confidence in his death. Rely on nothing else. Entrust yourself to his death entirely. Cover yourself over totally with his death alone; wrap yourself up in it completely. Should the Lord your God wish to judge you, then say, "O Lord, between your judgment and myself, I place the

---

47. Anselm, "Second Prayer."
48. Its reception by the Reformers as authentically Anselmic is attested by Martin Chemnitz in his *Examination of the Council of Trent*, discussed further below.

death of our Lord Jesus Christ. In no other way can I deal with you." Should God say that you are a sinner, then say, "O Lord, between my sins and you, I interpose the death of our Lord Jesus Christ." Should he say that you have merited condemnation, then say, "O Lord, between my evil merits and you, I place the death of our Lord Jesus Christ. I present his good merits which I ought to have, although I do not have them." Should he say he is angry toward you, then say, "O Lord, between your anger and me I place the death of our Lord Jesus Christ." And when you have said all this, say once again, "O Lord, I place the death of our Lord Jesus Christ between you and me."[49]

The influential post-Luther architect of the Lutheran tradition Martin Chemnitz—"the second Martin without whom the first would scarcely have endured"[50]—cited this and other passages from Anselm in his monumental *Examination of the Council of Trent* as proof that the marrow of justifying faith was sweetly present in the pre-Reformation church:

> There would be no end if I were to quote every instance of this kind which is found in the writings of the fathers. I have noted down these few in order to show that our teaching concerning justification has the testimony of all pious men of all times, and that not in rhetorical declamations nor in idle disputations but in the serious exercises of repentance and faith, when the conscience wrestles in trials with its own unworthiness, wither before the judgment of God or in the agony of death. For in this manner alone can the doctrine of justification be correctly understood as it is taught in Scripture.[51]

Bernard of Clairvaux (1090-1153)

If there was any medieval theologian to whom the Protestant Reformers appealed with emphasis and regularity, it was Bernard of Clairvaux, effective founder of the Cistercian order and one of the medieval West's most captivating preachers and spiritual writers—"the mellifluous, or honey-flowing, doctor," whose words dripped with the compassion of Christ for sinners. Within the medieval period, it was not thought at all strange in Dante's spiritual masterpiece of poetry, *The Divine Comedy*, that when Dante finally reached heaven, the figure that guided him through those most exalted realms was none other than Bernard of Clairvaux. For somewhat different reasons, the Reformers, too, seemed to sense in Bernard a kindred, heaven-oriented spirit, specifically in their overarching belief that salvation is by the free grace of God. Martin Luther famously extolled Bernard thus: "St. Bernard was a man of so elevated a spirit

---

49. From *Exhortation to a Dying Man*, or *Admonitio Sancti Anselmi*, traditionally ascribed to Anselm and found among his *Prayers and Meditations*. It may be read in its entirety in E. B. Pusey's older translation of the *Meditations and Prayers*, cited above.
50. Fred Kramer, "Martin Chemnitz," in *Shapers of Religious Traditions in Germany, Switzerland, and Poland, 1560–1600*, ed. Jill Raitt (New Haven, CT: Yale University Press, 1981), 51.
51. Martin Chemnitz, *Examination of the Council of Trent*, trans. Fred Kramer (Saint Louis, MO: Concordia, 1971), 1:512–13.

that I almost dare to rank him above all celebrated writers, whether from ancient or modern times."[52] John Calvin likewise quoted the great Cistercian multiple times, almost always favorably. Citing Bernard's handbook for his disciple Pope Eugenius, Calvin said that "Bernard speaks truth itself."[53] This acclaim reflects Calvin's general verdict on the teaching of Bernard. The Genevan Reformer quoted Bernard at some length in the *Institutes*, for instance, on the nature of true saving faith and evangelical repentance.[54]

Continuity with Augustine

Were the Reformers as right as they believed they were in their strong appeal to Bernard, especially with respect to the material principle of the Protestant Reformation, justification by faith? Any examination of Bernard's theology must certainly acknowledge at the outset that the medieval saint so loved by the Reformers was, if nothing else, an ardent and self-conscious disciple of Augustine. The eternal context of free, electing grace, which then fulfills itself in the experience of the redeemed, was as important to the honey-flowing doctor as to the bishop of Hippo. In Bernard's *On Grace and Free Choice*, approvingly quoted by Calvin in his *Institutes*, the Cistercian said,

> Whenever we experience the realities of salvation taking place deep within our hearts and with our lives, we must be scrupulous not to credit such things to our own human will, which lacks wellness, nor to any obligation on God's part, because he does not owe us a thing; but rather we must credit it to that grace alone of which God is the brimful source. It is grace that galvanizes our free choice, by sowing within us the seed of the good thought; it is likewise grace that brings wellness to our free choice, by changing its orientation. It is grace again that strengthens it, so as to steer it to action, and it is once more grace that keeps it from falling back into its old ways.
>
> When we speak about grace "cooperating" with free choice, we must remember that in salvation's beginning, grace runs ahead of free choice; but thereafter, grace runs alongside it. In fact, its very purpose in running ahead at the start is that it may cooperate with free choice thereafter. Consequently, what was begun by grace alone is then brought to mature fullness by grace and free choice together. They play their part in each new step in the spiritual life, yet they do not do this one at a time but rather jointly—not each by turns but simultaneously. It is not as if grace did fifty percent of the work, and free choice did the other fifty percent. Not at all! Each does the entire work according to its own special way of acting. Grace does the entire work, and free choice does the entire work. Yet we must add this one caveat—although the entire work is done *in* free choice, yet the entire work is done *from* grace.[55]

---

52. Martin Luther, *Sermon on the Gospel of St. John*, 33, in *LW* 22:388.
53. Calvin, *Institutes*, 4.11.11. According to Kirk Macgregor, Calvin cites Bernard forty-seven times, and forty-three of these citations are wholly positive. Macgregor, *A Central European Synthesis of Radical and Magisterial Reform: The Sacramental Theology of Balthasar Hubmaier* (Lanham, MD: University Press of America, 2006), 18.
54. See Calvin, *Institutes*, 3.2.25, 41; 3.3.15.
55. Bernard, *On Grace and Free Choice* 47. The treatise is quoted positively in Calvin, *Institutes*, 2.3.5.

Given Bernard's grace-centered Augustinianism, it is hardly surprising that he embraced Augustine's basic concept of God's *iustitia*, or righteousness, as salvifically self-communicative. God's righteousness in the gospel is not the righteousness that condemns but the righteousness that saves, by graciously imparting itself to the unrighteous. However, as far as the actual word "justification" (i.e., the Latin *iustificatio* and its cognates) is concerned, Bernard seems—like Anselm—to have followed Augustine's mainstream understanding that interpreted the gift of justifying righteousness as involving moral transformation. As the honey-flowing doctor typically stated, here in his *Sermons on the Song of Solomon*,

> Concerning your justice, so great is the bouquet it spreads that you are named not simply "just" but all the more "justice" itself, the justice that makes human beings just. Your power to make humans just is gauged by your liberality in pardoning. Therefore the human being who hungers and thirsts for justice through grief over sin, let him have faith in the one who transforms the sinner into a just person; then, considered righteous on the basis of this faith alone, he will enjoy peace with God.[56]

Continuity with the Reformers

For Bernard, then, the language of justification denotes moral transformation. "Justified by grace" means "morally transformed by grace." However, if we move beyond the specific verbal use of *iustificare* in the great Cistercian, we find a strong element of implicit teaching on justification that flows in the more "Protestant" channels we have already documented in Augustine. We could preface our examination of this body of teaching with one of those general statements by Bernard that sound this note clearly:

> No human being will be justified in the sight of God through the works of the law. ... Aware of our imperfection, we must cry to heaven—and God will show us mercy. On the last day, we will then know that God has saved us, not on the basis of good works done by ourselves but on the basis of his own mercy.[57]

Bernard, then, may not use the word "justify" often or consistently in a "Protestant" sense, but in other forms of language, he does teach that the sinner's sole hope is the sovereign mercy of God and the atoning work of Christ. When Bernard lay apparently dying in the year 1125, we are told by his contemporary biographer, William of Saint Thierry, that Bernard seemed to see himself standing before the judgment seat of God, where Satan hurled damning accusations against him. But the honey-flowing doctor had his reply to Satan ready:

> I acknowledge myself unworthy of heaven's glory, to which by my merits I can never attain. But my Lord possesses that glory by a double title: first, he is by nature the

---

56. Bernard, *Sermons on the Song of Solomon* 22.8 [PL 183:881]. Bernard seems to regard the divine gift of faith as bearing within itself the whole potency of moral transformation. Hence the believer is considered just or righteous on the basis of that very faith in itself. See the treatment of Thomas Aquinas below for the same view.

57. Bernard, *Sermons on the Song of Solomon* 50.2.

only-begotten Son of the eternal Father, possessing glory by right of inheritance, and second, he has purchased it by his precious blood. This second title he has conferred on me, and therefore I trust with assured confidence to obtain the glory of heaven through the praiseworthy merits of his suffering and death.[58]

This outburst of deathbed piety from Bernard is not isolated; it finds much resonance in the great Cistercian's writings. First, we find him warning against any religious trust in one's own righteousness:

What can all our own righteousness amount to in God's sight? Shall God not look on it as a filthy rag, as the prophet says? Indeed, if God judges it strictly, all our own righteousness will end up as unrighteousness and imperfection. How will it be, then, when it comes to our sins, if our very righteousness cannot even answer for itself? Let us therefore join with the prophet in crying out fervently, "Do not enter into judgment with your servant, O Lord!" [Ps. 143:2]. Rather let us humbly flee to God's mercy, for nothing else can save our souls.[59]

And again:

Your suffering and death are the final refuge, the only answer for sin. When human wisdom fails, when human righteousness proves inadequate, when the merits of human holiness collapse under the weight, then your suffering and death deliver us. What person will presume to find a sufficient source of salvation in his own wisdom, his own righteousness, or his own holiness? . . . Unless your blood interposes for me, I am not saved.[60]

Elsewhere, Bernard teaches that human merit has no place in securing God's favor. Rather, human acceptance with God lies wholly in God's free mercy or forgiveness, or more concretely, in the atoning work of Christ:

Why is the church anxious about merits? God deliberately provides her with a more stable and secure basis of confidence. There is no point in asking by what merits we may expect blessings, particularly when you take into consideration what the prophet says: "Thus says the Lord God, I do not do this for your sakes, O house of Israel, but for my own holy name's sake" (Ezek. 36:22, 32). It is enough for me to know that merits are insufficient.[61]

The earth beneath the agelong curse produced thorns and thistles, but now the church sees it rejoicing with flowers, renewed by the grace of a new blessing. Aware of the verse "My heart dances for joy, and in my song I will praise him" [Ps. 28:7], she refreshes herself with the fruits of his passion, gathered from the tree of the cross,

---

58. The sentiments of Bernard according to the biography of William of Saint Thierry, *Prima Vita* 1.12.
59. Bernard, *Festival of All Saints* 1.11.
60. Bernard, *Sermons on the Song of Solomon* 22.8.
61. Bernard, *Sermons on the Song of Solomon* 68.6.

and with the flowers of his resurrection, whose sweet odor invites the numerous visits of her Bridegroom. He then exclaims, "Behold you are fair, my beloved, you are pleasant: and our bed is green" [Song 1:16]. She manifests her desire for his coming, and the basis on which she hopes to obtain it: not on account of her own merits but because of the flowers of that God-blessed field.[62]

Bernard goes so far at times as to define human righteousness as nothing other than the individual's possession of God's unmerited mercy:

> Only they are righteous who, from God's mercy, have acquired the forgiveness of their sins.[63]

> The purpose of God remains secure, his verdict of peace on those who reverence him also remains secure, a verdict that covers over their bad qualities and rewards their good qualities, so that (in a marvellous way) not their good qualities alone but even their bad qualities work together for their good. Who, then, will bring any charge against God's chosen ones? It is enough for me that all my righteousness lies in having him propitiated against whom alone I have sinned. Everything he has decided not to impute to me is therefore as though it had never existed. God's own righteousness is to be free from all sin; human righteousness is simply the pure mercy of God.[64]

This line of thought is pithily summed up thus: "They only are righteous who from his mercy have received the forgiveness of their sins."[65]

Sometimes Bernard moved much closer to what would be a classical Protestant understanding of God's gift of righteousness in Christ to the sinner, namely, that it involves an imputation of Christ's righteousness. For example, he said,

> For what could humanity, enslaved by sin, held in the devil's strong grip, do of itself to regain the righteousness it had previously lost? Therefore the one who lacked righteousness had another's righteousness imputed to him. It was humanity that owed the debt; it was humanity that paid it [i.e., in the man Christ Jesus]. For as Paul says, if one died for all, then all died, so that as one bore the sin of all, the satisfaction made by one is imputed to all.[66]

There may perhaps be a similar line of thought woven into the language of his *Sermon on the Annunciation*:

> He did not understand that righteousness or holiness is God's gift rather than the fruit of human endeavor and that the one to whom the Lord does not impute iniquity is not only righteous but also blessed.[67]

---

62. Bernard, *On Loving God* 3. The "field" here refers to the resurrection of the crucified Redeemer.
63. Bernard *Sermons on the Song of Solomon* 22.11.
64. Bernard *Sermons on the Song of Solomon* 23.15. Cited with approval by Calvin, *Institutes*, 3.11.22.
65. Bernard, *Sermons on the Song of Solomon* 22.11.
66. Bernard, *Epistle* 190.6. This is at least a clear concept of the imputation of Christ's passive obedience.
67. Bernard, *Sermon on the Annunciation* 22.9.

When we consider these and analogous utterances of Bernard, it helps us understand how and why the sixteenth-century Reformers felt so comfortable in the Cistercian's writings. Bernard's disavowal of human merit in salvation, his insistence on God's mercy and forgiveness alone as the grounds of hope, and his construal of Christ's atoning death as the channel of divine grace to human faith—all these place the honey-flowing doctor in the same conceptual space as Luther and Calvin. Other historians of doctrine have duly noted this and come to the same conclusion.[68]

One point worth noting is that Bernard scarcely appears at all in Alister McGrath's all-but-definitive *Iustitia Dei*. The omission may have had its reasons (did McGrath regard Bernard as a mystical or devotional writer, rather than strictly and properly a theologian?). But in the present writer's opinion, the ultimate effect of the glaring omission is to make the Reformation doctrine of justification seem, in McGrath's weighty tome, far more of a theological *novum* than it actually was, especially given the Reformers' strong element of reliance on Bernard for their soteriology and the thoroughly defensible character of that reliance. There is thus greater medieval-Reformation continuity in the Western theological tradition, through the mediation of Bernard, than McGrath's *Iustitia Dei* might lead an unwary reader to think.

Peter Lombard (ca. 1096-1160)

Peter Lombard was an Italian of humble origins who rose to be a celebrated theologian in the Notre Dame cathedral school (immediate precursor of Paris University) and, at length, bishop of Paris. His significance for the development of Western medieval theology lay in his writing what became the standard textbook of medieval systematic theology, the *Libri Quatuor Sententiarum*, or *Four Books of Sentences*. The term *sentences* here does not bear a grammatical sense but could be translated "opinions," "thoughts," "sentiments," or, in a legal context, "definitive pronouncements."[69] From the early thirteenth century to the Protestant Reformation, Western theologians generally shaped their own doctrinal formulations by commenting on Lombard's *Sentences*. Lombard established the whole theological climate for following discussions.[70]

Given the formative influence of the *Sentences* on subsequent medieval theology, it is important to note the pervasive Augustinianism of the work. Almost 80 percent of the text of the *Sentences* is taken up with around a thousand citations from the writings of Augustine.[71] It often seems to the reader that Lombard does little more than string together passages from Augustine. For Lombard, these were pearls more demanding of reverence than interrogation. In his view, Augustine represented the entire Patristic era; one might with no exaggeration say that Augustine was *the* father in Lombard's mind.

---

68. See, e.g., Lane, *Justification by Faith in Catholic-Protestant Dialogue*; Franz Posset, *Pater Bernhardus: Martin Luther and Bernard of Clairvaux* (Kalamazoo, MI: Cistercian, 1999); Dennis E. Tamburello, *Union with Christ: John Calvin and the Mysticism of St. Bernard* (Louisville: Westminster John Knox, 1994).
69. Leo F. Stelten, *Dictionary of Ecclesiastical Latin: With an Appendix of Latin Expressions Defined and Clarified* (Peabody, MA: Hendricksen, 2008), 324.
70. See McGrath, *Iustitia Dei*, 53.
71. McGrath, *Iustitia Dei*, 56.

Although this did not guarantee that post-Lombard theology would be Augustinian in a monolithic sense, it did more generally set the tone for future generations of theological thinking. Subsequent theology would, through Lombard's work, be carried out in dialogue with Augustine as the perceived embodiment of Patristic tradition.[72]

Lombard followed Augustine in locating his soteriology within the framework of God's gracious predestination. God elects his people without any preceding merit or deserving on their part:

> Augustine, in the book *To Sixtus*. But if "we seek a deserving of obduracy and mercy, we find the deserving of obduracy; but we do not find a deserving of mercy, because there is no" deserving of mercy "lest grace be made empty, if it is not given freely, but is rendered for merits." Augustine, *Against Julian*: "He has mercy according to freely given grace, but he hardens according to the judgment which is rendered for merits." And so it is given to be understood that, as God's reprobation is to not will mercy, so for God to make obdurate is to not have mercy; not that anything is inflicted by him by which man is made worse, but only that that is not granted by which he may become better.[73]

Lombard likewise accepted Augustine's rejection of election according to foreseen faith. Rather, faith is itself the fruit of a merciful election:

> And so even the merit of faith comes from God's mercy. Therefore it is not because of faith or any merits that God has elected some from eternity or has conferred his grace of justification in time, but he has elected by his freely given goodness that they should be good. Hence Augustine, in the book *On the Predestination of the Saints*: "It was not because he foreknew that we would be such that he elected us, but in order that we should be such by the very election of his grace, by which *he granted us favour in his beloved Son*."[74]

We know, then, that as a faithful Augustinian, Lombard believed in justification by free grace, grounded in a gratuitous divine election from eternity.

Lombard's discussion of the meaning of justification itself is situated in a thoroughly Augustinian setting of the liberation of humanity's enslaved will and the accompanying polemical context of the refutation of Pelagianism. In other words, Lombard understood justification to be the divine work whereby a sin-bound will is transformed into a good, just, and godly will. He seemed to take it for granted that this is what the key term *justification* meant and cited Augustine to this effect without question or comment.[75] A typical quotation from Augustine reads,

---

72. McGrath, *Iustitia Dei*, 53.
73. Peter Lombard, *Sentences*, book 1, distinction 41, 1.1, in Peter Lombard, *The Sentences: Book 1, The Mystery of the Trinity*, trans. Giulio Silano, MST 42 (Toronto: Pontifical Institute of Mediaeval Studies, 2010), 224. The format of the quotation is Silano's.
74. Lombard, *Sentences*, book 1, distinction 41, 2.2, in Silano, *Sentences*, 226.
75. See Lombard, *Sentences*, book 2, distinctions 26–28. English translation in Peter Lombard, *The Sentences: Book 2, On Creation*, trans. Giulio Silano, MST 43 (Toronto: Pontifical Institute of Mediaeval Studies, 2012), 123–42.

> No merits precede the reception of that grace which heals the will of man so that, in its healed state, it may fulfil the law. For that is the grace by which the impious is justified, that is, the one who used to be impious is made pious.[76]

Here in pithy brevity is Augustine's prevalent understanding of justification as regeneration and its consequences. We find Lombard's Augustinian conception of justification set out at much greater length in book 3 of the *Sentences*, where the Italian schoolman deals with how Christ's death redeems us from the devil, sin, and punishment:

> QUESTION. But how are we released from our sins by his death? SOLUTION. Because by his death, as the Apostle says, God's charity toward us is commended, that is, God's charity toward us is revealed as most excellent and commendable, since he handed over his Son to death for the sake of us sinners. Since token of such great love toward us has been shown, we are moved to, and kindled with, love of God, who has done so much for us; in this way, we are justified, that is, we are released from our sins, and so we are made just. Indeed, Christ's death justifies us, as by it charity is kindled in our hearts.[77]

Lombard continued by noting that we are also justified by Christ's death in that it cleanses us from our sins, and he elucidated the nature of this cleansing by comparing it to the Israelites who were healed of the serpent's bite through gazing on the bronze serpent. The healing metaphor seemed to Lombard to indicate an inward and subjective cleansing of sin's depravity.[78] Lombard then spoke of justification as liberation from slavery to the devil. This, too, relates to the regeneration and sanctification of the elect, since Lombard described it in these terms:

> Because *a stronger one*, that is, Christ, coming *into the house of a strong one*, that is, into our hearts, where the devil had an abode, *bound the strong one*, that is, restrained him from the seducing of the faithful, so that seduction should not follow the temptation which is still allowed him.[79]

Lombard did relate redemption also to liberation from punishment. Christ's death sets believers free from the debt of punishment they owe to God's justice. Here Lombard espoused a penal-substitutionary model of the cross.[80] However, he did not describe this as "justification." The theological consequence is that he did have a clear notion of a status of "debts remitted" for the baptized convert,[81] but he located this reality outside his language of justification.

---

76. Lombard, *Sentences*, book 2, distinction 26, 7.1, in Silano, *Sentences*, 129.
77. Lombard, *Sentences*, book 3, distinction 19, 1.2, in Peter Lombard, *The Sentences: Book 3, On the Incarnation of the Word*, trans. Giulio Silano, MST 45 (Toronto: Pontifical Institute of Mediaeval Studies, 2010).
78. Lombard, *Sentences*, 1.3.
79. Lombard, *Sentences*, 1.3; italics original.
80. See Lombard, *Sentences*, 2.3–4. Alongside penal substitution, he also placed the old Patristic mousetrap model, where Christ's humanity is the bait for the devil, who is then crushed in the mousetrap, thus releasing sinners from his power. See Lombard, *Sentences*, 1.5.
81. Here is Lombard's own description: "All temporal punishment due for sin is entirely forgiven to the convert in baptism." Lombard, *Sentences*, 2.4.

Thomas Aquinas (ca. 1225–1274)

Thomas Aquinas hardly needs an introduction. By universal consent, his was the theological mastermind of the medieval era, at least in intellectual depth, creativity, and abiding power to stimulate, if not perhaps (in a Protestant assessment) in fidelity to Scripture.[82] In the aftermath of the Reformation, however, Aquinas's reputation suffered greatly among Protestants.[83] Even today his actual teaching can be misrepresented as merely an unbiblical antithesis to the purity of the Reformation gospel. There are noted Protestant scholars, however, who have sought to "demythologize" this ultrapolemical reading of Aquinas, resulting in a fairer portrait, wherein a classical Protestant can find many areas of sympathy and common concern across a broad range of Christian doctrines.[84]

Moral Transformation

Aquinas's understanding of justification in many respects follows the path we have already explored in the thinking of Augustine, Anselm, Bernard, and Lombard. Despite the claims of a few, there is no convincing reason to think that Aquinas broke with the basic Augustinian-transformative interpretation of *iustificare* and its cognates. The overwhelming majority report of Thomist scholarship is that when Aquinas spoke of "justification," he meant the moral and spiritual transformation of the sinner into a just or righteous person.[85] In the *Summa Theologiae*, Aquinas stated,

> If we regard justification in the strict sense, we must be aware that it can be considered either as lying in the habit[86] or as lying in the act. Consequently, we may understand justification in two ways. First, we may understand it in the sense of a human's being made just, by obtaining the habit of justice. Second, we may understand it in the sense of a human's performance of works of justice, and in this latter sense, justification is nothing other than the performance of justice. Now the term "justice," in the same way as the other virtues, may signify either the acquired virtue or the infused virtue. . . . The cause of the acquired virtue is works, but the cause of the infused virtue is God himself through his grace. This latter is true justice, which we are now considering, and it is in this respect that a man is said

---

82. As Protestants we might be tempted to bestow this last "award" on John Wycliffe (ca. 1330–1384), the "evangelical doctor."
83. Martin Luther in particular had a low estimate of Thomas Aquinas, identifying him with the "Aristotelian captivity of the Church," which Luther (like Erasmus) diagnosed as a chief problem of the day. Luther said, "Thus, like an infernal dog, the pope dares to subject God's Word to human creatures [papal decrees]. 'Tis just the same with Thomas Aquinas, who, in his books, argues, *pro et contra*, when he cites a passage in Scripture, he goes on: Aristotle maintains the contrary; so that the Holy Scripture must give place to Aristotle, a heathen. The world heeds not this abominable darkness, but condemns the truth, and falls into horrible errors." Luther, *The Table Talk of Martin Luther*, trans. William Hazlitt (London, 1848), utterance 476.
84. For a compelling introduction to this whole topic, see in particular Arvin Vos, *Aquinas, Calvin, and Contemporary Protestant Thought: A Critique of Protestant Views on the Thought of Thomas Aquinas* (Grand Rapids, MI: Eerdmans, 1985).
85. A good, relatively brief, scholarly summary and account of the majority view (the correct view, in the present writer's opinion) may be found in Bradley R. Cochran, "Justification in Aquinas," *Theophilogue* (blog), accessed May 10, 2017, https://theophilogue.files.wordpress.com/2012/01/justification-in-aquinas_1xxx_.pdf.
86. In Thomist vocabulary, the "habit" is a permanent inward disposition of the soul.

to be just before God, according to Romans 4:2: "For if Abraham was justified by works, he has something to boast about, but not before God."[87]

For Aquinas, the justification with which Abraham was justified before God was his obtaining the infused virtue of justice (or the condition of being just or righteous), where the source of the infusion is God himself through his grace. Justification is morally transformative. If this were our sole focus, we would find no basis for thinking that a Protestant could find any common ground with the angelic doctor.[88] Yet this would be as much a premature verdict as it would be with Augustine, Anselm, Bernard, and Lombard. Outside Aquinas's specific understanding of *iustificare*, there are notable elements in the architecture of his doctrine of justification that, so to speak, provide channels of continuity with a Pauline past and a Reformation future.

Predestination and Grace

First, we should never forget the basic Augustinianism of Aquinas. The angelic doctor was a doctor of grace. The salvation of all who would be saved, Aquinas held, lies ultimately in the free, electing grace of God. This position he set forth at length in the eight articles of question 23 of part 1 of the *Summa Theologiae*, titled *Of Predestination*. The following extract captures the drift of Aquinas's thinking on the predestination of grace:

> As we said previously, God's predestination involves his will. So we must seek the reason for predestination in the same way that we seek the reason for God's will. Now, as we have already shown, we cannot find any cause for God's will in his act of willing, but we can find a cause in the things that he wills. For God wills one thing on account of another thing. Therefore nobody has been mad enough to say that merits actually cause God to perform the act of predestination. But the question is whether his predestination has any cause in terms of one of its effects depending on another; or, in other words, whether God foreordained to give the final result of predestination to anyone on account of any merits.
>
> Some have thought that God foreordained the results of predestination for some people because of good things they had done in a previous life. This was the view of Origen, who held that human souls were created from all eternity and that according to their works God awarded them different conditions in the world when these souls were united to bodies. But the apostle disproves this view when he says, "Though they were not yet born and had done nothing either good or bad . . . not because of works but because of his call, she was told, 'The older will serve the younger'" (Rom. 9:11–12).
>
> Others said that the merits of good works we have already done in this present life are the reason and cause behind the results of predestination. The Pelagians taught that we ourselves take the first step in doing good, and God then brings it to

---
87. Aquinas, *Summa Theologiae* 2a.100.12.
88. The theological "nickname" of Aquinas.

completion. In this view, God gives the results of predestination to one person, and not to another, because the one took the first step by preparing himself, but the other did not. Against this, however, we must set what the apostle says: "Not that we are sufficient in ourselves to claim anything as coming from us" (2 Cor. 3:5).

It is impossible that the total result of predestination taken as a whole should have any cause in ourselves. For whatever is in a human being, disposing him toward salvation, is all included *within* the results of predestination. Even a person's preparing himself to receive grace is the effect of predestination; such preparation is impossible apart from divine assistance, as the prophet Jeremiah says, "Restore us to yourself, O LORD, that we may be restored!" (Lam. 5:21). In this way, as far as its results are concerned, the reason for predestination lies in the goodness of God. All the results of predestination are directed toward God's goodness as their end, and predestination proceeds from God's goodness as its first cause and principle.[89]

Whatever justification is for Aquinas, therefore, it flows from sovereign grace. Further, the angelic doctor focused his understanding of justification, transformative as it is, on the initial event rather than the ongoing process. In other words, when grace justifies a sinner, the reality in view is that transformative act of God in which he bestows the initial gift of faith on the unbeliever. This very act was intrinsically transformative for Aquinas, because he specifically regarded faith as a fundamental reorientation of the soul toward God as its true end.

The Gift and Role of Faith

To tease this out, we should first note that faith is indeed God's free gift to the soul in Aquinas's thinking. This follows naturally and inevitably from his predestinarian theology of grace, but it is helpful to have it spelled out:

Concerning human assent to the doctrines of the faith, we may note a double cause. There is a cause of outward stimulus, such as seeing a miracle or being given persuasive arguments by someone to accept the faith. But neither of these amounts to a sufficient cause, because the same people can see a miracle or hear the same sermon, and yet some of them believe, and others do not. Therefore we must posit another cause, an interior one, which moves a person inwardly to assent to the doctrines of faith.

The Pelagians taught that this inner cause was nothing other than human free will. Thus they said that the origin of faith lies with ourselves, since it is within our power to be willing to assent to the doctrines of faith, but that the perfecting of such faith lies with God, who gives us the truths we must believe. This, however, is untrue. A human being, by assenting to the truths of faith, is raised above his own natural powers; this must therefore be added to a person from some supernatural principle that moves him inwardly. This supernatural principle is God. Therefore faith, when

---
89. Aquinas, *Summa Theologiae* 1a.23.5.

we consider the assent that is the leading act of faith, comes from God, who moves human beings inwardly by grace.[90]

This grace-given gift of faith, bestowed through regeneration in time on those elected in eternity, is the sufficient principle of a sinner's justification, according to Aquinas. We must recollect at this point that Aquinas did not propound a forensic definition of justification—I am not endeavoring to portray him in that sense as an incipient Protestant or crypto-Lutheran. Yet within the framework of his Augustinian-transformative understanding of justification, it remains true that Aquinas presented faith as sufficient. In general, he affirmed that the way of salvation is single and indivisible across the whole of salvation history, consisting in faith in Christ—a faith sufficient to justify:

> Although the law of the old covenant was not sufficient for human salvation, another means of help from God other than the law was available to humanity, viz. faith in the Mediator, by which the fathers of the old covenant were justified, even as we were.[91]

> Scripture describes God's justice as existing in us through faith in Jesus Christ. This is not to imply that by faith we merit justification, as though faith comes from ourselves, and through this faith we merit God's gift of justice, as the Pelagians teach. Rather, God's justice exists in us through faith, because in that very justification by which God makes us just, the mind's first movement toward God is through faith: "Whoever would draw near to God must believe" (Heb. 11:6). Therefore faith, as the first element of justice, is given to us by God: "For by grace you have been saved through faith. And this is not your own doing; it is the gift of God" (Eph. 2:8).[92]

Such faith is sufficient to justify the sinner, according to Aquinas, because it redirects the whole soul away from false ends (created things) to God alone as the soul's true end. This revolutionary reorientation is accomplished through faith, not as bare intellectual belief (another Protestant caricature of Aquinas) but specifically as *willed* belief, voluntary belief in the truth of revelation, where the underlying character of belief is delight in the truth. Aquinas thus fused the intellectual and affective powers of the human soul in the act and state of faith. So conceived, faith is "the first element of justice," that is, the seed from whose innate potency all further justice (transformative righteousness) will grow.[93]

---

90. Thomas Aquinas, *Treatise on the Theological Virtues*, "On Whether Faith Is Infused into Man," 1.6.1.
91. Aquinas, *Summa Theologiae* 2a.98.2.
92. Thomas Aquinas, *Lectures on the Epistle to the Romans*, par. 302.
93. See Aquinas, *Lectures on the Epistle to the Romans*, par. 303–306 in Aquinas's commentary on Romans cited above. Where the affective aspect of faith is missing—where "faith" is merely intellectual belief in the truth without delight in the truth—there is found what Aquinas called "unformed faith," which is not justifying faith. Although the Thomist distinction between formed and unformed faith has traditionally been critiqued by Protestants, it is perhaps difficult to imagine any Protestant theologian classing as saving faith a bare intellectual belief in God's revealed truth devoid of any delight in that truth. Such loveless belief seems demonic in character (James 2:19). The affective element of faith, so important to the Reformers, is present in Aquinas precisely as "formed faith," belief in the truth allied to delight in the truth believed.

Faith and Merits

Protestants have often critiqued Aquinas's view that the Christian's merits are what acquire eternal life for him or her at the eschaton. It is true that Aquinas taught this idea. He argued that because the Holy Spirit is the source of the believer's virtues, these virtues possess the character of "condign merit"—genuinely and inherently worthy of divine reward. Aquinas thus distinguished between justification as he understood the term (the initial transformation of the unjust soul into a just soul by effectual grace) and entitlement to eternal blessedness (based on the acquired merits of the "justified" soul).[94] Protestant soteriology would relocate this entitlement to blessedness within the initial justification of the believer, alongside redefining that justification as forensic in nature.

While Aquinas clearly taught what Protestants have critiqued concerning the place of merit, what is often overlooked is his equally emphatic view that these merits are the necessary fruits of faith. As we have seen, Aquinas's view of faith is that its very bestowal fundamentally reorients the soul to God. The soul is thereby made inwardly just in principle. An inwardly just soul will then behave justly—that is, bear fruits of faith, which take the overall form of love. Aquinas was not prepared to dignify an unfruitful faith with the name or character of justifying faith. Such would have negated his whole conception of justification as transformative. Thus the "merits" of faith for Aquinas are the ensuing outward manifestations of the transformative power of justifying faith in its works.[95]

Instantaneous, Divine Act

We should further focus attention on the fact that the justification of the sinner by faith, in Aquinas's theology, is *primarily* a divine act at the very origin of a person's salvation rather than an ongoing process thereafter. The angelic doctor was quite straightforward about this in the *Summa Theologiae*:

> The cause of the ungodly's justification is the Holy Spirit's justifying grace. Now the Holy Spirit comes to human minds suddenly, as it says in Acts 2:2: "And suddenly there came from heaven a sound like a mighty rushing wind," concerning which the gloss says that "the grace of the Holy Spirit does not admit of any delayed efforts." Thus the justification of the ungodly is not consecutive, but instantaneous. . . . Because God's power is infinite, it can suddenly impose the proper form on any matter—and much more so in the case of human free will, whose movement is by nature instantaneous. It follows that God's justification of the ungodly occurs in an instant.[96]

---

94. For Aquinas's teaching on merit and its role in securing eternal blessedness for the justified soul, see his lengthy treatment in *Summa Theologiae* 2a.114.
95. In his *Lectures on the Epistle to the Romans*, Aquinas says that the justifying power of faith means that those good works a sinner could not previously do are now done, as it were, by instinct. These instinctual works of faith are the "merits" that at the eschaton God graciously rewards with eternal beatitude.
96. Aquinas, *Summa Theologiae* 1a2ae.113.7.

In light of the preceding discussion, it should be clear what Aquinas is saying. Justification means moral transformation; the interior quality in the soul by which it is transformed from an unjust to a just state is faith; faith is the gracious gift of God; therefore, the moment God bestows justifying faith on a human soul, it is instantaneously justified.

It must be conceded that critics may here be misled by thinking that if justification is moral transformation, and if such transformation is not complete in the sense of sinless perfection until the end of earthly life, then justification must necessarily for Aquinas be primarily an ongoing process. This, however, is to deny Aquinas's explicit teaching and to misapprehend entirely his view of justifying faith. As we have seen, Aquinas thinks that faith bears the interior potency by and from which all further "sanctification" (to employ the Protestant word and concept) comes about. Thus, the divine giving of faith is an act that inherently bestows justice on the soul, justice in potent seed, thereby making the soul essentially or substantially just—rightly oriented toward God as its supreme end. This justification is instantaneous, as Aquinas said consistently with his expressed soteriology. The soul, once alienated from God in its thoughts and affections, has now through faith been converted to him. Manifestly, then, for Aquinas, the gift of justification, bound up in the gift of faith, is an instantaneous event at the commencement of the Christian life: primarily an act rather than a process.

A sensitive Protestant student of Aquinas must take all the preceding factors of the angelic doctor's teaching into account:

- Justification flows from God's sovereign grace in eternity.
- Justification is only by faith in Christ, not by works or by human merit.
- Such justification by faith is the only way of salvation set forth in Scripture across the whole of salvation history.
- Justifying faith is the gracious gift of God to his elect.
- Justification is an instantaneous act at the commencement of the Christian life.

Once these factors have been taken into account, then it may be suggested that considerable common ground exists between the architecture of Aquinas's doctrine of justification and what I have called the Pauline past and the Protestant future, despite Aquinas's adherence to a transformative understanding of *iustificare*.[97]

---

[97]. It may be worth bearing in mind that Aquinas clearly endorsed a penal-substitutionary model of Christ's atoning death, most explicitly in his *Compendium of Theology*: "The apostle uses an even more astonishing expression in Galatians 3:13, saying that Christ 'was made a curse for us.' This is also why Christ is said to have assumed one of our obligations (that of punishment) in order to relieve us of a double burden, namely, sin and punishment.... To save us, consequently, Christ was not content merely to make our capacity to suffer his portion, but he willed actually to suffer, that he might satisfy for our sins. He endured for us those sufferings which we deserved to suffer in consequence of the sin of our first parent. Of these the chief is death, to which all other human sufferings are ordered as to their final term. 'For the wages of sin is death,' as the apostle says in Romans 6:23. Accordingly Christ willed to submit to death for our sins so that, in taking on himself, without any fault of his own, the punishment charged against us, he might free us from the death to which we had been sentenced, in the way that anyone would be freed from a debt of penalty if another person undertook to pay the penalty for him.... Christ wished to suffer not only death, but also the other ills that flow from the sin of the first parent to his offspring, so that—bearing in its entirety the penalty of sin—he might perfectly free us from sin by offering satisfaction." Thomas Aquinas, *Light of Faith: The Compendium of Theology*, trans. Cyril Vollert (New York: Book-of-the-Month Club by arrangement with the Sophia Institute, 1998), sec. 226–27, 231. This involves at least implicitly an imputation of Christ's satisfaction or passive obedience to the believer.

Gabriel Biel (ca. 1420-1495)

Gabriel Biel is generally regarded as the last great scholastic theologian prior to the Reformation. He was cathedral preacher in Mainz, theology tutor at the University of Tübingen, and a notable influence on the young Martin Luther before Luther came to reject Biel's thinking in favor of the neo-Augustinianism of his father-confessor within the Augustinian order, Johannes von Staupitz (ca. 1460–1524). Biel summed up the *via moderna* ("modern way") in Western medieval theology, which—in contrast to the *via antiqua* ("ancient way")—integrated into its understanding of divine grace a revolutionary new conception of the role of human free will in salvation.[98] Contemporary critics of the *via moderna*, notably Thomas Bradwardine of Canterbury (ca. 1290–1349), Gregory of Rimini (ca. 1300–1358), and John Wycliffe (ca. 1330–1384), called it pejoratively "the new Pelagianism," since they believed it essentially recapitulated that particular heresy condemned at the ecumenical Council of Ephesus in 431.

Biel himself countered this criticism within his own theology of grace by making extensive use of the concept of God's covenant (Lat. *pactum*).[99] He argued that God had graciously decreed a covenant with humankind, in which he promised to bestow supernatural grace on any human soul that "did its best" (*facere quod in se*, "doing what lies within one") to love God. Since God was under no obligation to make this covenant, its promulgation was an act of sheer grace. When, therefore, the soul complied with the covenant and did its best to love God by its own natural powers, this endeavor itself took place within the overarching framework of God's free and gracious covenant. The endeavor was a human response to God's prior grace in voluntarily choosing to commit himself to bestow grace on all who made this endeavor. This theological scheme sometimes enabled Biel to sound remarkably Augustinian. As Brian Gerrish notes,

> In a charming sermon preached in Mainz Cathedral (about 1460), for example, he confesses the marvel of grace and draws the inference that the heart of Christian piety is thankfulness. Grace is like a precious ring, given by a king to his subjects—a golden ring, studded with diamonds. "How could one ever praise highly enough the clemency and the preciousness of the gifts of such a king? Behold, such is our King and Savior! The gift is grace, which is bestowed abundantly on us."[100]

Some modern scholars judge that Biel's notion of God's prior covenant acquits him of Pelagianism, at least as understood in his own day.[101]

Biel certainly entertained the highest notions of what unregenerate human beings could accomplish by their natural powers. We can, he thought, love God supremely and

---

98. Thomas Aquinas is the classical representative of the *via antiqua* in scholastic theology.
99. See McGrath, *Iustitia Dei*, 87ff.
100. Brian Gerrish, "Sovereign Grace: Is Reformed Theology Obsolete?," *Int* 57, no. 1 (2003): 52. The quotation of Biel is taken from his sermon on Luke 2:21, in Heiko A. Oberman, *Forerunners of the Reformation: The Shape of Late Medieval Thought, Illustrated by Key Documents*, translations by Paul L. Nyhus (New York: Holt, Rinehart & Winston, 1966), 173.
101. Notably, McGrath, *Iustitia Dei*, 99ff. It seems that no one in Biel's own lifetime ever accused him of Pelagianism. The *via moderna* tradition out of which he grew, however, with its roots in the teaching of William of Ockham (ca. 1285–ca. 1349), had certainly been labeled Pelagian by its critics.

for his own sake by unaided free will. Should the modern student inquire in what sense salvation is even necessary if this is the case, Biel's answer was to employ the nominalist[102] distinction between obeying God's will *quoad substantiam actus* ("according to the substance of the act") and *quoad intentionem precipientis* ("according to the intention of the Lawgiver").[103] Humanity can love God by natural free will *quoad substantiam actus* but not *quoad intentionem precipientis*. This is because, according to the intention of the Lawgiver (God), we are to love him from within the fullness of the infused supernatural grace and life of Christ the God-man, the Mediator and head of the human race.

This, however, is wholly beyond the grasp of our natural capacity, according to Biel. We can love God, of ourselves, only from within our purely natural powers. Such a love may be according to the substance of the act, but Biel maintained that it falls radically short of the intention of the divine Lawgiver. For humanity to love God according to his intention, he must therefore step in and infuse into the soul the supernatural grace of which he alone is the wellspring. This instepping of God and infusion of supernatural grace is the "first grace," in Biel's terminology,[104] freely and mercifully promised by God to those who love him from their own natural powers. Biel believed he had preserved the gratuitous character of divine grace by situating its bestowal within this setting of a free and unconstrained commitment by God to give the first grace to those who loved him supremely by natural free will.

However, it should be recognized that for Biel, the divine covenant having been freely and graciously made, God is then obligated by his justice and faithfulness to observe its terms. Whenever any sinner does his or her best according to natural capacity and succeeds in loving God supremely, God is bound by his covenant to infuse grace into that sinner. Biel thus constructed a synthesis of mercy and justice, grace and works, that has struck more than one student as highly paradoxical.[105] It becomes even more so, from a later Reformation standpoint, when one considers that for Biel, the infusion of grace grants a meritorious character to a believer's works: he or she is now able, by grace, truly to merit final beatitude.

Within the structure of Biel's theology, justification remained largely tied to the characteristic medieval Latin understanding of the term as denoting regeneration and sanctification,[106] although Biel did also highlight the divine removal of guilt (*culpa*)

---

102. Nominalism signifies the late medieval school of philosophy and theology of which William of Ockham was the fountain. Nominalism was therefore closely associated with the *via moderna*. It lies beyond the scope of this chapter, however, to investigate the complexities of nominalism and its conflict with realism in the philosophical and theological arenas.

103. McGrath, *Iustitia Dei*, 101ff.; Heiko Oberman, *The Harvest of Medieval Theology: Gabriel Biel and Late Medieval Nominalism* (Cambridge, MA: Harvard University Press, 1963), 156ff.

104. Oberman, *Harvest of Medieval Theology*, 171.

105. Oberman, *Harvest of Medieval Theology*, 176ff. Oberman explains, "Biel has a remarkable doctrine of justification: seen from different vantage points, justification is at once *sola gratia* [by grace alone] and *solis operibus* [by works alone]! *By grace alone*—because if God had not decided to adorn man's works with created and uncreated grace, man would never be saved. *By works alone*—because not only does man have to produce the framework or substance for this adornment, but God ... is committed, even obliged [by the covenant] to add to this framework infused grace and final acceptation. Once man has done his very best, the other two parts follow automatically." *Harvest of Medieval Theology*, 176.

106. It may well be significant that in his commentary on Peter Lombard's *Sentences*, Biel located his discussion of justification in the context of the regenerating and sanctifying work of the Spirit. See G. R. Evans, "Robert Kilwardby, Gabriel Biel, and Luther's Saving Faith," chap. 21 in *The Medieval Theologians: An Introduction to Theology in the Medieval Period*, ed. G. R. Evans (Oxford: Blackwell, 2001), 361–62.

and penalty (*poena*), which are integral to the first grace.[107] It will be noted, however, that unlike the previous Western medieval thinkers considered here, Biel had abandoned the Augustinian backdrop of sovereign grace in the salvation of sinners. However he may have conceptualized predestination, Biel held to an exalted estimate of the natural powers of human free will that precluded him from believing in God's free, electing mercy as the sole source of a sinner's salvation. When the biblical language of justification is systematically misapprehended as a transformative "making righteous," it is the acceptance of what I have called an Augustinian backdrop of grace in God's eternal election that so often proves to be the saving grace (no pun intended) of Western medieval theology. The absence of this backdrop in Biel, its place taken by a purely general pact, or covenant, of God to infuse grace into those who by free will love him supremely, renders the whole fabric of Biel's theology unintentionally Pelagian.[108] It seems difficult not to go away from Biel without the impression that what God's grace does is enable sinners to save themselves.[109]

Biel gave a helpful summary of his thinking in his commentary on Peter Lombard's *Sentences*:

> Thus Augustine comments on 2 Tim. 2, "God cannot deny himself." Because he is just, he cannot deny his justice. Therefore, because he is compassionate, he cannot negate his own goodness and mercy, since he is more prone to give out of mercy and goodness than to punish out of justice. Now, if he is not able to deny his justice to malefactors, much less is he able to deny his goodness and compassion to those who beg for it. But he who does his very best [*facere quod in se*] begs for goodness and compassion. Therefore, God grants this to him. This gift is the infusion of grace. In this sense Augustine comments on Rom. 5:1: "Since we are justified by faith we have peace with God": God takes notice of those who seek their refuge with him. Otherwise there would be iniquity in him. But it is impossible that there should be iniquity in him. Therefore, it is impossible that he would not receive those who take refuge with him. But if one does his very best [*facere quod in se*], one does take refuge with him. Therefore, it is *necessary* that God receive him. This reception, now, is the infusion of grace.[110]

It may be of some consequence to note that when Martin Luther wrote his *Disputation against Scholastic Theology* in April 1517, the scholastic theology he chiefly had in mind was that of Gabriel Biel, against which Luther pitted Augustine's theology of unconditional, sovereign grace. It was the *via moderna*, in other words, and its perceived neo-Pelagianism that aroused Luther's wrath. Whether he would have reacted in

---

107. See Oberman, *Harvest of Medieval Theology*, 147ff.
108. Judged, that is, by the intrinsic character of Pelagianism, which is characterized by an autonomous conception of the nature of the human will (even after the fall), a consequent universal human ability to seek God, and the first actual movement of the will toward God occurring prior to God's acting within it by regenerating grace. A direct equivalence between ancient Pelagianism and the theology of Biel cannot be sustained, but there are family resemblances.
109. For a useful summary and critique from a Lutheran perspective, see Victor Shepherd, "Gabriel Biel," Sermons and Writings of Victor Shepherd, January 2000, http://victorshepherd.ca/gabriel-biel-2/.
110. As translated by Oberman, in *Harvest of Medieval Theology*, 174.

the same way had he been nurtured within the more Augustinian *via antiqua* is a moot point.[111]

Theophylact of Ochrid (ca. 1050-ca. 1109)

Compared with the attention paid by Western scholars to their own medieval traditions, far less has been given to the Eastern tradition—after the Great Schism of 1054, we may perhaps call it Eastern Orthodoxy, in the sense in which most would understand the name today. It is beyond the scope of this chapter to offer an extensive survey of Eastern thinking on justification. However, we may take as a very useful representative of Eastern medieval theologizing the great eleventh-century Greek Bible commentator Archbishop Theophylact of Ochrid, sometimes hailed as the Matthew Henry of the Eastern church.[112] Among other achievements as churchman and writer in his life and career, Theophylact's most noteworthy and enduring was his commentary on the whole New Testament (with the exception of the book of Revelation); from its first publication to the present, Theophylact's has been far and away the most widely studied Bible commentary among Eastern Orthodox people in Greece, Russia, Bulgaria, and Serbia. The commentary itself is a dexterous blending together of previous biblical writings by the early church fathers, particularly John Chrysostom, together with elucidatory remarks by Theophylact himself. He also penned Old Testament commentaries on Hosea, Jonah, Nahum, and Habakkuk. In a previous era of Protestant theology, Theophylact was well known to Protestant divines. Reference to the Bulgarian archbishop as a source of knowledge and wisdom is made in Calvin, Thomas Watson, John Owen, Matthew Henry, John Gill, Charles Hodge, and B. B. Warfield, among others.

Theophylact's commentary on Paul's letter to the Galatians is a convenient place from which to gauge the Greek archbishop's understanding of justification. In those passages in Galatians where Paul speaks of justification, Theophylact expounded the apostle's meaning in a way that leaves little obscurity. For example, consider Theophylact's interpretation of Galatians 2:16—"Yet we know that a person is not justified by works of the law but through faith in Jesus Christ, so we also have believed in Christ Jesus, in order to be justified by faith in Christ and not by works of the law, because by works of the law no one will be justified." In his comments, Theophylact affirmed that the reason why the law cannot "justify" a person is that it is impossible to obey all its commands. The sense of "justify" here seems pretty plainly to be "bestow a righteous status."[113]

In the next verse, Galatians 2:17—"But if, in our endeavor to be justified in Christ, we too were found to be sinners, is Christ then a servant of sin? Certainly not!"—

---

111. Calvin was also reared in the *via moderna* and consequently tended to lump all scholastic theology together as neo-Pelagian.
112. See the biography attached to the English translation of Theophylact's commentary on Galatians, *The Explanation of the Epistle of Saint Paul to the Galatians*, trans. Christopher Stade (House Springs, MO: Chrysostom, 2011).
113. Theophylact repeats his assertion about the law's inability to justify, based on the human inability to give perfect obedience to its commands, in several other places in his commentary, e.g., his comments on Gal. 2:19; 3:10, 13.

Theophylact represented Paul as saying that if the apostle's opponents were correct, Christ did not justify us but brought greater condemnation. The stark justify-condemn antithesis employed here shows that Theophylact had a forensic meaning in mind for the first term of the antithesis. In 2:20, Theophylact once again employed the justify-condemn antithesis: Christ by his death saved us from condemnation and justified us. The antithesis is indeed very pointed in the original Greek: Theophylact set the words κατάκρισις and δικαιωση directly alongside each other.[114] A little later, Theophylact likewise added that "faith in Christ . . . justifies us and rescues us from condemnation."[115] Following on from all this, in the next verse (2:21), Theophylact commented that by his death, Christ justified me apart from my works.[116] The meaning is plain: Christ's atoning death is the sole source of the believer's freedom from condemnation, apart from human deeds. Later in his comments on 3:13 (see below), Theophylact elaborated that the Savior's death liberates us from condemnation because in dying, he took our condemnation on himself, the innocent in place of the guilty.

In his exegesis of Paul's citation of Genesis 15:6 in Galatians 3:6—"Abraham believed God, and it was counted to him as righteousness"—Theophylact interpreted the phrase as meaning "justified by faith." He therefore clearly seemed to understand justification as equivalent to a counting or reckoning of righteousness to the believer. In other words, to justify means to put righteousness to a believer's account in the esteem or judgment of God.[117] The archbishop then applied Abraham's position before God to the believer under the new covenant: "If he [Abraham] who lived before grace [i.e., before the new covenant] is justified by faith, so much the more should they who are deemed worthy of grace cling to faith."[118] If justification—being counted righteous—by faith applied to Abraham before the new covenant was given, much more does it apply to the new covenant believer.

In discussing 3:9–13, Theophylact made a sustained contrast between the situation of being "cursed" and the situation of being "blessed/justified." For Theophylact, then, "justified" is the opposite of "cursed." In light of the archbishop's previous remarks, we seem fully warranted in concluding that he was contrasting two verdicts—the negative verdict of the curse (attached to the lawbreaker) and the positive verdict of justification or righteousness (attached to the believer in Christ). This is given further credibility by the way in which Theophylact meshed this contrast with a penal-substitutionary model of the atoning death of Christ:

> Paul demonstrates that the curse has been removed through Christ. He paid the price by himself becoming the curse and thereby redeeming us from the condemnation of

---

114. Perhaps to bring out this force, Stade renders δικαιωση in English as "counted righteous" rather than "justified," thus capturing the forensic sense. This translation was not dictated by confessional allegiance, as Stade is Eastern Orthodox.
115. Theophylact, *Galatians*, 45.
116. Stade once again adds the explanatory "counted me righteous" to the word "justified."
117. Stade again translates Theophylact's "justified" as "counted righteous": an interesting decision, when one again remembers that Stade is confessionally Eastern Orthodox.
118. Theophylact, *Galatians*, 49.

the law. Christ (in his human nature) escaped that curse [i.e., was not personally liable to it] by fulfilling the law, but we, unable to fulfil it, were guilty under the law. This is like an innocent man who chooses to die in the place of a guilty man condemned to death. Therefore Christ accepted the curse of being hung from a tree and thereby loosed the curse to which we were liable for not fulfilling the law.[119]

Christ the sinless Redeemer voluntarily took on himself the curse and condemnation of sinners, thereby justifying—freeing from condemnation—those who are united with him.

In 3:22—"The Scripture imprisoned everything under sin, so that the promise by faith in Jesus Christ might be given to those who believe"—Theophylact interpreted the function of the law as "enclosing" Israel in sin by revealing to the people beyond contradiction that they are sinners. The further purpose of this convicting work is to "compel them to seek the way of forgiveness. This way is faith in Christ, through whom we are blessed and counted righteous."[120] The phrase translated "counted righteous" is the Greek for "justified" (although I have no problem with the way the translator has rendered it). The whole complex of Theophylact's thought here is familiar to every Reformation Protestant: the divine law reveals our sin, convicts us of it, deprives us of any human means of escape from it, and thus compels us to seek God's forgiveness. This forgiveness is found in Christ, through whom we are justified by faith. Once again, the archbishop treated "blessed" and "justified" as virtual synonyms, pointing to their antonym, "cursed," and situating us in the realm of alternative verdicts. The translation of "justified" here as "counted righteous," therefore, seems unexceptionable.

Finally, in his comments on 5:5—"Through the Spirit, by faith, we ourselves eagerly wait for the hope of righteousness"—Theophylact glossed Paul's statement as meaning that the Holy Spirit, through faith as expressed or concretized in baptism, mediates to the believer the forgiveness of sins and justification. Since this section forms the archbishop's concluding statement on justification in his commentary on Galatians, we can only assume that "justification" here once again means the bestowal of a status before God, substantially equivalent to "forgiveness of sins." Theophylact's main point is actually to insist on the necessity and priority of faith. But once faith is present, then the Spirit is given, and in and with the gift of the Spirit, the person of faith obtains forgiveness and justification. In itself, his statement is less clear in its import for the meaning of justification as the Greek archbishop understood it, but when coordinated with his foregoing assertions in the commentary, there is little room for doubt that he was referring to a status of righteousness. This warrants the translator's decision once again to render "justified" as "counted righteous."[121]

The place accorded to the believer's justification (understood in a fundamentally forensic sense) in Theophylact's commentary on Galatians reflects its wider place in the

---

119. Theophylact, *Galatians*, 51.
120. Theophylact, *Galatians*, 54.
121. Theophylact, *Galatians*, 68. It should yet again be borne in mind that the translator has no Protestant ax to grind, as he is Eastern Orthodox.

Eastern tradition of theology.[122] That is, the doctrine is *there*, but it does not occupy anything like the central role it would play in Protestant models of soteriology. For the East, the central model would remain that of theosis, or deification. Yet this should not blind us to the fact that a close reading of a representative Eastern exegete like Theophylact reveals a clear acquaintance with the Pauline doctrine of justification by faith.[123]

Recommended Resources

Anselm. *Anselm of Canterbury: The Major Works*. Edited by Brian Davies and G. R. Evans. Oxford World's Classics. New York: Oxford University Press, 1998.

Augustine. *Anti-Pelagian Writings*. Vol. 5 of *Nicene and Post-Nicene Fathers of the Christian Church*. 1st series. Edited by Philip Schaff. 1886–1890. Reprint, Grand Rapids, MI: Eerdmans, 1956.

Bernard of Clairvaux. *On Grace and Free Choice*. Translated by Daniel O'Donovan. Rome: Cistercian, 1977.

Busenitz, Nathan. *Long before Luther: Tracing the Heart of the Gospel from Christ to the Reformation*. Chicago: Moody Publishers, 2017.

Chemnitz, Martin. *Examination of the Council of Trent*. Translated by Fred Kramer. Saint Louis, MO: Concordia, 1971.

Evans, G. R., ed. *The Medieval Theologians: An Introduction to Theology in the Medieval Period*. Oxford: Blackwell, 2001.

Franks, Robert S. *A History of the Doctrine of the Work of Christ in Its Ecclesiastical Development*. London: Hodder and Stoughton, 1930.

Gerrish, Brian. "Sovereign Grace: Is Reformed Theology Obsolete?" *Interpretation* 57, no. 1 (2003): 45–57.

Green, Bradley G., ed. *Shapers of Christian Orthodoxy: Engaging with Early and Medieval Theologians*. Downers Grove, IL: IVP Academic, 2010.

Lane, Anthony N. S. *Justification by Faith in Catholic-Protestant Dialogue: An Evangelical Assessment*. New York: T&T Clark, 2006.

———. "Ten Theses on Justification and Sanctification." In *Mission and Meaning: Essays Presented to Peter Cotterell*, edited by Antony Billington, Tony Lane, and Max Turner, 191–216. Carlisle, UK: Paternoster, 1995.

Lombard, Peter. *The Sentences*. Translated by Giulio Silano. 4 vols. Mediaeval Sources in Translation 42–43, 45, 48. Toronto: Pontifical Institute of Mediaeval Studies, 2007–2010.

Macgregor, Kirk. *A Central European Synthesis of Radical and Magisterial Reform: The Sacramental Theology of Balthasar Hubmaier*. Lanham, MD: University Press of America, 2006.

---

122. Outside Theophylact's commentary on Galatians, we find a similar understanding of δικαιόω in (for example) his exposition of the key dominical parable of the publican and the Pharisee. Theophylact once again employs "justify" as the antithesis of "condemn": "For everyone that exalteth himself shall be humbled and condemned by God; and he that humbleth himself when he is condemned by others shall be exalted and counted righteous [justified] by God." Theophylact, *The Explanation by Blessed Theophylact of the Holy Gospel according to Saint Luke*, trans. Christopher Stade (House Springs, MO: Chrysostom, 1997), 238.

123. Once again, we might note that this fact is underscored by the Eastern Orthodox translator Christopher Stade's decision to render δικαιόω as "to count righteous" in several places.

McCormack, Bruce L., ed. *Justification in Perspective: Historical Developments and Contemporary Challenges*. Grand Rapids, MI: Baker Academic, 2006.

McGrath, Alister E. "Forerunners of the Reformation? A Critical Examination of the Evidence for Precursors of the Reformation Doctrines of Justification." *Harvard Theological Review* 75, no. 2 (1982): 219–42.

———. *Iustitia Dei: A History of the Christian Doctrine of Justification*. 3rd ed. Cambridge: Cambridge University Press, 2005.

Oberman, Heiko A. *Forerunners of the Reformation: The Shape of Late Medieval Thought, Illustrated by Key Documents*. Translations by Paul L. Nyhus. New York: Holt, Rinehart & Winston, 1966.

———. *The Harvest of Medieval Theology: Gabriel Biel and Late Medieval Nominalism*. Cambridge, MA: Harvard University Press, 1963.

Osterhaven, M. Eugene. *The Faith of the Church: A Reformed Perspective on Its Historical Development*. Grand Rapids, MI: Eerdmans, 1982.

Posset, Franz. *Pater Bernhardus: Martin Luther and Bernard of Clairvaux*. Kalamazoo, MI: Cistercian, 1999.

Tamburello, Dennis E. *Union with Christ: John Calvin and the Mysticism of St. Bernard*. Louisville: Westminster John Knox, 1994.

Theophylact of Ochrid. *The Explanation of the Epistle of Saint Paul to the Galatians*. Translated by Christopher Stade. House Springs, MO: Chrysostom, 2011.

Thomas Aquinas. *Light of Faith: The Compendium of Theology*. Translated by Cyril Vollert. New York: Book-of-the-Month Club by arrangement with the Sophia Institute, 1998.

Vos, Arvin. *Aquinas, Calvin, and Contemporary Protestant Thought: A Critique of Protestant Views on the Thought of Thomas Aquinas*. Grand Rapids, MI: Eerdmans, 1985.

20

Can This Bird Fly?

The Reformation as Reaction to the *Via Moderna*'s Covenantal, Voluntarist Justification Theology

MATTHEW BARRETT

History is a series of turning points that hinge on decisions inherently theological in nature.[1] The publication and posting of the *Ninety-Five Theses* by Martin Luther in 1517 is, in the opinion of many historians, that turning point on which the entire modern era hinges. Historical inquiries into those theses naturally focus on Luther's growing discontent with the indulgence system. As Luther himself would increasingly discover, his own desire for reform would be pastorally motivated, troubled as he was by the way indulgences had swayed the average late medieval Christian to use what little money he had to secure the removal of temporal punishment for sins in purgatory. Tetzel's dramatic sermon pressuring the purchase of an indulgence only confirmed that Luther's fears were not unwarranted.[2]

Nevertheless, contemporary histories pay little tribute to the complicated medieval soteriology behind Luther's early outrage over indulgences in 1516 and 1517. The shape of late medieval soteriology, especially as it relates to a covenantal, voluntarist framework, has taken a backseat to the more conspicuous political, social, and ecclesiastical circumstances that surrounded October 31, 1517. For those unacquainted with the vortex of medieval soteriology, Luther's earliest polemics, which are filled with

---

[1]. This chapter is a revision of Matthew Barrett, "Can This Bird Fly? Repositioning the Genesis of the Reformation on Martin Luther's Early Polemic against Gabriel Biel's Covenantal, Voluntarist Doctrine of Justification," *SBJT* 21, no. 4 (2017): 61–101. Used by permission of *Southern Baptist Theological Journal*.
[2]. E.g., "Summary Instruction for Indulgence Preachers," and "John Tetzel: A Sermon [1517]," in Hans J. Hillerbrand, ed., *The Protestant Reformation*, rev. ed., DHWC (New York: Harper Perennial, 2009), 14–18, 19–21.

reactions against certain late medieval schoolmen, leave one mystified. Unfamiliar with late medieval justification theories, interpreters of Luther may come dangerously close to misunderstanding the Reformer's own reaction, which is no small danger considering the momentous weight Protestantism has placed on Luther's rediscovery of *sola fide* over against Rome.

What follows is a small contribution to remedy such an oversight and fill a historical lacuna. The purpose is methodologically motivated: I aspire to shift the spotlight off the usual storyline and shine it instead on Luther's polemical reaction to Gabriel Biel's covenantal, voluntarist doctrine of justification. More importantly, however, the argument is theological: apart from understanding *why* Luther reacted so negatively to Biel, one cannot, at least in full, do justice to Luther's own journey into an Augustinian justification theory and, eventually, beyond Augustinianism into a forensic view of justification, one that would characterize Protestantism for centuries to come.

What follows is not a claim to discover anything "new" so much as it is an attempt to move histories of the Reformation in a different direction, even, so to speak, turn the turning point, relocating the genesis of the Reformation within the late medieval context that defined the young Luther, almost successfully driving him into religious and psychological insanity. Luther's early academic life is instrumental, specifically his *Disputation against Scholastic Theology*, for there we discover a budding Augustinian theologian trapped in the categories of the *via moderna* until he can break free by means of a paradigm that, ironically enough, took the name of his own monastery. Should the story of the Reformation begin within that context, it becomes obvious why Luther's forensic doctrine of imputation is no mere modification of medieval soteriology but an entire paradigm shift, one that radically redefines covenantal, anthropological, and soteriological presuppositions.

The *Via Moderna* versus the *Schola Augustiniana Moderna*

Gabriel Biel (ca. 1420–1495), commonly recognized as the last of the scholastics, arrived on the eve of the Reformation. Yet the issues he was addressing originate before his time with the collision of two medieval schools of thought. Although Biel developed his own justification synthesis, his covenantal and voluntarist preunderstanding was not necessarily novel but inherent in the *via moderna*. Over the span of multiple centuries, the *via moderna* took form in the thought of William of Ockham (ca. 1285–ca. 1349), Robert Holcot (ca. 1290–1349), and Pierre d'Ailly (1350–1420), among others.[3]

Matriculating from universities such as Heidelberg, Biel was an engaged academic, yet his attention was particularly devoted to life in the church, being himself a priest and a known preacher. Such a pastoral emphasis stems from his background in the *Devotio Moderna*, the Brethren of the Common Life.[4] That fact is not irrelevant, for Biel's

---

3. For example, consult Robert Holcot, "Lectures on the Wisdom of Solomon," in *Forerunners of the Reformation: The Shape of Late Medieval Thought, Illustrated by Key Documents*, ed. Heiko A. Oberman (Philadelphia: Fortress, 1981), 142–50.
4. Oberman, *Forerunners*, 137.

insistence on man's ability, as captured in the slogan *facere quod in se est*, was pastorally motivated. Only if man possessed the spiritual ability "to do his very best," or, literally, "to do that which lies within him," could reconciliation with his Maker be attainable. As Heiko Oberman puts it, "Biel's concern is to provide a way to justification within the reach of the average Christian."[5]

The *schola Augustiniana moderna*, on the other hand, perceived the *via moderna* as a return to Pelagianism. The modern Augustinian school consisted of theologians such as Thomas Bradwardine (ca. 1290–1349), Gregory of Rimini (ca. 1300–1358), and Hugolino of Orvieto (after 1300–1373). Bradwardine is especially fascinating for his own conversion out of Pelagianism. A student-turned-lecturer at Merton College, Oxford University, he would later be chancellor of Saint Paul's, London, and eventually archbishop of Canterbury in Avignon. It was during his years at Saint Paul's that he wrote a book by the title *De causa Dei contra Pelagium* (*The Cause of God against Pelagius*), in 1344.[6] In that work, Bradwardine reflected on his own personal experience, having been absorbed by what he believed was Pelagianism at Oxford only to discover *sola gratia* through a text like Romans 9.[7] Bradwardine would be the formidable nemesis of Robert Holcot, whom the former encountered in Durham.[8]

Despite the force of Bradwardine, historians often point to another theologian from the Order of the Hermits of Saint Augustine at the University of Paris, Gregory of Rimini, as the man responsible for a revival of Augustinianism.[9] Frank James III notes how it was Rimini who reintroduced Augustine's predestinarianism, eventually influencing Peter Martyr Vermigli, the Italian Reformer whom Thomas Cranmer recruited to come to England (Bradwardine's influence on other Reformers, like Luther and Calvin, is contested).[10]

---

5. Heiko A. Oberman, *The Harvest of Medieval Theology: Gabriel Biel and Late Medieval Nominalism* (Grand Rapids, MI: Eerdmans, 1962), 157.

6. See Thomas Bradwardine, *De Causa Dei contra Pelagium*, ed. Henry Savile (Frankfurt: de Gruyter, 1964), 1.42. One of the best studies is Gordon Leff, *Bradwardine and the Pelagians: A Study of His "De Causa Dei" and Its Opponents*, CSMLT 5 (Cambridge: Cambridge University Press, 1957), 69.

7. Bradwardine wrote, "Idle and a fool in God's wisdom, I was misled by an unorthodox error at a time when I was still pursuing philosophical studies. Sometimes I went to listen to the theologians discussing this matter [of grace and free will], and the school of Pelagius seemed to me nearest the truth. . . . In the philosophical faculty I seldom heard a reference to grace, except for some ambiguous remarks. What I heard day in and day out was that we are masters of our own free acts, that ours is the choice to act well or badly, to have virtues or sins and much more along this line. . . . Every time I listened to the Epistle reading in church and heard how Paul magnified grace and belittled free will—as is the case in Romans 9, 'It is obviously not a question of human will and effort, but of divine mercy,' and its many parallels—grace displeased me, ungrateful as I was." Then something changed: "However, even before I transferred to the faculty of theology, the text mentioned came to me as a beam of grace and, captured by a vision of the truth, it seemed I saw from afar how the grace of God precedes all good works with a temporal priority [God as Savior through predestination] and natural precedence [God continues to provide for his creation as 'first mover']. . . . That is why I express my gratitude to him who has given me this grace as a free gift." Bradwardine, *De Causa Dei*, 2.32, p. 613, quoted in Oberman, *Forerunners*, 135.

8. All such details can be found in fuller form in Oberman, *Forerunners*, 136.

9. Heiko A. Oberman, *Masters of the Reformation: The Emergence of a New Intellectual Climate in Europe*, trans. Dennis Martin (Cambridge: Cambridge University Press, 1981), 70–71; Oberman, *Forerunners*, 151–64. Trapp calls Gregory of Rimini "the first Augustinian of Augustine." Damasus Trapp, "Augustinian Theology of the Fourteenth Century," *Augustiniana* 6 (1956): 181.

10. Frank A. James III, "Peter Martyr Vermigli," in *The Reformation Theologians: An Introduction to Theology in the Early Modern Period*, ed. Carter Lindberg (Oxford: Blackwell, 2002), 205. Also see John Patrick Donnelly, *Calvinism and Scholasticism in Vermigli's Doctrine of Man and Grace*, SMRT 18 (Leiden: Brill, 1976); James, *Peter Martyr Vermigli and Predestination: The Augustinian Inheritance of an Italian Reformer*, OTM (Oxford: Clarendon, 1998); James, "Peter Martyr Vermigli: At the Crossroads of Late Medieval Scholasticism, Christian Humanism, and

The influence of each school cannot be minimized. For instance, not only was the *via moderna* the position that Reformers like Luther and Calvin were taught to embrace, but representatives as late as Biel would leave a notable impression on sixteenth-century Roman theologians and councils as well. For example, Biel's soteriology is inherent within the theology of Luther's arduous opponent Johann Eck, as well as within the Council of Trent (1545–1563).[11] Writing to Frederick the Wise, Luther said concerning his 1519 debate at Leipzig with Eck, "In debating with me he [Eck] rejected Gregory of Rimini as one who alone supported my opinion against all theologians."[12] Aligning himself with an Augustinian like Gregory in 1519 was but the outcome of Luther's stance two years earlier as he rigorously set his aim on Biel, who serves in this chapter as the appropriate foil to understanding Luther's departure from the *via moderna*.

Biel's Covenantal, Voluntarist Account of Justification

The starting point to properly comprehending Biel's doctrine of justification is the divine *pactum*. Such a starting point may not be, at first glance, immediately relevant. For instance, in his sermon "Circumcision of the Lord," Biel spends most of his effort explaining infused grace and defining meritorious actions. Not until the end does he briefly introduce the "rule" or "covenant." Nevertheless, this covenant is critical to Biel's *processus iustificationis*.

According to Biel, "God has established the rule [covenant] that whoever turns to him and does what he can will receive forgiveness of sins from God. God infuses assisting grace into such a man, who is thus taken back into friendship."[13] The covenant established is voluntary on God's part and gracious in its inception. Recognizing that man has lost his way, God deliberates, leading him to initiate an agreement in which the possibility of eternal life might become a reality. Yet not only is the covenant voluntary in the sense that God chose to institute a rule he did not have to establish, but it is voluntarist in nature as well. The covenant is God's way of accepting man's works, even if they be unworthy in and of themselves. Biel puts forward a parable to convey this point:

> Let us say that there is a most lenient king who shows so much mercy to his people that he publishes a decree saying that he will embrace with his favor any of his enemies who desire his friendship, provided they mend their ways for the present and the future. Furthermore, the king orders that all who have been received in this

---

Resurgent Augustinianism," in *Protestant Scholasticism: Essays in Reassessment*, ed. Carl R. Trueman and R. Scott Clark, SCHT (Carlisle, UK: Paternoster, 1999), 62–78; James, "A Late Medieval Parallel in Reformation Thought: *Gemina Praedestinatio* in Gregory of Rimini and Peter Martyr Vermigli," in *Via Augustini: Augustine in the Later Middle Ages, Renaissance, and Reformation; Essays in Honor of Damasus Trapp*, ed. Heiko A. Oberman and Frank A. James III, SMRT 48 (Leiden: Brill, 1991), 157–88; Gordon Leff, *Gregory of Rimini: Tradition and Innovation in Fourteenth Century Thought* (Manchester, UK: University of Manchester Press, 1961). On Rimini's influence on Luther and Calvin, see Heiko A. Oberman, "Headwaters of the Reformation: *Initia Lutheri—Initia Reformationis*," in *Luther and the Dawn of the Modern Era*, ed. Heiko A. Oberman (Leiden: Brill, 1974), 40–88; Alister E. McGrath, "John Calvin and Late Medieval Thought: A Study in Late Medieval Influence upon Calvin's Theological Development," *ARG* 77 (1986): 58–78; Robert Spieler, "Luther and Gregory of Rimini," *LQ* 5 (1953): 160.

11. See Oberman, *Forerunners*, 137.
12. Martin Luther, "Letter from Luther to Spalatin concerning the Leipzig Debate," in *LW* 31:322.
13. Gabriel Biel, "The Circumcision of the Lord," in Oberman, *Forerunners*, 173.

fashion into his friendship will receive a golden ring to honor all who are dedicated to his regime, so that such a friend of the king may be known to all. *The king gives to such a man by way of delegation of his royal authority such a position that every work done to the honor of the king, regardless of where performed or how large or small it is, shall be rewarded by the king above and beyond its value.* And to give him extra strength to perform this kind of meritorious work, precious and powerful stones are inserted in the ring to encourage him who wears it, so that his body does not fail him when he needs it but increases in ability to gain further rewards the more the body is exercised and accustomed to resist every adverse force.[14]

That phrase "lenient king" is most telling. Leniency is the prime characteristic of the covenant that God inaugurates. His enemies deserve not his friendship. Nevertheless, should they be determined to "mend their ways," and should they perform works that honor the king to the best of their abilities, it matters not whether those works are inherently worthy, reaching the perfect standard of divine justice. The leniency of the king and his contract means that he will accept such works regardless. Such works may even be rewarded above and beyond any inherent value they possess. The king has that right or authority by virtue of his royal office. With that scheme in mind, it is appropriate to label Biel's covenantalism voluntarist in nature.

The Intellectualist Approach: Thomas Aquinas

The *via moderna* intentionally parted ways with the intellectualism of Thomas Aquinas (ca. 1225–1274), in which the divine intellect held primacy over the divine will. For the medieval intellectualist, prioritizing the divine intellect meant that the inherent value of man's merits mattered. God did not necessarily reward *above and beyond* the inherent value but *according to* the inherent value of one's works; otherwise, his own justice could be thrown into question. Approaching justification through an intellectualist framework avoided the charge that God's *liberum arbitrium* was arbitrary—a very dangerous and incriminating charge in the Middle Ages.[15]

Distinguishable, as well, is the *iustificationis* embraced by an intellectualist. For Aquinas, justification involved not merely the forgiveness of sins but an ontological transformation, one that involved the habit of grace being infused into man's soul, a habit necessary for man to be pleasing to God. With the habit of grace infused, man might cooperate (exercising his free will), being made righteous and in order to be made righteous.[16] As his nature is changed by habitual grace—a substance supernatural in

---

14. Biel, "Circumcision of the Lord," 173; italics added.
15. Why dangerous? McGrath answers, "Thomas rejected the opinion that *iustitia Dei* is merely an arbitrary aspect of the divine will. To assert that *iustitia* ultimately depends upon the will of God amounts to the blasphemous assertion that God does not operate according to the order of wisdom. Underlying *iustitia* is *sapientia*, discernible to the intellect, so that the ultimate standard of justice must be taken to be right reason." Alister E. McGrath, *Iustitia Dei: A History of the Christian Doctrine of Justification*, 3rd ed. (Cambridge: Cambridge University Press, 2005), 85.
16. "By every meritorious act," says Aquinas, "a man merits the increase of grace, equally with the consummation of grace which is eternal life." *Summa Theologiae* 1a2ae.114.8. I hesitate to use the word *cooperate* because it might give the impression that Aquinas is a synergist in the way that many in the late medieval or post-Reformation eras were. Aquinas's

orientation—man becomes more and more satisfactory in the eyes of God (i.e., *gratia gratis faciens*). Aquinas wrote in his *Summa Theologiae*, "God infuses a habitual gift into the soul," an infusion of "certain forms or supernatural qualities into those whom he moves to seek after supernatural and eternal good, that they may be thus moved by him to seek it sweetly and readily." The "gift of grace," he reasoned, "is a certain quality."[17] The ontological transformation that habitual grace manufactures is the preliminary ground on which God is then justified in his justification of the ungodly.

The main thrust of such a point can be simplistically pictured in figure 21.1, where such an infusion is presented as both gracious and prevenient. Enabled by infused grace, man's acquired merit is rewarded, complimented according to the measure of value it possesses. Justice is a priority in this schema; God is obligated to bestow the just reward every act of acquired merit deserves. Aquinas outlines the step-by-step logic of grace when he writes in his *Summa*, "The first is the infusion of grace; the second, the free-will's movement towards God; the third, the free-will's movement towards sin; the fourth, the remission of sin."[18]

Figure 21.1   Intellectualist Schema of Thomas Aquinas

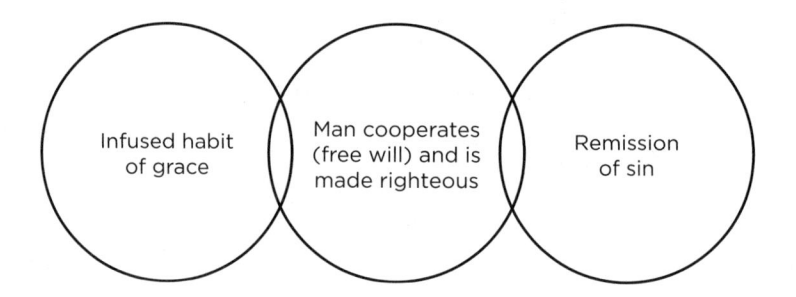

Infused habit of grace — Man cooperates (free will) and is made righteous — Remission of sin

Aquinas did not always prioritize grace over man's freedom. Earlier in his career, he wrote a commentary on Peter Lombard's *Sentences*, in which he (to be anachronistic) sounded like Biel centuries later. Man was to do his best, and his best would be rewarded by grace, a grace that would prepare him for justification. Man's best did not meet God's perfect standard, but God would accept it anyway because of his sovereign generosity.[19] Later on, as his *Summa Theologiae* and *Summa contra Gentiles* evidence, Aquinas would

---

predestinarian theology would preclude such an assumption. So the language of cooperation above is merely meant to acknowledge the role of man's acquired merits.

17. Thomas Aquinas, *Summa Theologiae* 1a2ae.110.2, in *Nature and Grace: Selections from the "Summa Theologica,"* trans. and ed. A. M. Fairweather, LCC (Louisville: Westminster John Knox, 1954), 159–60. For similar themes, see Aquinas, *Commentary on the Letter of Saint Paul to the Romans*, trans. F. R. Larcher, ed. J. Mortensen and E. Alarcón (Lander, WY: Aquinas Institute for the Study of Sacred Doctrine, 2012), 1.3, 1.6, 2.3. Also consult Brian Davies, *Thomas Aquinas's Summa Theologiae: A Guide and Commentary* (New York: Oxford University Press, 2014).

18. Aquinas, *Summa Theologiae* 1a2ae.113.8. Also see 1a2ae.113.7. Ozment pictures this logic in the following order: "(1) Gratuitous infusion of grace; (2) Moral cooperation: doing the best one can with the aid of grace; (3) Reward of eternal life as a just due." Steven Ozment, *The Age of Reform, 1250–1550: An Intellectual and Religious History of Late Medieval and Reformation Europe* (New Haven, CT: Yale University Press, 1980), 233.

19. E.g., Gabriel Biel, *In II Sententiarum*, d. 28, q. 1, a. 4 and 4um; Biel, *In IV Sententiarum*, d. 17, q. 1, aa. 3–4. See Biel, *Collectorium circa quattuor libros sententiarum*, ed. W. Werbeck and U. Hoffman, 4 vols. (Tübingen: Mohr, 1973–1984).

reverse the order, claiming instead that grace must come first if works are to follow at all.[20] It is essential to observe at this point that the *iustificationis* involves an *ordo* in which infused grace holds primacy to the movement of the will, thereby excusing Aquinas not only of Pelagianism but semi-Pelagianism as well.[21] As McGrath observes, *facere quod in se est* now takes on a different meaning: "doing what one is able to do when aroused and moved by grace."[22] Yet in contrast to the doctrine of the sixteenth-century Reformers, justification for Aquinas remained a transformation, one in which the individual was made righteous in his inner nature, not a forensic declaration, as the Reformers would argue at a much later date.[23]

The Voluntarist Approach: Scotus, Ockham, and Biel

By contrast, the voluntarist conception would differ completely. Duns Scotus (ca. 1266–1308) and English Franciscan William of Ockham believed that Aquinas had demolished God's freedom. The notion that God is restricted or obligated to reward works inherently worthy undermines God's freedom to reward works above and beyond what they are worth. God can and does reward however he sees fit; as God, he is free to do so. The freedom and sovereignty of the divine will entail that something is only good because God says it is good. If the liberality of God's choice is to be prioritized, then God is not to be held accountable to an external standard of justice, but justice itself is to be defined according to whatever God chooses to accept as just.[24]

In that vein came the perceived genius of Biel's covenantal conception, though its covenantal flavor is not original to Biel but is present in *via moderna* representatives like

---

20. Oberman, *Forerunners*, 130. Contrary to some who think Aquinas is contradicting himself, McGrath demonstrates that a change in Aquinas's view of nature and grace has occurred. See *Iustitia Dei*, 110–11.
21. E.g., Aquinas, *Summa Theologiae* 1a2ae.112.3; 1a2ae.109.6.ad2um.
22. McGrath, *Iustitia Dei*, 112.
23. McGrath stresses such a point, arguing that it is a misinterpretation of Aquinas to take that final step—remission of sin—and assume justification is forensic. "Some commentators have misunderstood Thomas' occasional definition of justification solely in terms of remission of sin, representing him as approaching a forensic concept of justification. It will be clear that this is a serious misunderstanding. Where Thomas defines justification as *remissio peccatorum*, therefore, he does not exclude other elements—such as the infusion of grace—for the following reasons. First, justification is thus defined without reference to its content, solely in terms of its *terminus*. Such a definition is adequate, but not exhaustive, and should not be treated as if it were. Second, Thomas' understanding of the *processus iustificationis* means that the occurrence of any one of the four elements necessarily entails the occurrence of the remaining three. The definition of *iustificatio* as *remissio peccatorum* therefore expressly *includes* the remaining three elements." The four elements McGrath references are (1) the infusion of grace, (2) the movement of the free will directed toward God through faith, (3) the movement of the free will directed against sin, and (4) the remission of sin. McGrath has in mind Aquinas, *Summa Theologiae* 1a2ae.113.8; 1a2ae.113.6; 1a2ae.113.6.ad1um. McGrath, *Iustitia Dei*, 64.
24. McGrath explains, "Gabriel Biel insists upon the priority of the divine will over any moral structures by declaring that God's will is essentially independent of what is right or wrong; if the divine will amounted to a mere endorsement of what is good or right, God's will would thereby be subject to created principles of morality. What is good, therefore, is good only if it is accepted as such by God. The divine will is thus the chief arbiter and principle of justice, establishing justice by its decisions, rather than acting on the basis of established justice. Morality and merit alike derive from the divine will, in that the goodness of an act must be defined, not in terms of the act itself, but in terms of the *divine estimation of that act*. Duns Scotus had established the general voluntarist principle, that every created offering to God is worth precisely whatever God accepts it for. . . . Applying this principle to the passion of Christ and the redemption of humankind, Scotus points out that a good angel could have made satisfaction in Christ's place, had God chosen to accept its offering as having sufficient value: the merit of Christ's passion lies solely in the *acceptatio divina*." McGrath, *Iustitia Dei*, 86. In view are the following works: Gabriel Biel, *Canonis missae expositio* 23E, ed. Heiko A. Oberman and William J. Courtenay, 4 vols. (Wiesbaden: Steiner, 1963–1967), 1.212; Biel, *In I Sententiarum*, d. 43, q. 1, a. 4 cor., in Biel, *Collectorium circa quattuor libros sententiarum*, 1:746.5–7; Biel, *In II Sententiarum*, d. 27, q. 1, a. 3, dub. 4, in Biel, *Collectorium circa quattuor libros sententiarum*, 2:253.7–9; Duns Scotus, *Opus Oxoniense*, bk. 3, d. 19, q. 1, n. 7. For an extended treatment of Scotus's position, see Richard Cross, *Duns Scotus*, Great Medieval Thinkers (Oxford: Oxford University Press, 1999). To see Ockham's position, consult his *Quodlibetal Questions*, vols. 1–2, *Quodlibets 1–7*, trans. Alfred J. Freddoso and Francis E. Kelley (New Haven, CT: Yale University Press, 1991).

Holcot. Through the establishment of a voluntary *pactum*, God obligates himself rather than being obligated by the inherent value of man's merit via habitual grace. That covenantal obligation preserves the freedom of his will, for he chooses if and how he will reward man's effort, and it need not be according to the weight of its value. In that sense, Biel believed his view to be *more* gracious than challenging views. If God is not bound to bestow the inherent value according to some external standard but is free to go above and beyond, then his reward for man's deeds can exceed their worth. The worth or value of man's merits is assigned or ascribed but cannot be inherent, innate, or inborn.

Furthermore, this view avoids Pelagianism since man doing his best is not meant to merit God's grace *de condigno*, as his deeds are unworthy in and of themselves, but rather *de congruo*. It is not

> that man's moral efforts unaided by grace are fully meritorious of God's rewards (*de condigno*) but rather that they are graciously regarded by God as half merits or merits in a metaphorical sense (*de congruo*). The relationship between God's bestowal of grace and sinful man's best effort rests on "contracted" rather than "actual" worth and is a result of God's liberality in giving "so much for so little."[25]

Nevertheless, there is a theological catch for Biel. The voluntarist nature of the covenant may mean God goes "above and beyond," but that is only true should one do his or her best. To be fair to Biel, the point is stated by him far more positively. All one must do is one's best to receive God's reward, even if one's best does not add up to God's perfect standard. Should one do his best, infused grace will subsequently matriculate. Hence we return to that previous statement from Biel: "God has established the rule [covenant] that whoever turns to him and does what he can will receive forgiveness of sins from God. God infuses assisting grace into such a man, who is thus taken back into friendship."[26] A more sophisticated, detailed diagram will be offered later, but for now, what's being outlined can be simplistically pictured, as in figure 21.2.[27]

Figure 21.2 Voluntarist Schema of Gabriel Biel

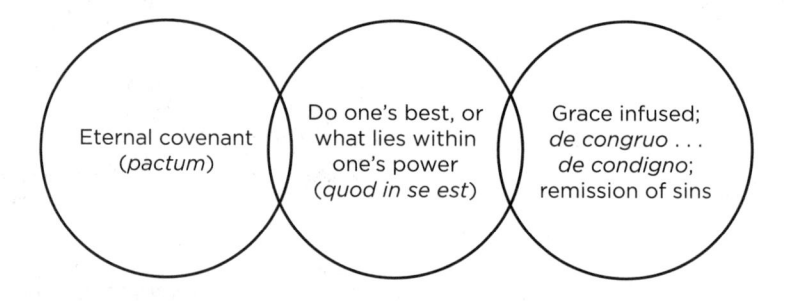

- Eternal covenant (*pactum*)
- Do one's best, or what lies within one's power (*quod in se est*)
- Grace infused; *de congruo* . . . *de condigno*; remission of sins

---

25. Oberman, *Forerunners*, 129.
26. Biel, "Circumcision of the Lord," 173.
27. Ozment offers a more detailed diagram of Ockham's and Biel's order: "(1) Moral effort: doing the best one can on the basis of natural moral ability; (2) Infusion of grace as an appropriate reward; (3) Moral cooperation: doing the best one can with the aid of grace; (4) Reward of eternal life as a just due." Ozment, *Age of Reform*, 234.

Biel's Anthropological Assumption: *Actum Facientis Quod In Se Est*

There is, however, one major assumption—and in the eyes of Biel's nemeses, the Achilles' heel of Biel's position—namely, that one is able to do one's best to begin with. Infused grace is a subsequent reality, conditioned on one doing what lies within. There is a strong anthropological optimism in Biel, one that would be characteristic of adherents to the *via moderna* system overall. God may graciously establish a covenant whereby he accepts man's best, however unqualified his best may be. Yet Biel assumes that man has a "best" to offer. Consider the power he credits to man's will in his work *In II Sententiarum*: The soul, by removing an obstacle toward a good movement to God through the free will, is able to merit the first grace *de congruo*. This is so because God accepts the act of doing "what lies within its powers" [*actum facientis quod in se est*] as leading to the first grace, which is thus not on account of God's generosity. The soul, by removing this obstacle, ceases from acts of sin and consent to sin; it thus elicits a good movement toward God as its principal end and does "what lies within its power" [*quod in se est*]. Therefore, God accepts, out of his generosity [*ex sua liberalitate*], this act of removing an obstacle and a good movement toward God as the basis of the infusion of grace.[28]

Such phrases as *actum facientis quod in se est* and *quod in se est*—phrases that originate not with Biel but with his Franciscan master Alexander of Hales—are revealing.[29] In man's power is the ability to "merit the first grace *de congruo*," a point we shall return to. Although the covenant may be prevenient, the first grace is subsequent to man's merit. Man's "good movement toward God" serves as the condition for future grace, the "basis of the infusion of grace." Free will, then, is very much alive, so much so that one wonders to what extent, if any, it has been affected by the fall.

To be accurate, however, Biel does believe man is a fallen creature, corrupt in his nature. Biel's emphasis on man's corruption is stronger than that of other medieval schoolmen. "More than Duns Scotus and Occam," says Oberman, "Biel stresses that man's original nature has been corrupted by original sin; man is not only *spoliatus a gratuitis* but also *vulneratus in naturalibus*." Oberman elaborates, "Man's miserable condition after the fall is not only due to a vertical imputation by God, but also to a horizontal continuation of infirmity, through an infection in which all mankind partakes and through which the will is wounded, so that it is more inclined to evil than to good deeds."[30]

Biel is, unfortunately, unclear as to the specifics. He "does not elucidate the exact relation of the potential disorder of man's created nature before the fall to the corruption of that nature—the law of the flesh reigning over man—after the fall."[31] What is

---

28. Gabriel Biel, *In II Sententiarum*, d. 27, q. unica, a. 3, c. 4, in Biel, *Collectorium circa quattuor libros sententiarum*, 2:517.1–8. The Latin translation comes from Alister E. McGrath, ed., *The Christian Theology Reader*, 4th ed. (Oxford: Wiley-Blackwell, 2011), 6.30.
29. Oberman, *Harvest of Medieval Theology*, 132. Hence Oberman summarizes Biel: "After the fall man is still able to detest sin and seek refuge with God with his own powers, without the help of any form of grace. This, of course, does not exclude God's general *concursus* in every deed, good, bad or indifferent, since without this 'natura' energy man would not be able to act at all." *Harvest of Medieval Theology*, 175.
30. Oberman, *Harvest of Medieval Theology*, 128.
31. Oberman, *Harvest of Medieval Theology*, 128.

clear is that the will is not so corrupted or wounded that it cannot perform meritorious acts. Man's will may be wounded and in need of repair, but it is not so wounded that freedom has been lost, that is, a freedom to act righteously, even if imperfectly. Apart from such freedom, man cannot do his best or what lies within him, which is necessary if he is to be rewarded with infused grace and merit divine justification. Original sin's grip, Oberman observes, is not ontological but psychological in its effect:

> Though man may be said to be in a miserable position, enslaved by the law of the flesh which requires that there be a healing aspect to the process of justification, his will is nevertheless free, original sin being a certain outgrowth of natural difficulties which can therefore be healed with natural medicines. Original sin has primarily a psychological, not an ontological impact on the free will of man; it destroys the pleasure of eliciting a good act and causes unhappiness and fear, thus changing the direction of the will. This does not, however, interfere with the freedom of the will as such. This presentation prepares us for Biel's psychological prescription for those who would like to reach the level of the *facere quod in se est* and thus dispose themselves for the infusion of grace.[32]

For that reason, Oberman seriously doubts that Biel is "Thomistic or Augustinian," an assertion Oberman finds "groundless," despite Biel's own claims.[33]

Grace Defined: The Impediment to Flight Lessened

Notwithstanding the heavy stress on the freedom of the will after the fall, Biel believed that he was far from bordering on Pelagianism. The grace God gives as a reward to those who do what lies within them originates not from man but from God.

After quoting Romans 11:6 in his sermon "The Circumcision of the Lord," Biel then claimed,

> Because nature cannot make something out of nothing, that which is created comes from God alone. If grace could come from the creature, a grace which would suffice unto salvation, then any creature would be able to save himself by his own natural powers, that is, do what only grace can do. That is the error of Pelagius.[34]

And again: "Now we must see just what this grace is by which the sinner is justified and what is actually accomplished in us. The grace of which we speak is a gift of God supernaturally infused into the soul. It makes the soul acceptable to God and sets it on the path to deeds of meritorious love."[35] Biel then proceeded to structure the majority of his sermon under three headings.

First, "God makes acceptable for this reason alone, that it is present in and is part of that nature which can be beatified, that is, man." Biel appealed to Scotus to explain how

---

32. Oberman, *Harvest of Medieval Theology*, 129.
33. Oberman, *Harvest of Medieval Theology*, 130–31.
34. Biel, "Circumcision of the Lord," 168.
35. Biel, "Circumcision of the Lord," 168.

grace is an enrichment of nature that is pleasing to God's will. Grace makes human nature acceptable to God by adorning it not with an ordinary acceptation but with that special acceptation by which man is according to God's decision ordained toward life eternal. For to be acceptable, to be beloved by God and to be His friend, means to be in such a state that one will attain eternal life unless one loses this state through sin.[36]

Second, "And because grace makes the sinner acceptable to God it follows that it also justifies him." Biel then broke justification down into two aspects: (1) "remission of guilt" and (2) "acceptation to eternal life, since it is impossible for one who is going to be accepted to eternal life to be at the same time condemned to eternal punishment." To be forgiven of one's guilt is, for Biel, a requirement of entering paradise.[37]

Biel did seem to distinguish between an infused grace that invites justification ("remission of guilt" and "acceptation to eternal life") and an infused grace that arrives after initial justification to continuously cultivate good works throughout the Christian life. Quoting Romans 3:24 to support his claim, Biel wrote,

> But if grace is infused into someone who is already justified, that which it accomplishes is not justification. An example would be the grace once given to the holy angels and now daily given to those who are upright of heart, who through their good works earn an additional gift of grace above and beyond the grace already in them.[38]

Third, "Thus God makes these our works meritorious and acceptable for eternal reward, not actually all our works but only those which have been brought forth by the prompting of grace."[39] If any act is to be ultimately meritorious, in Biel's framework, it must be, he says, "brought forth by the prompting of grace." Hence, not all acts qualify. But those acts prompted by grace should result in love for God above all else.[40]

Biel did follow in the footsteps of Lombard, listing two components of a meritorious act: *liberum arbitrium* ("free will") and the grace of God.

> There is no human merit that does not depend partly on free will. The principal cause of meritorious moral action, however, is attributed to grace. But grace does not determine the will. The will can ignore the prompting of grace and lose it by its own default. The prompting of grace is toward meritorious acts for the sake of God. Therefore, the act as such stems primarily from grace. This is the case because it is performed by someone who has grace in accordance with the prompting of grace.[41]

---

36. Biel, "Circumcision of the Lord," 168.
37. Biel, "Circumcision of the Lord," 169.
38. Biel, "Circumcision of the Lord," 169.
39. Biel clarified, "It is assumed of meritorious work that the person who performs it is accepted, since the acts of a person who has not been accepted or of an enemy cannot please God." "Circumcision of the Lord," 169.
40. Biel explained, "This grace prompts us to love God above all things and in all things, that is, to seek after the glory of God as the goal of every action, and to prefer the ultimate good, God, ahead of one's self and everything else. Therefore, all those things which are not directed consciously or unconsciously toward God do not come from the prompting of grace and therefore are surely not worthy of eternal life." "Circumcision of the Lord," 169.
41. And again: "Moreover, without grace it is absolutely impossible for him to love God meritoriously. Such is the rule established by God that no act should be accepted as meritorious unless it be prompted by grace." Biel, "Circumcision of the Lord," 170.

Indispensable to a meritorious act is *liberum arbitrium*. Biel did label grace essential, even the "principal cause of meritorious moral action." Nevertheless, he qualified that the will is never necessitated or determined by grace but can resist and defeat grace. Subsequent grace in the life of those who've done their best and been rewarded by infused grace can even be lost altogether. Grace may prompt but not efficaciously.[42]

Biel called grace the principal cause, but what exactly is grace? When Biel used the word *grace*, he had in mind "love" or "infused love." Love and grace, he said, "are exactly the same."[43] (On this point he differed, by his own admission, from Scotus, who distinguished love from grace.) Furthermore, grace is a "habit, although it is not acquired but infused." Biel explained,

> Grace accomplishes in the soul something similar to the effects of a naturally acquired habit, although in a far more perfect fashion than an acquired habit. The naturally acquired habit is a permanent quality in the power of the soul which stems from frequently repeated acts. This habit prompts and urges the man to repeat the same act. . . . But grace elevates human power beyond itself, so that acts which had been turned by sin toward evil or inward toward one's self now can be meritoriously redirected against the law of the flesh and toward God. Grace leads, assists, and directs in order that man may be prompted in a way which corresponds with divine charity. And thus grace weakens the remaining power of sin, not—as many doctors say—because it forgives or wipes out sins, but because it strengthens human power.[44]

The preacher that he was, Biel used the illustration of a bird trying to fly with a stone attached. Under such conditions, the creature can "scarcely fly away," but "if this bird's wings were strengthened, then we would say that the impediment to flight had been lessened, although the weight of the stone had not been lessened."[45] Similarly, grace infused into man strengthens him to overcome sin that weighs him down. Biel stressed, quite strongly, that this infused grace is a gift from the triune God: "By this grace we are able to remain without difficulty in His friendship, and to grow continually through good works. On such a foundation we can easily overcome the onslaughts of the devil, the world, and flesh, and gain a great reward in store for us."[46]

The Condition of the Covenant

Despite Biel's toil to emphasize the indispensability of God's infused, assisting grace, he ended his sermon, as noted earlier, with a *major* theological qualifier, brief though it may be: "Thus God has established the rule [covenant] that whoever turns to him and does what he can will receive forgiveness of sins from God. God infuses assisting grace into

---

42. Biel appealed to Augustine for support, especially Augustine's illustration of a rider and a horse. It is doubtful that Augustine would have agreed with how Biel appropriated him. Biel, "Circumcision of the Lord," 170.
43. Biel, "Circumcision of the Lord," 171.
44. Biel, "Circumcision of the Lord," 171.
45. Biel, "Circumcision of the Lord," 172.
46. Biel, "Circumcision of the Lord," 173.

such a man, who is thus taken back into friendship."[47] For a sermon that so stresses the import of infused grace, this may appear to be a surprising way to end. Infused, assisting grace may be necessary for justification, but owing to the covenantal arrangement, Biel viewed man doing what he can as a *preliminary step* toward the reception of such grace at all. If man "does what he can," then he "will receive forgiveness," and God will infuse "assisting grace" into him. That is the condition of the covenant, and the parable of the golden ring narrated already seems only to confirm that covenantal condition.

As gracious as it may be for God to infuse grace into man (like a bird suddenly strengthened in its wings by a power outside itself), nevertheless, whether man receives the infused grace at all depends on him doing his best. When Biel said that meritorious acts rely on two factors—*liberum arbitrium* and grace—the former, according to the nature of the covenant, is decisive for procuring the latter. Not only can the Christian lose grace after justification because of the stubborn disinclination of the will, but it would seem possible (likely?) that some may not receive infused grace at all should they not will to do their best in the first place, though Biel never said so in that many words. In short, as gracious as grace may be for Biel once the gift is given, whether the gift is given (and the covenant put into action) is an altogether different matter, one that depends entirely on man turning to God at the start.

From *Meritum De Congruo* to *Merita De Condigno*

Heiko Oberman, the leading medievalist historian to examine Biel's justification theory, has produced an elaborate chart that sets Biel's soteriology within an ecclesiastical framework (see table 21.1). For our purposes, it is the condition of the covenant (*facit quod in se est*) that is relevant and has thus been stressed in bold.

Oberman's visualization of Biel's justification process is illuminating for a variety of reasons. First, Oberman reminds interpreters that for Biel there is, in the sacrament of baptism, a habit of grace that is "infused and substituted for original righteousness." Tragically, man's "relapse" into a "state of mortal sin" undermines such a habit of grace. After baptism, grace is compromised, and a further infusion is needed, though one that depends on man doing his best according to the *pactum* arrangement.

Second, and perhaps most importantly, Oberman confirms that *facit quod in se est* is (ordinarily, *regulariter*) the *causa*, or basis, for infused grace in Biel's mind. Grace

> does not prepare the sinner for the reception of this justifying grace since *grace is not the root but the fruit of the preparatory good works*. . . . This *facere quod in se est* is the necessary disposition for the infusion of grace and implies a movement of the free will, which is at once aversion to sin and love for God according to Eph. 5:14.[48]

---

47. Biel, "Circumcision of the Lord," 173.
48. Oberman, *Harvest of Medieval Theology*, 140, 152. Oberman adds a key clarification as to how Biel understands "grace": "The most important point to be kept in mind for the further presentation of Biel's doctrine of justification is the conclusion that when Biel discusses the necessity of grace in the process of justification, its relation to man's free will, and its relation to the *ex opera operato* efficacy of the sacraments, he has always the *gratia gratum faciens* in mind—by which the sinner is made acceptable to God—and is not thinking of another kind of grace, traditionally often called *gratia gratis data*, the grace of divine vocation, by which the sinner is provided with the proper disposition for the reception of the *gratia gratum faciens*. Biel denies that the sinner would be incapable of providing such a disposition with his own power by doing good works." Oberman, *Harvest of Medieval Theology*, 140.

Table 21.1 [Oberman's] Schema 1: A Chart of the Interrelation of Justification and Predestination*

The Elect [*predestinati*]	Fall	Sacrament of Baptism	The Sinner's Disposition	Sacrament of Penance	Eternal Reward
Those foreknown to fulfill the requirements set in God's eternal decrees [*iustitia dei*]	Original sin [*spoliatus a gratuitis, vulneratus in naturalibus*]	Habit of grace	He does his very best [*facit quod in se est*]	The decisive transition	**Acceptation**
	State of mortal sin; the Virgin Mary exempted	Infused and substituted for original righteousness	**Not necessarily aided by prevenient grace** [*gratia gratis data*]	Confrontation with the preached Word [*ex nova*]	Good works produced in state of grace are necessarily by God's commitment—second decree—**accepted as full merits** [*merita de condigno*]
		Usually a relapse into a state of mortal sin	Ordinarily [*regulariter*] *facere quod in se est* is the basis [*causa*] for infusion	Acquired faith [*fides acquisita*]	They determine man's status in purgatory or heaven
			The Virgin Mary, the apostle Paul, and some others are exceptions to this rule	Supreme love for God [*amor dei super omnia*]	[N.B. The status in purgatory can also be influenced by indulgences acquired from the treasure of the church and applied to members of the church militant, which encompasses not only the living but also the dead who are not *beati*]
			God's general assistance [*influentia generalis*] is necessary for all acts, both good and evil	**God has committed himself—first decree—to reward those who are doing their best** Semi-merit [*meritum de congruo*]	Immediately or eventually *gloria*
				Restoration of the state of grace in anticipation of [*in proposito*] or at time of absolution [*gratia gratum faciens*] by infusion of faith, hope, and love	

* Oberman, *Harvest of Medieval Theology*, 194–95.

The Reprobate [*presciti*]	Fall	Sacrament of Baptism	The Sinner's Disposition	Sacrament of Penance	Eternal Word
Those foreknown not to fulfill the requirements set in God's eternal decrees [*iustitia dei*]	Original sin [*spoliatus a gratuitis, vulneratus in naturalibus*]	Habit of grace	He does not do his very best [*non facit quod in se est*]	*demerita*	Rejection
	State of mortal sin	Infused and substituted for original righteousness	Remains in a state of mortal sin; or if temporarily in a state of grace, he is in a state of sin at the time of his death		Guilt is punished by eternal damnation [*culpa pena damnationis*]
		Usually a relapse into a state of mortal sin	Guilt [*culpa*]		
			God's general assistance [*influentia generalis*] is necessary for all acts, both good and evil		

Within the context of the penance system, "God has committed himself—first decree—to reward those who are doing their very best."[49]

Such a "reward" produces *meritum de congruo*, and the "state of grace" is recovered—either before or during absolution "by infusion of faith, hope, and love." It is *meritum de congruo* that flowers into *merita de condigno*, as agreed on by God himself in his multilayered *pactum* (multilayered because *merita de condigno* is located in God's "second decree"). Therefore, the ordering of *meritum de congruo* and *merita de condigno* is critical, the former being conditioned on man's best works but the latter being acquired as one does one's best within a state of infused grace. Oberman explains,

> Once this genuine love for God's sake is reached, the last obstacle is removed and the road to acceptance is paved by the eternal decrees of God according to which this *facere quod in se est* is first *de congruo* rewarded with the infusion of grace, while then, secondly, acts performed in a state of grace are rewarded *de condigno* with acceptation by God.[50]

Pelagian or Semi-Pelagian? Biel's Interpreters

Since the covenantal condition (*actum facientis quod in se est*) results, if performed, in the gift of infused grace, some interpreters of Biel have labeled this grace a "reward" for prior merit. Though the following description by Steven Ozment focuses on Ockham (in contrast to Aquinas), it can be equally applied to Biel:

> In opposition to [Aquinas and company] making salvation *conditional* upon the presence of a *supernatural habit of grace*, Ockham argued that one could perform works acceptable to God simply *by doing the best one could with one's natural moral ability*. Not only did Ockham believe it possible for those lacking such a habit to love God above all things and detest sin, but he argued further that God found it "fitting" to *reward with an infusion of grace* those who did so. Whereas Aquinas . . . had required the presence of such grace *before* any positive relationship with God could exist, Ockham [and Biel] made the reception of grace a reward for *prior moral effort*. . . . Ockham appeared to free divine acceptance from absolute dependence on infused habits of grace only to make God's will dependent on the good works man could do in his natural moral state. Unassisted ethical cooperation now preceded, as a condition, the infusion of grace, which, with subsequent ethical cooperation, won man salvation. To the traditional mind such an argument was Pelagianism.[51]

Or consider Oberman, whose conclusion is just as affirmative though more nuanced. Oberman concludes that for Biel, "Sin has not made it impossible for man to act without the aid of grace."[52] Yet Biel "can speak in what appears to be such bold

---

49. Oberman, *Harvest of Medieval Theology*, 152.
50. Oberman, *Forerunners*, 184.
51. Ozment, *Age of Reform*, 41–42.
52. Oberman, *Harvest of Medieval Theology*, 164.

Pelagian language about the respective contributions of free will and grace as regards the moral quality of an act because he feels that he brings the full biblical doctrine of grace to bear on the relation of good deeds and meritorious deeds."[53]

Additionally, the *pactum*, by design, is meant to be gracious: "The gratuitous character of God's remuneration is therefore not based on the *activity* of the habit of grace nor on the *presence* of the habit of grace, but on God's decree according to which he has decided to accept every act which is performed in a state of grace as a *meritum de condigno*."[54] As Biel reveals in his commentary on the Mass,

> The infusion of grace is granted to the sinner when he does his very best, not on grounds of a previous pact, but on grounds of God's generosity. Biel invites his auditors and readers to find God's overriding love and sovereignty expressed in the most articulate way, not in the full merit of justice, but in the semi-merit of generosity.[55]

Given the complexity of the *pactum*—a *pactum* initiated by God out of his generosity yet conditioned for its success on man doing his best—Oberman believes he is warranted to conclude that Biel's doctrine of justification is "at once *sola gratia* and *solis operibus*!"

> *By grace alone*—because if God had not decided to adorn man's good works with created and uncreated grace, man would never be saved.
>
> *By works alone*—because not only does man have to produce the framework or substance for this adornment, but God by the two laws of grace is committed, even obliged to add to this framework infused grace and final acceptance. Once man has done his very best, the other two parts follow automatically.
>
> It is clear that the emphasis falls on "justification by works alone"; the concept of "justification by grace alone" is a rational outer structure dependent on the distinction between *potentia absoluta* and *potentia ordinata*.[56]

Oberman chides past historians (e.g., Vignaux, Weijenborg) for allowing Biel's "outer structure" (i.e., the *pactum*) to excuse the Pelagian feel of Biel's inner structure (i.e., man doing his very best). "*It is therefore evident*," Oberman says confidently, "*that Biel's doctrine of justification is essentially Pelagian.*"[57]

---

53. Oberman, *Harvest of Medieval Theology*, 166.
54. Oberman, *Harvest of Medieval Theology*, 170.
55. Strictly speaking, then, Biel "rejects the idea that a sinner is able to earn the first grace *de condigno*: neither with an act that precedes nor with an act caused by this first grace can he do so." We might add, according to Oberman's chart, that *meritum de congruo* is another matter. Oberman, *Harvest of Medieval Theology*, 171.
56. Oberman, *Harvest of Medieval Theology*, 176–77.
57. Oberman, *Harvest of Medieval Theology*, 177. Later, Oberman observes how Biel's Pelagianism makes a doctrine of predestination nonexistent: "As we can gather from the absence of any discussion of predestination in his sermons, this doctrine does not really function in Biel's theology. This should not surprise us. It is the traditional task of the doctrine of predestination proper to form a protective wall around the doctrine of justification by grace alone—a doctrine which does not necessarily imply justification by faith alone. Since we have found that Biel teaches an essentially Pelagian doctrine of justification, absolute predestination is not only superfluous but would even be obstructive. And seen against the background of his doctrine of justification, we can well understand that foreordination would in Biel's hands have to be transformed into foreknowledge." Oberman, *Harvest of Medieval Theology*, 196.

McGrath, however, could not disagree more with Oberman. To understand why, it is necessary to regress briefly into McGrath's portrait of Biel. According to McGrath, Biel's doctrine of *liberum arbitrium* can be summarized as follows:

1. The human free will may choose a morally good act *ex puris naturalibus*, without the need for grace.
2. Humans are able, by the use of their free will and other natural faculties, to implement the law by their own power but are unable to fulfill the law in the precise manner that God intended (that is, *quoad substantiam actus*, but not *quoad intentionem praecipientis*).
3. *Ex puris naturalibus* the free will is able to avoid mortal sin.
4. *Ex puris naturalibus* the free will is able to love God above everything else.
5. *Ex suis naturalibus* the free will is able to dispose itself toward the reception of the gift of grace.

In view of points one and five, why would McGrath disagree with Oberman? McGrath believes the *pactum* itself removes the Pelagian and semi-Pelagian charge, for the existence of the *pactum* is proof that God has taken the first initiative. All that is required of man is a "minimum human response to the divine initiative" in this *pactum*.[58] If the charge of Pelagianism or semi-Pelagianism means "that the *viator* can take the initiative in his own justification, the very existence of the *pactum* deflects the charge; God has taken the initiative away from humans, who are merely required to *respond* to that initiative by the proper exercise of their *liberum arbitrium*."[59]

Furthermore, the presence of the *pactum* itself in Biel's soteriology is absent in historic Pelagianism. Biel and Pelagius, therefore, cannot share a strict alignment. The Pelagian controversy did not have "so sophisticated a concept of causality as that employed by the theologians of the *via moderna*, expressed in the *pactum* theology, so that the applications of epithets such as 'Pelagian' to Biel's theology of justification must be regarded as historically unsound."[60]

Additionally, and perhaps most significantly for McGrath, the charge of Pelagianism is historically untenable since Biel himself was not under suspicion for heresy nor seen as contradicting prior councils. McGrath indirectly accuses Oberman of anachronism, judging it unfair of him to apply "one era's understanding of 'Pelagianism' to another."[61] What criteria would have been used in Biel's day to judge whether he was Pelagian? "The sole legitimate criteria . . . are the canons of the Council of Carthage—the only

---

58. McGrath explains, "As Biel himself makes clear, his discussion of the role of individuals in their own justification must be set within the context of the divine *pactum*. The requirement of a minimum response on the part of the humans of the divine offer of grace is totally in keeping with the earlier Franciscan school's teaching, such as that of Alexander of Hales or Bonaventure. Biel has simply placed his theology of a minimum human response to the divine initiative in justification on a firmer foundation in the theology of the *pactum*, thereby safeguarding God from the charge of capriciousness." *Iustitia Dei*, 100.
59. McGrath, *Iustitia Dei*, 101.
60. McGrath, *Iustitia Dei*, 101.
61. McGrath, *Iustitia Dei*, 100.

criteria which medieval doctors then possessed."[62] Biel simply did not have knowledge of or access to the minutes of the Second Council of Orange. McGrath concludes that if "Biel's theology is to be stigmatized as 'Pelagian' or 'semi-Pelagian,' it must be appreciated that he suffered from a historical accident which affected the entire period up to the Council of Trent itself."[63]

What is to be made of the McGrath-Oberman debate? On the one hand, McGrath makes a fine point about the Council of Carthage, as well as the Second Council of Orange. It would be unfair to hold an individual or movement accountable to documents not possessed. McGrath is also correct that Biel's introduction of the *pactum* defies a strict comparison between the *via moderna* and Pelagianism. The presence of a *pactum* does mean that God's initiation precedes man's, something that Pelagianism cannot say, at least not in the exact same way.

On the other hand, McGrath overlooks several factors and may be guilty of overreacting to Oberman. First, while McGrath accuses others of anachronism, McGrath himself does not entirely pay attention to the historical context and soil in which Biel's theology grew. If the *via moderna*, and with it the theology of the *pactum*, does not begin with Biel but can be traced back to Scotus, Ockham, and Holcot, then it is far too generous to conclude that the charge of Pelagianism crosses a line or would be foreign should it have been lobbed against Biel. One need only revisit the controversy between Holcot and Bradwardine to note the title of Bradwardine's polemical book of 1344: *De causa Dei contra Pelagium*. Even without access to documents from the Second Council of Orange, Bradwardine's work demonstrates that theologians in the fourteenth century (even before Biel) still assumed, and sometimes asserted outright, a certain criterion for whether one had crossed the heretical line. That is a reminder that even if confessional and conciliar documents are absent, the theological content of past theologians or movements is not necessarily lost but often continues. Furthermore, simply because Biel was not charged with the Pelagian heresy in his day does not mean his view is innocent. If that were a valid criterion, then any figure in the history of church to escape public accusations must be considered orthodox.

Second, and perhaps most vitally, is how McGrath downplays the role of *liberum arbitrium* in Biel's *processus iustificationis*. To call *quod in se est* a "minimum human response to the divine initiative," as if mankind is "merely required to *respond* to that initiative by the proper exercise of their *liberum arbitrium*," is not only to overplay the power of the *pactum* prior to infused grace but is also to underplay the magnitude of *liberum arbitrium*. McGrath believes that the positioning of the *pactum* at the start of the *processus iustificationis* eliminates Pelagian tendencies. Yet that is a failure to see how and when the *pactum* actually functions.

It is true that God has taken the initiative by establishing an agreement to reward man's very best. However, that is all it is—an agreement, a promise, a pledge—until man

---

62. McGrath, *Iustitia Dei*, 100.
63. McGrath, *Iustitia Dei*, 100.

does so. Stated otherwise, the *pactum*, as Oberman's chart demonstrates, is never actualized if *non facit quod in se est* ("he does not do his very best"). This is the most common oversight in those who believe Biel has escaped Pelagian or semi-Pelagian tendencies. It is the reason why Oberman admonished older historians. Seeing the "outer structure" (as Oberman calls it) of the *pactum*, they glossed over what we might label the "inner structure," namely, man doing his very best. As generous as the *pactum* may be, it is not and cannot functionally be applied until man does what lies within his power. In that sense, at least according to the "inner structure," it is man who is primary, not God, for God's *pactum* is conditioned on man's best.

It follows that although the *pactum* may have chronological priority, man's *liberum arbitrium* has causal priority, for whether God rewards man with infused grace depends entirely on man's undetermined choice. The *pactum* may issue a promise, but whether it is fulfilled or finds its application in man rests on *liberum arbitrium*—and not just any free act but man's *best* free act. Ironically, Biel's covenantal scheme may intend to protect a voluntarist conception of God, but in the end, it conditions divine sovereignty on human choice.

For that reason, the charge of Pelagianism is not far off the mark, even if the specifics of its alignment be contested. Suppose one softens the label to semi-Pelagianism because of the introduction of the *pactum*; it is still difficult to avoid just how conditioned that *pactum* is on man's best merits. Looking back on the *processus iustificationis* of the ungodly, one might conclude that only semi-Pelagianism applies to Biel since the *pactum* took effect when man did his very best. However, when one reflects on the pilgrimage of the *unjustified*, one realizes that as promising as the *pactum* may have sounded in theory, in reality it meant little since man never did his very best. To play off Biel's imagery, the bird never left the ground. Man's *liberum arbitrium* had the last word. Long before Biel, Aquinas identified the Pelagian heresy only to counter it by claiming that matter "does not move itself to its own perfection; therefore it must be moved by something else."[64] It is difficult to see how Biel could agree when the *pactum* does not actually move anyone but only promises divine movement should man move himself to the best of his abilities.

Luther's Revolt against Biel and the *Via Moderna*

Martin Luther's theological education was birthed out of the womb of the *via moderna*. While Luther was no doubt influenced by a variety of professors, one of the more significant was Johann Nathin. Scott Hendrix believes Nathin was a student of Biel himself, or at least a student who encountered Biel's teaching firsthand.[65] It was at Tübingen that Nathin completed his doctoral degree, and it is most probable that Nathin listened to Biel's lectures.

When Luther studied under Nathin, Nathin assigned to Luther Biel's commentary on the canon of the Mass.[66] Like his teacher, Luther absorbed Biel's soteriology in the

---

64. Thomas Aquinas, *Summa contra Gentiles*, book 3, *Providence*, trans. Vernon J. Bourke (Notre Dame, IN: University of Notre Dame Press, 1975), 3.149.1.
65. Scott H. Hendrix, *Martin Luther: Visionary Reformer* (New Haven, CT: Yale University Press, 2015), 36.
66. Hendrix, *Martin Luther*, 36.

process. So influential was Biel via Nathin that when Luther started lecturing on the Psalms (1513–1515), it was Biel's soteriological assumptions that rose to the surface. For instance, Luther wrote, "The doctors rightly say that, when people do their best, God infallibly gives grace. This cannot be understood as meaning that this preparation for grace is *de condigno* [meritorious], as they are incomparable, but it can be regarded as *de congruo* on account of this promise of God and the covenant [*pactum*] of mercy."[67] Yet Luther wrapped *quod in se est* within a righteousness framework as well:

> Righteousness [*iustitia*] is thus said to be rendering to each what is due to them. Yet equity is prior to righteousness, and is its prerequisite. Equity identifies merit; righteousness renders rewards. Thus the Lord judged the world "in equity" (that is, wishing all to be saved), and judges "in righteousness" (because God renders to each their reward).[68]

Progressively, sometimes slowly, Luther started to take issue with Biel, a turn that would occur as Luther transitioned from lecturing on the Psalms to lecturing on Romans (1515–1516), Galatians (1516–1517), and Hebrews (1517–1518).[69] His lectures at the University of Wittenberg on Romans were the first of the three to signal a shift. He did not speak of the *via moderna* as favorably as before, as Luther sounded considerably more Augustinian. The sinner is not active in the *via moderna* sense—doing his best, or doing what lies within—but passive in the reception of divine grace.[70]

Any hostility to the *via moderna* that remained in seed form in the years 1515–1516 reached its full potential by 1517. Luther went from skeptical to critical, believing the *via moderna* soteriology he had been fed was not only incompatible with a Pauline anthropology and soteriology but the root cause of his frustrations with the late medieval system. Although Franz Günther was to defend a set of theses that year as a requirement to earning his bachelor degree, it was Luther who wrote the theses for public appearance at the University of Wittenberg. These theses, which now bear the title *Disputation against Scholastic Theology*, were presented on September 4, 1517. Harold Grimm observes that they "grew out of" Luther's "commentary on the first book of Aristotle's *Physics*," which he wrote for the purpose of "dethroning the god of the scholastics."[71]

---

67. Martin Luther, *Psalmenvorlesung*, in WA 4:262.4–7 (cf. 3:288.37–289.4). This translation is McGrath's, in *Iustitia Dei*, 116. Cf. Martin Luther, *First Lectures on the Psalms II*, in LW 11:396.
68. Martin Luther, *Psalmenvorlesung (Glossen)*, in WA 55.1:70.9–11. McGrath comments, "Luther here produces the key aspects of Biel's understanding of *iustitia Dei*: *iustitia* is understood to be based upon divine equity, which looks solely to the merits of humans in determining their reward within the framework established by the covenant. The doctors of the church rightly teach that, when people do their best (*quod in se est*), God infallibly gives grace (*hinc recte dicunt doctores, quod homini facienti quod in se est, Deus infallibiliter dat gratiam*). Luther's theological breakthrough is intimately connected with his discovery of a new meaning of the 'righteousness of God,' and it is important to appreciate that his earlier works are characterized by the teaching of the *via moderna* upon this matter. Luther's later view that anyone attempting to do *quod in se est* sinned mortally remains notionally within this framework, while ultimately subverting its theological plausibility." McGrath, *Iustitia Dei*, 88–89. Cf. Luther, *Psalmenvorlesung*, in WA 4:262.4–5.
69. For an extensive study comparing Biel and Luther, see Leif Grane, *Contra Gabrielem: Luthers Auseinandersetzung mit Gabriel Biel in der Disputatio contra scholasticam theologiam, 1517*, ATDan 4 (Copenhagen: Gyldendal, 1962).
70. On this point, see Korey D. Maas, "Justification by Faith Alone," in *Reformation Theology: A Systematic Summary*, ed. Matthew Barrett (Wheaton, IL: Crossway, 2017), 517–18.
71. Harold J. Grimm, "Introduction" to *Disputation against Scholastic Theology*, in LW 31:6.

Disputation against Scholastic Theology (1517)

The *Disputation* begins with an outright contrast between Augustine and Pelagius, recognizing Pelagianism as heretical, a move that may have strategically cast Biel in an unorthodox shadow. The *Disputation* resembles Luther's future work *The Bondage of the Will* in countless ways, the first being Luther's opening theological claim that man is a "bad tree" and that on that basis he "can only will and do evil [cf. Matt. 7:17–18]."[72] That Luther chose man's corrupt identity, and with it his spiritual inability, as his point of departure, immediately situates him against the *via moderna*'s anthropological optimism. Luther thus precluded any attempt to attribute to man the initiation or cooperation of his conversion.

Moreover, Luther asserted not only that man "can only will and do evil" but also that such a necessity of man's inclination to evil is grounded in his nature. The image of a "bad tree" (Matt. 7:17–18) assumes the legitimacy of an Augustinian doctrine of original sin. The will's spiritual ineptitude is not the result of wicked decisions, but the will's perverse acts are due to corruption inherent within (i.e., man's nature). A "free" will was not, therefore, at all entertained by Luther, at least not in the sense it was by Biel. Captivity, on the other hand, is the choice word and concept: "It is false to state," Luther warned, "that man's inclination is free to choose between either of two opposites. Indeed, the inclination is not free, but captive. This is said in opposition to common opinion."[73] Acts that proceed from the will, in other words, should not be defined as if a choice can be made between two egalitarian options: imaginatively, sin or righteousness, or in Luther's world, the devil or God. The inclination of man is captivated, no doubt, by sin, the world, and Satan himself.

Any conception of an ability to do one's best by doing what lies within is nonsensical to Luther since what lies within is nothing but captivity to debauched inclinations. Luther said this much in his next thesis, not only naming Biel but Biel's forerunner, Scotus: "It is false to state that the will can by nature conform to the correct precept. This is said in opposition to Scotus and Gabriel."[74] Man cannot conform "by nature" to God's command since his nature is tainted by Adam's pollution to begin with, enslaving any inclination to righteousness. Unlike Scotus and Biel, Luther held that grace cannot merely be a reward for man doing his best but is necessarily a liberating force that precedes any willful action; in a depraved nature only grace can turn man's passivity into activity. "As a matter of fact," Luther corrected Scotus and Biel, "without the grace of God the will produces an act that is perverse and evil."[75] To qualify, Luther did not mean that the will in itself is evil, as if God created mankind with a skewed will from the start. The will is not, Luther clarified, "by nature evil," or "essentially evil," a view held by the Manichaeans.[76]

---

72. Martin Luther, *Disputation against Scholastic Theology*, in *LW* 31:9 (thesis 4).
73. Luther, *Disputation*, in *LW* 31:9 (thesis 5).
74. Luther, *Disputation*, in *LW* 31:9 (thesis 6).
75. Luther, *Disputation*, in *LW* 31:9 (thesis 7).
76. Luther, *Disputation*, in *LW* 31:9 (thesis 8).

Nevertheless, the will is "innately and inevitably evil and corrupt" and therefore "is not free to strive toward whatever is declared good"—again, a point that is "in opposition to Scotus and Gabriel."[77]

Do not the commands of God assume that one can do one's best or do that which lies within him? Prescription entails ability, does it not? To the contrary, says Luther, the will is not "able to will or not to will whatever is prescribed."[78] It is man's duty to love his Creator, but postfall it is "absurd to conclude that erring man can love the creature above all things," despite what "Scotus and Biel" claim.[79] If Jesus is right that man is a "bad tree," then it is not "surprising that the will can conform to erroneous and not to correct precept."[80] One must conclude, Luther insisted, that "since erring man is able to love the creature it is impossible for him to love God."[81] Luther could not state man's inability and captivity any stronger.

It may be tempting to think that Luther's concept of captivity eliminates the will altogether. That would be inaccurate. For Luther, the matter is not whether the will exists or acts but what it is *capable* of acting for or against. Desire is the issue. Whether the will desires to love God is what is impossible after the fall. The problem concerns what man does and does not *want*. Or as Luther explains, "Man is by nature unable to want God to be God."[82] Present in Luther's argument is a twofold emphasis: (1) man does not desire or want to love God, but (2) the corruption of his nature means he is unable and incapable of wanting to want to love God—"To love God above all things by nature is a fictitious term, a chimera, as it were."[83]

Biel used the concept of friendship to frame the covenant that God conditioned on man doing his best (i.e., *actum facientis quod in se est*). Luther, however, was convinced that Biel misunderstood *why* such friendship is possible to begin with. It has nothing to do with the capabilities of man's nature but is dependent entirely on divine grace: "An act of friendship is done, not according to nature, but according to prevenient grace. This in opposition to Gabriel." Luther further stressed the relation between will and nature when he concluded, "No act is done according to nature that is not an act of concupiscence against God."[84] For the unregenerate, will and nature work together in harmony prior to conversion, but such an agreement between the two is only in the direction of unrighteousness. Man's nature sets his will and the acts that follow on a course to destruction. No harmony exists, not yet at least, between nature and will that would lead the ungodly down the road of eternal life. Only divine grace can shift man's trajectory, for only grace can liberate man's nature, and the will with it, from not wanting God to be God.

---

77. Luther, *Disputation*, in *LW* 31:9 (theses 9, 10).
78. Luther, *Disputation*, in *LW* 31:10 (thesis 11).
79. Luther, *Disputation*, in *LW* 31:10 (thesis 13).
80. Luther, *Disputation*, in *LW* 31:10 (thesis 14).
81. Luther, *Disputation*, in *LW* 31:10 (thesis 16).
82. Luther, *Disputation*, in *LW* 31:10 (thesis 17).
83. Luther, *Disputation*, in *LW* 31:10 (thesis 18).
84. Luther, *Disputation*, in *LW* 31:10 (theses 20, 21). In thesis 23, Luther adds, "Nor is it true that an act of concupiscence can be set aright by the virtue of hope. This in opposition to Gabriel."

Luther named Biel eleven times in the *Disputation* (Scotus only four times). Biel is not named in the one thesis that most directly attacks the scholastic's soteriology, thesis 26: "An act of friendship is not the most perfect means for *accomplishing that which is in one*." Luther nearly quoted Biel's exact phraseology. Luther then wrote, "Nor is it the most perfect means for obtaining the grace of God or turning toward and approaching God."[85] Instead, "it is an act of conversion already perfected, following grace both in time and by nature."[86]

Yet does not a legion of passages prioritize man's effort—that is, "accomplishing that which is in one"—to return, draw near, and seek as that which is prerequisite to God responding with grace (cf. Jer. 29:13; Zech. 1:3; Matt. 7:7; James 4:8)? Luther warned that if such texts are interpreted in such a way, then we differ not from the "Pelagians" and what they "have said."[87] Rather than crediting man as he who does that "which is in" himself, clearly the motivating factor in God bestowing grace in Biel's soteriology, Luther bypassed man's will altogether and traveled back in eternity to credit the electing grace of God instead: "The best and infallible preparation for grace and the sole disposition toward grace is the eternal election and predestination of God."[88]

While Biel pointed to man's best as that which must precede the infusion of divine grace, Luther observed that if the spotlight is focused on man, all one will find is a will disinclined to God, inclined only to rebel against God: "On the part of man, however, nothing precedes grace except indisposition and even rebellion against grace."[89] Indisposition, not disposition, is the reason why God's predestining grace in eternity must be the cause of man's reception of grace in time and space. Appeal to predestination is the only way forward. It is but a false hope to think "that doing all that one is able to do"—again, Luther quoted Biel precisely—"can remove the obstacles to grace."[90] Despite what the "philosophers" imagine, we "are not masters of our actions, from beginning to end, but servants."[91] Servitude is what defines the will, but it is a matter of which master the will must serve.

Luther did not directly address Biel's covenantal conception. The closest he came is thesis 55: "The grace of God is never present in such a way that it is inactive, but it is a living, active, and operative spirit; nor can it happen that through the absolute power of God an act of friendship may be present without the presence of the grace of God. This in opposition to Gabriel."[92] Although Biel's *pactum* remained unnamed, Luther's language did seem to assume his knowledge of such a *pactum*. Identifying the "absolute power of God" (*potentia Dei absoluta*) is one indicator. When Luther denied

---

85. Luther, *Disputation*, in *LW* 31:10 (thesis 26).
86. Luther, *Disputation*, in *LW* 31:11 (thesis 27).
87. Luther, *Disputation*, in *LW* 31:11 (thesis 28).
88. Luther, *Disputation*, in *LW* 31:11 (thesis 29).
89. Luther, *Disputation*, in *LW* 31:11 (thesis 30).
90. Luther, *Disputation*, in *LW* 31:11 (thesis 33).
91. Luther, *Disputation*, in *LW* 31:11 (thesis 39).
92. Luther, *Disputation*, in *LW* 31:13 (thesis 55).

that absolute power can put forward a friendship without grace being actually present, he seemed to have in mind Biel's *ordo*, in which God proposes a "friendship" via the establishment of a *pactum* but does not actually bestow infused grace until man does his best. "Inactive" grace and grace not "present" are Luther's way of criticizing Biel's belief that God can look gracious by presenting a *pactum* while withholding infused grace until man does his best.

Despite thesis 55, Luther mostly focused on Biel's articulation of law and grace, which is unsurprising given how law and gospel would be defining characteristics of Luther's hermeneutic. Luther was persuaded not merely that Biel misunderstood the proper role of law and grace but that Biel turned grace into law, which is the same charge Augustine leveled against Pelagius and his disciples centuries earlier. In a series of theses, Luther explained his reasoning:

> 57. It is dangerous to say that the law commands that an act of obeying the commandment be done in the grace of God. This in opposition to the Cardinal and Gabriel.
> 58. From this it would follow that "to have the grace of God" is actually a new demand going beyond the law.
> 59. It would also follow that fulfilling the law can take place without the grace of God.
> 60. Likewise it follows that the grace of God would be more hateful than the law itself.
> 61. It does not follow that the law should be complied with and fulfilled in the grace of God. This in opposition to Gabriel.[93]

Thesis 59 was especially poignant for Luther. As much as God might establish a "friendship" by his absolute power, grace remains inactive and operationally absent if it is conditioned on man doing his best in obedience to the law. Luther countered by stressing not only the necessity of grace but also its prevenient character as long as man's inclinations follow his corrupt nature:

> 68. Therefore, it is impossible to fulfill the law in any way without the grace of God.
> 69. As a matter of fact, it is more accurate to say that the law is destroyed by nature without the grace of God.
> 70. A good law will of necessity be bad for the natural will.
> 71. Law and will are two implacable foes without the grace of God.
> 72. What the law wants, the will never wants, unless it pretends to want it out of fear or love.
> 73. The law, as taskmaster of the will, will not be overcome except by the "child, who has been born to us" [Isa. 9:6].
> 74. The law makes sin abound because it irritates and repels the will [Rom. 7:13].

---

93. Luther, *Disputation*, in *LW* 31:13.

75. The grace of God, however, makes justice abound through Jesus Christ because it causes one to be pleased with the law.
76. Every deed of the law without the grace of God appears good outwardly, but inwardly it is sin. This in opposition to the scholastics.
77. The will is always averse to, and the hands inclined toward, the law of the Lord without the grace of God.[94]

Then came Luther's most critical point:

79. Condemned are all those who do the works of the law.

Luther may not have been articulating his mature understanding of law and gospel (a point we will return to shortly). Nevertheless, the seed had been planted in these theses, and it was Biel who had watered the soil.

For Luther, law and will are antithetical *as long as* the will is captivated to Adam's nature. "Since the law is good," Luther later explained, "the will, which is hostile to it, cannot be good. And from this it is clear that everyone's natural will is iniquitous and bad."[95] The will can only be (and is only) reconciled with the law if grace itself mediates between the two.[96] In three consecutive theses, Luther corrected Biel:

90. The grace of God is given for the purpose of directing the will, lest it err even in loving God. In opposition to Gabriel.
91. It is not given so that good deeds might be induced more frequently and readily, but because without it no act of love is performed. In opposition to Gabriel.
92. It cannot be denied that love is superfluous if man is by nature able to do an act of friendship. In opposition to Gabriel.[97]

Biel believed that the will can act in love toward God, but Luther, with the full captivity of the will in mind, countered that the will is completely misdirected and will love God only if grace intervenes at the start. Biel assumed that the will can act, taking steps in a Godward direction, only for grace to then come along and spur the will on to take further steps. To play off Biel's previous illustration, the bird does the best he can to start flying, and if he does his best at flying, God will reward such effort by infusing strength into that bird's wings so that he might fly better and more acceptably.

Luther never addressed the bird illustration, but if he had, based on these theses, he might have colloquially quipped, "Biel, you make a moot point. This bird cannot fly. So damaged are its wings that this bird is grounded." Grace must be primary, prevenient, and, as Luther later came to state in his *Bondage of the Will*, effectual. Otherwise, the

---

94. Luther, *Disputation*, in *LW* 31:14.
95. Luther, *Disputation*, in *LW* 31:15 (theses 87, 88).
96. Luther, *Disputation*, in *LW* 31:15 (thesis 89).
97. Luther, *Disputation*, in *LW* 31:15.

will remains enslaved to its corrupt nature. Hence thesis 92: should man "by nature" be able to initiate friendship with God, then love itself is "superfluous."[98]

Facere Quod In Se Est, the Crisis of Assurance of Salvation, and the Necessity of *Amor Dei Super Omnia*

Luther's *Disputation* rarely, if ever, explores how Biel's soteriology might influence, or be influenced by, the atonement. While Luther's *theologia crucis* would be forcefully present in his other treatises, in this 1517 debate it was not at the forefront of Luther's argument.

Nevertheless, it is not unrelated, nor did Luther fail to connect one *locus* to another. Prior to 1517, not only was Luther raised on the *via moderna* in the classroom, but he also attempted to put it into practice in his own spiritual struggle to find a gracious God. Doing so, however, drove Luther to the edge of insanity. If the benefits of the cross—acceptance with God and infused grace—were withheld until one did one's best, then how was one to ever know if he had done his best? How would one know if *non facit quod in se est* was the real outcome of one's effort? That is a question Biel left unanswered, but one that drove Luther mad, unsure whether his assurance of salvation was justified or illegitimate. As Grimm clarifies,

> Although Luther thought highly of Ockham and Biel, he could not accept their doctrines of freedom of the will, good works, and justification. Ockham and Biel believed that man by nature could will to love God above all things and prepare the way for God's saving grace. Since, according to them, Christ's work of atonement became operative only after man had proven himself worthy of it, Luther could not be certain that he would be saved.[99]

One might be sure that God would reward grace if one did one's best, but one could never be sure that one had ever done one's best—that is, whether one's "best" really was one's best—in order to qualify for such a reward. Such a crisis over assurance can be traced back to the type of love that must be present in the act of doing one's best, namely, *super omnia*. Oberman explains:

> To desire God's help is doing one's very best, and those fallen Christians who in this way detest sin and adhere to God their creator may be certain that God will grant them grace, thus freeing them from the bonds of sin. But although a sinner may be certain of God's mercy in granting his grace to those who do their very best, he has no certainty that he has in fact done his very best. The standard required is a love of God for God's sake, that is, an undefiled love: *super omnia*. It is this last condition in particular which makes it practically impossible to know with certainty that one has really reached the stage of the *facere quod in se est*.[100]

---
98. Luther, *Disputation*, in *LW* 31:15.
99. Grimm, "Introduction," in *LW* 31:6.
100. Oberman, *Harvest of Medieval Theology*, 133.

Fast forward to Luther again: Luther's early struggle was one over *super omnia*. No matter how sincere his love for God or his repentance of sin, Luther never knew if his thoughts, words, and actions were truly conceived out of an "undefiled love." He could see a million ways, real and hypothetical, that his love might be defiled by the remaining residue of his sinful nature. That was an existential problem inherent in Biel's *pactum*. Supreme love for God—*amor Dei super omnia*—is essential, but Luther found it impossible to attain.

We might also add that Biel's voluntarist system only created further distress for those who so rigorously applied it to the Christian's trust in the character of a gracious God. Biel claimed that God was absolutely free (i.e., *potentia Dei absoluta*) to establish or not establish a covenant by which man might be accepted with God should he do his best. Nevertheless, once he entered into such a covenant, he was obligated to come through on the agreement of his *pactum* (i.e., *potentia Dei ordinata*, or ordinate power).

Or was he? Could God go back on his *pactum*? If God's will always has priority over his intellect, then what would stop God from prioritizing his absolute freedom rather than continuing with the *pactum* that binds him to certain salvific benefits? Could God decide, according to *potentia Dei absoluta*, that he might remove justifying grace at some point? Oberman and McGrath, both examining Biel's *pactum*, think not, and they would be right.[101] However, at a popular level people in late medieval Europe may not have been so careful with such nuances when applying the *via moderna*.

It is conceivable that for the average late medieval Christian, a voluntarist God would be difficult to reconcile with absolute assurance of salvation in the Christian life. Luther's existential crisis, he believed, was proof enough. And as he witnessed at the pastoral level, the combination of voluntarism and justification could potentially create untold angst in those seriously committed to doing their best. Would a lifetime of striving to achieve one's best be undermined should God change his will on a whim? Technically, based on Scotus, Ockham, and Biel, the answer was no. But pastorally, what was to keep the average medieval Christian from taking a voluntarist conception to its logical extreme, wondering (worrying) if God would, in the end, honor his *pactum*? These are the types of questions that rationally flowed out of a *via moderna* mentality, regardless of whether the *via moderna* really taught their validity. Lutheran theologian Korey Maas highlights just how problematic the situation had become in Luther's day:

> Thus, at least in theory, God could justify sinners even without the bestowal of his grace and their subsequent cooperation. Further, and more worryingly, the opposite was also understood to be the case: being bound by no necessity, God might deny salvation even to those who cooperate with the grace he has provided. Ockham's reasoning, following that of his predecessor Duns Scotus, was that "nothing created must, for reasons intrinsic to it, be accepted by God." That is, neither grace nor one's cooperation with it are deserving of salvation in and of themselves; they are accepted

---

101. Oberman, *Harvest of Medieval Theology*, 169–72; McGrath, *Iustitia Dei*, 87.

and rewarded only because God has voluntarily agreed to do so. Ultimately, then, one's salvation was understood to be dependent not only upon divine grace together with human cooperation but also, and most fundamentally, upon God's keeping his promise to regard these as meriting eternal life.[102]

Only when Luther abandoned the anthropological and soteriological presuppositions of the *via moderna* altogether and discovered instead that one is justified not by doing one's best but through faith alone did Luther then possess assurance of his right standing with God. Or as Grimm says,

> Such certainty came only with his discovery of justification by faith alone. This basic insight led him to repudiate scholasticism as a whole. Because he believed that it actually hindered God's work of saving man he vehemently attacked the schoolmen, Aristotle, and reason.[103]

One must forgive Luther if his rhetoric was aggressively antischolastic, for he felt a heavy sense of disgust for the way its schoolmen and their heirs had led not only Luther but the church to hell (Luther was convinced that heaven and hell hung in the balance). Luther had imbibed its theology, and his soul, by his own admission, was nearly damned in the process. Luther's breakthrough is often pictured in positive terms (he discovered *sola gratia* and *sola fide*), but it could equally be portrayed in negative terms (he discovered his reading of Paul had been skewed by the scholasticism others had taught him). While Luther's break with Biel may have had more to do with his understanding of law and gospel than a mature covenantalism, Luther had touched the raw nerve of the *via moderna*, exposing its instability.

In the variegated nexus of the Biel-Luther debate, that raw nerve and instability came down to one central issue: Biel assumed the power and freedom of the will. Lecturing on Romans, Luther came to a different conception of not only the righteousness of God but also the unrighteousness of man. Consequently, Luther's greatest argument against Biel was the same argument he would put forward against Erasmus: the will is captive.[104] Biel's entire covenantal, voluntarist view of justification crumbled with that one anthropological premise, a premise Luther was absolutely sure originated not merely from Augustine but from Scripture itself. And Scripture was, without a doubt, Luther's magisterial authority, as his turn to *sola scriptura* during those formative years manifests.[105]

Early Luther: Augustinian but Not yet Pauline

We would be mistaken to conclude, however, that in his 1517 *Disputation*, Luther had come to his mature understanding of forensic justification. Evidently, Luther had

---

102. Maas, "Justification by Faith Alone," 516.
103. Grimm, "Introduction," in *LW* 31:6.
104. See my lengthy treatment of the Luther-Erasmus debate: Matthew Barrett, "The Bondage and Liberation of the Will," in Barrett, *Reformation Theology*, 451–510. There I explore the type of freedom Luther affirmed. It was not Biel's "inalienable spontaneity," to use Oberman's phrase. Oberman, *Harvest of Medieval Theology*, 161.
105. See Matthew Barrett, *God's Word Alone: The Authority of Scripture; What the Reformers Taught . . . and Why It Still Matters*, Five Solas Series (Grand Rapids, MI: Zondervan, 2016), 33–52.

converted to a different tribe, shifting away from the *via moderna* to the *schola Augustiniana moderna* in some form. Doing so not only meant establishing the captivity of the will but recapturing the primacy, necessity, and sovereignty of grace.

Nevertheless, justification was still a *transformative process* in which man was *made* righteous in his nature. That belief—which all medieval Christianity assumed—would quickly disintegrate the closer Luther approached excommunication from Rome. Even so, in his *Disputation*, there were signs, though they be minuscule, that Luther had not yet reached his mature doctrine of justification. He wrote,

> 40. We do not become righteous by doing righteous deeds but, having been made righteous, we do righteous deeds. This in opposition to the philosophers.[106]

And,

> 54. For an act to be meritorious, either the presence of grace is sufficient, or its presence means nothing. This in opposition to Gabriel.[107]

One should not read too much into theses like these as Luther's intent is more polemical than didactic. At the same time, they do serve as benchmarks in Luther's journey to a forensic doctrine of justification, and it appears he had not yet arrived at this point. Grace may be prevenient, primary, and even effectual in the Augustinian sense, yet it does not exclude meritorious acts but instead enables them in the process of inner renewal. In a real sense, one must "become righteous."

Luther corrected Biel's *ordo*, crediting God, not man: "Having been made righteous, we do righteous deeds." The righteousness of God, therefore, is a gift, a notion present one or two years earlier in Luther's *Lectures on Romans* (1515–1516).[108] Still, justification is an intrinsic transformation, an assumption Luther would eventually abandon when, through Paul, he came to see that justification cannot be the renovation of one's nature. Instead, it is a change in one's status, a legal declaration that one is righteous on account of the righteousness of another, namely, Christ. If justification and sanctification were not always distinguished in medieval thought, the Reformers would refine the two, noting their distinction, though without sacrificing their inseparability. That started with Luther.

Exactly when Luther arrived at his mature, forensic doctrine of justification and imputation is disputed. In a recent study, however, Maas makes a strong case that it did not happen until 1518 or later. Maas supports his claim by pointing to Luther's *Lectures on Hebrews*, which, like his *Lectures on Romans*, still teaches a "progressive and sanative scheme formulated by Augustine and embraced by virtually all medieval theologians."[109] As Luther said in those lectures, the ungodly are righteous "not because they are, but because they have begun to be and should become people of this kind by

---

106. Luther, *Disputation*, in *LW* 31:12 (thesis 40).
107. Luther, *Disputation*, in *LW* 31:13 (thesis 54).
108. E.g., Martin Luther, *Lectures on Romans*, in *LW* 25:496.
109. Maas, "Justification by Faith Alone," 519.

making constant progress."¹¹⁰ By 1521, however, Luther switched his definition of grace from "an inherent quality or substance by which one is prepared to become righteous" to "favor of God," language present in Luther's work *Against Latomus*.¹¹¹

What pushed Luther beyond such an Augustinian conception of the medieval era to an altogether different paradigm? Maas is persuaded that it was the addition of Philipp Melanchthon to the Wittenberg faculty, a claim that strikes against twentieth-century Luther scholarship that attempted to read discontinuity between the two Reformers but one that is consistent with older Luther scholarship that defended continuity.

> The impetus for this sudden change almost certainly lay with the recently arrived Melanchthon, who from at least 1520 was making the case for understanding grace as God's favor or good will. He did so perhaps most clearly in the same year that Luther first embraced this definition, in the first edition of his *Loci Communes*, where he wrote that "the word 'grace' does not mean some quality in us, but rather the very will of God, or the goodwill of God toward us." This articulation in Melanchthon's *Loci* is significant not only because this work may justifiably be considered the first "systematic theology" of the Reformation but also because it profoundly influenced Luther, who regularly expressed his unreserved agreement with it, going so far as to assert hyperbolically that it deserved to be canonized.¹¹²

Maas goes on to give an extensive defense of this claim by appealing to Luther's dependence on Melanchthon for his interpretation of Hebrews 11, a chapter that would move Luther to rethink the biblical definition of πίστις ("faith").

As Luther progressively redefined grace and faith, as well as the righteousness of God, his doctrine of justification transitioned from a process to a declaration, from infusion to imputation, and from active to passive righteousness. Though ungodly, he who looks not to his own works but trusts (*sola fide*) in the perfect work of Christ alone (*solus Christus*) not only has the total penalty of his sins forgiven but has imputed to him a new status, namely, the righteous status of the infallible Mediator. With imputation, justification now became instantaneous and forensic, rather than a gradual, metaphysical renewal. Luther wrote in his 1535 *Lectures on Galatians*,

> But [contrary to the scholastics] this most excellent righteousness, the righteousness of faith, which God imputes to us through Christ without works, is neither political nor ceremonial nor legal nor work-righteousness but is quite the opposite; it is a merely passive righteousness, while all the others, listed above, are active. For here we work nothing, render nothing to God; we only receive and permit someone else to work in us, namely, God. Therefore it is appropriate to call the righteousness of faith or Christian righteousness "passive."¹¹³

---

110. Martin Luther, *Lectures on Hebrews*, in LW 29:139.
111. Maas, "Justification by Faith Alone," 520. See Martin Luther, *Against Latomus*, in LW 32:227.
112. Maas, "Justification by Faith Alone," 521, quoting Philipp Melanchthon, *Loci Communes Theologici* (1521), in *Melanchthon and Bucer*, ed. Wilhelm Pauck, trans. Lowell J. Satre, LCC 19 (Philadelphia: Westminster, 1969), 87.
113. Martin Luther, *Lectures on Galatians* (1535), in LW 26:5.

A forensic notion of imputation was the key that opened heaven's paradise because it provided Luther with the very thing he could not find no matter how many times he did his best, namely, Christian assurance:

> Therefore the afflicted conscience has no remedy against despair and eternal death except to take hold of the promise of grace offered in Christ, that is, this righteousness of faith, this passive or Christian righteousness, which says with confidence: "I do not seek active righteousness. I ought to have and perform it; but I declare that even if I did have it and perform it, I cannot trust in it or stand up before the judgment of God on the basis of it. Thus I put myself beyond all active righteousness, all righteousness of my own or of the divine Law, and I embrace only that passive righteousness which is the righteousness of grace, mercy, and the forgiveness of sins." In other words, this is the righteousness of Christ and of the Holy Spirit, which we do not perform but receive, which we do not have but accept, when God the Father grants it to us through Jesus Christ.[114]

After an early struggle attempting to apply Biel's justification theology to the Christian life, only to lose Christian assurance in the process, Luther had found peace with God and it came from outside himself (that is, *extra nos*), though never outside his Savior (*extra Christum*).

Facientibus Quod In Se Est Deus Non Denegat Gratiam: Good News?

Facientibus quod in se est Deus non denegat gratiam—"God does not withhold his grace from those who do their very best."[115] To Biel, that motto is good news. God will give grace; people just need to do their very best. For Luther, that motto is a death sentence, the worst news possible. Not only can one never know if he has done his best, but the scriptural witness is unambiguous: man lacks the spiritual ability to do his best to begin with. The only possible outcome is damnation. Luther hated God because God hung grace out like the sweet nectar of a flower in front of a hummingbird, an illustration Biel cherished in preaching to his parishioners. Yet Luther knew from watching his parishioners run to the indulgence tables what a false hope that proved to be. As promising as the nectar may have been, the bird could not fly.

For the bird to fly, an alternative paradigm was necessary, and it would prove revolutionary for Luther and all Protestantism to follow. Biel was correct that a divine *pactum* was essential if justification was to be gracious. However, Biel fundamentally erred by concluding that the *pactum* had to be contingent on man doing his very best, an impossibility for an enslaved will. Rather, the success of the *pactum* depended entirely on the best of another, one who could obey the law perfectly in the place of the ungodly. So worthy, so perfect, and so inherently valuable and sufficient were the

---

114. Luther, *Lectures on Galatians* (1535), in *LW* 26:5–6.
115. Or, *Facienti quod in se est Deus non denegat gratiam*—"God does not deny grace to the person who does what is in him."

works of this substitute that God need not turn a blind eye to justice or prioritize his will in order to accept that which was inherently unacceptable. The obedience of the Son was counted perfectly sufficient by the Father, enabling him, as Paul says, to be both "just and the justifier of the one who has faith in Jesus" (Rom. 3:26). Justification, in the end, was based on works, but contrary to Biel, Luther discovered that it was not the works of man but the works of the God-man, the sinless High Priest, the Lord Jesus Christ. In Christ alone was the gospel to be found. Should that good news be weighed down, even in the slightest way, by the works of man, it would cease to be good news at all:

> There is a clear and present danger that the devil may take away from us the pure doctrine of faith and may substitute for it the doctrines of works and of human traditions. It is very necessary, therefore, that this doctrine of faith be continually read and heard in public. . . . This doctrine can never be discussed and taught enough. If it is lost and perishes, the whole knowledge of truth, life, and salvation is lost and perishes at the same time. But if it flourishes, everything good flourishes—religion, true worship, the glory of God, and the right knowledge of all things and of all social conditions.[116]

Recommended Resources

Aquinas, Thomas. *Nature and Grace: Selections from the "Summa Theologica."* Edited by A. M. Fairweather, Library of Christian Classics 11. Louisville: Westminster John Knox, 1954.

Barrett, Matthew. "The Bondage and Liberation of the Will." In *Reformation Theology: A Systematic Summary*, edited by Matthew Barrett, 451–510. Wheaton, IL: Crossway, 2017.

Biel, Gabriel. *Canonis missae expositio.* Edited by Heiko A. Oberman and William J. Courtenay. 4 vols. Wiesbaden: Steiner, 1963–1967.

———. "The Circumcision of the Lord." In Oberman, *Forerunners*, 165–74.

Bradwardine, Thomas. *De Causa Dei contra Pelagium.* Edited by Henry Savile. Frankfurt: de Gruyter, 1964.

Davies, Brian. *Thomas Aquinas's Summa Theologiae: A Guide and Commentary.* New York: Oxford University Press, 2014.

Grane, Leif. *Contra Gabrielem: Luthers Auseinandersetzung mit Gabriel Biel in der Disputatio contra scholasticam theologiam, 1517.* Acta Theologica Danica 4. Copenhagen: Gyldendal, 1962.

Grimm, Harold J. "Introduction" to *Disputation against Scholastic Theology.* In *LW* 31:xv–xxii.

Hendrix, Scott H. *Martin Luther: Visionary Reformer.* New Haven, CT: Yale University Press, 2015.

Holcot, Robert. "Lectures on the Wisdom of Solomon." In Oberman, *Forerunners*, 142–50.

---

116. Luther, *Lectures on Galatians* (1535), in *LW* 26:3.

Leff, Gordon. *Bradwardine and the Pelagians: A Study of His "De Causa Dei" and Its Opponents*. Cambridge Studies in Medieval Life and Thought 5. Cambridge: Cambridge University Press, 1957.

Luther, Martin. *Lectures on Galatians* (1535). Vol. 26 of *LW*.

———. *Lectures on Hebrews*. In *LW* 29:107–241.

———. *Lectures on Romans*. Vol. 25 of *LW*.

———. *Luther's Works* (herein *LW*). Edited by Jaroslav Pelikan and Helmut T. Lehmann. American ed. 82 vols. (projected). Philadelphia: Fortress; Saint Louis, MO: Concordia, 1955–.

Maas, Korey D. "Justification by Faith Alone." In *Reformation Theology: A Systematic Summary*, edited by Matthew Barrett, 511–48. Wheaton, IL: Crossway, 2017.

McGrath, Alister E. *Iustitia Dei: A History of the Christian Doctrine of Justification*. 3rd ed. Cambridge: Cambridge University Press, 2005.

Melanchthon, Philipp. *Loci Communes Theologici* (1521). In *Melanchthon and Bucer*, edited by Wilhelm Pauck, translated by Lowell J. Satre, 1–151. Library of Christian Classics 19. Philadelphia: Westminster, 1969.

Oberman, Heiko A., ed. *Forerunners of the Reformation: The Shape of Late Medieval Thought, Illustrated by Key Documents*. Philadelphia: Fortress, 1981.

———. *The Harvest of Medieval Theology: Gabriel Biel and Late Medieval Nominalism*. Grand Rapids, MI: Eerdmans, 1962.

———, ed. *Luther and the Dawn of the Modern Era*. Leiden: Brill, 1974.

———. *Masters of the Reformation: The Emergence of a New Intellectual Climate in Europe*. Translated by Dennis Martin. Cambridge: Cambridge University Press, 1981.

Ozment, Steven. *The Age of Reform, 1250–1550: An Intellectual and Religious History of Late Medieval and Reformation Europe*. New Haven, CT: Yale University Press, 1980.

21

The First and Chief Article

Luther's Discovery of *Sola Fide* and Its Controversial Reception in Lutheranism

KOREY MAAS

Though it was not in fact Martin Luther—despite the still popular (mis)understanding—who coined the concise formula denominating justification as "the doctrine on which the church stands or falls,"[1] it remains true that this formula does indeed capture Luther's own thinking about what he would call "the first and chief article"[2] and the "central article of our teaching."[3] Also true, however, is that this was not always Luther's understanding of justification's place in the life and theology of the Christian church. Or at least this was not always his explicit and articulated understanding. It was certainly the case, as he would later recount, that even while a faithful friar of the Order of Augustinian Hermits, his most pressing and personal concern was to answer the question of how to find a gracious God.[4] Yet it was precisely the evident uncertainty concerning the answer to this question that prevented any early consideration of it being *the* central article of the Christian faith. Further militating against such a conclusion was, quite simply, its apparent novelty. A review of the standard theological texts in use in the late fifteenth and early sixteenth centuries yields the same conclusion at which

---

1. The earliest extant use of the phrase appears to be that of Johann Heinrich Alsted in 1618; see Alister E. McGrath, *Iustitia Dei: A History of the Christian Doctrine of Justification*, 2nd ed. (Cambridge: Cambridge University Press, 1998), 448n3. Luther does, however, use very similar formulas. See, e.g., his *Lectures on the Gradual Psalms* (1532–33), in WA 40.3:352.
2. "Smalcald Articles," 2, in *BOC*, 301.
3. Luther, *Lectures on the Gradual Psalms*, in WA 40.3:335.
4. See, e.g., Martin Luther, *Table Talk*, in *LW* 54:95 (no. 518).

Jesuit theologian Avery Dulles arrived upon reviewing those of the twentieth century: "Justification is not a central category in contemporary Catholic dogmatics."[5]

Despite frequent talk of Luther's "breakthrough" or "discovery," which can give the impression of an immediate moment of clarification, it was only a series of discoveries and a gradual development of his thought that allowed Luther finally to confess a doctrine of justification warranting its description as the central category of his own theology. In other words, justification's eventual *place* was entirely dependent on its *nature*. And the nature of Luther's mature doctrine of justification, that which would also become enshrined in the formal confessions of the Lutheran church, took shape over more than a decade of study, teaching, preaching, and debating. As R. Scott Clark has rightly emphasized, "Luther's doctrine of justification was one thing in 1513 and became another by 1536."[6] Even in 1513, though, Luther was not starting from scratch. Justification may not have been a "central category" in the theology of his late medieval milieu, but it was by no means an ignored or unimportant category. Indeed, at least partially responsible for Luther's own early uncertainty, and even despair, were the greatly diverse and intensely debated theologies of justification prominent in his day. Before taking up Luther and the Lutheran tradition, then, it is beneficial to survey at least briefly the complex theological context in which he lived and moved.

The Medieval Milieu

Scholastic Diversity

It has become customary—at least since Pope Pius V named him a "doctor of the church," and especially since Pope Leo XIII called on Roman Catholic theologians to "restore the golden wisdom of St. Thomas"[7]—to think of the thirteenth-century Dominican theologian Thomas Aquinas as the epitome and exemplar of medieval theology, especially the systematic "scholastic" theology of the universities. Though in some respects this is certainly true, it is also in important respects an anachronism that can obscure rather than clarify the theology of the medieval church and therefore the context out of which Luther's own theology gradually emerged. There is no doubt that, even in the later Middle Ages, Aquinas was an enormously respected and influential thinker, especially within his own Dominican order. Tendencies to view him as *the* representative of medieval orthodoxy, however, fail to appreciate what has rightly been described as a "lack of theological clarity"[8] and an "endemic doctrinal plurality in the later medieval period."[9] Illustrative confusion with respect to the evaluation of Aquinas himself

---

5. Avery Dulles, "Justification in Contemporary Catholic Theology," in *Justification by Faith*, ed. H. George Anderson, T. Austin Murphy, and Joseph A. Burgess, Lutherans and Catholics in Dialogue 7 (Minneapolis: Augsburg, 1985), 256.
6. R. Scott Clark, "*Iustitia Imputata Christi*: Alien or Proper to Luther's Doctrine of Justification," *CTQ* 70, nos. 3/4 (2006): 273.
7. Leo XIII, *Aeterni Patris*, in *Compendium of Creeds, Definitions, and Declarations on Matters of Faith and Morals*, compiled by Heinrich Denzinger, ed. Peter Hünermann with Helmut Hoping, Latin-English ed., 43rd ed. (San Francisco: Ignatius, 2012), 1880.
8. Joseph Lortz, "Why Did the Reformation Happen?," in *The Reformation: Basic Interpretations*, ed. Lewis W. Spitz, 2nd ed. (Lexington: D. C. Heath, 1972), 128.
9. Alister E. McGrath, *The Intellectual Origins of the European Reformation* (Grand Rapids, MI: Baker, 1995), 19.

is evident within a century of his death. Though he was declared a saint by Pope John XXII already in 1323, previously, in 1277, only three years after his death, the bishop of Paris had condemned 219 philosophical and theological theses, some of which, while not naming him, were understood by contemporaries to implicate conclusions held by Aquinas.[10]

The doctrine of justification itself, though not at issue in the condemnations of 1277, was by no means exempt from that late medieval "lack of theological clarity" acknowledged even by modern Catholic historians. Indeed, as Alister McGrath has suggested: "The uncertainty in the early decades of the sixteenth century in relation to the official teaching of the church on a number of matters is *particularly evident* in relation to the doctrine of justification."[11]

With an important qualification, this is unquestionably true. While there was a broad agreement on *what* happens in justification, there remained great—and growing—disagreement on *how* and *why* it happened. The point of agreement was in part predicated on a simple unpacking of the Latin term *iustificare*, itself a compound of *iustum* ("just" or "righteous") and *facere* ("to make"). As such, justification was understood literally as the process of "making righteous." That is, an individual's justification involved and was effected by a real moral and ontological transformation from being sinful to being just, righteous, or holy. Further, in light of the Pelagian controversy of late antiquity, there was broad agreement that divine grace was absolutely necessary for the effecting of this transformation. The nature, place, and role of God's grace in this process, however, was altogether less clear.

Some lack of consensus is evident already in the influential *Sentences* of Peter Lombard, which might be understood as having had a quasi-official status on account of its remaining the standard "textbook" of university theology from the thirteenth century well into the sixteenth. Though entertaining the possibility that saving grace was something created within the individual by God, Lombard dismissed this understanding and instead explained the salvation-effecting gift to be the living and active presence of the Holy Spirit himself.[12]

Thomas Aquinas, who well knew and wrote an influential commentary on Lombard's work, took issue with this interpretation in the next century. Such a view, he posited, would imply that the charity effected by such a gift "would cease to be voluntary and meritorious."[13] Such an objection highlights that, for Aquinas, grace retains its place of primary importance in the order of salvation but only grace understood in such a way that room is left for voluntary and meritorious human cooperation. Thus he could write, "The entire justification of the ungodly consists as to its *origin* in the

---

10. See, e.g., J. M. M. H. Thijssen, *Censure and Heresy at the University of Paris, 1200–1400*, Middle Ages Series (Philadelphia: University of Pennsylvania Press, 1998), 52.
11. McGrath, *Intellectual Origins*, 25; italics added.
12. Peter Lombard, *Sentences*, book 1, distinction 17, in Peter Lombard, *The Sentences: Book 1, The Mystery of the Trinity*, trans. Giulio Silano, MST 42 (Toronto: Pontifical Institute of Mediaeval Studies, 2007), 88–97.
13. Thomas Aquinas, *Summa Theologica*, trans. Fathers of the English Dominican Province (Notre Dame, IN: Christian Classics, 1981), 2a2ae.23.2.

infusion of grace," and could then continue: "For it is by grace that free-will is moved and sin is remitted."[14] In this light, Aquinas could conceive of justification as something like a three-step process. It originates with God's free and entirely unmerited infusion of grace. Having received divine grace, one is thereby empowered and moved to cooperate freely with it. Finally, then, this voluntary cooperation, being meritorious, disposes one to receive more grace and is ultimately rewarded with eternal life.[15] Simplifying even further, one might say that, for Aquinas, good works merit eternal life, but works are only good on account of their being done with the aid of unmerited grace. In his own words, "The very fact that we do what is good and that our works are worthy of eternal life is the result of God's grace."[16]

Just as Aquinas was concerned that Lombard's understanding of grace might leave too little room for the meritorious exercise of free will, subsequent *via moderna* ("new way") theologians such as William of Ockham and Gabriel Biel worried that even the *via antiqua* ("old way") scholastics like Aquinas gave free will too little credit. While maintaining, like Aquinas, that works aided by infused grace were meritorious, they also introduced the proposition that works even before and without divine grace are worthy of reward. Biel, for example, asserted that "the soul is able to merit the first grace *de congruo* by the removal of obstacles and by a good movement unto God produced by the free will."[17] In other words, even God's initial bestowal of grace can be earned. Thus emerged the phrase popularized by adherents of the *via moderna*: "God will not deny grace to those who do what is in them."[18] Further confusing matters, however, is the fact that this phrase, though popularized by *via moderna* theologians, was not novel to them. In fact, Aquinas himself had earlier endorsed it in his commentary on Lombard's *Sentences*. Though Aquinas moved away from this position in his later *Summa Theologiae*, many late medieval theologians continued to view his earlier commentary as authoritative.[19] Confusion regarding whether the "old" or "new" soteriology best represented orthodox opinion was thus further compounded by the fact that both "old" and "new" theologians could appeal to Aquinas for support.

If the scholastics of the *via moderna* (and even the early Aquinas) were eager to enlarge the role of man's free will in the order of salvation, they were also—and just as controversially—determined to expand and defend the scope of God's own free will. Though differing in their understandings of the nature of saving grace, Lombard and Aquinas were both emphatic in their insistence that one could not be saved without

---

14. Aquinas, *Summa Theologica* 1a2ae.113.7; italics added.
15. Aquinas, *Summa Theologica* 1a2ae.113–14.
16. Thomas Aquinas, *Commentary on the Letter of Saint Paul to the Romans*, trans. F. R. Larcher, ed. J. Mortensen and E. Alarcón (Lander, WY: Aquinas Institute for the Study of Sacred Doctrine, 2012), 176.
17. Gabriel Biel, *Collectorium circa quattuor libros sententiarum* (Tübingen: Mohr-Siebeck, 1973–1984), bk. 2, d. 27, q. 1, a. 2, c. 4K, quoted in Charles Raith II, *After Merit: John Calvin's Theology of Works and Rewards* (Göttingen: Vandenhoeck & Ruprecht, 2016), 61; italics added.
18. See, e.g., Gabriel Biel, "Doing What Is in One," in *The European Reformations Sourcebook*, ed. Carter Lindberg (Oxford: Blackwell, 2000), 17.
19. See Heiko A. Oberman, "'Iustitia Christi' and 'Iustitia Dei': Luther and the Scholastic Doctrines of Justification," in *The Dawn of the Reformation: Essays in Late Medieval and Early Reformation Thought*, ed. Heiko A. Oberman (Edinburgh: T&T Clark, 1992), 108.

this gift. William of Ockham, concerned that any talk of the "necessity" of grace would restrict God's freedom, would only affirm that it is "ordinarily" the case that God effects salvation by this means. In principle, however, Ockham insisted that "whatever God can produce by means of secondary causes he can directly produce and preserve without them."[20] That is, God, acting with complete freedom, might at least in theory choose to save some without the gift of infused grace and without the charitable habits and meritorious works enabled by it. In yet slightly different terms, God might *impute* righteousness to individuals even without having *infused* them with such.

Whatever pious intent lay behind this defense of divine freedom, it was, of course, a two-edged sword. If God was entirely free—free even to grant eternal life to those with neither grace nor charity—would he not also be free to deny eternal life to those with both grace and charity? Again, Ockham granted that, at least in theory, this was the case. As his fellow Franciscan Duns Scotus had posited previously, "Nothing created must, for reasons intrinsic to it, be accepted by God."[21] That is, neither the created grace inhering in an individual nor the love and good works effected by it are in and of themselves deserving of reward. Instead, God rewards them only because he has freely consented and covenanted to do so.

Still within the formal context of scholasticism, it is worth noting at least one further factor in the "lack of theological clarity" on the eve of the Reformation. Though the *via antiqua* and *via moderna*, which vied with one another for dominance in the late medieval universities, presented very different soteriological schemes, each appeared largely coherent on its own terms. These were by no means the only theological options on offer, however, and other contemporary *viae*, and the individuals associated with them, were sometimes happy to mix, match, and combine elements from these two most prominent schools of thought. Illustrative in this respect are representatives of what is often called the *schola Augustiniana moderna* (the "new Augustinian school"), theologians such as Thomas Bradwardine in England and Gregory of Rimini in France. Each, for example, was adamantly opposed to the *via moderna*'s notion that initial grace might be earned; the possibility of meriting any divine favor without the aid of grace veered, in their estimate, too close to the long-condemned error of Pelagius.[22] And yet proponents of the new Augustinianism could also make common cause with the *via moderna* in rejecting the *via antiqua*'s insistence on the soteriological necessity of created habits of grace.[23]

Popular Piety

As even this brief survey of some of the more prominent soteriological opinions makes evident, theological diversity was a hallmark of the later Middle Ages. What is more,

---

20. William of Ockham, *Quodlibeta* 6, q. 6, in William of Ockham, *Philosophical Writings: A Selection*, ed. Philotheus Boehner (Edinburgh: Nelson, 1957), 26.
21. Quoted in Steven Ozment, *The Age of Reform, 1250–1550: An Intellectual and Religious History of Late Medieval and Reformation Europe* (New Haven, CT: Yale University Press, 1980), 33.
22. See, e.g., Heiko A. Oberman, "Duns Scotus, Nominalism, and the Council of Trent," in Oberman, *Dawn of the Reformation*, 13.
23. See, e.g., McGrath, *Iustitia Dei*, 145–54.

the differences highlighted above are only some of those found within the confines of more formal scholastic theology. That is, they are differences between well-read and methodologically rigorous academic elites. And while the history of theology is often written with an exclusive focus on the treatises and commentaries produced by just such individuals, it would of course be incredibly naive to think that the religious views of the less educated laity—or even of the parish clergy—simply reflected those of university theology faculties. Pointedly stated, even the great theological variety evident among the church's respected theologians represents only a sliver of the diversity of thought that existed in the church at large.

Just how far pious lay thinking could diverge from that of the theologians is revealed in the heterodox Franciscan Paolo Ricci's 1540 testimony:

> I have heard with my own ears that most of the peasants and all the masses firmly believe that the blessed Mary is equal to Jesus Christ in power and bestowing grace, and some even believe that she is greater. This is the reason that they give: the earthly mother may not only ask but even compel her son to do something; and so the law of motherhood demands that the mother is greater than the son.[24]

Such sentiment may not have reflected university theology, especially that of the *via moderna* and its antipathy to the notion that God can be "compelled" at all in matters of grace and salvation. Yet one need not assume that Ricci's peasant masses arrived at such ideas wholly untutored. Indeed, in the course of an anti-Lutheran sermon from a decade later, one South German priest could, by comparison, make even the idea of compelling Christ appear tame:

> Now, my friends, be good enough to listen to me. The soul of a man who had died got to the door of heaven and Peter shut it in his face. Luckily, the mother of God was taking a stroll outside with her sweet Son. The deceased addressed her and reminds her of the Paters and Aves he has recited in her glory and the candles he has burnt before her images. Thereupon Mary says to Jesus, "It's the honest truth, my Son." The Lord, however, objected and addressed the suppliant: "Hast thou never heard that I am the way and the door and the life everlasting?" he asks. "If thou art the door, I am the window," retorted Mary, taking the soul by the hair and flinging it through the open casement. And now I ask you whether it is not the same whether you enter paradise by the door or by the window?[25]

Such examples, though not uncommon, should by no means be understood to suggest that these views would have fallen within the pale of orthodoxy, even granting the fluid doctrinal boundaries of the later Middle Ages. Instead, they simply serve to emphasize a point essential to understanding the origins and trajectory of Martin Luther's own

---

24. Quoted in Carlo Ginzburg, *The Cheese and the Worms: The Cosmos of a Sixteenth-Century Miller*, trans. John Tedeschi and Anne C. Tedeschi (New York: Penguin, 1982), 122.
25. Quoted in Preserved Smith, *The Social Background of the Reformation* (New York: Collier, 1962), 52.

contributions to an already diverse theological landscape. Not only did a number of divergent soteriologies exist side by side in the universities, making it all but inevitable that a university theologian such as Luther would wade into long-running and legitimate debates. But also, taking seriously his vocation as a theologian of the church, Luther well understood that he had not only the liberty but even the responsibility to address the often well-intentioned yet misinformed popular piety and folk theology of laity and clergy alike.

The Wittenberg Soteriology, 1513-1546
Luther and the Scholastic Traditions

As previously noted, Luther's theological development did not begin from scratch. Despite his 1505 vows as an Augustinian friar and his frequent and abundant praise of Augustine, it did not even begin with the so-called "Augustinian school." Instead, Luther's formal university education occurred firmly in the context of the *via moderna*. The University of Erfurt faculty of whom he spoke most frequently and, early on, most highly—men like Bartholomäus Arnoldi von Usingen and Jodokus Trutfetter—consciously upheld and advanced the intellectual tradition of Ockham and Biel.[26] Even Luther's monastic education, under Johann Nathin, continued in the same vein.[27] Indeed, so thoroughly was Luther steeped in the "modern way" that he seems to have had very little knowledge of Aquinas, Gregory of Rimini, or the alternative schools that they represented until he was several years into his own later tenure at the University of Wittenberg.[28] It is perhaps unsurprising, then, that when his Wittenberg colleague Philipp Melanchthon eventually penned a preface to the 1546 edition of Luther's writings, he would remark that Luther had not only preferred Ockham to Aquinas but that he could also recite Biel from memory.[29]

In this light it is also unsurprising that, upon his own appointment to a professorship at Wittenberg, Luther's earliest lectures, like those of Trutfetter, Arnoldi, and Nathin, would embrace and espouse the conclusions of the *via moderna*. This is clear, for example, in his 1513–1515 *Lectures on the Psalms*, in which he not only adhered to the broader medieval consensus on justification as a process of transformation by which one becomes righteous[30] but also explicitly endorsed the "modern" view that God's initial grace in renewal might be merited: "The teachers correctly say that to a man who does what is in him God gives grace without fail." But God does so "without fail" not because he is compelled by any necessity or by any worthiness intrinsic to human efforts; again in keeping with the *via moderna*, this is only the case on account of the "promise of God and the covenant of his mercy."[31]

---

26. Martin Brecht, *Martin Luther*, vol. 1, *His Road to Reformation, 1483–1521*, trans. James L. Schaaf (Philadelphia: Fortress, 1985), 36.
27. Brecht, *Martin Luther*, 1:91.
28. See, e.g., McGrath, *Intellectual Origins*, 109–13; Denis R. Janz, *Luther and Late Medieval Thomism: A Study in Theological Anthropology* (Waterloo, ON: Wilfrid Laurier University Press, 1983).
29. Philipp Melanchthon, *Preface to the Second Volume of Luther's Latin Writings* (1546), in *Philippi Melanthonis Opera*, in *CR* 6:159.
30. Martin Luther, *First Lectures on the Psalms*, in *LW* 10:191–92.
31. Luther, *First Lectures on the Psalms*, in *LW* 11:396–97.

Though briefly summarized, this emphasis on Luther's early training in and adherence to the *via moderna* is important in a number of respects. Most significant, perhaps, is the manner in which Luther's early influences might explain his later theological trajectory. Joseph Lortz, for instance, though more sympathetic to Luther than many Catholic scholars before the mid-twentieth century, gave voice to an enduringly popular trope when he suggested that if Luther had been "filled with the theology of St. Thomas [Aquinas] . . . his reformatory turn could never have taken place."[32] Instead and unfortunately, however, Luther had been schooled in a theology that was "no longer fully Catholic."[33] Lortz's judgment, however, is a clear case of the kind of historical anachronism alluded to previously. Whether Luther's reformation would have happened if he had been educated in the *via antiqua* is obviously a counterfactual question—the answer to which is therefore unknowable. But the implication that Aquinas was *the* representative of orthodoxy, while Biel and others were beyond the pale, was just as obviously not the settled opinion of the church in Luther's own day. Indeed, even the polemical Catholic historians Hartmann Grisar and Heinrich Denifle, both far less sympathetic to Luther than Lortz was, could evaluate Luther's Psalms lectures and conclude that even their clearly "modern" theology revealed no "deviation from the Church's faith," no "denial of Catholic doctrine," and "no teaching actually heretical."[34]

To be sure, Luther himself would eventually disagree with such an evaluation, and the earliest signs of revision to his soteriology appear precisely as rejections of emphases prominent in the *via moderna*. These revisions are evident, in fact, already in his next series of lectures at Wittenberg, the 1515–1516 lectures on Paul's epistle to the Romans. Here, for instance, he broke with the notion that "doing what is in one" might earn God's initial grace and instead insisted, as Aquinas and the "old" scholastics had, that this grace is received entirely passively.[35] This was certainly an important "breakthrough" or "discovery," as was his new understanding of the "righteousness of God," a biblical phrase with which Luther had wrestled for some time. Crediting Augustine, Luther now interpreted God's righteousness not as that which is intrinsic to his nature, nor in terms of a divine justice which would necessitate judging sinners as they deserve, but as the cause of salvation itself—the righteousness by which God himself justifies.[36]

Within the context of his *Lectures on Romans*, however, even these two breakthroughs together do not break through to anything like a doctrine of justification that Lutherans would recognize as their own or that Catholics would condemn as heterodox. The previously mentioned Denifle, for instance, abundantly demonstrated that Luther's supposedly "new" understanding of the righteousness of God was in fact entirely typical

---

32. Lortz, "Why Did the Reformation Happen?," 120.
33. Lortz, "Why Did the Reformation Happen?," 126.
34. Hartmann Grisar, *Luther* (London: Kegan Paul, Trench, Trübner, 1913), 1:74. Grisar here notes that this is also "Denifle's view," referring readers to Denifle, *Luther und Luthertum: Ergänzungen*, vol. 1, *Quellenbelege: Die abendländischen Schriftausleger bis Luther über Justitia Dei (Rom. 1,17) und Justificatio* (Mainz: Kirchheim, 1905).
35. Martin Luther, *Lectures on Romans*, in *LW* 25:496.
36. Luther, *Lectures on Romans*, in *LW* 25:151–52; cf. his "Preface to the Complete Edition of Luther's Latin Writings" (1545), in *LW* 34:337.

of his Roman predecessors.[37] Protestant theologian Alister McGrath similarly concludes that the theology evident in the *Lectures on Romans* was "well within the spectrum of contemporary catholic opinion."[38] This conclusion is further warranted in light of Luther's continued embrace of the scholastic understanding of "infused" grace, faith "formed" by love, and the medieval consensus regarding justification as a sanative or transformative process. As such, he could acknowledge that the sinner's justification *began* with God's unmerited grace, but he could not speak of the sinner having been justified per se. One might have the divine promise of health, but so long as one remained only partly righteous, that promise was not yet fulfilled.[39] This, together with the necessity of cooperating with grace in justification, remained unquestioned even in lectures Luther delivered two years after completing his course on Romans. In his 1518 *Lectures on Hebrews*, for example, he explained that Christians are called righteous "not because they are, but because they have begun to be and should become people of this kind by making constant progress."[40]

In light of the above discussion, it is warranted to speak of Luther's *Lectures on Romans* as revealing a "breakthrough" of sorts. Its nature, though, is best understood simply as a breaking away from the soteriology of the *via moderna* in which he was educated, a break which now brought him largely in line with the doctrine of the *via antiqua*.[41]

The Indulgence Controversy and Its Implications

Whether Luther's soteriological development would otherwise have ceased with his rejection of the "modern" theology is, of course, another counterfactual question. However, his continued movement was soon prompted less by his reflection on the intellectual tradition and its various iterations within the university than by the confusions and concerns attending popular piety. The piety in question was, of course, that which revolved around the sale of indulgences, and particularly those recently promulgated to fund the construction of Saint Peter's Basilica in Rome (and to repay the debt Albrecht of Mainz had incurred in purchasing his archbishopric).[42]

There is small irony in the modern remembrance of "Reformation Day" each October 31, the date on which Luther's *Ninety-Five Theses* concerning indulgences were made public in 1517.[43] For those who believe that justification by grace alone through faith alone on account of Christ's merits alone is indeed "the doctrine on which the

---

37. See Denifle, *Luther und Luthertum*.
38. McGrath, *Intellectual Origins*, 27.
39. Luther, *Lectures on Romans*, in *LW* 25:260, 434. Thus, in the same work he could bluntly state that "God has not yet justified us, that is, He has not made us perfectly righteous or declared our righteousness perfect, but He has made a beginning in order that He might make us perfect." Luther, *Lectures on Romans*, in *LW* 25:245.
40. Martin Luther, *Lectures on Hebrews*, in *LW* 29:139.
41. In this regard, cf. also Luther's 1517 *Disputation against Scholastic Theology*, in *LW* 31:9–16. Despite the title, the content makes clear that the "scholastics" at whom his criticisms are aimed are particularly the representatives of the *via moderna*, especially Gabriel Biel, who is by far the most frequently named.
42. See Martin Luther, *Against Hanswurst* (1541), in *LW* 41:233.
43. For the debate on whether the theses were actually "posted," see especially Volker Leppin and Timothy J. Wengert, "Sources for and against the Posting of the *Ninety-Five Theses*," *LQ* 29 (2015): 373–98.

church stands or falls," it can be a bit of a surprise to learn that Luther defended no such theology in his famous theses. Close attention to their content suggests rather that, while the theses do move away from a popular contemporary theology, they actually move, like his *Lectures on Romans*, in the direction of an older medieval theology. More provocatively stated, rather than articulating a distinctly "Reformation" theology, the *Ninety-Five Theses* defend much more traditional medieval conclusions. This is not to deny that the publication and wide dissemination of Luther's theses did in a very real sense begin the Reformation. Indeed, Luther himself consistently understood the course of the Reformation to have begun with the indulgence controversy.[44] But the theses themselves were, in the words of Kurt Aland, "just a spark; much more important was the chain reaction activated by them."[45] This is especially the case with respect to the doctrine of justification. As Lowell Green has persuasively argued, this original controversy "was the cause rather than the result of Luther's evangelical discovery of justification."[46]

Contextualizing this controversy requires recognizing that neither the theology of indulgences nor the critique of them was a novelty. The assertion that an indulgence—a remission of temporal punishment due on account of sin—might be granted by the church traces back at least to the eleventh-century context of the First Crusade, while criticism of indulgences was voiced by such popular medieval and Renaissance authors as Geoffrey Chaucer, Giovanni Boccaccio, and Desiderius Erasmus. Though not a recent novelty, indulgence theology did remain fluid and ambiguous.[47] More stable, however, was the tradition of penitential theology on which indulgences were built. As Luther rightly noted in a 1518 sermon on indulgences, the medieval tradition viewed the sacrament of penance in tripartite fashion.[48] Prerequisite was contrition, or sorrow, for one's sins. This was then followed by auricular confession to a priest and the pronouncement of absolution (typically understood as a single act). Finally, then, in accordance with clerical instructions, the penitent performed satisfaction, often in the form of charitable works such as prayer and almsgiving.[49] Though confession (or more precisely, the attendant absolution) was understood to forgive the *guilt* of sin, satisfaction was necessary for the remittance of the temporal *penalty* of sin. In view of the medieval doctrine of justification as a process of becoming righteous, what this meant was that those

---

44. See, e.g., Luther, "Preface to the Complete Edition," in *LW* 34:328–29; Luther, *Against Hanswurst*, in *LW* 41:231–34.

45. Kurt Aland, ed., *Martin Luther's 95 Theses: With the Pertinent Documents from the History of the Reformation* (Saint Louis, MO: Concordia, 2004), 18.

46. Lowell C. Green, *How Melanchthon Helped Luther Discover the Gospel: The Doctrine of Justification in the Reformation* (Fallbrook, CA: Verdict, 1980), xxiv.

47. The papal bull *Salvator noster*, for example, the first to speak of indulgences for the dead, was promulgated only in the decade before Luther's birth. The confusion it caused necessitated the subsequent papal encyclical *Romani Pontificis provida*. The officially defined doctrine of indulgences that "must be held and preached by all under penalty of *latae sententiae* [automatic] excommunication" was promulgated only after the start of the Luther controversy, in the 1518 decree *Cum postquam*. See the texts in Denzinger, *Compendium*, 353–54, 355–56, 362–63.

48. Martin Luther, *Sermon on Indulgences and Grace*, in WA 1:243.

49. In the twelfth of his ninety-five theses, Luther had rightly noted the different ordering of the early church, in which satisfaction of temporal penalties preceded the announcement of absolution. Martin Luther, *Ninety-Five Theses* (1517), in *LW* 31:26.

absolved would not face an eternal penalty—damnation—for their sin, but temporal penalties, either in this world or in purgatory, would still have to be satisfied before one was sufficiently purified to enjoy the beatitude of heaven. As Luther accurately noted in his 1518 sermon, traditional indulgence theology recognized indulgences to be relevant only with respect to satisfaction.[50] That is, contrary to frequent Protestant caricature, indulgences were not understood to forgive sins and so to provide salvation. Forgiveness itself was bestowed with prior priestly absolution. Indulgences merely mitigated or negated the necessity of subsequent penance, or satisfaction.

This is not to say, however, that those purchasing indulgences actually understood these nuances as the theologians did. Nor is it to suggest even that those clergy involved in the indulgence trade made any great effort to educate laypeople in the finer points of this traditional theology. The instructions regulating the sale of those indulgences to which Luther first objected, for example, described their first grace as "the plenary remission of all sins."[51] In his dramatic sermons, Johann Tetzel, the Dominican friar responsible for selling indulgences in the region nearest Luther, similarly proclaimed that those who confess and contribute money for an indulgence "will obtain complete remission of all their sins."[52]

Unsurprisingly, such ambiguity and its perceived effects attracted Luther's ire. Writing to Archbishop Albrecht of Mainz, who had issued the aforementioned instructions, Luther complained that the people were being led to understand that indulgences assured their salvation.[53] Though very likely the case, it must be observed that this was only a criticism of the manner in which indulgences were being misrepresented and misunderstood; it was not a rejection of indulgences or their theology as understood by the theologians.[54] Even more pertinent for grasping Luther's own soteriology at this point in time was his rationale for this criticism. He asserted that *no one* can be sure of salvation, not even "by the infusion of God's grace, because the Apostle orders us to work out our salvation constantly 'in fear and trembling.'"[55] Implicit here is still the traditional medieval belief that grace merely inaugurates and makes possible the cooperative process by which one is ultimately saved.[56]

---

50. Luther, *Sermon on Indulgences and Grace*, in WA 1:243.
51. Albert of Mainz, *Instructio summaria*, in *A Reformation Reader: Primary Texts with Introductions*, ed. Denis R. Janz (Minneapolis: Fortress, 1999), 53.
52. Johann Tetzel, "A Sample Sermon," in Lindberg, *European Reformations Sourcebook*, 31.
53. Martin Luther, "Letter to Albert of Mainz" (October 31, 1517), in *LW* 48:46.
54. In the same letter he also criticized what he took to be another misrepresentation of the church's more formal theology. He noted that Albrecht's instructions said that contrition and confession are not necessary prerequisites if one is purchasing an indulgence for one already in purgatory. Luther, "Letter to Albert of Mainz," in *LW* 48:47–48. In a sermon of the next year, Luther also questioned whether indulgences were even applicable to those in purgatory, stating that the church had not definitively established this position. Luther, *Sermon on Indulgences and Grace*, in WA 1:246. In this same year he noted in a letter to the pope himself that the church's decretals in fact denied this possibility. Martin Luther, "Letter to Pope Leo X" (May 1518), in WA 1:528; cf. Luther, *Against Hanswurst*, in *LW* 41:235. More explicitly indicative of how "traditional" Luther still remained at this juncture is that for some years after the indulgence controversy, he could still insist that "the existence of purgatory I have never denied. I still hold that it exists." Martin Luther, *Defense and Explanation of All the Articles* (1521), in *LW* 32:95.
55. Luther, "Letter to Albert of Mainz," in *LW* 48:46.
56. Quite possibly, Luther at this point still held to the traditional Catholic teaching that one cannot know with certainty even whether one has obtained God's grace. See, e.g., Aquinas, *Summa Theologica*, 1a2ae.112.5. By way of contrast, the "mature" Luther would pointedly insist that "we should make an effort to wipe out completely that wicked idea which

Indeed, it is precisely this traditional belief that undergirds the more substantive critique of indulgences found already in his *Ninety-Five Theses*. The first two of these do advertise a significant breakthrough, noting that the penitential concept of satisfaction itself rests largely on a faulty translation of Matthew 4:17. Where the Latin Vulgate had *paenitentiam agite* ("do penance"), Luther rightly observed that the original Greek term μετανοεῖτε actually means "repent," in the sense of "be contrite." Within the context of the medieval sacrament, therefore, Jesus's words would refer to initial and internal contrition rather than subsequent and external satisfaction.[57] Despite this discovery, however, Luther did not simply dismiss the necessity of satisfaction. Instead, and rather surprisingly, he immediately asserted that "such inner repentance is worthless unless it produces various outward mortifications of the flesh."[58] This, then, became the crux of Luther's critique of indulgences: "A Christian who is truly contrite seeks and loves to pay penalties for his sins."[59] The purchase of an indulgence, however, allows one to avoid making satisfaction. Luther deemed this reality problematic because it might thereby imply a lack of "true" contrition. Understanding that works of satisfaction are works of charity, or love, he further explained that "because love grows by works of love, man thereby becomes better. Man does not, however, become better by means of indulgences."[60]

In summary, then, the thrust of Luther's initial argument against indulgences betrays not a break with but a defense of traditional medieval doctrine. According to this doctrine, divine grace makes possible cooperative works of charity, which in turn merit salvation. Penitential satisfaction includes such charitable works, which contribute to the individual progressively being purified and "made righteous." The fundamental problem with indulgences, then, was that they undermined the charitable works that the "truly contrite" ought to do and therefore militated against one's becoming increasingly "better," or more just.[61] In this light, it is perhaps difficult to understand why the *Ninety-Five Theses* were so immediately controversial, especially since they nowhere went so far as to pronounce indulgences illegitimate but advised only that they "be preached with caution."[62] But controversial they were, and for the next two years, Luther was forced constantly to defend them in sermons, letters, treatises, and disputations.[63]

Revealingly, though, the earliest negative reactions to Luther's theses did not focus on the specifics of his assertions concerning indulgences. They instead highlighted a more

---

has consumed the entire world, namely, that a man does not know whether he is in a state of grace. For if we are in doubt about our being in a state of grace and about our being pleasing to God for the sake of Christ, we are denying that Christ has redeemed us and completely denying all His benefits." Martin Luther, *Lectures on Galatians* (1535), in *LW* 26:380.

57. Luther, *Ninety-Five Theses*, in *LW* 31:25.
58. Luther, *Ninety-Five Theses*, in *LW* 31:25.
59. Luther, *Ninety-Five Theses*, in *LW* 31:29.
60. Luther, *Ninety-Five Theses*, in *LW* 31:29.
61. One should note the contrast here with a history of scurrilous Roman polemic suggesting that Luther's aim was to make Christianity "easy" in order to justify libertinism. For example, *The Catholic Encyclopedia*, referring to what it calls Denifle's "masterpiece of critical erudition," endorses Denifle's conclusion that Luther's "immorality was the real source of his doctrine." *The Catholic Encyclopedia*, vol. 4 (New York: Robert Appleton, 1908), s.v. "Heinrich Seuse Denifle."
62. Luther, *Ninety-Five Theses*, in *LW* 31:29.
63. For a brief overview, see Brecht, *Martin Luther*, 1:202–21, 239–73.

general but all the more serious charge: to question indulgences was to question the power of the church—and the pope—which authorized them.[64] This was precisely the tack taken by Tetzel, whose indulgence sales were the most immediate precipitant of Luther's theses.[65] More significantly, it was also the emphasis of the theological opinion Pope Leo X solicited from his court theologian Sylvester Mazzolini of Prierio, which opinion became the basis for the official proceedings initiated against Luther at Rome.[66]

The question of papal power also came to the fore of the 1519 Leipzig Debate, the event that arguably concluded what some still believed was a controversy over indulgences.[67] Of the thirteen theses that the Ingolstadt Dominican Johann Eck had prepared for debate with Luther, all but one did, in fact, treat sin, penance, and indulgences. But the thirteenth, which addressed papal power and primacy, quickly overwhelmed the proceedings. Indeed, though it was the last of the topics listed for debate, it was taken up first and consumed fully half of what became a two-week debate. In his introductory remarks, Luther declared that he himself would "gladly have avoided this subject."[68] If rumor is to be believed, however, it is the only subject Eck was truly interested in debating. In private correspondence shortly after the debate, Luther wrote that Eck was "supposed to have said that if I had not questioned the power of the pope, he would readily have agreed with me in all matters." Similarly, Luther wrote concerning the second week of debate, "The debate over indulgences fell completely flat, for Eck agreed with me in nearly all respects."[69]

Though the drift of controversy from indulgences to ecclesiastical authority does not obviously or directly bear on soteriological questions, it is crucial to understanding Luther's development in a number of respects. First, in the early stage of the controversy, when Luther focused specifically on the theology and practice of indulgences, he revealed himself as still embracing a soteriology well within the bounds of medieval Catholicism. Unsurprisingly, then, his critics in these early years did not upbraid him for advancing a heterodox doctrine of salvation.

Second, as these critics steered the discussion toward questions of authority, Luther was compelled to throw himself into an increasingly intense study of these issues, especially in the historical record of the church's conciliar decisions, papal decrees, and canon law.[70] Already when he had publicized his original *Ninety-Five Theses*, he was aware that indulgences being applicable to the dead was not only a very recent idea but an idea contradicted by earlier decretals.[71] Nor was this a unique discrepancy. What was one to make, therefore, of authoritative ecclesiastical pronouncements apparently

---

64. See, e.g., Brecht, *Martin Luther*, 1:205–6.
65. See Brecht, *Martin Luther*, 1:209.
66. See Brecht, *Martin Luther*, 1:242–43.
67. For example, referring back to the *Ninety-Five Theses* of 1517, Kurt Aland writes, "Two years later people seldom thought of them, for in the meantime the controversy had arrived at an entirely different stage." Aland, *Martin Luther's 95 Theses*, 20.
68. W. H. T. Dau, *The Leipzig Debate in 1519: Leaves from the Story of Luther's Life* (Saint Louis, MO: Concordia, 1919), 131.
69. Martin Luther, "Letter to Georg Spalatin" (July 20, 1519), in *LW* 31:322.
70. See, e.g., Brecht, *Martin Luther*, 1:307.
71. See n. 54 above.

contradicting one another? Luther's answer to this question was finally—if hesitantly—delivered in the pressure of his exchanges with Eck at Leipzig: the church can err. Even the church's highest authorities—popes and councils alike—are fallible.[72] It was this open acknowledgment that not only foreordained Luther's eventual excommunication but also finally committed him to the conviction that theology could only be safely and certainly grounded in the infallible Word of God alone.

But the admission that all human authorities could err also confirmed an insight already evident in the *Ninety-Five Theses*: they could err even in their translations of Scripture itself. Luther's turn to *sola scriptura*, then, further strengthened his commitment to studying the Scriptures in their original languages. Fortunately—or providentially—the revival of classical and biblical languages and literature was central to the Renaissance humanism that had already begun to blossom at Wittenberg and that flowered especially with the arrival of Philipp Melanchthon in 1518, right in the midst of the indulgence controversy.

Melanchthon and the Humanist Contribution

Philipp Melanchthon's influence on sixteenth-century Lutheran debates about justification can hardly be overestimated. This is just as true with respect to intra-Lutheran conflicts as it is with respect to Lutheran-Catholic controversies. As a consequence, the relationship between the soteriologies of Melanchthon and Luther has become hotly contested.[73] Until the early twentieth century, it was typically assumed that their doctrines, at least during Luther's own lifetime, were fundamentally identical—not only with one another but also with the subsequent "Lutheran" doctrine given confessional status in the 1577 Formula of Concord. More recently, this long consensus has been questioned, though from diverging and even contradictory angles.

Bernhard Lohse, for example, follows the lead of Karl Holl, a central figure of the "Luther Renaissance" precipitated by the rediscovery of the above-mentioned *Lectures on Romans*. In their view, Luther's doctrine of justification is not simply forensic, defined by the forgiveness or nonimputation of sins and the imputation of Christ's own righteousness to the believer. Instead, even after his evangelical "breakthrough"—which Holl believed to have occurred as early as the 1515–1516 *Lectures on Romans*—Luther continued to understand justification as including the absolved sinner's progressive renewal, transformation, or sanctification. It was Melanchthon, in contrast to Luther, who restricted justification to imputation and thereby originated the misnamed "Lutheran" soteriology.[74] Similarly, in his influential work on the history of justification, Alister

---

72. See, e.g., Luther, "Letter to Georg Spalatin" (July 20, 1519), in *LW* 31:321–22, and the editorial introduction at 311.
73. Cf., e.g., Mark A. Seifrid, "Luther, Melanchthon, and Paul on the Question of Imputation: Recommendations on a Current Debate," in *Justification: What's at Stake in the Current Debates*, ed. Mark A. Husbands and Daniel J. Treier (Downers Grove, IL: InterVarsity Press, 2004), 137–52; Aaron O'Kelley, "Luther and Melanchthon on Justification: Continuity or Discontinuity?," in *Since We Are Justified by Faith: Justification in the Theologies of the Protestant Reformations*, ed. Michael Parsons, SCHT (Milton Keynes, UK: Paternoster, 2012), 30–43.
74. Bernhard Lohse, *Martin Luther's Theology: Its Historical and Systematic Development*, trans. and ed. Roy A. Harrisville (Minneapolis: Fortress, 1999), 262.

McGrath rightly recognizes that the distinction between justification and sanctification is the "essential feature of the Reformation doctrines of justification."[75] Yet elsewhere he asserts that "Luther himself did not teach a doctrine of forensic justification in the strict sense. The concept of a forensic justification necessitates a deliberate and systematic distinction between justification and regeneration."[76] If both of these statements were true, a surprising conclusion would follow, namely, that Luther did not embrace a "Reformation" doctrine of justification. Again, the doctrine eventually enshrined in the Lutheran confessions would instead be Melanchthon's.

Confusing matters even further is an alternative interpretation of divergence between Luther and Melanchthon. In this scenario, it is indeed Luther who teaches the "Lutheran" and "Reformation" doctrine of salvation. While Melanchthon's own doctrine might have been consonant with it for a period of time, he eventually betrayed justification by grace alone through faith alone on account of Christ's merits alone for a synergistic soteriology in which human cooperation was again deemed necessary.[77] Thus, the confession made formal in the Formula of Concord, after the deaths of both men, reiterated Luther's teaching and rejected Melanchthon's.

Needless to say, the constraints of this chapter prevent a thorough analysis of, or definitive conclusion to, these debates. It might be said at the outset, however, that if the soteriological doctrines of the two men were fundamentally discordant, it is exceedingly strange that neither of them seemed to have noticed or remarked on the fact during their many years of close cooperation at Wittenberg and elsewhere. What Luther himself did notice and remark on, almost from the moment of Melanchthon's arrival in Wittenberg, was that the young humanist's facility with the classical and biblical languages could only benefit the curricular and theological reforms taking place at the university.

There is some debate about the origins and extent of Luther's early familiarity with the humanist movement,[78] but his favorable impression was evident already before Melanchthon's arrival. The most famous of the northern European humanists, Desiderius Erasmus, had published his Greek edition of the New Testament in March 1516, and Luther had acquired a copy already by May of the same year and made use of it for the second half of his *Lectures on Romans*.[79] In discussions of curricular reform at the University of Wittenberg, Luther strongly encouraged the establishment of professorships in Greek as well as in Hebrew.[80] In recommending Melanchthon for the Greek professorship, the preeminent Hebraist Johannes Reuchlin confidently proclaimed that none except perhaps Erasmus himself could surpass him.[81] The inaugural address

---

75. McGrath, *Iustitia Dei*, 186.
76. Alister E. McGrath, "Forerunners of the Reformation? A Critical Examination of the Evidence for Precursors of the Reformation Doctrines of Justification," *HTR* 75, no. 2 (1982): 225.
77. See, e.g., John M. Drickamer, "Did Melanchthon Become a Synergist?," *Springfielder* 40, no. 2 (1976): 95–101.
78. For the status of humanism at Erfurt during Luther's studies there, see, e.g., Brecht, *Martin Luther*, 1:38–44.
79. Green, *How Melanchthon Helped Luther*, 112.
80. See, e.g., Martin Luther, "Letter to Georg Spalatin" (May 18, 1518), in *LW* 48:63.
81. Johannes Reuchlin, "Letter to Elector Frederick" (July 25, 1518), in *CR* 1:34.

Melanchthon delivered upon taking up the position in 1518 very clearly announced his Erasmian humanist agenda, explaining that a return to the direct study of the Greek and Hebrew Scriptures would free students from overdependence on scholastic commentaries.[82] He soon acknowledged that this was also Luther's agenda, ranking him together with Reuchlin and Erasmus in turning theology *ad fontes*, back "to the sources."[83] Luther repaid the compliment in turn, writing that Melanchthon "surpasses me even in theology"[84] and desiring that the whole church would imbibe his "pure theology."[85]

As such praise might suggest, Melanchthon's "pure theology"—made possible by his careful attention to the biblical texts and his facility with their original languages and linguistic contexts—had a profound influence on Luther's own understanding of Scripture and the doctrine of justification found therein. This is especially evident in Luther's shifting understanding of the biblical vocabulary with which that doctrine is defined. While neither Luther nor his medieval predecessors, for example, had ever denied the necessity of grace, as late as 1518, Luther continued to understand grace precisely as those predecessors had, namely, as an inherent quality by which one is divinely prepared to become righteous. Three years later, however, he had entirely abandoned this traditional view, defining grace now simply as the "favor of God."[86] That is, rather than a quality inhering in man, it is a disposition of God himself. Having rejected the notion of grace as a quality that makes possible the progressive "healing" of the sinner, he could now be so bold as to say, "Grace is a greater good than that health of righteousness. . . . Everyone would prefer—if that were possible—to be without the health of righteousness rather than the grace of God."[87] The significance of this shift becomes clearer when it is noted that only two years earlier Luther had not only not yet embraced this definition of grace but had explicitly rejected it.[88]

The impetus for this sudden change almost certainly lay with the recently arrived Melanchthon, who from at least 1520 was making the case for understanding grace as God's favor or goodwill.[89] He did so perhaps most clearly in the same year that Luther first embraced this definition, in the first edition of his *Loci Communes*, where he wrote that "the word 'grace' does not mean some quality in us, but rather the very will of God, or the goodwill of God toward us."[90] This articulation in Melanchthon's *Loci* is

---

82. Philipp Melanchthon, *On Correcting the Studies of Youth*, in *A Melanchthon Reader*, trans. Ralph Keen (New York: P. Lang, 1988), 48–57, esp. 55–56. Cf. Erasmus's own comment in the dedicatory epistle accompanying and explaining his Greek New Testament edition: "I perceived that that teaching which is our salvation was to be had in a much purer and more lively form if sought at the fountain-head and drawn from the actual sources than from pools and runnels." Erasmus, "Letter to Leo X" (February 1, 1516), in *Collected Works of Erasmus*, trans. R. A. B. Mynors and D. F. S. Thomson (Toronto: University of Toronto Press, 1976), 3:222.
83. Philipp Melanchthon, "Letter to Bernardo Mauro" (January 1519), in CR 1:63; cf. Melanchthon, "Letter to Georg Spalatin" (March 13, 1519), in CR 1:75.
84. Martin Luther, "Letter to Johann Lang" (December 18, 1519), in WABr 1:597.
85. Martin Luther, "Letter to Gerardus Listrius" (July 28, 1520), in WABr 2:149.
86. Martin Luther, *Against Latomus* (1521), in *LW* 32:227.
87. Luther, *Against Latomus*, in *LW* 32:227.
88. Martin Luther, *Lectures on Galatians* (1519), in *LW* 27:252.
89. Green, *How Melanchthon Helped Luther*, 159.
90. Philipp Melanchthon, *Loci Communes* (1521), in *Melanchthon and Bucer*, ed. Wilhelm Pauck, trans. Lowell J. Satre, LCC 19 (Philadelphia: Westminster, 1969), 87.

significant not least because Luther regularly expressed his unreserved agreement with the work, going so far as to assert hyperbolically that it deserved to be canonized.[91]

Luther was even more explicit about his debt to Melanchthon in arriving at his mature position on the biblical understanding of faith, which occurred during this same period. Following the Vulgate rendering of Hebrews 11:1, where faith is defined as "the substance [*substantia*] of things hoped for" (KJV), Luther, in harmony with the medievals, had long understood faith to be a quality present in those being made righteous. As a "substance," Luther had been taught, it was to be understood as a "possession."[92] Like grace, it played a necessary role in justification—but only as it became properly "formed." Hence, the medieval formula "faith formed by love" served to distinguish mere historical knowledge or intellectual assent from that faith joined with love and so contributing to righteousness. Perhaps taking his cue from Erasmus's own annotation of Hebrew 11:1, Melanchthon, from at least 1519, began to read the Greek πίστις ("faith") as synonymous with the Latin *fiducia* ("trust").[93] By the time he drafted the first edition of his *Loci*, he was insisting that, in accordance with ancient usage, the biblical uses of πίστις and its verbal form almost always mean "trust," rather than mere knowledge or assent.[94] Not only did Luther also embrace this definition, but he credited Melanchthon with correcting his earlier, traditional interpretation. With reference to his earlier understanding of *substantia* in Hebrews 11, Luther acknowledged that Melanchthon "did not allow me to understand it this way."[95] Instead, Melanchthon had explained that the underlying Greek term was better understood—and understood by church fathers such as John Chrysostom—as "essence" or "existence."[96]

Luther thus came to understand justifying faith not only as trust but trust that, on account of God's favor, the righteousness "hoped for" already existed. As such, Luther could now begin to speak of justification in the present tense, not merely as the future, hoped-for result of an ongoing process.[97] Most revealing of this new emphasis was the radical repurposing of that concept of which he had made use already in his earlier *Lectures on Romans*, that of the Christian being righteous and sinful at the same time. No longer did this formula simply express the idea that one was partly sinful and partly righteous or a present sinner with the future hope of being made righteous; the Christian now remained in himself wholly a sinner yet, by means of faith and in the eyes of God, wholly righteous.[98]

Finally, Luther began to insist that, since the Christian remains sinful in himself, righteousness received by grace and through faith must be understood as a necessarily extrinsic righteousness. Likewise, since it is not merely a partial righteousness but

---

91. Martin Luther, *The Bondage of the Will* (1525), in *LW* 33:16.
92. Luther, *Against Latomus*, in *LW* 27:377.
93. Green, *How Melanchthon Helped Luther*, 144.
94. Melanchthon, *Loci Communes* (1521), 92–102.
95. Luther, *Against Latomus*, in *LW* 27:377.
96. Luther, *Lectures on Galatians* (1519), in *LW* 27:377.
97. Martin Luther, "Two Kinds of Righteousness," in *LW* 31:298–99.
98. Cf., e.g., Luther, *Against Latomus*, in *LW* 32:172–73; Luther, *The Private Mass and the Consecration of Priests* (1533), in *LW* 38:158.

complete in the present, it could only be conceived of as a righteousness imputed or reckoned to the believer. Neither grace nor faith, therefore, are allowed to remain abstractions. God's favor is expressed in his unmerited imputing of Christ's righteousness to the believer, and it is in this that the believer trusts for his justification.[99] Thus understood, Luther could eventually state bluntly that "our righteousness is nothing other than the imputation of God."[100] The same conclusion came to the fore already in his famous dispute with Erasmus, where he emphasized that the Christian's righteousness is "reckoned" to him, while his sins are not "reckoned" to him.[101] Again, however, this emphasis on reckoning and imputation simply followed the lead of Melanchthon, who already in 1519—in a set of theses that Luther forwarded to his former confessor in Erfurt—was asserting that "all our righteousness is the gratuitous imputation of God."[102] There is, incidentally, some small irony in Luther's having pressed this point in his controversy with Erasmus, for it is likely that his and Melanchthon's initial insight into imputation derived from their reading of Erasmus. In his revised Latin translation of the New Testament at Romans 4:5, Erasmus had substituted *imputatum* for the Vulgate's *reputatum* and explained that this should be understood as the remission of an unpaid debt as if it had been paid.[103]

It is precisely this "forensic" doctrine of justification that would soon be explicated and defended not simply as Luther's or Melanchthon's but as the "Lutheran" doctrine. It was given confessional status, for example, already in the 1531 Apology of the Augsburg Confession, which explains that, in Scripture, "'justify' is used in a judicial [*forensi*] way to mean 'to absolve a guilty man and pronounce him righteous,' and to do so on account of someone else's righteousness, namely, Christ's, which is communicated to us through faith."[104] Before turning to the early confessional documents, however, it is worth briefly shifting once more from the rarified realm of academic inquiry and debate to the context of popular piety. Here, too, Erasmus's New Testament remains important, for from the second edition of this work, Luther would prepare his own vernacular translation of the New Testament.

As evidenced above, by 1521, Luther—with great assistance from Melanchthon—had drawn several independent discoveries together into a new and coherent articulation of the doctrine of justification. His articulation of salvation as "the gift of God," "by grace," and "through faith" was of course not new; this was simply the articulation of Saint Paul in Ephesians 2:8. What was new by 1521 was the manner in which Luther, drawn beyond scholastic commentary into the text and context of the New Testament itself, understood the meaning of such biblical terms as "grace" and "faith." Given these

---

99. See, e.g., Luther, *Lectures on Galatians* (1535), in *LW* 26:132: "These three things are joined together: faith, Christ, and acceptance or imputation."
100. Martin Luther, *Lectures on Isaiah* (1528), in *WA* 31.2:439.
101. See, e.g., Luther, *Bondage of the Will*, in *LW* 33:271.
102. Philipp Melanchthon, *Baccalaureatsthesen*, in *Melanchthons Werke in Auswahl*, vol. 1, *Loci Communes von 1521*, ed. Robert Stupperich (Gütersloh: C. Bertelsmann, 1951), 24.
103. See McGrath, *Iustitia Dei*, 211, 218.
104. "Apology of the Augsburg Confession" (quarto ed.), 4.305, in *The Book of Concord: The Confessions of the Evangelical Lutheran Church*, ed. and trans. Theodore G. Tappert (Philadelphia: Fortress, 1959), 154.

new understandings, he could now confess that justification consists in trusting that God is favorably disposed toward one on account of Christ, whose own perfect righteousness has been credited or imputed to the believer. Naturally, this is the doctrine that he desired even the laity to discern in their own reading of Scripture. Prerequisite, then, was that readers "have knowledge of its language."[105] Especially in the 1522 preface to his translation of Romans, Luther therefore took pains to clarify for his readers the biblical understanding of the central theological vocabulary with which Saint Paul proclaimed the doctrine of justification. "Faith," Luther there explained, "is a living, daring *confidence* in God's grace."[106] "Grace," in turn, "actually means *God's favor*, or the good will which in himself he bears toward us," and by which "we are *accounted* completely righteous before God."[107] Further, this righteousness accounted to the believer is the very "righteousness of God," but God in his mercy "*counts* it as [our] righteousness for the sake of Christ our Mediator."[108]

By 1522, then, Luther did appear clearly to embrace—along with Melanchthon—a forensic or imputative doctrine of justification.[109] If confusion remains on this point, it may be attributable at least in part to the manner and context in which Luther expressed himself still in this period. In the context of defining grace in his preface to Romans, for example, he compared and contrasted it with God's "gifts." As previously noted, he there explained that by grace "we are accounted completely righteous." By way of contrast, though, God's gifts "increase in us every day, but they are not yet perfect."[110] Though he did not here use what would later become the traditional vocabulary of *justification* and *sanctification*, the distinction between grace and gift seems quite clearly to express this very distinction, which McGrath notes to be definitive of the "Reformation" doctrine of "forensic" justification.

Perhaps even more confusing is what sounds like a devastatingly clear rejection of this doctrine in a sermon from the same year, in which Luther criticized "those who say that the forgiveness of sins and justification by grace lie completely in divine imputation; in other words, that all depends on the reckoning of God."[111] Contextual clues, however, offer good reasons to believe that Luther here was not in fact rejecting the "Reformation" doctrine. Specifically, he described those holding the criticized position as "the new teachers," which suggests that he had in view representatives of the *via moderna*, who did indeed teach a kind of justification by imputation. Since they held that God was bound by no necessity, God was (again, at least in principle) free to "reckon" one righteous even without the mediation of grace. But on the same principle

---

105. Martin Luther, "Preface to the Epistle of St. Paul to the Romans" (1522), in *LW* 35:366.
106. Luther, "Preface to Romans," in *LW* 35:370; italics added.
107. Luther, "Preface to Romans," in *LW* 35:369–70; italics added.
108. Luther, "Preface to Romans," in *LW* 35:371; italics added.
109. Noteworthy in this respect is also a comment Luther would make more than two decades later. Reviewing the course of events from his indulgence theses to his 1519 "breakthrough" regarding the "righteousness of God," he remarked on his delight in finding that Augustine had also understood this phrase as he now did. Nevertheless, he noted, Augustine "did not explain all things concerning imputation clearly." Luther, "Preface to the Complete Edition," in *LW* 34:337.
110. Luther, "Preface to Romans," in *LW* 35:369–70.
111. Martin Luther, *Sermon on Galatians 3:23–29* (1522), in WA 10.1.1:468.

of wholly arbitrary justification, wouldn't God thereby be free also to reckon individuals righteous even without the mediation of Christ himself? This was precisely the implication that Luther's sermon attacked: "If this were true, then the whole New Testament would be nothing and all in vain. Then Christ would have worked foolishly and vainly when he suffered for sin."[112] Clearly, this was not the doctrine of imputation embraced by Melanchthon or by the Lutheran confessions, to which we may now turn.

From Luther's Soteriology to Lutheran Soteriology

The Confession(s) at Augsburg

In the same few years during which Luther's soteriology was coming to maturity, the convictions of pope and emperor concerning Luther also reached their culmination. The papal bull finally excommunicating him in 1521 was quickly followed by the imperial Edict of Worms, which criminalized Luther, his books, and those who would harbor either. Throughout most of the decade, however, political complexities prevented the emperor from acting on the edict. To his great chagrin, this lack of action also allowed for the continued growth and spread of evangelical doctrine and practice. Thus, in 1530, when circumstances finally allowed, Emperor Charles V summoned representatives of the evangelical estates to answer for themselves at an imperial diet to be held in Augsburg.

Charles's summons had specifically requested an explanation of the practical and liturgical reforms introduced in his territories. When the evangelical rulers and their theologians arrived in Augsburg, however, they discovered that Luther's Leipzig opponent Johann Eck, at the instigation of the papal legate, had already circulated 404 theses condemning far more than evangelical liturgical practice.[113] Condemned, for example, was Luther's claim that "faith alone justifies; works do not," as well as Melanchthon's assertion that "love does not justify but rather faith justifies."[114] It became immediately apparent that the document that the Wittenberg contingent had previously prepared for the emperor would be wholly inadequate to the issues now mooted. Fortunately, in addition to this draft document, Melanchthon had also brought to Augsburg several other documents composed by Luther and with Luther's cooperation. With these at hand, Melanchthon set about to draft an entirely new document setting forth the Lutheran teaching. As he wrote to Luther on May 11, 1530, "I included almost all articles of faith, because Eck published most diabolical lies."[115]

Surprisingly, perhaps, not only does the article on justification itself consist of only two sentences,[116] but Melanchthon could say that it is "neither against nor contrary to the universal Christian church—or even the Roman church—so far as can be observed

---

112. Luther, *Sermon on Galatians 3:23–29*, in WA 10.1.1:468–69.
113. See Charles P. Arand, Robert Kolb, and James A. Nestingen, *The Lutheran Confessions: History and Theology of the Book of Concord* (Minneapolis: Fortress, 2012), 97–98.
114. Johann Eck, *Four Hundred Four Articles*, in SCBB, 55, 56.
115. Philipp Melanchthon, "Letter to Martin Luther" (May 11, 1530), in CR 2:45.
116. This is so in the original Latin and German editions of the texts, though not necessarily in their various English translations.

in the writings of the Fathers."[117] It is true that what came to be called the Augsburg Confession, presented before a political rather than ecclesiastical tribunal and with the primary goal of continued toleration, intentionally struck a conciliatory tone throughout. Nonetheless, even within two sentences, the Wittenberg soteriology is unambiguously articulated. The grace of justification is not a quality received into oneself; it is the very favor of God that one is instead "received into." God is graciously disposed, even toward sinners, "on account of Christ" (*propter Christum*), rather than on account of "their own powers, merits, or works." What later Lutheran theologians would call "objective justification" exists, therefore, even before one comes to faith; the forgiveness of sin is itself an objective reality already effected by Christ, whose "death made satisfaction for our sins." It is "through faith" (*per fidem*), then, that the individual believer receives unto himself the benefits of Christ's satisfaction; therefore, "God reckons [*imputat*] this faith as righteousness."[118]

Despite the clear exclusion of human "powers, merits, or works" in effecting justification, and insistence that this is wholly "a gift," the Augsburg Confession just as clearly denies that this doctrine implicates the Lutherans in antinomianism or in a dismissive attitude toward sanctification. Indeed, this was especially necessary because, as Melanchthon complained, "Our people are falsely accused of prohibiting good works."[119] To the contrary, he explained, justifying faith "is bound to yield good fruits."[120] It is therefore the case, he reiterated more than once, that "our people teach that it is necessary to do good works."[121] Just as consistently, however, he carefully clarified that such works are done not to merit an increase of grace or salvation itself. They are performed simply because "it is the will of God," while "it is only by faith that forgiveness of sins and grace are apprehended."[122]

Because the stipulations of the Edict of Worms would have prompted Luther's arrest had he been present at Augsburg, the drafting of the confession there fell primarily to Melanchthon. It would be a mistake, however, to understand it as uniquely representing Melanchthon's views. Throughout his time at Augsburg, Melanchthon not only consulted with the other evangelical theologians present but also maintained constant correspondence with Luther himself, who was safely ensconced a hundred and fifty miles away in Coburg. Moreover, as noted above, Melanchthon's work at Augsburg leaned heavily on a number of documents previously composed by or in cooperation with Luther. Thus, one modern authority could go so far as to assert that the materials with which Melanchthon "framed the fundamental symbol of the Lutheran Church were the thoughts and, in large measure, the very words of Luther."[123] Indeed, Luther, from the start, lavishly praised the document Melanchthon produced. It "pleases

---

117. "Augsburg Confession," concl. of part 1, 1, in *BOC*, 58.
118. "Augsburg Confession," 4, in *BOC*, 39–41.
119. "Augsburg Confession," 20.1, in *BOC*, 53.
120. "Augsburg Confession," 6.1, in *BOC*, 41; cf. 12.6, in *BOC*, 45.
121. "Augsburg Confession," 20.27, in *BOC*, 57; cf. 6.1, in *BOC*, 41.
122. "Augsburg Confession," 20.27–28, in *BOC*, 57; cf. 6.1–2, in *BOC*, 41.
123. F. Bente, *Historical Introductions to the Book of Concord* (Saint Louis, MO: Concordia, 1965), 17.

me extremely," he wrote to Melanchthon himself.[124] Writing to others, he referred to it as "this splendid confession"[125] and "altogether a most beautiful confession,"[126] and he remarked, "I do not know anything that can be improved or changed."[127] Before long he was referring to it as "our Confession."[128]

More surprisingly, even some who were decidedly not in the Lutheran camp reacted similarly. Following the public reading of the confession at Augsburg on June 25, 1530, the bishop of Augsburg himself is reported to have described what he heard as "the pure truth."[129] At the same time, Duke William of Bavaria upbraided Johann Eck for having so badly misrepresented the Lutheran teaching, and even the papal legate Campeggio averred that the teaching might be permitted if it wouldn't thereby set a precedent for tolerating other confessions.[130] Not all were so sanguine, however. Most significantly, the emperor himself—despite apparently having slept through the presentation of the confession[131]—ordered that it not be printed[132] and then appointed his own commission of theologians to draft a reply; the reply, he announced, would be issued in his own name, and submission to it would be enforced.[133]

It did not bode well for the Lutherans that Eck, who had already attempted to prejudice the proceedings with his 404 theses, would play a prominent role on the commission, together with Johannes Cochlaeus, who would later pen a scurrilous biography of Luther that concluded with demons dragging the Reformer into hell.[134] And in fact, the commission proved unwilling to countenance the Augsburg Confession's claim that its doctrine contained nothing "contrary to the universal Christian church—or even the Roman church." Responding bluntly to its confession of justification, the commission declared that "to reject human merit, which is acquired through the assistance of divine grace, is to agree with the Manichaeans and not the catholic church."[135] The Confutation of the Augsburg Confession would concede that "works of themselves have no merit"; nevertheless, "God's grace makes them worthy to earn eternal life."[136] Therefore, the confession of justification by faith alone "is wholly opposed to evangelical truth."[137] Instead, "justification pertains to faith *and* love," and even then, "love is the superior virtue."[138]

---

124. Martin Luther, "Letter to Philipp Melanchthon" (July 3, 1530), in WABr 5:435.
125. Martin Luther, "Letter to Justus Jonas" (July 9, 1530), in WABr 5:458.
126. Martin Luther, "Letter to Conrad Cordatus" (July 6, 1530), in WABr 5:442.
127. Martin Luther, "Letter to Elector John" (May 15, 1530), in WABr 5:319.
128. E.g., Luther, *Table Talk*, in *LW* 54:187 (no. 2974b).
129. Martin Luther, "Letter to Nikolaus Hausmann" (July 6, 1530), in WABr 5:440.
130. See Bente, *Historical Introductions*, 30, 19.
131. Johannes Brenz, "Letter to Johann Isenmann" (August 4, 1530), in CR 2:245.
132. Philipp Melanchthon, "Letter to Veit Dietrich" (June 26, 1530), in CR 2:142.
133. Arand, Kolb, and Nestingen, *Lutheran Confessions*, 119.
134. Johannes Cochlaeus, *The Deeds and Writings of Dr. Martin Luther*, in *Luther's Lives: Two Contemporary Accounts of Martin Luther*, trans. Elizabeth Vandiver, Ralph Keen, and Thomas D. Frazel (New York: Manchester University Press, 2002).
135. "The Confutation of the Augsburg Confession," 4, in *SCBC*, 108.
136. "Confutation," 4, in *SCBC*, 109. Cf. also article 20, where, responding to the claim that "good works do not merit the forgiveness of sins," the *Confutation* declares, "This teaching has been rejected and disapproved." In *SCBC*, 117.
137. "Confutation," 6, in *SCBC*, 109.
138. "Confutation," 6, in *SCBC*, 110; italics added.

Given the stipulations already announced by Emperor Charles V, the writing was now on the wall; the Lutherans had no more to gain at Augsburg. They could laugh openly as the Confutation was publicly read on August 3,[139] and they could complain to one another of its "puerile," "childish,"[140] and "most stupid"[141] nature, but they would not be allowed the opportunity of a formal response. Indeed, they would not even be allowed a copy of the document unless they agreed in advance to acknowledge the truth of its contents and refrain from replying to it—or even making its contents public.[142] Refusing these conditions, the Lutheran contingent departed Augsburg, and Melanchthon threw himself into the work of composing an extensive defense of the doctrine they had presented at the diet.[143]

The Defense of the Augsburg Confession

Despite being denied a copy of the Confutation, several of those present at its reading had taken copious notes; within a couple of months, someone had also "leaked" a complete copy to Melanchthon.[144] By the spring of 1531, he was thus able to publish the first edition of his Apology of the Augsburg Confession,[145] further explicating the confession at Augsburg and replying in detail to the objections raised by the Confutation. Immediately upon its publication, however, the work was circulated among the Wittenberg theologians and others, who consulted with Melanchthon and offered suggestions for revision. A second edition, which would remain the authoritative edition, therefore came off the press in September of the same year.[146] Unlike the Augsburg Confession and some of the earlier formulas on which it was based, formulas that had been commissioned by temporal authorities, the Apology was born as a "private" work of its author (though, again, being composed with the assistance of others—and being subsequently elevated to "confessional" status—it would be a mistake to view the Apology as merely expressing Melanchthon's own opinions). Also unlike the Augsburg Confession, the Apology forgoes any great efforts to be irenic, because "the opponents show by their actions that they care for neither truth nor concord; they want only our blood."[147]

Since the article on justification "deals with the most important topic of Christian teaching," and because "the opponents understand neither the forgiveness of sins, nor faith, nor grace, nor righteousness,"[148] Melanchthon would now make explicit the implications of what, in the context of the Augsburg Confession, might have appeared a

---

139. Arand, Kolb, and Nestingen, *Lutheran Confessions*, 121.
140. Philipp Melanchthon, "Letter to Martin Luther" (August 6, 1530), in *CR* 2:253.
141. Brenz, "Letter to Johann Isenmann" (August 4, 1530), in *CR* 2:245.
142. See Bente, *Historical Introductions*, 35, 38; cf. "Apology," preface, 1–4, in *BOC*, 109–10. Luther, in characteristic fashion, explained these conditions by writing, "Their conscience must sense instinctively that it is a flimsy, empty, and meaningless thing of which they would have to be ashamed if it were made public and examined in the light of day, or if it were to be answered." Martin Luther, *Dr. Martin Luther's Warning to His Dear German People* (1531), in *LW* 47:22.
143. The article on justification is the most dramatically expanded, from a mere two sentences to more than fifty pages in the most recent critical edition.
144. Arand, Kolb, and Nestingen, *Lutheran Confessions*, 123; cf. "Apology," preface, 14, in *BOC*, 110.
145. Often referred to as the "quarto" edition, on account of the size of its pages.
146. Being referred to as the "octavo" edition, again on account of the size of its pages.
147. "Apology," preface, 12, in *BOC*, 110.
148. "Apology," 4.2–3, in *BOC*, 120–21.

naively conciliatory claim: that the Lutheran doctrine does not contradict that of "the Roman church—so far as can be observed in the writings of the Fathers." Not only did he continue to deny that the Wittenberg theology was a novelty, he now also went on the offensive to argue that it was the contemporary Roman church that had departed both from Scripture and the church fathers to "miserably contaminate this article, obscure the glory and benefits of Christ, and tear away from devout consciences the consolation offered them in Christ."[149]

By way of preface, Melanchthon offered as a rule that "all Scripture should be divided into these two main topics: the law and the promises."[150] This is significant not only as an interpretive key for all that follows but also because it is this very distinction that Luther had identified as the culmination and capstone of his gradual evangelical breakthrough.[151] By the law is understood "the commandments of the Decalogue, wherever they appear in the Scriptures."[152] The promises of the gospel, by contrast, are those "concerning Christ" and that on account of Christ offer "the forgiveness of sins, justification, and eternal life."[153] On this distinction Melanchthon could then predicate a further consistent distinction between what he variously called the "righteousness of reason,"[154] "civil righteousness,"[155] or the "righteousness of the law,"[156] and what he referred to as "Christian righteousness"[157] and "spiritual righteousness."[158] Here is evident the distinction between the "two kinds of righteousness" that Luther was forwarding already as early as 1519[159] and that Melanchthon complained their opponents refused to grasp. Rejecting the distinction necessary "to recognize the benefits of Christ,"[160] the scholastic theologians "corrupt many passages, because they read into them their own opinions rather than deriving the meaning from the texts themselves."[161] The scholastic opinions read into Scripture, shaped largely by Aristotelian philosophy, teach "only a righteousness of the law and not the righteousness of the gospel."[162]

By no means, however, did Melanchthon reject Aristotelian philosophy or the righteousness of the law. Indeed, he was willing to acknowledge that "Aristotle wrote so eruditely about social ethics that nothing further needs to be added."[163] But however beneficial—and necessary—such righteousness is, it is not the uniquely Christian righteousness of justification, because

---

149. "Apology," 4.3, in *BOC*, 121.
150. "Apology," 4.5, in *BOC*, 121.
151. Luther, *Table Talk*, in *LW* 54:442 (no. 5518).
152. "Apology," 4.6, in *BOC*, 121. Thus, for example, in his discussion of Rom. 3:28, he rejected the Roman claim that Paul refers only to the "ceremonial" law of the Old Testament, and he cited Augustine in support. "Apology," 4.87, in *BOC*, 135–36.
153. "Apology," 4.5, in *BOC*, 121; cf. 4.43, in *BOC*, 127, where the gospel is succinctly defined as, "strictly speaking, the promise of the forgiveness of sins and justification on account of Christ."
154. "Apology," 4.9, in *BOC*, 121.
155. "Apology," 18.9, in *BOC*, 234.
156. "Apology," 4.21, in *BOC*, 124.
157. "Apology," 4.16, in *BOC*, 122.
158. "Apology," 18.9, in *BOC*, 234.
159. E.g., Luther, "Two Kinds of Righteousness," in *LW* 31:297–306.
160. "Apology," 4.184, in *BOC*, 149.
161. "Apology," 4.224, in *BOC*, 153.
162. "Apology," 4.47, in *BOC*, 127; cf. 4.9, in *BOC*, 121.
163. "Apology," 4.14, in *BOC*, 122.

God does not regard a person as righteous in the way that a court or philosophy does (that is, because of the righteousness of one's own works, which is rightly placed in the will). Instead, he regards a person as righteous through mercy because of Christ, when anyone clings to him by faith.[164]

This difference between the manner in which God and men regard individuals as righteous informed Melanchthon's careful and consistent use of the phrase "before God" when explaining the sinner's justification.[165] Similarly, his attribution of God's reckoning to mercy is synonymous with his attributing it to grace, that is, God's gracious disposition on account of Christ's atoning sacrifice. Certainly, Melanchthon recognized, Rome had not neglected to credit grace on account of Christ in articulating the doctrine of justification. But, he also noted, they both misplaced it and severely limited its role. They credited Christ "with meriting for us a certain disposition [*habitus*], or, as they call it, 'initial grace,' which they understand to be a disposition that inclines us to love God more easily. . . . Then they urge us to earn an increase of this disposition and eternal life by the works of the law."[166] Again, the reason they do so, according to Melanchthon, is that "human reason only focuses on the law and does not understand any other righteousness except obedience to the law."[167] Further problematic, he noted, is that even while explaining the nature and function of "initial grace," the scholastics "demand that people doubt whether this disposition is present."[168]

Following from his clarification of the nature of grace, Melanchthon was quick to explain that it cannot be understood in isolation: "Every time mercy is mentioned, we must bear in mind that faith is also required, for it receives the promised mercy." The converse is similarly true: "Every time we speak about faith, we want the object [of faith] to be understood as well, namely, the promised mercy."[169] The necessary interdependence of grace and faith he explained with reference to Romans 4:3, arguing that "Abraham realized that he had a gracious God only on account of God's promise. He assented to the promise."[170] Citing Romans 1:16 and 10:17, he further clarified: "If justification takes place only through the Word and the Word is grasped only by faith, it follows that faith justifies."[171] Summarizing, then, he bluntly asserted that "faith is that which grasps God's free mercy on account of God's Word. Whoever denies that this is faith completely misunderstands the essence of faith."[172]

Completely misunderstanding is precisely what Melanchthon charged Rome with doing. Once again, this is because they read into Scripture "their own opinions rather than deriving the meaning from the texts themselves." And once again, these opinions

---

164. "Apology," 4.283, in *BOC*, 165.
165. E.g., "Apology," 4.26, in *BOC*, 124: while judges or ethicists may regard men as righteous on account of their deeds, it is "false that people are accounted righteous *before God* because of the righteousness of reason" (italics added).
166. "Apology," 4.17–18, in *BOC*, 122–23.
167. "Apology," 4.229, in *BOC*, 154.
168. "Apology," 4.19, in *BOC*, 123; cf. 4.119, in *BOC*, 139–40.
169. "Apology," 4.55, in *BOC*, 129.
170. "Apology," 4.58, in *BOC*, 129.
171. "Apology," 4.67, in *BOC*, 131; cf. 4.50, in *BOC*, 128.
172. "Apology," 4.153, in *BOC*, 144.

had been shaped by an unwarranted intrusion of Aristotelian categories. As Melanchthon accurately noted, "The opponents imagine that faith is nothing more than a knowledge of history." That being the case, they suppose that it can coexist with mortal sin, and therefore it cannot save.[173] Instead, faith only becomes effectual for salvation when it is "formed" by love.[174] The concept of "form" here employed by the scholastic theologians is that of Aristotle, who had explained that every substance consists of both matter and form. Since the author of Hebrews had referred to faith as the "substance" of things hoped for, it was concluded that faith must also comprise matter (simple knowledge) and form (love). Though he was happy to concede that simple knowledge of the historical facts cannot effect salvation, Melanchthon insisted that the biblical use of the term "faith" connotes neither simple knowledge nor knowledge formed by love. Instead, as he had explained for more than a decade,[175] the faith to which Scripture consistently attributes justification must be understood as "assent to the promise,"[176] "trust in the promise,"[177] or "confidence in Christ."[178]

In light of the Roman insistence that faith by itself cannot save unless it is formed by love, Melanchthon exaggerated only slightly when he suggested that the opponents "do not in any way attribute justification to faith, but only to love."[179] That is, in light of his paradigmatic preface, they attribute it to the "law" rather than to "the promise." In doing so, "they thereby abolish the entire promise of the free forgiveness of sins."[180] By maintaining the distinction between law and promise, and between two kinds of righteousness, Melanchthon, on the other hand, was able to emphasize the necessity of love, good works, and "civil righteousness" without allowing them to obscure the biblical gospel of justification by grace alone through faith alone on account of Christ alone. In doing so he once again articulated—though again without using the later terminology—the fundamental distinction between justification and sanctification. Thus, though justification "apart from works of the law" (Rom. 3:28) must first be confessed, "later we add also the teaching of the law, not because we merit the forgiveness of sins by the law or because we are regarded as righteous on account of the law, . . . but because God requires good works."[181]

Indeed, the teaching of the law, which is fulfilled by love, must succeed the teaching of faith, because, as Melanchthon consistently reiterated, "it is necessary for love to follow faith."[182] As such, "it is impossible to separate love for God (however meager it may be) from faith."[183] This is the case, however, because love is a necessary consequence, rather

---

173. "Apology," 4.48, in *BOC*, 128.
174. "Apology," 4.109, in *BOC*, 138.
175. And also in the Augsburg Confession itself; see, e.g., 20.26, in *BOC*, 57.
176. "Apology," 4.48, in *BOC*, 128; cf. 4.113, in *BOC*, 139.
177. "Apology," 4.44, in *BOC*, 127.
178. "Apology," 4.82, in *BOC*, 134.
179. "Apology," 4.109, in *BOC*, 138. See, in this regard, the later 1539 claim by Roman Cardinal Jacopo Sadoleto that since faith includes and is formed by love, "love is essentially comprehended as the chief and primary cause of our salvation." Jacopo Sadoleto, *Letter to the Genevans*, in *A Reformation Debate*, ed. John C. Olin (Grand Rapids, MI: Baker, 1976), 36.
180. "Apology," 4.121, in *BOC*, 140; cf. 4.110, in *BOC*, 138–39.
181. "Apology," 4.188, in *BOC*, 150.
182. "Apology," 4.151, in *BOC*, 143.
183. "Apology," 4.141, in *BOC*, 142.

than a cause, of faith and justification. This must be understood as the case, Melanchthon noted, because "it is impossible to love God until the forgiveness of sins is first grasped by faith."[184] But the faith by which forgiveness is grasped necessarily then produces new life and brings forth fruit,[185] which thereby testify to the presence of faith.[186] Thus, while insisting that only faith justifies, Melanchthon could be equally insistent that faith not only justifies but also produces new and spiritual impulses, love, and obedience.[187]

If the Apology's clear and constant distinction between the two kinds of righteousness—of promise and law, faith and love, justification and sanctification—ever becomes potentially ambiguous, it is in those few places where it speaks of justification *making* one righteous and so is suggestive of the sanative view forwarded by the medieval theologians. Melanchthon could write, for example, that "'to be justified' means that out of unrighteous people righteous people are made."[188] He did so, however, immediately after declaring that, "properly and truly, by faith itself we are *regarded* as righteous for Christ's sake," and he acknowledged that "Scripture speaks both ways." Yet even here, he clarified that the formulation of being made righteous in this context ought not be understood in the medieval fashion, since "faith alone makes a righteous person out of an unrighteous one, *that is*, it alone receives the forgiveness of sins."[189] Further militating against reading the Apology as occasionally slipping back into a sanative soteriology is contemporary correspondence between its author and the Württemberg theologian Johannes Brenz, who had also been present with Melanchthon at Augsburg. In the very year that he composed the Apology, Melanchthon perceived that Brenz yet embraced the sanative doctrine, holding that one is justified because faith receives the Holy Spirit, who then enables one to become righteous by fulfilling the law. Melanchthon rejected this interpretation, reiterated the forensic nature of justification on account of the imputed righteousness of Christ, and counseled Brenz to examine the Apology on this doctrine further. Not insignificantly, Luther appended his own postscript to Melanchthon's letter, confirming its judgment.[190]

Despite its origins as a "private" work, Melanchthon's fellow Lutherans very quickly regarded the completed Apology not only as the definitive interpretation of the Augsburg Confession but also as having an authoritative status of its own. Luther could make combined reference to them as "our Confession and Apology," and both were subscribed to by the signatories to the 1536 Wittenberg Concord as well as by members of the Schmalkaldic League, the defensive alliance of Lutheran princes established in the aftermath of the 1530 Diet of Augsburg.[191] Half a century later, the drafters of the Formula of Concord regarded the Apology as part of "the unanimous consensus

---

184. "Apology," 4.36, in *BOC*, 126.
185. "Apology," 4.64, in *BOC*, 131.
186. "Apology," 4.188, in *BOC*, 150.
187. "Apology," 4.125, in *BOC*, 140.
188. "Apology," 4.72, in *BOC*, 132.
189. "Apology," 4.72, in *BOC*, 132; italics added.
190. Philipp Melanchthon and Martin Luther, "Letter to Johannes Brenz" (1531), in WABr 6:98–101. For further contextual insight into Melanchthon's soteriology at the time of the Apology's drafting, see his 1531 disputation "We Are Justified by Faith and Not by Love," in *SCBC*, 140–43.
191. Bente, *Historical Introductions*, 47.

and explanation of our Christian faith and confession."[192] Naturally, then, it would ultimately find a secure home with the Lutheran confessions bound together in the Book of Concord. Between its composition in 1531 and its inclusion in the 1580 Book of Concord, however, its doctrine of justification would prove to be anything but "the unanimous consensus and explanation," even among the Lutherans themselves.

Confusion, Contention, and Concord, 1547-1580

With the Augsburg Confession and its Apology, the Wittenberg soteriology was embraced not simply as Luther's or Melanchthon's but as the public confession of the Lutheran churches. While Luther lived, his personal authority served not only to unite the churches around these statements but also to quell any deviant interpretations or implications of the same. Even in the course of announcing the Reformer's death to the Wittenberg community in 1546, however, Melanchthon could make ominous reference to the "terrible calamity and great changes which will follow."[193] With astonishing speed, they did indeed follow, most immediately on account of dramatic changes in the political and ecclesiastical environment but also because these changes began to reveal—and enlarge—fault lines already present among Luther's former colleagues and students.

Six months after the long-delayed Council of Trent convened and only four months after Luther's death in 1546, pope and emperor entered an agreement to begin the suppression of Lutheranism by force.[194] The resulting Schmalkaldic War concluded in 1547 with the defeat of Lutheran estates and the emperor's attempt to impose what became known as the Augsburg Interim. Proclaimed law at Augsburg in 1548, the Interim, as its name suggests, provisionally defined imperial religious policy. Its definitions, the preface made clear, would eventually be superseded by those formulated by the Council of Trent, to which all imperial subjects would be expected to submit.[195] With respect to permissible soteriology, the Augsburg Interim unsurprisingly anticipated the conclusions of Trent. Justification was defined to include not only forgiveness but also renewal and sanctification, such that one is "made" righteous and possesses an "inherent righteousness." One is justified "to the extent that love is added to faith and hope," and so good works are deemed "necessary for the salvation of everyone justified." Finally, "people cannot believe without doubt that their sins are remitted."[196] Bluntly revealing the kind of confusion still existent in some Lutheran quarters, Johannes Agricola, who had been with Luther at the Leipzig Disputation and briefly taught at Wittenberg during Luther's tenure, interpreted the text of the Augsburg Interim to mean that "the Pope is reformed, and the Emperor is a Lutheran."[197] Melanchthon, the most obvious Wittenberg authority after Luther's death, more clearly recognized the doctrine for what it was and refused to assent to it.[198]

---

192. "The Epitome of the Formula of Concord," preface, 4, in *BOC*, 486–87.
193. Philipp Melanchthon, "On the Death of Luther" (February 19, 1546), in *CR* 6:59.
194. See "The Alliance between Emperor Charles V and Pope Paul III," in *Documents from the History of Lutheranism, 1517–1750*, ed. Eric Lund (Minneapolis: Fortress, 2002), 161–62.
195. "The Augsburg Interim," preface, in *SCBC*, 147.
196. "The Augsburg Interim," 4–8, in *SCBC*, 150–54.
197. Bente, *Historical Introductions*, 98.
198. See, e.g., Philipp Melanchthon, "Letter to Joachim Camerarius" (April 25, 1548), in *CR* 6:878.

Melanchthon, however, was in a tenuous position. The Schmalkaldic War had been lost, in part, because the Saxon Duke Moritz, nephew of the Elector John Frederick, abandoned the Schmalkaldic League and allied his troops with those of the emperor. In reward for his treachery, he was named Elector of Saxony in the place of his now imprisoned uncle; as such, he also controlled the University of Wittenberg. Though Moritz had received imperial assurance that he would not be forced to renounce his Lutheranism, he was now pressured to implement the Augsburg Interim in his territory.[199] Instead, he gambled on the production of a compromise document, with Melanchthon as its primary drafter. The resulting Leipzig Interim provoked an immediate backlash—not from the emperor but from Melanchthon's fellow Lutherans, many of them his former students. Though the document insisted that salvation was not merited on account of the worthiness of one's works, the language used in discussing justification and good works was otherwise ambiguous at best. Faith "alone," for example, received no mention. Indeed, the virtues of love and hope were also deemed "necessary for salvation," and without them "there is no reception of divine grace."[200] Similarly, in coming to faith the will was not described as remaining passive; it instead "cooperates."[201]

The sense of betrayal felt by many was only amplified by Melanchthon's cooperation with Moritz while John Frederick lingered in prison and hundreds of clergy were forced into exile for their refusal to compromise. Perhaps most significant for future controversies, Melanchthon's colleague and former student Matthias Flacius resigned his position at Wittenberg and moved to Magdeburg, where an organized resistance to both the Augsburg and Leipzig Interims was being mounted. Flacius there spearheaded a propaganda program directed not only at the Interims but at Melanchthon most specifically.[202] With Luther himself no longer available to mediate, the movement he birthed quickly divided into competing factions of so-called "Philippist" and "Gnesio" (i.e., genuine) Lutherans. With more than a little warrant, then, the later drafters of the Formula of Concord would call the controversies and divisions of the intervening years "a result of the Interim"—despite both Augsburg and Leipzig Interims quickly becoming dead letters.[203] Only four years after their imposition, further armed conflict routed the emperor and induced him to grant the Lutherans a qualified toleration with the Truce of Passau, which was followed three years later by the more equitable and permanent Peace of Augsburg. Suspicion of Melanchthon continued to simmer, however, and was given regular opportunity to boil over into outright hostility.

The Majoristic and Antinomian Controversies

The assertion of the Leipzig Interim, that virtues—and so even good works—were in some sense "necessary for salvation," was immediately and especially attacked by the

---
199. See Arand, Kolb, and Nestingen, *The Lutheran Confessions*, 177–78.
200. "The Leipzig Interim," in *SCBC*, 190.
201. "The Leipzig Interim," in *SCBC*, 185.
202. See, e.g., Oliver K. Olson, *Matthias Flacius and the Survival of Luther's Reform*, 2nd ed. (Minneapolis: Lutheran Press, 2011), 99–101, 124–27.
203. "The Solid Declaration of the Formula of Concord," preface, 19, in *BOC*, 530.

former Wittenberg professor Nikolaus von Amsdorf. Amsdorf took particular issue because it was the refusal to assent to this notion that had prompted Catholic authorities already in the 1520s to attempt to have him and his colleague George Major burned for heresy. Ironically, Major, who had joined the Wittenberg faculty in 1545, had not only made peace with the phrase but was now the first to defend it.[204]

Behind the immediate controversy, though, were conflicts precipitated more than a decade earlier. In his revised 1535 edition of the *Loci Communes*, Melanchthon had already referred to good works as "necessary to eternal life."[205] Amsdorf was among those who had expressed concern at the time, seeing the phrase as evidence that Melanchthon was departing from Luther's doctrine. Following an arranged dialogue between Luther, Melanchthon, and some of those who had expressed concern, Melanchthon could tell a correspondent that Luther had not appeared hostile.[206] Another present at the dialogue offered clarifying detail in his own correspondence: Luther did affirm that new obedience is an "effect necessarily following justification" but rejected the description of it as "necessary to salvation." The author of this letter further added his own impression that "Melanchthon was displeased with this."[207] If Melanchthon was indeed displeased, this might be partly explained by the fact that Luther himself had used precisely this formula only a year previously, saying that "works are necessary to salvation, but they do not cause salvation."[208] Whatever the case, Melanchthon did in fact scrub the offending phrase from subsequent editions of his *Loci*. Further, when it was revived with Major's defense of the Leipzig Interim, Melanchthon repeatedly advised Major against its use.[209] Major refused to relent, however, and the controversy continued until his death in 1574.

Unhappily, the unguarded polemic of this controversy also provoked yet another. In responding to critics such as Amsdorf and Flacius, Major and Melanchthon more than once counterattacked with accusations of antinomianism.[210] Whether such a label was technically accurate or not, it resonated in a context of fear that Luther's theology was, in his absence, being abandoned or distorted. The antinomian label inevitably called to mind the protracted series of "antinomian disputations" carried out at Wittenberg in the 1530s, in which Luther had thoroughly disproved and denounced the assumption that his teaching of justification *sola fide* exempted Christians from good works in obedience to God's law.[211] This controversy of the 1530s was again, though in a very different way, precipitated by Melanchthon's writing. In light of what he viewed as continuing libertinism in many parishes, Melanchthon's 1527 instructions for those examining congregations emphasized the ongoing necessity of preaching the law and so inducing

---

204. He did so by attempting to explain "necessary" not in a causal sense, however, but as referring to that which is inevitably present with salvation. See, e.g., his 1553 *Sermon on the Conversion of Paul*, in Lund, *Documents*, 194.
205. Melanchthon, *Loci Communes* (1535), in CR 21:429. But he, too, added "inasmuch as they must necessarily *follow* reconciliation" (italics added).
206. Philipp Melanchthon, "Letter to Veit Dietrich" (June 22, 1537), in CR 3:383.
207. Caspar Cruciger, "Letter to Veit Dietrich" (June 27, 1537), in CR 3:385.
208. Martin Luther, *Disputation concerning Justification* (1536), in LW 34:165.
209. See, e.g., Philipp Melanchthon, "Letter to Matthias Flacius" (September 5, 1556), in CR 8:842.
210. Arand, Kolb, and Nestingen, *Lutheran Confessions*, 192; Bente, *Historical Introductions*, 121.
211. The disputations are collected in *Only the Decalogue Is Eternal: Martin Luther's Complete Antinomian Theses and Disputations*, ed. Holger Sonntag (Minneapolis: Lutheran Press, 2008).

repentance.[212] The same Agricola who would later portray the Augsburg Interim as "Lutheran"—despite its insistence that love, good works, and inherent righteousness are necessary for salvation—accused Melanchthon of reverting from Luther's teaching to medieval legalism. In the series of disputations and publications that followed, however, Luther not only denied that Melanchthon had done any such thing but also took particular issue with Agricola's claim that his own opinion had Luther's approval.[213] That impression was decisively put to rest with Luther's 1539 treatise *Against the Antinomians*.[214]

Unfortunately, when Amsdorf was accused of antinomianism in the 1550s, he did little to deflect the charge. Indeed, he not only further encouraged it but did so, as Agricola had done unsuccessfully, by claiming Luther's sanction. Both missteps are most evident in the title of his 1559 treatise *That This Proposition, "Good Works Are Injurious to Salvation," Is a Correct, True, Christian Proposition, Taught and Preached by Sts. Paul and Luther*. In claiming that good works not only play no causal role in justification but even that they are detrimental to it, Amsdorf seemed clearly to embrace the "antilaw" sentiment his opponents attributed to him. He was, in a very narrow sense, correct that his proposition had been "taught and preached" by Luther. What he studiously avoided making clear, however, was that Luther consistently qualified the otherwise provocative thesis with the addition of "if [one] believes that he is justified by them."[215] So obviously distorting Luther's own position—as well as that of the Augsburg Confession and its Apology—such verbiage was succinctly denounced by Melanchthon as "filthy speech."[216] On this point, at least, he and his Gnesio-Lutheran critics could find common ground.

The Synergist Controversy

A united Philippist-Gnesio front against antinomianism was not enough to dampen suspicion of Melanchthon, however. Indeed, Melanchthon's eager defense of good works might even have heightened it, not least because by this time his influence was perceived to lay behind yet another controversy. This particular conflict, being the most subtle, was sparked by Moritz's theological adviser Johann Pfeffinger's 1555 publication of forty-one theses on free will. At issue was Pfeffinger's attempt to answer the thorny question of why some were saved and others damned. The difference between the redeemed and condemned, he concluded, must lie within the individuals themselves; namely, while the latter resisted the Holy Spirit's effecting of faith, the former actively assented to it.[217] In other words, the human will does not remain purely passive in justification. In a replay of the divisions triggered by the Leipzig Interim, Amsdorf, Flacius, and the Gnesio party immediately denounced this explanation, while Major and the Philippists

---

212. See Philipp Melanchthon, *Instructions for the Visitors of Parish Pastors in Electoral Saxony*, in LW 40:274–75.
213. Arand, Kolb, and Nestingen, *Lutheran Confessions*, 165–66.
214. Martin Luther, *Against the Antinomians* (1539), in LW 47:107–19.
215. E.g., Martin Luther, *The Freedom of a Christian* (1520), in LW 31:358.
216. Philipp Melanchthon, "Letter to Elector August of Saxony" (December 1557), in CR 9:407.
217. See Johannes Pfeffinger, *Five Questions on the Freedom of the Human Will*, in Lund, *Documents*, 197–98.

rose to its defense. Unsurprisingly, then, it was Melanchthon's own theology that was suspected of being propounded by Pfeffinger, a suspicion bolstered by Pfeffinger's claim that he was indeed following Melanchthon's lead.[218]

Especially from a post-Interim vantage point, it seemed clear that Melanchthon had increasingly shifted on the question of the will's cooperation in salvation. Revised editions of his *Loci Communes* in 1535 and 1543, for example, described the human will as one of justification's causes, together with the Word and the Holy Spirit.[219] That such explanations caused no immediate alarm, however, is evident in Luther's own claim about the 1535 *Loci*: "No better book has been written after the Holy Scriptures."[220] He could also still remark in 1544 that "I have absolutely no suspicion in regard to Philip."[221] Even the more provocative *Loci* edition of 1548—which explicitly affirmed the will's cooperation in conversion and identified this as the decisive difference between the saved and the condemned—received the initial praise of Flacius and other Gnesio-Lutherans who would later identify its theology as precipitating the synergist controversy.[222] Melanchthon's understanding of whether and how individuals cooperate in their justification may well have changed, but the more significant change explaining the controversy aroused by Pfeffinger was, again, that of the post-Interim environment of suspicion.

An effort toward reconciliation was eventually undertaken at Weimar in 1560, where the Jena professor and former Melanchthon student Viktorin Strigel defended the views of Pfeffinger and his former teacher, while Flacius represented the opposition. According to Strigel, his party acknowledged only that the will cooperates *after* the Holy Spirit initiates conversion. Though original sin has certainly damaged the will's power, he granted, it does not substantially change human nature or the nature of the will. Invoking Aristotelian categories, Strigel proposed instead that original sin is an "accident" of human nature. Flacius, to his discredit, embraced the Aristotelian terminology but retorted that original sin defined the "substance" of fallen humanity. Despite its antipathy to the Philippists, Flacius's own Gnesio party was quick to condemn this position as going too far. Flacius himself, however, refused to renounce it.[223]

The Osiandrian and Stancarian Controversies

The pattern of reaction and overreaction would play itself out once more in the 1550s. It would also afford another opportunity for Philippist and Gnesio factions to unite in opposition, this time to Andreas Osiander. Having lost his pastoral position in Nuremberg when the Augsburg Interim was imposed, Osiander fled to Königsberg and a post at its recently founded university. Understandably chagrined by the effects of the Augsburg Interim, he was perhaps just as understandably hostile to Melanchthon's compromise

---

218. Bente, *Historical Introductions*, 133.
219. Melanchthon, *Loci Communes* (1535), in CR 21:376.
220. Luther, *Table Talk*, in LW 54:440 (no. 5511).
221. Quoted in Drickamer, "Did Melanchthon Become a Synergist?," 99.
222. Drickamer, "Did Melanchthon Become a Synergist?," 99.
223. For this paragraph, see Arand, Kolb, and Nestingen, *Lutheran Confessions*, 206–8.

with it in the Leipzig Interim. Rather than critiquing the Leipzig document as evidence of Melanchthon's drift from the imputative doctrine of Luther and the Augsburg Confession, however, Osiander aimed directly at that doctrine itself.

In a series of disputations and publications from 1549 to 1551, Osiander argued that justification could not be attributed to an imputed righteousness but must be credited to an inherent righteousness. Fearing his doctrine had been misunderstood, Melanchthon clarified that his—and the Lutheran—teaching was not simply that righteousness was imputed for Christ's sake but that Christ's own righteousness was imputed to the believer.[224] But Osiander had not misunderstood. The only righteousness of Christ that suffices for justification, he insisted, was the divine righteousness "which is God himself." Our own righteousness, therefore, is that of "Christ dwelling in us . . . according to his divinity." Not only is the imputation of Christ's righteousness insufficient; so also is the nonimputation of sin. Instead, the forgiveness of sins, according to Osiander, is merely a "preparation" for justification.[225] Appealing to the now well-established distinction between two kinds of righteousness, between grace and gift, Melanchthon accused Osiander of erroneously commingling the two.[226] The confusion of justification and sanctification, as well as the assertion that faith and forgiveness merely prepare for justification, Melanchthon denounced as "false," "pernicious," "condemned," and, in effect, a return to the doctrine of the papacy.[227] The Gnesio party—and especially Flacius, who published no fewer than a dozen refutations of Osiander—could only agree.

Yet again, however, some refutations would veer wildly into equally erroneous conclusions. Francesco Stancaro's did exactly that. Also a Königsberg professor, Stancaro rightly noted the manner in which Osiander's emphasis on the essential righteousness of Christ's divine nature downplayed—and even made superfluous—the benefits of the incarnate Christ's active righteousness in fulfilling the law and dying in the stead of humanity. Rather than countering that justification is attributable to Christ's righteousness according to both his divine and human natures, Stancaro asserted that Christ saves *only* according to his human nature.[228] To Melanchthon's dismay, Stancaro even cited him in support.[229]

The Roman Reaction

In and of themselves the internecine feuds after Luther's death and provoked by the Augsburg and Leipzig Interims were a great embarrassment to the Lutheran churches. But they were all the more embarrassing because they were being played out in the shadow of the Council of Trent, where Rome was dogmatically defining its own

---

224. See, e.g., Philipp Melanchthon, *Commentary on II Corinthians*, preface, in CR 15:1200.
225. Quoted in Jaroslav Pelikan, *The Christian Tradition: A History of the Development of Doctrine*, vol. 4, *Reformation of Church and Dogma (1300–1700)* (Chicago: University of Chicago Press, 1985), 151.
226. Philipp Melanchthon, *Judgment concerning Osiander* (1552), in CR 7:893–94.
227. Philipp Melanchthon, "Confutation of Osiander" (1555), in Lund, *Documents*, 209.
228. Arand, Kolb, and Nestingen, *Lutheran Confessions*, 220.
229. McGrath, *Iustitia Dei*, 213.

doctrine of justification. No less than the Lutherans did the Tridentine fathers recognize the seriousness of the division concerning this doctrine. Already in an early report back to the Vatican, they acknowledged that "the importance of this council, regarding dogma, depends principally on the article of justification."[230] This being the case, Trent's "Decree on Justification"—going through nearly a dozen drafts over seven months—was given more attention than any other produced by the council. One draft of the decree made especially explicit the reason for this extended attention: "At this time nothing is more vexing and disturbing to the church of God than a novel, perverse, and erroneous doctrine concerning justification."[231] Though Luther himself had died just as the council was beginning, and though Trent's canons and decrees identify no Reformers by name, it is clear that the Wittenberger's soteriology was especially in view. As one Catholic historian concisely notes, "Luther set the agenda for the council."[232]

Though several prominent council members were not entirely antipathetic to the Lutheran articulation of justification, their views, perhaps unsurprisingly, were consistently sidelined.[233] And though, as noted above, some Lutherans could themselves misunderstand various implications of Luther's doctrine, Trent's ultimate rejection of that doctrine cannot be attributed simply to its own misunderstanding, to confusion regarding vocabulary, or to the parties talking past each other. As has often been noted, by freighting crucial terms such as *grace*, *faith*, and *justification* with their own long-standing definitions, the Tridentine theologians could very well have agreed with the confessional Lutheran definition of justification. Yet they rejected it precisely because they understood that these terms were defined very differently by the Reformers.[234]

Trent did distance itself, as had Luther, from the soteriology of the *via moderna*, rejecting the notion of meriting initial grace, and it clearly confessed that "the beginning of that justification must proceed from the predisposing grace of God."[235] At the same time, however, the council was equally clear in anathematizing all who would say that "the grace by which we are justified is only the good will of God."[236] Maintaining the understanding of grace as a quality within man, the "Decree on Justification" thus speaks of grace being bestowed and obtained, and thus of sinners being "made" just.[237] Further, the distinction between "predisposing grace" and the "grace of justification" allows for the insistence that the former is received without any merit on man's part, while the latter is obtained and increases by means of human cooperation and merit.[238]

---

230. *Concilium Tridentinum*, ed. Societas Goerresiana, 13 vols. (Freiburg: Herder, 1901–2001), 10:532 (no. 444).
231. *Concilium Tridentinum*, 5:420 (no. 179).
232. John W. O'Malley, *Trent: What Happened at the Council* (Cambridge, MA: Belknap Press of Harvard University Press, 2013), 12.
233. See, e.g., Hubert Jedin, *A History of the Council of Trent*, vol. 2, *The First Sessions at Trent, 1545–1547*, trans. Ernest Graf (Edinburgh: Thomas Nelson, 1961), 172–73, 181, 190–91, 279.
234. Cf. Robert Preus, *Justification and Rome* (Saint Louis, MO: Concordia, 1997), 27; Louis A. Smith, "Some Second Thoughts on the *Joint Declaration*," *LF* 31 (Fall 1997): 8.
235. *The Canons and Decrees of the Council of Trent*, trans. H. J. Schroeder (Rockford, IL: TAN Books, 1978), chap. 5 (31). Citations of Trent herein refer to the sixth session, "Concerning Justification"; decree chapters and canons are cited, with page numbers for the above translation included parenthetically.
236. *Canons and Decrees*, canon 11 (43).
237. Cf., e.g., *Canons and Decrees*, chap. 3 (31), canon 9 (43).
238. Cf., e.g., *Canons and Decrees*, canons 4 (42), 9 (43).

Because of this insistence on human cooperation in justification, any claims that the decrees of Trent are "not necessarily incompatible with the Lutheran doctrine of *sola fide*" remain highly questionable.[239] Again, the Tridentine fathers well understood what the Reformers meant when they spoke of justifying faith as "confidence in divine mercy," and they specifically condemned this meaning.[240] More pointedly rejected was the formula of "faith alone, meaning that nothing else is required to cooperate in order to obtain the grace of justification."[241] To be sure, Trent spoke just as highly of faith as of grace but, again, only in a qualified manner. Just as grace alone—without human cooperation—was deemed insufficient for justification, so too it was declared that faith cannot justify without the virtues of hope and love.[242] Retaining the view that justification was progressively sanative, the council could thus allow only that faith constitutes "the beginning of human salvation,"[243] a position emphatically rejected in the Apology of the Augsburg Confession.[244]

It was also this sanative understanding of justification that drove Trent's ultimate condemnation of any who would say that "men are justified either by the sole imputation of the justice of Christ or by the sole remission of sins."[245] Certainly, Trent did not condemn the proposition that God does indeed reckon or repute men righteous. Contrary to the Reformers, though, the council held that one is deemed righteous when and because one has inherently become so,[246] not only as the result of a divine infusion of righteousness but also, again, on the basis of human cooperation.[247] This is perhaps made most obvious in Trent's condemnation of the Reformers' insistence that rather than being a condition of justification, good works are simply the "fruits and signs of justification obtained."[248]

Such anathemas were not pronounced on straw men. The council fathers well understood the fundamental tenets of the Lutheran doctrine of justification. And while there may have been some confusion about the official Roman doctrine before Trent, its central features were now equally clear to Luther's theological heirs. Its formulation therefore gave rise to a new round of critique. Especially prominent in this regard is the work of Martin Chemnitz, a former student of Luther and Melanchthon who would play a key role in the drafting of Lutheranism's final confessional document, the Formula of Concord. In his multivolume *Examination of the Council of Trent*, Chemnitz suggested that Trent's "one chief argument" against the Reformation doctrine was the claim that since spiritual renewal is begun at the same time that sins are remitted,

---

239. "Justification by Faith (Common Statement)," §56, in Anderson, Murphy, and Burgess, *Justification by Faith*, 35.
240. *Canons and Decrees*, canon 12 (43).
241. *Canons and Decrees*, canon 9 (43).
242. *Canons and Decrees*, chap. 7 (34).
243. *Canons and Decrees*, chap. 8 (35).
244. "Apology," 4.71–72, in *BOC*, 132.
245. *Canons and Decrees*, canon 11 (43).
246. Cf. *Canons and Decrees*, chaps. 7 (33), 16 (41).
247. See, e.g., *Canons and Decrees*, chap. 7 (33–34). For brief commentary, see also Anthony N. S. Lane, *Justification by Faith in Catholic-Protestant Dialogue: An Evangelical Assessment* (New York: T&T Clark, 2002), 71–72, 74–75.
248. *Canons and Decrees*, canon 24 (45).

justification must be attributed to both.[249] By way of explaining the fundamental difference between Catholic and Lutheran doctrines, Chemnitz observed that the Roman theologians

> understand the word "justify" according to the manner of the Latin composition as meaning "to make righteous" through a donated or infused quality of inherent righteousness, from which works of righteousness proceed. The Lutherans, however, accept the word "justify" in the Hebrew manner of speaking; therefore they define justification as the absolution from sins, or the remission of sins, through imputation of the righteousness of Christ.[250]

This "Hebrew manner of speaking," Chemnitz demonstrated at length, is precisely the same manner in which the term "justify" is consistently used in both the sacred and profane literature of Greek antiquity.[251] In other words, Rome had long been misled by its dependence on deficient Latin translations of the Greek and Hebrew Scriptures. "Among the Greek authors, therefore, the word 'justify' is not used in that sense for which alone the papalists contend," Chemnitz concluded. Indeed, "its forensic meaning, as we commonly say, is so manifest" that even Trent's defenders found this difficult to deny.[252]

From Discord to (the Book of) Concord

While Trent formulated the soteriology around which Rome would unite, the Lutherans remained embroiled in the internecine feuds that had flared from the 1550s. Increasingly, however, the Lutheran quest for unity—a good in itself—was recognized also to be an urgent practical necessity. Princes and theologians alike desired consensus because they recognized that Rome's theologians could exploit not only the concessions made already with the Leipzig Interim but also the subsequent divisions among the Lutherans. The aborted 1557 Colloquy of Worms drove this point home. Convened by Ferdinand I, who had succeeded his brother Charles on the imperial throne, the Colloquy ended in embarrassment when, on account of disagreement between Lutheran factions, the Roman party concluded that it could not discern who represented true Lutheran doctrine. The confusion was no less problematic with respect to imperial politics. Because the 1555 Peace of Augsburg had decreed toleration only for those evangelicals adhering to the Augsburg Confession, some Catholic polemicists argued that intra-Lutheran dissension demonstrated an abandonment of that confession and so nullified the toleration of Lutherans.[253]

---

249. Martin Chemnitz, *Examination of the Council of Trent*, trans. Fred Kramer (Saint Louis, MO: Concordia, 1971), 1:579–80.
250. Chemnitz, *Examination*, 1:467.
251. See, e.g., Chemnitz, *Examination*, 1:470–76.
252. Chemnitz, *Examination*, 1:471. Robert Preus also notes that "as time went on Rome did not seriously dispute that the word *dikaioō* was a forensic term. The massive evidence for this fact brought forth by Chemnitz and the later Lutherans was utterly compelling." *Justification and Rome*, 68.
253. For this paragraph, see Bente, *Historical Introductions*, 239.

The above factors impressed on all parties the urgency of reconciliation and informed the diplomatically gifted Jacob Andreae's visits to nearly all Germany's evangelical courts, city councils, and university theology faculties.[254] On the basis of his intimate knowledge of the controverted matters, he published in 1573 *Six Christian Sermons concerning the Dissensions Which Have Gradually Arisen from 1548 to 1573*. As its title indicated, and similar to Martin Chemnitz's earlier *Judgment on Certain Controversies concerning Certain Articles of the Augsburg Confession*,[255] the work summarized the contentious questions and formulated more dispassionate answers than had sometimes been forwarded in the heat of debate. Though the publication was well received, a consensus also emerged that its sermonic form was not best suited to serve as a confession of faith. Andreae therefore reworked the sermons' content into what was dubbed the Swabian Concord.[256]

Like Chemnitz's *Judgment on Certain Controversies* and the Apology of the Augsburg Confession itself, the Swabian Concord was understood to serve as a commentary on the Augsburg Confession. Thinking in parallel with Chemnitz, with whom he had previously worked to introduce church reforms in Braunschweig, Andreae forwarded the document on to his former colleague for further feedback. Together with David Chytraeus, another former student of Luther and Melanchthon, Chemnitz reworked portions of Andreae's draft to produce what would now be called the Swabian-Saxon Concord of 1575. Keeping the princes abreast, the Swabians and Saxons forwarded their jointly agreed articles to the Saxon Elector August, who by this time had already appointed a commission of theologians to draft a similarly intended document. Upon receiving both the Swabian-Saxon Concord and the Maulbronn Formula he had commissioned, August convened a synod of theologians to meet at Torgau in 1576.[257]

On the bases of the Maulbronn Formula and Swabian-Saxon Concord, the theologians gathered at Torgau produced a comprehensive document that was first unimaginatively known as the Torgau Book but soon, with minor revisions, came to be known by its more descriptive and enduring title, the Formula of Concord. Though warmly greeted by the various political and theological authorities among whom it was circulated, concern about its ample size was regularly voiced. In the following year, then, as final revisions to the "Solid Declaration" of the Formula were made, an "Epitome" of this fuller document was also produced. Because the great majority of the Lutheran clergy and princes in Germany subscribed to it, the Formula thus finally established concord. Both the Solid Declaration and the Epitome would therefore find a home in the Book of Concord, the compilation of authoritative confessional documents officially published on June 25, 1580, the fiftieth anniversary of the original presentation of the Augsburg Confession.

Though the Formula largely concluded the controversies among sixteenth-century Lutherans, it has also served as the source of more than one contemporary debate. One of the most heated controversies concerns the question of how faithfully this Lutheran

---

254. Bente, *Historical Introductions*, 242.
255. Excerpted in *SCBC*, 200–219.
256. Arand, Kolb, and Nestingen, *Lutheran Confessions*, 270.
257. Arand, Kolb, and Nestingen, *Lutheran Confessions*, 271–72.

confession represents Luther's own confession of the doctrine of justification. Alister McGrath, for example, not only deems the Formula's soteriology more Melanchthonian than Lutheran but describes it as "the victory and consolidation of the critique of Luther from within Lutheranism itself." More specifically, he writes, "Luther's concept of justification [was] . . . rejected or radically modified."[258] This judgment is by no means unique to McGrath, however, and so others have objected that

> the constantly repeated assertion that FC [i.e., the Formula of Concord], unlike Luther, puts forward a merely imputational understanding of justification is manifestly untenable. What FC states is the same as that which Luther, Melanchthon, and Calvin held to be indispensable in this regard.[259]

At the very least, it can be said that the view of the Formula's own authors better accords with this latter sentiment than with McGrath's.

The Formula certainly does defend the forensic, imputational doctrine given confessional status already in Melanchthon's Augsburg Confession and its Apology.[260] As previously noted, however, this was precisely the doctrine embraced by Luther even before these confessions were drafted. It also remained his subsequent profession. Thus, when the Formula describes itself as an explication of the Augsburg Confession, it can also add that Luther—rather than that confession's actual author—was "the foremost teacher of the Augsburg Confession."[261] Indeed, in the revisions made between the Swabian-Saxon Concord and the final version of the Formula of Concord, the Swabian theologians were especially adamant that, whether or not Melanchthon was actually guilty of departing from the earlier theology that he and Luther held in common, any reference to Melanchthon's nonconfessional publications risked further controversy.[262] Thus, while Luther's own "private" publications are regularly cited throughout the Formula, Melanchthon's are nowhere quoted or referenced. Without mentioning Melanchthon by name, therefore, the questions at stake in the synergistic controversy are answered in accord with Luther's own consistent position and with frequent quotations from his writings. Sinners, it is explained, do not have "the ability, on the basis of their own powers, to help, act, effect, or cooperate—completely, halfway, or in the slightest, most insignificant way—in their own conversion."[263] Conversion is attributable "to divine activity and to the Holy Spirit alone."[264] Melanchthon's teaching that the will is one of the "causes" of conversion is therefore censured as misleading, while Luther's "pure[ly] passive" articulation is endorsed.[265]

---

258. McGrath, *Iustitia Dei*, 219.
259. Friedrich Beisser, "The Doctrine of Justification in the Formula of Concord," in *Justification by Faith: Do the Sixteenth-Century Condemnations Still Apply?*, ed. Karl Lehmann, Michael Root, and William G. Rusch (New York: Continuum, 1997), 156.
260. See, e.g., "Solid Declaration," 3.17, in *BOC*, 564.
261. "Solid Declaration," 7.34, in *BOC*, 598.
262. Bente, *Historical Introductions*, 244.
263. "Solid Declaration," 2.7, in *BOC*, 544.
264. "Solid Declaration," 2.25, in *BOC*, 549.
265. "Solid Declaration," 2.89–90, in *BOC*, 561.

In addressing the less subtle matters raised in the course of the Majoristic, Antinomian, Osiandrian, and Stancarian controversies, the Formula decisively rejects the errors resulting from opposite extremes. Good works, for example, are confessed to be neither "necessary for salvation" nor "harmful for salvation."[266] Even while it is acknowledged that "before this controversy many pure teachers used these and similar expressions," the propositions are condemned because their use and misuse have "resulted in all sorts of offensive exaggerations."[267] Positively confessed is, again, "what Dr. Luther correctly said," namely, that "faith alone lays hold of the blessing, apart from works, and yet it is never, ever alone."[268] Both the Osiandrian and Stancarian propositions that justification is attributable to only one of Christ's two natures are likewise condemned. Instead, righteousness is reckoned to sinners on account of "the obedience of the person [of Christ], who is at the same time God and a human being."[269] And while it is granted that Osiander was not wrong "regarding the indwelling of the essential righteousness of God in us," it is clarified—contra Osiander's teaching—that

> this indwelling of God is not the righteousness of faith, which St. Paul treats and calls *iustitia Dei* (that is, the righteousness of God), for the sake of which we are pronounced righteous before God. Rather, this indwelling is a result of the righteousness of faith which precedes it, and this righteousness [of faith] is nothing else than the forgiveness of sins and the acceptance of poor sinners by grace, only because of Christ's obedience and merit.[270]

Given the consistency with which the Formula restates the soteriology already articulated by Luther and Melanchthon a half century earlier and the clarity with which it explains and denounces erroneous interpretations or implications of that theology, it is not unreasonable to conclude that the Lutheran doctrine of justification was "set in stone" by 1580. Such a conclusion is all the more warranted with respect to the Catholic dogma defined in the irreformable canons and decrees of Trent. Worth noting in this respect is that the Formula of Concord, while certainly concerned to bring an end to intra-Lutheran disputes, did not limit its attention to these disputes. That is, like the Augsburg Confession, which it explicates, the Formula is concerned also to define the Lutheran doctrine vis-à-vis Roman theology, especially as now codified by Trent. Thus, the increasing clarity of positions developing through the sixteenth century might be characterized as reactionary, though very helpfully so. The Wittenberg soteriology first culminating in the Augsburg Confession and its Apology came to shape in the context of a real lack of clarity in the late medieval church. The Council of Trent went a great way also to clarify the confusions of late medieval soteriology

---

266. Cf. "Solid Declaration," 4.22–29, 37–40, in *BOC*, 578, 580–81.
267. "Solid Declaration," 4.36, in *BOC*, 580.
268. "Solid Declaration," 3.41, in *BOC*, 569.
269. "Solid Declaration," 3.58, in *BOC*, 572.
270. "Solid Declaration," 3.54, in *BOC*, 571–72.

but of course did so especially in reaction to the newly articulated Lutheran doctrine. And while the Formula of Concord necessarily addressed those confusions that had become evident even among the Lutherans, it also responded to the now clearly defined Roman dogma. It therefore bears repeating that, given the great lengths to which both Catholics and Lutherans went to articulate, explain, and defend their doctrines of justification, the divisive disputes of the sixteenth century cannot, especially after 1580, be waived away as the unfortunate result of unrecognized misunderstandings. Unfortunately, people attempt this approach too often. Perhaps especially exemplifying this move is the twentieth-century document intended and often understood to resolve those earlier disputes.

Conclusion: Contemporary Consensus or Continuing Conflict?

The suggestion that the Reformation controversies concerning justification largely resulted from a misreading or misunderstanding of important sources has become especially common over the last generation. What is often called the "Finnish" interpretation of Luther posits, for example, that both Lutherans and Catholics of the sixteenth century misunderstood Luther's soteriology. Rather than a forensic doctrine of imputation as articulated in the Lutheran confessions, Luther's doctrine is understood to define justification in terms of the sinner *essentially* being made righteous by means of his union with the indwelling Christ. While in some respects echoing the teaching of Osiander, and frequently compared with the Eastern Orthodox doctrine of theosis, such a reading also brings Luther much closer to the traditional Catholic dogma. Because chapter 23 in this volume treats this question in more detail, the conclusion of the present chapter will focus instead on a recent document that more explicitly forwards the thesis of a Catholic-Lutheran rapprochement, the 1999 *Joint Declaration on the Doctrine of Justification*.

Before the contents of this document are addressed, however, it deserves noting that, despite exaggerated claims that the signing of the *Joint Declaration* announced "the end of the Reformation,"[271] that "the Reformation is over," that "reconciliation has been achieved—time to return home [to Rome],"[272] the *Joint Declaration* does not in fact enjoy any authoritative status as Catholic doctrine. It certainly does not—and, in light of Catholic dogma respecting magisterial infallibility, *cannot*—trump the doctrines formally defined by the Council of Trent. Thus, its signing does not (and, again, cannot) mean, as one prominent convert erroneously declares, that "Catholicism and Lutheranism lifted their five hundred year-old mutual anathemas against each other."[273] Indeed, the fact that in the document's drafting Rome was represented by its Pontifical Council for Promoting Christian Unity rather than its Congregation for the Doctrine of the Faith—the body given responsibility for defining and defend-

---

271. Matthias Gierth, "A Time to Embrace," *Tablet* 253, no. 8309 (November 20, 1999): 6.
272. Christian Smith, *How to Go from Being a Good Evangelical to a Committed Catholic in Ninety-Five Difficult Steps* (Eugene, OR: Cascade Books, 2011), 83.
273. Smith, *How to Go from Being a Good Evangelical*, 81.

ing doctrine—is one clue that Rome in no way recognizes the *Joint Declaration* as signaling a change or "development" in its own dogma.[274]

Nevertheless, while acknowledging that sixteenth-century Catholic and Lutheran soteriologies were indeed "of a different character,"[275] the *Joint Declaration* proclaims that "our churches have come to new insights."[276] On account of these new insights, partially the result of two decades of ecumenical dialogue, the document claims finally to have articulated a "common understanding" and "consensus on basic truths of the doctrine of justification,"[277] such that the "doctrinal condemnations of the sixteenth century do not apply" any longer to the subscribing church bodies.[278] Whether this is entirely true, however, is cast into doubt both by the text of the *Joint Declaration* and by other contemporary documents. Avery Dulles, for example, a Catholic participant in the dialogues leading up to the production of the *Joint Declaration*, admitted in the course of them that "the theology of justification in Roman Catholic teaching has undergone no dramatic changes since the Council of Trent."[279] This observation is indeed borne out by the definition given to justification in the *Catechism of the Catholic Church*, which, unlike the *Joint Declaration*, does have authoritative standing. According to the *Catechism*, justification is not to be distinguished from sanctification and renewal; rather, it "includes the remission of sins, sanctification, and the renewal of the inner man."[280] In keeping with the *Catechism*, the *Joint Declaration* itself defines justification as both "forgiveness of sins *and* being made righteous" and accurately describes this definition as the "Catholic understanding."[281] But this is also the definition that the Lutheran signatories, unlike their sixteenth-century forebears, claim now to "confess together" with Rome.[282]

Conversely, the document nowhere engages, much less affirms, justification as the imputation of Christ's alien righteousness. The consistent Lutheran confession of sinners

---

274. Taking note of a number of serious questions raised about the document's contents, Catholic Cardinal Avery Dulles pointedly asked, "How could the Vatican agree to sign a document that it found so defective?" His own answer to the question emphasizes the *Joint Declaration*'s signing as a "symbolic event" with what might be called, frankly, utilitarian motives. Namely, in a "world that is so alien to the gospel, our churches are called to unite their forces in restoring missionary and evangelistic power." Avery Cardinal Dulles, "The Two Languages of Salvation: The Lutheran-Catholic Joint Declaration," *First Things* 98 (December 1999): 28, 29.

275. The Lutheran World Federation and the Roman Catholic Church, *Joint Declaration on the Doctrine of Justification* (Grand Rapids, MI: Eerdmans, 2000), 1 (9). Citations of the *Joint Declaration* refer to official paragraph numbers, with pages in the Eerdmans edition included in parentheses.

276. *Joint Declaration*, 7 (11).

277. *Joint Declaration*, 5 (10–11).

278. *Joint Declaration*, 13 (15). It must be observed, however, that the official Catholic response to the text of the *Joint Declaration* notes that the document's explanation of how Lutheranism understands the justified as *simul justus et peccator* ("at the same time righteous and a sinner") "is not acceptable," and thus "it remains difficult to see how [. . . it . . .] is not touched by the anathemas of the Tridentine decree." "Response of the Catholic Church to the Joint Declaration of the Catholic Church and the Lutheran World Federation on the Doctrine of Justification," Vatican, clarification 1, accessed July 25, 2018, http://www.vatican.va/roman_curia/pontifical_councils/chrstuni/documents/rc_pc_chrstuni_doc_01081998_off-answer-catholic_en.html.

279. Dulles, "Justification in Contemporary Catholic Theology," 256.

280. *Catechism of the Catholic Church* (New York: Image Books, 1995), par. 2019 (p. 544); cf. par. 2027 (p. 545): "Moved by the Holy Spirit, we can merit for ourselves and for others all the graces needed to attain eternal life."

281. *Joint Declaration*, 27 (20).

282. *Joint Declaration*, "Annex to the Official Common Statement," 2A (43); *Joint Declaration*, subheading 4.2 (18). This is the case even though the official Catholic response to the document, "meant to complete some of the paragraphs explaining Catholic doctrine," does so by clearly stating that "eternal life is, at one and the same time, grace and the reward given by God for good works and merits." *Response of the Catholic Church*, clarifications 5, 3.

being accounted, declared, or reckoned righteous is entirely absent in the *Joint Declaration*, which consistently "opts to use the word 'justification' in the Catholic sense."[283] It is difficult to view the "serious omission" of this central concept of Lutheran soteriology as anything but intentional.[284] The ambiguous employment of other key words appears similarly intentional. The term *grace*, for example, is frequently invoked, but whether this is to be understood as God's favor or as a quality in the soul is never indicated. Thus, the transposition of prepositions in describing justification as occurring "by faith and through grace"—rather than in the traditional Lutheran articulation, "by grace and through faith"—allows the impression that grace is the instrumental means of justification, while faith is its actual cause.[285] Such a reading is further made plausible by the document's definition of justifying faith in the traditional Roman sense, as *including* hope and love.[286]

Despite such ambiguities, omissions, and—especially on the part of the Lutheran signatories—concessions, it is not entirely unwarranted to believe that the *Joint Declaration* does speak accurately when it says that "the teaching of the Lutheran churches presented in this Declaration does not fall under the condemnations from the Council of Trent."[287] This is the case, however, only because the Lutheran teaching "presented in this Declaration" is neither the teaching of Luther himself, nor that of the confessional documents that formally define Lutheran doctrine. This being the case, it can only be concluded that the "controversial reception" of Luther's doctrine of justification by grace alone through faith alone on account of Christ's merits alone continues still today, even among some who identify as Luther's theological heirs. Even if controversially, however, it remains a doctrine the church must receive, for it is indeed the doctrine on which it stands or falls. Or, in Luther's own words, "If we lose the doctrine of justification, we lose simply everything."[288]

Recommended Resources

Primary Sources

The Canons and Decrees of the Council of Trent. Translated by H. J. Schroeder. Rockford, IL: TAN Books, 1978.

Chemnitz, Martin. *Examination of the Council of Trent.* Vol. 1. Translated by Fred Kramer. Saint Louis, MO: Concordia, 1971.

Kolb, Robert, and James A. Nestingen, eds. *Sources and Contexts of the Book of Concord.* Minneapolis: Fortress, 2001.

Kolb, Robert, and Timothy J. Wengert, eds. *The Book of Concord: The Confessions of the Evangelical Lutheran Church.* Minneapolis: Fortress, 2000.

---

283. Lane, *Justification by Faith in Catholic-Protestant Dialogue*, 157.
284. Lane, *Justification by Faith in Catholic-Protestant Dialogue*, 126, 158.
285. Department of Systematic Theology, Concordia Seminary, Saint Louis, "A Response to the *Joint Declaration on the Doctrine of Justification*," in *The Joint Declaration on the Doctrine of Justification in Confessional Lutheran Perspective* (Saint Louis, MO: Lutheran Church–Missouri Synod, 1999), 48n9.
286. *Joint Declaration*, 25 (19).
287. *Joint Declaration*, 41 (26).
288. Luther, *Lectures on Galatians* (1535), in *LW* 26:26.

Lund, Eric, ed. *Documents from the History of Lutheranism, 1517–1750*. Minneapolis: Fortress, 2002.

Luther, Martin. *D. Martin Luthers Werke, Kritische Gesamtausgabe, Schriften*. 73 vols. Weimar: Hermann Böhlaus Nachfolger, 1833–2009.

———. *Luther's Works*. Edited by Jaroslav Pelikan, Helmut T. Lehmann, and Christopher Brown. American ed. 82 vols. (projected). Philadelphia: Fortress; Saint Louis, MO: Concordia, 1955—.

———. *Only the Decalogue Is Eternal: Martin Luther's Complete Antinomian Theses and Disputations*. Edited by Holger Sonntag. Minneapolis: Lutheran Press, 2008.

Melanchthon, Philipp. *Loci Communes* (1521). In *Melanchthon and Bucer*, edited by Wilhelm Pauck, trans. Lowell J. Satre, 3–152. Library of Christian Classics 19. Philadelphia: Westminster, 1969.

———. *Philippi Melanthonis Opera*. Vols. 1–28 of *Corpus Reformatorum*. Edited by C. G. Bretschneider and H. E. Bindseil. Halle and Brunswick: Schwetschke, 1834–1860.

Secondary Sources

Anderson, H. George, T. Austin Murphy, and Joseph A. Burgess, eds. *Justification by Faith*. Lutherans and Catholics in Dialogue 7. Minneapolis: Augsburg, 1985.

Arand, Charles P., Robert Kolb, and James A. Nestingen. *The Lutheran Confessions: History and Theology of the Book of Concord*. Minneapolis: Fortress, 2012.

Bente, F. *Historical Introductions to the Book of Concord*. Saint Louis, MO: Concordia, 1965.

Brecht, Martin. *Martin Luther*. 3 vols. Translated by James L. Schaaf. Philadelphia: Fortress, 1985–1993.

Clark, R. Scott. "*Iustitia Imputata Christi*: Alien or Proper to Luther's Doctrine of Justification." *Concordia Theological Quarterly* 70, nos. 3/4 (2006): 269–310.

Drickamer, John M. "Did Melanchthon Become a Synergist?" *Springfielder* 40, no. 2 (1976): 95–101.

Green, Lowell C. *How Melanchthon Helped Luther Discover the Gospel: The Doctrine of Justification in the Reformation*. Fallbrook, CA: Verdict: 1980.

Lane, Anthony N. S. *Justification by Faith in Catholic-Protestant Dialogue: An Evangelical Assessment*. New York: T&T Clark, 2002.

Lehmann, Karl, Michael Root, and William G. Rusch, eds. *Justification by Faith: Do the Sixteenth-Century Condemnations Still Apply?* New York: Continuum, 1997.

The Lutheran World Federation and the Roman Catholic Church. *Joint Declaration on the Doctrine of Justification*. Grand Rapids, MI: Eerdmans, 2000.

McCormack, Bruce L., ed. *Justification in Perspective: Historical Developments and Contemporary Challenges*. Grand Rapids, MI: Baker Academic, 2006.

McGrath, Alister E. *Iustitia Dei: A History of the Christian Doctrine of Justification*. 2nd ed. Cambridge: Cambridge University Press, 1998.

22

The Ground of Religion

Justification in the Reformed Tradition

J. V. FESKO

The doctrine of justification *sola fide* is virtually synonymous with the Reformed tradition. "Justification is the article on which the church stands or falls" is a statement typically attributed to Martin Luther (1483–1546), but in actuality, a Reformed theologian stated it.[1] The fact that a Reformed theologian expressed the idea indicates how integral the doctrine of justification has been to the Reformed tradition. Given that the doctrine of justification was the material principle of the Reformation, this undoubtedly means that the doctrine has impacted the Reformed tradition in a significant way.[2] Reformed theologians joined Luther in his dissatisfaction with the prevailing medieval doctrine of justification. Reformed theologians embraced Luther's teaching and made it a chief foundation stone in its theological edifice, a stone that has endured into the present day. But even though many Reformed churches still profess the unreconstructed Reformed confessional doctrine of the sixteenth and seventeenth centuries, the doctrine neither emerged *ex nihilo* fully formed and fully developed nor has been equally received by all within the tradition. Skirmishes over the doctrine have at times appeared to threaten its well-being, but in the end, the overwhelming historical evidence reveals the tradition's unshakable commitment to this all-important doctrine, for which the Westminster Shorter Catechism offers an excellent and brief definition: "Justification is an act of

---

1. See Alister E. McGrath, *Iustitia Dei: A History of the Christian Doctrine of Justification*, 3rd ed. (Cambridge: Cambridge University Press, 2005), vii*n*1.
2. J. I. Packer, "Introductory Essay," in James Buchanan, *The Doctrine of Justification: An Outline of Its History in the Church and of Its Exposition from Scripture* (1867; repr., Edinburgh: Banner of Truth, 1991), vii.

God's free grace, wherein he pardoneth all our sins, and accepteth us as righteous in his sight, only for the righteousness of Christ imputed to us, and received by faith alone" (q. 33).[3]

To explore the historical origins, development, and reception of the doctrine, this chapter surveys its beginnings in the early Reformation with Luther and the host of theologians he influenced. The chapter then covers the periods of Early (1565–1630), High (1630–1700), and Late Orthodoxy (1700–1790) and the various debates that contributed to the doctrine's confessional codification and reception. The chapter then explores a number of key theologians in the nineteenth century, and its penultimate section delves into the doctrine's reception in the twentieth century. The chapter concludes with summary observations about the place of the doctrine of justification in the Reformed tradition.

Reformation (1517-1565)

Martin Luther

The common idea that Luther launched the Reformation when he tacked his famous *Ninety-Five Theses* to the Castle Church door at Wittenberg has more to do with myth than history. A close reading of the *Ninety-Five Theses* quickly reveals that nothing close to the Reformation doctrine of justification appears. As Luther later had time to reflect on various doctrines and scriptural texts, he eventually laid ax to the root of the medieval doctrine of justification. Luther opined in his 1517 *Disputation against Scholastic Theology*, "We do not become righteous by doing righteous deeds but, having been made righteous, we do righteous deeds. This in opposition to the philosophers."[4] Luther opposed the medieval idea that one becomes righteous through the acquisition of an infused habit and the subsequent exercise of this habit to acquire greater degrees of righteousness. He argued that such an idea originated with the philosophers, that is, Aristotle (384–322 BC). Instead, he argued, "The best and infallible preparation for grace and the sole disposition toward grace is the eternal election and predestination of God."[5] While Luther had not yet developed a full-fledged Protestant doctrine of justification, he was the first to break ground by rejecting medieval concepts connected with habitual righteousness. The rejection of habitual righteousness actually began nearly a decade earlier in his 1509 commentary on Lombard's *Sentences*.[6]

As Luther's thought continued to mature, he posited two kinds of righteousness, that which is internal and external to the redeemed sinner. In his famous 1519 sermon, he spoke of alien righteousness, "that is, the righteousness of another, instilled from without. This is the righteousness of Christ by which he justifies through faith."[7] The

---

3. Unless otherwise noted, all confession and catechism quotations and background information come from Jaroslav Pelikan and Valerie Hotchkiss, eds., *Creeds and Confessions of Faith in the Christian Tradition*, 3 vols. (New Haven, CT: Yale University Press, 2003).
4. Martin Luther, *Disputation against Scholastic Theology*, §40, in *LW* 31:12.
5. Luther, *Disputation*, §29, in *LW* 31:11.
6. Martin Luther, *Luthers Randbemerkungen zu den Sentenzen des Petrus Lombardus*, in WA 9:43 (comm. 1.17).
7. Martin Luther, "Two Kinds of Righteousness," in *LW* 31:297.

second type of righteousness is "our proper righteousness," which works and springs from the alien righteousness of Christ.[8] Luther employed another set of terms, namely, passive and active righteousness. Believers receive passive righteousness through imputation, and active righteousness is inherent.[9] In this move from a habitual to an alien righteousness, Luther finally broke from the medieval doctrine of justification by faith working through love. He instead argued that Christ was the form of faith—that is, only the alien righteousness received by faith alone justified sinners before the divine bar.[10]

Luther developed his mature doctrine of justification by faith alone by the alien imputed righteousness of Christ by 1535, well in advance of any significant engagement of the doctrine by a Reformed theologian.[11] John Calvin (1509–1564), for example, published the first edition of his famous *Institutes of the Christian Religion* in 1536, but he included no treatment of the doctrine of justification.

Huldrych Zwingli

Huldrych Zwingli (1484–1531) was undoubtedly aware of Luther's works but was a Reformer in his own right and developed his own theology independently from Luther.[12] Nevertheless, like Luther, Zwingli rejected the medieval doctrine of justification. In 1523, he presented his *Sixty-Seven Articles* as topics for discussion with the local bishop where he served as pastor in Zurich. Zwingli argued that rather than faith working through love as the means of justification, "our salvation is based on faith in the gospel, and our damnation on unbelief; for all truth is clear in it" (art. 15). Correlatively, Zwingli argued "that Christ is our righteousness, from which we conclude that our works are good in so far as they are of Christ; in so far as they are our works they are neither righteousness nor good" (art. 22). Zwingli flanked these claims with a rejection of papal authority, the Mass, and the intercession of the saints (art. 17–21). Like Luther, Zwingli spoke of two types of righteousness, the outward righteousness that we demonstrate to people and the inward righteousness by which we are pure before God. This righteousness comes from God through Christ by faith. In this sense Zwingli advocated imputed righteousness.[13]

Heinrich Bullinger

How Zwingli might have contributed to the refinement and further codification of the doctrine remains an unanswered question given his untimely death. Zwingli's successor, Heinrich Bullinger (1504–1575), took on the mantle of leadership at Zurich and contributed to the doctrine's development. When Pope Paul III (1468–1549) called for a church council in 1537 to address the burgeoning Protestant Reformation, the Lutheran

---

8. Luther, "Two Kinds of Righteousness," in *LW* 31:299.
9. Mark Mattes, "Luther on Justification as Forensic and Effective," in *The Oxford Handbook of Martin Luther's Theology*, ed. Robert Kolb, Irene Dingel, and L'ubomír Batka (New York: Oxford University Press, 2014), 264–73, esp. 263–66.
10. Martin Luther, *Lectures on Galatians* (1535), in *LW* 26:129; cf. Thomas Aquinas, *Summa Theologica* (Allen, TX: Christian Classics, 1948), 2a2ae.4.3.
11. Luther, *Lectures on Galatians* (1535), in *LW* 26:234.
12. W. P. Stephens, *The Theology of Huldrych Zwingli* (Oxford: Clarendon, 1986), 1.
13. Stephens, *Theology of Zwingli*, 160.

and Reformed churches responded. Bullinger, among others, drafted the First Helvetic Confession (1536). In line with the earlier sentiments of Luther and Zwingli, the confession explains that sinners do not obtain God's grace or sanctification through their own merit but "through faith which is a pure gift of God." And rather than personal merit as the means by which one grows in grace to attain justification, salvation rests entirely on the mercy of God and merit of Christ (chaps. 12–13). What lies somewhat vague in the confession receives fuller exposition in Bullinger's works, such as his famous *Decades*, fifty doctrinal sermons he published between 1549 and 1551.[14]

In these sermons Bullinger was very specific and defined justification as "the absolution of sins, for blessedness, and adoption into the number of the sons of God." He repeated the idea that justification is the remission or forgiveness of sins.[15] But it would be hasty to conclude that Bullinger defined justification only as the forgiveness of sins. Bullinger noted that justification is a legal term; its antonym is *condemnation*, which means that it is ultimately not a process but a divine act.[16] Bullinger expounded this idea when he excluded all the believer's good works from consideration in his justification.[17] The exclusion of works eliminated the possibility of a process whereby believers perform good works, which God then evaluates. Rather, faith in Christ brings justification to the believer because he lays hold of Christ's righteousness:

> There is that singular grace, whereby he doth, for his only-begotten Christ his sake, adopt us to be his sons: he doth not, I mean, adopt all, but the believers only, whose sins he reckoneth not, but doth impute to them the righteousness of his only-begotten Son our Saviour. This is that grace which doth alone justify us in very deed.[18]

A likely cause of Bullinger's greater clarity in comparison with the earlier statements of the First Helvetic Confession is that his sermons appeared after the initial pronouncements of the Council of Trent, which condemned the doctrine of imputed righteousness in its infamous sixth session, on January 13, 1547.[19]

The clearest and most succinct presentation of Bullinger's doctrine appears in the Second Helvetic Confession (1566), a document that he authored as a personal confession of faith but was later adopted by Zurich and Reformed churches across Europe, including Hungary, Scotland, Austria, and Poland. The confession was also widely circulated in France, England, and the Netherlands. There is a night-and-day difference between the inchoate statements of the First and the specificity of the Second Helvetic Confession. The Second defines justification as the remission of sins and the sinner being declared righteous on account of Christ. As with Bullinger's earlier writings, this statement defines justification as the absolu-

---

14. Joel Beeke and George Ella, "Henry Bullinger's *Decades*," in *The Decades of Henry Bullinger*, ed. Thomas Harding (1849–52; repr., Grand Rapids, MI: Reformation Heritage Books, 2004), 1:79.
15. Bullinger, *Decades*, 1:105–6 (1.4).
16. Bullinger, *Decades*, 1:106 (1.6).
17. Bullinger, *Decades*, 1:332 (3.9).
18. Bullinger, *Decades*, 1:330 (3.9).
19. Council of Trent, session 6 (January 13, 1547), in Pelikan and Hotchkiss, *Creeds and Confessions*, vol. 2, *Creeds and Confessions in the Reformation Era*, 826–39.

tion from sin but at the same time as bringing the imputed sufferings and righteousness of Christ. These redemptive benefits come by faith alone apart from works (chap. 15.1–4).

Juán de Valdés

Even though Zwingli represents a somewhat independent stream of doctrinal development, Luther did not recede to the background as the Reformed vessel left its moorings for the high seas of further doctrinal formulation. Zwingli may have formulated his doctrine of justification independently, but Bullinger was first drawn to Protestantism through the works of Luther and Philipp Melanchthon (1497–1560). He concluded that Luther and Melanchthon were in greater accord with Scripture than the teaching of the Roman church and hence embraced the Protestant Reformation.[20] A similar pattern unfolded with a little-known Spanish Reformer by the name of Juán de Valdés (ca. 1498–1541). Valdés remained within the Roman Catholic Church but still read and translated the works of Luther, which undoubtedly played a role in his development of a Protestant doctrine of justification.[21] Valdés first published *The Christian Alphabet* in 1536, the first work published in Italy that presented a Protestant doctrine of justification by faith alone.[22]

Why is Valdés significant for the Reformed doctrine of justification? He never left the Roman Catholic Church, so what role did he play? Valdés had a close circle of friends with whom he interacted, including Peter Martyr Vermigli (1499–1562), whom he convinced to join the Reformation.[23] Hence, Luther passed the baton to Valdés, who in turn made the handoff to Vermigli. This is not to say that Valdés and Vermigli merely repristinated Luther's views. Rather, Luther inspired other theologians to reformulate justification along forensic rather than ontological lines and to affirm it as a once-for-all divine act rather than a lifelong process. Valdés, for example, believed justification immediately entitled a person to eternal life, which stands in contrast to Roman views that claim that the process of justification only concludes at the final judgment.[24]

In contrast to Luther, Valdés also uniquely believed that Christ secured a general justification for all human beings but that people could only lay hold of this justification by faith in Christ.[25] This is not universalism but does bear the marks of a doctrine of universal satisfaction with a particular application only to those who believe. There is no parallel doctrine of this nature in Vermigli. In line with Luther, however, Valdés also affirmed the concept of two kinds of righteousness.[26] And he embraced Luther's doctrine of imputed

---

20. David C. Steinmetz, *Reformers in the Wings* (Grand Rapids, MI: Baker, 1971), 133–42.
21. Frank A. James III, "Juan de Valdés before and after Peter Martyr Vermigli: The Reception of *Gemina Praedestinatio* in Valdés' Later Thought," *ARG* 83 (1992): 183.
22. José C. Nieto, *Juan de Valdés and the Origins of the Spanish and Italian Reformation*, THR 108 (Geneva: Droz, 1970), 315.
23. Philip McNair, *Peter Martyr in Italy: An Anatomy of Apostasy* (Oxford: Clarendon, 1967), 148–49; Massimo Firpo, "The Italian Reformation and Juan de Valdés," *SCJ* 27, no. 2 (1996): 356.
24. Juán de Valdés, *Divine Considerations* (Cambridge: 1646), 242 (art. 69). For an overview of Trent's debates on justification, see Hubert Jedin, *A History of the Council of Trent*, vol. 2, *The First Sessions at Trent, 1545–1547*, trans. Ernest Graf (London: Thomas Nelson, 1958), 166–96.
25. Juán de Valdés, *Commentary upon St. Paul's Epistle to the Romans*, trans. John T. Betts (London: Trübner, 1883), 75–76.
26. Nieto, *Origins*, 320–21.

righteousness as the legal ground of justification within the context of the respective works of the first and last Adams.[27] One of Valdés's unique contributions was the degree to which he incorporated the doctrine of the covenants. He spoke of the new covenant, the covenant of justification, the covenant of resurrection, and the covenant of eternal life.[28]

Peter Martyr Vermigli

As Valdés inculcated him into the teachings of the Protestant Reformation, Vermigli developed the doctrine of justification in a number of ways.[29] In his early doctrine, he merged justification and sanctification, but in his mature formulations he distinguished them.[30] Vermigli's initial doctrine of justification echoed the views of Martin Bucer (1491–1551), a theologian he worked with in Strasbourg and England.[31] His mature doctrine embraced what was becoming the traditional elements of the Reformed doctrine, namely, that justification was not by works but by faith alone and that it brings the forgiveness of sins and the imputation of Christ's righteousness; it is not a process but a divine act.[32] In line with other Reformed views, Vermigli's insistence on *sola fide* did not sideline the importance of good works, which were the fruit of saving faith.[33] Vermigli believed that justification was not in the least inimical to good works: "This doctrine is the head, fountain, and mainstay of all religion."[34] As such, good works grow out of the root of this righteousness and are the immediate consequence of justification.[35]

By this point in the development of the doctrine, Vermigli, like other Reformed theologians, was responding to the Council of Trent. Vermigli explained how the Reformed view differed from the Roman view through the philosophical heuristic of Aristotelian fourfold causality:[36]

Table 23.1 Causality in Trent's View of Justification

Cause	Council of Trent
Efficient	Mercy of God
Meritorious (or material)	Christ's shed blood and the believer's good works
Formal	Justice of God
Final	Glory of God

---

27. Valdés, *Divine Considerations*, 416 (art. 108).
28. Valdés, *Divine Considerations*, 24–27 (art. 8).
29. Frank A. James III, "*De Iustificatione*: The Evolution of Peter Martyr Vermigli's Doctrine of Justification" (PhD diss., Westminster Theological Seminary, 2000).
30. Peter Martyr Vermigli, "Justification and Faith," in *The Peter Martyr Reader*, ed. John Patrick Donnelly, Frank A. James III, and Joseph C. McLelland (Kirksville, MO: Truman State University Press, 1999), 135–36.
31. James, "*De Iustificatione*," 194; McGrath, *Iustitia Dei*, 251–53; cf. Martin Bucer, *Common Places of Martin Bucer*, trans. and ed. David F. Wright, CLRC 4 (Appleford, UK: Sutton Courtenay, 1972), 160–69.
32. Peter Martyr Vermigli, *Predestination and Justification: Two Theological Loci*, trans. and ed. Frank A. James III, vol. 8 of *Peter Martyr Library*, SCES 68 (Kirksville, MO: Thomas Jefferson University Press, 2003), 96.
33. Vermigli, *Predestination and Justification*, 218.
34. Vermigli, *Predestination and Justification*, 96.
35. Vermigli, *Predestination and Justification*, 44, 151.
36. Vermigli, *Predestination and Justification*, 159.

Vermigli rejected this formulation because it mixes the good works of Christ and those of the believer, which is impossible to do. Not only are Christ's works eminently sufficient to secure the believer's salvation, but also the believer's works are always tainted by sin.[37] With Luther, Vermigli believed that to base justification on the combined good works of Christ and the believer amounted to a confusion of law and gospel.[38]

Vermigli's formulations played an important role in the development of the doctrine of justification because he was both a reception and transmission point. Vermigli made a significant impact on second-generation Reformer Zacharias Ursinus (1534–1583). Ursinus highly esteemed his mentor and praised his Romans commentary, in which Vermigli wrote on the doctrine of justification. Additionally, Vermigli carried on significant epistolary dialogue with Bullinger and Calvin.[39] In this epistolary venue, Bullinger sought Vermigli's approval for his Second Helvetic Confession.[40] This means that Vermigli was no minor player within the sixteenth-century Reformed tradition. Before we examine Ursinus's contribution, we explore how Calvin shaped the development of the doctrine.

John Calvin

As noted above, when Calvin first published his *Institutes of the Christian Religion* in 1536, he did not have a locus dedicated to the doctrine of justification. This changed when he revised the *Institutes* in 1539. Calvin added a discussion of the doctrine to the *Institutes* around the same time he was preaching through, teaching on, and writing his commentary on Romans.[41] Like other Reformed theologians, Calvin published his doctrine of justification in several venues: confessional documents, polemical works, sermons, commentaries, and doctrinal treatises. Even though Calvin's initial edition of the *Institutes* did not treat the doctrine, it was on his radar, albeit in inchoate form. In his 1536 Geneva Confession, for example, he stated that sinners receive the grace of God through the "intercession of Jesus Christ, so that by his righteousness and innocence we have remission of our sins, and by the shedding of his blood we are cleansed and purified from all our stains" (art. 7). Sinners receive these blessings by faith, and as such, they must look for saving righteousness solely in Christ and not at all in themselves (art. 9, 11). A major development in Calvin's treatment of the doctrine occurred in his response to the Council of Trent's canons on justification, which he wrote in 1547.[42]

In his response to Trent, Calvin meticulously engaged the council's canons and rejected most of their conclusions. He rejected the Roman Catholic notion of a twofold

---

37. Vermigli, *Predestination and Justification*, 159.
38. Vermigli, "Justification and Faith," 115.
39. Marvin W. Anderson, "Peter Martyr, Reformed Theologian (1542–1562): His Letters to Heinrich Bullinger and John Calvin," *SCJ* 4, no. 1 (1973): 42, 63–64.
40. John Patrick Donnelly, *Calvinism and Scholasticism in Vermigli's Doctrine of Man and Grace*, SMRT 18 (Leiden: Brill, 1976), 185.
41. Elsie Anne McKee, "Introduction," in John Calvin, *Institutes of the Christian Religion: 1541 French Edition*, trans. Elsie Anne McKee (Grand Rapids, MI: Eerdmans, 2009), vii.
42. John Calvin, *Canons and Decrees of the Council of Trent, with the Antidote* (1547), in *Tracts and Letters*, vol. 3, *Tracts, Part 3*, ed. and trans. Henry Beveridge (1851; repr., Edinburgh: Banner of Truth, 2009), 17–188.

justification, in which the first occurs in baptism and the second occurs at the final judgment.[43] He also explained the idea of the *duplex gratia*, or "twofold grace": when God redeems sinners, he does so through the twofold grace of justification and sanctification—two benefits that are inseparably united but nevertheless distinct.[44] In similar fashion to Vermigli, Calvin objected to Trent's confusion regarding the material cause of justification, which it attributed to Christ's and the believer's good works. Such a conclusion confuses the law and the gospel, according to Calvin.[45] The only source for a sinner's justification lies in the imputed righteousness of Christ.[46] Hence, Calvin believed that justification takes priority over good works: "It is necessary that the righteousness of faith alone so precede in order, and be so pre-eminent in degree, that nothing can go before it or obscure it."[47] To protect the integrity of justification, Calvin also stipulated that whenever he or the Reformed mentioned *sola fide*, they were not advocating a dead but lively faith that works by love (Gal. 5:6). And by this he meant, "It is therefore faith alone which justifies, and yet the faith which justifies is not alone."[48]

Beyond these engagements with the doctrine, Calvin made significant contributions to its development in two other publications: the final edition of his *Institutes* (1559) and the French Confession (1559), which he coauthored. Calvin's definitive edition of the *Institutes* is important because it represents the culmination of nearly twenty-five years of serving in pastoral ministry, lecturing through the biblical text, preaching, and debating on a host of polemical subjects. But what is especially noteworthy is Calvin's engagement with the erroneous views of Lutheran theologian Andreas Osiander (1498–1552). Osiander argued that when believers are justified, they receive through union with Christ his essential righteousness, not his imputed righteousness. Calvin added an entire new section to his locus on justification to deal with Osiander's views.[49]

Calvin's interaction with Osiander is important for at least three reasons:

1. Calvin rejected Osiander's doctrine of essential righteousness and held to the doctrine of imputed righteousness.
2. When Calvin might have been tempted to disconnect justification from union with Christ, to distance himself from Osiander's erroneous view, he continued to hold the two together as Reformed theologians had done.
3. This development represents a shift in the field of battle, for this was one of the first occurrences of intra-Protestant debate over justification. Up until this time the Reformed directed their polemical theology at Rome, especially the Council of Trent. But now there was debate within the Protestant camp. This third point represents a shift in the development of the doctrine, discussed further below.

---

43. Calvin, *Antidote*, 114.
44. Calvin, *Antidote*, 115–16.
45. Calvin, *Antidote*, 116.
46. Calvin, *Antidote*, 115.
47. Calvin, *Antidote*, 128.
48. Calvin, *Antidote*, 152.
49. John Calvin, *Institutes of the Christian Religion*, trans. Henry Beveridge (Grand Rapids, MI: Eerdmans, 1957), 3.11.5.

Calvin made a further contribution in a second work, the 1559 French Confession, a document he cowrote with Theodore Beza (1519–1605) and Pierre Viret (1511–1571). This confession was used among the French Reformed churches and also constituted the starting point for Guido de Bres's (1522–1567) Belgic Confession (1561). The French Confession offers one of the first full-fledged definitions and codifications of nearly thirty years of development, reflection, and debate:

> We believe that all our justification rests upon the remission of our sins, in which also is our only blessedness, as the Psalmist says. We therefore reject all other means of justification before God, and without claiming any virtue or merit, we rest simply in the obedience of Jesus Christ, which is imputed to us as much to blot out all our sins as to make us find grace and favor in the sight of God. (art. 18)

In addition to this statement, the confession explains that justification is by faith alone, which is the gratuitous gift of God given only to the elect, and that this holy faith enables justified Christians to live holy lives in the fear of God (art. 19–22). Similar statements appear in the Belgic Confession (art. 22–23). Through Calvin's confessional labors, he assisted in further defining and codifying the developing Reformed doctrine of justification. With Vermigli, who said that justification was the fountain and mainstay of all religion, Calvin wrote that justification "is the ground on which religion must be supported. . . . For unless you understand first of all what your position is before God, and what the judgment which he passes upon you, you have not foundation on which your salvation can be laid, or on which piety towards God can be reared."[50]

Zacharias Ursinus and the Heidelberg Catechism

Another noteworthy figure is Zacharias Ursinus, the author and chief expositor of the Heidelberg Catechism (1563). Ursinus is important for several reasons. First, as noted above, he sat at the feet of Vermigli and thought highly of his mentor's labors, particularly his commentary on Romans. Second, he also studied with Calvin and even wrote a compendium of his *Institutes*, which means he was intimately familiar with Calvin's theology.[51] Like Calvin, Ursinus also represents the reconnection of Reformed with Lutheran theology, owing to his time of study with Melanchthon. Third, as the author of the Heidelberg Catechism, Ursinus had the task of trying to unite the Reformed and Lutheran factions in Heidelberg behind a single confessional document. So at a number of points, the catechism represents the confluence of these different theological streams.

The catechism deals with the doctrine of justification by asking, How are you righteous before God? It answers,

---

50. Calvin, *Institutes*, 3.11.1.
51. Derk Visser, *Zacharias Ursinus: The Reluctant Reformer; His Life and Times* (New York: United Church Press, 1983), 3–143.

> Only by true faith in Jesus Christ. In spite of the fact that my conscience accuses me that I have grievously sinned against all the commandments of God, and have not kept any one of them, and that I am still ever prone to all that is evil, nevertheless, God, without any merit of my own, out of pure grace, grants me the benefits of the perfect expiation of Christ, imputing to me his righteousness and holiness as if I had never committed a single sin or had ever been sinful, having fulfilled myself all the obedience which Christ has carried out for me, if only I accept such favor with a trusting heart. (q. 60)

The catechism stipulates that this justification comes by faith alone and then notes that the sinner does not stand worthy before the divine bar by virtue of this faith but because this faith lays hold of "the satisfaction, righteousness, and holiness of Christ" (q. 61). In line with other Reformed theologians and confessional documents, the catechism explains that faith is a divine gift, and that while the believer produces good works by virtue of his or her union with Christ, such are not suitable to withstand divine scrutiny on the day of judgment because they are imperfect and defiled by sin. When God rewards believers, he does so by his grace, not on account of the supposedly meritorious nature of these works (qq. 62–65).

When he expounded these statements in his exposition of the catechism, Ursinus, as his predecessors, explained that Christ rendered satisfaction to the law in our place and did so through his humiliation, which lasted from his conception up to his glorification through his assumption of humanity, subjection to the law, poverty, reproach, sufferings, weakness, and death. In addition to all this, Christ fulfilled the law through his personal holiness and by his obedience, even unto death. Believers receive this threefold work of Christ (satisfaction, righteousness, and holiness) when God applies it to them by imputation, which believers receive through faith alone. Christ performs this work in the place of the redeemed sinner, and God accounts it to them as if it were theirs.[52]

By the end of the Reformation, Reformed theologians spent nearly a generation exegeting various biblical texts; writing commentaries, theological works, confessional documents; and engaging Roman Catholic theologians in debate. It was a settled fact that the doctrine of justification entailed the forgiveness of sins and the imputation of Christ's righteousness and that it was received by faith alone apart from works. Affirmation of justification *sola fide*, however, did not mean that Reformed theologians believed that good works were therefore superfluous. On the contrary, they believed that while justification was by faith alone, this faith was never alone but was always accompanied by the fruit of good works, which was by virtue of the believer's union with Christ. The Reformers laid the foundation, and subsequent generations of theologians guarded this deposit of truth, but development and refinement of the doctrine continued. The Osiander debate signaled that although the Reformed had established the broad parameters of the doctrine through the exegesis of Scripture and debates with

---

52. Zacharias Ursinus, *The Commentary of Dr. Zacharias Ursinus on the Heidelberg Catechism*, trans. G. W. Williard (1852; repr., Phillipsburg, NJ: P&R, n.d.), 327–33.

Rome, some details still required attention. This continued refinement surfaced in the Early and High Orthodox periods.

Early Orthodoxy (1565-1630)

The Piscator Controversy

The first significant intra-Reformed debate over the doctrine of justification surrounded the controversial views of Johannes Piscator (1546–1625). Throughout the sixteenth century, the confessional consensus was that justification consists in the forgiveness of sins and the imputation of Christ's righteousness.[53] Despite broad attestation, Piscator nevertheless rejected the doctrine of Christ's imputed righteousness. He believed that justification was merely the forgiveness of sins. Concerning Acts 13:38–39, Piscator wrote,

> The apostle in this place defines justification by forgiveness of sins only, is manifest partly by the consequence of sentences, whereof one is added to another, as explaining the same partly by the very phrase, *to be justified from sins*: which is no other thing, than to be absolved from sins committed, and by consequence, to obtain forgiveness of sins.[54]

Piscator held that Christ's personal obedience to the law was necessary to complete his work as Mediator but that God did not impute this obedience to the believer in justification.[55] Piscator believed that his views were not novel but rather a restatement of Calvin's doctrine of imputation.

Piscator's claims ignited an intra-Reformed debate over the question whether justification included Christ's imputed righteousness. David Pareus (1548–1622), a student of Ursinus, presented a taxonomy and defense of Piscator's doctrine. Piscator explained that all parties agreed on the meaning of the term *justify*, that it is *sola fide*, that God does not infuse believers with Christ's righteousness, and that Christ's alien righteousness justifies sinners. But the key point of contention surrounded the nature of Christ's merit. There were four different views:

1. Believers receive only the imputed passive obedience of Christ.
2. God imputes Christ's active law keeping to believers.
3. Believers receive only Christ's human righteousness.
4. Believers receive the essential or divine righteousness through union with Christ.

These views, according to Pareus, differed in terms of a single up to a fourfold imputation:

---

53. Cf., e.g., First Confession of Basel (1534), art. 9; Geneva Confession (1536), art. 7; Geneva Catechism (1541/1542), qq. 119–20; Forty-Two Articles (1553), 11; Belgic Confession (1561), art. 22; Heidelberg Catechism (1563), q. 60; Second Helvetic Confession (1566), chap. 15.3. The Reformed confessions moved from speaking of righteousness to imputed righteousness most likely because of the impact of the Tridentine condemnations of the doctrine.
54. Johannes Piscator, *A Learned and Profitable Treatise on Man's Justification* (London: 1599), 20.
55. Johannes Piscator, *Aphorismes of Christian Religion: or, A Verie Compendious Abridgement of M. I. Calvins Institutions* (London: Richard Field, 1596), 68 (13.7–8).

1. Single: passive obedience
2. Double: active and passive obedience
3. Triple: active, passive, and habitual obedience
4. Quadruple: divine and human righteousness, active and passive obedience

He also observed that these particular questions did not appear in the works of Luther, Melanchthon, Zwingli, Calvin, Vermigli, Wolfgang Musculus (1497–1563), or Andreas Hyperius (1511–1564).[56]

Pareus criticized the alternative views (double, triple, and quadruple imputation) and then defended his own view of single imputation of Christ's passive obedience. He rejected the other positions for nine reasons:

1. Promoters confuse Christ's personal righteousness with his merit, or more technically, they confound the efficient and material causes of justification.
2. Advocates impose false dilemmas on the theological question by employing binary categories of unrighteous and righteous, transgressing and fulfilling the law, dead and alive.
3. Why is Christ's passive obedience insufficient for justification?
4. If the forgiveness of sins is not the whole of our justification, then how can Romans 4:7, "Blessed are they whose lawless deeds are forgiven," be true?
5. If believers are not forgiven for their failure to obey the law through the passive obedience of Christ because such sins require the active obedience, how can it be true that "the blood of Jesus his Son cleanses us from all sin" (1 John 1:7)?
6. If we are justified by the active obedience of Christ, then what need was there for his death and suffering? His passive obedience is superfluous.
7. The division of Christ's righteousness into two or three parts derogates Christ's death and God's righteousness.
8. To seek our justification in different parts of Christ's work distracts our faith and robs us of comfort.
9. Nowhere does Scripture divide Christ's righteousness into two or three parts, and nowhere does it mention the imputation of Christ's holiness.[57]

In Pareus's mind, these reasons were sufficient grounds to reject double, triple, and quadruple imputation. He noted that, even though the Heidelberg Catechism (q. 60) appears to endorse triple imputation, Ursinus never intended to teach anything more than single imputation. To add further weight to his arguments, Pareus appealed to earlier confessional documents and theologians, such as Melanchthon, Calvin, and the French Confession (1559) to argue that they, too, only advocated justification as the forgiveness of sins.

Pareus believed, for example, that Calvin's famous definition of justification did not teach the imputation of Christ's righteousness. Calvin's definition reads, "Thus we

---

56. David Pareus, "The Epistle of D. David Parie to the Illustrious and Noble Count, Lord Ludovick Witgensteinius concerning Christ's Active and Passive Justice," in Zacharias Ursinus, *The Summe of Christian Religion*, ed. David Pareus (London: James Young, 1645), 792–93.
57. Pareus, "Christ's Active and Passive Justice," 795–96.

simply interpret justification, as the acceptance with which God receives us into his favor as if we were righteous; and we say that this justification consists in the forgiveness of sins and the imputation of the righteousness of Christ."[58] Pareus interprets the last phrase, "and the imputation of the righteousness of Christ," as explanatory of the "remission of sins." That is, Calvin's definition should read, "We say that this justification consists in the forgiveness of sins, which is the imputation of the righteousness of Christ."[59]

Piscator's formulations highlighted a new distinction in the Reformed doctrine of justification, namely, the active and passive righteousness of Christ. In other words, during the Reformation, theologians holistically conceived of Christ's righteousness as consisting in both his suffering and obedience to the law. Piscator, on the other hand, separated Christ's satisfaction (suffering the curse of the law) from his obedience to the law and argued that believers received only the former, not the latter. The unintended consequence of Piscator's rejection of the imputed active obedience of Christ (IAOC) was that he permanently etched the distinction into the Reformed doctrine of justification. Piscator's rejection of the IAOC created a firestorm of controversy.[60] In 1603, the Synod of Gap censured Piscator's views and warned him not to harass the Reformed churches with his "new-fangled Opinions." The synod also communicated with universities in England, Scotland, Leiden, Geneva, Heidelberg, Basel, and Herborn to request that they join the synod in their censure of Piscator. Local synods and consistories were urged to "have a careful Eye on those persons who be tainted with that Error, be they Ministers or private Christians, and . . . silence them; and in case of a willful stubborn persistency in their Error, to depose them, if they have a Pastoral Charge in the Church, from the Ministry."[61]

The synod did not hastily make this decision but instead relied on significant doctrinal precedent both within and without the Reformed churches. The Lutheran Formula of Concord (1577), for example, maintained that the obedience of Christ "consists not only in His suffering and death but also in the fact that He freely put himself in our place under the law and fulfilled the law with this obedience and reckoned it to us as righteousness."[62] Calvin argued that justification consisted in the forgiveness of sins *and* the imputation of Christ's righteousness.[63] Luther believed that sinners required an alien righteousness for justification.[64] Beza was explicit for the need of the IAOC in justification.[65] In fact, strong evidence points to the fact that Beza was the source of

---

58. Calvin, *Institutes*, 3.11.2.
59. Pareus, "Christ's Active and Passive Justice," 800.
60. For what follows, see Heber Carlos de Campos Jr., "Johannes Piscator (1546–1625) and the Consequent Development of the Doctrine of the Imputation of Christ's Active Obedience" (PhD diss., Calvin Theological Seminary, 2009), 13–18.
61. John Quick, ed., "The Acts and Decisions and Decrees of the XVII National Synod of the Reformed Churches of France, Held in the Town of Gap, and Providence of Dolphiny," in *Synodicon in Gallia Reformata* (London: Thomas Parkhurst, 1692), 1:227.
62. "The Solid Declaration of the Formula Concord," 3.15, in *The Book of Concord: The Confessions of the Evangelical Lutheran Church*, ed. Robert Kolb and Timothy J. Wengert (Minneapolis: Fortress, 2000), 564.
63. Calvin, *Institutes*, 3.11.2.
64. Luther, "Two Kinds of Righteousness," in *LW* 31:297–306.
65. Campos, "Johannes Piscator," 89–98.

the Heidelberg Catechism's threefold imputation, namely, the crediting of Christ's satisfaction, righteousness, and holiness in justification.[66] On this threefold imputation, Beza wrote,

> For our sinnes are defaced by the blood of Christ, and the guiltines of our corruption itself (which the Apostle calleth sinfull sinne) is healed in us by litle and litle, by the gift of sanctification, but yet lacketh besides that, an other remedie, to wit, the perfect sanctification of Christs owne flesh, which also is to us imputed.[67]

The Synod of Gap's speedy and forceful censure did not end the debate or eliminate Piscator's view. The delegates at the Synod of Dort (1618–1619) also debated this matter when the synod's president, Johannes Bogerman (1576–1637), tried to amend the Belgic Confession to accommodate both the critics and proponents of the IAOC. Article 24 of the Belgic states, "Jesus Christ is our righteousness in making available to us all his merits and all the holy works he has done for us." Bogerman tried to replace these words with the phrase "Christ's obedience," but the effort was nearly universally defeated when brought to a vote. Only two delegates voted in favor of the alteration. In fact, because of the efforts to reject the IAOC, the synod voted to add an explanatory phrase (italicized): "Jesus Christ is our righteousness in making available to us all his merits and all the holy works he has done for us *and in our place*." This change was nearly unanimously approved with only two dissenting votes.[68] A third layer of ecclesiastical denunciation appears in the Irish Articles (1615), which was written under the influence of James Ussher (1581–1656), the archbishop of Armagh and eventual primate over Ireland. The Articles specifically state, "He, for them, fulfilled the law in his life; that now, in him, and by him, every true Christian man may be called a fulfiller of the law" (art. 35). The Articles leave no room for Piscator's views, and Ussher was personally explicit in his affirmation of the IAOC.[69]

Jacobus Arminius, the Synod of Dort, and the Irish Articles

A second major Early Orthodox controversy over the doctrine of justification surrounded the views of Jacobus Arminius (1560–1609). Historians usually identify Arminius as the instigator of the debate in the Netherlands over the doctrine of predestination, but his doctrine of justification was also a flashpoint of controversy. Some historians see no difference between Arminius's view and the Reformed doctrine of justification, arguing that Arminius's doctrine of justification falls within

---

66. Campos, "Johannes Piscator," 92–98; Heidelberg Catechism, q. 61.
67. Theodore Beza, *The New Testament of Our Lord Jesus Christ*, trans. L. Tomson (London: Christopher Barker, 1586), comm. Rom. 8:2 (fol. 221v); Campos, "Johannes Piscator," 97n121.
68. Nicolaas H. Gootjes, *The Belgic Confession: Its History and Sources*, TSRPRT (Grand Rapids, MI: Baker Academic, 2007), 151–52.
69. Richard Snoddy, *The Soteriology of James Ussher: The Act and Object of Saving Faith*, OSHT (New York: Oxford University Press, 2014), 116–20.

historic confessional boundaries.[70] Recent analysis, however, presents compelling research to demonstrate that two of Arminius's critics, Franciscus Gomarus (1563–1641) and Sibrandus Lubbertus (ca. 1555–1625), believed his doctrine of justification departed from Reformed orthodoxy.[71] They contended that his views were closer to Socinianism than to a common Reformed understanding because he attributed justification to the human act of faith rather than to the merit of Christ.[72]

Arminius explained his understanding of faith and its role in justification:

> Faith is imputed to us for righteousness, on account of Christ and his righteousness. In this enunciation, faith is the object of imputation; but Christ and his obedience are the impetratory or meritorious cause of justification. Christ and his obedience are the object of our faith; but not the object of justification or divine imputation, as if God imputes Christ and his righteousness to us for righteousness.[73]

This is one of the clearest statements that explains Arminius's doctrine of faith. To be sure, Arminius believed that Christ is the object of faith, but faith is ultimately the basis of justification. God looks on the believer's faith as if it were righteousness. The historic Reformed view has always maintained that faith is instrumental, not foundational, in justification. We are justified *by* or *through* faith, not on the basis of faith.

Arminius's explanation was no slip of the pen, for he explicitly rejected faith as the instrumental cause of justification. He knew he was swimming against the Reformed stream of opinion:

> I wish therefore, that any man would reconcile for me, with this interpretation, that very common phrase in the Scriptures, when they are treating on Justification through Faith, which is *Faith imputed for righteousness*. If I understand at all, I think this is the meaning of the phrase, *God accounts faith for righteousness*: And thus justification is ascribed to faith, not because it accepts, but because it is accepted.[74]

Arminius continued and registered his dissatisfaction with the common Reformed doctrine of faith:

> But some one will reply, "Justification is attributed to faith, on account of the object which faith receives, and which is Christ, who is our righteousness." This is not

---

70. E.g., Roger E. Olson, *Arminian Theology: Myths and Realities* (Downers Grove, IL: IVP Academic, 2006), 200; Carl Bangs, *Arminius: A Study in the Dutch Reformation* (Eugene, OR: Wipf & Stock, 1998), 344–45; Keith D. Stanglin, *Arminius on the Assurance of Salvation: The Context, Roots, and Shape of the Leiden Debate, 1603–1609*, BSCH 27 (Leiden: Brill, 2007), 105–6; William den Boer, *God's Twofold Love: The Theology of Jacob Arminius (1559–1609)*, trans. Albert Gootjes (Göttingen: Vandenhoeck & Ruprecht, 2010), 203, 205–6.
71. Aza Goudriaan, "Justification by Faith and the Early Arminian Controversy," in *Scholasticism Reformed: Essays in Honour of Willem J. van Asselt*, ed. Maarten Wisse, Marcel Sarot, Willemien Otten, STR 14 (Leiden: Brill, 2010), 155–78.
72. Goudriaan, "Justification by Faith," 174.
73. Jacobus Arminius, "Letter to Hippolytus a Collibus, 8 April 1608," sec. 5, in Jacobus Arminius, *The Works of James Arminius*, trans. James Nichols and William Nichols (1828; repr., Grand Rapids, MI: Baker, 1996), 2:702.
74. Arminius, "Letter to Uitenbogaert, 10 Apr 1599," in Arminius, *Works*, 2:50n.

repugnant to my meaning, but it renders a reason why God imputes our faith to us for justification. But I deny that this expression is figurative, *We are justified by faith*, that is, by the thing which faith apprehends.[75]

Arminius was well aware of his divergence from commonly accepted Reformed norms, and this appears in the way he exegeted key texts. In his exegesis of Romans 4:3, "It was counted to him as righteousness," Arminius explained the difference between his own and the common Reformed interpretation:

> In this enunciation, "Faith is imputed to the believer for righteousness," is the word "faith" to be *properly* received as the instrumental act by which Christ has been apprehended for righteousness? Or is it to be *improperly* received, that is, by a metonymy, for the very object which faith apprehends?[76]

In technical terms, is faith the very thing that God receives as righteousness, or is *faith* a metonym for Christ and his righteousness? Arminius undoubtedly and clearly opted for the former. At this point in the development of the doctrine of justification, no major Reformed theologian or document advocated Arminius's view.[77] Given the common interpretation, it should come as no surprise that the ecclesiastical reception was swift and negative.

Again, the Synod of Dort famously issued its canons on predestination and related doctrines, but nestled in its deliverances was a rejection of Arminius's doctrine of faith:

> Having set forth the orthodox teaching, the synod rejects the errors of those who teach that what is involved in the new covenant of grace which God the Father made with men through the intervening of Christ's death is not that we are justified before God and saved through faith, insofar as it accepts Christ's merit, but rather that God, having withdrawn his demand for perfect obedience to the law, counts faith itself, and the imperfect obedience of faith, as perfect obedience to the law, and graciously looks upon this as worthy of reward of eternal life. (2.2, rej. of error 4)

News of Arminius's views and the rejection of them spread very quickly, and other ecclesiastical bodies added their dissent. The Irish Articles state,

---

75. Arminius, "Letter to Uitenbogaert, 10 Apr 1599," 2:50n.
76. Jacobus Arminius, *Certain Articles to be Diligently Examined and Weighed*, 22.16, in Arminius, *Works*, 2:728.
77. See, e.g., Lucas Trelcatius, *A Briefe Institution of the Common Places of Sacred Divinitie*, trans. John Gawen (London, 1610), 256 (2.9); Johannes Wollebius, *Compendium Theologiae Christianae*, in *Reformed Dogmatics*, ed. and trans. John W. Beardslee (New York: Oxford University Press, 1965), 165 (30.8); Johannes Polyander, Andreas Rivet, Antonius Walaeus, and Antonius Thysius, *Synopsis Purioris Theologiae / Synopsis of a Purer Theology*, ed. Henk van den Belt et al. (Leiden: Brill, 2016), 2:319 (33.27); Girolamo Zanchi, *De Religione Christiana Fides—Confession of Christian Religion*, ed. Luca Baschera and Christian Moser, SHCTr 135 (Leiden: Brill, 2007), 1:342–43 (19.6); William Perkins, *A Golden Chain, or, The Description of Theology* (1597; n.p.: Puritan Reprints, 2010), 172 (chap. 36); Theodore Beza, *The Christian Faith*, trans. James Clark (Lewes, UK: Focus Christian Ministries Trust, 1992), 17 (4.6); Heidelberg Catechism, qq. 60–61; Ursinus, *Commentary*, 328–29.

> When we say we are justified by faith only, we do not mean that the said justifying faith is alone in man without true repentance, hope, charity, and the fear of God (for such a faith cannot justify); neither do we mean that this, our act, to believe in Christ, or this, our faith in Christ, which is within us, does of itself justify us or deserve our justification unto us (for that were to account ourselves to be justified by the virtue or dignity of something that is within ourselves). (art. 36)

Ussher was one of the Articles' chief architects and was aware of Arminius's views as early as 1607, and other Irish officials also expressed concerns.[78] This would not be the last time theologians or confessional documents rejected Arminius's doctrine of faith. As discussed below, Reformed theologians during the High Orthodoxy era also registered their disapprobation.

High Orthodoxy (1630-1700)

The Westminster Confession

Reformed theologians of the High Orthodox period believed they had the responsibility to guard the truth that earlier generations entrusted to them. This is not to imply that the vibrant Reformed faith ossified into a hardened traditionalism—far from it. As with the first-generation Reformers, High Orthodox Reformed theologians were equally committed to the authority of Scripture and the primacy of exegesis in the formulation of doctrine.[79] Both the Synod of Dort and the Westminster Assembly produced commentaries on the whole Bible.[80] But at the same time, Reformed theologians believed that their forefathers bequeathed to them the treasure of the gospel, and so they sought to promote, codify, and defend this truth. In the preface to his work on justification, Westminster divine Anthony Burgess (1600–1663) captured this idea:

> Truth is a *depositum*. Aristotle doth rationally conclude, That it is a greater injustice to deny a little thing deposited, then a great summe that we are indebted for, because he that depositeth any thing in our custody, trusteth in us as a faithfull friend; the other expecteth only justice from us. Now of all points of Divinity, there is none that with more profit and comfort we may labour in, then in that of Justification, which is stiled by some, *articulus stantis & cadentis ecclesiae*, The Church stands or fals, as the truth of this is asserted, and a modest, sober vindication of this point from contrary errors, will not hinder, but much advantage the affectionate part of man, even as the Bee is helped by her sting to make honey.[81]

---

78. Alan Ford, *James Ussher: Theology, History, and Politics in Early-Modern Ireland and England* (Oxford: Oxford University Press, 2007), 162; Thomas Warren, "Letter XXXVI, Mr. Thomas Warren to Dr. James Ussher," in *The Whole Works of the Most Rev. James Ussher, D.D.*, ed. Charles R. Elrington and James H. Todd (Dublin: Hodges, Smith, 1829–1864), 15:141–42.
79. On the exegetical nature of Reformed theology, see Richard A. Muller, *Post-Reformation Reformed Dogmatics*, vol. 2, *Holy Scripture: The Cognitive Foundation of Theology*, 2nd ed. (Grand Rapids, MI: Baker Academic, 2003).
80. Theodore Haak, *The Dutch Annotations upon the Whole Bible . . . Ordered and Appointed by the Synod of Dort* (London: Henry Hills, 1657); John Downame, *Annotations upon All the Books of the Old and New Testament* (London: Evan Tyler, 1657).
81. Anthony Burgess, *The True Doctrine of Justification Asserted and Vindicated, from the Errours of Papists, Arminians, Socinians, and More Especially Antinomians* (London: Thomas Underhill, 1651), preface.

The title of Burgess's work reveals that he addressed a new threat that challenged the doctrine of justification. With the existing dangers of Pelagianism, Roman Catholicism, and Arminianism, Burgess discussed Antinomianism, the idea that God frees believers from the requirements of the moral law.

The Westminster divines saw the doctrine of justification imperiled on every side and thus sought to defend it. Evidence of their concerns appears in the way in which they carefully framed the doctrine in the Westminster Confession:

> Those whom God effectually calleth, he also freely justifieth: not by infusing righteousness into them, but by pardoning their sins, and by accounting and accepting their persons as righteous; not for anything wrought in them, or done by them, but for Christ's sake alone; nor by imputing faith itself, the act of believing, or any other evangelical obedience to them, as their righteousness; but by imputing the obedience and satisfaction of Christ unto them, they receiving and resting on him and his righteousness, by faith; which faith they have not of themselves, it is the gift of God. (11.1)

With each phrase of this statement, the divines established a defensive perimeter around the doctrine and at the same time set forth the common Reformed view (see table 23.2).

Table 23.2 Westminster Assembly's Rejection of Errors

Westminster Confession Statement	Rejection of Error
"Not by infusing righteousness into them"	Roman Catholic view of infused righteousness
"Not for anything wrought in them, or done by them"	Roman Catholic view that the believer's good works are necessary for justification
"Nor by imputing faith itself, the act of believing, or any other evangelical obedience to them, as their righteousness"	Arminius's doctrine of faith and other forms of neonomianism, or legalism

When we strip away these rejections of errors, the resulting positive definition of justification is this: "Those whom God effectually calleth, he also freely justifieth: by imputing the obedience and satisfaction of Christ unto them, they receiving and resting on him and his righteousness, by faith; which faith they have not of themselves, it is the gift of God."

In addition to rejecting common theological foes, the assembly targeted a number of forms of antinomianism. Some, like the assembly's prolocutor, William Twisse (1578–1646), believed that the elect were justified from eternity and that only when they made a profession of faith did they become aware of the status they already possessed. The divines specifically rejected this error without invoking Twisse's name: "God did, from all eternity, decree to justify all the elect, and Christ did, in the fullness of time, die for their sins, and rise again for their justification: nevertheless, they are not justified, until the Holy Spirit doth, in due time, actually apply Christ unto them" (11.4).[82] They also rebuffed the common accusation that justification led to apathy toward good works: "Faith, thus receiving and resting on Christ and his righteousness, is the alone instrument of justification: yet is it not alone in the person justified, but is ever accompanied with all other saving graces, and is no dead faith, but worketh by love" (11.2).

Additionally, they challenged the notion that, once God justified a sinner, he never saw any sin whatsoever in them. Rather,

> God doth continue to forgive the sins of those that are justified; and, although they can never fall from the state of justification, yet they may, by their sins, fall under God's fatherly displeasure, and not have the light of his countenance restored unto them, until they humble themselves, confess their sins, beg pardon, and renew their faith and repentance. (11.5)[83]

Correlatively, they maintained, "Good works . . . are the fruits and evidences of a true and lively faith" (16.2). This statement specifically addressed the errors of antinomianism, namely, those who misapplied the doctrine of justification to dismiss the believer's need to manifest good works.[84]

Burgess and other divines insisted on the importance and necessity of the imputed righteousness of Christ, but they had to defend this idea on two fronts: against the assaults of the antinomians and against the criticisms of those who rejected the IAOC. Even though the Reformed churches at the Synod of Gap and Synod of Dort rejected Piscator's views, they were still a live issue when the Westminster Assembly deliberated over the doctrine of justification. First, regarding antinomianism, Burgess believed that the doctrine of imputation did not lead to licentiousness: "The Imputation of Christs righteousnesse, the mistaking of which point, is no mean cause of Antinomianism."[85] Second, the divines extensively debated the IAOC. When Parliament first called the assembly, it originally commissioned it to revise the Thirty-Nine Articles. In the course of their labors, debate broke out when they arrived at the chapter on justification. A small but vocal minority of eight divines made 70 speeches against the IAOC. On the other side of the aisle, twenty divines made 181 speeches in favor of the IAOC.[86] Given the number of participants and speeches for and against, the outcome was predictable (see table 23.3).[87]

---

82. Cf. Burgess, *Justification*, 266–72. See Chad Van Dixhoorn, "The Strange Silence of Prolocutor Twisse: Predestination and Politics in the Westminster Assembly's Debate over Justification," *SCJ* 40, no. 2 (2009): 395–418.
83. Cf. Burgess, *Justification*, 24–95.
84. See Whitney G. Gamble, *Christ and the Law: Antinomianism at the Westminster Assembly* (Grand Rapids, MI: Reformation Heritage Books, 2018), 133–54.
85. Burgess, *Justification*, preface.
86. Chad Van Dixhoorn, "Reforming the Reformation: Theological Debate at the Westminster Assembly, 1642–1652" (PhD diss., Cambridge University, 2004), 1:332–34.
87. *The Proceedings of the Assembly of Divines upon the Thirty Nine Articles of the Church of England* (London, 1647), 8–9.

Table 23.3 Westminster Assembly's Revision of Thirty-Nine Articles, Article 11

Original Article 11	Revised Article 11
We are accounted righteous before God, only for the merit of our Lord and Savior Jesus Christ by faith, and not of our own works or deservings: Wherefore that we are justified by faith only is a most wholesome doctrine, and very full of comfort, as more largely is expressed in the Homily on Justification.	We are justified, that is, we are accounted righteous before God, and have remission of sins, not for nor by our own works or deservings, but freely by his grace, onely for our Lord and Saviour Jesus Christs sake, his *whole obedience and satisfaction* being by God imputed unto us and Christ with his righteousness, being apprehended and rested on by faith onely. The Doctrine of Justification by faith onely, is an wholsom Doctrine, and very full of comfort: *notwithstanding God doth not forgive them that are impenitent, and go on still in their trespasses.*

There are notable differences between the two statements, but the two italicized phrases deserve attention. The closing phrase rejects another tenet of antinomianism, namely, that once justified, believers can wantonly sin because they are justified. And in order to affirm the IAOC, the divines inserted the term "whole obedience" to denote both Christ's active and passive obedience.

The big question would come later, when the divines were given a new assignment of writing a new confession of faith and catechisms, namely, Why did the divines omit the phrase "whole obedience" in the Westminster Confession? Why did they refer only to the imputation of the "obedience and satisfaction of Christ unto" believers (11.1)? Some have argued that this omission was a deliberate accommodation of the anti-IAOC party.[88] They come to this conclusion in part because of the later alterations that Congregational theologians made to their version of the Westminster Confession, the Savoy Declaration, which specifically states, ". . . by imputing Christ's active and passive obedience to the whole law, and passive obedience in his death."[89] While this is a plausible explanation, the Westminster Standards on the whole provide an inhospitable environment for someone who denies the IAOC. In the broader context of the Standards, the Larger Catechism explains that Christ perfectly fulfilled the law (q. 48), which the catechism distinguishes from his death (qq. 49–50). And when the Larger Catechism unites its treatment of Christ's work (qq. 46–50) with justification (qq. 70–71), within the bicovenantal framework of the covenants of works and grace, it promotes the necessity of the IAOC. Other important considerations appear in the fact that proponents of the IAOC did not like the phrase "whole obedience."[90] Moreover, during this period "obedience and satisfaction" was a commonly used phrase to

---

88. Van Dixhoorn, "Reforming the Reformation," 1:323–30.
89. Van Dixhoorn, "Reforming the Reformation," 1:330.
90. Daniel Featly, *The Dippers Dipt; or, The Anabaptists Duck'd and Plung'd Over Head and Ears, at a Disputation in Southwark* (London: Richard Royston, 1647), 204–5.

denote the active and passive obedience of Christ.[91] The aggregated evidence, therefore, supports the claim that the divines codified the IAOC in a way that aligned with earlier Reformed ecclesiastical decisions.[92]

Richard Baxter

Beyond the assembly, there were other Reformed skirmishes over the doctrine of justification, most notably the debate between Richard Baxter (1615–1691) and John Owen (1616–1683). Many know Baxter through his practical works or his highly popular *Reformed Pastor*. Less known is that his peers were openly critical of his doctrine of justification. John Owen, for example, specifically wrote his work *The Doctrine of Justification* to refute Baxter. Baxter built his doctrine on a reconfigured understanding of the covenants of works and grace. In the covenant of works, God demanded perfect obedience, whereas in the covenant of grace, God lowered the standard and required only imperfect but nevertheless sincere obedience.[93] Within this reconfigured covenant of grace, the IAOC is not required for the believer. Rather, Christ's active obedience fulfills the demands of the covenant of works, and his passive obedience opens a platform on which believers can render their imperfect but sincere obedience to the law.[94] Baxter rejected the IAOC because he believed it would render the believer's good works in sanctification superfluous.[95] These systemic changes naturally rippled into Baxter's doctrine of justification.

Baxter did not affirm the common Reformed doctrine of justification, which taught that justification is a once-for-all act that is complete the moment a believer professes his or her faith in Christ. Samuel Rutherford (1600–1661), for example, offered a common explanation:

> (1) Justification is an indivisible act; the person is but once for all justified, by grace. But sanctification is a continued daily act. (2) Justification does not grow; the sinner is either freed from the guilt of sin, and justified, or not freed; there is not a

---

91. John Downame, *The Christian Warfare against the Devil, World, and Flesh* (London: William Stansby, 1634), 274 (2.2); William Perkins, *A Clowd of Faithfull Witnesses, Leading to the Heavenly Canaan: Or, a Commentarie upon the 11. Chapter to the Hebrewes*, in *The Workes of that Famous and Worthy Minister of Christ, in the Universitie of Cambridge, Mr. William Perkins* (London: Cantrell Legge, 1618), 5 (verse 2); Francis Cheynell, *The Rise, Growth, and Danger of Socinianisme, Together with a Plaine Discovery of a Desperate Designe of Corrupting the Protestant Religion* (London: Samuel Gellibrand, 1643), 41 (chap. 4); George Walker, *Socinianisme in the Fundamentall Point of Justification Discovered, and Confuted; or, an Answer to a Written Pamphlet Maintaining that Faith is in a Proper Sense without a Trope Imputed to Beleevers in Justification* (London: John Bartlet, 1641), 139, 232; James Ussher, *A Body of Divinitie, or The Summe and Substance of Christian Religion* (London: Tho. Downes and Geo. Badger, 1645), 171.

92. Alan D. Strange, "The Imputation of the Active Obedience of Christ at the Westminster Assembly," in *Drawn into Controversie: Reformed Theological Diversity and Debates within Seventeenth-Century British Puritanism*, ed. Michael A. G. Haykin and Mark Jones, RHT 17 (Göttingen: Vandenhoeck & Ruprecht, 2011), 31–51; Jeffrey K. Jue, "The Active Obedience of Christ and the Theology of the Westminster Standards: A Historical Investigation," in *Justified in Christ: God's Plan for us in Justification*, ed. K. Scott Oliphint (Fearn, Ross-shire, Scotland: Mentor, 2007), 99–130; Carl R. Trueman, "The Harvest of Reformation Mythology? Patrick Gillespie and the Covenant of Redemption," in Wisse, Sarot, and Otten, *Scholasticism Reformed*, 212.

93. Richard Baxter, *Aphorismes of Justification with Their Explication Annexed; Wherein Also Is Opened the Nature of the Covenants, Satisfaction, Righteousness, Faith, Works, etc.* (The Hague: Abraham Brown, 1655), 47–48.

94. Baxter, *Aphorismes of Justification*, 104.

95. Richard Baxter, *A Treatise of Justifying Righteousness in Two Books* (London: Nevil Simmons, 1676), 95.

third. But in sanctification, we are said to grow in grace (2 Pet. 3) and advance in sanctification: nor is it ever consummate and perfect, so long as we bear about a body of sin.[96]

The Westminster Shorter Catechism captures this point quite succinctly when it defines justification as an "act" of God's free grace, whereas sanctification is a "work" (qq. 33, 35). John Davenant (1572–1641), one of the Church of England's delegates to the Synod of Dort, similarly wrote, "Remission is perfect, and is instantly accomplished; sanctification, or the purification of corrupt nature, is effected by degrees, nor is it completed before death."[97] Davenant was simply advocating the position of the Thirty-Nine Articles (art. 11–13).

Baxter, on the other hand, divided justification into three stages. The first stage is *constitutive justification*, which is a "right to impunity, and to life or glory." Constitutive justification provides pardon of all past sins and occurs at the moment of conversion. In opposition to the common view, Baxter registered his disagreement: "And the saying of many that justification is perfect at first, and sanctification only by degrees, is a palpable error."[98] The second stage is *sentential justification*, or justification by sentence. This stage is "done by Christ as judge, and so is an act of his kingly office." This form of justification occurs throughout the believer's life. Whenever his conscience accuses him of sin, he can be reminded of his constitutive justification. Sentential justification ebbs and flows with the tides of a person's doubts and self-condemnation and may even cease when the believer sleeps or thinks of other things.[99]

The third and final stage is *executive justification*, which is the "public sentence and execution at the day of judgment." Baxter explains:

> In this sense to sanctify a man, is to justify him executively, and so sententially. For executive justification and pardon is the actual impunity, removing of deserved punishment, and actual giving possession of life and salvation, which constitutive justification gave us right to. And as our privation of the Spirit and holiness, and to be left in sin, is a great punishment; so to have the Spirit and holiness given us, is executive pardon and justification; and so will glorification much more.[100]

The first two forms of justification are mutable and defectible, whereas executive justification is immutable and indefectible. In order to receive this third and final stage of justification, the believer had to present his sincere but imperfect obedience before the divine bar to receive a favorable verdict. With his threefold doctrine of justification,

---

96. Samuel Rutherford, *Christ Dying, and Drawing Sinners to Himself* (Glasgow: Niven, Napier, and Khull, 1803), 313.
97. John Davenant, *A Treatise on Justification; or the Disputatio De Justitia Habituali et Actuali* (London: Hamilton, Adams, 1844), 1:27.
98. Richard Baxter, *The Second Part: Of God's Government and Moral Works* (London: Nevil Simmons, 1675), 85.
99. Baxter, *Of God's Government*, 85–86.
100. Baxter, *Of God's Government*, 86.

Baxter wrested the believer's justification away from the work of Christ and moved it to the believer's sanctification.[101]

In affirming his doctrine of threefold justification, Baxter departed from the Reformed confessional consensus and affirmed a view similar to that of Arminius. Arminius believed in a twofold justification, an initial justification by faith at conversion and a final justification at the final judgment. Like Baxter, Arminius also believed that justification was not indefectible until the verdict of the final judgment, because a person could apostatize and thus forfeit his justified status.[102]

As expected, Baxter's friends reacted negatively to his views. His peers told him he was propagating a dangerous error, which Baxter perceived as a hissing rebuke. Two of the Westminster divines, Richard Vines (ca. 1600–1656) and Anthony Burgess, also reacted disapprovingly. In fact, Burgess placed Baxter in the crosshairs in his work on justification.[103] John Brown of Wamphray (ca. 1610–1679) believed that Baxter "did corrupt the true Doctrine of Justification."[104] Owen took a similar view and penned his famous work *The Doctrine of Justification* specifically to refute Baxter.[105] Owen defended the common Reformed doctrine, which appears in chapter 11 of the Westminster Confession.

In addition to defending the common Reformed view, Owen engaged the question of twofold justification.[106] Owen rejected it and identified it with the twofold justification of Roman Catholicism. Burgess also engaged this issue but distinguished between an unorthodox and orthodox twofold justification. An unorthodox formulation rests the second justification on the believer's good works, as do Rome, Arminius, and Baxter. An orthodox second justification, according to Burgess, is an effect of the first justification. Concerning the views of Ludovicus de Dieu (1590–1642), Burgess wrote,

> The first he makes to be the imputing of Christs righteousness to us, received by faith, which is altogether perfect, and is the cause of pardon of sins: The second he makes an effect of the former, whereby through the grace of God regenerating, we are conformable unto that love in part, and are day by day more and more justified, and shall be fully when perfection comes.[107]

According to Burgess, de Dieu specifically distinguished his views from the Roman Catholic twofold justification. Speaking of a twofold justification was uncommon, but when theologians did affirm something of the idea, they were always careful to differentiate between justification *by faith* and the justification *of faith* by works. In other

---

101. Baxter, *Justifying Righteousness*, 7; Baxter, *Confession of His Faith: Especially concerning the Interest of Repentance and Sincere Obedience to Christ, in Our Justification and Salvation* (London: Thomas Underhill, 1655), 296.
102. Jacobus Arminius, *Private Disputations*, 48.12, in Arminius, *Works*, 2:407.
103. Hans Boersma, *A Hot Pepper Corn: Richard Baxter's Doctrine of Justification in Its Seventeenth-Century Context of Controversy* (Vancouver, BC: Regent College Publishing, 2004), 33–36.
104. John Brown (of Wamphray), *The Life of Justification Opened* (Utrecht, 1695), preface.
105. Carl R. Trueman, *John Owen: Reformed Catholic, Renaissance Man* (Aldershot, UK: Ashgate, 2007), 107–8.
106. John Owen, *The Doctrine of Justification by Faith*, in *The Works of John Owen*, ed. William H. Goold, vol. 5, *Faith and Its Evidences* (1850–1853; repr., Edinburgh: Banner of Truth, 1993), 137–40, 284–85.
107. Burgess, *Justification*, 257.

words, God justifies the *believer* by faith alone but justifies the believer's *faith* by his works, which is the evidence and fruit of his justification.

Francis Turretin (1623–1687) provided a common explanation when he wrote that justification

> is finished in one judicial act and brings to the believer the remission of all sins. Hence the Romanists (from their fictitious hypothesis concerning physical justification by an infusion of righteousness) falsely make it twofold: the first, that by which a man from being unjust is made just by an infusion of righteousness; the second, that which is from being just he is made more just by the increase of righteousness.[108]

Turretin went to great lengths to reject the Roman twofold justification. He acknowledged that justification makes an appearance at the final judgment, but this judgment "is not so much justification, as a solemn declaration of the justification once made, and an adjudication of the reward, in accordance with the preceding justification."[109] And whenever the believer's works enter the final judgment, they are a "sign and proof" of one's justified status. He averred, "Still falsely would anyone maintain from this a twofold gospel justification—one from faith in this life (which is the first); the other (and second) from works on the day of judgment (as some hold, agreeing too much with Romanists on this point)."[110]

The Neonomian-Antinomian Controversy

Despite the rejection of Baxter's views, his doctrine served as the seed for a controversy that erupted near the conclusion of the seventeenth century between neonomians and antinomians. The initial controversy broke out over the republication of notorious antinomian Tobias Crisp's (1600–1643) *Christ Alone Exalted*. To resolve the dispute, participants called on noted Dutch Reformed theologian Herman Witsius (1636–1708) to help them reconcile. In response, Witsius penned his *Irenical Animadversions* (1696).[111] In this debate there were opposing claims regarding the doctrine of justification. Richard Baxter, for example, accused Crisp of teaching justification from eternity, which in Baxter's view was a pillar of antinomianism.[112]

On the other side of the debate was one of the reputed neonomians, Daniel Williams (ca. 1643–1716). In many respects Williams promoted a common Reformed doctrine, but he did diverge at several key points, which drew criticisms from the reputed antinomians. Williams believed that in justification God imputed Christ's active and passive obedience but not his holiness: "Though Christ be perfectly holy, yet his holiness is not

---

108. Francis Turretin, *Institutes of Elenctic Theology*, trans. George Musgrave Giger, ed. James T. Dennison Jr. (Phillipsburg, NJ: P&R, 1992–1997), 16.10.5.
109. Turretin, *Institutes*, 16.9.11.
110. Turretin, *Institutes*, 16.10.8.
111. Herman Witsius, *Conciliatory, or Irenical Animadversions on the Controversies Agitated in Great Britain, under the Unhappy Names of Antinomians and Neonomians*, trans. Thomas Bell (Glasgow: W. Lang, 1807).
112. Baxter, *Aphorismes of Justification*, 60.

so imputed to us, as that we are therefore perfectly holy."[113] Williams rejected the view set forth in the Heidelberg Catechism, which holds that believers receive the imputed satisfaction, righteousness, and holiness of Christ (qq. 60–61). Williams made this claim for three reasons:

1. Holiness deals with sanctification, not justification.
2. Holiness is conformity to the law.
3. No person can be absolutely holy in this life.[114]

Williams appealed to Philippians 3:8–9 to argue that when Paul referred to his works as "dung," he meant his Jewish privilege, not gospel holiness. He therefore argued that in this passage Paul is not talking about the reception of Christ's imputed righteousness, which a person receives in his or her *first* justification, but rather the need for personal holiness beyond that imputation, which would ostensibly be evaluated at a *second* justification.[115] This naturally drew fire from the reputed antinomians; Samuel Crisp (1669–1704) accused Williams of presenting a "Romish gloss" of Philippians 3:8–9.[116] Crisp cited numerous Reformed exegetical authorities to prove that Williams erroneously exegeted Paul's text.[117] While Williams's formulation may have looked similar to Rome's twofold justification, in truth he was echoing the view of his colleague Baxter and his threefold justification. As the debate progressed, Williams appears to have retracted some of his statements and repeatedly affirmed his belief in justification *sola fide*.[118] In fact, Williams indicated that he would tremble at the thought that his works would serve as the basis of his sentential justification and only Christ's righteousness alone could serve as the legal basis.[119]

Witsius presented his own views in an effort to bring peace and did so, in his typically scholastic manner, through a number of carefully crafted theological distinctions. Witsius maintained the purity of justification by precluding the believer's good works from playing any role in justification—they contribute nothing.[120] Faith is not a condition of justification but rather its instrumental cause. Good works, however, are not superfluous but are the evidence that a person has been justified.[121] Witsius wrote,

> Since the learned men confess that sanctification is a consequence and an effect of justification, and such an effect indeed, which is inseparable from a consciousness of justification, it is strange why they deny that it is a certain sign of justification. Cannot therefore the

---

113. Daniel Williams, *Gospel-Truth Stated and Vindicated: Wherein Some of Dr. Crisp's Opinions Are Considered and the Opposite Truths Are Plainly Stated and Confirmed*, 2nd ed. (London: John Dunton, 1692), 38.
114. Williams, *Gospel-Truth*, 38.
115. Williams, *Gospel-Truth*, 176.
116. Samuel Crisp, *Christ Alone Exalted in Dr. Crisp's Sermons* (London: William Marshall, 1693), 2.
117. Crisp, *Christ Alone Exalted*, 4.
118. Daniel Williams, *A Defence of Gospel-Truth: Being a Reply to Mr. Chancey's First Part and as an Explication of the Points in Debate May Serve for a Reply to All Other Answeres* (London: John Dunton, 1693), 13–16.
119. Williams, *Defence of Gospel-Truth*, 15.
120. Witsius, *Animadversions*, 98 (8.16).
121. Witsius, *Animadversions*, 112 (10.8).

cause be known from its proper effects? From one of two inseparable benefits, cannot the other be inferred?[122]

In his response, Witsius essentially reiterated common elements of the traditional Reformed doctrine of justification, which holds justification and sanctification inseparably together but prioritizes the former over the latter to ensure that good works do not factor into a person's justification. He did not endorse Baxter's or Williams's earlier expressions regarding a first and second justification, but neither did he express agreement with the peculiar views of Tobias Crisp.

Part of the problem in the debate was that because some ministers republished Crisp's *Christ Alone Exalted*, others assumed that they agreed with his views. Debate participants such as Robert Traill (1642–1716) explicitly rejected this false assumption and aligned his views with Burgess and Rutherford, stalwarts of orthodoxy and fierce opponents of antinomianism: "Let not Dr. Crisp's Book be looked upon as the Standard of our Doctrine; there are many good things in it; and also many expressions in it, that we generally dislike."[123] Traill argued that he and his colleagues were simply maintaining the classic Protestant doctrine of justification. Quoting Foxe's *Book of Martyrs*, Traill invoked the name of Luther:

> But, saith he, Luther gave the stroke, and pluckt down the foundation, and all by opening one vein, long hid before, werein lieth the touchstone of all Truth and Doctrine, as the only Principle Origine of our Salvation, which is our free Justification by Faith only, in Christ the Son of God.[124]

Among the copious references to many Reformed theologians, he commended two books—Owen's *Doctrine of Justification* and Walter Marshall's *Gospel Mystery of Sanctification*—as two works that rightly addressed these issues and best explained the views of the so-called antinomians.[125]

Late Orthodoxy (1700-1790)

The Marrow Controversy

The Marrow Controversy in Scotland in 1717 and the republication of Edward Fisher's *Marrow of Modern Divinity* in 1718 once again fanned the embers of controversy into flame.[126] The book was originally published in 1645, when the Westminster Assembly was underway. The book even had an endorsement by one of the divines, Joseph Caryl (1602–1673). Scottish theologian Thomas Boston (1676–1732) discovered and greatly treasured the book. One of Boston's fellow ministers, James Hogg (ca. 1658–1734), republished the book in 1718, and Boston later published an annotated edition of

---

122. Witsius, *Animadversions*, 171–72 (16).
123. Robert Traill, *A Vindication of the Protestant Doctrine concerning Justification, and of Its Preachers and Professors, from the Unjust Charge of Antinomianism* (London: Dorman Newman, 1692), 10.
124. Traill, *Vindication*, 18.
125. Traill, *Vindication*, 34–35.
126. Edward Fisher, *The Marrow of Modern Divinity* (London: G. Calvert, 1645).

the same in 1726.[127] Due to the growing influence of Baxter's neonomian theology in England and Scotland, when Fisher's book was republished in 1718, it ignited significant controversy because it promoted justification *sola fide* by *sola gratia*.[128]

A contributing factor to the creation of the debate was Hogg's fiery preface to his 1718 edition. Hogg wrote,

> Behold! Evangelical light breaks forth in the midst of Papal darkness; and hereupon Antichrist's throne shakes, and is at the point of falling. Yet his wounds are cured, and he recovers new strength and spirits, thro a darkning of the glorious gospel, and perversion thereof, by anti-evangelical errors and heresies. That the tares of such errors are sown in the reformed Churches, and by men who profess reformed faith, is beyond debate; and these, who lay to heart the purity of Gospel-doctrine. Such dregs of Antichristianism do yet remain, or are brought in amongst us.[129]

Hogg believed the fox of neonomianism was in the hen house of the Reformed church, and thus he sounded the alarm. His remedy to this neonomian intrusion was to let the gospel loose on the Scottish kirk, and he believed he found the book to do it in Fisher's *Marrow of Modern Divinity*.

In the preface to his edition of the *Marrow*, Boston explicitly identified the specific source of what ailed the Scottish Kirk:

> Reader, lay aside prejudices, look and see with thine own eyes, call things by their own names, and do not reckon Anti-Baxterianism or Anti-Neonomianism to be Antinomianism; and thou shalt find no Antinomianism taught here; but thou wilt be perhaps surprised to find that the tale is told of Luther, and other famous Protestant divines, under the borrowed name of the despised Mr. Fisher, author of the "Marrow of Modern Divinity."[130]

Boston, Hogg, and other marrow men argued that justification in no way includes any works, but in a context where the prevailing winds blew in neonomian directions, the marrow men were unsuccessful in redirecting opinions.[131] Baxter's neonomianism presupposed the necessity of good works for justification; hence, the gospel preaching that grew out of such soil naturally produced trees that bore the fruit of legalism.

One of the marrow men, Ralph Erskine (1685–1752), refuted neonomianism through his poetry. He disparaged legalistic preaching:

> Let all that love to wear the legal dress
> Know that as sin, so, bastard righteousness

---

127. Joseph H. Hall, "The Marrow Controversy: A Defense of Grace and the Free Offer of the Gospel," *MJT* 10 (1999): 243.
128. Hall, "Marrow Controversy," 245.
129. James Hogg, "Preface," in Edward Fisher, *The Marrow of Modern Divinity: The First Part* (Edinburgh: R. Drummond, 1745), xiii–xiv.
130. Thomas Boston, ed., *The Marrow of Modern Divinity*, in *The Whole Works of the Late Reverend Thomas Boston of Ettrick*, ed. Samuel McMillan (Aberdeen: George and Robert King, 1859), 7:148.
131. Boston, *Marrow of Modern Divinity*, 247.

> Has slain its thousands, who in tow'ring pride
> The Righteousness of Jesus Christ deride
> A Robe divinely wrought, divinely won,
> Yet cast aside by men for robes that are their own.
> But some to legal works seem whole deni'd
> Yet would by gospel works be justifi'd,
> By faith, repentance, love, and other such:
> These dreamers being righteous overmuch,
> Like Uzza, give the ark a wrongful touch.[132]

Erskine did not specifically name Baxter, but this poem certainly struck his neonomian views dead center. The marrow men affirmed justification *sola fide*, which earned them the censure of the church and proscription of the *Marrow of Modern Divinity*. This eventually led to the formation of the Secession Church in 1733.[133]

Jonathan Edwards

In one sense, the Marrow Controversy was a carryover of issues that boiled over from the cauldron of seventeenth-century theology, such as the neonomian-antinomian controversy. But at the same time, a different philosophical breeze blew throughout the Western world when the ascendant Aristotelian cosmology and metaphysics fell out of favor for other Enlightenment views. This shift originated in part with the philosophy of René Descartes (1596–1650). Among the tenets of his philosophy was a rejection of Aristotelian fourfold causality. Descartes scuttled final, material, and instrumental causes and only acknowledged efficient causes. Initially, this may not appear to have had a significant effect on theology, let alone the doctrine of justification, until we consider the fact that Reformed theologians since the earliest days of the Reformation designated faith as the instrumental cause of justification. The metaphysical distinctions that Reformed theologians once regularly employed were deemed outdated and intellectually insufficient to bear theological freight.[134] Some Reformed theologians were persuaded by this philosophical turn of events, including Jonathan Edwards (1703–1758).

At first glance, Edwards has what appears to be a common Reformed doctrine of justification. He speaks of justification by faith alone, the forgiveness of sins, and imputed righteousness.[135] But upon closer inspection, at least two things stand out. First, nineteenth-century Reformed theologians such as Charles Hodge (1797–1878), Robert Dabney (1820–1898), James Thornwell (1812–1862), and John Girardeau (1825–1898) accused Edwards of violating the Reformed confessional boundaries with his views on

---

132. Ralph Erskine, *Gospel Sonnets: or, Spiritual Songs* (Pittsburgh: Luke Loomis, 1831), 58–59.
133. Thomas Boston, *An Explication of the Assembly's Shorter Catechism*, in McMillan, *Whole Works*, 7:91–100; Hall, "Marrow Controversy," 240, 243.
134. See, e.g., Roger Ariew, *Descartes and the Last Scholastics* (Ithaca, NY: Cornell University Press, 1999), 15–16.
135. Jonathan Edwards, "Justification by Faith Alone," in *The Works of Jonathan Edwards*, vol. 19, *Sermons and Discourses 1734–38*, ed. M. X. Lesser (New Haven, CT: Yale University Press, 2001), 150.

causation, the freedom of will, contingency, pantheism, and imputation.[136] So for whatever contemporary popularity Edwards enjoys as a garden-variety Reformed theologian, his immediate reception was rather different. Second, Edwards's unique theology did have an impact on his doctrine of justification—his doctrine did not follow standard Reformed confessional norms. Edwards was well aware of historic Reformed theology, given his knowledge of the Westminster Confession and Reformed luminaries such as William Ames (1576–1633), Francis Turretin, and Petrus van Mastricht (1630–1706).[137] In short, there are at least two areas where Edwards diverged from Reformed confessional norms: (1) the doctrine of faith and (2) a twofold justification.[138]

Space prohibits a detailed examination of each of these points given the complexity of the issues and the ocean of secondary literature. Nevertheless, a brief account of each point can illustrate Edwards's departure from the Reformed confessional norms. First, given the philosophical changes and the rejection of instrumental causality, Edwards refused to define faith as the instrumental cause of justification. This definition of justification was a settled and unquestioned fact for the Reformed tradition. Edwards was aware of this but nevertheless insisted on eliminating it.[139] Instead of designating faith as the instrumental cause, he distinguished between *natural* and *moral* fitness. A nut and bolt are naturally fit objects because they are made for one another. Moral fitness, on the other hand, is when something is commendable because of its moral excellence, such as when a person obeys the law and merits reward.[140] These terms were unprecedented in the Reformed tradition and owe their origin to Edwards. Nevertheless, he blanketed his doctrine of faith under the rubric of natural fitness—faith is the naturally fit companion to justification. It is not morally fit; otherwise, it would fall under the category of merit, which would violate the idea of justification *sola fide*. This move was arguably benign, but when Edwards combined this distinction with his definition of faith, other complications arose.

Unlike the earlier tradition, which distinguished between faith and its evidences, Edwards conflated them. The Westminster Confession, for example, identified the principal acts of saving faith as resting on, receiving, and accepting Christ alone for justification (14.2). The confession distinguished between faith, which chiefly receives, rests,

---

136. On Edward's reception, see, e.g., Sean Michael Lucas, "'He Cuts Up Edwardsism by the Roots': Robert Lewis Dabney and the Edwardsian Legacy in the Nineteenth-Century South," in *The Legacy of Jonathan Edwards: American Religion and the Evangelical Tradition*, ed. D. G. Hart, Sean Michael Lucas, and Stephen J. Nichols (Grand Rapids, MI: Baker Academic, 2003), 200–216. On matters related to contingency and free choice and the broader reception of Edwards's views, see Richard A. Muller, "Jonathan Edwards and the Absence of Free Choice: A Parting of the Ways in the Reformed Tradition," *JES* 1, no. 1 (2011): 3–22; Paul Helm, "A Different Kind of Calvinism? Edwardsianism Compared with Older Forms of Reformed Thought," in *After Jonathan Edwards: The Courses of the New England Theology*, ed. Oliver D. Crisp and Douglas A. Sweeney (New York: Oxford University Press, 2012), 91–106. Regarding imputation, see Oliver D. Crisp, *Retrieving Doctrine: Essays in Reformed Theology* (Downers Grove, IL: InterVarsity Press, 2010), 47–68.
137. John Dykstra Eusden, "Introduction," in William Ames, *The Marrow of Theology*, trans. John Dykstra Eusden (Grand Rapids, MI: Baker, 1968), 10–11; Gerald R. McDermott, "Jonathan Edwards on Justification by Faith—More Protestant or Catholic?," *PE* 17, no. 1 (2008): 105.
138. For a positive assessment of these points and one who argues that Edwards was within Reformed doctrinal boundaries, see Douglas A. Sweeney, *Edwards the Exegete: Biblical Interpretation and Anglo-Protestant Culture on the Edge of the Enlightenment* (New York: Oxford University Press, 2016), 202–18.
139. Edwards, "Justification by Faith Alone," 153.
140. Edwards, "Justification by Faith Alone," 159.

and accepts (i.e., language that denotes trust), and its fruit, namely, love and obedience (11.2). Edwards did not distinguish the principal from the secondary acts of saving faith. Rather, he wrote, "Even faith, or a steadfastly believing the truth, arises from a principle of love."[141] In contrast, Reformed theologians such as Turretin argued that *trust* was the essence of saving faith—faith is the cause, and love is the effect.[142] Edwards reversed this, which means that the believer's love is at the foundation of justification rather than the righteousness of Christ.[143] When Edwards rejected the instrumentality of faith, it removed an important exegetical and theological guardrail that prevented faith from becoming foundational in justification.

Things only become more problematic when we consider the second point of Edwards's divergence, his twofold justification. Edwards posited something quite different from earlier Reformed formulations that characterized the "orthodox second justification" as the evidence or effect of the first justification. He argued that God considered a believer's perseverance in his justification: "For though a sinner is justified on his first act of faith, yet even then, in that act of justification, God has respect to perseverance, as being virtually in that first act; and 'tis looked upon as if it were a property of the faith, by which the sinner is justified."[144] According to Edwards, God factors the believer's perseverance in his justification, albeit a virtual perseverance. In other words, God takes the believer's perseverance into account even though he has not yet persevered—it is virtually present. By contrast, the Westminster Confession does not locate the efficacy of the believer's perseverance in his own efforts but in the immutability of God's decree, the efficacy of Christ's merit, and the abiding presence of the Spirit (17.2).

Other complications arise in his explanation of the role of works in justification. Edwards wrote, "Our act of closing with and accepting of Christ is not in all respects completed by our accepting him with our hearts till we have done it practically too, and so have accepted him with the whole man: soul, spirit, and body." In other words, a person's justification is incomplete until his faith gives birth to works: "Indeed, as soon as we had done it in our hearts, the first moment our hearts had consented, we should be entitled in some sense; but we should not look on fulfillment of the condition as being all respected, till we had also actually done it."[145] In Edwards's scheme, faith is the naturally fit component to justification, and hence it is nonmeritorious. Nevertheless, unlike the earlier Reformed confessional tradition, Edwards cannot claim that justification is *sola fide* in the historic sense but only according to his redefined doctrine of faith, a doctrine that conflates faith, works, and love.

---

141. Jonathan Edwards, "Miscellanies," no. 411, "Faith," in *The Works of Jonathan Edwards*, vol. 13, *The "Miscellanies," Entry Nos. a–z, aa–zz, 1–500*, ed. Thomas A. Schafer (New Haven, CT: Yale University Press, 1994), 471.
142. Turretin, *Institutes*, 15.13.6.
143. For further argumentation and documentation, see J. V. Fesko, *The Covenant of Redemption: Origins, Development, and Reception* (Göttingen: Vandenheock & Ruprecht, 2016), 127–39, esp. 133–36.
144. Jonathan Edwards, "Miscellanies," no. 729, "Perseverance," in *The Works of Jonathan Edwards*, vol. 18, *The Miscellanies: 501–832*, ed. Ava Chamberlain (New Haven, CT: Yale University Press, 2000), 354.
145. Jonathan Edwards, "Miscellanies," no. 996, "How We Are Justified by Works," in *The Works of Jonathan Edwards*, vol. 20, *The Miscellanies: 833–1152*, ed. Amy Plantinga Pauw (New Haven, CT: Yale University Press, 2002), 324–25.

Given this conflation, it is unsurprising that Edwards held to a twofold doctrine of justification—one by faith and the other by works. Edwards rejected what he called a "conditional pardon or justification," in which the person's legal standing hangs in the balance. Edwards likely rejected this view because it placed works and justification in a cause-and-effect relationship and represented a scheme of moral rather than natural fitness. Nevertheless, Edwards averred,

> But not to dispute about this, we will suppose that there may be something or other at the sinner's first embracing the gospel, that may properly be called justification or pardon, and yet that final justification, or real freedom from the punishment of sin, is still suspended on conditions hitherto unfulfilled.[146]

Edwards's formulation was unique and ultimately did not find widespread acceptance within the eighteenth-century American Reformed tradition. The same can also be said of the European Reformed tradition.[147] Edwards stands in stark contrast to the doctrine of justification espoused by the marrow men.

Nineteenth Century

Old Princeton

Further evidence of the rejection of Edwardsian theology appeared in the changing of the guard at the College of New Jersey (now Princeton University) when John Witherspoon (1723–1794) took the helm of the institution. Witherspoon subscribed to the Westminster Standards *ex animo*, a practice that continued throughout the nineteenth century at Princeton Theological Seminary. In other words, he professed the Westminster Standards from the heart and without mental reservation. The Edwardsian faculty eventually departed because they were out of step with Witherspoon, who did not share Edwards's philosophical outlook.[148]

Archibald Alexander (1772–1851) served as Princeton's first seminary professor from 1812 to 1851 and embraced a traditional Reformed confessional doctrine of justification.[149] Appealing to Luther, Alexander maintained that justification was the article on which the church stands or falls.[150] As with the classic confessional doctrine, Alexander argued that the believer receives two inseparable but nevertheless distinct benefits, justification and sanctification, which come through the believer's union with Christ (cf. Westminster Larger Catechism, q. 77).[151] And this justification includes the pardon of sin and the imputation of Christ's righteousness.[152] Likewise, he believed that

---

146. Edwards, "Justification by Faith Alone," 168.
147. See, e.g., John Brown (of Haddington), *Questions and Answers on the Shorter Catechism* (1846; repr., Grand Rapids, MI: Reformation Heritage Books, 2006), 156–61.
148. Mark Noll, *Princeton and the Republic, 1768–1822* (Vancouver, BC: Regent College Publishing, 1989), 38.
149. Archibald Alexander, *A Treatise on Justification by Faith* (Philadelphia: Presbyterian Tract and Sunday School Society, 1837).
150. Alexander, *Justification by Faith*, 4.
151. Alexander, *Justification by Faith*, 8–9.
152. Alexander, *Justification by Faith*, 10.

"evangelical obedience was the fruit and consequence of our justification, [rather] than that evangelical obedience is the condition of our justification."[153] Good works could never stand the scrutiny of God's judgment because of their inherent imperfection; hence, believers require a more faithful legal foundation, which comes only through Christ's imputed active obedience.[154]

While Alexander did not specify any polemical targets (e.g., Rome, Arminius, Baxter, Edwards), he nevertheless devoted a section in his work to the idea of a twofold justification. Alexander first identified his conceptual target, namely, that justification is first by faith and second by works, to which he responded,

> If our evangelical obedience is truly the ground of our justification, what is called the first justification is no justification at all. How can a man be justified until the obedience is rendered which constitutes his justifying righteousness? If a man become truly justified in the sight of God, he needs no second justification.[155]

Alexander allowed for the fact that, at the final judgment, the believer's justified status would be revealed through his works, to prove he belonged to Christ. "But I repeat it again," wrote Alexander, "there cannot be a twofold justification of the sinner, unless the first should be annulled."[156] Alexander repositioned the confessional Reformed doctrine of justification as the norm, and the subsequent line of Charles Hodge, A. A. Hodge (1823–1886), B. B. Warfield (1851–1921), and Caspar Wistar Hodge Jr. (1870–1937) resolutely defended this view well into the twentieth century.[157]

James Buchanan

Across the Atlantic Ocean, another theologian defended the confessional Reformed doctrine, namely, James Buchanan (1804–1870). In many respects his work *The Doctrine of Justification* has become a contemporary classic—a definitive exposition of the classic Reformed confessional doctrine.[158] Within Buchanan's historical context, he was responding to the Oxford movement (1833–1845), which was led in part by John Henry Newman (1801–1890). Newman and other Tractarians of the Oxford movement were hostile to the Reformed doctrine of justification and sought to present Richard Hooker (1554–1600) as a forerunner of their own *via media* between the Reformation and Roman Catholicism.[159] One of the chief means by which Newman sought to make his

---

153. Alexander, *Justification by Faith*, 16.
154. Alexander, *Justification by Faith*, 23, 27.
155. Alexander, *Justification by Faith*, 17.
156. Alexander, *Justification by Faith*, 17; see also 36.
157. See, e.g., Charles Hodge, *Systematic Theology* (1872; repr., Grand Rapids, MI: Eerdmans, 1993), 3:41–212; A. A. Hodge, *The Confession of Faith* (1869; repr., Edinburgh: Banner of Truth, 1958), 179–90; B. B. Warfield, "Justification," in *The Selected Shorter Writings of Benjamin B. Warfield*, ed. John E. Meeter (Phillipsburg, NJ: P&R, 2001), 1:283–84; Caspar Wistar Hodge Jr., "Imputation," in *The International Standard Bible Encyclopedia*, ed. James Orr (1939; repr., Grand Rapids, MI: Eerdmans, 1974), 3:1462–66.
158. Buchanan, *Justification*.
159. C. Brad Faught, *The Oxford Movement: A Thematic History of the Tractarians and Their Times* (University Park, PA: Pennsylvania State University Press, 2003); Peter B. Nockles, *The Oxford Movement in Context: Anglican High Churchmanship, 1760–1857* (Cambridge: Cambridge University Press, 1994).

case was through a series of lectures on the doctrine of justification and through several key tracts.[160] Three chief elements in Newman's doctrine of justification set him apart from the historic Reformed consensus.

First, Newman believed that justification entailed the real presence of the Trinity within the soul of the justified sinner. Newman wrote, "This is to be justified, to receive the Divine Presence within us, and be made a Temple of the Holy Ghost."[161] The divine indwelling was the essence of what it meant to be counted righteous. Second, Newman conflated justification and sanctification. The divine indwelling constituted this double benefit.[162] Third, Newman rejected the common Reformation definition of faith, namely, as trust. Rather, faith had to work through love; he thus maintained that justification included faith and works.[163] These three elements are a melding of Protestant and Roman Catholic points. Newman tried to read article 11 of the Thirty-Nine Articles, on justification, in a manner consistent with his doctrine to prove that there was a distinct Anglican doctrine of justification. Newman's efforts, combined with a resurgence of Scottish Episcopalianism, fueled Scottish theologians such as Buchanan to respond.[164]

Buchanan responded to these developments in his lectures from a confessional and ecclesiastical vantage point.[165] He started with the history of the doctrine in seven lectures and then devoted eight more lectures to the doctrine itself. In his historical survey, he placed Luther at the foundation of the Reformation's doctrine, arguing that the other Reformers were in fundamental agreement with him.[166] He surveyed numerous divergent views, such as Socinianism, Arminius, Piscator, Neonomianism, and the Marrow Controversy, as well as Newman's views.[167] Over and against these opposing views Buchanan set forth the common confessional doctrine.[168] And with the historic tradition, Buchanan maintained that good works are the "effects and evidences of faith, and, as such, the signs or tokens of justification." He did not believe they could "form any part of the ground on which faith relies, or on which Justification depends."[169] In brief, Buchanan affirmed justification *sola fide*.[170] Buchanan rejected Newman's efforts to minimize the differences between the Roman Catholic and Reformed doctrines of justification. The final exclamatory coda of his lectures was his emphatic agreement with the Westminster Shorter Catechism's definition of justification (q. 33).[171]

---

160. John Henry Newman, *Lectures on Justification* (London: J. G. & F. Rivington, 1838).
161. John Henry Newman, *Lectures on Justification*, 3rd ed. (1874; Eugene, OR: Wipf & Stock, 2001), 144; McGrath, *Iustitia Dei*, 297.
162. McGrath, *Iustitia Dei*, 298.
163. McGrath, *Iustitia Dei*, 298–99.
164. Carl R. Trueman, "A Tract for the Times: James Buchanan's *The Doctrine of Justification* in Historical and Theological Context," in *The Faith Once Delivered: Essays in Honor of Dr. Wayne R. Spear*, ed. Anthony T. Selvaggio, WARF (Phillipsburg, NJ: P&R, 2007), 33–43.
165. Trueman, "Tract for the Times," 44.
166. Buchanan, *Justification*, 153.
167. Buchanan, *Justification*, 161–64, 170–73, 175, 177–78, 182–88, 213–16.
168. Buchanan, *Justification*, 229–33, 250–54, 264–67, 277–88, 322–38.
169. Buchanan, *Justification*, 358.
170. Buchanan, *Justification*, 384.
171. Buchanan, *Justification*, 411.

Twentieth Century

Machen and Liberalism

In the twentieth century, adherents to the traditional doctrine of justification continued to press their case for the doctrine's exegetical accuracy and theological necessity. J. Gresham Machen (1881–1937) stood in a long line of Princetonian professors who maintained the traditional doctrine, which he carried with him when he left Princeton to found Westminster Theological Seminary in Philadelphia, Pennsylvania. Machen's arena of intellectual combat, however, was not the world of intra-Reformed debates but the wider church and culture in the modernist-fundamentalist controversies at the close of the nineteenth and beginning of the twentieth centuries. By this point in church history, many liberal theologians had scuttled the doctrine of justification and with it the gospel. The most infamous example comes from Presbyterian missionary Pearl S. Buck (1892–1973), who denied the necessity and exclusivity of the gospel. This sentiment appeared in a published report titled *Re-Thinking Missions*. This report claimed, "Whatever its present conception of the future life, there is little disposition to believe that sincere and aspiring seekers after God in other religions are to be damned."[172] This abandonment of the gospel stoked Machen's fire to respond. He never wrote a doctrinal treatise on justification, but in his most famous book, *Christianity and Liberalism*, Machen presented liberalism not as a variant form of Christianity but as an altogether different religion. Within the scope of his critique, he marched out the doctrine of justification. Machen appealed to and defended the doctrine of the Westminster Confession and argued, "At the centre of Christianity is the doctrine of 'justification by faith.'"[173]

Machen, however, was not merely rehashing a stagnant traditionalism but rather was forging his view in the furnace of his own exegetical labors. In his work on Galatians, for example, Machen exegeted 3:10–14 and explained the juxtaposition between Paul's quotation of Habakkuk 2:4 and Leviticus 18:5 in the following manner:

> [By these words,] "he who has done them shall live in them," Paul means to say, "describe the nature of the law. It requires *doing* something. But faith is the opposite of doing. So when the Scripture says that a man is justified by faith, that involves saying that he is *not* justified by anything that he does. There are two conceivable ways of salvation. One way is to keep the law perfectly, to *do* the things which the law requires. No mere man since the fall has accomplished that. The other way is to *receive* something, to receive something that is freely given by God's grace. That way is followed when a man has faith. But you cannot possibly mingle the two."[174]

---

172. William Ernest Hocking, *Re-Thinking Missions: A Layman's Inquiry after One Hundred Years* (New York: Harper & Brothers, 1932), 19; cf. J. V. Fesko, *Spirit of the Age: The Nineteenth-Century Debate over the Holy Spirit and the Westminster Confession* (Grand Rapids, MI: Reformation Heritage Books, 2017), 96–98.

173. J. Gresham Machen, *Christianity and Liberalism* (1923; repr., Grand Rapids, MI: Eerdmans, 1999), 141.

174. J. Gresham Machen, *Machen's Notes on Galatians*, ed. John H. Skilton (Philadelphia: Presbyterian and Reformed, 1972), 178.

Machen believed that Galatians was crucial for a proper understanding of the doctrine because as Luther and Calvin expounded this Pauline epistle, it became "the Magna Charta of Christian liberty."[175] Machen firmly believed in justification *sola fide* and that this was not Luther's invention but a rediscovery of Paul and ultimately the teaching of Jesus.[176]

The Shepherd Controversy

Despite Machen's promotion of the classic Reformed doctrine, Westminster Theological Seminary professor Norman Shepherd (1933–) created controversy when he denied key elements of the doctrine. Shepherd's views developed during the mid-1970s, when he first presented a series of lectures for a meeting of the Presbytery of Ohio of the Orthodox Presbyterian Church on February 7, 1975. Shepherd's views came to light when a young licentiate failed his exams over views he attributed to Shepherd. The controversy has many twists and turns, but in brief, Shepherd's position included three defining beliefs.

First, he believed that the Reformed doctrine of justification was markedly different from the Lutheran doctrine.[177] Shepherd would later write, "Here we see the characteristic difference between the Reformed and the Lutheran ways of understanding the nature of justifying faith. For Calvin, justifying faith is an obedient faith. For Luther faith *becomes* an obedient faith *after* it has justified."[178] Shepherd went on to describe the supposed differences between Luther and Calvin by arguing that Calvin did not hold to *sola fide*: "The Lutheran doctrine of justification by faith alone excludes the Reformed doctrine of justification by a penitent and obedient faith."[179] Hence, Shepherd rejected *sola fide* and instead maintained a view of justification by faith working through love.[180]

Second, Shepherd was accused of denying that Christ's righteousness was the exclusive legal ground for justification. In his "Thirty-Four Theses on Justification," Shepherd argued that Christ's obedience was the exclusive ground of justification but that the believer's good works were necessary to continue in a state of justification and that they are necessary for his or her justification at the final judgment.[181]

Third, critics suspected that Shepherd denied the doctrine of the imputed active obedience of Christ, a chief pillar within the doctrine of justification. While there is question regarding the timing and development of his views, there is no question regarding

---

175. Machen, *Christianity and Liberalism*, 144.
176. Machen, *Notes*, 148; Machen, *God Transcendent* (1949; repr., Edinburgh: Banner of Truth, 1982), 88; Machen, *Christianity and Liberalism*, 144.
177. A. Donald MacLeod, *W. Stanford Reid: An Evangelical Calvinist in the Academy* (Montreal: McGill-Queen's University Press, 2004), 264.
178. Norman Shepherd, "Justification by Faith in Pauline Theology," in *Backbone of the Bible: Covenant in Contemporary Perspective*, ed. P. Andrew Sandlin (Nacogdoches, TX: Covenant Media Press, 2004), 92n3.
179. Norman Shepherd, "Justification by Works in Reformed Theology," in Sandlin, *Backbone of the Bible*, 111.
180. Norman Shepherd, *The Call of Grace: How the Covenant Illuminates Salvation and Evangelism* (Phillipsburg, NJ: P&R, 2000), 16, 19, 36, 39, 47, 49, 50, 63.
181. Norman Shepherd, "Thirty-Four Theses on Justification," cited in MacLeod, *W. Stanford Reid*, 266.

the final outcome.¹⁸² Like Piscator, Shepherd denied the IAOC and claimed Calvin and Ursinus as patriarchs of his view.¹⁸³

The controversy ended with Shepherd's dismissal from the seminary and move from the Orthodox Presbyterian Church to the Christian Reformed Church before his presbytery could prosecute charges against him.¹⁸⁴

The Federal Vision and the New Perspective on Paul

Despite Shepherd's termination from Westminster Theological Seminary, his views were eventually promoted by a group that called itself the Federal Vision, which originated at a theology conference at Auburn Avenue Presbyterian Church in Monroe, Louisiana. The Federal Vision promoted a wide-ranging series of views on justification, covenant, ecclesiology, and the sacraments. But with regard to justification, the Federal Vision followed and promoted the views of Shepherd, particularly in the denial of the IAOC.¹⁸⁵

In addition to Shepherd's views, proponents of the Federal Vision appealed to New Testament scholars associated with the New Perspective on Paul. Advocates of the New Perspective maintained that the Reformation created a Paul of faith and that the church had to return to the Paul of history. In other words, rather than read Paul's letter through the lens of Luther and the sixteenth-century Reformers, the church needed to read Paul in his first-century Jewish context. The literature on the New Perspective on Paul is legion, so at this point its relevance is of interest only insofar as it intersects with the Federal Vision. In this case, N. T. Wright's rejection of the doctrine of imputation served as one of the load-bearing pillars for Federal Vision claims. Wright argued that the doctrine of imputation is superfluous in light of the believer's union with Christ. Moreover, Wright claimed that the doctrine is largely absent from Paul's epistles.¹⁸⁶

Reaction against the Federal Vision was prompt. Numerous books, articles, and official denominational responses rejected their views and affirmed the classic Reformed confessional doctrine of justification.¹⁸⁷

---

182. Shepherd, "Justification by Faith," 88.
183. Shepherd, "Justification by Works," 105–6, 112, 115; also see Shepherd, "The Imputation of Active Obedience," in *A Faith That Is Never Alone: A Response to Westminster Seminary California*, ed. P. Andrew Sandlin (La Grange, CA: Kerygma, 2007), 249–78.
184. For an overview of the controversy, see MacLeod, *W. Stanford Reid*, 257–79.
185. Steve Wilkins and Duane Garner, eds., *The Federal Vision* (Monroe, LA: Athanasius Press, 2004).
186. N. T. Wright, *What Saint Paul Really Said: Was Paul of Tarsus the Real Founder of Christianity?* (Grand Rapids, MI: Eerdmans, 1997), 118–20, 125–31; Wright, Romans, in *The New Interpreter's Bible*, vol. 10 (Nashville: Abingdon, 2002), 485, 491; Wright, "The *RRJ* Interview with N. T. Wright, pt. 1," *RRJ* 11, no. 1 (2002): 128–30.
187. Denominational reports include the following: *Report of the Synodical Study Committee on the Federal Vision and Justification* (United Reformed Churches of North America, 2009); *Report of the Special Committee to Study Justification in Light of the Current Justification Controversy: Adopted by the 258th Synod of the Reformed Church of the United States, May 10–13, 2004* (Reformed Church of the United States, 2004); *Justification: A Report from the Orthodox Presbyterian Church* (Glenside, PA: Committee on Christian Education of the Orthodox Presbyterian Church, 2007); *Report of Ad Interim Study Committee on Federal Vision, New Perspective, and Auburn Avenue Theology*, in *Minutes of the General Assembly of the Presbyterian Church in America* (Atlanta, GA: Presbyterian Church in America, 2007). Seminary responses include the following: R. Scott Clark, ed., *Covenant, Justification, and Pastoral Ministry: Essays by the Faculty of Westminster Seminary California* (Phillipsburg, NJ: P&R, 2007); *Doctrinal Testimony regarding Recent Errors* (Dyer, IN: Mid-America Reformed Seminary, 2007).

Conclusion

The Reformed tradition has historically and consistently affirmed justification *sola fide*, a truth first learned from Luther but then wholeheartedly embraced as its own. The history of the doctrine of justification *sola fide* in the Reformed tradition is the valiant battle to defend the truth from the errors of neonomianism and antinomianism. These twin threats present twisted teachings to lead Christ's disciples astray so that they either elevate their own works and give them equal footing with Christ's or denigrate God's grace and live with wanton disregard for the moral law. Both errors are gross distortions of the doctrine of justification and the gospel. The tradition's unending war against these errors and fidelity to justification *sola fide* only heightens the desire for Christ's return. In the words of Samuel John Stone's (1839–1900) hymn "The Church's One Foundation,"

> Though with a scornful wonder the world see her oppressed,
> By schisms rent asunder, by heresies distressed,
> Yet saints their watch are keeping; their cry goes up: "How long?"
> And soon the night of weeping shall be the morn of song.

Until that glorious day, the prayer for the future of the Reformed tradition should be that it would remain a faithful sentry on the ramparts of the church and defend justification *sola fide* so that the world always knows that right standing with God comes only by faith alone in Christ alone through God's grace alone. Only in God's act of justification can fallen humans receive pardon of sin and the imputed righteousness of Jesus Christ, which alone, indefectibly, immutably, and irreversibly grants them right and title to the blessings of eternal life.

Recommended Resources

Alexander, Archibald. *A Treatise on Justification by Faith*. Philadelphia: Presbyterian Tract and Sunday School Society, 1837.

Buchanan, James. *The Doctrine of Justification: An Outline of Its History in the Church and of Its Exposition from Scripture*. 1867. Reprint, Edinburgh: Banner of Truth, 1991.

Burgess, Anthony. *The True Doctrine of Justification Asserted and Vindicated, from the Errours of Papists, Arminians, Socinians, and More Especially Antinomians*. London: Thomas Underhill, 1651.

Calvin, John. *Canons and Decrees of the Council of Trent, with the Antidote* (1547). In *Tracts and Letters*. Vol. 3, *Tracts, Part 3*, edited and translated by Henry Beveridge, 17–188. 1851. Reprint, Edinburgh: Banner of Truth, 2009.

Goudriaan, Aza. "Justification by Faith and the Early Arminian Controversy." In *Scholasticism Reformed: Essays in Honour of Willem J. van Asselt*, edited by Maarten Wisse, Marcel Sarot, Willemien Otten, 155–78. Studies in Theology and Religion 14. Leiden: Brill, 2010.

Hodge, Caspar Wistar, Jr. "Imputation." In *The International Standard Bible Encyclopedia*, edited by James Orr, 3:1462–66. 1939. Reprint, Grand Rapids, MI: Eerdmans, 1974.

Owen, John. *The Doctrine of Justification by Faith*. In *The Works of John Owen*. Edited by William H. Goold. Vol. 5, *Faith and Its Evidences*, 1–400. Edinburgh: Banner of Truth, 1993.

Traill, Robert. *A Vindication of the Protestant Doctrine concerning Justification, and of Its Preachers and Professors, from the Unjust Charge of Antinomianism*. London: Dorman Newman, 1692.

Vermigli, Peter Martyr. *Predestination and Justification: Two Theological Loci*. Translated and edited by Frank A. James III. Vol. 8 of *Peter Martyr Library*. Sixteenth Century Essays and Studies 68. Kirksville, MO: Thomas Jefferson University Press, 2003.

Witsius, Herman. *Conciliatory, or Irenical Animadversions on the Controversies Agitated in Great Britain, under the Unhappy Names of Antinomians and Neonomians*. Translated by Thomas Bell. Glasgow: W. Lang, 1807.

23

Not by Faith Alone?

An Analysis of the Roman Catholic Doctrine of Justification from Trent to the *Joint Declaration*

LEONARDO DE CHIRICO

Justification by faith was the matter of the Reformation five hundred years ago, but does it matter in the same way in the present-day ecumenical climate?[1] In responding to the Protestant account of justification, the Council of Trent (1545–1563) understood it inside a synergistic dynamic of the process of salvation. This understanding of grace appears in an updated form in the *Joint Declaration on the Doctrine of Justification* (*JDDJ*), signed in 1999 by the Roman Catholic Church and the Lutheran World Federation. The *JDDJ* is a clear exercise in an increased "catholicity" (i.e., the ability to absorb ideas without changing the core) on the part of Rome, which has not become more evangelical in the biblical sense.

Justification by faith alone has been a cause of rupture between Protestantism and the church of Rome since the sixteenth century, and this is an unchangeable fact with important theological and symbolic significance. The present-day *status quaestionis* of the debate is a contested issue. Roughly speaking, there are two ways of coming to terms with its contemporary relevance. According to mainstream ecumenical theology, "the doctrine of justification should not be, today, an element of division between churches."[2] This does

---

[1]. Parts of this opening section are adapted from Leonardo De Chirico, "140. Is the Roman Catholic Church Now Committed to 'Grace Alone'?," *Vatican Files* (blog), August 1, 2017, http://vaticanfiles.org/en/2017/08/140-is-the-roman-catholic-church-now-committed-to-grace-alone/; De Chirico, "68. 2017: From Conflict to Communion?," *Vatican Files* (blog), November 15, 2013, http://vaticanfiles.org/en/2013/11/68-2017-from-conflict-to-communion/. Used by permission of the author.

[2]. Fulvio Ferrario and William Jourdan, *Per grazia soltanto: L'annuncio della giustificazione* (Torino: Claudiana, 2005), 111.

not mean that all differences and distinctions have been overcome, but it does mean that today they are no longer considered impediments to the unity of the church, at least to a certain extent. This is the basic line of argumentation that drives the 2013 Roman Catholic–Lutheran document *From Conflict to Communion*, prepared for the joint commemorations of the fifth centenary of the Protestant Reformation.[3] It is a ninety-page joint statement between the Vatican and the Lutheran World Federation that attempts to summarize what happened in the sixteenth century, the controversies that arose, and the reinterpretation of the whole in light of pressing ecumenical concerns.

After providing a carefully written summary of the main issues that divided the (Lutheran) Reformation and Roman Catholicism, the document ends by suggesting five imperatives for preparing for the commemoration. The first is the following: "Catholics and Lutherans should always begin from the perspective of unity and not from the point of view of division in order to strengthen what is held in common even though the differences are more easily seen and experienced."[4] Unity, not truth in love, is the main and driving motive. The first imperative is unity above all else. This, however, is not the best way of honoring the Reformation, nor is it a biblical approach to Christian unity. Despite its many shortcomings, the Reformation was nonetheless a cry to have one's own conscience and the church bound to God's Word alone. *Sola scriptura* was the "first imperative" of the Reformation from which all else followed, unity included. It is telling that after five hundred years, ecumenical unity is now the top priority, replacing the authority of God's Word. There is the risk of elevating "unity" to the absolute principle, a little "god" claiming preeminence. Perhaps this is the ecumenical idol of the day that needs to be addressed in a "Protestant" way, that is, recasting unity under the Word of God and not the other way around.

On the other hand, there is a significant segment of contemporary evangelical theology that continues to see the doctrinal issue epitomized in the sixteenth-century debates on justification as still standing theologically, even though it is presented in more nuanced and graceful ways by the ecumenical climate that has characterized the twentieth and early twenty-first centuries. Salvation in Christ alone by grace alone through faith alone according to Scripture alone remains a point of separation between the evangelical Protestant reading of justification and the Roman Catholic one.

To underscore the point, several hundred evangelical scholars and leaders around the world signed the 2016 document *Is the Reformation Over? A Statement of Evangelical*

---

3. Lutheran–Roman Catholic Commission on Unity, *From Conflict to Communion: Lutheran-Catholic Common Commemoration of the Reformation in 2017*, Vatican, accessed July 28, 2018, http://www.vatican.va/roman_curia/pontifical_councils/chrstuni/lutheran-fed-docs/rc_pc_chrstuni_doc_2013_dal-conflitto-alla-comunione_en.html. Notice that the chosen word is not "celebration" but "commemoration." Celebration would have implied an element of sober feasting in remembering the Reformation with an attitude of thanksgiving, while not hiding the "dark pages" of Protestant history. On the contrary, in spite of all that is said in Roman Catholic circles about Luther being "a witness of Jesus Christ," ecumenism cannot celebrate the Reformation. Official Roman Catholicism, even the post–Vatican II and ecumenically minded versions of it, can only commemorate it. It can only remember, ponder, and reflect on it. Yet is the standing legacy of the Reformation to be commemorated only? Is the call to go back to the Scriptures not to be celebrated? Is a Christ-centered, grace-dependent, God-exalting faith not to be celebrated but only remembered? This chapter and this volume answer by saying that celebration is rightly in order.
4. Lutheran–Roman Catholic Commission on Unity, *From Conflict to Communion*, 6.239.

Convictions.⁵ This statement is characterized by a biblical parrhesia, namely, the bold conviction that derives from being persuaded by the gospel truth, which, after all, was recovered at the Reformation. The post–Vatican II Roman church, while being more open and nuanced toward biblical authority and salvation by faith alone, still retains a significantly different theological orientation from the classical understanding of Scripture and salvation represented during the Reformation. *Dei Verbum* (the Vatican II dogmatic constitution on divine revelation) is a masterful exercise of theological *aggiornamento* (i.e., modernizing) according to the "both-and" pattern of Roman Catholicism at its best. Still, it is not what the Reformation understood concerning *sola scriptura*. The 1999 *Joint Declaration on the Doctrine of Justification*, signed by Roman Catholics and Lutherans, comes close to what the Reformation stood for in recovering the good news of salvation as a Christ-given gift, but it tends to blur the lines on significant points. The document reaffirms that on the two basic issues (i.e., the supreme authority of Scripture and justification by faith alone), the Reformers were simply recovering the biblical gospel, which Rome rejected and still does, although in more nuanced and suffused forms.

The comparison between the two readings is the tip of the iceberg of divergent theological orientations, and the fifth centenary of the Protestant Reformation is a welcomed opportunity to study afresh and in depth the whole topic. A modest contribution to the ongoing reflection can be briefly summarized by recalling the steps that led to the present-day ecumenical reinterpretation of the old controversy. To do so, in this chapter the texts of the Council of Trent are examined, as they represent the main Roman Catholic response to the challenges posed by the Protestant Reformation on the doctrine of justification. Trent framed the Roman Catholic understanding of justification for subsequent centuries and thus became a strong reference point for Catholic identity in modern times. This sketched study of the Tridentine view of justification is followed by a bird's-eye view on the twentieth century's ecumenical trajectory in which Rome was involved (e.g., Second Vatican Council, Hans Küng, Otto Pesch, Evangelicals and Catholics Together) and that eventually resulted in the *JDDJ*, providing a theological assessment of the main tenets of this important ecumenical document. In conclusion, some critical remarks are presented concerning the correlation between Trent and present-day discussions of Rome's position on justification by faith.

The Council of Trent (1545-1563) and the Fixation of the Roman Catholic Doctrine on Justification

It took more than twenty years for Rome to process what was going on with the Protestant Reformation and to agree on the best possible way to respond. The Council of Trent was convened between 1545 and 1563, many years after the publication and circulation of Luther's early writings on justification. If one bears in mind that by the

---

5. *Is the Reformation Over? A Statement of Evangelical Convictions*, http://www.isthereformationover.com. This website contains the document translated in eight languages and the press release highlighting its main points.

end of the council more than forty years had gone by since the beginning of the Reformation, Rome's slowness to respond and the resulting negative consequences cannot be overlooked. According to Hubert Jedin, the greatest modern historian of the Council of Trent, the delay was motivated by a twofold reasoning:

1. The political situation in Europe was such that the conflict between different interests paralyzed action. Emperor Charles V was in favor of a council because the political unity of the empire needed the realignment of its religious unity, whereas Francis I was against it because a conciliatory council would have strengthened the power of the empire at his expense.
2. The Reformers' request for a "free" council—that is, free from papal control—was not something that could have been easily accepted by any pope. Understandably, the pope wanted to be the supreme judge of the matter and not the accused party before a church court.[6]

It is no surprise that justification was dealt with during the first session of the council. The session lasted seven months (from June 21, 1546, to January 13, 1547), and it was the most intense topic that the council addressed. Since the issue of justification had never been studied or dogmatized by any preceding council, the task was not to polish or refine previously promulgated pronouncements but to craft them almost from scratch.[7] The scholastic treatments of justification generally relegated it to the appendix on the doctrine of grace and the sacraments, without giving it a central place in the theological system. Given the relatively minor status that justification had in medieval theology, it is easy to see why Trent produced a lengthy doctrinal text ("decree") that was divided into sixteen chapters, while also drafting thirty-three "canons"—that is, summary formulations singling out heretical views on justification—coupled with the "anathema" for those who held them.[8]

The conciliar debates focused on two major points: the issue of "double justification," as it had been treated at the Colloquy of Regensburg (1541), and the issue of the certainty of grace.[9] On the former, theologians like Girolamo Seripando[10] were openly in favor of reiterating what had been agreed on by the Protestants, namely, the acceptance of both inherent and imputed righteousness (thus the expression "double justification") on the basis of the imperfection of our inherent righteousness and thus

---

6. Hubert Jedin, *A History of the Council of Trent*, trans. Ernest Graf, 2 vols. (London: T. Nelson, 1957–1961). For a more recent treatment on Trent, see John W. O'Malley, *Trent: What Happened at the Council* (Cambridge, MA: Belknap Press of Harvard University Press, 2013).
7. An in-depth study of the history of the doctrine of justification can be found in Alister E. McGrath, *Iustitia Dei: A History of the Christian Doctrine of Justification*, 2nd ed. (Cambridge: Cambridge University Press, 1998) esp. chaps. 2–4.
8. The texts of the Council of Trent can be found in *Canons and Decrees of the Council of Trent*, trans. H. J. Schroeder (London: Herder, 1941). Quotations are cited parenthetically by chapter or canon.
9. On the importance of the Colloquy of Regensburg and its relationship to the Council of Trent, see Anthony N. S. Lane, "A Tale of Two Imperial Cities: Justification at Regensburg (1541) and Trent (1546–1547)," in *Justification in Perspective: Historical Developments and Contemporary Challenges*, ed. Bruce L. McCormack (Grand Rapids, MI: Baker Academic, 2006), 119–45.
10. On the role of Seripando at the Council of Trent, see Michele Cassese, "Girolamo Seripando il Concilio di Trento e la riforma della Chiesa," in *Geronimo Seripando e la Chiesa del suo tempo*, ed. Antonio Cestaro (Rome: Edizioni di Storia e Letteratura, 1997), 189–225.

the need for Christ's righteousness to be imputed. Other theologians, like the Jesuits Alfonso Salmeron and Diego Laynez, were opposed to it and were able to convince the majority of the council not to endorse double justification. As for the latter, the Lutheran insistence on linking justification to the objective and subjective certainty of faith was a matter of concern for the council and caused it to debate whether the justified person could have attained the total certainty of being in a state of grace. Their answer was in the negative. The council wanted to emphasize the role of human freedom in responding to God's grace, and therefore the importance of the theme of "cooperation" and the value of merits, although considering both as gifts of God. There can be no certainty of faith if the ground of it also depends on human freedom and its cooperation with God's grace.

If before Trent justification had not been a central locus of Catholic soteriology, with the Council of Trent justification entered Roman Catholic theology as a specific doctrinal topic in the context of the Catholic teaching on grace and the sacraments. This was in distinction from the Reformation emphasis that justification is a legal pronouncement by God and received by faith alone by the sinner.[11]

The Three States of Justification

In approaching the topic, Trent distinguished between three states or stages of justification.

The first state deals with the initial justification of adults (chaps. 1–8). It begins with the moment and event when a person receives justification for the first time. Trent endorsed the Augustinian view that all people are unrighteous because they have been born in Adam and are in need of being reborn in Christ. This change can take place only with baptism or the desire for it. God's predisposing grace initiates the move, and then human free will needs to assent to this grace and cooperate with it. It can also reject it. The process of justification is thought of in terms of five causes borrowed from Aristotelian language: final, efficient, meritorious, instrumental, and formal causes. The final cause is the glory of God, the efficient cause is the merciful God, the meritorious cause is the Lord Jesus Christ, the instrumental cause is baptism, and the formal cause is the righteousness of God. Justification is programmatically defined as "not only in the forgiveness of sins but also in the sanctification and renewal of the inward being."[12] So the formal cause of justification refers both to God and to man. As canon 10 states,

> If anyone says that people are justified without the justice of Christ by which he gained merit for us; or that they are formally just by his justness itself; let him be anathema.[13]

---

11. For a detailed Roman Catholic study of the theological meaning of justification according to Trent, see G. Colzani, "La nozione di 'giustificazione': Il senso del suo impiego nei dibattiti tridentini, la verifica di un modello di comprensione," in *La giustificazione*, ed. Giovanni Ancona (Padova: Messaggero, 1997), 65–111.

12. Jaroslav Pelikan and Valerie R. Hotchkiss, eds., *Creeds and Confessions of Faith in the Christian Tradition*, vol. 2, *Creeds and Confessions in the Reformation Era* (New Haven, CT: Yale University Press, 2003), 829.

13. Pelikan and Hotchkiss, *Creeds and Confessions*, 2:837.

Here the two sides of righteousness are evident: God's and ours. And they cannot be separated.

The second state deals with progression in justification, that is, how an already justified person ought to preserve the received justification and make progress in it by working hard to maintain it to the end (chaps. 7, 10–11, 16). This state concerns the life of the justified man in the context of his Christian journey.

According to Trent, once justified, we are called to keep the commandments and preserve our righteousness spotless through faith and works. In this way we grow in righteousness, increasing it and anticipating a reward. In other words, salvation is not by faith *alone*; in the end eternal life is both a grace promised and a reward given for good works and merits.

The third state focuses on the loss and recovery of justification (chaps. 13–15) and describes what happens when the justified person falls into sin and therefore prescribes what needs to be done in order to recover justification. After falling into sin, justification can be regained through the sacrament of penance, which involves the sacramental confession of one's own sins, priestly absolution, and making satisfaction. The first justification needs to be supplemented by the reenactment of the application of the merits of Christ to the sinner through the sacramental system of the church.

From the start, then, instead of treating justification as a divine legal pronouncement that declares a definitive and permanent change of the sinner's status before God, Trent nuanced justification, making it dependent on the particular state in which the person finds himself. Justification is subject to certain human and sacramental conditions and does not entirely stem from a forensic speech act of God. Justification is seen as a synergistic process combining God's and man's involvement, rather than a divine act changing the state of affairs and causing man to change accordingly. Justification is therefore "dialectical" in that it oscillates between the pole of God's imputation and the pole of man's contribution.[14] It is never a given *status* received from outside; it is rather a *process* always in progress.

According to Trent, justification is far more extensive than the forensic understanding of the Reformers, embracing the whole scope of the Christian life. By blurring the lines between justification and sanctification, Trent inflated justification with meanings that bypassed the legal framework and included the transformative aspect of the Christian life.

Moreover, whereas Protestant accounts of justification were theocentric in their approach, in that the focus was on the triune God working out his work of salvation in favor of the sinful creature, Trent's theological angle had a more anthropocentric focus, thus concentrating on man's role and contribution in salvation. The center of gravity differed significantly. The God who justifies by imputing his righteousness by faith alone to the sinner is the point of departure for the Reformers. The affirmation of man's

---

14. The "dialectical" aspect of justification in Trent is argued by Giovanni Iammarone, *Il dialogo sulla giustificazione: La formula "simul iustus et peccator" in Lutero, nel Concilio di Trento e nel confronto ecumenico attuale* (Padova: Messaggero, 2002), 69–82.

capacitas to cooperate with God's grace in the transformative process of justification was the pervasive presupposition of Trent. The word *justification* was the same, but the theological frameworks were different, and the semantic import of the word contained mutually excluding elements.

The Reformers' Alleged Errors

It is now possible to see why the Council of Trent wanted to denounce what was perceived as the heretical significance of the Protestant doctrine of justification. It is useful to highlight its numerous aspects over against Trent's theory of the three stages of justification.[15]

As for the first stage of justification, Trent took issue with these elements:

- Free will after Adam's fall is only an empty word, or better, a word detached from a standing and permanent anthropological reality (canon 5).
- In justification it is God alone who works it out, being that it is a God-given gift from beginning to end. Man does not cooperate in any way; he only passively receives it (canon 4). Trent could not cope with the notion that "no other cooperation is required for him to obtain the grace of justification" (canon 9).[16]
- We are justified by faith alone even before charity begins to work in us and without counting on our inherent righteousness. Assurance of salvation rests therefore on divine mercy, and the forgiveness of sin is granted by the righteousness of Christ being imputed to us when we were unrighteous (canon 12).
- For justification to take place and prior to receiving it, any human effort or disposition is in fact sinful (canons 7, 8).

As for the second stage, Trent strongly criticized the following points:

- All works of the justified person are sinful and deserve hell (canon 25).
- All works done with the hope of glory or out of fear of eternal penalty are evil (canon 31).
- No good works following justification can merit any increment in justification (canon 24).
- The justified person is bound to believe that he is in a state of grace, that his sins are no longer imputed to him, and that he is predestinate (canons 13, 14, 15).

Finally, Trent condemned the following concerning the third stage of justification:

- The justified person cannot lose his righteousness (canon 23). In contrast, Trent held that since justification is a process involving man's participation, the final outcome must be open ended.
- Confession is not necessary and does not forgive sin (canons 9, 12, 14).

---

15. A reliable and stimulating guide in this topic is Bernard Sesboüé, *Sauvés par la grâce: Les débats sur la justification du XVIe siècle à nos jours* (Paris: Éditions Facultés de Paris, 2009). I had access to the Italian edition of the book: *Salvati per grazia: Il dibattito sulla giustificazione dalla Riforma ai nostri giorni*, trans. Rita Simionati (Bologna: EDB, 2012), 67–143.
16. Pelikan and Hotchkiss, *Creeds and Confessions*, 2:837.

Whether these representations and interpretations of the Reformation's doctrine of justification are correct is dubious. In many instances they seem to be caricatures rather than fair descriptions. However, they certainly single out the main points of difference between the two readings, namely, the divergent accounts of the way justification is conceived and received. According to Trent, *faith alone* is an anthropological impossibility in that it denies man's inherent *capacitas* to contribute to the process of salvation. *Faith alone* is also a soteriological conundrum in that it provides a certainty that cannot be attained if salvation secondarily but fundamentally rests on man's participation in salvation. On top of that, *faith alone* excludes the primary and necessary sacramental mediation of the church in administering God's grace. The theological structure of Trent's understanding of justification is significantly different from that of the Reformation.

Justification by Faith as an Unresolved Ecumenical Issue[17]

Theologically, historically, symbolically, and emotionally, justification has been the chief point of controversy between Protestant theology and Tridentine Catholicism. For centuries, the debate was characterized by clashes and oppositions. Each part repeated, like refrains, arguments in support of its vision and demolished those of others as inherently tainted by fatal mistakes. Not much movement occurred in either camp. The standard Tridentine account of justification remained the magisterial teaching of the Catholic Church and was no longer subject to intense work. But something entirely different occurred in the twentieth century with the rise of the ecumenical movement.

Before influencing individual points of discussion, ecumenism changed the rules of engagement for the discussion itself, gradually transforming a spiritual battle with a winner and a loser into a friendly game where in the end everybody wins in one way or another. Ecumenism marked the end of the confrontation as a clash between two alternative versions of Christianity and introduced a compatibility and complementary mode between the Catholic and evangelical accounts of Christianity, which in the past had been considered mutually exclusive. More specifically, justification by faith, which had been the point of the conflict, became a broad doctrinal topic that was stretched and smoothed in order to make room for the legitimacy of different interpretations.[18]

The gradual penetration of an ecumenical sensitivity made justification a field where cross-fertilization of interpretations was possible and even commendable. The result was the cleaning of a theater of war, which led to the achievement of a broad consensus, right where there had been a battle line drawn for centuries. At the same time, the ecumenical rereading of the doctrinal locus attributed a weightier understanding to the historical context in which the doctrinal formulations had been shaped and worded. The age of the Reformations was a century of strong passions and powerful concerns that were overtheologized, becoming self-contained ideologies and reaching peaks of

---

17. This section is based on my article "La giustificazione come questione ecumenica irrisolta," *SdT* 53, no. 1 (2015): 99–118. Used by permission of *Studi di teologia*.
18. This point is made by Angelo Maffeis, "La dottrina della giustificazione da K. Barth a oggi," in Ancona, *La giustificazione*, 113–94.

argumentative paroxysm. After many centuries of dispute, it was possible to look with greater detachment at the theological issues, the protagonists involved, and the events surrounding them, reaching a greater awareness of the role of nontheological factors and a more relaxed view of the theme of justification as a whole.[19]

Then, attention was given to the driving concerns underlying the positions taken by the Reformation and by Rome on justification. The Reformers wanted to safeguard the primacy of God's grace in the work of salvation, while Rome wished to protect the role of the church and human participation in salvation. The newly discovered ecumenical sensitivity attempted to grasp each other's legitimate concerns and points of view in order to reassemble them into a broader context that would be capable of affirming both. As a result, modern observers could see that both sides had reasonable arguments that their opponents simply did not grasp and that this lack of understanding gave rise to emotional resentment and ecclesiastical condemnation. Centuries later, the different perspectives could finally be valued without being disqualified, endorsed in the context of their mutual compatibility.

In addition, serious work was done on the theological semantics of the language used in the controversy (e.g., righteousness, justice, faith, grace, works, concupiscence, original sin, imputation, sacraments, *solus/sola*). This awareness of the subtleties of the meaning of words could explain the roots of such deep and mutual misunderstandings running through the use of a similar vocabulary. The Latin language was formally the same, but the theological meaning of the terms and expressions was different, and this opened the way to shortcuts and failures in communication. These problems became increasingly evident and were further accentuated with the use of various modern European languages.

The mutual excommunications were then reinterpreted in the light of a complex hermeneutic that tried to keep in mind all these external influences that had produced polarizations and conflicts. On top of this massive work of reinterpretation, there were also the controversial outcomes pertaining to the New Perspective on Paul, which added further developments in the realignment of the once mutually exclusive positions. In the years when the ecumenical reconsideration of justification reached its peak, the New Perspective suggested that while the debate had come to a standstill over Paul's view and language of justification, Protestants and Catholics could find a way forward by recognizing that the sixteenth-century accounts (i.e., salvation by grace or salvation by works) were actually caricatures of what the apostle meant in dealing with the question of justification. According to the New Perspective, Luther and, consequently, the Council of Trent had built their conflict on a tragic misunderstanding of the biblical text. Paul did not intend to address "how are we saved" (either by faith alone or by faith and works)

---

19. Accounts of the ecumenical reinterpretation of justification by faith can be found in Klaas Runia, "Justification and Roman Catholicism," in *Right with God: Justification in the Bible and the World*, ed. D. A. Carson (Carlisle, UK: Paternoster, 1992), 197–215; Angelo Maffeis, *Giustificazione: Percorsi teologici nel dialogo tra le chiese*, UT 63 (Cinisello Balsamo, Italy: San Paolo, 1998); Paweł Holc, *Un ampio consenso sulla dottrina della giustificazione: Studio sul dialogo cattolico-luterano*, TGST 53 (Rome: Editrice Pontificia Università Gregoriana, 1999).

but "who belongs to the covenant community," which does not appear to address the sixteenth-century dispute between imputation and infusion. Therefore, these scholars concluded, the *casus belli* of the Reformation was essentially a hoax, and the resulting controversy could have been immediately solved in a friendly manner.[20]

Second Vatican Council, Hans Küng, and Otto Pesch

The hermeneutics of the ecumenical movement gradually proceeded to dismantle piece by piece the traditional theological controversy through the process of historical detachment (i.e., looking at the controversy in its context and leaving entrenched emotional factors outside) and resignification of the debate (i.e., deconstructing thought forms and theological constructions in order to show degrees of compatibility). The outcome was that the remaining differences could be ascribed to a physiological dialectic of legitimate disagreements within a plural Christianity.

Even before the opening of the ecumenical movement by the Catholic Church at the Second Vatican Council (1962–1965), it was Hans Küng, a Catholic theologian who took part at the Council, who made a significant contribution to the reframing of the issue. In his landmark book on justification, published in German in 1957, he strongly argued for compatibility between the official teaching of the church of Rome and the exposition of justification made by the Protestant theologian Karl Barth.[21] Notice the chosen word: compatibility (a buzzword of ecumenical theology!), not sameness, not equal import. Whether or not Barth's doctrine of justification coincided with that of the Reformers,[22] what is really at stake with Küng's book is that it delivers less than what is promised. As Alister McGrath rightly observes, rather than demonstrating the compatibility of Barth and Catholicism, Küng showed only the anti-Pelagian common basis of the two understandings of justification, giving the impression of forcing the data on the bigger and deeper issues in order to make them compatible.[23]

Ten years later, it was Otto Pesch who, in the context of a study of Martin Luther and Thomas Aquinas on justification, suggested that the differences that had crystallized in the sixteenth century arose from the different matrices for their respective theologies: an "existential" matrix shaping Luther and a "sapiential" matrix characterizing Aquinas's thought.[24] The theological effort to be made was therefore to consider them as two complementary perspectives, rather than conflicting ones. This reconstruction certainly

---

20. The impact of the New Perspective on the debates over justification is aptly assessed by Philip Eveson, *The Great Exchange: Justification by Faith Alone in the Light of Recent Thought* (Bromley, UK: Day One, 1996), 110–57.
21. Hans Küng, *Justification: The Doctrine of Karl Barth and a Catholic Reflection*, trans. Thomas Collins, Edmund E. Tolk, David D. Grandskou (London: Burns & Oates, 1964).
22. It is in fact dubious, to say the least. The fact that Barth differs from the Reformers even on justification is maintained by Paul G. Schrotenboer, ed., *Roman Catholicism: A Contemporary Evangelical Perspective* (Grand Rapids, MI: Baker, 1988).
23. Alister E. McGrath, "Justification: Barth, Trent, and Küng," *SJT* 34, no. 6 (1981): 517–29. Cf. Trevor Hart, "Barth and Küng on Justification: 'Imaginary Differences'?," *ITQ* 59, no. 2 (1993): 94–113; Vittorio Subilia, *La giustificazione per fede*, BCR 27 (Brescia, Italy: Paideia, 1976), passim.
24. Otto Hermann Pesch, *Theologie der Rechtfertigung bei Martin Luther und Thomas von Aquin: Versuch eines systematisch-theologischen Dialogs*, WSAMA 7 (Mainz: Matthias-Grünewald Verlag, 1967). Pesch has an updated version of the thesis of this book in his more recent introduction to Martin Luther: *Hinführung zu Luther* (Mainz: Matthias-Grünewald Verlag, 2004).

contained useful elements; however, it did not properly account for the forensic framework of Luther's theology of justification, which created the context for his existential appropriation of the doctrine. Moreover, Pesch's insistence on the sapiential tradition of Thomism did not properly explain the fact that the Council of Trent responded to Luther using other categories (e.g., sacramental, juridical) rather than insisting on the sapiential ones. In other words, Pesch rightly stressed the importance of theological frameworks, but this point, though important, did not prove to be the decisive one in coming to terms with the complexity of the doctrinal dispute over justification.

The works by individual theologians like Hans Küng and Otto Pesch opened a season of dialogues on justification between ecclesiastical bodies. Among the fruits of this dialogue were the North American document *Justification by Faith* (1983)[25] and the international dialogue on *Church and Justification* (1993),[26] in which the theologians of the Lutheran and the Roman churches insisted on the newly discovered compatibility between the two accounts. These dialogues formed the background to and were case studies in preparation for the *Joint Declaration on the Doctrine of Justification* (1999). In the decade between these two dialogues, the thorny issue of the mutual excommunications in German history was addressed. The attempt was to come to an ecumenical understanding of these objective and symbolic obstacles to Christian unity. A meticulous work of clarification and contextualization of the anathemas suggested the possibility of not considering the excommunications valid for the current interlocutors.[27] A question mark still remained on their historical value as far as they related to those involved in the controversy over the centuries. All these debates came to fruition in the *JDDJ*.

Evangelicals and Catholics Together

As part of an informal dialogue among some Roman Catholics and some evangelicals in the USA, a faint echo of these discussions on justification was heard in the document "The Gift of Salvation" (1997).[28] Born as part of the Evangelicals and Catholics Together initiative, which aimed at building a platform for dialogue between theologically conservative cultures in the context of a highly secularized society, the aforementioned document came to support the newly found agreement on the fundamental understanding of justification based on a minimalist and generic soteriological basis. Without even making explicit reference to the previously mentioned international dialogues, the document appears to have been marked by a hasty pragmatic agenda that betrayed success. With a couple of short paragraphs on justification, the document presumed to have solved the centuries-long controversy. The whole issue of imputed versus transformative

---

25. H. George Anderson, T. Austin Murphy, Joseph A. Burgess, eds., *Justification by Faith*, Lutherans and Catholics in Dialogue 7 (Minneapolis: Augsburg, 1985).

26. Lutheran–Roman Catholic Joint Commission, *Church and Justification: Understanding the Church in the Light of the Doctrine of Justification* (Geneva: Lutheran World Federation, 1994).

27. Karl Lehmann and Wolfhart Pannenberg, eds., *The Condemnations of the Reformation Era: Do They Still Divide?*, trans. by Margaret Kohl (Minneapolis: Fortress, 1990).

28. "The Gift of Salvation," *First Things*, January 1998, https://www.firstthings.com/article/1998/01/001-the-gift-of-salvation.

righteousness that had been discussed for five centuries was considered a secondary point still to be explored but not belonging to the "fundamental truths" on justification that already united the signatories. It is perhaps no coincidence that the criticism raised after the release of "The Gift of Salvation" revealed the several flaws of the whole Evangelicals and Catholics Together initiative.[29]

The 1999 Lutheran-Catholic *Joint Declaration on the Doctrine of Justification*

If the preparatory season took half a century to move the first steps of the ecumenical reflection, it was through the *JDDJ* that ecumenical dialogue reached a level of maturity that made it possible for some Roman Catholics to commit themselves to a cosigned document with another ecclesial body, the Lutheran World Federation.[30] The celebration of the official signing took place on October 31, 1999, the day of the conventional anniversary of the Protestant Reformation (October 31, 1517), and in the city of Augsburg, where in 1530 the Augsburg Confession, the manifesto of Lutheran faith, had been signed.

In ecumenical circles, the *JDDJ* was greeted with great enthusiasm, as if it were a watershed event that simultaneously healed the old controversy in the Western church, while having also accelerated the path toward a more full unity. It must be borne in mind, though, that the chorus of praise was not unanimous. In fact, there was no lack of critical voices among German academic theologians raising several points of concern.[31] The Roman Catholic Church itself, after signing the *JDDJ* by the Pontifical Council for Promoting Christian Unity, needed further "clarifications" through the intervention of the Congregation for the Doctrine of the Faith. An "Annex"[32] to the *JDDJ* was added to provide these elucidations, as well as a Roman Catholic "Response,"[33] which was formally issued to overcome any possible misunderstanding.

Theological Analysis

The Joint Declaration presents "a consensus in basic truths on the doctrine of justification" between Lutherans and Catholics (art. 40).[34] Notice the careful wording of the statement. There is no consensus on justification as a whole, but there is a degree of

---

29. For further study on the subject, allow me to refer to my essay "Christian Unity vis-à-vis Roman Catholicism: A Critique of the Evangelicals and Catholics Together Dialogue," *ERT* 27, no. 4 (2003): 337–52.
30. This section is adapted from Leonardo De Chirico, "140. Is the Roman Catholic Church Now Committed to 'Grace Alone'?," *Vatican Files* (blog), August 1, 2017, http://vaticanfiles.org/en/2017/08/140-is-the-roman-catholic-church-now-committed-to-grace-alone/. Used by permission of the author.
31. See the Italian translation, "Presa di posizione dei 139 professori di teologia sulla Dichiarazione congiunta sulla dottrina della giustificazione," in *Il consenso cattolico-luterano sulla dottrina della giustificazione: Documenti ufficiali e commenti*, ed. Fulvio Ferrario and Paolo Ricca, PBT 50 (Torino: Claudiana, 1999), 81–85.
32. Vatican, "Annex to the Official Common Statement," accessed July 30, 2018, http://www.vatican.va/roman_curia/pontifical_councils/chrstuni/documents/rc_pc_chrstuni_doc_31101999_cath-luth-annex_en.html.
33. Vatican, "Response of the Catholic Church to the Joint Declaration of the Catholic Church and the Lutheran World Federation on the Doctrine of Justification," accessed July 30, 2018, http://www.vatican.va/roman_curia/pontifical_councils/chrstuni/documents/rc_pc_chrstuni_doc_01081998_off-answer-catholic_en.html.
34. Quotations from the *JDDJ* are marked by article number and come from Lutheran World Federation and the Roman Catholic Church, *Joint Declaration on the Doctrine of Justification* (Grand Rapids, MI: Eerdmans, 2000).

consensus on some foundational truths about justification. The consensus is on a significant part of the doctrine that is considered "basic" but not on the whole doctrine. After a preamble that recalls the central importance of the issue for the Protestant Reformation and the Council of Trent and a summary of the ecumenical journey that led to the drafting of the document, the first section deals with the biblical message of justification. It is telling to read of the need to listen "to the word of God in Scripture" (art. 8). It would seem a promising commitment if it were not marked by a reductive understanding of the Word of God, which is "in" the Bible but does not coincide with all the Scriptures. Here Catholics and Lutherans converge: the Word of God is in the Bible, but the Bible is not the Word of God *sic et simpliciter*. The Bible contains the Word without identifying with it. For Catholic theology, the Word of God "exceeds" Scripture, and the Magisterium is therefore necessary to listen to its fullness; for post-liberal Protestant theology, the Word of God "happens" in Scripture when God speaks through it. In both cases, this does not appear to be a solid basis on which to construct a theological consensus. The *JDDJ* testifies to a rhetorical willingness to listen to the Word of God, but at the same time, it expresses a desire to hear a word that only in one remote sense is connected to the whole of the Bible: the Word of God is "in" the Bible. Evangelical theology cannot but point to this significant shortcoming in the theological foundation of the *JDDJ*'s ecumenism, *evidencing its departure from sola scriptura*.[35]

A long section then deals with "a common understanding of justification" structured in such a way as to have a joint statement from both parties followed by an explanation from each of them, the Catholic and the Lutheran. In this way, the *JDDJ* tries to find a unitary formulation and also makes room for a differentiated interpretation of it. Typically, the sections held in common are carefully worded so that none of the decisive questions are explicitly touched on, while the claims of each group emphasize the specific nature of their theological tradition.

Many commentators with good intentions, even on the evangelical side, have rightly given attention to what seems to be the heart of the *JDDJ*, article 15, which solemnly says,

> By grace alone, in faith in Christ's saving work and not because of any merit on our part, we are accepted by God and receive the Holy Spirit, who renews our hearts while equipping and calling us to good works.

If read out of context and in a theologically naive way, this sentence could be a relevant and pointed summary of the biblical message concerning the mode of justification (by grace only and not based on merits), the means of justification (by faith alone), the ground of justification (the saving work of Christ), and the consequences of justification (divine adoption and the gift of the Holy Spirit, the renewal of the heart and the activation of the Christian life). Every sound exercise in theological hermeneutics, however,

---

35. On this strategic point for evangelical theology, see Pietro Bolognesi, "La Bibbia è la Parola di Dio?," *SdT* 47, no. 1 (2012): 28–44.

including the reading of ecumenical documents, must take into account the immediate and more general context, the meaning of the words used, and the consequences of what is being claimed. Taken out of context, article 15 would make much sense from an evangelical perspective, yet it must be considered an integral part of the *JDDJ* and therefore must be understood in relationship to the whole document.

Presenting the various aspects of the doctrine, the Catholic and Lutheran representatives agreed on a sacramental understanding of grace. It is this sacramental framework that qualifies the reference to the expression "by grace alone" contained in article 15. Together, in fact, they declare that "by the action of the Holy Spirit in baptism, they [the sinners] are granted the gift of salvation" (art. 25), thus undermining the idea that God saves sinners by grace alone through faith alone. Lutheran theology, with its theology of baptismal regeneration, actually runs this risk. Later, in article 28, the *JDDJ* states (always with both parties affirming this together) that "in baptism the Holy Spirit unites one with Christ, justifies, and truly renews the person." It is not surprising, however, that the Catholic clarification on this point forcefully underlines that "persons are justified through baptism as hearers of the word and believers in it" (art. 27). On the one hand, then, the *JDDJ* wants to affirm the importance of the declaration of the righteousness of God received by faith; on the other hand, it reiterates the need for sacramental action through the mediation of the church that is essential in justification and therefore for salvation. How the baptized infant is considered a "hearer" of the Word and a "believer" in it is objectively difficult to reconcile with a biblical vision of the proclamation and the hearing of the gospel while maintaining a realistic view of the baby's cognitive and responsive condition. Regardless, the Catholic point is further reinforced when it is also claimed that Catholics hold that the grace of Jesus Christ is "imparted" in baptism (art. 30).[36] According to this view, grace is not received by faith alone but is granted by God through the church that administers it in baptism. This statement cannot be reconciled with the evangelical belief that salvation is by grace alone, apart from works, even sacramental ones. Despite all the good intentions expressed and the admirable effort in dialogue, the result does not meet expectations and is beyond a faithful adherence to the biblical Word of God. In contemporary Roman Catholicism, we see a total consistency with respect to the traditional doctrine—that is, justification occurs at baptism by a sacramental act.

For the Catholic Church, "by grace alone" (art. 15) means that grace is intrinsically, constitutionally, and necessarily linked to the sacrament, to the church that administers it, and then to the works implemented by it. In this view, salvation cannot be by grace alone but only by grace organically incorporated into the sacrament of the church. We are evidently in the presence of a different concept of grace. In the *JDDJ* there is an attempt to redescribe this theological understanding of salvation in a language that looks like the

---

36. This point is further stressed in the *Response of the Catholic Representatives*, where we read that "in baptism everything that is really sin is taken away" (art. 1). Recalling Trent, the *JDDJ* reinforces the idea that it is baptism that saves and the sacrament of penance where "the sinner can be justified anew [*rursus iustificari*]" (art. 4). Rome therefore can speak of "grace alone" but always intending sacramental grace in the contest of an ongoing process.

Lutheran one and is appropriated by the Catholic Church (such as the use of the expression "by grace alone" in art. 15 and the recognition that works "follow justification and are its fruits" in art. 37), without giving the impression to have really moved away from Tridentine theology. According to Trent, grace is necessarily sacramental and seen inside a synergistic, dynamic process of salvation. This understanding of grace, which is part of the "basic truths of the doctrine of justification," appears to be more in line with the Catholic heritage of the Council of Trent, in an updated form, than with classic Protestant theology. In this sense, the *JDDJ* is a clear exercise of an increased "catholicity" on Rome's part but without becoming more evangelical in the biblical sense.

Disappointments

In addition to these reservations to the overall meaning of the *JDDJ*, another list of considerations needs to be presented. What practical, ecclesial, and spiritual consequences may have a similar pronouncement by the Catholic Church? This is also a way to test the specific import of this ecumenical document. It is surely too soon to make definitive judgments, but it is certainly possible to catch a glimpse of what is *not* happening.

The year after the signing of the *JDDJ*, the church of Rome celebrated the Great Jubilee of 2000, which had as its corollary a massive offering of indulgences, a triggering factor in the sixteenth-century Reformation and a concentration of a synergist, sacramental, and ecclesiocentric theology. After consenting to such a view of divine grace as captured in the *JDDJ*, the church of Rome reopened the holy doors, dusted off purgatory, and invested in the more anti-Protestant devotion at its disposal, that is, the holy year and the issuing of indulgences. It seemed as though the loud-sounding words of the *JDDJ* on justification by faith were disproved by the practice of Roman Catholic life, at least as it is perceived by evangelical theology.

The other disappointment that was felt especially in ecumenical circles was the Catholic resistance toward granting "eucharistic hospitality" (i.e., the partaking of the Eucharist) to non-Catholic Christians. After Rome reached a broad consensus on justification and dropped the anathemas on present-day Lutherans, many Protestants were expecting it to implement ecclesiological consequences and relax the traditional rigidity of eucharistic doctrine and practice against non-Catholics. Nothing of this sort happened.

Dominus Iesus (2000)

But there is something more to be added to the picture. A year after the *JDDJ*, the Congregation for the Doctrine of the Faith, the same Vatican office that had written the "clarifications" and the "Response" to the document, released the declaration *Dominus Iesus* (2000), signed by the then Cardinal Joseph Ratzinger.[37] This document was a real shock for ecumenical supporters who believed that 1999 had been a positive point of

---

37. Congregation for the Doctrine of the Faith, "Declaration '*Dominus Iesus*' on the Unicity and Salvific Universality of Jesus Christ and the Church," Vatican, accessed July 30, 2018, http://www.vatican.va/roman_curia/congregations/cfaith/documents/rc_con_cfaith_doc_20000806_dominus-iesus_en.html.

no return and a push toward full unity. With great intellectual honesty, *Dominus Iesus* clarified that the Roman Catholic Church, in opening to the ecumenical dialogue, did not renounce any significant point of its self-identity, especially in the area of ecclesiology. Rome, which had apparently come closer to Protestant sensitivities on justification, would not become "Protestant" but would remain strongly committed to its foundational doctrinal core. Rome would only engage in ecumenism in the fullness of her self-consideration as the Holy Roman Catholic Church, safeguarding the integrity of her ecclesiology and distinguishing herself from the Christian communities that are not *cum Petro et sub Petro* (i.e., "with Peter and under Peter," including the Lutheran churches that had signed the *JDDJ* in 1999). These communities, according to *Dominus Iesus*, are "ecclesial communities," not churches in the proper sense.

Rome had signed the *JDDJ*, but obviously, this signature and the contents of the document did not result in any substantial change in her self-understanding and in the consideration of other Christian churches. Individuals were lifted from the excommunications as people, but their communities were not recognized as true and real churches. For these reasons, in the ecumenical world there are those who still wonder if the *JDDJ* has been a "milestone in the history of Western Christianity" or if there is the risk of it becoming "the monument of a great illusion and of its subsequent delusion."[38]

Standing Theological Issues on Justification

Immediately after the publication of the *JDDJ*, some evangelical voices expressed critical views on historical, theological, ecclesiastical, pastoral, and spiritual aspects emerging from the document. The reception by evangelicals was marked by general skepticism.[39] The word that best describes the evangelical perception was *ambiguity*. Henri Blocher puts it in the context of the Roman Catholic "grand hermeneutical tradition of paradoxical subtlety."[40]

Ambiguities in the equivocal meaning of words; ambiguity in the juxtaposition of different theological understandings; ambiguity in the posture of the church of Rome that seems to say one thing and then contradicts it; ambiguity in the lack of practical consequences to the intentions expressed—is it possible to identify the really decisive issues? And then, on the basis of this recognition, is it feasible to suggest a theological analysis to determine the specific systemic weight of the issues at stake?

---

38. Paolo Ricca, "Le ragioni dell'evangelo," in Ferrario and Ricca, *Il consenso cattolico-luterano*, 10.

39. For example, E. Hahn, "Rapprochement between the Roman Catholic and Protestant Churches in the Doctrine of Justification: Danger or Hope?," *EuroJTh* 7, no. 1 (1998): 9–14; W. Robert Godfrey, "Lutheran–Roman Catholic Joint Declaration," *Banner of Truth* 436, no. 17 (2000): 17–20; Gerald Bray and Paul Gardner, "The Joint Declaration on the Doctrine of Justification," *Chm* 115, no. 2 (2001): 110–27; David Estrada, "The Joint Declaration on the Doctrine of Justification by the Lutheran World Federation and the Catholic Church," *CS* 11, no. 1 (2001): 12–17; T. M. Dorman, "The Joint Declaration on the Doctrine of Justification: Retrospect and Prospects," *JETS* 44, no. 3 (2001): 421–34; Albert Greiner, "Que se passe-t-il entre catholiques et luthériens?," *FR* 51–52, nos. 2–3 (2000): 4–21; David Vaughn, "Déclaration commune sur la doctrine de la justification de la fédération luthérienne mondiale et de l'église catholique romaine," *RRef* 216, no. 1 (2002): 43–64; José Moreno Barrocal, "La Declaracion Conjunta sobre la Justificacion," *Nueva Reforma* 50 (2000): 4–9; Leonardo De Chirico, "Più che pietra miliare, pietra d'inciampo," *Ideaitalia* 3, no. 6 (1999): 3.

40. Henri A. Blocher, "The Lutheran-Catholic Declaration on Justification," in McCormack, *Justification in Perspective*, 201.

The evangelical scholar Anthony Lane, after a meticulous study of the *JDDJ*, identified fifteen key issues that are at stake in the dialogue between Catholics and Protestants on justification:

1. The status of theological language
2. Taking charge of the biblical tension
3. The interpretation of historical precedent
4. The role of justification in the overall theological system
5. The consideration of human inability
6. The definition of justification
7. Imputation
8. The permanence of sin in the Christian
9. Faith alone
10. Baptism
11. Law and gospel
12. Lapse and the restoration
13. Merit and reward
14. Assurance of salvation
15. Magisterium[41]

Justification lies at the intersection of all these critical points. The word *justification* has specific preunderstandings that are stratified in history and theology, and it opens complex theological maps that lead to different orientations. The awareness of the "systemic" nature of theology, of its being an interconnected whole, can only help the dialogue, preventing it from referring to theological fragments in a superficial and atomistic manner, while encouraging serious engagement on core points at the service of truth in love. In dialogue we often limit ourselves to the use of an "ecumenically correct" code, but in reality, this approach conceals the true questions and then builds on a shaky foundation. If practiced in this ecumenically correct way, ecumenism becomes a game where, in spite of the formal kindness and diplomatic procedures, it ultimately ends with little change of any meaning and doctrinal significance.

Entering into the labyrinth of each issue at stake with justification is an objectively difficult task. It could be helpful, though, to concentrate the analysis around the two fundamental axes that lie at the core of the Roman Catholic vision and that can serve as a prism for a deeper understanding. The two axes of Roman Catholicism are the nature-grace relationship and the sacramental nature of the church, or, following the recent terminology suggested by Gregg Allison, "nature-grace interdependence" and "Christ-Church interconnection."[42] After all, the various constitutive elements of the problem could be

---

41. Anthony N. S. Lane, *Justification by Faith in Catholic-Protestant Dialogue: An Evangelical Assessment* (London: T&T Clark, 2006).
42. Gregg R. Allison, *Roman Catholic Theology and Practice: An Evangelical Assessment* (Wheaton, IL: Crossway, 2014), 42–67. For further details on these two axes, see my book *Evangelical Theological Perspectives on Post–Vatican II Roman Catholicism*, RD 19 (Oxford: Peter Lang, 2003), 217–83.

placed on these two axes and find their theological sense and weight. Here we can suggest a preliminary attempt.

The 1992 *Catechism of the Catholic Church* (chap. 1) opens with a programmatic statement that man is *capax Dei*, "capable of God," inherently opened and oriented to God.[43] It is not only the recognition of the religious man but the inherent openness of man to God. For Roman Catholicism, divine grace finds in the very being of man the necessary code to be activated. Divine action presupposes the intrinsic capability of man not only as recipient but as coworker of grace.

Indeed, the human being in his natural capacity for God is constitutively innervated by the desire for God and oriented to him. Certainly, Roman Catholic theology recognizes the debilitating effects of sin but not to the point of undermining man's inherent *capacitas Dei*. Catholicism has a softened hamartiology, a milder view of sin. Sin is to be taken seriously, but it is not spiritually fatal. It is no coincidence that the Catholic understanding of salvation has always privileged "participatory" categories that presuppose man's cooperation and has always refused the "declarative" ones, which focus on the primacy of grace alone. Man does not have to be declared righteous from his radical injustice but can participate in becoming righteous if his involvement is properly solicited. In contrast to this view, the Reformation insisted on the *coram Deo* dimension of life. Man is before God, whose presence cannot be avoided whenever he tries to escape from him. He is always inexcusable. Man has radically and permanently lost his natural *capacitas Dei* because of sin. The covenant was broken, and man is under the judgment of God without any possibility and ability to cope with it, let alone to bypass it. Here is a first crossroad that radically separates the two perspectives, the Catholic and the evangelical. What is the anthropological presupposition of justification? If it is that of the ongoing *capacitas Dei* of the Catholic view, justification will always be looking for a point of contact, an area of collaboration, a framework for synergy between divine grace and human contribution. In this view, grace in some way is already present in nature, which is always inherently "capable" of grace.

Roman Catholic theology soaked in the anthropology of *capax Dei* is not found in the evangelical vision of the radical nature of sin and of the tragic condition of man in his "natural" condition as sinner and covenant breaker. This is the reason why Catholic theology cannot accept the concept of an "alien" righteousness—that is, the righteousness of Jesus Christ and him only, which is "imputed" by grace alone to the sinner. For the evangelical faith, it is an alien righteousness, external to man, that saves him. Man does not "participate" in his righteousness by his own efforts, but he is "declared" righteous by the power of God and not out of his own righteousness. And in fact, even with all the wise use and blending of theological expressions, the *JDDJ* lacks any reference to the alien righteousness of Christ that is imputed to man in justification. In fact, this central point of the 1530 Augsburg Confession (art. 4) is simply

---

43. *Catechism of the Catholic Church* (Vatican City: Libreria Editrice Vaticana, 1993), accessed July 30, 2018, http://www.vatican.va/archive/ENG0015/_INDEX.HTM.

and tragically absent from the *JDDJ*, and this is not by accident. The Catholic system is viscerally reluctant to undermine the human *capacitas Dei*—and rightly so, from its point of view; it sees imputation of an alien righteousness as opposition to its moderate anthropological optimism. The fact that the Lutheran signatories of the *JDDJ* have abandoned this crucial theological point is telling, exposing the loss of a major pillar in theological heritage.

On this point, what Eberhard Jüngel argues is helpful. For him, the fact that many Protestants have substantially lost the radicalism of an evangelical anthropology is due to Immanuel Kant and his rather optimistic anthropology.[44] In endorsing a Kantian anthropology more than a biblical one, modern Lutherans have come close to the Tridentine view of justification, losing sight of the radical effects of sin and dropping the imputation of an alien righteousness. Protestantism was brought toward Trent's moderate synergism and cautious optimism not via Thomas Aquinas but through Kant. In the *JDDJ* Rome has embraced the use of a kind of language that seems close to the Protestant heritage, considering it is complementary to its own, but not at the price of accepting the questioning of its own version of the interdependence of nature and grace, which, in fact, in the end came out to be reinforced by the *JDDJ*. Indeed, Rome has succeeded in removing alien righteousness and its imputation to the sinner even in an official Lutheran document like the *JDDJ*! What is at stake is not just an issue about words but a profoundly theological issue. *The final result is very clearly in favor of Roman Catholicism.*

With the door left open by the anthropology of the *capax Dei*, the sacramentality of the church also enters as a necessary instrumentality of grace to make nature participate in its original and inherent desire for God. In this sense, the Catholic system, whereby nature and grace are interdependent, also connects this interdependence to the interconnection between Christ and the church. In addition to the emphasis on the alien character of Christ's righteousness imputed by grace alone, the Reformation emphasized the declaratory and forensic aspect of justification. God declares us righteous in Christ with a pronouncement that has a legal nature and legal effects. Justification is a performative act of God by which the righteousness of Christ is accounted to the sinner. The use of legal categories that evoke the courtroom is not the decision of the Reformers; it is instead inherent to the biblical message of salvation and emerges out of the covenantal matrix of biblical revelation.[45] God's covenantal dealings with the world and in salvation always have a legal aspect, and the new covenant that Jesus inaugurated keeps this irrepressible forensic dimension.

Being "in Christ" is possible thanks to a declaration of God with legal effects on the status of the sinner who is justified. The evangelical faith has linked the doctrine of imputation (as seen) to justification in a declarative and legal sense but also to the

---

44. Eberhard Jüngel, *Justification: The Heart of the Christian Faith*, trans. Jeffrey F. Cayzer (London: T&T Clark, 2006), 200.
45. See D. A. Carson, "Reflections on Salvation and Justification in the New Testament," *JETS* 40, no. 4 (1997): 581–608; Carson, "The Vindication of Imputation: On Fields of Discourse and Semantic Fields," in *Justification: What's at Stake in the Current Debates*, ed. Mark A. Husbands and Daniel J. Treier (Downers Grove, IL: InterVarsity Press, 2004), 46–80.

assurance of salvation in a covenantal context.[46] Considering that salvation is the gift of the external righteousness of Christ imputed to the sinner by faith, this divine utterance is sure, stable, and firm. Thanks to its legally binding covenantal character, it is possible to have confidence in God and in his purpose of salvation. Otherwise, as it happens in the Catholic perspective, justification is understood primarily in participatory categories to the life of God through the sacramental nature of the church. Man is not "declared" righteous with a righteousness that is not his own but is constantly "transformed" in his inner righteousness by the infusion of divine grace. Righteousness, already inherent in his being *capax Dei*, even if polluted by sin, is pumped into the dynamics of the Christian life and is expected to increase with participation in the sacramental life of the church. At baptism, as it is taught by the Catholic Church, man is justified. With the sacrament of reconciliation, righteousness is restored, and so on. The system needs a church that bestows grace and that thinks of herself as an organ that cannot be separated from the transmission of divine grace. God does not utter his pronouncement that justifies once and for all but infuses his righteousness through the sacraments of the church. Justification is not declared as once and forever guaranteed by the promise of God but as having an incremental dynamic governed by the church as the universal sacrament of salvation. Even viewed from this angle, the controversy over justification is not reducible to two complementary versions that can be rearranged into a higher synthesis. It goes straight to the very core of two theological accounts of the Christian life that are fundamentally and irreducibly *different*.

The sixteenth-century Reformers believed that justification was the article on which the church stands or falls.[47] In other words, they attributed to justification a fundamental epistemic role for the faith and decisive spiritual significance for the overall stability of biblical Christianity. Their insistence was not based on an obsession with a favorite theological *locus*; on the contrary, they could see that justification contained *in nuce* or *in extenso* all the reasons why the church needed a reformation according to the gospel. Based on the biblical Word of God, the confusions surrounding this doctrine and the extrabiblical intrusions and devotional developments that the church had accumulated on the doctrine of salvation were in need of clarification and correction.[48] The recovery of the doctrine of justification had a liberating effect on the toxins accumulated over the centuries: from the defective precision of Augustine on the distinction between justification and sanctification to the medieval "invention" of purgatory and indulgences. Acknowledging the role of the Scriptures as the "formal" criterion of faithfulness to the gospel, the Reformers also recognized the "material" principle that should have

---

46. Michael S. Horton convincingly stresses the covenantal dimension of being in Christ, distinguishing it from the participatory dimension (which is not covenantal) of Roman Catholicism. *Covenant and Salvation: Union with Christ* (Louisville: Westminster John Knox, 2007).
47. The quotations of Luther, Calvin, and other Reformers who use this or other similar expressions are given by Lane, *Justification by Faith in Catholic-Protestant Dialogue*, 140–42.
48. An excellent collection of sources and study of the Patristic doctrine of justification is found in Thomas Oden, *The Justification Reader* (Grand Rapids, MI: Eerdmans, 2002). This book shows how the assumptions of the evangelical insistence on "grace alone" were not an invention of the Protestant Reformation but belonged to the tradition of the "catholic" church, which recognized the primacy of God's grace in salvation.

contained the fundamental elements of the Christian view of salvation: the state of the human condition irremediably fallen in sin, the just judgment of God pending on sinners, the atoning significance of the cross of Christ, the gratuitousness of salvation given by faith alone without any human merit or participation, the legal framework of God's covenant expressed in the imputation of Christ's righteousness to the sinner. Even if today all this creates ecumenical embarrassments and anxieties,[49] this is the gospel in essence; this is the backbone of the biblical message of salvation: man is sinful and lost, God is a righteous and merciful covenant God, Christ is the one who is righteous and has taken the place of sinners, the grace of righteousness is received by faith alone, there is no participation by man's cooperation, and there is no other mediator apart from the Lord Jesus Christ. Salvation is a gift, that's the point: this is justification by grace alone through faith alone. And it is this justification that must be continually preached, lived out, and proclaimed as the core of the Christian faith.

Assessing Rome's Unfolding Trajectory on Justification

Having surveyed the teachings of the Council of Trent on justification as it is now reinterpreted by the *JDDJ*, we can now consider some concluding remarks to help us evaluate the present-day Roman Catholic trajectory on justification and answer the question whether Rome upholds a "faith alone" understanding of justification.[50]

Hope of Reconciliation

To understand the 1999 *Joint Declaration*, we need a little historical context. The already quoted *Is the Reformation Over?* statement summarizes the issues this way:

> On the doctrine of salvation, many are under the impression that there is a growing convergence regarding justification by faith and that tensions between Catholics and Evangelicals have eased considerably since the sixteenth century. At the Council of Trent (1545–1563), the Roman Catholic Church reacted strongly against the Protestant Reformation by declaring "anathema" (cursed) those who upheld justification by faith alone, as well as affirmed the teaching that salvation is a process of cooperating with infused grace rather than an act grounded in grace alone by faith alone.

---

49. The "ecumenically correct" formulation of today is that justification is *a* criterion of faithfulness to the gospel that is necessary but not sufficient in itself. See George Vandervelde, "Justification between Scripture and Tradition," *ERT* 21, no. 2 (1997): 128–48. The distinction between "necessary" and "sufficient" may be plausible, although it does not capture the compelling point of the Reformers, and it opens the door to other criteria that are "ecumenically acceptable," such as, for example, the sacramental nature of the church, owing to the insufficiency of justification. Not by accident, the *JDDJ* speaks of justification as an "indispensable" criterion (art. 18) but not as the most crucial for the Christian faith. Formally, the language is "correct," but theologically, the meaning is to suggest that the concerns of the Reformation were necessary, indispensable, but in need of a "Catholic" supplement to become sufficient.

50. This section was researched and written in collaboration with my colleague and friend Greg Pritchard and originally published in an article responding to criticism raised against the *Is the Reformation Over?* statement: Leonardo De Chirico and Greg Pritchard, "The Need for Clarification: Is the Reformation Over?," World Reformed Fellowship, June 1, 2017, http://wrfnet.org/articles/2017/06/wrf-members-continue-debate-reformation-over#.WWcYllFLfIU. Used by permission of World Reformed Fellowship. Parts of this section are also adapted from Leonardo De Chirico, "70. Trent, 450 Years Later," *Vatican Files* (blog), December 16, 2013, http://vaticanfiles.org/en/2013/12/70-trent-450-years-later/. Used by permission of the author. Greg Pritchard and I also collaborated on the article "What Do You Think about Pope Francis?," Evangelical Focus, September 24, 2015, http://evangelicalfocus.com/blogs/1000/What_do_you_think_about_Pope_Francis_.

Until recently, there has never been a serious claim that the five-hundred-year Reformation divide has been mended. Only in recent years have some leaders from significant Christian bodies proposed that this division has been healed. As noted above, the most influential and official discussion has been between the Roman Catholic Pontifical Council for Promoting Christian Unity and the Lutheran World Federation. The ecumenical world was excited when these groups released their *JDDJ* in 1999. As the *Is the Reformation Over?* statement explains,

> Some argue that the Joint Declaration on the Doctrine of Justification signed by the Roman Catholic Church and the Lutheran World Federation in 1999 has bridged the divide.

In fact, that was the very claim of the *Joint Declaration* itself, which explained that the Lutherans and Catholics were "now able to articulate a common understanding of our justification by God's grace through faith in Christ" (art. 5).

It is here that understandings begin to differ. We attempt to summarize both the positive and the critical evaluations of the *JDDJ*. There are certainly parts of the *JDDJ*, such as article 9, that use some of the biblical language of salvation, including the Protestant-sounding phrase "'justification' of sinful human beings by God's grace through faith (Rom 3:23–25), which came into particular prominence in the Reformation period." This sort of language allows an ecumenically eager reader to conclude that we have a different Roman Catholic Church, which now agrees with the Protestant Reformers that we are saved by faith alone.

Protestant-Evangelical Response

In sharp contrast, mainstream evangelicals understand the *Joint Declaration* as an attempt by Catholics to use some biblical language but to integrate this within a Catholic framework. We quoted above a portion of article 9 in the *JDDJ* that sounds like it affirms the Protestant-evangelical conviction of justification by faith alone. But article 11 articulates a traditional Catholic understanding of justification that provides the framework for interpreting the preceding article:

> Justification is the forgiveness of sins (cf Rom 3:23–25; Acts 13:39; Lk 18:14), liberation from the dominating power of sin and death (Rom 5:12–21) and from the curse of the law (Gal 3:10–14). . . . It occurs in the reception of the Holy Spirit in baptism and incorporation into the one body (Rom 8:1f, 9f; I Cor 12:12f).

As Michael Reeves explains,

> Quite clearly, justification is here said to include the process of inner transformation, and not include the imputation of Christ's righteousness. . . . Any theology that makes the believer's inner transformation a constituent part (instead of a

consequence) of justification is at odds with the material principle of the Reformation (justification by faith alone).[51]

Reeves and other mainstream evangelical critics all believe that the Roman Catholic and evangelical understanding of justification cannot be integrated together.[52] You cannot have a round square. You cannot have a married bachelor. Justification cannot be simultaneously a divine declarative act and an internal process of sanctifying transformation. The biblical language in the *JDDJ* is interpreted within the historic Catholic teaching of Trent. In short, the statement conflates elements of sanctification (the process of growing in holiness) with the categories of justification and embeds all of them in a sacramental framework so that justification fits within the Catholic teaching of baptismal regeneration and access to grace by means of the sacraments.

The Lutheran Church–Missouri Synod provided one of the most substantial early critiques of the *JDDJ* in 1999. They concluded,

> Although change has taken place in the Roman Catholic Church since Vatican II, JDDJ shows how very little headway has been made toward a genuine resolution of the differences between Lutherans and Roman Catholics on justification. This statement is not a "breakthrough."
>
> JDDJ does not settle the major disagreement between Lutheran theology and Roman Catholic theology on justification. Lutherans teach that justification is essentially a declaration of "not guilty" and "righteous" pronounced by God on a sinner because of Christ and His work. Roman Catholics teach that justification involves an internal process in which a believer is transformed and "made" more and more righteous. The non-settlement of this issue forms the chief defect of JDDJ.[53]

Lutheran Reverend Paul T. McCain, who participated in formulating the Missouri Synod's critical evaluation of the *JDDJ*, described the situation more bluntly:

> Ten years after it appeared, we still continue to hear that the Joint Declaration on the Doctrine of Justification was a "breakthrough" between the Roman Catholic Church and the Lutheran Church. The media loves to perpetuate this myth. In fact, the Joint Declaration on the Doctrine of Justification is a fraud. It was a sell-out by revisionist Lutherans to Rome.[54]

---

51. Michael Reeves, "The Joint Declaration on the Doctrine of Justification: A Curtain on the Reformation?," Reformanda Initiative, accessed July 30, 2018, http://reformandainitiative.org/the-joint-declaration-on-the-doctrine-of-justification-a-curtain-on-the-reformation/.
52. See Gregg Allison's popular article, "Has Rome Really Changed Its Tune? The Catholic Church—500 Years Later," desiringGod, September 24, 2016, http://www.desiringgod.org/articles/has-rome-really-changed-its-tune; and Garry J. Williams's more academic summary of the areas that separate Catholics and evangelicals, "The Five Solas of the Reformation: Then and Now," *Unio cum Christo* 3, no. 1 (2017): 13–34.
53. The Lutheran Church–Missouri Synod (1999), "The Joint Declaration on the Doctrine of Justification in Confessional Lutheran Perspective" (St. Louis, MO: Commission on Theology and Church Relations, 1999), points 13, 4.
54. Paul T. McCain, "A Betrayal of the Gospel: The Joint Declaration on the Doctrine of Justification," *First Things*, March 12, 2010, https://www.firstthings.com/blogs/firstthoughts/2010/03/a-betrayal-of-the-gospel-the-joint-declaration-on-the-doctrine-of-justification.

The title of McCain's article, "A Betrayal of the Gospel," says it all; he described the liberal Lutherans who signed the *JDDJ* as "fundamentally dishonest" because they compromised on basic Lutheran convictions. McCain did not blame Catholics for this fraud. "Rome is not to be faulted in any of this. The Papacy maintained the historic position of the Roman Church, and did not change it." He put the blame squarely on the Lutherans, whose liberal church had slowly moved away from biblical teaching throughout the twentieth century: "Mainline liberal Lutherans, however, compromised the key doctrine of the Scriptures and the very heart of the Lutheran Confessions."[55]

Reformed theologian Michael Horton concluded that "calling bad news [i.e., *Joint Declaration*] good news is destructive . . . of the prospects for genuine long-term ecclesiastical reconciliation."[56] Michael Reeves writes, "For all attempts to find wording that fits both Roman Catholic and evangelical views of justification, there remains a material and momentous difference between them."[57]

The *Is the Reformation Over?* statement summarized why the *JDDJ* does not teach the historic evangelical perspective:

> While the document is at times friendly towards a more biblical understanding of justification, it explicitly affirms the Council of Trent's view of justification. All of its condemnations of historic Protestant/Evangelical convictions still stand; they just do not apply to those who affirm the blurred position of the Joint Declaration.
>
> As was the case with Trent, in the Joint Declaration, justification is a process enacted by a sacrament of the Church (baptism); it is not received by faith alone. It is a journey that requires contribution from the faithful and an ongoing participation in the sacramental system. There is no sense of the righteousness of God being imputed by Christ to the believer, and thus there can be no assurance of salvation.

Where evangelicalism (or at least that segment that affirms Reformation convictions) views justification as a divine declarative act whereby God pronounces the sinner righteous in Christ, Rome still sees justification as an ongoing, transformative, and cooperative process.[58] The *JDDJ* uses more nuanced language in its attempt to accommodate the Lutheran position. The more dynamic categories of Rome can find room for some of the forensic language of the Reformation, but the reverse is not possible. The gulf is still there.

---

55. McCain, "Betrayal of the Gospel." Another Lutheran evaluation of the *JDDJ* is Lutheran Pastor Mark D. Menecher's "Ten Years After JDDJ: The Ecumenical Pelagianism Continues," *Logia* 18, no. 3 (2009), http://www.ccmverax.org/documents/LOGIAXVIII-3Menacher.pdf. One of the most significant criticisms of the *JDDJ* when it was released was more than 150 German university professors who signed a statement to publically reject the *JDDJ* as inconsistent with historic Lutheranism. See the brief description of the *JDDJ* in Erwin Fahlbusch, Jan Milic Lochman, Jaroslav Pelikan, John Samuel Mbiti, and Lukas Vischer, eds., *The Encyclopedia of Christianity* (Grand Rapids, MI: Eerdmans, 2003), 3:72–73.

56. Michael S. Horton, in "Now No Condemnation?," *World*, December 25, 1999, 20.

57. Reeves, "Curtain on the Reformation?"

58. An evangelical evaluation of the section on justification of the *Catechism of the Catholic Church* (§§1987–2005) is given by Allison, *Roman Catholic Theology*, 431–47.

Roman Catholic Response

In the face of this consistent mainstream evangelical perspective that the *Joint Declaration* does not teach what historic Protestants have always believed, some may think that the *JDDJ* does not affirm the doctrine of the Council of Trent. The problem is that this is simply not the case, and this time we should listen to the authoritative voice of the Vatican to underline this mistake.[59] At the time of the *JDDJ*'s announcement, Vatican leaders quickly clarified that the *Joint Declaration* had not denied or departed from the Council of Trent, which remains binding dogma for the Roman Catholic Church. Cardinal Cassidy, president of the Pontifical Council for Promoting Christian Unity and the individual leading Rome's involvement in the *Joint Declaration*, made this point clearly at a press conference that was held when the *JDDJ* was signed:

> Asked whether there was anything in the official common statement contrary to the Council of Trent, Cardinal Cassidy said: "Absolutely not, otherwise how could we do it? We cannot do something contrary to an ecumenical council. There's nothing there that the Council of Trent condemns."[60]

So we see clearly that from the Catholic perspective, the Council of Trent's pronouncements have not changed. What does Trent affirm about justification (from the sixth session)?

> Canon IX: If anyone says that the sinner is justified by faith alone, meaning that nothing else is required to cooperate in order to obtain the grace of justification . . . let him be anathema [condemned].
>
> Canon XII: If anyone says that justifying faith is nothing else than confidence [trust] in divine mercy, which remits sins for Christ's sake, or that it is this confidence [trust] alone that justifies us, let him be anathema [condemned].
>
> Canon XIV: If anyone says that man is absolved from his sins and justified because he firmly believes that he is absolved and justified . . . and that by this faith alone absolution and justification are effected, let him be anathema [condemned].

As already noted in the section on the Council of Trent, Trent's clear and unmistakable teaching is that salvation by faith alone is a heresy that should be condemned.

We also see this same clear message in the *Catechism of the Catholic Church* (1992), which articulates the Catholic doctrine of justification formulated at the Council of Trent. In the nineteen years since the *JDDJ*, we have not seen a new Catholic catechism published that updates the Catholic doctrinal position. This is because their position is still consistent with the authoritative Council of Trent: "We cannot do something contrary to an ecumenical council." Catholics have found a way to pacify liberal Lutherans and absorb some of the biblical language into their teaching

---

59. The following paragraphs closely follow McCain's well-articulated argument in "Betrayal of the Gospel."
60. McCain, "Betrayal of the Gospel," quoting Stephen Brown, "Lutheran-Catholic Declaration a 'Fine Way of Dialogue,' Says Cassidy," *Ecumenical News Bulletin*, November 1, 1999, 36.

and language through the *JDDJ*, but their position and commitment to Trent have not changed.

We see this same affirmation of Trent in the official Vatican response to the *JDDJ* written by Pope Benedict before he was chosen as pope. This official Vatican document criticizes some of the elements of the *JDDJ* and argues that Trent's condemnations still stand. As McCain explains,

> The Vatican's response clearly affirms Rome's historic position that justification is a process involving both God's grace and the good works of human beings, in other words, the classic Roman position that salvation is not by grace through faith alone, but by grace plus human merit and good works.

Thus, the Roman Catholic system of sacramental distribution of grace through physical objects has not changed. As the *Is the Reformation Over?* statement explains,

> The Roman Catholic Church's view is revealed by its continued use of indulgences (i.e., the remission of the temporal punishment for sin allotted by the Church on special occasions). It was the theology of indulgences that triggered the Reformation, but this system has been invoked most recently by Pope Francis in the 2015–2016 Year of Mercy.
>
> This shows that the Roman Catholic Church's basic view of salvation, which is dependent on the mediation of the Church, the distribution of grace by means of its sacraments, the intercession of the saints, and purgatory, is still firmly in place, even after the Joint Declaration.

The tone of the *Joint Declaration* is certainly different from that of Trent, but the theological content of the Council of Trent has neither been superseded nor bypassed.

We see one last problem in the current Catholic approach to justification. The same pope who said at the ecumenical ceremony in Lund that "the doctrine of justification expresses the essence of human existence before God," thus seeming to be in accord with what evangelicals might want to say on the doctrine, wrote very different things in a more authoritative statement. In his widely acclaimed 2013 exhortation "The Joy of the Gospel," the programmatic document of his pontificate, Francis wrote, "Non-Christians, by God's gracious initiative, when they are faithful to their own consciences, can live justified by the grace of God."[61]

---

61. Pope Francis, "Apostolic Exhortation Evangelii Gaudium of the Holy Father Francis to the Bishops, Clergy, Consecrated Persons, and the Lay Faithful on the Proclamation of the Gospel in Today's World" (no. 254), Vatican, accessed July 30, 2018, http://w2.vatican.va/content/francesco/en/apost_exhortations/documents/papa-francesco_esortazione-ap_20131124_evangelii-gaudium.html. This section of the exhortation deals with ecumenical and interreligious dialogue in the context of mission. According to Pope Francis, non-Catholic Christians are already united in baptism (244), Jews don't need to convert (247), and with believing Muslims, the way is "dialogue" because "together with us they adore the one and merciful God" (252, a quotation of *Lumen gentium*, 16). Other non-Christians are also "justified by the grace of God" and are associated to "the paschal mystery of Jesus Christ" (254). The gospel appears not to be a message of salvation from God's judgment but instead is a vehicle to access a fuller measure of a salvation that is already given to all mankind.

Pope Francis also argued for the importance of the atheist's own conscience in an interview in the Italian newspaper *La Repubblica*:

> You ask me if the God of Christians forgives one who doesn't believe and doesn't seek the faith. . . . The question for one who doesn't believe in God lies in obeying one's conscience.[62]

What is the pope saying in his apostolic exhortation? He is using the language of justification to speak about non-Christians and to argue that if they are faithful to their consciences, they can be justified. This is totally contrary to even the minimum core definition of justification given by the Bible and historically affirmed by evangelicals. Here we are confronted with completely different theological categories that make it possible for the pope to use the language of "justification" when he deals with Protestants and the same language of "justification" when he speaks about non-Christians.

Conclusion

Five centuries after the Protestant Reformation, the Roman Catholic Church has definitely adopted a different pastoral and ecclesial "style" than that of Trent, but it has not substantially changed it, nor denied it in whole or in part. There is no point at which Vatican II moves away from the dogmatic teaching of the Council of Trent. At Vatican II, Trent was kept in the background and remained within the framework of Roman Catholicism. The Tridentine paradigm was put, so to speak, in historical perspective, but it was neither forsaken nor forgotten. Vatican II has metabolized Trent but in no way abandoned it.[63]

With the 1999 *JDDJ*, Trent was updated in its language and emphases but reiterated in its substance. The Catholic and Lutheran positions were juxtaposed and held compatible, thus working with a "both-and" scheme that is quintessentially the Roman Catholic way of developing its doctrinal system. The Tridentine "anathemas" were lifted for those who hold the doctrines of the Reformation if reinterpreted ecumenically, but the theological core of contemporary Catholicism is still steeped in its Tridentine content: it is the institutional church that mediates the grace of God through its sacramental system. Grace alone was and is still rejected. A clear indication of this is the fact that nothing has changed in important areas like indulgences, purgatory, the sacramental prerogatives of the church, the cult of the saints, and so forth.

A final comment: On the occasion of the official celebration in Trent of the 450th anniversary of the Council of Trent (December 1, 2013), Pope Francis sent a special envoy to Trent together with a letter.[64] In it he said that the anniversary

---

62. "Pope Francis writes to *La Repubblica*: 'An open dialogue with non-believers,'" *La Repubblica*, September 11, 2013, http://www.repubblica.it/cultura/2013/09/11/news/the_pope_s_letter-66336961/.
63. On the relationship between Trent and Vatican II, see Raymond F. Bulman and Frederick J. Parrella, eds., *From Trent to Vatican II: Historical and Theological Investigations* (New York: Oxford University Press, 2016).
64. The Latin text of the letter can be found at the Vatican website: https://w2.vatican.va/content/francesco/la/letters/2013/documents/papa-francesco_20131119_brandmuller-450-chiusura-concilio-trento.html.

behooves the Church to recall with more prompt and attentive eagerness the most fruitful doctrine which came out of that council. Certainly not without cause, the Church has for a long time already accorded so much care to the Decrees and Canons of that Council that are to be recalled and observed.

"No doubt," the letter continued, "with the Holy Ghost inspiring and suggesting, it especially concerned the Fathers not only to guard the sacred deposit of Christian doctrine, but also to more clearly enlighten mankind." The same Spirit, according to the pope, now guides the church "to restore and meditate upon the most abundant doctrine of Trent." Quoting Pope Benedict XVI, Francis ended the letter by saying that the church "is a subject which increases in time and develops, yet always remains the same, the one subject of the journeying People of God." It is the pope that affirmed the continuity between Trent and the present-day Roman Catholic Church. It is not a static continuity in that the church "develops" over time but is a continuity in which the church changes while always remaining the same.

In terms of the doctrine of justification by faith, the clear opposition of Trent to "faith alone" has become a milder, softer, and more nuanced position. Yet it has not crossed the Rubicon that the Reformers had crossed in recovering the gospel of Jesus Christ received by grace alone through faith alone, based on Scripture alone, and focused on Christ alone for the glory of God alone. Rome is still on the other side.[65]

Recommended Resources
General
Carey, G. L. "Justification and Roman Catholicism." In *Here We Stand: Justification by Faith Today*, edited by J. I. Packer et al., 120–36. London: Hodder & Stoughton, 1986.

McGrath, Alister E. *Iustitia Dei: A History of the Christian Doctrine of Justification*. 2nd ed. Cambridge: Cambridge University Press, 1998. Esp. chaps. 2–4.

O'Collins, Gerald, and Oliver P. Rafferty. "Roman Catholic View." In *Justification: Five Views*, edited by James K. Beilby and Paul Rhodes Eddy, 265–90. Spectrum Multiview Books. Downers Grove, IL: IVP Academic, 2011.

Pesch, Otto Hermann. *Theologie der Rechtfertigung bei Martin Luther und Thomas von Aquin: Versuch eines systematisch-theolischen Dialogs*. Walberberger Studien der Albertus-Magnus-Akademie 7. Mainz: Matthias-Grünewald Verlag, 1967.

Preus, Robert. *Justification and Rome*. Saint Louis, MO: Concordia, 1997.

Runia, Klaas. "Justification and Roman Catholicism." In *Right with God: Justification in the Bible and the World*, edited by D. A. Carson, 197–215. Carlisle, UK: Paternoster, 1992.

---

65. The Five Solas Series is an excellent resource to help readers appreciate the tenets of the biblical gospel as it was recovered by the Reformation in the context of past and present-day controversies with the Roman Catholic Church. See Thomas Schreiner, *Faith Alone: The Doctrine of Justification; What the Reformers Taught . . . and Why It Still Matters* (Grand Rapids, MI: Zondervan, 2015); David VanDrunen, *God's Glory Alone: The Majestic Heart of the Christian Faith and Life; What the Reformers Taught . . . and Why It Still Matters* (Grand Rapids, MI: Zondervan, 2015); Matthew Barrett, *God's Word Alone: The Authority of Scripture; What the Reformers Taught . . . and Why It Still Matters* (Grand Rapids, MI: Zondervan, 2016); Stephen Wellum, *Christ Alone: The Uniqueness of Jesus as Savior; What the Reformers Taught . . . and Why It Still Matters* (Grand Rapids, MI: Zondervan, 2017); Carl R. Trueman, *Grace Alone: Salvation as a Gift of God; What the Reformers Taught . . . and Why It Still Matters* (Grand Rapids, MI: Zondervan, 2017).

Sesboüé, Bernard. *Sauvés par la grâce: Les débats sur la justification du XVIe siècle à nos jours*. Paris: Éditions Facultés de Paris, 2009.

On Trent

Colzani, G. "La nozione di 'giustificazione': Il senso del suo impiego nei dibattiti tridentini, la verifica di un modello di comprensione." In *La giustificazione*, edited by G. Ancona, 65–111. Padova: Edizioni Messaggero Padova, 1997.

Lehmann, Karl, and Wolfhart Pannenberg, eds. *The Condemnations of the Reformation Era: Do They Still Divide?* Translated by Margaret Kohl. Minneapolis: Fortress, 1990.

Pelikan, Jaroslav, and Valerie R. Hotchkiss, eds. *Creeds and Confessions of Faith in the Christian Tradition*. Vol. 2, *Creeds and Confessions in the Reformation Era*. New Haven, CT: Yale University Press, 2003.

Waltz, A. "La giustificazione tridentina: Note sul dibattito e sul decreto conciliare." *Angelicum* 28 (1951): 7–138.

On the *Joint Declaration on the Doctrine of Justification*

Blocher, Henri A. "The Lutheran-Catholic Declaration on Justification." In *Justification in Perspective: Historical Developments and Contemporary Challenges*, edited by Bruce L. McCormack, 197–218. Grand Rapids, MI: Baker Academic, 2006.

Holc, Paweł. *Un ampio consenso sulla dottrina della giustificazione: Studio sul dialogo cattolico-luterano*. Tesi Gregoriana, Serie Teologia 53. Rome: Editrice Pontificia Università Gregoriana, 1999.

Lane, Anthony N. S. *Justification by Faith in Catholic-Protestant Dialogue: An Evangelical Assessment*. London: T&T Clark, 2006.

24

The Eclipse of Justification

Justification during the Enlightenment and Post-Enlightenment Eras

BRUCE P. BAUGUS

According to the magisterial Reformers and their orthodox heirs, justification is an act of grace in which God forgives believing sinners and counts them righteous through faith in Jesus Christ alone. More precisely, they generally agreed that justification is a forensic or judicial act of God (*actus forensis*) in which he does two inseparable things: negatively, he pardons or forgives individual believers of all their sins (*iustificatio negativa*), and positively, he counts or declares them righteous in his sight (*iustificatio activa*). Believing sinners are pardoned and declared righteous by a single judicial act of grace that, contrary to all cooperative or synergistic formulations, does not take into account or leave room for any active contribution on the part of the justified (*sola gratia*). The righteousness that God credits to the believer is entirely Christ's (*iustitia aliena*), whose satisfaction (*satisfactio vicaria*) of the guilt and penalty due to sinners (*obedientia passiva*) and fulfillment of the law (*obedientia activa*) on behalf of his people is imputed (*imputatio*) to those who trust Christ. Justification is received or appropriated only through the instrumental means of faith that rests in Jesus Christ alone for salvation (*sola fide*).

This formulation of the biblical teaching on justification, often abbreviated as *sola fide*, represents a broad Protestant consensus from the opening of the Reformation to the eve of the Enlightenment.[1] This consensus stands in direct contrast to the

---

1. James Buchanan observes, perhaps a touch too strongly, that "few things in the history of the Church are more remarkable than the entire unanimity of the Reformers on the subject of a sinner's Justification before God." *The Doctrine of Justification: An Outline of Its History in the Church and of Its Exposition from Scripture* (1867; repr.,

predominant family of medieval views that considered justification a process through which God infuses justifying or sanctifying grace into the soul of cooperative sinners, thereby making them intrinsically righteous to some degree and thus acceptable to God.[2] Lutheran and Reformed theologians elaborated and refined Luther's insight into the soteriological heart of the gospel with remarkable unanimity on what Scripture taught and its vital significance for the life and health of the church; in the main, they did not alter or modify the point in their elaboration and codification of it and successfully rejected formulations that did.[3] While important differences emerged around the edges of justification—on the imputation of Adam's sin, the ground of Christ's infinite merit and scope of his vicarious satisfaction, the proper use of the law by the justified, and so on—they carefully expounded and vigorously defended *sola fide* as a defining doctrine not just of Protestantism but of the faith "once for all delivered to the saints" (Jude 3).

As James Buchanan observed, "Luther knew human nature too well to suppose that the truth" about "the substance" of the doctrine of justification *sola fide* "could be preserved in its purity without constant conflict with error; and he predicted more than once the gradual declension even of the Protestant Churches from this fundamental article of faith."[4] History has proved Luther right. This chapter traces some of the many ways that subsequent Protestant theology permitted justification *sola fide* to be eclipsed by the rise of Enlightenment thought from Reformed orthodoxy to neoorthodoxy.

Justification on the Eve of Enlightenment

Two noteworthy contextual factors fired the pre-Enlightenment development of this doctrine: positively, the magisterial success of both the Lutheran and Reformed branches of Protestantism across most of northwestern Europe (including several emerging colonial powers), and here and there throughout the rest of the Continent; negatively, objections from Roman Catholic and radical quarters and challenges from within Lutheran and Reformed quarters. Together, these factors drove demand for detailed and orderly expositions of justification *sola fide* set within systematic summaries of the faith to support the didactic and polemic needs of the church and academy in Protestant lands.

Edinburgh: Banner of Truth, 1984), 151. Alistair E. McGrath similarly describes the Protestant "consensus" that existed "over the period 1530–1730" on "the *nature* of justification" as a "forensic *declaration*," distinct from regeneration and sanctification, in which "the alien righteousness of Christ" is imputed to believers as "a *synthetic* rather than *analytic*" judgment. *Iustitia Dei: A History of the Christian Doctrine of Justification*, 3rd ed. (Cambridge: Cambridge University Press, 2005), 212–13.

2. McGrath observes that in the medieval era, "justification is invariably understood to involve a real change in the sinner, . . . [and] this change was generally regarded as involving the infusion of a supernatural habit of grace into the souls of humans." Yet, he notes, certain questions, such as "the relationship between . . . the infusion of supernatural habits" and "the divine acceptance," remained contentious into the sixteenth century. *Iustitia Dei*, 176.

3. Despite recognizing the broad Protestant consensus on the nature of justification throughout the era of Protestant orthodoxy, McGrath follows the discredited characterization of the robust scholastic development of this doctrine within the Reformed tradition as "a significant shift from Calvin's position on a number of matters of importance." Chief among them, he suggests, is that Calvin's "Christological emphasis" is "replaced by a theocentric emphasis, as the basis of theological speculation shifts from an inductive method based upon the Christ-event to a deductive method based upon the divine decrees of election." This, he claims, led to the formulation of "a doctrine of limited atonement" and reinterpretation of "predestination . . . as an aspect of the doctrine of *God*, rather than as an aspect of the doctrine of *salvation.*" *Iustitia Dei*, 266. Cf. Richard A. Muller, *After Calvin: Studies in the Development of a Theological Tradition* (New York: Oxford University Press, 2003), 3–102.

4. Buchanan, *Justification*, 153.

Tridentine Roman Catholicism

The situation was rather different in large swaths of Roman Catholic Christendom, of course, where counter-Reformation measures, on doctrinal and institutional fronts at least, led Pope Paul III to convene a general council to consolidate Rome's strained communion. The council took up justification in its sixth session (1546–1547) and condemned *sola fide* despite the diversity of opinions within Rome represented at Trent and the efforts of Reginald Pole, Giulio Contarini, and others to restrain the council from doing so.[5] Specifically, the council anathematized anyone who dared to claim (1) "that the sinner is justified by faith alone, meaning . . . no other cooperation is required for him to obtain the grace of justification"; (2) that "people are justified . . . solely by the attribution [i.e., imputation] of Christ's justice, . . . to the exclusion of the grace and charity which is poured forth in their hearts by the Holy Spirit and abides in them"; or (3) "that the faith which justifies is nothing else but trust in the divine mercy, which pardons sins" for Christ's sake, "or that it is that trust alone by which we are justified."[6] At Trent, Rome doubled down on what Protestants viewed as a confusion of justification and sanctification, maintaining that sinners must become righteous by cooperating with the infusion of grace into their soul before they are or can be declared righteous by God, much less enjoy any present assurance of being justified in his sight.

While Rome's recalcitrance at Trent (and inquisitorial ruthlessness) rather effectively checked any openness to justification *sola fide* within her communion, Tridentine justification was not the only alternative to *sola fide* on the scene by the dawn of the Enlightenment.[7] Among the radical Reformers—a diverse lot who were often less clear or precise than their magisterial contemporaries—many rejected Rome's sacerdotal and progressive construal of justification as well as the merely instrumental view of faith in forensic justification. While some radical thinkers adopted the language of "faith alone," they tended to define justifying faith as something active through love, and thus comprehending personal piety or good works, as the basis of justification. Others explicitly denied *sola fide* and argued that sinners are justified by faith and love or good works or on the basis of some transformation of the sinner (regeneration). In other words, while radical writers sometimes affirmed that justification is by grace alone through faith alone, they generally advocated some version of an ontological concept of justification in which the sinner is

---

5. On the diversity of Roman Catholic opinions leading up to Trent, see McGrath, *Iustitia Dei*, 309–24; on maneuvers at Trent to exclude and suppress views reminiscent of Lutheran justification, see Christopher Ocker, "Explaining Evil and Grace," in *The Oxford Handbook of the Protestant Reformations*, ed. Ulinka Rublack (Oxford: Oxford University Press, 2017), 34–38. Leopold von Ranke counts three bishops and five theologians who resisted the condemnation of justification *sola fide* out of the perhaps seventy members of the council. *History of the Popes: Their Church and State*, trans. E. Fowler, rev. ed. (New York: Colonial Press, 1901), 1:138.

6. Excerpts from session 6, canons 9, 11, and 12, in Jaroslav Pelikan and Valerie R. Hotchkiss, eds., *Creeds and Confessions of Faith in the Christian Tradition*, vol. 2, *Creeds and Confessions in the Reformation Era* (New Haven, CT: Yale University Press, 2003), 837. Other canons of the sixth session object to real or supposed errors relating to the freedom of the will, use of the law, merit and necessity of good works, possibility and ground of assurance, and the necessity of penance and purgatory, among other things.

7. The Spanish Reformer Juán de Valdés (ca. 1498–1541), who held a Lutheran view of justification and yet remained in communion with Rome, died before the council was convened. Peter Martyr Vermigli (1499–1562) sparked a wave of Italian refugees when he fled to Protestant territory in 1542. Under the Spanish inquisition, the loyal Bartolomé Carranza (1503–1576), archbishop of Toledo and participant at Trent, was suspected of Lutheran sympathies in 1558 and arrested, removed from his see, and threatened with death. Though finally acquitted in 1576, he died only days afterward.

graciously made intrinsically right rather than the forensic concept in which the alien righteousness of Christ is imputed to the sinner.[8]

Socinianism

Among the radicals, the Polish Brethren are particularly interesting given their doctrinal affinities with the dawning Enlightenment. The Brethren denied the Trinity and separated from the Reformed Church of Poland in 1565. They subsequently embraced and advanced the anti-Trinitarian theology that the exiled Italian humanist Faustus Socinus (1539–1604) developed out of his well-traveled uncle Laelius's notions about Christ and salvation. From 1602, the Racovian Academy in southern Poland taught Socinianism as set out in the Racovian Catechism (1605) until it was shut down in 1638. According to this catechism, the Father alone is God, the Holy Spirit is an impersonal power, and Jesus Christ, who has no prior existence, is God's son only insofar as he was conceived by divine power.[9] Jesus, who is an exceptionally holy and authoritative human being, is not divine. By setting an example of self-denying obedience, he shows others the only way to be saved and is properly and necessarily praised as the Savior.

There is, however, no vicarious satisfaction for sin and no need for such in the Socinian soteriological scheme; God forgives sin out of sheer mercy, and people are justified as they strive to follow Christ's example. Though no one else is as holy as Jesus, our "faith renders our obedience more estimable and more acceptable in the sight of God," the catachism claims, and it "supplies the deficiency of our obedience, and causes us to be justified by God." What is more, "that faith to which alone and in reality salvation is ascribed [includes] not only trust, but obedience also."[10] Like many other radicals who rejected forensic justification, Socinians believed that their view better promoted personal piety and conformed to the practical emphasis of Christianity.

Socinianism, and Unitarian thought in general, proved remarkably influential across Enlightenment Europe and America. Racovian writings were circulated among dissenting groups throughout the Continent, including Remonstrants in Holland, where many

---

8. Alvin J. Beachy, *The Concept of Grace in the Radical Reformation*, BHR 17 (Nieuwkoop: De Graaf, 1976), esp. 25–34; Egil Grislis, "The Meaning of Good Works: Luther and the Anabaptists," *Word and World* 6, no. 2 (1986): 170–80. Beachy studies seven radical thinkers and argues that there is a discernible and shared concept of grace across radical thought that underlies an ontological concept of justification. Chester David Hartranft argues that the role of love in Schwenckfeld's view renders it "personal" rather than "forensic." Hartranft, ed., *Corpus Schwenckfeldianorum*, vol. 1, *A Study of the Earliest Letters of Caspar Schwenckfeld von Ossig* (Leipzig: Breitkopf & Härtel, 1907), 476. While many radical thinkers shared a concern over forensic justification's perceived effects on personal piety, Grislis admits the difficulty of summarizing radical thought owing to the great diversity of opinions in these circles and relative marginalization of justification among them. Suggestions that many radical writers were not more explicit on *sola fide* because they assumed agreement with the magisterial Reformers on this point are unconvincing since they were subjected to withering criticism by Lutheran and Reformed polemicists.

9. An Arian alternate to strict Socinianism affirmed the preexistence of Christ as a created being. Despite their Christological differences, both rejected vicarious satisfaction and forensic justification.

10. Thomas Rees, trans. and ed., *The Racovian Catechism with Notes and Illustrations* (London: Longman, Hurst, Rees, Orme, and Brown, 1818), 321–22 (5.9). Buchanan summarizes the Socinian view of justification "as amounting, in substance, to this—that sinners obtain pardon and acceptance with God, through His mere mercy, on the ground of their own repentance and reformation." *Doctrine of Justification*, 162.

Socinians found refuge and continued to write and publish after the close of the Racovian Academy and especially their expulsion from Poland twenty years later, in 1658.[11] Socinus's collected works were published by his grandson in Amsterdam in 1668 and were read widely and with interest by many Enlightenment thinkers who often developed Unitarian views along deistic lines, which "had no other doctrine of Justification than that of pardon on repentance and reformation," or even along more pantheistic lines, which "had no room even for pardon or repentance."[12] Nevertheless, notable Unitarian associations arose in England and America, where Congregational Unitarians eventually won the battle for Harvard with the appointment of Henry Ware to the prestigious Hollis Chair of Divinity in 1805.

As the Enlightenment progressed, Socinus was increasingly memorialized as a pioneering freethinker who dared to let reason trump authority in religion.[13] Though exaggerated, there is some truth to the claim. While Socinus and most early Socinians continued to argue, often on the basis of miracles, that Scripture (especially the New Testament) was divine revelation of the only way of salvation, they also rejected traditional interpretations of key passages supporting cardinal articles of the faith such as the Trinity, original sin, and incarnation as "repugnant . . . to right reason."[14] This line of criticism, granting to human reason a more magisterial role in biblical hermeneutics and theology, implicated vicarious satisfaction and justification *sola fide* as well. "Socinianism can thus be characterized," Andrew Fix explains, "as a biblically based creed with a pronounced rationalistic inclination."[15] It was this rationalistic inclination that interested Enlightenment thinkers, many of them riding one form or another of rational Unitarianism (Socinian, Arian, deist, panentheist) out of the orthodox corral, leaving *sola fide* in the dust behind them.[16]

---

11. Earl Morse Wilbur traces an active and, on the Socinian side at least, sympathetic correspondence between the Remonstrants and Polish Brethren from at least the 1610s. *A History of Unitarianism*, vol. 1, *Socinianism and Its Antecedents* (Cambridge, MA: Beacon, 1945), 573–87. This was no doubt awkward for Remonstrants, who denied Socinian tendencies even as both Socinian and orthodox writers claimed numerous points of agreement. The orthodox accused various Remonstrants of holding Socinian views beginning with professor Conrad Vorstius's appointment at Leiden. While Hugo Grotius rejected such accusations (see, e.g., his *Defensio Fidei Catholicae de Satisfactione Christi adversus Faustum Socinum Senensum*, 1617), Johannes Pelt set Remonstrant and Socinian passages in parallel columns to display their similarities in *Harmonia Remonstrantium et Socinianorum* (1633). See also Andrew Cooper Fix, *Prophecy and Reason: The Dutch Collegiants in the Early Enlightenment* (1990; repr., Princeton, NJ: Princeton University Press, 2016), 135–61.

12. Buchanan, *Doctrine of Justification*, 165. In Holland, Socinians fell in with Remonstrants and other dissenters, including Benedict de Spinoza briefly, in the "colleges" that emerged after the Synod of Dort (see Fix, *Prophecy and Reason*, 144–61); in England, Socinianism was promoted by John Biddle, among others, and both John Locke and Isaac Newton read Socinian works and held similar views of God and Christ, as did many deists. The first openly Socinian congregation in London was established in 1774 and in Boston about 1784, though there were also many Arian Unitarians (and deists) already in these cities as well.

13. This assessment is reflected, for example, on the 1879 memorial to Laelius and Faustus Socinus in Siena, Italy, which lauds the pair as "avengers of human reason against the supernatural" and Socinianism as the champion of "modern rationalism for three centuries." This is ludicrous: Faustus Socinus advanced and defended a thoroughly supernatural worldview on the basis of divine revelation confirmed through miracles.

14. Rees, *Racovian Catechism*, 45 (3.1).

15. Fix, *Prophecy and Reason*, 137.

16. Paul Tillich begins his discussion of the Enlightenment development of Protestant theology with Socinianism, declaring this theological movement "one of the sources of the Enlightenment" and "more important than either the repetition of it in English deism, where it was radicalized, or in modern liberal theology, . . . where it was carried through." *A History of Christian Thought: From Its Judaic and Hellenistic Origins to Existentialism* (New York: Simon and Schuster, 1968), 287. Adolf von Harnack concludes that Socinianism represents "the *self-disintegration* of dogma" and in this sense an end of Christian dogmatics. *History of Dogma*, trans. Neil Buchanan (Boston: Little, Brown, 1900), 7:165–67.

Displacing and Dismantling Justification *Sola Fide*

The two theologically tumultuous centuries between Socinus's death in Raków in 1604 and Harvard's embrace of Unitarianism in 1805 are marked by at least two significant trends for justification *sola fide*: (1) the rise and spectacular collapse of a grand yet unorganized Enlightenment project to refound Christianity, or religion in general, on principles that are supposed to be universally accessible and compelling to human reason alone, and (2) the appearance and spreading influence of Pietism, whose slow fade is still working itself out on the religious landscape today. In the quest for a universal religion of reason or nature, as rational theologians conceived it, great violence was done to the integrity of the Christian faith as one point of the gospel after another was found to be either unsupportable or superfluous by autonomous reason. Meanwhile, certain German theologians and pastors started voicing their suspicion that justification *sola fide* was breeding spiritual and moral lethargy throughout the Lutheran church. While space does not permit a full recounting of the scores of writers and thinkers who contributed to these developments, a select account of each suffices to trace the contours of their oddly similar rationalistic-moralistic critiques of justification *sola fide*.

Rational Theology

Against the backdrop of the Thirty Years War (1618–1648), the well-educated and widely traveled Welsh mercenary and ambassador to Paris Edward Lord Herbert of Cherbury wondered aloud in *De Veritate* about the plight of "the wretched terror-stricken mass" of humanity in Europe who were torn between warring factions divided, largely, along religious lines.[17] They "have no refuge," he lamented, "unless some immovable foundations of truth resting on universal consent are established, to which they can turn amid the doubts of theology and philosophy."[18] In theology, Herbert identified five "common notions" that can be strung together: (1) there is one God (2) who ought to be revered by all people by leading (3) virtuous and (4) repentant lives (5) in view of divine judgment in this world and the next. These five articles, he argued, are the fundamental principles of the religion of nature universally accessible to reason alone and agreed to by all rational people. Whatever goes beyond this in religion is at least unessential and perhaps false, arising primarily from corrupt imaginings and self-serving priests.[19]

Conspicuously absent from this summary of the supposed universal religion of reason are the doctrines of the Trinity, original sin, incarnation, vicarious satisfaction, and the justification of sinners through faith alone. By adopting "universal consent" as the

---

17. It is undeniable that religious commitments played a critical role throughout the Thirty Years War and featured prominently in the Peace of Westphalia at its conclusion. That said, religion was also exploited or sometimes even ignored, as by France who sided with Protestants against fellow Roman Catholics, since political self-interest ultimately trumped everything else.
18. Lord Herbert of Cherbury, *De Veritate*, trans. Meyrick H. Carré (1624; 3rd ed., 1645; repr. Bristol: University of Bristol, 1937), 117.
19. Herbert of Cherbury, *De Veritate*, 118. Herbert developed these themes further in *De Causis Errorum* and *De Religione Laici*, and attempts to demonstrate these five articles are held by common consent in *De Religione Gentilium*.

criterion for determining what is true, Herbert precluded the very possibility of anything exclusively Christian, much less distinctly Protestant, being judged essential. "Some doctrines due to revelation may be, some ought to be, abandoned," he reasoned.[20] Indeed, the only category of divine revelation he permitted was directly to the rational individual; Scripture is merely a report by ancient authors who claimed such revelation for their writings and is at best merely probable. What is required, he suggested, is a rational principle to distinguish the kernel of truth from the husk of particular religious beliefs and practices that either cannot be known to be true or can even be known to be false. Herbert's doctrine of "common notions" became that principle of rational criticism, distinguishing what is essential from what is unessential in Scripture, theology, and religious practice.[21]

Herbert is often considered, retrospectively, the father of English deism since he was perhaps the first to articulate the five articles that came to define this stripped-down religious offspring of the Enlightenment. At the time, however, it was not clear just where this equally audacious and naive embrace of the magisterial use of reason would lead. Many thinkers of the era pursued rational theology into a more fully developed moralistic deism that was indeed characterized by Herbert's five articles. John Toland (1670–1722), Matthew Tindal (ca. 1657–1733), and Thomas Chubb (1679–1747) advanced this widely influential brand of deism in England; the thinking of Voltaire (1694–1778) and other *philosophes* ran along similar lines in France; and so did the thinking of higher-critical pioneers Hermann Samuel Reimarus (1694–1768) and Johann Salomo Semler (1725–1791) in Germany, under the more pronounced influence of a post-Cartesian brand of rationalism worked out by Benedict de Spinoza (1632–1677) and Gottfried Leibniz (1646–1716).

None of these Enlightenment thinkers found any place in their rational religious schemes for justification *sola fide*, arguing instead that one is right with God through a combination of a moral life and repentance, as opposed to participating in religious ceremonies or believing claims that could be known only from supposed sources of special revelation. While many admitted the possibility of divine revelation, they broadly agreed that morality is the essence of religion and so also of Christianity, rightly interpreted, and that the content of morality, which is all that is religiously required of humans, can be known by reason without resorting to special revelation. Special revelation, on this view, is redundant at best. Some argued that justification *sola fide* (especially the imputation of an alien righteousness) is rationally unsupportable and obscures the moral simplicity of the religion of reason. All agreed that humans are acceptable to God only on the basis of a moral and repentant life.[22]

---

20. Herbert of Cherbury, *De Veritate*, 289.
21. "In this connection," Herbert wrote, "the teaching of Common Notions is important; indeed, without them it is impossible to establish any standard of discrimination in revelation or even in religion." Herbert of Cherbury, *De Veritate*, 289.
22. McGrath develops this insight from the work of Thomas Chubb. *Iustitia Dei*, 363–64. He could have easily developed the point from the works of earlier writers, such as John Toland's *Christianity Not Mysterious* (1696) or Matthew Tindal's *Christianity as Old as the Creation* (1730).

Others, however, such as William Chillingworth (1602–1644), John Tillotson (1630–1694), and John Locke (1632–1704) in Britain and Christian Wolff (1679–1754) and arguably Gotthold Ephraim Lessing (1729–1781) on the Continent, defended Christianity, or at least some fuller approximation of it than deism, on rational grounds. In *Religion of Protestants*, for instance, Chillingworth assumed that all Christians, or at least all Protestants, agree that the Bible is the Word of God, and he argued that all God requires is that we merely accept Scripture as his Word and strive to understand it rightly and live by it. If one started with Scripture, reason could lead the rest of the way to a free and harmonious religious order beyond all the divisive, tyrannical abuses of competing confessions and communions.[23]

Although Tillotson was raised in a Puritan home, he, too, was taken by the prospects of rational theology and convinced that revealed religion rests on the principles of natural religion and does little more than confirm what reason knows is our duty toward God and others.[24] The future archbishop of Canterbury asserted that "nothing ought to be received as a revelation from God which plainly contradicts the principles of natural religion."[25] It was on this principle that he famously rejected transubstantiation, in which the Communion elements are supposedly transformed into the actual body and blood of Christ while seemingly remaining bread and wine to our senses.[26]

Tillotson consistently argued that Christianity is the superior religion, but this is only because it offers a clearer revelation of what is already known to reason from nature, which gives us a "more certain and perfect law for the government of our lives."[27] As for how a sinner is justified before God, he spoke only of the necessity of repentance in view of the coming judgment and the power of the "best religion in the world" to "make us good" and thereby acceptable in God's sight.[28] Though no deist—Tillotson defended the reality of special revelation partly on the basis of miracles—there appears to be no more room in his system for the imputation of an alien righteousness than there is for transubstantiation.

The displacement of *sola fide* among the less radical rational theologians is evident in another son of Puritan parents, John Locke, who graduated from Oxford's college of Christ Church, then under the deanship of John Owen. In *The Reasonableness of Christianity* (1695), Locke developed the rational trajectory established by Tillotson, building on his distinction between propositions that are according to reason, contrary to reason, and above reason. Any proposition that is according to reason may be known to be true by reason; any proposition that is contrary to reason may be known to be false on that account; but "propositions whose truth or probability we cannot by reason derive from those principles"—referring to the principles of his empirical

---

23. Chillingworth's views shifted significantly throughout his life and carried him from his youthful Laudian Anglicanism to Jesuit Roman Catholicism and eventually back again by the time he wrote *The Religion of Protestants* in 1637.
24. See, among many other places, John Tillotson, *The Works of the Most Reverend Dr. John Tillotson, Late Lord Archbishop of Canterbury*, vol. 1, *The Excellency of the Christian Religion* (London: Ware et al., 1742), 128–51.
25. John Tillotson, *A Discourse against Transubstantiation* (London: Brabazon Aylmer and William Rogers, 1684), 37–43.
26. Tillotson, *Works*, vol. 2, *Of the Trial of the Spirits*, 33.
27. Tillotson, *Excellency of the Christian Religion*, 129.
28. Tillotson, *Excellency of the Christian Religion*, 151.

rationalism—may nevertheless be revealed by God and rational to believe if sufficiently attested by God through miracles.[29]

Despite his apparent defense of Protestant principles, however, Locke maintained that there are only two things necessary to be accepted by God: to believe that Jesus Christ is God's Messiah and to live a righteous and repentant life. On the first point, "all that was to be believed for justification," he argued, "was no more but this single proposition; that *Jesus of Nazareth was the Christ, or the Messiah.*"[30] As for the second, he held that Paul's actual teaching is that sinners are justified through "faith working by love. And that faith without works, i.e. the works of sincere obedience to the law and will of Christ, is not sufficient for our justification, St. James shows at large." He continued, echoing the misguided analysis of earlier critics of *sola fide*:

> Neither indeed could it be otherwise; for life, eternal life, being the reward of justice or righteousness only, appointed by the righteous God (who is of purer eyes than to behold iniquity) to those only who had no taint or infection of sin upon them, it is impossible that he should justify those who had no regard to justice at all whatever they believed. This would have been to encourage iniquity, contrary to the purity of his nature; and to have condemned that eternal law of right, which is holy, just, and good; of which no one precept or rule is abrogated or repealed; nor indeed can be; whilst God is an holy, just, and righteous God, and man a rational creature.[31]

Locke's confession of Jesus as the Messiah did not embrace his divine nature as the eternal Son of God, much less the Trinity. Locke largely passed over these articles of orthodoxy, leaving his critics to fill in the broadly Arian blanks. When it came to the sinner's justification, however, he explicitly rejected *sola fide* as pernicious to the order of justice and morality as the rational theologians in the late seventeenth century conceived it.[32]

While the less radical rational theologians of the era differed from their more deistic counterparts on some important points—especially the epistemic justification of beliefs based on divine revelation that were otherwise unknown to reason—they generally agreed that one is justified before God on the broad basis of two kinds of works: moral goodness and sincere repentance for any failures. These works were sometimes traced to faith as a kind of spring from which they flowed, especially among the less radical set, but the emphasis fell consistently on works of rational morality and simple moral repentance. While works of mere religious ceremony were excluded from justification as pure vanity, the evangelical principle that sinners are justified by the gracious imputation of Christ's alien righteousness to those who believe was displaced by a supposedly rational and universal principle of works—grace assisted or otherwise.

---

29. Tillotson held essentially the same line. For Locke's general religious epistemology, see book 4 of *An Essay Concerning Human Understanding*, ed. Peter H. Nidditch (Oxford: Oxford University Press, 1979).
30. John Locke, *Reasonableness of Christianity*, ed. John C. Higgins-Biddle (Oxford: Oxford University Press, 1999), 33.
31. Locke, *Reasonableness of Christianity*, 118, 119.
32. The common tendency of rational theologians to deny Christ's eternal deity and the Trinity alongside their rejection of imputed righteousness led many of the era's defenders of *sola fide*, such as John Owen, to brand them "Socinian," even though some, like Locke, appear more Arian in their Christological views.

Pietism

While justification *sola fide* was being displaced by a vague moralistic religion of reason among rational theologians, a sizable pietistic contingent was dismantling *sola fide* among Lutheran evangelicals. As a self-conscious movement within Lutheranism, Pietism is usually traced to Philipp Jakob Spener's publication of *Pia Desideria* in 1675, though certain mystical and devotional writers such as Jakob Böhme and Johann Arndt had already sounded several of the same notes. A number of German theologians and pastors shared Spener's concern over the apparent spiritual lethargy of orthodox Lutheran churches and followed his lead in crafting a theology designed to awaken the drowsy to a new spiritual vibrancy in their faith.

A concern for personal holiness cultivated and expressed through pious devotion is clearly evident in many Reformed champions of *sola fide*, especially among Puritan and *Nadere Reformatie* pastors and teachers, throughout the seventeenth and early eighteenth centuries. But in Lutheran circles, the quest for a more vibrant pietistic practice took a decidedly different turn. Although Arndt clearly and strongly affirmed justification *sola fide* throughout his highly influential devotional work *True Christianity* (1606–1610), he also stressed the active nature of saving faith and the pious and repentant life of faith as the defining and necessary marks of a true Christian, demonstrating one's justifying faith, with such force that subsequent Pietists began to argue that one's piety and repentance somehow factored into God's justification of the sinner.[33]

They went even further than this, however. Rather than adhering to *sola fide* while drawing on the priority of the believer's union with Christ over the *duplex gratia* of justification and sanctification or developing a more robust sense of the third use of the moral law, Pietist authors concluded that *sola fide* was an integral part of the problem of impiety in Lutheran pulpits and pews. The notion that believing sinners are counterfactually declared righteous before God apart from any consideration of either their regenerate nature or the activity of saving faith working through love was judged destructive to the very piety that is the essence of the Christian life. It is a familiar critique, echoing objections to Luther sounded by some Roman Catholics and radical Reformers from the start but now being made with a distinctly pietistic twist from within Lutheranism.

The Pietist critique of *sola fide* obviously demanded a reformulation of the doctrine of justification on some grounds other than the imputation of Christ's righteousness to the believing sinner. While Pietism was always a diverse movement, with some strands accenting mystical and others moralistic themes, in general they crafted their view of justification around the two most defining points of Pietist soteriology: the necessity of moral regeneration and the active nature of saving faith. The reformulated doctrine of justification maintained that sinners are judged right before God in

---

33. For places where Arndt affirms justification *sola fide*, see Johann Arndt, *True Christianity: A Treatise on Sincere Repentance, True Faith, the Holy Walk of the True Christian, etc.*, trans. A. W. Boehm (1712; repr., Philadelphia: Smith, English, 1868), xli, 1.5, 1.19, 1.41, 2.1–3.

view of their moral regeneration, through which they become partakers of the divine nature, and the pious acts of their lively faith.[34]

By the opening decades of the eighteenth century, Pietism was becoming a significant force throughout Lutheran lands, and its influence was spreading to other branches of Protestantism. Through the German noble Nikolaus Ludwig von Zinzendorf, Pietism exerted a particularly significant influence on Moravian and Wesleyan thought and practice. Moravians and Wesleyans diverged over their respective views of justification, however, as the former tended to develop the mystical strands of Pietism's emphasis on becoming a partaker of the divine nature through regeneration in a more quietist direction, even as John Wesley renounced supposed Moravian antinomianism and embraced the Pietist critique of the imputation of Christ's active obedience as destructive to Christian piety.

Meanwhile, in centers such as the University of Halle, Pietism developed in ways that highlighted the odd affinity between the pietistic and rationalistic critiques of *sola fide*. As McGrath notes,

> Many representatives of the German Enlightenment (*Aufklärer*) were of Pietist origins, and appear to have been familiar with the standard Pietist critique of the "*als-ob*" theologies of justification of Protestant (especially Lutheran) orthodoxy—namely, that they were ultimately fictitious rather than actual, and did not encourage moral regeneration. This emphasis upon the moral dimension of justification, and the rejection of the view that justification entailed a synthetic, rather than an analytic, judgement, is also characteristic of the early *Aufklärung*.[35]

As we have seen, rationalist versions of this essentially moralistic critique of *sola fide* were already current within rational theology. The moralist aspect of both critiques, therefore, formed a common link between rationalism and Pietism for many German Enlightenment thinkers, and Pietism continued to make significant contributions to the eclipse of *sola fide* into the early nineteenth century.

The Pietist dismantling of *sola fide* even penetrated pockets of orthodox Lutheranism. Though from a Huguenot background and aligned with the Lutheran establishment, Johannes Franciscus Buddeus (1667–1729) was influenced by leading Pietists such as Spener, August Hermann Francke (1663–1727), and Zinzendorf; he also mentored August Gottlieb Spangenberg (1704–1792) while the latter was a student at Jena.[36] Between his two stints on the faculty at Jena, however, Buddeus taught moral philosophy at Halle (1693–1705) and later appeared to accommodate a Pietist formulation of

---

34. On this view, the very notion of vicarious satisfaction is subjected to the same critique as justification and dismantled by the same pietistic logic. As McGrath observes, this line of critique in the Pietist tradition "can be instanced from the writings of Spener, although it is particularly associated with John Wesley," who was greatly influenced by Pietist thought. *Iustitia Dei*, 293.
35. McGrath, *Iustitia Dei*, 364.
36. Buddeus inspired Spangenberg to abandon law for theology and apparently introduced him to Pietism and Zinzendorf when he once visited Buddeus in Jena. After Jena, Spangenberg initially settled in Halle but eventually became a devoted Moravian, the leading expositor of their doctrine (see *Idea Fidei Fratrum*, 1782), and Zinzendorf's biographer and apologist.

justification when addressing the "justification of the sinner before God" in his *Institutes of Dogmatic Theology* (1724). In line with pietistic accounts generally, Buddeus viewed justification as the forensic declaration of the sinner as righteous before God but concluded that the divine verdict presupposes and is ultimately vindicated by the moral transformation of the sinner through regeneration.[37] Similarly, the eminent Lutheran historian Johann Lorenz von Mosheim "explicitly stated the transformational concept of justification underlying his moralist soteriology," defining justification as "an act of God, by which God changes an unrighteous person so that he becomes righteous."[38]

By mid-century, the University of Halle, the academic center of German Pietism, had fully embraced the German Enlightenment, signaled by the return of Christian Wolff in 1740. Disturbed by Wolff's Leibnizian brand of rationalism, Francke had orchestrated his expulsion from the faculty just seventeen years before. During the intervening years, however, and partly owing to the attention his expulsion attracted, Wolff rose to become perhaps the most popular and influential German philosopher of his generation; in 1743, the prodigal professor, three years into his second stint on faculty, became Halle's new chancellor.

Although many have interpreted Wolff's return to Halle as a triumph of Enlightenment rationalism over a pietistic strand of Protestant orthodoxy, this reading of the event is too coarse. Despite significant and sometimes sharply contended differences between them, both rationalist and Pietist theologians were clearly willing to revise some of the most defining doctrines of Protestant orthodoxy in whatever way they deemed necessary to support, respectively, the priority of rational morality or Christian piety to religion.

Similarities between rationalist and Pietist theological programs are not merely structural either. Among several places where the content of their theologies coincide are their respective critiques of justification *sola fide*. Both critiques turn on the necessity of good works, which the orthodox maintain is the only ultimate alternative to *sola fide*. For rational theologians, those works are the works of the universal moral order plus simple repentance; for early Pietists, general moral goodness is supplemented by particular acts of religious devotion. In both cases, one is justified by acts of love, actual or presupposed, rather than by the imputation of Christ's righteousness. As time went by, Pietists tended to reduce their concept of piety to simple moral goodness, and as McGrath observes, "in many respects, the early German Enlightenment (*Aufklärung*) paralleled later Pietism in its theology of justification, retaining the concept of justification as *actus forensis Dei*, while substituting an analytic concept of divine judgement in place of orthodoxy's synthetic equivalent."[39] Kantian scholar Theodore M. Greene goes further: "The influence of pietism upon Germany was considerable; in its individualism, its emphasis upon the practical side of religion, and its opposition to the

---

37. Johannes Franciscus Buddeus, *Institutiones Theologiae Dogmaticae: Variis Observationibus Illustratae* (Leipzig: Thomas Fritsch, 1724), 4:955–56 (4.4). See also McGrath, *Iustitia Dei*, 365.
38. McGrath cites Johann Lorenz von Mosheim's *Elementa Theologiae Dogmaticae* (1758). *Iustitia Dei*, 365.
39. McGrath, *Iustitia Dei*, 365.

dogmatism of the church, it helped to prepare the way for, and indeed formed part of, the *Aufklärung*." In this sense, he argues, the *Aufklärung* assumed "two main forms, evangelical pietism and rationalistic deism."[40]

Although it would be too much to suggest that Pietism simply merged with Enlightenment rationalism at Halle or elsewhere—perhaps it was more like a hostile takeover— a theological confluence did occur.[41] Pietism was not so much displaced by rationalism at Halle (and elsewhere) as absorbed into it. This is represented by the career of Siegmund Jakob Baumgarten (1706–1757). Baumgarten was born into a Pietist family and was himself a devoted Pietist who studied at Halle as a student, became minister of the most prominent church in town in 1728, and then was appointed professor of theology at the university in 1730. He also, however, showed a clear interest in English deism, embraced Wolff's rationalist philosophy without any apparent conflict with his Pietist theology, and after Wolff's return to Halle, became rector of the university in 1748.[42]

One of Baumgarten's students at Halle was Johann Gottlieb Töllner (1724–1774), who eventually became professor of theology and then also of philosophy at Frankfurt. Töllner's main contribution to German Enlightenment theology reflected the confluence of rationalist and Pietist thought in his training. Neither rationalist nor Pietist formulations of justification had any apparent use for an imputed alien righteousness, and Töllner naturally extended the critique of *sola fide* to the role of Christ's active obedience in his mediatorial work of satisfaction. Contrary to Lutheran orthodoxy, Töllner argued in *Der Thätige Gehorsam Jesu Christi Untersucht* (1768) that Christ was under the law and thus had to fulfill the law for himself. As such, there is no clear reason to assume that his satisfaction of the law was on behalf of others.[43] In a variation of the moral-influence theory, Töllner then argued that the saving benefit of Christ's sinless life is as a moral example that "inspires a corresponding moral quality within humans—upon the basis of which they are forgiven and justified"—and that his crucifixion is a mere assurance of God's gracious disposition toward us. So in Töllner's hands, the confluence of German rationalism and Pietism led back to a Socinian-like dismissal of the ground of *sola fide* in the vicarious satisfaction of Jesus Christ.[44]

Gotthilf Samuel Steinbart (1738–1809) developed Töllner's "insights," leading him to reject Augustine's "arbitrary hypotheses" of original sin, predestination, and vicarious satisfaction, along with "the Protestant doctrine of imputation of the righteousness of Christ."[45] By this point the Pietist-rationalist critique of justification *sola fide* was nearly complete, having dismantled not just the point itself but the theological structure

---

40. Theodore M. Greene, "The Historical Context and Religious Significance of Kant's *Religion*," introduction in Immanuel Kant, *Religion within the Limits of Reason Alone*, trans. Theodore M. Greene and Hoyt H. Hudson (New York: Harper and Row, 1960), ix, xiv.
41. Pietism's willingness to revise orthodoxy reflects not only its priority on personal piety over doctrine but also a broad devaluation of doctrine relative to orthodoxy.
42. Greene observes that Baumgarten "seems to have reviewed almost every English deistic and apologetic work" as they came out, often introducing them to his German audience. "Religious Significance," xv.
43. Johann Gottlieb Töllner, *Der Thätige Gehorsam Jesu Christi Untersucht* (Breslau: Johann Ernst Meyern, 1768).
44. McGrath, *Iustitia Dei*, 368–69.
45. McGrath, *Iustitia Dei*, 369.

that framed it. "According to Steinbart," McGrath writes, "Christ redeemed humanity from false understandings of God—such as the idea of God as wrathful, as a tyrant, or as one who imposed arbitrary penalties or conditions upon his creation." What is more, Steinbart dismissed "questions such as the necessity and significance of Christ's passion and death as beyond meaningful discussion, and irrelevant to human happiness and moral perfection." In the end, the very "concept of vicarious satisfaction is both impossible theologically and unnecessary practically."[46]

By the 1780s, when Steinbart published his three eudaemonist booklets under the title *Philosophische Unterhaltungen zur weiteren Aufklärung der Glückseligkeitslehre*, the doctrine of justification *sola fide* appeared to be completely eclipsed within Enlightenment theology.[47] Although orthodox Lutheran and Reformed evangelicals still defended *sola fide* and flourished in many places throughout the world as they continued to hang religion on this hinge, it was clear that the doctrine would have to be completely reimagined and reappropriated, as it were, if there was going to be any future for it within Enlightenment and post-Enlightenment theology. That, however, is precisely what happened.

Reinterpreting Justification

The rational-theology project was naive from the beginning and destined to collapse eventually. The honor of pushing it over, however, fell as much to David Hume (1711–1776) as to any other writer of the era, and the fatal shove he gave it was his witty and posthumously published *Dialogues concerning Natural Religion* (1779, though written around 1750). Hume, who was raised Presbyterian but who cultivated a skeptical inclination, playfully pretended to relay a conversation between an apparently orthodox believer named Demea, a Lockean-like rational theist named Cleanthes, and a seeming skeptic named Philo. By the end of the discussion Demea has excused himself, and Cleanthes's position is in shambles. Philo, however, does not claim the victory for atheism but instead, in an infamous *volte-face* that has perplexed many interpreters, suggests in language reminiscent of Calvin that "no man can be so hardened in absurd systems as at all times to reject" entirely "the sense of religion impressed upon his mind ... as the divine Being ... discovers himself to reason, in the inexplicable contrivance of nature."[48] Hume's point about natural religion, or at least Philo's version of it, is not that religious belief in general is baseless but that the rational-theology project of founding religion on rational intuition and demonstration is impossible because human reason is simply not up for the task.[49]

---

46. McGrath, *Iustitia Dei*, 370.
47. Gotthilf Samuel Steinbart, *Philosophische Unterhaltungen zur weiteren Aufklärung der Glückseligkeitslehre* (Züllichau, 1782–1786).
48. David Hume, *Dialogues concerning Natural Religion*, 2nd ed. (Indianapolis: Hackett, 2007), 77; see also his 1757 essay *The Natural History of Religion*, in *A Dissertation on the Passions, The Natural History of Religion: A Critical Edition*, ed. Tom L. Beauchamp (Oxford: Clarendon, 2007).
49. For a fuller development of the line of interpretation represented here, see Lee Hardy, "Hume's Defense of True Religion," in *The Persistence of the Sacred in Modern Thought*, ed. Chris L. Firestone and Nathan A. Jacobs (Notre Dame, IN: University of Notre Dame Press, 2012), 251–72.

All this is in line with the broader criticisms of rationalist and empiricist presumptions that Hume develops most fully in *An Enquiry concerning Human Understanding* (1748).[50] This work called into question the very possibility of metaphysics on the grounds of Enlightenment rationalism and empiricism. That, in turn, is what Immanuel Kant picked out in his *Prolegomena to Any Future Metaphysics* (1783) when he confessed that reading "David Hume was the very thing which many years ago first interrupted my dogmatic slumber."[51]

Immanuel Kant

Immanuel Kant (1724–1804) was born and raised and spent nearly his entire life in the Prussian city of Königsberg. Like many other German cities at that time, Königsberg had a strong Pietist influence through the opening decades of the eighteenth century that slowly gave way to Wolffian rationalism after 1730. Kant was born into a devoutly Pietist household and in 1732 began his childhood studies at the leading Pietist school in the city, under the direction of Franz Albert Schultz. He went on to study under Martin Knutzen at the University of Königsberg. Schultz and Knutzen, both prominent men in Königsberg, were devoted Pietists who embraced Wolffian rationalism and tried to harmonize it with their Pietist convictions.[52]

Through these two men, and perhaps especially the latter, Kant was taught a Wolffian brand of Pietism founded on *a posteriori* arguments for God's existence and divine revelation and a thoroughly Pietist doctrine of justification in which Christ's death, as a demonstration of both the holiness and love of God, inspires the kind of moral regeneration to a virtuous life of faith working through love that alone satisfies divine justice.[53]

Despite his Pietist upbringing and his sincere devotion to his parents and teachers, after observing the hypocrisy of his childhood classmates, Kant "acquired a lasting abhorrence of all religious emotion and would have nothing to do with prayer or the singing of hymns the rest of his life."[54] Nevertheless, he admired the moral integrity and genuine love for others he observed in sincere Pietists such as his mother and Schultz and attached himself to the theology faculty as a university student, though he ended up reading far more philosophy than theology. In all his studies, however, he was not jarred out of his "dogmatic slumber" in Wolffian rationalism until he encountered David Hume.[55]

After reading Hume's criticisms of prior Enlightenment thought, Kant realized their radical epistemic implications not just for Wolffian rationalism but for the very

---

50. David Hume, *An Enquiry concerning Human Understanding* (Oxford: Oxford University Press, 1999).
51. Greene argues that "the chief difference between" John Locke and Christian Wolff is "the fact that Locke was an empiricist while Wolff was a dogmatic rationalist." Whereas Locke believed that "our knowledge of God rests on empirical evidence from which certain conclusions may be drawn," Wolff rested "his belief in God almost entirely on the *a priori* proofs." "Religious Significance," xvii.
52. Greene, "Religious Significance," xxiv–xxv.
53. See Martin Knutzen, *Philosophischer Beweis von der Wahrheit der Christlichen Religion*, RFN 1 (Nordhausen: Traugott Bauts, 2005).
54. Greene, "Religious Significance," xxviii.
55. Kant had offered a rational proof of God's existence, *The Only Possible Argument in Support of a Demonstration of the Existence of God*, as late as 1763.

possibility of metaphysics. At the same time, he refused to accept the severe epistemic restrictions Hume's criticisms entailed. Most famously, if Hume was right, then concepts as basic to empirical science as causality could not be known. This was untenable to Kant, who set out to save metaphysics from skepticism—and rational religion along with it.

His "Copernican" proposal is expounded across his corpus, chiefly in his *Critique of Pure Reason* (1781), *Critique of Practical Reason* (1788), and *Critique of Judgment* (1790). While the details of Kant's epistemology are beyond the scope of this chapter and readily accessible elsewhere, the uptake for theology is that we cannot know God or have any knowledge of God—either that he exists or that he does not exist—because God is not a sensible object.

Theology is not out of business, however. As Kant explained in his preface to the second edition of *Critique of Pure Reason* (1787),

> I cannot even *assume God, freedom and immortality* for the sake of the necessary practical use of my reason unless I simultaneously *deprive* speculative reason of its pretension to extravagant insights; because in order to attain to such insights, speculative reason would have to help itself to principles that in fact reach only to objects of possible experience, and which, if they were to be applied to what cannot be an object of experience, then they would always actually transform it into an appearance, and thus declare all *practical extension* of pure reason to be impossible. Thus I had to deny *knowledge* in order to make room for *faith*.[56]

Some things impossible to know through speculative reason, in other words, must be presupposed by practical reason. Those things include God, freedom, and immortality, which happen to be the pillars of rational religion.

What is more, not just any view of God or the afterlife satisfies the demands of practical reason. So humans find themselves in a peculiar situation in which we must not only presuppose a God whose existence cannot be known but must also presuppose some things about what this God is like. Similarly, we must not only presuppose human immortality but must also presuppose a just eschaton in which moral goodness and personal happiness meet. So on Kant's account, a certain style of theology and kind of rational-moral religion are not just possible but rationally necessary.

That said, theology and religion are also entirely determined by the demands of practical reason. True religion is the religion of rational-moral faith alone; everything that goes beyond whatever practical reason demands is not only uncertain or superfluous to true religion but an obstacle to further enlightenment. Kant allowed that the unenlightened masses may need to rely for a time on the positive forms of historical religions, such as the doctrines and practices of Christianity, but only temporarily and only insofar as these religious forms lead their adherents to the purity of rational-moral faith.

---

56. Immanuel Kant, *Critique of Pure Reason*, trans. and ed. Paul Guyer and Allen W. Wood (Cambridge: Cambridge University Press, 1998), 117 (B:xxix–xxx).

Eventually, he reasoned, they must be stripped of their emotional appeals, ceremonial rites, ecclesiastical orders, and whatever doctrines are not capable of being reinterpreted according to the principles of his rational-moral faith.

What is required for the progress of enlightenment in Christendom, therefore, is a reinterpretation of the whole system of Christian doctrine according to just the moral principles that practical reason demands. That is the project he took up late in his life in *Religion within the Limits of Reason Alone* (1793). Here Kant wrestled with and offered new interpretations of a number of Christian doctrines, including justification.

Justification, he proposed, is "the idea . . . of a human being who is indeed guilty but has passed into a disposition well-pleasing to God."[57] On the surface, this strikes one as precisely the sort of Pietist view Kant had learned from childhood. Kant was convinced that humans were theoretically capable of fulfilling the demands of practical reason—of being morally worthy of divine approval—yet he also accepted the presence of radical evil in our wills, rendering us morally guilty. The problem of justification, then, is how one whose will is radically evil can become worthy of divine approval.

Kant identified several difficulties that must be overcome if the sinner is to be justified:

> The first difficulty which makes doubtful the possibility of realizing in us the ideal of a humanity well-pleasing to God, . . . [is that] the distance between the goodness which we ought to effect in ourselves and the evil from which we start is . . . infinite, and . . . is not exhaustible in any time.[58]

There is, Kant contended, no possibility of humans ever achieving perfection in our deeds when measured against the perfect standard of the moral law, not in this age or the endless age to come.

What is possible, however, is for the sinner to adopt a right disposition toward the moral law and the duty of perpetual moral renewal. "This is a change of heart which must itself be possible because it is a duty," he reasoned. The question becomes, "How can this disposition count for the deed itself, when this deed is *every* time . . . defective?" Kant's "solution" was in part that the good disposition is evident in "the infinite progression of the good toward conformity to the law" such that we can "expect to be *generally* well-pleasing to God" after adopting the good disposition despite our continuing deficiencies.[59]

Many Pietist accounts would rest just about there—that we are judged right by God in view of our present or potential moral regeneration. For Kant, however, this general acceptance does not remove "the actual evil in this infinite series" or the "debt" resulting from a sinner's start in evil, "which is impossible for him to wipe out."[60] Even if, "after his change of heart, he has not incurred new debts," this is not "equivalent to his

---

57. Immanuel Kant, *Religion within the Boundaries of Mere Reason; and Other Writings*, trans. and ed. Allen W. Wood and George Di Giovanni, CTHP (Cambridge: Cambridge University Press, 1998), 6.76.
58. Kant, *Religion*, 6.66.
59. Kant, *Religion*, 6.67.
60. Kant, *Religion*, 6.67n, 6.72.

having paid off the old ones. Nor can he produce," he continued, "in the future conduct of a good life, a surplus over and above what he is under obligation to perform each time; for his duty at each instant is to do all the good in his power."[61]

Here one might expect from a more orthodox-minded author an appeal to vicarious satisfaction and imputed righteousness. Kant, however, ruled this out. This debt, he argued,

> cannot be erased by somebody else. For it is not a *transmissible* financial debt (where it is all the same to the creditor whether the debtor himself pays up, or somebody else for him), but the *most personal* of all liabilities, namely a debt of sins which only the culprit, not the innocent, can bear, however magnanimous the innocent might be in wanting to take the debt upon himself for the other.[62]

Kant's religion instead reduced Christ to an aspirational personification of the moral ideal we affirm and must believe is possible but nevertheless fail to realize. Christ is necessary for us as a model, in other words, but is stripped of the redemptive glory of his vicarious satisfaction and resurrection.

The punishment owed to the sinner, which consists in the "moral consequence of his earlier disposition," is not "fully exacted" prior to his conversion; neither can it "be considered appropriate to his new quality" as one who is now "well-pleasing to God," he reasoned. Nevertheless, he insisted that "satisfaction must be rendered," and that left him with little choice. So "the punishment must be thought as adequately executed in the situation of the conversion itself."[63]

How so? Appropriating Paul's language in Romans 6, Kant maintained that

> the emergence from the corrupted disposition into the good is in itself already sacrifice (as "the death of the old man," "the crucifying of the flesh") and entrance into the long train of life's ills which the new human being undertakes . . . simply for the sake of the good, yet are still fitting *punishment* for someone else, namely the old human being (who, morally, is another human being).—Physically . . . he is still the same human being liable to punishment, and he must be judged as such before a moral tribunal of justice. . . . Yet, in his new disposition, . . . in sight of a divine judge for whom the disposition takes the place of the deed, he is morally another being.[64]

The imaginary personification of this idea, Kant claimed, is the doctrine of vicarious satisfaction made on our behalf by the Son of God. Insofar as Christians imagine Christ's single sacrifice as sufficient for all, they are merely projecting the satisfaction rendered through the conversion of all humanity onto this one man. Christians must then suppose that the benefit of his work is imputed to us by grace. What is actually being "imputed" in Kant's view, however, is the moral quality of the convert's unending future of living

---

61. Kant, *Religion*, 6.72.
62. Kant, *Religion*, 6.72.
63. Kant, *Religion*, 6.73.
64. Kant, *Religion*, 6.74.

as one well pleasing to God. This, he contended, is credited "to us as if we already possessed it here in full."[65]

Kant still interpreted justification as a matter of divine judgment rendered in view of the sinner's moral conversion and the quality of the new life, stretching into eternity, lived by the good disposition. Thus far, his views displayed his Pietist background. But he went well beyond Pietist formulations, not just criticizing the orthodox soteriological points of imputation and vicarious satisfaction but reinterpreting them as imaginary personifications and unnecessary or even misguided projections of rational-moral principles. Kant's reinterpretation of justification was so far removed from Protestant orthodoxy that he saw no positive use for this doctrine at all. Instead of being the hinge on which all true religion turns, he found only the negative use of stripping away every hope of forgiveness not tied to rational morality.[66] In the end, Kant could only urge his readers to strive as though their eternal happiness depended entirely on their good works, in "hope that they [would] appear justified before their judge," who they might discover is nothing more than the personification of their own practical reason.[67]

Friedrich Schleiermacher

Friedrich Schleiermacher (1768–1834), the preeminent Romantic churchman and theologian of Berlin, was no more satisfied by Kant's sophisticated attempt to found religion on the dictates of practical reason—on morality or the will—than he was by the rational-theology program attempting to do so on pure reason. In his estimation, both erred in reducing religion to something else: for Kant, that something else was ethics; for rational theology, it was metaphysics. For Schleiermacher, who was raised in Moravian Pietism but fell under the influence of higher criticism while studying at Halle, religion was its own affair and demanded its own seat at the table of human life.[68]

Despite this, Schleiermacher devised his own reinterpretation program. At its essence, he argued, religion does not consist in the externalities of ceremonial practices and systems of theology. These make up the husk of religion; the kernel hidden within the husk is the soul-consuming "immediate feeling of the Infinite and Eternal."[69] Religion, in other words, is rooted in human nature and the immediacy of self-consciousness before a sense of the "Infinite" in the world; it is not the deliverance or conclusion of

---

65. Kant, *Religion*, 6.74–75.
66. Kant, *Religion*, 6.76–77.
67. Robert Merrihew Adams observes that Kant is just as capable of framing this issue in terms of "the judge within" as he is in terms of the divine Judge above: "When he asks, as he does, 'How can I be well-pleasing to God?' the question is explicitly one that does not lose its interest for Kant if God is not there to do anything about it" in the end. In other words, Kant's doctrine of justification is completely ruled by the practical demands of rational morality, even though it is couched in theological language and offered as an interpretation of Christianity. "Introduction," in Kant, *Religion*, xvi.
68. Friedrich Schleiermacher, *On Religion: Speeches to Its Cultured Despisers*, trans. John Oman (Louisville: Westminster John Knox, 1994), 37–38. By Schleiermacher's own confession, Moravian Pietism and higher criticism would remain major influences on his life and thought. In a letter to George Reimer on April 30, 1802, Schleiermacher reflected on his course thus far and credited his Moravian upbringing for helping him weather "all the storms of skepticism," and he famously remarked "that after all I have passed through I have become a Herrnhuter again, only of a higher order." Friedrich Schleiermacher, *Life of Schleiermacher as Unfolded in Autobiography and Letters*, trans. Frederica Rowan (London: Smith, Elder, 1860), 1:283–84.
69. Schleiermacher, *On Religion*, 15–16.

a rational process or something we learn by memory or acquire secondhand but the self-consciousness of our "absolute dependence on God"—that we live and have our being in and through him.[70]

Schleiermacher, however, did not advocate discarding the husk of religion, as though public worship and theology have no place in an authentically religious life. On the contrary, the husk is "absolutely unavoidable" whenever our consciousness of being in relation to God "is made the subject of reflection and comparison."[71] Those who are truly moved by the ultimately ineffable sense of their dependence on God are compelled to give some expression to it. As they do, they engage in external forms of worship and testimony. This is the source of all the externalities of religion, and although the religious sense is entirely mystical and thus profoundly personal, what we feel is at some level objective, and hence our various expressions of it resonate with others who have felt the same. For this reason, "religion is essentially social, for that is our nature. Each individual's deeply felt religious sentiments cry out to be shared."[72]

Schleiermacher's metatheory of religion thus established a hermeneutic of doctrine in which the church's teachings, not excluding Scripture, must be reinterpreted as expressions of the religious sense of absolute dependence on God. In his systematic theology, *The Christian Faith* (1821–1822; rev. 1830–1831), Christianity is romantically rendered. The task of theology, he contended, is to give lucid linguistic expression to this prior and ultimately ineffable religious feeling. He then proceeded to reorganize and reinterpret the whole scope of Protestant theology, point by point, under this controlling principle.

From the perspective of religious self-consciousness, he explained, justification is the same thing as conversion with one difference: whereas conversion is the expression of "self-consciousness passing into movement of will," justification is the expression of "self-consciousness at rest in contemplation."[73] Just like the two aspects of conversion (repentance and faith working through love), so also each aspect of justification (forgiveness and adoption, in his scheme) "expresses merely the relation of the man to God" in the Christian's consciousness as he passes from "the common life of sinfulness" to "living fellowship with Christ" through faith.[74]

As Schleiermacher puzzled over how this can be, he first observed that "the longer and more uninterruptedly we come under the sway of Christ, the sooner do we forget sin, because it no longer emerges; and if sin does not come into consciousness, neither does the sense of guilt and of deserving punishment." The consciousness expressed as

---

70. Schleiermacher, *On Religion*, 49–50; Schleiermacher, *The Christian Faith*, ed. H. R. Mackintosh and J. S. Stewart (Edinburgh: T&T Clark, 1968), 12.
71. Schleiermacher, *On Religion*, 87–88.
72. James C. Livingston, *Modern Christian Thought*, vol. 1, *The Enlightenment and the Nineteenth Century*, 2nd ed. (Minneapolis: Fortress, 2006), 98. Schleiermacher believed that all religions have this expressive dynamic in common. Although all religions are valid, not all are equal. Like Kant before him and his contemporary Georg Wilhelm Friedrich Hegel, Schleiermacher argued that Christianity is superior to all other religions precisely because in Christology, it has achieved a fuller realization of the religious ideal.
73. Livingston, *Modern Christian Thought*, 1:497.
74. Livingston, *Modern Christian Thought*, 1:498.

justification, however, is not just a matter of forgetting sin, nor does it lie at the far end of progressive sanctification; it is rather a "present possession." As such, "justification and conversion are simultaneous." The consciousness of "forgiveness" exists "even while sin and the consciousness of it are also present."[75]

In a move remarkably similar to Kant's, reflecting their respective Pietist roots, Schleiermacher turned to the dynamics of conversion to account for the consciousness expressed contemplatively in justification. He related conversion to justification in this way:

> Repentance, as the self-consciousness moved by the consciousness of sin, comes to rest in forgiveness in the same way as the faith, which from its birth is active through love, is in thought the consciousness of being a child of God, and as this itself is identical with the consciousness of living fellowship with Christ.[76]

The one who, in repentance, "has let himself be taken up into living fellowship with Christ"—that is, the one who has "come under the sway" of his "absolutely powerful God-consciousness"—is "a new man," and "sin in the new man is no longer active; it is only the after-effect of the old man."[77]

Justification, therefore, as a form of self-consciousness, expresses the changed relationship to God of one who is converted—who has repented of sin and is therefore dead to sin and "lays hold believingly on Christ" and is therefore alive to Christ.[78] As Schleiermacher explained,

> The new man thus no longer takes sin to be his own; he indeed labours against it as something foreign to him. The consciousness of guilt is thus abolished [and] his penal desert must vanish with this. . . . And in regard to the second element of conversion, Christ cannot live in us without His relation to His Father being formed in us also and making us sharers in His sonship; this is the power to be children of God that flows from Him, and it includes the guarantee of sanctification.[79]

Although Schleiermacher's Romantic framework led to a different understanding of the nature of conversion and thus the change that occurs in the person, the structure of his doctrine of justification nonetheless presupposed a change in the believer. As McGrath remarks, there is no "reintroduction of an objective dimension to the doctrine of justification. Justification was still seen essentially in terms of human transformation."[80]

Schleiermacher openly admitted that his view of the matter was "readily liable to the misconstruction that each man justifies himself."[81] He denied that this is the case but

---

75. Livingston, *Modern Christian Thought*, 1:498.
76. Livingston, *Modern Christian Thought*, 1:498.
77. Livingston, *Modern Christian Thought*, 1:498.
78. Livingston, *Modern Christian Thought*, 1:503. Schleiermacher also denied that people are objects of wrath prior to conversion.
79. Livingston, *Modern Christian Thought*, 1:499.
80. McGrath, *Iustitia Dei*, 382.
81. Schleiermacher, *Christian Faith*, 499–500.

not on the basis of any appeal to the passivity of faith as an instrument of reception or the nature of justification as a divine declaration. Schleiermacher denied these points as well.[82] He argued instead that by grounding justification in conversion and conversion in the historical influence of Christ over the Christian's self-consciousness, his view of justification really did depend on divine action insofar as only divine action could bring about the necessary change.[83]

Georg Wilhelm Friedrich Hegel

Georg Wilhelm Friedrich Hegel (1770–1831), a graduate of Tübingen's Protestant seminary and a colleague of Schleiermacher at Berlin, offers a strikingly different, absolute-idealist rendering that represents an apex in late-Enlightenment reinterpretations of Christianity. In his distinct brand of panentheism, the Absolute, or Spirit, is coming to full self-consciousness through the dialectical unfolding of world history. Religion, in this scheme, is "the knowledge which Spirit has of itself as Spirit." In other words, both "the subject as well as the object" of religious consciousness "is Spirit."[84] Spirit's consciousness of itself as Spirit is therefore identical with the collective human religious consciousness of Spirit itself. The knowing Spirit within humanity is none other than the Spirit known by humanity.

The fundamental problem of the religious way of knowing Spirit is that the "the social or collective subject of religious knowledge is not immediately aware of its identity with its object" but continues to project what it knows onto "God" as if Spirit were a different object.[85] In religion, Spirit may be conscious of Spirit as Spirit but is not conscious of the fact that the Spirit it knows as Spirit is itself. Spirit is conscious of Spirit but not self-conscious of being Spirit. Given this lack of self-consciousness, religions trade in pictorial ideas (*Vorstellung*, in Hegel's jargon) rather than philosophical concepts (*Begriff*). The difference between the religious and the philosophical ways of knowing is the difference between consciousness and self-consciousness as just described. What religion knows as the other, idealist philosophy knows as itself; where religion can only ever rise to mere consciousness of Spirit as Spirit, philosophy arrives at self-consciousness of Spirit as Spirit.

Religious knowledge, therefore, always retains a projection dynamic in which Spirit objectifies itself as another. In order to transcend this dynamic and arrive at full self-consciousness, religious ideas have to be translated into pure philosophical concepts. (This also means religious communities have to become philosophical communities—communities that no longer trade in religious ideas but in philosophical concepts.) For

---

82. Schleiermacher represented faith as always active through love. His denial of its instrumentality in justification, however, took a curious turn: "We bring with us nothing except our living susceptibility, which is the real receptive organ." Schleiermacher, *Christian Faith*, 504.
83. Schleiermacher, *Christian Faith*, 499–500.
84. Merold Westphal, *History and Truth in Hegel's "Phenomenology,"* 3rd ed. (Bloomington: Indiana University Press, 1998), 194. For more on Hegel's panentheism, see John W. Cooper, *Panentheism: The Other God of the Philosophers; From Plato to Present* (Grand Rapids, MI: Baker Academic, 2006), 107.
85. Westphal, *History and Truth*, 194.

Hegel, that means Christianity will inevitably and necessarily be transcended as Spirit achieves fuller self-consciousness through world history. Christianity as we know it may survive for a long time, but its contribution to the progress of world history and Spirit's self-consciousness will be dialectically sublated in a new stage of development just as Christianity transcended and sublated Judaism.

Although Christianity continues to trade in terms of religious ideas instead of philosophical concepts, it has come closer than any other religion to transcending the problematic projection dynamic inherent in the religious way of knowing. This is why Hegel deemed Christianity the consummate religion. In Christianity, "the *implicit* unity of God and humanity is made *explicit* in . . . *the historical fact* of the Incarnation."[86] Rendering the implicit union between Spirit and humanity explicit, however, requires Spirit to undergo the extreme measure of finitude. In Hegel's words,

> The deepest need of spirit is that the antithesis within the subject itself should be intensified to its universal, i.e., its most abstract, extreme. . . . What satisfies this need is the consciousness of atonement, of the sublation, the nullification of the antithesis, so that the latter is not the truth. Rather, the truth is the attainment of unity through the negation of the antithesis; this is the peace, the reconciliation, that the need demands.[87]

For the implicit unity between Spirit and humanity to become fully explicit, "it must take on radical finitude, which includes estrangement and death. Otherwise, God is not fully manifested in finite existence. . . . Absolute Spirit must, in other words, lose its life before it can fully realize itself."[88]

The death of Christ is that extremity of finitude in which Spirit becomes fully explicit to itself as Spirit and the union between Spirit and humanity realized. In this light, "the resurrection and ascension into Heaven is the pictorial representation of the truth that Spirit sacrifices its particular embodiment" in Christ "and thereby initiates the advent of Absolute Spirit, the coming of the Holy or Universal Spirit" into the world and thus into concrete reality. Pentecost, therefore, "represents the universal reconciliation of the divine and human that was implicit from the beginning" and this moment ushers in a new universal humanity and spiritual community marked by freedom and justice.[89]

For Hegel, therefore, the death of Christ is a necessary stage in the progressive development of Absolute self-consciousness in world history in which the negation of the individuality of Christ results in the realization of the identity of Spirit with universal human consciousness. What was confined to the consciousness of a single individual in Jesus Christ is now, by the death of that individual, universalized. This is his interpretation of the doctrine of reconciliation or atonement. For Hegel, the very history

---

86. Livingston, *Modern Christian Thought*, 1:124.
87. Georg Wilhelm Friedrich Hegel, *Lectures on the Philosophy of Religion*, vol. 3, *The Consummate Religion*, ed. Peter C. Hodgson, trans. R. F. Brown, P. C. Hodgson, and J. M. Stewart (Berkeley: University of California Press, 1988), 452 (B.2.a).
88. Livingston, *Modern Christian Thought*, 1:124.
89. Livingston, *Modern Christian Thought*, 1:123, 125.

of the world is the history of reconciliation as it is being realized in universal human consciousness, which is ultimately Absolute Spirit's self-consciousness.

It is not surprising that justification is almost unrecognizable in Hegel's mature writings. Hegel viewed sin as the consciousness of alienation that Adam, a mythical character who represents universal humanity, falls into when he awakens from an unreflective animal-like state of mere consciousness to a reflective state of self-consciousness as an individual, finite creature: "The apple of knowledge which kills the happy ape in the garden brings to life the man, with his pain, his self-seeking, his evil—and his destiny of self-conscious reconciliation with God."[90]

In Judaism, Hegel argued, the consciousness of sin—"the consciousness of the self as a negation of itself, sinful"—reaches an "excruciating pitch" as it is fully internalized and thereby becomes a world-historical development. In Christianity, however, this consciousness is finally sublated through the realization of the consciousness of reconciliation. "The extreme of alienation," Crites notes, "is the basic step toward reconciliation."[91]

This reconciliation is a universal, world-historical moment in the dialectical development of Spirit's self-consciousness. "In his view," Crites explains, "the death and resurrection of Christ has . . . abolished the merely finite standpoint according to which Christ and the recipients of his grace are merely separate individuals living at distinct times." He continues,

> Within this finite standpoint, each man would have to bear the consequences of his own deeds alone; for one man's goodness, one man's suffering, to suffice for all would be morally indefensible. But it is just that finite standpoint which has been *aufgehoben* in the work of Christ. . . . [Now,] to believe in Christ is to believe in the identity of God and man in general, and thus to know one's own identity with God. . . . The sensuous certainty of the divine-human identity in Christ must give way to the attestation of this truth in and for itself in the life of every man, in its intrinsic necessity; that is, the reconciling work of Christ must be fulfilled in the "outpouring of the Spirit." . . . Just as Christ has divested himself of his estranged finitude, so must we![92]

Hegel's absolute-idealist construal of justification, if that is what it is, amounts to the believer dialectically sublating the consciousness of sin, which just is the consciousness of finite estrangement, through the negation of that consciousness, which is historically realized and modeled for us in the death of Jesus Christ. This occurs through the realization of the universal identity between Spirit and humanity now, after the ascension, concretely realized in the world. As such, justification is a determination of universal consciousness that the believer in Jesus appropriates to himself in community with other believers.

---

90. Stephen D. Crites, "The Gospel according to Hegel," *JR* 46, no. 2 (1966): 251–52.
91. Crites, "Gospel according to Hegel," 253, 257.
92. Crites, "Gospel according to Hegel," 258.

Ferdinand Christian Baur

Ferdinand Christian Baur (1792–1860), a left-wing Hegelian and pioneering higher critic of the so-called Tübingen school, adhered closely to the structure of Hegel's philosophy of history and even to the supposed dialectical relation between Judaism and Christianity.[93] The former he adopted as the structure of his own thought, and the latter he developed into a basic critical principle in his study of Scripture and early Christianity. These also shaped his thoroughly Hegelian interpretation of Paul's doctrine of justification, which he developed primarily in *Paul, the Apostle of Jesus Christ* (1845) and *Lectures on New Testament Theology* (posthumously, 1864).[94] Although his interpretation of Paul, along with the higher-critical debates over Paul's doctrine of justification, are beyond the scope of this chapter, Baur's influential work is of interest because it so clearly outlines the idealist reinterpretation of justification and the idealist critique of *sola fide*.

According to Baur, the Pauline doctrine of justification by faith alone was formulated as a polemic against the Judaizing party within the early church. Paul's polemic drove him to make strong claims regarding works, though the apostle is capable of representing faith as "working through love." Nevertheless, "the Apostle's major thesis . . . is that human beings are justified by faith and not by works of the law." Paul develops this thinking, Baur continued, "as the antithesis to the thesis of Judaism" that one is justified by works of the law. Following Hegel, Baur argued that Judaism prepared the way for Christianity as an intensification of the consciousness of sin.[95] Indeed, "sinfulness is the character" of all religious consciousness in "the ante-Christian time." Though adherents of Judaism sought justification, they failed to achieve it because they sought it under the consciousness of sin and therefore as if it were by works of the law, which only intensified the consciousness of sin.[96]

In Christianity—the absolute religion for Baur as for Hegel—the thesis of Judaism is dialectically negated by the consciousness of union with Spirit achieved, objectively, through the incarnation, death, and ascension of Christ but realized within each individual through faith. As such,

> the highest expression of the Pauline concept of justification is therefore . . . the law of the spirit of life (Romans 8:2). The law of the spirit, that is, spirit as the principle determining a human being's entire orientation, is the principle of Christian consciousness as the life-principle for those who, believing in Christ, can have the principle of their spiritual life in him alone.[97]

---

93. Livingston notes that Baur had formed many of his views prior to Hegel's influence on his thought and was even critical of Hegel on certain points. *Modern Christian Thought*, 1:127. That said, the influence of Hegel on his thought was profound, especially on the points under consideration here.
94. Ferdinand Christian Baur, *Paul the Apostle of Jesus Christ: His Life and Work, His Epistles and Teachings*, trans. Allan Menzies (London: Williams and Norgate, 1875), 2:115–289, 297–313; Baur, *Lectures on New Testament Theology*, ed. Peter C. Hodgson, trans. Robert F. Brown (Oxford: Oxford University Press, 2016), 153–94.
95. Baur, *New Testament*, 189.
96. Baur, *Paul*, 120.
97. Baur, *New Testament*, 190.

For Baur, faith is "the necessary presupposition of this spirit," and yet "faith fundamentally relates to spirit simply as form relates to content. In the spirit, faith first becomes the living reality of the Christian consciousness filled with its positive content."[98]

The positive content of the Christian consciousness is the consciousness of being united with Spirit—spirit with Spirit—which is understood here in a distinctly dialectical manner, à la Hegel. Paul's law of the spirit, according to Baur, establishes "the moral idea" of justification:

> The entire process of justification is first consummated in the spirit. Being declared righteous in a truly Christian sense is then no longer a being declared righteous by faith in the sense in which, for someone . . . trusting in him who justifies the ungodly, that person's faith is . . . only something reckoned as righteousness. In [that sense] the justified person's relation to God still always rests on a merely represented righteousness, to the extent that someone who is ungodly in himself is . . . only looked upon as a righteous person and declared to be such.[99]

Here the idealist critique of *sola fide* comes into view. The idealist construal of justification is entirely in terms of the believer's consciousness of being in union with universal Spirit realized through the death and ascension of Christ. A fundamental problem with the orthodox doctrine, on this view, is that it turns on a "merely represented righteousness." In other words, an imputed alien righteousness remains an objectified righteousness of another—a righteousness that does not belong to the believer's inner self in the form of self-consciousness but is projected onto another who is the believer's object of consciousness, not self-consciousness.

There must, therefore, be some sense—"the moral idea"—in which the believer is actually right with God, if you will, and not merely declared right with God. To say the same thing in Hegelian terms, that means there must be some ground of the self-consciousness of being one with Spirit in the believer. Baur put it like this:

> The truly Christian sense [of being declared righteous] is an authentically just being-declared-righteous because, in the law of the spirit, in the spirit as the principle operative within someone, that person, in fact and in truth, is placed in the relation to God that befits the moral idea. In the faith counted as righteousness, what is still merely an external relationship has become a truly inner relationship through the mediation of . . . the Spirit, a mediation in which God imparts his Spirit to human beings; . . . a relation of spirit to the Spirit. In this relationship the human spirit, as the principle of subjective consciousness, comes together in oneness with its objective ground, with the Spirit of God, as the Spirit of Christ.[100]

And so the form of faith is only justifying in so far as it is filled with the content of the consciousness of being in a new inner relation to what is ultimately, for the absolute idealist, universal Spirit.

---

98. Baur, *New Testament*, 190.
99. Baur, *New Testament*, 190.
100. Baur, *New Testament*, 190.

In this way, Baur proposed, "the antithesis between works of the law and faith is cancelled out from both sides. The two together . . . are the subjective requisite without which it is not possible to be declared righteous." The problem with the principle of justification through works of the law is that "the abstract nature of the concept is simply so fixated on the actual fulfilling of what the law commands that one's disposition gets almost no consideration." Conversely, the problem with the principle of *sola fide* is that faith is conceived as "abstract and contentless, as though it were not the inner disposition animating human beings, the one by which, first and foremost, a human being's moral worth is determined." In their "abstract generality," these two principles are "mutually exclusive," but "as soon as it becomes concrete actuality" in historical consciousness, "then they must counterbalance each other in order to be practical." Accordingly, "works" no longer refer to works of the law but to the inner moral disposition of the one in union with Spirit, and faith is no longer conceived as a contentless instrument of reception but as the form of consciousness in union with universal Spirit. For this reason, one may say that "anyone who does what is right, is acceptable to God."[101]

Traces of Kant and Schleiermacher and even hints of Pietism are present in Baur's distinctly Hegelian account of justification, which demands some real change in the believer's consciousness as the moral ground of the declaration that one is right with God. But in the idealist reinterpretation of justification as a determination of consciousness, something else arguably comes into view as well. Not only does the idealist reinterpretation of justification have no use for certain objective elements of *sola fide*, such as the forensic imputation of an alien righteousness and the purely objective declaration of the sinner as righteous before God, but also these elements are positively problematic insofar as they perpetuate an objectification that interferes with the self-conscious realization of being in union with universal Spirit.

An imputed alien righteousness is nothing more than merely representational righteousness, which is objectified righteousness. But now, through the achievement of Christ's death, in an absolute-idealist perspective, the objectifying dynamic has been sublated. According to Hegel, Jesus Christ died to finite particularity, with its consciousness of sin or estrangement from Spirit, and thereby achieved self-consciousness as universal Spirit. The objectifying dynamic involved in the imputation of an alien righteousness, therefore, has been sublated along with the consciousness of estrangement or sin that was maximally intensified under the law.

Whatever has been sublated, however, has been irretrievably eliminated as such (via dialectical negation) and is only carried forward under a new form—a new religion, perhaps—from the perspective of the world-historical development of Spirit's self-consciousness. Just as Judaism continues to be observed in the world, so also orthodox formulations of *sola fide* will continue to be maintained by some, but Spirit has

---

101. Baur, *New Testament*, 194–95.

achieved a higher self-consciousness, and that cannot be reversed. Whatever the future of Protestant orthodoxy, the future of spiritual consciousness in the world belongs to absolute idealism.

Albrecht Ritschl

Just then, however, absolute idealism both predictably and yet inexplicably collapsed.[102] Although Hegel's influence over subsequent Western thought, including theology, is enormous—in addition to F. C. Baur, Hegel influenced thinkers as diverse as David Strauss, Ludwig Feuerbach, Karl Marx, Søren Kierkegaard, Paul Tillich, Wolfhart Pannenberg, Jürgen Moltmann, and Jacques Derrida—the generation of scholars after Baur, including his own student, Albrecht Ritschl (1822–1889), approached Hegel's system as vultures to a carcass.

With the demise of Hegel's absolute idealism, many young German scholars turned to Kant's critical alternative. According to Kant, we can only know the sensible world and only insofar as our experience of it is structured by the categories of our mind. Yet the world, which in itself is unknown to us, cannot be reduced to consciousness as it could for Hegel. Rather, our consciousness is of our subjectively structured experience of the world. "The rejection of philosophical speculation," therefore, led to a renewed Kantian "concentration on the empirical and historical. Even our moral judgments do not emerge in a vacuum," neo-Kantians insisted, "but are mediated to us through our participation in a historical tradition and social experience." Likewise, "Christian experience is only appropriated through particular historical events mediated through a community."[103]

Operating in this milieu, Ritschl turned his full attention to soteriology in his three-volume *The Christian Doctrine of Justification and Reconciliation* (1870–1874). Here he worked out his views on theology as the investigation of the objective historical consciousness (faith) of the religious community (church). He attempted an empirical study of the history of justification and reconciliation free from the *a priori* Hegelian prejudice that marred his mentor's treatment and "was able to demonstrate that, contrary to Baur's axiom, elements eliminated from the doctrine of reconciliation by one generation had subsequently been reappropriated by another."[104] This put supposedly sublated features of the doctrine of justification back on the table.

Though Ritschl aimed to free himself from Hegelian prejudice, he was not free from every prejudice, and he argued that the gospel of primitive Christianity—the proclamation of "the mighty works of God" in redemptive history (Acts 2:11)—had been transformed into a speculative metaphysical message under the corrupting influence of Hellenistic philosophy. He was sure that this supposed development represented a *corruption* of primitive Christianity, rather than a mere elaboration, for example, be-

---

102. Karl Barth's musings on what Hegel's idealistic system represented to Enlightenment thought, the diversity of reactions to it, and its demise are insightful on several levels. See Karl Barth, *Protestant Theology in the Nineteenth Century: Its Background and History*, trans. Brian Cozens and John Bowden (Grand Rapids, MI: Eerdmans, 2002), 370–407.
103. Livingston, *Modern Christian Thought*, 1:270.
104. McGrath, *Iustitia Dei*, 382–83.

cause he was *a priori* convinced, on neo-Kantian grounds, that humans cannot know metaphysical reality. Our knowledge of God is restricted to just the relative value judgments we make about his redemptive acts in history and their significance to us. (The incarnation, for example, is a value judgment we make regarding the revelatory significance we find in the work of Jesus of Nazareth and not, strictly speaking, a metaphysical claim about the divine person of the Son.) Anything that goes beyond this is merely metaphysical speculation.

If theology rests on the value we find in God's redemptive acts, then it must be centered on soteriology or the doctrine of reconciliation.[105] For Ritschl, the necessary presupposition of reconciliation is justification. "Justification," he wrote, "as the religious expression of that operation of God upon men which is fundamental in Christianity, is the acceptance of sinners into that fellowship with God in which their salvation is to be realized and carried out into eternity." Justification can be viewed "as the removal of guilt and the consciousness of guilt," or it can be "viewed as effective" and thus "as reconciliation."[106] All knowledge of God, therefore, begins with the religious value judgment we make of the effects of his justifying act for us. "Apart from this value-judgment of faith," he concluded, "there exists no knowledge of God worthy of this content. . . . The truth rather is that we know the nature of God and Christ only in their worth for us."[107]

Notably, Ritschl's emphasis on value judgments we make about the effects of God's redemptive acts on us does not result in an orthodox construal of justification and its relation to reconciliation. Within Protestant orthodoxy, God is reconciled to sinners through Christ's satisfaction, and sinners are justified through faith as Christ's satisfaction is graciously imputed to them. For Ritschl, reconciliation is the effect of justification, something achieved through the divine act of forgiving sin and declaring the sinner righteous before him. This represents a complete reconstruction of the doctrine of reconciliation and its relation to justification. Here God is reconciling sinners to himself through a justifying act rather than being reconciled to sinners through Christ's propitiatory act. What is more, the law does not have to be satisfied before God can forgive sinners. God is not alienated from sinners; they are alienated from him. The objective ground of reconciliation is located not in Christ's satisfaction, therefore, but in the justifying act of God's declaration, subjectively apprehended through faith.

McGrath suggests that Ritschl's argument at this point can be viewed as an extension of Hugo Grotius's Arminian critique of forensic justification. The point is well taken. Ritschl argued, by way of analogy, that the law is a judicial instrument ordered to some teleological end higher than itself, which is human well-being. Established law does not, therefore, represent a strict standard of justice that must be adhered to or satisfied. In

---
105. Ritschl maintains that soteriology is the preoccupation of all religions but construes salvation in terms of experiencing spiritual freedom over nature through some kind of divine help.
106. Albrecht Ritschl, *The Christian Doctrine of Justification and Reconciliation*, trans. H. R. Mackintosh and A. B. Macauley (Edinburgh: T&T Clark, 1902), 3:85.
107. Ritschl, *Justification and Reconciliation*, 3:212.

cases where human well-being is at odds with whatever the law commands, the moral end of human well-being trumps the judicial demand of enforcing the law. The law exists to serve the common good: ordinarily, the moral good of the people is realized by way of upholding the law, but exceptions arise. Whenever upholding the law conflicts with the moral good of the people, the moral trumps the merely judicial. In such cases, extrajudicial acts are permissible to achieve the higher moral good.[108]

For Ritschl, therefore, justification, as an act of pardon and declaration of a sinner as righteous, is just such an extrajudicial act of God. In justification God is not declaring a righteous person righteous but a sinner righteous. Self-consciously breaking with the long run of rationalist and Pietist formulations of justification, Ritschl insisted, in his Kantian terminology, that God renders a synthetic rather than analytic judgment when he justifies the sinner. As such, the judgment itself cannot be according to the strict application of the law because it adds the otherwise counterfactual predicate "righteous" to the believing sinner. (As we have seen, rationalist and Pietist alternatives to *sola fide* ordinarily argue that God's judgment presupposes some grounding condition in the one being justified.) Rather ironically, from an orthodox perspective, Ritschl's insistence on a synthetic divine judgment that establishes what it declares is the very reason he also insisted that this judgment must not be judicial or forensic in nature.[109]

Ritschl's antimetaphysical, socially oriented, profoundly subjective, and thoroughly practical theology drew heavily but selectively on ideas advanced by Kant and Schleiermacher. It proved highly influential over a rapidly ascending Protestant liberalism in the post-Enlightenment era from the publication of *The Christian Doctrine of Justification and Reconciliation* in 1874 to the advent of World War I in 1914. Some of the era's most influential religious voices—Wilhelm Hermann, Adolf von Harnack, Walter Rauschenbusch, and Ernst Troeltsch, for instance—were self-consciously Ritschlian in their views. There were, however, more independent voices in the era too. One, Martin Kähler, made justification at least as central to his theological system as Ritschl had.

Martin Kähler

Martin Kähler (1835–1912) is remembered today mostly for his insightful and broadly existential critique of higher criticism's quest for the historical Jesus, *The So-Called Historical Jesus and the Historic, Biblical Christ* (1892). We must abandon the quest, he argued, not only because we lack sufficient resources to piece together Christ's biography but also because we do not need his biography. All we actually need, religiously and subjectively, is to know that Jesus died for our sins, which is objectively proclaimed in the Scriptures and pulpits of the church whatever "the correctness of the . . . literary-historical details" of the biblical account may be.[110]

---

108. Notably, Ritschl's theory of independent value judgments maintains that they are nothing other than perceptions of how well something serves this moral end.
109. Ritschl, *Justification and Reconciliation*, 3:79–85; see also McGrath, *Iustitia Dei*, 386.
110. Martin Kähler, *The So-Called Historical Jesus and the Historic, Biblical Christ*, trans. Carl E. Braaten (Philadelphia: Fortress, 1964), 114.

This critique, and the underlying method of correlating the subjectivity of human experience with the objectivity of the biblical account of Christ, would have profound influence on Rudolf Bultmann and Paul Tillich. It also signaled the rise of a new theological and soteriological perspective that would lead to a reappropriation of the doctrine, or at least the concept, of justification in the twentieth century.

Kähler "understood the problem of doubt," Tillich argues, because he understood that "doubt is an element in the continuous human situation which we cannot simply overcome by putting everything into the subjectivity of experience."[111] The Enlightenment seemed to strip theology of everything but the subjectivity of the theologian's personal religious experience, displacing the formal principle of Scripture with the subjective experience of the theologian or community of faith and the material principle of *sola fide* with the content of our consciousness. On this point, Kähler saw little difference between Ritschl, Schleiermacher, and earlier Enlightenment theologians.

While Kähler had no interest in denying the subjectivity of human experience, Tillich notes, he did argue that we must "combine" our subjectivity "with the objectivity of the biblical witness," or what Bultmann would later call the "kerygma." Combining our subjective personal experience with the objective biblical witness, however, "means that we cannot reach absolute certainty."[112] Like Kierkegaard, Kähler was convinced that epistemic certainty about the historicity of the biblical witness is impossible to achieve through historical-critical research. Any view, such as Ritschl's and Hermann's, that rests faith entirely on the historical Jesus is tendentious and inadequate. In this sense, Tillich concludes that for Kähler, doubt—including doubts about Scripture arising from historical-critical scholarship—cannot be eliminated from faith through historical scholarship or any other means. The Christian is always a believing doubter and doubting believer.

Kähler considered the paradoxical situation of being a believing doubter and doubting believer as the epistemic counterpart to being simultaneously saint and sinner (*simul iustus et peccator*). Breaking with Ritschlian theology, Kähler insisted that reconciliation through the death of Christ is an objective reality achieved by grace alone and not the subjective effect of the justifying act. This means for him that our doubt is no more an obstacle to our being reconciled to God than other kinds of sin. To be justified, an individual must subjectively appropriate *by faith* the proclaimed objective reality of being reconciled to God through Christ—faith being the only possible way to do so. Being justified by grace alone through faith alone, on this view, amounts to accepting the news that one is in fact reconciled to God despite one's present and continuing consciousness of sin and doubt and estrangement from God.

While in some respects Kähler's exposition of justification falls along more traditional Lutheran lines than many of his liberal predecessors, the effect of his appropriation of the concept of justification is more than a mere reaffirmation of *sola fide* as

---

111. Tillich, *History of Christian Thought*, 509.
112. Tillich, *History of Christian Thought*, 509; cf. 450.

the material principle of Protestantism, at least insofar as it functioned as such for the Reformers and their orthodox heirs. In his treatment, justification by grace through faith in Christ is not just a distinguishing soteriological point of the evangelical faith but "the basic article" (*grundartikel*) of Christian theology (as Ritschl had also suggested, in his own way) and therefore the organizing principle of the whole theological encyclopedia, unifying its apologetic, systematic, and ethical dimensions.[113] In this thinking, Kähler went beyond Lutheran orthodoxy; in his hands, justification became a model for combining the objective biblical witness with subjective religious consciousness. It also began to acquire the characteristics of a formal principle for theology insofar as justification functions as both the vital perspective through which the whole theological encyclopedia can be viewed in its internal coherence and the hermeneutic principle of doctrine through which every teaching is related and interpreted.[114] As Karl Barth noted, "With the possible exception of M. Kähler, no one dares actually to plan and organize Evangelical dogmatics around the doctrine of justification as a centre. It is a matter for reflection that neither in the older or more recent Lutheranism has this ever been done."[115]

Paul Tillich

Kähler's theology, especially his correlation of subjectivity and the objective proclamation of Christ and his defense of that proclamation as beyond the reach of higher-critical research, sounded certain existential themes that attracted admiring attention from fellow Germans like Rudolf Bultmann (1884–1976) and Paul Tillich (1886–1965). The latter, a critic of National Socialism, moved to America in 1933 after being dismissed from his post at Frankfurt. Later he would freely and fondly admit the profound impact that his mentor had on him, and he encouraged a modest postwar revival of interest in Kähler's work.

Tillich, however, developed his own "method of correlation" that went far beyond anything Kähler appears to have contemplated. Still, the basic outlines remain. According to Tillich, human existence implies questions that theology answers. Because existence merely *implies* questions—inescapable, angst-inducing, existential questions—theology's first task is to identify and explicitly state these questions for each generation. The questions are not from theology, however, but from human existence. Theology then answers these questions out of the symbols offered in the Christian message. So "the method of correlation explains the contents of the Christian faith through existential questions and theological answers in mutual interdependence."[116]

---

113. Martin Kähler worked out this systematic perspective in *Die Wissenschaft der christlichen Lehre*, 3rd ed. (Waltrop: Spenner, 1994).
114. Kähler, *Die Wissenschaft der christlichen Lehre*, 69. As Eberhard Jüngel notes, Kähler did not argue that we can deduce the whole system of doctrine from this single article. Nevertheless, Kähler did appropriate justification both as an epistemic paradigm and formal principle of his system. Eberhard Jüngel, *Justification: The Heart of the Christian Faith*, trans. Jeffrey F. Cayzer (2001; repr., London: T&T Clark, 2014), 24–25.
115. Karl Barth, *Church Dogmatics*, vol. 4, bk. 1, *The Doctrine of Reconciliation, Part 1*, ed. G. W. Bromiley and T. F. Torrance, trans. G. W. Bromiley (Edinburgh: T&T Clark, 1956), 522.
116. Paul Tillich, *Systematic Theology*, vol. 1, *Reason and Revelation; Being and God* (Chicago: University of Chicago Press, 1967), 60.

Tillich argued that systematic theology has always employed this method, just more or less consciously over time (he cited the opening of Calvin's *Institutes* as a more conscious example). As the theologian analyzes the human situation to identify and formulate the questions, he "employs material made available by man's creative self-interpretation in all realms of culture . . . and organizes these materials in relation to the answer given by the Christian message." In doing so, he works as a philosopher. But as he turns to "the revelatory events on which Christianity is based" to answer these questions, he works as a theologian. All theology is fundamentally apologetic: the form or structure of any given system will be determined by the questions implied by the present human situation, but the content of the answers will be drawn from the Christian message.[117]

According to Tillich, the question implied by the human situation in mid-twentieth-century America was no longer driven by anxiety about one's moral finitude, expressed in the consciousness of guilt and fear of condemnation, as it was in Luther's day, but by our existential finitude, expressed in the consciousness of estrangement and despair over meaning and purpose.[118] Because of this cultural sea change, the orthodox formulation of the doctrine of justification *sola fide* had become practically unintelligible. The theological task was obvious: the doctrine of justification had to be reformulated in existentialist rather than moral-forensic terms.[119]

Tillich attempted to do just this by working out the doctrine within a system of panentheitic idealism reminiscent of the views we encountered in Hegel and Baur above.[120] According to Tillich, "In the overwhelming majority of occasions in which the word 'salvation' . . . is used, it refers to salvation from . . . ultimate negativity."[121] Although "ultimate negativity" can be and historically has been described in many different ways, including "condemnation" and "eternal death," Tillich described it as the "ultimate consequence" of "existential estrangement."[122] This description is central to his existential reinterpretation of soteriology in general—for example, this understanding of "ultimate negativity" is what Christ is viewed as enduring on the cross—and justification in particular. "The tremendous weight of the question of salvation is rooted in this understanding of the term," he concluded. "It becomes the question of 'to be or not to be.'"[123]

Tillich answered Hamlet's question in terms of "participation in the New Being" through "absolute faith." Absolute faith, George Lindbeck explains, "is preconceptual and can be present even in the absence of any identifiable object of belief or trust."[124] Accordingly, absolute faith may acquire the form of explicit faith in Jesus Christ or

---

117. Tillich, *Systematic Theology*, 1:60, 63–64.
118. Paul Tillich, *The Courage to Be*, 2nd ed. (New Haven, CT: Yale University Press, 1952), 60–67.
119. See Paul Tillich, *The Protestant Era*, trans. James Luther Adams (Chicago: University of Chicago Press, 1948), 185–86.
120. Cooper argues that Tillich's "existential panentheism" is closer to Schelling's brand of idealism than Hegel's, but the family resemblance is strong. *Panentheism*, 194–212.
121. Tillich, *Systematic Theology*, vol. 2, *Existence and the Christ*, 165.
122. Tillich, *Systematic Theology*, 2:155.
123. Tillich, *Systematic Theology*, 2:165.
124. George Lindbeck, "Justification and Atonement: An Ecumenical Trajectory," in *By Faith Alone: Essays on Justification in Honor of Gerhard O. Forde*, ed. Joseph A. Burgess and Marc Kolden (Grand Rapids, MI: Eerdmans, 2004), 193–94.

some other theistic rendering of "the ground of being" but need not do so; even an avowed atheist may have this faith. In *The Courage to Be*, Tillich identified three "elements" that constitute absolute faith: (1) an experience of the power of being, (2) an experience of the dependence of nonbeing on being, and (3) "the acceptance of being accepted."[125] This consciousness—of the power of being, of the relation of nonbeing to being, and of acceptance—is consciousness of "God," whom Tillich represented as the ground of being who comprehends all being and nonbeing in himself, as existentially sufficient for us.

The third element of absolute faith is the necessary subjective corollary to the objective "eternal act of God by which . . . he accepts as not estranged those who are indeed estranged from him by guilt and the act by which he takes them into the unity with him which is manifest in the New Being in Christ."[126] One is not justified before God unless one accepts that God has accepted him. The acceptance of being accepted is justifying faith, the faith through which one receives the eternal acceptance of God for oneself. As such, justifying faith may be nothing more than a condition of finite consciousness. As noted, it does not depend on explicit faith in Jesus Christ or any other theistic representation of the ground of being. That said, the specifically Christian consciousness of salvation "can be known fully and definitively only through Jesus," even if it is possible to be justified through absolute faith without reference to the Christian symbols of Christ, cross, resurrection, and so on.[127]

To be justified by grace alone, according to Tillich, indicates that God accepts the unacceptable; to be justified through faith alone indicates that we must accept that we are accepted despite our unacceptability. There is never a question about whether we are accepted; there is only the need to accept that we are accepted. Accepting that we are accepted, however conscious we may be of our unacceptability, is the confidence to live under the consciousness of our existential finitude, haunted as it is by nonbeing, meaninglessness, and despair. The justified, therefore, live courageously by this confidence, and so all who are justified are also sanctified.

Karl Barth

As Tillich was working out an existential reinterpretation of justification *sola fide* suitable for the mid-twentieth century situation, his Swiss contemporary Karl Barth (1886–1968) was busy doing the same. Tillich and Barth belonged to a tangle of twentieth-century thinkers who shared certain theological sensibilities as they sought to revitalize Christianity in Protestant liberalism's moment of crisis, each in his own dialectical way.

In a 1916 address titled "The Righteousness of God," Barth signaled his break with Ritschlian liberalism's social-moral project by drawing a sharp contrast between the

---

125. Tillich, *Courage to Be*, 177.
126. Tillich, *Systematic Theology*, 2:178–79.
127. Lindbeck, "Justification and Atonement," 194.

righteousness of God and the righteousness of humanity. Protestant liberalism tended to view history as the progress of civilization toward the realization of the kingdom. In back of this view was an apparent desire for the righteousness of God to be realized on earth, in human society, and an assumed harmony between the righteousness of God and the righteousness of humanity.

Barth admitted, "We yearn for the righteousness of God," but he lamented, "We do not let it into our lives and our world." Our desire for the righteousness of God is superficial, he argued. We desire relief from injustice in various forms, but at the decisive moment when the righteousness of God is about to arrive, "we come to our own rescue. It is as if," he wrote with Kierkegaardian suspicion, "we were afraid of an all too real and complete fulfillment of our longing." We do not really want the righteousness of God to fully come into our lives and the world, he suspected, because it must come on its own terms, not ours. In doing so, it exposes our supposed righteousness, the contribution we are determined to make, as vanity and unrighteousness—so many bricks for Babel, whether made of moral, legal, or religious mud and straw.[128]

His diagnosis of Protestant liberalism was clear as he directed his audience, at the height of the Great War, away from self-righteousness to the "inner way" of "simple faith" in Jesus Christ:

> One cannot say that humanity has already exhausted the possibilities of this way. We have made many things out of Jesus. But we have not yet comprehended the simplest thing, that he is the Son of God and that we may go with him on the way. . . . It remains to be seen whether the quaking of the Tower of Babel which we are now experiencing is strong enough to bring us a little bit closer to the way of *faith*. An opportunity to do so has now arrived. It may or may not happen. But sooner or later it will happen. There is no other way.[129]

As McGrath remarks, one could think "that Barth's . . . theology . . . might represent a recovery of the Reformer's insights into the significance of the *articulus iustificationis*. In fact, this is not the case."[130] Barth actually proceeded to criticize the centrality of *sola fide* to Christian theology and to recast justification in terms of revelation, correlating what is objectively disclosed in Christ with the subjective recognition and apprehension of it.

Barth acknowledged that justification has sometimes "been asserted as *the* Word of the Gospel," or "it has been adopted as *the* theological truth." He even granted that "there have been times when this has been not merely legitimate but necessary." But he also contended that theology must take a wider view than just what the current situation requires. Looking beyond the Reformation, for example, we see that justification "has not always been the Word of the Gospel, and it would be an act of narrowing

---

128. Karl Barth, "The Righteousness of God," in *The Word of God and Theology*, trans. Amy Marga (London: T&T Clark, 2011), 6.
129. Barth, "Righteousness of God," 13.
130. McGrath, *Iustitia Dei*, 394.

and unjust exclusiveness to proclaim and treat it as such." It may even be appropriate, he suggested, for justification to assume a low profile in the church's teaching at times. Justification is not the one necessary thing the church must always, at all times, and in all places treat as "the centre or culminating point of the Christian message."[131]

Barth's emphatic argument may seem a strange obsession—it was not as though *sola fide* was receiving undue attention in Protestant liberalism in his day. His contention was with Ernst Wolf, however, and while Barth may have gone too far and not done justice to Wolf's views, some of Barth's points are roughly in line with Protestant orthodoxy. Orthodox statements on the significance of justification to the gospel, church, or religion, for example, were never intended to transform justification into a formal principle of theology or a norm of doctrine. Justification is just one point in the *ordo salutis*. That said, orthodoxy has always insisted that justification *sola fide* is vital to the church on earth and glory of Christ in the proclamation of the gospel, points he seemed to admit.[132] Barth's dislodging bump of justification was not about correcting Wolf's supposed exaggerations so much as setting up his own recasting of this doctrine in terms of divine revelation in Jesus Christ.[133]

The emphasis on revelation and thus knowledge in Barth's doctrine of justification makes sense from within his system. Barth argued that God has elected all humanity in Christ and that Christ acted on behalf of all humanity in his death and resurrection:

> The grace of God in which it [i.e., the new reconciled being] comes and is made over to us is the grace of Jesus Christ, that is, the grace in which God from all eternity has chosen man (all men) in this One, in which He has bound Himself to man—before man even existed—in this One. He, Jesus Christ, is the One who accomplishes the sovereign act in which God has made true and actual in time the decree of his election by making atonement, in which he has introduced the new being of all men.[134]

Not all men, Barth noted, have the confidence and joy that comes from knowing this, but it is nevertheless "the being of the new man reconciled with God which in Him has truly and actually been appropriated to them and to all men" by God.[135]

So all humanity is elect in Christ and has been reconciled with God in Christ, who made atonement for all people. To be justified by grace alone means we make no contribution whatsoever to our right standing before God or his vindication as the just justifier of sinners. Faith does not contribute to our justification, and unbelief cannot prevent it. The new being "has truly and actually been appropriated to . . . all men." All this taken together suggests the possibility—some claim necessity—of universalism. Barth implied as much and seemed eager to leave the possibility on the table. At the

---

131. Barth, *Church Dogmatics*, 4.1:522–24.
132. Cf. McGrath, *Iustitia Dei*, 400. Here, once again, McGrath follows a thoroughly discredited reading of "Reformed orthodoxy" as displacing the Reformers' "analytic and inductive method" focused on the concrete event of justification of the sinner in Christ" with "a synthetic and deductive method" centered on "the divine decree to elect."
133. Barth, *Church Dogmatics*, 4.1:527–28.
134. Barth, *Church Dogmatics*, 4.1:91–92.
135. Barth, *Church Dogmatics*, 4.1:92.

same time, he yielded to God's freedom to save whomever he wants and refused to draw this conclusion explicitly.[136]

The justification of sinners before God, therefore, occurs in Christ's death and resurrection, as opposed to the sinner's coming to faith. Barth wrote,

> Justification definitely means the sentence executed and revealed in Jesus Christ and His death and resurrection, the No and Yes with which God vindicates Himself in relation to covenant-breaking man, with which He converts him to Himself and therefore reconciles him with Himself. He does it by the destruction of the old and the creation of the new man.[137]

This destruction of the old and creation of the new occurs in the death and resurrection of Christ, which is actually effective for all people. The divine declaration of the sinner as righteous is no mere "verbal action, with a kind of bracketed 'as if,' as though what is pronounced were not the whole truth about man." On the contrary, "it is a declaring righteous which without any reserve can be called a making righteous" precisely because "it is a declaration about man fulfilled and therefore effective in this event."[138]

For both Tillich and Barth, everyone is already justified objectively. Not just satisfaction as the ground of justification but also humanity's actual justification has already been revealed in Christ. As such, "Christian faith . . . believes in a sentence which is absolutely effective, so that man is not merely called righteous before God, but is righteous before God." The sentence has already been "executed and revealed in Jesus Christ."[139] And yet for Barth, as for Tillich, there is a necessary subjective corollary to this revelation: faith.

The sinner's justification revealed in Christ "calls for faith in every man as a suitable acknowledgment and appropriation and application."[140] Justifying faith is not necessary in order to be justified but "to do justice to the sovereign self-demonstration of the justified man," who is Jesus Christ.[141] This faith "that recognizes and apprehends man's justification, is the obedience of humility." It "denies the competence, the relevance, the power and the value of all human action," including the act of faith itself.[142] This is the humility of faith and precisely why we must affirm *sola fide*. The obedience of humility, therefore, is nothing other than faith's clinging to "the self-demonstration of the justified man," by which Barth meant "the crucified and risen Jesus Christ who lives as the author and recipient and revealer of the justification of all men."[143]

In the end, both Tillich and Barth advanced broadly universalist formulations of justification in which all people are already objectively justified by God but ignorant

---

136. See, for example, Karl Barth, *Humanity of God* (Richmond: John Knox, 1960), 61–62.
137. Barth, *Church Dogmatics*, 4.1:96.
138. Barth, *Church Dogmatics*, 4.1:95.
139. Barth, *Church Dogmatics*, 4.1:95.
140. Barth, *Church Dogmatics*, 4.1:514.
141. Barth, *Church Dogmatics*, 4.1:514.
142. Barth, *Church Dogmatics*, 4.1:626–27.
143. Barth, *Church Dogmatics*, 4.1:629.

of this reality. What is required, therefore, is the revelation of this fact and "the faith which recognizes and apprehends" it. Though their accounts of that faith differ, the effects are similar in that faith produces an altered consciousness in the individual that allows the believer to begin enjoying what in fact was already true.

Conclusion

The historical survey offered above has been selective, to be sure, but it is also broadly representative, focusing on major contributions and developments in the history of this doctrine. While I have mostly ignored the many advocates and defenders of *sola fide* active throughout the era, many of whom are covered in other chapters, it is worth pondering this observation: everyone included in this survey, however devout or brilliant, understood himself to be offering the best interpretation of Christianity and understanding of the Christian message yet achieved, even though none of them adhered to or defended justification *sola fide* in the robust sense outlined at the beginning of this chapter.

Calvin is surely right: the doctrine of justification "is the main hinge on which religion turns"; he is also surely right that we must therefore "devote the greater attention and care to it."[144] This chapter makes the same point, negatively—and demonstrates that Luther was right to forecast constant conflict with error and a gradual declension of *sola fide* even within Protestant churches. From the faint glow of the Enlightenment's dawn in Europe's eastern, Socinian skies to the fading light of Protestant liberalism across the Atlantic far to the west, the story told above is the tale of *sola fide*'s almost total eclipse across large swaths of Protestantism. I am grateful it is only part of a much larger story to be told and that the doctrine of justification by grace alone through faith alone in Christ alone is being taught and believed by orthodox evangelicals throughout the world today.

Recommended Resources

Barth, Karl. *Church Dogmatics*. Vol. 4, bk. 1, *The Doctrine of Reconciliation, Part 1*. Edited by G. W. Bromiley and T. F. Torrance. Translated by G. W. Bromiley. Edinburgh: T&T Clark, 1956.
Baur, Ferdinand Christian. *Lectures on New Testament Theology*. Edited by Peter C. Hodgson. Translated by Robert F. Brown. Oxford: Oxford University Press, 2016.
Beachy, Alvin J. *The Concept of Grace in the Radical Reformation*. Bibliotheca Humanistica et Reformatorica 17. Nieuwkoop: De Graaf, 1976.
Buchanan, James. *The Doctrine of Justification: An Outline of Its History in the Church and of Its Exposition from Scripture*. 1867. Reprint, Edinburgh: Banner of Truth, 1984.
Crites, Stephen. "The Gospel according to Hegel." *Journal of Religion* 46, no. 2 (1966): 246–63.
Hardy, Lee. "Hume's Defense of True Religion." In *The Persistence of the Sacred in Modern Thought*, edited by Chris L. Firestone and Nathan A. Jacobs, 251–72. Notre Dame, IN: University of Notre Dame Press, 2012.

---

144. John Calvin, *Institutes of the Christian Religion*, ed. John T. McNeill, trans. Ford Lewis Battles, LCC 20–21 (Louisville: Westminster, 1960), 3.11.1.

Hegel, Georg Wilhelm Friedrich. *Lectures on the Philosophy of Religion*. Vol. 3, *The Consummate Religion*. Edited by Peter C. Hodgson. Translated by R. F. Brown, P. C. Hodgson, and J. M. Stewart. Berkeley: University of California Press, 1988.

Herbert of Cherbury. *De Veritate*. Translated by Meyrick H. Carré. 1624. 3rd ed., 1645. Reprint, Bristol: University of Bristol, 1937.

Kant, Immanuel. *Critique of Pure Reason*. Translated and edited by Paul Guyer and Allen W. Wood. Cambridge: Cambridge University Press, 1998.

———. *Religion within the Boundaries of Mere Reason; and Other Writings*. Translated and edited by Allen W. Wood and George Di Giovanni. Cambridge Texts in the History of Philosophy. Cambridge: Cambridge University Press, 1998.

Livingston, James C. *Modern Christian Thought*. 2 vols. 2nd ed. Minneapolis: Fortress, 2006.

Locke, John. *Reasonableness of Christianity*. Edited by John C. Higgins-Biddle. Oxford: Oxford University Press, 1999.

McGrath, Alistair E. *Iustitia Dei: A History of the Christian Doctrine of Justification*. 3rd ed. Cambridge: Cambridge University Press, 2005.

Pelikan, Jaroslav, and Valerie R. Hotchkiss, eds. *Creeds and Confessions of Faith in the Christian Tradition*. 3 vols. New Haven, CT: Yale University Press, 2003.

Ritschl, Albrecht. *The Christian Doctrine of Justification and Reconciliation*. Vol. 3. Translated by H. R. Mackintosh and A. B. Macauley. Edinburgh: T&T Clark, 1902.

———. *A Critical History of the Christian Doctrine of Justification and Reconciliation*. Translated by John S. Black. Edinburgh: Edmonston and Douglas, 1872.

Schleiermacher, Friedrich. *The Christian Faith*. Edited by H. R. Mackintosh and J. S. Stewart. Edinburgh: T&T Clark, 1968.

———. *On Religion: Speeches to Its Cultured Despisers*. Translated by John Oman. Louisville: Westminster John Knox, 1994.

Tillich, Paul. *A History of Christian Thought: From Its Judaic and Hellenistic Origins to Existentialism*. New York: Simon and Schuster, 1968.

———. *Systematic Theology*. Vol. 1, *Reason and Revelation; Being and God*. Chicago: University of Chicago Press, 1967.

Tillotson, John. *The Works of the Most Reverend Dr. John Tillotson, Late Lord Archbishop of Canterbury*. 12 vols. London: Ware et al., 1742.

Tindal, Matthew. *Christianity as Old as the Creation: Or, the Gospel a Republication of the Religion of Nature*. London, 1730.

Toland, John. *Christianity Not Mysterious: Or, a Treatise Shewing That There Is Nothing in the Gospel Contrary to Reason, Nor above It*. 2nd ed. London: Sam. Buckley, 1696.

Westphal, Merold. *History and Truth in Hegel's "Phenomenology."* 3rd ed. Bloomington: Indiana University Press, 1998.

Wilbur, Earl Morse. *A History of Unitarianism*. 2 vols. Cambridge, MA: Beacon, 1945.

PART FOUR

JUSTIFICATION IN PASTORAL PERSPECTIVE

25

Justification and Conversion

Attractions and Repulsions to Rome

CHRIS CASTALDO

As the sun descended on the Middle Ages, the church floundered in mediocrity.[1] A papacy engrossed in political affairs, splendid in most things except religion, induced a certain discontent, an ecclesial malaise that left hungry souls wanting. But these grains of discontent would eventually fall to the ground as seeds of renewal—a spiritual transmutation that would germinate, grow, and blossom, bearing fruit in a series of Reformations.[2]

The movement of Christian renewal that started in the sixteenth century has continued through the generations, a process that extends to the present. However, it should be noted that religious reform was not limited to Protestants. In the Council of Trent (1545–1563), the Catholic Church enacted a variety of new initiatives. Because of those who implemented these measures, not least the Jesuits, the tide of Protestant conversions was stemmed, and some of the previously converted Protestants returned to Rome.

The centuries-long confluence of Christian conversions to and from Rome has fomented ecclesial white water. If these converts were swimmers on the Roman Tiber—the river that leads directly into (or away from) the arms of Saint Peter's Basilica—they would form a mass of converts churning frenetically in both directions, each one

---

1. Portions of this chapter are a revision of Chris Castaldo, *Justified in Christ: The Doctrines of Peter Martyr Vermigli and John Henry Newman and Their Ecumenical Implications* (Eugene, OR: Pickwick, 2017). Used by permission of Wipf and Stock Publishers, www.wipfandstock.com. Also, some sections are adapted from Chris Castaldo, "Why Catholics and Protestants Convert," *Chris Castaldo* (blog), November 20, 2012, http://www.chriscastaldo.com/2012/11/20/why-catholics-and-protestants-convert/. Used by permission of the author.
2. Carter Lindberg provides reasons for the plurality of Reformation movements in *The European Reformations*, 2nd ed. (Malden, MA: Wiley-Blackwell, 2010), 11–22.

swimming for his (eternal) life. Faced with these roiling waters of theological ideas and ecclesial commitments, as anathematizing canons are launched overhead from shore to shore, we have to eventually ask why. In other words, what motivates men and women to swim the Tiber (in either direction)?

Of the many converts from Reformed theology to Roman Catholicism during the modern period, the most notable is unarguably John Henry Newman (1801–1890), the nineteenth-century Anglican-divine-turned-Catholic. After converting in 1845, Newman was made a cardinal by Pope Leo XIII in 1879 and, more than a century later, was beatified by Pope Benedict XVI in 2010. Regarded by many as the eminent and most creative English theologian of the nineteenth century, Newman is variously remembered: leader of the Oxford movement, Victorian sage, educational theorist, poet, satirist, preacher, and forerunner of Vatican II. Library shelves around the globe are weighed down by the several hundred volumes dedicated to his life and thought. Perhaps most of all, however, Newman is known as the quintessential *convert* to Catholicism.

It is noteworthy, for instance, that the title of Professor Thomas Howard's conversion testimony, *Lead, Kindly Light*,[3] is taken from Newman's hymn by the same name:

> Lead, kindly Light, amid th'encircling gloom,
>   Lead Thou me on!
> The night is dark, and I am far from home;
>   Lead Thou me on!
> Keep Thou my feet; I do not ask to see
>   The distant scene; one step enough for me.[4]

Newman originally penned this hymn during his visit to southern Europe in 1833, far from his English homeland and terribly ill. His words would also describe his religious conversion to the Roman church.

In what follows, we accompany Newman on his journey to full communion with Rome, giving particular attention to the way the Protestant doctrine of justification motivated his decisions. In doing so, we seek to understand the chief reasons why he chose and why others like him choose to cross the Tiber in favor of Rome. We then contrast Newman's experience with that of a prominent Catholic leader who traversed the Tiber in the opposite direction to become a leading light among sixteenth-century Reformed theologians, Italian theologian Peter Martyr Vermigli (1499–1562). While modern readers have sometimes identified Vermigli as the "Italian Calvin," on account of his friendship with and similar theology to the Geneva Reformer, this description is inadequate. If we had been living in Oxford in 1549, when Vermigli singlehandedly debated a team of three Catholic apologists in the famous disputation on the Eucharist, we might have been tempted to describe Calvin as the "French Vermigli," so penetrating was Vermigli's theological acumen. Here we see that Newman and Vermigli were

---

3. Thomas Howard, *Lead, Kindly Light: My Journey to Rome* (San Francisco: Ignatius, 2004).
4. John Henry Newman, "Lead, Kindly Light" (also, "The Pillar and the Cloud"), 1833.

motivated by a common concern, namely, *How does one encounter the saving presence of Christ?* With such an understanding in view, we then consider where the basic lines of doctrinal agreement and difference fall between Roman Catholics and Reformed Protestants. Finally, we identify principles that help us understand reasons and attendant circumstances surrounding such conversions.

John Henry Newman
Newman Questions His Evangelical Assumptions

When Newman became a fellow at Oriel College at the University of Oxford in April 1822, he expected that colleagues would challenge his Calvinist creed.[5] He was right. Discussion in the Oriel common room often turned to theology, with particular scrutiny aimed at Newman. When Newman was confronted by this offensive, his Reformed doctrine of predestination was the first piece of his theology to crumble.[6] The noetic triumvirate of Thomas Arnold (1795–1842), Richard Whately (1787–1863), and Edward Hawkins (1789–1882) imposed sustained pressure, forcing Newman to retreat from his assumptions and reevaluate his religious convictions.

Newman maintained the core of his Calvinist creed, at least for the time being. Walter Mayers, Newman's evangelical mentor (until his untimely death in 1828), persuaded Newman to take holy orders, and in 1824, he was ordained deacon. The following year he was ordained to the Anglican priesthood. After becoming curate of Saint Clement's, a working-class parish in east Oxford, Newman engaged in pastoral ministry with great enthusiasm. It was at this time that Newman started to question a *sine qua non* of evangelicalism: the distinction between "nominal" and "real" Christians.

The importance of this tenet among evangelicals was fundamental. As David Newsome explains,

> Time and time again the Evangelicals would stress that there were two kinds of Christian—the *nominal* Christian and the "truly religious" or "real" Christian, a distinction which gained currency with the publication of Joseph Milner's *Church History*, which appeared in stages during the 1790's and the following decade, and with Wilberforce's own *Practical View*. . . . This distinction was soon recognised as stock Evangelical phraseology—and indeed its acceptance rapidly became a sort of party shibboleth.[7]

The question whether such a distinction is pastorally defendable asserted itself in Newman's mind in the summer of 1824. With many of the academic fellows away from campus, Newman spent more time with Edward Hawkins, who advised the young protégé on his parochial duties, particularly on his preaching. Hawkins roundly criticized

---

5. Newman seemed to have anticipated this critique when he attributed his reticence to "the result of his Calvinistic beliefs." Newman, *Autobiographical Writings*, ed. Henry Tristram (London: Sheed and Ward, 1956), 65–66.
6. Newman, *Autobiographical Writings*, 4.
7. David Newsome, *The Parting of Friends: The Wilberforces and Henry Manning* (Grand Rapids, MI: Eerdmans, 1966), 47.

Newman's first sermon, which, by its evangelical denigration of baptismal regeneration, "divided the Christian world into two classes, the one all darkness, the other all light."[8] According to Newman, Hawkins chided him by explaining,

> Men are not either saints or sinners; but they are not so good as they should be, and better than they might be. . . . Preachers should follow the example of St Paul; he did not divide his brethren into two, the converted and unconverted, but he addressed them all as "in Christ" . . . and this, while he was rebuking them for irregularities and scandals which had occurred among them.[9]

To emphasize his point, Hawkins gave Newman a copy of John Bird Sumner's *Apostolical Preaching*, which argued that Paul addressed the visible church as a collective body of Christians who categorically possessed the Holy Spirit (and not two distinct groups of converted and unconverted).[10] This work, coupled with an active routine of pastoral visitation, effectively dented Newman's distinction between real and nominal Christians.[11] Thinking through these concepts, especially in conversation with Edward Pusey, would eventually lead Newman to question his doctrine of imputation.[12] In his own words, writing in January of 1825, "I think, I am not certain, I must give up the doctrine of imputed righteousness and that of regeneration apart from baptism."[13]

While Hawkins reoriented Newman's understanding of the doctrine of imputation, he influenced him in yet another far-reaching way, namely, by insisting that sacred tradition is a necessary accompaniment to Scripture.[14] This occurred at a crucial moment as Newman was trying to give an answer for the Patristic hope within him. While Anglican tradition would not provide the connection to the early church for which he was searching (his conversion to Catholicism would be fueled by the Roman church's ability to account for sacred tradition from the earliest centuries),[15] his acceptance of tradition at this point under Hawkins, which started in 1825, was a critical departure from his evangelical background, as Newman himself explained:

> He [Hawkins] lays down a proposition, self-evident as soon as stated, to those who have at all examined the structure of Scripture, viz. that the sacred text was never

---

8. Newman, *Autobiographical Writings*, 77.
9. Newman, *Autobiographical Writings*, 65.
10. John Bird Sumner, *Apostolical Preaching Considered, in an Examination of St. Paul's Epistles* (London: J. Hatchard, 1815). Newman studied the work of Sumner, the evangelical bishop of Chester, early in his life before delving into his *Apostolical Preaching*.
11. About this experience, Newman writes (referring to himself in the third person), "It was during these years of parochial duty that Mr. Newman underwent a great change in his religious opinions." Newman, *Autobiographical Writings*, 73. Later in his memoir, he explains that "the religion which he had received from John Newton and Thomas Scott would not work in a parish; that it is unreal; that this he had actually found as a fact, as Mr. Hawkins had told him beforehand; that Calvinism was not a key to the phenomena of human nature, as they occur in the world." Newman, *Autobiographical Writings*, 79.
12. Newman, *Autobiographical Writings*, 203.
13. Newman, *Autobiographical Writings*, 203.
14. Years later, Newman would refer to this as "the *quasi*-Catholic doctrine of Tradition." Newman, *Autobiographical Writings*, 78.
15. Newman tells this story in his *Apologia Pro Vita Sua: Being a History of His Religious Opinions* (London: Longmans, Green, 1882), 127–237.

intended to teach doctrine, but only to prove it, and that, if we would learn doctrine, we must have recourse to the formularies of the Church; for instance to the Catechism, and to the Creeds. He considers, that, after learning from them the doctrines of Christianity, the inquirer must verify them by Scripture.[16]

Newman's commitment to tradition would eventually lead to a doctrinal impasse. To the extent that he studied the history of the early church, he saw what appeared to be the universal practice of infant baptism. Newman reasoned that if baptism constitutes the rite of initiation into Christ, and not simply the *visible* church, as evangelicals were inclined to see it, it would therefore be possible for infants to be regenerated. He was not yet fully prepared to accept this conclusion. Instead, he opted for the position of Mayers, which viewed baptism as planting the seed of grace. But make no mistake about it: as Newman modified his views on justification and the authority of tradition, he found himself traveling along a new religious path.

"Shreds and Tatters" of Evangelicalism

Books played a crucial role in Newman's conversion. In addition to Sumner's *Apostolical Preaching*, Joseph Butler's *Analogy of Religion* (1736) also exerted influence.[17] Above all, Butler's work cast aspersions on the chief tenets of evangelicalism, portraying it as "an emotional religion [with which Newman] could have little sympathy."[18] This especially affected Newman's view of the Protestant doctrine of *sola fide*, about which he would soon write that "the Church considers the doctrine of justification by faith only to be a *principle* and the religion of the day takes it as a *rule of conduct*."[19] The tragic effect, from Newman's point of view, was to reduce Christian faith to a subjective experience and to undermine the urgency of obedience. In other words, Newman feared that evangelical faith led inexorably to antinomianism. It was for these reasons, according to Newman, that he "had taken the first step towards giving up the evangelical form of Christianity; however, for a long while certain shreds and tatters of that doctrine hung about his preaching."[20]

Recounting in his *Apologia* the factors that most significantly swayed him during this period, Newman highlighted two. The first was his interest in liberalism, which preferred intellectual to moral excellence.[21] This interest, however, was only short lived on account of his emotional breakdown as an examiner of schools and the sudden death of his favorite sister, Mary. The other factor was John Keble's *Christian Year* (1827), particularly its sacramental impulse, which brought to mind principles that he had

---

16. Newman, *Apologia*, 9.
17. Joseph Butler, *The Analogy of Religion, Natural and Revealed, to the Constitution and Course of Nature* (London: John and Paul Knapton, 1736).
18. Newman, *Autobiographical Writings*, 78.
19. John Henry Newman, *Lectures on the Doctrine of Justification*, 3rd ed. (London: Rivington, 1874), 333. Hereafter, page numbers to the first edition (1838) are listed in brackets.
20. Newman, *Autobiographical Writings*. This step occurred shortly after his ordination to the priesthood on May 29, 1825.
21. Newman, *Apologia*, 14. Cf. Vincent Ferrer Blehl, *Pilgrim Journey: John Henry Newman, 1801–1845* (London: Burns & Oates, 2001), 77.

previously learned from Butler. In Newman's words, "[It] was what may be called, in a larger sense of the word, the Sacramental system, that is, the doctrine that material phenomena are both the types and the instruments of things unseen."[22] Newman went on to explain that sacraments are not simply signs directing the faithful to the mysteries of faith (as many of his evangelical contemporaries asserted); they are also the *instrumental means* by which one encounters them.[23]

As Newman rejected evangelicalism's "subjective" basis for church membership in favor of an objective sacramental foundation, there was a decisive turning point in the development of his thought.[24] Momentum was added to this movement in 1831 when, having been relieved from his teaching duties, Newman received a commission to compose a history of the church councils. For various reasons, however, his attention was diverted to another project, his first great work, *The Arians of the Fourth Century* (1833).[25] Research for this volume strengthened Newman's commitment to the principles of regeneration understood in the context of sacramental objectivity and the authority of the church institution. Ian Ker summarizes Newman's position on ecclesial authority after completing his study of the fourth-century church:

> Nor did the early Church use the Bible to teach the faith; it was the Church that taught what had to be believed, and it only appealed to "Scripture in vindication of its own teaching"; heretics, on the other hand, like the Arians, relied on a "private study of Holy Scripture" to elicit a "systematic doctrine from the scattered notices of the truth which Scripture contains." The parallel with the contemporary situation was obvious.[26]

Through this new lens, Newman's reflection on Christian initiation led him to a heartened vision of the sacramental church in which one experiences union with Christ in baptism. With this new appreciation for ecclesial authority, he moved away from the doctrine of Scripture alone to a combination of Scripture and tradition under the aegis of an authoritative church institution. In this way, he sought to protect the doctrinal fidelity of the contemporary Church of England (since large segments were falling for liberalism) by embracing the beliefs and practices of the ancient church vis-à-vis oral tradition and the efficacy of sacramental mediation.[27]

---

22. Newman, *Apologia*, 18. The second principle that Newman learned from Butler is "probability [in the service of faith and love] as the guide of life." Newman, *Apologia*, 19.

23. Newman, *Apologia*, 18.

24. Newman, *Apologia*, 49. Newman's sermon titled "Holiness Necessary for Future Blessedness" makes explicit his repudiation of the evangelical doctrine of sudden conversion: "It follows at once, even though Scripture did not plainly tell us so that no one is able to prepare himself for heaven, that is, make himself holy in a short time; . . . there are others who suppose they may be saved all at once by a sudden and easily acquired faith." Newman, *Parochial and Plain Sermons* (San Francisco: Ignatius, 1997), 10.

25. John Henry Newman, *The Arians of the Fourth Century: Their Doctrine, Temper, and Conduct, Chiefly as Exhibited in the Councils of the Church, between A.D. 325 & A.D. 381* (London: C. J. G. & F. Rivington, 1833). For an assessment of Newman's work, see Rowan Williams, *Arius: Heresy and Tradition* (London: Darton, Longman and Todd, 1987), 3–6, 147, 158.

26. Ian Ker, *John Henry Newman: A Biography* (New York: Oxford University Press, 2009), 52.

27. Frederick H. Borsch explains how such an approach infused Tractarian spirituality with a measure of mysticism, often leading to an emphasis on the Eucharist. Borsch, "Ye Shall Be Holy: Reflections on the Spirituality of the Early Years of the Oxford Movement," *AThR* 66, no. 4 (1984): 356.

Approaching the Tiber

After John Keble's famous sermon "National Apostasy" from the pulpit of Saint Mary's on July 14, 1833, the so-called Oxford movement was underway and increasingly reaching greater numbers with its essays on theological and ecclesial issues (eventually collected in *Tracts for the Times*). The tracts had two primary targets: the "high and dry" establishment, which sought to promote the marriage of state and church, and the Nonconformist churches (consisting largely of evangelicals), which had grown in membership throughout Britain. Newman became so involved in the Oxford movement that he would eventually edit, publish, or contribute to thirty of the ninety tracts. Like Athanasius of old, Newman regarded himself as a defender of the church against the threat of heresy—the liberal heresy of Erastianism (that the state has authority over the church in ecclesiastical matters) and the subjective heresy of evangelicals.[28]

Of the various criticisms leveled against the tracts, the most common was its agenda to undermine the Protestant character of the Church of England. John Bowden, for example, had warned Newman in a letter dated July 14, 1834, that the tracts "will be one day charged with rank Popery" and recommended that Newman publish a tract to preempt the charge.[29] In response to this critique, Newman composed two tracts ("Tract 38" and "Tract 41") suggesting that the Church of England had in fact become more Protestant than it had previously been. The genuine trajectory of Anglicanism, argued Newman, is a *via media* between Protestantism and the Roman Catholic Church.[30] His case culminated in 1837 with his *Lectures on the Prophetical Office of the Church* (first published on March 11, 1837), a work that systematized the teaching of Anglican Divines of the seventeenth century, originally delivered in the Adam de Brome chapel of Saint Mary's Church.[31]

Newman's *via media* distinguished the so-called episcopal tradition, which grew explicitly out of the Catholic creeds and was passed through generations by a succession of bishops, from the prophetical tradition, which was located in the broader development of the church's theological reflection.[32] In his *Lectures on the Prophetical Office*, Newman emphasized the necessity of this prophetical tradition, drawing attention to the growth of Christian teaching beyond the primitive creeds, an emphasis that effectively

---

28. Avery Cardinal Dulles, *John Henry Newman* (London: Continuum, 2011), 5. Newman narrates his role in the movement up to his eventual disenchantment with the *via media* in his *Apologia*, 101–46.
29. John Henry Newman, *Letters and Diaries of John Henry Newman*, ed. Charles Stephen Dessain et al., vol. 4, *The Oxford Movement: July 1833 to December 1834* (London: T. Nelson, 1961–1977), 304.
30. Unlike other expressions of Anglo-Catholicism, which borrowed wholesale from the Roman Catholic Church, the Tractarians were more cautious in such identification. W. S. F. Pickering, *Anglo-Catholicism: A Study in Religious Ambiguity* (London: Routledge, 1989), 41.
31. John Henry Newman, *Lectures on the Prophetical Office of the Church: Viewed Relatively to Romanism and Popular Protestantism*, 2nd ed. (London: C. J. G. & F. Rivington, 1838). In December 1876, Newman organized this work into a two-volume set titled *The Via Media*. The first volume consisted of the third edition of the *Lectures on the Prophetical Office of the Church*. The second volume comprised eleven more occasional pieces, including his tracts on the Church Missionary Society of 1830, documentation of "Tract 90," and his retraction of anti-Catholic statements in 1841. Newman wrote a new preface, which serves as his last word on the concept of an Anglican *via media*. Newman, *The Via Media of the Anglican Church* (London: Pickering, 1877).
32. Newman, *Lectures on the Prophetical Office*, 304–13. In Newman's thought, these two traditions generally corresponded to the *lex credendi* (the episcopal tradition's dogmatic formulations) and the *lex orandi* (the prophetical tradition's development of doctrine).

moved the purview of apostolic faith closer to Roman Catholicism. Statements such as the following illustrate how Newman's logic drove him in this direction:

> What is meant by the Church Catholic at this day? Where is she? What are her local instruments and organs? how does she speak? when and where does she teach, forbid, command, censure? how can she be said to utter one and the same doctrine every where, when we are at war with all the rest of Christendom, and not at peace at home? In the Primitive Church there was no difficulty, and no mistaking; then all Christians every where spoke one and the same doctrine, and if any novelty arose, it was at once denounced and stifled. The case is the same, indeed, with the Roman Church now; but for Anglo-catholics so to speak, is to use words without meaning, to dream of a state of things long past away from this Protestant land.[33]

It is worth noting that in this second edition of the *Lectures* (1840), following the above emphasis on visible authority, Newman renamed "Anglicanism" "Anglo-Catholicism." In this vein, Newman and his fellow Tractarians contended that it was necessary to look back *before* the sixteenth-century context of Thomas Cranmer, Hugh Latimer, and Nicholas Ridley in appreciation of the Catholic deposit of the early church.[34] With such a vision, Newman sought to strengthen the church to withstand the theological perils of the moment by inculcating an informed commitment to "Apostolical Succession" and "the Liturgy."[35]

While limitations of space do not permit us to explore the development of Newman's *via media* through the Oxford movement, I would argue that by July 1833, when the movement started (dated from Keble's assize sermon),[36] Newman already possessed the fundamental convictions that would lead him to Rome. This basically consisted of regeneration understood in the context of sacramental objectivity and the authority of the church institution. Therefore, we now switch gears from presenting this portion of Newman's historical narrative to considering the specific forces that motivated his conversion to Rome.

Crossing the Tiber

Newman's conversion to Roman Catholicism in 1845, like all spiritual conversions, consisted of a "push" and a "pull." There was a certain discontent with Anglicanism, which effectively pushed him into the Tiber River, and a thirst for what Catholicism had to offer, which pulled him to the other side. To be sure, he faced obstacles along the way but none so great as to deter his progress. We now consider each of these actions in turn: a major push, a pull, and a formidable deterrent that he overcame.

---

33. Newman, *Lectures on the Prophetical Office*, 317–18.
34. Newman's infamous opposition to the construction of the Martyrs' Memorial, the broad contours of which are helpfully outlined by Ian Ker, bears eloquent testimony to this fact. Ker, *John Henry Newman*, 172–73.
35. Thomas L. Sheridan, *Newman on Justification: A Theological Biography* (New York: Alba, 1967), 214.
36. Keble's sermon underscored the struggle for church identity in the face of government intervention, a theme that would remain central to the Tractarian movement. Geoffrey Rowell, *The Vision Glorious: Themes and Personalities of the Catholic Revival in Anglicanism* (New York: Oxford University Press, 1983), 4.

As noted, through his study of the post-Nicene Fathers, Newman grew uncertain about whether Anglicanism could be properly called "catholic." Was it *truly* universal? These doubts took root in 1839, when he read an article by Roman Catholic Cardinal Nicholas Wiseman in the *Dublin Review* in which he compared Anglicans to African Donatists during the time of Augustine—a splinter group that was more parochial than catholic. Reflecting on this question over time, Newman began to correlate the Church of England with the heretical Arians of the fourth century. In Newman's mind, Anglicanism failed the catholic test. Here is how Newman put it:

> My stronghold was Antiquity; now here, in the middle of the fifth century, I found, as it seemed to me, Christendom of the sixteenth and the nineteenth centuries reflected. I saw my face in the mirror, and I was a Monophysite. The Church of the Via Media [*sic*] was in the position of the Oriental communion, Rome was, where she now is; and the Protestants were the Eutychians.[37]

With regard to Catholicism's pull, several features of the Roman church attracted Newman: the church's claim on catholicity, a rich and textured liturgy, clerical celibacy (a discipline to which he had committed himself at a young age), and an authoritative magisterium. Most of all, perhaps, Newman was attracted to the objective character of sacramental rites, an attraction that had been building for many years in opposition to his personal experience of evangelical Protestantism.[38]

Newman also faced obstacles in his conversion to Rome. A part of Catholicism that deeply troubled Newman was its subbiblical "superstition" and religious accretions such as papal primacy, devotion to the Blessed Virgin and the saints, veneration of relics, purgatory, monastic vows, and the like. For instance, writing in his journal from Palermo on June 13, 1833, Newman recorded the following impression of the Catholic Church during his visit to Italy as an Anglican:

> Oh that thy creed were sound!
>   For thou dost soothe the heart, Thou Church of Rome
> By thy unwearied watch and varied round
> Of service, in thy Saviour's holy name.[39]

This author read the above lines a few years ago when visiting Rome. Like Newman, I, too, was struck by the city's beauty and significance, if only I could be persuaded of its Roman Catholic theology. Well, Newman found a way. In his *Essay on the Development of Christian Doctrine*, which he wrote in 1845 (the year of his conversion), Newman addressed his doubt by reasoning that external religious traditions develop gradually, like an acorn becoming a tree. Similar to what Charles Darwin would say in

---

37. Newman, *Apologia*, 116.
38. According to Ian Ker, "The blame [for reducing faith to unhealthy subjectivity] is laid squarely on Evangelical Christianity, which directs 'its attention to the heart itself; not to anything external to us, whether creeds, actions, or ritual,' and which is really a specious form or trusting man rather than God." Ker, *John Henry Newman*, 122.
39. John Henry Newman, *Verses on Various Occasions* (London: Longmans Green, 1903), 153.

his classic work *On the Origin of Species*, Newman explained how a subject develops and matures.[40] This enabled him to embrace the Catholic tradition in those places where it seemed to lack explicit biblical witness.

So what were the specific forces that motivated Newman's conversion to Rome? In summary, they were twofold: ecclesiology and soteriology. In the first place, he was attracted to the Christian institution that he found to have the most legitimate claim to apostolic succession. Concerning the latter, he embraced a sacramentally objective system of salvation that stressed internal sanctification (as opposed to what Newman regarded as the subjective and lackadaisical doctrine of imputation and *sola fide*). In reaching these conclusions, Newman jettisoned his *via media* for a *via Romana*.

Peter Martyr Vermigli

A fascinating contrast to Newman's story can be seen in the conversion experience of Peter Martyr Vermigli. Interestingly, Vermigli's pursuit of Christ's saving presence surfaces the same two concerns seen in Newman—the appropriation of apostolic authority and the precise way sinners experience saving faith. However, unlike Newman, Vermigli concluded that the supreme form of Christian authority is *sola scriptura* (Scripture alone) and that the means by which one receives Christ's righteousness is *sola fide* (faith alone). Here is a brief look at how Vermigli's conversion occurred.

Vermigli's Conversion from Roman Catholicism

On October 28, 1542, Martin Bucer wrote a letter to John Calvin announcing, "A man has arrived from Italy who is quite learned in Latin, Greek, and Hebrew and well skilled in the Scriptures. . . . His name is Peter Martyr."[41] From north of the Alps, it may have appeared that Peter Martyr Vermigli emerged on the scene *ex nihilo*. However, by this time (at age forty-three), the curriculum vitae of Italy's foremost theologian and exegete was extensive, and as Bucer and Calvin would soon discover, it was already rooted in Reformed theology.

Born in Florence in 1499, Peter Martyr Vermigli acquired his name from the thirteenth-century Dominican martyr of Verona. Thus, contrary to what one would naturally assume, our Peter Martyr was in fact not a martyr but was simply named after one. He went against his father's wishes by joining an Augustinian order in 1514. On account of his intellectual promise, Vermigli was transferred in 1519 to a monastery near Padua, where he graduated as a doctor of divinity in 1526. Immediately after graduation, he was employed as a public preacher in Brescia, Pisa, Venice, and Rome. In his intervals of leisure, he mastered the languages of Greek and Hebrew. So distinguished did Vermigli's ministry become that his Augustinian order described him

---

40. Avery Cardinal Dulles rightly cautions us against drawing too close a connection to Darwin's work since Newman opposed the "transformist" notion that Christianity is in flux and accommodates itself. *John Henry Newman*, 74.
41. "Advenit ex Italia vir quidam graece, hebraice et latine admodum doctus, et in scripturis feliciter versatus. . . . Petro Martyri nomen est." Martin Bucer to John Calvin, 28 October 1542, in Jean Calvin, *Ioannis Calvini opera quae supersunt omnia*, ed. Guilielmus Baum, Eduardus Cunitz, and Eduardus Reuss, vol. 11, CR 39 (Brunsviga: C. A. Schwetschke, 1873), sec. 430.

as *Predicatorem eximium* ("an exceptional preacher").[42] Philip McNair suggests that it was during this period that the activity of preaching and teaching started him on a trajectory that would eventually estrange Vermigli's mind from his scholastic training:

> From the Schoolmen he turned to the Fathers, from the Fathers to the Vulgate, and from the Vulgate to the Source itself—the lively Oracles of God in their original expression. At Padua he had learned Greek to read Aristotle: at Bologna he learned Hebrew to read Scripture.[43]

As his name grew famous in the largest Italian cities, Vermigli was promoted to an even higher position. He was assigned to a new post as abbot of San Pietro ad Aram in Naples. Josias Simler (1530–1576), Vermigli's eventual successor at Zurich and biographer, identifies Naples as the place where Vermigli's theological journey turned an evangelical corner: "In this city the grace of divine illumination began to shine on him more brightly and clearly."[44] According to Frank James, "There is little doubt that [Simler's account] understood this 'greater light of God's truth' to be the doctrine of justification by faith alone."[45] Interestingly, Simler also notes that during this time in Naples, Vermigli "fell into a serious and deadly sickness."[46] We can only speculate how this may have factored into his conversion.

In Naples, Vermigli belonged to a group of evangelical disciples consisting of high-ranking Italian prelates, women of nobility, and literati who gathered to study the Bible with particular attention to justification by faith alone.[47] Pietro Carnesecchi, who was part of this circle, described these gatherings as *regno di Dio* ("the kingdom of God").[48] According to Simler, it was at this time that Vermigli acquired books by Reformed theologians such as Martin Bucer and Huldrych Zwingli.[49] As his study of Reformed theology developed, so did his public exposition of Scripture.[50] His gift for biblical preaching drew a great deal of attention, especially when it occasionally clashed with common interpretations of the Catholic tradition. Here is how Simler describes one such incident from the Neapolitan period:

> For he began to interpret publicly Saint Paul's first letter to the Corinthians and did so with great fruit. Not only the fellow members of the community listened to him but

---

42. Philip McNair, *Peter Martyr in Italy: An Anatomy of Apostasy* (Oxford: Clarendon, 1967), 192.
43. McNair, *Peter Martyr in Italy*, 124–25.
44. Josias Simler, "Oration on the Life and Death of the Good Man and Outstanding Theologian, Doctor Peter Martyr Vermigli, Professor of Sacred Letters at the Zurich Academy," in *Life, Letters, and Sermons*, trans. and ed. John Patrick Donnelly, vol. 5 of *Peter Martyr Library*, SCES 42 (Kirksville, MO: Thomas Jefferson University Press, 1999), 19.
45. Frank A. James III, "*De Iustificatione*: The Evolution of Peter Martyr Vermigli's Doctrine of Justification" (PhD diss., Westminster Theological Seminary, 2000), 1. James is echoing the assessment of McNair, who states that the dawning light of God's truth was "the doctrine of justification by Faith alone in a crucified yet living Christ. The acceptance of this vital doctrine entailed so drastic a reorientation of heart and mind that it amounted to conversion." McNair, *Peter Martyr in Italy*, 179.
46. Simler, "Life," 22. The disease is thought to have been malaria.
47. Paul F. Grendler, "Religious Restlessness in Sixteenth-Century Italy," *Canadian Catholic Historical Association* 33 (1966): 27.
48. José C. Nieto, *Juan de Valdés and the Origins of the Spanish and Italian Reformation*, THR 108 (Geneva: Librairie Droz, 1970), 148.
49. Simler, "Life," 20.
50. Simler, "Life," 20–21.

also some bishops and many nobles, for as you know that city was always the place of residence for noble and famous men. But when the words of Paul found in the third chapter of his letter, "Fire will test what sort of work each one has done . . . ," he interpreted them contrary to the received opinion, [thus stirring] up against him many adversaries and enemies. The common view was that by these words the fires of purgatory were established and confirmed.[51]

With this new, Protestant theology, Vermigli moved northward in May 1541 to become prior of the rich and influential monastery on Saint Frediano in the Republic of Lucca. It was there that he initiated a series of educational and ecclesiastical reforms that, in the words of McNair, amounted to an "ideological revolution," so much that "Lucca came perilously near to civic reformation on the pattern of Calvin's Geneva."[52] But after a mere fifteen months of such reform, Pope Paul III hastened its demise by reinstituting the Roman Inquisition. Recognizing discretion as the better part of valor, Vermigli renounced his vows and made the difficult decision to flee his homeland.[53] When he finally crossed through the Rhaetian Alps and arrived at Zurich in the fall of 1542, he was welcomed by Heinrich Bullinger (1504–1575) and company. Unfortunately, there were no positions open in Zurich. Eventually, Vermigli accepted an invitation to teach in Strasbourg, where he succeeded the late Wolfgang Capito as professor of divinity.

Vermigli the Reformed Theologian

Simler explains that it was "that good and learned man" Martin Bucer who arranged for Vermigli's academic appointment to the College of Saint Thomas at Strasbourg.[54] The Italian exile was expected to "teach sacred letters," which he proceeded to do from the twelve books of the Minor Prophets, Lamentations, Genesis, Exodus, and a large part of Leviticus.[55] James notes, "Certainly, upon his arrival, Vermigli's theological perspective was judged acceptable to the Reformers of Strasbourg."[56] It wasn't long before Vermigli's notoriety as a teacher of Reformed theology ascended to the stature of Bucer and, in the estimation of some, even surpassed him.[57]

---

51. Simler, "Life," 21.
52. Philip McNair, "Biographical Introduction," in *Early Writings: Creed, Scripture, and Church*, ed. Joseph C. McLelland, trans. Mariano Di Gangi, vol. 1 of *Peter Martyr Library*, SCES 30 (Kirksville, MO: Truman State University Press, 1994), 7.
53. It was on the basis of Matt. 10:23, which provides sanction for Christians to flee persecution, that Peter Martyr and Bernardino Ochino chose to leave their beloved homeland. Joseph C. McLelland, *The Visible Words of God: An Exposition of the Sacramental Theology of Peter Martyr Vermigli, A.D. 1500–1562* (Edinburgh: Oliver & Boyd, 1957), 9. For an interesting treatment of Vermigli's theology of exile, see Jason Zuidema, "Flight from Persecution and the Honour of God in the Theology of Peter Martyr Vermigli," *RRR* 15, no. 1 (2013): 112–16.
54. Simler, "Life," 28.
55. Simler, "Life," 28. In a personal letter to Heinrich Bullinger in 1551, Vermigli corroborated Simler's account by mentioning these books vis-à-vis his Strasbourg lectures (except for Lamentations). About them he wrote, "But if it please God to spare my life, and I should obtain leisure, I shall not object to publish them." Peter Martyr Vermigli, "Letter CCXXXII, Peter Martyr to Henry Bullinger," in *Original Letters Relative to the English Reformation, 1531–1558*, ed. Hastings Robinson (Cambridge: Cambridge University Press, 1846–1847), 2:499.
56. James, *"De Iustificatione,"* 155.
57. In Simler's words, "[Vermigli] seemed in the judgment of all not just to match Bucer but to surpass him." "Life," 29.

After five fruitful years of teaching in Strasbourg (where he also married a former nun from Metz named Catherine Dammartin), Vermigli recognized the potential threat of doctrinal censuring (in what was to become the Augsburg Interim).[58] Thankfully, liberation soon arrived in the form of an invitation from Archbishop Thomas Cranmer to help fortify the nascent Church of England with Protestant theology. Shortly after Vermigli arrived in England, King Edward VI approved him as Regius Professor of Divinity at Oxford University and bestowed on him the honor of doctor of divinity.[59] Along with Martin Bucer (who arrived in the autumn of 1549 to occupy the Regius Chair at Cambridge),[60] Vermigli was chosen for the express purpose of implementing a Reformed vision.[61]

With this brief look at Vermigli's background, we now examine the motivational underpinnings of his conversion in terms of his "push" and his "pull," to see where the lines of continuity and difference fall compared to Newman. Perhaps the biggest push for Vermigli was his troubled conscience in having to teach and observe unbiblical "superstitions" over Scripture. He made this point, for example, in a letter dated December 25, 1542, to Italian friends whom he left behind in Lucca after fleeing the peninsula:

> Besides, you are hardly unaware of the tortures which tormented my conscience because of the way of life which I was following [as a Catholic priest]. I had to live with countless superstitions every day; not only did I have to perform superstitious rites, but also I had to demand harshly that others do many things which were contrary to what I was thinking and teaching. I was your pastor; I did what I was able to accomplish by sermons and lectures since I was not able to govern the church in the way that Christian truth demands. I thought it better to leave such a demanding profession and to betake myself to a place from which I could at least encourage you by letter rather than to remain.[62]

A few years later, on February 14, 1556, Vermigli made a similar point in a letter to leaders of the Reformed church in Poland. He sought to encourage his brethren in the gospel as they faced active opposition from the Catholic majority and from radical Protestants by underscoring the biblical orientation of Christian faith:

> When I say *faith*, I do not understand by it that faith which people have fabricated by their cleverness, by a figment of their imagination, or a judgment of human prudence. I mean a faith which, as Paul taught, comes from hearing, not just any hearing, but only that of God's word, as we already have gathered by God's grace in the divine letters. I add this because there are people about everywhere who are not ashamed to dilute and adulterate it.[63]

---

58. Charles V's victory at Mühlberg on April 24, 1547, over the Lutheran Schmalkaldic League was probably the writing on the wall. The Augsburg Interim became imperial law on June 30, 1548.
59. Claire Cross, "Oxford and the Tudor State, 1509–1558," in *The Collegiate University*, ed. James McConica, vol. 3 of *The History of the University of Oxford*, ed. T. H. Aston (Oxford: Oxford University Press, 1986), 133–35.
60. Cross, "Oxford and the Tudor State," 134.
61. This was especially true with regard to the doctrine of the Eucharist. McLelland, *Visible Words of God*, 16.
62. Vermigli to the Church at Lucca, December 25, 1542, in Donnelly, *Life, Letters, and Sermons*, 19, 100.
63. Vermigli to the Reformed Church in Poland, February 14, 1556, in Donnelly, *Life, Letters, and Sermons*, 143.

You don't have to read much Vermigli to realize that his entire ministry revolved around the exposition of Scripture. Hans Asper's painting of Vermigli, which hangs in the National Portrait Gallery in London, testifies to this fact. In it, Vermigli's penetrating eyes look to the distance beyond the gilded frame while he points to a single book in his hand: the Bible. If we were to place a statement on Vermigli's lips, it would perhaps be his exhortation for youth to study Scripture above all else. In Vermigli's words, "Let us immerse ourselves constantly in the sacred Scriptures, let us work at reading them, and by the gift of Christ's Spirit the things that are necessary for salvation will be for us clear, direct, and completely open."[64] When the order of Scripture and tradition is confused, as Vermigli perceived to be the case among his interlocutors, he objected in forceful terms. Thus, he wrote, "We have certain adversaries who judge little or nothing at all on the basis of the Holy Scriptures, but measure all their religion by the Fathers and councils, so much that they can be called *Patrologi* instead of *Theologi*."[65] With regard to church councils, Vermigli asserted that they "should not be heard without selectivity and judgment. We ought to receive and reverence only those councils which have kept their doctrine within the rule of Holy Scriptures."[66]

A major pull for Vermigli revolved around his sense of calling to preach the gospel scripturally and to equip pastors for the same. The following quotation from his *Locus on Justification* elucidates this point. Notice how it contrasts Vermigli's gospel-centered ministry from the Catholic approach he had left behind vis-à-vis the "keys" of the kingdom:

> The preaching of the word of God concerning the forgiveness of sins to be obtained by Christ is the only key to open the kingdom of heaven, and if he who hears this Word also joins it with a true faith and fully assents to these words, then he adds the other key. By these two keys the kingdom of heaven is opened and the forgivness of sins obtained. Therefore, sending forth his apostles, Christ said: "Go and preach the Gospel," then added, "He who believes shall be saved." By these few words he describes the keys which he delivered to the church. In these words one will find no work done (*opus operantum*), as they call it, for Christ commends only the faith of the hearers and the word of God by which faith is preached.[67]

Reflecting on Vermigli's conversion, McNair has memorably stated that during his Neapolitan residency, Vermigli was "half mortified by fever [but] . . . wholly justified

---

64. Peter Martyr Vermigli, "Exhortation for Youths to Study Sacred Letters," in Donnelly, *Life, Letters, and Sermons*, 281.
65. Pietro Martire Vermigli, *In epistolam S. Pauli apostoli ad Romanos commentarii*. . . . (Basel: Petrum Perna, 1560), 1236. For the English translation, see Peter Martyr Vermigli, *Predestination and Justification: Two Theological Loci*, trans. and ed. Frank A. James III, vol. 8 of *Peter Martyr Library*, SCES 68 (Kirksville, MO: Truman State University Press, 2003), 143. Hereafter, Vermigli's *Locus on Justification* is listed as *Romanos*, followed in brackets by pages from James's English translation.
66. Vermigli, *Romanos*, 1245–47 [152–55]. Because Vermigli's central concern is the problem of Pelagianism, he cites councils that explicitly renounce it, namely Milevis (AD 416) and the Second Council of Orange (AD 529).
67. Vermigli, *Romanos*, 1235 [141–42]. To get a sense of Martyr's commitment to training pastors and church leaders in this gospel-centered approach, see his orations to students in *Life, Letters, and Sermons*, where Donnelly has translated two speeches from Oxford (287–308), one from Strasbourg (309–20), and Martyr's inaugural oration from Zurich (321–34).

by faith."[68] It was from this turning point that Vermigli crossed the Tiber to the shore of Reformed theology without looking back.

To what extent, however, did Vermigli retain Catholic doctrine as a Protestant Reformer? Surely he didn't jettison all of it. And for that matter, how much Reformed theology did Newman bring with him into the Catholic Church? Answers to such questions promise insight into specific areas where contemporary Catholics and Reformed may agree and where we must necessarily disagree. In the following sections, therefore, we seek to gain such insight by comparing Newman and Vermigli[69] with occasional reference to the Council of Trent's "Decree on Justification" and the modern *Catechism of the Catholic Church*.

Doctrinal Agreement among Catholics and Protestants

The conversion experiences of Newman and Vermigli reflect the realities of their respective faith journeys, which boil down to a longing to encounter the saving presence of Christ. This melodic line runs through the whole of their lives. It is captured, for instance, in the slogan of Newman's coat of arms, *cor ad cor loquitur* ("heart speaks to heart"), in which his emphasis on the incarnation and divine presence leads him to accent a heart-to-heart relationship with God through his church.[70] And it is also observed in Vermigli's pursuit of union with Christ, or *Christoformia*, as he called it in a letter to Calvin in 1555.[71] Because of this desire, the Catholic Newman and the Reformed Vermigli maintained an important set of common commitments.

First, the continuity between them consists in a commitment to finding and propagating Christian faith in its most biblically rooted, historically attested, and philosophically coherent form. Such a vision motivated their exegesis of Scripture, always sensitive to the larger context of Christian tradition, a tradition that foregrounded justification's Trinitarian shape—that the Father declares sinful man to be righteous on the merits and saving grace of Christ by the regenerating work of the Holy Spirit.[72] And they recognized the aim of salvation to be the realization of holiness by the power of the Spirit in service of the glory of God.[73]

Probing into some of the issues that motivated their crossing the Tiber, we find Newman and Vermigli both opposing *cheap grace*. Since Newman read the Protestants of his day as reducing the entire doctrine of justification to *merely* imputation, he emphasized the importance of virtue, an inner renewal that generates spiritual fruit.[74] The reason for the Protestant error, according to Newman, was the popular belief in justification

---

68. McNair, *Peter Martyr in Italy*, 179.
69. An excellent place in which to examine Vermigli's theological priorities is his commentary on *Romans*. Following chap. 11 is his *Locus on Justification*, where he articulates his Reformed creed in opposition to the Council of Trent. As it turns out, Newman also wrote a treatise on justification, in which he likewise articulates his position over against the tradition from which he had come. Therefore, we draw primarily from these texts in our comparison.
70. Charles Stephen Dessain, *The Spirituality of John Henry Newman* (Minneapolis: Winston, 1980), 33–34.
71. McNair, "Biographical Introduction," 24.
72. *Catechism of the Catholic Church*, 2nd ed. (Vatican City: Libreria Editrice Vaticana, 1997), §§1988–95.
73. *Catechism of the Catholic Church*, §1992.
74. Newman, *Justification*, 63 [112].

by *sola fide*, which he regarded as a direct route to antinomianism.[75] For Vermigli, *sola fide* was not the problem but the solution, as his doctrine of justification labors to prove. Nevertheless, while arguing for faith alone, Vermigli simultaneously insisted (with other Reformers) that such faith can never *remain* alone:[76]

> We do not say that faith through which we are justified is in our minds without good works, though we do say that the same "only" is that which takes hold of justification and the remission of sins. The eye cannot be without a head, brains, heart, liver, and other parts of the body, and yet the eye alone apprehends color and light. Therefore, those who reason against us in this way commit the error of false argument: faith (as they say) justifies; but faith is not alone; ergo faith alone does not justify.[77]

Furthermore, Vermigli, like Calvin, affirmed that the virtuous life (or good works) of the one who is justified is acceptable to God: "We have never denied that the works of those now justified are acceptable to God."[78] According to Vermigli, God accepts[79] and rewards[80] Christian works as the fruit of final justification, an understanding that resonates with Calvin's conviction: "For we dream neither of a faith devoid of good works nor of a justification that stands without them."[81] Having entered into union with Christ, one undergoes the sanctifying work of the Spirit, which results in a virtuous life.

Anthony Lane has explained the logic of this doctrine, the so-called "double justification," noting that "God both accepts and rewards the good works of the justified believer, in addition to accepting the believer himself."[82] As such persons are engrafted into Christ, their blemished works are covered by Christ's perfection, which causes the shortcomings of those works to be expunged. In addition to explaining how genuinely good (but flawed) works may be pleasing to God,[83] the doctrine of double justification enabled Calvin and Vermigli to explain the range of biblical data, including the teaching of James, which portrays God as rewarding human works. The difference between them, however, is that while Calvin does not employ justification language to describe internal renewal or the rewarding of human works (Calvin categorically distinguishes the event of justification from the process of sanctification, his so-called

---

75. Sheridan, *Newman on Justification*, 26–29, 265.
76. Vermigli, *Romanos*, 1307 [212]. Quoting Jerome, Vermigli writes, "'If love is absent, faith also departs with it.' These words clearly declare that his judgment was that true faith cannot be divided from love, something we also teach and defend."
77. Vermigli, *Romanos*, 1312 [218].
78. Vermigli, *Romanos*, 1227–28 [134]. Cf. John Calvin, *Institutes of the Christian Religion*, ed. John T. McNeill, trans. Ford Lewis Battles, LCC 20–21 (Philadelphia: Westminster, 1960), 3.17.5, 10.
79. Vermigli, *Romanos*, 1227–28 [134]; cf. *In Selectissimam D. Pauli Apostoli Priorem ad Corinthios Epistolam Commentarii* (Zurich: Christophorum Froschouerum, 1579), 19.
80. Vermigli, *Romanos*, 1288 [195].
81. Calvin, *Institutes*, 3.16.1. Or the Westminster Confession states, "Faith, thus receiving and resting on Christ and His righteousness, is the alone instrument of justification: yet is it not alone in the person justified, but is ever accompanied with all other saving graces, and is no dead faith, but works by love." Westminster Confession of Faith 11.2.
82. Anthony N. S. Lane, *Justification by Faith in Catholic-Protestant Dialogue: An Evangelical Assessment* (London: T&T Clark, 2002), 33.
83. While Calvin does not speak of believers as "justified by work," he describes acceptance "by reason of works." *Calvin's Commentaries: The Acts of the Apostles 1–13*, trans. John Fraser and W. J. G. McDonald, ed. David W. Torrance and Thomas F. Torrance (Edinburgh: Saint Andrews Press, 1965), 308–9.

"double grace"), Vermigli is quite comfortable using justification language in this sense.[84] James helpfully summarizes:

> In sum, Vermigli embraces both a narrower and stricter forensic understanding of justification, as well as a broader moral understanding, which stresses the necessary relationship between forensic justification and its accompanying benefits of regeneration and sanctification. Forensic justification, which is based on the imputed righteousness of Christ alone, is necessarily accompanied by the regenerative work of the Holy Spirit, which produces a moral transformation in the sinner, which in turn inevitably produces sanctification and good works.[85]

In addition to opposing cheap grace, Newman and Vermigli also repudiated *works righteousness*. From Newman's perspective, Roman Catholic soteriology was vulnerable to this critique. He regarded the doctrine of *gratia inhaerens* ("inherent grace") as potentially reducing justification to a matter of meritorious works, a move that he considered detrimental to the development of personal faith.[86] We must acknowledge, however, that Trent was likewise concerned to avoid works righteousness. Chapter 8 of the Council's "Decree on Justification," for instance, explicitly states that justification comes as a "free gift," and does so on the perennial consent of the Catholic Church, on the basis of faith, "without which 'it is impossible to please God'" (Heb. 11:6).[87]

Concern for the practical liabilities of meritorious works vis-à-vis unhealthy introspection was unsurprisingly shared by Vermigli:

> Certainly no one understands except those who have experienced how difficult it is for a bruised heart, dejected and weary with the burden of sins to find comfort. . . . If we, like the Sophists, commanded a person to have regard for his own works, then he would never find comfort, would always be tormented, always in doubt of his salvation and finally, be swallowed up with desperation.[88]

In addition to cautioning against the danger of falling in "desperation" beneath the righteous requirement of God, Vermigli and Newman also identified the tendency toward impersonal worship in the Catholic tradition. For instance, Newman viewed much of popular Romanism as promoting a sort of religious transaction, an exchange of "the [mere] influence of grace, not as the operations of a living God, but as something to bargain about, and buy, and traffic."[89] Vermigli also addressed what he regarded as the impersonal nature of the Roman Catholic system when he contrasted the ritualistic

---

84. Cornelis P. Venema, "Calvin's Understanding of the 'Twofold Grace of God' and Contemporary Ecumenical Discussion of the Gospel," *MJT* 18 (2007): 67–105.
85. Frank A. James III, "Romans Commentary: Justification and Sanctification," in *A Companion to Peter Martyr Vermigli*, ed. W. J. Torrance Kirby, Emidio Campi, and Frank A. James III, BCCT 16 (Leiden: Brill, 2009), 314.
86. Newman, *Justification*, 190 [220].
87. "Decree on Justification," chap. 8, in *Decrees of the Ecumenical Councils*, ed. Norman P. Tanner, vol. 2, *Trent to Vatican II* (London: Sheed and Ward, 1990), 674.
88. Vermigli, *Romanos*, 1208 [114].
89. Newman, *Justification*, 186–87 [216–17].

function of the Petrine "keys" with the preaching of the word, appropriated by personal faith.[90]

Newman and Vermigli were also concerned to protect the dignity of the "church." However, their understanding of the church, particularly how it functions as the organ of divine authority and revelation, differed significantly. From his early days at Oriel College and into Catholicism, Newman located authority in the church hierarchy—an authority that he regarded as having come through apostolic succession.[91] As noted earlier, it was under Edward Hawkins's influence that Newman came to regard doctrinal instruction as primarily residing in the formularies of the church, that is, the catechism and the creeds.[92] Thus, whereas Vermigli looked supremely to Scripture as the locus of divine authority and revelation, Newman emphasized the church's hierarchically derived mission.[93] The fundamental nature of this distinction is of such profound importance for understanding many of the differences between Roman Catholics and Reformed Protestants that we must consider it more carefully.

The Church as Organ of Authority and Revelation

The Catholic tradition articulates Newman's emphasis on ecclesial authority by invoking the concept of "continuous incarnation,"[94] a term that describes the way Christ's authority subsists in and extends through her teaching and sacramental life, that is, how the incarnated presence of Jesus (the "Head") is manifested or prolongated in his church (the "members").[95] "Incarnation," in this sense, is not simply a historical event from two millennia ago; it is, according to Rome, the continuous bond that makes the church a single subject with Christ.[96]

During the sixteenth century, Catholic thinkers addressed the notion of ecclesial incarnation by describing their church as a perfect society (*societas perfecta*) or a specific type of human community (*coetus hominum*).[97] In this vein, Robert Bellarmine contrasts his Catholic definition of the church over against five "heretical" models of the church promulgated by various Protestants. He writes, "The one true Church is the community

---

90. Vermigli, *Romanos*, 1234–35 [141–42].
91. Avery Cardinal Dulles provides an incisive overview of Newman's ecclesiology in "Authority in the Church," in *The Cambridge Companion to John Henry Newman*, ed. Ian Ker and Terrence Merrigan, CCR (Cambridge: Cambridge University Press, 2009), 170–88.
92. Newman, *Apologia*, 9.
93. Newman's sermon "The Visible Church an Encouragement to Faith," a message published in 1836, makes this point. *Parochial and Plain Sermons*, 633–43. See also Newman's sermon "The Communion of Saints." *Parochial and Plain Sermons*, 839–49. Newman understood the church and the kingdom of God to be synonymous. Philip Flanagan, *Newman, Faith, and the Believer* (Westminster, MD: Newman Bookshop, 1946), 285, 311.
94. Sebastian Tromp, *Corpus Christi, Quod Est Ecclesia*, trans. Ann Condit (New York: Vantage, 1960), 194.
95. A contemporary example is found in Robert Barron, *Catholicism: A Journey to the Heart of the Faith* (New York: Image Books, 2011), 3. An older work that develops this idea is Émilien Lamirande, *The Communion of Saints*, trans. A. Manson (New York: Hawthorn Books, 1963), 73.
96. While Catholic theologians have employed the term "simple subject," it should be noted that it is not a single subject simply speaking. For instance, one cannot attribute the sins of the church to Christ. Joseph Cardinal Ratzinger, *Principles of Catholic Theology: Building Stones for Fundamental Theology*, trans. Mary Frances McCarthy (San Francisco: Ignatius, 1987), 44–47, 245. Some works that draw on this theme are Henri de Lubac, *Catholicism: A Study of Dogma in Relation to the Corporate Destiny of Mankind*, trans. Lancelot C. Sheppard (London: Burns, Oates & Washbourne, 1950); David Tracy, *The Analogical Imagination: Christian Theology and the Culture of Pluralism* (New York: Crossroad, 1981); Tromp, *Corpus Christi, Quod Est Ecclesia*.
97. "Perfect society" does not mean moral perfection. It refers to a society containing within it everything necessary for its life.

of men brought together by the profession of the same Christian faith and conjoined in the communion of the same sacraments, under the government of the legitimate pastors and especially the one vicar of Christ on earth, the Roman pontiff."[98] Please note how Bellarmine's definition eliminates from the church everyone who is not in visible communion with the Roman pontiff.

The institutional self-understanding of the Catholic Church reached its apex in Vatican I (1869–1870), which more explicity emphasized the concept of a perfect society:

> We teach and declare: The Church has all the marks of a true Society. Christ did not leave this society undefined and without a set form. Rather, he himself gave its existence, and his will determined the form of its existence and gave it its constitution. The Church is not part nor member of any other society and is not mingled in any way with any other society. It is so perfect in itself that it is distinct from all human societies and stands far above them.[99]

As decades unfolded into the twentieth century, the church's institutional conception was augmented by the idea of mystical communion. This emphasis came to a head in 1943 when Pope Pius XII published his encyclical *Mystici Corporis Christi* (*On the Mystical Body of Christ*). In this vision, the image of the body of Christ on earth coalesces with the societal concept, highlighting the unity of its members. As in the institutional model, however, there remain clear lines of demarcation separating insiders from outsiders: "Actually only those are to be included as members of the Church who have been baptized and profess the true faith, and who have not been so unfortunate as to separate themselves from the unity of the Body, or been excluded by legitimate authority for grave faults committed."[100] But within a few decades, Vatican II's *Lumen gentium* would speak about this body without asserting that it is necessarily coterminous with the Roman Catholic Church.[101]

How did Vermigli respond to the Catholic Church's claim to institutional authority? Two brief quotations on this point must suffice, both taken from his *Schism and the True Church*, in which he gives an answer for his ecclesial hope as a Reformed Protestant:

> Let not our adversaries put their confidence in the perpetual continuity of the Church of Rome.[102]

---

98. Roberto Bellarmino, *Disputationum de controversiis Christianae fidei*, vol. 2, bk. 3, *De ecclesia militante*, chap. 2, "De definitione Ecclesiae" (Ingolstadt: David Sartorius, 1588), 147–48.

99. This quotation is taken from Vatican I's preparatory statement on the constitution of the church, translated by Josef Neuner and Heinrich Roos, *The Teaching of the Catholic Church as Contained in Her Documents*, ed. Karl Rahner, trans. Geoffrey Stevens (Staten Island: Alba House, 1967), 213–14.

100. Pope Pius XII, *Mystici corporis Christi* (*Mystical Body of Christ*), sec. 22, Vatican, June 29, 1943, accessed August 15, 2018, http://w2.vatican.va/content/pius-xii/en/encyclicals/documents/hf_p-xii_enc_29061943_mystici-corporis-christi.html.

101. Second Vatican Council, *Lumen gentium* (*Light of the Nations*), sec. 9, Vatican, November 24, 1964, accessed August 15, 2018, http://www.vatican.va/archive/hist_councils/ii_vatican_council/documents/vat-ii_const_19641121_lumen-gentium_en.html. Ian Ker explains that Newman's vision of the church as an organic communion, defined primarily in sacramental terms, anticipated the teaching of the Second Vatican Council. "The Church as Communion," in Ker and Merrigan, *Cambridge Companion to John Henry Newman*, 152–53.

102. Vermigli, *Schism and the True Church*, in McLelland, *Early Writings*, 213.

In parting company with the Romanists, therefore, we have not forsaken the Church but have fled from an intolerable yoke and conspiracy formed against the doctrine of the Gospel.[103]

As one might expect, we find Vermigli giving priority to the sacred Scriptures, accenting the gospel-centered nature of orthodox faith. This leads us to the second fundamental difference between Catholics and Protestants.[104]

The Doctrine of Justification[105]

According to Alister McGrath, the chief elements of the evangelical Protestant outlook on justification coming out of the sixteenth century are threefold: First, justification involves a "forensic *declaration* that the Christian is righteous," that is, a change in one's legal status before God (as opposed to a process of internal renewal by which one is *made* righteous). Second, there is a "deliberate and systematic distinction" between the forensic activity of justification and the internal process of sanctification or regeneration. Third, "justifying righteousness or the formal cause of justification" is alien, external, and imputed.[106]

On the other side of the ecclesial divide, the Roman Catholic Church responded to Protestants by convening the Council of Trent (1545–1563), where it defined its doctrine in the "Decree on Justification" (1547). Repudiating the Protestant view of "faith alone" grounded in the forensic imputation of Christ's righteousness, the Roman church chose to emphasize the "process" of justification in which the gift of righteousness is internally "infused" through her sacraments, a process involving moral virtues and good works as the condition for man's final absolution.[107] As for the contemporary significance of Trent's teaching, Avery Cardinal Dulles explains that the "theology of justification in Roman Catholic teaching has undergone no dramatic changes since the Council of Trent."[108]

---

103. Vermigli, *Schism and the True Church*, 214.

104. Philip Schaff's popular distinction between the "material" and "formal" causes of the Reformation, that is, the doctrine of justification (*principium essendi*) and the normative authority of Scripture (*principium cognoscendi*) helpfully delineates these fundamental differences. *The Principle of Protestantism as Related to the Present State of the Church*, trans. John W. Nevin (Chambersburg, PA: Publication Office of the German Reformed Church, 1845), 54–94.

105. Newman's *Lectures on the Doctrine of Justification*, first published in 1838 while he was an Anglican and later republished in 1874 when he was a Catholic, postures itself as a *via media* between what he perceived to be the extremes of the Protestant and Catholic traditions. Because Newman's doctrine of justification differs from the standard teaching of both traditions (and because space limits us from doing justice to its complexity), we do not address it here except for a few places where he clearly agrees with Trent.

106. Alister E. McGrath, "Forerunners of the Reformation? A Critical Examination of the Evidence for Precursors of the Reformation Doctrines of Justification," *HTR* 75, no. 2 (1982): 219–42; cf. Alister E. McGrath, *Iustitia Dei: A History of the Christian Doctrine of Justification*, 2nd ed. (Cambridge: Cambridge University Press, 1998), 212–13. Berndt Hamm's conclusions support this taxonomy vis-à-vis the ground of justification, imputation, and distinction of justification from sanctification. *The Reformation of Faith in the Context of Late Medieval Theology and Piety*, ed. Robert J. Bast, SHCT 110 (Leiden: Brill, 2004), 192, 194, 196. For the historical antecedents to these characteristics, see Lane, *Justification by Faith*, 138–40.

107. Chapter 7 of the "Decree on Justification" explains "what the justification of the sinner is and what are its causes." In Tanner, *Decrees*, 2:673.

108. Avery Cardinal Dulles, "Justification in Contemporary Theology," in *Justification by Faith*, ed. H. George Anderson, T. Austin Murphy, and Joseph A. Burgess, Lutherans and Catholics in Dialogue 7 (Minneapolis: Augsburg, 1985), 256. I take Dulles's word "dramatic" to mean "substantive." According to Lane, even if the *Joint Declaration on the Doctrine of Justification* (1999) is taken into account, the positive exposition of the Tridentine decree remains incompatible with a Protestant understanding, even though the gap is narrower than it was previously. Lane, *Justification by Faith*, 223.

When comparing the Roman Catholic and Reformed Protestant doctrines of justification, it is clear that the decisive difference comes down to the ground or reason for God's favor, the fundamental cause of divine acceptance.[109] From a Catholic point of view, this is typically described in terms of the "formal cause." By way of definition, the formal cause is an intrinsic component of a subject,[110] the fundamental reality that makes it what it is.[111] Taking its cues from Aristotle's list of four "causes,"[112] the Council of Trent explicated justification's formal cause as follows:

> Finally, the one formal cause [*unica formalis causa*] is the justness of God: not that by which he himself is just, but that by which he makes us just and endowed with which we are renewed in the spirit of our mind, and are not merely considered to be just but are truly named and are just.[113]

The Protestant Reformers were also keen to define salvation's causes.[114] In his *Locus on Justification*, Vermigli agrees with the overall causal framework of Trent in terms of the "final" cause (the glory of God), the "efficient" cause (divine mercy), and the "meritorious" cause (the death and resurrection of Christ).[115] Vermigli then explains that the point of contention is particularly the "formal cause."[116] Unlike Trent, which defined justification's cause in terms of righteousness with which one is counted *and made* just, Vermigli, with Reformed Protestantism, strictly limited the ground of justification to the forensic attribution of righteousness: "Therefore, we say that justification cannot consist in that righteousness and renewal by which we are created anew by God. For it is imperfect because of our corruption, so that we are not able to stand before the judgment of Christ."[117] Peter Toon helpfully summarizes how fundamental is this difference between Catholics and Protestants:

---

109. Edward Yarnold, "*Duplex Iustitia*: The Sixteenth Century and the Twentieth," in *Christian Authority: Essays in Honour of Henry Chadwick*, ed. G. R. Evans (Oxford: Clarendon, 1988), 208; Lane, *Justification by Faith*, 72; Newman, *Justification*, 343; Vermigli, *Predestination and Justification: Two Theological Loci*, 159; Peter Toon, *Evangelical Theology, 1833–1856: A Response to Tractarianism* (London: Marshall, Morgan and Scott, 1979), 145–46.

110. Yarnold, "*Duplex Iustitia*," 208.

111. Lane, *Justification by Faith*, 70. Or as Newman suggests in his extended appendix on the topic, the formal cause comprises a subject's basic constitution. The first edition of Newman's *Lectures on the Doctrine of Justification* (1838) contains a fifty-two-page appendix titled "On the Formal Cause of Justification." Newman, *Justification*, 1st ed., 391–443. The sixty-one-page appendix of the third edition is essentially the same, apart from a few explanatory notes (on pp. 343, 348–49, and 353).

112. In seeking to explain the "why" of a thing, that is, its cause, Aristotle explains changes of movement in terms of its material, formal, efficient, and final causes. *The Physics* 2.3, trans. Philip H. Wicksteed and Francis M. Cornford, LCL 228 (Cambridge, MA: Harvard University Press, 1968), 1:128–31.

113. Tanner, *Decrees*, 673. The causal scheme of Trent, which develops the final, efficient, meritorious, instrumental, and formal causes, varies somewhat from the Aristotelian taxonomy.

114. Richard A. Muller, *Dictionary of Latin and Greek Theological Terms: Drawn Principally from Protestant Scholastic Theology* (Grand Rapids, MI: Baker, 1985), 61. For an explanation of how John Calvin's causal scheme relates to Trent, see Lane, *Justification by Faith*, 68–72.

115. In this section of the *Locus*, Vermigli does not mention Trent's "instrumental cause," namely, the sacrament of baptism. This would have been another point of sharp disagreement since here Vermigli is concerned to uphold faith as the sole means of appropriating the divine forgiveness. *Romanos*, 1252 [159].

116. Vermigli, *Romanos*, 1252 [159].

117. Vermigli, *Romanos*, 1251–52 [159]. Outside of his response to Trent's causal framework, in which he identifies justification's ground as the imputation of Christ's righteousness (1251–52 [159]), Vermigli does not explicitly address the *causa forma*.

On the *formal cause* of justification, that by which God actually pronounces and accepts a sinner as righteous, there had never been agreement. The traditional Roman Catholic position was that at baptism God infuses into the soul his divine grace and that this grace purifies the soul. On seeing this infused righteousness in a human being God accepts him or justifies him. This new grace of the soul is thus the *formal cause* of justification and is at the same time the means of sanctification. With this view Protestant scholars had no sympathy. They argued that once God's grace enters the soul it becomes a human righteousness and no human righteousness is sufficient in quality to be the basis for justification and full acceptance with the eternal God. So they pointed to the external righteousness of Christ the Mediator and argued that his righteousness was imputed or reckoned to the Christian as the *formal cause* of acceptance of justification. Within both of these camps, the Roman and the Protestant, there was a limited variety of teaching within the fixed limits of either the infused, inherent righteousness or the external righteousness of Christ, as the *formal cause*.[118]

Moving beyond conversion into the larger experience of one's justification, Vermigli agreed with Rome that those who have been justified still struggle with "concupiscence"; that is, Christians still possess an inclination toward evil despite the indwelling presence of the Spirit.[119] His difference from Rome on this point centers on the question of its status. Is concupiscence simply an inclination to sin, or is the inclination itself a sin? Vermigli insisted on the latter, recognizing sin as an ongoing obstacle to fellowship with God, which only Christ's imputed righteousness can remedy.[120] By contrast, the Council of Trent, in its "Decree on Original Sin," unequivocally asserted the former—that concupiscence tends toward evil but does not constitute sin.[121]

Disagreement over the status of concupiscence has bearing on another difference between Catholics and Protestants: the instrumental cause or means by which one is justified. Whereas Rome maintains baptismal regeneration as the way a person initially receives forgiveness, Vermigli asserted that forgiveness is accessed by faith alone. Because Rome teaches that in baptism one receives "the forgiveness of all sins and the gift of new life,"[122] it is impossible, in its view, for concupiscence to constitute sin, since two contradictory states cannot simultaneously coexist in a baptized person: the righteousness of God and mortal sin. But for Vermigli, who affirmed the idea of *simul iustus et peccator* (that justified persons are simultaneously righteous and sinner), the only way to appropriate forgiveness is by faith.[123]

---

118. Toon, *Evangelical Theology*, 145–46. It should be pointed out that if one understands the "formal cause" in its Aristotelian sense, as an intrinsic component of a subject, it does not quite correctly describe the Reformed position, which views Christ's righteousness as forensic (and thus not substantial).

119. For instance, Vermigli makes this point from the Lord's Prayer: "Moreover, the Son of God commanded believers to say in their prayers, 'Forgive us our trespasses.' This shows that the faithful also need forgiveness for the things they do, for our works are not perfect nor are they able to satisfy." Vermigli, *Romanos*, 1206 [113].

120. From the beginning of his *Locus*, Vermigli asserts that "'to justify' comes by way of judging or accounting, to ascribe righteousness to someone and not make him just in reality." Vermigli, *Romanos*, 1183 [88–89]; cf. 1194 [100].

121. "Decree on Original Sin," chap. 5, in *Catechism of the Catholic Church*, §1426.

122. *Catechism of the Catholic Church*, §1427.

123. For Vermigli, baptism functions as a covenantal sign akin to circumcision in God's covenant with Israel. *Romanos*, 1251 [158].

Vermigli's wholehearted defense of *sola fide* illustrates its central importance for Reformed Protestantism.[124] His conviction grew out of the belief that one's good works in no way cause justification.[125] It should be noted that contemporary Catholicism is sometimes willing to use the *sola fide* formula in this respect—that God is to be relied on for salvation over oneself.[126] But this should not be confused with the same position for which Vermigli and his fellow Reformers contended. With Trent, modern Catholic thought is eager to uphold the need for a faith formed by love (*fides formata caritate*) in a sacramental framework beginning with baptism. As the *Catechism of the Catholic Church* states, "The grace of the Holy Spirit confers upon us the righteousness of God. Uniting us by faith and Baptism to the Passion and Resurrection of Christ, the Spirit makes us sharers in his life."[127] Simply put, Rome teaches that justifying faith is "alone" over against relying on one's human ability, but it is nevertheless always embedded in meritorious works in the context of sacramental life. In the final analysis, while *sola fide* is not quite as basic a difference as is justification's ground (i.e., the issue of imputation), it remains a major point of division between Catholics and Protestants.

All these differences naturally lead the pilgrim and scholar alike to the matter of assurance. Apart from the possibility of receiving insight through special revelation, the Tridentine fathers denied that one can be assured of persevering to the end.[128] It is only with the special help of God that one can indeed persevere,[129] and present perseverance is always tinged with the possibility of falling away from grace.[130] This notion is reiterated in the *Catechism of the Catholic Church*: "*Mortal sin* destroys charity in the heart of man by a grave violation of God's law; it turns man away from God, who is his ultimate end and his beatitude, by preferring an inferior good to him."[131]

In contrast to the Catholic position, Vermigli argued that one who is justified will most assuredly persevere to the end:

---

124. The third and final section of Vermigli's *Justification Locus* agues that justification "is by faith alone." Vermigli, *Romanos*, 1312–24 [218–30].

125. Vermigli, *Romanos*, 1321 [227]. In his words, "And when we say that one is justified by faith alone we obviously say nothing else than that one is justified only by the mercy of God and by the merit of Christ, which we cannot grasp by any other instrument than faith alone."

126. This is true in Catholic biblical studies and theology alike. Joseph A. Fitzmyer, for instance, argues in his exegesis of Rom. 3:28 that "in this context Paul means [to teach justification] 'by faith alone.'" Fitzmyer also provides support for *sola fide* from Patristic and medieval interpreters. Joseph A. Fitzmyer, *Romans: A New Translation with Introduction and Commentary*, AB 33 (New York: Doubleday, 1993), 360–63. Then in his sermon on justification in Saint Peter's Square on November 19, 2008, Pope Benedict XVI said, "Being just simply means being with Christ and in Christ. And this suffices. Further observances are no longer necessary. For this reason Luther's phrase: 'faith alone' is true, if it is not opposed to faith in charity in love." Pope Benedict XVI, *Saint Paul* (San Francisco: Ignatius, 2009), 82. A week later, on November 26 in the Paul VI Audience Hall, the pontiff continued this emphasis: "Following Saint Paul, we have seen that man is unable to 'justify' himself with his own actions, but can only truly become 'just' before God because God confers his 'justice' upon him, uniting him to Christ his Son. And man obtains this union through faith. In this sense, Saint Paul tells us: not our deeds, but rather faith renders us 'just'" (84). Finally, there is the annex (§2C) to the *Joint Declaration on the Doctrine of Justification*, which states that "Justification takes place 'by grace alone' . . . , by faith alone; the person is justified 'apart from works.'" The Lutheran World Federation and the Roman Catholic Church, *Joint Declaration on the Doctrine of Justification* (Grand Rapids, MI: Eerdmans, 2000), 45.

127. *Catechism of the Catholic Church*, §2017.

128. "Decree on Justification," chap. 13, canon 15, in Tanner, *Decrees*, 2:676, 680.

129. "Decree on Justification," canon 22, in Tanner, *Decrees*, 2:680.

130. "Decree on Justification," canon 23, in Tanner, *Decrees*, 2:680.

131. *Catechism of the Catholic Church*, §1855. For Newman there was also no perseverance. Just as possessing the Spirit amounts to justification, losing the Spirit means that one has jeopardized justification. *Justification*, 151 [168].

In general, it may be stated that faith cannot be completely extinguished because serious sins are committed by the justified and those destined to salvation. In such cases, faith is lulled to sleep and lies hidden and does not burst forth into action unless awakened again by the Holy Spirit. In such fallen ones, the seed of God remains, although for a time it produces no fruit.[132]

If perseverance can hang in the balance, then justification must be subject to contingency. According to Newman, meritorious works can indeed increase as one's apprehension of justification itself (by a greater manifestation of the Spirit).[133] For Trent, it is on account of the merits of Christ being poured into the hearts of those who are justified.[134] In this instance, as with Newman's position, the *process* of justification entails an ongoing appropriation of divine righteousness by which one is increasingly justified. As the *Catechism of the Catholic Church* puts it, "Moved by the Holy Spirit, we can merit for ourselves and for others all the graces needed to attain eternal life."[135]

For Vermigli and the Reformed tradition, the notion that one can in some way merit divine favor before God (*coram Deo*) is unacceptable: "Therefore, we must take away all merit, not only in those who are not yet justified, but also in those who have been justified."[136] To his mind, it is only by the merit of Christ (*solus Christi merito*) that one is accepted by the Father,[137] a conviction that found expression in Vermigli's dying words. According to Simler, in Vermigli's final moments of life, with Heinrich Bullinger and a small band of friends before him, Vermigli "was silent in deep personal reflection; then he turned to us and stated with a rather clear voice that he acknowledged life and salvation in Christ alone, who had been given by the Father to the human race as its only savior."[138] In this Reformed gospel Peter Martyr Vermigli lived and died.

Conversion in Pastoral Perspective

This chapter has noted how conversions across the Tiber are embedded in concrete experiences that are deeply personal, they respond to both push and pull, and they encounter obstacles along the way. These obstacles are challenges that either keep us contained within or catapult us out of a theological system. When a doctrinal position has the power to withstand objections, it undergirds faith as a foundation. On the other hand, when that formulation crumbles in the face of scrutiny, it becomes a doorway.

Recognizing that no two persons share identical conversions, we have nonetheless observed in the experiences of Vermigli and Newman principles that offer insight into the contemporary pattern of conversion, a pattern that is illuminated by the doctrine of justi-

---
132. Vermigli, *Romanos*, 1278 [186].
133. Newman, *Justification*, 151–52 [168–69]. Because justification and sanctification are united in Newman's doctrine and grow together in proportion to God's manifest presence, the believer's meritorious works likewise grow.
134. "Decree on Justification," chap. 7, in Tanner, *Decrees*, 2:673–74.
135. *Catechism of the Catholic Church*, §2027.
136. Vermigli, *Romanos*, 1289 [195].
137. Vermigli, *Romanos*, 1321 [227].
138. Vermigli, *Life, Letters, and Sermons*, 60.

fication. It is the familiar experience of guilt, alienation, and shame in search of a gracious God, a search that reaches back not only to the Reformation but to the garden of Eden, where alienation was born. In this way, the question of Vermigli and Newman—How does one encounter the saving presence of Christ?—proves to be the question of the ages, and the question of every aching heart.

There is, of course, a great deal more that can be said on the subject.[139] As Lewis Rambo explains in his classic work *Understanding Religious Conversion*, the dynamics of conversion are complex, involving a multifaceted process of change with personal, cultural, social, and religious implications.[140] We have focused on the theological and personal dimensions of such movement. In this vein, the following principles are intended to provide insight into the reasons and attendant circumstances of conversion across the Tiber and thus enrich our ability to serve men and women who have undergone such an experience.

Conversion usually consists of twists and turns. As pilgrims on a journey, we often walk through different seasons of belief before landing on a particular position. Newman is said to have experienced three distinct conversions: to evangelicalism (1816), briefly to a Latitudinarian (or Broad Church) form of liberalism (1828), and finally to the Roman Catholic Church (1845). Vermigli also underwent a process of conversion as his thinking and reflection led him to eventually embrace the principles of the Protestant Reformation.

Conversion is deeply personal. This is true on a vertical plane, as seekers make discoveries before the face of a personal God. It also happens horizontally, as men and women develop their thoughts among mentors, friends, and those whom they serve.

Trusted friends exert significant influence on one's conversion. Newman's schoolmaster Walter Mayers was instrumental in his initial conversion and embrace of Calvinism, and Charles Russell facilitated his conversion to Rome. Similarly, Vermigli had the likes of Juán de Valdés, Bernardino Ochino, Giulia Gonzaga, and Pietro Carnesecchi. Furthermore, such friends often provide books that influence the journey. In addition to Mayers feeding Newman the writings of Thomas Scott, it was most likely Russell who introduced Newman to *The Spiritual Exercises of Saint Ignatius*. It was with Valdés that Vermigli devoured the pseudonymous writings of Zwingli and Bucer.

Conversion generally follows a careful evaluation of truth claims. Vermigli and Newman investigated the traditions from which they came and found them wanting. By means of an intellectual assessment, genuine conversion penetrates through mere appetite, inclination, or preference into the realm of propositional truth.

The destination of one's conversion is largely connected to the place where he or she locates apostolic authority. If one looks for authority in apostolic succession and

---

139. This is especially true of Newman. For more on this topic, see Ian Ker, ed., *Newman and Conversion* (Edinburgh: T&T Clark, 1997).
140. Lewis R. Rambo, *Understanding Religious Conversion* (New Haven, CT: Yale University Press, 1993). In addition to taking a much broader sampling, a comprehensive study would also draw from the insights of psychology, sociology, anthropology, history, and missiology.

tradition, he is likely to end up a Catholic (notwithstanding, perhaps, some High Church Anglicans). The one who finds supreme authority in the text of Scripture will be inclined toward Protestantism.

Value is placed on the universality of the church, albeit differently. Catholics such as Newman agree with Bellarmine that universality is found in a common profession of faith, conjoined in the communion of the Catholic sacraments under the authority of bishops, particularly the vicar of Christ. Reformed Protestants such as Vermigli are also keen to base universality on a common profession (with the gospel of Christ at the forefront), sacramental framework (baptism and the Lord's Supper), and visible authority (elders of the church), as long as these practices are consistent with the teaching of Scripture, which alone is infallible.

There is a natural desire to construct an apologetic that explains the intellectual and theological cogency of one's conversion. Newman's spiritual autobiography, *Apologia Pro Vita Sua* (1864), is a supreme example but not the only one. His first major publication as a Roman Catholic, *Loss and Gain* (1848), a witty satire that narrates the theological journey of a certain Charles Reding from Oxford to Rome, is another classic example.[141] Vermigli wrote his *Schism and the True Church*, in which he offers his apologetic for Reformed ecclesiology. My own work *Holy Ground: Walking with Jesus as a Former Catholic* is a modern expression of the same impulse.[142]

Converts often employ rhetoric that demonizes, or at least casts aspersions on, the church they have left. Vermigli's *Locus on Justification* and Newman's *Lectures on the Doctrine of Justification* contain many colorful examples.

Conversion often creates turmoil in one's own family. For example, in 1891, the year after Newman's death, his brother, Francis Newman, scandalized readers with his *Contributions Chiefly to the Early History of the Late Cardinal Newman*.[143] It was an ugly screed, apparently intended to prove that Newman was a thoroughgoing papist long before his conversion in 1845. Such dissension (not always with this degree of acrimony) is common. Vermigli's conversion required him to leave Italy (on account of the Catholic Inquisition), never to see his family again.

Conversion carries a cost. To the extent that we anchor our conviction in the Catholic or Protestant traditions, we inevitably alienate ourselves from certain individuals and communities. Vermigli and Newman lived in the crucible of criticism and exile for the remainder of their lives.

It is common for converts to retain affection for the community of colleagues and friends from which they have come. An example of this is found in Newman's classic sermon "The Parting of Friends"—preached on September 15, 1843, at Littlemore after he resigned from Saint Mary's—in which he expressed love for his Oxford movement

---

141. The subject of conversion is also central to another of Newman's novels: *Callista: A Sketch of the Third Century* (London: Burns and Oates, 1856).
142. Chris Castaldo, *Holy Ground: Walking with Jesus as a Former Catholic* (Grand Rapids, MI: Zondervan, 2009).
143. Francis William Newman, *Contributions Chiefly to the Early History of the Late Cardinal Newman: With Comments* (London: K. Paul, Trench, Trübner, 1891).

companions. Vermigli exhibited this tendency in his correspondence with the church at Lucca after his exile.

The question of how to encounter the saving presence of Christ is an overriding concern. One becomes a Catholic when one recognizes the sacramental presence of Christ embodied in an institutional church, receiving from it sanctifying grace that leads to salvation. On the other hand, one becomes an evangelical Protestant when one embraces Scripture as the supreme authority and has a born-again experience that appropriates justifying grace by faith alone.

Thankfully, our day is different from the period in which the sixteenth-century Reformers lived and wrote. Since religious solidarity and national destiny no longer go hand in hand to the same degree as they did for Vermigli and his European contemporaries, we can now disagree with Roman Catholics in a charitable manner. This, however, is not to say that the Reformation is over. Far from it. The same fundamental differences separating Catholics and Protestants in previous centuries continue to exist. But instead of showing open hostility toward our Catholic conversation partners, we can now enjoy a cup of coffee with them, pray for their families, and cherish them as friends.

This, in my humble opinion, is the opportunity facing those of us who identify with contemporary Reformed theology: to approach Catholics with a thoughtful balance of grace *and* truth, manifesting Christ's love while preaching the gospel of grace as though life depends on it. Because it does.

Recommended Resources

Primary Sources

Newman, John Henry. *Apologia Pro Vita Sua: Being a History of His Religious Opinions*. London: Longmans, Green, 1882.

———. *Autobiographical Writings*. Edited by Henry Tristram. London: Sheed and Ward, 1956.

———. *Letters and Diaries of John Henry Newman*. Edited by Charles Stephen Dessain et al. Vol. 4, *The Oxford Movement: July 1833 to December 1834*. London: T. Nelson, 1961–1977.

Tanner, Norman P., ed. *Decrees of the Ecumenical Councils*. Vol. 2, *Trent to Vatican II*. London: Sheed and Ward, 1990.

Vermigli, Peter Martyr. *Early Writings: Creed, Scripture, and Church*. Edited by Joseph C. McLelland. Translated by Mariano Di Gangi. Vol. 1 of *Peter Martyr Library*. Sixteenth Century Essays and Studies 30. Kirksville, MO: Truman State University Press, 1994.

———. *Life, Letters, and Sermons*. Translated and edited by John Patrick Donnelly. Vol. 5 of *Peter Martyr Library*. Sixteenth Century Essays and Studies 42. Kirksville, MO: Thomas Jefferson University Press, 1999.

———. *The Peter Martyr Reader*. Edited by John Patrick Donnelly, Frank A. James III, and Joseph C. McLelland. Kirksville, MO: Truman State University Press, 1999.

———. *Predestination and Justification: Two Theological Loci*. Translated and edited by Frank A. James III. Vol. 8 of *The Peter Martyr Library*. Sixteenth Century Essays and Studies 68. Kirksville, MO: Truman State University Press, 2003.

———. *Sacred Prayers Drawn from the Psalms of David*. Translated and edited by John Patrick Donnelly. Vol. 3 of *Peter Martyr Library*. Sixteenth Century Essays and Studies 34. Kirksville, MO: Thomas Jefferson University Press, 1996.

Secondary Sources

Castaldo, Chris. *Holy Ground: Walking with Jesus as a Former Catholic*. Grand Rapids, MI: Zondervan, 2009.

———. *Justified in Christ: The Doctrines of Peter Martyr Vermigli and John Henry Newman and Their Ecumenical Implications*. Eugene, OR: Pickwick, 2017.

Ker, Ian. *John Henry Newman: A Biography*. Oxford: Oxford University Press, 2009.

Lane, Anthony N. S. *Justification by Faith in Catholic-Protestant Dialogue: An Evangelical Assessment*. London: T&T Clark, 2002.

McNair, Philip. *Peter Martyr in Italy: An Anatomy of Apostasy*. Oxford: Clarendon, 1967.

Newsome, David. *The Parting of Friends: The Wilberforces and Henry Manning*. Grand Rapids, MI: Eerdmans, 1966.

Rambo, Lewis R. *Understanding Religious Conversion*. New Haven, CT: Yale University Press, 1993.

Steinmetz, David C. *Reformers in the Wings*. Philadelphia: Fortress, 1971.

26

The Ground on Which We Stand

The Necessity of Justification for Pastoral Ministry

SAM STORMS

This book is devoted to a searching examination of justification from a historical, biblical, and theological perspective. In this chapter our attention focuses on the necessity of justification for pastoral ministry in the local church. But is it really "necessary"? Is it not enough that we understand what the Bible says about justification, its theological implications, and how its truth served to shape the development of Christianity through the centuries? No, it isn't. Justification is the doctrine on which the "church" stands or falls, and the church is not primarily an institution or denomination but the people of God, the living stones that "are being built up as a spiritual house, to be a holy priesthood, to offer spiritual sacrifices acceptable to God through Jesus Christ" (1 Pet. 2:5).

One may not immediately recognize the truth of justification in this passage, but its presence is both conspicuous and foundational. All that we are as "a chosen race, a royal priesthood, a holy nation, a people for [God's] own possession," who exist to "proclaim the excellencies of him" who called us "out of darkness into his marvelous light" (2:9), is *through Jesus Christ* (2:5). This is simply a short summation of the truth that our salvation from a well-deserved damnation and our status as "God's people" (2:10) are solely because of who Jesus is and what he has achieved on our behalf in his life, death, and resurrection. Peter can declare without hesitation that we "are able to offer spiritual sacrifices acceptable to God" because who we are and how God now views us is something that has come to pass "through Jesus Christ." Is this not the reality of justification made simple? Do we not, in this singular prepositional phrase, find the basis on which we approach God in confidence and joy and offer up our praise and adoration?

There is little hope that the people of God will worship, give, serve, and love one another in a way that the excellencies of God are honored and made known until they acknowledge that it is entirely due to, or to use Peter's preposition, "through" Jesus Christ. Take as but one example the membership covenant that men and women enter into at Bridgeway Church in Oklahoma City where I serve as pastor. Our membership document makes clear that the commitment that each "living stone" makes to one another, to the elders, and to God himself

> is not undertaken that we might gain God's favor, but because we already have it. We do not promise to fulfill our covenant responsibilities in order that we might be forgiven or gain entrance into God's kingdom, but because through the finality and all-sufficiency of what Jesus Christ has accomplished on our behalf, we have already been forgiven and are already heirs of God's kingdom.[1]

Does that not itself make clear that our justification by grace alone through faith alone in Christ alone is the foundation and the sustaining energy by which we live out our lives in community in the body of Christ, the local church?

I first heard this distinction from Tim Keller.[2] Our church summarizes his persuasive argument in our membership covenant as follows:

> Many Christians live in an *"if / then"* relationship with God. *If* I do what is right, *then* God will love me. *If* I give extra money to missions, *then* God will provide me with a raise at work. *If* I avoid sinful habits, *then* I will be spared suffering and humiliation, etc. It's a *conditional* relationship that is based on the principle of *merit*. The gospel [of justification by faith alone] calls us to live in a *"because / therefore"* relationship with the Lord. *Because* we have been justified by faith in Christ, *therefore* we have peace with God (Rom. 5:1). *Because* Christ died for us, *therefore* we are forgiven. *Because* Christ has fulfilled the law in our place, *therefore* we are set free from its demands and penalty, etc. This is an *unconditional* relationship that is based on the principle of *grace*. The difference between these two perspectives is the difference between *religion* (*"if / then"*) and the *gospel* (*"because / therefore"*). The "religious" life is not the "gospel-centered" life.[3]

All this is to say, again in Peter's words, that our hope for reconciliation with God and fruitful ministry for his sake is from beginning to end "through Christ"!

In our local church, as in countless others around the world, we insist that

> no one should embrace . . . covenant [membership] without a clear understanding of this truth. We are happy to commit ourselves in covenant one with another because God has already committed himself in covenant to us in [or "through"] the

---

1. "Covenant Membership," Bridgeway Church, accessed March 9, 2018, http://www.bridgewaychurch.com/covenant-for-membership.
2. The most extensive treatment of this issue by Timothy Keller is found in his book *Center Church: Doing Balanced, Gospel-Centered Ministry in Your City* (Grand Rapids, MI: Zondervan, 2012), 27–85.
3. "Covenant Membership," Bridgeway Church.

person of his Son, Jesus Christ. Thus, the principles of our membership covenant are not a legalistic code by which we judge our worth or hope to gain God's approval. Rather, these principles are an expression of our joyful recognition that our worth and approval in the sight of God are already rooted in Christ and established by his redemptive work on our behalf.

Therefore, as we seek to walk in obedience to the biblical obligations of [our] covenant, we understand and freely confess that it is only the grace of God working in us that will empower us to fulfill our responsibility and delight as Christians. Apart from God's grace, all we can expect from ourselves is a life of failed attempts at righteousness, but in light of the gospel, and with the empowering grace of God by the Holy Spirit, we seek to walk in grace-motivated obedience while God works in us "both to will and to work for his good pleasure" (Phil. 2:12–13).

On those occasions when we fail to live up to the commitments we . . . make (and we *will* fail), we pray that God would grant us quick and unmistakable conviction of our sin and a repentant heart that turns from self-centered and idolatrous living to a robust confidence and joy in the truth of the Gospel and the power of the Holy Spirit.[4]

This is what justification does for us. This is how it inserts itself into the life not simply of the individual believer but also of the corporate body of Christian men and women who by God's grace strive together to "proclaim the excellencies" of the one who called us "out of darkness into his marvelous light" (1 Pet. 2:9).

Justification by faith alone is far more than a foundation for the people of God living in covenant community one with another. It is assuredly that, but it is no less the truth that gives shape to the superstructure and serves to bring coherence and consistency to all we do as the people of God. In other words, the gospel of justification is more than simply the message we "received" when Christ was proclaimed to us. It is also the gospel "in which [we] stand" and "by which [we] are being saved" (1 Cor. 15:1–2). There is little hope for success in gospel ministry if the people of God strive in a power of their own making. To the extent that we mistakenly believe that our efforts, in any shape or form, are the foundation on which the life of the church is built, we are doomed to abject failure. Our doing is merely the fruit of God's doing in and "through" Jesus Christ.

The apostle Paul spoke very personally of this truth but also on behalf of every born-again believer when he declared that his (our) desire was to "be found" in Christ, "not having a righteousness of my [our] own that comes from the law" (Phil. 3:9). This aspiration of Paul's is articulated in the wake of his own confession to having achieved as much by the force of his own will and flesh as any human possibly could. He had a righteousness that came from the law (Phil. 3:6), but it availed for nothing! It gave him no confidence in God's presence. But why not? Because no matter how much he might obtain, he could never know if it was enough.

---

4. "Covenant Membership," Bridgeway Church.

After all, God requires absolute and utter perfection. Furthermore, even if we think ourselves to have succeeded in observing the law and performing good works in the past, there is no guarantee that we will continue to do so into the future. And how would one even know whether the righteousness one thinks he has produced is precisely the righteousness that God requires? It's all hopeless! Our righteousness simply must come from another source besides and beyond ourselves. It must come "through Jesus Christ" (1 Pet. 2:5). Thus, "man is justified by laying hold of a righteousness which is not, and can never be, his own—the *iustitia Christi aliena*, which God mercifully 'reckons' to man."[5]

Paul longs for a righteousness "which comes through faith in Christ" (Phil. 3:9). He does not say we gain righteousness because of faith or on the basis of faith, as if faith were the God-approved substitute for good works. Faith is not an alternative way of earning God's favor. Faith is the very antithesis of merit. Faith is our confession that we are unable to do anything to win God's approval. Faith always looks away from itself and to its object, to that in which the human soul has placed its trust and hope and confidence. And this righteousness, he declares, ultimately comes "from God" (Phil. 3:9), as a gift of his grace. Thus we must always hold firmly that the value of faith is not in itself as a human act but in its divine object: the righteousness of Jesus Christ graciously and freely imputed to the believer.

Clearly, then, Paul conceives of two sorts of righteousness. On the one hand is that (so-called) righteousness that a person achieves through good works. On the other hand is that righteousness that God gives through faith. One is a righteousness based on human effort. The other is a righteousness received as a divine gift. On the former Paul pours contempt. It is the object of his most intense and fervent hatred. Those who promote it he calls dogs and evildoers (3:2). On the other Paul heaps effusive praise. For it he gives thanks to God, and on it he has staked his eternal life.

It is as a result of this newfound relationship with Jesus Christ that Paul wants to experience the very power that raised Jesus from the dead (3:10; cf. Rom. 8:11; Eph. 1:19–21). This word "know" goes beyond mere intellectual understanding. It is surely a function of the mind but also, and no less, an experience of the heart. Paul wants to feel and be energized by this power so that he can say no to sin and temptation and devote himself fully to the worship and service of Christ. Simply put, Paul isn't saying he wants to know more *about* the resurrection of Jesus, as if he were hungry for knowledge about its circumstances or the people who witnessed it. He is saying, *"I want to feel the power by which Christ defeated death and sin and Satan! I want to live daily in conscious awareness of and dependence on this power that now works in me."*

And lest we think that Paul is some sort of crass triumphalist, we observe that he also wants to "share his sufferings, becoming like him in his death" (Phil. 3:10). From power to persecution, from the strength of the risen Christ to the suffering of the crucified

---

5. Alister E. McGrath, *Iustitia Dei: A History of the Christian Doctrine of Justification*, vol. 2, *From 1500 to the Present Day*, 1st ed. (Cambridge: Cambridge University Press, 1986), 12.

Christ, Paul's desire is to live in such vital and inseparable union with Jesus that the same abuse and persecution that fell on his Lord might now fall on him as well. It isn't that Paul wants to experience the redemptive and saving sufferings of Jesus. He simply wants to stand in precisely that relation to the world in which Christ himself stood, such that whatever affliction the world sought to impose on Christ might yet fall on him. If the world hated Jesus, then by all means let it hate me. If the world rejected Jesus, then I am willing to endure its rejection as well.

This is the message the world needs to hear from the church. One day we will stand in his presence. We will be clothed, either in the so-called righteousness of our own making or in the glorious righteousness of Christ Jesus that has been granted to us "through Christ Jesus." Those are the only two possibilities. And the so-called righteousness or goodness of our own making is worse than nakedness. It is filthy rags. It is a repulsive garment that brings only death and condemnation. Our only hope is to renounce our trust in anything other than Christ and his righteousness. We must invest ourselves wholly in who Jesus is and what he has done in his sinless life and what Jesus endured on the cross and what Jesus achieved by his resurrection from the grave.

A Brief Summation of the Meaning of Justification

An extensive biblical and theological articulation of the meaning of justification has already been supplied in the preceding chapters of this book.[6] But a brief summation of the salient points proves helpful as we consider the place and power of this doctrine in the life and ministry of the local church pastor. So please take note of the following eight brief points.

First, contrary to the Roman Catholic view, justification means that we are *declared* righteous, not made righteous. It is a change in our status, not our nature. That doesn't mean that justification has no relationship to progressive sanctification, in which we are gradually, by grace, transformed inwardly into the very image of Jesus himself. These are distinct spiritual realities but by no means separable. Those who are truly justified will be sanctified. This radical and fundamental distinction between justification as a status obtained by initial faith and the subsequent sanctification or transformation of one's nature through grace was a profound insight of the Protestant Reformers and a return to the biblical doctrine itself.

Second, and directly related to the previous point, justification is *objective*, not subjective. That is, it is something done *for* us, or on our behalf, not in us. Or to say much the same thing, justification is *forensic*, not experiential. Justification, then, is a *legal act*, not an emotional feeling. While we do not feel justification when it occurs, once we comprehend what God has done, there may be great exhilaration of soul and spirit.

Thus, the differences between the Protestant and Roman Catholic views on justification are unmistakable. In Protestantism, justification is extrinsic (not intrinsic), alien

---

6. This section is adapted from Sam Storms, "The Doctrine of Justification," Enjoying God, accessed March 9, 2018, http://www.samstorms.com/all-articles/post/the-doctrine-of-justification. Used by permission of the author.

to us (not inherent within us), objective or for us (not subjective or in us), punctiliar (occurring at a point in time, when we believe, not progressive), forensic (not experiential), and declarative (not transformative); it entails the imputation of righteousness to us (not the impartation or infusion of righteousness in us), issues in (but is not the same as) sanctification, and pertains to our status (not our being) as we are reckoned righteous (not made righteous).

Third, justification is both *acquittal* and *acceptance*. That is, it involves both the forgiveness of sins and the receiving of the righteousness of Christ. God not only declares us "Not guilty!" but he also declares us "Righteous!" by imputing or reckoning to us the righteousness of Jesus (what theologians refer to as the "active obedience" of Christ). Mere pardon would leave us spiritually naked with no righteousness. Pardon might save us from hell, but it won't get us into heaven.

Fourth, justification is both *exclusive* and *extensive*. By exclusive, I mean that there is no middle ground: you either are or are not justified. It is not something you attain by degrees (contra Rome) but is a standing that is yours by divine decree. By extensive, I mean that *all* sins are dealt with, whether past, present, or future.

Fifth, justification is both *instantaneous* and *irreversible*. It is a position or status to which we are elevated. It is not a process. Furthermore, it is irreversible. It cannot be lost. God's verdict will never be appealed to a higher court (cf. Rom. 8:31–34).

Sixth, justification is received by *faith*, being *freely* bestowed by God (3:24). Thus the sinner is justified *per fidem propter Christum*, "through faith on account of Christ," rather than *propter fidem per Christum*, "on account of faith through Christ." We are not justified because we believe. Faith is not a human work that somehow merits justification. We are justified on account of or because of Christ, whose righteousness we receive passively, through faith.

Seventh, justification is by faith *alone*, but the faith that justifies is never alone. In other words, the person who is justified *will be* sanctified. *Sola fides iustificat, sed non fides quae est sola*, or "faith alone justifies, but not the faith that is alone." Thus, whereas we are not justified by works, neither are we justified without works, for in the faith that justifies lies the seed of that sanctification of life apart from which no one shall see God. Korey D. Maas has articulated this idea well in his explication of Luther's understanding of justification. The crucial distinction, he notes, is "between good works being necessary (as a consequence) *to* but not (as a condition) *for* justification."[7]

Finally, justification by faith alone is grounded in our union with Christ. What we receive from God by grace is the indwelling of Christ himself, into whose risen life we are incorporated. As Alister McGrath says, "Justification is still treated as the external pronouncement of God that we are right in his sight—but the pronouncement is made on the basis of the presence within us of the living Christ."[8]

---

7. Korey D. Maas, "Justification by Faith Alone," in *Reformation Theology: A Systematic Summary*, ed. Matthew Barrett (Wheaton, IL: Crossway, 2017), 531.

8. Alister E. McGrath, *Justification by Faith* (Grand Rapids, MI: Academie Books, 1990), 58.

The Relationship between Faith and Works in the Christian Life

Essential to all pastoral ministry is the communication to God's people of the truth of both the gratuitous nature of our justification and the necessity of obedience to all that Scripture commands.[9] But if we refuse, and rightly we should, to sever justification from sanctification by insisting that, although we are not saved by works, neither are we saved without them, how do we avoid falling into the error of making our acceptance with God in some measure meritorious? This is an issue that every local church pastor must address with his people. The problem is raised in several New Testament texts, nowhere more explicitly than in Romans 2–3. There Paul posits what appears to some as mutually exclusive propositions:

> For by works of the law no human being will be justified in his sight, since through the law comes knowledge of sin. (3:20)

This seems clear enough, until we compare it with several statements made earlier in Romans 2:

> To those who by patience in well-doing seek for glory and honor and immortality, he will give eternal life. (2:7)

> But glory and honor and peace for everyone who does good, the Jew first and also the Greek. (2:10)

> For it is not the hearers of the law who are righteous before God, but the doers of the law who will be justified. (2:13)

Romans 2:7, 10, and 13 appear to say that eternal life is the reward to those who persevere in doing good deeds, in evident contradiction to what Paul would later declare in 3:20. There have been numerous efforts to harmonize these seemingly disparate declarations, the most persuasive of which (in my opinion) follows.

In Romans 3:20, Paul has in mind one's initial entrance into salvation, that inaugural event when God declares one righteous in his sight through faith in Christ. In 2:13 (based on 2:7, 10), on the other hand, he refers to the final judgment when one's works or good deeds, being the evidence or fruit of saving faith, will vindicate the individual or reveal him or her to be in right standing before God. According to this view, Paul is advocating a judgment based on works (cf. 1 Cor. 6:9–10; Gal. 5:21; 6:8; Eph. 5:5–6). The point is that good works secure entrance into eternal life *insofar as they are the product of a true saving faith*. A mere profession of faith in Christ without perseverance in good deeds will not avail on the day of judgment. As Thomas Schreiner points out, "Paul's statements in Romans 2 are not merely hypothetical;

---

9. This section is adapted from Sam Storms, "Romans 2:1–3:20," Enjoying God, accessed March 9, 2018, http://samstorms.com/all-articles/post/romans-2:1-3:20; Storms, "Are We Justified by Faith or by Works? Yes!—James 2:14–26," Enjoying God, accessed March 9, 2018, http://samstorms.com/all-articles/post/are-we-justified-by-faith-or-by-works-yes—james-214-26. Used by permission of the author.

those who fail to do good works will face judgment, while those who practice good works will experience eternal life."[10] He explains this in more detail:

> Even though Paul asserts that no one can attain salvation by good works [which is his point in 3:20], he also insists that no one can be saved without them, and that they are necessary to obtain an eschatological inheritance [which is his point in 2:7, 10, 13]. The Spirit's work in a person produces obedience to the law (Rom. 2:26–29). The saving work of Jesus Christ radically changes people so that they can now obey the law they previously disobeyed (see Rom. 8:1–4). The works that are necessary for salvation, therefore, *do not constitute an earning of salvation but are evidence of a salvation already given*. The transforming work of the Spirit accompanies and cannot be separated from, the justifying work of God. Such good works manifest the work of the Holy Spirit in the believer's life. We should also stress that Paul is not demanding perfect obedience, but obedience that is significant, substantial, and observable.[11]

The New Testament is clear on this point. Faith alone is the condition of salvation, but works are the consequence of it. The absence of works likely betrays the superficial and spurious nature of one's profession of faith. The regenerate life that is experienced by the one who is justified by faith necessarily yields the fruit of daily repentance and a commitment to practical holiness. The faith that justifies is the cause of which works are the effect. Thus, whereas we aren't saved *by* works, we most assuredly are saved *for* works. This fundamental principle is the point of what James says concerning the relation of faith to works.

There simply is no more eternally important or pastorally urgent question that any man or woman can ask and then answer than this: "How might I, a hell-deserving sinner, be reconciled to God and made acceptable in his sight?" Or we might pose the question in yet another way: "How might I, a man or woman who is undeniably unrighteous and thus deserving of eternal judgment, be made righteous in the sight of God?" Other questions might feel more pressing or more practical, but rest assured that nothing else in all of life matters much in comparison with the issue of how we can be made right with God and thus assured of eternal life in his presence. To put it another way, what is it that commends us to God? On what grounds or for what reason does God receive us as his children and look on us with a smile of approval and joy?

Some continue to insist that Paul and James supply us with conflicting answers. They envision the apostle Paul and James standing face-to-face, doing all they can to refute and overturn the other's view. After all, when we put their respective statements on justification side by side, they appear to be contradictory and mutually exclusive. You can't affirm one view without denying and rejecting the other. Or so it seems. Paul writes,

---

10. Thomas R. Schreiner, *The Law and Its Fulfillment: A Pauline Theology of Law* (Grand Rapids, MI: Baker, 1993), 187.
11. Schreiner, *Law and Its Fulfillment*, 203–4; italics original.

> For by works of the law no human being will be justified in his [God's] sight. (Rom. 3:20)
>
> For we hold that one is justified by faith apart from works of the law. (3:28)
>
> Yet we know that a person is not justified by works of the law but through faith in Jesus Christ, so we also have believed in Jesus Christ, in order to be justified by faith in Christ and not by works of the law, because by works of the law no one will be justified. (Gal. 2:16)

It is hard to imagine anyone stating a position with any greater clarity. But how, then, can James assert the following?

> What good is it, my brothers, if someone says he has faith but does not have works? Can that faith save him? (James 2:14)
>
> Was not Abraham our father justified by works when he offered up his son Isaac on the altar? (2:21)
>
> You see that a person is justified by works and not by faith alone. (2:24)

We must begin with the recognition that Paul and James are not waging theological war against each other. They are not to be thought of as standing face-to-face but rather as standing back-to-back. Neither of them disagrees with the other. They are in fact responding to the errors of different theological opponents. Paul is confronting the legalist, more specifically, a person who believes that acceptance with God, being in the right with God, is dependent on doing works of religious obedience. Good deeds save us. I call him a "legalist" because he loves all things legal or relating to the law of God. "Do the works of the law, and you will be saved." This is the person whom Paul confronts and engages in theological debate. Paul stands face-to-face and nose-to-nose with this person and says without qualification that "by works of the law no one will be justified" (Gal. 2:16).

James also confronts a theological enemy: the antinomian, the sort of person who says, "Well, if I'm justified by faith alone, as Paul says, it doesn't matter how I live my life. I can sin all I want. I don't need to worry at all about obeying God's will. He has accepted me on the grounds of my faith in Christ. So I'll ignore the law of God, I'll play fast and loose with his commandments, I don't have to worry about good works at all. Simply put, sanctification is optional." James stands back-to-back with Paul but face-to-face with the antinomian. And he says to him, "Sir, you are horribly misinformed. Whereas it is true that we are justified by faith alone, we are not justified by the faith that is alone. That is, the faith that alone justifies or makes us acceptable in God's sight is the sort or kind of faith that then will work and obey and happily do the things that God has commanded."

Paul is responding to the legalist, who thinks that doing good deeds is the basis or foundation of our acceptance with God. James is addressing the antinomian, who thinks that good works have no place at all in the Christian life. Since we are justified by faith alone, we need not worry about practical obedience. Thus when we realize who the opponents are, we see that Paul and James actually concur on this vital issue. They are simply arguing against different distortions of the gospel of Jesus Christ. Both men agree that justification is by faith alone. But both also agree that the faith that alone justifies is not a faith that is alone. It is a faith that obeys.

Not All "Faith" Is Saving Faith

Another key to understanding James is found not only in the recognition that he and Paul are arguing against different theological opponents but also in the knowledge that they are talking about two different kinds of so-called faith.

Imagine for a moment that I have in my hand two small objects, both of which I claim are seeds. If you were to take them in your hand, you probably couldn't tell any difference between the two. They weigh the same, smell the same, feel the same, and look the same. But only one of them is truly a seed. The other is a pebble, a lifeless, inert piece of matter that resembles a seed and could for a time pass as a seed. But merely *claiming* it to be a seed does not make it one. Merely *saying* it is a seed doesn't transform its nature. I might insist that this object is a seed and in time will bring forth plant life of some sort. But it won't.

So how do you know which one is the seed and which is the pebble? You plant them in the ground and water them and make sure that they receive plentiful sunlight. The seed will eventually grow and produce a plant or fruit or perhaps a flower. The pebble will lie lifeless in the ground and produce nothing. "Ah," you say, "now I know which one is the seed. I draw my conclusion based on the fruit it produces. I know that the other object was a lifeless pebble, no matter how loudly someone insists that it is really a seed. And I know this because it produces nothing."

This is what James is saying about the nature of that faith that alone brings us justification in the sight of God. And Paul would say it as well. Some people have a religious experience and call it faith. Some people are raised in church all their life and refer to their Sunday routine as faith. Some people sign a decision card or even get baptized and point to each and call it faith. But James says that if this thing you call "faith" doesn't produce works of obedience, it's probably a pebble. Real faith, the sort of faith that justifies and saves and reconciles us to God, is like a seed: when planted and watered, it produces fruit; it produces a life in which one's heart loves the things of God and desires to walk in obedience to the revealed will of God. It doesn't produce perfection, but it does result in passion for God and a pursuit of holiness. Jonathan Edwards speaks of this transformation in his twelfth sign of genuine religious affections:

> If God dwells in the heart, and be vitally united to it, he will shew that he is a God, by the efficacy of his operation. Christ is not in the heart of a saint, as in a sepulcher, or as a dead Saviour, that does nothing; but as in his temple, and as one that is alive

from the dead. For in the heart where Christ savingly is, there he lives, and exerts himself after the power of that endless life, that he received at his resurrection. Thus every saint that is the subject of the benefit of Christ's sufferings, is made to know and experience the power of his resurrection. . . . Hence saving affections, though oftentimes they don't make a great noise and show as others; yet have in them a secret solidity, life and strength, whereby they take hold of, and carry away the heart, leading it into a kind of captivity (II Cor. 10:5), gaining a full and steadfast determination of the will for God and holiness. . . . And thus it is that holy affections have a governing power in the course of a man's life.[12]

The point that James and Paul (and Edwards) are making is that not everything that calls itself faith or passes itself off as trust in Christ is the sort of "faith" that justifies and saves. Some so-called experiences of "faith" are nothing more than *intellectual assent*. By this I have in view the cognitive consent of one's mind to the truth of some claim or some event. Other experiences that people call "faith" are nothing more than *emotionally charged reactions to a moment of religious euphoria*. Perhaps you attended a worship service and were deeply moved by the music; you were swept up in the highly charged atmosphere of the evening. You may even have wept and felt the presence of the Holy Spirit. But unless that experience leads to genuine repentance from sin and active, joyful, sincere trust in who Jesus is and what he has done on the cross for sinners, it's no different from the pebble in my hand. It accomplishes nothing. It saves no one. Not the loudest protests in the world will change that. Not the most vigorous declarations that this person has believed in Jesus will change that pebble into the seed of saving faith.

And the only ultimate test for whether this thing you call "faith" is in fact saving, justifying faith is what happens when you plant it and water it and make certain that the sun shines on it. Likewise, the only ultimate test for whether this experience of yours is true faith, the faith that Paul says alone can justify the sinner in the sight of God, is whether it produces a life of obedience and love for holiness.

In James 2:14–17, he labors to demonstrate that a so-called faith that does not produce works of obedience and compassion and generosity and kindness is not saving faith. What good is it, he asks, if you *say* you have faith but there are no works? "Can *that* faith save him?" (2:14). No, says James, "that" kind of faith is not saving faith, and we know it isn't saving faith because it is not a working faith. James isn't saying that you need works as the *cause* of your justification. He is saying that you need works as the *consequence* of your justification.

In 2:18–19, he provides yet another line of evidence to make his point. He puts forth a hypothetical discussion between two people. The principle here is the same: How do I know that you have faith in the absence of works? If you have no works, if you have no desire to obey Jesus, if you fail to display the fruit of the Holy Spirit, such as love, joy, peace, patience, kindness, and so on, how am I supposed to know that you really

---

12. Jonathan Edwards, *The Works of Jonathan Edwards*, vol. 2, *Religious Affections*, ed. John E. Smith (New Haven, CT: Yale University Press, 1969), 392–93.

have faith? Do you expect me simply to believe because you say so? Instead, let me demonstrate to you the reality of my faith precisely in the works that I love to do for the sake of God's glory.

But someone objects, "Wait a minute. I have true beliefs about God, just like you. I affirm that there is only one God and not many. Isn't that good enough to prove that my profession of faith is real and saving?" No, says James, for "even the demons believe" that God is one. And they not only believe it, they are terrified by it. They tremble when they think of God. They fear the coming judgment that God will impose on them. But their knowledge of who God is does not change the fact that they are still demons! And your knowledge of who God is does not by itself mean you are not still an unbeliever and lost in your sin.

Orthodoxy severed from orthopraxy proves nothing. Having right beliefs and sound, scriptural theology is vitally important. But merely asserting in your mind and giving intellectual assent to the truth of what the Bible says does not in itself mean you are in good standing with God. Faith certainly involves believing truths about God, sin, Christ, and the cross. But if you don't actually and authentically trust in, rely on, and put your hope in who Christ is and what he has done, your theology amounts to nothing. And the way we can know that you have authentically trusted in, relied on, and put your hope in Jesus is whether this so-called faith gradually and incrementally transforms how you live.

So I conclude that James is not arguing for works without faith. Rather, he is arguing against faith without works. Or again, James is not saying that saving faith without works is dead but that faith without works is not a saving faith. To the person who asks, "Is it faith that justifies us, or is it works?" the apostle Paul replies, "Faith alone justifies, without works." When that same person asks again, "But does all faith justify?" James replies, "No, the faith that is alone, the faith that does not work, does not justify."

The Practical and Pastoral Implications of Justification by Faith Alone

The glorious truth of our justification was never intended by God to remain solely a topic for theological conversation and controversy.[13] The imputation of the righteousness of God the Son to otherwise fallen humanity, through faith alone and not in consequence of any work performed, is the foundation and controlling principle that governs the Christian life and provides hope not only for our practical transformation but also for a joyful communion with the risen and exalted Savior. Justification by faith alone is consistently portrayed in the New Testament as the ground for any and every appeal to sanctified living. This is seen in numerous texts of Scripture, several of which are noted below.

We might also approach this topic by asking the question, What is the greatest challenge facing the local church pastor? No doubt countless answers could be given,

---

13. This section is adapted from Sam Storms, "Romans 5:1–21," Enjoying God, accessed March 9, 2018, http://samstorms.com/all-articles/post/romans-5:1-21. Used by permission of the author.

but I want to argue that preeminent among them is the struggle in the hearts of God's people to confidently rest in the truth of justification. The average Christian, when honest and vulnerable, will confess to battling anxiety, doubt, fear, self-contempt, a lingering sense of guilt, and what can only be called a defiled conscience. Needless to say, this is not conducive to a vibrant, joy-filled, peaceful experience of the salvation that has been secured in Christ. That being said, the remainder of this chapter is devoted to a brief examination of what several New Testament texts tell us concerning the spiritual, emotional, and relational blessings that come to God's children when they fully embrace and find their rest in the truth of their justification by faith in Christ.

Perhaps the best place to begin is with Calvin's definition of justification and the practical conclusion that he draws from it:

> But we define justification as follows: the sinner, received into communion with Christ, is reconciled to God by his grace, while, cleansed by Christ's blood, he obtains forgiveness of sins, and clothed with Christ's righteousness as if it were his own, he stands confident before the heavenly judgment seat.[14]

If Calvin is correct, and I believe he is, justification by faith alone is the ground on which the believer "stands confident before the heavenly judgment seat." As noted above, perhaps the greatest struggle in the Christian's life is doubt and the anxiety it produces: "Am I truly saved? Does God really love me? I feel so unworthy, if not altogether worthless. How can a righteous God look with anything other than disgust and disappointment on a sinner such as myself? What hope is there for me to accomplish anything of benefit in the body of Christ? My conscience constantly stings me with accusations of failure and hypocrisy and lingering guilt. I feel paralyzed in my relationship with Christ. What possible use can I be to him?"

This, then, is the principal challenge to every pastor, to speak and apply God's truth in such a way that by the Spirit's power the child of God can overcome these debilitating fears and, as Calvin said, "stand confident before the heavenly judgment seat." But on what is our confidence based? What reason do we have to be confident in the presence of an infinitely holy God? To what might we appeal? Surely, it is not our own inherent righteousness but rather the alien, imputed, perfect righteousness of Christ himself in which we are "clothed." This truth is present in countless New

---

14. John Calvin, *Institutes of the Christian Religion*, ed. John T. McNeill, trans. Ford Lewis Battles, LCC 20–21 (Philadelphia: Westminster, 1975), 3.17.8. Elsewhere, Calvin writes, "Justified by faith is he who, excluded from the righteousness of works, grasps the righteousness of Christ through faith, and clothed in it, appears in God's sight not as a sinner but as a righteous man. Therefore, we explain justification simply as the acceptance with which God receives us into his favor as righteous men. And we say that it consists in the remission of sins and the imputation of Christ's righteousness." *Institutes*, 3.21.2. Whereas Calvin recognized the formal distinction between justification and sanctification, he refused to separate them. Whereas we are not justified by works, neither are we justified without works, for in the faith that justifies is that sanctification of life apart from which no one shall see God. Calvin also writes, "We dream neither of a faith devoid of good works nor of a justification that stands without them. This alone is of importance: having admitted that faith and good works must cleave together, we still lodge justification in faith, not in works. . . . Because by faith we grasp Christ's righteousness, by which alone we are reconciled to God. Yet you could not grasp this without at the same time grasping sanctification also." *Institutes*, 3.16.1.

Testament texts. A few words about how Paul addresses this matter in Romans is our first order of business.

Justification the Ground for Holiness and Hope

The failure to embrace the truth of justification and be susceptible to its transforming power is one of the principal reasons why so many Christians languish in hopelessness and have consigned themselves to what they believe is the inevitability of remaining forever in the same condition in which they find themselves today.[15] They don't openly and angrily defy God but simply slip ever so slowly into spiritual lethargy. They have long since abandoned hope that life will be meaningful and fruitful. They hope only to survive one day to the next without falling into openly scandalous and shameful sin.

What is it that has the power to awaken such folk from their slumber and apathy? What is it that has the power to ignite a fire of passion and renew an awareness of eternal value in their lives? The answer is justification. The one constant in the Christian religion that serves to inspire and energize otherwise lifeless souls is the simple declaration that there is "now no condemnation for those who are in Christ Jesus" (Rom. 8:1). What feels like an unshakable sense of guilt, shame, and self-contempt is overcome when the minds of men or women are quickened by the Spirit of God to know—not hope or wish or speculate about but know—that whatever may come their way from this day into eternity, condemnation will never fall on them. And the reason is because it has already fallen on their sacrificial substitute, Jesus Christ. Paul's ringing proclamation in Romans 8:1 does not emerge in a vacuum but is the inescapable consequence of what he has said repeatedly in the preceding chapters of his epistle (see esp. 1:16; 3:21–24, 26, 28; 4:4–5; 5:1, 9; 6:22).

The only thing that will shatter the hard shell of hopelessness that so often envelops the human heart is the truth that God justifies the "ungodly" (4:5). The paralysis of sin and shame is lifted with the realization that one stands before an infinitely holy God clothed in the very righteousness of that same God, a righteousness that this infinitely holy God freely bestows in response not to works or moral improvement or an impressive résumé but to simple faith in Jesus Christ.

This condemnation that will never, ever descend on the one who trusts in Jesus does not magically disappear. It does not vanish at the wave of a sorcerer's wand or slowly dissipate as we replace our disobedience by obedience. It is very real and ineffably painful. But it has been laid on another in our stead. Justification comes as we look to this other in trust. When he becomes our only hope, we can rest assured, confident that the condemnation we so richly deserved has been laid on him, and the righteousness we could never attain on our own, his righteousness, is now reckoned to be ours. That is the consequential force of that glorious word "therefore." "There is *therefore* now no condemnation for those who are in Christ Jesus" (8:1). This is the truth that every

---

15. This section is adapted from Sam Storms, "Romans 5:1–21," Enjoying God, accessed March 9, 2018, http://samstorms.com/all-articles/post/romans-5-1-21. Used by permission of the author.

pastor must know and embrace and treasure for himself and faithfully proclaim and happily declare to his people.

As we continue to explore the far-reaching, life-changing implications of justification for both a local church pastor and the people of God to whom he ministers, we need to take note of Paul's comments in Romans 5, particularly verses 1–5:

> Therefore, since we have been justified by faith, we have peace with God through our Lord Jesus Christ. Through him we have also obtained access by faith into this grace in which we stand, and we rejoice in hope of the glory of God. Not only that, but we rejoice in our sufferings, knowing that suffering produces endurance, and endurance produces character, and character produces hope, and hope does not put us to shame, because God's love has been poured into our hearts through the Holy Spirit who has been given to us.

To be at peace with God as a result of justification implies that *prior* to justification, we were *at war* with him. Without the righteousness that alone avails in God's presence, we were at enmity with him, subject to his holy wrath (see John 3:36; Rom. 5:10; Eph. 2:3). To be at peace with God implies a *cessation* of the hostilities (cf. Col. 1:19–22). But being at peace with God is more than a cessation of hostilities. It is the inauguration of intimacy, friendship, and love. The peace with God that justification establishes issues in the more subjective, experiential peace of God that now rules in our hearts.

Justification and our being at peace with God also issues in a new presence. This grace that brought us the righteousness of Christ is something "in which we stand" (Rom. 5:2). I suspect that Paul envisions the once-alienated person now standing confidently in God's gracious presence (cf. Eph. 2:18; 3:12). We are surrounded, upheld, and guarded by this grace of God, which sets in motion, as it were, a chain reaction that consummates in the unspeakable joy of experiencing the reality of God's unfailing love in our hearts.

Because we have been justified by faith, we are at peace with God, in whose holy presence we stand without fear or anxiety. This simple reality in turn awakens joy in the "hope" that we will both see and forever bask in the beauty of God's scintillating glory (Rom. 5:2).[16] This verse is made all the more remarkable when it is read in the light of what Paul says in Romans 1:21–23 and 3:20. We who once scorned God's glory and exchanged it for a pathetic creaturely substitute (1:21–23), we who once fell short of God's glory in failing to ascribe to him the praise of which he is worthy, are now promised a future share in it!

Although the ESV renders 5:2 with the word "rejoice," a more accurate translation would be that we "boast" in this hope of God's glory. Boasting is always criticized when

---

16. As R. Michael Allen has pointed out, "Justification brings peace and grants access, but it is the glory of God that is the hope of the Christian." *Justification and the Gospel: Understanding the Contexts and Controversies* (Grand Rapids, MI: Baker Academic, 2013), 15.

it has an improper object, such as human effort, accomplishment, or wisdom (Rom. 3:27; 4:2; 1 Cor. 1:29; 3:21; 4:7; 2 Cor. 11:18; Gal. 6:13; Eph. 2:9). But boasting in God or his gracious work in and through us is entirely appropriate (1 Cor. 1:31; 2 Cor. 10:17; Gal. 6:14; Phil. 3:3).

The same word "boast" is used in Romans 5:3 to describe our response to suffering. Thus we do not merely rejoice or boast in the hope of God's glory to come, but even now, in the present moment, we "rejoice in our suffering" (5:3). Few things run as counter to the intuitive instincts of a man or woman than that we should find anything other than discomfort and disillusionment in suffering. But Paul wants us to understand that being reckoned as righteous in God's glorious presence reconfigures our attitude toward suffering for Christ's sake. He isn't suggesting that pain is magically transmuted into pleasure. Paul was, if anything, a realist about the hardships of life, especially for those who have made peace with God. Although the latter is foundational to our existence as God's children, we are still at war with the world, and the suffering it imposes on those who name the name of Jesus is inescapable and undeniably agonizing.

But the foundational reality of justification enables the believing saint to joyfully endure (5:3) rather than quit in bitterness and disillusionment. What I'm suggesting, then, is that the supernatural capacity to rejoice (boast) not simply "in" our suffering but even because of it is not the deranged thinking of a religious masochist. It is the spiritual fruit of knowing that we have been justified through faith in Christ and thus are at peace with God. Suffering does not destroy faith but serves to refine and purify it, similar to the effect of fire on gold (1 Pet. 1:7). Just as the dross and alloy is removed from the precious metal by the literal fire of a furnace, so also the "various trials" of life reveal the "genuineness" of our faith (1:6–7), issuing in an intensified love for Jesus and a joy that is "inexpressible and filled with glory" (1:8). This is why Paul could speak of joy in the midst of suffering, because he knew that the endurance it produces in us yields the sweet fruit of transformed "character" (Rom. 5:4). Paul comes full circle, arguing that this proven and purified character itself sustains and expands the kind of hope that "does not put us to shame" (5:5). Our shameless confidence in God's presence is not the result of human engineering or mere will power but the fruit of that hope produced in us by the Holy Spirit as he reinforces in our conscious experience the profound truth that this infinite and immeasurably holy God genuinely loves us (5:5).

There is yet one more nagging question that Paul addresses: How do we know that our hope in Christ won't fall apart? How do we know that it all won't fizzle out in the end or be consumed by the fires of God's wrath on the final day? We know, says Paul, by virtue of the action God has taken to assure us of his eternal and unchanging love, revealed principally in the provision of a God-given righteousness through the life, death, and resurrection of Jesus. The sensible awareness of this love he poured out into our hearts through the Holy Spirit (5:5). Paul is emphasizing the bountiful lavishness with which God has flooded our hearts with a sense of his love for us. "The hearts of believers," writes John Murray, "are regarded as being suffused with the love of God; it controls and captivates their hearts."[17]

This is an exuberant communication of God's love. God wants *your* heart to be inundated by wave after wave of his fatherly affection, so effusively poured out that you feel compelled to request that he pull back lest you drown in his passion! Paul is not talking "of faint and fitful impressions," says J. I. Packer, "but of deep and overwhelming ones."[18] Packer also points out the significance of Paul's use of the perfect tense of the verb, which implies

> a settled state consequent upon a completed action. The thought is that knowledge of the love of God, having flooded our hearts, *fills them now*, just as a valley once flooded remains full of water. Paul assumes that all his readers, like himself, will be living in the enjoyment of a strong and abiding sense of God's love for them.[19]

In other words, God's love doesn't leak! Unlike the waters of Noah that receded after a time, God's love remains perpetually at flood stage in our souls. And the Holy Spirit works to evoke and stimulate in your heart the overwhelming conviction that God loves you. The amplitude and immensity of God's devotion is not abstract and generic but concrete and personal. It is not indiscriminately for everyone in general but for God's elect in particular.

It is difficult to describe more precisely what Paul is saying here. Perhaps this is because he's not talking about knowledge that we gain by inference from a body of evidence. Neither deduction nor induction can account for what he has in mind. Empirical observation doesn't yield the assurance of being God's beloved. The *objective* proof of God's love is the sacrificial gift of his Son (see Rom. 5:6–8). But the phenomenon portrayed in Romans 5:5 is altogether *subjective* in nature. This is an assurance of being God's beloved that is fundamentally *intuitive*. One knows it to be true because the internal work of the Spirit assures one that it is true.

The point in unpacking this remarkable paragraph is simply that none of this is even remotely possible apart from our grasp of justification. If we are still at war with God, we can hardly hope for anything other than eternal exclusion from his presence and the suffering of his righteous wrath.

Justification and the Certitude of our Salvation

Justification by faith also addresses and provides the only lasting remedy to what may be the greatest single fear and source of anxiety in the hearts of most Christians in our world.[20] It is not the threat of terrorism or nuclear holocaust or even a diagnosis of terminal cancer. It is the fear that God's love for us in Christ won't last. There is a

---

17. John Murray, *The Epistle to the Romans: The English Text with Introduction, Exposition and Notes*, NICNT (Grand Rapids, MI: Eerdmans, 1968), 1:165.
18. J. I. Packer, *Knowing God* (1973; repr., Downers Grove, IL: IVP Books, 1993), 118.
19. Packer, *Knowing God*, 118; italics original.
20. This section is adapted from Sam Storms, " Romans 8:31–39," Enjoying God, accessed March 9, 2018, http://www.samstorms.com/all-articles/post/romans-8-31-39. Used by permission of the author.

fear that no matter how good it may be *now* to reflect on God's love for us, it is likely only temporary. No matter how heart-warming it may be to think of God's affection and delight for me, hell-deserving sinner that I am, there's likely coming a day when it will all end. No matter how often I remind myself that God is good and that he always keeps his promises, I am stuck with the inescapable reality of my own sinful soul and the countless times I treat God's grace and love with contempt. Surely, or so I say to myself, God will one day get fed up with me and pull the plug on my salvation. And honestly, I would not blame him if he did.

When I ask people why they struggle with this fear, among the many answers given, three often stand out. It is common for people to say, first, my enemies are too many and too powerful. The deck is stacked against me. There are powerful people and even spiritual forces that threaten to expose me as the fraud that I am. They step in between me and God and threaten to tell him how pathetic I am when it comes to loving him and obeying him. It may be people who pass themselves off as my friends. It may be a family member. It may be someone who really hates me. And Satan is surely there all the time seeking to undo what God's grace has done.

Then, second, my needs are just too many; they are, quite simply, overwhelming. To stay the course, to persevere in faith, to find the strength not to quit, requires so much that I seriously doubt if God is either able or willing to keep on supplying me with what I need. Surely at some point, the well is going to run dry. Surely at some point, God will put a plug on the fountain of mercy and grace that has flowed so freely for so long.

Third, and finally, even if something can be done about my enemies, and even if I can be convinced that God can meet my needs, my sins are simply too numerous. I keep doing the same stupid, selfish things over and over and over again. When I think of how ungrateful I am, how prone I am to repeat past failures, how prideful and lustful and weak and addicted I am, I find it almost impossible to believe that a God worth his salt would bother to put up with me any longer and continue to invest his energy in my life.

So how long will God's love last? A lot of Christians, when asked that question, shrug their shoulders in ignorance or cringe in fear that it won't last much longer. These concerns, these anxieties, these reasons why we doubt the durability of God's love aren't theological abstractions concocted by some pointy-headed apostle who got bored sitting in his first-century ivory tower. They are all too real, and we each face them in our own ways almost daily. Each one of these three fears that leads to doubt and anxiety and, in some people, despair, are raised by Paul here in Romans 8 and then carefully and thoroughly refuted by him. So let's follow the apostle as he takes up, one by one, each of our fears and finally and forever puts them to rest by telling us what God has done and will do for us in Jesus Christ.

Overwhelmed by Enemies

First of all is this objection: "My enemies are too numerous and so committed to undoing everything God has done, I don't think I stand much of a chance in the long run.

Satan is too clever, my enemies are too many, and others hate me so deeply that I'm not sure I can hold up much longer. I'm surrounded by people who would love nothing more than to see me fail miserably."

Paul's response to this is simple and straight to the point: "If God is for us, who can be against us?" (Rom. 8:31).[21] In asking this question, Paul is not suggesting that we have no adversaries. He himself had dozens, perhaps hundreds, of them. They beat him, flogged him, stoned him, threw him in prison, and did everything they could to undermine his work and ministry. Paul lists our adversaries and the opposition we face in 8:35–36. You will never reach a level of maturity in the Christian life in which you no longer have enemies or face opposition. In fact, with spiritual increase and success, our enemies often multiply.

Paul's point is simply that no adversary or enemy is of any account since God is for us. Because God is for us, to use the words of Romans 8:28, all things work together for our ultimate spiritual good, even those things that our enemies intend for our harm. No enemies can ever achieve what they arrogantly claim when they attack us. Notice also that Paul doesn't simply ask the question, "Who is against us?"; his question is, "If God is for us, who can be against us?" That is, if the God who, according to Romans 8:29–30, foreknew and predestined and called and justified and glorified us, if *that* God is for us, who can be against us (see also Isa. 46:9–10; Dan. 4:34–35)?

The reason Paul gives voice to this rhetorical question is that he is confronting our fear of the collective power of the many forces and enemies amassed against us. Paul knows that there will always be a person or people whose ridicule and hostility and rejection you feel unable to face. Paul knows how inhibiting and paralyzing such fear can be. So he calls on us to think: Think about all your enemies and all their disdain for you and put it on one side of the scales of balance. Now put "this" God on the other side. Who is weightier? Who is mightier? Who is more powerful? "He who is in you," said the apostle John, "is greater than he who is in the world" (1 John 4:4).

Overwhelmed by Needs

Paul may have made his point. Maybe my enemies are no match for God, but what about my needs? This brings us to our second concern and the apostle's response. "My needs are so many and so deep and so diverse that I live in constant fear that I'm going to come up short. I need faith that God is going to do what he promised he would do. I need strength to resist temptation. I need wisdom to navigate through some really tough decisions that are ahead of me. I need joy in Jesus to keep me from seeking satisfaction in what the world offers."

Yes, I know, says Paul. But just as your fear of your enemies and adversaries led me to ask you a question, so too does your fear that your needs are too many. You fear that God either can't or won't supply you or provide you with what you need every day to

---

21. I refer you to Packer's excellent treatment of this theme in *Knowing God*, 253–79.

stay true to him. Well, here's my question for you: "He who did not spare his own Son but gave him up for us all, how will he not also with him graciously give us all things?" (Rom. 8:32). Now again, if Paul had merely asked, "Will God give us all things?" we might have wondered. We might have said in response: "Well, you know, I need so many things, big things, important things; how can I be certain God will provide them? I'm not saying he lacks the power to do so, but what if he lacks the will?"

But look again at how Paul phrases the question. The God who Paul says will graciously give us all things is *the God who "did not spare his own Son but gave him up for us all!"* In other words, the God about whom we ask if he will give us all things we need is the very God, the only God, who has already given us his very own beloved Son, Jesus Christ. This is the same point Paul made earlier in 5:9–10: "Since, therefore, we have now been justified by his blood, much more shall we be saved by him from the wrath of God. For if while we were enemies we were reconciled to God by the death of his Son, much more, now that we are reconciled, shall we be saved by his life." That is, since God has done the unspeakably and indescribably great and costly thing, namely, sacrifice for us his only begotten Son, we may be fully confident that he will do what is by comparison infinitely less. The point is this: If God would do the greatest thing for you, he will certainly do all lesser things. You live in fear that God won't do all lesser things and meet all these many needs you have to stay faithful to him. No! In comparison with giving Christ Jesus, it's a foregone conclusion. Giving you all things is easy. This is the unbreakable, unshakable logic of heaven.

Negatively, God did not "spare" his own Son. Parents, we "spare" our children when we refrain from inflicting on them all the discipline that their disobedience calls for. Judges "spare" criminals when they reduce or suspend a sentence. But this is precisely what God did *not* do with Jesus. He did not withhold one stroke of his holy wrath in punishing Jesus for what we have done. No mitigation, no lessening of the penalty, no suspension of the sentence, no leniency.

Positively, he "gave him up" for us all, or better still, he "delivered" him up. As someone has insightfully asked, Who delivered up Jesus, and why? Was it Judas Iscariot, and did he do it for thirty pieces of silver? No. Was it the Jewish religious leaders, and did they do it out of jealousy? No. Was it Pontius Pilate, and did he do it out of fear of the crowds? No. It was God the Father, and he did it because of love for you and me.

Therefore, God will do what is by comparison infinitely easier. He will give us "all things" we need for spiritual success. Whatever is necessary for you to make it to the end of life still faithful and still trusting Christ, God will give you. Whatever is necessary for you to be conformed to the image of his Son and to resist temptation, he will give you.

Packer issues us a challenge in the light of Romans 8:32.[22] Think about what kind of person you would be and the kind of life you would live if you really believed all this. You know that Jesus calls on us to deny ourselves, take up our cross, and follow him

---

22. Packer, *Knowing God*, 260–77.

daily. You know that he calls on us to lay up for ourselves treasure in heaven and not on earth. You know that he warns us that if we follow him, we will suffer persecution, whether slander or gossip or injustice or mockery or imprisonment or death. You know that we are called by our Lord to embrace humility and meekness and gentleness and to pursue purity of life. So why don't we do it? The biggest reason is fear. We are afraid of being stranded and left to ourselves and being trampled on and exploited and taken advantage of and left with nothing. The bottom line is that we are not persuaded that God really will provide us with all that we need to live the life that he's called us to live. Our fear is fueled by unbelief.

Overwhelmed by Sins

We've come now to the third and final reason why we fear that God's love just won't last, that somehow, someday, in some way or other God will pack up and leave us to ourselves, forever. The protest in our hearts goes something like this: "My sins are too numerous, too many, too great, too severe, too regular. And the guilt and shame and the feeling of being disqualified are so overwhelming that it doesn't make sense to pretend any longer." Paul's answer not only is profound but also alerts us to why the truth of our justification is the underlying or foundational warrant for everything Paul says in this paragraph:

> Who shall bring any charge against God's elect? It is God who justifies. Who is to condemn? Christ Jesus is the one who died—more than that, who was raised—who is at the right hand of God, who indeed is interceding for us. (Rom. 8:33–34)

Paul is not saying that people won't charge us with wrongdoing. They do it all the time. He's not suggesting that Satan won't make every effort to condemn us by bringing up to God and to our own consciences the many ways we fall short. But all such charges fall short. All such accusations are to no avail. Why? Is it because we are innocent of what they accuse us of? No. In fact, we are probably guilty of a lot more than they can think of or find time to mention. They are to no avail because "Christ Jesus is the one who died" (8:34) for us. The penalty that those sins call for, whether they be past, present, or yet future, has already been paid in full. How can anyone condemn you when Christ has already been condemned in your place? What is left for you to suffer? What guilt or penalty remains that might damage your relationship with God?

And it does not stop there. He not only died but was raised from the dead to testify to the sufficiency and perfection of what he accomplished for you on the cross. And he not only was raised from the dead but was exalted to the right hand of God the Father, the place of supremacy and authority and honor and power. But he was exalted not only that he might demonstrate his power and authority but also that he might intercede on your behalf (8:34). Each time an accusation is brought against you, Jesus turns to the Father and says, "I was reckoned guilty for that sin. I died for it. Your justice has been satisfied." Over and over and over and over again.

This is the basis or ground on which Paul declares in 8:33, "It is God who justifies." God is the one who declares that you are righteous in his sight, no matter how loudly your enemies may say that you are guilty, no matter how viciously Satan may attack you, no matter how painfully your own conscience may scream in protest. It is God who justifies you. Who, then, could possibly bring a charge against you that might stick?

And when, exactly, did God do this? According to 4:5, God justifies the "ungodly." God passed a favorable sentence on your behalf in full view of your moral failures, in full view of your shortcomings. God justified you with his eyes wide open. He knew the very worst about you at the time he accepted you for Jesus's sake. God didn't wait until you were "godly" and then justify you on the basis of what you had achieved. He looked at you in full and exhaustive awareness of every sin you would ever commit, and because of what Jesus achieved, he declared you righteous in his sight.

Packer once pointed out that there are two kinds of sick consciences.[23] There is first the conscience that is not sufficiently aware of sin, the conscience that is hardened and virtually oblivious to failure and fault. These are the people who persist in spiritual rebellion and immorality and never think twice about it. But then there is the conscience that is not sufficiently aware of forgiveness. It is to this second sort that Paul is speaking in Romans 8. He knows how easily the consciences of some Christians can become sensitive—that is, self-condemning—and insecure. So, says Packer, Paul here speaks

> directly to the fear (to which no Christian is a total stranger) that present justification may be no more than provisional—that it may one day be lost by reason of the imperfections of one's Christian life. Paul does not for a moment deny that Christians can fail and fall, sometimes grievously. . . . But Paul denies emphatically that any lapses now can endanger our justified status. The reason, he says in effect, is simple: nobody is in a position to get God's verdict reviewed![24]

These are the three primary reasons so many Christians live in anxiety and fear about their future with God: too many enemies, too many needs, too many sins. But Paul has silenced all three by grounding our relationship with God and his treatment of us in the truth of our justification in his sight through faith in his Son.

Justification and the Insecure Pastor

We turn now from a consideration of how justification serves the body of Christ to its function in the life of the local church pastor.[25] First, consider the devastating effects of insecurity in a pastor and how justification alone can provide a healing remedy. A crippling sense of insecurity in a pastor can wreak havoc in the local church. The only lasting solution is a deep and abiding conviction that one is altogether justified in the sight of God through faith alone in Christ alone. Consider the nature and consequences of insecurity.

---

23. Packer, *Knowing God*, 272.
24. Packer, *Knowing God*, 272.
25. This section is adapted from Sam Storms, "Insecurity and Pastoral Bullies," Enjoying God, April 18, 2013, http://www.samstorms.com/enjoying-god-blog/post/insecurity-and-pastoral-bullies. Used by permission of the author.

Insecurity makes it difficult for a pastor to acknowledge and appreciate the accomplishments of others on staff (or in the congregation). In other words, the personally insecure pastor is often incapable of providing genuine encouragement to others. Their success becomes a threat to him, his authority, and his status in the eyes of the people. Thus, if you are insecure, you will not likely pray for others to flourish.

Related to the above is the fact that an insecure pastor will likely resent the praise or affirmation that other staff members receive from the people at large. For the insecure pastor, constructive criticism is not received well but is rather perceived as a threat or outright rejection. Because the insecure pastor is incapable of acknowledging personal failure or lack of knowledge, he is often *unteachable*. He will always be resistant to those who genuinely seek to help him or bring him information or insights that he lacks. His spiritual growth is therefore stunted.

The insecure pastor is typically heavy handed in his dealings with others. The insecure pastor is often controlling and given to micromanagement. The insecure pastor will rarely empower others or authorize them to undertake tasks for which they are especially qualified and gifted. He will not *release* others but rather restrict them. The insecure pastor is often given to outbursts of anger.

At its core, insecurity is the fruit of pride. In other words, at its core, insecurity is the result of not believing the gospel that we are justified by faith alone. Thus, the antidote to feelings of insecurity is the rock-solid realization that one's value and worth are in the hands of God, not other people, and that one's identity is an expression of who one is in Christ through faith, not through ministerial success. Only as we deepen in our grasp of his love for us and his sacrifice on our behalf will we find the freedom and confidence to affirm and support others while never fearing either their success or threats.

Justification and Pastoral Bullies

In his instructions to elders/pastors, Peter insists that they must not lead for love of power, which is to say that they must not "domineer" those in their charge, but rather, they must be "examples" to them (1 Pet. 5:3).[26] How might a pastor or elder "domineer" his flock? In other words, what makes a man a pastoral bully? And what would be the most effective remedy for this problem in local church leadership? I'm persuaded that a robust and biblically rooted understanding of how a pastor, like all other Christians, is justified by faith alone in Christ alone is the perfect antidote to this recurring problem that seems to plague so many in pastoral ministry. But first, what is a pastoral "bully"? What does Peter mean when he speaks of local church leaders "domineering" their flock?

A man can "domineer," or "lord it over," his flock by intimidating them into doing what he wants done or by holding over their heads the prospect of loss of stature and position in the church. A pastor domineers whenever he threatens them with stern

---

26. This section is adapted from Sam Storms, "Pastoral Bullies," Enjoying God, April 17, 2013, http://www.samstorms.com/enjoying-god-blog/post/pastoral-bullies. Used by permission of the author.

warnings of the discipline and judgment of God even though there is no biblical basis for doing so. This also occurs whenever he threatens them with public exposure of their sin should they not conform to his will.

A pastor domineers whenever he uses the sheer force of his personality to overwhelm others and coerce their submission or when he uses slick verbiage or eloquence to humiliate people into feeling ignorant or less competent than they really are. A pastor is a bully whenever he presents himself as superspiritual. (His views came about only as the result of extensive prayer and fasting and seeking God; how could anyone, then, possibly disagree with him?)

If a pastor or elder should ever exploit the natural tendency people have to elevate their spiritual leaders above the average Christian, they may prove guilty of domineering their flock. That is, many Christians mistakenly think that a pastor is closer to God and more in tune with the divine will. The pastor often takes advantage of this false belief to expand his power and influence.

A pastor domineers whenever he gains a following and support against all dissenters by guaranteeing those who stand with him that they will gain from it, either by being brought into his inner circle or by some form of promotion. On occasion, this can also happen when he intentionally widens the alleged gap between "clergy" and "laity." In other words, he reinforces in them the false belief that he has a degree of access to God that they do not.

Related to the former is the way some pastors will make it appear that they hold sway or power over the extent to which average laypeople can experience God's grace. He presents himself in subtle (not overt) ways as the mediator between the grace of God and the average believer. In this way, he can secure their loyalty for his agenda. He also domineers by building into people a greater loyalty to himself than to God. Or he makes it appear that not to support him is to work at cross-purposes with God.

I often hear of local church leaders who domineer by teaching that they have a gift that enables them to understand Scripture in a way that the ordinary person cannot. People are led to believe that they cannot trust their own interpretive conclusions and must yield at all times to that of the lead pastor of a church.

Yet another characteristic of pastoral bullying is when a man short-circuits due process by shutting down dialogue and discussion prematurely or by not giving all concerned an opportunity to voice their opinion. This sort of leader domineers by establishing an inviolable barrier between himself and the sheep. He either surrounds himself with staff who insulate him from contact with the people or withdraws from the daily affairs of the church in such a way that he is unavailable and unreachable.

Related to the above is the practice of some in creating a governmental structure in which the senior pastor is accountable to no one, or if he is accountable, it is only to a small group of very close friends and fellow elders who stand to profit personally from his tenure as pastor. He domineers by viewing the people as simply a means to the achieving of his own personal ends. Ministry is reduced to exploitation. The people exist to "serve his vision" rather than he and all the people together existing to serve the vision of the entire church.

He bullies people by making them feel unsafe and insecure should they desire to voice an objection to his proposals and policies, or by convincing them, ever so subtly, that their spiritual welfare is dependent on his will. To cross him is to cross God.

He domineers by "ministering" in such a way that people are led to believe that the pastor is special and need not be held accountable to the biblical standards of moral conduct in the way that all others are. Or he can gravitate to the other extreme by building a culture of legalism rather than one of grace. People are thus motivated to embrace his authority and bow to his will based on extrabiblical rules that supposedly are the criteria for true spirituality.

Peter would also have in mind the sort of pastor who domineers by arguing or acting as if his movements and decisions are ultimately determinative of the spiritual welfare of others (cf. 2 Cor. 1:23–24). He domineers when he leads people to believe that their faith hinges (i.e., rises or falls) on his life and decisions, as well as when he uses people as a means to his own satisfaction rather than enabling them to experience satisfaction in Christ alone.

So how does a sincere belief in the reality of justification by faith serve to correct these destructive tendencies in a local church pastor? It isn't hard to see. Confident that my acceptance with God is not dependent on my earthly fame or ministerial success, I am free to speak the truth of Scripture without hesitation and without turning an eye to what the wealthy and powerful might think. Knowing that my value as a man is grounded in what God has done and is for me in Jesus Christ, I am released from the pressure to gain the praise of others for my pastoral accomplishments. If the righteousness of Jesus Christ is truly mine through faith, I have no need to build a platform for my own praise or use God's people to bolster a sagging ego.

How did Peter and Paul, for example, overcome the allure of public acclaim and promotion? Was it not by looking on all human achievement and comparing it with the glory of knowing Christ, being found in him, and being clothed with the righteousness that God imputes through faith (see Phil. 3:1–10)? When the heart of a man is captivated by this unspeakably glorious truth that he is accepted in the beloved, that he is wholly forgiven of all sin and seen now as in Christ and enveloped by his righteousness, then is the grip of human accolade broken; then is the seductive appeal to use people to promote oneself conquered; then is the temptation to manipulate others and put them down so that he might be elevated in their opinion rendered powerless. The reality of justification undercuts all fleshly ambition, for who would seek the praise of men when he knows he has the approval of God? It undermines and eviscerates self-seeking and prideful self-assertion.

The man whose heart is not saturated with this truth of justification by faith alone is susceptible to all manner of temptation from the world, the flesh, and the devil. That isn't to say that justification as a doctrine automatically prevents temptation from coming our way. Rather, a heart captivated by this truth is strengthened and motivated to resist any alluring or seductive prospect that might confront him in the course of pastoral ministry.

One of the more popular worship songs in our day is "In Christ Alone," written by Keith Getty and Stuart Townend. Of the numerous deeply theological lyrics in the song, none strikes home quite like the declaration that because of Christ there is "no guilt in life, no fear in death." On what basis can this claim be defended? The answer again is that the believer is justified by faith alone. Justification is the remedy for the guilt-ridden conscience. Whatever guilt we have incurred has been imputed to Christ. He has suffered its penal consequences for us and in our place. And is not the fear of death fueled by the prospect of standing before a holy God unforgiven and condemned? How far removed this is from the confidence of Jude, who extolled the God "who is able to keep you from stumbling and to present you blameless before the presence of his glory," not with fear or uncertainty but "with great joy" (Jude 24). We are "blameless" because the stain and shame of our sins have been laid on Christ, and we will stand in the "presence of his glory with great joy" because his righteousness is now ours by a marvelous imputation. It is simply staggering to consider the impact on a lost and dying world if God's people lived in the transforming truth of having been justified by faith in Christ. Would that pastors might happily and passionately proclaim this truth.

Conclusion

John Bunyan speaks vividly of his futile effort to establish a righteousness of his own that might prevail in the presence of God. He writes,

> One day as I was passing into the field . . . this sentence fell upon my soul. Thy righteousness is in heaven. And methought, withal, I saw with the eyes of my soul Jesus Christ at God's right hand; there, I say, was my righteousness; so that wherever I was, or whatever I was doing, God could not say of me, he wants [lacks] my righteousness, for that was just before him. I also saw, moreover, that it was not my good frame of heart that made my righteousness better, nor yet my bad frame that made my righteousness worse, for my righteousness was Jesus Christ himself.[27]

Is there a more powerful remedy than this for diseased souls that anxiously strive to find acceptance with a God whom they know will settle for nothing less than perfection? Whatever peace prevails in our hearts, whatever joy energizes our efforts, whatever confidence we may ever hope to attain will come only as we, like Bunyan, can say, "For my righteousness was Jesus Christ himself."

John Piper's counsel for pastors is that they hold forth this singular truth to their flocks as the only hope for happiness in this life and assurance of the next:

> For Martin Luther and John Bunyan the discovery of the imputed righteousness of Christ was the greatest life-changing experience they ever had. Luther said it was

---

27. John Bunyan, *Grace Abounding to the Chief of Sinners* (1666; repr., Hertfordshire, UK: Evangelical Press, 1978), 20.

like entering a paradise of peace with God. For Bunyan it was the end of years of spiritual torture and uncertainty. Brothers, what would your people give to know for sure that their acceptance and approval before God was as sure as the standing of Jesus Christ, His Son?[28]

My primary concern in this chapter has been to draw attention to the numerous ways in which the doctrine of justification serves both as the foundational principle on which Christian living is based and the sustaining power by which we pursue a life of holiness. But I wish to close by directing our attention to the fact that justification has profoundly political implications as well. I was alerted to this by something John Piper wrote with regard to William Wilberforce. The role Wilberforce played in bringing the slave trade to an end is well known, but less known is the influence exerted on him by the truth of justification by faith alone. In fact, Wilberforce attributed much of the moral lethargy of his day to the separation of Christian obedience from Christian doctrine. When one asks what could possibly have energized this man to withstand eleven parliamentary defeats over the span of twenty years of hostile opposition, the answer is quick in coming. It was primarily the truth of justification. As Piper notes, "The indomitable joy that perseveres in the battle for justice is grounded in the experience of Jesus Christ as our righteousness."[29]

This was the power that impelled Wilberforce to endure unimaginable opposition in his pursuit of social justice. The people of his day, he complained (to use Piper's words),

> pursued morality without first relying utterly on the free gift of justification by grace alone through faith alone on the basis of Christ alone. They got things backward. First they strived for moral uplift, and then they appealed to God for approval. That is not the Christian gospel. And it will not transform a nation.[30]

The true Christian, said Wilberforce, knows "that this holiness is not to precede his reconciliation to God, and be its cause; but to follow it, and be its effect. That, in short, it is by faith in Christ only that he is to be justified in the sight of God."[31]

Whether it be fighting for abolition of the slave trade or resisting sexual temptation or the allure of money and power, the truth of justification, rooted in the trusting human heart, is the only hope for sustained commitment and success.

Recommended Resources

Allen, R. Michael. *Justification and the Gospel: Understanding the Contexts and Controversies*. Grand Rapids, MI: Baker Academic, 2013.

Buchanan, James. *The Doctrine of Justification: An Outline of Its History in the Church and of Its Exposition from Scripture*. 1867. Reprint, Grand Rapids, MI: Baker, 1977.

---

28. John Piper, *Brothers, We Are Not Professionals: A Plea to Pastors for Radical Ministry* (Nashville: Broadman, 2002), 31–32.
29. John Piper, "Abolition and the Roots of Public Justice: The Public Power of Protestant Justification," in *A Godward Heart: Treasuring the God Who Loves You* (Colorado Springs: Multnomah Books, 2014), 190.
30. Piper, "Abolition," 191.
31. Quoted in Piper, "Abolition," 191.

Carson, D. A., ed. *Right with God: Justification in the Bible and the World*. Grand Rapids, MI: Baker, 1992.

Gaffin, Richard B., Jr. *By Faith, Not by Sight: Paul and the Order of Salvation*. 2nd ed. Phillipsburg, NJ: P&R, 2013.

Johnson, Marcus Peter. *One with Christ: An Evangelical Theology of Salvation*. Wheaton, IL: Crossway, 2013.

McGrath, Alister E. *Justification by Faith*. Grand Rapids, MI: Academie Books, 1990.

Piper, John. *The Future of Justification: A Response to N. T. Wright*. Wheaton, IL: Crossway, 2007.

Schreiner, Thomas. *Faith Alone: The Doctrine of Justification; What the Reformers Taught . . . and Why It Still Matters*. Five Solas Series. Grand Rapids, MI: Zondervan, 2015.

Seifrid, Mark A. *Christ, Our Righteousness: Paul's Theology of Justification*. New Studies in Biblical Theology 9. Downers Grove, IL: InterVarsity Press, 2000.

Sproul, R. C. *Faith Alone: The Evangelical Doctrine of Justification*. Grand Rapids, MI: Baker, 1995.

Waters, Guy Prentiss. *Justification and the New Perspective on Paul: A Review and Response*. Phillipsburg, NJ: P&R, 2004.

White, James R. *The God Who Justifies: The Doctrine of Justification: A Comprehensive Study of the Doctrine of Justification*. Minneapolis: Bethany, 2001.

Wilson, Jared C. *The Pastor's Justification: Applying the Work of Christ in Your Life and Ministry*. Wheaton, IL: Crossway, 2013.

Contributors

Matthew Barrett (PhD, Southern Baptist Theological Seminary) is associate professor of Christian theology at Midwestern Baptist Theological Seminary, as well as the founder and executive editor of *Credo Magazine*. He is the author of *Surprised by God: Discovering the Classical Attributes of God*; *40 Questions about Salvation*; *God's Word Alone: The Authority of Scripture*; and *Salvation by Grace: The Case for Effectual Calling and Regeneration*; coauthor (with Michael A. G. Haykin) of *Owen on the Christian Life*; and the editor of *Reformation Theology: A Systematic Summary*.

Bruce P. Baugus (PhD, Calvin Theological Seminary) is associate professor of philosophy and theology at Reformed Theological Seminary in Jackson, Mississippi. He serves as a teaching elder in the Presbyterian Church in America and is the editor of *China's Reforming Churches: Mission, Polity, and Ministry in the Next Christendom*.

Gerald Bray (DLitt, University of Paris-Sorbonne) is research professor of divinity, history, and doctrine at Beeson Divinity School and director of research for the Latimer Trust. He is the author of *The Doctrine of God*; *God Is Love: A Biblical and Systematic Theology*; *God Has Spoken: A History of Christian Theology*; and *The Church: A Theological and Historical Account*.

Robert J. Cara (PhD, Westminster Theological Seminary) is the Hugh and Sallie Reaves Professor of New Testament and provost and chief academic officer at Reformed Theological Seminary in Charlotte, North Carolina. He is the author of *Cracking the Foundation of the New Perspective on Paul: Covenantal Nomism versus Reformed Covenantal Theology*.

Chris Castaldo (PhD, London School of Theology) is lead pastor of New Covenant Church in Naperville, Illinois. He is the author of *Talking with Catholics about the Gospel: A Guide for Evangelicals*; and *Holy Ground: Walking with Jesus as a Former Catholic*; and he is also coauthor (with Gregg Allison) of *The Unfinished Reformation: What Unites and Divides Catholics and Protestants after 500 Years*.

Brandon Crowe (PhD, Edinburgh) is associate professor of New Testament at Westminster Theological Seminary in Glenside, Pennsylvania. He is the author of *The Message* of the General Epistles in the History of Redemption: Wisdom from James, Peter, John, and Jude;* and *The Last Adam: A Theology of the Obedient Life of Jesus in the Gospels.* He is also coeditor (with Carl R. Trueman) of *The Essential Trinity: New Testament Foundations and Practical Relevance.*

Leonardo De Chirico (PhD, King's College London) is the pastor of Breccia di Roma and vice chairman of the Italian Evangelical Alliance. Additionally, Leonardo is lecturer of historical theology at Istituto di Formazione Evangelica e Documentazione and director of the Reformanda Initiative. He is the author of *A Christian Pocket Guide to the Papacy: Its Origin and Role in the 21st Century;* and *A Christian Pocket Guide to Mary: Mother of God?*

Stephen Dempster (PhD, University of Toronto) is professor of religious studies at Crandall University in Moncton, New Brunswick, Canada. He is the author of *Dominion and Dynasty: A Theology of the Hebrew Bible;* and *Micah: A Theological Commentary.*

J. V. Fesko (PhD, University of Aberdeen) is academic dean and professor of systematic theology and historical theology at Westminster Seminary California in Escondido, California. He is the author of *Justification: Understanding the Classic Reformed Doctrine; Death in Adam, Life in Christ: The Doctrine of Imputation;* and *The Trinity and the Covenant of Redemption.*

Allan Harman (ThD, Westminster Theological Seminary) is research professor of Old Testament at Presbyterian Theological College in Melbourne, Australia. He is the author of *The Psalms; Isaiah: A Covenant to Be Kept for the Sake of the Church;* and *Exodus: God's Kingdom of Priests.*

Timo Laato (ThD, University of Åbo Academy, Turku, Finland) is senior lecturer in New Testament at Församlingsfakulteten in Göteborg, Sweden. He is the author of *Paul and Judaism: An Anthropological Approach;* and "Justification according to James: A Comparison with Paul."

Korey Maas (DPhil, University of Oxford) is assistant professor of history at Hillsdale College in Hillsdale, Michigan. He is the author of *Making the Case for Christianity: Responding to Modern Objections; Justification and Sanctification: The Lutheran Difference;* and *Law and Gospel: The Lutheran Difference.*

Dan McCartney (PhD, Westminster Theological Seminary) is professor of New Testament interpretation at Redeemer Seminary in Dallas. He is the author of *James* in the Baker Exegetical Commentary on the New Testament series and coauthor (with Charles Clayton) of *Let the Reader Understand: A Guide to Interpreting and Applying the Bible.*

Jason Meyer (PhD, Southern Baptist Theological Seminary) is the pastor for preaching and vision at Bethlehem Baptist Church and associate professor of preaching at Bethlehem College and Seminary in Minneapolis, Minnesota. He is the author of *The End of the Law: Mosaic Covenant in Pauline Theology*; and *Preaching: A Biblical Theology*.

Andrew David Naselli (PhD, Bob Jones University; PhD, Trinity Evangelical Divinity School) is associate professor of New Testament and theology at Bethlehem College and Seminary. He is the author of *How to Understand and Apply the New Testament: Twelve Steps from Exegesis to Theology*; *From Typology to Doxology: Paul's Use of Isaiah and Job in Romans 11:34–35*; and *No Quick Fix: Where Higher Life Theology Came From, What It Is, and Why It's Harmful*.

Nicholas Needham (PhD, University of Edinburgh) is minister of Inverness Reformed Baptist Church in Inverness, Scotland, and lecturer in church history at Highland Theological College in Dingwall, Scotland. He is the author of the four-volume series *2000 Years of Christ's Power*.

David A. Shaw (MTh, Oak Hill College) is the theological adviser to the Fellowship of Independent Evangelical Churches, as well as the editor of *Primer*. He is a PhD candidate at Cambridge University under Simon Gathercole and tutor of New Testament at Oak Hill Theological College.

R. Lucas Stamps (PhD, Southern Baptist Theological Seminary) is assistant professor of Christian studies at Anderson University in Anderson, South Carolina. He serves as an executive director for the Center for Baptist Renewal, a fellow for the Research Institute of the Ethics and Religious Liberty Commission, and a senior fellow for the Center for Ancient Christian Studies.

Sam Storms (PhD, University of Texas at Dallas) is the lead pastor for preaching and vision at Bridgeway Church in Oklahoma City, Oklahoma, and serves as the president of Enjoying God Ministries. He is the author of *Chosen for Life: The Case for Divine Election*; *Kept for Jesus: What the New Testament Really Teaches about Assurance of Salvation and Eternal Security*; and *Kingdom Come: The Amillennial Alternative*.

Mark Thompson (DPhil, University of Oxford) is the principal of Moore College in Sydney, Australia. He is the author of *Engaging with Calvin: Aspects of the Reformer's Legacy for Today*; *A Clear and Present Word: The Clarity of Scripture*; and *A Sure Ground on Which to Stand: The Relation of Authority and Interpretive Method in Luther's Approach to Scripture*.

David VanDrunen (PhD, Loyola University Chicago) is the Robert B. Strimple Professor of Systematic Theology and Christian Ethics at Westminster Seminary California in Escondido, California. He is the author of *God's Glory Alone: The Majestic Heart of Christian Faith and Life*; *Living in God's Two Kingdoms: A Biblical Vision for*

Christianity and Culture; and *Divine Covenants and Moral Order: A Biblical Theology of Natural Law*.

Willem A. VanGemeren (PhD, University of Wisconsin) is professor emeritus of Old Testament and semitic languages at Trinity Evangelical Divinity School in Deerfield, Illinois. He is the author of *The Progress of Redemption: The Story of Salvation from Creation to the New Jerusalem*; and *Interpreting the Prophetic Word: An Introduction to the Prophetic Literature of the Old Testament*. He is also the general editor of *The New International Dictionary of Old Testament Theology and Exegesis* (NIDOTTE).

Brian Vickers (PhD, Southern Baptist Theological Seminary) is professor of New Testament interpretation and biblical theology in Louisville, Kentucky. He is the author of *Jesus' Blood and Righteousness: Paul's Theology of Imputation*; and *Justification by Grace through Faith: Finding Freedom from Legalism, Lawlessness, Pride, and Despair*.

Stephen J. Wellum (PhD, Trinity Evangelical Divinity School) is professor of Christian theology at the Southern Baptist Theological Seminary in Louisville, Kentucky. He is the author of *God the Son Incarnate: The Doctrine of Christ*; *Kingdom through Covenant: A Biblical-Theological Understanding of the Covenants*; and *Christ Alone: The Uniqueness of Jesus as Savior*. He is also coeditor (with Brent E. Parker) of *Progressive Covenantalism: Charting a Course between Dispensational and Covenantal Theologies*.

General Index

Abegg, M. G., Jr., 164n72
abiding in Christ, 210
Abraham, 41–65
   faith counted as righteousness, 54–57, 224
   faith of, 33, 52–54, 59, 193, 249–51, 255, 395, 432, 565–68
   faith results in faithfulness, 63
   as father of many nations, 50, 64, 395, 397
   justice of, 113–14
   justification of, 225, 280–82, 394, 395
   justified by works, 281–82
   as new Adam, 64
   obedience of, 59–60, 274, 290–91
   Pauline and Philonic interpretations of, 43, 63
   sacrifice of son, 59
   suffering of, 114
Abrahamic covenant, 43–44, 58, 69, 395–97, 539
à Brakel, Wilhelmus, 422–23, 476–77
"absolute faith" (Tillich), 801–2
absolute idealism, 796
acorn-tree analogy, 819
acquittal, 352
active obedience of Christ, 14, 27, 31, 208–9, 232, 354, 364, 374, 393, 399, 401, 442, 485, 490–96, 711, 712, 713
   bound up with passive obedience, 461
   definition of, 442–43
   resistance to, 446
   and right to eternal life, 452
active righteousness (Luther), 703
Acts
   on gospel to the Gentiles, 201–2
   and Isaiah, 113
   on obedience of Christ, 467
Adam
   covenant with, 23–24, 378–79, 444, 448n34
   failure to obey, 26
   fall of, 24
   as federal head, 24, 227, 445
   historicity of, 269, 379n130, 456

   imputation of sin of, 446, 494–95n126
   sin of, 227, 380–81, 448, 449, 458
   state before the fall, 26
Adam-Christ typology, 364, 447, 458, 462, 464, 527
adoption, 261, 412, 413, 437, 502n147
Agricola, Johannes, 684, 687
Aland, Kurt, 666, 669n67
Albrecht of Mainz, 665, 667
Alexander, Archibald, 731–32
Alexander, Philip S., 166n79
Alexander of Hales, 631
alien righteousness, 225, 343, 446n24, 509, 575, 830, 851
   incompatible with Roman Catholic anthropology, 756
   Luther on, 435–36, 506, 514, 517, 523, 577, 702–3
   prefigured in Augustine, 594, 595
Allen, R. Michael, 337n48, 338, 341n69, 343, 853n16
Allison, Dale C., Jr., 274n5, 275n10, 276, 277n17
Allison, Gregg, 755
already–not yet, 216n8, 413
Alsted, Johann Heinrich, 35, 657n1
Ambrose, 581
Ambrosiaster, 581–83, 584
Ames, William, 729
Ammi, 129–32, 133, 135
Amos, 121
Amsdorf, Nikolaus von, 686–87
Andreae, Jacob, 693
Anglicanism
   as "catholic," 819
   as *via media*, 817–18
Anglo-Catholicism, 817n30, 818
Anselm, 427, 587
   on atonement, 361–62
   on imputed righteousness, 598
   on justification, 596–601
   on satisfaction, 598, 600

antinomianism, 31–32, 267, 515–16, 520, 530
  antinomian-neonomian controversy, 724–26
  Augsburg Confession on, 677
  Lloyd-Jones on, 556–57
  Lutheran controversy, 686–87, 695
  Newman on, 815, 826
  Westminster Assembly on, 718–19
apocalyptic reading of Paul, 148n3, 327, 331–34, 346
apologetic, for conversion, 836
Apology of the Augsburg Confession, 679–84, 687, 691, 693
apostolic authority, 835–36
apostolic succession, 818
Aquinas. *See* Thomas Aquinas
Arianism, 772n9, 777
Aristotelian causality, 706, 728, 831
Aristotelian philosophy, 680, 682, 702
Aristotle, 422
Arminianism, 366, 372–73, 394n8, 718, 797
Arminius, Jacobus, 714–16, 723, 733
Arndt, Johann, 778
Arnold, Thomas, 813
Ashby, Stephen M., 366n70
Asper, Hans, 824
assensus (assent), 433, 516
assurance, 234, 437, 582, 654
Assyria, 122, 137, 138, 144
asyndeton, 48–49
Athanasius, 363n56, 817
atheism, 405
atonement, 27, 29, 197–98, 355, 358, 360, 363–76, 791
Attridge, Harold, 463n113
Aufklärung, 780–81
Augsburg Confession, 674, 677–79, 687, 692, 694, 750, 756
Augsburg Interim, 684–85, 687, 688, 823n58
Augustine, 150n14, 218, 434, 511, 581, 584, 587, 644, 647, 652, 664
  against Pelagius, 644, 647
  on atonement, 361, 597–98n40
  on justification, 589–96, 758
Aulén, Gustaf, 363n56
autonomy, 144, 145

Baalism, 134, 136, 139
Baal Peor, 138n75
Babylonians, 122
baptism, and justification, 743, 758
baptismal regeneration, 752, 814, 815, 832–33
Barclay, John M. G., 263, 295–96, 298, 318–24, 338, 339n60, 341
Barr, James, 42, 63, 534n4

Barth, Karl, 410–11, 421, 424, 432, 748, 796n102, 800, 802–6
Bartimaeus, healing of, 192–93
Baruch, 314
Bates, Matthew, 282–83n34
Baumgarten, Jakob, 781
Baur, Ferdinand Christian, 793–96, 801
Bavinck, Herman, 388, 444–45, 460n96, 461n101, 479, 529–30
Baxter, Richard, 721–24, 727
Bayer, Oswald, 119
Beachy, Alvin J., 772n8
Beatitudes, 182
"because / therefore" relationship with God, 840
Becker, Otto, 540
Belgic Confession (1561), 709, 714
belief and unbelief, in Mark, 193–98
believing and obeying, 63
Bellarmine, Robert, 828
Benedict XVI, Pope, 764, 766, 812, 833n126
Berkhof, Hendrikus, 101–2
Berkhof, Louis, 400, 470n2, 524–25
Bernard of Clairvaux, 587, 601–6
bestiality, 548
Bethel, 138–39n75
Beza, Theodore, 709, 713–14
biblical theology, and interpretation of Paul, 270
Biddle, John, 773n12
Biel, Gabriel, 427–28, 587, 615–18, 624–27, 628, 629–30, 642–45, 654, 660, 663, 664
Billerbeck, Paul, 297n10
Billings, J. Todd, 473n6, 506n3, 527
Bird, Michael, 470, 491–96
bird trying to fly (Biel illustration), 634, 648, 654
Blazosky, Bryan, 220n28
Blenkinsopp, Joseph, 107n12
blessing, 47, 79
Blocher, Henri, 754
boasting, 223, 853–54
Boccaccio, Giovanni, 666
Bockmuehl, Markus, 159n53
Boers, Hendrikus, 397
Bogerman, Johannes, 714
Böhme, Jakob, 778
bondage of the will, 644–49, 651
Book of Common Prayer (1552), 429
Book of Concord (1580), 684, 693
"Book of Consolation," 537
Borsch, Frederick H., 816n27
Boston, Thomas, 726–27
"both-and" scheme, and Roman Catholic development of doctrine, 765

boundary markers, 204, 229, 246–48
  works of the law as, 284n39
Bowden, John, 817
Boyd, Gregory, 363n56
Bradwardine, Thomas, 615, 625, 641, 661
bread of life, 208
Brenz, Johannes, 683
Bridgeway Church (Oklahoma City), 840–41
broken spirit, 81
Brown, John, of Haddington, 477–78
Brown, John, of Wamphray, 723
Brunner, Emil, 430
Bryan, Steven M., 309n89, 315
Bucer, Martin, 706, 821, 822, 823, 835
Buchanan, James, 732–33, 772n10
Buck, Pearl S., 734
Buddeus, Johannes Franciscus, 779–80
Buddhism, 14
Bullinger, Heinrich, 432, 438, 703–5, 707, 822, 834
Bultmann, Rudolf, 331, 333n26, 338, 554, 799, 800
Bunyan, John, 864–65
Burgess, Anthony, 717–18, 723
Butler, Joseph, 815

Calvin, John, 35, 249, 343, 422n14, 423, 435n61, 707–9
  on atonement, 363
  definition of faith, 434
  definition of justification, 851
  on *duplex gratia*, 474–75, 506
  on good works, 292, 571
  on the heart, 134n65
  on the Holy Spirit, 522
  incarnational analogy of, 521
  on inseparability of justification and sanctification, 519–20
  on James, 571–72
  on justification, 429, 438, 507–8
  on justification as "main hinge," 518, 524, 588n6, 806
  on obedience of Christ, 445, 521
  on Osiander, 512–13, 517, 522
  on resurrection of Christ, 408–9
  on suffering of Christ, 27
  as "theologian of the Holy Spirit," 510
  on Theophylact, 618
  on two-Adam typology, 364
  on twofold meaning of justification, 290
  on union with Christ, 474–75, 509–10
  and Vermigli, 707
  and *via moderna*, 618n111
"Calvin vs. the Calvinists," 507n6

Campbell, Constantine R., 471n3
Campbell, Douglas A., 221n36, 335–38, 340, 342, 446–47n29
Campeggio, 678
Canaanites, 47
capax Dei, 756–58
Capito, Wolfgang, 822
Carnesecchi, Pietro, 821, 835
Carranza, Bartolome, 771n7
Carson, D. A., 133, 181n4, 182n8, 206n41, 207n46, 221–22, 224–25, 382n144, 437n66, 547n54
Caryl, Joseph, 726
Catechism of the Catholic Church (1992), 697, 756, 763, 825, 833, 834
causes of justification, 743–44
Celsus, 574
certainty of faith, 742–43
chain of salvation, 228. See also *ordo salutis*
Charles V, Emperor, 676, 678–79, 742
Chaucer, Geoffrey, 666
cheap grace, 825, 827
Chemnitz, Martin, 429, 435, 600n48, 601, 691–92, 693
"children of the living God," 132–33, 144
"children of whoredom," 127
Childs, Brevard, 110, 117n37
Chillingworth, William, 776
Christ. *See* Jesus Christ
Christ-church interconnection, in Roman Catholicism, 755
Christian initiation, Newman on, 815–16
Christian liberty, 475
Christian life
  faith and works in, 845–48
  and Mosaic law, 544–50
Christian righteousness, 680
Christians, real and nominal, 813–14
Christology, and justification, 14
Christus Victor, 363, 364, 366, 369, 375
Chrysostom, John, 361, 422, 581, 618, 673
Chubb, Thomas, 775
church
  as "continuous incarnation," 828
  dignity of, 828
  as organ of authority and revelation, 828–29
  unity of, 740
  universality of, 836
church fathers
  on atonement, 360–61
  on justification, 563–85
"Church's One Foundation, The" (hymn), 737
Chytraeus, David, 693

circumcision, 62, 64, 196, 223, 229, 263, 275, 288, 553
  as covenant sign, 58
  as Jewish identity marker, 305, 306, 523
circumcision of the heart, 62, 64, 100, 124, 184, 553
"Circumcision of the Lord" (Biel sermon), 427–28, 626–27, 632–35
City of God, 116
civil righteousness, 680, 682
Clark, R. Scott, 658
classical realist epistemology, 513
cleansing from sin, 75–76, 81
Clement of Alexandria, 567
Clement of Rome, 565–66
Clines, David, 82n21, 93
clothing imagery for righteousness (Augustine), 595
Cochlaeus, Johannes, 678
College of New Jersey, 731
Colloquy of Regensburg (1541), 742
Colloquy of Worms, 692
Colossians, justification in, 265
common notions, 775
compassionate justice, 107, 113–14, 117
concupiscence, 645, 832
condemnation, 227, 352, 390, 403, 430–31, 436, 489, 508, 704
conditional grace, 340–41
confidence before God, 851
Confutation of the Augsburg Confession, 678–79
conscience, 860
consciousness of God, Tillich on, 802
constitutive justification (Baxter), 722
Contarini, Giulio, 771
contrition, 81, 668
conversion, 203, 554
  to and from Roman Catholicism, 811–13, 834–37
  Schleiermacher on, 789–90
convicted of righteousness, 206
Cooper, John W., 801n120
coram Deo, 756, 834
Corban, 196
corporate exile position (works of the law), 250–51
corporate unity with Christ (Powers), 482–83
Council of Carthage (397), 640–41
Council of Constantinople (553), 579n53
Council of Ephesus (431), 321, 615
Council of Milevis, 824n66
Council of Orange (529), 641, 824n66

Council of Trent (1545–1563), 423n14, 575, 626, 684, 689–92, 695, 698, 704, 739, 771–72, 811
  on alleged errors of Reformers, 745–46
  anathemas of, 742, 765
  "Decree on Justification," 690, 825, 827, 830
  "Decree on Original Sin," 832
  on fourfold causality of justification, 706
  on imputed righteousness of Christ, 711n53
  on justification, 511–12, 707–8, 763
  synergism of, 757
  on three stages of justification, 743–44
counted as righteous, 225, 394, 436, 769
covenant
  Biel on, 615–16
  and promise, 539
  in the Psalms, 69–70, 82
  as relational and legal, 472
  and righteousness, 534–35
covenantal nomism, 148–49, 296–98
  and social function of the law, 304–5
  as synergistic, 298, 301, 302–4
covenantal, voluntaristic framework of justification, 623–27, 629–30
covenant faithfulness, 163, 330, 357
  righteousness as, 156n42, 217, 260, 352n6, 358, 375, 378, 495n129
covenant membership, 148, 305, 307, 330
covenant of creation, 24, 26
covenant of grace, 472
covenant of peace (Isaiah), 115–16
covenant of redemption, 378, 510n20. See also *pactum salutis*
covenant of works, 340–41, 455
covenants, Valdés on, 706
covenants of promise, 539
covenant sons, failure of, 383
covenant terminology, in Paul, 534
covenant with creation (Noah), 46
covering of sin, in the Psalms, 79–80
Cranfield, C. E. B., 279n22
Cranmer, Thomas, 429, 438–39, 818, 823
creation
  renewal of, 134–35
  violation of, 46
Creator-creature distinction, 377
Crisp, Oliver D., 356n23, 367, 368–69n79, 370
Crisp, Tobias, 515, 724
Crites, Stephen D., 792
cross of Christ, 27, 257, 259, 437
  centrality of, 442, 449
  and entire obedience of Christ, 447
  necessity of, 381–82
Crowe, Brandon, 393

cup of God's wrath, 28, 29, 391
curse, 46, 249–51, 254, 538
Cyprian, 571, 574, 584

Dabney, Robert, 728
d'Ailly, Pierre, 624
Damascus Document (CD), 157
Damascus road, 34
Darwin, Charles, 819–20
Das, Andrew, 542
Daunton-Fear, Andrew, 569n18
Davenant, John, 722
David
    looks ahead to future deliverance, 463
    prophesied resurrection of Christ, 406–7
    sin with Bathsheba, 80
Davidic covenant, 69, 71
Davidic king, 115
Davis, Dale Ralph, 87
Davis, Peter H., 275n7
Day of Atonement, 69, 87, 203, 484
"day of Jezreel," 131
day of punishment, 138
day of the Lord, 120–22, 353
de Boer, Martinus, 332–34, 335
de Bres, Guido, 709
Decades (Bullinger), 704
de Campos, Heber Carlos, 437n66, 713n60
decree, 510n20
decretal union, 510, 521, 524
de Dieu, Ludovicus, 723
definitive sanctification, 258, 437, 499, 500n141, 508
deification, 513
Deines, Roland, 186n13
deism, 775, 776
Demarest, Bruce, 371
demons, faith of, 280
Denifle, Heinrich, 664, 668n61
Denney, James, 67, 74
DeRouchie, Jason, 548
Derrida, Jacques, 796
Descartes, René, 596, 728
Deuteronomistic Books, 100
Deuteronomistic theology, 125
Deuteronomy, 100
Diaspora, as exile, 312–13
Dibelius, Martin, 279n24
Diet of Augsburg, 676, 683
discipleship, 207, 569
disciples of Jesus, 200n35
Disputation against Scholastic Theology (Luther), 617, 624, 643–49, 651–52, 665n41, 702

distributive justice, 367
divine-human agency, as zero-sum game, 340–41
divine oath, 59
divine voluntarism, 368
Divine Warrior, 110, 111
doctrine, development of, 588
doers of the law, 219–20
Dominus Iesus (2000), 753–54
"double assurance of grace" (Augustine), 595–96
double grace. See *duplex gratia*
double imputation, 341n69, 712
double justification, 742, 826
doubt, 278, 799
Dulles, Avery Cardinal, 658, 697, 820n40, 830
Dunn, James D. G., 147, 147n3, 148n4, 148n6, 161, 163, 240n5, 246n37, 246n40, 295–96, 300n29, 302–6, 322, 323–24, 330, 514
    on covenant in Paul, 534nn3–4
    on Spirit-letter contrast, 553n67
Duns Scotus, 368n77, 428, 629, 631, 644–45, 646, 661
duplex gratia, 32, 475, 506, 518, 527, 708, 778, 827

Early Orthodoxy (1565–1630), 702, 711–17
Eastern Christianity, 510n21, 513, 618–21, 696
"easy believism," 571
Eaton, John, 515
"ecclesial communities" vs. churches in proper sense, 754
Ecclesiastes, 95–96
ecclesiology, of Newman, 820
Eck, Johann, 626, 669, 676, 678
economic Trinity, 401
ecumenical theology, 748
    on justification by faith, 746–47
    on the Reformation, 739–40
ecumenic justice. See transcultural (ecumenic) justice
Edict of Worms, 676, 677
Edomites, 121
Edwardian theory, 367n74
Edwards, Jonathan, 104n6, 402, 421, 728–31, 848–49
effectual calling, 529n91
efficacy, of gift, 318, 319, 321
efficient cause, of justification, 743
Egypt, 137, 138, 144n79
"Egyptian treatment" of sin, 87
election
    Augustine on, 589–90
    Peter Lombard on, 607

election in Christ, 521
Eliezer, 50
emptiness, 96
empty hand (metaphor for faith), 434–35
Enlightenment, 774
    and eclipse of justification, 770
    influence of, 772–73, 775
    subjectivity of, 799
entire obedience of Christ, 442, 446, 447–50, 456, 458–59, 460–62, 464, 521
Epaphroditus, 460
Ephesians
    justification in, 261–63
    as Pauline, 240
Ephraim, 126, 142
episcopal tradition, 817
Epistle of Diognetus, 270, 361, 569
Epstein, Isidore, 164–65
Erasmus, Desiderius, 651, 666, 671, 674
Erastianism, 817
Erskine, Ralph, 727–28
eschatological community, 103, 106, 107, 114–15
eschatological day, in Hosea, 130, 132, 134–35
eschatology, 264, 327–28
Eskola, Timo, 158n49
eternal justification, 515, 530
eternal life, requires perfect obedience, 208, 210, 444, 445, 449, 450, 451, 453–56
eternal security, 516, 519
ethical righteousness, 156n42, 181, 464
ethics, and justification, 344–46
"eucharistic hospitality," 753
Eusebius, 360–61
evangelical obedience, 373, 732
evangelicals
    ambiguity toward *Joint Declaration on the Doctrine of Justification*, 754
    anthropology of, 756–57
    on the Reformation, 740
Evangelicals and Catholics Together, 741, 749–50
everlasting covenant, 383
exceeding righteousness, 180–82
executive justification (Baxter), 722
exile, 133, 308–16
Exodus creed, 68–69
exorcisms, 188
Ezekiel, 102–3, 104, 552
Ezra, 310

faith
    always accompanied by other saving graces, 719
    as antithesis of merit, 842
    as confidence in God's grace, 675
    contrasted with works, 249–51, 344, 432, 537
    as faithfulness, 514–15
    formed and unformed distinction (Aquinas), 612n93
    fulfills the law, 224
    as a gift, 434–35
    and healing, 192–93
    and holiness, 849
    importance in Torah, 61–62
    imputed for righteousness, 715–16
    instrumentality of, 31, 33, 64, 225, 226, 232, 406, 522, 715
        denied by Edwards, 729–30
    and justification, 193
    as a life orientation, 283
    and obedience, 64, 849
    as only instrument of justification, 769–70
    as "outward referring," 433
    Paul on, 282–85
    and resurrection of Christ, 406, 408
    and works, 274–92, 845–48
faith alone, 31, 409, 433, 759, 844. See also *sola fide*
faith formed by love, 665, 673, 682, 833
faithfulness, 139, 203, 514–15
faith, hope, and love, 578–79
faith in Jesus Christ (genitive construction debate), 221n35, 244, 266
faith of demons, 850
faith without works, 280, 848–50
faith working through love, 288, 703, 735, 793
fake faith, 280, 282
false righteousness, 180, 206–7
fasting, 203
Father
    free and electing mercy, 520
    vindication of the Son in resurrection, 402–3
favoritism, 279
fear of God, 73, 91, 94–95, 96, 108, 139
Federal Vision, 736
Feldmeier, Reinhard, 42
Ferguson, Sinclair B., 502n146, 515
Fesko, J. V., 400, 405, 414–15, 437n66, 473n6, 506n3, 512
feudalism, 361
fiducia (trust), 433, 516, 673
final cause, of justification, 743
final justification, 235
Finney, Charles, 372n92
"Finnish" interpretation of Luther. *See* New Finnish Interpretation of Luther
1 Clement, 275n8
1 Corinthians, justification in, 257–59
First Crusade, 666

First Helvetic Confession (1536), 704
1 Timothy, justification in, 266–68
Fisher, Edward, 726–27
Fitzmyer, Joseph A., 833n126
Fix, Andrew, 773
Flacius, Matthias, 685, 686, 687–88, 689
flesh, 286
flesh heart, 552
flood, as exile, 46
food laws, 196, 229, 305, 523
forensic justification, 360, 487–89, 509, 524, 772
   in Formula of Concord, 694
   in Luther, 651–52, 674, 675
forensic union, 510, 521, 524
forgiveness of sin, 85, 187, 193–94, 230, 265, 338, 360, 769
   in Augustine, 593–94
   as benefit of justification, 444–45, 462, 467
   collective, 88–90
   in Galatians, 245–48
   in the Old Testament, 75
   and passive obedience of Christ, 393, 452
   in the Psalms, 77–86
   in Theophylact, 620
forgiving one another, 265
formal cause, of justification, 743, 831
Former Prophets, 100–101
form of a servant, 27
Formula of Concord, 507, 670, 671, 683, 685, 691, 692–96, 713
Forward Theory, 335n35
4 Baruch, 311
4 Ezra, 150–51, 177
Frame, John, 356
France, R. T., 180, 187n16, 197n29
Francis, Pope, 764–66
Francke, August Hermann, 779–80
freedom
   from bondage of the law, 255–56, 528
   for gazing on the glory of God, 554
Freedom of a Christian (Luther), 523, 528
freedom of the will, 660
   Biel on, 632–34, 635, 639, 640, 641, 651
   in Judaism, 297
   Luther on, 649
free-grace-theology movement, 516
French Confession (1559), 709, 712
friendship, 645
fruit of the Spirit, 145
"fulfilling all righteousness," 465–66
fulfillment of the law. *See* active obedience of Christ
Furnish, Victor Paul, 553
future of justification, 235

Gaffin, Richard B., Jr., 268, 289n47, 388n3, 414, 459, 466, 470, 497–99, 506n3, 545
Galatians
   justification in, 242–57
   Machen on, 735
   vs. Romans, 328–29, 333
Garcia, Mark A., 506n3, 517–18
Garvie, Alfred E., 291
Gathercole, Simon, 155, 171n92, 246–47, 459n91
Gaventa, Beverly, 334–35
general justification, Valdés on, 705
Geneva Confession (1536), 707
Gentile believers, 144–45, 329
Gentiles
   gospel to, 201–2
   have law written on hearts, 219, 390
   inclusion of, 132–33, 182n9
   justified by faith, 223
   righteousness of, 229
Gentry, Peter J., 45n28
George, Timothy, 218, 363n59
German Christian pietism, 331
German Enlightenment, 779–81
Gerrish, Brian, 615
Getty, Keith, 864
Gibeah, 139n75
gift, Barclay on, 318–22
"Gift of Salvation" (Evangelicals and Catholics Together), 749–50
Gilead, 139n75
Gilgal, 139n75
Gill, John, 618
Girardeau, John, 728
global justice, 107
glorification, 412, 437
glory of God, 853
   as final cause of justification, 743
   as goal of justification, 235
Gnesio-Lutherans, 685, 687–88, 689
gnostics, 278
God
   ad extra work, 438
   aseity of, 356
   as "bloodthirsty tyrant," 340n64
   character of, 103, 124
   compassion of, 85, 87, 89, 123, 128, 132, 141, 143
   covenantal condescension of, 455
   covenantal love of, 82, 85, 89
   covenant faithfulness of, 260, 330, 357, 358, 374–75, 378
   as Father, 140–43
   freedom of, 423–24, 661

glorifying self as highest good, 356
grace of, 132, 423–24
holiness of, 70–72, 76, 96, 140–43, 356–58, 484
honor of, 361
inscrutable to human mind, 93
as Judge, 355–56
judgment and salvation of, 120
justice of, 72, 107–9, 118, 138, 140, 423–24, 425, 484
as the law, 362, 370
lordship of, 378
love of, 140, 338, 357–58, 362, 425–26
mercy of, 76, 90
monergistic promises of, 124, 129, 131, 134–35, 140
as moral standard of universe, 357
as not the law, 368, 370
overlooked "former sins," 375
patience of, 138
requires absolute and utter perfection, 842
righteousness of, 72, 425–26
sovereignty of, 109, 110–11, 119, 377
triunity of, 376–78
God-law-sin relationship, 362, 364–65, 367, 372, 374, 382
godliness, 90
Gomarus, Franciscus, 715
Gomer, 127, 134
Gonzaga, Giulia, 835
Goodwin, Thomas, 451, 454
good works
  church fathers on, 574, 576
  as fruit and evidence of saving faith, 292, 520, 706, 710, 724, 733
  in Heidelberg Catechism, 710
  Luther on, 517, 686
  necessary corollaries to justification, 259, 884
  necessary for salvation, 685–86
  performed after justification, 583
  rewarding of, 826
  Thomas Aquinas on, 660
  Vermigli on, 826
  Westminster Confession on, 719
Gorman, Michael, 342–44, 470, 486–89
gospel, and justification, 243–48
Gospels
  on active and passive obedience of Christ, 464–67
  on justification, 179–216
  resurrection accounts, 467
governmental view of the atonement, 363, 364, 366–70, 372–76

grace
  Biel on, 632–42
  in *Joint Declaration on the Doctrine of Justification*, 698
  sacramental understanding of, 752–53
  in Second Temple Judaism, 298
  See also habit of grace
grace alone. See *sola gratia*
grace and works, as mutually exclusive, 523
grace vs. gift, 675
gratia inhaerens, 827
Great Schism (1054), 618
Grech, Prosper, 575–76
greed, 144
Green, Lowell, 666
Green, William Henry, 92n39
Greene, Theodore M., 780–81, 783n51
Gregory of Nyssa, 363n56
Gregory of Rimini, 615, 625–26, 661, 663
Grider, J. Kenneth, 372
Grimm, Harold, 643, 649
Grisar, Hartmann, 664
Grotius, Hugo, 363n56, 366, 773n11, 797
Groves, J. Alan, 79
Grudem, Wayne, 231n64, 232
Gundry, Robert H., 198n31, 494–95n126
Günther, Franz, 643

Ha, John, 51
Habakkuk, 122
habit of grace, 627–28, 634
Hagar, 256
Haggai, 123, 311
Handel, George Frideric, 93
hardening, Isaiah's ministry of, 105–6
Harnack, Adolf von, 773n16, 798
Harris, Murray J., 554
Hartranft, Chester David, 772n8
Harvard College, 773
Hawkins, Edward, 813–14, 828
Hays, Richard, 339–40, 553
healing, in Mark, 188–93, 195
healing metaphor, in Peter Lombard, 608
heart, 134n65
heart change, in new covenant, 184–85, 551–54
Hebrews, on obedience of Christ, 462–63
Hegel, Georg Wilhelm Friedrich, 790–92, 793, 796, 801
Heidelberg Catechism (1563), 345, 363–64, 444, 709–10, 712
  threefold imputation in, 710, 714, 725
Hellenistic philosophy, 796
Helm, Paul, 507n6
Helyer, Larry, 161

Hendrix, Scott, 642
Hengel, Martin, 198n32, 276
Henry, Matthew, 618
Herbert, Peter Lord, 774–75
Hermann, Wilhelm, 798, 799
"High Calvinism," 515
higher criticism, 793
higher life theology, 234
High Orthodoxy (1630–1700), 702, 717–26
High Priestly Prayer, 26, 210
Hillel, house of, 174–75
Hillel the Elder, 171
Hinduism, 14
historia salutis, 23, 389, 402, 518
   link with *ordo salutis*, 34–35, 404, 410, 413, 416
   and *pactum salutis*, 400–401
historical Adam, 269, 359, 379n130, 456
historical Jesus, 799
historical psalms, 88–89
Hodge, A. A., 732
Hodge, Caspar Wistar, Jr., 732
Hodge, Charles, 231, 478–79, 618, 728, 732
Hodges, Zane, 516
Hogg, James, 726–27
Holcot, Robert, 624, 641
holiness, 71–72, 527, 852–55
   growth in, 258, 261, 508, 519. *See also* sanctification
   and imputation, 724–25
   and sin, 95
Holl, Karl, 670
Holmes, Stephen R., 359n39
Holy One of Israel, 71, 105, 108, 114, 116, 141
Holy Spirit, 111–13, 116
   application of redemption to elect, 521–22
   gift of, 521
   and union with Christ, 472, 510, 530
honor, Anselm on, 361
Hooker, Richard, 732
hope, 852–55
   in Isaiah, 106, 115
   in Old Testament, 101
Horton, Michael S., 27, 354, 472n4, 506n3, 528–30, 758n46, 762
Hosea, 43, 102, 104, 119, 123–43
Howard, Thomas, 812
humanist movement, 671–72
human justice, 107, 109–10, 118
human race, unity of, 456
humble, exalting of, 205
Hume, David, 782–84
humility, 109
Hwang, Yohan, 56n61

Hyperius, Andreas, 712
hypocrites, hypocrisy, 196, 278–79

Iammarone, Giovanni, 744n14
identity and idolatry, 126–27
idolatry, 126–27, 144, 145
"if / then" relationship with God, 840
Ignatius, 241n11, 569
illusory righteousness, 430
imago Dei, 23
imitation of Christ, 569
Immanuel, 104, 128, 141
impersonal worship, 827
implied-premise view (works of the law), 249–51
impurity, 144
imputation of active obedience of Christ, 372, 490–96, 769
   denied by Shepherd, 735–36
   jettisoning of, 470
   rejected by Piscator, 713
   in Westminster Confession, 719–21
imputation of Adam's sin, 446, 494–95n126
imputation of Christ's righteousness, 30, 34, 205, 230–31, 257, 264, 289n48, 353–55, 356, 358, 360, 388, 436, 437, 438, 605, 830
   in Anselm, 598
   Augustine on, 595, 675n109
   condemned by Council of Trent, 711n53
   missing in *Joint Declaration on the Doctrine of Justification*, 697
   Luther on, 674
   Paul on, 224–25
   rationalists' rejection of, 773, 776
   rejected by Piscator, 711–13
   Valdés on, 705–6
imputation of Christ's satisfaction
   in Bernard, 605
   in Thomas Aquinas, 614n97
"in Adam," 359, 380
incarnation, 355, 360, 362, 363, 380, 797
"in Christ," 228, 257, 286, 343, 415, 471, 510, 520, 757, 758n46
"In Christ Alone" (hymn), 864
incongruity, of gift, 318, 319, 320
"incorporation," as enjoying blessing of justification, 492–93
incorruption, Paul on, 407
indicative-imperative structure in Paul, 262
indulgences, 665–70, 753, 758
infant baptism, 815
infused grace, 511, 665
   Biel on, 626, 633–35
   Thomas Aquinas on, 628

infused righteousness, 217, 446n24
inherent grace, 827
iniquity, 78–80, 86
initial justification (Roman Catholic Church), 743
inner righteousness, Zwingli on, 703
Institutes of the Christian Religion (Calvin)
    final edition (1559), 708
    first edition (1536), 707
instruction, Isaiah's ministry of, 106–7
instrumental cause, of justification, 743
"internal mechanism" of the cross, 363, 364, 366
Irenaeus, 363n56, 452, 563, 567, 570
Irish Articles (1615), 714, 716–17
Irons, Charles Lee, 156n42
Isaac, 58–59, 256
Isaiah, 102, 104–19
Isaianic servant, 454
Ishmael, 58, 256
Israel
    apostasy of, 126
    continual exile of, 307, 308–16, 317
    covenant infidelity of, 25, 119, 136–37
    false piety of, 136, 137
    guilt and complicity of, 103
    injustice of, 105n6
    national righteousness of, 116–17
    prostitution of, 104, 138–40, 144
    restoration of, 134, 311
    spiritual adultery of, 126
    syncretism of, 136–37
Israel (northern kingdom), 105, 120, 126n49, 129, 136, 141
"it is necessary" statements, 466
iustificatio activa, 769
iustificatio negativa, 769
iustitia aliena, 769, 842. *See also* alien righteousness

Jacob, 142
Jairus, 190–93
James
    on faith and works, 433, 846–50
    on justification, 42, 290–91, 826
    on the law, 285–88
    and Paul, 274–78, 433
    Luther on, 273–74
James, Frank A., III, 625, 821, 822, 827
Jansenist movement, 590
Jedin, Hubert, 742
Jenni, Ernst, 53
Jeremiah, 102–3, 104, 551–52
Jeroboam II, 128

Jerusalem, 123
Jerusalem Council (AD 49), 243, 277
"Jesus, Thank You" (song), 235–36
Jesus Christ
    ascension of, 409, 521
    baptism of, 465–66
    circumcision of, 444
    as covenant head, 353, 355, 360, 363
    crucifixion of, 25
    deity of, 365, 564, 581, 777n32
    divinity and humanity hypostatically united, 521
    exaltation of, 460, 521
    federal headship in the resurrection, 403, 406
    as firstborn from the dead, 413
    as glorious image of God, 118
    holiness of, 710
    human holiness of, 711
    humiliation of, 458, 460, 710
    justification of, 267–68
    as last Adam, 25, 26, 208, 210, 354n16, 355, 360, 379–80, 446, 450, 454, 458–59
    learned obedience, 27
    life as redemptive, 26
    as Mediator, 267, 353, 354, 362, 380, 442
    as meritorious cause of justification, 743
    as moral example, 782
    obedience of. *See* obedience of Christ
    ongoing priestly work of, 521
    recapitulates history of Israel, 27
    represents those who receive gift of righteousness by faith, 227
    resurrection of, 394
        as dawn of new age, 393–97, 402
        and justification, 226, 231, 259, 397, 459, 460, 490
        and union with Christ, 472
        as vindication, 29, 458–59
    sacrifice of, 463
    saving presence of, 837
    session of, 521
    substitutionary atoning death of, 28, 197–98, 223
    suffering of, 401, 443, 444, 465. *See also* passive obedience of Christ
    temptation of, 465
    threefold office of, 364
    victory of, 29
    vindication of, 399–403
"Jesus-righteousness," 186n13
Jewish apocalyptic eschatology, 332
Jewish soteriology, as synergistic, 323–24
Jews
    included in Zion, 117
    justified by faith, 223

Jezreel, 127–28, 129–31, 135
Job, 91–94
Joel, 121
John, Gospel of, 206–10
John Frederick, Elector, 685
Johnson, Marcus Peter, 232, 470n2, 480n58, 493n124, 501n144
John XII, Pope, 659
Joint Declaration on the Doctrine of Justification (1996), 696–98, 739, 743, 749, 750–65, 833n126
Jonah, 121
Josephus, 305, 315
Judah (southern kingdom), 105, 120, 136, 141–42
Judaism
    as intensification of consciousness of sin, 792, 793
    as synergistic, 323
Judaizers, 276, 305
judgment, 389–90
    according to works, 259, 520
judgmentalism, 345
judgment-day justification, 290n49
judicial righteousness, 156n42
Julian of Eclanum, 591
Jüngel, Eberhard, 423, 424–25, 757
justice, 425
    in Isaiah, 107–10
justification
    as act of grace, 120
    active and passive, 529
    as acquittal and acceptance, 844
    as article on which church stands or falls, 13, 15, 19, 505, 657, 701, 731, 758
    based on righteousness of Christ, 231
    Baur on, 794
    Baxter's three stages of, 722–23
    blessings of, 851
    built on entire obedience of Christ, 446, 456
    centrality of, 35–36
    and certitude of salvation, 855–60
    as cleansing and renewal, 511
    in Colossians, 265
    in Corinthian correspondence, 257–61
    as corporate and ecclesiological, 330
    as declaration, 288, 436, 507, 757, 762, 830, 843–44
    as "dialectical," 744
    and elements of soteriology, 758–59
    Enlightenment eclipse of, 770
    in Ephesians, 261–63
    as eschatological, 247n45, 413–15, 437
    ethics of, 344–46
    as exclusive and extensive, 844
    as extrinsic, 843
    in 1 Timothy, 266–68
    as folly to many today, 36–37
    as forensic, 230, 288, 289, 290–91, 342, 344, 351–52, 358, 470, 474, 475, 476–77, 480, 481, 505–6, 757, 769, 780, 830, 843–44
    and forgiveness of sins, 230, 245–48, 507
    future of, 235
    goal of, 235
    and good works, 719
    Gorman on, 487
    and the gospel, 243–48
    as gracious gift, 232
    grounded in work of Christ, 29
    as ground of religion, 15
    Hegel on, 792
    and holiness, 852–55
    and hope, 852–55
    as horizontal, 231, 246, 262–63
    includes imputation, 230–31, 353–55, 507
    by infused grace, 511
    and life, 247–48
    loss and recovery of, 744
    in the Lutheran tradition, 657–98
    as "main hinge on which religion turns," 518, 524, 588n6, 806
    as merely imputation, 825
    as moral transformation, 591–93, 597, 659, 758, 760–62, 778–79, 780
        in Bernard, 603
        in early Luther, 652–54
        in Thomas Aquinas, 609–10, 614
    necessity of, 231
    and new covenant, 533, 534–36
    and new life in Christ, 268–69
    not a legal fiction, 432, 496, 518
    as objective, 843–44
    objective and subjective, 529–30
    in the Old Testament, 41, 75
    as participation in Christ, 343, 482–83
    in Pastoral Epistles, 266–69
    and pastoral ministry, 839–65
    in Philemon, 265–66
    in Philippians, 263–65
    present and future, 290n49
    in Prison Epistles of Paul, 261–66
    prophetic nature of, 403–5
    and propitiation, 430–31
    as proving or manifesting righteousness, 289, 290
    in the Psalms, 67, 70–79
    as punctiliar and complete, 523
    received by faith, 844
    as reconciliation, 797

as rectification, 374
in the Reformed tradition, 701–37
as religious consciousness, 800
and revelation, 803–6
as "rightwised" with God, 373
Ritschl on, 797
in the Roman Catholic Church, 739–66
sacramentalism of, 301
and sanctification, 233, 505–30
2 Timothy, 268
as self-consciousness, 789–90
Shepherd on, 735–36
source in God, 438
subject to contingency, 834
as synergistic process, 744
as theosis, 342–43, 486
in Thessalonian correspondence, 260–61
in Titus, 268–69
as transformative, 342, 505–6
two benefits of, 442–47, 462, 467
twofold meaning of the word, 288–89, 290
as vertical, 231, 262–63
and vindication, 399–400
in Wisdom Literature, 67, 90–96
without ethnic distinction, 233
by works of the law, 255–57
justification and sanctification, 14, 270
  Calvin on, 708
  conflation of, 511–15, 522
    by Newman, 733
    by Osiander, 689
    by Trent, 744
  as distinct benefits, 31, 436–37, 522–23, 524–25
  as distinguishable yet inseparable, 556–58, 708
  as inseparable gifts, 32–33, 519–22
  integration of, 516–18
  justification as foundational for sanctification, 234, 475, 497, 499
  Melanchthon on, 682–83
  priority of justification over sanctification, 473, 475–82, 497, 499, 506, 517, 524–30
  separation of, 515–16
  simultaneity of, 498–99
justification of faith by works, 724
"Justification Theory" (Campbell), 335–37, 446–47n29
justified, as opposite of cursed, 619
"justified by his blood," 226, 535
Justin Martyr, 251, 566–67

Kähler, Martin, 798–800
Kaiser, Walter C., Jr., 94
Kant, Immanuel, 757, 783–87, 795, 796, 798
Käsemann, Ernst, 13, 324, 331–32, 333n26, 342
Keble, John, 815, 817
Keller, Timothy, 840
kenosis, 107, 109, 113–15, 119
Ker, Ian, 816, 818n34, 819n38
kernel and husk of religion (Schleiermacher), 787–88
Ketubim (Writings), 99
Kierkegaard, Søren, 796, 799
kingdom of God, 109n15, 179, 186–87
  welcomes all, 200
kingdoms of the world, evil of, 121
Kittel, Gerhard, 318–19, 320–21
Klein, Ralph W., 45n28
Kline, Meredith G., 53n49, 541n30
Klink, Edward W., III, 206n45
knowing Christ, 842
Knox, Broughton, 435
Knutzen, Martin, 783
Koch, Klaus, 331
Koet, Bart J., 118
Kruse, Colin G., 226n51
Küng, Hans, 741, 748–49
Kuyper, Abraham, 434n53

Laato, Timo, 298–99n23
Lancaster, Robert, 515
land of promise, 47, 52
Lane, Anthony, 755, 826
Lane, William L., 190, 462n111
Late Orthodoxy (1700–1790), 702, 726–31
Latimer, Hugh, 818
Latter Prophets, 101, 102–4
law
  and common good, 798
  demands of, 443
  freedom from, 233
  not intrinsic or essential to God's nature, 368, 370
  not of faith, 252, 254
  requires perfect obedience, 252–53, 256–57
  third use of, 161
  See also Mosaic law
law and gospel, 680
  as covenantal contrast, 537–43
  Luther on, 651
law and grace, Biel on, 647–68
law court metaphor, 217, 351, 359n39, 757
law-covenant, 540–42
lawlessness, 278, 287
law of Christ, 286, 288, 549

Laynez, Diego, 743
"Lead, Kindly Light" (hymn), 812
Lectures on Romans (Luther), 664–65, 673
legalism, 144, 204, 249
legalistic preaching, 727–28
legalistic works righteousness, 149–50
"legal voluntarism," 368n79
Leibniz, Gottfried, 775
Leipzig Debate, 626, 669, 676, 684
Leipzig Interim, 685, 686, 687, 689, 692
lenient-king parable (Biel), 626–27
Leo X, Pope, 669
Leo XIII, Pope, 658, 812
leper, healing of, 189
lepers, 200n34
Lessing, Gotthold Ephraim, 776
Letham, Robert, 370
letter-Spirit contrast, 553–54, 556
Levenson, Jon, 42–43, 46n30, 63–64
lex credendi and *lex orandi*, 817n32
liberalism. *See* Protestant liberalism
liberal-postmodern view of the atonement, 364
libertinism, 668n61
liberum arbitrium. *See* free will
life, from adherence to the law, 253
life in the Spirit, 546
life under the law, 546
Lindbeck, George, 801
Lloyd-Jones, D. Martyn, 556–58
Lo-Ammi, 127, 129–32, 135, 138, 144
Loci Communes (Melanchthon), 653, 672, 686, 688
Locke, John, 773n12, 776, 777, 783n51
Lohse, Bernhard, 670
Longacre, Robert E., 54n54
Longenecker, Bruce W., 151n17
Longenecker, Richard N., 442n3, 462n108
Lord (divine name), 68
Lord's Prayer, 832n119
Lortz, Joseph, 664
Lo-Ruhamah, 127, 128–30, 135, 138, 144
love
   for God, 346
   for neighbor, 203, 346, 547–49
Lubbertus, Sibrandus, 715
Luke, Gospel of
   and Isaiah, 113
   "it is necessary" statements, 466
   on justification of sinners, 198–206
Lumen gentium, 764n61
Luther, Martin, 24, 31, 35, 36, 119, 217–18, 220–21, 249, 419, 425, 702–3, 712, 864–65
   on alien righteousness, 435–36, 506, 517, 523

   antischolasticism of, 651
   on atonement, 363
   on bondage of the will, 651
   disputation, 624
   Disputation against Scholastic Theology, 617, 643–49, 651–52, 665n41, 702
   forecast constant conflict with *sola fide*, 806
   on forensic justification, 514, 588n6, 624, 651–52, 671, 674, 675
   and Formula of Concord, 694, 695
   on good works, 517, 571
   Heidelberg Disputation, 428
   on James, 273–74, 276
   Lectures on Romans, 664–65, 673
   Ninety-Five Theses, 623, 665–70, 702
   on Paul, 324
   on "Pauline psalms," 77–83
   on "proper righteousness," 517, 523
   on psychological benefits of justification, 528
   reading of church fathers, 584
   and scholasticism, 663–65
   on substitutionary atonement, 431
   on two kinds of righteousness, 517, 523, 680, 702, 703
   on union with Christ, 512, 514, 524
   on *via moderna*, 642–44
Lutheran Church–Missouri Synod, 761
Lutheranism
   on baptismal regeneration, 752
   on justification, 657–98
Lutheran orthodoxy, 517
Lutheran World Federation, 739–40, 750, 760
"Luther vs. the Lutherans," 507n6

Maas, Korey D., 508n8, 513, 650–51, 652–53, 844
MacArthur, John, 217n12, 232
Macaskill, Grant, 472n5
Maccabees, books of, 314–15
McCain, Paul T., 761–62, 764
McComiskey, Thomas Edward, 131n57
McCormack, Bruce, 528–29
McFarland, Orrey, 47n36
McGrath, Alister, 564, 627n15, 629, 659, 675, 770nn1–3, 830, 844
   on Augustine, 591–92
   on Barth, 803
   on Biel, 640–41, 643n68, 650
   on Formula of Concord, 694
   on German Enlightenment, 780
   on Küng, 748
   on Luther, 665
   omission of Bernard, 606
   on Pietism, 779

on Reformation doctrine of justification, 505, 509, 588–89, 670–71
on Reformed Orthodoxy, 804n132
on Ritschl, 797
on Steinbart, 782
Machen, J. Gresham, 232, 236, 374, 734–35
McKenzie, Steven L., 551n58
Macleod, Donald, 362, 373–74
McNair, Philip, 821–22, 824–25
Major, George, 686, 687, 695
Major Prophets, 103
Malachi, 123, 144
Manichaeans, 644, 678
Mannermaa, Tuomo, 513
Marcion, 278
Marcionism, 338
Marius Valentinus, 584
Marius Victorinus, 581
Mark, Gospel of, 186–98
  on victory of Jesus over all opposition, 464–65
marriage to foreigners, 309, 310
Marrow Controversy, 515, 726–28, 733
Martyn, J. Louis, 148n3, 332–34, 341
marvelous exchange. See wonderful exchange
Marx, Karl, 796
Matlock, R. Barry, 245n30, 337n48
Matthew, Gospel of
  fulfillment-formula quotations, 465
  on love and obedience, 466–67
  on righteousness, 180–86
Maulbronn Formula, 693
Mayers, Walter, 835
Mayhue, Richard, 217n12, 232
Mayor, J. B., 275n9, 276n11
Mazzolini, Sylvester, 669
mediator of the covenant, 540
  and justification, 267
medieval theology, 575, 623
  on atonement, 361–62
  continuity with Reformation, 587–88, 606
  on sin, 427–28
Melanchthon, Philipp, 35, 273, 508n8, 517, 575, 653, 663, 670–76, 705, 712
  and Apology of the Augsburg Confession, 679–84
  and Augsburg Confession, 676–78
  and the Formula of Concord, 694–95
  on union with Christ, 512
Melchizedek, 48
"men from James," 276–77
mercy and sacrifice, 466–67
mercy of God, 87
  as efficient cause of justification, 743

merit, 577, 583, 630, 743, 834, 842
  Anselm on, 599
  Bernard on, 604–5
  church fathers on, 573–74
  not basis of standing before God, 29
  rabbinic doctrine of, 43
  Thomas Aquinas on, 613
merita de congruo, 630, 631, 638, 643, 660
merit of Christ
  four views on, 711
  through sacramental system of the church, 744
meritum de condigno, 613, 630, 638, 639, 643
meritorious cause, of justification, 743
Messiah, 111, 123, 383, 384
method of correlation (Tillich), 800–801
Meyer, R., 53
Micah, 122
Miley, John, 363n56, 366, 367
Minor Prophets. See Twelve, the (Minor Prophets)
Miqsat Ma'ase Ha-Torah (4QMMT), 161–64, 177
Mishnah, 165–69
Mizpah, 139n75
Moberly, Walter, 43, 44, 45n28, 64–65
Molnar, Paul, 410
Moltmann, Jürgen, 796
Moo, Douglas J., 216, 244n22, 275n9, 337n48, 352n5, 381n139, 382, 538n20, 546, 553n65
moral fitness, 729
moral-influence view of the atonement, 366, 371
moral naturalism, 358–59
Moravians, 779
Moritz, Duke of Saxony, 685, 687
Morris, Leon, 221, 420
mortal sin, 833
mortification and vivification, 415, 509
Mosaic covenant, as administration of covenant of grace, 453
Mosaic law, 124, 264, 536–37
  and Christian life, 544–50
  moral, ceremonial, and civic distinctions, 453n62
  necessity of perfect obedience to, 453
  not designed to bring justification, 539–43
  not ladder of good works, 455
  provisional character of, 253–54
  and salvation in covenantal nomism, 298
Moses, 61–62, 99–101
  as fountainhead of prophets, 124–25
  as mediator, 540
Mosheim, Johann Lorenz von, 780

Muller, Richard A., 365, 400, 473n6, 507n6
Murray, John, 73, 231, 236, 374, 443, 458n87, 461n106, 470n1, 527n81, 855
   on definitive sanctification, 500n141
   on union and justification, 480–81
Musculus, Wolfgang, 712
mystical union, 469–70n1, 510, 521, 524–25
mysticism, 343
   in Paul, 329

Nadere Reformatie, 778
Nahum, 122
nakedness, 309–10
Nathin, Johann, 642–43, 663
nations, inclusion of, 116–17
natural fitness, 729
nature-grace interdependence, in Roman Catholicism, 755
Nazi Germany, 331
needy and oppressed, 109
Nehemiah, 310
neonomianism, 724–26, 727–28, 733
neoorthodoxy, 36
Neusner, Jacob, 165, 297n11
Nevi'im (Prophets), 99
new age, 328
new Augustinianism. See *schola Augustiniana moderna*
"New Being" (Tillich), 801–2
"new" commandment, 549
new covenant, 381, 383–84, 463
   brings justification, 537
   fruit bearing in, 555
   glories of, 551–56
   and gospel, 535
   in Hosea, 132
   in Jeremiah, 102
   as ministry of justification, 535
   righteousness in, 184–85
new creation, 384
New Finnish Interpretation of Luther, 36, 513–14, 696
new Jerusalem, 384
Newman, John Henry, 36, 588n4, 732–33, 812–20, 825–30, 834–37
newness of life, 415–17
newness of the Spirit, 555–56
"new Pelagianism," 615
New Perspective on Paul, 36, 42n11, 147–48, 176, 289n46, 295–325, 352n6, 374, 378, 736, 747–48
   conflation of justification and sanctification, 514–15, 523
   on eschatological nature of justification, 413–14

   on justification as horizontal, 231, 538
   on the law, 390
   limited Pauline corpus of, 240
   as offspring of Albert Schweitzer, 327, 330
   on works of the law, 220, 262
Newsome, David, 813
new song, 68
Newton, Isaac, 773n12
Newton, John, 814n11
Nickelsburg, George W. E., 148n7, 159
Ninety-Five Theses (Luther), 623, 665–70, 702
Nineveh, God's compassion toward, 121
Noah
   covenant with, 46
   righteousness of, 56, 57
nominalism, 616
nomism, 297
noncircularity, of gift, 318, 341
North Galatian theory, 242
notitia (knowledge), 433, 516

Obadiah, 121
obedience, 96, 219
   and discipleship, 207
   evangelical vs. legal, 373
   and life, 208–9
   in new covenant, 545–50
   See also perfect obedience, requirement for eternal life
"obedience and satisfaction" of Christ, 720–21
obedience of Christ, 30, 208–10, 265, 268, 382–83, 441
   brings righteousness and life, 448, 449
   as lifelong, 442, 452
   in state of humiliation, 458
   Turretin on, 457–58
   unity of, 450, 451, 467–68
   unto death, 459–61
   See also active obedience of Christ; passive obedience of Christ
obedientia activa, 769. *See also* active obedience of Christ
obedientia passiva, 769. *See also* passive obedience of Christ
Oberman, Heiko, 616n105, 625, 631–32, 635–39, 649, 650
objective justification, 677
Ochino, Bernardino, 835
Oden, Thomas, 758n48
old covenant, 302
   as ministry of condemnation, 535, 537–38
   and Mosaic law, 536–37
   prophesied dawning of new covenant, 381
   transition to new covenant, 543–44

Old Princeton, 731–32
Old Testament
  justification language in, 488
  sacrifices, 222–23, 484
"one act of obedience," 451–52
Onesimus, 266
oracles of judgment, in Hosea, 136–37
"order of nature," 475
ordo salutis, 23, 32n11, 389, 402, 501–2
  challenge to, 470
  link with *historia salutis*, 34–35, 410, 413
  logical priorities in, 525
  and *pactum salutis*, 400
  validity of, 518
Origen, 563, 564, 567–68, 572–74, 584
  on imputed and imparted righteousness, 575–78
  on merit, 574
original righteousness, 26
original sin, 632, 644
ornithological imagery, 126
Orr, James, 599
Ortlund, Raymond C., Jr., 236
Osiander, Andreas, 512–13, 517, 522, 525, 688–89, 695, 696, 708, 710
outer righteousness, Zwingli on, 703
Ovey, Michael, 427–28
Owen, John, 362, 388, 400, 421, 509n15, 618, 721, 723, 777n32
Oxford movement, 732, 817–18
Ozment, Steven, 638

Packer, J. I., 394n8, 855, 858, 860
pactum (Biel), 615, 626, 630, 635, 639–42, 646–47, 650, 654
pactum salutis, 25–26, 27, 378, 399–401, 462n110, 510n20
panentheism, 790, 801
Pannenberg, Wolfhart, 425–26, 796
paralytic, healing of, 189–90
Pareus, David, 711–13
Park, E. A., 367n74
partiality, 279
participation, 299, 486
  and eschatology, 299, 335n35, 337
  justification through, 482–83, 513
  in Roman Catholicism, 758n46
  in Sanders, 299–301
passive obedience of Christ, 14, 31, 208–9, 232, 364, 374, 393, 399, 401, 442, 485, 490–96, 711–12, 713
  bound up with active obedience, 461
  definition of, 442–43
  and forgiveness of sins, 452

  as lifelong, 452
  not passivity, 443
passive righteousness (Luther), 703
Passover, 88
pastoral bullies, and justification, 861–64
Pastoral Epistles, justification in, 266–69
pastoral insecurity, and justification, 860–61
patriarchs, 100
Paul
  on Abraham, 43, 63
  appropriates message of the Twelve, 144
  on centrality of the cross, 442, 447, 449
  Christology of, 301–2
  on covenant, 534
  as devout Pharisee, 316
  Dunn on, 303–4
  eschatology as cosmological not forensic, 333
  ethics of, 329
  on faith, 282–85
  on faith and works, 274
  forensic notions on the law, 389
  on imputation, 224–25
  introspective conscience of, 316
  and James, 274–78, 433, 572
  on justification, 239–42, 289–90, 488–89, 508
  on the law, 285–88, 389
  on law and gospel, 537–43
  life under Jewish law, 263
  monergism of, 301
  as mystic, 329
  on obedience of Christ, 447–62
  on resurrection, 397–98, 407
  on righteousness by faith, 33–34
  on termination of the law, 543–44
  on works of faith, 285
  on works of the law, 284–85, 305
Paul III, Pope, 703, 771, 822
Pauline corpus, 13, 240–42, 266, 269
Pauline Epistles, justification in, 239–70
"Pauline psalms," 77–83
Peace of Augsburg, 685, 692
Peace of Westphalia, 774n17
peace with God, 233, 526, 853
Pelagianism, 150, 154, 160, 164–65, 176, 333, 402, 580, 584, 591, 611, 629, 630, 718, 824n66
  of Biel, 615, 616, 625, 632, 639–42, 661
Pelagius, 150n14, 303, 580n55, 644, 647
Pelt, Johannes, 773n11
penal substitution, 359–64
  in Anselm, 600
  and justification, 363–64, 369, 376
  in Peter Lombard, 608
  Theophylact on, 619–20

in Thomas Aquinas, 614n97
and Trinity, 378
penance, 668, 744
penitential psalms, 82, 83–84
Pennington, Jonathan T., 181n7
perfect obedience, requirement for eternal life, 252–53, 269, 372, 373, 378–79, 444, 445, 451, 452–56
perichoresis, 118–19
perseverance, 516, 519, 526
in justification (Edwards), 730
Roman Catholics on, 833–34
personal righteousness, 203
Pesch, Otto, 741, 748–49
Pesher Habakkuk (1QpHab), 160–61, 177
Peter Abelard, 365
Peter Lombard, 587, 606–8, 616n106, 628, 659–60
Peterson, David, 508n10
Pfeffinger, Johann, 687–88
Pharisee and tax collector, parable of, 190n23, 198–99, 202–5, 429–30
Pharisees, 125, 194, 195
Philemon, 265–66
Philippians, justification in, 263–65
Philippists, 685, 687–88
Philo exegesis of Abraham, 43, 63
Phinehas, 43, 55–56
Pictet, Benedict, 425
Pietism, 774, 778–82
of Kant, 785–87
Piper, John, 233, 864–65
Piscator, Johannes, 437n66, 711, 733, 736
Pius V, Pope, 658
Plato, 589
Pole, Reginald, 771
Polycarp, 241n11, 570
Pontifical Council for Promoting Christian Unity, 696, 750, 760, 763
poor, salvation for, 200–201
Porter, Stanley E., 534, 539, 540n26
postexilic Judaism, 123
postmodern theology, 366
post-Vatican II Catholicism, 36
potentia Dei absoluta, 639, 646, 650
potentia Dei ordinata, 639, 650
Powers, Daniel, 470, 482–85
Pratt, Jonathan R., 234
predestination
in Lombard, 607
Thomas Aquinas on, 610–11
preservation, 413
prevenient grace, 628
priestly absolution, 744

Princeton Theological Seminary, 731
prioritization thesis, 517–18
priority, of gift, 318, 319, 321
Prison Epistles of Paul, justification in, 261–66
proclamation of good news, 112–13
prodigal children, 141, 143
prodigal son, parable of, 204–6
progression in justification, 744
progressive sanctification, 233–34, 258, 508, 519, 551, 554, 789, 843
promise, delayed fulfillment of, 47–50
promises and law of God, 539–43
proper righteousness, 517, 523, 703
prophet, as God's watchman, 138
prophetic tradition, 817
prophet like Moses, 104
prophets, metaphors and imagery of, 125–26
propitiation, 29, 222–23, 231, 338, 357, 391–92, 394, 412, 429–32, 437, 438, 494
Prosper of Aquitaine, 589
prostitution metaphor, 104, 126, 145
Protestant liberalism, 36, 365, 371, 405, 411, 734–35, 802–4, 806
Proverbs, 94–95
Psalms of Solomon, 155–57, 177
Psalter, 67, 70–79, 96
punishment of Yahweh, severity of, 139
"pure gift," 321
purgatory, 577, 758
Pusey, Edward, 814

quadruple imputation (divine and human righteousness, active and passive obedience), 712
Quarles, Charles, 180n3
Qumran community, 157–60, 162, 241, 246–47, 297

rabbinic literature, works righteousness in, 164–76
Racovian Academy, 772
Racovian Catechism (1605), 371n87, 772
Rahab, 281n29, 282, 290–91
Rahner, Karl, 410–11
Rambo, Lewis, 835
ransom, 84, 197–98
ransom theory of the atonement, 363
rational theology, 774–77
Ratzinger, Joseph, 753
Rauschenbusch, Walter, 798
recapitulation, 363, 364, 366, 369, 452, 570
reconciliation, 13, 141, 233, 260, 411–12, 449, 527, 853
Hegel on, 791–92
Ritschl on, 797

rectitude, 424
rectoral justice, 367–68, 369–70, 374
redemption, 82, 87, 103, 221–22
   accomplished and applied, 23
   through justification, 233
   as liberation from punishment, 608
   as liberation from slavery, 334
redemptive history, 397
Reeves, Michael, 760–61, 762
Reformation
   "creative genius" of, 588–89
   formal and material causes of, 830n104
   introspective turn in, 330, 336
   on penal substitution, 362
   view of justification, 148, 149, 176, 701–37
Reformed Orthodoxy, 702, 711–31, 804n132
Reformed tradition, on justification, 701–37
refuge, 83
regeneration, 505, 508, 528–29, 558n82
   Augustine on, 591
   Calvin on, 475n14
   Peter Lombard on, 608
Reimarus, Hermann Samuel, 775
rejoicing, in justification, 233
religious self-consciousness (Schleiermacher), 788–90
remembering, in Old Testament, 384n147
remission of sins, as element of justification, 438
remnant, 123, 144
Remonstrants, 773n12
repentance, 144, 187
results, of justification, 228
resurrection
   covenantal nature of, 394–97
   forensic, prophetic power of, 404
   as ground of justification, 406–8
   horizontal and vertical ramifications, 403
   and justification, 226, 259, 387–417
   as object of saving faith, 405–8
   and reconciliation, 411–12
   and soteriology, 405, 415
   as source of faith, 408–11
   in systematic theologies, 387–88
   ushers in new era, 415
   as vindication, 235, 404, 449, 458–59
resurrection life, 264–65
retributive justice, 358–59, 367–68, 370, 389–90
Reuchlin, Johannes, 671–72
reward, 50, 58, 826
Ricci, Paulo, 662
Ridley, Nicholas, 818
righteousness, 13, 56–57, 139
   and covenant, 46, 534–35
   as covenant faithfulness, 378
   as evidence of the "righteous," 185
   as forensic, 216n8
   as gift, 495
   as inherent and imputed, 742
   in the Psalms, 72
   as rectification, 334
   and relationship, 56
   in Romans, 214
   stems from obedience of Christ, 393
   as transformative, 216n8
   two kinds of, 680
   of unbelieving Israelites, 229
   in Wisdom Literature, 91
righteousness by works of the law, 144, 229–30, 263–64, 680. *See also* works righteousness
righteousness of Christ, 260, 710
   basis of justification, 231
   divine and human, 711–12
   See also imputation of Christ's righteousness
righteousness of God, 185–86, 264, 496
   Augustine on, 675n109
   as Christological righteousness, 461
   as covenant faithfulness, 217
   as formal cause of justification, 743, 831
   as a gift, 391–92
   Luther on, 664, 675n109
   in Romans, 216–17
   Wright on, 491
righteousness of reason, 680
righteousness through faith, 229, 230, 842–43
"Righteous One," 424, 431
right to eternal life, 444, 452, 462, 467
Ritschl, Albrecht, 371, 796–98, 799
ritual cleansing, 76
Robar, Elizabeth, 54
Robinson, John A. T., 276n11
"Rock of Ages" (Toplady hymn), 435, 520
Roman Catholic Church
   anthropology of, 756–57
   on the church, 828–29
   conflates justification and sanctification, 511–12
   evangelical trajectory of, 741
   on justification, 233–34, 739–66
   on Scripture, 751
Romans, on justification, 213–36
romanticism, of Schleiermacher, 788–89
Rosner, Brian S., 547nn54–55
"royal law," 286, 287–88
royal-priestly servant, 115
Rufinus, 574, 579n53, 584
Ruhamah, 129–32, 133, 135
Rule of the Community (1QS), 157–60, 177

Russell, Charles, 835
Rutledge, Fleming, 374, 376n124
Ryrie, Charles, 516

Sabbath, 194–95, 229, 305, 523
sacramental system of the church, 744, 755, 758
sacraments, Newman on, 816
sacrifice, 69
sacrifice and obedience of Christ, 462–63
sacrificial giving, 550
Sadducees, 125
Sailhamer, John, 62
Salmeron, Alfonso, 743
Saltmarsh, John, 515
salvation
   individual vs. cosmic, 328–29
   in Isaiah, 118
   is God's alone, 108
   for outsiders, 199–201
   Sanders on, 298
   of Yahweh alone, 113
salvation belongs to the Lord, 121
Salvator noster (papal bull), 666n47
Samaritans, 199–200
sanctification, 31–32, 258, 261, 413, 554–56
   Augsburg Confession on, 677
   Augustine on, 591
   as gradual and partial, 523
   and the law, 546
   Newman on, 820
   as process, 32
   as the purpose of justification, 500–503
   and resurrection of Christ, 404–5, 412
   as transformative, 508–9
   See also definitive sanctification; justification and sanctification; progressive sanctification
Sanders, E. P., 147–48, 151, 152, 155, 156, 158, 163, 164, 166–67, 169, 171, 173–77, 295–302, 323–24, 330, 335n35, 413, 514, 536
sapiential justice, 107, 113–14
Sarah, 48, 58, 256, 396
satisfaction of Christ, 710, 769
satisfactio vicaria, 769
saving faith, 279, 405–6, 408, 434, 516, 729–30, 848–50
Savoy Declaration, 720
Schaff, Philip, 830n104
Scheck, Thomas P., 572n29, 575, 578
Schelling, Friedrich, 801n120
Schleiermacher, Friedrich, 787–90, 795, 798, 799
Schliesser, Benjamin, 47n36
Schmalkaldic League, 683

Schmalkaldic War, 684–85
Schmitt, Hans Christoph, 62
schola Augustiniana moderna (new Augustinian school), 625, 652, 661
scholasticism, 617, 618n11, 661
Schreiner, Thomas R., 216, 217n16, 219n23, 219n25, 230, 396–97, 398, 403–4, 452n59, 457n82
Schultz, Franz Albert, 783
Schweitzer, Albert, 299, 327–29, 330, 331, 336, 337n47, 340, 342
Scott, James M., 308n84, 314n106
Scott, Thomas, 814n11, 835
scribes and Pharisees, 180–82, 193n27, 195–96, 207
Scripture
   Roman Catholic Church on, 751
   Vermigli on, 824, 828, 830
Sczebel, Pat, 235–36
Secession Church (Scotland), 728
2 Baruch, 152–53, 177
2 Corinthians, justification in, 259–61
Second Helvetic Confession (1566), 438, 704–5, 707
2 Peter, on obedience of Christ, 463–64
Second Temple Judaism, 147–77, 298, 302n42, 303, 514
2 Timothy, justification in, 268
Second Vatican Council, 741, 748, 765, 812
Seebass, Horst, 56n61
seed of Abraham, 52
seed of the woman, 383
Seifrid, Mark A., 202n36, 305, 315n116
self-consciousness of Spirit (Hegel), 790–92
self-consciousness (Schleiermacher), 788–90
self-justification, 203
self-righteousness, 207, 229, 286, 345–46, 515
semi-Pelagianism, 150, 159–60, 163, 164, 169, 176, 629
   of Biel, 641–42
Semler, Johann Salomo, 775
Sentences (Peter Lombard), 606–8, 616n105, 628, 659–60
sentential justification (Baxter), 722
Serapion of Antioch, 241n9
Seripando, Girolamo, 742
Sermon on the Mount, 180–82, 184
servant of the Lord, 112, 118. *See also* suffering servant
servants of the Lord, 112, 115, 116
sexual immorality, 144, 494, 548
shalom, 134
Shammai, house of, 174–75
Shelton, R. Larry, 372, 373

Shema, 61
Shepherd, Norman, 735–36
Shepherd of Hermas, 275n8
shepherds, 199
shield, 50, 58
Silva, Moisés, 149n12, 250, 540–41n29
Simler, Josias, 821, 822n55, 834
Simon, Marcus, 580n54
simul iustus et peccator, 225, 436, 577, 832
sin
   in apocalyptic reading of Paul, 339–40
   of commission and omission, 450
   as context of justification, 426–29
   covering of, 79–80
   and death, 247–48, 427
   forensic consequences of, 426–27
   guilt of, 666
   and holiness, 95
   inclination toward, 832
   individual and corporate, 74
   as missing the mark, 78–80, 86
   noetic impact of, 427
   overwhelmed by, 859–60
   penalty of, 666–67
   and punishment, 370
   as repudiation of word of God, 427
   universality of, 390, 430
sinfulness of humanity, 96, 484
   depth of, 428
   in the Psalms, 70, 72–74
single imputation (passive obedience of Christ), 711–12
singularity, of gift, 318
sinners and tax collectors, 200
sins, cast into depths of the sea, 87
Sirach, 151–52, 177
Sixty-Seven Articles (Zwingli), 703
slavery to the law, 528
slave to righteousness, 227
slave to sin, 227
slave trade, 865
Smalcald Articles, 35
Smith, Barry D., 160n55
social justice, 118, 865
Socinian-classic, liberal-postmodern view of the atonement, 364–66, 369, 370–71
Socinianism, 365, 368, 370, 733, 772–73, 777n32, 781, 806
Socinus, Faustus, 365, 772–73
Socinus, Laelius, 772, 773n13
Sodom and Gomorrah, 104n6
sola fide, 23, 31, 33, 34, 35, 36, 37, 342, 394, 395, 624, 653, 769–70
   and antinomianism, 826

   constant conflict on, 806
   dismantled by Pietists, 778–82
   dismantled by rationalists, 775–77
   eclipsed in much of contemporary Protestantism, 806
   and good works, 686, 706, 710
   a lively faith, not a dead faith, 708
   rejected by radical Reformers, 773
   Trent on, 746, 766, 771
   Vermigli on, 832–33
sola gratia, 31, 37, 411, 639, 769
   not the invention of the Reformation, 758n48
sola scriptura, 651, 670, 740, 751
soli Deo gloria, 342
solis operibus, 616n105, 639
solus Christi merito, 834
solus Christus, 23, 35, 653
Son, obedience of, 655. *See also* obedience of Christ
song of Moses, 88
song of the Lamb, 88
Song of Witness, 88
Son of David, 192, 384
South Galatian theory, 242–43
sovereign grace
   abandoned by Biel, 617
   Augustine on, 589–90
   Thomas Aquinas on, 611
Spangenberg, August Gottlieb, 779
Spanish Inquisition, 771n7
speech-act theory, 529
Spieckermann, Hermann, 42
Spinoza, Benedict de, 773n12, 775
Spirit (Hegel), 790–92
Spirit of God, 111–13, 116. *See also* Holy Spirit
spiritual Christians, vs. carnal Christians, 516
spiritual righteousness, 680
Sprinkle, Preston M., 159n50, 161, 164n71, 298–99n23
Spurgeon, Charles, 404
Stancaro, Francesco, 689, 695
steadfast love, 82, 85, 86, 87, 89–90
Steinbart, Gotthilf Samuel, 781–82
Stendahl, Krister, 247, 330, 336, 514, 564
stewardship, 550
Stockhausen, Carol, 551
Stone, Michael, 151
Stone, Samuel John, 737
stone heart, 552
Stott, John R. W., 217, 218–19, 222, 362n55
Strauss, David, 796
Streck, Odil Hannes, 317n120
Strigel, Viktorin, 688
striving, faith as, 292

Stuart, Douglas, 126n50
Stuhlmacher, Peter, 160n55, 300n29
substitution, 360
    and participation in Christ, 485
substitutionary atonement, 431, 483–85
    jettisoning of, 470, 482–83
    and union with Christ, 485
suffering, 109, 113–14, 854
suffering servant, 28, 110, 115, 117, 465
summum bonum, 14
Sumner, John Bird, 814, 815
superabundance, of gift, 319, 321
Swabian Concord, 693
synecdoche, 575
synergist controversy (Lutheranism), 671, 687–88
Synod of Dort (1618–1619), 714, 716, 717, 719
Synod of Gap, 713, 714, 719
systematic theology, 270

Tabor, 139n75
Tan, Kim Huat, 535n10
tax collector (parable), 198–99, 204–5
tax collectors, 200
Taylor, Willard, 373
temple, 71
Tertullian, 241n9, 563, 571, 584
    on atonement, 361
    on merit, 573
Testament of Abraham, 153–55, 177
Tetzel, Johann, 667, 669
Theobald, Michael, 245n32
theologia crucis (Luther), 649
theologians of glory, 24, 29
theology proper, and justification, 355–59, 420–22
Theophylact, 587, 593n21, 618–21
theosis, 342–43, 486, 513, 696
Thessalonians, on justification, 260–61
thief on the cross, 573
Thielman, Frank, 536
third stage of justification (Roman Catholic Church), 744, 745
Thirty-Nine Articles (1571), 719–20, 722, 733
Thirty Years War, 774n17
Thistelton, Anthony C., 283n37
Thomas Aquinas, 421, 432, 587, 589, 658–60, 664
    on four necessary elements of justification, 423n14
    on good works, 660
    intellectualism of, 627–29
    on justification, 609–14
Thomism, sapiential tradition of, 748–49

Thornwell, James, 728
threefold imputation, in Heidelberg Catechism, 710, 714, 725
three stages of justification (Baxter), 722–23
three stages of justification (Roman Catholic Church), 743–44
Tillich, Paul, 773n16, 796, 799, 800–802, 805
Tillotson, John, 776, 777n29
Tindal, Matthew, 775
Tipton, Lane G., 470n2, 498n137, 500n141
tithe commandment, 550
Titus, 240, 268–69
Toland, John, 775
Töllner, Johann Gottlieb, 781
Toon, Peter, 515, 831–32
Toplady, Augustus M., 435, 520
Torah (Pentateuch), 99, 125
Torgau Book, 693
Torrance, James B., 340
Torrance Thomas F., 521n62
Tosefta, works righteousness in, 169–76
Townend, Stuart, 864
Tractarians, 732, 817n30, 818
Tracts for the Times, 817
tradition, development of, 819
traditions, scribes and Pharisees on, 195–96
transcultural (ecumenic) justice, 104, 114, 116, 118
transgression, 78–80, 86
transitoriness, 96
transubstantiation, 776
Travis, Stephen, 382n144
tree
    and obedience of Christ, 451
    and sin of Adam, 451
tree of life, 95, 379, 448n34
tree of the knowledge of good and evil, 379
trespasses, as forensic terminology, 398
Tridentine Roman Catholicism. *See* Council of Trent (1545–1563)
Trinity, 522, 777
    in justification and sanctification, 558
triple imputation (active, passive, and habitual obedience), 712
Troeltsch, Ernst, 798
Truce of Passau, 685
Trueman, Carl R., 514n35
trust, 283
    as essence of saving faith, 730
Trutfetter, Jodokus, 663
Tübingen school, 790, 793
Turretin, Francis, 362, 452n60, 475–76, 729, 730
    on obedience of Christ, 457–58
    on twofold justification, 724

Twelve, the (Minor Prophets), 103–4, 120, 144
Twisse, William, 718
two-Adam structure. *See* Adam-Christ typology
twofold justification
    of Edwards, 730–31, 732
    of Roman Catholic Church, 707–8, 723
two horizons, of justification, 182
two kinds of righteousness, 517, 523, 680, 683, 689, 702, 703, 705

undefiled love, 649–50
Union school, 334. *See also* apocalyptic reading of Paul
union with Christ, 32, 34, 118, 207, 210, 221n36, 232, 239, 260, 265, 289n48, 353, 355, 360, 413, 416, 517, 826, 842, 844
    as central idea in soteriology, 497
    as controlling concept, 470, 471
    and divine righteousness, 711
    and forensic justification, 486–90
    in Heidelberg Catechism, 710
    and imputation of active obedience of Christ, 490–96
    and justification, 533, 559
    as means of justification (Finnish interpretation), 696
    as mutual indwelling, 509–10
    mutually determining and illuminating with justification, 469, 470, 472, 481, 502
    and *ordo salutis*, 496–502
    and substitutionary atonement, 485
Unitarianism, spread of, 772–73
universal blessing, 44–46
universal consent, 774
universalism, in apocalyptic reading of Paul, 337n47
universal satisfaction, 705
University of Berlin, 790
University of Erfurt, 663
University of Halle, 779–81
University of Wittenberg, 663, 671–72
unrighteous, will not inherit kingdom of God, 258–59
unrighteousness, 214, 216, 258, 494
Upper Room Discourse, 206, 210
Ursinus, Zacharias, 433n49, 707, 709–10, 712, 736
Ussher, James, 714, 717

Valdés, Juán de, 705–6, 771n7, 835
VanDrunen, David, 30nn8–9
vanity, 95
VanLangingham, Chris, 155, 159n52

van Mastricht, Petrus, 729
Vatican II. *See* Second Vatican Council
vegetative imagery, 126
veil, removal of, 554–55
Venema, Cornelis, 518
Vermigli, Peter Martyr, 35, 625, 705, 706–7, 709, 712, 771n7, 812, 820–25
    on authority of the church, 829–30
    conversion of, 834–37
    on Scripture, 824, 828, 830
    on *sola fide*, 832–33
via antiqua (old way), 615, 617, 618, 624–26, 631, 641, 642–44, 650–51, 660–61, 664–65
via media, 732, 817–18, 820, 830n105
via moderna (new way), 615, 617, 618n111, 624–26, 631, 641, 642–44, 649, 650–51, 660–62, 675, 690
    and training of Luther, 663–65
via Romana, 820
vicarious atonement, 198n31, 483–44
    rejected by radical Reformers, 772
vicarious repentance, 366
Vickers, Brian, 224n45, 227n54, 231n64, 394
Vignaux, Paul, 639
vindication, 352, 399–400
Vines, Richard, 723
Viret, Pierre, 709
voluntarism, 629–30
von Rad, Gerhard, 42–43
von Ranke, Leopold, 771n5
von Staupitz, Johannes, 615
Vos, Geerhardus, 403, 404, 444, 467, 470n1, 479–80
Vulgate, 668

Wagner, J. Ross, 117
waiting for the Lord's justice, 115
Wallace, Daniel B., 541n34
Waltke, Bruce K., 80, 94, 308n85
Walton, John H., 451n52
Ward, R. B., 281n29
Ware, Henry, 773
Warfield, B. B., 134n65, 150n14, 510, 618, 732
Watson, Francis, 161n57, 552
Watson, Richard, 372–73n96
Watson, Thomas, 618
Watts, Rikki E., 188n18
Webster, John, 420, 422
Weijenborg, Reynold, 639
Weinandy, Thomas, 415n45
Weinfeld, Moshe, 94
Wesley, John, 779

Wesleyanism, 779
Westerholm, Stephen, 260–61, 339n58, 546n50
Westminster Confession of Faith, 717–21, 729, 734
  on condescension of God, 455n74
  on faith accompanied by other saving graces, 826n81
  on good works, 719
  on imputation of active obedience of Christ, 719–21
  on justification, 354, 507, 718
  on Mosaic law, 453n62, 455n71
  on obedience of Christ, 441n1
  on perseverance, 730
  rejection of errors, 718
  on sanctification, 509
  on saving faith, 729
  on union and justification, 473
Westminster Larger Catechism
  on distinction between justification and sanctification, 731
  on exaltation of Christ, 460n96
  on faith as outward referring, 433
  on imputation of active obedience of Christ, 720
  on obedience of Christ, 441n1
  on union and justification, 473–74
Westminster Shorter Catechism
  on justification, 701–2, 733
  on justification and sanctification, 722
  on obedience of Christ, 441n1
Westminster Theological Seminary, 734, 735–36
Whately, Richard, 813
Whitehead, Alfred North, 589
wholeness, 187–89
"whole obedience" of Christ, 720
Wilberforce, William, 865
Wilbur, Earl Morse, 773n11
Wildberger, Hans, 63n76
wilderness wandering, 126
Wiley, H. Orton, 372
William of Bavaria, Duke, 678
William of Ockham, 368n77, 615n101, 616n102, 629, 631, 649, 660–61, 663
William of St. Thierry, 603
Williams, Daniel, 724–25
Williams, Garry, 358–59, 366n70
Williamson, Paul R., 535n9, 536
wisdom, 107
Wisdom Books, 90–91, 96
wise and foolish, 95
Wiseman, Nicholas, 819

Witherspoon, John, 731
Witsius, Herman, 510n20, 724, 725–26
Wittenberg Concord, 683
woe oracles, 105n6
Wolf, Ernst, 804
Wolff, Christian, 766, 780, 781, 783
Wolff, Hans Walter, 137
Wolterstorff, Nicholas, 105n6
woman with hemorrhage, healing of, 190–93
"wonderful exchange," 29–30, 431, 599
Word and faith, 119
work of Christ, as "double cure," 520
works, and final judgment, 259
works of the law, 220, 249–51, 262, 263, 268–69, 284–85, 288, 352
  as Jewish identity markers, 246–48, 304–6, 317, 322, 514, 523
  as perfect obedience, 252–53
works righteousness, 842–43
  in 4 Ezra, 150–51
  as legalism, 149–50
  in Miqsat Ma'ase Ha-Torah (4QMMT), 161–64
  in Mishnah, 165–69
  in Pesher Habakkuk (1QpHab), 160–61
  of Pharisee (parable), 203–4
  in Psalms of Solomon, 155–57
  in rabbinic literature, 164–76
  repudiated by Newman and Vermigli, 827
  in Rule of the Community (1QS), 157–60
  in 2 Baruch, 152–53
  in Second Temple Judaism, 147–77, 514
  in Sirach, 151–52
  in Testament of Abraham, 153–55
  in Tosefta, 169–76
world
  false righteousness of, 206–7
  lies under curse, 46
world religions, *sola fide* and *sola gratia* in, 232n72
worldview, and justification, 14–15
wrath of God, 28, 103, 122, 138, 142, 233, 254, 255, 262, 265, 338, 353, 357, 360, 375, 391–92, 430–31, 494
wrath to come, 412
Wrede, William, 327, 328n3, 329n13, 330n14, 337n47
Wright, David, 591, 596
Wright, N. T., 147, 148, 149n11, 161, 163–64, 240nn5–6, 241, 295–96, 306–18, 323–24, 330, 338n54, 339, 340n62, 340n64, 514
  on atonement, 363n56
  on covenant faithfulness of God, 374–75
  on faith and obedience, 514n39

on imputation, 375, 470, 491–96, 736
on justification, 247n45, 352n6, 413–14
on Mosaic covenant, 536
on obedience of Christ, 452n59, 454–55
on resurrection and ecclesiology, 415
on righteousness of God, 260, 374–75, 491
on works, 259n111
Writings, 125
Wycliffe, John, 615

Yinger, Kent L., 148n4

Zahn, Theodore, 276
Zechariah, 123
Zephaniah, 122–23
Ziesler, John, 382n144
Zinzendorf, Nikolaus Ludwig von, 779
Zion, 116, 117, 123
Zwingli, Huldrych, 703, 705, 712, 821, 835

Scripture Index

Genesis
book of 41, 43, 44, 52, 53n50, 55, 56n61, 57, 59, 63, 63n76, 91, 274, 822
1 ....46n31, 139n77
1–2........377
1–3........454
1–5........456n79
1–11........44
1–Ex. 19....60
1:2 47
1:3 44
1:27 23
1:31 380
2 95
2:1–3 377
2:4 ....57n64
2:15–17....379
2:16–17....24, 362
2:17 ....427, 449, 456
2:23 ....57n64
3 ....13, 24, 26, 380, 391
3–11 46
3:1 44
3:5 ....424, 427
3:6 ....380, 427
3:13 427
3:14 46
3:15 ....380, 382
3:17 46
3:19 85
3:21–24....380
3:22 ....379, 456
3:23–24....46
4:9 44
4:10–16....46
4:11 46
5:1 ....57n64
5:29 46
6 ....46n31
6–9 46
6:5 ....380, 390
6:5–8 46
6:9 ....46, 55, 56, 57, 57n64
7:1 ....46, 56
8:1 ....384n147
8:21 46
9:25 46
10:1 ....57n64
11:1–9 46
11:4 24
11:8–9 46
11:27 ......47n37, 57n64
11:31–32 ...47
12 ....48n38, 59
12–22 63
12:1 ....45, 45n29, 47n37
12:1–2a....45
12:1–3 45
12:2–3 .....46, 47
12:2b–3....45
12:3 46
12:4 ....47n37, 54
12:4–15:21 .45
12:6 47
12:8 ....43n19
12:10–20 ...47
13:12–13 ...48
13:14–17 ...51
13:18 ......43n19, 54
14 ....48, 49
14:14 48
14:19–20 ...48
14:20 50
14:23 50
15 ....43, 43n17, 44, 48, 48n38, 49, 50, 51, 52, 56n61, 58, 59, 61, 63, 64, 277, 281, 290, 393
15:1 ....44, 48, 49, 50, 52, 58
15:1–6 .....49, 52
15:2–3 .....44, 52
15:3 50
15:4 ....49, 50
15:4–5 52
15:5 54
15:6 ....33, 41, 42, 42n10, 44n23, 49, 51, 52, 54, 54n54, 55, 56n61, 59, 63, 64n82, 79, 162, 162n64, 163, 193, 224, 249, 251–52, 274, 275, 275n10, 276, 277, 281, 291, 344, 381, 381–82, 494n126, 566, 619
15:6a 52
15:6b 52, 57
15:7 ....48n38, 49, 51, 52, 54n54
15:7–17.....51, 52
15:7–21.....49, 51
15:8 ....49, 52
15:9 52
15:10–12 ...52
15:11–16 ...64
15:13–16 ...44, 49
15:13–17 ...52
15:18 ......44, 48, 48n38, 49, 52
15:18–21...44n23, 51, 52
16 ....48n38, 50, 58, 341
16:1–22:23 .45
17 58
17:1 ....57, 113
17:1–14.....33
17:5 116
17:6 50
17:10 ......57n64
17:16 116
17:17 ......48, 48n39
17:17–18 ...44
18:12 ......48, 48n39
18:18 47
18:19 ......57, 106, 113
18:22–33 ...33
18:23 57
18:23–33 ...56, 113
18:24 57
18:25 ......57, 355, 359, 422, 423, 484
18:26 57
18:28 57
19 48
21 ....49, 49n40
21:24 54
22 ....43, 43n17, 45, 49, 49n40, 62, 63, 277, 281, 290
22:1 ....44n23
22:1–19.....33
22:2 ....45n29, 46
22:13 92
22:16 113
22:16–18 ...44n22
22:17 131

22:18.......46, 47, 63, 116
22:18–19...44n23
23..........47
24:1–28.....33
25:26.......142
26..........63
26:3–5......60
26:4........47
26:5........42, 64, 64n80, 64n82
28:14.......47
31:15.......55
31:54.......92
32:22–32...142
35:15.......138n75, 142
38:15.......55, 57
38:26.......352n5
41:52.......142
42:20.......52
44:16.......352n5
44:30–31...54
45:26.......52

Exodus
book of.....69, 70, 87, 197, 822
Ex.–Deut....86n28
2:11–14.....100
3:5–6.......356
4...........62
4:1.........61, 62
4:5.........61
4:8.........61, 62
4:9.........61, 62
6:2.........106
6:6.........106
6:8.........106
8:31........220n27
9:6.........220n27
10:19.......220n27
12:22.......81
12:26–27...88
14:14.......61
14:31.......53, 61, 579
15:4–5......87
15:10.......87
15:11.......356
19–Num. 10
..........63
19:9........61
19:23–25...356
20–Num. 10:11
..........60
20:12.......547
23:6........488
23:7........224, 352n5, 484, 488, 494
24..........60n72
24:12.......551n60
29:14.......198n30, 260
29:36.......198n30
30:12.......84
32–34.......60n72
32:1–35.....86

32:32.......75
33..........86
33:13.......68, 86
33:17–34:9 .86
33:18.......68
33:19.......68, 128
34..........68, 86
34:1–4......551
34:6........69, 70, 87, 174
34:6–7......68, 124, 132, 358
34:7........357, 422
34:9........87
34:10–28...87

Leviticus
book of.....70, 75, 197, 822
1:4.........484
4:3.........198n30
4:4.........484
4:8.........198n30, 260
4:14........198n30
4:20–21.....260
4:24........260
4:28........198n30
4:29........260
4:34........260
5:8.........198n30
5:11........198n30
5:12........198n30
7:18........55
9–10........60n72
9:2.........198n30
9:7.........198n30
9:10........198n30
11:44.......356, 377
11:44–45...71
14:4........81
14:6........81
14:49.......81
14:51.......81
14:52.......81
16..........69, 87, 88, 203, 392
16:3........198n30
16:6........198n30
16:9........198n30
16:21.......484
16:27.......198n30
17:4........55
18..........308, 450n45, 538
18:1–5......538n21
18:3........538
18:5........156, 156n38, 252, 252n76, 253, 256, 450, 450n45, 453, 538, 538n21, 734
18:24–28...310
18:28.......538
18:28–29...539n21
18:29.......538, 539n21
19..........105
19:1........356
19:2........71, 357n30

19:18.......287, 443, 547, 548
20..........308
20:3........357n30
20:7........71
20:9–21.....539n21
20:22–24...310
20:26.......71, 357n30
21:6........71
21:8........71
24:10–14...60n72
26..........308, 309
26:31.......310
26:32–39...309
26:33–34...309
26:34–35...310
26:40–45...309
26:42.......309

Numbers
book of.....197
5:11–31.....167
5:12........167n83
5:18........167
5:19........167n83
5:20........167n83
5:22........52n47
5:26–27.....167
5:29........167n83
6:11........198n30
6:16........198n30
7:22........198n30
7:34........198n30
7:46........198n30
8:8.........198n30
8:21........198n30
10:12–36:13
..........60
11:19.......220n27
11:29.......106
12:7........52
14:11.......61
14:18.......68
15..........60n72
18–19.......60n72
20:12.......61
25..........138n75
25:1–18.....126

Deuteronomy
book of.....60, 60n71, 61, 88, 89, 91, 94, 100, 104, 132, 185, 453
1–34........60
1:9–18......94
1:21........94
1:29........94
1:33........106
3:2.........94
3:22........94
3:24........89
4:2.........94
4:10........106
4:13........551n60, 552

4:30–31 . . . . . 140, 143
4:34 89
5:15 89
5:22 . . . . 551n60
5:29 106
6:1–9 94
6:2 94
6:4 . . . . 223n41, 280
6:4–5 61
6:5 . . . . 100, 105, 443
6:13 94
6:21 89
6:24 94
6:25 56
7:7–8 69
7:8 89
7:9 . . . . 52, 72
7:18–19 94
7:19 89
8:6 94
9:9 . . . . 551n60
9:10 . . . . 551n60
9:11 . . . . 551n60
9:23 . . . . 61, 62
9:26 89
10 184
10:12 . . . . . . 94, 100, 105
10:12–13 . . . 62
10:16 . . . . . . 62, 106, 124, 180, 184
10:17 484
10:20 94
11:1 . . . . 60n70
11:2 89
12:9–10 100
13:1 94
13:4 94
14:23 94
16:18–20 . . . 94
16:19 279
16:20 124
17 462
17:14–20 . . . 61
17:18 107
18:15 104
19:14 94
21:10–14 . . . 61
21:23 . . . . . . 255, 255n91, 598n40
22:8 548
24:1–5 61
24:13 56
25:1 . . . . 352, 352n5, 488
25:13–16 . . . 94
26:8 89
26:15 . . . . . . 357n29
27 250
27–30 308
27:15–26 . . . 52n47
27:26 . . . . . . 246, 249, 250, 252, 252n76, 453
28 . . . . 309, 310
28:21 309
28:25 309

28:32 309
28:36–37 . . . 309
28:41 309
28:49–52 . . . 309
28:63–68 . . . 309
29:21 538
30:1–8 106
30:3 . . . . 140, 143
30:3–4 132
30:6 . . . . 61, 62, 106, 124, 180, 185
30:10–15 . . . 109
30:11–14 . . . 124
30:19–20 . . . 100
30:20 100
31–32 100
31:16 104
31:16–18 . . . 127
31:19 . . . . . . 88, 107
31:22 88
31:27 105
31:30–32:47
. . . . 88
32 . . . . 88, 106, 309n89
32:1 104
32:4 358
32:5 104
32:20 104
32:32 104
32:44 88
34:10 104

Joshua
book of 99, 100, 282
2:1–11 290
2:9–13 282
6:21–25 291
10:8 . . . . 220n27
15:7 125
21:44 . . . . . . 220n27
23–24 100
23:14 . . . . . . 220n27
24:2–3 . . . . . 47n36, 224
24:19 . . . . . . 357n30

Judges
book of 99, 100
4–5 . . . . 139n75
5:26 . . . . 53n50
19–21 . . . . . 139n75

Ruth
book of 99
4:16 52

1 Samuel
book of 99, 100
1:13 . . . . 55, 57
1:17 84
1:19 . . . . 384n147
2:2 356
2:6 . . . . 174, 175
6:20 . . . . 357n30

10:17–27 . . . 139n75
11:14–15 . . . 139n75
15:21–23 . . . 139n75
15:22 . . . . . . 453n62, 463
21:1–6 194
26:23 57
27:12 53

2 Samuel
book of 80, 99, 100
7 71
8:15 172
11–12 80
11:3 . . . . 81n20
12:13 80
13:30 220
15:12 . . . . . . 81n20
19:19 . . . . . . 55, 56
22:21 57
23:34 . . . . . . 81n20

1 Kings
book of 99, 100
1:36 . . . . 52n27
3:6 57
8:27 377
8:32 . . . . 56, 352n5

2 Kings
book of 62, 99, 100
9:11 138
10:1 52
16:7 69
17:14 62
18:16 52
21:1–18 173
23:26 173
24:3 173
25 100
25:25 101
25:27–30 . . . 101

1 Chronicles
book of 91, 99
1:1 . . . . 456n79
16:10 . . . . . . 357n29
16:34 90
16:35 . . . . . . 357n29
29:16 . . . . . . 357n29

2 Chronicles
book of 91, 99
5:13 90
6:23 . . . . 352n5
6:40 81
7:3 90
7:14 . . . . 190n21
19:7 279
20:21 90
30:18–19 . . . 76
33:1–20 173
33:12–13 . . . 173
33:13 173

Scripture Index 897

33:18–19 ...173
33:19 173

Ezra
book of 99, 144, 310
4:1–6:22 310
9–10 310
9:6–9 308
9:8–9 312
9:10–15 310
10:8 310

Nehemiah
book of 99, 144, 310
1:6 81
1:11 81
3:17–6:19 ...310
4:5 75
5:13 ....52n47
9:8 63
9:15 207
9:17 ....68, 82
9:32–37 308
9:36–37 312
13:1–6 310
13:10–12 ...550
13:15–22 ...310
13:17–18 ...310
13:23–31 ...310

Esther
book of 99

Job
book of 90, 91, 92, 92n38, 93,
            93n43, 95, 96, 99
1:1–2:13 92
1:5 92
9:15 ....352n5
13:24 55
18:3 55
19:11 55
19:15 55
19:23–24 ...93
19:23–27 ...93
33:10 55
37:14–24 ...92
38 92
38–41 ......92, 92n40
38:1 92
38:8 92
38:12 92
38:31 92
42:1–3 93
42:1–6 92
42:5 93
42:7–17 92
42:8 92

Psalms
book of 13, 56, 67, 68, 69, 70,
           71, 72, 73, 74, 75, 77,
           90, 91, 96, 99, 218,
           390, 595, 643, 664
1:1 78

2 123
2:7 ....400, 407
3 592
3:4 ....357n29
5:4 93
5:9 390
6 ....83, 84
6:1 83
6:4–5 84
6:8–10 84
7:11 422
7:17 377
8 ....458, 462n111
9:2 377
9:5–6 358
9:15–20 358
9:17 ....174, 175
10:14–18 ...144
11:4 ....357n29
14 73
14:1–3 .....25, 390
14:3 75
15 71
15:2–5 71
16:8–11 406
16:10 ......406, 407, 467
20:6 ....357n29
21:7 377
22:2 ....198n32, 431n45
22:2–3 71
22:3 ....357n29
24 71
24:3 ....71, 82, 357n30
24:4 72
24:5 72
25:11 75
28:2 ....357n29
28:7 604
31:1 ....72, 358
32 ....75, 77, 78, 79, 80, 83,
           84, 86
32:1 ....79, 508
32:1–2 .....77, 79, 80, 225, 382
32:2 ....55, 56
32:3–4 77
32:3–5 78
32:5 ....78, 79
33:16–22 ...143
33:21 71
36:1 ....73, 390
36:10 358
37 90
38 ....83, 84
38:1 83
38:18 84
38:22 84
40 ....462, 462n112, 463
40:2 74
40:6–8 .....453n62, 462, 463
40:7–8 .....400n20
40:7–9 .....462n109
40:8 463
40:12 463
40:13–17 ...463

41:4 190
44 67
46:4 71
48:1 ....357n29
49 ....84, 143
49:3–4 84
49:7 84
49:8 84
50:12–14 ...377
51 ....72, 75, 76, 77, 78, 80,
           81, 83, 84, 86, 87
51:1 75
51:1–2 .....80, 87
51:2 ....75, 76
51:4 ....75, 80, 81, 289
51:5 81
51:7 ....75, 76, 80, 87
51:7–10 81
51:9 ....75, 80, 87
51:10 76
51:14 72
51:17 81
53:1–3 390
53:3 75
58:10–11 ...484
60:6 ....357n30
65:3 70
65:4 ....70, 71, 357n29
68:5 144
69:2 82
69:14 82
71 71
71:2 358
71:22 71
72 ....155n37
72:13 595
73 90
73:13 ......288n43
74 67
78 ....67, 70, 74, 88, 126n49,
           128n55
78:2 88
78:8 88
78:38 ......70, 89
78:41 71
78:42 70
78:52 70
78:54 70
79:9 70
82:3 ....144, 352n5
85:2 79
85:9–11 72
86 ....68, 83
86:5 68
86:15 68
88:12 57
89 69
89:16 72
89:18 71
89:35 ......357n30
90 ....67, 85
93:2 377
94:7–9 358
95 100

Scripture Index   899

96 90	130:5–6. 82	4:12 170
97:9 377	130:7–8. 82	6–9 96
98:2 57	130:8 82	7:20 428
99 . . . . .71n4, 76	132 69	9:18 . . . . . . .169, 170
99:3 . . . . . . .76, 356	135 . . . . .88, 89	12:8–14. 95
99:4 76	135:3 89	12:13 . . . . . . .95, 96
99:5 . . . . . . .76, 356	135:15–18. . .89	
99:8 76	136 . . . . .88, 89, 90	*Song of Songs*
99:9 . . . . . . .76, 356	136:1–3. 90	book of 90, 99
102 . . . . .83, 84	136:4 90	1:5 90
102:13. 84	136:12 89	1:16 605
102:16. 84	136:25 90	3:7 90
102:21. 84	139:1–4. 377	3:9 90
103 . . . . .68, 84, 86, 87, 88	139:1–10 . . .377	3:11 . . . . .86, 90
103:1 71	139:16 . . . . . .377, 378	7:1 52
103:1–2. . . . .85, 86n27	140:3 390	8:11–12. 90
103:3 . . . . . . .75, 86, 87, 190n21	140:6 83	
103:4 . . . . . . .85, 87	141:1 83	*Isaiah*
103:6–19 . . .86	142:5 83	book of 56n61, 57, 71, 99, 102, 104, 107, 110n25, 113, 117, 118, 119, 187, 187n17, 188, 190, 197, 198, 200, 344
103:7 . . . . . . .85, 86	143 . . . . .77, 82, 83, 84	
103:7–8. 68	143:1 72	
103:8 . . . . . . .68, 85, 86	143:1–6. 83	
103:8–19 . . .85	143:2 . . . . . . .74, 75, 82, 83, 344, 604	
103:9 85	143:6 83	
103:9–10 . . .85	144:3 . . . . . . .57n64	1 . . . . .105n8
103:10. . . . . .85, 86	145:8 . . . . . . .68, 69	1–39 128
103:11. . . . . .85, 87	145:17. . . . . .357n30, 358	1:2 104
103:12. . . . . .69, 85, 86, 87	145:21. 71	1:2–3 104
103:13. 87	146 143	1:3 114
103:15–16 . .85	147:3 . . . . . . .86, 190n21	1:4 . . . . .104, 105, 105n6, 105n8, 116
103:17. . . . . .72, 85, 87		
103:17–19. . .85	*Proverbs*	1:4–20. 356
103:18. 85	book of 90, 91, 94, 95, 96, 99, 151	1:5–6 137
103:20–22. . .85		1:5–8 106
105 . . . . .69, 74, 88, 89, 90	1:7 . . . . .91, 95	1:9 . . . . .104n6, 105n8
105:3 71	2:16–17. 94	1:10 . . . . .104, 104n6, 105, 105n8
105:5 89	3:1–10 94	1:10–15. 105
105:8 89	3:11–12. 95	1:11 . . . . .453n62
105:42. 89	3:18 95	1:11–15. . . . .104n6
106 . . . . .74, 88, 89, 90	4:18 95	1:16 . . . . .104n6
106:4 89	8:35 593	1:16–17. 114
106:6 74	9:10 91	1:17 . . . . .104n6
106:7 89	11:30 95	1:18 . . . . .81, 87, 104n6, 106, 110
106:13. 89	13:12 95	1:21 . . . . .104, 104n6, 117
106:21. 89	14:5 52	1:23 . . . . .104n6
106:30–31. . .43	15:4 95	1:26 . . . . .105n7, 110
106:31. . . . . .55, 162, 163	17:15 . . . . . . .217n12, 224, 352, 484, 488, 494	2:2–4 116
106:45. 89		2:3 117
106:47. 71	17:28 55	2:5 106
107 89	20:23 94	2:9–21 108
107:1 89	21:3 463	2:10–22. 353
109:14. 75	22:10 94	2:11 107
110 . . . . .382, 400, 458	24:12 358	2:12 107
110:1 . . . . . . .384, 406	24:23 94	2:17 107
111:9 . . . . . . .71, 82	24:24 224	4:2 117
111:10. 91	28:4 94	4:2–6 . . . . . . .108, 110
116:1 174	28:21 94	4:4 117
118:9 143	30:5–6 94	4:6 109
126 67	30:9 94	5 . . . . .105n8
130 . . . . .77, 81, 82, 83, 84		5:1–7 . . . . . . .104, 105
130:1 74	*Ecclesiastes*	5:7 57
130:2 81	book of 90, 91, 95, 96, 99	5:8 . . . . .105n6
130:3 82	1:1–11 95	5:8–10 . . . . . .105n6
130:4 . . . . . . .75, 82, 419n1	1:12–12:7. . .95	5:11–17. . . . .105n6
		5:14 107

5:16 . . . . 105n6, 107, 357n30
5:18–19. . . . . 105n6
5:20 . . . . 105n6
5:21 . . . . 105n6
5:22–23. . . . . 105n6
5:23 . . . . 224, 352n5
5:24 . . . . 105, 105n6, 105n8,
                106, 114, 116
6 107
6:1 . . . . 357n29, 377
6:1–3 377
6:1–5 356
6:3 117
6:10 105
6:13 113
7–11. 105
7:3 . . . . 107n13
7:14 . . . . 128, 141
8:1 . . . . 107n13
8:3 . . . . 107n13
8:6 116
8:8 141
8:8–10. 128
8:10 141
8:12 105
8:13–14. . . . . 107, 108
8:16 . . . . 107, 114
8:17 . . . . 107, 114
8:18 . . . . 107n13
8:31 105
9 . . . . 110, 115
9:6 . . . . 112, 384, 647
9:6–7. 110
9:7 . . . . 111, 384
9:8 110
10:1–4. . . . . . 105n6
11 . . . . 110, 115
11:1 384
11:1–2. . . . . . 111, 112
11:1–5. . . . . . 112, 384
11:1–9. . . . . . 110, 112
11:9 117
12:1 . . . . 102, 143
12:1–6. 113
12:6 . . . . 102, 108, 141
13:6–11. 353
14:32. 109
16:5 111
19:22. . . . . . . 190n21
24:16. 424
25:1–8. 108
25:6–9. 384
25:9 108
26:8–9. 114
26:9–10. 114
26:11. 110
28 . . . . 105n6
28–33 . . . . . . 105n6
28:5–6. . . . . . 111, 113, 117
28:9 106
28:17. 108
28:29. 113

29 . . . . 105n6
29:9–14. 105
29:11–12 . . . 107
29:13. . . . . . . 106, 196, 463, 466
29:18. . . . . . . 105, 200
30–31 . . . . . . 105n6
30:8–11. 107
30:12. 116
30:18. . . . . . . 110, 115, 117
30:19–26 . . . 115
30:20. 115
30:23–26 . . . 115
30:27–28 . . . 108
30:27–33 . . . 115
30:29. . . . . . . 108, 115
30:30. . . . . . . 108, 115
31:2 113
32:1–2. 108
32:1–4. . . . . . 105n6
32:1–5. 111
32:15–20 . . . 105n6, 111
33 . . . . 105n6
33:2 115
33:5 . . . . 107, 108, 113, 117
33:10. 107
33:14. 108
33:14–15 . . . 188
33:15. 109
33:15–16 . . . 108
33:16. 108
33:17. . . . . . . 108, 111, 188
33:17–24 . . . 117
33:18–22 . . . 111
33:20. 188
33:20–24 . . . 108
33:22. . . . . . . 108, 111, 188
33:24. . . . . . . 108, 115, 188
34 110
35:1–6. 188
35:1–10. 117
35:3 200
35:5 105
35:8 356
35:10. 116
36–37 . . . . . . 106, 138, 141
36–39 . . . . . . 112, 115
37:4 . . . . 104n6
37:31–32 . . . 104n6
37:32. 110
38:17. . . . . . . 190n21
40 . . . . 115, 187
40–66 112
40:1 . . . . 102, 113
40:1–5. 117
40:3 187
40:3–5. 115
40:5 . . . . 104, 117
40:10–11 . . . 115
40:12–26 . . . 357n29
40:12–31 . . . 92, 92n40
40:25–26 . . . 115
40:31. . . . . . . 86, 115

41:1 112
41:4 112
41:9 116
42 115
42:1 112
42:1–4. 115
42:2–4. 112
42:6 201
42:6–7. 112
42:7 115
42:13. 110
42:21. 117
43 115
43:8 105
43:10. 115
43:12. 115
43:25. . . . . . . 82, 87
44:2–5. 112
44:8 115
45–48 110
45:8 358
45:11. . . . . . . 357n29
45:17. 111
46:9–10. 857
46:9–11. 377
46:13. . . . . . . 57, 358, 381n139
47:4 . . . . 357n29
48 115
48:16b. 112, 115
48:17. . . . . . . 357n29
48:17–20 . . . 106, 109
48:18–20 . . . 106
49 115
49:2–9. 112
49:6 . . . . 115, 201
49:6–9. 112
49:6–12. . . . . 400n20
49:21. 116
50 115
50:4 112
50:5–8. . . . . . 381n139
50:5–9. 112
50:6–9. 112
50:8 . . . . 352n5, 488, 489, 490
51 115
51:1 116
51:1–3. 116
51:2–5. 114
51:4–5. 117
51:4–8. 358
51:5–6. 111
51:7 116
51:8 57
51:10. 82
51:11. 116
52 115
52–53 . . . . . . 115, 465
52:7 . . . . 112, 116
52:10. . . . . . . 357n29
52:13. 117
52:13–53:12
        112

Scripture Index 901

53 . . . . .79, 197, 226n50, 382, 465
53:3 28
53:3–4 . . . . . .57n64
53:4 465
53:4–5 28
53:4–6 484
53:5 . . . . .86, 110
53:5–6 370
53:8 370
53:10 110
53:10–12 . . .197, 226n50
53:11 . . . . . . .79, 384, 424
53:12 . . . . . . .79, 110, 398, 474
54–66 115
54:4 115
54:5 . . . . .357n29
54:10 116
54:11–12 . . .116
54:11–17 . . .112, 116
54:13 . . . . . . .112, 116
54:17 112
55:1 116
55:1–3 143
55:3 407
55:3–5 112
55:5 . . . . .357n29
55:6–7 143
56 115
56:1 109
56:1–2 116
56:2 116
56:2–7 116
56:4 116
56:6–7 116
56:7 117
56:10 105
57:1 109
57:11–13a . .108
57:13 116
57:13b 108
57:13–15 . . .357n29
57:15 . . . . . . .116, 356
57:17 110
57:18 . . . . . . .190n21
58–59 115
58:5–12 109
58:6–7 105
58:6–10 116
58:6–12 109
58:8 111
58:13–14 . . .116
58:14 117
59:1–2 357
59:1–15 109
59:4 116
59:7–8 73
59:10 105
59:14–15 . . .109, 116
59:15 116
59:16–17 . . .113
59:16–20 . . .110
59:17 110
59:19 . . . . . . .111, 116
59:20 116
59:21 . . . . . . .112, 113, 116, 117
60 . . . . .110, 113, 116
60:1 111
60:1–14 116
60:1–22 117
60:1–63:7 . . .110
60:2 111
60:3 . . . . .115, 201
60:10 . . . . . . .110, 116
60:13 111
60:14 . . . . . . .105n7, 116
60:16–18 . . .116
60:19 111
60:19–20 . . .115, 116
60:20 116
60:21–22 . . .116
60:22 113
61 . . . . .115, 116, 200
61–62 . . . . . .115, 116
61:1 112
61:1–2 . . . . . .112n28
61:1–3 113
61:3 113
61:8 . . . . .105, 107, 112
61:8–9 116
62:1–12 117
63:1–6 110
63:3 110
63:6 110
63:7–64:12 . . . . .104n6, 110
63:10 . . . . . . .357n29
63:15 110
63:17 105
64:4 109
64:5–6 109
64:6 . . . . .207n45, 428
64:8 109
64:9 . . . . .109, 110
64:10–12 . . .106
65–66 . . . . . .110, 117
65:2–3 110
65:14 117
65:18 110
65:23 113
65:25 110
66 . . . . .115, 116
66:2 . . . . .116, 117
66:5 117
66:7–15 116
66:15 110
66:15–16 . . .108
66:18 111

Jeremiah
book of 75, 87, 99, 119, 185, 286, 551, 552
1–25 537
2:22 75
3:1 104
3:11 . . . . .141, 289, 352n5
3:14 102
3:20 102
3:22 . . . . .190n21
3:23 103
4:1–2 104
4:4 . . . . .453n62, 463
4:14 . . . . .75, 453n62
6:17 138
6:21–24 463
7:1–34 . . . . . .453n62, 463
9:25 463
11 102
11:5 . . . . .52n47
14:1 . . . . .49n41
23:5–6 384
23:9 . . . . .357n30
25:30 . . . . . . .357n29
29:12–14 . . .103
29:13 646
30–33 537
30:17 103
31 . . . . .285n40, 383, 552
31:31–32 . . .566n5
31:31–34 . . .463
31:32 . . . . . . .102, 134
31:32–33 . . .535n9
31:33 . . . . . . .102, 184, 551, 552
31:34 . . . . . . .87, 102, 382, 383, 384, 384n147, 551
32:40 551
34 102
36:32 152
38 551
38:33 554
39 551
46:10 353
51:56 484

Lamentations
book of 99, 822, 822n55
5:17–18 84
5:21 611

Ezekiel
book of 99, 104, 119, 185, 551, 552n64, 554
1 103
1–3 356
1:3 . . . . .49n41
3:17 138
10 103
11 . . . . .103, 551
11:19 . . . . . . .535n9, 552
11:19–21 . . .62
11:23 103
14:14 . . . . . . .63n76
16:8 103
16:15–29 . . .104
16:36 308
16:51–52 . . .352n5
16:52 . . . . . . .352n5

16:60......103
16:62......103
16:63......103
18:5–9......63n76
18:5–27....57
18:14–17...63n76
18:20......63n76
20:5......104
20:30......104
22:8......357n30
22:26......357n30
27:34......82
28:14......357n29
33:2......138
33:6......138
33:7......138
33:12......170
34:25......103
34:30–31...103
36.........551
36:22......357n30, 604
36:25–27...184
36:26......62, 551, 552
36:26–27...535n9
36:27......551, 553, 556
36:32......604
37.........169
37:1–23....384
37:3......554
37:6......554
37:12–14...131n58
37:26–28...103
39:7......357n30
39:29......103
40–48......103, 104
48:35......103

Daniel
book of.....99, 99n2
4:34–35.....857
7..........197, 454n64
9..........308, 311, 313
9:9........82
9:18.......207n45
9:24.......111
12:2.......174, 384

Hosea
book of.....102, 104, 119, 120,
           125, 126, 127, 133,
           141, 144, 618
Hos.–Mal...103
1..........127
1–3........124, 126, 140, 141
1:1........125
1:2........126, 127
1:4........127
1:4–5......131
1:6........127
1:6–7......131
1:6–8......135n70
1:7........124, 128, 138, 141
1:9........127, 129

1:10......129, 131, 132, 133, 144
1:10–11....129, 130, 131
1:10–2:1...135
1:11......125, 129, 131
2:1........129, 133, 133n64,
           135n70
2:1–13.....130
2:1–15.....131
2:2–6......134
2:2–13.....134
2:3........134
2:4........127
2:6........133
2:7–13.....134
2:8........136
2:9........133
2:10.......308
2:12–23....143
2:13.......134, 136
2:14.......126, 133, 134
2:14–15....130, 134, 141
2:14–22....129
2:14–23....129, 131
2:15.......125, 134, 135
2:15–16....135
2:16.......129, 134
2:16–17....130, 134
2:17.......134, 136
2:18.......129, 130, 134, 135
2:19.......129, 140
2:19–20....130, 135, 139, 140
2:19–21....136
2:20.......129, 135
2:21.......129
2:21–22....131, 132, 135
2:21–23....129, 130, 135, 143
2:22.......129, 131
2:22–23....129, 131, 140
2:23.......129, 131, 132, 144
3:5........123, 124, 125
4–8........135
4–10.......140
4–14.......136, 142
4:1........136
4:1–3......128, 140
4:1–4......137
4:2........139
4:3........136
4:4........136
4:4–6......140
4:5........133, 136, 138
4:6........136
4:6–12.....129
4:7........136
4:7–10.....140
4:9........136
4:15.......126n50, 139n75
5:1........136, 139n75
5:1–4......140
5:1–15.....128
5:5–7......140
5:6........136

5:6–12.....137
5:7........136
5:8........139n75
5:8–12.....140
5:9........129, 138
5:9–12.....136
5:10.......139
5:13.......136
5:13–14....136
5:13–15....140
5:14–15....137
5:15.......137
6:1–3......137, 143
6:4........137, 142
6:5........137, 141
6:6........137, 144, 443, 453n62,
           463, 466, 467
6:6–11.....137
6:7........137, 448n34, 456n79
6:7–11.....137, 138
6:7–11a....140
6:8........139n75
6:9........136
6:11–7:1...128, 129, 137
6:11b–7:16
          140
7:1–16.....137
7:3........136
7:5........136
7:7........136, 139
7:10.......137
7:11.......136, 137
7:13.......137
7:14.......137
7:14–16....140
7:15.......137
7:16.......137, 138, 139
8:1........137
8:1–14.....140
8:2........137, 144
8:4........136
8:4–6......137
8:5........137, 143
8:7........128
8:7–10.....137
8:9........136
8:11–13....137
8:13.......138, 144
8:14.......138, 142
9–10.......138
9:1........138
9:1–6......138
9:1–17.....140
9:3........144
9:4........144
9:4–6......138
9:6........138
9:7........129, 138
9:7–8......138
9:7–17.....128
9:8........138, 138n74, 141
9:9........139n75

9:9–10......138n75	13:2.........142	6:5.........57
9:10........126, 139, 141	13:3.........142	7:9.........381n139
9:10–13.....126	13:4.........134	7:18.........70
9:11.........126	13:4–6......141, 142	7:18–20......101, 122
9:13.........126	13:4–8......142	7:19.........87
9:15.........126, 126n50, 139, 139n75	13:7–8......142	
10...........140	13:9.........142	*Nahum*
10:1.........126, 139, 141	13:9–10......142	book of.....120, 121, 618
10:1–3......139	13:10......136, 139	1:2–6.........122
10:1–12......140	13:11......139, 142	1:3.........68
10:1–15.....128	13:14......131, 131n57, 142	1:7.........122
10:3.........139	13:15......131n57, 142	
10:4.........139	13:16......142	*Habakkuk*
10:5.........136, 138n75	14...........140, 141	book of.....120, 121, 160, 161, 618
10:5–6......139, 144	14:1–9......143	1:1–2:20.....160
10:7.........139	14:2–3......144	1:6.........160
10:7–8......139	14:3.........140, 144	1:12–13.....356
10:8.........139n75	14:3–4......124, 143	2:3b.........160
10:9.........139n75	14:4.........120, 143, 190n21	2:4.........31, 122, 161, 251, 252, 344, 453, 535, 571, 734
10:9–10......139	14:4–7......143	2:4a.........160
10:12......128, 139	14:7.........126	2:4b.........160
10:13......128, 139	14:7–8......143	2:14.........122
10:13–15...139, 140	14:9.........133	2:16.........160
10:14.........142		2:17.........161
10:15.........139	*Joel*	3:18–19.....122
11...........140, 141	book of.....120	
11–14......140, 141	2...........406	*Zephaniah*
11:1.........141	2:1.........357n29	book of.....120, 121
11:1–2......137	2:13.........68	1:14–2:3...353
11:2.........136	2:28–32.....121	3:9.........123
11:3.........141	3:16.........121	3:12.........123
11:5.........136, 144	3:17.........121	3:17.........123
11:5–6......141		
11:7.........141	*Amos*	*Haggai*
11:8.........102, 105, 140, 141, 143	book of.....120	book of.....120, 123, 144, 311
11:8–11......142	1:3–3:2.....358	1:10.........311
11:9.........141, 143, 357, 357n30, 377	2:7.........357n29	1:12.........123
	4:2.........357n30	1:14.........123
11:9–11.....124	4:12–13......121	2...........311n91
11:10–11...141	5...........121	2:2.........123
11:11.........129	5:4.........121	2:3.........311
11:11–12...126	5:19–20......353	2:7.........311
11:12.........136	5:21–24......463	2:9.........311
11:12–12:1 141	5:24.........121	2:19.........311
11:12–12:14 128	9:11–12......121	
	9:13–15......121	*Zechariah*
12:1.........136		book of.....120, 123, 144
12:2.........142	*Obadiah*	1:1.........49n41
12:3–5......142	book of.....120, 121	1:3.........646
12:4.........138n75	15..........353	2:13.........357n29
12:6.........142	17..........121	4:6.........123
12:7–8......142		6:13.........400
12:9.........134, 141, 142	*Jonah*	7:1.........49n41
12:10......138, 141, 142	book of.....120, 121, 125n47, 618	8:3.........123
12:11......126n50, 139n75	3:10.........121	13:9.........174, 175
12:12......134, 142	4:2.........68	14:9.........223n41
12:13......134, 138, 141, 142		
12:14.........142	*Micah*	*Malachi*
13...........141	book of.....120, 121	book of.....120, 123, 144
13:1.........136, 142	3:11.........122	1–3.........144
	3:12.........122	1:2–3.........126
	4–5.........122, 123	1:6.........144
	4:1.........122	

1:11 144
1:14 144
2:9 279
2:11 . . . . 357n30
3:16 123
3:18 . . . . 123, 144

Matthew
book of 26, 180, 181, 181n6,
  181n7, 182, 183,
  183n11, 184, 185, 186,
  186n13, 186n15, 465
1:1–17 183
1:11–12 316
1:17 316
1:21 . . . . 25, 111, 112, 426, 465
1:23 25
2:1–12 183
2:15 141
3:3 187
3:7–12 183
3:13–14 465
3:15 . . . . 26, 181, 355, 465, 466,
  521
4:1 27
4:2 27
4:10 27
4:17 . . . . 182, 668
5:1–10 182
5:3 200
5:6 . . . . 180, 181, 182
5:10 181
5:17 . . . . 125, 180
5:17–20 . . . . . 182n8, 443
5:19 180
5:20 . . . . 180, 181, 181n4, 186
5:21–22 180
5:27–28 180
5:28 443
5:32 548
5:39 182
5:43 287
5:44 182
5:48 . . . . 181n7
6:1 181
6:2 157
6:25–34 182
6:33 . . . . 180, 181, 185
7:7 646
7:7–8 182
7:12 443
7:16 282
7:17 182
7:17–18 644
7:20 282
7:24 180
8 465
8:5–10 201
8:10–12 183
8:17 465
8:28–34 201
9:9 200

9:13 . . . . 443, 466
9:36 . . . . 118, 425
10:23 . . . . 822n53
11:19 . . . . 289, 489n98
11:20–24 . . . 183
12 . . . . 194n28
12:7 . . . . 443, 466
12:37 288
13:18–23 . . . 578
14:14 118
15:1–28 183
15:8 466
15:32 118
19:4 . . . . 456n79
20:28 25
20:34 118
21:32 181
21:43 183
22:1–14 143
22:37 445
22:37–38 . . . 443
22:37–39 . . . 466
22:39 287
22:41–46 . . . 384
23 . . . . 149n9
23:13 157
23:23 466
24:2 . . . . 220n27
24:36 . . . . 191n24
25:31–46 . . . 279n25
26:28 467
26:39 . . . . 437, 452
26:42 437
28:18–20 . . . 201, 377

Mark
book of 26, 186, 187, 189,
  190, 192, 193, 193n27,
  194, 198, 464, 465,
  467n132
1 465
1:1 198
1:3 187
1:4 187
1:12 . . . . 465n124
1:12–13 464
1:15 . . . . 186, 187, 188, 283
1:24–25 194
1:25 188
1:30–31 188
1:32 186
1:34 186
1:40 192
1:40–45 189
1:41 . . . . 118, 189
2 . . . . 189, 192, 193
2:1–10 189
2:1–12 193
2:5 189
2:7 . . . . 189, 194, 196
2:8 191
2:8–11 194

2:10–11 190
2:16 187
2:16–17 193
2:17 . . . . 187, 196, 207
2:23–24 194
2:23–28 . . . . . 194, 195
2:28 194
3 . . . . 195, 464, 465
3:1–6 195
3:2 195
3:4 195
3:22 196
3:22–30 464
4:1–32 186
4:39 186
5 192
5:1–21 201
5:22–43 190
5:23 190
5:26 190
5:27 190
5:27–28 191
5:30 191
5:31 191
5:33 191
5:34 191
5:36 191
5:38 191
5:39 191
5:41 191
6:34 118
7 195
7:1–15 195
7:2 195
7:3–4 195
7:6 157
7:6–7 196
7:9 196
7:9–13 196
7:15 196
7:19 196
8:29 192
8:31 . . . . 467n132
8:31–9:1 192
8:34 283
9:5 192
9:30–50 192
9:31 . . . . 467n132
10:6 . . . . 456n79
10:32–45 . . . 192
10:34 . . . . 467n132
10:45 . . . . 187, 187n16, 197, 198,
  198n31, 198n32, 431,
  483n74, 485
10:46–52 . . . 192
10:47–48 . . . 192
10:49 192
10:51 192
10:52 192
11:21 192
11:22 . . . . 278n20
13:32 . . . . 191n24

Scripture Index   905

14:24 . . . . 187n16, 198n32
14:36 452
14:45 192
15:38f. 198n32
16:6–7 . . . . . . 467n132
16:8 . . . . 467n132

Luke
book of 26, 112n28, 113,
    182n9, 198, 199, 200,
    200n33, 466
1:46–55 . . . . . 85n24
2:1–20 199
2:21 . . . . 615n100
2:32 201
2:49 . . . . 466, 466n131
3:4 187
3:38 . . . . 456n79
4 . . . . 112n28
4:18–19 200
5:32 25
6:15 200
6:20 200
7:1–10 201
7:22 200
7:29 . . . . 488, 508
7:35 . . . . 489n98, 508
7:36–50 571
7:41–43 501
7:47 501
8:26–39 201
9:22 466
9:52–53 199
10:25 252
10:29 594
10:30–35 199
12:6 . . . . 220n27
12:49–50 466
13 466
13:10–17 466
13:16 466
13:24 292
13:31–35 466
13:32–33 466
13:33 466
14:15–24 143
14:26 126
15:1 200
15:2 204
15:11–32 . . . . 143, 204
15:21 . . . . 204, 205
15:22–24 205
15:29–30 204
16:29 125
16:31 125
17:10 455
17:15–16 199
17:25 466
18 . . . . 186, 190n23
18:9 . . . . 202, 207, 284, 430
18:9–14 . . . . . 149n9
18:11 . . . . 202, 202n38

18:13 . . . . 202n38, 430
18:14 . . . . 198, 205, 289, 760
19:5 200
19:10 25
22:29 400
22:37 466
22:42 . . . . 28, 452
23:30 139
23:43 573
24:7 466
24:26 466
24:27 125
24:44 125
24:44–47 466
24:46–47 201

John
book of 25, 26, 189, 206, 207,
    207n46, 283n36
1:1 377
1:1–4 377
1:9 25
1:14 . . . . 103, 377, 424
1:18 424
1:23 187
1:29 443
2:11 . . . . 189n19
2:13–23 . . . . . 207n46
3:3 268
3:16 . . . . 378, 426
3:16–18 35
3:27 574
3:35 426
3:36 . . . . 357, 853
4:34 . . . . 209, 452
4:54 189
5:19 401
5:20 426
5:30 400
5:36 . . . . 26, 401, 426
5:43 400
6 207
6:14–15 . . . . . 207n48
6:31 207
6:35 208
6:37–40 208
6:38 209
6:38–40 . . . . . 26, 400
6:48 208
6:51 208
6:53–54 208
6:56 208
6:64 208
6:68–69 208
7:19 . . . . 207n46
8:12 25
8:28–29 209
8:29 . . . . 426, 437
9:39 207
10:15 209
10:17–18 209
10:20–21 210

10:26–27 . . . 283
12:32 . . . . 460n96
12:42–43 . . . 207n46
12:49–50 . . . 210
13:34 . . . . 547, 549
14–16 206
14:15 549
14:30–31 . . . 210
15:10 437
15:13 549
15:15 426
16:8 206
16:8–11 206
16:10 206
16:16–22 . . . 136
17 210
17:2 210
17:4 210
17:4–8 26
17:4–12 400
17:5 210
17:8 426
17:12 . . . . 220n27
17:14 426
17:17 . . . . 210, 509
17:21–23 . . . 210
18:9 . . . . 220n27
21:25 211

Acts
book of 112n28, 113, 201,
    240n7, 243, 243n19,
    248, 248n50, 269,
    277n16, 406, 407, 462,
    464, 467
1:7 111
1:8 201
2 408
2:2 613
2:11 796
2:22 406
2:23 406
2:24 406
2:24–28 . . . . . 449n39
2:27 467
2:29 406
2:30–35 406
2:36 407
2:36–38 123
2:37 407
2:38 407
3:14–15 467
3:15 427
4:32 . . . . 220n27
5:30–31 409
7:52 . . . . 424, 431, 437
9:2 34
10 . . . . 244n21
10–11 183
10:9–17 196
10:34 279
13 . . . . 255, 407, 408

13:14–14:23
..........243
13:16–41 ...240n7, 248
13:23.......407
13:26.......407
13:27.......407
13:29.......255, 255n91, 407
13:30.......407
13:31.......407
13:32–33 ...407
13:34.......407
13:36.......407
13:36–39 ...259
13:37.......407
13:38–39 ...240n7, 248, 255, 407, 711
13:39.......202, 353, 760
13:48–50 ...409
15 ....183, 243
15:6–11.....256n101
15:10.......201
15:11.......256n101
15:15–19 ...121
17:24–25 ...377
17:28.......377
17:31.......437
22:14.......424, 437

Romans
book of 13, 33, 34, 74, 77, 183n10, 202n36, 213, 214, 216, 216n8, 217, 218, 220, 230, 235, 239, 240, 242, 242n12, 266, 269, 275, 277n17, 278, 284, 288, 289, 289n46, 306, 316, 319, 320, 323, 325, 328, 329, 334, 335, 345, 388, 394, 420, 426, 427, 450, 451, 454, 488, 489, 493, 494n126, 499, 500n141, 526, 535, 564, 566, 567, 579n53, 581, 582, 584, 612n93, 643, 651, 664, 665, 675, 709, 852
1 218
1–3.........301, 389, 391, 526
1–4.........300n30, 330, 335, 335n35, 336, 337n49, 339, 339n59, 344, 345, 397
1–5.........329
1–8.........235, 335
1:1 ....420, 535n8
1:2 344
1:3 ....179, 420, 424
1:3–4 ......270n159, 459
1:4 ....393, 409, 459n89, 472
1:5 283
1:9 ....535n8
1:16 ....183, 257, 420, 442, 681, 852
1:16–17.....216, 391
1:17 ....122, 161, 214, 216, 217, 218, 230, 231, 232, 391, 424, 491, 535, 571, 592
1:17–32.....215
1:17–10:10
..........215
1:18 ....24, 214, 216, 334n31, 339, 389, 430, 493, 494
1:18–21.....337n44
1:18–32.....258, 357, 360
1:18–3:20...185, 214, 221, 231, 337, 358, 381, 391, 430, 489n99, 493
1:20–21.....342
1:21 427
1:21–23.....853
1:21–32.....494
1:23 389
1:24 389
1:24–25.....389
1:25 389
1:26–32.....389
1:29 ....214, 412
1:32 ....214, 334n31, 357
2 ....148, 215, 219n25, 285, 389, 845
2–3.........845
2:1 389
2:1–3:8 219
2:2 ....389, 422
2:3 389
2:4 ....266, 389
2:5 ....214, 389, 412, 422
2:5–16......219, 232
2:6 ....259, 389, 412
2:6–7.......219
2:6–11......219n22
2:6–16......219
2:7 ....219, 845, 846
2:8 ....214, 389
2:8–16......357
2:10 ....219, 845, 846
2:11 ....279, 389
2:11–4:25...328
2:12 ....389, 489
2:12–13.....219
2:12–16.....251
2:12–29.....389
2:13 ....214, 215, 219, 220, 235, 285, 352, 389, 489, 489n99, 494, 494n125, 594, 845, 846
2:14–16.....219
2:15 ....285n40, 390, 489
2:16 ....390, 489
2:26 ....214, 495n126
2:26–29.....846
2:29 553
3 ....73, 74, 390, 391, 393, 394, 420, 423, 435
3–4.........275, 526
3–5.........185, 274, 471, 557
3:1–8.......390
3:1–20......215
3:1–5:21....328
3:3 283
3:4 ....81, 215, 289, 489
3:5 ....214, 215, 216, 251, 390
3:6 390
3:7–8.......390
3:8 ....215, 277, 287, 390
3:9 ....251, 334
3:9–10......25, 390
3:9–20......219, 220, 232, 381
3:10 ....214, 220, 231, 380, 390, 494
3:10–12.....426, 450, 484
3:10–18.....73, 489
3:11–18.....494
3:12 ....75, 220, 339
3:12–18.....450
3:13–14.....73
3:15–17.....73
3:18 ....73, 390
3:19 ....73, 215, 390, 426, 431, 494
3:19–20.....489
3:19–21.....233
3:19–24.....500
3:20 ....25, 74, 82, 162, 215, 220, 303n49, 344, 352, 390, 391, 392, 393, 402, 494, 845, 846, 847, 853
3:20–30.....523
3:21 ....31, 214, 216, 221, 224, 233, 235, 381, 392, 494, 582n58
3:21–22.....222, 230, 495
3:21–24.....852
3:21–26.....13, 34, 220, 221, 223, 231, 236n87, 334, 352n6, 355, 357, 375, 377, 380–81, 381, 381n136, 382, 384, 391, 392, 393, 430
3:21–31.....185
3:21–4:25...214, 215, 220, 226
3:21–5:21...500
3:22 ....29, 31, 214, 216, 221, 232, 245n28, 393, 464n119
3:22–23.....221, 233
3:22–25.....289n48
3:22–26.....420
3:23 ....29, 251, 360, 380, 391, 426, 450
3:23ff......221n31
3:23–25.....760

Scripture Index 907

3:24 . . . . .181, 215, 221, 232, 233, 391, 392, 471, 490, 633, 844
3:24–25. . . . .29, 34, 300, 431
3:24–26. . . . .363, 484
3:25 . . . . . . .29, 214, 216, 222, 225, 232, 334, 382, 391, 398, 412, 425, 437, 492, 494
3:25–26. . . . .222, 231, 381, 392, 431
3:26 . . . . .31, 214, 215, 216, 219, 222, 223, 289, 420, 508, 655, 852
3:27 . . . . . . .223, 854
3:27–28. . . . .31, 223, 224, 232
3:27–31. . . . .223, 224, 225
3:28 . . . . . . .215, 274, 291, 352, 430, 433, 572, 680n152, 682, 833n126, 847, 852
3:29 183
3:29–30. . . . .223, 224, 225, 233
3:30 . . . . . . .215, 223n41, 352
3:31 . . . . . . .224, 233, 286
4 . . . . .148n5, 193, 202n36, 224, 227n54, 286, 381, 393, 395, 420, 432, 492, 494, 494n126, 495
4–5 289
4:1–5 . . . . . .185, 232, 494, 523
4:1–8 . . . . . .205, 224, 230, 231, 232, 380
4:1–25. 33
4:2 . . . . .215, 220n29, 224, 224n44, 232, 352, 353, 567, 610, 854
4:2–3 582
4:2–4 . . . . . .284n39
4:2–6 29
4:3 . . . . .41, 162, 193, 214, 224, 681, 716
4:3–5 . . . . . .181, 232
4:4 . . . . .224, 494, 494n126, 582n61
4:4–5 . . . . . .303, 303n49, 495, 508, 852
4:4–6 354
4:4–8 . . . . . .248n52, 257
4:5 . . . . .214, 215, 224, 230, 232, 289, 289n48, 353, 355, 358, 363, 420, 432, 435, 494, 494n126, 495n126, 499, 674, 852, 860
4:5–8 508
4:6 . . . . .214, 220n29, 231, 436, 494, 494n126, 495, 496
4:6–7 353
4:6–8 . . . . . .225, 230
4:7 . . . . .225, 712
4:7–9 231
4:8 . . . . .494n126

4:9 . . . . .41, 214, 494n126, 495n126, 579
4:9–13. 225
4:9–17. . . . . .224, 225, 233
4:9–25. 232
4:11 . . . . . . .214, 225, 395, 494n126, 496
4:11–12. 395
4:13 . . . . . . .214, 395
4:13–21. . . . .539n22
4:14 395
4:14–15. 225
4:16 . . . . . . .395, 432
4:16–17. 225
4:17 225
4:18–21. 225
4:18–22. 396
4:18–25. 225
4:19 . . . . . . .225, 341
4:20 342
4:21 432
4:22 . . . . . . .41, 214, 225, 394, 414, 579
4:23–24. 394
4:23–25. 226
4:24 224
4:24–25. . . . .231, 394
4:25 . . . . . . .29, 37, 215, 224, 226, 226n51, 259, 289, 397, 398, 399, 408, 411, 414, 432, 441, 449, 459, 472, 484, 485, 492, 521
5 . . . . .26, 215, 226, 393, 403, 404, 447, 448, 450, 452, 454, 454n66, 455, 455n71, 456, 457, 458, 459n91, 459n93, 495, 526, 527, 853
5–8 . . . . .334n30, 335, 335n35, 343, 487
5:1 . . . . .215, 226, 233, 344, 352, 353, 355, 414, 436, 617, 840, 852
5:1–2 . . . . . .232, 354, 380, 411
5:1–5 . . . . . .526, 853
5:1–11. 226
5:1–21. 214
5:1–8:30 228
5:2 . . . . .226, 233, 346, 853
5:2–11. 233
5:3 . . . . .583n62, 854
5:3–5 115
5:3–10. . . . . .226, 233
5:4 854
5:5 . . . . .576, 854, 855
5:6 411
5:6–8 . . . . . .338, 855
5:6–11. . . . . .339, 527
5:7 214
5:8 . . . . .255, 344, 411, 484, 485
5:8–11. 452

5:9 . . . . .215, 226, 231, 353, 412, 535, 570n24, 852
5:9–10. . . . . .441, 527, 858
5:9–11. 380
5:9–21. 353
5:10 . . . . . . .344, 412, 413, 449, 853
5:10–11. . . . .412, 582n60
5:11 . . . . . . .226, 233
5:12 . . . . . . .81, 96, 335, 427, 447, 450
5:12–13. 251
5:12–21. . . . .24, 185, 210, 224, 232, 354, 359, 379, 380, 381, 447, 449, 450n48, 452, 456, 462, 527, 760
5:13–17. 447
5:14 . . . . . . .379, 461
5:15 495
5:15–16. 450
5:15–19. . . . .227, 230, 231, 232, 496
5:15–21. . . . .227, 495n127
5:16 . . . . . . .32, 214, 448, 489, 495
5:16–17. . . . .227, 232
5:17 . . . . . . .214, 495
5:17–21. . . . .452, 456
5:18 . . . . . . .30, 214, 215, 226n51, 227, 230, 235, 393, 415, 441, 441n2, 447, 448, 448n33, 449, 449n35, 451, 451n54, 457n82, 457n83, 495
5:18–19. . . . .181, 208, 380, 448, 449, 451, 452, 457, 457n82, 492–93
5:18–21. 402
5:19 . . . . . . .30, 214, 227, 227n54, 231, 352n4, 354n16, 393, 415, 447, 448, 449, 450, 451n54, 457, 495, 576
5:20–21. . . . .227, 393, 415
5:21 . . . . . . .214, 227, 449, 468
6 . . . . .185, 215, 222, 234, 251n70, 300n30, 487, 492, 500, 500n141, 527, 557, 786
6–7 . . . . .500n141, 501, 546
6–8 . . . . .329, 557
6:1 . . . . .390, 500, 557
6:1–4 521
6:1–11. . . . . .301, 527
6:1–23. . . . . .214, 233
6:1–7:6 485
6:1–8:1 328
6:2 415
6:2–4 500
6:3 415
6:3–4 471
6:3–5 471
6:4 . . . . .322n145, 415, 471
6:5 416
6:5–12. 405

6:6 118
6:6–11 416
6:7 . . . . .215, 248n49, 485
6:8 478
6:9 416
6:11 416
6:12–13 185
6:12–14 . . . . .251, 417
6:12–23 227
6:13 214
6:14 . . . . .477, 500
6:14–15 . . . . .544, 546
6:15–22 287
6:16 . . . . .118, 214, 281
6:16–22 485
6:17 185
6:18 . . . . .118, 214
6:19 214
6:20 214
6:22 852
6:23 . . . . .96, 360, 362, 368n79, 380, 427, 449, 450, 614n97
7 . . . . .215, 436, 501, 545, 557
7:1–3 485
7:1–13 286
7:1–25 . . . . . .214, 233
7:4 . . . . .405, 477, 501, 555, 556
7:4–6 478
7:5 . . . . .545, 555, 555n72, 556
7:6 . . . . .477, 485, 500, 544, 545, 553, 555, 556
7:7–13 284
7:8–11 . . . . . .284, 501
7:12 . . . . .214, 284, 286, 358
7:13 647
8 . . . . .185, 215, 228, 284n39, 527, 557, 856, 860
8:1 . . . . .30, 32, 224, 227, 230, 232, 300, 335, 352, 353, 471, 490, 496, 852
8:1f. 760
8:1–4 . . . . . . .224n42, 227, 846
8:1–7 527
8:1–17 32
8:1–39 214
8:2 . . . . .286n41, 793
8:2–4 281
8:3 . . . . .227, 370, 426, 490
8:3–4 . . . . . . .501n142
8:3–6 33
8:4 . . . . .185, 214, 224, 227, 233, 286n41, 546
8:7 337
8:9f. 760
8:9–10 472
8:10 . . . . .32, 214
8:11 842
8:14–15 . . . . .502n147
8:14–39 354
8:15 521
8:15–17 . . . . .471, 530
8:28 . . . . .590, 857
8:28–30 228
8:28–39 234
8:29 . . . . .437, 509, 521
8:29–30 857
8:30 . . . . .215, 235
8:31 . . . . .228, 235, 857
8:31–34 844
8:31–39 . . . . .228, 235
8:32 . . . . .228, 360, 858
8:32–34 235
8:33 . . . . .215, 217, 228, 860
8:33–34 . . . . .227, 230, 288, 335, 352, 430, 489, 490, 508, 859
8:34 . . . . .179, 228, 405, 409, 859
8:35–36 857
8:35–39 228
9 . . . . .625, 625n7
9–11 . . . . . . .117, 148, 148n5, 235, 316, 335n35, 535
9:1–4 229
9:1–29 215
9:1–11:36 . . .214
9:4 . . . . .534, 539
9:8 . . . . .495n126
9:11–12 . . . . .303n49, 610
9:14 214
9:15–26 . . . . .132, 144
9:18 597
9:20–31 128
9:24–25 183
9:30 . . . . .132, 144, 214, 229
9:30–10:4 . . .224
9:30–10:5 . . .232
9:30–10:6 . . .228, 229
9:30–10:13
 . . . . .228, 229, 231, 232, 233
9:30–10:21
215
9:31 . . . . .132, 144, 214, 229
9:31–33 284
9:32 . . . . .220n29, 229, 267
9:32–33 229
10 230
10:1 . . . . .229, 434
10:1–5 229
10:2 229
10:2–4 303
10:3 . . . . .207, 214, 216, 229, 230, 284
10:3–4 523
10:4 . . . . .214, 229, 264
10:5 . . . . .156n38, 214, 229, 230, 450, 453
10:5–13 . . . . .124, 229
10:6 . . . . .214, 229
10:9 . . . . .406, 408
10:9–10 229
10:10 . . . . . . .214, 406
10:11–13 233
10:12–13 233
10:17 681
11 215

11:6 . . . . .220n29, 523, 568, 632
11:15 131
11:17 510
11:25–32 . . . .132, 144
11:26–28 133
11:27 534
11:28 133
11:29 . . . . . . .133, 590
11:33–36 . . . .235, 377
11:35 597
11:36 235
12 215
12:1–15:13
214
12:19 215
13 215
13:4 215
13:8 . . . . .546, 548
13:8–10 224
13:9 548
13:9–10 287
13:10 . . . . . . .288, 546, 548
14 215
14:7 . . . . .220n27
14:17 . . . . . . .179n1, 214
14:17–19 . . . .109n15
15 215
15:12 179
15:16 . . . . . . .535n8
15:19 461
16 215
16:25–26 344
16:25–27 235
16:26 283

1 Corinthians
book of 240, 242, 257, 269, 277n17, 285, 821
1:4–5 471
1:17–2:5 257
1:18 . . . . .257, 263, 442
1:18–19 257
1:18–31 . . . . .259n111
1:22–23 257
1:23 . . . . .36, 37
1:24 257
1:25 36
1:29 . . . . .257, 854
1:30 . . . . .224, 300, 353n10, 462, 521, 530, 557
1:30–31 257
1:31 . . . . .257, 854
2:2 442
2:8 25
3 822
3:21 854
4 258
4:1 258
4:4 258
4:7 854
4:20 . . . . .179n1
5:7 443
6 . . . . .258, 437

Scripture Index 909

6:9 . . . . .179n1, 186
6:9a 258
6:9b–10. 258
6:9–10. . . . .258, 285, 845
6:9–11. 258
6:10 . . . . . . .179n1, 186
6:11 . . . . . . .248, 258, 300, 301, 436, 519
6:15–19. . . . .471, 472
7:19 288
8:5–6 377
9 . . . . .286n41
9:13–14. 550
9:21 . . . . . . .286, 286n41
10:16–17 . . .301, 471
11:2 261
11:23–29 . . .301
11:25 . . . . . .534, 535
12:12f. 760
13 579
13:2 285
13:13 578
15 . . . . .259, 456, 456n77, 458, 459, 459n89, 459n91
15:1 259
15:1–2. . . . .243, 841
15:1–3. 339
15:1–4. . . . .259, 261, 261n126
15:2 . . . . . . .259, 261
15:3 . . . . . . .255, 370, 431, 458
15:3–4. 344
15:4 259
15:4–8. 458
15:10 568
15:12–28 . . .259
15:13–14 . . .259
15:17 . . . . . .231, 259, 399, 404, 408, 414, 415, 459
15:20 . . . . . .413, 459
15:21 . . . . . .268, 458
15:22 . . . . . .24, 456n79
15:24 . . . . . .179, 179n1
15:25–27 . . .458
15:42–58 . . .259
15:45 . . . . . .402, 456n79, 458
15:46 458
15:47 . . . . . .426, 458
15:50 . . . . . .179n1
15:54–55 . . .131, 142
15:54–57 . . .458
15:56 . . . . . .284, 501
15:58 345
16:2 550

2 Corinthians
book of. 34, 240, 242, 259, 269, 535
1:20 432
1:23–24. 863
3 . . . . .286, 551, 552, 552n64
3:1–6 551
3:3 . . . . .535n9, 551, 552
3:3–6 551

3:4 264
3:5 611
3:6 . . . . .534, 535, 552, 553, 554
3:7–11. . . . .537, 551
3:9 535
3:12–18. . . . .551, 554
3:14 . . . . . . .534, 554, 555
3:15 554
3:17 554
3:18 . . . . . . .437, 555
4:1–6 340
4:3–4 535
4:3–6 . . . . . .25, 535n9
4:6 . . . . .301, 552, 555
5 . . . . .260, 260n115
5:10 . . . . . . .259, 438, 520
5:12–15. . . . .259n111
5:14 483
5:14–15. 416
5:14–21. . . . .343, 487
5:17 . . . . . . .259, 301
5:18 259
5:18–19. 260
5:19 . . . . . . .259, 353–54
5:20 260
5:21 . . . . . . .30, 34, 181, 224, 255, 260, 300, 353, 354, 360, 437, 462, 471, 483, 490, 493, 496
6:8 287
8–9 550
8:1 550
8:2 550
8:3 550
8:9 550
9:8 345
9:8–9 285
10:5 849
10:17 854
11:18 854
12:20 287
13:4 424
13:14 377

Galatians
book of. 34, 216n8, 218, 240, 242, 243, 243n16, 246, 247, 248, 250, 251, 254, 255, 256, 256n101, 257, 262, 263, 264, 266, 269, 274, 275, 276, 284, 285, 288, 289n46, 316, 319, 320, 323, 325, 328, 333, 462, 462n108, 523, 527, 539, 541n31, 542, 544n44, 618, 618n112, 620, 621n122, 643, 734, 735
1 . . . . .265, 544n44
1–2. 242
1:2 242

1:4 . . . . .242, 248, 255, 265, 333, 334, 339, 344n84, 370, 490
1:6–9 . . . . . .34, 35
1:8–11. 243
1:14 316
2 . . . . .243, 246, 247, 248, 284, 544n44
2–3. . . . . . . .274, 284
2:6 279
2:11–14. . . . .244, 245
2:12 . . . . . . .275, 276, 277
2:14 247
2:15–16. . . . .31, 181
2:15–16a 341
2:15–3:29 . . .35
2:16 . . . . . . .74, 82, 162, 244, 245, 245n32, 247, 248, 251, 255, 264, 264n138, 344, 352, 523, 618, 847
2:17 . . . . . . .247, 289n48, 300, 471, 490, 618
2:17–18. 247
2:18 247
2:19 . . . . . . .247, 618n113
2:19–20. 462
2:20 . . . . . . .247, 257, 301, 322, 322n145, 338, 442, 483, 521, 619
2:21 . . . . . . .31, 247, 248, 540, 540n28, 542, 619
3 . . . . .202n36, 245, 248, 250, 252, 450n45, 472, 538, 540n29, 544n44
3–4. . . . . . . .286, 543
3–5. 148
3:1–9 . . . . . .248, 249
3:1–14. 537
3:2 . . . . .249, 341, 538
3:2–3 527
3:3 522
3:5 . . . . .249, 250n68, 538
3:5–9 . . . . . .250n65
3:6 . . . . .41, 162, 249, 250n68, 619
3:6–9 . . . . . .250, 253, 255, 543
3:6–14. 255
3:7 . . . . .250, 538
3:8 352
3:9 34
3:9–13. 619
3:10 . . . . . . .31, 246, 249, 250, 250n65, 251, 252, 253n81, 254, 255, 255n92, 255n95, 445, 453, 538, 618n113
3:10–12. . . . .250n65, 254, 537
3:10–13. 254
3:10–14. . . . .34, 248, 249, 250n67, 252, 255, 453, 453n61, 462, 500, 538, 734, 760
3:10–20. . . . .537, 537n17

3:11........31, 122, 161, 251, 252, 453, 535, 538
3:11a......538
3:11b......538
3:11–12.....538
3:11–14.....251
3:12........156n38, 252, 253, 256, 450n45, 453, 538
3:12a......538
3:12b......538
3:13........252, 252n75, 253, 254, 255, 255n92, 353, 360, 370, 490, 538, 597n40, 614n97, 618n113, 619
3:13–14.....254, 501n142
3:14........32, 254, 255, 544
3:14a......254
3:14b......254
3:15........534, 539, 539n22
3:15–20.....539
3:17........224n44, 249n54, 253, 534, 539, 543
3:17–18.....540
3:18........538, 540, 540n28, 541, 541n30
3:19........253, 256, 540n26, 543, 544
3:19–20.....540, 540n26
3:20........540n26
3:21........538, 540
3:22........251, 255, 541n32, 543n40, 620
3:22–24.....253, 541n32
3:22–4:5....462
3:23........247, 254, 255
3:23–24.....544
3:23–26.....543
3:24........300, 352, 541n32, 543n40
3:24–27.....301
3:25........328, 543
3:25–29.....471
3:26........300
3:27........510
3:28–29.....183, 254
3:29........34, 35
4...........544n44
4–6.........255
4:1–2.......544
4:1–7.......543, 544
4:1–9.......284, 542n36
4:2.........544
4:3–4.......544
4:3–5.......27
4:4.........521, 544
4:4–5.......253, 255, 450n48
4:4–7.......354, 355
4:5.........255, 328, 544
4:10........246n38
4:19........461
4:21........256

4:21–31.....256, 341
4:24........534
4:25........256, 316
4:25–26.....256
4:26........256
5...........545, 546
5:1.........255, 256
5:1–4.......542n35
5:2.........256, 453
5:2–4.......542
5:3.........252, 284
5:3–4.......256
5:4.........538, 542, 542n35
5:5.........620
5:6.........204, 283, 285, 288, 708
5:13........255, 256, 501n142
5:14........287, 546, 548
5:18........544, 545, 546
5:19–21.....258
5:21........179n1, 186, 285, 845
5:22........301
5:22–23.....145, 545
5:23........545
5:25........545
6:2.........288, 549
6:7–8.......139
6:8.........845
6:12–14.....256
6:13........854
6:14........247, 257, 263, 394, 442, 854
6:15........204
6:15–16.....288

Ephesians
book of.....240, 241, 241n11, 242, 261, 263, 265, 269, 304, 433, 434, 462, 570
1...........400
1:3–6.......590
1:3–14......261, 510
1:4.........261, 262, 378, 520
1:4–12......400
1:5.........261, 521
1:6.........521
1:7.........248, 261, 265
1:10........458n88, 462, 570
1:11........377, 378
1:13........248, 354
1:14........510
1:15........261
1:19–21.....842
1:20........179
1:20–22.....462
1:21........179
2...........262, 263, 337
2:1.........262, 428
2:1–2.......24
2:1–3.......340, 484
2:1–4.......360
2:1–9.......262

2:1–10......262, 339
2:3.........262, 853
2:4–5.......262
2:5.........262, 428
2:6.........428, 472
2:8.........612, 674
2:8–9.......262, 304, 462, 570
2:8–10......149n9, 262, 322, 323, 352, 409, 433, 523, 583, 583n63
2:9.........323, 581, 854
2:10........262, 345
2:11–22.....262
2:12........534, 539
2:13–14.....263
2:14........284
2:15........265
2:15–17.....263
2:16........394, 442
3:6–7.......535n8
3:11........400
3:12........264
4–6.........262, 263
4:6.........377
4:13........437, 461
4:15........509
4:28........443
4:31........287
4:32........248, 263, 265
5–6.........286
5:2.........483n74, 485
5:3–7.......258
5:3–17......145
5:5.........145, 179n1, 186
5:5–6.......845
5:14........635
5:15........547n55
5:25–33.....485
5:26........258, 509
5:26–27.....263
6:1–2.......547n55
6:1–3.......547
6:9.........279

Philippians
book of.....30, 34, 118, 230, 240, 242, 263, 269, 460, 492
1:6.........95
1:22........535n8
1:29........434
1:29–30.....409
2...........265n141, 459, 459n93, 460, 460n97, 461
2:1–8.......119
2:3.........460
2:4.........460
2:5.........460
2:6–11......264, 265, 380, 459
2:8.........28, 30, 30n9, 354n16, 355, 437, 442, 459, 460, 460n98, 461

2:8b......461
2:9......460, 460n96
2:9–11......30
2:12......571
2:12–13......265, 841
2:14......460
2:15......460
2:30......460
3......148, 230, 263, 264, 265, 266, 267, 461
3:1–9......354
3:1–10......863
3:2......842
3:2–3......263
3:2–9......229
3:3......263, 854
3:3–4......264
3:4–6......33, 263
3:5......263
3:6......195, 230, 263, 266, 316, 841
3:6–9......207
3:7......264
3:7–8......264
3:7–9......34, 303
3:8......34
3:8–9......435, 725
3:9......30, 181, 210, 224, 229, 230, 264, 284, 300, 343, 471, 490, 492, 496, 841, 842
3:10......842
3:10–11......34
3:11......264
3:12......264
3:13......265
3:14......471

Colossians
book of......240, 242, 265
1:4......265
1:5......278
1:10......345
1:13......179n1, 265
1:13–14......265, 384
1:14......248, 265
1:16......427
1:18......413
1:19–22......853
1:23......535n8
2:10......179
2:11–12......471
2:12......409
2:13......248, 415
2:13–14......265
2:13–15......360, 384
2:14......265
3–4......286
3:1......179, 472
3:1–2......415
3:1–4......405, 416
3:4......415

3:5......145
3:5–7......265
3:5–8......258
3:8......287
3:8–11......118
3:10–12......145
3:12......118, 145
3:13......248, 265
3:25......279
4:11......179n1

1 Thessalonians
book of......240, 242, 260, 261, 262, 269
1:3......283, 285
1:3–5......472
1:9–10......261, 412
2:12......179n1
2:16......261
4:3–8......258
4:6......261
5:1–11......261
5:9......578
5:10......483
5:23......508, 519

2 Thessalonians
book of......240, 242, 260, 261
1:5......179n1
1:5–10......261
1:8–9......261
1:11......283, 285
2:10......261
2:12......261
2:13......261, 400, 509
2:13–15......261, 261n126
2:15......261

1 Timothy
book of......240, 241n11, 242, 266, 267, 268
1:1......269
1:5......267
1:6–11......267
1:8......267
1:8–10......258
1:15......266, 338
1:16......267
2:2......267
2:5......267
2:6......483n74, 485
2:13......456n79
3:16......85n26, 259, 267, 268, 289, 352n7, 399, 459, 472, 490
4:7–8......267
5:21......279
6:3......267
6:6......267
6:11......267
6:14......461

2 Timothy
book of......240, 241n11, 242, 268, 268n155
1:1......269
1:8–10......149n9
1:8–14......268
1:9......263, 268, 322, 400
1:9–10......400
1:10......268
2......617
2:8......179
2:9......461
3:1–9......258
3:5......285
4:1......179n1
4:18......179n1

Titus
book of......240, 242, 268, 268n155, 269
1:1......269
1:16......285
2:14......483n74, 485
3......269
3:3–7......258
3:4–7......149n9, 268, 269
3:5......207, 258, 263, 268, 269, 322, 522
3:5–7......72, 462
3:7......181, 268

Philemon
book of......240, 242, 265, 269
3......266
5......266
8......266
10......266
11......266
16......266
20......266
23......266

Hebrews
book of......13, 28, 218, 239n2, 273n2, 403, 409, 462n111, 463, 463n113, 463n116, 484, 643, 682
1:3......118
2......462n111
2:3......239n2
2:5–18......360
2:10......110
2:17......28
4–10......403
4:14......292
4:15......437, 463
4:15–16......27
5:1–10......380
5:8–9......27, 354n16, 355
6:4–8......578
7–10......409
7:26......357n30

7:27 ....463, 485
8:1–2 463
8:6 ....540n25
8:7 463
9–10 431
9:14 463
9:15 ....540n25
9:28 360
10 ....462, 466
10:1 484
10:1–18 355
10:4 ....382, 463
10:5 ....462, 463
10:5–7 ......453n62, 462, 463
10:7 ....400n20
10:10 463
10:12 485
10:14 ....437, 463
10:26–31 ...463n116
10:38 ....122, 161
11 ....281, 653, 673
11:1 ....409, 673
11:6 ....612, 827
11:7 ....495n128
12:10 ....357n30
12:24 ....431, 540n25
12:28 356
12:28–29 ...114
13:15–16 ...159

James
book of 14, 273, 273n2, 274,
            275, 276, 276n11, 277,
            277n17, 278, 278n21,
            288, 289n48, 291,
            291n54, 433, 846
1:3 ....278n21
1:5–6 278
1:6–8 278
1:12 ....279n24, 291
1:14–15 278
1:15 ....281, 287
1:18 278
1:21 ....279n24, 291, 291n54
1:22 ....279, 292
1:22–25 285
1:25 286
2 ....274, 275, 278, 279,
            282, 286, 288, 290
2:1 ....278, 279
2:1–13 279
2:2–7 275
2:5 400
2:8 ....286, 287

2:9 286
2:10 ....445, 450
2:10–11 284
2:12 286
2:14 ....279, 280n26, 291, 847,
            849
2:14–17 .....279, 849
2:14–25 279
2:14–26 .....501n143
2:15–16 279
2:17 ....280, 280n26
2:18–19 849
2:18–20 280
2:19 ....280, 612n93
2:20 ....280, 286n41
2:21 ....280, 288, 291, 489n98,
            847
2:21–26 .....280, 571, 572
2:22 281
2:23 ....42, 281, 291
2:24 ....274, 433, 489n98, 847
2:25 ....282, 291
2:26 ....280, 282, 433
3:1 ....291n53
3:17 280
4:1–4 286
4:8 646
4:11 287
4:11–12 286
4:12 422
5:4–6 286
5:15 ....278, 279
5:20 ....279n24, 291

1 Peter
1:2 400
1:3 408
1:6–7 854
1:7 854
1:8 854
1:10–12 .....121, 123
1:15–16 .....356, 357n30
1:17 520
1:18–19 431
1:20 378
1:21 ....283, 409
1:23 529
2:3 266
2:5 ....839, 842
2:9 ....839, 841
2:10 ....132, 144, 839
2:21 283
2:24 ....370, 484
3:18 ....360, 472

4:1–5 258
5:3 861
5:8 36

2 Peter
book of 464
1:1 ....409, 463, 464, 464n119
1:5–9 258
1:11 464
2:5–8 464
2:21 464
3 722
3:9 110
3:13 464

1 John
1:1–9 35
1:5 356
1:7 712
1:8–10 82
2:1–2 357
2:2 ....28, 35
3:16 549
3:24 549
4:4 857
4:8–10 357
4:9–10 35
4:10 ....28, 425–26

Jude
book of 273n2
3 ....37, 770
14 ....456n79
16 279
21 464
24 864

Revelation
book of 273n2, 618
1:5 413
2:10 ....461n104
4 356
4:3 377
6:16 139
12:11 ....461n104
15:3–4 88
15:4 ....357n30
19–20 358
21 116
21–22 110
21:3–4 384
21:8 258
22 ....139n77
22:14–15 ...258
22:17 143